ATLAS OF CANADA

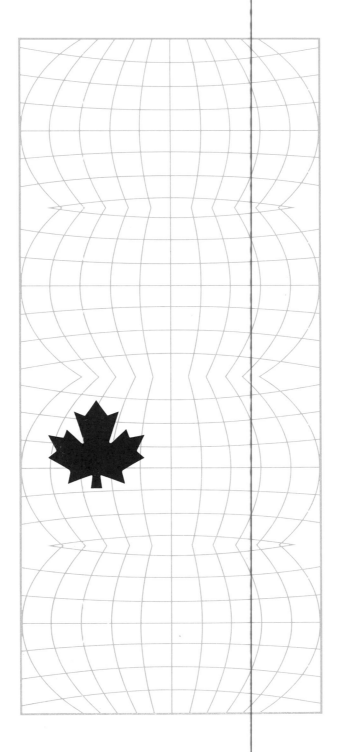

Published by The Reader's Digest Association (Canada) Ltd. in conjunction with the Canadian Automobile Association

First Edition

ISBN 0-88850-096-3

Printed in Canada 81 82 83/6 5 4 3 2 1

ACKNOWLEDGMENTS

General consultant

Dr. Henry W. Castner,
Associate Professor of Geography,
Queen's University, Kingston

Special consultants

Dr. W. P. Adams,
Professor of Geography,
Trent University, Peterborough

James S. Beckett,
Senior Policy/Program Adviser,
Fisheries Research Branch,
Fisheries and Oceans Canada

Dr. Norbert Berkowitz,
Professor of Mining Engineering,
University of Alberta, Edmonton

Dr. Andrew Burghardt,
Professor of Geography,
McMaster University, Hamilton

Dr. A. C. Carlisle,
Project Leader,
Petawawa National Forestry Institute,
Chalk River, Ontario

Dr. Alan Cooke,
Consultant, Centre for Northern Studies
and Research,
McGill University, Montréal

Dr. David Douglas,
Assistant Professor of Geography,
University of Ottawa

Dr. Leonard Gertler,
Professor, School of Urban
and Regional Planning,
University of Waterloo,
Waterloo, Ontario

Dr. Leonard Guelke,
Professor of Geography,
University of Waterloo,
Waterloo, Ontario

Dr. C. Richard Harington,
Curator of Quaternary Zoology,
Paleobiology Division,
National Museum of Natural Sciences,
National Museums of Canada, Ottawa

Dr. Alexander Himelfarb,
Associate Professor of Sociology,
University of New Brunswick, Fredericton

T. Ainslie Kerr,
Consultant to the transportation and
communications industry, Montréal

Dr. G. A. MacEachern,
President,
Agricultural Economics Research Council
of Canada, Ottawa

Dr. J. R. Mallory,
Professor of Political Science,
McGill University, Montréal

Dr. J. K. Morton,
Professor of Biology,
University of Waterloo,
Waterloo, Ontario

David Phillips,
Head, Developmental Climatology,
Central Services Directorate,
Atmospheric Environment Service,
Downsview, Ontario

Dr. C. James Richardson,
Associate Professor of Sociology,
University of New Brunswick, Fredericton

Dr. E. S. Rodgers,
Curator, Department of Ethnology,
Royal Ontario Museum, Toronto

Dr. Dale Russell,
Chief, Paleobiology Division,
National Museum of Natural Sciences,
National Museums of Canada, Ottawa

Dr. John Theberge,
Professor, Faculty of Environmental Studies,
University of Waterloo,
Waterloo, Ontario

Morley K. Thomas,
Director General, Central Services Directorate,
Atmospheric Environment Service,
Downsview, Ontario

William Trimble,
Past Vice-President, Academic,
Humber College of Applied Arts and Technology,
Toronto

Dr. John Udd,
Director, Mining Program,
Department of Mining
and Metallurgical Engineering,
McGill University, Montréal

Dr. P. B. Waite,
Professor of History,
Dalhousie University, Halifax

Dr. J. Tuzo Wilson,
Director General,
Ontario Science Centre, Toronto

The Gazetteer maps and index contained in the Reader's Digest *Atlas of Canada* are derived from those prepared for the *Canada Gazetteer Atlas* by the Surveys and Mapping Branch, Energy, Mines and Resources Canada, and are published here under a license agreement with the Canadian Government Publishing Centre, Supply and Services Canada. Additional information on roads and tourist attractions has been added by the publisher.

The Publishers wish to express their gratitude to Statistics Canada, the McGill University Libraries, and the Westmount Library.

Reader's Digest staff

EDITOR: A. R. Byers
DEPUTY EDITOR: Kenneth Winchester
ART DIRECTORS: Lucie Martineau,
John McGuffie, Val Mitrofanow
ART DIRECTOR (maps): Pierre Léveillé
ASSISTANT EDITORS: David Dunbar,
Barbara Peck
STAFF WRITERS: Patricia Derrick,
Lynda Dickson, Horst D. Dornbusch,
Patricia Sylvester
ASSISTANT DESIGNERS (maps): Mary Ashley,
Guylaine Mongeau, Jean-Claude Paré,
Anne Racine, Alex Wallach
ASSISTANT DESIGNERS: Michel Rousseau,
Lyne Young
TEXT RESEARCH: Risë Segall (chief),
Caroline Miller
PHOTO RESEARCH: Rachel Irwin (chief),
Michelle Turbide
COPY PREPARATION: Peter Madely (chief),
Betty Dunn, Francis Legge, Debby Seed
PROJECT COORDINATOR: Nicole Samson-Cholette
PRODUCTION: Holger Lorenzen
ADMINISTRATOR: Denise Rainville

C O N T E N T S

Atlas of Canada is divided into four parts: thematic pages (6 to 59); *Facts About Canada,* a compendium of basic knowledge (60 to 76); the maps of Canada (77 to 177); and the Gazetteer Index to the maps (178 to 219). The thematic pages cover the principal themes of Canada's geology, geography, history, society and economy. Each theme is treated in a self-contained two-page unit, the headings of which are given below. Under each heading, the main topics are listed, followed by references to related subjects on other thematic pages and in *Facts About Canada.*

A Nation of Superlatives

He shall have dominion also from sea to sea, and from the river unto the ends of the earth.   —Psalms 72:8

"When you see [this country] for the first time, all of it . . . you say to yourself. 'My God, is all this ours!' "
      —Hugh MacLennan, *Two Solitudes*

From a geographic viewpoint, Canada bulks large. With a land area of 9,992,330 square kilometres, it spreads over half a continent, covering nearly seven percent of the earth's surface. The largest country in the Western Hemisphere, Canada rests on the Americas like a giant capstone. It is, in fact, the largest country in the world after the Soviet Union. Among the rest, only Australia, Brazil, China and the United States rival its territorial extent. There is no other nation that could not be accommodated comfortably within Canada's boundaries. France and Germany could be fitted into the interior of Quebec, leaving room for Poland, and Czechoslovakia. Belgium and the Netherlands together would not cover New Brunswick.

More than 4600 kilometres separate Canada's northern extremity, Cape Columbia on Ellesmere Island, from Point Pelee in the southernmost tip of Ontario. Seen from a northern perspective, Canada's only land neighbor, the United States, with which it shares a boundary of 8892 kilometres, almost disappears from view.

Even greater than the north–south span of Canada is the distance from east to west. St. John's on the Atlantic coast is 5047 kilometres from Victoria, on the Pacific. Alberta is as far to the west of Newfoundland as Germany is to the east. Vancouver is closer to Mexico City, and to the Arctic coast, than it is to Halifax.

No wonder the vision of this nation, stretching from sea to sea, captured the imagination of the Fathers of Confederation, inspiring Sir Samuel Leonard Tilley of New Brunswick to suggest "Dominion" for Canada's baptismal name.

The physical diversity of the country is remarkable: towering mountains, great plains, fertile lowlands, northern wilderness and tundra. Few nations can match Canada's abundance of minerals, forests and bodies of waters. The lakes, scattered so liberally across the land, contain some of the world's greatest stores of fresh water. Majestic rivers, pathways of the fur trade and of settlement, set amid landscapes of ineffable beauty, everywhere evoke sentiments of grandeur and abundance. The most famous of our river systems, the St. Lawrence–Great Lakes, is the cardinal fact of Canadian geography. Along this route the nation had its origins, as adventurers and missionaries penetrated the interior of the continent.

But Canada's landforms have combined with its climate to confine development. Above the thin line of settlement along the country's southern edge loom the Precambrian Shield, which reaches down to the St. Lawrence between Lake Ontario and Montréal, and the Arctic. Four-fifths of Canada has never been settled permanently and, of all the provinces, only Prince Edward Island is completely inhabited. The largest unbroken tract of mixed rural and urban settlement is the Prairies, which account for slightly more than six percent of Canada's area. Most of the nation's 24 million people live in urban communities that take up only one percent of the land, of which the heaviest concentration is to be found in the industrial heartland stretching from Québec to Windsor.

Yet the distances separating Canada's major cities are vast. In no other country, save Australia, is there a comparable scattering of centers of population without continuous settlement. Thus development of transportation systems, particularly the railways, has been of special importance in Canada's history. Without the 1127-kilometre Intercolonial Railway, completed in 1871 between Québec and Halifax, there could have been no sense of physical union between Upper Canada and the Maritime Provinces. And only that epic of nation-building, the Canadian Pacific Railway, 27,487 kilometres across prairie and forest, mountain and muskeg, from the Maritimes to the Fraser delta, made "dominion from sea to sea" truly possible. To seal this bond, nearly a century later, came the Trans-Canada Highway between Victoria, B.C., and St. John's, Nfld., at 7770 kilometres the world's longest national road.

The three global views at right present Canada as it might be seen from high above the North Atlantic (top), the mid-Pacific (middle), and the high Arctic (bottom). Bounded by these three vast bodies of water, Canada has the longest ocean coastline in the world: 241,402 kilometres.

On the Atlantic shore, the direct distance between the Bay of Fundy and Hudson Strait (separating northern Quebec and Baffin Island) is about 1600 kilometres. But the true measure of this shoreline, with its numerous estuaries, inlets and capes, is ten times as great. Facing eastward to Europe and northward to Greenland, Atlantic Canada is bypassed by the Gulf Stream which warms the coast of northern Europe. The chill Labrador Current, flowing down from between Baffin Island and Greenland, meets the Gulf Stream off the coast of Newfoundland. Canada's Atlantic coast was the first to become known to Europeans. Norse explorers briefly settled the northern tip of Newfoundland in the 11th century. Five hundred years later, when European exploration began in earnest, Jacques Cartier discovered the St. Lawrence—the gateway to the interior of North America.

Canada's Pacific coast was charted by the Royal Navy in the 18th century. Here the mountain ranges rise sheer from the sea, creating a formidable barrier to the interior. The length of this precipitous shore is 7022 kilometres. For most of its distance it is deeply indented by fjords and studded with islands, the largest of which are Vancouver Island and the Queen Charlottes. This coastline, warmed by the Alaska Current, is temperate and, except for sheltered inlets, its waters are ice-free. The 30,000-kilometre coastline of the Arctic and Hudson Bay is the longest in Canada and, because the ocean is perpetually covered with drifting ice, the least accessible. Locked in the Arctic ice is one of the world's largest archipelagoes, with a land area of over 1,250,000 square kilometres. The centuries-old search for a passage through these hazardous waters ended in 1906 with the successful voyage of Roald Amundsen. Today icebreakers and other vessels with modern navigation aids make the passage from Baffin Bay to the Beaufort Sea in late summer and early autumn. Year-round Arctic shipping, spurred by northern oil discoveries, may be a possibility in the 1980s.

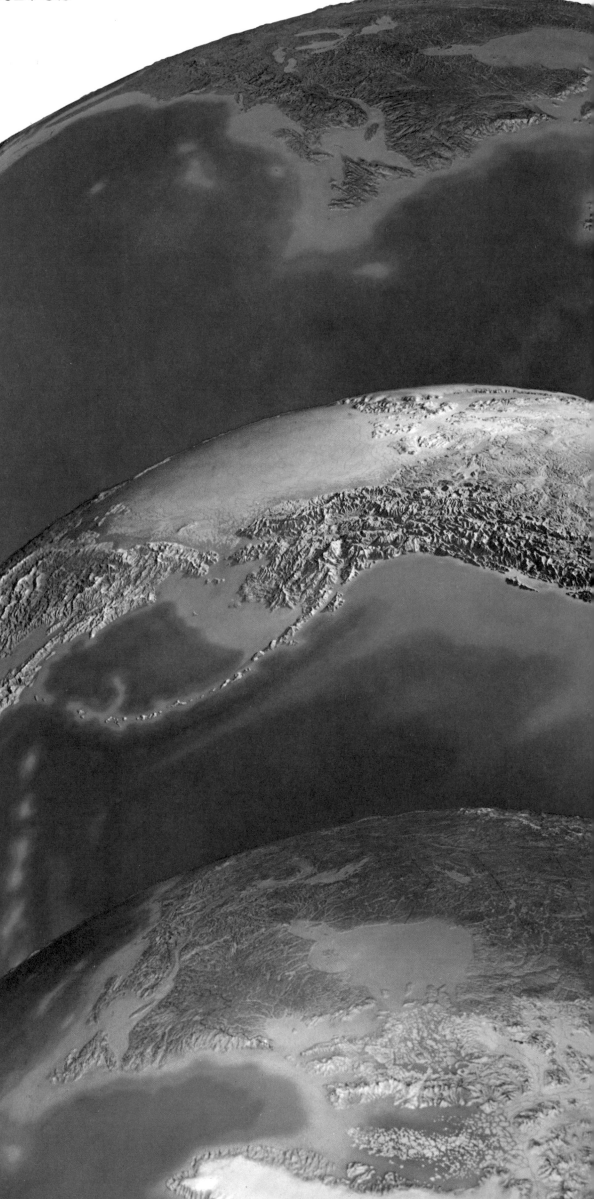

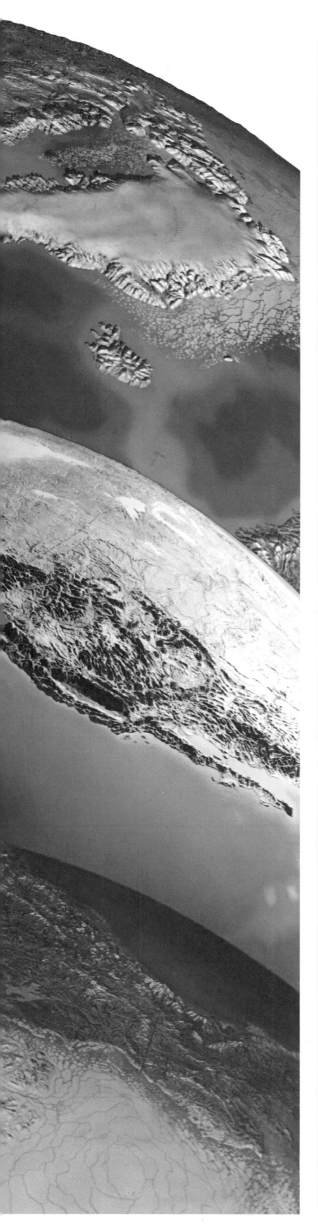

Too Much Geography?

Prime Minister Mackenzie King once remarked that while some countries had too much history, Canada had too much geography. One way of appreciating Canada's vast size is to superimpose its territorial outlines on a map of Europe, which, at 9.9 million square kilometres, occupies less area than our country. As the map (1) indicates, if the upper British Columbia coast lies on Spain and the Bay of Biscay, then Winnipeg is in the Balkans, Montréal is in the Caucasus and the Maritime Provinces reach into Asiatic Russia.

Canada's largest province, Quebec, is almost equal in size to the area encompassed by the European Economic Community, which consists of Belgium, Denmark, France, Great Britain, Ireland, Italy, Luxembourg, the Netherlands and West Germany (2). These nine countries cover an area of 1,512,143 square kilometres, compared to Quebec's 1,540,687, which accounts for only 15 percent of Canada.

Ontario, the second-largest province at 1,068,587 square kilometres is almost double France's 551,000 square kilometres. And British Columbia, occupying less than a tenth of Canada, rivals Egypt in area: 950,000 square kilometres to one million (3). Newfoundland, covering four percent of Canada, is larger than Japan: 405,000 square kilometres to 380,000 (4). But Japan is inhabited by 115 million people, compared to Newfoundland's 500,000.

In Numbers of People, A Different Story

In contrast to its immense physical size, Canada's population of 24 million—less than half of one percent of the world total—is but a thin slice atop the familiar outline of the United States in the cartogram below. Each country on the map below has been enlarged or reduced in proportion to the number of inhabitants. In five countries—China, India, the Soviet Union, the United States and Indonesia—live half the world's 4.9 billion people. China, with an estimated population of almost a billion people, is home to one out of every five persons on earth.

Population distribution has always been uneven, and it appears likely to stay that way. In Canada the rate of natural increase (the difference between the number of births and deaths per thousand people) is low, which also means that the average age is increasing. Due to improved health standards, countries such as Mexico, Iran, Kenya and Indonesia have rapid growth rates, burgeoning populations and a declining average age.

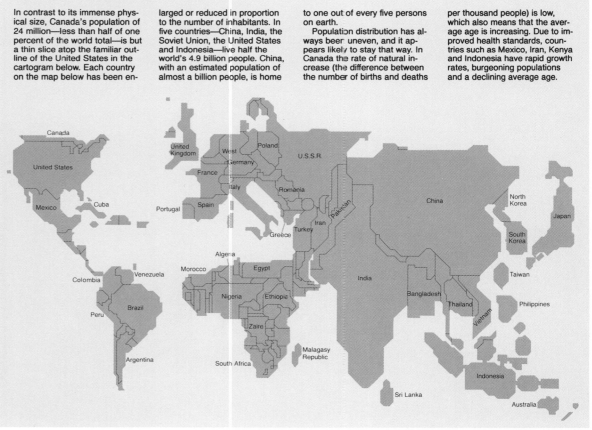

The Making of Our Land

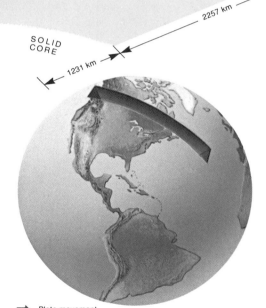

NORTH AMERICAN PLATE
NORTH AMERICAN CONTINENT

CONTINENTAL CRUST
UPPER MANTLE
Convection Currents
ASTHENOSPHERE

SEDIMENT
OCEAN CRUST

OCEAN

LOWER MANTLE

LIQUID CORE

SOLID CORE

1231 km
2257 km
2533 km
340 km
10 km
Not to scale

Plate movement
Spreading rift
Subduction zone
Transform fault
Uncertain or generalized boundary

The earth was formed more than 4.5 billion years ago. From whirling clouds of cosmic gas and dust, a knot of particles gathered, then compacted into a spinning, solid globe. Intense heat was produced, both from the impact of material falling onto the growing sphere and from decaying radioactive materials trapped in its depths. Gradually the mass melted, churned and settled into layers. Heavier matter, rich in iron and nickel, sank to form a core. Complex magnesium silicates formed a thick, surrounding mantle. Lighter materials, richest in silica, rose to the surface, eventually forming a crust. Volcanoes spewed molten rock, gases and water vapor, slowly giving birth to land, air and seas.

The slow sorting of the earth into layers is still going on. At the earth's center, the inner core burns at a white-hot 4000°C, but pressures up to 3.5 million times the normal surface atmospheric pressure compress it to a solid ball. The molten outer core flows around it, rippling with currents caused by the earth's rotation. This fluid core behaves like a dynamo, turning the earth into a gigantic magnet with north and south poles. The solid mantle is composed of three zones: a rigid lower layer; the soft asthenosphere, eddying slowly like liquid simmering in a pot; and a rigid upper layer. The upper layer of the mantle together with the crust forms the rigid lithosphere: a thin, brittle layer some 100 kilometres thick which floats on the asthenosphere. The lithosphere is cracked into a mosaic of huge plates of irregular size and shape. The crust includes the continents and ocean basins—less than one percent of the earth's bulk. The continental crust, formed of relatively light granitic rock up to 40 kilometres thick, floats higher in the asthenosphere than the heavier ocean floors. Basaltic ocean crust averages only ten kilometres in thickness, but sags to form deep basins that fill with seawater.

Our restless planet is never still. Over billions of years, parts of it have been uplifted, then ground flat again, washed by seas and sculpted by erosion, thrust up into belts of rugged mountains and worn down into plains and gently rolling hills.

Drifting Plates, Colliding Continents

The earth is a geologic jigsaw puzzle broken into 20 or more plates up to 100 kilometres thick, all driven by currents in the asthenosphere. Earthquakes and volcanoes outline the plate boundaries and give awesome testimony to the forces beneath our feet.

Where plates pull apart, as at the mid-Atlantic rift, molten rock oozes up onto the seafloor, creating three centimetres of new bottom each year. Where plates push together—off Canada's west coast, for example—one may be forced under the other, eventually to soften in subduction zones and melt in the hot interior. The westward-creeping American plate is bulldozing over the small Juan de Fuca and Explorer plates. Molten rock from the descending plate edge once fueled active volcanoes throughout British Columbia, and its heat produced a solid granite spine 2000 kilometres long underlying the

Coast Range. Where two continents collide, the ocean floor separating them crumples and is pushed up into mountain peaks. Some 250 million years ago, such continental collision produced the Appalachians of eastern Canada. At certain plate boundaries, called transform faults, plates grind past each other, triggering earthquakes. California's San Andreas Fault is cne of these.

Ocean floor spreading pushes Canada and Europe farther apart by three centimetres a year. At the same time, the Pacific plate is shrinking, and British Columbia and Japan draw 12 centimetres closer every year. In 42 million years, if drift continues, North and South America will separate, Africa will break apart, the Mediterranean will be squeezed into a large lake and California west of the San Andreas Fault—including Los Angeles—will have drifted off Canada's west coast.

The Violent Birth of the Continents

200 million years ago

135 million years ago

65 million years ago

Some 200 million years ago, the continents formed one landmass, *Pangaea* (Greek for "all lands"), with what is now Canada at its northwest corner. About 135 million years ago this continent began ripping apart, dividing into southern Gondwanaland and northern Laurasia, which included an embryo North America ("Laurentia"). As the Atlantic Ocean developed, Canada's east coast pulled apart from southern Europe, and North America swiveled before separating from Scandinavia.

The jigsaw-puzzle fit of both sides of the Atlantic, and the similarity of fossils and mineral deposits on widely separated continents support the theory of continental drift. Scientists have found proof that seafloors are older the farther they are from mid-ocean rifts. This enables them to map how the earth's oceans grew, and to determine in which direction and how fast each plate is moving.

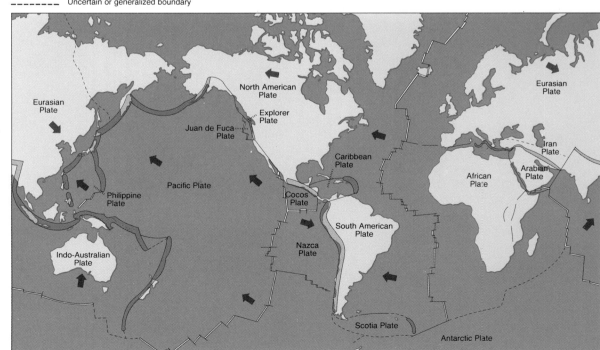

Eurasian Plate
North American Plate
Explorer Plate
Juan de Fuca Plate
Eurasian Plate
Iran Plate
Caribbean Plate
African Plate
Arabian Plate
Philippine Plate
Pacific Plate
Cocos Plate
South American Plate
Indo-Australian Plate
Nazca Plate
Scotia Plate
Antarctic Plate

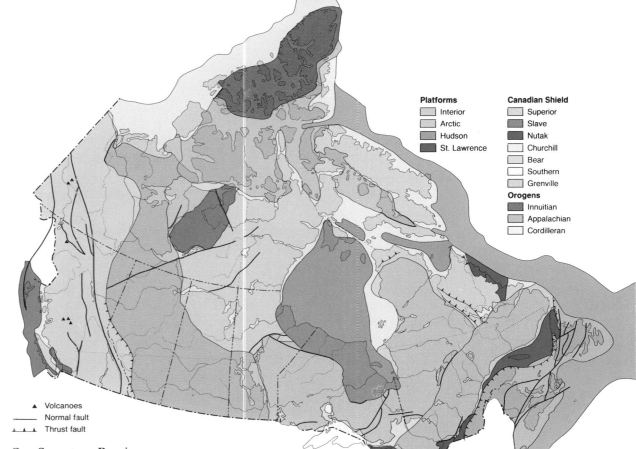

Pent-Up Pressures That Cause Quakes

Plate movements, where rock grinds against rock, create immense pressures. Ninety-five percent of earthquakes occur at plate boundaries such as the Pacific "Ring of Fire," the rest along inland fault lines. Sometimes the rock masses move imperceptibly. When they resist, pressures may build. Rock bends until pent-up strain overcomes friction, then moves suddenly and violently—an earthquake. There are more than a million quakes each year, 300 in Canada.

Parts of Quebec and British Columbia lie in zones most susceptible to quakes, but damage would be most severe in major cities, in coastal areas vulnerable to tidal waves from offshore quakes, and in areas where loose, clay-based soils may shift or even liquefy. Earthquakes measuring seven or more on the Richter scale, powerful enough to bend steel rails and topple all but the strongest buildings, have happened in Canada (see map), although never in densely settled areas. Large and small, all quakes are monitored, since repeated shuddering is a clue that the pressure is building.

Risk of earthquake damage

- No damage
- Minor damage
- Moderate damage
- Major damage

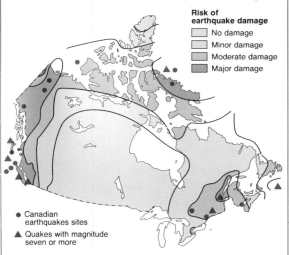

- ● Canadian earthquakes sites
- ▲ Quakes with magnitude seven or more

Platforms
- Interior
- Arctic
- Hudson
- St. Lawrence

Canadian Shield
- Superior
- Slave
- Nutak
- Churchill
- Bear
- Southern
- Grenville

Orogens
- Innuitian
- Appalachian
- Cordilleran

- ▲ Volcanoes
- —— Normal fault
- ▲▲▲ Thrust fault

Coastal shelves and plains
- Arctic
- Atlantic
- Pacific

Our Seventeen Provinces

Canada has 17 geologic provinces or landform regions. The nucleus of the continent is the Canadian Shield, the ancient, eroded landmass cradling Hudson Bay. The seven provinces of the Shield formed during three surges of mountain-building over two billion years. Near its edges, the Shield disappears under the plateaus, plains and lowlands of the four platform provinces, built from layers of sediments. At the Shield's edges are belts of unstable younger mountains—the three orogen provinces. In the youngest of the orogens, the Cordilleran, a few volcanoes remain. Although all are dormant, several Canadian volcanoes are thought to have erupted as recently as 200 years ago. On the fringes of the orogens, new sediments are accumulating in the continental shelves of the three coastal provinces.

Erosion and Uplift Transform the Land

Wind, rain and frost gnaw at the Canadian landscape, working to level it. Rocks split from jagged peaks, then shatter; boulders slowly disintegrate. Grains of sand are ground to silt. The loose, eroded sediments are pounded by rains and peppered by grit-laden winds. Streams and rivers carry them to the sea. While these forces are constantly wearing down the land, others are rebuilding it. As rock is worn away, other rock moves up to replace it. More rock pushes from the sides, sometimes causing warping and fracturing. At such lines of fracture, called faults, one side of the break may sink downward (normal fault), or overlap the other (thrust fault). Molten rock oozes upward along dikes (cracks in older rock), then solidifies. Near the collision zone between two plates, uplift builds mountains such as the Canadian Rockies and the Coast Range. Farther from plate boundaries, the earth is quieter. The flat grasslands of the Prairies, the rolling hills of the Shield and the broad, submerged continental shelf beneath Newfoundland's Grand Banks show that forces of erosion may be winning.

YOUTH

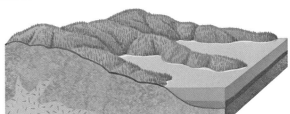

MATURITY

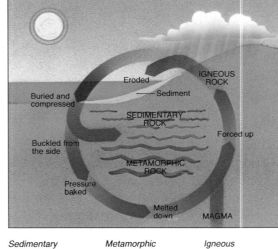

- Folded layers of rock
- Normal fault
- Magma pocket
- Dormant volcano
- Thrust fault
- Landslide
- Exposed igneous rock
- Sedimentary rock layer
- Eroding river
- Shingle beach
- Spit
- Offshore sediments
- Tombolo
- Island
- Hook

Sandstone, Gneiss and Granite: The Three Phases of Rock Formation

SEDIMENTARY rock—shales, limestones and sandstones—is formed from particles of other rock, or from the fossil shells of tiny marine animals. They accumulate in layers, often trapping larger plant and animal fragments, and are compressed and cemented together by water-soluble minerals. Forming at or near the earth's surface, they make up only eight percent of the crust, but 75 percent of its topmost layer. As surface rocks, they erode easily and are ground back to loose sediments. The sculpted coulees and hoodoos of western Canada's badlands show how poorly sandstones and shales resist erosion.

METAMORPHIC or altered rocks are formed when older rocks, chiefly sedimentary, are baked by volcanic heat, or are buried deep in the earth and steeped in hot, chemically active groundwater. These new rocks may form without melting, but the process takes millions of years.

Minerals separate into bands of long, stretched-out crystals; pebbles flatten; crystals lock together. Metamorphized marbles, granites and gneisses lie in mountain belts and in the Canadian Shield.

IGNEOUS or fire-formed rocks harden from pockets of magma (older rock which has melted), rising from 40–60 kilometres underground. If it reaches the surface while hot and still liquid, it is called lava. Magma may also be forced through cracks in older rocks to harden as sheets or vertical dikes of igneous rock. Larger masses may crystallize underground in coarse, grainy blocks. Eventually all are exposed as softer surrounding rocks wear away.

However they form, most rocks contain silica and a few other minerals. The photographs (right) show a silica compound as it might appear at each major step of the rock cycle—as sandstone, gneiss and granite.

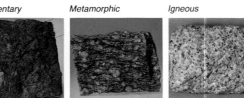

Sedimentary Metamorphic Igneous

OLD AGE

Where Restless Waves Carve and Age an Ever-Changing Shoreline

These views show a slowly sinking coast. In the seacoast's youth, river-carved valleys have been drowned by rising sea levels to form deep bays and estuaries, while the sea pounds against former inland hills. Waves gnaw at steep promontories, cut cliffs on their seaward sides, and flush away rock and soil. A coast of this type provides excellent natural harbors.

As the seacoast matures, headlands slowly erode, and sandbar spits and crescents of shingle beach are built from sediments sorted by the sea. More sediment accumulates in the shallow, sheltered waters of the bay.

As the seacoast ages, sandbars may transform bays into silt-choked lagoons, and eventually into tidal mud flats. Parts of New Brunswick's coast have reached this stage. Relentless pounding by waves breaks up offshore islands and washes them away. Eventually the sinking coastline will be worn nearly straight, far inland from the original shorelines.

The Panorama of Ages Past

Peeled back, the layers of Canada's surface should reveal the rocks of earlier ages as neat chapters of geologic history. But the layers were seldom left in peace. Molten rock pierced and tilted them. Folding and faulting sandwiched and inverted them. Parts of the continent rose and sank, and whole pages of the story were destroyed by erosion. Piecing together this fragmented record, geologists have drawn speculative maps of Canada in past ages: a drifting land rent by earthquakes, engulfed by oceans, uplifted by mountain building and worn down by wind and water.

Like the story of the changing land, the history of life is written in the rocks, in remnants called fossils. Mineral-rich groundwater may petrify plants, animal bones and shells, turning them to stone. Shells often leave their imprints in casts or molds. Animal remains have been preserved in dry caves or acidic peat bogs. These remains not only reveal what lived in the past, but provide clues to our planet's age, the evolution of its life, and climate conditions that existed in the past.

The story begins with the first stirrings of life in Precambrian seas, where organic molecules joined to form amino acids—building blocks of life—and finally living cells. As the fossil record shows, the road was long and tortuous: the evolution of single-celled organisms from organic compounds took far longer than the development from single cell to *Homo sapiens*. Early life, cradled by warm, shallow seas, burgeoned in the Cambrian Period some 550 million years ago. Species diversified and, following evolutionary trends toward complexity and specialization, eventually spread from sea to land.

Each era had its own most successful types. The hard-shelled trilobites and other arthropods of the Paleozoic were dominant for 300 million years. They were superseded by the reptiles of the Mesozoic, whose rule on earth lasted 150 million years. When the dinosaurs fell 65 million years ago, they were succeeded by the more efficient and adaptable warm-blooded animals of the Cenozoic, which quickly diversified to fill niches left empty. As the once-unified continents slid farther apart on their moving plates, each landmass drifted through its own sequence of environmental changes. Over the epochs and the Ice Age, modern mammals evolved, joined at last by a recent immigrant to North America—man.

THE RIBBON OF TIME

The entire span of earth's history is divided into four unequal portions called eras—the Precambrian, stretching from earth's formation to 570 million years ago; the Paleozoic ("ancient life"); Mesozoic ("middle life"); and Cenozoic ("recent life"). Each is further divided into periods and epochs, including the Pleistocene, or Ice Age, and the Holocene, the last 10,000 years. Life has evolved slowly since the first single-celled organisms appeared in the late Precambrian. If this time scale were compressed into a single day, man would appear only in the final few seconds.

PRECAMBRIAN

PALEOZOIC
1 Cambrian
2 Ordovician
3 Silurian
4 Devonian
5 Carboniferous
6 Permian

MESOZOIC
7 Triassic
8 Jurassic
9 Cretaceous

CENOZOIC
10 Tertiary
11 Quaternary

570 475 425 413 355 265 230 185 130 65 2 (million years ago) Present

Marine deposits	Ocean	Terrestrial deposits	Island arcs	Land

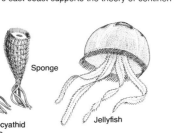

Early Cambrian (550 million years ago). Continental shields, low and barren, drifted about the globe, and climates were mild during the Cambrian Period. In a burst of evolution, animals with hard parts began replacing simple, soft-bodied organisms. In warm, shallow seas swam the earliest invertebrates: crustaceans and mollusks, worms and jellyfish. The similarity of fossils found in western Europe and North America's east coast supports the theory of continental drift.

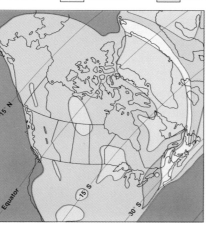

Sponge

Jellyfish

1 Archeocyathid
2 Trilobite
3 Arthropod
4 Annelid worm
5 Sea cucumber

1 2 3 4 5

Late Ordovician (440 million years ago). As North America slowly rotated toward Eurasia, shallow tropical seas flooded the continents. An arc of volcanic islands along Canada's east coast preceded the uplift of an eastern mountain chain. Two marine animal groups dominated the period: bryozoans, plantlike creatures of various shapes from stems to mosslike colonies; and brachiopods or "lamp shells," once numbering 30,000 species. In placid shallows appeared jawless fishes, the first vertebrates.

Brachiopod

1 Solitary coral
2 Gastropod
3 Trilobite
4 Cephalopod
5 Colonial coral

Graptolite

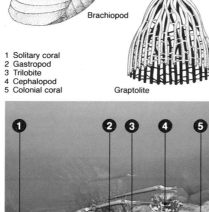

1 2 3 4 5

Late Devonian (360 million years ago). The triumph of the vertebrates began with the Devonian "age of fishes." Five classes had evolved: the jawless fishes, represented today only by lampreys and hagfishes; the jawed armored fishes and spiny sharks, both extinct; the true sharks, skates and rays; and the bony fishes. On land, small plants and rootless trees crowned with leaflike fronds sprouted in abundance. Lush swamps left a legacy of coal, oil and natural gas which underlies much of North America. Forests teemed with air-breathers, such as spiders, ancestral dragonflies and some 800,000 species of insects that survive today.

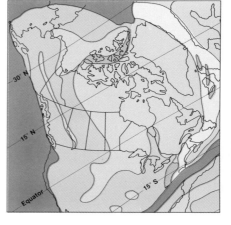

Armored fish

Giant fern

1 Lungfish
2 Cephalopod
3 Early shark
4 Solitary coral

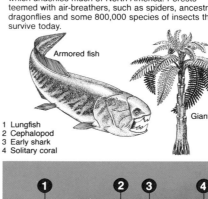

1 2 3 4

Permian (230 million years ago). The drifting continents came together to form the single supercontinent Pangaea. A jarring collision with northern Africa uplifted North America's east coast, where volcanoes towered over baking deserts. Previously isolated faunas came into contact, causing competition and widespread extinctions. The union of the continents drained shallow seas, exposing continental shelves and reducing favored marine environments. As marine species waned, land-dwelling amphibians and reptiles such as *Dimetrodon* (below) diversified.

Conifer

Cordaites

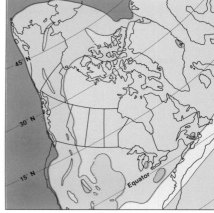

10

The Climatic Pendulum

Fossil evidence shows that world temperatures have swung many times during past ages (*below*). The coalfields of British Columbia, Saskatchewan and Nova Scotia, and the oil reserves of Alberta and the North are evidence of a much warmer and wetter climate during several past epochs; southern Ontario's moraines and drumlins mark the paths of great glacial ice sheets that covered North America in other ages.

These temperature changes were never large, but the earth's climate is so finely tuned that a shift of a few degrees could upset the balance. A rise of 5°C would melt polar ice caps, drowning the continents; a 5°C fall could lock the earth in an ice age. Fluctuations are normal—scientists calculate that ice ages have occurred at least four times

in the last billion years, perhaps coinciding with some greater galactic cycle.

Earth's climate is influenced by even minute variations in solar activity, atmospheric conditions and shifts in the earth's orbit or tilt, as well as developments on its surface. In the Precambrian, seas were shallow and landmasses low, and both precipitation and the sun's warmth spread easily around the globe. The uplift of mountain ranges and the draining of vast inland seas in later ages brought about today's complex weather patterns and diverse climatic zones.

Canada's climate has swung more drastically than the chart indicates. Propelled by sluggish currents in the upper mantle, North America has drifted through various latitudes, from the equator to the North Pole.

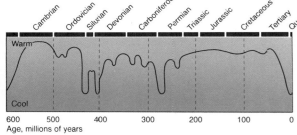

Dykes, Faults and Dormant Volcanoes

Igneous and plutonic rocks
- Acidic rocks
- Basic rocks
- Anorthosite
- Granitic gneiss
- Granulite
- Gabbro dyke

Sedimentary and volcanic rocks
- CENOZOIC
- MESOZOIC
- Cretaceous
- PALEOZOIC
- Late Paleozoic
- Devonian
- Early Paleozoic
- Proterozoic and Paleozoic
- PROTEROZOIC
- HADRYNIAN
- HELIKIAN
- Neohelikian

- ▲ Volcano
- Thrust fault
- Normal fault

- Paleohelikian
- APHEBIAN
- ARCHEAN

The geologic map of Canada shows the age of surface rocks. Canada's oldest rocks, Precambrian granites and gneisses, are found in the stable Laurentian Shield; the youngest are being deposited in the deltas of such eroding waterways as the Mackenzie and Fraser rivers.

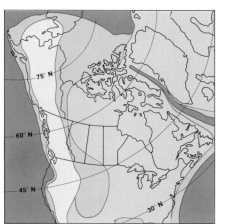

Late Jurassic (150 million years ago). The age of reptiles began as the great landmass of Pangaea began the slow breakup into the continents of today. Dinosaurs evolved in bewildering variety: long-necked vegetarians such as *Brachiosaurus* (*below*), fierce predators, leather-winged gliders, bizarre creatures with bony armor. They found living room and plentiful food supplies on Jurassic plains and in widespread tropical jungles dominated by tall conifers, delicate tree ferns and mosses, and palmlike cycads.

Plesiosaur

Early Tertiary (50 million years ago). In North America, the Rockies rose, high plains formed in the Midwest, and forests gave way to spreading grasslands. Oaks, maples and hickories joined the rich forests of pines, palms and cycads. Huge lakes flooded the plains, teeming with perches, gars and other forerunners of modern freshwater fishes. The 100-million-year reign of the dinosaurs had ended abruptly. In their place emerged a new group: warm-blooded mammals, such as *Uintatherium* and primitive horses (*below*), descendants of shrewlike Jurassic ancestors. On North American plains roamed ancestral hyenas, marmots, squirrels and *Smilodectes*, an early primate.

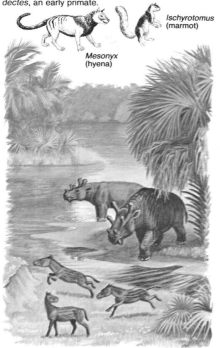

Ischyrotomus (marmot)

Mesonyx (hyena)

When Reptiles Ruled

The Mesozoic Era was an age of giants, especially in subtropical North America where dinosaurs grew to unprecedented size—ranging in length up to 25 metres. Reptiles, unlike earlier species, were not dependent on water for reproduction, and moved freely inland. Most were vegetarians, browsing on the lush greenery of cypress swamps and conifer forests; others preyed on their more peaceable cousins. *Tyrannosaurus rex* stood 6 metres high, the largest predator ever to walk on land, and had teeth the size of railway spikes. *Apatasaurus* was 15 metres long and weighed as much as 10 large elephants.

Giant reptiles also ruled the seas, including the seaway that bisected the continent. Long-necked plesiosaurs sculled slowly along the surface. Below swam marine lizards called mosasaurs, fishlike ichthyosaurs and giant turtles.

Suddenly, 65 million years

Struthiomimus

Albertosaurus

Triceratops

Lambeosaurus

ago, the dinosaurs were gone. Their extinction—whether from climatic change, continental drift, competition from mammals, or celestial phenomenon such as an exploding supernova—remains one of nature's greatest mysteries.

Alberta's Red Deer Badlands (left), once a land of forests and floodplains, now yield fossil treasures. Here roamed the beaked "ostrich-mimic" Struthiomimus; the ferocious predator Albertosaurus; armor-plated Triceratops; and duck-billed Lambeosaurus, whose skeleton (above) was discovered near Manyberries, Alta.

How the Ice Age Shaped Canada

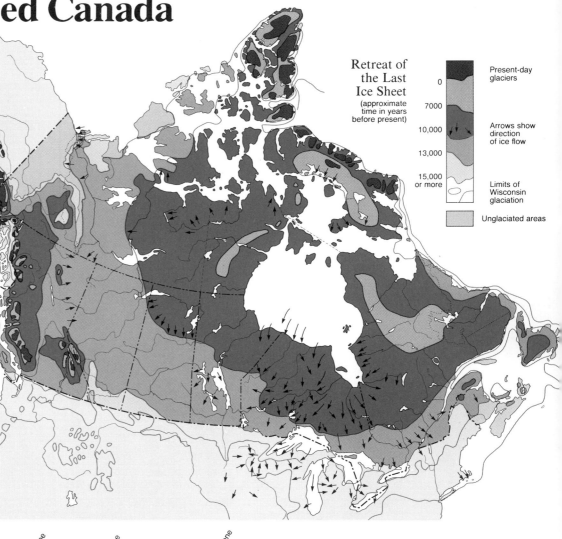

Almost two million years ago, an icy shroud of white spread across Canada as the Northern Hemisphere slipped into the Ice Age. During the Pleistocene Epoch, continental ice sheets surged at least four times, then retreated during long, warm interglacial periods.

The last of the great advances, the Wisconsin glaciation, began 25,000 years ago in Canada, from centers in the Ungava and Keewatin lowlands, the Western Cordillera, and islands in the eastern Arctic. At its zenith 20,000 years ago, the Laurentide ice sheet covered the entire Canadian Shield to depths of up to three kilometres. In the west, the smaller Cordilleran glacier complex stretched from the Rockies to the Pacific. The glaciers met, and for centuries formed an awesome barrier from coast to coast.

Both coming and going, the ice reshaped Canada. Advancing slowly but irresistibly, it ground rocks into pebbles and pebbles into clay, and bulldozed tremendous quantities of rock and earth over the land. As temperatures warmed and the ice retreated at a sluggish 30 kilometres per century, embedded debris was exposed and dropped in the wake of the melting mass. Ice-gouged river channels and lake bottoms flooded with meltwater, and many of today's familiar landmarks were created—the Great Lakes, Niagara Falls, Lake Winnipeg and Atlantic Canada's rocky coast.

The Ice Age also influenced animal life in Canada. The glacial barrier and intense cold squeezed life zones southward into narrowing bands, and withdrew water from the oceans, lowering the global sea level by 120 metres. A broad land connection emerged where now the Bering Strait separates Eurasia from North America. Earlier, plate movements had raised the Panamanian Isthmus, creating a land bridge to South America. Animals—including man—could now migrate freely between the continents.

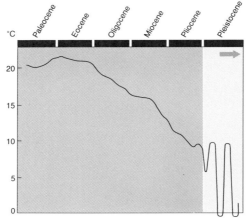

Why the Ice Came; Will It Return?

Slowly, during the late Tertiary, temperatures veered downward. In the North, ice caps grew larger as winter snowfall outpaced summer melting. Under the pressure of its own weight, the ice spread from centers in Canada, Greenland, Northern Europe and Siberia.

Scientists can only speculate why the earth's climate suddenly shifted. Continental drift, which affects ocean and atmospheric circulation, and the amount of solar radiation reaching the earth, may have initiated the cooling trend. Perhaps the sun temporarily dimmed, either from its own internal processes or from the passing of an interstellar dust cloud. Other theories include shifts in the earth's orbit or tilt, meteorite impact, the position of the solar system, and polar wandering.

The earth may be due for another glacial advance. Some scientists believe that today's warmer weather is only an interglacial reprieve, and that the ice may surge again within 10,000 years.

Bridges and Refuges: Nature's Truce With Ice

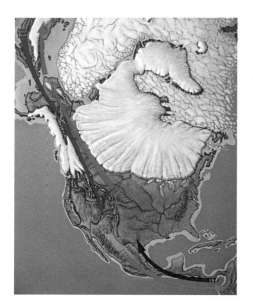

Across the Bering and Panamanian land bridges coursed a two-way traffic of Pleistocene animals. From Eurasia came the bulk of ice-age megafauna, including many species now considered "native": musk-ox, wapiti, moose, caribou, bear and wolf. From South America arrived ground sloths and armadillos. Some indigenous species, such as ancestral camels and horses, migrated north and south to other continents, only to die out in North America.

Sheltered by the mountains from the ice that blanketed much of North America, Beringia was one of several *refugia* where ice-age mammals thrived. The grasslands of the Yukon and interior Alaska provided a natural haven for men and beasts, some of which are depicted (in greater-than-life concentration) at right.

1 Arctic ground squirrel	12 Musk-ox	21 Wolverine
2 Caribou	13 Large-horned bison	22 Grizzly bear
3 Brown lemming	14 Musk-ox	23 Lionlike cat
4 Red fox	15 Ground sloth	24 Stag-moose
5 Horse	16 Man	25 Yak
6 Badger	17 Moose	26 Musk-ox
7 Saiga antelope	18 Woolly mammoth	27 Wapiti
8 Dall sheep	19 Great North	(American elk)
9 Arctic fox	American short-	28 Camel
10 Alaskan tundra hare	faced bear	29 American mastodon
11 Lynx	20 Wolf	30 Saber-toothed cat

How the Ice Changed the Land

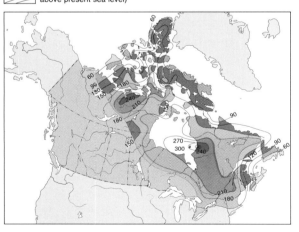

1 Marginal lake
2 Submerged river
3 Ice sheet
4 Meltwater stream
5 Outwash plain
6 Ice blocks

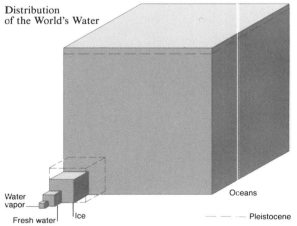

1 Lake bottom plain
2 Kame terrace
3 Esker
4 Moraine
5 Drumlin
6 Outwash plain
7 Kettle lake

Glacial Geology

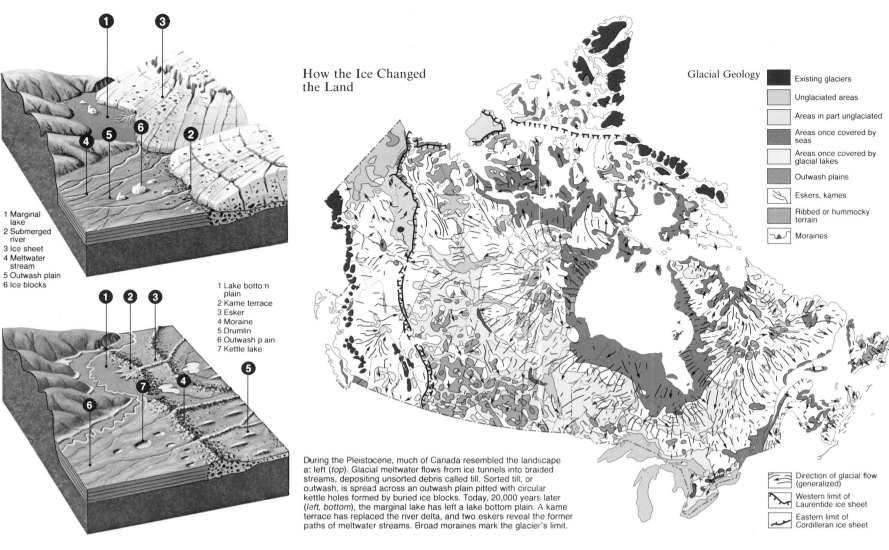

■	Existing glaciers
	Unglaciated areas
	Areas in part unglaciated
	Areas once covered by seas
	Areas once covered by glacial lakes
	Outwash plains
	Eskers, kames
	Ribbed or hummocky terrain
	Moraines

Direction of glacial flow (generalized)

Western limit of Laurentide ice sheet

Eastern limit of Cordilleran ice sheet

During the Pleistocene, much of Canada resembled the landscape at left (*top*). Glacial meltwater flows from ice tunnels into braided streams, depositing unsorted debris called till. Sorted till, or outwash, is spread across an outwash plain pitted with circular kettle holes formed by buried ice blocks. Today, 20,000 years later (*left, bottom*), the marginal lake has left a lake bottom plain. A kame terrace has replaced the river delta, and two eskers reveal the former paths of meltwater streams. Broad moraines mark the glacier's limit.

Rebounding Land, Rising Seas

Millions of tonnes of ice covered Canada during the Wisconsin glaciation—a burden so massive that it pushed the rock foundations of the crust down into the plastic mantle on which they float. For every 3.6 metres of ice above it, the crust sagged approximately one metre.

Relieved of this tremendous burden as glaciers receded, the crust began to spring back to its present position. This rebound is still going on (*below, left*). The north shore of Lake Ontario is rising above the south shore at

the rate of ten centimetres per century. Hudson Bay, where the ice first accumulated and disappeared last, will eventually re-emerge as dry land.

Glaciers also alter nature's balance by locking up vast amounts of water as ice. Today's glaciers hold less than two percent of the earth's water supply (*below, right*); Pleistocene ice sheets held more than five percent—an extra 40.5 million cubic kilometres. Sea levels dropped by some 120 metres worldwide, draining much of the

shallow continental shelves.

As the ice waned, meltwater swelled rivers and lakes, altering drainage patterns and raising sea levels. Glacial Lake Agassiz once covered most of Manitoba and filled the Red River valley of Minnesota and North Dakota. (Lake Winnipeg is a remnant, as is the flat, fertile soil of the Prairies.) The sediments of other ancestral lakes, into which glacial streams and the newly exposed land drained, form the lake plains of the Great Lakes region today, including all of

southwestern Ontario. Bond Lake, north of Toronto, was left by a single block of melting ice.

The most spectacular monument to the action of the ice is the Great Lakes. All four glacial advances played a part in producing them, each gouging the basins deeper until the earth's largest bodies of fresh water were formed. Niagara Falls was born as receding glaciers revealed a channel between Lakes Erie and Ontario. Erosion will eventually reduce the falls to low cataracts.

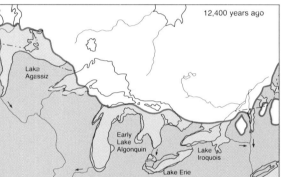

About 12,400 years ago, the ancestral Great Lakes discharged to the south—down the Illinois River to the Mississippi.

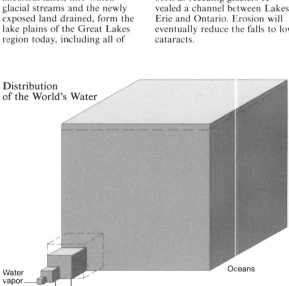

210 Maximum height of post-glacial rebound (in metres above present sea level)

Distribution of the World's Water

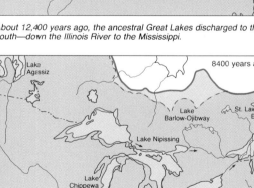

Water vapor
Fresh water
Ice
Oceans

Pleistocene

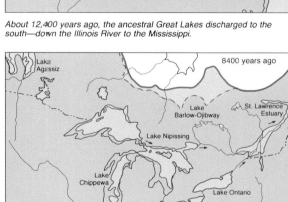

By 8400 years ago, drainage patterns had changed and the lakes discharged to the sea via the St. Lawrence Estuary.

Anatomy of a River of Ice

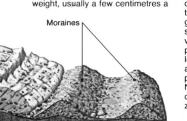

Snow crystals

Firn (granular snow)

Glacier ice

A glacier is a mass of permanent land ice that sometimes moves. Fresh snow feeds a glacier, but only snow that survives from winter to winter is transformed into granular *firn*. After many years, pressure changes the snow crystals into glacier ice. This mass begins to flow under the pressure of its own weight, usually a few centimetres a

day, but sometimes "galloping" at 10 to 100 times its normal rate. Above its firn line, which advances and retreats in response to climate, the glacier grows. Below, it wastes away as new snow evaporates or tumbles down in avalanches. The upper surface, rent with crevasses, flows slightly faster than the lower portion, which grinds against the land. Rockslides pile rubble on the advancing glacier; beneath, pieces of bedrock are plucked, locked in the ice and dragged along. Gradually, the debris is plowed forward into moraines. Near the glacier's rubble-choked snout is the ablation zone, or area of melting.

Firn line
Accumulating snow
Crevasses
Shear fracture
Evaporation
Moraines

What Makes Us Cold—or Warm

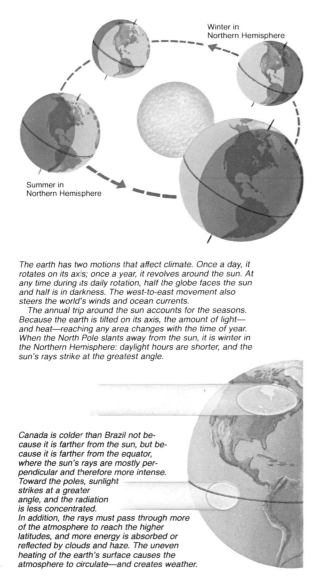

The earth has two motions that affect climate. Once a day, it rotates on its axis; once a year, it revolves around the sun. At any time during its daily rotation, half the globe faces the sun and half is in darkness. The west-to-east movement also steers the world's winds and ocean currents.

The annual trip around the sun accounts for the seasons. Because the earth is tilted on its axis, the amount of light—and heat—reaching any area changes with the time of year. When the North Pole slants away from the sun, it is winter in the Northern Hemisphere: daylight hours are shorter, and the sun's rays strike at the greatest angle.

Canada is colder than Brazil not because it is farther from the sun, but because it is farther from the equator, where the sun's rays are mostly perpendicular and therefore more intense. Toward the poles, sunlight strikes at a greater angle, and the radiation is less concentrated.

In addition, the rays must pass through more of the atmosphere to reach the higher latitudes, and more energy is absorbed or reflected by clouds and haze. The uneven heating of the earth's surface causes the atmosphere to circulate—and creates weather.

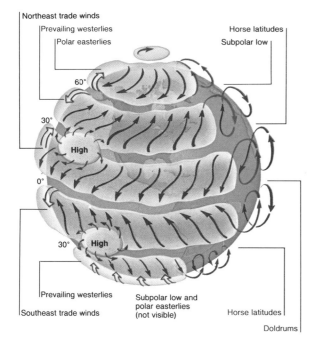

Great Rivers of Air

The earth's average temperature is a mild 14°C, but actual temperatures vary widely: flowers bloom all winter in Victoria, but the sun barely shines in Inuvik.

Canada loses more heat to space each year than it receives from the sun. Despite this loss, the weather does not get colder and colder each year because the circulation of the atmosphere constantly redistributes heat.

Hot air in the tropics expands and rises, creating a low-pressure area around the equator (the hot, humid doldrums). Heavier, cooler air from high-pressure areas to the north and south sweeps in toward the equator, producing the steady, gentle trade winds.

Warm equatorial air cools as it flows toward the poles.

Around latitude 30° N and S it begins to sink to earth, creating belts of alternating calm air and weak breezes called the horse latitudes. Here, centered over the oceans, are large "cells" of high pressure where air spirals outward. On the eastern side of the cells the air flows toward the equator; on the western side it flows poleward, joining the changeable westerlies.

Heavy, frigid polar air flows toward the equator. Areas where polar easterlies and prevailing westerlies clash—the subpolar lows—are among the stormiest on earth.

The earth's spin deflects the movement of all air currents—in the Northern Hemisphere to the east, and in the Southern Hemisphere to the west.

Climate affects every aspect of life in Canada. Fogs shrouding the coast of Newfoundland often disrupt fishing and shipping for days. Toronto can be a steam bath in July, a deep freeze in January. Heavy rainfalls produce lush forests that supply jobs in logging for more than a fifth of British Columbia's work force.

The Canadian climate—its sun and rain, blistering heat and bone-chilling cold—is a combination of the four main factors that determine global climate: the sun, the earth's position in space, the earth's atmosphere and its landforms.

The sun is one natural resource man will never exhaust. In five billion years this thermonuclear furnace will still radiate as much energy as it does today. Most of the radiation disappears into space, but the amount reaching this planet—about one two-billionth—provides more energy in a minute than all mankind uses in a year. The earth itself influences the climate by its orbit, its tilt and its daily rotation. These determine how much sunlight—and heat—the earth receives, and where.

The Atmospheric Engine

Although solar rays travel 150 million kilometres to reach the earth, barely half penetrate the protective blanket that surrounds the planet. Averaged worldwide, the atmosphere's ozone, water vapor and dust absorb about 17 percent of the sun's rays (1), including most of the lethal ultraviolet rays. Approximately 32 percent of the rays are returned unused to space. Some are scattered by dust (2), but most bounce off the upper surface of clouds (3). The earth's surface reflects an average two percent of the sun's rays (4), but actual amounts vary with ground cover. A dense forest soaks up almost all the sunlight that reaches it; fresh snow may reflect 90 percent.

About 19 percent of the sun's direct rays are finally absorbed by the earth (5). A further 28 percent reach the ground as diffused light, filtered through clouds (6) or dust (7).

Once absorbed, the sun's rays are converted to heat, which warms the earth and is radiated into the atmosphere. Some heat energy escapes into space (8), but most is captured by water vapor and carbon dioxide (9), then reradiated back to earth (10).

The atmosphere plays a crucial role in regulating climate. Heat is distributed unequally about the earth, and the atmosphere's attempt to redistribute it, through massive movements of air, results in the daily phenomenon called weather. (While weather constantly changes—all too unpredictably—climate is dependable, the average pattern of weather observed over many years.) The atmosphere's thin veil shuttles water vapor about the globe, and insulates the earth from the cold of space and the scorching rays of the sun.

One final factor influences climate: the earth's mountains, plains, lakes and oceans. Canada's vast size and varied landscape result in weather that swings from one extreme to another. One summer day is warm and breezy, the next oppressively hot and humid. In a few hours, winter's blue skies and crisp, clean air can give way to bitter cold and howling winds. But just when the weather makes Canada seem uninhabitable, it turns delightful again. This is the climate Canadians endure—and appreciate.

Meanwhile, winds (11) and ocean currents (12) redistribute the sun's warmth.

About a third of the heat is lifted into the atmosphere (13), either by air currents or by evaporation (see Water's Endless Cycle, opposite page).

Eventually, every ray of sunlight the earth receives is radiated back into space (14). But before this energy leaves the atmosphere, it has changed from light to heat to motion—the winds and water currents.

Radiation from the sun

Radiation from the earth

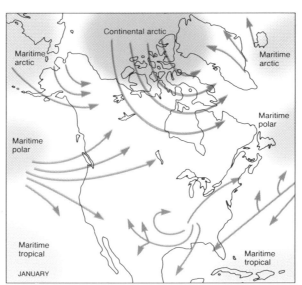

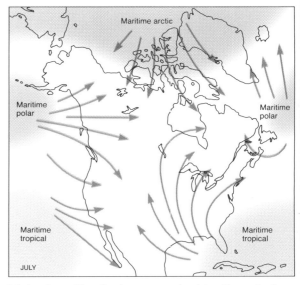

Winds carry great bodies of air across land and sea. Each air mass has uniform temperature and moisture throughout, taking these characteristics from the area over which it forms: usually a vast landmass or an ocean. In the maps above, colored areas show the sources of air masses that affect Canada; arrows indicate their most frequent direction of flow.

Winter winds transport continental arctic air masses to much of Canada, bringing clear, cold weather. In summer, cool, moist maritime arctic air sweeps down to provide relief from heat waves. Mild, humid maritime polar air delivers rain and snow to the Rocky Mountains, occasional fog and cloud to the East Coast. Maritime tropical air from the Pacific seldom reaches Canada, but to the east, warm, humid air masses from the Gulf of Mexico sometimes bring snowstorms in January and hot, muggy weather in July.

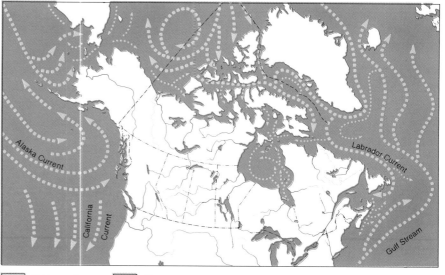

JANUARY:
Average daily temperature (°C)

−35 −25 −15 −5 0

Drastic temperature changes mark Canada's seasons. The interior has a continental climate—colder than coastal regions in winter, warmer in summer. Only southwestern British Columbia is temperate—temperatures here rarely fall below freezing.

JULY:
Average daily temperature (°C)

5 10 15 20

The Rockies protect the West Coast from the Arctic's chilly blasts, but they also funnel cold northern air toward the south and east, making Prairie winters long and bitterly cold. Snow cover sends temperatures lower by reflecting great amounts of sunshine. For their latitudes, southern Ontario and Quebec rank among the earth's coldest places. Even so, cactuses grow on Canada's southernmost tip, Point Pelee in Ontario.

Canada's coldest spot is Ellesmere Island, near the North Pole, where the January temperature averages −37.5°C.

Cold currents   Warm currents

The Weather-Making Oceans

Water heats up more slowly than land but retains its warmth longer. Thus oceans can absorb heat in tropical zones and transfer it, by means of ocean currents, to cooler lands.

Both wind and the earth's rotation push much of ocean currents on their global journeys. The earth's spin causes the currents to move in great circular eddies.

The Alaska Current tempers the climate of British Columbia and Alaska. Huge masses of warm water bring mild winters unusual for such high latitudes.

The climate in the Atlantic Provinces is harsher than that of the West Coast, since prevailing winds blow much of the mild maritime air out to sea. The Labrador Current brings frigid Arctic water—and icebergs—past Baffin Island to Labrador and Newfoundland. Off the Grand Banks, the current collides with the warm Gulf Stream and fog results.

Smaller bodies of water also affect climate. The Great Lakes and Hudson Bay moderate winter temperatures in adjacent areas by warming the air. But additional moisture due to evaporation is transported to land, and heavy snowfalls result.

Water's Endless Cycle

The amount of water on earth is approximately 1.36 billion cubic kilometres. Water in ice caps and glaciers may remain frozen for centuries, but the rest of the world's supply, in oceans, lakes, rivers and the atmosphere, is constantly recycled.

The water cycle transforms salt water (97 percent of the earth's water) into fresh. Water evaporates from the oceans, and the circulation of the atmosphere sweeps moist air over land. There the water vapor condenses and falls as rain or snow.

Some precipitation evaporates while falling; some is caught by vegetation and held until it evaporates. Water in the soil either evaporates or is taken in by plants, which transfer it to the air (transpiration).

As runoff, some water joins streams and rivers; some seeps down to become groundwater. Both eventually drain to the sea.

Water vapor helps redistribute the sun's warmth. Tropical heat causes much evaporation. The resulting water vapor, transported poleward, carries with it heat. As it cools and condenses, great quantities of heat are released.

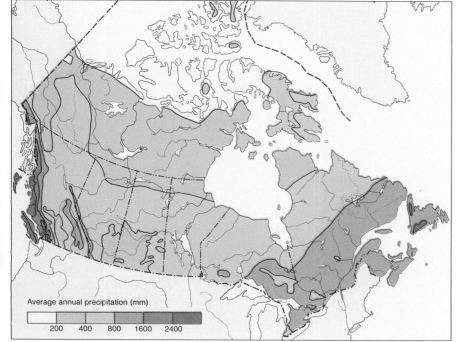

Average annual precipitation (mm)

200 400 800 1600 2400

Patterns of Rain and Snow

Canada's heaviest precipitation falls on the Pacific and Atlantic coasts. (Figures for precipitation—rain and snow—are the sum of total rainfall plus one-tenth the depth of freshly fallen snow.) Parts of British Columbia receive more than 3200 millimetres a year. The mountains here wring so much moisture from the air that on their leeward sides, in the rain shadow, luxuriant forests give way to sagebrush and cactus.

The rain shadow effect also produces occasional droughts on the Prairies. However, this region's heaviest rainfall usually comes in May and June, when wheat needs it most.

Most precipitation in the Arctic—Canada's driest area—falls in summer showers. Winter snowfall is surprisingly light.

Moist air from exotic climes—the Gulf of Mexico and Caribbean Sea—causes abundant rain and snow to fall on most of eastern Canada.

The Ingredients of Precipitation

Precipitation occurs when moist air is lifted and cooled, causing water vapor to condense and fall. Three common conditions produce precipitation over land. The first is brought about by the earth's landforms. Here (above) a moisture-laden wind encounters a mountain and is forced upward. The air cools as it rises, and precipitation results. On the lee side of slopes, the air descends, warms and is able to hold more water. This often brings a dramatic reduction in rainfall—the rain shadow effect.

Second, a layer of cold air can trigger precipitation. Since cold air is denser than warm, it remains close to the ground. Warm air colliding with it is pushed upward and rain occurs where the two air masses meet.

Uneven heating of the ground often causes air to rise spontaneously—a third cause of precipitation. The sun warms a field, for instance, more quickly than it does a forest. A balloon of hot air begins to rise, cooling as it ascends. Condensation then releases heat, which sends the balloon even higher, until cold air causes moisture to fall as rain.

The Zigs and Zags of Our Weather

Weather lore has been passed from generation to generation through stories and proverbs, some less reliable than others. No one would really pack his winter coat away if the groundhog missed its shadow on February 2, or buy more heating oil according to the layers of an onion. But often there is more than a grain of truth in weather lore, legend and litany. It is true, for example, that "the moon with a circle brings water in her beak." High cirrus clouds—which can form a halo around the moon or sun when ice crystals scatter light—are usually forerunners of rain or storm.

Scientific forecasting started to replace folklore in the 19th century. A network of stations across Canada began to issue storm warnings in the 1870s. When widespread telegraph lines made distributing information easier, forecasts were printed in morning newspapers. Ship's captains and, later, airplane pilots especially needed reliable weather reports.

Computers, their memory banks loaded with data from around the world, now help predict the weather. Satellites send pictures of cloud formations from vantage points in space. But science has not made us masters of the weather. Farmers still plant, irrigate and harvest according to reports of rainfall, drought and frost. Construction workers stop pouring concrete when the temperature dips below freezing. Even the baseball manager's choice of a pitcher is influenced by weather: curveballs are more easily thrown when air pressure is high; low pressure is better for fastballs. Unable to control the weather, neither can man predict it with much certainty. Although he can be reasonably sure of tomorrow's weather, long-range forecasts—even a week ahead—are still beyond man's grasp.

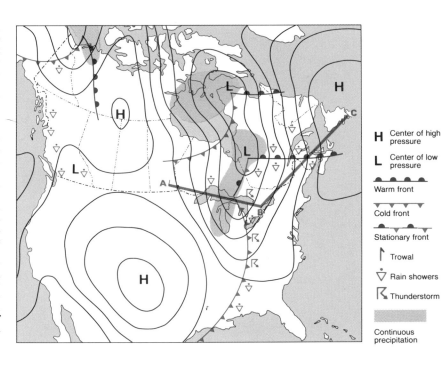

H	Center of high pressure
L	Center of low pressure

Warm front

Cold front

Stationary front

Trowal

Rain showers

Thunderstorm

Continuous precipitation

Fair Weather or Foul? Reading a Weather Map

At least four times a day, more than 250 observers across Canada record atmospheric pressure, cloud cover, winds, precipitation, temperature and humidity: information used to compile a weather map, and to make the next day's forecast.

Differences in the weather are the result of different air masses. Generally, cold air sweeps down from the north, warm air moves up from the south; moist air comes from the ocean, dry air from the land. Most weather changes occur along the fronts where two air masses collide. Cold air is heavy; where it meets warm air, it nudges—or shoves—the warm air aloft. Clouds that appear when rising air cools and condenses may produce rain, snow or thunderstorms.

A weather map's curving black lines, called isobars, link all points of equal pressure, the

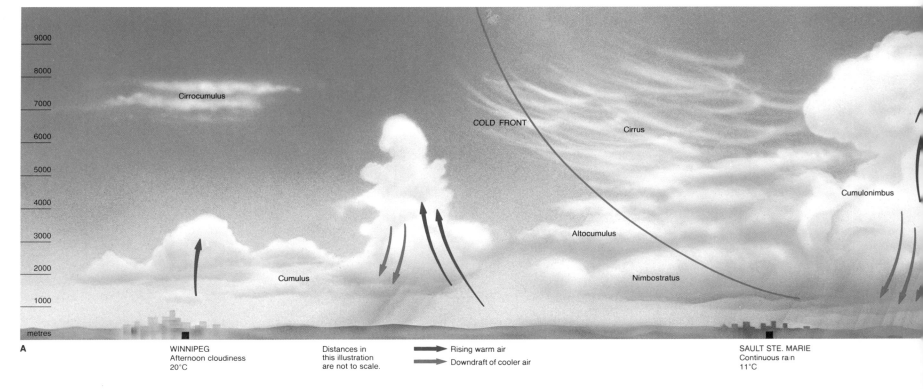

A

WINNIPEG
Afternoon cloudiness
20°C

Distances in this illustration are not to scale.

→ Rising warm air
→ Downdraft of cooler air

SAULT STE. MARIE
Continuous rain
11°C

Days of Warmth and Sunshine

Canadians must cope with cold and snow, sealing homes against chilly blasts and venturing out in heavy clothes. Despite a love for winter sports, most Canadians welcome the warmth and sunny skies of summer.

Temperature is a good indicator of vacation weather: in high summer, that period when the daily maximum is above 18°C, swimming and other outdoor recreations are popular. The map of annual hours of bright sunshine shows Canada's sunniest spots. July is the sunniest month for most of Canada.

In coastal British Columbia, a long, mild summer with gentle breezes brings ideal boating weather to the Strait of Georgia. But farther north is Canada's cloudiest city, Prince Rupert, where the sun shines an average 120 hours in July—and 24 hours in December.

The Prairies have long, hot summers. Canada's highest temperature ever was recorded here in 1937: 45°C at both Midale and Yellow Grass, Sask.

Uncomfortable, humid heat occurs mostly in the large cities of the East. Ideal cottage country is found around the Great Lakes and the thousands of smaller lakes in southern Ontario and Quebec. Summers here are usually warmer than anywhere else in Canada.

In the Atlantic provinces, warm days are fewer due to the icy Labrador Current, and skies are dimmed by fogs that roll in off the ocean. Parts of northern Canada have no high summer at all: despite 24-hour sunshine, cold northern seas and permafrost keep the summer months chilly.

Days of Rain and Storm

Rain revives parched gardens, but spoils picnics and sometimes washes topsoil away. When rainstorm turns into thunderstorm, nature can be truly destructive. Lightning sparks forest fires that destroy half a million hectares of trees in Canada each year; deluging rains, combined with snowmelt, can cause peaceful waterways such as the St. John and Red rivers to flood thousands of homes.

Most thunderstorms occur in summer, triggered by heat that causes moist, unstable air to rise. Rainy periods vary throughout Canada. The Pacific Coast has pronounced wet and dry seasons. During sodden Vancouver winters, rain falls a third of the time, and the ground is seldom dry.

Thunderstorms are rare on the West Coast, but frequent during hot Prairie summers. Those with hail are so common in Alberta

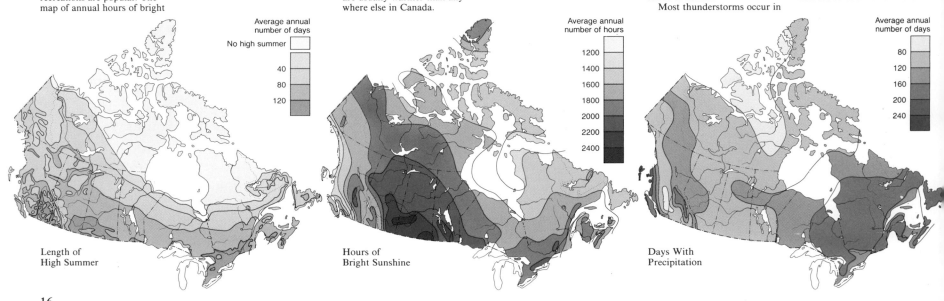

Average annual number of days

No high summer

40

80

120

Length of High Summer

Average annual number of hours

1200
1400
1600
1800
2000
2200
2400

Hours of Bright Sunshine

Average annual number of days

80
120
160
200
240

Days With Precipitation

same way lines on a contour map join points of equal elevation. Winds blow along the isobars. The closer the lines, the stronger the winds.

The arrival of a high-pressure region generally means sunny weather. Low-pressure areas, or depressions, bring unstable, rising air currents that cause rain and snow. Much of Canada's unsettled weather is brought by vast depressions advancing from west to east.

The map at left describes the weather on an actual day in June; the illustration below depicts that weather between Winnipeg and St. John's.

A weak low-pressure area lies over the West Coast—"weak" because a lack of isobars indicates that pressure is almost uniform throughout. Skies are clear over all three Prairie provinces—weather usually associated with a high. Cumulus clouds over Winnipeg are caused by afternoon heat and warm air billowing upward.

Much of Ontario and Quebec

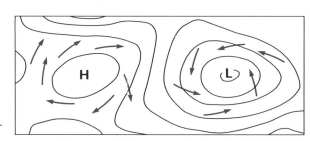

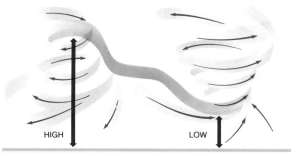

Low-pressure areas are also called cyclones — not tropical storms, but depressions that bring changeable weather. Winds whirl around a pressure system; in the Northern Hemisphere, they spiral counterclockwise toward the center of a cyclone. An anticyclone is a high-pressure system where winds whirl outward in a clockwise direction.

HIGH   LOW

is experiencing bad weather from a large trough of low pressure. Two centers can be seen; a third is forming over Sault Ste. Marie. A thunderstorm rages in this area, where warm and cold air masses meet. Air shoots upward, then is dragged downwind to form an anvil-shaped thunderhead on the ominous cumulonimbus clouds. Behind the thunderstorm, the air is cold and a continuous rain falls from low, gray nimbostratus clouds. Farther west, altocumulus and cirrus clouds dim the sky.

Cloud formations could act as a storm warning to observant Montrealers, now enjoying warm, humid weather with mostly clear skies. Wispy cirrus clouds mean increasing moisture aloft, and signal possible rain. Most of the Maritimes is experiencing intermittent showers associated with a warm front. Altocumulus clouds threaten to bring showers to Charlottetown, while St. John's, under the influence of a high-pressure area, has sunny skies.

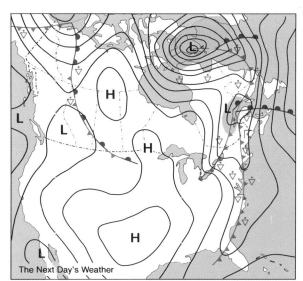

The Next Day's Weather

Weather in Canada never stays the same for long. In 24 hours the high over the Prairies has shifted east, bringing clear weather to Ontario. A new low-pressure center has formed over Sault Ste. Marie, and merged with the center farther north; this system is now causing rain over northern Quebec. A trowal—"trough of warm air aloft"—in the deep low over Baffin Island is also producing precipitation.

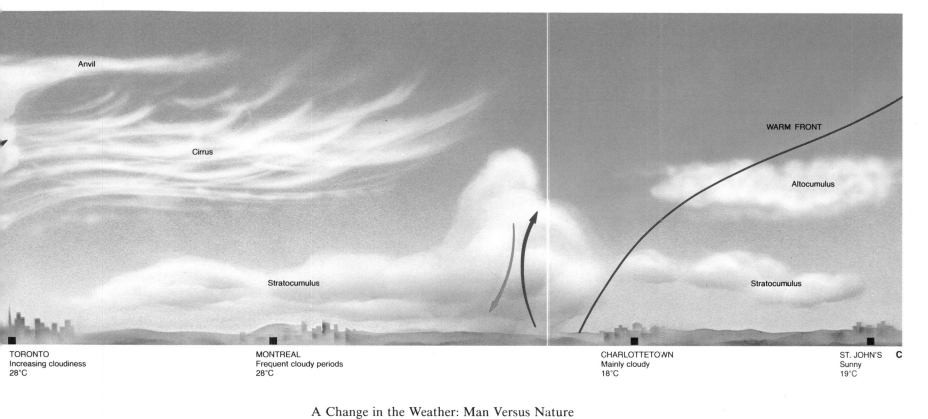

Anvil

Cirrus

Stratocumulus

WARM FRONT

Altocumulus

Stratocumulus

TORONTO
Increasing cloudiness
28°C

MONTREAL
Frequent cloudy periods
28°C

CHARLOTTETOWN
Mainly cloudy
18°C

ST. JOHN'S
Sunny
19°C C

A Change in the Weather: Man Versus Nature

that the area between Calgary and Edmonton is called "hailstone alley." Tornadoes also occur: 60 to 100 are reported each year, most in the Prairies and southern Ontario. Hurricanes cause occasional damage, but few reach Canada with their destructive power intact.

Winters are dry on the Prairies, but in southern Ontario and Quebec both long dry and long wet spells are rare. Southwestern Ontario has the most thunder

and lightning: more than 30 days a year.

Though rainfall increases toward the east, the number of thunderstorms drops. Remnants of hurricanes may travel up the Atlantic coast, but Newfoundland averages only two to six thunderstorms a year.

The Arctic has the fewest days of rain; in some areas, thunderstorms have never been recorded. Here dryness and low temperatures keep air stable.

Man has always longed to change the weather. In early days he modified his environment by huddling around fires and making clothes to keep warm. Modern man, having learned how to predict at least short-term weather, now seeks ways to change it.

Besides devising such creature comforts as central heating and air conditioning, man is also trying to modify weather for the benefit of agriculture. He plants rows of trees to shield crops from wind, or sets out smudges when frost threatens his orchards. The most ambitious venture is rainmaking: injecting silver iodide into clouds to provide nuclei for raindrops. But its success is still hard to measure. In Alberta, where hailstorms destroy crops every year, meteorologists are studying the use of cloud seeding to suppress hail. The technique may also modify thunderstorms.

Scientists conceive of long-range plans to change the earth's climate permanently. But even if their plans could be carried out, the consequences must first be predicted. Weather is the result of subtle interactions of oceans, atmosphere, landforms and living creatures. A change in one element would surely change the whole.

Upside-Down Air Causes Urban Pollution

Winds usually disperse polluted air. But when cool air is trapped near the ground by a layer of warm air—a phenomenon known as temperature inversion—pollutants can accumulate. Toronto often suffers from smog while windier cities on the Prairies enjoy cleaner air.

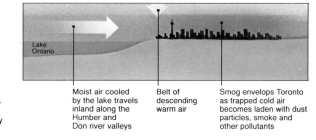

Lake Ontario

Moist air cooled by the lake travels inland along the Humber and Don river valleys

Belt of descending warm air

Smog envelops Toronto as trapped cold air becomes laden with dust particles, smoke and other pollutants

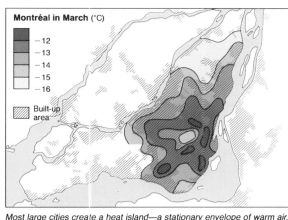

Montréal in March (°C)

-12
-13
-14
-15
-16

Built-up area

Most large cities create a heat island—a stationary envelope of warm air. Heat escapes from buildings, is released by car exhausts and spewed out of factories. Bricks and concrete retain warmth longer than trees and soil; Mount Royal Park (above) remains a cool basin.

Man's greatest influence on the weather is unintentional. Polluted air reflects the sun's rays and cools the earth. Acid rains, carrying chemicals emitted by industrial plants, are harming forests and crops, and destroying aquatic life in thousands of lakes. Burning fossil fuels release carbon dioxide, causing the atmosphere to trap more heat radiated from the earth, and raising temperatures.

Long-term weather changes are still impossible to predict. Perhaps cooling caused by air pollution and heating caused by carbon dioxide will cancel each other out. A temperature increase of only a few degrees could melt polar ice caps and cause wide-scale flooding. But colder temperatures could devastate Canadian crops.

Average annual number of days

1
5
10
15
20
25
30
35

Days With
Thunderstorms

Living With Snow

"A few acres of snow" is how Voltaire described Canada. Summer always comes, but for many months snow does predominate, influencing our economy, recreation and culture. From back-breaking work with a shovel to the sophisticated equipment that keeps airport runways clear, countless dollars and hours of effort are spent in overcoming snow. Millions of dollars more are spent enjoying snow: on snowmobiles, ski vacations and the latest in winter fashions.

Despite the quantities of snow Canadians must deal with, few people know much about it. Most know what kind of snow is good for snowballs or skiing, but the English language, born in a moderate climate, has no way to express it.

The Inuit, whose lives are linked with snow, have a more intimate knowledge of it. To them, the snow that collects on trees is *qali*; snow on the ground, *api*; and dense, wind-packed snow, *upsik*. *Tumarínyiq* is their word for ripple marks sculpted by the wind. They know how snow varies in texture from place to place, and use this knowledge to survive. For centuries the Inuit have fashioned sleds and snowshoes to travel over snow, and cut blocks of it to build winter houses.

Though most southern Canadians don't think of snow as useful, like the Inuit they would find life difficult without it. Farmers appreciate the insulating value of snow, which limits frost penetration. Snow also acts as a natural fertilizer, spreading nourishing minerals over the soil. Pulp and paper companies make use of snow in the North to build thousands of kilometres of snow roads each winter. Some northern communities, isolated in summer, are easily accessible by snowmobile in winter. In spring, the melting of snowfields irrigates farms and replenishes town and city reservoirs. Animals use snow for its insulating qualities: many make their winter homes in snug burrows beneath its surface. And some creatures enjoy snow for its own sake. Bears and otters delight in snowslides; mink and weasels leap in and out of snowbanks like dolphins in water.

Snow transforms drab, leafless landscapes into scenes of still and silent beauty. Seldom is it white: it glitters on a cold, bright day, lies dull gray under overcast skies or urban grime, or deep purple in a shadowed drift. Snow is always changing, from a light shawl of delicate flakes to a mass of icy pellets. Each spring it melts; just as inevitably, it falls again next winter.

World Snow Cover

- Permanent snow and ice
- Stable snow cover forms every year
- 8 — Duration of snow cover, in months
- Unstable snow cover forms most years
- No snow cover

A snowfall map is never exact, since snow is difficult to measure. It drifts and blows, or melts as it hits the ground. Annual snowfalls in any one location vary widely: more snow may fall in one day than fell in the entire previous winter. An area southeast of Kitimat has the highest snowfalls: an average 1071 centimetres a year. Far to the north, on Ellesmere Island, Eureka averages only 38 centimetres of snow a year—but it falls year round.

Average annual snowfall (cm)

80 160 280 400

Blizzards, Chinooks and an Arctic Semidesert

Canada's highest and lowest snowfalls occur in British Columbia. Parts of Vancouver Island's mild west coast often receive less than 30 centimetres of snow a year, and rain soon clears the ground. Entire winters may pass without snow cover.

But when moist air from the Pacific Ocean is forced up by coastal and interior mountain ranges, record snowfalls result. Near Revelstoke, 2446 centimetres of snow fell during the winter of 1971-72.

Glaciers grow from snow that accumulates from one year to the next. Many form in Canada's loftiest range, the St. Elias Mountains of northwestern British Columbia and the Yukon, where snowfields lie year round.

Snowfall on the Prairies is

comparatively light, but blizzards—with bitter cold, high winds and driving snow—are common. Southwestern Alberta is often released dramatically from winter's grip by the wind known as a chinook (also called a "snow eater"). Warm, dry air descending from the Rockies can suddenly raise temperatures 20 degrees.

The Great Lakes trigger heavy snowfalls. Moisture evaporating from these vast bodies of water rises, condenses over the cold terrain, and deposits a belt of deep snow downwind. But southernmost Ontario has a low annual snowfall: mild temperatures often bring rain instead of snow.

Both southern Ontario and Quebec lie in the path of most major winter storms crossing

Average annual snowfall (cm)

400
300
200
100
0

52.4 — Vancouver
119.4 — Yellowknife
131.1 — Edmonton
114.8 — Regina
131.3 — Winnipeg

Measurements of snow cover help provide snow-load estimates for builders, and also help predict spring runoff. The yearly flow, vital to power plants, farms and reservoirs, is less welcome when it causes rivers to flood fields and houses. Each spring, melting of the deep snowpack that accumulates on British Columbia mountain slopes—as much as six metres—turns great rivers such as the Fraser and Skeena into raging torrents.

Average maximum depth of snow (cm)

50 100 160

Most Canadian cities must wage campaigns against snow each winter. Fredericton snow is often heavy and wet, Québec plows must negotiate steep, narrow streets; in Saskatoon light snow is blown into hard, packed drifts. Montréal spends more than $33 million to clear almost 1700 kilometres of streets, while Vancouver spends an average $400,000 on 1400 kilometres.

The heavy work is done in a long procession: plows and graders scrape the snow into windrows; a blower scoops it up and discharges it into trucks, which haul the snow away to dumps or sewers. Despite this army of machines, few winters pass without one blizzard that strands airline passengers, jams traffic and brings unscheduled school holidays.

Salting the roads eases winter transportation in some cities, but creates other problems. Salt can harm plants and trees and contaminate water supplies; it also causes millions of dollars worth of damage by corroding vehicles.

This map shows the length of time the depth of snow is 2.5 centimetres or more. It matters to many: skiers, farmers, those who use snow roads in the North. The snow season's onset varies from the end of August in the Queen Elizabeth Islands to the end of December on the coasts of British Columbia, Nova Scotia and Newfoundland. Snow in the Arctic may linger until June, further delaying the coming of summer by reflecting much of the sun's radiation.

Length of snow cover season (average annual number of days)

80 120 160 200 240 280

Winter's Many Faces, Delightful and Destructive

Canadian winters shape Canadian living. Car owners spend millions each year on snow tires, antifreeze and repairs to salt-rusted vehicles. One Canadian, determined to overcome snow, invented the snowmobile: a tracked power toboggan that cruises over snowbanks. Canadians also pioneered development of snowplows, making winter highway and rail travel possible.

Canadian architects design for a northern climate. A structure's exterior walls must be insulated against bitter cold, its roof solid enough to withstand heavy snow loads.

To aid construction, the Canadian building code provides estimates of snow loads across the country. Climatic records are used to determine the most likely maximum depth of snow. The weight of this much snow is calculated, using an average density, and to this is added the weight of any rain the snow might absorb—a particular hazard in spring.

Certain structures create snowdrifts. Porches or balconies

beside higher roofs can collapse from collected snow. Poor design of large buildings may produce winds that deposit snow in towering piles that obstruct walks and entrances. Snow fences are sometimes used to collect snow before it reaches traveled areas, but barriers placed too close to a road can make drifting worse.

Engineers in Canada are studying snowdrift patterns. They build scale models of buildings, then simulate drifting with fine white sand carried by water as wind would carry snow. Their tests solve problems with existing buildings and help design new structures better suited to Canadian winters.

Snow load in a sheltered area

Wind

Snowdrift on a porch roof

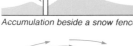
Accumulation beside a snow fence

Accumulation between barriers

Snowdrifts can form wherever wind speed drops. Above, an obstacle such as a wall or building disrupts the wind flow, causing turbulence on its leeward side. Here downdrafts produce snow accumulation.

Fragile Works of Art in Ice

Snow crystals form when water vapor in the atmosphere freezes around microscopic particles such as dust or salt. Like human fingerprints, no two crystals are alike. Most are hexagonal, but few are perfectly symmetrical.

In cold, dry weather, snow crystals are usually small, simple plates or columns. Crystals formed in warmer, moister clouds sprout intricate branches. Hundreds may stick together to form huge, feathery snowflakes. Other crystals, battered by winds, land as ragged fragments.

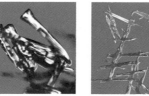
Hexagonal plates

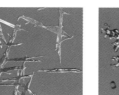

Stellar crystal

Hexagonal columns — *Needles* — *Spatial dendrite* — *Capped column* — *Irregular crystal*

North America. Eastern Canada's heaviest snowfall occurs north of the Gulf of St. Lawrence, where moist air is forced upward by steep slopes. Snow accumulates here because of constant low winter temperatures; in parts of central Quebec and Labrador snow may lie two metres deep by March.

Although snowfall is high in much of Atlantic Canada, the ocean's warming influence brings frequent mild spells to the coast, melting snow or causing precipitation to fall as rain.

The treeless tundra of the Northwest Territories actually has one of Canada's lowest snowfalls, and snow drifts so much that ground is often bare. Despite long, cold winters, the air in the semidesert Arctic Islands holds too little moisture to produce much snow.

[Bar chart values:] 239.6 — 326.7 — 280.4 — 299.9 — 305.0 — 363.8
[Cities:] Montréal — Québec — Fredericton — Halifax — Charlottetown — St. John's

Wildlife in Winter: Adapt, Migrate or Sleep

Winter is a hard season for most animals. Water is scarce; snow covers food caches and makes travel difficult. Many die of cold or starvation, or fall victim to hardier predators.

The snowshoe hare is designed for snow country. It skims over deep snow on wide, heavily furred feet, with a white winter coat for camouflage.

Moose are adapted to winter in another way: long, stilt-like legs permit them to wade through all but the deepest snowbanks. Deer usually spend winter months grouped together in yards—treed areas where snow is trampled down—where they browse on trees and shrubs. If severe weather confines them too long, many die of starvation.

Some animals cope with winter by hibernation, entering a sleeplike state in which their body temperatures drop, their heartbeat and breathing rates slow down, and their need for food is drastically reduced.

Other creatures survive winter by finding shelter in snow. Mice, shrews and voles dig snowy tunnels which hold their body heat and deflect harsh winter winds. In this damp, silent world the temperature remains just below freezing, no matter how frigid the air above.

Animals whose habits or anatomy cannot adapt to snow find a way to avoid winter altogether: each fall millions of birds and butterflies migrate to southern skies.

Moose

Cottontail rabbit

White-footed mouse — *Masked shrew* — *Meadow vole*

Snow cleared from the streets must be put somewhere else. Montréal, with more snow than any other large city in the world, has four ways to dispose of it. Some snow is dumped into the St. Lawrence River, some into sewers through special chutes. Huge loads are melted in pits by hot water from oil-fired burners, and the rest, piled in vacant lots, is left to the sun and rain. The last is the slowest method: outside Ottawa, such piles often linger until June, as dirt and debris slow down melting while valuable land goes unused. Salt and garbage in snow dumped into rivers can also cause environmental problems.

When blizzards sweep the Prairies, tales are told of pioneer farmers who perished midway between house and barn. Even today a traveler stranded in a blizzard may be in great danger.

But the greatest loss of life from snow is due to avalanches. In Canada, most occur in British Columbia's interior mountain ranges, where average snowfalls can exceed 900 centimetres. A single slide—carrying as much as 22,000 tonnes of snow—can strip a mountainside of trees.

Concrete snowsheds cover the Trans-Canada Highway at danger spots; earth dams and barriers of rubble divert small slides. At Rogers Pass, one of the world's worst avalanche zones, winter observers watch for dangerous buildups. Then an artillery crew fires howitzer shells into unstable snow to trigger a controlled avalanche.

Victims of a heavy snowslide once stood little chance of survival, but today many people who work or ski in avalanche-prone areas wear electronic beacons that will help searchers to locate them if buried.

The pleasures of the season: Striking out for the wilderness (above), a skier seeks the snowy solitude of winter. Right, riders glide along a lakeside trail. About one in eight Canadians owns a snowmobile.

Skiers keep a watchful eye on winter weather, lamenting warm, moist winds or light rainfall that covers slopes with a hard, unskiable crust. Heavy snowfalls and long winters make two areas in Canada ideal for alpine skiing: the high slopes of British Columbia and Alberta, and the rolling hills of Quebec's

Eastern Townships and Laurentian regions. Cross-country skiing can be enjoyed wherever snow lies several centimetres deep—almost anywhere in Canada in winter.

Man can modify ski conditions. When natural snowfall is insufficient, ski-area owners manufacture their own, spraying

a mixture of air and water over the slopes with special nozzles. Near Saskatoon, Mount Blackstrap, a 91-metre mountain, was man-made for the 1971 Canada Winter Games.

Canadians are said to spend more on skiing than on snow removal. Snowmobiling is another popular sport that consumes vast sums of money. Snowshoes are one less expensive way to explore the tranquil beauty of a

winter landscape. But however they do it, many Canadians find some way to make fun of snow.

Avalanche! Treacherous snow thunders down a slope in the Yukon's St. Elias Mountains. A slide may be set off by an earth tremor, falling cornice (overhanging drift) or skiers' weight.

Natural Regions: The Five/Far West

Canada's vast landscape contains natural "provinces" as distinctive as its political divisions: the coastal rain forest, interior plateau and towering mountains of the Western Cordillera; the patchwork grasslands; the evergreen arch of the boreal forest; the diverse mixed forest of the East; and the harsh, treeless tundra.

Occasionally, climate, soil and topography draw clear boundaries, as in southwestern Alberta where the high spine of the Rocky Mountains soars above the grasslands. More often, natural provinces blend together in transition zones called *ecotones*, which abound in plants and animals from adjoining regions.

Each province is composed of ecosystems—associations of plants and animals living in a relationship not only to each other, but also to the rocks and soil. Ecosystems may be as small as a Pacific tidal pool brimming with more than 40 species of plants and animals, or as vast as the boreal forest, dominated by a dozen types of trees throughout its 6000-kilometre span.

Each type of organism has a role essential to the entire community. Through photosynthesis, green plants transform water, oxygen, minerals and the sun's energy into living matter that provides food for animals. Herbivores (plant eaters) consume this vegetation and are, in turn, consumed by carnivores (meat eaters) in a sequence of eating and being eaten known as the food chain. Since most organisms consume more than one type of plant or animal, simple chains combine to form complex food webs. Even when an organism dies, it remains part of the community. Bacteria and other microorganisms decompose dead organic matter and return its minerals to the soil, where they again become available to plants.

Canada's natural regions began to assume their present character about 10,000 years ago when belts of flora, like fauna, shifted north in the wake of receding glaciers. Tundra vegetation colonized the Arctic barrens, while conifers covered the boreal forest and much of the Western Cordillera. Seeds of broad-leaved and evergreen trees were carried by wind and water from southern refuges to form eastern Canada's mixed forest. Grasses invaded the Prairies and thrived in clay soils—once the beds of glacial lakes.

The landscape was dominated by large mammals, most of which migrated from Asia across the Bering land bridge. Yet, within a few thousand years of the last glaciation, some 70 percent of this megafauna—the ground sloths, mammoths, mastodons, native camels and horses—had vanished. Most species could not adapt to climatic changes at the end of the Pleistocene. Man, another recent immigrant to North America, may have accelerated these extinctions by hunting large herbivores into oblivion, depriving carnivores of prey.

Man's impact is still being felt. Grasslands, where 60 million bison once thundered, are now checkered with farms and ranches. Man's imprint, in the form of oil rigs, pipelines and mines, has even scarred Canada's last frontier, the North. Parks and sanctuaries—only five percent of Canada's total area—preserve much of what remains of its primeval landscapes.

Legend:
- Western Cordillera
- Grasslands
- Boreal forest
- Mixed forest
- Tundra
- Transition zones

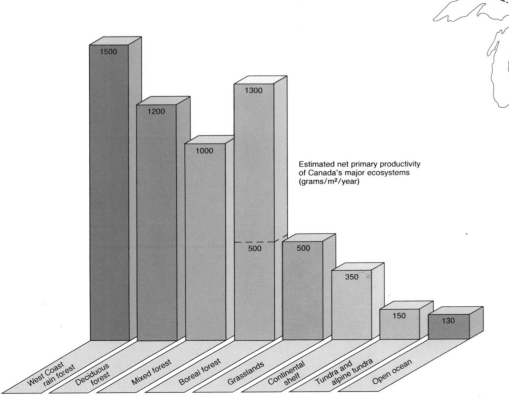

Estimated net primary productivity of Canada's major ecosystems (grams/m²/year)

West Coast rain forest · Deciduous forest · Mixed forest · Boreal forest · Grasslands · Continental shelf · Tundra and alpine tundra · Open ocean

(1500, 1200, 1000, 1300, 500, 500, 350, 150, 130)

Fertile Rain Forests, Arctic Barrens

All living things depend on the ability of plants to capture and convert light energy from the sun into biomass, or living matter. Canada's natural regions vary in productivity, due mainly to differences in climate and soil on land, and currents and light penetration in the ocean.

The graph (*left*) illustrates the amount of biomass, estimated in grams per square metre, produced annually by Canada's natural regions. Most of this biomass is plant tissue, less than one percent of which is converted into animal tissue by herbivores in the first link of a food chain. The rest dies and decays; its energy is lost to the environment as heat. Canada's most productive region, the humid coastal forest of the Western Cordillera, yields about ten times more biomass annually per square metre than the Arctic tundra. The boreal forest, Canada's largest natural region, varies in productivity from about 500 grams of biomass per square metre near the tundra to about 1300 grams in the coniferous forests of northeastern British Columbia and northwestern Alberta.

Oceans, which cover three quarters of the earth's surface, contribute only about a quarter of its biomass yield. Shallow, nutrient-rich continental shelves produce abundant sea life, but the deep, open ocean is as barren as a terrestrial desert. Pockets of productivity called fishing banks yield twice as much as other parts of the continental shelf and four times as much as the high seas. At the Grand Banks off Newfoundland, where the cold Labrador Current and the warm Gulf Stream mix, plankton upwells and nourishes schools of cod, herring, mackerel and haddock. Yet, only a few hundred kilometres southeast, the Atlantic yields less than the Arctic.

20

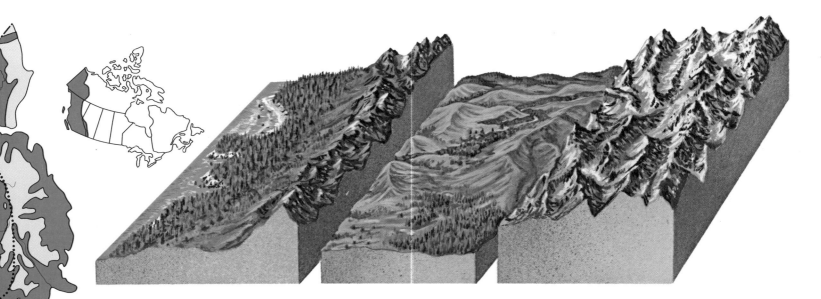

The Western Cordillera: Between Seashore and Summit

The Western Cordillera has Canada's wettest climate, highest mountains and densest forests. More species of plants and animals live here, in a greater diversity of habitats, than in any other part of the country. This land of superlatives comprises three regions: the Pacific Coast (*above, left*), the interior plateau (*above, center*) and the interior mountains (*above, right*).

Along the Pacific Coast, Canada's longest growing season and up to 3200 millimetres of precipitation nourish dense rain forests of Sitka spruce, western red cedar, western hemlock and majestic Douglas fir. Coast deer and Roosevelt elk, found nowhere else in Canada, prefer clearings and meadows to dark forests; their chief predators are the cougar, North America's counterpart to the African lion, and the wolf.

More than 300 species of fish and 20 kinds of marine mammals, including seals, whales and sea lions, are found in waters off the convoluted coastline. On seaside cliffs nest shorebird colonies: guillemots, murres, cormorants and storm petrels, whose six-day feeding flights may take them hundreds of kilometres out to sea.

In the dry "rain shadow" of the Coast Mountains lies an interior plateau creased by valleys and rumpled with low mountains. In semiarid southern valleys some 230 millimetres of annual precipitation support sagebrush, bitterroot and grasslands of rough fescue and blue grama, home to badgers and white-tailed jackrabbits.

Lakes in the plateau teem with rainbow trout; migratory salmon battle up their native rivers to spawn and die, or fall prey to grizzly bears and otters. North of Kamloops, blue Douglas fir predominates in rolling rangeland. Subalpine forests of Engelmann spruce, lodgepole pine and alpine fir grow as far north as the arid Stikine Plateau; beyond is the boreal forest of the Yukon highlands.

East of the interior plateau rise the Rockies and their associated ranges: the Columbias in southeastern B.C., and the Mackenzie, Richardson and British ranges north of the Liard River. To scale these peaks is to pass through different life zones. The average temperature drops 1.9°C with each 300 metres of altitude, a change that profoundly influences plant growth. Transitions in vegetation that normally occur over thousands of kilometres are compressed into a few thousand vertical metres.

Mountain caribou roam subalpine forests between 1800 and 2300 metres, also the haunt of grouse and golden eagles. Wapiti browse in flower-dotted meadows, along with hoary marmots and Columbian ground squirrels fattening up for hibernation on grasses, bulbs and seeds.

Above 2300 metres even the hardiest trees begin to thin out, the survivors twisting into stunted shapes. Beyond the tree line grow ground-hugging mosses, lichens and Arctic shrubs. Most alpine plants take 15 years to bloom; a clump of moss campion may be a century old.

Few animals live year round above the tree line, including only one kind of bird, the ptarmigan. Bighorn sheep descend in autumn to sheltered meadows; only fierce storms drive mountain goats from the summits.

Map legend

- Glaciers and ice fields
- Alpine tundra
- Boreal forest
- Coastal and interior "wet-belt" forest
- Coastal subalpine forest
- Interior subalpine forest
- Plateau-montane forest
- Grassland and parkland

1 Pacific Coast
2 Interior plateau
3 Interior mountains

Mountain goat

Bighorn sheep

Wapiti

Cougar

Grizzly bear

Golden eagle

White-tailed ptarmigan

Hoary marmot

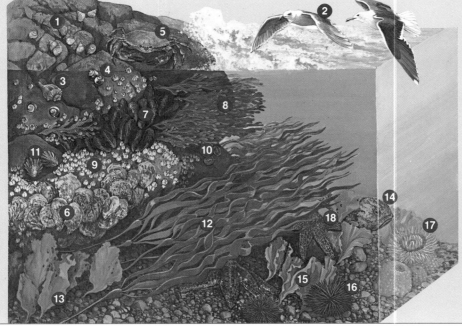

Turbulent Life Between the Tides

Where the sea meets the land, life is linked to the rise and fall of tides. Along the shore are three distinct habitats: the splash zone, high on the rocks; the intertidal zone, where tides ebb and flow twice daily; and the subtidal zone, usually covered with water.

Plants and animals in these turbulent realms have adapted to battering waves, exposure to air and submersion. Organisms anchored to rocks depend on the sea to bring water-borne food. Some creatures are active at low tide when their prey is exposed; others take refuge in shallow tide pools that seldom dry up.

Marine life on the West Coast, whose habitat is warmed by the Alaska Current, is more varied than in any other temperate waters. There are some 90 types of North Pacific starfish, but only about 20 varieties at similar latitudes in the Atlantic, which is chilled by the Labrador Current.

Splash Zone
Life here relies on spray for its seawater needs, and tough coverings to withstand lengthy exposure to air. The checkered periwinkle (1) obtains oxygen directly from the air; its young develop, complete with shell, inside the female's shell. This snail eats minute blue-green algae which it scrapes from rocks with an abrasive, tonguelike radula that is longer than the periwinkle's body. Glaucous gulls (2) patrol shores for dire whelks (3) and turban snails (4); gull eggs and shore crabs (5) often fall prey to minks. Black oyster catchers open the shells of mussels and oysters with a chisel-like bill.

Intertidal Zone
Resisting pounding surf is the key to survival here. Olympia oysters (6) cement themselves into dense colonies; females release 100 million eggs two or three times a year into the hostile sea, but few offspring survive. Sticky threads anchor California mussels (7) among rubbery fingers of bladder wrack (8). Acorn barnacles (9) spend three months as floating larvae, then attach their shells to rocks. Four plates atop the shell close to retain moisture when the tide is out; when submerged, the plates open and the barnacle sweeps in plankton with its feathery feet. The shell of the chiton (10) is composed of eight plates that allow the mollusk to curl into a protective ball. The chiton grazes over its base rock and, although sightless, always returns to the same spot before daylight; the limpet (11) has similar feeding habits.

Subtidal Zone
Broad-bladed ribbon kelp (12) sprout from rocks patched with sea lettuce (13); rootlike holdfasts anchor kelp, whose fronds stream in and out with the surf. Sculpins (14) lurk among the purple laver (15). Sea urchins (16), anchored with hundreds of sucker-tipped feet, swivel threatening spines to confront attackers. Tentacles of the green sea anemone (17)—in appearance more floral than animal—capture prey with poison-tipped stingers. A purple starfish (18) pries open shellfish with suction-cup feet, inserts its stomach and digests the prey within.

Natural Regions: Grasslands, Boreal Forest

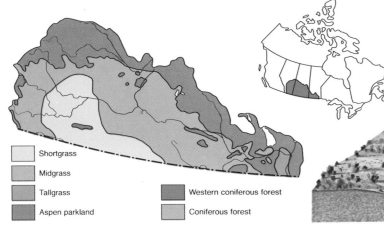

Shortgrass
Midgrass
Tallgrass
Aspen parkland
Western coniferous forest
Coniferous forest

The Patchwork Grasslands

Climate and soil define four grassland regions: shortgrass, midgrass and tallgrass prairie, and aspen parkland where plains yield to boreal forest.

The shortgrasses—mainly blue grama, wheatgrass and needle-grass—grow to half a metre in light-colored, often sandy soil with 250 millimetres of annual precipitation. Sagebrush, buckbrush and hay grass stabilize the semiarid Great Sand Hills of southwestern Saskatchewan.

In the midgrass prairie, 400 millimetres of precipitation and dark brown soil support more luxuriant, metre-high western wheatgrass, needle and thread, and little bluestem.

Tallgrasses up to 2.5 metres high once flourished in the rich, black topsoil of southern Manitoba. Patches of big bluestem and Indian grass still grow along roadsides and in river valleys.

Trembling aspen predominates in the parklands; Manitoba maple and bur oak are scattered throughout moist regions of eastern Saskatchewan and southwestern Manitoba. Silvery lupine, bunchberry and lodgepole pine—common in Rocky Mountain foothills—grow in the cool, moist Cypress Hills. Balsam fir and white spruce, usually found

in the boreal forest, carpet much of Manitoba's Riding Mountain.

Large animals of the grasslands survive on the margins of cultivated land, or like the bison, in parks and sanctuaries. Mule deer, pronghorn antelope and sharp-tailed grouse find refuge in badlands and sandhills. Burrowing rodents such as the ground squirrel are found throughout the region; their tunnel systems have several entrances as protection from badgers, weasels and coyotes.

Waterfowl offer the most spectacular wildlife displays. More than eight million potholes and sloughs provide breeding grounds for half of North America's ducks, geese, swans and pelicans.

Most grassland soil is chernozem (Russian for "black earth"). Its layers, or horizons, usually consist of a surface mat of humus; a layer of topsoil mixed with roots, dead plant matter and microorganisms; and a mineral horizon of lime particles.

The tallgrass prairie and aspen parkland have black, humus-rich soil laced with fibrous roots that absorb water and nutrients from moist clays in the subsoil.

Midgrass prairie soil is relatively shallow. The mineral horizon, mixed with clay, is within reach of metre-deep root systems.

Humus-poor sandy soil about a half-metre deep lies below the shortgrass prairie. The lime layer marks the depth to which rainwater and roots penetrate. Below, the subsoil is permanently dry.

Dry subsoil | Humus | Topsoil | Moist subsoil
Lime layer
SHORTGRASS | MIDGRASS | TALLGRASS

Coyote

Mule deer

Bison

Richardson's ground squirrel

Sharp-tailed grouse

Pelican

Pronghorn antelope

Mallard

Flexible, Durable Grass

More than 100 grass species carpet Canada. Typical features are shown in a single stylized plant (*right*).

Spikelets of grass flowers are exposed only once for pollination—usually for an hour—when temperature, humidity and sunlight trigger the opening of a protective capsule.

Hollow stems (culms) and solid joints (nodes) give grasses strength and flexibility. Leaves grow at the nodes; the sheath wraps around the stem and unfurls a narrow blade.

Root systems penetrate the soil to a depth of up to six metres. Tallgrasses usually reproduce by underground stems called rhizomes; short- and midgrasses propagate by surface runners called stolons.

Spikelet
Culm
Node
Sheath
Blade
Stolon
Rhizome
Roots

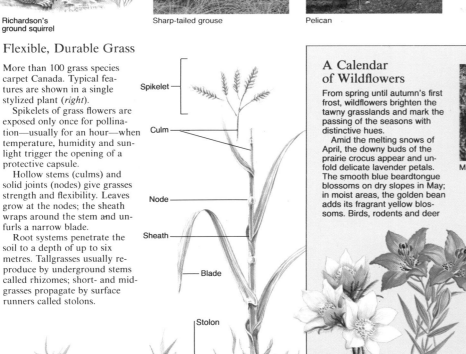

A Calendar of Wildflowers

From spring until autumn's first frost, wildflowers brighten the tawny grasslands and mark the passing of the seasons with distinctive hues.

Amid the melting snows of April, the downy buds of the prairie crocus appear and unfold delicate lavender petals. The smooth blue beardtongue blossoms on dry slopes in May; in moist areas, the golden bean adds its fragrant yellow blossoms. Birds, rodents and deer

feed on the seeds of the prairie sunflower, a two-metre-high annual that blooms in June.

By midsummer, eastern Prairie thickets are ablaze with wild bergamot. The western red lily highlights meadows and open woodlands with flame-red flowers. On foothill slopes, late summer brings gaillardia's distinctive flower head—a purplish disc surrounded by yellow petals.

The blazing star's dense

clusters of rose-purple flowers spike sandy hillsides from July to September. In early autumn many-flowered asters spangle the grasslands with white or pinkish blossoms that usually face the same direction.

Many-flowered aster

Wild bergamot

Blazing star

Prairie crocus

Western red lily

Gaillardia

Prairie sunflower

Golden bean

Smooth blue beardtongue

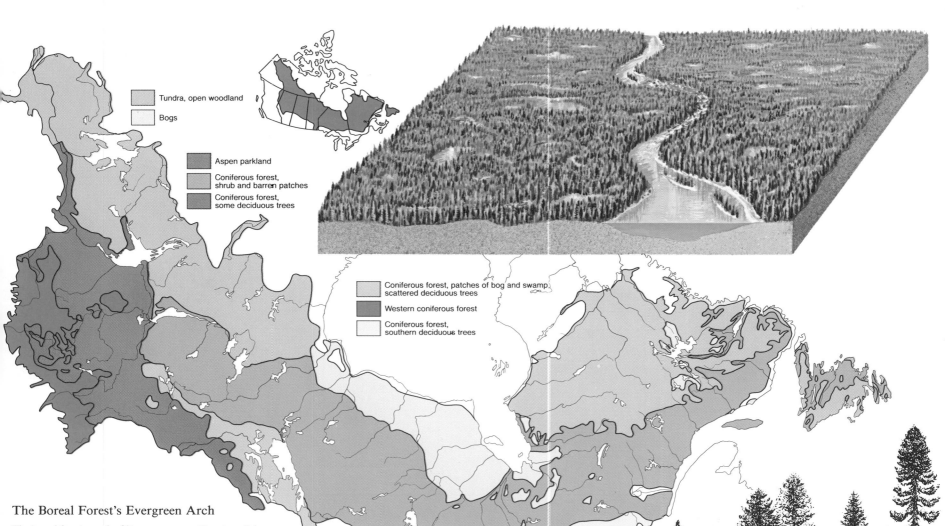

The Boreal Forest's Evergreen Arch

The boreal forest, much of it wilderness, covers more than a quarter of Canada. Its vegetation is remarkably uniform: mainly balsam fir, spruce, jack pine and tamarack. Willows and alders grow in sheltered river valleys, and aspen and birch invade logged or burned-over areas.

In the northern boreal forest, thin, acidic soil underlaid with patches of permafrost supports impenetrable thickets of tamarack and black spruce.

Near the tree line, the stunted trees of the open woodlands average 12 metres; lichens carpet the forest floor. Clumps of birch and dwarf willow grow farther apart and gradually thin out. Beyond lies the treeless tundra.

Most of Canada's animals are found in the boreal forest. The beaver fells about 300 trees a year for food and building material for dams. Carnivorous fur bearers such as martens, weasels and fishers feed on porcupines, squirrels and mice. The mink kills even when not hungry; carcasses cached in dens often remain uneaten. Wolves usually hunt in packs of six to ten for moose, deer and woodland caribou, culling the old, young and sick from herds.

The moose, largest member of the deer family, browses wetlands for water lily roots in summer, then retreats to forests in winter to feed on bark and twigs. Shrews, voles and chipmunks store winter food supplies. Red squirrels cache nuts, mushrooms and pine cones, occasionally in middens one metre high.

Warblers, most of which migrate south in autumn, comprise nearly half the summer bird population, and feed on the scourges of the boreal forest—mosquitoes and some 60 species of blackflies.

Jack pine

White spruce

Balsam fir

Black spruce

Beaver

Moose

Wolf

Porcupine

Yellow warbler

Life in a Bog: Cold, Wet and Acidic

Most of Canada's 1.3 million square kilometres of wetlands are found in the boreal forest, where Ice Age glaciers gouged countless stagnant, water-filled depressions.

Bogs are the most common type of wetland in northern forests. These poorly drained patches of land are pocked with pools of open water colonized by floating plants such as the water lily and pondweed. The remains of these aquatic species form a fine, soft layer called a "false bottom" which gradually rises as sediment accumulates.

Reeds, sedges and marsh cinquefoil grow in the shallows; buckbean sends "runners" along the surface to form a floating mat. Sphagnum, a moss that absorbs 20 times its weight in water, fills the spaces between plants. The mat thickens and may form hummocks and ridges that support shrubs such as leatherleaf, Labrador tea, sweet gale and bog rosemary, which are less tolerant of water. Scattered clumps of black spruce and tamarack grow between the bog and the surrounding forest of spruce, balsam fir and birch.

Different zones of vegetation—sedge, sphagnum, shrubs and trees—deposit distinctive types of peat, occasionally to a depth of 30 metres. This partially decomposed organic matter releases acids that stain bog water brown.

The landscape is brightened with orchids: dragon's tongue, lady's slipper, spotted coralroot, grass pink, and twayblade orchid, which takes years to flower.

Carnivorous pitcher plants and round-leaved sundews obtain nutrients from insects. Down-pointed bristles on the inner surface of pitcher plant leaves trap insects, which drown in a mixture of rainwater and enzyme-rich secretions. The plant then digests its victim. Sundew leaves have hundreds of sticky red hairs that entangle insects. The plant then slowly closes, suffocating its prey.

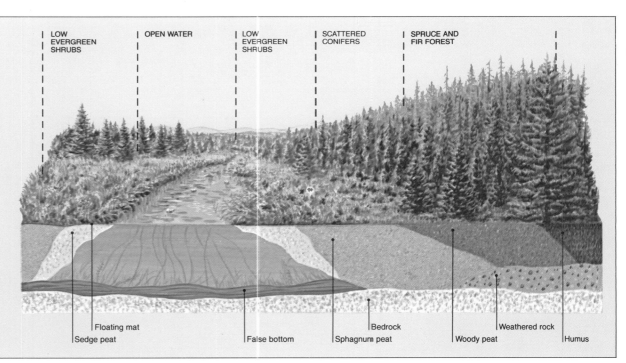

LOW EVERGREEN SHRUBS | OPEN WATER | LOW EVERGREEN SHRUBS | SCATTERED CONIFERS | SPRUCE AND FIR FOREST

Floating mat

Sedge peat

False bottom

Sphagnum peat

Bedrock

Woody peat

Weathered rock

Humus

Natural Regions: Eastern Forest, Tundra

The Mixed Forest: Woodlands and Wetlands

Almost none of the original mixed forest that confronted Canada's pioneers survives today. Agriculture and urban sprawl have swallowed most of the woodlands; logging, mining and fire have altered much of the rest.

Hardwoods more typical of the United States grow in southwestern Ontario, including hickory, sassafras, pawpaw and tulip tree—species found nowhere else in Canada.

In the Great Lakes-St. Lawrence region, sugar maple and beech dominate mature forests; sun-loving red and white oak, basswood, white elm and black cherry thrive in younger woodlands. Coniferous species, mainly white and red pine and eastern hemlock, are scattered throughout stands of deciduous trees.

The Acadian forest of the Maritimes has hardwoods similar to those in the Great Lakes-St. Lawrence region. Boreal trees, especially red and black spruce and balsam fir, fringe the coastlines and carpet the highlands of Cape Breton Island and the Gaspé Peninsula.

Wildlife in the mixed forest is most abundant in freshwater marshes and wooded swamps. Plankton-rich waters and aquatic plants such as cattails, duckweed and loosestrife anchor food chains and sustain wetland creatures. The sleek otter pursues sunfish, minnows and game fish such as perch and bass. Painted turtles sun on mossy rocks and logs. The bobcat prowls wetland margins for rabbits and rodents, and earns its reputation for ferocity when treed or cornered.

Thousands of monarch butterflies congregate at Point Pelee on Canada's southernmost tip each autumn before flying south. The region also shelters the opossum, Canada's only marsupial. This primitive mammal, which has changed little in 70 million years, bears up to 20 young, and nourishes them for about six weeks in a pouch.

Deciduous trees

Deciduous trees; scattered conifers

Deciduous and coniferous trees

Conifers; scattered deciduous trees

Conifers

Monarch butterfly

Opossum

Swainson's hawk

Otter

Bobcat

Arctic tern

Brant

Largemouth bass

Midland painted turtle

Migration by Land, Stars, Sun and Sound

Two thirds of North America's 660 bird species migrate in twice-yearly journeys along four main flyways. More than 200 species pass over Point Pelee, where the Mississippi and Atlantic flyways overlap.

But no one is certain why birds migrate, although food shortages are a factor. Most species fly much farther than necessary to avoid winters that the stay-at-homes survive. The arctic tern wings 35,000 kilometres on round trips between the polar regions.

How they migrate is also a mystery. Birds sense changes in the length of daylight and add layers of fat to fuel their impending flights. Night migrants are believed to navigate in part by the stars. Nestlings learn the rotation of the heavens, and later recognize constellations. Day migrants steer by the sun, and follow coastlines, mountain ranges and rivers.

Orientation may also involve ultraviolet and polarized light, even the earth's magnetic field in combination with gravity. Homing pigeons can hear infrasound, noise that carries tremendous distances in the atmosphere. The sound of breakers pounding a distant shore may guide a seabird to a tiny mid-ocean island.

Migration is risky. In North America, 100 million waterfowl wing south each fall. Only 40 million return. Hunters kill 20 million; the rest succumb to predators, accidents and disease.

White trillium

Highbush cranberries

Tulip tree flower

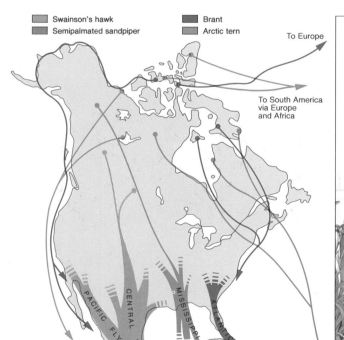

Swainson's hawk

Semipalmated sandpiper

Brant

Arctic tern

To Europe

To South America via Europe and Africa

To South America and Antarctica

PACIFIC FLYWAY

CENTRAL FLYWAY

MISSISSIPPI FLYWAY

ATLANTIC FLYWAY

Urban Animals: The Wildlife Among Us

The wildlife that most Canadians encounter is found in our cities, where animals thrive in seemingly hostile environments. The familiar rock dove, or pigeon, has been urbanized since the time of ancient Egypt, and lives in parks and downtown areas, where it flourishes on human handouts. Nighthawks nest on flat roofs, the urban equivalent of gravelly beaches; city lights allow them to hunt all night, rather than just at dawn and dusk. Gray squirrels, notorious panhandlers in parks, seem to prefer manmade nesting boxes to natural cavities in trees. The Norway rat prowls waterfronts and rundown neighborhoods, feeding mainly on garbage.

Some species prefer residential areas and suburbs. Winter feeding stations attract chickadees, grosbeaks, blue jays and house wrens. Aggressive species such as starlings and sparrows pirate nests from woodpeckers and bluebirds. Gardens provide bountiful larders of vegetables and tender greens for cottontail rabbits and woodchucks. The garter snake, one of the few urbanized reptiles, slithers after wood frogs chorusing in moist, shady nooks. Moles furrow lawns, gardens and golf courses for grubs and earthworms. Raccoons and skunks raid garbage cans at night and during the day den in trees, garages, culverts and chimneys.

24

The Tundra's Brief Season of Life

North of the tree line, as far as the Arctic Ocean, lies the tundra, a vast plain carpeted with sedge and grass hummocks and mats of dwarf willow and birch. Glaciers and rock deserts, hospitable only to avens, lichens and saxifrage, cover much of the Arctic islands.

The tundra receives about 250 millimetres of annual precipitation—scarcely more than deserts—but frozen ground (permafrost) prevents drainage and leaves a sodden summer landscape. But from June until August, a sun that never sets unfolds almost 900 species of flowering plants. The arctic poppy flowers and goes to seed in less than a month. Willows and sedges start summer growth while still buried in metre-deep snowbanks.

Timing is also crucial for the birds that congregate here in summer from all over the Western Hemisphere. Mating often occurs during migration; eggs are laid by mid-June so parents can rear offspring in time for the August exodus.

The tundra shelters tremendous concentrations of wildlife. Prince Leopold Island hosts a vast seabird colony in summer; for a few days each year thousands of beluga whales calve in the warm shallows of Cunningham Inlet on Somerset Island. Between 300,000 and 500,000 caribou in five main herds wander between summer feeding grounds on the tundra, then winter in the sheltered boreal forest. Musk-oxen, found mainly in the Arctic islands, graze in valley meadows, then shift in winter to windswept hummocks and mountain slopes with light snow cover.

Polar bears winter along oceans and bays near the breathing holes of ringed seals. The walrus uses its tusks to rake the bottom for shellfish, open breathing holes in the ice, haul itself up on floes and fight enemies—polar bears on land and killer whales at sea.

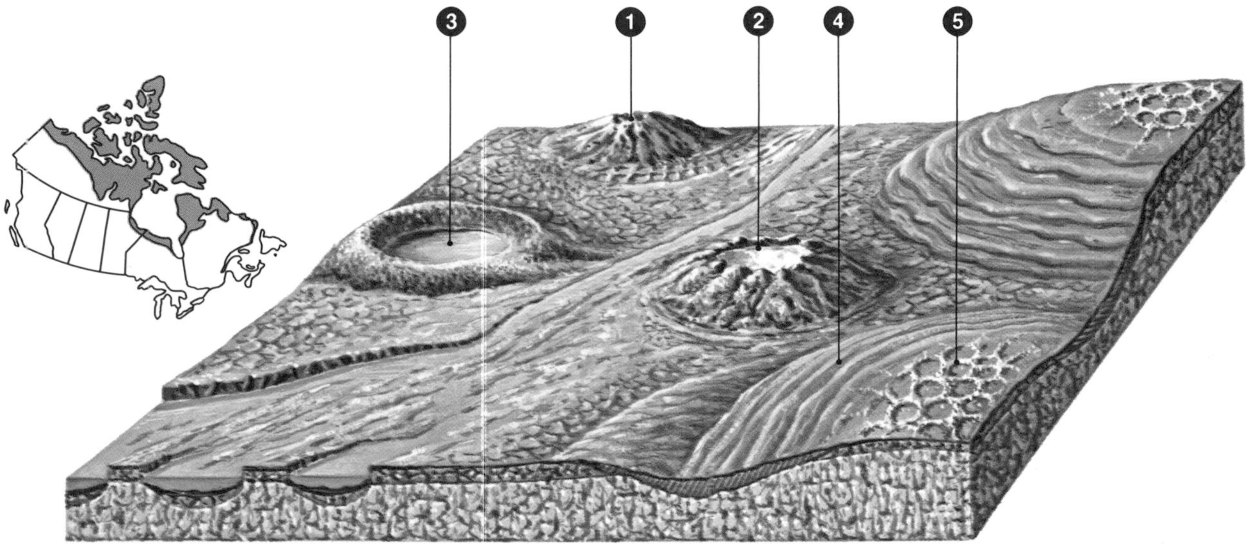

Poor in variety but rich in numbers, the tundra supports tremendous concentrations of wildlife near nutrient-rich ocean currents or in lush feeding grounds known as polar oases.

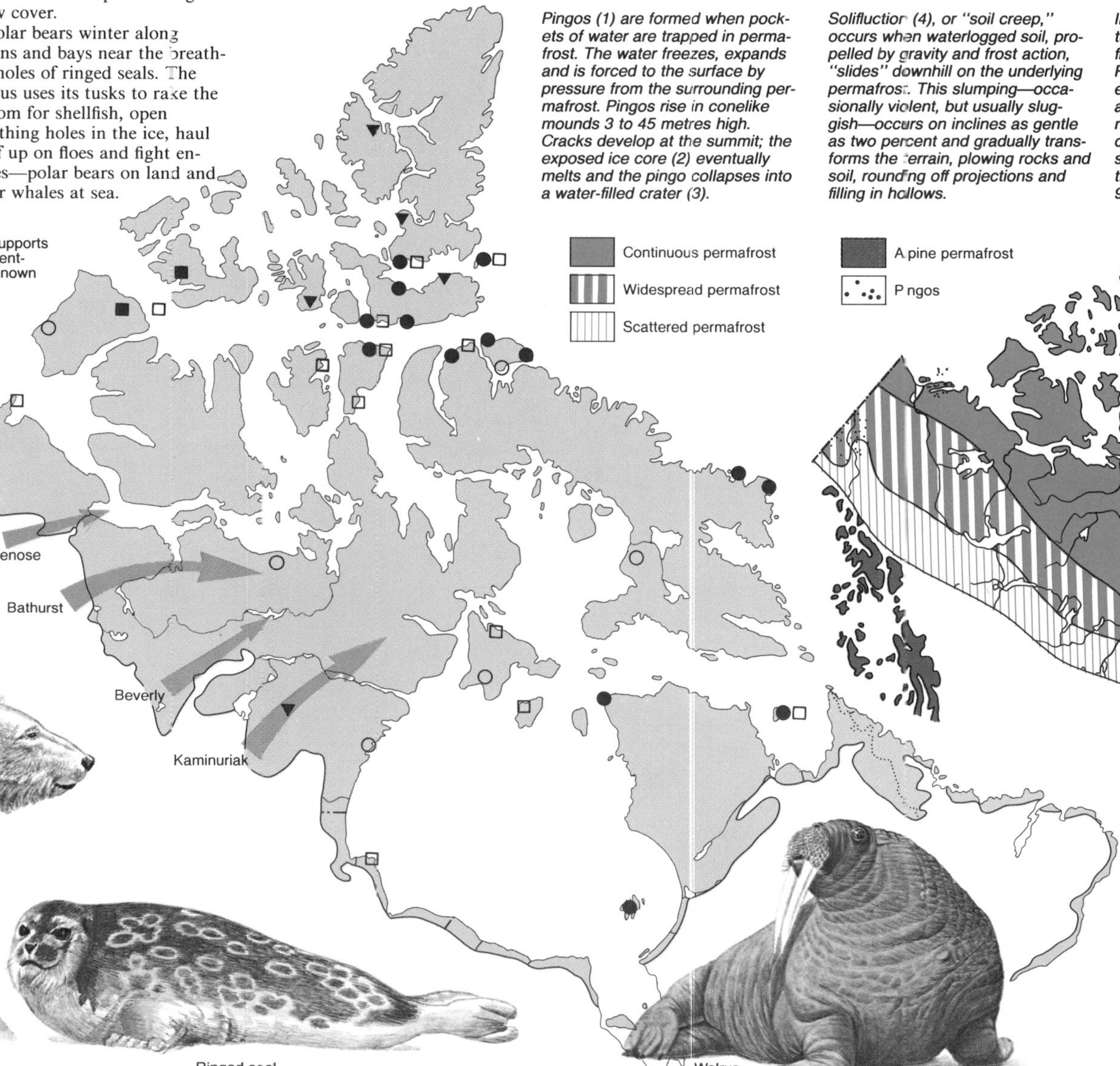

→ Migration routes of barren-ground caribou herds

■ Other terrestrial mammals (musk-oxen, foxes, hares)

□ Marine mammals (polar bears, seals, walrus, whales)

● Seabirds and waterfowl (fulmars, murres, kittiwakes, gulls, guillemots, ducks, whistling swans)

○ Geese (Canada, lesser and greater snow, brant, Ross's)

▼ Polar oases (concentrations of diverse species)

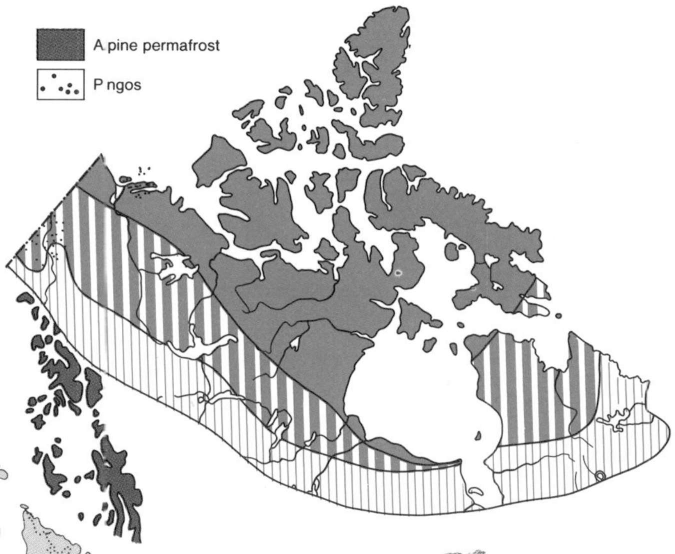

Porcupine

Bluenose

Bathurst

Beverly

Kaminuriak

Pingos (1) are formed when pockets of water are trapped in permafrost. The water freezes, expands and is forced to the surface by pressure from the surrounding permafrost. Pingos rise in conelike mounds 3 to 45 metres high. Cracks develop at the summit; the exposed ice core (2) eventually melts and the pingo collapses into a water-filled crater (3).

Solifluction (4), or "soil creep," occurs when waterlogged soil, propelled by gravity and frost action, "slides" downhill on the underlying permafrost. This slumping—occasionally violent, but usually sluggish—occurs on inclines as gentle as two percent and gradually transforms the terrain, plowing rocks and soil, rounding off projections and filling in hollows.

Intense cold contracts the soggy tundra soil, and forms fissures that fill with water during spring thaws. Repeated freezing and thawing expands the openings. Eventually, after several years, this produces networks of geometric fractures called polygons (5). The more severe and rapid the freeze-up, the larger the polygon; some are 90 metres across.

▨ Continuous permafrost

▥ Widespread permafrost

▤ Scattered permafrost

▨ Alpine permafrost

⦂ Pingos

Captions (animal illustrations)
Polar bear

Ringed seal

Walrus

Musk-ox

The Lichen— Two Plants in One

Deserts, mountain peaks, tundra: lichens grow almost anywhere, often where nothing else can survive. These primitive, rootless plants need no soil, few minerals and little moisture and sunlight.

A lichen is two primitive plants in one: an alga and a fungus that combine in a beneficial relationship called mutualism. The fungus lacks chlorophyll to produce its own food, but absorbs moisture vital to the millions of algal cells enmeshed in its tangled network of strands. The algae, in turn, photosynthesize food for the entire organism.

Lichens have a variety of appearances. Crustose lichens are crusty mats embedded in wood and rocks by tiny threads that penetrate as much as one centimetre. Foliose lichens attach small, leafy lobes to rocks, soil and trees with a rootlike anchor called an umbilicus. Fruticose lichens include trumpet-shaped fairy cups, red-capped British soldiers and reindeer moss, which forms spongy mats 25 centimetres thick in open woodlands near the tree line and provides winter fodder for caribou.

Lichens remain dormant during drought and intense heat and cold. Even in hospitable climates they grow slowly—at most one millimetre a year—but steadily; some colonies are thought to be 4,000 years old.

Reindeer moss

Fairy cups

British soldiers

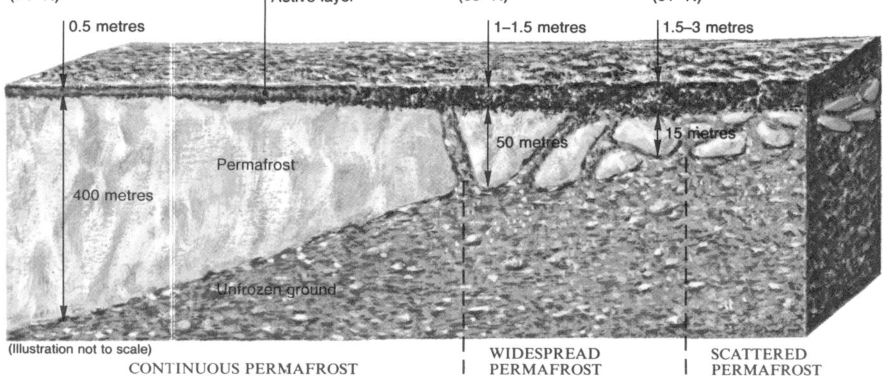

The Power of Permafrost

The "active layer" of the shallow tundra soil thaws each spring; below lies permafrost, ground frozen year round. Almost half of Canada, including mountain summits in the Western Cordillera and eastern Arctic islands, lies within zones of continuous or discontinuous permafrost.

Permafrost is formed when the ground temperature, determined mainly by air temperature, soil, drainage and snow cover, remains below 0°C. Ground temperature is usually 1° to 5° warmer than the average air temperature, so permafrost extends to areas with an average temperature of about –1°C. The colder the ground temperature, the deeper the permafrost. At Hay River, N.W.T., a ground temperature slightly below freezing produces patches of permafrost 1.5 to 15 metres deep. Resolute, N.W.T., with an average ground temperature of –13.3°C, rests on permafrost about 400 metres deep.

Permafrost and powerful frost action, called "cryoplanation," shape the Arctic landscape more than erosion. Cryoplanation forces soil to the surface in circular frost boils, or fractures the terrain into polygons—geometric scars that cover hundreds of square kilometres. Permafrost melts when its insulating mantle of vegetation is removed, and the ground fractures and slumps.

Resolute, N.W.T. (74° N)

Active layer

Norman Wells, N.W.T. (65° N)

Hay River, N.W.T. (61° N)

0.5 metres

1–1.5 metres

1.5–3 metres

Permafrost

400 metres

50 metres

15 metres

Unfrozen ground

(Illustration not to scale)

CONTINUOUS PERMAFROST

WIDESPREAD PERMAFROST

SCATTERED PERMAFROST

Our Great Outdoors

To Canada's early settlers, the wilderness was a place of hardship and an inexhaustible source of raw materials, land and wealth. But the land had another face, as author-pioneer Susanna Moodie observed in 1853: "Beautiful—most beautiful in her rugged grandeur is this vast country. How awful is the sublime solitude of her pathless woods! What eloquent thoughts flow out of the deep silence that broods over them." Today, much of that grandeur has been cleared and cut, mined, dredged and dammed. Only about 10 percent of the provinces can be considered truly wild. The picture brightens when the North is included, but there too, wilderness is shrinking in the wake of industry and development.

Hundreds of hiking trails and canoe routes, 28 national parks, more than 600 provincial parks and scores of wildlife refuges and wilderness areas seek to preserve what remains of Canada's wild lands. They comprise a majestic array of landscapes: the wave-sculpted shore of Vancouver Island, northern Saskatchewan's mosaic of rivers and lakes, the twisted shapes of Alberta's Red Deer Badlands, Cape Breton's rugged highlands and the exotic plant and animal life where Point Pelee juts into Lake Erie.

More than 20 million park visitors each year present a challenge: how to invite people into parks and still preserve them. New parks are one answer: since 1970 more than 50,000 square kilometres have been added to the national park system alone. Nearer home, managers seek to make better use of older parks. Pollution-free shuttle buses have replaced cars in some parks, enabling both visitor and vegetation to breathe easier. Interpretive programs, museums, canoe routes and self-guiding nature trails transform spectators into participants, and broaden the park experience beyond a blurred vision through a speeding car window.

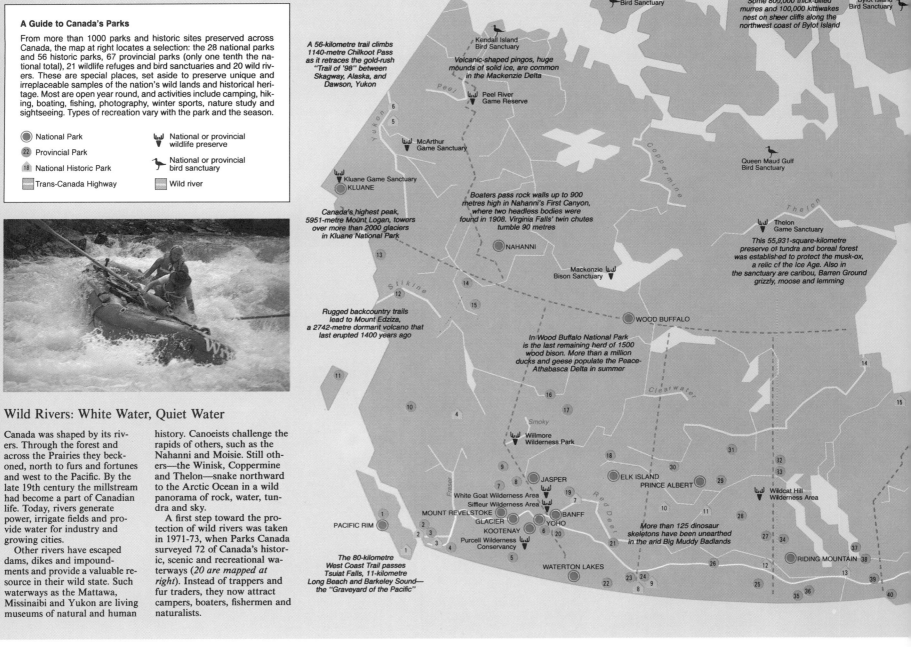

A Guide to Canada's Parks

From more than 1000 parks and historic sites preserved across Canada, the map at right locates a selection: the 28 national parks and 56 historic parks, 67 provincial parks (only one tenth the national total), 21 wildlife refuges and bird sanctuaries and 20 wild rivers. These are special places, set aside to preserve unique and irreplaceable samples of the nation's wild lands and historical heritage. Most are open year round, and activities include camping, hiking, boating, fishing, photography, winter sports, nature study and sightseeing. Types of recreation vary with the park and the season.

- ⓝ National Park
- ㉒ Provincial Park
- ⑱ National Historic Park
- ▭ Trans-Canada Highway
- ⱳ National or provincial wildlife preserve
- ⌁ National or provincial bird sanctuary
- ▭ Wild river

A 56-kilometre trail climbs 1140-metre Chilkoot Pass as it retraces the gold-rush "Trail of '98" between Skagway, Alaska, and Dawson, Yukon

Volcanic-shaped pingos, huge mounds of solid ice, are common in the Mackenzie Delta

Some 800,000 thick-billed murres and 100,000 kittiwakes nest on sheer cliffs along the northwest coast of Bylot Island

Banks Island Bird Sanctuary

Bylot Island Bird Sanctuary

Kendall Island Bird Sanctuary

Peel River Game Reserve

McArthur Game Sanctuary

Queen Maud Gulf Bird Sanctuary

Kluane Game Sanctuary
KLUANE

Canada's highest peak, 5951-metre Mount Logan, towers over more than 2000 glaciers in Kluane National Park

Boaters pass rock walls up to 900 metres high in Nahanni's First Canyon, where two headless bodies were found in 1908. Virginia Falls' twin chutes tumble 90 metres

NAHANNI

Thelon Game Sanctuary

This 55,931-square-kilometre preserve of tundra and boreal forest was established to protect the musk-ox, a relic of the Ice Age. Also in the sanctuary are caribou, Barren Ground grizzly, moose and lemming

Mackenzie Bison Sanctuary

Rugged backcountry trails lead to Mount Edziza, a 2742-metre dormant volcano that last erupted 1400 years ago

WOOD BUFFALO

In Wood Buffalo National Park is the last remaining herd of 1500 wood bison. More than a million ducks and geese populate the Peace-Athabasca Delta in summer

Willmore Wilderness Park

JASPER

White Goat Wilderness Area
Siffleur Wilderness Area

ELK ISLAND
PRINCE ALBERT

Wildcat Hill Wilderness Area

MOUNT REVELSTOKE
GLACIER
BANFF
YOHO
KOOTENAY
Purcell Wilderness Conservancy

More than 125 dinosaur skeletons have been unearthed in the arid Big Muddy Badlands

PACIFIC RIM

WATERTON LAKES

RIDING MOUNTAIN

The 80-kilometre West Coast Trail passes Tsuiat Falls, 11-kilometre Long Beach and Barkeley Sound—the "Graveyard of the Pacific"

Wild Rivers: White Water, Quiet Water

Canada was shaped by its rivers. Through the forest and across the Prairies they beckoned, north to furs and fortunes and west to the Pacific. By the late 19th century the millstream had become a part of Canadian life. Today, rivers generate power, irrigate fields and provide water for industry and growing cities.

Other rivers have escaped dams, dikes and impoundments and provide a valuable resource in their wild state. Such waterways as the Mattawa, Missinaibi and Yukon are living museums of natural and human history. Canoeists challenge the rapids of others, such as the Nahanni and Moisie. Still others—the Winisk, Coppermine and Thelon—snake northward to the Arctic Ocean in a wild panorama of rock, water, tundra and sky.

A first step toward the protection of wild rivers was taken in 1971-73, when Parks Canada surveyed 72 of Canada's historic, scenic and recreational waterways (*20 are mapped at right*). Instead of trappers and fur traders, they now attract campers, boaters, fishermen and naturalists.

Provincial Parks—Picnic Sites to Primeval Domains

Canada's provincial parks range in size from a few hectares to many thousands of square kilometres. They protect wild lands and habitats, and provide outdoor recreation for more than 20 million visitors each year. Many have a small entry charge and, where applicable, a camping fee. There are numerous private camping and picnic grounds in the Yukon and Northwest Territories but no areas that correspond to provincial parks. Most of Nova Scotia's fine parkland is divided between provincial wildlife areas and two national parks. Prince Edward Island has an extensive system of recreation areas from day-use-only picnic sites to campgrounds.

Mount Robson (B.C.)

Dinosaur (Alta.)

Cypress Hills (Sask.)

Algonquin (Ont.)

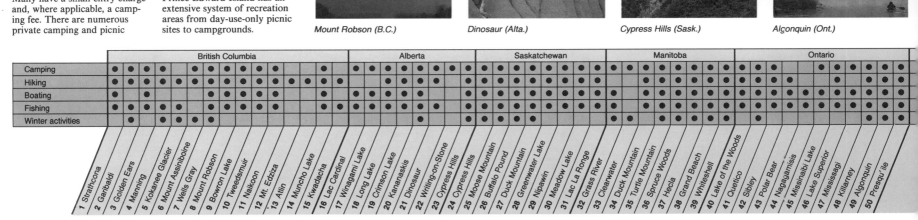

	British Columbia																Alberta								Saskatchewan									Manitoba								Ontario									
Camping																																																		
Hiking																																																		
Boating																																																		
Fishing																																																		
Winter activities																																																		

1 Strathcona · 2 Garibaldi · 3 Golden Ears · 4 Manning · 5 Kokanee Glacier · 6 Mount Assiniboine · 7 Wells Gray · 8 Mount Robson · 9 Bowron Lake · 10 Tweedsmuir · 11 Naikoon · 12 Mt. Edziza · 13 Atlin · 14 Muncho Lake · 15 Kwadacha · 16 Lac Cardinal · 17 Winagami Lake · 18 Long Lake · 19 Crimson Lake · 20 Dinosaur · 21 Dinosaur · 22 Writing-on-Stone · 23 Cypress Hills · 24 Cypress Hills · 25 Moose Mountain · 26 Duck Mountain · 27 Buffalo Pound · 28 Greenwater Lake · 29 Nipawin · 30 Meadow Lake · 31 Lac La Ronge · 32 Grass River · 33 Clearwater · 34 Duck Mountain · 35 Turtle Mountain · 36 Spruce Woods · 37 Hecla · 38 Grand Beach · 39 Whiteshell · 40 Lake of the Woods · 41 Quetico · 42 Sibley · 43 Polar Bear · 44 Nagagamisis · 45 Missinaibi Lake · 46 Lake Superior · 47 Mississagi · 48 Killarney · 49 Algonquin · 50 Presqu'ile

A Place to Grow in Canada's Wildlife Preserves

In the beginning, the purpose of national and provincial wildlife preserves was clear-cut: to protect game animals and birds, especially migratory waterfowl, from the devastating effects of a growing society. Now a wider view of the role of refuges has emerged. Legislation has dealt not only with game animals but with all threatened wildlife, including Canada's 34 endangered species (*right*).

Improving or expanding wildlife habitats involves more than buying up pristine land. Much of the property is overgrazed, logged, drained or burned, requiring investment in dams, fences, reforestation and other expensive rehabilitation.

Roadless and resortless, wildlife refuges may restrict visitors to daylight hours or ban them completely so that the fauna will not be disturbed. But for the most part these wild lands are open and beckoning.

BIRDS
Eastern peregrine falcon
Arctic peregrine falcon
Whooping crane
Eskimo curlew
Greater prairie chicken

FISH
Longjaw cisco
Atlantic whitefish
Silver chub
Gravel chub
Pugnose minnow
Banff longnose dace
Black redhorse
Shorthead sculpin
Aurora brook trout

Arctic peregrine falcon

REPTILES AND AMPHIBIANS
Timber rattlesnake
Blue racer
Lake Erie water snake
Pacific gopher snake
Pigmy short-horned lizard
Eastern tiger salamander
Small-mouthed salamander
Blanchard's cricket frog

MAMMALS
Vancouver Island marmot
Black-tailed prairie dog
Eastern cougar
Black-footed ferret
Sea otter
Northern kit fox

Northern Rocky Mountain wolf
Wood bison
Blue whale
Humpback whale
Right whale
Grey whale

Lake Erie water snake

Wilderness "Unimpaired": the National Parks

Some 80,000 square kilometres of the Canadian landscape are preserved in 28 national parks. By law these parks are "dedicated to the people . . . for their benefit, education and enjoyment" and must remain "unimpaired for future generations." They range from the oldest, Banff, to the newest, Auyuittuq (the world's first north of the Arctic Circle); from the world's largest, 27,700-square-kilometre Wood Buffalo, to Canada's smallest, the 400-hectare St. Lawrence Islands park. There are the rugged coastal cliffs of such eastern parks as Terra Nova, Gros Morne (*right*) and Cape Breton Highlands; parks fronting lovely beaches, especially the Prince Edward Island and Pacific Rim parks; and the great parks of the Prairie grasslands and western mountains.

As pressures on the national parks increased, the federal government—in cooperation with the provinces—responded with more parks (ten since 1968). At some time in the future it is hoped that Canada will have 55 parks, the greatest park system in the world.

Mantling Auyuittuq is the 5720-square-kilometre Penny Ice Cap. Among 38 bird species are the endangered peregrine falcon and whistling swan

AUYUITTUQ

Dewey Soper Bird Sanctuary

The world's largest goose colony protects one million Canada geese, lesser snow geese and black brants

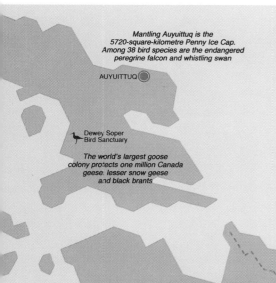

Polar bears, arctic foxes and caribou roam the park, one of the world's most southerly extensions of arctic tundra

Akimiski Island Bird Sanctuary

Canoeing is popular in Chibougamau Provincial Park, where the Chamouchouane River plunges 33 metres over Chaudière Falls and churns through a series of rapids. Pike, trout, walleye, otter and beaver inhabit the many lakes

La Mauricie has campsites, beaches, wilderness and wildlife areas, and 154 lakes. A 23-kilometre scenic road divides the park

PUKASKWA

Along the Bruce Peninsula are eroded limestone "flowerpots," rare orchids and 400-million-year-old fossils embedded in shale bluffs

GEORGIAN BAY ISLANDS

POINT PELEE

Some 300 bird species have been sighted on the 17-kilometre sandspit at the southernmost tip of mainland Canada, also a haven for rare plants and animals

TERRA NOVA
GROS MORNE
Avalon Wilderness Area
Wilderness Area

Arctic hare and Newfoundland caribou inhabit this park, named for 806-metre Gros Morne Mountain. Tidal pools teem with sea urchins, sponges and sea anemone

FORILLON
CAPE BRETON HIGHLANDS
PRINCE EDWARD ISLAND
Plaster Rock-Renous Game Refuge
Kedgwick Game Management Area
KOUCHIBOUGUAC
Canaan Game Management Area
Chignecto Game Sanctuary
FUNDY
Lepreau Game Management Area
KEJIMKUJIK
Tobeatic Game Sanctuary

In Kejimkujik are Indian petroglyphs and one of Canada's most varied reptile and amphibian populations

Coves and inlets cut into steep sandstone cliffs along Fundy's 13-kilometre shoreline. Beachcombers can explore coves and tidal pools; amateur naturalists can watch for some of the park's 185 bird species

ST. LAWRENCE ISLANDS

	Power boating	Canoeing	Hiking trails	Nature trails	Fishing	Horseback riding	Winter sports	Museum	Camping	Trailer park	Accommodations in park
Kluane (Yukon)	●	●	●	●	●		●		●		●
Nahanni (N.W.T.)	●	●	●		●				●		
Pacific Rim (B.C.)	●	●	●	●	●	●		●	●		●
Mount Revelstoke (B.C.)			●	●	●		●	●	●		
Glacier (B.C.)			●	●	●		●	●	●	●	
Yoho (B.C.)		●	●	●	●	●	●	●	●	●	●
Kootenay (B.C.)			●	●	●	●	●	●	●	●	●
Jasper (Alta.)	●	●	●	●	●	●	●	●	●	●	●
Banff (Alta.)	●	●	●	●	●	●	●	●	●	●	●
Waterton Lakes (Alta.)	●	●	●	●	●	●	●	●	●	●	●
Elk Island (Alta.)	●	●	●	●	●		●		●	●	●
Wood Buffalo (Alta.-N.W.T.)	●	●	●		●				●		
Prince Albert (Sask.)	●	●	●	●	●	●	●	●	●	●	●
Riding Mountain (Man.)	●	●	●	●	●	●	●	●	●	●	●
Pukaskwa (Ont.)		●	●	●	●				●		
Georgian Bay Islands (Ont.)	●	●	●	●	●				●		
Point Pelee (Ont.)	●	●	●	●	●		●	●			
St. Lawrence Islands (Ont.)	●	●	●	●	●			●	●		
La Mauricie (Que.)	●	●	●	●	●		●		●		
Forillon (Que.)		●	●	●	●	●	●	●	●	●	
Kouchibouguac (N.B.)	●	●	●	●	●	●	●		●		
Fundy (N.B.)	●	●	●	●	●	●	●	●	●	●	●
Kejimkujik (N.S.)	●	●	●	●	●		●		●		
Cape Breton Highlands (N.S.)	●	●	●	●	●	●	●	●	●	●	●
Prince Edward Island (P.E.I.)	●	●	●	●	●			●	●		●
Gros Morne (Nfld.)	●	●	●	●	●			●	●		
Terra Nova (Nfld.)	●	●	●	●	●		●		●	●	●
Auyuittuq (N.W.T.)		●	●		●						

National Historic Parks: Preserving Our Past

The 56 national historic parks commemorate people, places and events that have shaped Canada's history. Historians, archeologists and anthropologists are active in the excavation and restoration of these sites. Fur-trade posts such as Lower Fort Garry have been restored with care; battlements, towers and historic houses rebuilt and refurnished in the style of the 17th, 18th and 19th centuries. The Fortress of Louisbourg, built in 1720 and abandoned for two centuries, is Canada's biggest historical reconstruction. The 52-square-kilometres park includes some 50 buildings, the blackened shells of other structures and extensive stone fortifications. Today these parks are more than monuments and repositories. Many have museums, costumed guides and sound-and-light shows recreating the past.

Yukon Historic Sites

Fort Lennox (Que.)

1 Fort Rodd Hill
2 St. Roch
3 Fort Langley
4 Fort St. James
5 Yukon Historic Sites
6 Robert Service Cabin
7 Rocky Mountain House
8 Fort Walsh
9 Cypress Hills Massacre
10 Battleford
11 Batoche
12 Fort Esperance
13 Lower Fort Garry
14 Fort Prince of Wales
15 York Factory
16 Fort St. Joseph
17 Fort Malden
18 Woodside
19 Fort George
20 Queenston Heights and Brock's Monument
21 Butler's Barracks
22 Bethune Memorial House
23 Kingston Martello Towers
24 Bellevue House
25 Battle of the Windmill
26 Fort Wellington
27 Rideau Canal
28 Fort Témiscamingue
29 Maison Sir Wilfrid Laurier
30 Coteau-du-Lac
31 Fort Chambly
32 Fort Lennox
33 Les Forges du Saint-Maurice
34 The Fortifications of Québec
35 Artillery Park
36 Cartier-Brébeuf National Historic Park
37 National Battlefields Park
38 St. Andrews Blockhouse
39 Carleton Martello Tower
40 Port Royal Habitation
41 Prince of Wales Martello Tower
42 Fort Edward
43 Fort Anne
44 York Redoubt
45 Halifax Citadel
46 Grand Pré
47 Fort Beauséjour
48 Province House
49 Fort Amherst
50 Alexander Graham Bell National Historic Park
51 Fortress of Louisbourg
52 Castle Hill
53 Cape Spear Lighthouse
54 Signal Hill
55 L'Anse aux Meadows
56 Port au Choix

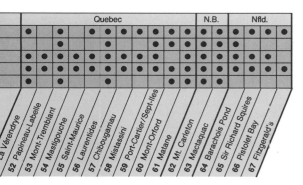

	Quebec									N.B.		Nfld.	
	●	●	●	●	●	●				●	●	●	●
		●				●	●				●		●
	●		●	●	●			●		●	●	●	●
		●		●		●	●		●	●	●	●	●
	●	●	●	●	●	●				●	●		●
				●									

La Vérendrye
52 Papineau-Labelle
53 Mont-Tremblant
54 Mastigouche
55 Saint-Maurice
56 Laurentides
57 Chibougamau
58 Mistassini
59 Port-Cartier/Sept-Îles
60 Mont-Orford
61 Matane
62 Macpès
63 Maclaquac
64 Barachois Pond
65 Sir Richard Squires
66 Pistolet Bay
67 Fitzgerald's

The First Canadians

Ice-age glaciers created a land bridge between Siberia and Alaska, providing a means of passage for the first immigrants to North America. But scholars disagree as to when man first traversed it. Recent finds in the Yukon's Old Crow Basin—ice-free during most of the Pleistocene—support a date of at least 27,000 B.P. (before present). Evidence from Alberta may push that date back even farther, perhaps to 40,000 B.P.

Whenever they came, the first Canadians were neither explorers nor settlers nor adventurers. They were simply hungry nomads following the game upon which their survival depended. These ancestors of today's Indians and Inuit needed intelligence and imagination to adapt to the wondrous, variegated new continent. They had to learn to live on frozen tundra, in forests, on grassy plains and high mountains, and along rugged coastlines.

To survive in these environments, the people developed weapons and techniques for hunting, learned to farm and forage, and used the natural medicines the earth provided. They built dwellings, from simple windbreaks to huge wooden buildings, for many climates, and watercraft for everything from river travel to whale hunting. Clothing was made from the cured skins of animals, and even the woven bark of trees. Tools were essential, and were fashioned from rock, wood, bone and copper.

As the people spread over the continent, languages and lifestyles developed which were as diverse as those of Europe. Indians of the Subarctic and the Plains, where game was plentiful, became hunters. The rich resources of the sea made fishing the mainstay of West Coast and maritime Woodland tribes. When good soil and ample water were available, as in the woodlands of southern Ontario, several tribes turned to farming. Other groups acted as middlemen in the exchange of goods among tribes.

Social and political structures also varied. Iroquoians of the populous Eastern Woodlands felt intense tribal loyalty, but the concern of nomads in the sparsely populated Subarctic did not extend beyond the family. The Inuit were a democratic people; among the West Coast tribes, individuals were rigidly ranked by lineage and wealth.

Despite this remarkable diversity, the Indians and Inuit existed in rare harmony with their environment, holding that all living things—plants as well as animals—had souls and were to be shown respect. They had no theories about ecology, but did have a basic appreciation of the interdependence of all living things—an attitude still only dimly understood by modern man.

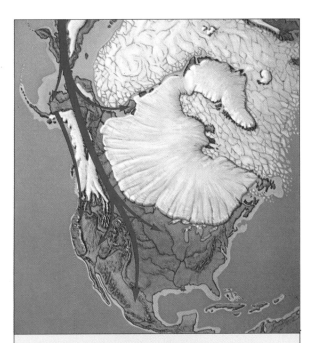

Across an Arctic Bridge Glaciers penetrated deep into the Northern Hemisphere during the Pleistocene, locking up so much water that sea levels dropped some 120 metres. Beringia, the land bridge between Siberia and Alaska (lightly shaded area in map above), vanished and reappeared with the ebb and flow of the glaciers, but was exposed for two extended periods: between 34,000 and 30,000 B.C. and again between 26,000 and 11,000 B.C. Migrating Asian hunters followed such game as mammoths and caribou down ice-free corridors (arrows) to the heart of the continent, perhaps as early as 40,000 years ago.

25,000 B.C.	Caribou bone scraper, Yukon—earliest evidence of man in North America.	
10,000	Paleo-Indians hunt giant ice-age mammals.	
8000	Ancestors of Subarctic Indians move north in wake of receding ice sheet.	*Caribou bone scraper*
7000	First settlements along Pacific Coast.	
4000	Last of the ice-age megafauna disappear.	*Stone mortar and pestle*
2000	Copper is mined on the upper Great Lakes.	
2000	First wave of immigration to Arctic (Small Tool Tradition) begins.	*Copper blade*
1000	Pottery made in eastern Canada.	*Bone harpoon head*
A.D. 300	Village Tradition settlements begin to dot Prairies.	
500	Beans, maize and squash cultivated in Eastern Woodlands.	*Reed duck decoy*
1000	Thule—ancestors of present-day Inuit—replace Dorset culture across Arctic.	*Ivory snow goggles*
1400	West Coast tribes establish vast trade network.	
1600	Mohawk, Oneida, Onondaga, Cayuga and Seneca form powerful Iroquois confederacy.	*Carved owl's head*

WEST COAST
Traders and Artisans

As Pacific salmon returned generation after generation to spawn in native rivers, so came West Coast Indians to ancestral fishing grounds. A few weeks of feverish activity in summer and fall would yield enough salmon—filleted, smoked and stored—to last through the wet, stormy winter.

Cod and halibut could be taken with hook and line throughout the year. Ocean and shore yielded abundant shellfish and edible kelp. Sea mammals provided both food and furs. In the thickly forested mountains abutting the narrow beaches were deer, elk, mountain goat, wolf,

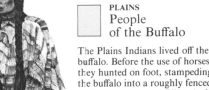

Kwakiutl

A mild climate and abundant salmon fostered a leisure class among West Coast tribes. Huge winter houses sheltered some half-dozen related families whose quarters were arranged according to status.

bear, beaver and marten.

Cedar grown huge in the mild, damp climate made dugout canoes up to 22 metres long in which paddlers would hunt whales or trade with neighboring tribes. Cedar posts and beams framed houses 20 metres wide and more than 90 metres long. The wood, easily split with stone tools, made planks to sheath houses; its shredded bark was woven into rain cloaks, mats and conical hats..

So much wealth so easily obtained left little time for artistic expression. Brightly colored designs and stylized animal forms were woven into blankets of dog and goat hair. Festive and utilitarian objects of wood were decorated with elaborate, carved designs: this sculpture in wood is one of Canada's finest arts.

Because the Coastal people had an abundance of necessities, seaboard trade centered on luxuries. The Nootkas offered whale products, for example, in exchange for ceremonial canoes built by the Haidas of the Queen Charlotte Islands. Slaves—considered the ultimate sign of wealth—were a major item of barter. There was also much trade with the tribes of the interior, the Kwakiutls and Tlingits acting as middlemen.

No occasion was more important among most West Coast Indians than the potlatch, an elaborate ceremony given by one clan to humble another. Such ceremonies offered the hosts an opportunity to display their wealth—thus confirming their status—through lavish gifts and the destruction of valuable possessions.

PLATEAU
Fishermen and Foragers

Wedged between the Coast Mountains and the Continental Divide, the interior Plateau formed a cul-de-sac into which migrant people of various languages and customs moved over many centuries.

The Columbia and Fraser rivers were the arteries of this landlocked region. They were the avenues of trade and travel and, in season, a source of food in migrating salmon. Their banks provided homesites for countless small tribes speaking dialects of four major languages.

Most Plateau people spent

Spears in hand, Plateau Indians fish for salmon on the Columbia.

summers in lodges constructed of bulrush mats layered over cottonwood frames. In winter they lived in semiunderground earthen lodges, entered by way of a notched log ladder through a central roof opening. Early spring found them combing the

Plateau

ground for wild carrots, wild onions, bitterroot and camas root. The starchy bulb of the camas, a variety of lily, was eaten raw, roasted, or pulverized into cakes that were then boiled. Fish, berries and wild game rounded out the Plateau diet. The cold climate and poor soil prevented widespread agriculture.

Trade thrived throughout the river-laced Plateau region. Dugouts brought merchants from the West Coast bearing sea otter pelts, decorative shells and baskets; along with material goods, they passed on their love of wealth, status and power. Plateau traders paddled pine and cottonwood dugouts downstream to barter fur pelts, copper, jadeite and herbs with coastal tribes.

Most Plateau groups had few, if any, political ties outside their loosely organized villages; their culture was essentially a patchwork quilt with the pieces provided by their neighbors. Religion, dress, customs, housing—all reflected regions bordering the Plateau.

PLAINS
People of the Buffalo

The Plains Indians lived off the buffalo. Before the use of horses, they hunted on foot, stampeding the buffalo into a roughly fenced enclosure or over a cliff—a buffalo jump.

Virtually every part of the buffalo was utilized. Meat was dried on racks and made into jerky, or pounded together with fat and berries to make pemmican, a concentrated, high-protein food carried on the trail. Hides were made into leggings, dresses and moccasins. Skins taken in autumn and winter, when the hair was long and thick, served as blankets and robes. Buffalo hair, woven, became strong rope; loose, it stuffed cradleboards, moccasins

[Map with labels: MACKENZIE, KUTCHIN, HARE, TUTCHONE, KASKA, TAHLTAN, TSETSAUT, SEKANI, CARRIER, TSIMSHIAN, HAIDA, BELLA BELLA, BELLA COOLA, KWAKIUTL, COMOX, NOOTKA, COWICHAN, CHILCOTEN, SHUSWAP, INTERIOR SALISH, NICOLA, KOOTENAY, SARCEE, YELLOWKN, DOGRIB, SLAVE, BEAVER, BLACKFO]

Copper

ARCTIC
Survivors in an Icy Realm

From the eastern tip of Siberia, across Alaska and Canada to Greenland, Inuit territory stretched more than 8000 kilometres. Their homeland was the tundra: rocky, rolling plains bearing little vegetation other than mosses, lichens and low-lying bushes; a bitter, snowbound world in winter, a mosquito-infested quagmire in summer.

Along the Arctic Coast, seals, whales and walruses were hunted with spear and lance. Fish was an important food, especially when meat supplies ran low. The land yielded other game—from caribou and an occasional polar bear to burrowing voles and lemmings. Birds were snared with seal-thong nets or felled by darts, sticks and stones.

Blubber, meat and fish were eaten when raw (and most nutritious), and partially digested lichen from a caribou's stomach was a delicacy. Driftwood—the only wood available—was carved and pegged to make harpoons and sleds. Where there was no wood, caribou antlers were pieced together. In an emergency, Inuit built sleds of frozen fish or hides—sleds which could be eaten if necessary.

As autumn waned, many Inuit gathered in groups of 100 or more on the sea ice to build winter snowhouse villages. When stormbound, an entire village might gather in a large snowhouse to take part in a drum dance, watch wrestling matches or witness a shaman's attempt to quell a storm.

The Inuit had 100 words for various types of snow but not one word for chief. Power lay in the community's acceptance or rejection of its members. There were no bad hunters, just "unlucky" ones. When all luck ran out, people died.

Intensely spiritual, all Inuit shared an unshakable belief in the supernatural, and their daily lives were directed by concerns over human and animal souls, monsters and deities. They relied on shamans and medicine men to protect them from evil spirits.

Despite their constant struggle for survival, the Inuit lived life one day at a time, with constant cheerfulness that puzzled early European explorers—but for which the Inuit had an explanation: "If you knew what horrors we often have to live through, you would understand why we are so fond of laughing."

Evidence of the antiquity of Northern art, this shaman's mask (left) dates back 1000 years. Ivory goggles (below) shielded eyes from the sun's glare, preventing snow blindness. In a 19th-century engraving (bottom), a lone Inuit hunter sits patiently beside a seal hole, watching for signs of his prey. He would then harpoon the seal sight unseen and chop the hole large enough to land it.

Labrador

Canada in 1500

By 1500, Indian population patterns in Canada were well established. The map (left) locates major tribal groups at the beginning of the 16th century. Names within each color-coded cultural zone place the Indians according to historical evidence. Because of shifting of tribes, some locations are only approximate. Groups often moved from place to place as climate changed, game migrated or dwindled, or hostile neighbors threatened—a situation that accelerated as European settlement spread.

Naskapi

Assiniboine

Iroquois

SUBARCTIC
Nomads of the Northern Forest

Athapaskan-speaking tribes of the western Subarctic were nomadic hunters whose lives revolved around the caribou. They ate its flesh, made tools from its bones and antlers, and converted its skin into clothing and shelter. During the spring and fall, hunting was a communal effort. Large numbers of caribou were driven into surrounds—corrals of wooden posts—or killed at river crossings.

When traveling, the band carried the entire camp on its backs. Women and children shouldered loads of up to 60 kilograms while men ranged through the woods in constant search of game.

Like the Woodland Algonkians farther south, Algonkians of the eastern Subarctic fished, foraged and hunted a variety of game. Meat and fat were used for food, bones for making implements. From hide, women sewed clothing, using tendons as thread. Moose and caribou stomachs were made into cooking pots, and glands were valued as medicine. From the wood, bark and roots of trees were made canoes and conical wigwams, snowshoes and toboggans.

In winter, three or four families frequently trekked and camped together. In summer, several groups hunted and fished cooperatively. During such gatherings, berry picking, dancing, storytelling and gambling alternated with the tanning of hides and construction of birchbark canoes.

Large animals were easy prey to Subarctic hunters on snowshoes.

dwelling, it was also a sacred place. The floor was the earth on which the Indians lived; the sides, vaulting to a peak, the sky. The tepee's roundness was a reminder of the sacred life circle, with no beginning or end, and behind the hearth, in even the most modest of tepees, was an earthen altar where incense was burned and prayers intoned.

Tribes left the open grasslands in late autumn, setting up winter camps along broad, timbered river valleys and scattering their tepees among the trees. Men drove buffalo into hobbling snowdrifts or stalked deer and elk. But severe winters thwarted even small-game hunting, and when dried meat and pemmican ran out, there was starvation.

In summer, when life was easy, the Plains people gave thanks to the Great Spirit through such rituals as the Sun Dance, which included feats of endurance and self-mutilation.

Flailing furiously with webbed sticks, Plains Indians play a version of today's lacrosse.

and pillows. At birth, the Indian was often swaddled in the soft skin of a young calf; in death, a buffalo robe became his shroud.

Without buffalo skins there could have been no tepees. Not only was the tepee a movable

EASTERN WOODLANDS
Woodsmen and Warriors

As early as A.D. 1000, the woodlands of eastern Canada began to show unmistakable signs of human presence. There were green squares of maize and tobacco, as well as patches of ground farmed into sterility and then abandoned. Fishing camps dotted the riverbanks, and hunting paths were hardened into well-trodden trails.

Food was bountiful and life matched the seasons: in winter, Algonkian-speaking northern tribes hunted deer, caribou and moose; in spring and summer, they ate fish, beaver and the flesh and eggs of birds, and gathered roots and berries, drying the surplus for periods of shortage; in the fall, they returned to hunting. Coastal, lake and river tribes also found a bounty in shellfish and marine mammals.

Despite Algonkian predominance, these tribes faced a formidable foe in the Iroquois Confederacy, whose homeland spread inland through the forests surrounding Lakes Ontario, Huron and George. Iroquoians, such as the Hurons of southern Ontario, depended heavily on agriculture and grew beans, maize and squash—the "Three Sisters"—and tobacco, which had profound religious significance.

The Woodland people made good use of the materials at hand: clay, wood and bark for cooking utensils; bark for torches, canoes, dishes, wigwams and longhouses; rushes for mats and bags. They used some 270 species of plants for medicine, 130 for food, 27 for "tobacco," 25 for dyes.

Warfare was a part of life for the Wood and tribes. Although most confrontations were on a small, raiding-party scale, local rivalries were deep-rooted and intense. In these raids, enemies were slain, and captives and goods taken. Prisoners were sometimes tortured and killed, but often they were adopted into the captors' tribe to replace men who had died.

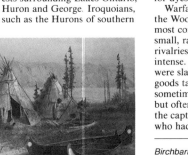

Birchbark canoes and wigwams identify a Woodland Indian camp of the 19th century.

Exploration From Sea to Sea

"Between Spain and India there is a small sea which may be crossed in a matter of a few days." So wrote Christopher Columbus, planning his 1492 voyage westward to Asia. Like most knowledgeable men of his time, Columbus believed that the world was round. But no one knew its size. He calculated that a mere 4400 kilometres of ocean lay between Europe and Asia. In fact, the distance was 16,000 kilometres—and a vast obstacle, the North American continent, blocked the way.

Legends hint at much earlier visits to the unknown continent: pilgrims from Britain in A.D. 75, the sixth-century missionary Saint Brendan seeking a "land of promise," Irish monks living along the St. Lawrence toward the end of the ninth century. Certainly Norwegian Vikings had reached North America 500 years before Columbus, but their settlements disappeared and Europe had forgotten the New World.

In the 15th century it was the dream of a sea route to the spices, silks and jewels of the Orient that lured Europe's kings and merchants to send explorers westward into the Sea of Darkness. These riches were available in Middle East markets, but Arab traders and Italian middlemen controlled all trade routes. By the end of the century, better ships and navigation aids had made long ocean voyages possible. The new Portuguese caravels combined Arab lateen (triangular) sails for speed with the deep, sturdy hull of North European trading ships. Instruments that helped determine latitude gave sailors confidence on the open sea.

Adventurers set out across the Atlantic and found, not Asia, but North America. Columbus believed until his death that he had reached the East Indies. In the summer of 1497 John Cabot, a Venetian in the service of England's Henry VII, became the first explorer since the Vikings to set foot on this continent. His exact landfall is not known. It may have been Cape Breton Island. He found no land of silks and spices. His reports of the teeming Grand Banks fishing grounds, however, brought European fishing vessels to Canada's coast in the following years. Still convinced he had found Asia, Cabot set out again in 1498 in search of Japan, but never returned.

Gaspar Corte-Real, sailing from Portugal, landed in Labrador in 1501. His three ships separated near the Strait of Belle Isle, and Corte-Real was never seen again. In 1524 Giovanni da Verrazzano, in the service of France, landed near Cape Fear, North Carolina, and sailed north to Newfoundland. Gradually an accurate view of the new continent's coast emerged. However, it was not until Jacques Cartier, sent by Francis I of France, landed on Canadian shores in 1534 that Newfoundland was discovered to be an island. On his second visit, in 1535, the existence of the St. Lawrence River—the key to the interior—became known.

The search for ways around or through the continent took explorers and traders farther inland as the New World revealed its real riches: furs. Rival European traders fighting for new territory moved gradually westward. But the exploration of Canada was to take three centuries to complete. Not until 1793, when the young Scottish fur trader Alexander Mackenzie reached the Pacific overland from Montréal, was the country finally crossed from sea to sea.

John Cabot's discovery of Canada and the Grand Banks in 1497 made him England's hero. "He goes dressed in silk," wrote a contemporary, "and these English run after him like mad." But Henry VII, who had hoped for gold, not fish, was less impressed. He paid Cabot £10. Cabot set out again, in 1498, to find the Orient, but never returned.

Jacques Cartier was contemptuous of the land (probably Labrador) he first saw in 1534, describing it as "the land God gave to Cain." In 1535 he discovered the St. Lawrence, and traveled 1300 kilometres up what he thought was a waterway to the Orient to the Iroquois village of Hochelaga, where eventually Montréal would grow.

A Race for Furs— and a Continent Spanned

No silks or spices filled the holds of European ships returning from the new land. Explorers found only fish off Canada's shores, and the search for a passage to Asia continued. Only slowly did Europe realize that the furs for which fishermen bartered with the Indians could be as valuable as the riches of the Orient.

Led by the visionary Samuel de Champlain, the French returned to North America in the 17th century. Champlain traveled inland from the St. Lawrence, charting much of the Great Lakes region. In 1615 he followed the waterways to Georgian Bay, pioneering the main fur-trade route to the West.

Traders, missionaries and explorers extended the horizons of New France. In 1672 the Jesuit Charles Albanel traveled north to Hudson Bay. Fur trader René-Robert Cavelier de La Salle traced the Mississippi to the Gulf of Mexico, and in 1682 claimed its enormous watershed in the name of Louis XIV. In the early 1700s, Pierre de La Vérendrye and his sons reached the Prairies, establishing a chain of trading posts as they went.

Meanwhile, the English Hudson's Bay Company was establishing a stronghold in the north. Pierre-Esprit Radisson

Using John Cabot's information, Columbus's shipmate Juan de la Cosa drew the first map (left) depicting North America in 1500.

and Médard Chouart des Groseilliers, disenchanted with the French governor in Québec, had found backers in the court of England's Charles II for their scheme to take furs out by sea from the great uncharted "Bay of the North." In 1670 the company was granted a trade monopoly in the bay.

Company policy was to trade only from its bayside posts, but individuals roamed the interior to persuade Indians to desert French traders and bring their furs to the bay. In 1691 Henry Kelsey reached the plains of northern Saskatchewan. In 1754 Anthony Henday, a company laborer, became probably the first white man to see the Canadian Rockies.

The HBC was forced to abandon its "long sleep by the Frozen Sea" when aggressive Scots traders moved into Québec after the British

conquest and allied themselves with French-Canadian *voyageurs* to take over the French trade. Its monopoly thus challenged, the HBC sent traders inland. Indian reports of vast copper deposits sent Samuel Hearne to the Coppermine River in 1771. He was the first white man to reach the Arctic Ocean by land.

As competition sharpened, the Montréal traders joined forces in 1787 to form the North West Company. Seeking a passage through the Rockies, Nor'Wester Alexander Mackenzie discovered the river that bears his name in 1789. In 1793 he reached the Pacific— the first European to cross the continent.

In the race for new sources of fur, in a double line of advance from Montréal and Hudson Bay, the Canadian West had been explored and mapped.

Cabot 1497
Corte-Real 1501
Verrazzano 1524

Through Arctic Ice—Triumph and Tragedy of a Legendary Passage

By the mid-1500s, explorers had found that the land barrier separating Europe from Asia presented a continuous coastline from the Arctic to Cape Horn. The remote, stormy Strait of Magellan to the south was Spanish territory. English explorers headed north into Arctic waters.

Adventurer Martin Frobisher, sent by Queen Elizabeth I, pioneered the search for a navigable, ice-free route around the north of the continent in 1576. He sailed west to Baffin Island and discovered Frobisher Bay, an inlet he mistakenly hoped was a strait leading to Asia.

Henry Hudson's ill-fated 1610 voyage took him through Hudson Strait to discover Hudson Bay (which he thought was the Pacific), before his mutinous crew set him adrift in a small boat.

Concluding that there was no way out of Hudson Bay to the west, William Baffin

circumnavigated Baffin Bay in 1616. This took him farther north than anyone else was to go for more than two centuries. On his return he discovered Lancaster Sound, but the importance of his discovery was not recognized. Only in the 19th century was this proven to be the entrance to the passage.

After wintering in James Bay in

HMS Investigator in pack ice north of Banks Island during Comdr. Robert McClure's unsuccessful 1850-54 search for the Franklin expedition.

1631, Thomas James wrote a grimly discouraging account of his experiences. "In all probability," he concluded, "there is no northwest passage to the south sea." His backers gave up.

Two hundred years passed before the Royal Navy resumed the task. After the Napoleonic wars, Britain had men and ships to spare,

and in 1819 Arctic ice conditions were favorable. In that year Lieut. Edward Parry sailed into Lancaster Sound, through Barrow Strait and Viscount Melville Sound, farther west than anyone before him.

The most significant of 19th-century British Arctic ventures, the Franklin expedition, ended in tragedy. Sir John Franklin and his men were never heard from again after they left England in 1845. In the futile search for the Franklin party, however, most of Canada's Arctic coastline was charted, and much of the Arctic archipelago added to the map.

A route through the polar ice cap had now been revealed, but remained to be proved navigable. In 1903-06 Norwegian Roald Amundsen, in his converted fishing smack, *Gjøa*, made his way in ice-strewn waters through Lancaster Sound and the maze of Arctic islands into the Beaufort Sea. The Northwest Passage had finally been conquered.

Canada From the West

Canada's Pacific coast was all "uncertainty and conjecture" in 1778 when **Capt. James Cook** (*right*) anchored in Nootka Sound and became the first European to go ashore. Cook had surveyed the St. Lawrence and made his reputation as a mathematician and astronomer. He volunteered to search for a waterway through North America from the Pacific, eventually concluding that it did not exist.

Capt. George Vancouver, a 20-year-old midshipman on Cook's voyage to the Pacific, made a second survey of the coast in 1791-95, exploring inlets Cook had missed. In June 1793, he discovered the outlet of the Bella Coola River, just seven weeks before Alexander Mackenzie reached the same spot, and by 1795 had disproved the theory of a low-latitude Northwest Passage.

A reputation for daredevil seamanship gained **Martin Frobisher** the blessing of Queen Elizabeth I for his expedition to find the Northwest Passage. Sailing into a large body of water off Baffin Island in July 1576, he confidently named it "Frobisher's streytes." His straits, however, proved to be only a bay, and later voyages became futile treasure hunts.

In December 1770, **Samuel Hearne,** a 24-year-old clerk for the Hudson's Bay Company, was sent on a 1400-kilometre trek to locate a northern river and its rumored wealth of copper. In July 1771, he discovered the Coppermine River—where copper was present but scarce— and continued on to become the first to reach the Arctic Ocean overland.

Hoping to blaze a fur-trading trail across the Rockies to the west coast, Scots-born **Alexander Mackenzie** followed an outlet from Great Slave Lake in 1789. When he found that it led instead to the Arctic Ocean, he named the river Disappointment. But in 1793, he finally succeeded in reaching the Pacific by land via the Peace and Parsnip rivers.

In 1819, while seeking the Northwest Passage, British naval officer **Edward Parry** forced his ketches *Hecla* and *Griper* into Lancaster Sound and beyond. Stopped by ice at Melville Island, he had nevertheless gone farther west than anyone before him. Parry's Arctic exploration methods and survival techniques became standard procedure.

Sir John Franklin's ships *Erebus* and *Terror* left England in 1845 to search for the Northwest Passage, but were never seen again. In the hunt for Franklin and his men, 40 search parties charted thousands of kilometres of Arctic coastline. In 1859, a message found in a cairn on King William Island told of Franklin's death in 1847.

In 1903-06, sailing with a six-man crew, Norwegian **Roald Amundsen** realized the goal of generations of explorers when he fought his way through shallow waters, drifting ice and dense fogs to navigate the Northwest Passage. In 1911 he became the first to reach the South Pole. But in 1928, while leading a rescue party in the Arctic, Amundsen vanished.

The major routes of more than four centuries of Canadian exploration are shown here in three phases. Only the most significant expeditions have been mapped, and where a succession of explorers followed the same route, only one is shown. The first globe traces the discovery and exploration of North America's east coast in the 15th and 16th centuries. (Because of conflicting evidence, early routes are approximate.) The center globe shows early searches for the Northwest Passage, and the exploration of the interior as far west as the Prairies. West coast expeditions, later searches for the Northwest Passage, and the charting of the Canadian North are mapped below.

John Cabot's historic 1497 voyage was made in the barque Matthew, less than 23 metres long, with canvas that included a triangular sail copied from Arab spice traders. Improved navigation aids had made the crossing possible.

Birchbark canoes, from 5 to 10 metres long, carried explorers into Canada's interior on waterways unnavigable to conventional craft.

Roald Amundsen's Gjøa, the first ship to sail the Northwest Passage, was a converted herring smack 22 metres long and 3 metres wide. Packed with scientific instruments and supplies for the voyage, Gjøa barely rode above the waterline, but made the passage where larger ships had failed.

Jacques Cartier 1535-36
Martin Frobisher 1576-77
John Davis 1585
Samuel de Champlain 1608-09, 1615-16
Henry Hudson 1610-11
Etienne Brûlé 1615-16, 1621
Robert Bylot, William Baffin 1616
Thomas James 1631-32
Médard Chouart des Groseilliers 1654-56
Pierre-Esprit Radisson, Médard Chouart des Groseilliers 1659-60
René-Robert Caveller de La Salle 1669, 1678-80
Charles Albanel 1672
Henry Kelsey 1689, 1690-92
William Stuart 1715
Pierre de La Vérendrye 1731-41
Louis-Joseph, François de La Vérendrye 1742-43

Anthony Henday 1754-55
Samuel Hearne 1770-72
James Cook 1778-79
Peter Pond 1778-88
Alexander Mackenzie 1789, 1793
George Vancouver 1792-94
David Thompson 1796
Simon Fraser 1808
John Ross 1818, 1829-33
William Edward Parry 1819-20, 1821-22
John Franklin 1819-22, 1825-27, 1845-47
William Hendry 1828
George Back 1833-34
John Rae 1846-47, 1854
Robert Campbell 1851
Roderick Ross MacFarlane 1857
Charles Francis Hall 1871-73
George Strong Nares 1875-76
Albert Peter Low 1892-95
Otto Neumann Sverdrup 1898-1902
Roald Amundsen 1903-06
Robert Edwin Peary 1908-09
Vilhjalmur Stefansson 1913-18

A New World Settled, a New Country Founded

THE people of present-day Canada had little say in deciding the shape of their country. The settlements, from which Canada and the United States of America evolved, started off perched on the Atlantic shores and worked their way west. As this westward expansion went on, the boundary developed sector by sector. Treaties were made—and boundaries settled—between the United States and a distant Britain interested mainly in the fur-trading routes to the west and north. By the time Canada became a Confederation, her southern boundaries had been fixed from coast to coast.

Struggle for Survival—The Age of New France

France's empire in the New World began in 1605 with the tiny colony of Port Royal in Nova Scotia. Three years later Samuel de Champlain built his *Habitation* at Québec, its great shadowing rock a symbol of his determination and a destination for Indians traveling downriver with pelts to barter.

Both Acadia, on the Atlan-

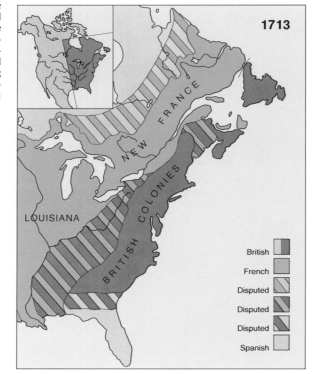

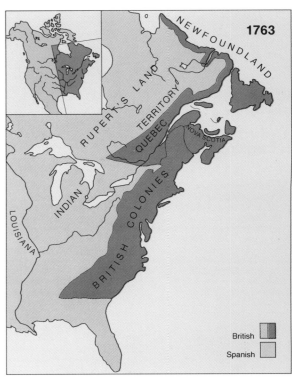

1713

1763

British
French
Disputed
Disputed
Disputed
Spanish

British
Spanish

By 1700, Indians were trading 100,000 beaver pelts each year

tic, and Canada, along the St. Lawrence, were founded as fur-trading ventures. The quality of northern furs, the Grand Banks cod fisheries, territorial claims laid for France by Jacques Cartier, Spanish and English strength in the south—all contributed to the choice of a New France in the north. But as England and France warred in Europe, the territories France had chosen began to be contested.

As early as 1613, a party of English raiders from Virginia burned Port Royal. In 1627 the monopolistic Company of One Hundred Associates was set up to govern New France, promising to defend the colony and to send 200 settlers each year. But the next year, freebooting Englishmen intercepted the Company's first convoy of settlers and supplies and besieged Québec, forcing Champlain to surrender. Québec was returned to France in 1632 but the Company, interested only in fur profits, neglected colonization. The tiny settlements, isolated and poorly defended, were fre-

quently attacked by Iroquois tribes. Alienated by Champlain's support of their Algonkin and Huron enemies, the Iroquois had become allies of the English. Their hostility to the French was the cause of the death by torture of six Jesuit missionaries.

When Louis XIV established royal government in New France in 1663 there were fewer than 3000 inhabitants. He set up a sovereign council composed of a governor, the bishop, an intendant (administrator), and five colonists. Jean Talon, the first intendant, arrived in 1665. To encourage immigration, he paid passages and provided land, supplies and tools. Bachelors were penalized—denied fishing, hunting and trapping rights—while parents of 10 or more children received 300 livres ($750) a year. Talon imported "king's girls"—orphans and farmers' daughters—to become wives and mothers. By 1673 the population had more than doubled.

Seigneurs, "persons of rank," were granted waterfront land which they had to fill with tenant farmers. New France's first professional fighting force, the *Troupes de la Marine,* arrived from France in 1683 and, along with the colonial militia, checked the Iroquois threat for a time. Talon started a shipbuilding industry and a brewery, and encouraged farmers to grow hops, and hemp for thread, cloth, rope and sails.

But the furs demanded by European fashion remained the economic backbone of the colony—and many of New France's young men defied government and church decrees to take to the forest as *coureurs de bois.* They traded with Indians, and their forays into the interior opened up the country. Montréal became the great entrepôt for the fur trade. Annual fairs were established, and bartering, feasting and brandy attracted hundreds of Algonkins, Hurons and Ottawas with their pelt-laden canoes.

By the 1680s the empire claimed by France extended beyond Lake Superior, and down the Mississippi to the Gulf of Mexico. But it was thinly held and most of its inhabitants

lived along the St. Lawrence between Québec and Montréal. The English colonies to the south, by contrast, had a population of 250,000. Their farmers and merchants enjoyed a flourishing trade with Europe and the West Indies. They had year-round access to the sea and a range of climates that favored varied and plentiful crops. To the north of New France, the English Hudson's Bay Company, formed in 1670, had claimed the whole of the Hudson Bay drainage basin as its territory.

The great imperial struggle for the continent began in 1689, when England joined a European alliance against Louis XIV. In North America, English and French colonists used Indian allies in guerilla attacks on each other's forts and settlements. Québec withstood a siege in 1690, but this series of wars went badly for France. The Treaty of Utrecht in 1713 gave the Hudson Bay territory, Newfoundland and mainland Acadia to England. Some 1700 Acadians were forced to choose allegiance to the British Crown or exile. Most chose to stay on the fertile Fundy lowlands.

Left with an unpopulated Cape Breton Island as the last Atlantic approach to New France, the French built the massive Fortress of Louisbourg to protect it. The fortress was captured by New England forces in 1745 but was returned three years later. The British founded Halifax in 1749 to rival Louisbourg.

Farms in New France were laid out in narrow strips so that each seigneurial tenant had river frontage. Cool in summer and warm in winter, farmhouses were made of stone with metre-thick walls for stability. Steep gable roofs limited snow buildup; dormers were added as growing families needed top stories for bedrooms.

Formidable but undermanned, isolated fortress Louisbourg guarded New France's Atlantic approach

The thirteen colonies had a population of 1.2 million by 1750; New France, only 55,000. But the English, hemmed in along a strip of Atlantic coastline, were prevented from ex-

panding beyond the Appalachians by France's claim to the midwest. The decisive conflict came with the Seven Years' War (1756-63).

Both the French and the British reinforced their colonial armies for this climactic struggle. France sent one of its ablest generals, the Marquis de Montcalm, as commander-in-chief. But the British sent more troops, their regulars numbering 23,000 in 1757, as opposed to 6800 for the French. Louisbourg fell to the British in June 1758. A year later, Gen. James Wolfe arrived off Québec with 168 ships. On Sept. 13, 1759, he led his men up an undefended cliff to the Plains of Abraham. Both Wolfe and Montcalm were killed. Montréal's frail defenses fell a year later. In 1762 Louisiana was ceded to Spain and in 1763, the Treaty of Paris made Canada a British colony. New France was no more.

Montcalm's death in 1759 sealed the fate of New France

1600	1610	1620	1630	1640	1650	1660	1670	1680	1690	1700	1710	1720
			• Kirke brothers capture French convoy in Gulf of St. Lawrence	• Maisonneuve brings first colonists to Montréal		• Royal government established at Québec		• La Salle claims Louisiana for France		• Iroquois sign peace treaty with New France		• French begin construction of Fortress Louisbourg
	• Québec founded by Champlain		• English capture Québec	• Iroquois destroy Jesuit missions to the Hurons; five priests martyred		• Hudson's Bay Company founded		• Lachine Massacre triggers new series of Iroquois raids		• Port Royal surrenders for last time to English		
	• First Jesuits arrive in New France		• Treaty of St. Germain-en-Laye restores Québec to France		• Laval becomes first bishop of Québec		• La Salle builds *Griffon,* first ship launched on Great Lakes		• Frontenac dies		• A 12,000-man British force from Boston out to conquer Québec is shipwrecked in the Gulf of St. Lawrence	
	• Recollet missionaries arrive in New France		• Champlain dies at Québec			• Jean Talon becomes first intendant of New France. Canada's earliest sponsored immigrants, the *filles du roi,* arrive		• British capture Port Royal but fail to take Québec			• Treaty of Utrecht cedes Hudson Bay, Newfoundland and mainland Acadia to Britain	
	• Port Royal sacked by Virginians		• Port Royal re-established at present-day Annapolis Royal, N.S.				• Frontenac appointed Governor of New France		• French attack and destroy British settlements in Newfoundland			
	• Louis Hébert and family first settlers at Québec					• Fort Frontenac (Kingston) founded		• Treaty of Ryswick restores Acadia to France				
	• James VI of Scotland grants Nova Scotia to Sir William Alexander											

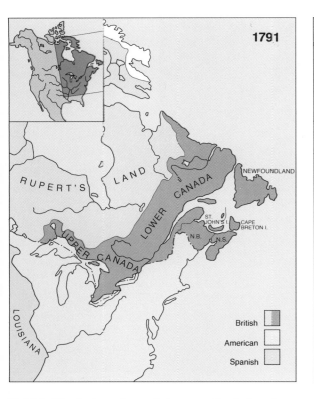

1791

NEWFOUNDLAND

RUPERT'S LAND

LOWER CANADA

UPPER CANADA

LOUISIANA

ST. JOHN'S I.
CAPE BRETON I.
N.B.
N.S.

British
American
Spanish

1866

RUPERT'S LAND

CANADA

NEWFOUNDLAND

P.E.I.
N.B.
N.S.

British
American

Métis massacred 20 outmaneuvred Red River settlers and Assiniboia Governor Robert Semple at Seven Oaks in 1816

British North America—Colony to Confederation

Following the Treaty of Paris, some 60,000 French Canadians faced life in a continent that was British from the Gulf of Mexico to Hudson Bay. They were under military government until 1774, when the British Parliament's Quebec Act granted them political rights and religious freedom as Catholics, and confirmed the system of French civil law and seigneurial land ownership.

After the outbreak of the American Revolution in 1775, British regulars and Canadian militia stood against invading American armies. When a second Treaty of Paris ended the war in 1783, the first boundary between Canada and the United States was fixed from the Atlantic to Lake of the Woods. Americans who supported the British during the revolution called themselves Loyalists. Others branded them traitors and hounded them off their land. Some 50,000 Loyalists fled northeast, to found New Brunswick, or north into the St. Lawrence Valley and the Great Lakes region. Their new land was forbidding and lonely—"the roughest I ever saw," said one. Those transported into the "Western Settlements" of Quebec lived in tents until they could build log cabins. Difficult adjustments had to be made between two quite different peoples and their legal, religious and social systems. The problem was partly solved in 1791 by the division of Quebec

into Lower and Upper Canada, each with its own legislature and legal system.

By 1812, a half-million people were spread thinly over the Maritimes, and Lower and Upper Canada. In that same year, the vast plains of the West received their first European settlers as the Red River Settlement was established by the philanthropic Earl of Selkirk. But this venture angered the Métis, the mixed descendants of Indians and French and Scots fur traders, who considered the region their own. The new colonists also came into conflict with the North West Company, whose main trade route crossed Selkirk's land. Attacks on settlers by Métis and Nor'Westers resulted in the death of 20 settlers at the Seven Oaks Massacre in 1816. Reprisals followed. Five years later the Nor'Westers merged

Lord Durham found "two nations warring" in Canada and proposed change in his 1839 report

with the Hudson's Bay Company. The Red River Settlement survived, grew and prospered.

After the indecisive War of 1812, British North America

Some 14,000 Loyalist refugees landed at Saint John in 1783

experienced an expansion of trade with Britain, the West Indies and the Mediterranean countries. The timber trade and shipbuilding flourished. Upper Canada had 2000 sawmills by 1845 and British North America's merchant fleet grew into the third largest in the world. Montréal and Québec were busy commercial centers. York (renamed Toronto in 1834) grew into the business center of Upper Canada. Halifax was a major seaport and garrison town; Saint John, the trading center of a prosperous New Brunswick.

But the growing colonies were still ruled by governors accountable only to the British government. Executive councils controlled administrative appointments, banking and land grants. Unrest grew as Maritimers and Canadians became dissatisfied with the colonial constitutions and social structure.

Demands for reform were intense in both the Canadas. In Upper Canada they were prompted by abuses in government and the courts, and the power of the Anglican Church. In Lower Canada the struggle was also a social and religious one, French Canadians fighting for control of an English Executive Council. In 1837 armed rebellions broke out in both provinces. They were put down by British troops and militia—but they dramatized the need for change.

Lord Durham was sent out in 1838 to report on the rebel-

lions and to suggest solutions. His 1839 *Report on the Affairs of British North America* led to the union of Upper and Lower Canada in 1841, and to the introduction of responsible government—but not before this latter goal was achieved in Nova Scotia. There, editor-orator Joseph Howe led a long battle against the local oligarchy and the British government. In 1848 his province formed the first responsible government in the overseas Empire. In the same year the Province of Canada also achieved responsible government, and by 1855, so had Newfoundland, Prince Edward Island and New Brunswick. In 1858 the Crown Colony of British Columbia was created.

Lord Durham had written that, "The North American colonist needs some nationality of his own," and now there was serious consideration of union among the colonies. When the American Civil War broke out in 1861, unease over the threat of an American invasion increased. At the same time, Britain, increasingly reluctant to spend money on the defense of British North America, was encouraging its colonies to move toward union and self-government.

In June 1864, a coalition of the Liberal-Conservative and Reform parties in the Province of Canada was formed to promote a confederation of all the colonies. The Maritimes, already considering their own

union, were doubtful. At the Charlottetown conference in 1864, Canada held out to the Maritimers the prospects of an intercolonial railway, assumption of their public debts, allowance for new debts, legislatures for local affairs, representation by population in an elected House of Commons and Maritime representation equal to that of the Canadas in an appointed Senate. But no resolution was passed.

In October of that year, the Québec Conference elaborated the Confederation scheme, and in 1865, the Canadian legislature voted in favor of it. Opposition was growing in the Maritimes, particularly Nova Scotia—but the British government wanted the colonies to unite.

The threat from the United States seemed greater after the North's victory in the Civil War in 1865. And in 1866, the Fenian Brotherhood made armed attacks across the border from New York State in an effort to foment rebellion against British rule. These attacks convinced some doubters in New Brunswick and Nova Scotia that Confederation was necessary to their survival.

The British Parliament passed the British North America Act in 1867, and on July 1, the new country came into being with four provinces: Nova Scotia, New Brunswick, Quebec and Ontario—"One Dominion under the Name of Canada."

Rough-hewn but practical, a typical Upper Canadian homestead was built of squared logs cleared from the fields. Other lumber went into snake fences that were "horse-high, bull-strong and skunk-tight." A settler might take three years to clear 30 acres. Until they were pulled, burned or rotted, stumps made one third of the cleared land useless.

1740	1750	1760	1770	1780	1790	1800	1810	1820	1830	1840	1850	1860

- First road from Québec to Montréal, Chemin du Roi, opened
- First Canadian iron foundry, Les Forges du Saint-Maurice, established at Trois-Rivières
- King George's War
- Louisbourg surrenders to New England expedition
- Louisbourg returned to French by Treaty of Aix-la-Chapelle
- Halifax founded by the British
- Canada's first newspaper, the Halifax Gazette, is published
- Deportation of the Acadians
- Seven Years' War begins between England and France
- British capture and destroy Louisbourg
- New France ceded to Britain by Treaty of Paris
- Wolfe defeats Montcalm at Québec
- Montréal surrenders to the British
- Quebec Act guarantees civil and religious rights to French Canadians; extends Quebec's boundaries to include Labrador, Anticosti Island, the Magdalens and Indian territory southwest to the junction of the Ohio and Mississippi rivers, and north to Hudson's Bay Company lands
- Scottish emigration to Canada begins as 300 dispossessed Highlanders come to Prince Edward Island
- American invasion of Canada stopped at Québec
- Montréal fur traders form partnerships leading to North West Company
- King's College, founded in Windsor, N.S., first university in Canada
- York (Toronto) founded
- Alexander Mackenzie explores the "River Disappointment" (Mackenzie River) to the Arctic Ocean
- Arrival of the Loyalists; refugees from new American republic, in New Brunswick, Nova Scotia and Quebec
- U.S.-Canada boundary fixed from Atlantic to Lake of the Woods
- Quebec split into Provinces of Lower and Upper Canada
- Captains Vancouver and Quadra meet at Nootka Sound to settle British and Spanish claims to Pacific Coast
- Alexander Mackenzie, commissioned by the North West Company, crosses continent to Pacific
- St. John's Island renamed Prince Edward Island
- Labrador Act transfers Labrador coast from Lower Canada to Newfoundland
- War of 1812; Americans raid York, British raid Washington
- Lord Selkirk's Scottish settlers arrive at Red River
- First Canadian steamer begins service from Montréal to Québec
- Beginning of heavy immigration from Britain
- Rush-Bagot Agreement ends naval armament on the Great Lakes
- Boundary between U.S. and Canada west of Lake of the Woods fixed on 49th parallel to Rockies
- Welland Canal opened
- Hudson's Bay Company absorbs North West Company
- Lachine Canal opens
- Bytown (Ottawa) founded
- Howe, elected to Nova Scotia Assembly, begins agitation for responsible government
- Rebellions against autocratic government, led in Lower Canada by Louis-Joseph Papineau, in Upper Canada by William Lyon Mackenzie
- Editor Joseph Howe wins landmark freedom of the press case against magistrates of Halifax
- Upper Canada and Lower Canada united into Province of Canada
- Canada's first railway opens between Laprairie and Saint-Jean in Quebec
- Oregon Treaty sets 49th parallel as Canada's southwestern boundary.
- Nova Scotia gains responsible government
- Lord Durham investigates 1837 rebellions, writes Report for British government
- Gold discovered in Columbia, Thompson and Fraser rivers
- Famine in Ireland brings 80,000 immigrants to British North America
- Mainland colony of British Columbia proclaimed
- Vancouver Island founded as a Crown Colony
- Webster-Ashburton Treaty sets Maine-New Brunswick boundary

Triumphs and Trials of Nationhood

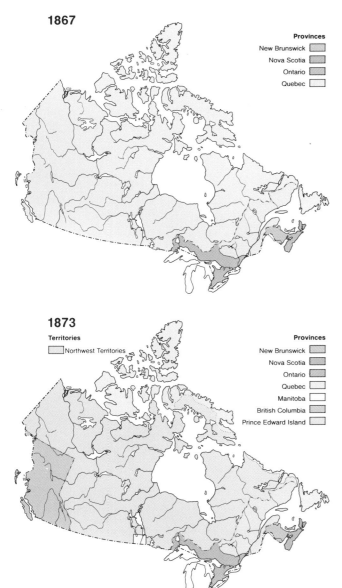

Provinces
New Brunswick ☐
Nova Scotia ☐
Ontario ☐
Quebec ☐

Territories
☐ Northwest Territories

Provinces
New Brunswick ☐
Nova Scotia ☐
Ontario ☐
Quebec ☐
Manitoba ☐
British Columbia ☐
Prince Edward Island ☐

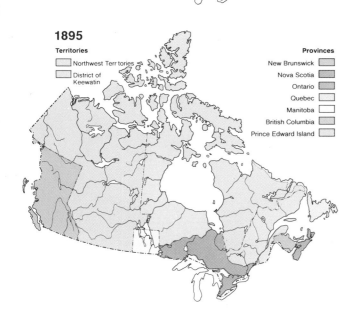

Territories
☐ Northwest Territories
☐ District of Keewatin

Provinces
New Brunswick ☐
Nova Scotia ☐
Ontario ☐
Quebec ☐
Manitoba ☐
British Columbia ☐
Prince Edward Island ☐

On July 1, 1867, the new Dominion of Canada was born. Its first prime minister was Sir John A. Macdonald who, apart from a five-year break, was to remain in power until his death in 1891. But the Dominion he was to govern was incomplete. Prince Edward Island and Newfoundland had refused to join, the vast prairie lands to the west and north belonged to the Hudson's Bay Company, and British Columbia seemed remote.

The first step toward forming a nation from sea to sea was the acquisition of the Northwest Territories from the Hudson's Bay Company. Manitoba, carved out of this area, became the fifth province in 1870. British Columbia, promised a railway link to the east, joined Confederation a year later. Prince Edward Island came into the Dominion in 1873 after a federal promise to establish permanent communication with the mainland and to assume the island's crippling railway debts.

The West now had to be governed and protected. American fur traders had begun to move into the Canadian Prairies, and after the Cypress Hills massacre in May 1873, when Montana wolf hunters killed a group of Assiniboine Indians, the North West Mounted Police were organized. Treaties were negotiated with Plains Indians for their land. In September 1877, leaders of the Blackfoot Confederacy, the last of the Prairie Indians to surrender their lands, signed Treaty No. 7 and ceded 130,000 square kilometres of what is now southern Alberta to the federal government.

The railways were the links that united the young nation. The Intercolonial Railway between Halifax and Québec went into operation in July 1876. As for the transcontinental route to British Columbia, the Macdonald government, realizing that the estimated costs of more than $100 million would consume much of Canada's available capital, decided to allow a private company to build the railroad.

Two rival groups, in Toronto and Montréal, applied for the charter. The Montrealers were

After 30 months and three conferences, the Fathers of Confederation created the new four-province country which became, by royal proclamation, "One Dominion under the Name of Canada." On July 1, 1867, in Ottawa, Scots-born Sir John A. Macdonald (standing, center) was sworn in as Prime Minister with his cabinet.

The CPR's Pacific Express, Canada's first transcontinental passenger train, arrived at Port Moody, B.C., from Montreal on July 4, 1886.

awarded the contract—until it was revealed that they had subsidized Macdonald's reelection in 1872. The ensuing Pacific Scandal brought down the Conservative government in 1873.

Under the new Liberal government of Alexander Mackenzie, government-supervised construction began between Fort William, Ont., and Winnipeg. Five years later the Conservatives were returned to office, but progress on the railway was hampered by lack of funds. Finally, in February 1881, a private company was formed—the Canadian Pacific Railway. The CPR's dynamic general manager, William Cornelius Van Horne, achieved what had been

thought impossible. Regular service was inaugurated on June 28, 1886, when the Pacific Express left Montréal for Port Moody, B.C. It arrived at noon on July 4, six days and 4652 kilometres from Montréal.

The CPR enabled the government to transport troops west to defeat the combined Métis-Indian forces in the Northwest Rebellion of 1885. The Métis leader, Louis Riel, had demanded self-government and recognition of their title to the land, proclaiming a provisional government and threatening the North West Mounted Police with a "war of extermination."

The execution of Louis Riel stirred great controversy. The government was caught between those who demanded Riel's death and others who felt that the government had provoked the rebellion.

The Conservatives, in power for 24 of the Dominion's first 29 years, fell in 1896 on the Manitoba Schools Question. Roman Catholics felt that the province's "nondenominational" schools were a Protestant system in disguise. But the federal Tories were divided on the issue and in 1896 they were beaten by the Liberals under Sir Wilfrid Laurier.

During his 15-year administration, Laurier presided over

dramatic changes in Canada. Industrial development, begun in the 1880s and spurred by Macdonald's National Policy, encouraged a shift of population toward the cities. Technological change improved communications. The Laurier years were an age of massive immigration to the West. Canada's population in 1901 was 5.4 million. Ten years later it was 7.2 million, with the largest growth in the West. In 1913 alone more than 400,000 immigrants arrived in Canada, many of whom went west to take up farming. On the treeless grasslands toward the U.S. border, settlers built houses of sod—"prairie shingles." Wheat production leaped from 56 million bushels in 1901 to 231 million in 1912. Alberta and Saskatchewan became separate provinces in 1905. The borders of Ontario, Manitoba and Quebec were extended north to their present limits in 1912, but the Quebec–Labrador boundary remained unsettled until 1927.

Those buoyant years had ended, however, by 1914, when the British Empire went to war against Germany. In October of that year, 33,000 Canadian troops sailed overseas; at least 400,000 others were to follow. By 1917, the rate of Canadian casualties—10,000 at Vimy Ridge alone—was causing a crisis at home. The toll of dead and wounded was outstripping enlistments, and Sir Robert Borden's Conservative government introduced conscription. By the end of the war in 1918, more than 60,000 Canadians had died.

Borden accompanied British leaders to Versailles and took an active part in the peacemaking of 1919. At his insistence, Canada signed the peace treaties separately and with that, achieved its first significant recognition as an autonomous nation, a status ultimately confirmed by the Statute of Westminster in 1931.

In the postwar years, automobiles became common. Women now had the vote. Prohibition, temporarily successful during

Ottawa was chosen as Canada's capital in 1857. Two years later, ground was broken for the Parliament Buildings.

1860	1865	1870	1875	1880	1885	1890	1895	1900	1905	1910	1915

• Sir John A. Macdonald first prime minister

• Colonies of Vancouver Island and British Columbia combined

• Hudson's Bay Company cedes territorial rights to Crown

• Red River Rebellion, led by Louis Riel, resists Ottawa's plans for new government; military expedition under Col. Garnet Wolseley restores order

• British North America Act establishes the Dominion of Canada with four provinces: Nova Scotia, New Brunswick, Quebec, Ontario

• Prince Edward Island enters Confederation

• Charlottetown and Québec Conferences discuss the confederation of British North American colonies

• Manitoba becomes the fifth province

• British dominion over Arctic islands passes to Canada

• British Columbia, promised transcontinental railway in ten years, joins Confederation

• Intercolonial Railway opened between Halifax and Québec

• District of Keewatin created from part of Northwest Territories

• Second Macdonald administration

• Administration of Alexander Mackenzie, first Liberal prime minister

• North West Mounted Police formed

• 15,000 Chinese laborers imported to work on the Canadian Pacific Railway

• Canadian Pacific Railway completed

• Secessionist government elected in Nova Scotia, but fails to take action

• Northwest Rebellion erupts over land and hunting grievances; Louis Riel forms provisional government, but yields to military force and is hanged

• Blackfoot Confederacy last of Indian tribes to surrender prairie lands in exchange for reserves

• Last British troops (except for small garrisons at Halifax and Esquimalt, B.C.) leave Canada

• First use of secret ballot in federal general election

• Wheat first exported from Manitoba to Britain

• Manitoba law abolishes denominational schools and use of French as legislative language, creates nondenominational school system

• Series of short-lived governments, headed successively by John Abbott, John Thompson, Mackenzie Bowell and Sir Charles Tupper

• Heavy immigration from Europe until World War I

• Sir John A. Macdonald dies

• First Ukrainian settlers arrive

Canada-Alaska boundary fixed •

• Yukon District becomes a separate territory

• Canadian soldiers take part in Boer War

• Klondike Gold Rush

• Doukhobors settle in the West

Administration of Sir Wilfrid Laurier

• Provinces of Alberta and Saskatchewan formed

• Northwest Territories divided into Mackenzie, Keewatin and Franklin districts

Early-maturing Marquis • wheat introduced

Mariner Joseph-Elzéar • Bernier affirms Canadian sovereignty in Arctic by erecting a plaque on Melville Island

First manned flight in • British Empire, at Baddeck, N.S., by J. A. D. McCurdy

Conservative administration of Sir Robert Borden

Royal Canadian Navy formed •

Battles of Vimy Ridge, • Hill 70, Passchendaele

World War I •

Britain declares war on Germany. More than 30,000 Canadian volunteers leave for England

Empress of Ireland • sinks in St. Lawrence, 1015 die

Conscription and personal income tax introduced

Halifax Explosion kills • nearly 2000 people and levels north end of city

• Ontario, Manitoba and Quebec boundaries extended north to present limits

Severe immigration restrictions begin (preferred countries include Belgium, France, Britain, Germany, Holland, Switzerland and Scandinavia)

Bankrupt railroads amalgamated into publicly owned Canadian National Railways

Canada, as separate state, signs Treaty of Versailles ending World War I

Union government led by Borden

Slabs of sod, held together by wheatgrass roots and often thatched with grass, made the first homes of many Prairie settlers.

the war years, was gradually lifted by the introduction of government-owned liquor stores. At home and abroad, stock markets soared—and their disastrous crash in 1929 led to the Great Depression. The Conservatives, under R. B. Bennett, defeated the Liberals in 1930 but inherited mass unemployment. Trade and the gross national product declined. By 1933, one quarter of Canada's labor force was out of work. The world price of wheat plummeted, and a series of droughts in 1931 and 1934 ruined thousands of western farmers. Mackenzie King's Liberals, reelected in 1935, started an inquiry into constitutional powers, for the Depression was demonstrating that the federal government lacked the power to deal with such an emergency. By the time a Royal Commission recommended changes in 1940, the country was again at war.

Canada had made its own declaration against Germany on Sept. 10, 1939, seven days after Britain. In five years the British Commonwealth Air Training Plan graduated 131,553 airmen at 97 flying schools across Canada. The Royal Canadian Navy helped convoy merchant ships through a North Atlantic infested with U-boats. The Royal Canadian Air Force became one of the Allies' largest. Canadian soldiers fought in Hong Kong, Italy and Western Europe.

The war made Canada an industrial power. Canadian citizenship was proclaimed in 1947. The Supreme Court of Canada became the court of last resort when appeals to Britain's Privy Council were abolished in 1949. Mackenzie King retired in 1948 after 22 years as prime minister—a British Commonwealth record—and was succeeded by Louis St. Laurent, who welcomed Newfoundland as the tenth province in 1949.

Oil discoveries provided a major impetus to the Canadian economy in the immediate postwar years. In February 1947, Leduc No. 1 came in south of Edmonton, the first major indication of Alberta's huge reserves of oil and natural gas. Iron ore was exploited in Ungava, along the Quebec–Labrador boundary, and the need to facilitate ore shipments spurred the construction of the St. Lawrence Seaway. The most controversial project was a natural gas pipeline from Alberta to Montréal, the financing of which became a hotly debated issue and

contributed to the St. Laurent government's fall in 1957. John Diefenbaker, Canada's first western prime minister, led the Tories back to power and, in an election the following year, obtained the largest majority of any party in Canadian history: 208 out of 265 Commons seats.

The 1960s saw a resurgence of nationalism in Quebec, characterized by the development of a separatist movement and the emergence of a new pro-Confederation group led by Pierre Elliott Trudeau. After the federal Liberals, led by Lester B. Pearson, were returned to office in 1963, they appointed a Royal Commission on Bilingualism and Biculturalism to examine the whole field of French–English relations, then took its advice by initiating measures to expand federal government services in French for French-speaking Canadians. When he replaced Pearson in 1968, Trudeau continued this policy, and the Official Languages Act of 1969 promoted the use of French in the federal public service.

Separatist strength grew in Quebec, culminating in the triumph of the Parti Québécois under René Lévesque in the election of 1976. Lévesque told the voters of Quebec he would seek a special mandate in a referendum before taking any steps toward independence or "sovereignty-association" with Canada. Before this took place, Trudeau's administration, beset by the nation's problems of infla-

Canadians who stormed Vimy Ridge gave the British Empire its first major victory in World War I.

tion and unemployment, fell when the 1979 national election brought to power the Conservatives under Joe Clark, Canada's 16th prime minister. Clark's government fell nine months later over the proposed budget, and the Trudeau administration was returned with a strong majority in February 1980.

Canadian Immigration and Emigration, 1871-1978

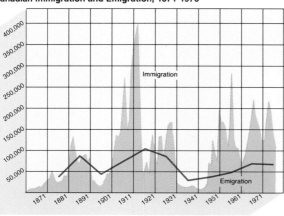

Growth of a Nation: From First Arrivals to Postwar Baby Booms . . .

Year	Population
1978	23,481,000
1971	21,568,311
1961	18,238,247
1951	14,009,429
1941	11,506,655
1931	10,376,786
1921	8,787,949
1911	7,206,643
1901	5,371,315
1891	4,833,239
1881	4,324,810
1871	3,689,257

Yukon and Northwest Territories · British Columbia · Alberta · Saskatchewan · Manitoba · Ontario · Quebec · New Brunswick · Nova Scotia · Prince Edward Island · Newfoundland

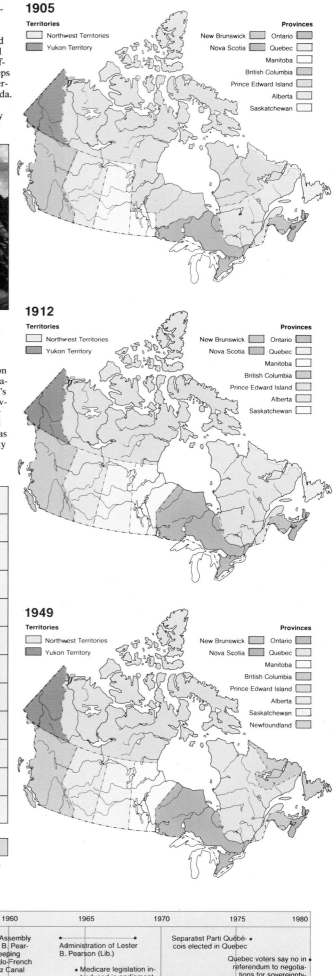

1905

Territories: Northwest Territories · Yukon Territory

Provinces: New Brunswick · Nova Scotia · Ontario · Quebec · Manitoba · British Columbia · Prince Edward Island · Alberta · Saskatchewan

1912

Territories: Northwest Territories · Yukon Territory

Provinces: New Brunswick · Nova Scotia · Ontario · Quebec · Manitoba · British Columbia · Prince Edward Island · Alberta · Saskatchewan

1949

Territories: Northwest Territories · Yukon Territory

Provinces: New Brunswick · Nova Scotia · Ontario · Quebec · Manitoba · British Columbia · Prince Edward Island · Alberta · Saskatchewan · Newfoundland

---

Timeline: 1925 – 1980

- First administration of Arthur Meighen
- First administration of W. L. Mackenzie King
- Drs. F. G. Banting and C. H. Best discover insulin
- Canada signs Halibut Treaty with U.S.—first bilateral treaty signed independently of Britain
- Group of Seven at peak of artistic fame
- Royal Canadian Air Force created
- Imperial conference defines Dominion autonomy within British Commonwealth
- Quebec-Labrador boundary settled by Privy Council

- Administration of R. B. Bennett
- Bank of Canada founded
- Wall Street Crash marks beginning of ten Depression years
- Statute of Westminster gives Canada and other Dominions complete autonomy
- Canada joins the League of Nations
- Second Meighen administration
- Unemployment reaches Depression peak
- Second Mackenzie King administration
- Dionne quintuplets born in Callander, Ont.
- Canada agrees with United States to build St. Lawrence Seaway
- Canadian Radio Broadcasting Commission formed

- World War II. Canadians play naval role in Battle of the Atlantic, 1939-45
- Unemployment insurance introduced
- Third Mackenzie King administration
- Canada declares war on Japan following Pearl Harbor attack. Canadian force taken prisoners in fall of Hong Kong
- Canadian Army fights in Western Europe, 1943-45
- Trans-Canada Airlines inaugurates transcontinental service
- Canadians suffer heavy casualties in Dieppe raid on coast of France
- King George VI first reigning monarch to visit Canada

- Heavy postwar immigration begins
- Family allowances introduced
- Canadian forces fight in Korean War under United Nations authority
- First major oil discovery in Alberta
- Newfoundland joins Confederation
- RCAF joins Bomber Command assault on Germany, 1942-45
- Collapse of Germany and Japan

- Stratford Shakespearean Festival launched
- Administration of Louis St. Laurent
- Supreme Court of Canada becomes court of last resort. Appeals to Privy Council in London abolished
- Hungarian revolution: 37,000 flee to Canada
- Vincent Massey becomes first Canadian-born Governor-General

- U.N. General Assembly adopts Lester B. Pearson's peacekeeping plan after Anglo-French attack on Suez Canal
- Conservatives under Diefenbaker win greatest election victory in Canadian history: 208 seats out of 265 in House of Commons
- Administration of John Diefenbaker
- St. Lawrence Seaway opens
- Lester B. Pearson wins Nobel Peace Prize
- Beginning of "Quiet Revolution" ushers in era of social reform in Quebec

- Medicare legislation introduced in parliament
- Administration of Lester B. Pearson (Lib.)
- Official Languages Act promotes use of French in federal public service
- Medicare becomes nationwide as Quebec joins plan
- Expo '67 in Montréal highlights Confederation Centenary
- American draft resistors seek asylum in Canada
- Administration of Pierre Elliott Trudeau reelected 1980

- Separatist Parti Québécois elected in Quebec
- Quebec voters say no in referendum to negotiations for sovereignty-association
- Olympic Games in Montreal
- Conservative government elected under Joe Clark, but defeated over budget. Trudeau administration returned to power in 1980.

Social Trends, Social Profiles

Facts and figures gathered in Canada's major census—a massive undertaking held every ten years—help paint a picture of contemporary Canada. The 1871 census was compiled by 50 clerks; the 1981 census involved seven years of planning and 42,000 employees. Information gathered on housing, occupations, languages and education helps determine how our society is changing. Governments consult census data in planning roads, schools and hospitals; businesses review statistics when choosing new sites and evaluating markets. Interim information is provided by a smaller census, held midway between major enumerations.

Census statistics reveal a society that is rapidly changing. The cost of living is rising steadily; women are working in greater numbers; the birthrate is falling; families are smaller than ever before. But increasing numbers of young, well-educated workers—the generation born in the immediate postwar years—are entering a job market that has not kept pace with their needs. Canadians' life expectancies continue to rise as infant mortality rates are reduced by better medical care, hygiene and diet. Immigrants still come to Canada from all over the world, adding their own heritage to the social diversity that characterizes this country.

Births and Deaths

The shaded area in the top graph (right) shows the difference between Canada's birthrate (number of births per 1000 people) and death rate (deaths per 1000 people); thus, the natural increase in population. The downward trend in the death rate is testimony to steadily improving health care, hygiene and diet, while the fluctuating birthrate reflects more complex social changes. The birthrate was low between 1929 and 1945 but with postwar prosperity, the rate climbed. Those born in the baby boom of 1947–61 crowded Canadian schools until recently, and are swelling the work force today.

Fertility rates (near right)—the average number of children a woman bears—also reflect social conditions. The postwar trend toward large families has given way to a 1979 average of 1.7—the lowest in Canadian history.

Canada's rate of infant mortality (far right)—a good indicator of a society's general welfare—is among the world's lowest, and good health care and living conditions have kept the rate falling steadily.

Education

In 1800, at least one out of three Canadians was illiterate. But by 1900 school attendance was compulsory, and today most Canadian children stay in school until they are 15 or 16. Levels of education still vary from province to province (below, top): in general, provinces with relatively high proportions of rural residents and of elderly people have the lowest levels of formal schooling.

Retention rates (below, left) compare a province's enrollment in Grade 12 with the Grade 2 enrollment ten years earlier. (In Quebec and Newfoundland, Grade 11 lists are compared with Grade 2.) It is apparent that students in rural areas, especially the Northwest Territories, the Yukon and the Maritimes, leave school at a much earlier age than those in British Columbia, Alberta and Quebec.

The labor force graph (below, right) shows, by level of education, the proportion of men and women in the work force in 1979. Men's rates generally vary little, but the higher a woman's level of education, the more likely she is to hold a job.

Marriage, Divorce and the Family

About nine out of ten adults in Canada marry, but marriages were not always so common: in 1901 just over half of Canadian adults had taken husbands or wives.

The effects of World War II on the marriage rate (marriages per 1000 people) are evident in the top graph (above). The wartime economy was strong, and thousands of servicemen were wed before heading overseas. Their return triggered another few years of high marriage rates, but also resulted in numerous divorces. After 1963 the marriage rate showed a slight upward turn, as the baby-boom generation reached marriageable age.

The divorce rate (above, left), shown as divorces per 100,000 people, leaped from 54.8 in 1968 to 124.2 in 1969, when a new act liberalized Canada's divorce laws. Although the rate has continued to climb, less than two percent of Canadians over 15 are divorced, while 64 percent are married. And just as there have been more divorces in recent years, there have also been more remarriages, since most divorced people stay single less than three years.

But one in ten families has only one parent (above, right). And in 83 percent of these families, that single parent is the mother. (Men have a shorter life expectancy, and children usually live with their mother if marriages break up.)

Population Growth

The percentages of men and women in different age groups (top, left) influence the population growth rate. Even though most new families are small, Canada's population is rising because of the large number of women of childbearing age: the baby-boom generation. As predicted here (far left), the population may top 31 million by the year 2001 (assuming an average family size of 2.1 children in 1991, and net migration—immigration minus emigration—of 100,000 persons a year). The same graph also forecasts an increase in the proportion of persons over age 65 due to high birthrates in the early 1900s, the flood of young immigrants into Canada in 1911–31, and a general rise in life expectancy.

Like infant mortality rates, life expectancies reflect a country's general standard of living. In three quarters of the world, life expectancy is still below 55 years. But a boy born in Canada today will enjoy an average life span of 70 years, while a girl's is 77.5 years. Expanding government medicare programs and improved medical technology are allowing Canadians to live longer. As late as Confederation, the average life expectancy in Canada was only 40 years; then the leading causes of death were old age, consumption, diphtheria and lung disease. Today the major causes have become the diseases of affluence: heart attack, cancer and stroke.

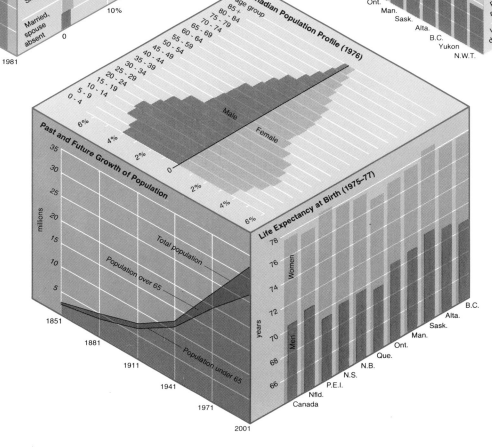

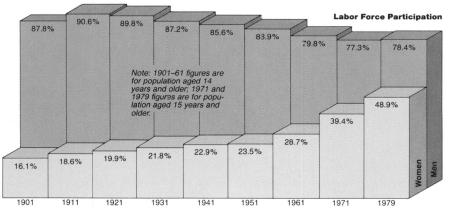

Labor Force Participation

1901	1911	1921	1931	1941	1951	1961	1971	1979
87.8%	90.6%	89.8%	87.2%	85.6%	83.9%	79.8%	77.3%	78.4%
16.1%	18.6%	19.9%	21.8%	22.9%	23.5%	28.7%	39.4%	48.9%

Women / Men

Note: 1901–61 figures are for population aged 14 years and older; 1971 and 1979 figures are for population aged 15 years and older.

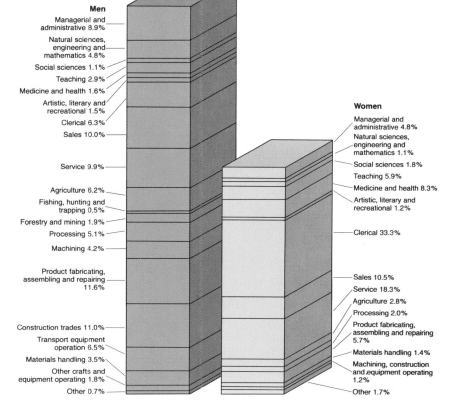

Men
- Managerial and administrative 8.9%
- Natural sciences, engineering and mathematics 4.8%
- Social sciences 1.1%
- Teaching 2.9%
- Medicine and health 1.6%
- Artistic, literary and recreational 1.5%
- Clerical 6.3%
- Sales 10.0%
- Service 9.9%
- Agriculture 6.2%
- Fishing, hunting and trapping 0.5%
- Forestry and mining 1.9%
- Processing 5.1%
- Machining 4.2%
- Product fabricating, assembling and repairing 11.6%
- Construction trades 11.0%
- Transport equipment operation 6.5%
- Materials handling 3.5%
- Other crafts and equipment operating 1.8%
- Other 0.7%

Women
- Managerial and administrative 4.8%
- Natural sciences, engineering and mathematics 1.1%
- Social sciences 1.8%
- Teaching 5.9%
- Medicine and health 8.3%
- Artistic, literary and recreational 1.2%
- Clerical 33.3%
- Sales 10.5%
- Service 18.3%
- Agriculture 2.8%
- Processing 2.0%
- Product fabricating, assembling and repairing 5.7%
- Materials handling 1.4%
- Machining, construction and equipment operating 1.2%
- Other 1.7%

Making a Living

The Canadian labor force has changed dramatically since we were a nation of farmers. The chart above shows the change in the labor force *participation rate*: the proportion of working-age men and women either employed or looking for work. In 1901, 88 percent of men and only 16 percent of women worked outside the home; today 78 percent of men and almost 50 percent of women are in the labor force.

The fall in the rate for men is largely explained by longer school attendance and earlier retirement. The leap in the rate for women reflects greater social changes. Economic pressures have sent more women outside the home to earn money to support their families. The falling birthrate means more women are available to work.

The diagram at right shows the participation of today's workers in various occupations.

As recently as 1941, one out of four people worked on farms; today farmers make up only five percent of the labor force. Most workers are employed in "white-collar" occupations as professionals, managers, clerks and salespeople. But while women have more than doubled their participation in the work force since 1931, most are still employed in education, clerical jobs and the service industries.

Average Unemployment Rate, 1979
- 15 %
- 12 %
- 10 %
- 5 %

Out of Work

This map of Canada's estimated average unemployment rates (in 1979) reveals marked variations across the country. Seasonal fluctuations are not shown—Canada's climate makes certain outdoor work unfeasible in winter.

Regional variations—in climate, types of industry, economic development, and the age and education level of the work force—contribute to different levels of unemployment. In recent years the rate has remained highest in most parts of Quebec and the Atlantic provinces (where average earnings are the lowest). Ontario and the Prairies have enjoyed the lowest

rates of unemployment. Even in 1973, a year when the national economy was booming, the unemployment rate in Atlantic Canada reached nine percent, while Ontario's rate was only four percent. In some Newfoundland communities, the rate may reach 50 percent in winter.

These days, young people suffer the highest unemployment. In 1979, workers 24 and younger made up almost half the ranks of the unemployed. Many must spend time after leaving school to find work. Others leave jobs to search for work they find more satisfying.

Canada Moves

The 1976 census revealed that almost half the population aged five and over had moved within the last five years. In 1966–74 (*below*) the populations of Ontario and British Columbia grew the fastest, net interprovincial migration averaging more than 20,000 people a year. But economic growth in these two provinces has slowed, and since 1974 Alberta has lured more and more Canadians from other parts of the country.

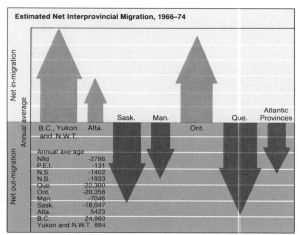

Estimated Net Interprovincial Migration, 1966–74

Net in-migration / Net out-migration / Annual average

B.C., Yukon and N.W.T. — Alta. — Sask. — Man. — Ont. — Que. — Atlantic Provinces

Annual average
Nfld.	-2786
P.E.I.	-131
N.S.	-1402
N.B.	-1933
Que.	-22,300
Ont.	-20,358
Man.	-7046
Sask.	-16,047
Alta.	5423
B.C.	24,980
Yukon and N.W.T.	884

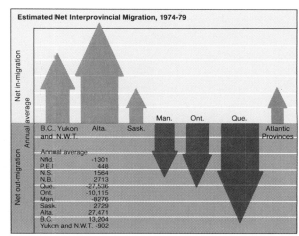

Estimated Net Interprovincial Migration, 1974–79

Net in-migration / Net out-migration / Annual average

B.C., Yukon and N.W.T. — Alta. — Sask. — Man. — Ont. — Que. — Atlantic Provinces

Annual average
Nfld.	-1301
P.E.I.	448
N.S.	1564
N.B.	2713
Que.	-27,536
Ont.	-10,115
Man.	-8276
Sask.	2729
Alta.	27,471
B.C.	13,204
Yukon and N.W.T.	-902

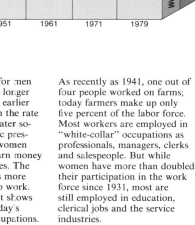

Canada

United States (mainland) — Others — Hawaii — Caribbean — Europe — Nfld. / P.E.I. / N.S. / N.B. — Que. — Ont. — Man. — Sask. — Alta. — B.C. — Yukon and N.W.T.

Vacation Travel

Vacation patterns are changing as declines in the value of the Canadian dollar and higher prices abroad keep Canadians closer to home. An estimated 62 percent of vacation trips made in 1979 (*left*) were confined to Canada. One quarter of Canadians' vacation trips were made to the United States. As many trips were made to Florida (seven percent) as to the Caribbean, Bermuda and Hawaii combined.

Melting Pot or Mosaic?

Canada's population has mushroomed from an estimated 200,000 Indians and Inuit in the year 1600 to more than 23 million people from many ethnic groups.

Wars, white man's diseases, dwindling herds and changes in traditional ways of life took a heavy toll on the native population, which fell to 100,000 by the year 1900. Today improved medical services have helped reverse this attrition.

Settlers from Great Britain and France formed the base of the early European population. But today the English-speaking

population so outnumbers the French that the fear of cultural assimilation is a continuing concern. The Quebec government has passed several acts encouraging the use of French as the official language of education and commerce.

From the early 1900s, settlers began to flood into Canada, clearing the vast Prairie farmlands and swelling city populations. Many immigrants have sought to preserve some of their distinct cultural heritage—and Canada's image as an ethnic mosaic rather than a melting pot.

Population by Ethnic Group
- Indian and Inuit
- French
- British
- Asian
- Dutch
- German
- Greek
- Hungarian
- Italian
- Jewish
- Polish
- Scandinavian
- Ukrainian
- Other

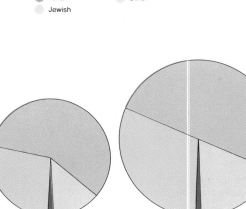

1700 (est.)	1790 (est.)	1810 (est.)	1830 (est.)	1850 (est.)	1871	1901	1921	1941	1971
200,000	404,500	696,000	1,291,500	2,581,200	3,689,257	5,371,315	8,787,949	11,506,655	21,568,311

Our Urban Society

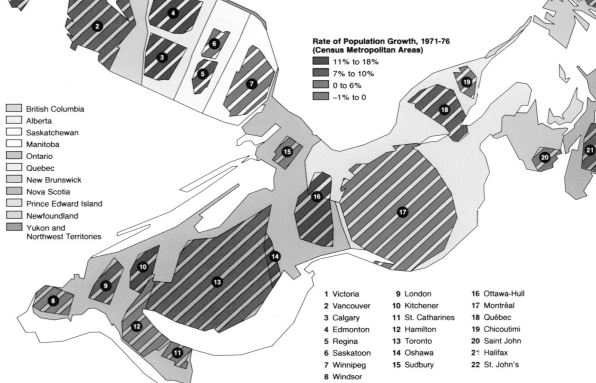

Canada's earliest cities were founded where water was deep or land was high. In the 1500s, the snug harbor of St. John's, Nfld. became a favored resting place for fishermen, who anchored there to repair their ships, replenish stocks of water and wood, and dry their catches of cod. The site of Québec, founded in 1608, was so defensible that Jesuit journals called it "the key to North America . . . because it is first a rock, secondly a height, thirdly a promontory; and, lastly, because it is fortified by two rivers in a manner of a trench and a moat." Montréal's strategic location at the confluence of the St. Lawrence and Ottawa rivers made it the outfitting center for fur-trading expeditions to the interior. Hull began where the Chaudière Falls forced a portage on the Ottawa River—a spot that became a meeting place for Indians, explorers, trappers, traders and loggers.

Even the sites of some Western cities were chosen for defensive purposes. In 1875, the North West Mounted Police built a garrison post called Fort Calgary at the junction of the Bow and Elbow rivers as part of their battle against whiskey traders. Soon after, the railroad began to influence the growth of Western cities. Towns along the Canadian Pacific route, such as Calgary and Vancouver, boomed when the transcontinental line was completed in 1885.

Its location can affect a city's growth in other ways. The flat land around such Prairie cities as Regina and Edmonton encourages urban sprawl; cities built on islands grow up, not out, as in the case of Montréal. Not until the construction of the Lion's Gate Bridge in 1938 did West Vancouver's rapid expansion begin.

The map at right, where cities and provinces are shown in proportion to their populations, is striking proof that we are an urban society: three out of four Canadians live in cities. Colors indicate the rates of growth among urban centers (*top, right*).

British Columbia
Alberta
Saskatchewan
Manitoba
Ontario
Quebec
New Brunswick
Nova Scotia
Prince Edward Island
Newfoundland
Yukon and Northwest Territories

Rate of Population Growth, 1971-76 (Census Metropolitan Areas)
11% to 18%
7% to 10%
0 to 6%
–1% to 0

1 Victoria
2 Vancouver
3 Calgary
4 Edmonton
5 Regina
6 Saskatoon
7 Winnipeg
8 Windsor
9 London
10 Kitchener
11 St. Catharines
12 Hamilton
13 Toronto
14 Oshawa
15 Sudbury
16 Ottawa-Hull
17 Montréal
18 Québec
19 Chicoutimi
20 Saint John
21 Halifax
22 St. John's

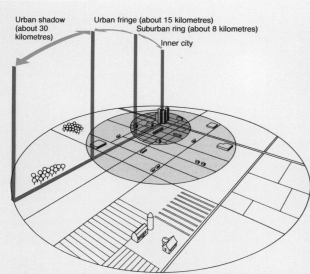

Urban shadow (about 30 kilometres)
Urban fringe (about 15 kilometres)
Suburban ring (about 8 kilometres)
Inner city

The city casts a broad shadow over its rural environs. At its core are a tightly packed business district and high-density housing. The suburban ring, with single-family dwellings, may extend eight kilometres past the core of a medium-sized city. The urban fringe beyond, often a haphazard mixture of urban blight and uncultivated fields, can extend twice as far. The edge of the urban shadow, as far as 30 kilometres away, also feels the city's impact.

North Vancouver's Marine Drive illustrates a familiar Canadian problem: urban sprawl.

Paradise Paved: How City Invades Countryside

Canada's cities were compact in the days when people traveled on foot or by horse-drawn carriage. In the 1880s streetcars began to expand metropolitan boundaries, but it was the mass-produced automobile that started the flight to the suburbs.

The very qualities that make land suitable for agriculture—mild climate, fertile and well-drained soil, sufficient water and flat surface—also make it ideal for development. Canada's fast-growing cities are gradually encroaching upon some of the country's most valuable farmland, notably in the Niagara fruit belt and the lower Fraser Valley.

City dwellers wanting country homes in these areas escalate property values, inducing farmers to sell out. Not all the land is used for residences: some is needed for airports, dams and expressways; some is bought by speculators anticipating the city's growth.

Strict zoning laws can preserve agricultural land and set areas aside for green belts, parks, and planned urban and industrial development. But Canadian housing preferences contribute to urban sprawl, since many parents prefer detached homes over apartments. A return to higher-density living would restrain urban expansion. Low-rise housing is more land- and energy-efficient than a detached house on a large lot, and could provide an alternative to the high-rise apartment. Other solutions to urban sprawl include use of empty space in existing neighborhoods, and redevelopment of old, underused industrial land.

Housing Types in Selected Census Metropolitan Areas

(St. John's, Montréal, Toronto, Thunder Bay, Winnipeg, Saskatoon, Edmonton, Vancouver — 10% to 100%)

Thunder Bay has the highest proportion of households in single detached homes, Montréal the highest in apartments.

Single detached
Single attached
Apartment
Duplex
Mobile home

Nature Tamed: Urban Green Spaces

Fortunately, most early planners of Canadian cities recognized the need for urban green spaces as antidotes to city noise and bustle. But green wasn't always available. Regina, founded in 1882, stood on a dry, treeless plain. Farsighted city fathers dammed the muddy trickle called Wascana Creek to create a lake, and established what is now Wascana Centre: a verdant playground complete with formal gardens, fountains and cycling paths.

Other cities had more scenic settings. Montréal's Mount Royal Park was established in 1860 on a thickly wooded hill overlooking the city and the St. Lawrence River. The park's grassy slopes, lookouts and Beaver Lake were designed by the master of urban landscaping, Frederick Law Olmsted, an American architect who also planned New York's Central Park and Winnipeg's Kildonan Park.

Through judicious use of green space, Ottawa has acquired a beauty that befits the nation's capital. A green belt (an average of four kilometres wide) encloses the city, thwarting urban sprawl.

Vancouver 35.8%
Winnipeg 6.9%
Edmonton 23.1%
Halifax 32.9%
Regina 10.8%
St. John's 37.7%

Early morning mist shrouds a lagoon in Jericho Park, not far from downtown Vancouver. This 50-hectare urban oasis shelters more than 150 varieties of birds. The park's other attractions include a fine bathing beach, sailing center and playing field.

Cubes (left) show green space in proportion to a city's total area. (Parks, golf courses and cemeteries are included as green space.)

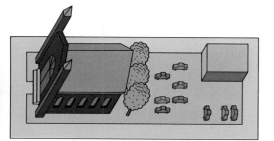

Here, a church occupies half a lot (top) in an area zoned for a floor/area ratio of five: that is, the floor space may not exceed five times the lot's area. Thus, a five-story building may be constructed on the entire lot (above). But to encourage preservation of the church, the city may disregard the church's floor space, and allow a ten-story building to be put up on half the lot (right).

The Shifting Patterns of City Skylines

The heart of a city is constantly changing: growing, deteriorating, redeveloping. In the 1960s, when progress meant skyscrapers, dozens of high office towers sprang up in larger Canadian cities. Such buildings make optimum use of valuable downtown land, and many add open space with landscaped plazas.

Although city revenues benefit from skyscrapers, people may not. High-rise construction often forces the demolition of entire blocks of low-rent housing.

Today many Canadian cities are moving toward development on a more human scale. *Downzoning* is one way to control new construction: most cities are reducing the allowable floor area of new buildings, as well as encouraging developers to add housing space to new structures.

Restorations can revitalize older neighborhoods: Victoria's Bastion Square and Vancouver's Gastown emerged from elderly, rundown districts. The charm of these historic areas can add more to a city's character than slabs of concrete and glass.

Urban renewal is also brought about by redevelopment or by rehabilitation. Some cities award grants and loans so that landlords and homeowners in designated areas can repair and renovate their own buildings.

Once a waterfront slum (right, top), Vancouver's historic Gastown district now hums with new life as old buildings are restored and refurbished (right).

From Traffic Jam to Rapid Transit

The automobile is firmly implanted in the Canadian way of life. Travel by car can be convenient, but heavy traffic cannot circulate in dense urban areas without expressways that appropriate valuable space, mar city landscapes and contribute to noise and air pollution.

Public transit can alleviate these problems, but only in city centers. Convenient bus routes through sprawling suburbs prove almost impossible to plan. Even in the city, the flood of cars often makes buses slow and inefficient. As fewer people use public tran-sit, fares rise, routes are cut, vehicles become overcrowded.

Modifications to public transit systems can increase their effectiveness. Several Canadian cities, such as Québec, speed up service with reserved bus lanes; others, like Montréal and Ottawa, offer reduced fares with monthly passes. Toronto's system combines a subway, buses, trolleybuses, commuter trains and streetcars. Outside peak hours, a telephone call from Regina's suburbs can summon a Telebus, which provides door-to-door transfer to main bus lines.

In Vancouver, vessels called Sea-Buses link North Vancouver with downtown transit, ferrying rush-hour passengers across Burrard Inlet.

Some commuters provide their own pollution-free rapid transit. Victoria's network of bicycle routes encourages pedaling to work, while Ottawa's frozen canal provides a healthy—if seasonal—mode of travel by skate.

The legacy of the automobile: landscapes laced with concrete.

Use of Public Transit by Type of Vehicle

Millions of passengers
1945 1950 1955 1960 1965 1970 1975
1600
1400
1200
1000
800
600
400
200
0

- Total
- Streetcar
- Diesel bus
- Trolleybus
- Subway

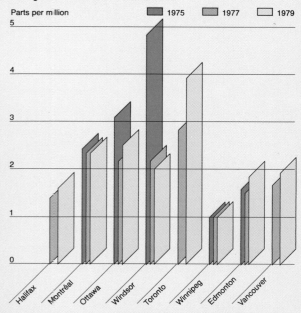

Average Carbon Monoxide Levels in the Air

Parts per million — 1975 / 1977 / 1979
5
4
3
2
1
0

Halifax, Montréal, Ottawa, Windsor, Toronto, Winnipeg, Edmonton, Vancouver

Polluted air is one of the greatest hazards of city living. Motor vehicles produce 60 percent of the poisonous carbon monoxide in our air. Some levels have fallen recently, due to catalytic reactors that convert exhaust fumes into carbon dioxide and water.

Passenger travel on public transit decreased almost continuously from the end of World War II until 1971. Since then, rising gasoline prices have been making travel by bus and subway more attractive. Even so, 72 percent of commuter trips in Canada in 1976 were made by car—carrying an average 1.26 persons apiece.

Six Canadian Cities: A Profile

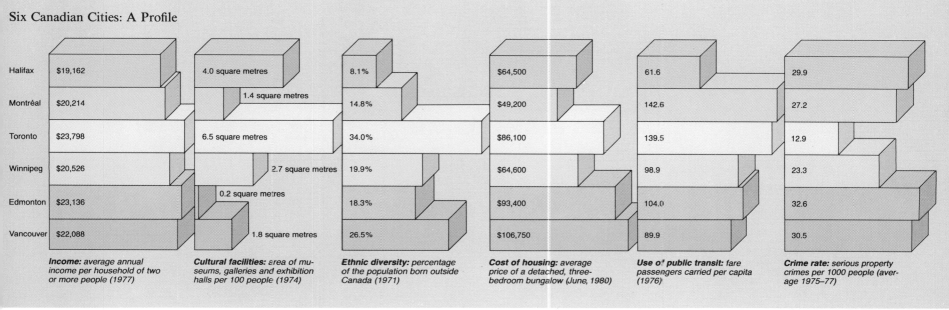

	Income	Cultural facilities	Ethnic diversity	Cost of housing	Use of public transit	Crime rate
Halifax	$19,162	4.0 square metres	8.1%	$64,500	61.6	29.9
Montréal	$20,214	1.4 square metres	14.8%	$49,200	142.6	27.2
Toronto	$23,798	6.5 square metres	34.0%	$86,100	139.5	12.9
Winnipeg	$20,526	2.7 square metres	19.9%	$64,600	98.9	23.3
Edmonton	$23,136	0.2 square metres	18.3%	$93,400	104.0	32.6
Vancouver	$22,088	1.8 square metres	26.5%	$106,750	89.9	30.5

Income: average annual income per household of two or more people (1977)

Cultural facilities: area of museums, galleries and exhibition halls per 100 people (1974)

Ethnic diversity: percentage of the population born outside Canada (1971)

Cost of housing: average price of a detached, three-bedroom bungalow (June, 1980)

Use of public transit: fare passengers carried per capita (1976)

Crime rate: serious property crimes per 1000 people (average 1975–77)

How We Are Governed

Canada is a constitutional monarchy, a parliamentary democracy with responsible government, and a federal union.

As a constitutional monarchy, Canada is headed by a monarch who has no real power but who represents the permanence and continuity of the state. All power is exercised in the monarch's name. The monarch also symbolizes the common political heritage of the member states of the British Commonwealth.

Canada has a system of responsible government: our public affairs are conducted by an executive responsible to a popularly elected legislature. Nova Scotia became, in 1848, the first British colony overseas to have this system, which replaced a council appointed by the governor. It spread quickly to the rest of British North America and, at Confederation on July 1, 1867, Canada achieved nationhood as a full-fledged parliamentary democracy.

On that date, Canada also became a federal union. There were four provinces at first—Nova Scotia, New Brunswick, Quebec and Ontario—but provision was made for the admission of others. Today all ten provinces possess certain sovereign powers.

The distribution of powers between federal and provincial governments is specified in the British North America (BNA) Act of 1867, which is our written constitution and the cornerstone of Canadian government. The BNA Act conferred the residual powers, those that were not clearly spelled out, upon the federal government. Over the years, however, judicial interpretations have increased provincial authority at the expense of the federal.

Canada also has an unwritten constitution, the legacy of usages and conventions acquired from Great Britain. This unwritten constitution is what sanctions the office of prime minister, the institution of the Cabinet or chief executive body, the existence of political parties and the formal division between government and opposition in the House of Commons.

The Governor General

For practical purposes, Canada's head of state is the governor general, who represents the Queen except on those rare occasions when she is on Canadian soil. The governor general is appointed by the Queen for a five-year term on the advice (always accepted) of the prime minister of Canada. The term may be extended.

Although symbolic, the position of the governor general is one of honor and dignity. It is the embodiment of the nation, standing above considerations of party and politics. The governor general's presence lends a sanction to events that none other can give. His signature makes laws official. He opens and closes Parliament. His administration of the oath of allegiance allows Cabinet ministers to assume their offices. He alone can accept the prime minister's resignation. (If he is incapacitated, his functions are exercised by the

Chief Justice of the Supreme Court of Canada.)

At one time, the Canadian prime minister always recommended the appointment of a British notable to this viceregal post. But this practice ceased in 1952, when Vincent Massey, a distinguished career diplomat and chairman of the Royal Commission on National Development in the Arts, Letters and Sciences, became the first Canadian-born governor general.

The last British governor general was Field Marshal the Earl Alexander of Tunis, one of the great Allied commanders of World War II, a man under whose leadership many Canadian soldiers went into battle.

The Big Business of Public Administration

Fast as Canada has grown, it has not grown as fast as its government. In 1980, one in every five employed Canadians was working for government at the federal, provincial or local level. The total government wage bill was more than $10 billion annually.

In the federal public service

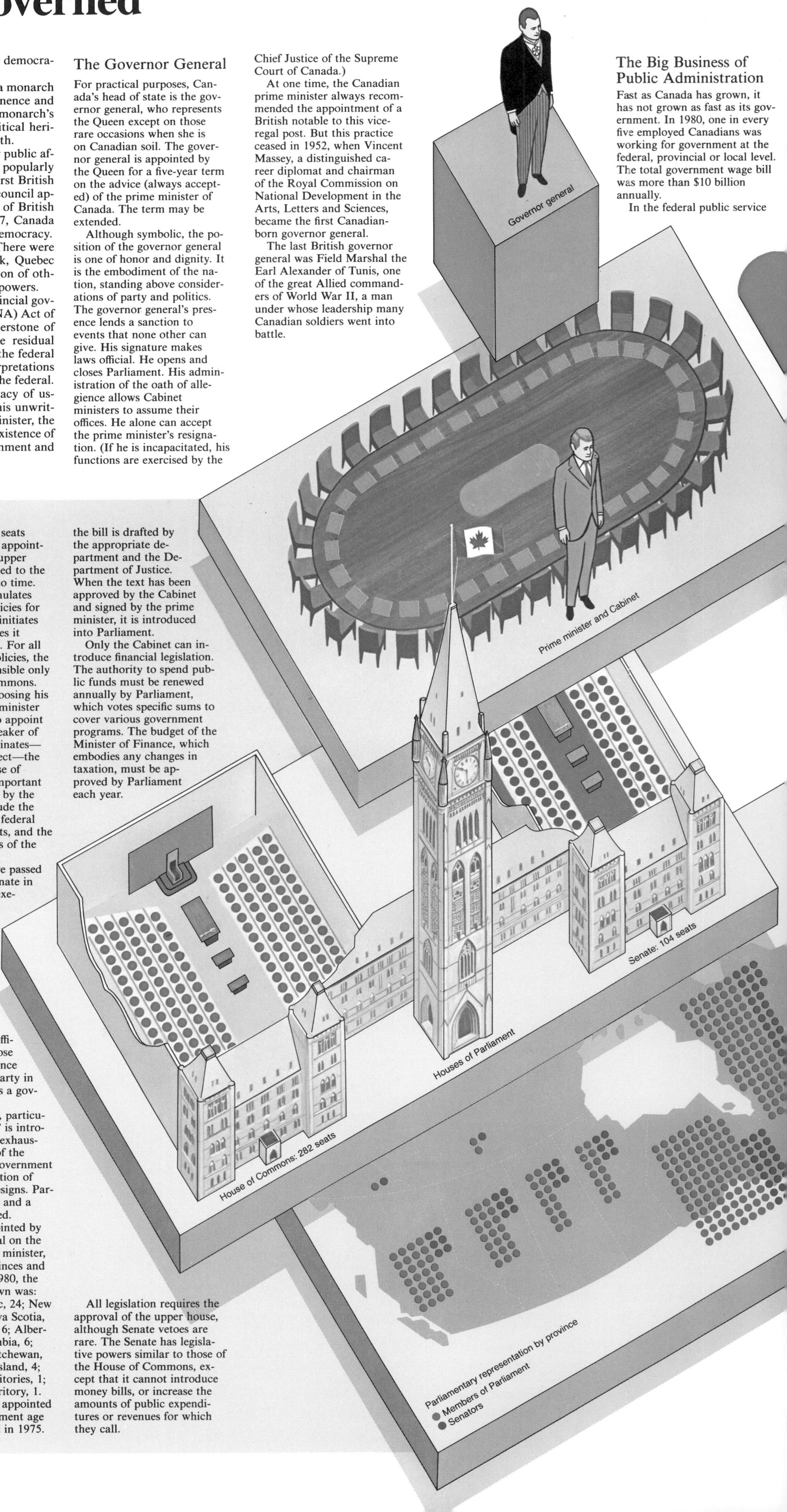

Prime Minister and Cabinet

In theory, the prime minister advises the Crown on measures to be taken for the good of Canada. In practice, however, the prime minister and his Cabinet are the real executive of the country.

The prime minister's tenure of office lasts as long as he remains party leader and retains the support of a majority in the House of Commons. By law, the life of Parliament may not exceed five years. But, if he wishes to strengthen his position in the House, or if he has been defeated on a vote of confidence, he can bring about a general election at any time by asking the governor general to dissolve Parliament.

One of the first acts of a new prime minister is the selection of his Cabinet: the ministers who head the departments and agencies that provide public services. Because these ministers are collectively responsible to the House of Commons,

they generally hold seats there. Senators, the appointed members of the upper house, are also named to the Cabinet from time to time.

The Cabinet formulates and implements policies for governing Canada, initiates legislation and guides it through Parliament. For all their actions and policies, the ministers are responsible only to the House of Commons.

In addition to choosing his Cabinet, the prime minister also has the right to appoint senators and the speaker of the Senate. He nominates—but the members elect—the speaker of the House of Commons. Other important appointments made by the prime minister include the chief justices of the federal and provincial courts, and the lieutenant governors of the provinces.

Most bills that are passed by Parliament originate in the Cabinet. Once executive support has been granted,

the bill is drafted by the appropriate department and the Department of Justice. When the text has been approved by the Cabinet and signed by the prime minister, it is introduced into Parliament.

Only the Cabinet can introduce financial legislation. The authority to spend public funds must be renewed annually by Parliament, which votes specific sums to cover various government programs. The budget of the Minister of Finance, which embodies any changes in taxation, must be approved by Parliament each year.

House of Commons and the Senate

The House of Commons is the lower house of the Canadian Parliament. Its members are elected for maximum terms of five years from electoral districts known as constituencies or ridings.

Representation in the House of Commons is based on population and is apportioned by province. In 1980, the provincial breakdown of members was: Ontario, 95; Quebec, 75; British Columbia, 28; Alberta, 21; Manitoba, 14; Saskatchewan, 14; Nova Scotia, 11; New Brunswick, 10; Newfoundland, 7; Prince Edward Island, 4; the Northwest Territories, 2; and the Yukon Territory, 1.

If a single political party wins more than half the seats in the House of Commons, it forms a majority government. Otherwise, the party with the largest number of seats will usually form a minority government and carry on until it is defeated in the House.

The party that wins the second-largest number of seats becomes the official opposition, whose duty is both to balance and challenge the party in power, and to act as a government-in-waiting.

Major legislation, particularly "money bills," is introduced and debated exhaustively on the floor of the House. When the government is defeated on a motion of nonconfidence, it resigns. Parliament is dissolved and a new election is called.

The Senate, appointed by the governor general on the advice of the prime minister, represents the provinces and the territories. In 1980, the provincial breakdown was: Ontario, 24; Quebec, 24; New Brunswick, 10; Nova Scotia, 10; Newfoundland, 6; Alberta, 6; British Columbia, 6; Manitoba, 6; Saskatchewan, 6; Prince Edward Island, 4; the Northwest Territories, 1; and the Yukon Territory, 1. Senators were once appointed for life, but a retirement age of 75 was instituted in 1975.

All legislation requires the approval of the upper house, although Senate vetoes are rare. The Senate has legislative powers similar to those of the House of Commons, except that it cannot introduce money bills, or increase the amounts of public expenditures or revenues for which they call.

Governor general

Prime minister and Cabinet

Senate: 104 seats

Houses of Parliament

House of Commons: 282 seats

Parliamentary representation by province

● Members of Parliament
● Senators

alone, there were 299,991 employees in 1980, carrying out tasks of government that ranged from the daily emptying of bureaucratic wastebaskets to representing Canada in the world's major capitals.

The service is organized basically into departments, each headed by a deputy minister who is its permanent chief. His superior is the particular Cabinet minister who is accountable to the House of Commons for the department's work. But the number of ministers in the Cabinet usually exceeds the number of government departments. Some ministers are given the duty of administering special agencies such as the Canadian Wheat Board, or of executing special programs, as in the area of multiculturalism. In 1980, the number of ministerial positions (*below*) was 33.

Federal and provincial powers were originally defined in the BNA Act. Those assigned to the federal government include the regulation of trade and commerce, "any mode or system of taxation," the postal services, defense, navigation, fisheries, currency, banking, naturalization, criminal law, and jurisdiction over railways,

Sir John A. Macdonald had a Cabinet of 13.

canals and telegraphs extending beyond the limits of a province.

Provincial powers include education, law enforcement, roads, natural resources, municipal affairs, and property and civil rights. There are areas of divided jurisdiction, notably agriculture, labor and health. All powers not specified in the BNA Act were granted to the federal government, although the trend in judicial interpretation has been to expand the role of the provinces.

Provincial administrations are similar in structure to the federal. But they range in size from Quebec's 26-member executive to Prince Edward Island's Cabinet of ten.

In addition to the departments of government, a large number of nondepartmental agencies and Crown corporations (publicly owned businesses) operate under the government's jurisdiction, particularly at the federal level. Crown corporations most familiar to the public are Air Canada, the Canadian National Railways and the Canadian Broadcasting Corporation. Rivaling these federal corporations are such provincial ones as Ontario Hydro, Hydro-Québec and the Saskatchewan Telephone Company.

Minister of Finance	Department of Consumer and Corporate Affairs	Department of Communications	Department of National Revenue
Department of Transport	Department of Veterans Affairs	Department of National Defence	Minister of State (Finance)
Department of Justice	Department of Energy, Mines and Resources	Department of Regional Economic Expansion	Minister of State (Small Businesses)
Department of Social Development	Department of Fisheries and Oceans	Minister of State (Canadian Wheat Board)	Minister of State (Trade)
Department of Indian Affairs and Northern Development	Department of State for Science and Technology	Department of Labour	Treasury Board Secretariat
Department of State for Economic Development	Department of the Environment	Department of External Affairs	Department of Employment and Immigration
Department of Industry, Trade and Commerce	Department of National Health and Welfare	Solicitor General	Department of Public Works
Department of Agriculture	Department of Supply and Services	Minister of State (Multiculturalism)	Minister of State (Mines)

How Laws Are Made

Every proposed law, or bill, goes through three readings in Parliament (see chart, *right*) to ensure that it has been fully understood and debated. Once the draft of a bill has been approved by the prime minister, the sponsoring minister will introduce it in either the House of Commons or the Senate, usually the former. A bill must pass both houses before it becomes law.

At the first reading, the minister offers a brief explanation of the bill. Then a printed copy is distributed to members for their examination. The second reading involves a debate and a vote on the bill's general principles. Next, the bill is examined in detail by a parliamentary committee, which either approves the bill or recommends changes and additions. The committee's report is followed by a third reading and a debate that leads to the final vote on the bill. The bill is then referred to the other house, where the entire procedure is repeated.

When the bill has been passed by both the House and the Senate, it must be signed into law by the governor general: the granting of royal assent.

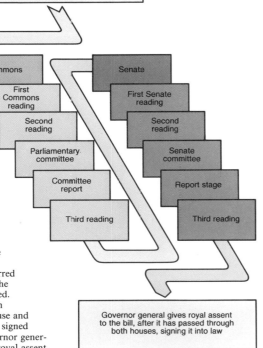

Cabinet approval of the bill, or proposed law, prepared by the sponsoring minister and the Department of Justice

Commons — First Commons reading — Second reading — Parliamentary committee — Committee report — Third reading

Senate — First Senate reading — Second reading — Senate committee — Report stage — Third reading

Governor general gives royal assent to the bill, after it has passed through both houses, signing it into law

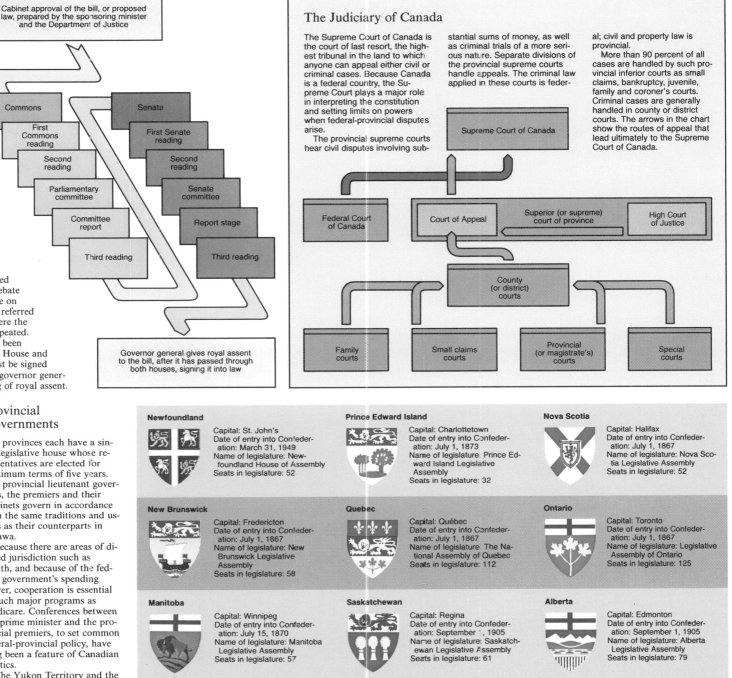

The Judiciary of Canada

The Supreme Court of Canada is the court of last resort, the highest tribunal in the land to which anyone can appeal either civil or criminal cases. Because Canada is a federal country, the Supreme Court plays a major role in interpreting the constitution and setting limits on powers when federal-provincial disputes arise.

The provincial supreme courts hear civil disputes involving substantial sums of money, as well as criminal trials of a more serious nature. Separate divisions of the provincial supreme courts handle appeals. The criminal law applied in these courts is federal; civil and property law is provincial.

More than 90 percent of all cases are handled by such provincial inferior courts as small claims, bankruptcy, juvenile, family and coroner's courts. Criminal cases are generally handled in county or district courts. The arrows in the chart show the routes of appeal that lead ultimately to the Supreme Court of Canada.

Supreme Court of Canada

Federal Court of Canada | Court of Appeal — Superior (or supreme) court of province | High Court of Justice

County (or district) courts

Family courts | Small claims courts | Provincial (or magistrate's) courts | Special courts

Parliamentary Representation

The number of members that each province can elect to the House of Commons is based primarily on population. The last redistribution, made in 1976, provided the Commons with 282 members. At Confederation there were 181 MPs. Since then, membership in the Senate has grown from 72 to 104. Northern Canada was not represented in the Senate until 1976, when one seat was granted to each of the territories.

Provincial Governments

The provinces each have a single legislative house whose representatives are elected for maximum terms of five years. The provincial lieutenant governors, the premiers and their Cabinets govern in accordance with the same traditions and usages as their counterparts in Ottawa.

Because there are areas of divided jurisdiction such as health, and because of the federal government's spending power, cooperation is essential in such major programs as Medicare. Conferences between the prime minister and the provincial premiers, to set common federal-provincial policy, have long been a feature of Canadian politics.

The Yukon Territory and the Northwest Territories fall largely under the direct jurisdiction of the federal government, and enjoy only a limited degree of self-government. A federally appointed commissioner for each territory heads a legislative council and reports to Parliament in Ottawa.

Newfoundland
Capital: St. John's
Date of entry into Confederation: March 31, 1949
Name of legislature: Newfoundland House of Assembly
Seats in legislature: 52

Prince Edward Island
Capital: Charlottetown
Date of entry into Confederation: July 1, 1873
Name of legislature: Prince Edward Island Legislative Assembly
Seats in legislature: 32

Nova Scotia
Capital: Halifax
Date of entry into Confederation: July 1, 1867
Name of legislature: Nova Scotia Legislative Assembly
Seats in legislature: 52

New Brunswick
Capital: Fredericton
Date of entry into Confederation: July 1, 1867
Name of legislature: New Brunswick Legislative Assembly
Seats in legislature: 58

Quebec
Capital: Québec
Date of entry into Confederation: July 1, 1867
Name of legislature: The National Assembly of Quebec
Seats in legislature: 112

Ontario
Capital: Toronto
Date of entry into Confederation: July 1, 1867
Name of legislature: Legislative Assembly of Ontario
Seats in legislature: 125

Manitoba
Capital: Winnipeg
Date of entry into Confederation: July 15, 1870
Name of legislature: Manitoba Legislative Assembly
Seats in legislature: 57

Saskatchewan
Capital: Regina
Date of entry into Confederation: September 1, 1905
Name of legislature: Saskatchewan Legislative Assembly
Seats in legislature: 61

Alberta
Capital: Edmonton
Date of entry into Confederation: September 1, 1905
Name of legislature: Alberta Legislative Assembly
Seats in legislature: 79

British Columbia
Capital: Victoria
Date of entry into Confederation: July 20, 1871
Name of legislature: Legislative Assembly of British Columbia
Seats in legislature: 57

Yukon Territory
Capital: Whitehorse
Date of proclamation as a separate territory under federal jurisdiction: June 13, 1898
Name of legislature: Yukon Legislative Council
Seats in legislature: 16

Northwest Territories
Capital: Yellowknife
Date of proclamation as a separate territory under federal jurisdiction: July 15, 1870
Name of legislature: Council of the Northwest Territories
Seats in legislature: 22

Money and the Economy

Canada's economic history is a tale of expansion and contraction, of boom and bust, of conservatism and innovation. The reasons for the low points in the cycle have varied, from unwise speculation and overoptimism to the complex web of social, political and economic events that led to the New York stock market crash of 1929. Yet, despite some backward steps and the persistent problems of inflation and unemployment, Canadians enjoy one of the highest standards of living in the world.

Canada's transition from a nation of farmers to a major industrial power took less than a century. Pre-Confederation Canada was a collection of isolated colonies of Great Britain—suppliers of raw materials and consumers of imported goods. After Confederation, domestic markets were widened by a growing transportation and communications network. The National Policy of protective tariffs further encouraged fledgling Canadian industry to compete in world markets.

The 20th century has witnessed major changes in the structure of the Canadian economy. Despite revivals of economic nationalism, the country's economic health, including the value of the Canadian dollar, has become closely tied to that of the United States. Economic trends in Canada (see chart, *below*) generally mirror American events and policy. In the 1920s and 1930s, labor unions gained strength and successfully demanded a larger share of Canada's business profits for their workers. Free enterprise had been gospel in North America, but an increasingly urban, industrialized society prompted government attempts to regulate the cycles of boom and bust. With the Depression, and the instability that has marked more recent years, most Canadians have taken for granted active government involvement in the economy.

From pelts to plastic; anything that is used by people as a standard of value and a medium of exchange is money. Many forms have been used in Canada (*right*), with widely ranging liquidity, risk and return.

Material goods such as **beaver pelts** *were the basis of barter.*

Silver **sols**, *the coinage of New France, were imported.*

Made beavers *were minted by the Hudson's Bay Company.*

Playing-card money *was issued during an 18th-century coin shortage.*

Private **bank notes** *reflected the lack of official currency.*

Canada's present currency system dates from 1934.

Credit cards *are symbols of today's "cashless society."*

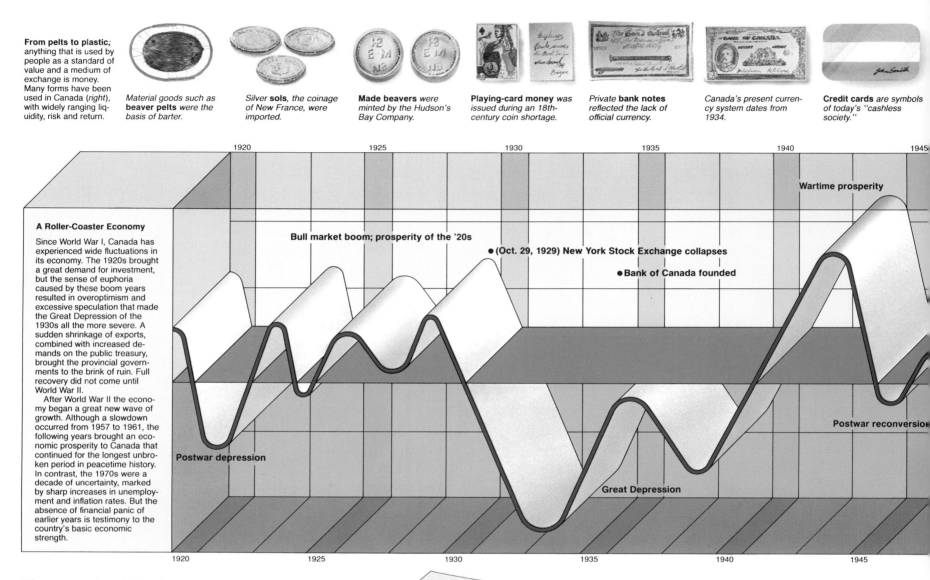

A Roller-Coaster Economy

Since World War I, Canada has experienced wide fluctuations in its economy. The 1920s brought a great demand for investment, but the sense of euphoria caused by these boom years resulted in overoptimism and excessive speculation that made the Great Depression of the 1930s all the more severe. A sudden shrinkage of exports, combined with increased demands on the public treasury, brought the provincial governments to the brink of ruin. Full recovery did not come until World War II.

After World War II the economy began a great new wave of growth. Although a slowdown occurred from 1957 to 1961, the following years brought an economic prosperity to Canada that continued for the longest unbroken period in peacetime history. In contrast, the 1970s were a decade of uncertainty, marked by sharp increases in unemployment and inflation rates. But the absence of financial panic of earlier years is testimony to the country's basic economic strength.

Bull market boom; prosperity of the '20s

● **(Oct. 29, 1929) New York Stock Exchange collapses**

● **Bank of Canada founded**

Wartime prosperity

Postwar depression

Great Depression

Postwar reconversion

The Geography of Wealth

In 1979 the total Canadian national income was $210 billion, or about $8800 for each man, woman and child. But the economic pie is not sliced into equal portions. Illustrated at right is the material standard of living across Canada (estimated by dividing Gross Provincial Product—the value of all goods and services produced within each province—by provincial population). The map dramatizes an historic problem in Canadian politics and economics: regional disparities of wealth.

Underlying these geographical differences are differences in industry. The economies of the Atlantic Provinces depend heavily on fishing, forestry and mining—industries vulnerable to cycles of unemployment and changing world markets. In contrast, Ontario and Quebec have diversified, tariff-protected economic bases: about 80 percent of all Canadian manufacturing is concentrated along the Great Lakes-St. Lawrence industrial heartland. The farming provinces of Manitoba and Saskatchewan, where provincial incomes have traditionally been slightly lower than the rest of Canada, enjoy generally higher employment levels. In the 1970s, Alberta passed Ontario and British Columbia in per capita wealth. Its dramatic growth has been due largely to its vast mineral reserves, particularly oil and gas. British Columbia's economy is balanced among re-

source industries, foreign trade and a growing manufacturing sector.

The relative cost of living also varies across Canada (*below*), although not to the same extent as wealth. The selected components of the chart make up more than half of the average urban consumer's budget. The greatest difference is in the cost of housing (not charted), which in 1980 was twice as high in booming Edmonton as in Montréal.

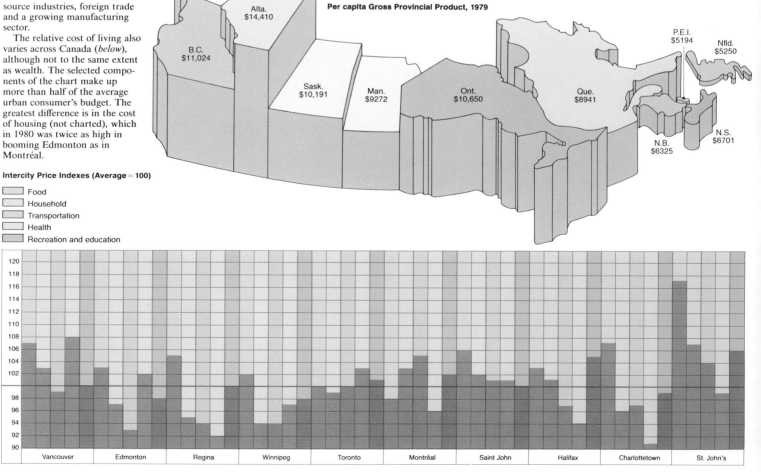

Per capita Gross Provincial Product, 1979

- Alta. $14,410
- B.C. $11,024
- Sask. $10,191
- Man. $9272
- Ont. $10,650
- Que. $8941
- P.E.I. $5194
- Nfld. $5250
- N.B. $6325
- N.S. $6701

Intercity Price Indexes (Average = 100)

- Food
- Household
- Transportation
- Health
- Recreation and education

Vancouver · Edmonton · Regina · Winnipeg · Toronto · Montréal · Saint John · Halifax · Charlottetown · St. John's

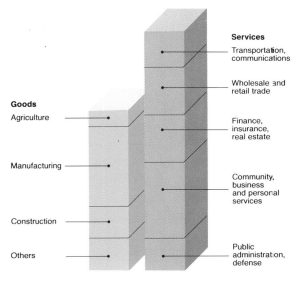

Goods

Agriculture

Manufacturing

Construction

Others

Services

Transportation, communications

Wholesale and retail trade

Finance, insurance, real estate

Community, business and personal services

Public administration, defense

Goods and Services

At the turn of the century, workers employed in the goods-producing industries—agriculture, fishing, forestry, mining, construction and manufacturing—outnumbered service workers two to one. By 1980, more than half of all the workers in Canada were producing services rather than goods, with services contributing 60 percent of the Gross National Product (*left*). Much of the remarkable growth of services is the result of government involvement—federal, provincial and local—in the economy. Government spending as a percentage of the GNP has doubled from 20 percent in the early 1950s to about 40 percent today.

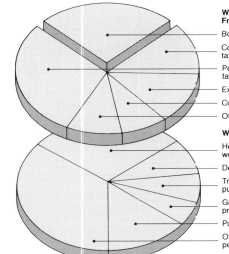

Where It Comes From:

Borrowed 25¢

Corporate income taxes 13¢

Personal income taxes 30¢

Excise taxes 13¢

Customs duties 8¢

Other 11¢

Where It Goes:

Health and welfare 28¢

Defense 8.5¢

Transportation and public works 7¢

Grants to provinces 6.5¢

Public debt 15¢

Other federal expenses 35¢

The Federal Dollar

About 20 percent of all spending in Canada is done by the federal government, which raises money in four main ways: through bank and individual loans (such as bonds), by increasing the money supply, and by collecting taxes. In 1941 the federal income tax of all citizens averaged $22.50; by 1980 it totaled more than $600.

In 1931 the government spent $42.56 per person. Today that figure has climbed to $2000. In 1979, federal expenditures reached an awesome $47 billion, compared to an income of $37 billion. This deficit—25 cents per budget dollar—must be borrowed, adding to the national debt.

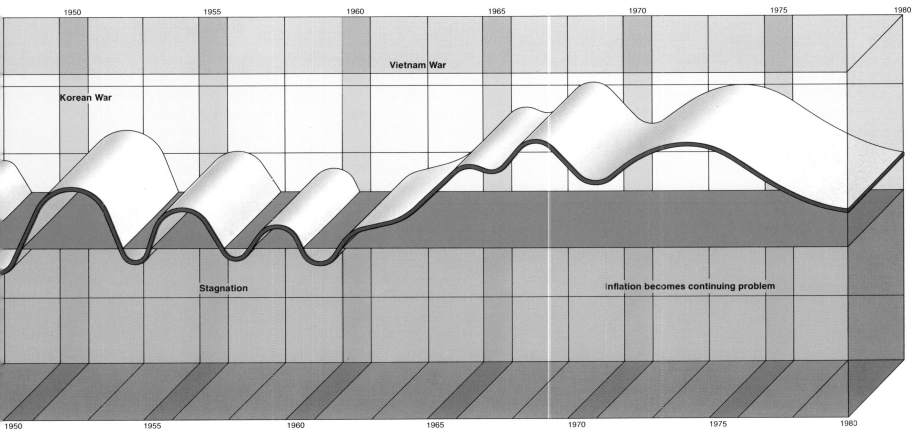

Korean War

Vietnam War

Stagnation

Inflation becomes continuing problem

1950 1955 1960 1965 1970 1975 1980

Pull Plus Push Equals Inflation

Inflation, long summed up as "too much money chasing too few goods," shows itself as a sustained rise in prices or fall in the value of money.

Inflation falls into two broad categories. *Demand-pull* inflation occurs when there is too much money available in the form of credit, when governments spend more than they collect in taxes, and when expectations of rising prices trigger speculative buying. *Cost-push* inflation is fueled by rising costs in raw materials, capital or labor, which in turn force consumer prices to rise.

Primary inflation-fighting weapons are in the hands of government. The federal government, which directs fiscal policy, can reduce its spending, raise taxes, establish wage and price guidelines or legislate mandatory wage and price controls. The Bank of Canada, which regulates the money supply, can restrict borrowing by raising the interest rates on loans, by varying the reserve ratio (the amount of money which must be held on deposit by the chartered banks), by buying and selling securities (open-market transactions), and by influencing foreign-exchange rates.

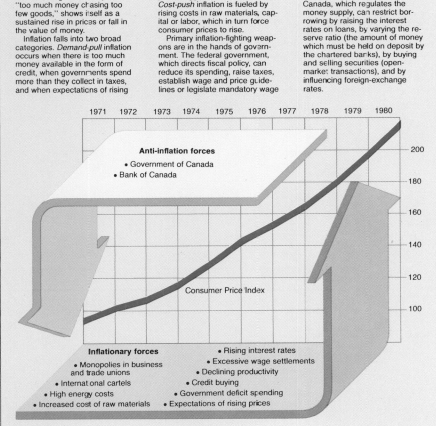

1971 1972 1973 1974 1975 1976 1977 1978 1979 1980

Anti-inflation forces
• Government of Canada
• Bank of Canada

Consumer Price Index

200
180
160
140
120
100

Inflationary forces
• Monopolies in business and trade unions
• International cartels
• High energy costs
• Increased cost of raw materials
• Rising interest rates
• Excessive wage settlements
• Declining productivity
• Credit buying
• Government deficit spending
• Expectations of rising prices

Swelling Prices, Shrinking Dollar

The same "basket" of goods and services that cost $100 in 1970 cost the consumer $132.40 in 1975, and $201.80 in February 1980. In effect, the 1980 dollar has shrunk to 50 cents.

To measure the impact of inflation on Canadians, Statistics Canada periodically updates the 300 components in the Consumer Price Index (CPI), from dental fillings to haircuts. The recent price histories of major consumer goods and services are charted at right.

The price index measures movements rather than actual price levels. If the index price of milk is 110 and butter 105, it does not mean that milk is more expensive than butter, but that the price of milk has increased twice as much since 1971, the base period. The survey also "weights" the items in the CPI on the basis of their importance. A five percent rise in gasoline, for example, would have a greater impact than even a 50 percent rise in pepper.

A large number of goods and services have risen far more than 100 percent since 1971, while others have gone up much less. Only one item—long-distance phone calls—has actually declined in price. Nationally, the steepest rises have come in life's necessities: food, clothing and shelter, which represent 65 cents of the average family's budget dollar.

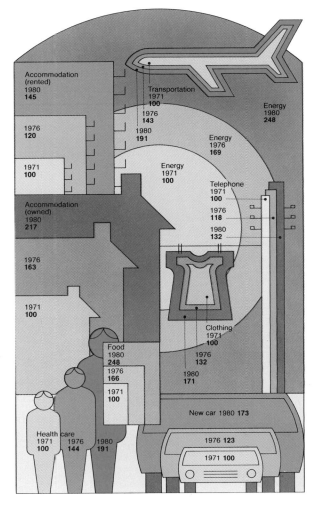

Accommodation (rented)
1980 145
1976 120
1971 100

Accommodation (owned)
1980 217
1976 163
1971 100

Transportation
1971 100
1976 143
1980 191

Energy
1980 248
1976 169
1971 100

Telephone
1971 100
1976 118
1980 132

Clothing
1971 100
1976 132
1980 171

Food
1980 248
1976 166
1971 100

Health care
1971 100
1976 144
1980 191

New car 1980 173

1976 123
1971 100

Working Our Land: The Farms

Only one eighth of Canada's land is suitable for agriculture. On this small area along the southern border, farmers raise a variety of produce: apples and asparagus, cattle and wheat, grapes to make wine and sunflowers for oil, potatoes for chips and hogs for *tourtière*.

Though today only five percent of Canada's labor force works on the farm, this country was settled by farmers. Indians were the first to cultivate the soil. They cleared land by cutting trees and burning the stumps, then planted hills of corn, beans and squash. In the rich soil and mild climate of southwestern Ontario, Indians grew tobacco for religious ceremonies and barter.

The first Europeans to reach these shores were more interested in fish and furs than farming. But once settlements were established, one family came to New France in 1617 and cleared ten acres of forest with axe, pick and spade to plant grain and a vegetable garden for Champlain's colony at Québec.

Early in the 19th century, agriculture had spread to the Prairies with the Selkirk colony—a group of Scottish farmers—in Manitoba's Red River Valley. Late in the century, waves of im-

migrants moved west and agriculture boomed. The government lured prospective farmers with pamphlets printed in 20 languages and distributed across the United States and Europe. A man could earn a homestead—160 acres of empty prairie—with three years' clearing, breaking and residence.

The Canadian Pacific Railway also encouraged immigration, to help fill its trains and sell its real estate in the West. Advertisements touted "25,000,000 acres of the richest soil, the healthiest climate, and the cheapest farming land in the world." Photographs depicting this paradise were always taken in summer. Though bitter Prairie winters tested their fortitude, those early settlers took possession of a vast expanse of deep topsoil which had been covered for centuries with a dense growth of mixed grasses. Layer upon layer of decaying vegetation had produced a fertile, water-retentive soil, ideal for growing wheat.

Pioneer farmers struggled against wind, hail, frost and drought, insects, weeds and disease. But above all there was the weary isolation of frontier life. To fight loneliness, farm families formed close-knit groups, gathering for religious meetings, community suppers and sports days. Harvest bees and barn raisings

were organized to help neighbors; "beef rings" were set up to share one family's slaughtered steer among others, making fresh meat available every few weeks.

Agricultural fairs became a necessary social event. Farmers exhibited their finest crops, fattest sows and strongest draft horses; competed in plowing matches and tugs-of-war; and traded advice with neighbors. Farm women displayed their best quilts, preserves and baked goods. Today, these fairs give many city dwellers their only glimpse of rural Canada.

Many time-honored farming methods have gone the way of the hand-held plow and milking stool. Where once a farmer tethered his bull through a ring in its nose, today's cattle breeder houses high-priced livestock in a spotless barn, where they are monitored by closed-circuit television and even vacuumed every day. Maple sap, once collected in galvanized buckets and drawn by wagon to the sugarhouse, now flows through plastic tubing to a central vat. In place of horses, farmers ride tractors equipped with tape decks and air conditioning. But no matter how sophisticated their methods, farmers still have one thing left to worry about: the weather.

Canadian Born and Bred

One of Canada's greatest agricultural achievements helped to open up the West. In the early 1900s, the Prairies were accessible by rail, but a short growing season made farming risky. Then, in 1904, a chemist at the Dominion Experimental Farm in Ottawa discovered a

Marquis wheat

cross between hardy Red Fife wheat and an Indian variety called Red Calcutta. This was the earliest maturing wheat ever developed: 100 days from seed to harvest. In time, the variety named Marquis wheat made Canada one of the world's great grain producers.

When Marquis eventually succumbed to the disease called rust, farmers turned to newer varieties. Today, scientists continue to breed resistant strains of wheat, since rust keeps reappearing in new forms.

Canada's apples are also world famous, because of the fruit that started as "Granny McIntosh's apple." In 1811

a settler discovered a remarkable apple tree on his homestead in Ontario's Dundas County. Its crisp, juicy apples became known throughout the district, but since apple seeds do not produce a tree of the same variety, no one could share his fortune. Finally, the family learned how to graft a branch onto another tree to produce the original fruit. Orchards descended from this single tree spread throughout the county, then across Canada.

Today, horticulturalists search for fruit and vegetable hybrids best suited to Canada's various climates and soils. They also look for hardy types that can be harvested by machine, or shipped bruise-free across the continent.

Other researchers work to

McIntosh apple

breed livestock suited to a northern environment. Canadian holsteins are an adaptable breed with exceptional milk production. A top breeding bull can sell for as much as $600,000 and, with artificial insemination, can sire thousands of offspring.

Holstein cow

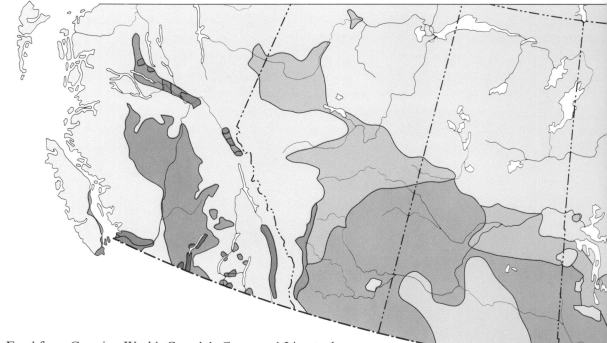

Food for a Growing World: Canada's Crops and Livestock

In British Columbia, scenery is plentiful but land to grow food is scarce. Less than five percent of the province is good farmland. However, Canada's longest growing season makes the southern coast ideal for raising vegetables and fruit. Irrigation has transformed the arid Okanagan Valley into lush orchards.

Great herds of dairy and beef cattle once grazed the interior foothills of British Columbia and Alberta. Today beef cattle still roam the vast ranches, but most are prepared for market by feed-lot finishing—"finished" on a rich diet of feed grains that increases each animal's weight by

as much as a kilogram a day.

Canadians eat an average 50 kilograms of beef per person each year. We prefer grain-fed beef, and Alberta's source of cattle feed is close at hand in Prairie grainfields. "Canada's breadbasket" is a vast tract of land where long summer days, moderate temperatures and limited rainfall produce some of the world's best wheat. The level land is ideally suited to the heavy machinery that makes large-scale grain farming profitable.

Wheat, barley, oats and rye grow well here. A newer crop is oilseed, such as rape and flax.

Few farmers planted rapeseed in the 1950s; today more than eight million acres bloom with its bright yellow flowers.

Since milk is difficult to transport long distances, most of Canada's dairy farms are located near their urban markets in southern Ontario and Quebec. Ontario also has the most livestock farms, many of them highly mechanized "food factories" where hogs and chickens are raised. The southern region's rich soil and mild temperatures favor such high-value crops as corn, grapes and tobacco.

Many Quebec farms raise both livestock and field crops. But

more than half the province's farms are dairy farms, producing milk and supplying ingredients to butter and cheese factories.

Both Ontario and Quebec grow apples, but neither province's crop is as famous as that of Nova Scotia's Annapolis Valley. In other parts of Nova Scotia are dairy, livestock and poultry farms, while potatoes grow well in the slightly acidic red soil of New Brunswick and Prince Edward Island. Farmers in Newfoundland, where the soil is rocky and the climate harsh,

---

1 Feeding reel
2 Sickle
3 Auger
4 Threshing cylinder
5 Wing beater
6 First separator
7 Second separator
8 Straw and chaff
9 Fan
10 Cleaning shoe
11 Grain bin
12 Unloading tube

Prairie Gold—From Kernel to Kitchen

After choosing a variety suited to local soil and climate, a Prairie wheat farmer sows his crop in May, as soon as threat of frost is past. The steel blades of a tractor-drawn discer comb furrows eight centimetres deep into

which seeds are dropped every 2.5 centimetres. With enough rain, green shoots appear within a week. Most farmers rely on chemicals to fertilize the soil and kill weeds. During the summer they make two or more applications.

Harvesting begins in mid-August, when the tall, golden stalks are heavy with kernels. Timing is crucial: late summer wind or rainstorms can be harmful; hail, frost or tornadoes disastrous.

Some farmers cut wheat with a swather and lay it in metre-wide windrows to dry and harden in the sun. Others harvest with a combine (*below*): the self-propelled machine that revolu-

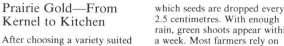

tionized grain farming when it was developed in Canada in 1938. The combine cuts the stalks, threshes the wheat (knocks the kernels from the head), separates the grain from the stalks, cleans it by screening out chaff and delivers grain ready for storage. One person can combine 50 acres in a day—

once the work of 200 men.

Most Prairie wheat is trucked to grain elevators, where it is weighed and graded. From there it travels by boxcar to West Coast ports, to Churchill or to Thunder Bay, where it is stored in huge terminal elevators, or poured into ships bound for eastern Canada or foreign ports.

Canada's chief customers are the European Economic Community, China and Japan. The world's leading wheat producer, the Soviet Union, is also a major buyer of Canadian wheat.

More than a quarter of the crop is consumed here, as livestock feed and a substantial part of Canadians' diets.

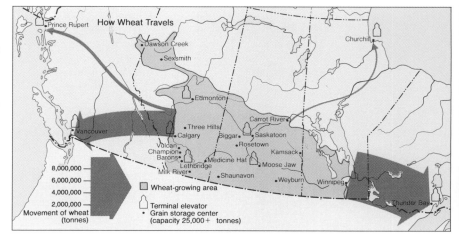

How Wheat Travels

Prince Rupert
Dawson Creek
Sexsmith
Churchill
Edmonton
Three Hills
Carrot River
Vancouver
Calgary
Biggar
Saskatoon
Volcan
Champion
Barons
Rosetown
Kamsack
Medicine Hat
Moose Jaw
Lethbridge
Milk River
Shaunavon
Weyburn
Winnipeg
Thunder Bay

8,000,000
6,000,000
4,000,000
2,000,000
Movement of wheat (tonnes)

☐ Wheat-growing area
⌂ Terminal elevator
• Grain storage center (capacity 25,000+ tonnes)

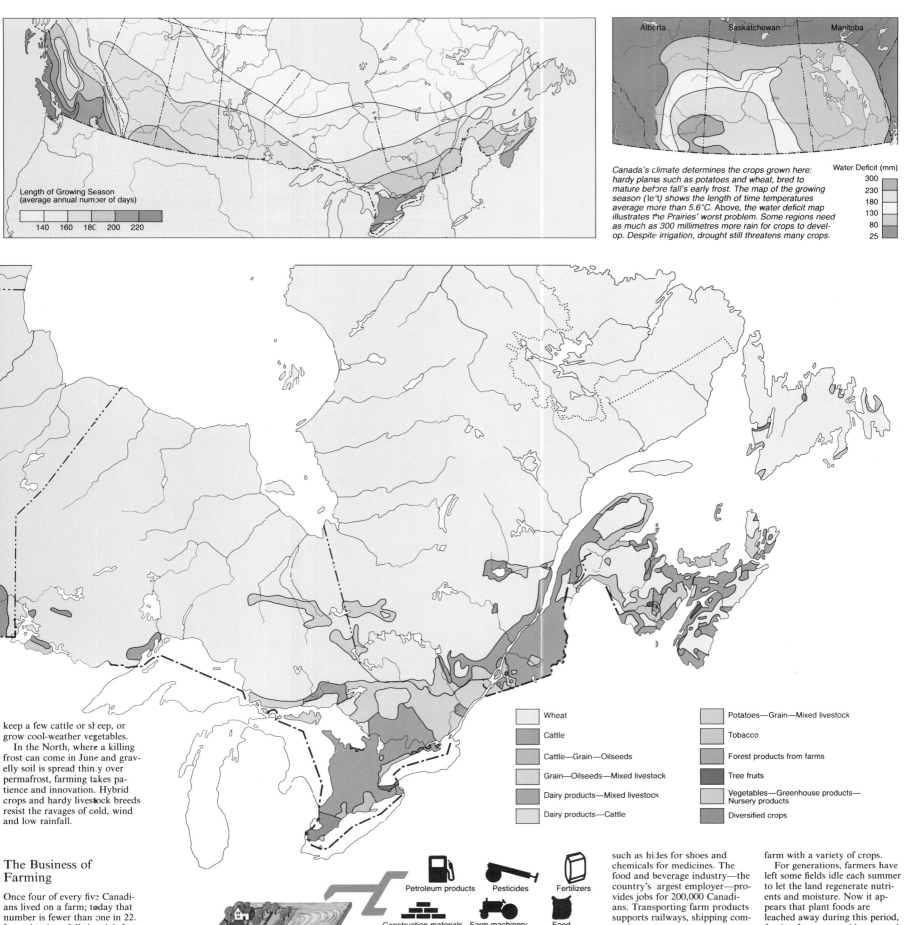

Length of Growing Season
(average annual number of days)

140 160 180 200 220

Canada's climate determines the crops grown here: hardy plants such as potatoes and wheat, bred to mature before fall's early frost. The map of the growing season (left) shows the length of time temperatures average more than 5.6°C. Above, the water deficit map illustrates the Prairies' worst problem. Some regions need as much as 300 millimetres more rain for crops to develop. Despite irrigation, drought still threatens many crops.

Water Deficit (mm)

300
230
180
130
80
25

Wheat
Cattle
Cattle—Grain—Oilseeds
Grain—Oilseeds—Mixed livestock
Dairy products—Mixed livestock
Dairy products—Cattle

Potatoes—Grain—Mixed livestock
Tobacco
Forest products from farms
Tree fruits
Vegetables—Greenhouse products—Nursery products
Diversified crops

keep a few cattle or sheep, or grow cool-weather vegetables.

In the North, where a killing frost can come in June and gravelly soil is spread thinly over permafrost, farming takes patience and innovation. Hybrid crops and hardy livestock breeds resist the ravages of cold, wind and low rainfall.

The Business of Farming

Once four of every five Canadians lived on a farm; today that number is fewer than one in 22. It used to be a full-time job for a farmer and his family to produce enough food to eat; now a single farm worker produces food for 55 people.

Technology has dramatically increased the farmer's reach. In the last century, a man with two horses could plow two acres in a day; now, with giant tractor-pulled plows, he can work as many as 120 acres. Machines dig potatoes, sort fruits and grade eggs. In dairying, almost everything but the cow is automated.

Science has produced new ways to increase yields. Pesticides limit the ravages of insects and weeds; chemical fertilizers, hybrid seeds and new farming methods have more than doubled wheat yields per acre.

In the process of modernization, agriculture has changed from a way of life to big business. One trend is toward fewer

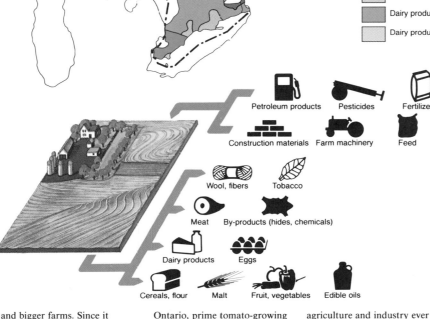

Petroleum products   Pesticides   Fertilizers

Construction materials   Farm machinery   Feed

Wool, fibers   Tobacco

Meat   By-products (hides, chemicals)

Dairy products   Eggs

Cereals, flour   Malt   Fruit, vegetables   Edible oils

and bigger farms. Since it doesn't pay to use costly equipment on small areas, farmers must expand to compete. Specialization is also more profitable. Most successful farmers concentrate on large-scale livestock raising or a single crop.

Skyrocketing land prices discourage part-time farming. In

Ontario, prime tomato-growing land was selling for as much as $5000 an acre in 1980. Those who would cultivate such valuable property must follow price and market trends as closely as businessmen or investors.

Increasing mechanization, specialization and massive investments of money have linked

agriculture and industry ever more closely together. No longer self-sufficient, farmers are major consumers of fuels, chemicals and building materials. Yearly sales of farm machinery total well over a billion dollars. In turn, farms supply cereals, fruit and vegetables, dairy products, meat and animal by-products

such as hides for shoes and chemicals for medicines. The food and beverage industry—the country's largest employer—provides jobs for 200,000 Canadians. Transporting farm products supports railways, shipping companies and ports.

But the land itself is the basis for all agriculture, and critics feel that some farming practices are destroying that precious resource. Heavy machines compact the earth so that water cannot penetrate. Pesticides kill many nutrient-producing micro-organisms in the soil as well as harmful ones. Increasing amounts of pesticides are needed to protect the single-crop farm, which is far more vulnerable to infestation or disease than a

farm with a variety of crops.

For generations, farmers have left some fields idle each summer to let the land regenerate nutrients and moisture. Now it appears that plant foods are leached away during this period, forcing farmers to add more and more fertilizer, and that as the soil deteriorates, it holds less water. Thus, valuable topsoil sifts away in the wind.

Even more soil is lost each year to pavement, as cities encroach upon choice farmland. The fertile Niagara Peninsula, situated in Canada's most populous area, is slowly being engulfed by roads and buildings. Will Canadians someday be forced to choose between home-grown fruit and autoroutes?

How farmers expanded—or gave up

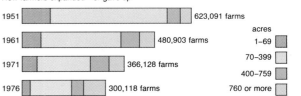

1951   623,091 farms
1961   480,903 farms
1971   366,128 farms
1976   300,118 farms

acres
1–69
70–399
400–759
760 or more

Working Our Land: The Forests

The forests that cover one third of Canada present some of the country's most familiar landscapes: shadowed woods thick with evergreens, lightened here and there by gleaming trunks of white birch; the flaming foliage of autumn maples; the slender stems and flickering leaves of an island of aspens in a sea of grass. Traditionally, wood has been the country's greatest source of wealth. Even today, in a world of steel and plastics, thousands of Canadians depend on wood and wood products for their livelihood.

As Canada's forests are almost all publicly owned, every Canadian holds eight hectares of productive forest land. The forests are administered by the provinces, which lease them to lumber and pulp and paper companies. In the past, when Canada's trees grew thick and tall at every doorstep, loggers cut without a

thought for the future. But a tree that can be felled in minutes takes 50 to 100 years to grow. Canada still has thousands of hectares of untouched forest, but much of it lies in remote areas, or too far north to grow to a usable size. Timber suitable for the mills is disappearing faster than it is growing back.

Forests supply more than wood. They limit erosion and regulate streamflow, and provide habitat for wildlife. They are also recreational havens from the tumult of city life.

But trees must be cut. Wood is an essential raw material for everything from houses to hockey sticks, telephone poles to writing paper. As logging costs rise and conservation problems become more apparent, foresters are more aware of the need for responsible harvesting and reforestation. Well-planned logging

roads need not gouge and erode the soil. If harvested areas are shaped to blend with natural landforms, the visual impact of clear-cutting is minimized. Planting and cultivation can vastly increase the yield from accessible areas. Short rotation crops, such as hybrid poplars, produce logs in less than ten years.

As the demand for forest products grows, better use is made of wood. Machines turn trees into chips for pulp right in the forest, so no waste is left behind. Researchers are investigating new uses for wood, such as animal feed made from residue.

Canada's wilderness is shrinking, and loggers, naturalists and vacationers may never be entirely compatible. But farsighted management can provide Canadians with forests that yield not only jobs and products, but a beautiful, living natural resource.

Logging Techniques from Coast to Coast

Vast differences in Canadian climate and topography have resulted in eight distinct forest regions. Just as the forests vary, so do the methods used to harvest them.

British Columbia's lush coastal climate supports Canada's tallest trees: Douglas fir, which tower as high as 90 metres, western red cedar and western hemlock. These are softwoods prized for lumber. Tall, straight trunks with few limbs make them easy to harvest and mill; the wood is strong for its weight, and easy to saw and nail.

Trees are felled with a chain saw and bucked: sawed into shorter lengths. Throughout mountainous West Coast logging areas, a system called cable yarding is used to drag the timber to a loading point. A tall

mast, or spar, is set in a clearing; cables attached to its top and powered by a diesel engine draw the logs to its foot.

At one time the spar was a tree, but today it is usually a tubular steel telescopic tower mounted on a vehicle that drives from site to site. Bulldozers clear logging roads through even the roughest terrain; trucks transport the logs to mills.

Mechanization has brought even greater changes to logging east of the Rockies. The softwood trees of the boreal forest are smaller and easier to harvest than those on the West Coast, and make excellent pulp. The wood's long fibers produce the high-quality newsprint for which Canada is famous.

In the black spruce stands of eastern Canada, a harvesting machine cuts trees as large as 40 centimetres in diameter in a single bite, nipping them off at the ground with hydraulic shears. The same machine severs the branches, cuts the trunk into sections, and measures, bundles and stacks the wood.

Trucks, trains, barges and

ships are used to transport timber, but rivers are still the cheapest way. At spring break-up, waterways from British Columbia to Newfoundland are thick with logs. Timber transported through calmer water in lakes and wide rivers can be held together by linked floating booms, and hauled downstream by tugboats to the mills.

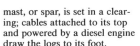

Legend

- **Boreal.** White and black spruce, balsam fir, jack pine, white birch, balsam poplar
- **Subalpine.** Engelmann spruce, alpine fir, lodgepole pine
- **Montane.** Douglas fir, lodgepole and ponderosa pine, trembling aspen
- **Coast.** Western red cedar, western hemlock, Sitka spruce, Douglas fir
- **Columbia.** Western red cedar, western hemlock, Douglas fir
- **Deciduous.** Beech, maple, black walnut, hickory, oak
- **Great Lakes-St. Lawrence.** Red pine, eastern white pine, yellow birch, maple, oak
- **Acadian.** Red spruce, balsam fir, maple, yellow birch
- **Grasslands.** Trembling aspen, willow, bur oak
- **Barren**
- ▲ Sawmill (200+ employees)
- ● Pulp and paper mill (500+ employees)

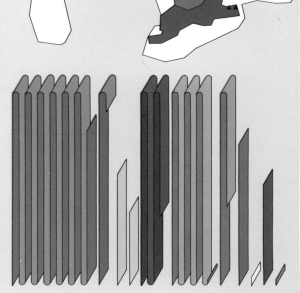

Average Annual Timber Harvest

British Columbia, with only one sixth of Canada's forested land, usually produces more than half of all the wood harvested. The province's mild weather and heavy rainfall promote rapid growth: east of the Rockies, a conifer might grow to 18 metres in 75 years; in British Columbia, a tree could soar to 40 metres in the same period.

(cubic metres)
B.C.:	63,959,000
Alta.:	5,524,000
Sask.:	2,869,000
Man.:	1,895,000
Ont.:	18,245,000
Que.:	30,119,000
N.B.:	7,947,000
N.S.:	3,653,000
P.E.I.:	166,000
Nfld.:	2,631,000
Yukon and N.W.T.:	149,000

40 metres

25 metres

20 metres

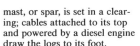

Western hemlock: Important to British Columbia. Strong white wood used for pulp and in flooring, siding, crates and plywood

White spruce: Light, resilient wood used in construction. White color of pulp produces the finest newsprint

Jack pine: Moderately hard wood used in construction, siding and pulp. Also good for railway ties, posts and mine timbers

Balsam fir: A staple of the pulp and paper industry. Also used for construction, plywood and packaging, and as Christmas trees

White birch: Strong, fine-textured, whitish wood that makes excellent plywood. Solid birch used in furniture and cabinets

Sugar maple: Valuable hardwood used in furniture, flooring and plywood. Sap is boiled down to make maple syrup and sugar

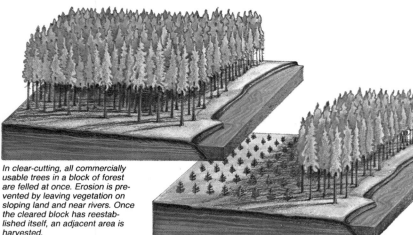

In clear-cutting, all commercially usable trees in a block of forest are felled at once. Erosion is prevented by leaving vegetation on sloping land and near rivers. Once the cleared block has reestablished itself, an adjacent area is harvested.

In selection cutting, only individually chosen trees of a desired size and species are felled. The practice is usually confined to mixed forests of hardwoods and softwoods of uneven ages; less than 20 percent of Canada's trees are harvested this way. Natural reseeding usually ensures regeneration. Harvesting expenses are greater, since care is needed to avoid damaging trees left standing.

Cash Crop or Renewable Resource?

Most trees in Canada are harvested by clear-cutting: all the timber in an area—which may be as large as 400 hectares—is cut down and removed. This method is widely used in the boreal forest, where natural stands often consist of a single species of uniform age.

After the cutting, bare ground may be prepared for new growth by burning the slash (debris) and applying herbicides, or by scarification: breaking up the surface to expose mineral soil. Adjacent stands of trees may then reseed the site naturally, but the resulting forest may not be of commercial value. Seeding or replanting by hand or machine, though expensive, does ensure the growth of usable species.

Careless clear-cutting can be disastrous. Wildlife suffers from loss of habitat; water catchment areas are affected when forests disappear. Removing trees from the banks of waterways can bring soil erosion, flooding and silting of streams and rivers.

Selection cutting—harvesting single trees or small groups of trees—disturbs the environment less but is not always practical. When an area's tree cover is not fully removed, new growth must be capable of developing in shade. Trees that are not shade-tolerant, including many softwoods, fare poorly under these conditions.

But thinning by selection cutting does benefit remaining trees, allowing them more sunlight, water and nutrients. The practice also preserves scenic forest landscapes and wildlife habitats.

In the past, timber was "mined" as a nonrenewable resource. Today, foresters try to maintain a *sustained yield* of wood, ensuring new growth by replacing harvested trees. However, these efforts at reforestation have not made up for past wastefulness. Wood for mills must be hauled greater and greater distances to fill demands. *High-yield* forestry would improve the situation, but more money must be devoted to silviculture, or "farming" trees. Better soil preparation, planting of healthy seedlings from the best parent trees, weeding, thinning and fertilizing can more than double forest yields—and ensure supplies of wood for future generations.

The Life of a Lumberjack

Canada's earliest pioneers considered trees an obstacle rather than a resource. Settlers used some wood for fuel and for building cabins and boats, but most trees were simply destroyed in giant bonfires as the land was cleared for farms.

Then, late in the 18th century, the Royal Navy began to buy Canada's wood. Tall white pines proved ideal for ships' masts. Square timbers—massive logs with straight-hewn sides—were also shipped overseas.

Soon the woods around the St. John, Miramichi and Ottawa rivers rang with the sound of axes. But felling trees was brutal work. Loggers worked in pairs, taking alternate swings at tree trunks perhaps two metres in diameter. Skilled axmen could predict a tree's fall with amazing accuracy.

A shantyman's winter home was a "camboose," a crowded log cabin without windows or chimney. A fire blazed in the center of the floor: some of the smoke—and much of the heat—escaped through a hole in the roof. Amusements were few, and cooks served the same meal three times a day: bread, pork, beans and tea.

Shantymen at season's end, released with pockets full of cash from their dangerous, back-breaking labor, wreaked havoc in town. Some acquired enduring reputations, such as Joe Montferrand (called Joe Mufferaw by the English), a brawling raft foreman from Montréal. Agile, belligerent and strong as a bear, Montferrand could kick so high that he left heel marks on tavern ceilings with his hobnailed boots.

By 1860, massive white pines were becoming scarce in eastern Canada, and loggers were forced to cut smaller trees or other species—or to move west, where giant Douglas fir still stood. In 1866, a mill was built at Valleyfield, Quebec, which ground wood into pulp for paper. Canada was on its way to becoming the world's greatest producer of newsprint.

Making the Most Out of Wood

Almost half the wood cut in Canada is used for lumber. Some 1100 sawmills across the country slice and plane softwoods like spruce, hemlock and Douglas fir, and hardwoods such as birch and maple, to produce boards of varying dimensions. Each year Canada exports enough lumber to build 1.3 million three-bedroom houses.

Other primary wood products are plywoods, shingles (mostly cut from easy-splitting western red cedar) and veneers. Further processing turns wood into moldings, kitchen cabinets, doors, sashes and prefabricated buildings.

As costs rise, mills find ways to use wood that once was wasted. Some is sold for pulp chips or fuel. Sawdust and wood shavings are coated with adhesive and pressed into sheets to form cheap, sturdy particle board for cabinet and furniture cores. Waferboard, made from wood flakes, is as strong as plywood.

The pulp and paper industry, long one of Canada's leading manufacturers, provides an endless stream of wood pulp, paperboards, paper products such as boxes and bags, and by-products such as turpentine, rayon and artificial sponges. The most important product is newsprint: our mills turn out 40 percent of the world's supply. Journalism's appetite is insatiable—a single edition of a major Canadian newspaper consumes more than eight hectares of trees.

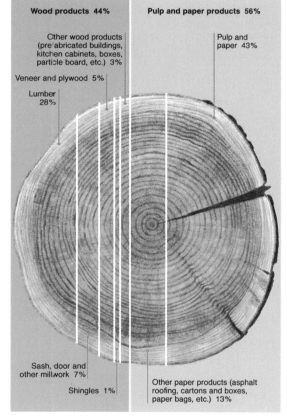

Percentage Value of Forest Products

Wood products 44%

Other wood products (prefabricated buildings, kitchen cabinets, boxes, particle board, etc.) 3%

Veneer and plywood 5%

Lumber 28%

Sash, door and other millwork 7%

Shingles 1%

Pulp and paper products 56%

Pulp and paper 43%

Other paper products (asphalt roofing, cartons and boxes, paper bags, etc.) 13%

Risk of Forest Fire

- Very low
- Low
- Moderate
- High
- Very high
- Extreme

Enemies of the Forest

Fires caused by lightning were part of the forest cycle long before man's arrival, periodically removing overmature trees to clear the way for vigorous new growth. Many plants flourish in direct sunlight and the mineral-rich soil left by fire.

But nature's way is not always convenient to man. Each year fires in Canada destroy more than a million hectares of trees and cause untold damage to soils and wildlife. Lightning sets off only one quarter of the fires; most are caused by man—with a smoldering cigarette butt or untended campfire.

Fire risk can be reduced by prescribed (deliberate) burning of slash and by closing the woods to the public in times of high fire hazard. The map above combines information on temperature, humidity, wind speed and rainfall to gauge forest fire risk.

Some fires are fought on the ground, by men pumping water from tanks on their backs or clearing fire lines and trenches. Aircraft bomb some blazes with tankfuls of water scooped from nearby lakes or rivers.

Pests and diseases also take their toll of Canada's trees. Spruce budworm, the most voracious of all insect pests, lays waste to forests in New Brunswick, Quebec and Ontario. Though aerial spraying is widely used to control these insects, some fear that chemical pesticides may harm people and the environment. Scientists are seeking biological pest controls, such as viruses, bacteria or parasitic insects.

Even chemicals cannot stop the spread of some forest diseases. Heartrot destroys some 28 million cubic metres of timber annually. In its slow procession across the country, Dutch elm disease has killed many of the stately shade trees lining city streets in eastern Canada.

Infrared, or false-color, photography can be used to detect forest damage not visible to the naked eye. Since chlorophyll in healthy trees is a strong reflector of infrared, variations in chlorophyll content show up in aerial photographs. Above, healthy early autumn foliage on deciduous trees ranges from magenta to pink to yellow in infrared colors. A plantation of healthy red pines appears reddish, but a small patch of bright yellow-green (circled) reveals a stand of damaged trees.

Working Our Waters: Fishing

John Cabot, returning to England from the New World in 1497, told of a sea so thick with fish that they could be dipped out of the water with a net. This was the vast range of submerged plateaus and plains that stretches 1600 kilometres between Cape Cod and Labrador. Over these submarine fields, fertilized by great rivers and enriched by nutrients churned up by Atlantic currents, swarm billions of fish. On the Pacific Coast, where the rich continental shelf extends to 100 kilometres from land, salmon and herring gather in estuarial waters by the millions every year. Inland, the fishery is dispersed over myriad lakes and rivers.

From these vast resources Canadian fishermen annually harvest more than one million tonnes of fish, of which Atlantic cod, American lobster and Pacific salmon are the most important varieties. Canada ranks among the top ten fishing nations in the world, and fishing provides about 82,000 people with full or seasonal employment. With more than two-thirds of its catch sold in foreign markets, Canada in 1979 became the world's largest fish exporter.

Dwindling stocks and a severe decline in the fishing industry prompted Canada to extend its offshore limits to 200 miles in January 1977. The value of some species, such as scallop and cod, has since quadrupled. Herring prices have risen tenfold, and other species such as squid, once fished only for bait, suddenly became costly. Despite these favorable signs, the industry faces stiff competition on world markets, and the constant danger of overfishing. A moratorium on commercial fishing of Atlantic salmon was imposed in 1972, but poaching, pollution and overfishing in the North Atlantic are resulting in the continual decline of the species. On the opposite coast, a $150 million Salmonid Enhancement Program was launched in 1977 to reverse declines in Pacific salmon stocks, the mainstay of the prosperous West Coast fishery.

A more promising trend is the growth of aquaculture, or fish farming. Worldwide, more than six million tonnes of seafood are grown this way. Successful Canadian operations include trout farming in Prairie potholes, the culture of oysters in the Maritimes and salmon "ranching" in British Columbia.

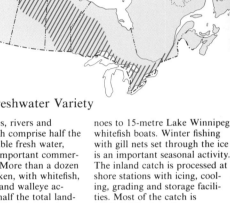

Freshwater catch by value, 1978 (thousand dollars)

Canada 32,959
Man. 9644
Alta. 646
Que. 979
Sask. 2629
Ont. 17,161
North 1541
N.B. 359

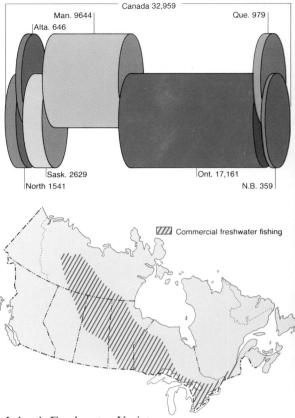

Commercial freshwater fishing

British Columbia: Salmon Story

The five Pacific salmon—Chinook, coho, chum, pink and sockeye—dominate Canada's Pacific fishery, accounting for about 70 percent of British Columbia's $200 million annual catch. Until 1968, huge catches of herring were processed into fish meal and oil, but due to a drastic reduction in stocks, only herring used for human consumption can currently be harvested. Of lesser importance are the groundfish: ling, gray and black cod. Clams, crabs and oysters also provide fishing revenue.

Fish of "mysterious comings and goings," salmon are hatched in cold, clear rivers often hundreds of kilometres from the sea, then spend up to a year, depending on species, in freshwater lakes. As fingerlings, they enter the Pacific and gain weight rapidly in the rich depths of the open ocean. The salmon return to their native rivers, usually in the fourth year, then spawn and die. (Unlike the Pacific species, the Atlantic salmon may spawn more than once.) Only one in a thousand eggs will produce a salmon that will reach maturity.

Most West Coast fishing is carried on within sight of land. But even small boats, highly powered and equipped with sophisticated mechanical gear, navigational aids and fish-finding sonar, travel great distances along the coast following the seasonal movements of fish. The bulk of the catch is canned; the remainder is sold fresh, frozen or mild-cured.

- Pacific salmon
- Pacific herring
- 200-mile limit

Value (thousand dollars)

56,817
55,181
33,336
29,461
27,269
12,835

Pacific herring | Sockeye | Coho | Chinook | Chum | Pink

Catch (tonnes)

7887
9152
15,331
15,885
22,321

81,400

Trolling: Tall poles reaching up from behind the wheelhouse and bow identify Pacific trollers (left). Baited hooks or lures are dragged behind the boat, their depth controlled by the speed of the boat or by large sinkers called cannonballs. When a fish strikes, the line is drawn in by a power "gurdy," or reel. The catch, mostly Chinook and coho salmon, is gutted, cleaned and stored in ice.

Sockeye salmon (sea-run)
Oncorhynchus nerka
24 in. (610 mm), 5 lb. (2.3 kg)

Male sockeye in spawning colors

Female sockeye in spawning colors

Inland: Freshwater Variety

Canada's lakes, rivers and streams, which comprise half the world's available fresh water, also support important commercial fisheries. More than a dozen species are taken, with whitefish, yellow perch and walleye accounting for half the total landed value. Locally important species include Manitoba saugers, Ontario lake trout and Quebec eels.

The inland lakes are fished in summer with gill and pound nets and a variety of craft from canoes to 15-metre Lake Winnipeg whitefish boats. Winter fishing with gill nets set through the ice is an important seasonal activity. The inland catch is processed at shore stations with icing, cooling, grading and storage facilities. Most of the catch is marketed fresh or frozen.

Commercial fishing has declined or disappeared in certain areas, not due to lack of fish, but to environmental and economic problems. Chemical pollutants, some of them transported from the United States as acid rain, have contaminated many stocks. And despite the establishment in 1969 of the Freshwater Fish Marketing Corporation to stabilize prices, low profitability plagues small-scale and part-time operations.

Gill netting: The gill net (left) is "set" in the water to form either a fixed or drifting wall of fine nylon netting. It is buoyed by floats on the top line, weighted by lead sinkers on the bottom line, and marked by a surface buoy. Fish attempting to swim through the net are caught by their gills and entangled. One disadvantage is that the fish deteriorate unless the catch is emptied frequently.

Walleye
Stizostedion vitreum
16 in. (406 mm), 1.5 lb. (0.7 kg)

Yellow perch
Perca flavescens
7 in. (178 mm), 8 oz. (0.2 kg)

Lake whitefish
Coregonus clupeaformis
15 in. (381 mm), 1.5 lb. (0.7 kg)

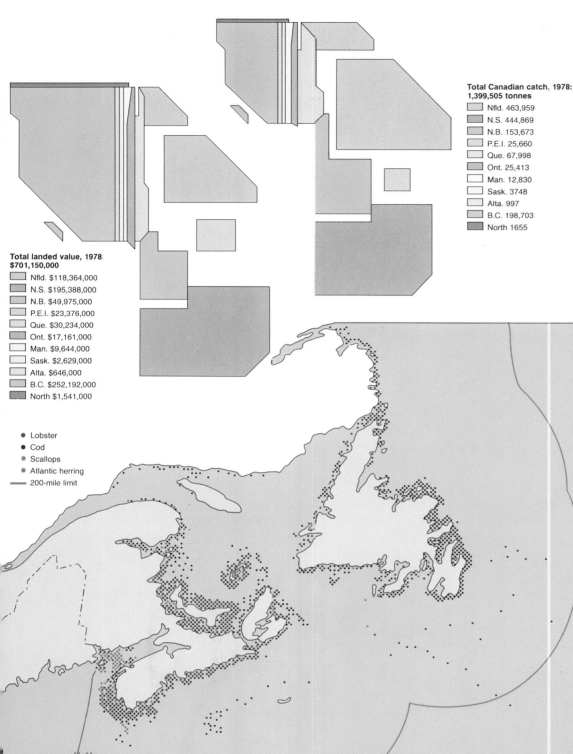

Total Canadian catch, 1978: 1,399,505 tonnes

Nfld.	463,959
N.S.	444,869
N.B.	153,673
P.E.I.	25,660
Que.	67,998
Ont.	25,413
Man.	12,830
Sask.	3748
Alta.	997
B.C.	198,703
North	1655

Total landed value, 1978: $701,150,000

Nfld.	$118,364,000
N.S.	$195,388,000
N.B.	$49,975,000
P.E.I.	$23,376,000
Que.	$30,234,000
Ont.	$17,161,000
Man.	$9,644,000
Sask.	$2,629,000
Alta.	$646,000
B.C.	$252,192,000
North	$1,541,000

- ● Lobster
- ● Cod
- ● Scallops
- ▲ Atlantic herring
- — 200-mile limit

Out of the Water: Tonnes and Dollars

Tiny Prince Edward Island dwarfs Ontario in these cartograms (*left*) depicting the provinces' contribution to Canada's total 1978 fish production.

The Atlantic Provinces and Quebec accounted for 83 percent of the fish landed in Canada, and almost two-thirds of the total landed value. Lobsters—less than two percent of the Atlantic catch—brought 18 percent of the landed value.

Inland, the fishery is dispersed across seven provinces and the number of tonnes of fish taken is low. However, the relatively high value of fresh-water fish makes inland commercial fishing profitable.

High-priced Pacific salmon account for the West's share of the market: 14 percent of the national catch and 36 percent of landed value.

Value (thousand dollars)

86,382
75,591
63,482
43,279
24,317
13,066

Cod | Herring | Small flatfish | Scallops | Redfish | Lobster

Catch (tonnes)

19,179
77,076
109,176
109,404
246,132
296,859

Atlantic: Bounty From the Banks

More than 30 kinds of fish, shellfish and marine mammals are harvested from the rich North Atlantic. The most valuable catches are cod and lobsters. Taken with cod are other groundfish (so called because they feed on the sea bottom), including haddock, pollock, hake, cusk, redfish, and the flatfishes.

Important shellfish are clams, quahogs, oysters and scallops. Of schooling ("pelagic") and estuarial fish, herring dominate the catch.

The traditional shore fishery is carried on within 20 kilometres of land, using traps, handlines and trawl lines with individually baited hooks. Mackerel and herring are landed with seine, trap and gill nets; lobsters are trapped in "pots." Special rakes or tongs are used to gather oysters; scallops are harvested with dredges.

Offshore, trawlers and draggers tow huge otter trawls (*below*) or other nets; long-liners haul thousands of baited hooks.

Much of the groundfish catch is still salted and dried for export. In North America these species are marketed chilled or frozen. Lobsters are sold live; canning is the main method of processing other species.

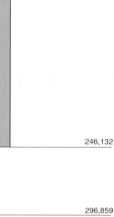

Otter trawl: *Groundfish on both coasts are often taken by trawlers, or "draggers," using the otter trawl (below): a long, wedge-shaped net that narrows into a "cod end." Two ironclad wooden "doors" keep the mouth of the trap open as it is towed along the ocean floor, scooping up fish. As the trawl is drawn in, the fish are forced into the cod end, which is hoisted on to the ship's deck and emptied.*

Lobster trap: *Hydraulic winches and echo sounders have replaced brawn and intuition in lobster fishing, but the basic trap (left) remains little changed. Lobsters enter the "pot" lured by bait in the first compartment or "kitchen." The entrance is a funnel of netting that allows entry but prevents exit. Passing through a second hole to the "bedroom," the lobster is trapped.*

Purse seine: *One end of the large, small-meshed purse seine (left) is secured to a small skiff. The seiner then encircles a school of fish, returning to the skiff, where the two ends of the seine are joined. The purse line is tightened, drawing the bottom of the net together to form a huge bag where the fish are trapped. The seine is then hauled aboard.*

Lobster
Homarus americanus

Atlantic herring
Clupea harengus harengus
To 17 in. (431 mm), 1.5 lb. (0.7 kg)

Giant scallop
Placopecten magellanicus

Atlantic cod
Gadus morhua
25 in. (635 mm), 5 lb. (2.3 kg)

Redfish
Sebastes marinus
12 in. (304 mm), 2 lb. (0.9 kg)

49

Working Our Land: Mining

Mining in Canada dates back almost 1000 years, to Norsemen who dug iron ore from a bog near present-day L'Anse aux Meadows, Nfld., and forged it into crude tools. Five centuries later, Jacques Cartier mined what he thought were diamonds and gold near Quebec City; in France, the minerals were found to be quartz and iron pyrite. In the 1570s, Martin Frobisher also confused pyrite with gold, and shipped tonnes of worthless "blacke stone" to England from mines on Baffin Island.

An accidental discovery ushered in Canada's modern mining era. In 1883, workmen blasting a route for the Canadian Pacific Railway through northern Ontario ripped into copper and nickel deposits near Sudbury. This bonanza spurred other discoveries nearby: silver at Cobalt; gold at Kirkland Lake and Timmins; and, in the 1920s, copper and gold in Quebec's Abitibi region.

Today, the industry is nationwide and employs 160,000 workers to prospect, mine and smelt 60 kinds of minerals—the world's most diversified output. Canada is third in total production (after the United States and the Soviet Union), and ranks first in the mining of zinc; second in asbestos, nickel and potash; third in gold and silver; and fourth in copper and lead.

Mining is risky and expensive. Canadian oil companies spend as much as $2 billion a year drilling some 7800 exploratory oil and natural gas wells, but few prove commercially successful. It costs an average $25 million to find a mineral deposit in Canada rich enough to mine, and takes up to six years of planning and construction before ore is extracted. New discoveries are usually made in remote regions, and the resulting mines require townsites for workers and transportation links to refineries and markets. All new railroad construction in Canada since World War II has been associated with mineral development. The tremendous deposits of iron ore first reported along the Quebec-Labrador border in 1894 achieved economic importance only in the 1950s, after completion of the St. Lawrence Seaway, a 560-kilometre railroad and new ports to handle 200,000-tonne freighters.

Mining is a once-only harvest, but Canada seems blessed with an abundant supply of most minerals. At 1975 consumption rates, estimated reserves of iron ore will last 240 years; copper, 140 years; uranium, 190 years. Additional reserves are added as new discoveries and technology, along with higher prices, turn low-grade, less accessible deposits into producing mines.

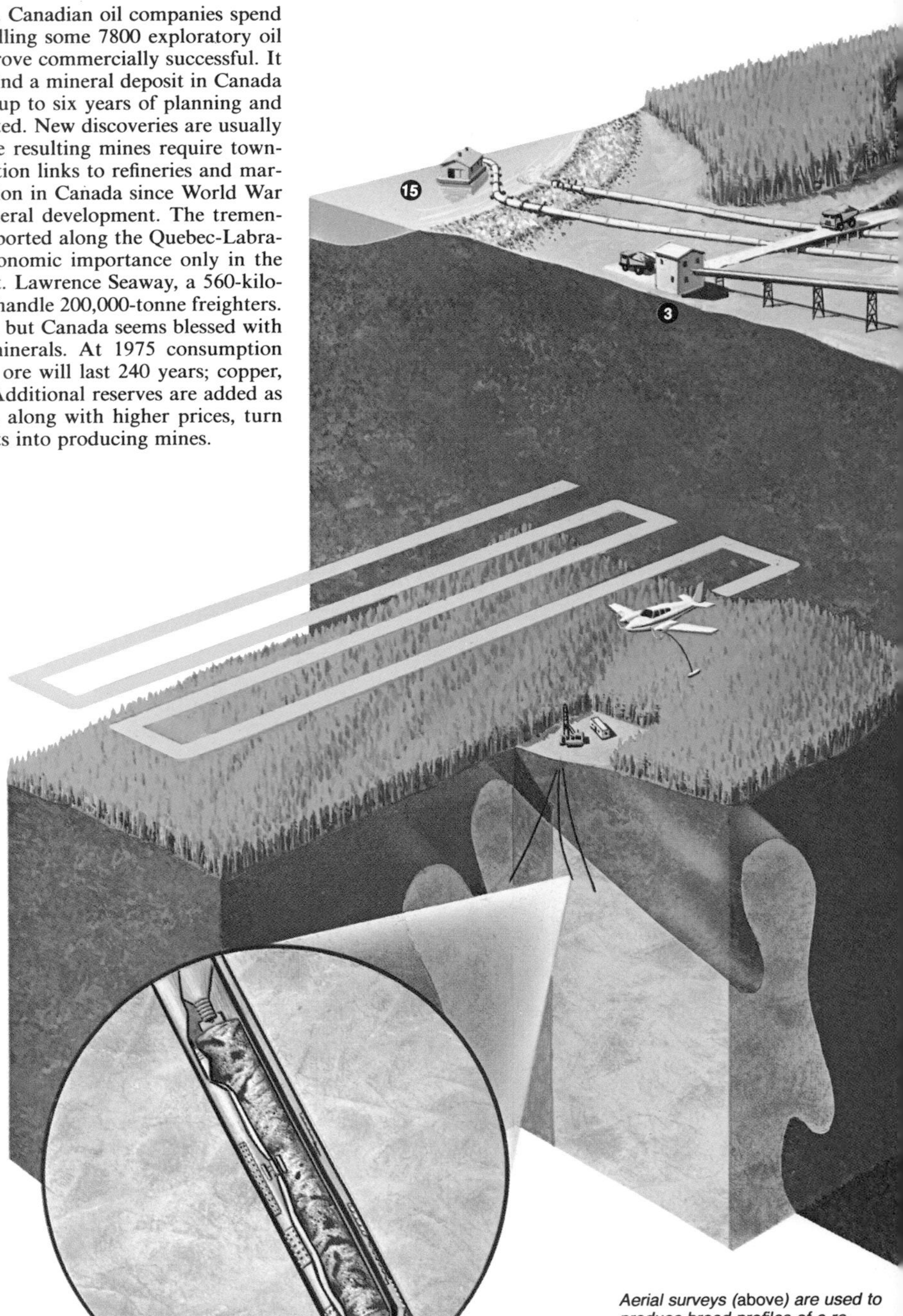

Geologic regions
- Cordilleran
- Interior plains
- Canadian Shield
- Appalachian
- Innuitian

Industrial minerals
- Asbestos
- Salt
- Gypsum
- Potash

Metals
- Copper-molybdenum
- Nickel-copper
- Copper-zinc
- Copper-gold-silver
- Lead-zinc
- Iron
- Molybdenum
- Precious metals

Mineral fuels
- Oil
- Oil and natural gas
- Natural gas
- Uranium
- Coal

Aerial surveys (above) are used to produce broad profiles of a region's geophysical properties. Ground survey teams then compile more detailed information on areas with potential ore-bearing rock. Cylindrical core samples obtained from diamond drilling indicate the size, shape and grade of a deposit. A core sample (left) from the Shield contains light gray host rock (quartzite) embedded with chalcopyrite, a common copper-iron sulfide; pyrrhotite, a magnetized iron sulfide often present in nickel deposits; and sphalerite, a zinc-bearing mineral usually associated with lead.

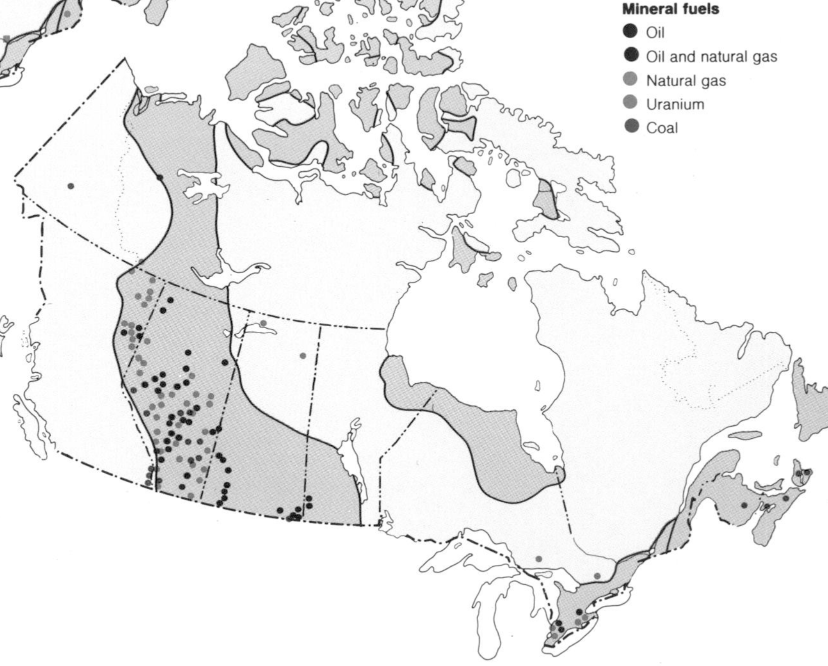

Canada's Widespread Mineral Wealth

Almost every part of Canada contributes to the $26 billion mining industry. Western provinces dominate the mineral fuels. Alberta produces about 85 percent of Canada's oil and 90 percent of its natural gas from more than 130 fields. Saskatchewan and British Columbia are the other main producers. Almost a fifth of Canada's current output of coal comes from a mine near Sparwood, B.C.; in all, the province contributes 40 percent to the total output. Other principal coal-producing provinces are Alberta (30 percent) and Nova Scotia (15 percent). More than half of Canada's uranium, a metal used as a fuel for nuclear power, comes from five mines in Ontario; five mines in northern Saskatchewan produce the rest.

Metal ores are found in the Precambrian Shield, the Western Cordillera and the Appalachian region of the East. Although the entire Shield is often thought of as a vast storehouse of minerals, much of it is barren granite and gneiss. About 30 mines concentrated between Sudbury and Timmins, Ont. and Val d'Or, Que. produce more than 15 kinds of metals, mainly nickel, copper, zinc, gold and silver. Mines along the Labrador-Quebec border, the other great mining area in the Shield, produce three quarters of Canada's iron ore.

The Western Cordillera yields 90 percent of Canada's molybdenum, a metal used to strengthen steel, more than 40 percent of its copper and almost 20 percent of its zinc. The giant Sullivan mine at Kimberley, B.C., taps the world's largest single source of lead, zinc and silver—metals often found in the same ore body.

Industrial minerals are more widespread. About 85 percent of Canada's asbestos comes from nine mines in southeastern Quebec. All of Canada's potash, the second most valuable industrial mineral, is mined in Saskatchewan. Nova Scotia produces two thirds of our gypsum; Ontario mines two thirds of our salt.

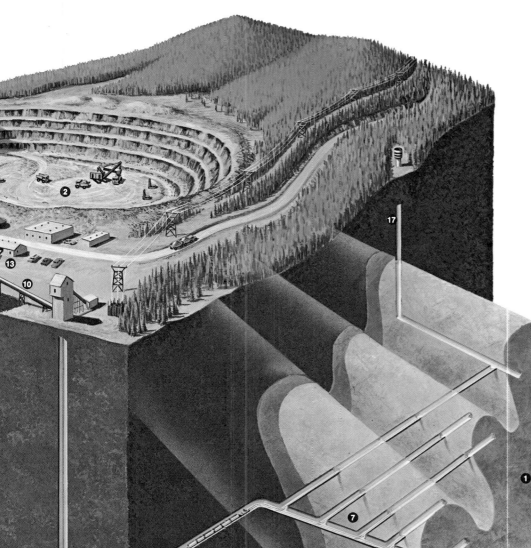

The Search for Deposits; Getting Out the Ore

Mining companies locate anomalies (geologic irregularities that may contain minerals) using federal and provincial geophysical maps and through exploration. Deposits are then pinpointed with aerial and surface surveys. The density, magnetism and conductivity of rocks, recorded by magnetometers, gravimeters and other electromagnetic instruments, determine the depth and composition of an ore body buried beneath barren rock. Geochemical surveys trace concentrations of minerals from soil, water and plants to a deposit. Geobotanists look for "indicators": vegetation patterns and individual plants affected by minerals. Natural radiation from uranium, for example, sometimes produces local mutations: blueberries with unusual shapes, and white flowers on normally purple fireweed.

The illustration (*left*) shows a typical mine working a metal-bearing ore body (1). Vegetation, soil and barren rock are removed, and the exposed ore is recovered from an open-pit mine (2). The rock is loosened with explosives, scooped into trucks by electric shovels, and transported to a primary crusher (3).

When the cost of removing the overburden and waste rock exceeds the value of the recovered ore, an underground mine (4) may be developed. A shaft (5) houses the mine's elevator for workers, machinery and ore. Tunnels, called drifts (6), branch off the shaft and parallel the ore body; crosscut tunnels (7) intersect the deposit. In this type of mine, ore is usually loosened with explosives from stopes, or working areas, between the levels. The broken rock is transported to a primary crusher (8). An ore skip (9) hoists the rock to the surface, where conveyors (10) transport it to a storage pile (11). Another conveyor system (12) feeds a secondary crusher (13) that reduces the ore to pebble size; grinding mills pulverize the ore to a sand-like consistency. A concentrator (14) separates the ore from waste minerals, or tailings, which are pumped to a storage pond (15). The mineral concentrate is then shipped to smelters for further refining.

Other mine structures include maintenance shops (16), warehouses, offices and a ventilation shaft (17), which supplies fresh air to the mine and doubles as an emergency exit.

Mining coal once meant abusing the land, but now stringent environmental laws demand reclamation in most areas of Canada. At this strip mine 200 kilometres southeast of Edmonton (above), scrapers have shoved topsoil into mounds on the left for later reclamation. The cranelike dragline removes the overburden, or spoil, and dumps it into the excavation left by the previous cut as the mining operation moves from right to left. An electric shovel loads the exposed coal into a 60-tonne truck for transport to the generating station seen in the background.

Two years later at the mined-out seam (left), the spoil piles have been leveled, and the topsoil replaced and seeded with wheat and forage crops. The following July, yields were about average for the region.

Rocks to Riches

Mining contributes more than ten percent of Canada's Gross National Product. Mineral fuels comprise 58 percent of the total production value (*right*). Major metals produce about 20 percent and leading industrial minerals, 8 percent. The "others" category is dominated by structural minerals. The value of sand, gravel and quarried stone is almost twice as much as gold, which is extracted mainly as a refining by-product of other metals.

Alberta has led mineral production in Canada since 1960 (*left*); mineral fuels comprise 97.5 percent of its total. Six metals—nickel, uranium, copper, iron, zinc and gold—contribute almost two thirds of Ontario's diversified output

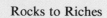

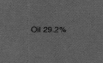

Oil 29.2%
Natural gas 18%
Iron 7.2%
Copper 5.8%
Natural gas by-products 5.2%
Zinc 4.2%
Coal 3.3%
Nickel 3.2%
Cement 2.8%
Potash 2.7%
Uranium 2.5%
Asbestos 2.5%
Others 13.4%

Alberta (49.4%)
Ontario (12.5%)
British Columbia (10.5%)
Quebec (8.6%)
Saskatchewan (7%)
Newfoundland (4.2%)
Manitoba (2.2%)
New Brunswick (2%)
Northwest Territories (1.6%)
Yukon (1.2%)
Nova Scotia (0.8%)
P.E.I. (less than 1%)

Rx for the Environment: Recycle and Reclaim

Canada's 280 mines disturb about 65,000 hectares, or .006 percent of the landscape (highways cover 1.4 percent). The effects of mining, however, are often widespread: rivers and lakes contaminated by acidic mine water; air polluted with dust and gases from refining and smelting; and remote regions invaded by the highways, railroads and townsites that accompany mineral development.

Today, companies prepare extensive studies on a projected mine's environmental and social impact to comply with the regulations of local, regional, provincial and federal agencies. Land reclamation is now mandatory in most of Canada, with the stipulation that the land be returned as closely as possible to its original condition. At the Luscar coal mine in Alberta, 500 hectares have been landscaped and replanted with 29 varieties of grasses, legumes and shrubs.

Stringent regulations have led to innovative antipollution controls and a cleaner environment. Special bacteria, developed to neutralize acidic mine water, turn soluble iron into an insoluble form, which settles out in holding basins. Limestone is added and the neutralized, iron-free water is returned to the environment. Some mines recycle up to three quarters of the 60 million litres of water used daily at large operations.

Canadian mines process 600 million tonnes of rock annually. It takes about 50 tonnes of ore, for example, to produce one tonne of refined copper. Some of the tailings, or waste rock, is used to support underground mines, but most of it is stored in ponds that eventually dry up and are eroded by wind and water. Many mines in Canada now stabilize tailings with vegetation. At a uranium mine near Elliot Lake, Ont., wastes from sawmills and nearby towns were mixed with tailings and topsoil, and a former slurry pond has become a field of grain.

Energy: Problems and Prospects

Canada consumes more energy per person than any other nation except Luxembourg: the equivalent of nine tonnes of oil annually for each man, woman and child. With its vast distances and extremes of climate, Canada expends tremendous amounts of energy on transportation, heating and cooling. The energy industry itself accounts for almost 20 percent of our total consumption of energy. The petrochemical and pulp and paper industries also use vast quantities of energy: much of the 105,000 cubic metres of oil that Canada imports daily is used in the production of plastics, fertilizers and paper for export. But our voracious appetite for energy is largely due to inefficiency and waste—legacies from the days of cheap fuel.

How much energy is left in Canada? Reserves are difficult to estimate, or even to define. They refer to the amounts of coal, oil, natural gas and uranium that are not only recoverable at commercial rates from proven deposits, but also close enough to a transportation system that can deliver the resource to markets. Using this definition, Canada's coal will last about 200 years at 1979 production rates; uranium, about 30 years. In 1976 it was estimated that our marketable natural gas would last 26 years; but more recent discoveries have increased reserves to 31 years at 1979 production rates.

Canada gets half of its energy from conventional oil, but without major new discoveries, our reserves may run out by 1990. In 1970 reserves of conventional crude were almost 1.7 billion cubic metres. Ten years later they had dwindled to less than 1.1 billion, as oil was pumped faster than new reserves were found. Both improved recovery methods for established fields and new discoveries may extend reserves. However, the 1977 strike in West Pembina, Alta., was the first major oil discovery in Canada since 1965.

More than 159 billion cubic metres of oil lie in the oil sands and heavy oil deposits of northern Alberta—more than all the reserves of the Middle East—but only about 15 percent can be recovered with open-pit mining, the present method of extraction. To exploit more of this vast resource, much of which lies 300 metres belowground, will require the perfection of new technology to heat the oil in place to make it flow into wells. This method will extract only about another 15 percent. An estimated 70 percent of the oil may never leave the ground.

Where Canada's Energy Comes From, Where It Goes

The chart below shows the amount of energy fed into the economy by our main fuels.

Some energy is exported; the rest is divided among five main users. The chart also shows how efficiently these consumers transform energy into usable heat, light and motion, and the vast amount that is wasted in transmission losses, mechanical inefficiencies and incomplete combustion.

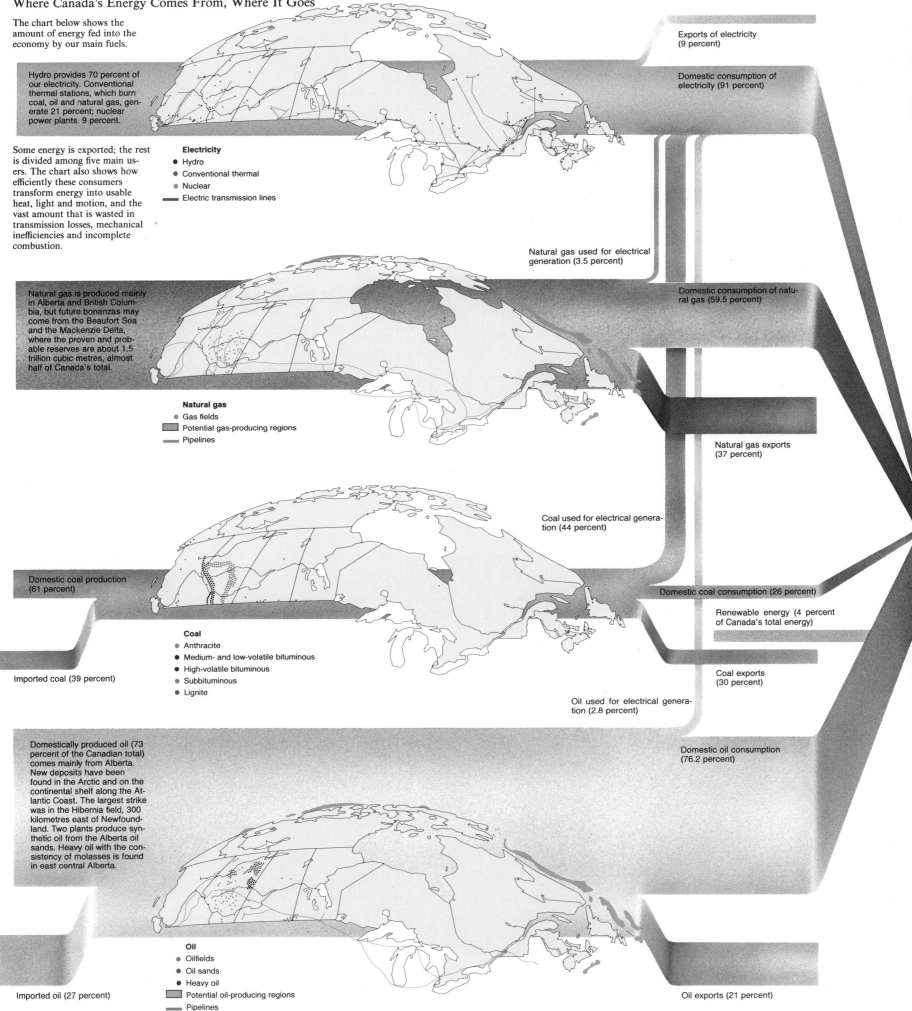

Hydro provides 70 percent of our electricity. Conventional thermal stations, which burn coal, oil and natural gas, generate 21 percent; nuclear power plants, 9 percent.

Electricity
- Hydro
- Conventional thermal
- Nuclear
- Electric transmission lines

Natural gas is produced mainly in Alberta and British Columbia, but future bonanzas may come from the Beaufort Sea and the Mackenzie Delta, where the proven and probable reserves are about 1.5 trillion cubic metres, almost half of Canada's total.

Natural gas
- Gas fields
- Potential gas-producing regions
- Pipelines

Domestic coal production (61 percent)

Imported coal (39 percent)

Coal
- Anthracite
- Medium- and low-volatile bituminous
- High-volatile bituminous
- Subbituminous
- Lignite

Domestically produced oil (73 percent of the Canadian total) comes mainly from Alberta. New deposits have been found in the Arctic and on the continental shelf along the Atlantic Coast. The largest strike was in the Hibernia field, 300 kilometres east of Newfoundland. Two plants produce synthetic oil from the Alberta oil sands. Heavy oil with the consistency of molasses is found in east central Alberta.

Imported oil (27 percent)

Oil
- Oilfields
- Oil sands
- Heavy oil
- Potential oil-producing regions
- Pipelines

Exports of electricity (9 percent)

Domestic consumption of electricity (91 percent)

Natural gas used for electrical generation (3.5 percent)

Domestic consumption of natural gas (59.5 percent)

Natural gas exports (37 percent)

Coal used for electrical generation (44 percent)

Domestic coal consumption (26 percent)

Renewable energy (4 percent of Canada's total energy)

Coal exports (30 percent)

Oil used for electrical generation (2.8 percent)

Domestic oil consumption (76.2 percent)

Oil exports (21 percent)

Fuels of the Future

Some experts believe that our energy needs will double by the year 2000, and increase another 25 percent by 2025. Electricity will supply half of our energy—

roughly the present figure for oil. Nuclear power may increase sevenfold and replace hydro as our main source of electricity.

By 2025 about half of the present oil consumption will have shifted to more abundant resources. For example, thermal generating stations will burn coal in place of oil, which will be reserved for transportation and the petrochemical industry,

where substitution is more difficult. Coal may also be refined into synthetic petroleum products and petrochemical feedstocks.

Alternative resources may satisfy about ten percent of our energy needs by 2025. Passive solar heating, using proper insulation and south-facing homes to capture, store and distribute the sun's radiation, could slash residential energy bills in half.

Abundant but unreliable wind power could supply electricity to remote areas. On the Magdalen Islands, where wind speeds aver-

age 32 kilometres an hour, a 37-metre windmill with vertical "eggbeater" blades generates part of the local electricity.

Biomass energy can be released from garbage and from agricultural and forest wastes by burning them to generate electricity or converting them for use as solid, liquid or gaseous fuels. In the Bay of Fundy, the awesome power of 15-metre tides channeled through generators could displace 950,000 cubic metres of imported oil a year by 1990, but the environmental cost may be high: damming a section of the bay might create a vast mud flat.

With our inefficient use of energy, it is cheaper to save power than to find new sources. By the year 2000, we could cut our domestic and commercial heating bills an average 50 percent over projected demand by upgrading insulation and lighting.

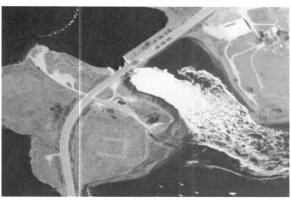

Prince Edward Island's innovative Ark (above) is a self-contained complex where renewable energy is used in daily life.

The power of the world's highest tides (below) has been tapped in this prototype hydro generator near Annapolis Royal, N.S.

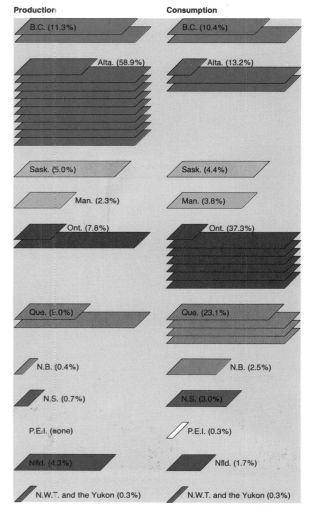

This 37-metre high wind turbine (above) can generate up to 200 kilowatts of electrical power for the Magdalen Islands.

1975 (8 quads)
Electricity (35%)
Nuclear (5%)
Coal (33%)
Hydro (62%)

Natural gas (19%)

Oil (46%)

2000 (16 quads)
Renewables (2.5%)

Electricity (47.5%)
Nuclear (31%)
Coal (28%)
Hydro (33%)
Renewables (6%)
Others (2%)

Natural gas (20%)

Oil (30%)

2025 (20 quads)
Renewables (5%)

Electricity (52%)
Nuclear (34%)
Coal (24%)
Hydro (26%)
Renewables (8%)
Others (8%)

Natural gas (18%)

Oil (25%)

Balancing future energy budgets will require more electricity and less oil and natural gas, according to the federal government projections shown above. Units of energy at this scale are expressed in quads, or quadrillions, of British thermal units. (It takes 170 supertankers to haul one quad of oil.) About half of the renewable energy will be used for electricity; the rest will provide heating.

Western Production, Eastern Consumption

The graphs below show the regional imbalance between Canada's production of primary energy (fossil fuels and hydro and nuclear electricity), and consumption of primary and secondary energy (refined petroleum products and thermal electricity).

Three quarters of our primary energy comes from the West, mainly in the form of fossil fuels. Oil constitutes half of Alberta's production, natural gas more than 40 percent. British Columbia produces almost 30 percent

of its primary energy from coal, and about 40 percent from natural gas.

All of Quebec's production, and half of Ontario's, come from hydroelectricity, the main form of primary energy in eastern Canada. Prince Edward Island has no source of primary energy; it produces all of its electricity from imported oil.

Only Alberta, Saskatchewan and British Columbia produce

more energy than they consume. Ontario uses 37.3 percent of Canada's total energy; however, the province also contains 36 percent of Canada's population. Industry uses 45 percent of Ontario's energy—more than five times the primary energy used in Atlantic Canada.

Three quarters of Alberta's primary energy is exported to the United States or to other provinces.

Residential/farming uses 28 percent of Canada's energy for lighting, heating, cooling and cooking. This section also includes commercial and governmental consumers.

Industry—mining, manufacturing and other processes—consumes 41 percent of our energy. Also included here are energy supply industries, which use energy to refine and transport more energy.

Transportation—Canada's planes, ships, boats, trucks, buses and 13 million cars use 22 percent of our energy. Road transportation comprises more than three quarters of the total in this sector.

Electrical generation and transmission consumes 7 percent of our energy.

Coal, oil and natural gas stockpiles maintained by steelmakers, utilities and other industries comprise 2 percent.

Usable energy is obtained from 60 percent of the available energy. It heats and lights our homes and powers our industry and automobiles. The residential/farm sector gets useful work from 75 percent of the energy it consumes; industry, 85 percent; transportation, 20 percent; and electrical generation, 33 percent.

Waste energy, which does no useful work, accounts for the remaining 40 percent. Some waste is unavoidable. When one form of energy is converted into another, some energy is lost to friction and heat absorption. Half of the waste in transportation, however, could be saved with more energy-efficient cars and drivers.

This section of the chart shows the total amount of available energy. Electricity contributes 21 percent; natural gas, 21 percent; coal, 4 percent; oil, 50 percent; renewable energy, 4 percent. Renewable energy is produced mainly from waste wood, which is burned by the forestry industry for heating.

Production	Consumption
B.C. (11.3%)	B.C. (10.4%)
Alta. (58.9%)	Alta. (13.2%)
Sask. (5.0%)	Sask. (4.4%)
Man. (2.3%)	Man. (3.8%)
Ont. (7.8%)	Ont. (37.3%)
Que. (6.0%)	Que. (23.1%)
N.B. (0.4%)	N.B. (2.5%)
N.S. (0.7%)	N.S. (3.0%)
P.E.I. (none)	P.E.I. (0.3%)
Nfld. (4.3%)	Nfld. (1.7%)
N.W.T. and the Yukon (0.3%)	N.W.T. and the Yukon (0.3%)

Made in Canada: Primary Products, Finished Goods

A single glove means jobs for at least 60 Canadians. They tan, cut and stitch hides. They spin cotton into thread and weave thread into lining, assemble sewing machines, cast steel into girders, mix cement for the factory walls and lay asphalt for the roof. Manufacturing employs 1.3 million people, produces more than 10,000 items, and accounts for nearly 25 percent of all Canadian production.

Before Confederation, Canada fueled the industrial revolutions of Great Britain and the United States with such raw materials as lumber and furs, and looked abroad for finished goods. Sir John A. Macdonald's National Policy of protective tariffs and the success of the railways encouraged domestic manufacturers to compete with foreign companies for a larger share of Canadian markets.

The prosperity of the early 20th century brought a great demand for investment to build electric power plants and factories, especially for automobiles and electrical appliances. But with the Great Depression of the 1930s, investment plummeted and unemployment rose to include one in four Canadians. Full recovery did not come until World War II, when massive government spending on war materials brought a new surge of economic vigor. Canadian production increased dramatically: agricultural products, 40 percent; iron and steel, 100 percent; aluminum, 500 percent.

After the war, the economy began a great new wave of peacetime growth. Many industries looked beyond labor-intensive processing to automated, capital-intensive production. Today, American-controlled subsidiaries—branch plants set up to breach the tariff "wall"—account for approximately 40 percent of Canadian production. Eighty percent of the country's manufacturing is concentrated along the St. Lawrence River and Great Lakes, bounding North America's industrial heartland.

Les Forges du Saint-Maurice (left), Canada's first heavy industry, produced stoves, plowshares, tools and anchors by 1738. At peak production, 300 men worked around the clock, many on six-hour shifts stoking the cold-air blast furnaces. The forges closed down in 1883 when the supply of local bog iron ran out.

Most pre-Confederation manufacturers employed fewer than five workers per shop and supplied local markets with furniture, shoes, flour and farm equipment. Industry was dependent on water for power and transportation; millponds and riverside factories were part of the 19th-century landscape.

A GUIDE TO CANADIAN MANUFACTURING

Canada's six economic regions and their key local factories, regional industries and industrial giants are located on the map at right. The goods they produce—from paper and petroleum to light bulbs and potato chips—are grouped within 23 industrial classifications which are listed below and symbolized on the map.

- The North
- British Columbia
- The Prairies
- Ontario
- Quebec
- Atlantic Provinces

- Automobiles
- Chemicals
- Dairy products
- Electrical products
- Fabricated metals
- Fertilizers
- Foods and beverages
- Furniture
- Leather products
- Machinery
- Meats
- Primary metals
- Printed matter
- Processed fish
- Processed fruits and vegetables
- Pulp and paper
- Refined oil
- Rubber products
- Ships
- Textiles
- Tobacco
- Transportation equipment
- Varied products

The North

Remote and sparsely settled, the Yukon and Northwest Territories have only 25 manufacturing industries. Still, some of Canada's most luxurious goods—gold, fur clothing and native art—are made here. Mackenzie-area mills saw poles, piling and lumber for the region's mines. Petroleum refineries in Whitehorse and Norman Wells produce gasoline, stove oil, and diesel and industrial fuels for local markets.

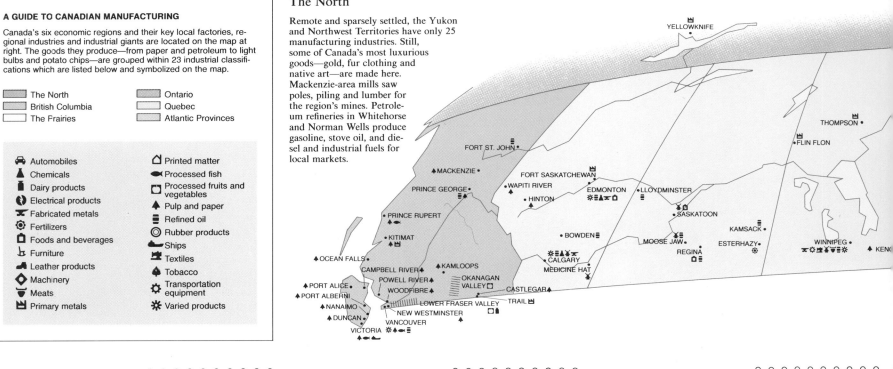

British Columbia

As its forests tower over British Columbia's landscape, so the forest industry dominates provincial manufacturing. Pulp and paper, lumber, veneer and plywood mills account for half of provincial production, and employ four in ten of B.C.'s manufacturing workers. From the province's mills comes one third of Canada's pulp and paper, and enough lumber each year to build one million houses.

The railway opened eastern markets to western raw materials in the late 19th century. Primary manufacturing, particularly sawmills, spread rapidly. Improvements in technology and transportation—larger oceangoing ships, freight airplanes and container handling—raised B.C. industries to world scales and made foreign trade profitable.

Today British Columbia is Canada's most active exporting province. Nearly 40 percent of its manufactured goods leave the country, including most of its pulp, newsprint, lumber and fish products.

Vancouver, trade gateway to the Pacific, is Canada's third largest manufacturing center. The city's diverse industries include machinery, motor

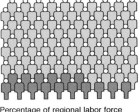

Percentage of regional labor force employed in manufacturing

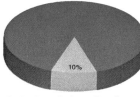

10%

Regional contribution to Canadian manufacturing

vehicles and appliances.

Resource-based and single-industry "company towns" are characteristic of B.C. manufacturing. Towns such as Powell River depend on pulp and paper mills. Trail's smelters and refineries process locally mined silver, lead and zinc ores. Kitimat's massive aluminum complex and its wealth of hydroelectric power have helped to bring billions of dollars of new industry into the province in pulp and paper, fishing and tourism.

The Prairies

Land grants and rail links opened the western frontier to settlers in the late 19th century. Burgeoning Prairie towns provided new markets for the products of B.C. sawmills, Ontario tool factories and Nova Scotia ironworks and steelworks.

By 1929, the Prairie provinces had meat slaughtering and packing facilities, flour mills, breweries, printing plants, and electrical generating stations. Winnipeg became the hub of a Western transportation network. The growing petroleum industry centered in Alberta. Winnipeg, Regina, Saskatoon, Calgary, Edmonton and Medicine Hat produced a wide range of products for local markets. Expansion was accelerated by the discovery of rich oil, natural gas and potash deposits after World War II. These large-scale extraction industries attracted workers and investors and spurred the growth of related industries.

Saskatchewan, once a wheat-producing province with little major industry, became a world supplier of processed potash to agriculture and industry. A giant plant in Esterhazy is the largest of 18 in the province. Regina and Saskatoon, whose populations doubled between

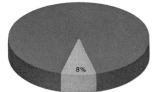

Percentage of regional labor force employed in manufacturing

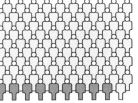

8%

Regional contribution to Canadian manufacturing

1941 and 1966, diversified into the manufacturing of steel pipes, cement, chemicals and fertilizers.

Soaring symbols of oil-fueled progress, Calgary and Edmonton grew from frontier garrisons into major centers in less than a century. More than 400 companies in Calgary alone are directly involved in the booming petroleum industry. Refineries and petrochemical plants in turn have attracted such dependent industries as plastics and textiles.

Ontario

Pickles, automobiles, toys, radar—from Ontario comes 55 percent of Canada's manufactured goods. Ontario produces 90 percent or more of Canada's motor vehicles, farm machinery, tobacco products and soap, and 80 percent of its rubber goods, wine, carpets, batteries, tanned leather and breakfast foods.

In the industrial heartland of southern Ontario, half the country's manufacturing labor force, working in half of Canada's factories, produces most of Canada's manufactured goods.

No other province offers Ontario's spectrum of attractions to industries: a large labor pool and consumer market; proximity to markets, raw materials and hydroelectric power; and key rail, water and highway links.

Along the north shore of Lake Ontario, stretching east from Niagara Falls, is the province's "Golden Horseshoe" of plants extending up the St. Lawrence to Cornwall. Major manufacturing centers around the lake include St. Catharines, Hamilton, Oakville, Toronto, Oshawa, Belleville, Kingston and Brockville. The concentration extends west from Toronto to Windsor and includes Brant-

Percentage of regional labor force employed in manufacturing

51%

Regional contribution to Canadian manufacturing

ford, London, St. Thomas and Chatham.

In Hamilton, where lake freighters unload coal and iron ore, half the manufacturing work force is employed by three steelworks. Canada's seventh largest city produces about 80 percent of the country's steel. Some of the processed iron ore remains in Hamilton, to be used by metal fabricating industries in tools, furnaces, wire and stamped metal plates. The production chain continues through transportation and

---

Acres of machinery grind wood chips, then roll and dry pulp at a Powell River newsprint mill, one of the world's largest. More than 2000 workers oversee this capital-intensive manufacturing process.

Packers slaughter, dress, split into sides and hang beef in this refrigerated room at a Winnipeg meat plant. A government inspector later grades each side before it is butchered.

After a "heat" of steel is produced in the furnaces of this Hamilton mill, it is tapped every four hours into ladles which then pour the molten metal into ingot molds.

Manufacturing Labor Force
Most industries locate near major consumer markets and labor pools, as the map of the manufacturing labor force (right) illustrates. Four out of five Canadian workers live between Windsor and Québec. Of the remaining 20 percent, three quarters live in the West and the rest in the Atlantic Provinces. Southern Ontario and Quebec form the northern part of the populous North American industrial heartland. Across the "invisible border" with the United States flows a two-way traffic in raw materials and finished goods. British Columbia manufacturers look overseas to Pacific markets.

250,000 Manufacturing workers

200,000

150,000

100,000

50,000

◄ 1,000

Production (current $) 2962%

Production (constant $) 696%

Labor force 285%

1920 1930 1940 1950 1960 1970 1980

Production: More, Faster, Cheaper
In 1920 some 600,000 Canadian workers produced $3.7 billion worth of manufactured goods. By the late 1970s, 1.3 million workers—almost three times as many as 1920—made more than $110 billion worth of goods ($26 billion when adjusted for inflation). Technological advances, mechanization and automation are largely responsible for this dramatic increase in production.

LABRADOR CITY
WABUSH

SEPT-ÎLES
POINTE-NOIRE
PORT-CARTIER
BAIE-COMEAU

CORNER BROOK
CARBONEAR
HARBOUR GRACE
COME BY CHANCE
ST. JOHN'S

LEBEL-SUR-QUÉVILLON

KAPUSKASING
DOLBEAU
ALMA
MURDOCHVILLE
CHANDLER
RED ROCK
MARATHON
THUNDER BAY
TERRACE BAY
IROQUOIS FALLS
CHICOUTIMI-JONQUIÈRE
CLERMONT
RIVIÈRE-DU-LOUP
DALHOUSIE
CARAQUET
EDMUNSTON
BATHURST
NEWCASTLE
GRAND FALLS
GRAND BANK
LA TUQUE
QUÉBEC
TÉMISCAMING
DONNACONA
ST-MAURICE VALLEY
SAULT STE. MARIE
SUDBURY
FALCONBRIDGE
ESPANOLA
COPPER CLIFF
MATTAWA
STE-THÉRÈSE
LOUISEVILLE
SOREL-TRACY
MONCTON
AMHERST
TRENTON
SYDNEY
POINT TUPPER
PORT HAWKESBURY
GATINEAU
MONTRÉAL
OTTAWA-HULL
CORNWALL
BEAUHARNOIS
EASTERN TOWNSHIPS
BLACKS HARBOUR
SAINT JOHN
TRURO
HALIFAX
ANNAPOLIS VALLEY
LUNENBURG
BRAMPTON
OAKVILLE
GUELPH
PETERBOROUGH
KINGSTON
BELLEVILLE
YARMOUTH
SHELBURNE
OSHAWA
PORT HOPE
KITCHENER-WATERLOO
STRATFORD
TORONTO
ST. CATHARINES-NIAGARA
SARNIA
HAMILTON
NIAGARA PENINSULA
LONDON
WELLAND
WINDSOR
PORT COLBORNE
CHATHAM

appliance manufacturers, who use stamped steel parts in products ranging from toys to truck bodies.

Toronto, Windsor, St. Catharines, Kitchener and London are all large consumers of iron and steel. Metal plate, fabricated metal, machinery and automobile-parts makers dominate manufacturing in these cities. Similarly, Sarnia's oil refineries—Canada's largest—have attracted such related industries as plastics, fertilizers, pharmaceuticals, paints, soaps, cosmetics and industrial chemicals.

From Toronto comes 20 percent of the country's manufactured goods—including machinery, transportation equipment and electrical, rubber, wood, metal and plastic products. Raw material shortages and sluggish specialized markets, devastating to single-industry towns, have less impact on Toronto's diversified economy.

Dotted across northern Ontario are pulp and paper mills. In this area, the other important primary manufacturing industry is metal refining, concentrated around Sudbury.

Quebec

Quebec, the second most important manufacturing province, produces about 30 percent of the country's manufactured goods. The province's major industry is pulp and paper, followed by primary metals. Other important products are electrical and transportation equipment, textiles, clothing, fabricated metals and chemicals. Key local industries include cabinetmaking, petroleum refining, pharmaceuticals, iron ore and asbestos processing.

Industrial growth in Quebec coincided with the decline of small family farms. Such labor-intensive industries as textiles, clothing and furniture making attracted the rural population to Montréal, Québec and Trois-Rivières.

Maritime trade and cheap power further encouraged Quebec's growth. Port-oriented in-

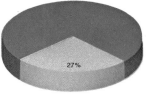
Percentage of regional labor force employed in manufacturing

27%

Regional contribution to Canadian manufacturing

dustries using imported raw materials mushroomed along the St. Lawrence. Québec added paper mills and garment factories. Generating stations attracted large textile plants, pulp and paper mills and aluminum refineries.

By World War II, electrical power had replaced steam, and electrometallurgy offered new industrial prospects. Huge new mining operations in Chibougamau, Matagami, Schefferville, Gagnon, Wabush, Labrador City and Lake Allard produced gold, silver, copper, lead and zinc for Montréal refineries.

Today, Quebec's 50 pulp and paper mills make one third of Canada's pulp and newsprint. From eight refineries comes 20 percent of the nation's processed petroleum. Forty percent of Canada's fabricated metals is manufactured in Quebec.

Montréal's industries, ranging from food, beverage and pharmaceutical companies to transportation equipment and appliance makers, account for half of Quebec's work force, factories and output. The city's largest employer is the clothing industry, vulnerable to seasonal slumps and unpredictable markets.

Atlantic Provinces

The Atlantic Provinces have traditionally looked to the sea. In the mid-1800s, 200 shipyards exported $2.5 million worth of vessels. From nearly 2000 sawmills came lumber for boats, barrels and casks.

But from 1876 to 1900, the export of ships dropped 90 percent as iron replaced wood in hulls and steam engines made canvas sails obsolete. Textile and dairy plants did spring up in Nova Scotia and Prince Edward Island, however. And by the end of the century, growing New England markets sought Maritime processed fish. Investments in Cape Breton iron and steel mills led to new rolling mills and wire-, nail- and bolt-making facilities.

For a time, Sydney's iron and steel mills were the country's largest, and eastern wool, cotton and canvas mills prospered. But by the 1920s, heartland factories had overshadowed eastern mills. Hamilton's steel facilities were outproducing Sydney's. The Maritime textile industry was eroded by Quebec's.

Percentage of regional labor force employed in manufacturing

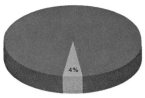
4%

Regional contribution to Canadian manufacturing

In more recent times, provincial governments in the Atlantic Provinces have sought to stimulate late industrial growth. Food processing in particular has enjoyed relative prosperity. The pulp and paper industry has expanded to meet British and American newsprint demands. And energy resources and the promise of offshore oil are attracting new industry to Newfoundland—traditionally one of Canada's "have-not" provinces.

Assembly lines at this Oshawa car plant produce more than 800 cars daily. While some workers assemble chassis, others weld and paint bodies. These sections will be bolted together elsewhere in the plant.

Lightning-fast fingers attach zippers; others stitch on buttons; still more sew the seams of pants at this Montréal garment factory. Piecework means speed and precision in such a labor-intensive industry.

Skilled packers at this Blacks Harbour sardine cannery in New Brunswick sort, clean and pack 2500 sardines an hour. The filled tins are sealed and sterilized automatically.

Transportation and Communications

Canada became a nation in spite of its geography. Its boundaries, set by treaties in distant Europe, cut across the natural north–south grain of the continent. To fulfill the political dream of nationhood, Canadians were forced to ignore the shorter and easier river and coastal trade routes to the south. But as they forged new links westward across vast, desolate stretches of snow, bog, and granite and the formidable western mountains, they staked their claim to the land and its wealth.

Roads, canals and railway tracks reached out across the land, etching a skeleton of lines that determined the shape of today's inhabited part of the country. Settlers came, building homes and villages along the rights-of-way. Cities grew and industry flourished where one form of transportation met another. Trade promoted industrial development and diversification.

In the space of just a few generations, technology has dramatically and irreversibly changed the way we keep in touch with one another. Once travel was hazardous and bone-jarring; messages arrived only with time and a good deal of luck. Today's traveler may lean back in comfort, watching the scenery whiz past. Communications flash along wires or airwaves, giving instant contact by voice, printed word or televised image. But new problems replace those that have been solved. Rising fuel costs, a rugged land and a harsh climate can ground planes, fell wires, and block roads, bringing the most advanced technology to a standstill. Tying this immense land together remains a great and uniquely Canadian challenge.

Most of Canada's rail, road, water and air routes serve a narrow strip along the United States border, and cities in this corridor are gateway centers. Smaller routes fan out from them, giving access to the country's hinterlands. Travel density over this network varies widely. Depending on how large and how close two centers are, traffic between them may travel by superhighways and hourly air departures, or by a simple two-lane road.

More than 872,000 kilometres of roads and streets serve Canada's 12.9 million motor vehicles. The Trans-Canada Highway, longest national road in the world, spans a distance of 7821 kilometres, passing through all ten provinces.

Laced with some 70,000 kilometres of main-line track, Canada has grown along the railways laid down in the late nineteenth and early twentieth centuries. Its network is exceeded in size only by those of the United States and the Soviet Union.

International trade accounts for over three-fifths of the shipping handled by Canadian ports, most of it low-value bulk goods such as wheat and ores. Much of coastal Canada is dependent on this industry; two oceans, the Great Lakes and Hudson Bay provide major ports in all provinces except Prince Edward Island, Alberta and Saskatchewan.

Canada's size makes domestic air service more important than in most countries. Some 130,000 kilometres of controlled airways arc across the land, connecting widely separated cities and penetrating areas, particularly the North, that are inaccessible to ground transport .

Moving People

About 80 percent of Canadian households own automobiles. In 1979, private cars made 84 percent of all intercity passenger trips, and consumed more than half the fuel used in transportation. As travelers prefer the flexibility, freedom and convenience of the automobile, bus and train travel have consequently declined in popularity, and compete with each other for a shrinking market. Air travel still accounts for only 12.5 percent of travel. While the airplane's speed has cut travel time drastically (see map, below), higher costs are a deterrent. At-

tempting to lure people back to the more energy-efficient forms of transportation, federal and local governments are making some effort to revitalize train travel and public transit. Duplicate services such as transcontinental trains have been combined, while other services have been eliminated.

Toronto International Airport

Don Valley Parkway, Toronto

A Shrinking Country

Speed of travel has shrunk Canada's immense distances to a manageable size. This map dramatizes how technology has reduced the time needed to travel between Montréal and Vancouver.

- 1893 Steam (wood and coal) train 115 hours
- 1935 Steam (coal) train 90 hours
- 1971 Diesel train 60 hours
- 1939 Propeller-driven aircraft 18 hours
- 1971 Jet aircraft 5 hours

Bringing Canadians Together

- ■ Census metropolitan area
- +—+ Canadian Pacific
- +—+ Canadian National
- Trans-Canada Highway
- Macdonald Cartier Freeway
- Yellowhead Route
- Alaska Highway
- ▲ Northern airport
- ● Telesat receiving station
- ● Telesat receiving station (major)

Airport passenger density

- 10,000,000
- 5,000,000
- 2,500,000
- 1,000,000
- 500,000
- 250,000
- 100,000

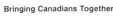

Seagoing Workhorses

Linking islands and mainland and serving Pacific coastal settlements as far north as Prince Rupert, British Columbia's fleet of 24 ferries hauls cars, buses and truckloads of consumer goods. About 200 vehicles can be loaded in a matter of minutes stacked up to three decks high.

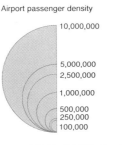
B.C. ferry, Queen of Cowichan

Booms and Barges

Logging trucks can seldom carry more than a few dozen logs at a time, but a single boat can handle hundreds. From a harvest site, logs are hoisted or trucked out, then tumbled into the sea. Rounded up and se-

Self-dumping log barge, B.C.

cured to form large raftlike booms, they are towed down the coast to the mill.

Self-dumping log barges can move logs farther and through rougher water than traditional booms. Cranes on board the barges load the logs. At the mill, tanks on one side are flooded, tipping the barges and dumping their load with a splash.

Superport

In Roberts Bank, B.C., a thin, 2-kilometre-long strip of landfill and concrete juts out from shore, ending in a bulb-shaped artificial peninsula that gives deepwater berths for huge tankers and bulk carriers. Loading

and unloading is almost completely automated. A huge rotary dumper lifts coal cars from the track every 100 seconds, tips them, and sets them neatly down again. The coal is whisked along a conveyor belt to stockpiles or poured directly onto a waiting ship.

Over the Rockies

Road-building through mountains means chiseling ledges along steep slopes, blasting tunnels and raising bridges. Costs often exceed $600,000 per kilometre. At Kicking Horse Pass (1625 metres), the highest point on the Canadian Pacific Railway, two spiral tunnels twist

Logging truck, Vancouver Island

through adjoining peaks to permit trains a slow, steady climb. Wind and cold, however, make avalanches and rockslides a constant concern. Snow fences and concrete snowsheds shelter tracks and highways at their most vulnerable points. In avalanche season in Rogers Pass (1320 metres), small falls are triggered by an artillery crew to prevent dangerous buildups of snow and ice.

Rail Freight

The simple boxcar is being replaced by double-deck and three-level vehicle carriers, container cars, flatcars with tie-downs for heavy equipment or

Symington Yards, Winnipeg

side supports for logs, refrigerator ("reefer") and cushioned freight cars. Livestock cars water and feed en route, "prairie schooners" have removable gondola lids, and tank cars carry everything from acid to molasses. To get each car to its destination, freight trains must be broken up and sorted when they reach a major rail yard. Some, such as Winnipeg's Symington Yards, put a computer to work sorting up to 6000 cars a day. Incoming trains are scanned on a monitor, which records each car's code number for the computer. A yard locomotive nudges the train over a small "hump" toward a fan of 62 lines of track. As the cars roll

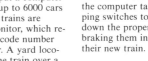
Grain depot, Carmangay, Alta.

downhill—four each minute—the computer takes over, flipping switches to send them down the proper track, then braking them in time to join their new train.

Ships Built Like Cigars

Low, skinny and shallow, ten times as long as they are wide, Canada's fleet of 150 lake freighters is built especially for bulk-cargo service in the sheltered waters of the St. Lawrence Seaway and the Great Lakes. Shaped like the canal locks they must pass through, the lakers' ungainly length and shallow draft would make them unsafe in rough ocean waters.

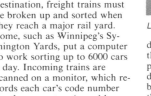
Lake freighter, Welland Canal

Moving Things

The railroad is still the preferred way of shipping domestic freight, but the trucking industry is the fastest growing. By carrying lighter, more valuable goods, it already leads in freight revenues earned.

Water transport is by far the cheapest transportation method. On average, it costs five times more to move goods by train than by ship; five times more by truck than by train; and nearly three times more by plane than by truck. But water transport, limited to coastal areas and the St. Lawrence–Great Lakes system, comes to a halt when ice chokes the ports. Bulk goods such as wheat or ore can travel by any mode, but manufactured goods, perishables and rush orders require special handling. Weight, size, handling and the availability of return cargoes all determine the methods by which products move.

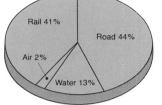

Rail 41%
Road 44%
Air 2%
Water 13%

Spiral railway tunnel near Field, B.C.

Communications for a Vast Land

Alexander Graham Bell placed the world's first long-distance telephone call between Brantford and Paris, Ont., in 1876. Still a leader in telecommunications, Canada launched *Anik I* (Inuit for brother) in 1972, its first communications satellite, and the world's first to give long-distance telephone service. Orbiting 35,900 kilometres above the earth, "talking bird" satellites such as *Anik* also relay computer data, and radio and television signals. Before *Anik*, signals had to travel through strands of wire or via a series of 60-metre-high microwave relay stations strung out every 50 kilometres. Telephone and television services were impossible; the North talked to the rest of Canada, when static permitted, over high-frequency radio.

At least one telephone sits in 96 percent of Canadian homes—more than one for every two people; each person makes an average 1000 calls a year. Technological advances have made those calls

Awkward-looking but efficient, Anik B was launched in 1978, the fourth of Canada's communications satellites. Anik is part of the Telesat system, which includes repeater satellites in stationary orbits, a control center, tracking and command facilities and more than 120 earth stations (below). Signals beamed to the satellite are amplified and rebroadcast to earth stations tuned to the particular channel.

☐ B.C. Tel
☐ Alberta Government Telephones
☐ SASK Tel
☐ Manitoba Telephone System
■ Bell Canada
☐ NBTe
☐ Maritime Tel & Tel
☐ Island Tel, PEI
☐ Newfoundland Telephone
■ Other companies

Microwave Routes:
— TCTS Dataroute
— Datapac Network
— TCTS Microwave

clearer, faster and cheaper than ever before. Automated switching has almost eliminated the operator, just as transmission relay towers replaced intercity cables. The latest advance, fiber optics, may soon replace electric currents with pulses of light moving along hair-thin glass fibers.

Postal service is still an important form of communication. Canada's 8000 post offices handle more than six billion pieces a year with automated sorting machines that "read" coded mail electronically.

Mass media—radio and television—have a formidable reach in Canada, giving an instant view of people, politics and problems from coast to coast. Some 98 percent of Canadian homes have radios; 97 percent have television, most of them color. One house in three is hooked up to a cable service. Heavily settled parts of the country have a wide choice of programs from local stations and Canada's two national networks; in addition, 73 percent of viewers have direct access to the immense American system and its three major networks.

Moving North

It has generally been easier for Canadians to travel to Europe than to the Yukon and Northwest Territories, where a population of 64,900 is scattered across some 4 million square kilometres. Permanent roads are few and generally unpaved; most serve the southwestern Yukon and the Mackenzie Valley. The only railway lines in the territories connect Whitehorse with the Alaska panhandle and Hay River, N.W.T.; and Great Slave Lake with northern Alberta. Building permanent road or rail routes is expensive. Spongy tundra and muskeg can swallow roadbeds, and frost heave can lift bridge pilings right out of the ground. The terrain is difficult and construction materials such as timber and crushed gravel are scarce.

Without permanent roads, the seasons dictate how the northern people and goods

Arctic tug, Beaufort Sea

move. In winter, frozen lakes are potential landing strips, and families use snowmobiles the way southerners use cars. Tractor-trains haul strings of freight sleds over winter roads of packed snow. In summer, airplane skis are replaced with pontoons, and tugs, barges and freighters take to the waters. They hurry, because the season is short—only five to seven weeks for much of the Arctic Coast. In the spring and summer, overland travel in much of the North comes to a halt, and only air cargo travels quickly. Food, fuel and heavy freight for the eastern Arctic's coastal settlements must wait until government supply ships can pick a way among the treacherous summer ice floes. Western Arctic supply convoys leave the railhead in Hay River for the 1720-kilometre trip down the Mackenzie River. As many as a dozen 1300-tonne barges are lashed together and nosed ahead by a tugboat. The trip north to Tuktoyaktuk takes nine days; returning empty against the fast-flowing current takes two weeks.

Water Key to Canada

The St. Lawrence Seaway became a reality in 1959, opening a 3700-kilometre route from the Atlantic to the head of Lake Superior, and giving ocean vessels access to North America's industrial and agricultural heartland. The Seaway bypassed a rapid-strewn, 293-kilometre stretch of the St. Lawrence River, enlarged existing canals around Niagara Falls, and forced relocation of 6500 people in eastern Ontario as five new dams flooded eight towns and 22 farms. Today, ships pass through 16 locks as they climb 183 metres from sea level to Lake Superior. Prairie grain moves from the western Great Lakes to markets in the east and overseas; returning ships carry iron ore from Labrador and northern Quebec to steel mills in Ontario. Ships of more than 30 nations pick up and deliver general cargoes, many of them containerized. Contrary to expectations, however, Seaway tolls are not covering construction costs. Winter ice limits the shipping season to 250 days a year, and the Seaway's 8-metre draft limitation bars many vessels.

Breaking the Ice

In winter and early spring, Canada's reinforced-hull icebreakers clear channels in Atlantic shipping lanes and the Gulf of St. Lawrence and keep ports ice-free as far inland as Montréal. In summer they do duty in the eastern Arctic. Even the passenger ferries making regular trips to Prince Edward Island, Newfoundland and Labrador risk meeting icebergs or being trapped by drifting floes. In spring, ice jams in the Seaway and Great Lakes must be cleared to prevent flooding upriver.

Containerports

At such modern containerports as Bruntern in Saint John, N.B., the shipping of manufactured goods has been revolutionized by use of the container, a standard-sized box that locks onto trucks and railway cars and can be stacked neatly in ship holds and storage areas. Tall, fixed gantry cranes can unload a 500-container ship in just 24 hours; conventional freighters may take five days to unload.

Parting the Seas

Tethering the island of Cape Breton to mainland Nova Scotia, the 1370-metre Canso

Halifax containerport

FROBISHER BAY
Sept-Îles
CHICOUTIMI-JONQUIERE
Bagotville
THUNDER BAY
Sault Ste. Marie
SUDBURY
QUEBEC
Fredericton
Moncton
Charlottetown
Sydney
Gander
ST. JOHN'S
OTTAWA-HULL
MONTREAL
SAINT JOHN
HALIFAX
HARRIETSFIELD
ALLAN PARK
TORONTO
OSHAWA
KITCHENER
ST. CATHARINES–NIAGARA
LONDON
HAMILTON
WINDSOR

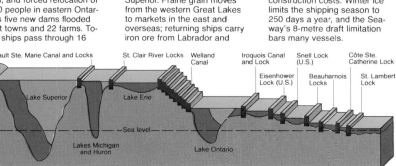

Sault Ste. Marie Canal and Locks | St. Clair River Locks | Welland Canal | Iroquois Canal and Lock | Eisenhower Lock (U.S.) | Snell Lock (U.S.) | Beauharnois Locks | Côte Ste. Catherine Lock | St. Lambert Lock
Lake Superior | Lake Erie | Sea level | Lakes Michigan and Huron | Lake Ontario

Icebreaking air-cushion vehicle on the St. Lawrence River, Que.

Causeway is the deepest in the world. Its 243-metre-wide base tapers to just 24 metres at its top, 66 metres above the sea floor. The causeway carries the Trans-Canada Highway, a railway track and a pedestrian walkway. The 25-metre-wide Canso Lock permits freight, fishing and pleasure craft to sail through at the Cape Breton end. An electronically operated swing bridge clears a passage for taller boats. Point Tupper, once the terminus of a rail ferry, now has a deepwater terminal dock built in the causeway's sheltered waters that handles some of the world's largest supertankers.

Canada Among the Nations

Although Canada became a self-governing country in 1867, its real declaration of independence is the Statute of Westminster, which defined the status of the British Dominions as "autonomous communities" in 1931. This declaration recognized an evolution that had been taking place in the British Empire in the 20th century, with Canada conspicuously in the vanguard. In the first half century of Canadian nationhood, Canada's interests were clearly subordinated to those of Britain. In 1914, when Britain declared war on Germany, Canada was automatically at war, too. However, emboldened by this country's sacrifices in that war, the Canadian delegation to the peace conference insisted on signing the Treaty of Versailles in 1919 as representatives of a separate state.

The League of Nations accepted this claim to sovereign status and admitted Canada to its ranks. In 1923, the British government allowed the Dominion to sign its first treaty, the Halibut Fisheries Treaty with the United States, without Britain's customary cosignature. By the end of the 1920s, Canada had sent its first diplomats to Washington, Paris and Tokyo. Canada made its own declaration of war in 1939, and played a leading part in the founding of the United Nations. The last vestige of British rule disappeared in 1949, when appeals to the Imperial Privy Council were abolished and the Supreme Court of Canada became this nation's highest court of appeal.

While retaining its Commonwealth status, Canada has broadened its international role since World War II. It has become a major source of aid to underdeveloped countries outside as well as within the Commonwealth. It has taken an active part in United Nations peacekeeping and welfare-promoting activities. Lester B. Pearson won the Nobel Peace Prize for defusing the Suez Canal crisis in 1956, and his successor, Paul Martin, led the hasty organization of a UN force that averted war in Cyprus in 1964.

Having marshaled the third-strongest navy and fourth-strongest air force among the Allied powers by 1945, Canada reduced its armed forces drastically after World War II. It chose the path of collective security by joining the United States and west European countries in the North Atlantic Treaty Organization in 1949. This, and the North American Air Defense system, are our major military commitments.

As a country of vast and varied resources, and relatively small population, Canada has always been a major trading nation. Traditionally, its main partners have been the United States and Great Britain, but trade with other countries has grown substantially in the last quarter century.

Ottawa is the center of the world in this Lambert Equal Area projection. It reveals that the shortest route from Ottawa to Singapore is over the North Pole, and that a direct route from Ottawa to Tokyo passes over the Yukon. Concentric circles on the map make it clear that Honduras is as close to Ottawa as Whitehorse, that Brasilia is slightly closer than Hawaii, and that the most distant city in the world is Canberra, Australia.

Goods, Services and the Wealth of Nations

Canadians enjoy one of the highest material standards of living in the world, as can be seen from this comparison with a list of selected countries representing all continents. The chart compares per capita Gross Domestic Product (GDP): the total annual output of goods and services per person. Fifteen countries, including the United States, annually produce more goods and services per person than does Canada. Four countries—the United States, the Soviet Union, Japan and West Germany—produce half the world's GDP.

Distributing the global value of goods and services would provide every person with about $1500—equal to the standard of living in Argentina, or 15 times that of Ethiopia.

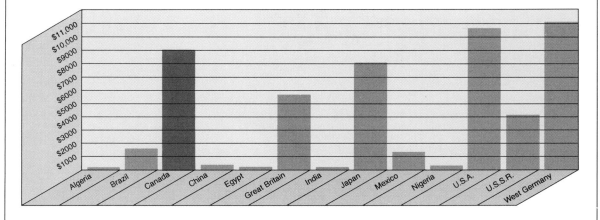

Imports and Exports: Barley to Blue Jeans

One half of all the goods produced in Canada is shipped abroad. The world's top exporter of newsprint, nickel, silver, asbestos, wheat, barley and fish, Canada is among the world's first ten trading nations—and one of only four countries that export more than they import. Because national income levels closely follow exports, trade is essential to Canadian prosperity.

For 200 years, Canada's major trading partners have been Great Britain and the United States. Since 1882, the United States has been more important in terms of total trade. But Britain remained the foremost market for Canadian exports until the late 1940s.

Trade between Canada and the United States is greater than that between any other two countries. Since the Canada–U.S. Automotive Products Agreement of 1965, motor vehicles and parts have become Canada's most profitable exports, accounting for nearly one out of every four export dollars earned. The traditional major exports—fabricated materials such as lumber, newsprint and chemicals, and raw commodities such as wheat, metal ores and crude petroleum—bring in most of the rest. In effect, these goods are exchanged for a wide range of manufactured imports, from aircraft engines to plastic trinkets, farm machinery to blue jeans, that help Canada to maintain its high material standard of living.

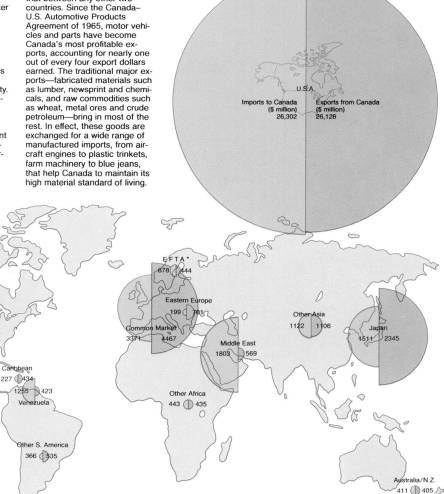

Imports to Canada ($ million) 26,302
Exports from Canada ($ million) 26,128

U.S.A.

EFTA*
678 / 444

Eastern Europe
199 / 701

Common Market
3371 / 4467

Other Asia
1122 / 1106

Japan
1511 / 2345

Middle East
1803 / 569

Caribbean
227 / 434
1255 / 423
Venezuela

Other Africa
443 / 435

Other S. America
366 / 535

Australia/N.Z.
411 / 405

*European Free Trade Association

This global projection, centered on Canada, illustrates the breadth of the nation's many external ties. Diplomatic and consular representation keeps Canada in touch with almost every other country. Our membership in the Commonwealth and NATO, and our UN peacekeeping role and external aid programs have all forged substantial links around the world.

*The **North Atlantic Treaty Organization** comprises 15 countries in North America and Europe that are bound together for mutual defense under a treaty signed, partly at Canadian instigation, in 1949. Canada's NATO commitment is executed by army and air force units stationed in West Germany and by a fleet based mainly in Halifax.*

PAPUA – NEW GUINEA

AUSTRALIA

NAURU

Canberra

FIJI

SAMOA

TONGA

NEW ZEALAND
Wellington

8000 km
10,500 km
12,000 km
13,500 km
15,000 km
16,500 km
18,000 km

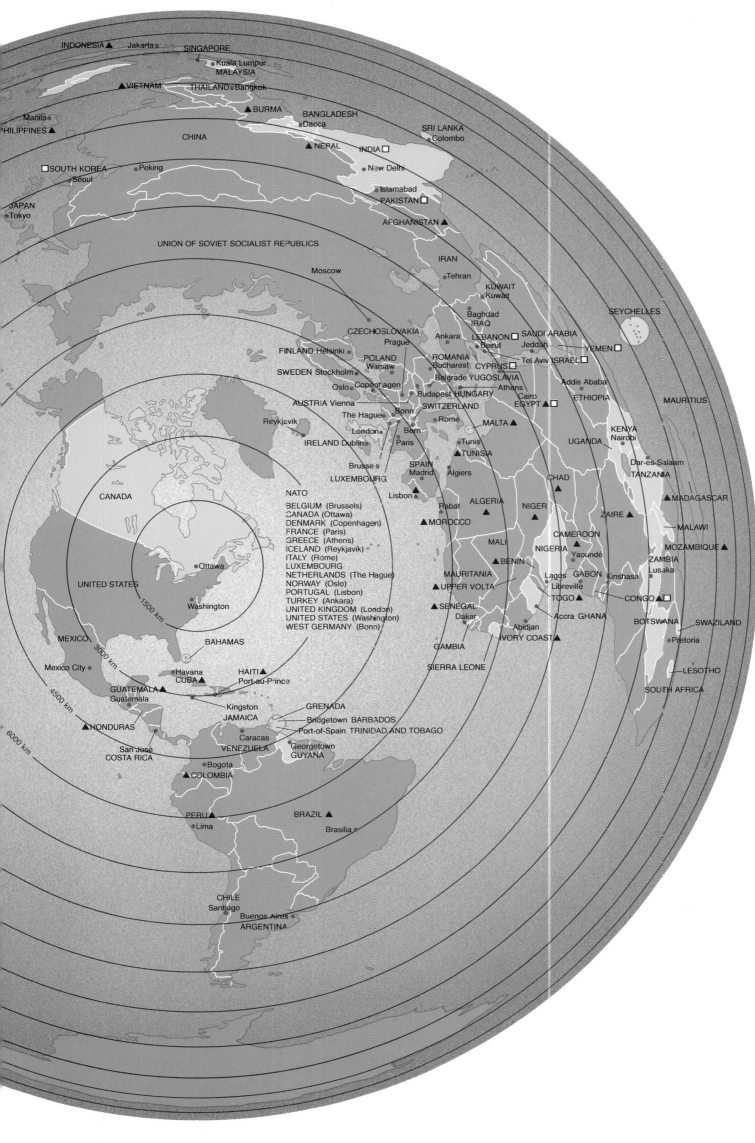

Foreign Aid and Investment

Canadian money—either as external aid or as business investment—finances projects in more than 70 countries on four continents. Half of this aid (more than one billion dollars) is sent directly to the governments of recipient countries, in the form of food, building materials, industrial and agricultural equipment, or technology. The Canadian International Development Agency (CIDA) distributes another 40 percent of its funds among some 60 international organizations, many of them United Nations agencies. This money helps to finance programs undertaken by such agencies as UNICEF (the United Nations International Children's Emergency Fund) and the World Bank.

Canada's external aid program was initiated in 1950 as part of the Commonwealth's Colombo Plan. For 14 million Canadians in 1950, the $200,000 worth of wheat donated to India, Pakistan and Ceylon represented a penny-a-person sacrifice. By the end of the 1970s, Canada's donations to more than 70 countries amounted to more than $40 from every Canadian.

Direct Canadian investment in business abroad has also increased significantly, jumping from $3.7 billion in 1966 to more than $13 billion in 1977. The United States was the largest beneficiary of these investment dollars ($7 billion, or 52 percent of the total), followed by the United Kingdom and Brazil, each with a $1.4-billion, ten-percent share.

Foreign Aid

1. Other countries 2%
2. Latin America 7%
3. Commonwealth: Caribbean 7%
4. Commonwealth: Africa 18%
5. Francophone Africa 19%
6. Asia 47%

Foreign Investment

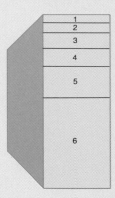

1. Australia 4%
2. Africa, Asia, South America 6%
3. North America 9%
4. Brazil 10%
5. Europe 18%
6. United States 53%

NATO
BELGIUM (Brussels)
CANADA (Ottawa)
DENMARK (Copenhagen)
FRANCE (Paris)
GREECE (Athens)
ICELAND (Reykjavik)
ITALY (Rome)
LUXEMBOURG
NETHERLANDS (The Hague)
NORWAY (Oslo)
PORTUGAL (Lisbon)
TURKEY (Ankara)
UNITED KINGDOM (London)
UNITED STATES (Washington)
WEST GERMANY (Bonn)

The member states of the **Commonwealth of Nations** are all former colonies of the British Empire. Allied by sentiment, by tradition and by assent to the Statute of Westminster, they cover one quarter of the earth's landmass and are home to a similar proportion of its people. The heads of the Commonwealth governments meet periodically to discuss matters of common concern. In addition, the member governments hold some 50 conferences yearly on topics such as education, science and health. Canada provides development assistance to four out of five Commonwealth nations; the Caribbean members receive the highest share on a per capita basis.

Canada maintains **permanent representatives** in 74 countries. They are called ambassadors or, in the case of Commonwealth countries, high commissioners. Some 300 consulates are located in cities, other than national capitals, where Canadians have trade and travel interests, extending Canada's diplomatic reach even farther.

Canada is the only country in the world to have participated in all of the **United Nations peacekeeping missions** undertaken since World War II. At the end of the 1970s, Canadian troops or official military observers were stationed in the Middle East, in Kashmir along the India–Pakistan border and in Cyprus.

Canada's **foreign aid** extends beyond the Commonwealth to about 32 countries. Latin American states and former French colonies in Africa are increasingly significant beneficiaries as Canada expands its cultural and trade ties. The map shows the worldwide distribution of Canadian aid, in the form of food, loans or grants, as of 1980.

59

FACTS ABOUT CANADA

Canada: Apparently derived from the Iroquoian *kanata*, meaning "village" or "community," the name Canada first appears in Jacques Cartier's description of the Indian village of Stadacona (later Québec) in 1534.

The Nation and the Provinces

CANADIAN SUPERLATIVES

Largest island: Baffin (N.W.T.), 507,451 km²
Longest river: Mackenzie, 4241 km
Largest lake within Canada: Huron (Ont.). Area in Canada: 36,001 km². (Total area of the lake, including U.S. area: 59,570 km²)
Highest mountain: Mount Logan (Yukon), 5951 m
Highest lake: Chilco (B.C.), 1171 m
Rainiest place: Seymour Falls (B.C.), 3504.5 mm/year
Highest waterfall: Takakkaw Falls (B.C.), 503 m
Greatest waterfall by volume: Niagara (the Canadian Horsehoe Falls, Ont.), 5365 m³/second
Largest metropolitan area (1976 census): Ottawa-Hull (Ont. & Que.), 3998.9 km²
Longest bridge: The Pierre Laporte Suspension Bridge, Québec (Que.), 668 m
Longest tunnel: Connaught Railway Tunnel at Rogers Pass (B.C.), 8.08 km
Highest dam: Mica, Columbia River (B.C.), 244 m
Coldest city: Yellowknife (N.W.T.). Mean annual temperature: –5.6°C
Warmest city: Vancouver (B.C.). Mean annual temperature: 9.8°C
Northernmost point: Cape Columbia, Ellesmere Island (N.W.T.), 83°07′N
Northernmost town: Alert, Ellesmere Island (N.W.T.), 82°30′N
Southernmost point: Middle Island, Lake Erie (Ont.), 41°41′N
Southernmost town: Pelee Island Sound (Ont.), 41°45′N
Westernmost point: Mount St. Elias (Yukon), 141°W
Westernmost town: Beaver Creek (Yukon), 142°52′W
Easternmost point: Cape Spear (Nfld.), 52°37′W
Easternmost town: Blackhead, St. John's South District (Nfld.), 52°39′W
Highest city: Rossland (B.C.), 1056 m
Highest town: Lake Louise (Alta.), 1540 m
Highest tide: The Bay of Fundy at Burncoat Head (N.S.), 14.25 m (mean spring range)

AREA OF THE PROVINCES AND TERRITORIES

Province or territory:	Land (km²)	Freshwater (km²)	Total (km²)	Percent of total area
Newfoundland	370,485	34,032	404,517	4.1
Prince Edward Island	5657	—	5657	0.1
Nova Scotia	52,841	2650	55,491	0.6
New Brunswick	72,092	1344	73,436	0.7
Quebec	1,356,792	183,889	1,540,681	15.5
Ontario	891,195	177,388	1,068,583	10.8
Manitoba	548,495	101,592	650,087	6.5
Saskatchewan	570,269	81,631	651,900	6.6
Alberta	644,389	16,796	661,185	6.6
British Columbia	930,529	18,068	948,597	9.5
Yukon Territory	478,034	4481	482,515	4.9
Northwest Territories	3,246,392	133,294	3,379,686	34.1
CANADA	9,167,170	755,165	9,922,335	100.0

POPULATION BY PROVINCE (thousands)

Province or territory	1961	1971	1976	1978	1979 (July)
Newfoundland	458	522	558	569	574
Prince Edward Island	105	112	118	122	123
Nova Scotia	737	789	829	841	847
New Brunswick	598	635	677	695	701
Quebec	5259	6028	6234	6285	6301
Ontario	6236	7703	8264	8444	8505
Manitoba	922	988	1022	1032	1030
Sask.	925	926	921	947	957
Alberta	1322	1628	1838	1950	2014
British Columbia	1629	2185	2467	2530	2570
Yukon	15	18	22	22	21
Northwest Territories	23	35	42	44	43

POPULATION: How Canada may grow

Year (as of June 1)	Total (thousands)	Percent change	Age groups: 0–14	15–24	25–44	45–64	65+
1971	21,563.3	6.60	6380.9	4003.8	5415.9	4023.3	1744.4
Projected:							
1981	24,573.5	6.88	5691.8	4712.4	7232.5	4622.7	2314.1
1991	28,091.9	6.69	6668.0	3893.8	9312.4	5218.7	2999.0
2001	30,980.7	4.51	6849.9	4519.2	9217.9	6931.3	3462.3

POPULATION OF CENSUS METROPOLITAN AREAS

Census Metropolitan Area	1951	1956	1961	1966	1971	1976	1978
Calgary	142,315	201,022	279,062	330,575	403,319	469,917	504,900
Chicoutimi–Jonquière	91,161	110,317	127,616	132,954	133,703	128,643	129,700
Edmonton	193,622	275,182	259,821	425,370	495,702	554,228	581,400
Halifax	138,427	170,481	193,353	209,901	222,637	267,991	271,200
Hamilton	281,901	341,513	401,071	457,410	489,523	529,371	536,300
Kitchener	107,474	128,722	154,864	192,275	226,846	272,158	280,100
London	167,724	196,338	226,669	253,701	286,011	270,383	274,100
Montreal	1,539,308	1,830,232	2,215,627	2,570,982	2,743,208	2,802,485	2,823,000
Oshawa					120,318	135,196	139,300
Ottawa–Hull	311,587	367,756	457,038	528,774	602,510	693,288	726,400
Quebec	289,294	328,405	379,067	436,918	480,502	542,158	554,500
Regina	72,731	91,215	113,749	132,432	140,734	151,191	160,000
Saint John, N.B.	80,689	88,375	98,083	104,195	106,744	112,974	117,200
St. Catharines–Niagara	189,046	1233,034	257,796	285,453	303,429	301,921	306,000
St. John's, Nfld.	80,869	92,565	106,666	117,533	131,814	143,390	146,500
Saskatoon	55,679	72,930	95,564	115,900	126,449	133,750	139,200
Sudbury	80,543	107,889	127,446	136,739	155,424	157,030	155,000
Thunder Bay	73,713	87,624	102,085	108,035	112,093	119,253	120,700
Toronto	1,261,861	1,571,952	1,919,409	2,289,900	2,628,043	2,803,101	2,856,500
Vancouver	586,172	694,425	826,798	933,091	1,082,352	1,166,348	1,173,300
Victoria	114,859	136,127	155,763	175,262	195,800	18,250	222,500
Windsor	182,619	208,456	217,215	238,323	258,643	247,582	246,300
Winnipeg	257,229	412,741	476,543	508,759	540,262	578,217	589,100

POPULATION: Canada and the world

Rank	Country	Population (Jan. 1, 1980)	Density/km²
1.	China	969,650,710	101
2.	India	660,002,000	200
3.	Soviet Union	264,803,970	12
4.	United States	221,089,000	24
5.	Indonesia	153,535,228	75
6.	Brazil	119,501,000	14
7.	Japan	118,258,000	317
8.	Bangladesh	89,278,137	620
9.	Pakistan	81,455,500	101
10.	Nigeria	71,507,300	77
11.	Mexico	70,405,500	36
12.	West Germany	61,703,500	248
13.	Italy	57,439,300	191
14.	Great Britain	55,721,100	228
15.	France	54,210,700	99
16.	Vietnam	51,423,700	156
17.	Philippines	47,805,300	159
18.	Thailand	47,191,200	92
19.	Turkey	44,921,300	58
20.	Egypt	41,515,448	41
21.	South Korea	39,872,500	405
22.	Spain	37,359,500	74
23.	Iran	36,890,200	22
24.	Poland	35,484,300	113
25.	Burma	33,458,700	49
26.	Ethiopia	30,618,900	25
27.	Colombia	29,916,700	26
28.	Zaire	28,057,600	12
29.	Argentina	26,911,600	10
30.	South Africa	24,708,651	22
31.	CANADA	23,690,500	2
32.	Romania	22,210,300	93
33.	Yugoslavia	22,210,200	87
34.	Afghanistan	21,635,800	33
35.	Morocco	19,646,400	28
36.	North Korea	19,010,500	158
37.	Algeria	18,226,500	8
38.	Peru	17,530,500	14
39.	Sudan	17,527,800	7
40.	Taiwan	17,432,200	484

POPULATION: Where the growth will be

Province	1976 Census (thousands)	% increase by 2001
Newfoundland	557.7	11.2
Prince Edward Island	118.3	12.3
Nova Scotia	828.6	12.5
New Brunswick	677.2	15.4
Quebec	6234.5	22.1
Ontario	8264.5	44.2
Manitoba	1021.4	16.0
Saskatchewan	921.4	5.1
Alberta	1838.0	54.2
British Columbia	2466.6	56.6
Yukon Territory	21.8	104.6
Northwest Territories	42.6	108.0
CANADA	22,992.6	34.7

SURFACE AREA: The largest countries

Rank	Country	Area (thousand km²)
1.	Soviet Union	22,402
2.	Canada	9922
3.	China	9596
4.	United States	9363
5.	Brazil	8511
6.	Australia	7686
7.	India	3287
8.	Argentina	2766
9.	Sudan	2505
10.	Algeria	2381
11.	Zaire	2345
12.	Saudi Arabia	2149
13.	Mexico	1972
14.	Indonesia	1919
15.	Libya	1759
16.	Iran	1648

ALBERTA

The wealthiest of Canada's provinces, Alberta was named after Queen Victoria's daughter, the wife of the Marquis of Lorne, governor-general from 1878 to 1883. La Vérendrye was probably the first European to set foot in Alberta in 1751. In 1754, Anthony Henday was sent by the Hudson's Bay Company to establish contact with the Blackfoot Indians. By 1774, Peter Pond had established a trading post on Lake Athabasca. But it was not until the District of Alberta was created in 1882, and the railway pushed through, that a steady flow of immigrants came from Europe, the United States and eastern Canada. Marquis wheat, and oil and gas discoveries have contributed to the province's prosperity.

Capital: Edmonton
Motto: None
Flower: Wild rose (also known as prickly rose)
Date of entry into Confederation: September 1, 1905
Total area: 661,185 km²
Percentage of Canada: 6.66%
Length of boundaries: 3926 km
Length of coastline: 0 km
Population (July, 1979): 2,014,000
Percentage of national population: 8.5%
Urban population (1976): 75%
Population density (1977): 3.0/km²
Per capita provincial income: $14,410

Events: Calgary Stampede, Calgary (July); Klondike Days, Edmonton (July); Banff Festival of the Arts (May–Aug.).

Historic Sites: Fort Macleod; Card's Cabin, Cardston; Fort Dunvegan at Dunvegan.

Natural Attractions: Dinosaur Provincial Park; Valley of the Dinosaurs near Drumheller; Red Deer River Valley; Willmore Wilderness Park; Canadian Rockies; Columbia Icefield.

BRITISH COLUMBIA

Exploration of Canada's most westerly province brought Britain and Spain close to war. Spaniards were in the area as early as 1774. Captain Cook visited the coast in 1778. In 1792, Captain Vancouver was sent by the Royal Navy to survey the territory a year before Alexander MacKenzie reached the Pacific overland. Spain withdrew in 1795, and by 1821, the Hudson's Bay Company controlled the territory. Vancouver Island and the mainland became two separate crown colonies, but were joined in 1866. Five years later, the united colonies joined Confederation on the promise of a railway. Immigration surged when the rail line was completed, and again after a drought in the Prairies and during World War II. Queen Victoria christened the province in 1858, changing the proposed name of New Caledonia to avoid confusion with a French island of the same name in the Southwest Pacific.

Capital: Victoria
Motto: *Splendor Sine Occasu*
(Splendor without diminishment)
Flower: Pacific dogwood
Date of entry into Confederation: July 20, 1871
Total area: 948,597 km²
Percentage of Canada: 9.5%
Length of boundaries: 30,801 km
Length of coastline: 25,726 km
Population (July, 1979): 2,570,000
Percentage of national population: 10.8%
Urban population (1976): 76.9%
Population density (1977): 2.8/km²
Per capita provincial income: $11,024

Events: Pacific National Exhibition, Vancouver (Aug.); Abbotsford International Air Show (Aug.); International Bathtub Race Celebrations, Nanaimo (July); Vancouver Sea Festival (July).

Historic Sites: Barkerville, former gold-rush capital of the Cariboo; Fort Steele, Fort Steele Historic Park; CPR "Last Spike" cairn, Eagle Pass, Craigellachie; RCMP schooner, *St. Roch*, Vancouver Maritime Museum; Craigflower School, Victoria.

Natural Attractions: Gulf Islands; the fjords of the Pacific Coast; Cathedral Grove, MacMillan Provincial Park; Pacific Rim National Park; Della Falls, Strathcona Provincial Park; Takakkaw Falls, Yoho National Park; Okanagan Valley; Glacier National Park; Canadian Rockies.

MANITOBA

Cree, Salteaux and Assiniboines inhabited the area now known as Manitoba when the first European, Sir Thomas Button, wintered on Hudson Bay in 1612. Fur trading soon began and in 1670, Charles II of England granted the entire watershed to the Hudson's Bay Company. York Factory, later Port Nelson, was founded in 1682. In 1812, Lord Selkirk brought Scottish crofters to the Red River Valley near present-day Winnipeg to provide agricultural products for the fur traders. In 1869, Canada purchased the land for 300,000 pounds, and in 1870, Manitoba became the fifth province of the Dominion. Manitoba was once known as "Lake of the Prairies;" its name is possibly derived from two Indian words: "Minne Toba," meaning "water prairie." English-speaking Canadians, British, Icelandic, Ukrainian and Mennonite peoples were the main settlers before the 1900s.

Capital: Winnipeg
Motto: None
Flower: Prairie crocus
Date of entry into Confederation: July 15, 1870
Total area: 650,087 km²
Percentage of Canada: 6.5%
Length of boundaries: 4063 km
Length of coastline: 917 km
Population (July, 1979): 1,030,000
Percentage of national population: 4.3%
Urban population (1976): 69.9%
Population density (1977): 1.9/km²
Per capita provincial income: $9272

Events: Folklorama, Winnipeg (Aug.); Festival du Voyageur, St. Boniface (Feb.); National Ukrainian Festival, Dauphin (July–Aug.); Beausejour Winter Carnival, Beausejour (Feb–Mar.); Gimli Icelandic Festival, Gimli (Aug.).

Historic Sites: St. Michael's Ukrainian Orthodox Church, Gardenton; Great Stone of Remembrance World War I memorial, Winnipeg; St. Boniface Museum, Winnipeg; Fort Prince of Wales, Churchill.

Natural Attractions: Baldy Mountain, Duck Mountain Provincial Park; Carberry Sandhills, Spruce Woods Provincial Park and Forest; Lake Winnipeg.

NEW BRUNSWICK

French-speaking settlers were the first European inhabitants in New Brunswick. Da Verrazano and Cartier explored the coast in the 16th century, and Champlain established the first Canadian settlement on Ile Ste. Croix in 1604. France relinquished its control to Britain in 1713 and in the wake of the American Revolution, United Empire Loyalists streamed in. In 1784, the area was separated from Nova Scotia, becoming the colony of New Brunswick in honor of Britain's reigning House of Brunswick. In the 1800s thousands of immigrants came from the British Isles. Saint John is the oldest incorporated city in Canada, and Mount Allison University in Sackville was the first university to confer a degree on a woman, in 1867.

Capital: Fredericton
Motto: *Spem Reduxit* (Hope was restored)
Flower: Purple violet
Date of entry into Confederation: July 1, 1867
Total area: 73,436 km²
Percentage of Canada: 0.7%
Length of boundaries: 3078 km
Length of coastline: 2269 km
Population (July, 1979): 701,000
Percentage of national population: 2.95%
Urban population (1976): 52.3%
Population density (1977): 9.5/km²
Per capita provincial income: $6325

Events: Acadian Festival, Caraquet (Aug.); Loyalist Days, Saint John (July); Atlantic National Exhibition, Saint John (Aug.); Moncton Railroad Days (July); Campbellton Salmon Festival (June).

Historic Sites: Champlain monument, Saint John; Martello Tower, Saint John; Trinity Anglican Church, Kingston, Acadian Historical Village, near Caraquet.

Natural Attractions: Sugarloaf Peak, Sugarloaf Provincial Park; Grand Falls; Kouchibouguac National Park; Grand Manan Island.

NEWFOUNDLAND

The oldest English dependency in the New World and possibly the home of the first European child born in North America, Snorre Karlsefni (b. 1013), is the youngest province of Canada. Newfoundland's history is a blend of legend and high adventure. Bristol merchants from England were engaged in lucrative fishing off the Grand Banks as early as 1481, and in 1502 King Henry VII referred to it as "newe founde launde." Morris Dancers from England performed in St. John's in 1583, but it was not until 1610 that the first organized colony was established by John Guy. In 1855, it became a self-governing dominion, and in 1949, joined Confederation. It has the highest birthrate and lowest death rate in Canada.

Capital: St. John's
Motto: *Quaerite prime Regnum Dei*
(Seek ye first the Kingdom of God)
Flower: Pitcher plant
Date of entry into Confederation: March 31, 1949
Total area: 404,517 km²
Percentage of Canada: 4.5%
Length of boundaries: 33,479 km
Length of coastline: 28,957 km
Population (July, 1979): 574,000
Percentage of national population: 2.4%
Urban population (1976): 58.9%
Population density (1977): 1.5/km²
Per capita provincial income: $5250

Events: St. John's Regatta, (Aug.); Annual Kite Festival, St. John's (June–July); Eastport Summer Festival of the Arts, Eastport (early summer); St. John's Summer Festival (July–Aug.).

Historic Sites: Viking settlement at L'Anse aux Meadows; Cabot Tower, St. John's; Signal Hill, St. John's.

Natural Attractions: Gros Morne National Park; Long Point, near Twillingate; Conception Bay; Terra Nova National Park.

NOVA SCOTIA

It may be that Celtic monks from Iceland settled on Cape Breton Island in 875 A.D., and the Norseman Thorfinn Karl Sefne lived for a time around 1008 on the mainland coast. Historians agree that John Cabot visited Nova Scotia in 1497 and Portuguese fishermen likely wintered there. But the first permanent settlement was built in 1605 when de Monts and Champlain founded Acadia near Port Royal. One year later, Champlain encouraged the formation of Canada's first social club, the "Ordre de Bon Temps". In 1621, Nova Scotia was granted to Sir William Alexander for settlement, and his charter bears the name "New Scotland" in Latin. In 1848, it was the first British colony to have responsible government. English, Germans, Scots and Loyalists were the main settlers. Possessor of a great seafaring tradition, Nova Scotia is still called "the wharf of North America."

Capital: Halifax
Motto: *Munit Haec et Altera Vincit*
(One defends and the other conquers)
Flower: Mayflower
Date of entry into Confederation: July 1, 1867
Total area: 55,491 km²
Percentage of Canada: 0.6%
Length of boundaries: 7613 km
Length of coastline: 7579 km
Population (July, 1979): 847,000
Percentage of national population: 3.57%
Urban population (1976): 55.8%
Population density (1977): 15.8/km²
Per capita provincial income: $6701

Events: Annapolis Valley Apple Blossom Festival (May–June); Antigonish Highland Games, Antigonish (July); Lunenburg Fisheries Exhibition and Fishermen's Reunion (Sept.); Gathering of the Clans and Fishermen's Regatta, Pugwash (June–July).

Historic Sites: Port Royal National Historic Park, Port Royal; Fort Anne National Historic Park, Annapolis Royal; Fortress of Louisbourg, Louisbourg; Canada's oldest lighthouse (1759), Sambro Island; *Bluenose II*, Halifax; Cape Breton Miners' Museum, Glace Bay; Grand Pré National Historic Park, Grand Pré; Alexander Graham Bell National Historic Park, Baddeck.

Natural Attractions: Giant's Causeway, Brier Island; Kejimkujik National Park; Annapolis Valley; Five Islands Provincial Park; Joggins fossils, Chignecto Bay; Margaree Valley; Cabot Trail, Cape Breton Island.

ONTARIO

An old Iroquois word meaning "the shining waters," Ontario has one quarter of all the available fresh water in the world. In the early 17th century, Etienne Brûlé, a 16-year-old lieutenant of Champlain, explored as far as western Ontario before he was killed by the Hurons. Henry Hudson claimed the northern part for the British Crown in 1610. In 1791, the province of Upper Canada was formed, and William Lyon MacKenzie was instrumental in gaining power for the legislative assembly following an unsuccessful rebellion in 1837. English, Germans, Dutch, Scots, Irish and runaway slaves from the United States were Ontario's earliest immigrants, and since 1881 other Europeans have added their heritage to this prosperous province.

Capital: Toronto
Motto: *Ut Incepit Fidelis Sic Permanet*
(Loyal she began and loyal she remains)
Flower: White trillium
Date of entry into Confederation: July 1, 1867
Total area: 1,068,583 km²
Percentage of Canada: 10.8%
Length of boundaries: 6263 km
Length of coastline: 1210 km
Population (July, 1979): 8,505,000
Percentage of national population: 35.9%
Urban population (1976): 81.2%
Population density (1977): 9.1/km²
Per capita provincial income: $10,650

Events: Stratford Festival (June–Nov.); The Shaw Festival, Niagara-on-the-Lake (May–Oct.); The Canadian National Exhibition, Toronto (Aug–Sept.); Oktoberfest, Kitchener-Waterloo (Oct.); Mariposa Folk Festival, Toronto (summer).

Historic Sites: Reconstruction of Fort William, Thunder Bay; Drummond Hill Cemetery, Niagara Falls; Fort George, Niagara-on-the-Lake; Fort Henry, Kingston; Bytown Museum, Ottawa; Parliament Hill, Ottawa; Laurier House, Ottawa; Stephen Leacock Memorial Home, Orillia; Upper Canada Village, Morrisburg; Dundurn Castle, Hamilton.

Natural Attractions: Kakabeka Falls, Kakabeka Falls Provincial Park; Lake of the Woods; Ouimet Canyon, Ouimet Canyon Provincial Park; Agawa Bay, Lake Superior Provincial Park; Manitoulin Island; Killarney Provincial Park; Horseshoe Falls; Algonquin Provincial Park; Thousand Islands; Georgian Bay Islands National Park; Pukaskwa National Park.

PRINCE EDWARD ISLAND

Canada's smallest and most densely populated province is an island of picturesque beauty. The Micmac Indians called it *Abegweit*, a "home cradled on the waves." The French established an outpost in 1663 and named it Ile St. Jean. Conquered by the British in 1758, it was renamed St. John's Island, and later Prince Edward Island after Edward, Duke of Kent, father of Queen Victoria. Loyalists settled here during the American Revolution, and Scottish settlers, led by Lord Selkirk, arrived in 1803. Agriculture, tourism and fishing are the Island's main industries today.

Capital: Charlottetown
Motto: *Parva Sub Ingenti*
(The small under the protection of the great)
Flower: Lady's slipper
Date of entry into Confederation: July 1, 1873
Total area: 5,657 km²
Percentage of Canada: 0.1%
Length of boundaries: 1260 km
Length of coastline: 1260 km
Population (July, 1979): 123,000
Percentage of national population: 0.51%
Urban population (1976): 37.1%
Population density (1977): 20.2/km²
Per capita provincial income: $5194

Events: Charlottetown Festival, Charlottetown (June–Sept.); Old Home Week, Charlottetown (Aug.); Acadian Festival, Abrams Village (Aug.).

Historic Sites: Province House, Charlottetown; Green Park Provincial Historic Park, Port Hill; Micmac Indian Village, Fort Amherst National Historic Park, Rocky Point.

Natural Attractions: Prince Edward Island National Park; Basin Head; Bonshaw Hills.

QUEBEC

An Indian settlement, Stadacona, was the site of the trading post founded by Champlain in 1608 and called "Québec": an Indian name meaning "the place where the water narrows." In 1642, a French civil servant, Sieur de Maisonneuve, organized a settlement on the site of an older Indian village, Hochelaga. Today it is Montréal, Canada's second largest metropolis. By 1663, "Canada" had become a province of France, following the Seven Years War, and 100 years later it was ceded to Britain. In 1791, the territory was divided into Lower and Upper Canada (Quebec and Ontario). Reunited in 1841, they were once again separated in 1867. In the late 18th and 19th centuries, there was an influx of Loyalist and British settlers, but this province remains uniquely French-Canadian.

Capital: Québec
Motto: *Je me souviens* (I remember)
Flower: Madonna lily (fleur de lis)
Date of entry into Confederation: July 1, 1867
Total area: 1,540,681 km²
Percentage of Canada: 15.5%
Length of boundaries: 20,683 km
Length of coastline: 13,773 km
Population (July, 1979): 6,301,000
Percentage of national population: 26.59%
Urban population (1976): 79.1%
Population density (1977): 4.6/km²
Per capita provincial income: $8941

Events: Western Festival, Saint-Tite (Sept.); Québec Winter Carnival, Québec (Jan–Feb.); World Film Festival, Montréal (Aug.); Les Floralies (International Flower Show), Montréal (May–Sept.); Saint-Jean Baptiste Day festival—province-wide (June 24).

Historic Sites: Replica of "La Grande Hermine," Cartier-Brébeuf National Historic Park, Québec; Reconstruction of Canada's first trading post, Tadoussac; Cape Redoubt, Québec; National Battlefields Park, Québec; Fort Chambly, Chambly; The Château de Ramezay, Montréal; The Citadel, Québec; Les Forges du Saint-Maurice National Historic Park, Trois Rivières; Wolfe-Montcalm monument, Québec.

Natural Attractions: The Laurentians; Eastern Townships; Montmorency Falls; Baie-Saint-Paul; Lac St. Jean; Parc de la Gaspésie; Gaspé Peninsula.

SASKATCHEWAN

Half the improved land in Canada is located in Saskatchewan, whose name derives from "Kisiskatchewan," a Cree word meaning "the river that flows swiftly." Paleo-Indians may have roamed here 20,000 years ago; later it became the home of the Chippewa, Blackfoot and Assiniboines. Samuel Hearne set up Cumberland House in 1774 for the Hudson's Bay Company, but within a century, the fur-trading era had ended. Beginning in 1872, settlers were lured by free land, and in 1882, Pile of Bones—later called Regina—was founded beside a vast midden of buffalo bones.

Capital: Regina
Motto: None
Flower: Western red lily (also known as prairie lily)
Date of entry into Confederation: Sept. 1, 1905
Total area: 651,900 km²
Percentage of Canada: 6.6%
Length of boundaries: 3571 km
Length of coastline: 0 km
Population (July, 1979): 957,000
Percentage of national population: 4.03%
Urban population (1976): 55.5%
Population density (1977): 1.6/km²
Per capita provincial income: $10,191

Events: Saskachimo Exposition, Saskatoon (July); Frontier Days, Swift Current (July).

Historic Sites: RCMP Museum, Regina; Church of Saint-Antoine-de-Padoue, Batoche; John Diefenbaker's boyhood home, Wascana Centre, Regina.

Natural Attractions: Otter Rapids, Lac la Ronge Provincial Park; Cypress Hills Provincial Park; Big Muddy Badlands; Qu'Appelle River Valley.

YUKON TERRITORY

Capital: Whitehorse
Motto: None
Flower: Fireweed
Date of entry into Confederation: June 13, 1898
Total area: 482,515 km²
Percentage of Canada: 4.9%
Length of boundaries: 4409 km
Length of coastline: 343 km
Population (July, 1979): 21,000
Percentage of national population: 0.08%
Urban population (1976): 61.0%
Population density (1977): 0.04/km²
Per capita income: $10,853 (Yukon and N.W.T.)

Events: Sourdough Rendezvous, Whitehorse (Feb.); Discovery Days, Dawson City (Aug.); Frantic Follies (vaudeville), Whitehorse (May–Sept.); Gaslight Follies (vaudeville), Dawson City, (May–Sept.).

Historic Sites: Robert Service's Cabin, Dawson; Old Log Church, Whitehorse; Restoration of stern-wheeler S. S. *Klondike*, Whitehorse.

Natural Attractions: Kluane National Park.

NORTHWEST TERRITORIES

Capital: Yellowknife
Motto: None
Flower: Mountain avens
Date of entry into Confederation: July 15, 1870
Total area: 3,379,686 km²
Percentage of Canada: 34.1%
Length of boundaries: 165,389 km
Length of coastline: 161,764 km
Population (July, 1979): 43,000
Percentage of national population: 0.18%
Urban population (1976): 49.7%
Population density (1977): 0.01/km²
Per capita income: $10,853 (Yukon and N.W.T.)

Events: Caribou Carnival, Yellowknife (Mar.); Delta Daze, Inuvik (Sept.); Trans-Arctic Games, Inuvik (July).

Historic Sites: Franklin expedition cenotaph, Beechey Island; Victoria Point, King William Island, where the Franklin expedition abandoned ship.

Natural Attractions: Wood Buffalo National Park; The Pingos of Tuktoyaktuk; Alexandra Falls, Hall River; Nahanni National Park, Auyuittuq National Park.

CANADIAN "FIRSTS"

Permanent settlement—Port Royal, 1605
Incorporated city—Saint John, N.B., 1785
Homestead—John Sanderson, Delta, Man., 1872
Coal mine—Cape Breton Island, N.S., before 1677
Textile factory—Mme. de Repentigny, Montréal, 1703
Iron smelter—Les Forges du Saint-Maurice, near Trois-Rivières, Que., 1737
Commercial oil well—Oil Springs, Ont., 1857
Paper mill—Lachute, Que., 1803
Hydroelectric plant—Niagara Falls, Ont., 1905
Nuclear power station—Rolphton, Ont., 1962
Paper money—playing cards, Québec, 1686
Bank—Bank of Montreal, 1817
Decimal currency—1858
Insurance company—Canada Life Assurance Company, Hamilton, Ont., 1847
Postal service—Montréal to Québec, 1721
Post office—Halifax, 1755
Airmail postal service—1928
Telegraph—Montréal to Québec, 1847
Long-distance telephone call—Brantford-Paris, Ont., 1876
Regular radio programming—CFCF, Montreal, 1920
Television broadcast—Montréal, 1952
Horse—brought to Québec, 1647
Ship—built at Québec, 1669
Lighthouse—Louisbourg, 1734
Road—Digby Cape to Port Royal, 1606
Gas station—Vancouver, 1908
Steamship—Montréal, 1809
Canal—Coteau-du-Lac, Que., 1780
Railway—Saint-Jean to La Prairie, Que., 1836
Flight—J.A.D. McCurdy, Baddeck, N.S., 1909
Commercial jet transport—Jetliner, 1949
Polar air service—Vancouver-Amsterdam, CP Air, 1955
Street railway—Toronto, 1861
Subway—Toronto, 1954
Hospital—Hôtel-Dieu de Québec, 1639
Pharmacist—Louis Hébert, Port Royal, 1606
Woman doctor—Emily Howard Stowe, Ontario, licensed 1880
Woman dentist—Emma Casgrain, Quebec, licensed 1898
School—Port Royal, 1606
Institution of higher education—Québec Seminary, Québec, 1668
Chartered university—King's College, Windsor, N.S., 1799
Martyr—René Goupil, 1642
Marriage—Québec, 1654
Divorce—Halifax, 1750
Protestant church—St. John's, Nfld., 1720
Synagogue—Montréal, 1777
Official flag—Union Jack, 1763
Trade agreement with the United States—Elgin-Marcy Treaty, 1854
Protective tariff—Galt tariff, 1859
Woman Member of Parliament—Agnes Macphail, 1921
Woman cabinet minister—Ellen Fairclough, 1957
Indian Senator—James Gladstone, 1958
Curling club—Montréal, 1807
Tennis court—Montréal, 1836
Hockey game—Kingston, Ont., 1855
Queen's Plate winner—James White on Don Juan, 1860
Stanley Cup winner—Montreal Amateur Athletic Association, 1893
Olympic gold medal winner—Etienne Desmarteau (hammer throw), 1904
Live hockey broadcast—Foster Hewitt, 1923

THE GOVERNORS GENERAL OF CANADA

VISCOUNT MONCK (1867-68)

Sir Charles Stanley, 4th Viscount Monck, played a major role in the Confederation of the British North American colonies and served as the first Governor General of the Dominion of Canada on July 1, 1867. He had to tread a fine line in fulfilling his new job, respecting the powers of the new government without compromising the prerogatives of the Crown.

Born in 1819 and educated at Trinity College, Dublin, he entered the British House of Commons in 1852 and served as Lord of the Treasury in the Palmerston cabinet. In 1868, he returned to Ireland, where he was Lord Lieutenant of County Dublin for 20 years. He died there in 1894.

BARON LISGAR (1868-72)

Baron Lisgar was Governor General during the Red River Rebellion of 1870, and the Fenian border raids, where his wisdom and administrative experience aided in the resolution of these conflicts. In a fishing-rights dispute with the United States, however, Baron Lisgar made little effort to defend Canada's interests, as his overriding concern was to maintain good relations between London and Washington. As a result, the 1871 Reciprocity Treaty on fishing and navigational rights was highly favorable to the United States.

A thoughtful, practical man, he was born into an Irish family in India in 1807. He led a relatively secluded life as Governor General, but did undertake several official tours. He died in Ireland in 1876.

THE EARL OF DUFFERIN (1872-78)

Canada's third Governor General, Frederick Temple Blackwood, the Earl of Dufferin, was a charming and enthusiastic man who inaugurated a period of vitality and enterprise at Rideau Hall. Though he used his eloquence to advance the cause of Canadian unity, he ran into conflict with the Canadian government. In 1875 the Earl exercised his right of clemency by lifting the death sentence imposed on Louis Riel's adjutant general, who had been accused of murdering Thomas Scott. Justice Minister Edward Blake opposed the Earl's acting without the advice of the Canadian cabinet. As a result of this conflict, future governors general were instructed to act on the advice of their Canadian ministers.

Born in 1826, Dufferin had a noteworthy career in the British public service. In Canada, he and his remarkable wife, Hariot, hosted countless parties, cultural events and sport activities. In 1875, he persuaded Québec citizens to preserve their city walls, then threatened by demolition.

After his departure from Canada in 1878, Dufferin served as Britain's ambassador to Russia, Turkey, Italy and France, and as Viceroy of India. He died in 1902.

THE MARQUESS OF LORNE (1878-83)

Sir John Douglas Sutherland Campbell, the Marquess of Lorne, was the husband of Queen Victoria's daughter Louise. Their chief influence was in the field of arts and letters: they helped found Royal Canadian Academy of Arts, from which grew the National Gallery of Canada, and the Royal Society of Canada.

In 1878, Lorne took Prime Minister Sir John A. Macdonald's advice by dismissing Lieutenant Governor Letellier de Saint–Just of Québec, although Lorne personally disagreed with the decision. Again, to enhance the position of the Governor General above politics, he approved the creation of the office of High Commissioner to represent Canada's interests in London. Born in 1845, son of the Duke of Argyll, he succeeded to his father's title in 1900. He died in 1914.

THE MARQUESS OF LANSDOWNE (1883-88)

A controversial figure, Henry Charles Keith Petty-Fitzmaurice, 3rd Marquess of Lansdowne, was a member of the Gladstone cabinet from 1868 to 1872, and in 1880 was appointed Secretary for India. He resigned from that post over a disagreement with Gladstone about Irish Home Rule.

Lansdowne's vice-regency was an eventful time for Canada: in the spring of 1885, the second Riel Rebellion erupted in the Northwest, followed by a fisheries dispute with the United States, but Lansdowne was able to intercede on Canada's behalf with the British Colonial Office. In his farewell speech in 1888, he noted with pride the "peaceful progress of industry, education and art" during his tenure. He was Viceroy of India from 1888 to 1893, and served from 1900 to 1905 as Foreign Secretary. Born into Irish nobility in 1845, he died in 1927 at Clonmore, Ireland.

BARON STANLEY OF PRESTON (1888-93)

Sir Frederick Arthur Stanley was born in 1841, the younger son of the British Prime Minister, the Earl of Derby. A man of tact and good judgment, he was a Member of Parliament and held several cabinet posts, including that of Colonial Secretary, before coming to Canada.

Baron Stanley's term in Canada was marked by his strong support of culture and sports: he is particularly remembered for his institution of the Stanley Cup. After his departure, Baron Stanley served as Lord Mayor of Liverpool and as first Chancellor of the University of Liverpool. He died in 1908.

THE EARL OF ABERDEEN (1893-98)

Upon their arrival in Canada, John Campbell Gordon, 7th Earl of Aberdeen, and his wife declared their goals to be to "sweeten and elevate public life" and became involved in social and philanthropic work. Lady Aberdeen founded the YWCA in Ottawa, the Canadian branch of the Boys' Brigade (which served both Christian and Jewish children), the Ottawa Maternity Hospital, the National Council of Women and the Victorian Order of Nurses. She also organized relief for famine victims in India, clubs for newsboys and the prison reform movement. Lord Aberdeen withheld approval in 1896 of what he called some "lame duck" political appointments, though it cost him the friendship of Prime Minister Sir Charles Tupper.

Born in 1847, Lord Aberdeen was Lord Lieutenant of Ireland, before and after his term in Canada. He was raised to Marquess of Aberdeen and Temair in 1915, and died in 1934.

THE EARL OF MINTO (1898-1904)

Gilbert John Elliott, the 4th Earl of Minto, came to Rideau Hall as a veteran of the Russo-Turkish War of 1877, the Afghanistan War of 1879 and the Egyptian campaign of 1882. A military man, he was a staunch supporter of Canadian participation in the Boer War. His chief interest as Governor General, however, lay in the establishment of a system of national parks. He also urged the government to safeguard Indian culture and to redress injustices that had been dealt to the native peoples. As well, he persuaded the government to build the Public Archives in Ottawa. From 1905 to 1910 Lord Minto was Viceroy of India. He died in 1914.

THE EARL GREY (1904-11)

Albert Henry George Grey, 4th Earl Grey, started a movement for the preservation of the Plains of Abraham as a national park, and for the restoration of the Fortress of Louisbourg. He also donated the Grey Cup, the nation's premier football trophy, led a campaign for better treatment of tuberculosis, presided over the 1905 ceremonies creating the provinces of Saskatchewan and Alberta, and established the Department of External Affairs in 1909.

Born in 1851, he was elected to the British House of Commons in 1880 and entered the House of Lords in 1894. An ardent imperialist and lifelong friend of King Edward VII, Lord Grey regarded Canadians as unenthusiastic about the Empire, but he supported the growth of Canadian nationalism. He died in 1917.

THE DUKE OF CONNAUGHT (1911-16)

The first royal Governor General was Prince Arthur, the Duke of Connaught, son of Queen Victoria, and husband of Princess Luise of Prussia. During the First World War, the Duke was active in auxiliary war services and charities, while his wife worked for the Red Cross.

As war casualties mounted, life at Rideau Hall grew increasingly austere. Nearly all the members of the Duke's household staff were killed, and the Duke presented a memorial window to St. Bartholomew's, the parish church across the park, to commemorate them. He died in England in 1942, the last surviving child of Queen Victoria.

THE DUKE OF DEVONSHIRE (1916-21)

The last Governor General to be appointed without the Canadian Prime Minister's consultation, Victor Christian William Cavendish, Duke of Devonshire, arrived in time for the conscription crisis of the First World War. Conscription was enforced, and a bitter controversy followed, but Devonshire was careful not to interfere in domestic political matters. He gained the confidence of Prime Minister Sir Robert Borden through simple dignity, wisdom and geniality. He had a special interest in Canadian agriculture and was also a great hockey fan.

Born in 1868, he began working in business and reading law in London. Elected to Parliament in 1891, he succeeded to the dukedom in 1908, then served as First Lord of the Admiralty before his appointment to Canada. When he returned to Britain in 1921, Devonshire was appointed Colonial Secretary. He died in 1938.

ENGLISH AND FRENCH MONARCHS OF CANADA

FRENCH

François I	1515-1547
Henry II	1547-1559
François II	1559-1560
Charles IX	1560-1574
Henry III	1574-1589
Henry IV	1589-1610
Louis XIII	1610-1643
Louis XIV	1643-1715
Louis XV	1715-1774

ENGLISH

Henry VII	1485-1509
Henry VIII	1509-1547
Edward VI	1547-1553
Mary I	1553-1558
Elizabeth I	1558-1603
James I	1603-1625
Charles I	1625-1649
Charles II	1660-1685
James II	1685-1688
William III	1689-1702
Mary II	1689-1694
Anne	1702-1714
George I	1714-1727
George II	1727-1760
George III	1760-1820
George IV	1820-1830
William IV	1830-1837
Victoria	1837-1901
Edward VII	1901-1910
George V	1910-1936
Edward VIII	1936-1936
George VI	1936-1952
Elizabeth II	1952-

EARLY GOVERNORS

FRENCH

Samuel de Champlain	1612-1629, 1633-1635
(New France under British occupation)	1629-1632
Charles Huault de Montmagny	1636-1648
Louis d'Ailleboust de Coulonge	1648-1651
Jean de Lauzon	1651-1656
Pierre de Voyer, vicomte d'Argenson	1658-1661
Pierre Dubois, baron d'Avaugour	1661-1663
Augustin Saffray, chevalier de Mézy	1663-1665
Daniel de Rémy de Courcelle	1665-1672
Louis de Buade, comte de Frontenac	1672-1682, 1689-1698
Joseph-Antoine Lefebvre de La Barre	1682-1685
Jacques-René de Brisay, marquis de Denonville	1685-1689
Louis-Hector, chevalier de Callières	1699-1703
Philippe de Rigaud, marquis de Vaudreuil	1703-1725
Charles, marquis de Beauharnois	1726-1747
Jacques-Pierre Taffanel, marquis de La Jonquière	1749-1752
Ange, marquis Duquesne de Menneville	1752-1755
Pierre de Rigaud, marquis de Vaudreuil-Cavagnal	1755-1760

BRITISH

James Murray	1764-1766
Sir Guy Carleton	1768-1770, 1774-1778
Frederick Haldimand	1778-1784
Sir Guy Carleton, Lord Dorchester	1786-1791 1793-1796
Robert Prescott	1797-1799
Sir James Henry Craig	1807-1811
Sir George Prevost	1812-1815
Sir John Coape Sherbrooke	1816-1818
Duke of Richmond	1818-1819
Lord Dalhousie	1820-1828
Lord Aylmer	1831-1835
Lord Gosford	1835-1838
Lord Durham	1838-1838
Sir John Colborne	1838-1839
Charles Poulett Thomson (Lord Sydenham)	1839-1841
Sir Charles Bagot	1842-1843
Sir Charles Metcalfe	1843-1845
Lord Cathcart	1846-1847
Lord Elgin	1847-1854
Sir Edmund Head	1854-1861
Lord Monck	1861-1867

INTENDANTS OF NEW FRANCE

Jean Talon	1665-1668, 1670-1672
Claude de Bouteroue	1668-1670
Jacques Duchesneau	1675-1682
Jacques de Meulles	1682-1686
Jean Bochart de Champigny	1686-1702
François de Beauharnois	1702-1705
Jacques Raudot	1705-1711
Antoine Denis Raudot	1705-1710
Michel Bégon	1710-1726
Claude Thomas Dupuy	1726-1728
Gilles Hocquart	1731-1748
François Bigot	1748-1760

GOVERNORS OF ACADIA

By the 1713 Treaty of Utrecht, France ceded mainland Acadia to England. It became the British colony of Nova Scotia. Civil government was established in 1749, and there were seven governors from that date until 1786, when Nova Scotia came under the jurisdiction of the governor at Québec.

Edward Cornwallis	1749-1752
Peregrine Thomas Hopson	1752-1753
Charles Lawrence	1756-1760
Montague Wilmot	1764-1766
William Campbell	1766-1773
Francis Legge	1773-1776
John Parr	1782-1786

BARON BYNG OF VIMY (1921-26)

Julian Hedworth George Byng was the central figure in the King-Byng Crisis of 1926. He refused to dissolve Parliament when Prime Minister Mackenzie King wanted to evade a vote on a motion of censure. Byng instead called on Arthur Meighen to form a government. When the Tory leader failed to gain a majority, Byng granted his request for dissolution. King fought and won the ensuing general election on the grounds that Byng had meddled in politics. Historians have generally agreed, however, that he was justified in refusing King's request.

A career soldier, Byng gained renown as commander of the Canadian Corps at Vimy Ridge in 1917. He was elevated to the peerage in 1919. When Byng returned to Britain in 1926, he was created viscount and promoted to field marshal. From 1928 to 1931 he was commissioner of the London Metropolitan Police. He died in 1935.

VISCOUNT WILLINGDON OF RATTON (1926-31)

Viscount Willingdon, a diplomat by experience and temperament, was an ideal Governor General at a time when Canada was taking the final steps toward autonomy. These years saw the opening of our first foreign diplomatic missions and the definition, in the Statute of Westminster, of the British Dominions as fully autonomous states.

Born Freeman Freeman-Thomas in 1866, Willingdon was lord-in-waiting to King George V from 1911 to 1913. From 1913 to 1924 he was governor of Bombay and Madras respectively. After leaving Canada in 1931, Willingdon returned to India as Viceroy. He died in 1941.

THE EARL OF BESSBOROUGH (1931-35)

Sir Vere Brabazon Ponsonby, the 9th Earl of Bessborough, arrived in Canada in the midst of the Depression and voluntarily refunded a tenth of his stipend. Despite the economic difficulties of the time, the Bessboroughs initiated the Dominion Drama Festival and generally encouraged the arts. That same year witnessed the creation of the Canadian Radio Broadcasting Corporation, the forerunner to the CBC. A shy man with a high sense of duty and a stiff manner, Bessborough was less popular than his French wife, Roberte de Neuflize. Newspapers criticized him for rebuking the mayor of Toronto on the grounds that the latter was discourteous to him, the King's representative.

Born in 1880, he entered business life in London. A Member of Parliament from 1913 to 1920, he served in France and Gallipoli during the First World War. He succeeded to the earldom in 1920. Bessborough returned to London's business world in 1935. During the Second World War, he set up a division to aid French refugees in Britain. He died in 1956.

BARON TWEEDSMUIR OF ELSFIELD (1935-40)

Lord and Lady Tweedsmuir had little interest in "society," preferring the company of intellectuals. Together they established a proper library at Rideau Hall and instituted the Governor General's Awards for literature. Born John Buchan in 1875, the son of a clergyman, Tweedsmuir was himself a writer of distinction who published histories, biographies, and novels. His well-known novel, *The Thirty-Nine Steps*, was made into a film by Alfred Hitchcock. During World War I, he was a *Times* correspondent in France. From 1927 to 1935, he represented the Scottish universities in the House of Commons.

Devoted to the cause of Canadian unity, he spoke eloquently against religious and racial barriers, publicly deploring narrow provincial policies that ignored the nation as a whole. Conscious of the prestige of his position, he traveled extensively. In 1939, King George VI and Queen Elizabeth made a tour of Canada; World War II broke out the same year. The strain of these events put great pressure on Tweedsmuir's frail health: he died in Montréal on Feb. 11, 1940—the first Governor General to die in office.

THE EARL OF ATHLONE (1940-46)

The Earl of Athlone arrived in Canada early in World War II, at a time when many were calling for a Canadian Governor General. But Athlone and his wife, Princess Alice, were a dignified couple who helped to provide needed stability during the war years. They showed great interest in Can-

ada's war effort, inspecting military bases and training schools, and visiting hospitals and factories.

Born Prince Alexander of Teck in 1874, Athlone was a career soldier who joined the British Army in 1894 and served in the Boer War and World War I. In 1917 he relinquished his German title and was made Earl of Athlone. He was promoted to major general in 1923, when he began an eight-year term as Governor General of South Africa. Lord Athlone died in England in 1957.

VISCOUNT ALEXANDER OF TUNIS (1945-52)

The last British Governor General appointed to Canada, Sir Harold Alexander came here with a secure reputation as one of the greatest military leaders in his country's history. Commissioned in 1910, he commanded a battalion and was wounded in World War I. A major general when World War II broke out, he commanded the 1st Division in France and directed the evacuation of Dunkirk in 1940; the last man to leave the beach. He was commander in chief in the Middle East in 1942 and in 1943 led the invasion of Italy. In 1944, following the capture of Rome, he was made field marshal. For the next two years, he was the Supreme Allied Commander in the Mediterranean, after which he was raised to the peerage.

In Canada, Lord and Lady Alexander made long, arduous tours of the country, but lived a simple and informal private life away from the glare of publicity. After leaving Canada, Alexander served as Minister of Defence in the last Churchill cabinet. He died in 1970.

VINCENT MASSEY (1952-59)

Long before he became the first Canadian-born Governor General, Vincent Massey was one of the nation's most eminent public servants. He opened the Canadian legation in Washington in 1926, becoming the first diplomat to represent this country in a foreign land. From 1936 to 1947 he was High Commissioner in London. From 1949 to 1951 he was chairman of the Royal Commission on National Development in the Arts, Letters and Sciences, whose report led to creation of the Canada Council.

Born in Toronto on Feb. 20, 1887, Massey studied at the University of Toronto and at Oxford. He became a history professor at the University of Toronto in 1913, then entered the Canadian public service. His autobiography, *What's Past is Prologue*, appeared in 1963. He died on Dec. 30, 1967, at his home near Port Hope, Ont.

GENERAL GEORGES-PHILIAS VANIER (1959-67)

A handicapped veteran with a distinguished war record, General Georges Vanier displayed remarkable energy in the role of Governor General. He travelled widely, kept in touch with the life of the nation at many points and, in 1964, called a national conference that resulted in the creation of the Vanier Institute of the Family.

Born in Montréal on Apr. 23, 1888, Georges Vanier graduated from Laval University as a lawyer. His destiny was changed by the First World War, in which he lost his right leg. From 1925 to 1928 he commanded Quebec's famous Royal 22nd Regiment, and then became Canada's representative on the Permanent Advisory Commission of the League of Nations for Military, Naval and Air Questions. From 1931 to 1938 he was secretary at the Office of the Canadian High Commissioner for Canada in London. In 1939 he became Canadian minister to France, returning to Canada after the fall of France in 1940 to command the Quebec Military District. In 1943 he was named Canadian minister to the Allied governments-in-exile in London, and Canadian representative to the French Committee of National Liberation the same year. In 1944 he was named ambassador to France, serving in that post for nine years. One of the most widely admired men ever to serve as Governor General, he died at Rideau Hall on Mar. 5, 1967.

ROLAND MICHENER (1967-74)

Roland Michener began his term as Governor General by introducing the Order of Canada, the first exclusively Canadian system of honors for exemplary merit and achievement. He became the Order's first chancellor and principal companion.

Born in Lacombe, Alta., on Apr. 19, 1900, Michener was educated at the University of Alberta. He served in the Royal Air Force in 1918. In 1920 he went to Oxford as a Rhodes Scholar, and began practicing law in Toronto four years later. He was elected to the Ontario legislature in 1945, serving as Provincial Secretary until 1948. From 1957 to 1962 he was Speaker in the House of Commons and in 1964 was appointed Canada's High Commissioner to India.

The first Governor General to pay state visits to other countries, he was especially suited to this task by his extensive background in law, politics and diplomacy. His personal interests were sports and physical fitness, and he was devoted to youth groups. He retired from his post in 1974, and settled in Toronto.

JULES LÉGER (1974-79)

A few months into his term as Governor General, Jules Léger suffered a stroke that impaired his ability to speak and partially paralyzed his right arm. He offered to resign but was asked by the government to remain. After his convalescence, he traveled across the country, meeting people on the job, presenting citizenship certificates personally to new Canadians, and issuing written messages to the press. His main concern was preserving Canadian unity, and he showed great interest in contemporary trends.

Born in St. Anicet, Que., on Apr. 4, 1913, Léger studied law at the University of Montréal and won a doctorate from the Sorbonne. He was assistant editor of *Le Droit* in Ottawa for a year before joining the Department of External Affairs. From 1943 to 1947 he served with the Canadian legation in Chile, and in 1948 acted as adviser to the Canadian delegation to the United Nations General Assembly. In 1950, he was made Assistant Under Secretary of State for External Affairs. Three years later he was appointed ambassador to Mexico. Promoted to Under Secretary of State for External Affairs in 1954, he was in that post for four years. Subsequently he was ambassador to Italy, France, Belgium and Luxembourg. Admired for his courageous battle against his illness, Léger stepped down as Governor General in 1979.

EDWARD SCHREYER (1979-)

Edward Richard Schreyer, Canada's 22nd Governor General, was born in Beausejour, Man., on Dec. 21, 1935. He studied at the University of Manitoba, and at one point considered professional baseball as a career. Instead, he graduated with a Master's Degree in political science and economics, and taught at St. Paul's College in Winnipeg. In 1960, he married Lily Schulz.

He became the youngest member of the Manitoba Legislature when first elected in 1958. Seven years later, he won the seat for Springfield in the House of Commons. Schreyer did not like Ottawa, however: he returned home to become leader of the New Democratic Party in Manitoba and then premier of the province from 1969 to 1977. His government amended the Public Schools Act to permit full-time instruction in either English or French, and he championed Ottawa's efforts to promote bilingualism.

In January, 1979, Ed Schreyer became the first Governor General from the West. His tenure of Rideau Hall has been marked by a friendly and informal atmosphere, his four young children enlivening the official residence.

THE PRIME MINISTERS OF CANADA

SIR JOHN A. MACDONALD

Born in Glasgow, Scotland, on Jan. 11, 1815, John Alexander Macdonald arrived in Canada five years later. The son of a cotton broker, he was articled to a young Kingston lawyer at the age of 15 and called to the bar in 1836. He made a name for himself by acting for the defense in unpopular cases, and, because of his wit and graciousness, acquired a reputation as a dandy as well. He married his cousin, Isabella Clark, in 1843. The following year, he was elected Tory representative for Kingston to the Legislative Assembly, a seat he would hold almost continuously until his death in 1891. He became Receiver General in the Draper administration in 1847 and later Attorney General for Upper Canada. He played a leading role in the formation of the Great Coalition of 1864, which led to Confederation three years later. He was the chief architect of the union of Canada and became Canada's first Prime Minister.

Macdonald, a staunch defender of the Crown, opposed reciprocity with the United States. He introduced a system of protective tariffs known as the National Policy, and is credited with the creation of the Canadian Pacific Railway. His administration saw the Red River Rebellion of 1870-71, as well as the Fenian raids of the same period.

He lost the 1873 elections over the Pacific Scandal, but was returned to power five years later and remained leader of the country until his death. An adroit political opportunist, he was master of the art of managing people and considered ethical niceties subordinate to political necessity. He died while in office on June 6, 1891.

ALEXANDER MACKENZIE

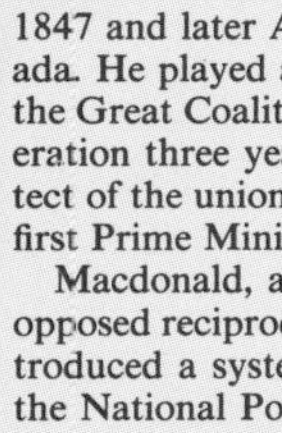

Alexander Mackenzie was born on Jan. 28, 1822 near Dunkeld, Scotland, and came to Canada at the age of 20. A builder and contractor by trade, he married Helen Neil in 1845. From 1852 to 1854, he was editor of the *Lambton Shield*, a crusading reform newspaper that failed after a Tory minister sued for libel.

Mackenzie entered politics to support his brother's ambitions, but was himself elected to the Legislative Assembly in 1861. A good organizer and a strong debater, he won a seat in the House of Commons six years later. He reluctantly became leader of the Liberal party in 1872; Macdonald's defeat the following year made him Prime Minister.

In 1874 he introduced a bill that led to the creation of the North West Mounted Police. He served as public works minister while in office, and applied himself, to the point of illness, to the building of the CPR.

A cautious, strict man of stubborn honesty, he lacked Macdonald's bold imagination and breadth of vision. He was defeated in the 1878 election, but remained party leader for another three years, despite the Liberals' protests. After stepping down, he stayed on as a member of Parliament until his death on Apr. 17, 1892, in Toronto.

SIR JOHN J.C. ABBOTT

The son of an English Missionary, John Abbott was born on Mar. 12, 1821, at St. Andrews, Lower Canada (later Quebec). He enrolled as a student in McGill's law faculty at the age of 22, and became its Dean in 1855. Elected as the Conservative member for Argenteuil, Abbott sat in Parliament for 14 years. In 1862, he served briefly as Solicitor General. In 1887 he was named to the Senate; that same year he was also elected Mayor of Montreal.

He was closely involved with the construction of the Canadian Pacific Railway and played a key role in the Pacific Scandal. A reluctant Prime Minister, he was pressed into service as a "caretaker" when Macdonald died in 1891. However, Abbott resigned the following year due to illness. Canada's first native-born prime minister died in Montréal on Oct. 30, 1893.

SIR JOHN S.D. THOMPSON

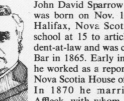

John David Sparrow Thompson was born on Nov. 10, 1844, in Halifax, Nova Scotia. He left school at 15 to article as a student-at-law and was called to the Bar in 1865. Early in his career, he worked as a reporter for The Nova Scotia House of Assembly. In 1870 he married Annie Affleck, with whom he had five children. A dedicated public servant, he served as chairman of the Board of School Commissioners in Halifax before being elected to the House of Assembly as the Conservative member for Antigonish in 1877. The following year he was made Attorney General of Nova Scotia, and in 1882 he became Premier. In the election later that year, however, the Conservatives were defeated, and while he retained his seat, he resigned soon after to become judge in the Nova Scotia Supreme Court.

Macdonald persuaded him to become Canada's Justice Minister in 1885; two years later, he played a major role in negotiating the fishing rights Treaty of Washington. He became Prime Minister following Abbott's resignation and was responsible for bringing a great deal of new legislation before Parliament. A politician of great ability and high character, he won the respect of his fellow legislators and countrymen. His premature death occurred in December, 1894. He had been at Windsor Castle in England, just after having been sworn in as member of the Privy Council, when he suddenly collapsed. All mourned the lucid, puckish, faithful John Thompson.

SIR MACKENZIE BOWELL

Born in Suffolk, England, on Dec. 27, 1823, Mackenzie Bowell came to Canada with his father in 1833. Soon after, he was apprenticed to the publisher of the *Belleville Intelligencer*, a job he kept until the age of 18, when he left for school in Upper Canada. Six months later, he returned to the position of foreman at the paper. In 1847, he married Harriet Louise Moore, and, around the same time, bought the *Intelligencer*. He founded the Belleville Rifle Company, and became a member of the Orange Order, a fraternal group hostile to French Canadians and Roman Catholics, and eventually became its Grand Master.

He ran as the Conservative candidate for Belleville in 1863 and lost, but four years later won a federal seat for Hastings North and sat in Parliament until 1892. He was appointed to the Cabinet as Minister of Customs in 1878, where he implemented the National Policy. He served as Minister of Militia under Sir John Abbott and as Canada's first Minister of Trade in the Thompson administration. In 1892 he was appointed to the Senate, and two years later, became Prime Minister following Thompson's sudden death. His Cabinet forced his resignation over the Manitoba schools crisis, but he remained in the Senate from 1896.

Noted for his penchant for arguing and capacities as critic, Bowell was nevertheless considered a mediocre administrator. He died in Belleville, Ontario, on Dec. 10, 1917.

THE FATHERS OF CONFEDERATION

Between 1864 and 1866, 36 delegates from the British North American colonies attended one or more of three conferences held in Charlottetown, Québec and London, England. The result was the drawing up of the articles of Confederation; given Royal Assent Mar. 29, 1867 to take effect July 1, 1867.

Canada
Etienne Paschal Taché
John A. Macdonald
George Etienne Cartier
William McDougall
William P. Howland
George Brown
Alexander Tilloch Galt
Alexander Campbell
Oliver Mowat
Hector L. Langevin
James Cockburn
Thomas D'Arcy McGee
Jean Charles Chapais

Nova Scotia
Charles Tupper
William A. Henry
Robert B. Dickey
Jonathan McCully
Adams G. Archibald
John W. Ritchie

New Brunswick
Samuel Leonard Tilley
John M. Johnson
Robert D. Wilmot
Peter Mitchell
Charles Fisher
Edward B. Chandler
William H. Steeves
John Hamilton Gray

Newfoundland
Frederick B.T. Carter
Ambrose Shea

Prince Edward Island
John Hamilton Gray
Edward Palmer
William H. Pope
George Coles
Thomas Heath Haviland
Edward Whelan
Andrew A. Macdonald

SIR CHARLES TUPPER

The son of a Baptist minister, Charles Tupper was born in Amherst, Nova Scotia on July 2, 1821. He studied medicine at Edinburgh University, graduated at the age of 22, and practised in rural Nova Scotia. In 1846 he married Frances Amelia Morse. He was elected to the province's House of Assembly in 1855 as the Tory member for Cumberland. Two years later, he was appointed Provincial Secretary. He became Premier of Nova Scotia in 1864, and helped plan the Charlottetown Conference that led to Confederation.

He lost the provincial election of 1867, and rather than press a claim for high office in the newly formed Federal government, sat as a private member in the House of Commons. In 1870 he entered the Cabinet, then became President of its Privy Council. He was Minister of Inland Revenue in 1872 and Minister of Customs the following year. In 1878, he was appointed Minister of Public Works and was responsible for building the transcontinental railway. As Minister of Finance in 1887, he helped negotiate the Canada-U.S. fishing treaty, for which he was rewarded with a baronetcy the next year. He served as Canada's High Commissioner in London from 1883 until 1896, when he became Secretary of State.

Tupper took over as Prime Minister in 1896, but lost the federal election three months later. He remained leader of the Conservatives until after the elections of 1900, where the party again faced defeat. He died at Bexley Heath, England, on Oct. 30, 1915.

SIR WILFRID LAURIER

Wilfrid Laurier, the son of a land surveyor, was born in St. Lin, Quebec, on Nov. 20, 1841, the son of a land surveyor. He graduated from McGill with a law degree in 1864, and practised in Montréal for two years before moving to Arthabaska because of his health. While there, he also edited *Le Défricheur*, which folded in 1867. The following year he married Zoë La-

fontaine. He was elected to the Quebec legislature in 1871, but resigned three years later to represent Drummond-Arthabaska as a Liberal Member of Parliament. In 1877 he was appointed Minister of Inland Revenue, and that same year made a speech that has since become a classic statement of Canadian liberalism.

A brilliant orator, handsome, stately, and charming Laurier won wide acclaim. When he was elected Prime Minister of Canada in 1896, he assembled a brilliant cabinet. The country entered into the "Sunshine Years:" the economy flourished, and thanks to an aggressive immigration policy, the population boomed.

Laurier is also credited as the author of Canadian independence: British troops were withdrawn from Canadian soil and the militia came under Canadian command; the Navy was founded and Canada won the right to negotiate its own trade treaties. In 1909 the Department of External Affairs was established.

Laurier was reelected in 1900, 1904 and 1908, but was defeated over the reciprocity treaty with the United States in 1911. He supported Canada's war commitment in 1914, but would not enter into a coalition with Borden over the conscription issue in 1916. In the elections of the following year, he won Quebec but lost the rest of the country. Laurier remained in the House of Commons until his death on Feb. 17, 1919.

SIR ROBERT BORDEN

Born June 26, 1854, at Grand Pré, Nova Scotia, Robert Laird Borden was teaching classics and mathematics at a local school at the age of 14. In 1874, he entered law school in Halifax and was called to the bar four years later. He married Laura Bond in 1879. By 1882, he was a junior partner in the largest legal practice in the Maritimes. He entered politics out of a sense of public duty, winning the seat for Halifax in the House of Commons in 1896, and became Conservative leader in 1901. As Prime Minister from 1911 through the war years, he insisted that Canada have a voice in the conduct of the war.

In 1917 he formed a coalition without Laurier and won the federal election over the conscription issue. At the Peace Conference following the First World War, he won the right of separate representation for Canada.

Borden resigned from government in 1920 because of poor health. He had been Chancellor of McGill University from 1918 to 1920, and from 1924 to 1930 he served in the same capacity at Queen's University in Kingston, Ontario. He died on June 10, 1937, in Ottawa.

ARTHUR MEIGHEN

Born June 16, 1874, near Anderson, Ontario, Arthur Meighen studied mathematics at the University of Toronto, where he graduated with First Class Honours in 1896. He then taught school for a year, but quit over disagreements with the trustees. After investing in a small business that later failed, he moved to Manitoba, where he again taught for a time. He then studied law, was called to the bar in 1903, and steadily became a successful and prosperous lawyer. The following year he married Isabel Cox.

He was elected to the House of Commons in 1908 as the Conservative representative for Portage la Prairie, and was appointed Solicitor General five years later. He entered the Privy Council, became Secretary of State, and in 1917, Minister of the Interior. Despite opposition from the Cabinet, Borden appointed Meighen his successor in 1920. The new Prime Minister became leader of the Opposition less than eighteen months later, when the Conservatives lost the 1921 election. Meighen was restored briefly to power when the Governor General, Lord Byng, asked him to form a government in 1926. But this administration became involved in a crisis over parliamentary procedure, and called an election, which it lost, only three months later.

CANADA AT WAR

Canada's first army, a small volunteer force, was established a decade before Confederation. Until then, British North America depended entirely on British garrisons comparable in strength to the regular U.S. Army. In 1870, Britain began to withdraw its forces, leaving only the naval bases and a few soldiers at Halifax and Esquimault until the formation of the Royal Canadian Navy in 1910. In 1871, two batteries of Canadian artillery were formed, and in 1883, cavalry and infantry units were raised.

Between 1899 and 1902, 7300 Canadians fought in the Boer War at the battles of Paardeberg, Wolve Spruit and Leliefontein. There were 476 Canadian casualties, including 224 dead.

Together with Britain, Canada entered World War I on Aug. 4, 1914, and the first Canadian contingent, 30,808 strong, sailed for England on Oct. 3. By August, 1916, four Canadian divisions were fighting in Europe, and in 1917 the army experienced its first major victory, at Vimy Ridge. In June of that year, the Canadian Corps was placed under its first Canadian commander, Lt. Gen. Sir Arthur Currie. By August, 1918, the Canadians, along with other Allied forces, were finally on the advance. When the Armistice came in November, they were in Mons, Belgium.

World War I claimed the largest number of Canadians of any war: 59,544 fatalities and 172,950 wounded from the Army; 225 dead from our small Navy; and 1600 killed from among those serving with the British Royal Flying Corps and the Royal Naval Air Service.

Canada entered World War II on Sept. 10, 1939. The Navy was in action on convoy routes from the beginning; the 1st Division went overseas before the end of 1939; and Air Force units were posted to Britain in 1940. The whole population was mobilized for a prodigious war effort, which included the manufacture of 16,000 aircraft, 1000 ships, 8000 small craft, 50,000 tanks and gun carriers and 800,000 army trucks.

The Royal Canadian Navy grew from 1585 men at the start of the war to 106,522 men and women during the war and, by the end of the war, had a fleet of 404 warships and 566 auxiliary vessels. The Navy's main role was the protection of Allied shipping in the North Atlantic, but it also saw action in European waters and the Pacific.

Canadian troops fought in the unsuccessful defense of Hong Kong against the Japanese in December, 1941, and led the raid on the French coast at Dieppe in August, 1942. The next year, the 1st Division took part in the invasion of Sicily, and fought its way up the Italian mainland with the British 8th Army. By the end of 1943, there was a Canadian Corps in Italy. The 3rd Division stormed ashore at Normandy in June, 1944, and soon the 1st Canadian Army, commanded by Lt. Gen. H.D.G. Crerar, became operational on the Western front. Canadian soldiers fought their way along the coast of the English Channel during the Allied offensives of 1944 and 1945, and were largely responsible for the liberation of the Netherlands in 1945.

Canada's air force became the fourth largest among the Allied Powers during World War II. Canadian airmen fought in the Battle of Britain, patrolled the north Atlantic and joined in the massive bomber assault on Germany from 1942 to 1945. The largest Canadian formation overseas was the No. 6 R.C.A.F. Group, attached to the R.A.F. Bomber Command.

Canadian forces also fought in the Korean War, 1950-53. A destroyer flotilla, dispatched to Korean waters in July, 1950, remained on duty there throughout the war. One R.C.A.F. transport squadron assisted in the trans-Pacific airlift of supplies, and a small number of combat pilots saw duty with the United Nations. On the ground, a Canadian brigade was in action under UN command.

Meighen returned to a career in investment banking in 1926. He made a brief reappearance in politics, but lost a by-election in 1942. He returned to Toronto, where he died on Aug. 5, 1960.

WILLIAM LYON MACKENZIE KING

The grandson of the 1837 reform leader William Lyon Mackenzie, King was born Dec. 17, 1874, in Kitchener, Ontario. A graduate of the University of Toronto, he studied sociology at Harvard and worked for a year in Chicago. He was appointed deputy minister of Laurier's newly-created Labour Department in 1900, and was elected the Member of Parliament for Waterloo eight years later. From 1909—the same year that he was awarded his Ph.D.—to 1911, he was Minister of Labour. He succeeded Laurier as Liberal leader in 1919 and became Prime Minister with a minority government two years later. The Liberals barely made it to power in 1925, and resigned one year later only to return in three months by means of a forced election. Except for the 1930 election, which King lost by misjudging the severity of the Depression, he was to remain Prime Minister for a total of 22 years, returning in 1935 and serving until 1948. During that long period, he played a role in the Allied war effort and prevented a breach between English and French Canadians over conscription.

In 1948, he passed the party leadership on to Louis St. Laurent. King, a lifelong bachelor who believed in the supernatural and visited mediums, died at Kingsmere, Quebec, in July, 1950.

RICHARD BEDFORD BENNETT

Richard Bennett was born on July 3, 1870, in Hopewell, New Brunswick. The son of a shipbuilder, he became a school teacher, then principal, before he was 20, then studied law at Dalhousie University in Halifax. He began his practice in Chatham, New Brunswick, and was elected to its town council in 1896. The following year he moved to Calgary, where he became a successful corporation lawyer. He was elected to the Northwest Territories Legislature in 1898, and in 1909 won a seat in Alberta's legislature. He resigned two years later to sit in the House of Commons as the Conservative representative for Calgary East. He served briefly as Minister of Justice and Attorney General in 1921, and in 1926, as Minister of Finance. He was chosen party leader the following year and won a landslide victory in 1930.

Until 1934, the government had adopted a laissez-faire approach to the Depression. Bennett proposed legislation on minimum wages, maximum hours, pensions, price controls and unemployment and health insurance. He created the Canadian Wheat Board, the Bank of Canada and the forerunners of both the CBC and Air Canada.

Bennett lost the 1935 election but remained leader of the Opposition until 1938, when he retired in England. He was later appointed to the British House of Lords as Viscount Bennett. He died in England on June 26, 1947.

LOUIS ST. LAURENT

Louis St. Laurent was born in Compton, Quebec, on Feb. 1, 1882. He began training for the priesthood at St. Charles-Boromée Seminary, but switched to studying law at Laval University. Refusing a Rhodes Scholarship, he began his career in 1905, the year he married Jeanne Renault. He had a flourishing law practice and lectured at Laval. He became head of the Quebec Bar in 1929 and President of the Canadian Bar Association the following year.

In 1941, he was asked to join King's cabinet, where he served as Justice Minister and Attorney General. Toward the end of the war, he acted as Prime Minister whenever King left the country, and was appointed chairman of the Canadian delegation to the founding conference of the United Nations. After the war, he became Secretary of State for External Affairs and was one of the original advocates of the North Atlantic Pact.

He was chosen as King's successor in 1948; soon after, he was elected Prime Minister. He brought Newfoundland into Confederation in 1949, saw the St. Lawrence Seaway built and the Trans-Canada highway begun, and established the Canada Council. He helped to make the Supreme Court the final court of appeal and to establish Canada as a respected international power. St. Laurent lost the 1957 elections, retired the same year, and died in Québec on July 25, 1973.

JOHN GEORGE DIEFENBAKER

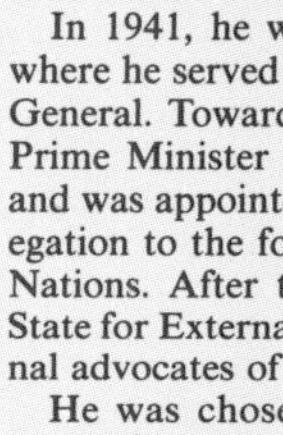

Born in Grey County, Ontario, on Sept. 18, 1895, John Diefenbaker moved with his family to rural Saskatchewan in 1903. He studied at the University of Saskatchewan, where he distinguished himself as both an orator and a practical joker, and went off to war in 1916. Later he became a lawyer, creating a reputation for himself as a brilliant criminal defense counsel. He ran for Parliament in 1925 and again the following year, losing both times. In 1929 he married Edna Bower. After successive attempts to win office, he finally became Member of Parliament in 1940, then Conservative leader 16 years later. Two years after his wife's death in 1951, he married Olive Palmer.

In 1957, Diefenbaker was elected Prime Minister of Canada. He introduced the Bill of Rights in 1960 and set up federal agencies to help both the western and Atlantic provinces. He also moved to expel South Africa from the Commonwealth. He initiated grain sales to mainland China and maintained trade and diplomatic links with Cuba after the 1961 Missile Crisis.

Despite having united the West into a coherent political force, he was defeated in 1963 due to his inability to build support in Quebec, as well as by his uncertainty over defense issues.

Diefenbaker then became leader of the Opposition until he lost the party leadership in 1967. "The Chief" continued as a vigorous and outspoken Member of Parliament until his death in August, 1979.

LESTER BOWLES PEARSON

Son of a Methodist minister, "Mike" Pearson was born in Toronto on Apr. 23, 1897. He began studying at the University of Toronto, but enlisted in 1915. He was awarded a degree in history in 1919, then attended Oxford, where he distinguished himself as an athlete. He returned to teach history at the University of Toronto in 1923 and married Maryon Elspeth Moody two years later.

At the age of 32, he joined Canada's infant foreign service. He was appointed first secretary to the High Commissioner in London in 1935, was posted to the Canadian embassy in Washington in 1941 and became ambassador to the United States four years later. He played an important role in establishing the United Nations.

In 1946 he returned to Canada as under secretary for External Affairs; two years later he was appointed minister. He served as both President of the United Nations General Assembly and Chairman of the NATO council in 1952. He won the Nobel Prize for Peace in 1957.

The Liberal leader from 1958, Pearson won both 1963 and 1965 elections with a minority government. His administration introduced Medicare and the Canada Pension Plan, and legislated today's Canadian flag during the Centennial. Pearson resigned in 1968. He died in Ottawa on Dec. 27, 1972.

PIERRE ELLIOTT TRUDEAU

Born into a wealthy Montréal family on Oct. 18, 1919, Pierre Trudeau attended Jean de Brébeuf College and studied law at the University of Montréal. After being called to the bar, he studied political economy at Harvard, Paris and London, and traveled widely. He entered Parliament as the Liberal member for Mount Royal in 1965. Two years later he was Justice Minister and Attorney General. He succeeded Lester Pearson as Liberal Party leader in 1968, winning a decisive victory in the federal election that year.

In 1970, the October Crisis erupted in Quebec, and Trudeau invoked the emergency War Measures Act to maintain order. The elections in 1972 resulted in a minority government for the Liberals, and revealed regional hostilities growing out of cultural and economic differences. In 1974, Trudeau regained a strong majority. The Liberals lost the 1979 contest, but returned to power early in 1980. In May, 1980, Trudeau led the federalist forces to victory in Quebec's referendum on sovereignty-association.

The Trudeau administration has been responsible for the Official Languages Act, the early recognition of the People's Republic of China, temporary wage and price controls, and the extension of the offshore fishing limit to 200 miles.

JOE CLARK

Charles Joseph Clark was born in High River, Alberta, on June 5, 1939. He attended the University of Alberta and Dalhousie, and was National President of the Progressive Conservative Student Federation from 1963 to 1965. In 1967, Clark served as Advisor to Davie Fulton and Executive Assistant to Robert Stanfield for the following three years. First elected to the House of Commons in 1972, he became Conservative party leader four years later, succeeding Robert Stanfield.

Clark served as Prime Minister of Canada for six months following the Conservative victory in the June, 1979 elections. His minority government fell, over its first budget, and he was defeated at the polls in February, 1980. He subsequently became leader of the Opposition.

PARTY REPRESENTATION BY REGIONS 1949-1980

	1949	1953	1957	1958	1962	1963	1965	1968	1972	1974	1979	1980
CANADA												
Liberal	193	171	105	40	100	129	131	155	109	141	114	147
Conservative	41	51	112	208	116	95	97	72	107	95	136	103
New Democratic	13	23	25	8	19	17	21	22	31	16	26	32
Social Credit	10	15	19	—	30	24	(4	14	15	11	6	0
Other	5	5	4	—	—	—		1	2	1	0	0
ONTARIO												
Liberal	56	51	21	15	44	52	51	64	36	55	32	52
Conservative	25	33	61	67	35	27	25	17	40	25	57	38
New Democratic	1	1	3	3	6	6	9	6	11	8	6	5
QUEBEC												
Liberal	68	66	62	25	35	47	56	56	56	60	67	74
Conservative	2	4	9	50	14	8	8	4	2	3	2	1
Social Credit	—	—	—	—	26	20	9	14	15	11	6	0
ATLANTIC												
Libertal	26	27	12	8	14	20	15	7	10	13	12	19
Conservative	7	5	21	25	18	13	16	25	22	17	17	13
New Democratic	1	1	—	—	1	—	—	—	—	1	2	0
WESTERN												
Liberal	43	27	10	1	7	10	9	27	7	13	3	2
Conservative	7	9	21	66	49	47	46	25	42	49	60	49
New Democratic	11	21	22	5	12	11	12	16	19	6	18	26
Social Credit	10	15	19	—	4	4	5	—	—	—	—	0

100 NOTABLE CANADIANS OF THE PAST

François Amyot: (1904-1962) Six times Canadian canoeing champion, Olympic gold medalist (1936).
Brother André: (1845-1937) Religious mystic; builder of a shrine to St. Joseph on Mount Royal, Montréal.
Sir Frederick Banting: (1891-1941) Physician and scientist, winner with Dr. J.J.R. Macleod of the 1923 Nobel Prize for the discovery of insulin.
Big Bear: (d. 1888) Chief of the Plains Cree Indians during the Northwest Rebellion, 1885.
Julia Beckwith: (1796-1867) Novelist, published the first novel in Canada, *St. Ursula's Convent* (1824).
George Stansfeld Belaney (Grey Owl): (1888-1938) Author and wildlife conservationist.
W.A.C. Bennett: (1900-1979) Social Credit premier of British Columbia (1952-1972).
Charles Best: (1899-1978) Biochemist, codiscoverer of insulin with Sir Frederick Banting and Dr. J.J.R. Macleod.
Norman Bethune: (1890-1939) Surgeon, organizer of the world's first mobile blood-transfusion service.
William Avery (Billy) Bishop: (1894-1956) First World War air ace; Victoria Cross winner.
Paul-Emile Borduas: (1905-1960) Painter and author.
Henri Bourassa: (1868-1952) Politician; founder and editor of the Montréal newspaper, *Le Devoir* (1910).
Marguerite Bourgeoys: (1620-1700) Founder of the Montréal Congregation of Notre Dame.
Ignace Bourget: (1799-1885) Roman Catholic Bishop of Montréal (1840-1876).
Joseph Brant: (1742-1807) Mohawk chief and principal chief of the Six Nations Indians, whom he led on the British side during the Seven Years War.
Jean de Brébeuf: (1593-1649) Jesuit missionary and martyr.
Samuel Bronfman: (1891-1971) Industrialist, president of Distiller's Corporation-Seagram's Ltd. (1928-1971).
Tommy Burns: (1881-1955) Boxer, Canada's only world heavyweight champion (1906).
Franklin Carmichael: (1890-1945) Artist, member of the Group of Seven.
Emily Carr: (1871-1945) Painter and author.
Noël Chabanel: (1613-1649) Jesuit missionary and martyr.
Lionel Conacher: (1900-1954) Canada's all-round athlete of the first half century.
Octave Crémazie: (1827-1879) Poet, the "father of French-Canadian poetry."
Henry Crerar: (1888-1965) General, Commander-in-Chief, First Canadian Army, Second World War.
Sir Samuel Cunard: (1787-1865) Halifax merchant and shipowner. founder of the Cunard steamship lines.
Sir Arthur Currie: (1875-1933) General, commander of the Canadian Corps, First World War.
Louis Cyr: (1863-1912) Weightlifter and legendary strongman.
John Dafoe: (1866-1944) Journalist, editor-in-chief of the *Winnipeg Free Press* (1901-1944).
Antoine Daniel: (1601-1648) Jesuit missionary and martyr.
Mazo De La Roche: (1879-1961) Novelist and playwright, author of the 24 *Jalna* novels.
Etienne Desmarteau: (1877-1905) Canada's first Olympic gold medalist (hammer throw, 1904).
Adam Dollard des Ormeaux: (1635-1660) Pioneer leader massacred by Iroquois at the Long Sault, 1660.
Sir James Douglas: (1803-1877) Governor of Vancouver Island (1851-1863) and British Columbia (1853-1864).
Gabriel Dumont: (1838-1906) Military leader of the Northwest Rebellion of 1885.
Maurice Duplessis: (1890-1959) Union Nationale premier of Quebec (1936-1939; 1944-1959).
Timothy Eaton: (1834-1907) Merchant, founder of T. Eaton and Company (1869).
Sir Sandford Fleming: (1827-1915) Civil engineer, inventor of international standard time and designer of Canada's first stamp.
Simon Fraser: (1776-1862) Fur trader and explorer.
Charles Garnier: (1606-1649) Jesuit missionary and martyr.
Abraham Gesner: (1797-1864) Doctor, geologist, author, inventor of kerosene (1852).
George (Mooney) Gibson: (1880-1967) Baseball star.
James Gladstone: (1887-1971) Canada's first Indian senator.
Charlies Gorman: (1897-1940) Speed skater, world champion (1926-1927).
René Goupil: (1608-1642) Jesuit missionary and martyr.
Médard Chouart, sieur des Groseilliers: (1818-1696) Fur trader and explorer.
Lionel Groulx: (1878-1967) Historian.
Sir Casimir Gzowski: (1813-1898) Civil engineer and financier; builder of the Grand Trunk railway from Toronto to Sarnia, Ont.
T.C. Haliburton: (1796-1865) Judge and author of humorous fiction under the pseudonym Sam Slick.
Edward (Ned) Hanlan: (1855-1908) Six times world rowing champion.
Lawren Harris: (1885-1970) Artist, member of the Group of Seven.
Louis Hébert: (d. 1627) Canada's first farmer.
C.D. Howe: (1886-1960) World War II federal cabinet minister; contributed to establishing the Canadian Broadcasting Corporation.
Joseph Howe: (1804-1873) Nova Scotia journalist and politician.
A.Y. Jackson: (1882-1974) Artist, member of the Group of Seven.
Isaac Jogues: (1607-1646) Jesuit missionary and martyr.
Pauline Johnson: (1862-1913) Indian poet.
Frank (or Franz) Johnston: (1888-1949) Artist, member of the Group of Seven.
Paul Kane: (1810-1871) Artist, known for paintings of Indians and the West.
Cornelius Krieghoff: (1815-1872) Artist.
Father Albert Lacombe: (1827-1916) Roman Catholic missionary to the Canadian West.
Jean de La Lande: (d. 1646) Jesuit missionary and martyr.
François-Xavier Laval-Montmorency: (1623-1708) First Roman Catholic bishop of Quebec.
Calixa Lavallée: (1842-1891) Composer of Canada's National Anthem, "O Canada."
Pierre de la Vérendrye: (1685-1749) Fur trader and explorer.
Stephen Leacock: (1869-1944) Humorist, educator and author.
Arthur Lismer: (1885-1969) Artist, member of the Group of Seven.
J.E.H. MacDonald: (1873-1932) Artist, member of the Group of Seven.
Sir Alexander Mackenzie: (1764-1820) Fur trader and explorer.
William Lyon Mackenzie: (1795-1861) Politician, leader of Upper Canada's Rebellion of 1837.
Agnes Macphail: (1890-1954) First woman Member of Parliament (1921-1940).
Nellie McClung: (1873-1951) Author, feminist and suffragette.
John McCrae: (1872-1918) Physician and poet, author of "In Flanders Fields."
J.A.D. McCurdy: (1886-1961) Air pioneer; made the British Empire's first airplane flight, in the *Silver Dart* (1909).
James McGill: (1744-1813) Montréal merchant and philanthropist.
James McGuigan: (1894-1974) Archbishop and cardinal.
R.S. (Sam) McLaughlin: (1871-1972) Manufacturer and philanthropist; first president of General Motors of Canada (1918-1945).
Honoré Mercier: (1875-1937) Lawyer and politician; Liberal premier of Quebec (1887-1891).
Lucy Maud Montgomery: (1874-1942) Novelist, creator of *Anne of Green Gables.*
Emily Murphy: (1868-1933) Author and the British Empire's first woman magistrate.
Leonard Warren Murray: (1896-1972) Rear Admiral, Commander in chief, Canadian Northwest Atlantic, Second World War.
James Naismith: (1861-1939) Professor of physical education, inventor of basketball (1891).
Sir William Osler: (1849-1919) Physician and author.
Louis-Joseph Papineau: (1786-1871) Politician; leader of French-Canadian reformers, *les patriotes*, in the 1837 rebellion.
Wilder Penfield: (1891-1976) Neurosurgeon, founder of the Montreal Neurological Institute.
Poundmaker: (1826-1886) Cree Indian chief; took part with Louis Riel in the second Northwest Rebellion (1885).
Pierre Radisson: (1636-1710) Fur trader and explorer.
James Armstrong Richardson: (1885-1939) Financier, pioneer in Canadian aviation development.
Louis Riel: (1844-1885) Métis leader of the Northwest Rebellions (1870, 1885).
Fanny (Bobbie) Rosenfeld: (1903-1969) Sportswriter and athlete; voted Canada's best woman athlete of the half century.
Adolphus Egerton Ryerson: (1803-1882) Methodist minister and educator.
Laura Secord: (1775-1868) Heroine of the British-American War (1813).
Robert Service: (1874-1958) Poet and novelist of the North.
Ernest Thompson Seton: (1860-1946) Artist, naturalist and author.
Vilhjalmur Stefansson: (1879-1962) Arctic explorer.
Emily Stowe: (1831-1903) Canada's first woman doctor and a leading female suffragist.
Kateri Tekakwitha: (1656-1680) Christian Convert, first Indian to be named venerable by the Roman Catholic Church.
David Thompson: (1770-1857) Geographer and explorer; first white man to descend the Columbia River.
Tom Thomson: (1877-1917) Artist.
Sir William Van Horne: (1888-1910) President and chairman of the board of directors of the Canadian Pacific Railway.
Fred Varley: (1881-1969) Artist, member of the Group of Seven.

The Physical Environment

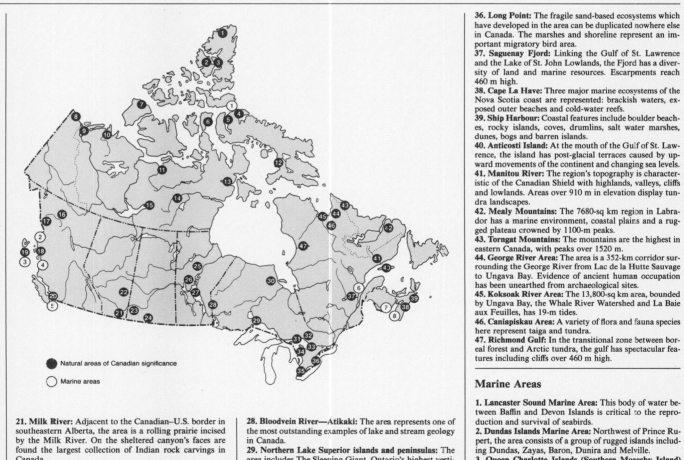

Natural Areas of Canadian Significance

1. Northern Ellesmere Island: The high plateau surrounding Lake Hazen has mountains reaching 2590 m, the highest in the Arctic islands.
2. Axel Heiberg Island: Dominated by a range of ice-capped mountains, the second highest in the Arctic archipelago (up to 2290 m), the coasts are indented by fjords and are icebound most of the year.
3. Fosheim Peninsula: An excellent example of a high Arctic ecosystem, the landscape has rolling hills and a mild climate for the latitude (80° N).
4. Bylot Island—Eclipse Sound: A rectangular island off the coast of Baffin Island, with mountains rising to 1830 m.
5. Western Borden Peninsula: Precambrian and Paleozoic bedrock have given the Peninsula a varied topography, including a vast polar desert with little vegetation.
6. Creswell Bay: Rock deserts and diverse rock types have produced varied floral varieties.
7. Northern Banks Island: The island varies from a ravined Devonian plateau to coastal lagoons and supports the most vigorous muskox population in the Arctic.
8. Northern Yukon: This area of diverse environments is of critical importance as the habitat for Arctic mammals and birds.
9. Caribou Hills—Napoiak Channel: At the outer delta of the MacKenzie River, land and sea support varied plants and animals.
10. Horton—Anderson Rivers: Brock River Canyon, 16 km long with vertical walls up to 110 m, and the Smoking Hills with their burning bituminous beds are features of the area.
11. Bathurst Inlet: Penetrating 160 km south into the Canadian Shield, the Inlet is a submerged rift valley. Wilberforce Falls (50 m) are the highest north of the Arctic Circle.
12. Foxe Lowlands: The Great Plain of Koukdjuak supports the largest goose colony in the world.
13. Wager Bay: A submerged rift valley penetrating 160 km north into the Canadian Shield on the west coast of Hudson Bay.
14. Thelon Game Sanctuary: Remarkable for its variety of tundra vegetation and concentration of wildlife, including the largest surviving mainland population of muskox.
15. East Arm Great Slave Lake: Artillery Lake lies across the transition zone between taiga and tundra and supports diverse flora and fauna.
16. Spatsizi Plateau: The Plateau is part of the more extensive Stikine Plateau and contains the headwaters of the Stikine River, one of the most spectacular in northern British Columbia.
17. Mt. Edziza—Coast Mountains: Lava flows, cinder cones and breccia pipes are found near Mt. Edziza, a composite volcano. Colored, altered lavas coat the Spectrum Range.
18. Northern Coast of British Columbia: A diverse biological and geological region representative of the Pacific coast.
19. Queen Charlotte Islands: Plants that occur nowhere else in the world are evidence of a pleistocene glacial refuge on the islands.
20. Gulf Islands—Saltspring Island—Cowichan Estuary: In the Straights of Georgia, the Islands have a remarkable biological diversity.

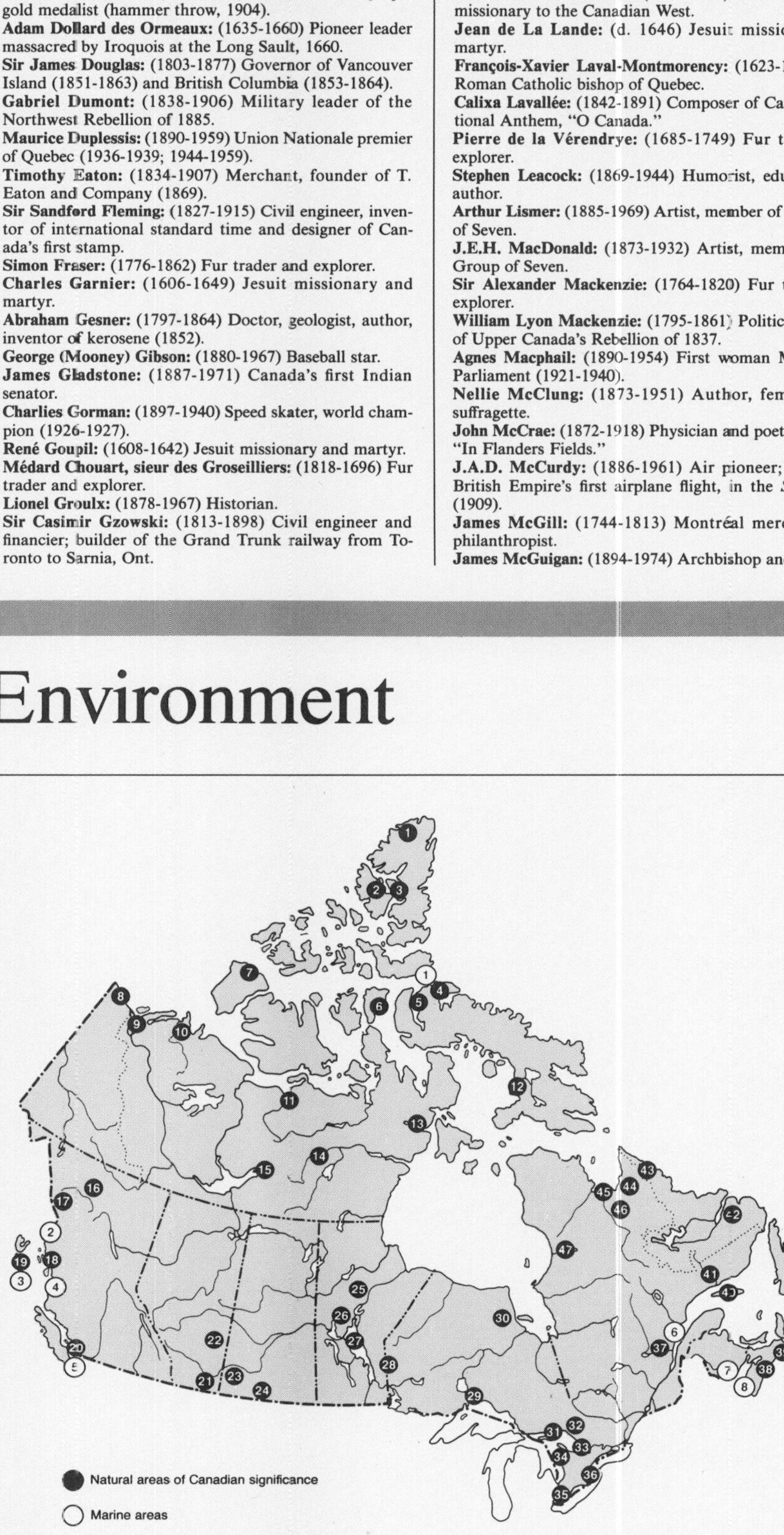

21. Milk River: Adjacent to the Canadian–U.S. border in southeastern Alberta, the area is a rolling prairie incised by the Milk River. On the sheltered canyon's faces are found the largest collection of Indian rock carvings in Canada.
22. Suffield: An area of tremendous archaeological potential containing ancient Indian cairns, tepee rings and medicine wheel sites.
23. Cypress Hills: The treeless prairie is broken here by the Cypress Hills, a flat-topped plateau rising 760 m.
24. Grasslands: The Val Marie-Killdeer area of southern Saskatchewan is broken by the bizarre landforms of the Killdeer badlands. Dinosaur remains were discovered here in 1874.
25. Churchill River: Among the resources of this forested Precambrian lake country are aboriginal rock paintings considered sacred.
26. Little Limestone Lake: In the northern part of the Manitoba Lowlands, the area displays varied landforms such as flood plains, sinkholes and meandering rivers.
27. Long Point: Both Silurian and Ordovician geological themes are found in the area, also famous for migrating raptors, waterfowl and shorebirds.
28. Bloodvein River—Atikaki: The area represents one of the most outstanding examples of lake and stream geology in Canada.
29. Northern Lake Superior islands and peninsulas: The area includes The Sleeping Giant, Ontario's highest vertical cliffs, 11 km long and rising to 300 m. Nearby Ouimet Canyon is a 110 m-deep gorge, 150 m wide and 3 km long.
30. Attawapiskat River—Akimiskitwin Island Area: The area spans several transitional zones and has excellent examples of delta vegetation and marine ecology.
31. Manitoulin Island: Lying in the northern part of Lake Huron, Manitoulin is said to be the largest freshwater island in the world.
32. French River: The river's forested mouth is one of the most spectacular stretches of the Great Lakes.
33. Parry Sound: Several rare plant species and virtually every species of wildlife in the region are found here.
34. Bruce Peninsula: The rugged peninsula is on an extension of the Niagara Escarpment Cuesta. Bluffs rise 90 m above the Georgian Bay shoreline.
35. Point Pelee: Canada's southernmost point is a haven for birds and birdwatchers. A large part of the point is below water level and marshy.
36. Long Point: The fragile sand-based ecosystems which have developed in the area can be duplicated nowhere else in Canada. The marshes and shoreline represent an important migratory bird area.
37. Saguenay Fjord: Linking the Gulf of St. Lawrence and the Lake of St. John Lowlands, the Fjord has a diversity of land and marine resources. Escarpments reach 460 m high.
38. Cape La Have: Three major marine ecosystems of the Nova Scotia coast are represented: brackish waters, exposed outer beaches and cold-water reefs.
39. Ship Harbour: Coastal features include boulder beaches, rocky islands, coves, drumlins, salt water marshes, dunes, bogs and barren islands.
40. Anticosti Island: At the mouth of the Gulf of St. Lawrence, the island has post-glacial terraces caused by upward movements of the continent and changing sea levels.
41. Manitou River: The region's topography is characteristic of the Canadian Shield with highlands, valleys, cliffs and lowlands. Areas over 910 m in elevation display tundra landscapes.
42. Mealy Mountains: The 7680-sq km region in Labrador has a marine environment, coastal plains and a rugged plateau crowned by 1100-m peaks.
43. Torngat Mountains: The mountains are the highest in eastern Canada, with peaks over 1520 m.
44. George River Area: The area is a 352-km corridor surrounding the George River from Lac de la Hutte Sauvage to Ungava Bay. Evidence of ancient human occupation has been unearthed from archaeological sites.
45. Koksoak River Area: The 13,800-sq km area, bounded by Ungava Bay, the Whale River Watershed and La Baie aux Feuilles, has 19-m tides.
46. Caniapiskau Area: A variety of flora and fauna species here represent taiga and tundra.
47. Richmond Gulf: In the transitional zone between boreal forest and Arctic tundra, the gulf has spectacular features including cliffs over 460 m high.

Marine Areas

1. Lancaster Sound Marine Area: This body of water between Baffin and Devon Islands is critical to the reproduction and survival of seabirds.
2. Dundas Islands Marine Area: Northwest of Prince Rupert, the area consists of a group of rugged islands including Dundas, Zayas, Baron, Dunira and Melville.
3. Queen Charlotte Islands (Southern Moresby Island) Marine Area: The area is renowned for its diversity of invertebrates and seaweed.
4. Calvert Island—Hunter Island Marine Area: The area includes Calvert, Hunter and Goose Islands and smaller surrounding islands. With their exposed coastlines, the Goose and Calvert islands have diverse flora and fauna.
5. Gulf Islands Marine Area: An archipelago dominated by a mild, dry, Mediterranean-type climate, wave action has worn the coastal sandstone into striking caves.
6. Tadoussac—Les Escoumins Marine Area: The last remaining stronghold of the declining population of Beluga (white) whales.
7. Deer Island Archipelago Marine Area: Cold saline water supports abundant zooplankton life, while islands and islets shelter seabird colonies.
8. Brier Island Marine Area: One of the richest biological areas in the Bay of Fundy, with undisturbed shoreland bogs that support unique Atlantic flora and fauna.

LAND AND FRESHWATER AREAS

Province or Territory	Land (km²)	Freshwater (km²)	Total (km²)
Nfld.	370,485	34,032	404,517
Island of Nfld.	(106,614)	(5685)	(112,299)
Labrador	(263,871)	(28,347)	(292,218)
P.E.I.	5657	—	5657
N.S.	52,841	2650	55,491
N.B.	72,092	1344	73,436
Que.	1,356,791	183,889	1,540,680
Ont.	891,194	177,388	1,068,583
Man.	548,495	101,592	650,087
Sask.	570,269	82,631	651,900
Alta	644,389	16,796	661,185
B.C.	930,528	18,068	948,597
Yukon	478,034	4481	482,515
N.W.T.	3,246,390	133,294	3,379,686
CANADA	9,167,165	755,165	9,922,330

HIGHEST POINTS

Province and point:	Elevation (m)
Newfoundland Unnamed peak, Torngat Mountains	1652
Prince Edward Island Highest point, Queen's County	142
Nova Scotia Highest point, Cape Breton	532
New Brunswick Mount Carleton	820
Quebec Mont D'Iberville	1652
Ontario Highest point, Temiskaming District	693
Manitoba Baldy Mountain	832
Saskatchewan Cypress Hills	1392
Alberta Mount Columbia	3747
British Columbia Fairweather Mountain	4663
Yukon Mount Logan	5951
Northwest Territories Mount Sir James MacBrien	2762

LAND USE, 1976 (km²)

Status	Nfld.	P.E.I.	N.S.	N.B.	Que.	Ont.	Man.	Sask.	Alta.	B.C.	Yukon	N.W.T.	CANADA
Federal Crown lands other than national parks, Indian reserves and forest experiment stations	440	16	181	1489	1295	1158	259	5452	2896	904	513,193	3,340,849	3,868,132
National parks	2339	21	1331	433	790	1922	2978	3875	54,084	4690	22,015	35,690	130,168
Indian reserves	—	8	114	168	4077	6703	2383	5688	6566	3390	5	135	29,237
Federal forest experiment stations	—	—	—	91	28	103	138,008	—	155	—	—	—	377
Privately owned land or land in process of alienation from the Crown	17,788	4944	37,438	39,754	112,664	119,023	—	247,662	181,925	55,040	168	72	795,800
Provincial or territorial area other than provincial parks and provincial forests	382,842	435	2652	28,495	1,210,799	891,261	482,204	34,758	63,525	539,280	943	2937	3,621,560
Provincial parks	805	31	109	215	194,249	48,412	10,230	4944	7700	41,629	—	—	308,187
Provincial forests	303	202	13,665	2792	16,778	—	14,025	349,521	344,334	303,663	—	—	1,084,669
Total area	404,517	5657	55,490	73,437	1,540,680	1,068,582	650,087	651,900	661,185	948,596	536,324	3,379,683	9,976,138

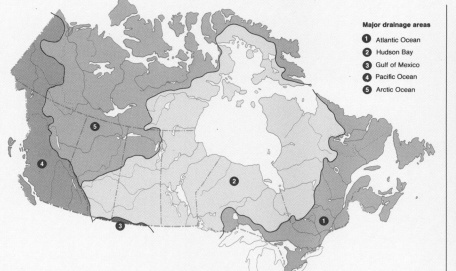

Major drainage areas

1. Atlantic Ocean
2. Hudson Bay
3. Gulf of Mexico
4. Pacific Ocean
5. Arctic Ocean

GLACIERS

Arctic Islands	Ice Area (km²)	No. of Glaciers surveyed
Axel Heiberg	11,383	1121
Baffin	35,890	10,526
Bylot	4851	579
Coburg	218	106
Devon	15,714	1907
Ellesmere	77,596	N/A
Ice shelf	484	N/A
Meighen	83	N/A
Melville	155	N/A
North Kent & Calf	148	68
	146,522	14,307
Mainland		
Into Nelson River	319	1616
Into Yukon River	10,246	N/A
Into Great Slave Lake	606	N/A
Into Pacific Ocean	36,527	N/A
Into Arctic Ocean	816	N/A
Into Atlantic Ocean	N/A	N/A
All glaciers in Labrador	23	N/A
	48,537	1616

Key: N/A = not available
Estimate of total ice cover in Canada: 195,059 km²

ISLANDS

Region and island	Area (km²)
Baffin Island	507,451
QUEEN ELIZABETH ISLANDS	
Ellesmere	196,236
Devon	55,247
Axel Heiberg	43,178
Melville	42,149
Bathurst	16,042
Prince Patrick	15,848
Ellef Ringnes	11,295
Cornwallis	6996
Amund Ringnes	5255
Mackenzie King	5048
Borden	2795
Cornwall	2258
Eglinton	1541
Graham	1378
Lougheed	1308
Byam Martin	1150
Ile Vanier	1127
Cameron	1059
ARCTIC ISLANDS SOUTH OF QUEEN ELIZABETH ISLANDS	
Victoria	217,290
Banks	70,028
Prince of Wales	33,338
Somerset	24,786
King William	13,111
Bylot	11,067
Prince Charles	9521
Stefansson	4463
Richards	2165
Air Force	1720
Wales	1137
Rowley	1090
HUDSON BAY AND HUDSON STRAIT	
Southampton	41,214
Coats	5499
Mansel	3181
Akimiski	3002
Flaherty	1585
Nottingham	1373
Resolution	1015
PACIFIC COAST	
Vancouver	31,284
Graham	6361
Moresby	2608
Princess Royal	2251
Pitt	1375
ATLANTIC COAST	
Newfoundland and Labrador	
Newfoundland (main island)	108,860
South Aulatsivik	456
Killinek	269
Fogo	254
Random	249
Gulf of St. Lawrence	
Cape Breton	10,311
Anticosti	7941
Prince Edward	5657
Bay of Fundy	
Grand Manan	137

RIVERS

Drainage basin and river	Length (km)
FLOWING INTO THE PACIFIC OCEAN	
Yukon (mouth to head of Nisutlin)	3185
(International Boundary to head of Nisutlin)	1149
Columbia (mouth to head of Columbia Lake)	2000
(International Boundary to head of Columbia Lake)	721
Fraser	1368
Skeena	579
Stikine	539
Thompson	489
FLOWING INTO THE ARCTIC OCEAN	
Mackenzie (to head of Finlay)	4241
Back (to outlet of Muskox Lake)	974
Coppermine	845
Anderson	692
Horton	618
FLOWING INTO HUDSON BAY AND HUDSON STRAIT	
Nelson (to head of Bow)	2575
(to outlet of Lake Winnipeg)	644
Churchill (to head of Churchill Lake)	1609
Severn (to head of Black Birch)	982
Albany (to head of Cat)	982
Thelon	904
La Grande-Rivière (Fort George River)	893
Koksoak (to head of Caniapiscau)	874
Nottaway (via Bell to head of Mégiscane)	776
Rupert (to head of Témiscamie)	763
Eastmain	756
Attawapiskat (to head of Bow Lake)	748
Kazan (to head of Ennadai Lake)	732
Grande rivière de la Baleine (Great Whale)	724
George	563
Moose (to head of Mattagami)	547
Harricanaw	533
Hayes	483
Aux Feuilles (Leaf)	480
Winisk	475
Broadback	451
A la Baleine (Whale)	428
de Povungnituk	389
FLOWING INTO THE ATLANTIC OCEAN	
St. Lawrence River	3058
Ottawa River	1271
Saguenay (to head of Peribonca)	698
Saint-Maurice	563
Manicouagan (to head of Mouchalagane)	560
aux Outardes	499
Romaine	496
Betsiamites (to head of Kanouanis)	444
Moisie	410
Bersimis	386
St-François	280
St-Augustin	233
Chaudière	193
Richelieu (to mouth of Lake Champlain)	171
Churchill (to head of Ashuanipi)	856
Saint John	673
du Petit-Mécatina	547
Natashquan	410
Exploits	246
Eagle	233
Miramichi	217
Gander (to head of Northwest Gander River)	175

LAKES

Province and lake	Elevation (m)	Area (km²)
NEWFOUNDLAND AND LABRADOR		
Ashuanipi	529	598
Atikonak	518	433
Grand	87	539
Joseph	518	451
Melville	tidal	3069
Michikamau	460	2031
Lobstick	457	510
Ossokmanuan Reservoir	479	834
Smallwood Reservoir	471	6475
NOVA SCOTIA		
Bras d'Or	tidal	1098
QUEBEC		
Albanel	389	445
Bienville	427	1248
Cabonga Reservoir	361	679
Dozois Reservoir	346	404
Eau Claire	241	1383
Evans	241	546
Gouin Reservoir	404	1570
Kaniapiskau	564	471
Leaf	tidal	453
Lower Seal	262	578
Manouane	494	585
Minto	168	761
Mistassini	372	2336
Payne	130	534
Pipmuacan	396	979
Saint-Jean	98	1002
Sakami	195	593
ONTARIO		
Abitibi	265	932
Big Trout	213	660
Lake of the Woods (total 4,349)		
Canadian part 3,149	323	3149
Nipigon	261	4848
Nipissing	196	831
Rainy (total 932)		
Canadian part 741	338	741
St. Joseph	371	492
Sandy	276	526
Seul	357	1658
Simcoe	219	743
Trout (English River)	394	414
MANITOBA		
Cedar	253	1352
Cross	207	756
Dauphin	260	521
Gods	178	1150
Granville	258	490
Island	227	1222
Manitoba	248	4659
Molson	221	399
Moose	255	1368
Oxford	187	401
Playgreen	217	658
Sipiwesk	183	456
Southern Indian	255	2248
Winnipeg	217	24,390
Winnipegosis	253	5374
SASKATCHEWAN		
Amisk	294	430
Athabasca	213	7936
Black	281	464
Churchill	421	559
Cree	487	1435
Deschambault	324	541
Doré	459	642
Frobisher	421	515
Ile à la Crosse	421	391
La Ronge	364	1414

Province and lake	Elevation (m)	Area (km²)
Montreal	490	456
Peter Pond	421	777
Pinehouse	385	404
Primrose	599	448
Reindeer	337	6651
Scott	444	394
Tazin	344	391
Wollaston	398	2681
ALBERTA		
Bistcho	552	427
Claire	213	1437
Lesser Slave	577	1168
BRITISH COLUMBIA		
Atlin	668	774
Babine	711	495
Kootenay	532	407
Ootsa	853	404
Williston	664	1761
YUKON TERRITORY		
Kluane	781	409
NORTHWEST TERRITORIES		
Aberdeen	80	1101
Amadjuak	113	3116
Angikuni	257	510
Artillery	365	552
Aubry	258	391
Aylmer	375	847
Baker	2	1888
Bluenose	557	401
Buffalo	265	614
Clinton Colden	375	736
Colville	245	456
Contwoyto	445	958
De Gras	416	632
Des Bois	297	469
Dubawnt	236	3833
Ennadai	311	681
Eskimo North	0.3	839
Eskimo South	2	629
Faber	213	440
Ferguson	11	588
Garry	148	976
Great Bear	156	31,328
Great Slave	156	28,570
Hall	6	492
Hazen	158	541
Hottah	180	917
Kamilukuak	266	635
Kaminak	53	601
Kaminuriak	92	549
Kasba	336	1342
Keller	247	394
La Martre	265	1777
Mac Alpine	176	448
Mackay	431	1062
Mallery	158	479
Netilling	29	5543
Netsilik	8	391
Nonacho	319	785
Nueltin	278	2279
Point	375	702
Princess Mary	116	523
Selwyn	398	717
Snowbird	359	505
South Henik	184	513
Takiyuak	381	1080
Tathlina	280	572
Tebesjuak	146	575
Tehek	133	482
Trout	503	505
Tulemalu	279	668
Wholdaia	364	679
Yathkyed	141	1448

THE GREAT LAKES

Lake	Elevation (m)	Length (km)	Breadth (km)	Maximum depth (m)	Total area (km²)	Area on Canadian side of boundary (km²)
Superior	183	563	257	405	82,103	28,749
Michigan	176	494	190	281	57,757	—
Huron	176	332	295	229	59,570	36,001
St. Clair	175	42	39	6	1114	694
Erie	174	388	92	64	25,667	12,769
Ontario	75	311	85	244	19,011	10,049

CLIMATE

City	Hours of bright sun-shine	Days with no sun-shine	Days with measur-able precipi-tation	Days with measur-able snowfall	Days with freezing precipi-tation	Days with snow cover of 1 or more inches	Mean daily minimum temper-ature in January	Mean daily maximum temper-ature in July	Days with minimum temper-ature below 0°C	Hours with temper-ature greater than 30°C	Hours with temper-ature below -20°C
Toronto	2046	65	134	45	10	62	-10.5	27.0	154	72.8	32.1
Montreal	1959	67	163	60	14	116	-14.3	26.3	153	30.5	130.2
Vancouver	1931	76	161	12	1	7	-0.4	22.2	57	1.3	0
Ottawa	1995	69	152	60	16	116	-15.6	26.4	166	48.8	190.1
Winnipeg	2232	48	121	58	11	126	-23.2	25.9	195	56.2	884.0
Edmonton (municipal airport)	2246	44	121	60	6	121	-19.4	23.4	192	15.1	517.3
Québec	1827	81	164	67	16	139	-16.2	25.1	177	16.6	232.0
Hamilton (Royal Botanical Gardens)	2035	62	125	38	12	–	-8.6	27.2	134	–	–
Calgary	2207	41	113	61	3	99	-16.7	23.5	201	17.0	415.0
Kitchener	1950	–	113	31	–	–	-9.9	26.9	154	–	–
London	1929	69	165	66	12	–	-9.9	26.4	152	35.0	31.7
Halifax (Shearwater)	1945	77	142	36	17	60	-7.8	21.9	142	2.0	7.8
Windsor	–	–	137	42	8	43	-7.8	27.8	135	80.5	7.7
Victoria (Gonzales Heights)	2183	51	142	9	<1	5	+1.9	20.8	18	1.3	0
Sudbury	–	–	155	73	19	139	-18.4	24.8	183	15.9	396.0
Regina	2278	45	114	58	12	130	-22.6	26.2	207	91.4	744.0
St. John's	1458	108	210	85	36	120	-7.0	20.1	177	0	2.1
Oshawa (Pickering)	–	–	122	32	–	–	-10.9	25.7	–	–	–
Saskatoon	2402	44	103	54	9	130	-23.9	25.9	206	64.8	845.9
Saint John	1819	88	164	58	11	82	-12.6	22.3	175	1.9	92.0
Sherbrooke	1901	72	170	63	9	–	-17.8	24.6	161	12.9	292.7
Trois-Rivières	–	–	152	53	7	–	-17.4	26.2	177	–	–
Kingston	2113	51	130	39	–	–	-11.6	25.0	148	–	–

WINDCHILL

The combination of near-freezing temperatures with strong winds can have the same chilling effect as a much lower temperature on a windfree day. For example, a -15°C temperature with a 40 km/h wind has a cooling effect on the skin similar to that of a -40°C temperature in calm conditions.

The windchill factor is a measure of the combined chilling effect of wind and temperature. The calculation of the factor—based on the rate at which water will cool in combined low temperature and wind conditions—applies equally to the human body. Since the combination of wind and low temperatures can cause frostbite on exposed skin and a life-threatening loss of body heat (hypothermia), the chart of windchill factors below, accompanied by the conditions they produce, will serve as a guide for necessary precautionary measures.

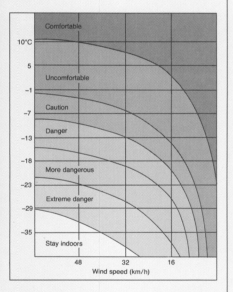

HUMIDITY AND COMFORT

When high temperatures and high humidity (large amounts of water vapor in the air) combine, hot, muggy, and often oppressive weather conditions are the result. On the chart below, the degrees of such discomfort are expressed numerically. The "humidex" reading relates humid air to dry air equivalent on a comfort/discomfort scale. If 75 percent relative humidity is combined with a temperature of 32°C, then the humidex reading equals an uncomfortable 46°C.

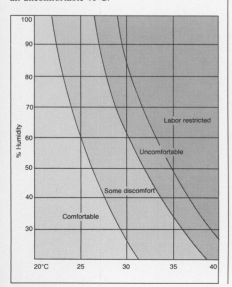

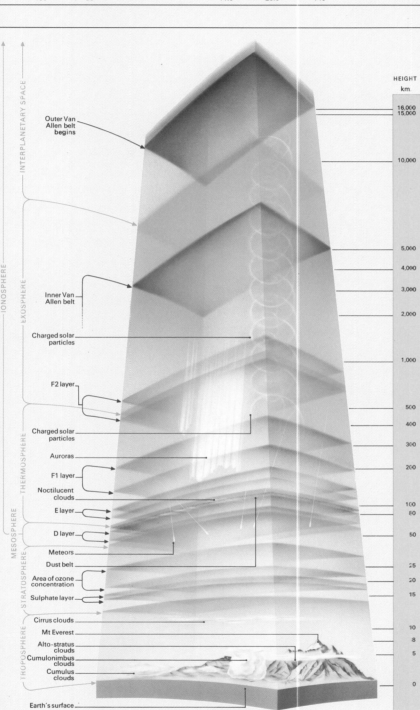

ZONES OF THE ATMOSPHERE

The earth's atmosphere consists of several gaseous layers called the troposphere, the stratosphere, the mesosphere, and the thermosphere and exosphere, also known as the ionosphere. The layers interact not only with one another, but also with the sun's radiation which passes through them. They differ greatly in temperature and are subject to constant chemical and physical change.

The **troposphere** is not warmed directly by the sun's heat, which travels in wavelengths too short to be absorbed by the carbon dioxide and water vapor composing this layer. Instead, it receives indirect heat which bounces off the earth's surface in longer infrared wavelengths. Temperature falls in the troposphere by about 6°C for every kilometre rise in altitude.

In contrast with the troposphere, the temperature of the **stratosphere** increases with height (from about -60°C to 0°C). Ozone, a poison formed by the reaction of oxygen atoms with ultraviolet radiation,

is present in the stratosphere in large quantities. The ozone layer has two important effects: it traps weather in the troposphere, since convection currents cannot rise through the warmer air above it, and it blocks out ultraviolet radiation from the sun, which would otherwise destroy all living organisms.

From 50 km to 80 km, in a layer called the **mesosphere**, the temperature cools again so that it reaches -100°C at its outer boundary. Beyond is the **ionosphere**, composed of nitrogen and oxygen broken down into atoms by intense solar radiation. The atoms, once stripped of their electrons, produce electrically charged particles (ions), which interact with each other as well as with Earth's gravity and magnetic field.

The ionosphere and interplanetary space interact as well. The latter is affected by the earth and its magnetic field. This field deflects the constant barrage of electrically charged particles from the sun to form a region called the **magnetosphere**.

THE WANDERING NORTH POLE

Centuries of conjecture and exploration preceded the discovery of the north magnetic pole. Today we know that electric currents deep within the earth's molten core produce the planet's magnetic field. But in the Middle Ages a legend arose that a huge magnetic mountain far in the north attracted compass needles and any ships unfortunate enough to pass close by. It was found that the compass did not point exactly to the true north, but a little to one side. In a 1546 map, Gerardus Mercator erroneously located a magnetic pole near Bering Strait, while his world map of 1569 offered two positions.

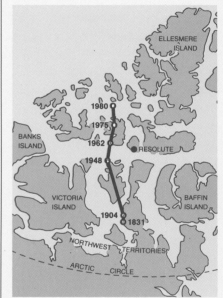

Track of the north magnetic pole, 1831 to 1980

In 1600, English physician William Gilbert first put forth the theory that the earth itself was the magnet and that this explained the action of the compass and not the far-off mountain. After years of polar exploration, the north magnetic pole was finally located by James Ross in 1831—fully 2100 km from the geographic north pole. But, like the travelers it has guided, the magnetic pole is in continuous motion, and the cairn Ross built at Cape Adelaide no longer marks the spot. The pole's average daily movement is clockwise in an ellipse centered on its mean position, which drifts from year to year. It is now some 1400 km from the north geographic pole.

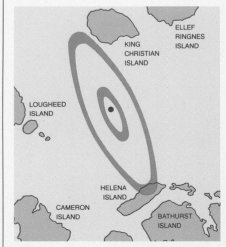

Daily motion of the north magnetic pole in early 1980: inner ring, movement on a magnetically quiet day; outer ring, movement on an active day.

METEORITES

Meteorites are fragments of rock or metal which have fallen to earth from space. Most have formed in a zone located between Mars and Jupiter, the product of collisions between hundreds of planet-like bodies called asteroids. They vary in size from that of a pinhead to masses of several tonnes.

Meteorites are of three types: stony, stony iron and iron. The stony specimens resemble ordinary rocks and are the most commonly found. The stony irons are an almost equal mix of metal and silicate minerals, while the iron meteorites are generally heavy masses of metal containing smaller amounts of silicate minerals.

Though all meteorites resemble natural rocks and minerals, they have distinctive features which aid in their identification. They generally possess a fusion crust, a soft outer layer dull black to brown in color. Stony meteorites contain metallic iron and rounded granules of silicate minerals called chondrules, while iron and stony iron meteorites contain large amounts of nickel and are strongly magnetic.

Almost a third of the world's largest meteorite craters (measuring a kilometre or more in diameter) have been found in this country. In 1979, the Canadian inventory of such craters was 24.

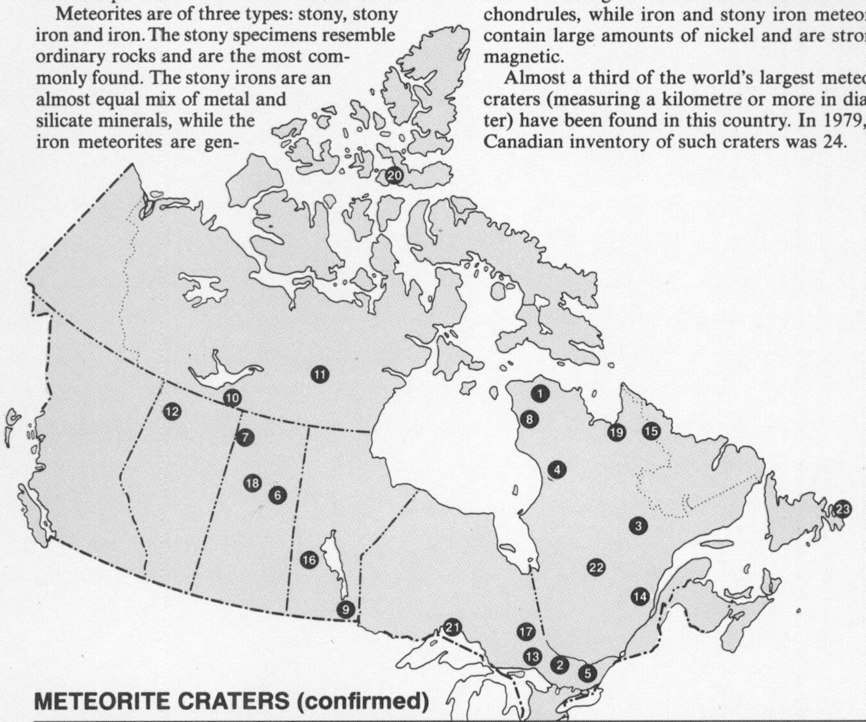

METEORITE CRATERS (confirmed)

Location	Diameter (km)	Age (million years)	Surface features
1. New Quebec Crater, Que.	3.2	5	rimmed circular lake
2. Brent, Ont.	3.8	450 ± 30	sediment-filled, shallow depression
3. Manicouagan, Que.	70	210 ± 4	circumferal lake, central elevation
4. a) Clearwater East, Que.	22	290 ± 20	circular lake
b) Clearwater West, Que.	32	290 ± 20	island ring in circular lake
5. Holleford, Ont.	2	550 ± 100	sediment-filled, shallow depression
6. Deep Bay, Sask.	12	100 ± 50	circular bay
7. Carswell, Sask.	37	485 ± 50	discontinuous circular ridge
8. Lac Couture, Que.	8	420	circular lake
9. West Hawk Lake, Man.	2.7	100 ± 50	circular lake
10. Pilot Lake, N.W.T.	6	<300	circular lake
11. Nicholson Lake, N.W.T.	12.5	<450	irregular lake with islands
12. Steen River, Alta.	25	95 ± 7	none, buried to 200 metres
13. Sudbury, Ont.	140	1840 ± 150	elliptical basin
14. Charlevoix, Que.	46	360 ± 25	semi-circular trough, central elevation
15. Mistastin Lake, Labrador	28	38 ± 4	elliptical lake and central island
16. Lake St. Martin, Man.	23	225 ± 40	none, buried and eroded
17. Lake Wanapitei, Ont.	8.5	37 ± 2	lake-filled, partly circular
18. Gow Lake, Sask.	5	<200	lake and central island
19. Lac La Moinerie, Que.	8	400	lake-filled, partly circular
20. Haughton, N.W.T.	20	15	shallow, circular depression
21. Slate Islands, Ont.	30	350	islands are central uplift of submerged structure
22. Ile Rouleau, Que.	4	<300	island is central uplift of submerged structure
23. Conception Bay, Nfld.	?	500	4 localities of shocked rock

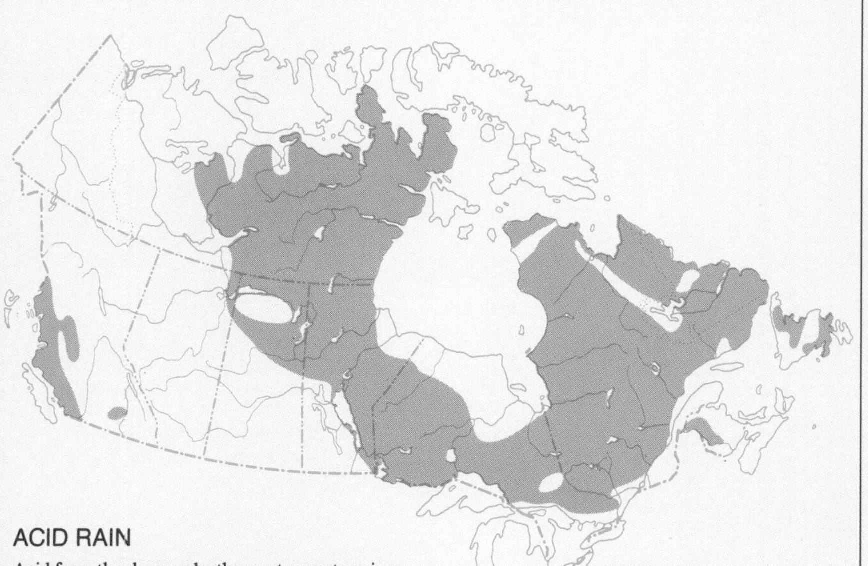

ACID RAIN

Acid from the sky may be the most urgent environmental problem in North America today. It corrodes metals, damages forests, crops and soils, and kills lakes by halting the spawning of fish and destroying other aquatic organisms. A serious health hazard, it can damage throat and lung tissues.

Acid precipitation is caused largely by the burning of fossil fuels. When sulphur dioxide and nitrogen oxide are emitted, a chemical reaction with water vapor in the atmosphere produces corrosive nitric and sulphuric acid that falls as rain or snow. The stronger the acid, the lower the pH. Water has a pH of about 5.6; the acid rain that falls on Canada may be as low as 3 (about as acidic as vinegar).

The industries of eastern North America produce a quarter of the world's man-made sulphur dioxide emissions. Smelting ore, generating power, refining petroleum and manufacturing pulp and paper all contaminate the air with pollutants that can travel thousands of kilometres from their source. some of Canada's acid rain has thus come all the way from Pennsylvania steel mills, while we export a portion of our acid rain to the eastern United States. Some may even be carried as far as Greenland.

Lakes situated on limestone basins are able to neutralize acid rain, but many Canadian lakes lie on granite rocks unable to counteract acidity. Ontario has been the province hardest hit, with some 140 dead or dying lakes and many more threatened. Western Canada has been little affected to date, but lakes in Quebec and the Maritimes are starting to show damage. The best game fish are usually the first to disappear: acid rain has killed all the salmon in seven Nova Scotia rivers.

Control of sulphur dioxide emissions is the only long-term solution to acid rain. Processes have been developed for reducing pollutants, such as washing coal before burning it, or trapping harmful emissions during combustion. But many industries resist expensive innovations until they are forced by government to implement them, and many laws concerning emissions are ambiguous and ineffective. Before the problem of acid rain is solved, international agreements will have to be reached, for this danger threatens the global environment.

WIND: THE BEAUFORT SCALE

In 1805 and 1806, British Admiral Sir Francis Beaufort developed a scale from 0 to 12 to indicate wind strength (originally on ships' sails). Hurricane strength (force 12) he described in fitting naval terms as "that which no canvas could withstand." The scale has since been modified for use on land. Beaufort number 6, for example, is a strong breeze (40 to 50 km/h), which causes umbrellas to turn inside out and large tree branches to sway.

Beaufort Number	Wind Name	Speed (km/h)	Observed Effect of Wind
0	Calm	0–1	Calm. Smoke rises straight up into the air.
1	Light Air	2–5	Weather vanes remain motionless. Smoke drifts slightly with the wind.
2	Light Breeze	6–11	Weather vanes active. You can feel the wind on your face. Leaves rustle.
3	Gentle Breeze	12–19	Light flags fill out with wind. Twigs on trees move.
4	Moderate Breeze	20–29	The wind picks up dust and loose paper. Small tree branches sway.
5	Fresh Breeze	30–39	Waves break on inland waters. Small trees sway in the wind.
6	Strong Breeze	40–50	Using an umbrella becomes difficult. Large tree branches sway.
7	Moderate Gale	51–61	Walking against the wind is difficult. Entire large trees sway.
8	Fresh Gale	62–74	Walking against the wind is almost impossible. Twigs break off trees.
9	Strong Gale	75–87	Shingles blown off house roofs. Some damage to buildings.
10	Whole Gale	88–102	Entire trees blown over and uprooted. Much damage to buildings.
11	Storm	103–118	Severe damage to crops, trees, and property.
12	Hurricane	119+	Widespread, violent destruction.

THE RICHTER SCALE

The Richter scale, devised in 1935 by the American scientist Charles F. Richter, is a measure of the magnitude of an earthquake—an index of each quake's energy at its source.

Though the scale is not a damage indicator as such, the destructiveness of a quake generally coincides with the amount of energy released. Most devastation occurs at the quake's epicentre (the point of the earth's surface directly above the quake). The damage lessens as distance increases from the epicentre.

The Richter scale is graded logarithmically. An increase of one point on the scale indicates a tenfold jump in earthquake magnitude. Magnitude 4, for example, signifies earth tremors of sufficient strength to close open doors and awaken sleepers. Magnitude 5, however, with ten times greater force than 4, denotes vibrations capable of overturning furniture and cracking masonry.

The Modified Richter Scale of Magnitude

Magnitude	Estimated number recorded each year	Estimated damage
10	Possible but never recorded	Would be felt all over the earth
9	"	Felt in most parts of the globe
8 to 8.6	Occur infrequently	Very great damage
7.4 to 7.9	4	Great damage
7.0 to 7.3	15	Serious damage, railway tracks and bridge members bent
6.2 to 6.9	100	Widespread damage to most structures
5.5 to 6.1	500	Moderate to slight damage
4.9 to 5.4	1400	Felt by everyone within the affected area
4.3 to 4.8	4800	Felt by most
3.5 to 4.2	30,000	Felt by a few
2.0 to 3.4	More than 150,000	Not felt but recorded

JET STREAM

Jet streams are tubular ribbons of high-speed winds circling the earth in wavelike patterns generally from west to east. Like narrow currents in a river, jet streams always travel at greater speeds than the air surrounding them. Formed in the tropopause zone of the atmosphere, they may be 450 km wide and 6 km high. Wind speeds can better hurricane intensities, often reaching 400 km/h and more at the core, with velocities decreasing outwards from the centre.

The streams vary in number and differ in the paths they take over the globe according to the earth's seasons. One major jet stream over Canada (*see chart below*) follows a path over Vancouver, Winnipeg, Montréal and Halifax. Eastbound aircraft heading into this stream gain the added push of these strong winds, allowing them to cross the continent at least an hour faster than the same flight westwards.

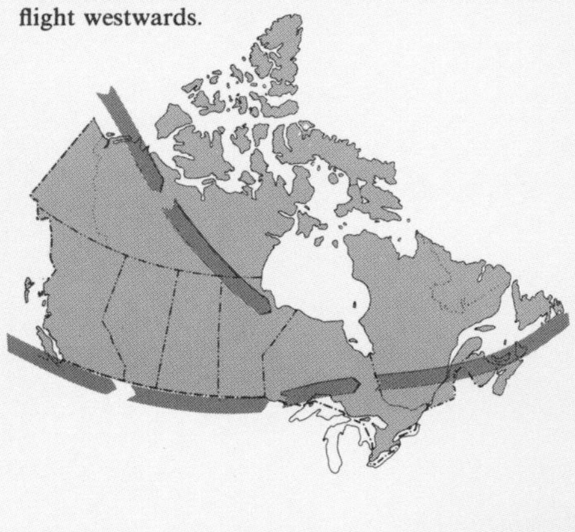

DISCOVERING NATURE

Museums of Natural History

The Provincial Museum of Alberta, Edmonton.
British Columbia Provincial Museum, Victoria.
Manitoba Museum of Man and Nature, Winnipeg.
The New Brunswick Museum, Saint John.
Newfoundland Museum, St. John's.
Nova Scotia Museum, Halifax.
Royal Ontario Museum, Toronto.
Saskatchewan Museum of Natural History, Regina.

Aquaria

Vancouver Public Aquarium, Vancouver.
The Huntsman Marine Laboratory and Aquarium, St. Andrews, N.B.
Fisheries Museum of the Atlantic, Lunenburg, N.S.
Northumberland Fisheries Museum, Pictou, N.S.
Aquarium de Montréal, Montréal.

Botanical Gardens

Devonian Botanic Garden, University of Alberta, Edmonton.
Botanical Gardens, St. George's Island, Calgary, Alta.
Nikka Yuko Centennial Garden, Lethbridge, Alta.
Vandusen Botanical Display Garden, Vancouver.
The Butchart Gardens, Victoria, B.C.
Royal Roads Botanical Garden, Victoria, B.C.
The Botanical Garden, University of British Columbia, Vancouver.
Agriculture Canada Research Station, Morden, Man.
Allan Gardens, Toronto.
Centennial Conservatory, Thunder Bay, Ont.
Royal Botanical Gardens, Hamilton, Ont.
Botanical Gardens of the Federal Government, Central Experimental Farm, Ottawa.
Jardin Botanique de Montréal, Montréal.
Patterson Park Botanical Garden, University of Saskatchewan, Saskatoon, Sask.

Arboreta

Crown Zellerbach Arboretum and Museum, Ladysmith, B.C.
Queen Elizabeth Arboretum, Vancouver.
Woody Plant Test Arboretum, University of Manitoba, Winnipeg.
University of Guelph Arboretum, Guelph, Ont.
Plum Grove Arboretum, Kakabeka Falls, Ont.
Niagara Parks Commission, School of Horticulture, Niagara Falls, Ont.
The Arboretum, Applied Arts Division, Humber College, Rexdale, Ont.
The Arboretum, Lakehead University, Thunder Bay, Ont.
Morgan Arboretum, Macdonald College of McGill University, Ste. Anne de Bellevue, Que.

Zoological Gardens

Calgary Zoo Conservatory, St. George's Island, Calgary, Alta.
Edmonton Valley Zoo, Edmonton.
Kamloops Wildlife Park, Kamloops, B.C.
Stanley Park Zoological Gardens, Vancouver.
Assiniboine Park Zoo, Winnipeg.
Wildlife Park, Shubenacadie, N.S.
Bronte Creek Children's Farm, Burlington, Ont.
Chippewa Park Zoo, Thunder Bay, Ont.
Wasaga Beach Wildlife Park, Wasaga Beach, Ont.
Toronto Island Park and Farm, Toronto Island, Toronto.
Metro Toronto Zoo, West Hill, Ont.
Prince Edward Island Wildlife Park, North Rustico, P.E.I.
Jardin zoologique de la Gaspésie, Bonaventure, Que.
Jardin zoologique de Québec, Charlesbourg, Que.
Société zoologique de Granby, Granby, Que.
Jardin zoologique de Montréal, La Ronde, Ile Sainte-Hélène, Montréal.
Société zoologique de Saint-Félicien Incorporée, Saint-Félicien, Que.
Sleepy Hollow Museum and Game Farm, Abernethy, Sask.
Moose Jaw and District Wild Animal Park, Moose Jaw, Sask.
Forestry Farm Animal Park, Saskatoon, Sask.

Source: Canadian Museums Association

People and Society

HEALTH: Principal causes of death

Heart disease	34.8%
Cancer	21.5
Stroke	9.3
Accidents	6.7
Respiratory	6.5
Arterial disease	3.4
Suicide	1.9
Diabetes	1.8
Cirrhosis of the liver	1.6
Nervous system	1.0
Congenital anomalies	0.9
Other	10.6

LIFE EXPECTANCY, 1977

At birth	Male 70.19 years	Female 77.48 years
1 year	70.24	77.41
2	69.31	76.49
3	68.37	75.53
4	67.42	74.57
5	66.46	73.60
10	61.57	68.71
15	56.70	63.80
20	52.09	58.95
25	47.55	54.10
30	42.90	49.25
35	38.21	44.43
40	33.59	39.67
45	29.11	35.02
50	24.86	30.51
55	20.88	26.14
60	17.23	21.96
65	13.95	18.00
70	11.05	14.33
75	8.55	11.03
80	6.44	8.15
85	4.73	5.81
90	3.39	4.03
95	2.39	2.74
100	1.68	1.84

Population by mother tongue, 1976

Language	No.	%
English	14,122,765	61.4
French	5,887,205	25.6
Baltic	34,190	0.1
Celtic	10,060	—
Chinese	132,560	0.6
Croatian, Serbian, etc.	77,570	0.3
Czech and Slovak	34,955	0.2
Finnish	28,470	0.1
German	476,715	2.1
Greek	91,530	0.4
Indo-Pakistani	58,420	0.3
Inuit (Eskimo)	15,900	0.1
Italian	484,045	2.1
Japanese	15,525	0.1
Magyar (Hungarian)	69,305	0.3
Native Indian	117,110	0.6
Netherlandic and Flemish	122,555	0.5
Polish	99,845	0.4
Portuguese	126,535	0.5
Romanian	8755	—
Russian	23,480	0.1
Scandinavian	59,410	0.3
Semitic languages	37,100	0.2
Spanish	44,130	0.2
Ukrainian	282,060	1.2
Yiddish	23,440	0.1
Other	63,950	0.3
Not stated	445,020	1.9
Total	22,992,605	100.0

Dominant Mother Tongue, 1976

Province or Territory	Language	%
British Columbia	English	84.8
	German	3.4
	Chinese	1.9
	French	1.6
Alberta	English	82.4
	German	4.4
	Ukrainian	3.6
	French	2.5
Saskatchewan	English	79.0
	German	6.8
	Ukrainian	5.1
	French	2.9
	Native	2.3
Manitoba	English	72.7
	German	7.3
	Ukrainian	6.0
	French	5.5
	Native	2.5
Ontario	English	79.7
	French	5.7
	Italian	3.8
	German	1.9
Quebec	French	81.5
	English	13.1
	Italian	2.0
New Brunswick	English	65.4
	French	33.6
Prince Edward Island	English	93.6
	French	5.6
Nova Scotia	English	93.8
	French	4.5
Newfoundland	English	98.8
	French	0.5

POPULATION: Estimated population by province, June 1, 1976 (thousands)

Province or Territory	0-4 years Male	0-4 years Female	5-9 years Male	5-9 years Female	10-14 years Male	10-14 years Female	15-19 years Male	15-19 years Female
Newfoundland	29.7	28.1	32.1	30.8	34.3	32.7	32.1	30.6
Prince Edward Island	5.0	4.6	5.4	5.1	6.8	6.3	6.5	6.4
Nova Scotia	33.7	31.9	36.9	34.9	44.1	42.2	44.6	42.1
New Brunswick	29.7	28.5	31.7	29.8	37.6	35.8	38.0	35.8
Quebec	227.3	215.4	248.6	237.0	318.7	303.4	338.4	327.9
Ontario	311.7	295.5	342.0	325.8	409.3	389.5	412.7	395.3
Manitoba	42.5	39.8	43.3	41.6	49.8	48.0	51.0	49.3
Saskatchewan	38.0	36.7	39.9	38.1	48.6	46.8	49.4	47.5
Alberta	78.4	74.6	83.5	79.5	95.6	91.6	99.0	94.3
British Columbia	88.6	84.6	99.2	94.8	116.2	111.7	121.0	116.9
Yukon Territory	1.1	1.0	1.1	1.0	1.2	1.1	1.1	1.0
Northwest Territories	2.8	2.7	2.9	2.7	2.7	2.6	2.2	2.1
CANADA	886.6	843.4	966.7	921.1	1164.6	1111.7	1196.0	1149.3

Province or Territory	20-24 years Male	20-24 years Female	25-34 years Male	25-34 years Female	35-44 years Male	35-44 years Female	45-54 years Male	45-54 years Female
Newfoundland	26.0	26.1	41.6	40.4	26.9	25.1	23.4	22.0
Prince Edward Island	5.0	5.0	8.3	8.3	6.0	5.7	5.3	5.3
Nova Scotia	38.2	37.2	62.3	60.4	42.9	42.0	39.1	40.8
New Brunswick	32.0	31.8	51.1	48.7	33.5	33.1	31.1	32.3
Quebec	229.2	299.3	515.6	514.2	363.9	365.0	330.3	346.3
Ontario	368.3	376.1	652.0	650.2	488.0	476.5	466.1	470.8
Manitoba	47.0	47.0	75.8	74.0	53.0	51.8	52.0	54.5
Saskatchewan	41.7	39.7	59.3	56.7	45.9	44.9	48.6	48.3
Alberta	94.6	91.4	150.0	144.0	106.0	99.8	93.2	90.2
British Columbia	110.3	111.2	200.8	194.9	144.8	135.1	134.4	134.3
Yukon Territory	1.2	1.2	2.5	2.2	1.5	1.1	1.1	0.8
Northwest Territories	2.2	2.1	4.0	3.5	2.4	2.0	1.6	1.3
CANADA	1065.8	1068.0	1823.2	1797.3	1314.9	1282.1	1226.2	1246.8

Province or Territory	55-64 years Male	55-64 years Female	65-69 years Male	65-69 years Female	70 + years Male	70 + years Female	All ages Male	All ages Female
Newfoundland	20.0	19.0	7.0	6.8	10.2	12.6	283.4	274.3
Prince Edward Island	5.0	5.3	2.1	2.1	3.9	5.1	59.3	59.0
Nova Scotia	36.2	38.3	14.0	14.5	22.0	30.3	414.2	414.4
New Brunswick	27.3	28.5	10.6	11.1	16.8	22.6	339.3	337.9
Quebec	237.9	264.7	84.5	101.6	120.3	175.0	3084.6	3149.8
Ontario	336.5	359.2	120.5	140.4	189.8	288.2	4096.9	4167.6
Manitoba	45.8	48.6	17.5	19.3	30.4	39.4	508.0	513.5
Saskatchewan	44.1	45.0	17.4	17.4	31.9	35.5	464.8	456.6
Alberta	66.4	68.2	23.9	24.6	41.8	47.6	932.4	905.7
British Columbia	107.3	118.4	40.7	44.2	69.2	88.0	1232.5	1234.1
Yukon Territory	0.6	0.4	0.2	0.1	0.2	0.2	11.7	10.1
Northwest Territories	0.9	0.7	0.3	0.2	0.3	0.3	22.4	20.2
CANADA	928.1	996.4	338.5	382.3	536.9	744.6	11,449.5	11,543.1

Demographic profile, 1977

Province or Territory	Marriages	Divorces	Births	Deaths
Newfoundland	3895	456	11,110	3323
Prince Edward Island	892	136	1969	1095
Nova Scotia	6304	1802	12,374	6955
New Brunswick	5275	961	11,515	5202
Quebec	47,230	14,501	95,690	43,011
Ontario	67,730	19,735	122,758	60,645
Manitoba	8238	2085	16,716	8262
Saskatchewan	7237	1474	16,547	7809
Alberta	17,976	5843	34,401	11,584
British Columbia	21,540	8251	36,030	18,788
Yukon Territory	204	59	432	123
Northwest Territories	266	67	1191	212
CANADA	186,787	55,370	360,733	167,009

Families and persons per family, 1966, 1971 & 1976

Province or Territory	1966 Families	1971 Families	1976 Families	1966 Persons per family	1971 Persons per family	1976 Persons per family
Newfoundland	97,011	107,960	124,655	4.6	4.4	4.0
Prince Edward Island	22,728	24,170	27,560	4.2	4.0	3.7
Nova Scotia	166,237	179,595	200,480	4.0	3.8	3.5
New Brunswick	129,307	139,720	162,035	4.3	4.0	3.7
Quebec	1,229,301	1,353,655	1,540,400	4.2	3.9	3.5
Ontario	1,657,933	1,877,055	2,104,540	3.7	3.6	3.4
Manitoba	222,735	234,595	251,975	3.8	3.6	3.4
Saskatchewan	216,674	241,840	225,685	3.9	3.7	3.5
Alberta	331,158	380,220	448,765	3.9	3.7	3.5
British Columbia	445,297	530,830	628,445	3.6	3.5	3.3
Yukon Territory	7885	10,530	4930	4.5	4.3	4.3
Northwest Territories			8425			
CANADA	4,526,266	5,053,170	5,727,875	3.9	3.7	3.5

Population: urban and rural

Province or Territory	Urban No.	Urban %	Rural nonfarm No.	Rural nonfarm %	Farm No.	Farm %	Total rural No.	Total rural %	Total population No.
Newfoundland	328,270	58.9	228,365	40.9	1095	0.2	229,460	41.1	557,725
Prince Edward Island	43,880	37.1	62,155	52.6	12,190	10.3	74,345	62.9	118,220
Nova Scotia	462,590	55.8	353,815	42.7	12,170	1.5	365,985	44.2	828,510
New Brunswick	354,420	52.3	311,150	46.0	11,685	1.7	322,835	47.7	677,220
Quebec	4,932,755	79.1	1,110,580	17.8	191,110	3.1	1,301,690	20.9	6,234,445
Ontario	6,708,520	81.2	1,276,890	15.4	279,055	3.4	1,555,945	18.8	8,264,465
Manitoba	714,480	69.9	205,570	20.2	101,455	9.9	307,025	30.1	1,021,510
Saskatchewan	511,330	55.5	217,425	23.6	192,570	20.9	409,995	44.5	921,325
Alberta	1,379,165	75.0	269,225	14.7	189,650	10.3	458,875	25.0	1,838,035
British Columbia	1,897,085	76.9	525,950	21.3	43,575	1.8	569,525	23.1	2,466,605
Yukon Territory	13,310	61.0	8525	39.0	—	—	8525	39.0	21,835
Northwest Territories	21,165	49.7	21,435	50.3	10	—	21,445	50.3	42,610
CANADA	17,366,970	75.5	4,591,070	20.0	1,034,560	4.5	5,625,630	24.5	22,992,605

ETHNIC GROUPS, 1971

Country of origin	No.	%
British Isles	9,624,115	44.6
French	6,180,120	28.7
Other European	4,959,680	23.0
Austrian	42,120	0.2
Belgian	51,135	0.2
Czech and Slovak	81,870	0.4
Danish	75,725	0.4
Finnish	59,215	0.3
German	1,317,200	6.1
Greek	124,475	0.6
Hungarian	131,890	0.6
Icelandic	27,905	0.1
Italian	730,820	3.4
Jewish	296,945	1.4
Lithuanian	24,535	0.1
Netherlands	425,945	2.0
Norwegian	179,290	0.8
Polish	316,425	1.5
Portuguese	96,875	0.4
Romanian	27,375	0.1
Russian	64,475	0.3
Spanish	27,515	0.1
Swedish	101,870	0.5
Ukrainian	580,660	2.7
Yugoslavian	104,950	0.5
Other	70,460	0.3
Asiatic	285,540	1.3
Chinese	118,815	0.6
Japanese	37,260	0.2
Other	129,460	0.6
Other	518,850	2.4
Eskimo	17,550	0.1
Native Indian	295,215	0.2
Negro	34,445	0.2
West Indian	28,025	0.1
Other and not stated	143,620	0.7
Total	21,568,310	100.0

INDIAN POPULATION, 1977

Province or Territory	Number of Bands	Membership
Atlantic	29	11,093
Quebec	39	30,175
Ontario	115	66,057
Manitoba	57	43,349
Saskatchewan	68	44,986
Alberta	41	35,162
British Columbia	194	54,318
District of Mackenzie	16	7541
Yukon	14	3217
CANADA	573	295,898

INUIT POPULATION, 1979

Northwest Territories	15,712
Rest of Canada	7580
CANADA	23,292

CANADIAN COLLEGES AND UNIVERSITIES

(including founding dates and enrolment)

Acadia University; Wolfville, N.S.; 1838 (3489).
Alberta, The University of; Edmonton, Alta.; 1906 (22,006).
Athabasca University; Edmonton, Alta.; 1970 (2273).
Bishop's University; Lennoxville, Que.; 1843 (983).
Brandon University; Brandon, Man.; 1899 (2044).
Brescia College (Univ. of Western Ontario); London, Ont.; 1919 (340).
British Columbia, University of; Vancouver, B.C.; 1890 (25,355).
Brock University; St. Catharines, Ont.; 1964 (4803).
Calgary, The University of; Calgary, Alta.; 1945 (13,682).
Campion College (Univ. of Regina); Regina, Sask.; 1917 (19).
Cape Breton, College of; Sydney, N.S.; 1974 (1530).
Carleton University; Ottawa, Ont.; 1942 (14,642).
Concordia University; Montréal, Que.; 1974 (21,968).
Dalhousie University; Halifax, N.S.; 1818 (8924).
Collège Dominicain de Philosophie et de Théologie; Ottawa, Ont.; 1900 (836).
Guelph, University of; Guelph, Ont.; 1964 (10,416).
Huron College (Univ. of Western Ontario); London, Ont.; 1863 (587).
King's College, University of (Dalhousie Univ.); Halifax, N.S.; 1789 (361).
King's College (Univ. of Western Ontario); London, Ont.; 1966 (1022).
Lakehead University; Thunder Bay, Ont.; 1946 (4121).
Laurentian University of Sudbury; Sudbury, Ont.; 1960 (6002).
Laval, Université; Québec, Que.; 1852 (23,872).
Lethbridge, University of; Lethbridge, Alta.; 1967 (2070).
Luther College (Univ. of Regina); Regina, Sask.; 1926 (226).
McGill University; Montréal, Que.; 1821 (19,956).
McMaster University; Hamilton, Ont.; 1887 (13,315).
Manitoba, The University of; Winnipeg, Man.; 1877 (19,370).
Memorial University of Newfoundland; St. John's, Nfld.; 1949 (9385).
Moncton, Université de; Moncton, N.B.; 1963 (6449).
Montréal, Université de; Montréal, Que.; 1876 (35,566).
Mount Allison University; Sackville, N.B.; 1843 (1416).
Mount Saint Vincent University; Halifax, N.S.; 1925 (2289).
New Brunswick, University of; Fredericton, N.B.; 1785 (7907).
Nova Scotia Agricultural College; Truro, N.S.; 1905 (462).
Nova Scotia College of Art and Design; Halifax, N.S.; 1887 (565).
Nova Scotia Technical College; Halifax, N.S.; 1907 (752).
Ontario Institute for Studies in Education, The; Toronto, Ont.; 1965 (enrollment included with Univ. of Toronto).
Ottawa, University of; Ottawa, Ont.; 1848 (18,705).
Prince Edward Island, University of; Charlottetown, P.E.I.; 1969 (2206).
Québec, Université du Québec; Que.; 1968 (42,673).
Queen's University at Kingston; Kingston, Ont.; 1841 (12,864).
Regina, The University of; Regina, Sask.; 1974 (7004).
Royal Military College of Canada; Kingston, Ont.; 1874 (717).
Ryerson Polytechnical Institute; Toronto, Ont.; 1948 (11,291).
Sainte-Anne, Université; Church Point, N.S.; 1890 (650).
St. Francis Xavier University; Antigonish, N.S.; 1853 (2894).
St. Jerome's College, The University of (Univ. of Waterloo); Waterloo, Ont.; 1864 (1010).
St. John's College (Univ. of Manitoba); Winnipeg, Man.; 1849 (enrollment included with Univ. of Manitoba).
St. Mary's University; Halifax, N.S.; 1802 (3736).
St. Michael's College, University of (Univ. of Toronto); Toronto, Ont.; 1852 (2730).
St. Paul University; Ottawa, Ont.; 1965 (730).
St. Paul's College (Univ. of Manitoba); Winnipeg, Man.; 1926 (enrollment included with Univ. of Manitoba).
St. Thomas More College (Univ. of Saskatchewan); Saskatoon, Sask.; 1936 (680).
St. Thomas University; Fredericton, N.B.; 1910 (1219).
Saskatchewan, The University of; Saskatoon, Sask.; 1907 (13,371).
Sherbrooke, Université de; Sherbrooke, Que.; 1954 (9763).
Simon Fraser University; Burnaby, B.C.; 1963 (11,637).
Sudbury, The University of; Sudbury, Ont.; 1913 (enrollment added with Laurentian Univ.).
Toronto, University of; Toronto, Ont.; 1837 (47,166).
Trent University; Peterborough, Ont.; 1963 (3254).
Trinity College, University of (Univ. of Toronto); Toronto, Ont.; 1852 (1074).
Victoria, University of; Victoria, B.C.; 1963 (7746).
Victoria University (Univ. of Toronto); Toronto, Ont.; 1836 (2893).
Waterloo, University of; Waterloo, Ont.; 1959 (19,248).
Western Ontario, The University of; London, Ont.; 1878 (21,293).
Wilfred Laurier University; Waterloo, Ont.; 1973 (5978).
Windsor, University of; Windsor, Ont.; 1963 (10,219).
Winnipeg, The University of; Winnipeg, Man.; 1967 (deriving from Manitoba College, 1871, and Wesley College, 1877), (4650).
York University; Downsview, Ont.; 1959 (22,842).

Source: Association of Universities and Colleges of Canada.

EDUCATION: Schools, teachers and enrolment

	Canada	Nfld.	P.E.I.	N.S.	N.B.	Que.	Ont.	Man.	Sask.	Alta.	B.C.	Yukon	N.W.T.
No. of Schools:													
Elementary/secondary	15,442	688	76	617	484	2990	5186	824	1064	1529	1881	22	70
Post-secondary:													
Non-university	186	6	2	14	9	73	30	8	3	20	21	—	—
University	65	1	1	10	4	7	22	7	3	5	5	—	—
Total	15,693	695	79	641	497	3070	5238	839	1070	1554	1907	22	70
No. of Teachers:													
Elementary/secondary	269,768	7711	1426	11,083	7812	68,514	97,526	12,460	11,392	22,590	28,035	271	667
Post-secondary:													
Non-university	19,678	225	70	368	208	9500	5004	356	367	1867	1713	—	—
University	32,634	791	120	1635	1073	7340	12,803	1648	1405	2842	2977	—	—
Trade	6112	602	129	696	344		1997	370	252	730	992	—	—
Total	328,192	9329	1745	13,782	9437	85,354	117,330	14,834	13,416	28,029	33,717	271	667
Enrolment:													
Elementary/secondary	5,286,017	153,565	27,853	196,811	160,673	1,297,419	1,981,826	232,470	220,979	447,249	545,062	5247	12,903
Post-secondary:													
Non-university	247,034	1960	770	2768	1656	136,123	64,499	3019	2397	17,063	16,779	—	—
University	367,973	6161	1390	17,932	10,904	84,017	154,396	17,017	14,446	31,171	30,539	—	—
Total	5,901,024	161,686	30,013	217,511	173,233	1,517,559	2,200,721	252,506	237,822	495,483	592,380	5247	12,903

RELIGION IN CANADA

The history of religion in Canada dates back to the summer day in 1534 when Jacques Cartier planted a 9-metre wooden cross on the Gaspé Coast on behalf of the King of France and in the name of Christ. Since then, the growth of Canada has been intertwined inextricably with the development of its religious faiths.

Missionary activity did not begin, however, until Champlain's arrival in 1603, and it was only on June 24, 1615, that the Roman Catholic Church held its first recorded celebration of the mass in New France, on the Island of Montréal. In spite of hardships and the brutal martyrdom of some of the early missionaries, men and women of the Récollet, Jesuit, Capuchin and Grey Nun Orders came to the New World to spread the faith, teach and heal.

Canada's largest religious faith is Roman Catholicism. There are 10,202,625 Roman Catholics in Canada (1971 Census). The Roman Catholic hierarchy in Canada consists of an Apostolic Delegate representing the Pope; archbishops appointed to supervise the ecclesiastical provinces, of whom the most eminent are Cardinals; and bishops appointed to govern the dioceses. In modern Canada, the Roman Catholic Church has played an important role in education, and social movements.

Protestantism traces its Canadian beginnings to the late 16th and early 17th centuries when French Huguenots settled on the shores of the St. Lawrence River and the Bay of Fundy. A number of Congregationalists came to Nova Scotia from New England between 1749 and 1752. The Methodist population was significant by 1772, and most of the early Methodist clergy were circuit riders. Church services were conducted either by these itinerant ministers or by lay preachers.

Denomination	1951 No.	1951 %	1971 No.	1971 %
Adventist	21,398	0.2	28,590	0.1
Anglican Church of Canada	2,060,720	14.7	2,543,180	11.8
Baptist	519,585	3.7	667,245	3.1
Christian Reformed	—	—	83,390	0.4
Greek Orthodox	172,271	1.2	316,605	1.5
Jehovah's Witnesses	34,596	0.2	174,810	0.8
Jewish	204,836	1.5	276,025	1.3
Lutheran	444,923	3.2	715,740	3.3
Mennonite	125,938	0.9	181,800	0.8
Mormon	32,888	0.2	66,635	0.3
Pentecostal	95,131	0.7	220,390	1.0
Presbyterian	781,747	5.6	872,335	4.0
Roman Catholic	6,069,496	43.3	9,974,895	46.2
Salvation Army	70,275	0.5	119,665	0.6
Ukrainian (Greek) Catholic	191,051	1.4	227,730	1.1
United Church of Canada	2,867,271	20.5	3,768,800	17.5
Other	317,303	2.2	1,330,480	6.2
Total	14,009,429	100.0	21,568,310	100.0

The largest Protestant denomination, the United Church of Canada with 3,768,800 members, is an amalgamation of Methodist, Presbyterian and Congregationalist churches. The government of the United Church is presbyterial; its presbytery and conference courts consisting equally of ministerial and lay representatives. The chief executive officer, called a moderator, is elected biennially at a General Council.

The Anglican Church of Canada is part of the international Anglican communion, which became a separate stream in Christendom in the 16th century. Anglican church government, like Roman Catholic, is episcopalian; it is structured into ecclesiastical provinces which are divided into dioceses. One of the archbishops is designated Primate of All Canada, but the real authority rests in each diocese. The head of each diocese is a bishop in apostolic succession elected by lay and clerical representatives of all parishes at a diocesan synod. The church has 2,543,180 members in Canada.

The earliest recorded church service in Canada was an Anglican Eucharist celebrated by Robert Wolfall aboard explorer Martin Frobisher's ship off Baffin Island in the summer of 1578. A few years later, in 1583, Sir Humphrey Gilbert claimed Newfoundland for England, and the Church of England became its official church. Anglican clergy were associated with the Hudson's Bay Company in 1683, but it was apparently not until the early 18th century that permanent church buildings appeared—in Newfoundland and Nova Scotia. The Canadian Anglican communion became an autonomous church in 1893.

The fourth largest denomination in Canada is the Presbyterian Church, comprising 872,335 members. When the United Church of Canada was formed, one Presbyterian in three remained out of union, thus preserving a distinct Canadian Presbyterian denomination. Presbyterianism is a form of church government in which the church is administered by presbyters or elders. In Canada, the Presbyterian Church is headed by a moderator, committees of a general assembly, and eight synods.

The Lutheran Church, also a product of the Reformation, appeared early in Canada. Capt. Jens Munck and 36 men from Denmark, including Rev. Rasmus Jensen, landed on Hudson Bay near the Churchill River in August, 1619. By Easter, only three had survived an outbreak of scurvy. In 1740, however, Lutheran services began in Nova Scotia. More Lutheran immigrants from the United States and Europe settled in the Maritimes, Ontario and the West in the 19th century. The church's creed is based on the theology of 16th-century reformers Martin Luther and Philip Melanchthon. In Canada, there are three branches, unified by a Lutheran Council, each with a president as its chief officer. There are 715,740 members.

HOUSING

Housing type		1966	1971	1976
Total occupied private dwellings:	No.	5,180,475	6,034,510	7,166,095
	%	100.0	100.0	100.0
Single detached	No.	3,234,125	3,591,770	3,991,540
	%	62.4	59.5	55.7
Single attached	No.	401,755	679,590	587,180
	%	7.8	11.3	8.2
Apartment and duplex	No.	1,516,420	1,699,045	2,412,660
	%	29.3	28.2	33.7
Mobile	No.	28,180	64,105	174,710
	%	0.5	1.1	2.4
Tenure:				
Owned	No.	3,269,970	3,636,925	4,431,235
	%	63.1	60.3	61.8
Rented	No.	1,910,505	2,397,580	2,734,860
	%	36.9	39.7	38.2

TYPE OF DWELLING, BY PROVINCE AND CITY, 1976

Province or Territory	Total private dwellings	Single detached	Apartments, row houses and duplexes	Single detached	Apartments
Newfoundland	131,665	95,925	31,455	72.9	23.9
Prince Edward Island	32,930	24,315	7000	73.8	21.3
Nova Scotia	243,000	162,550	66,570	66.9	27.4
New Brunswick	190,435	125,830	52,585	66.1	27.6
Quebec	1,894,110	745,595	1,120,630	39.4	59.2
Ontario	2,634,620	1,494,465	1,117,365	56.7	42.4
Manitoba	328,005	219,950	100,140	67.1	30.5
Saskatchewan	291,155	224,510	55,755	77.1	19.2
Alberta	575,280	372,420	174,610	64.7	30.4
British Columbia	828,290	516,485	268,690	62.4	32.4
Yukon Territory	6495	3425	2165	52.7	33.4
Northwest Territories	10,020	6070	2865	60.6	28.7
CANADA	7,166,095	3,991,540	2,999,840	55.7	41.9
Metropolitan area:					
Calgary, Alta.	155,155	90,765	62,475	58.5	40.3
Chicoutimi, Que.	33,850	16,165	17,080	47.8	50.5
Edmonton, Alta.	179,635	100,345	77,350	55.9	43.1
Halifax, N.S.	81,845	39,335	39,030	48.1	47.7
Hamilton, Ont.	172,510	101,470	70,805	58.8	41.0
Kitchener, Ont.	87,880	47,305	40,455	53.8	46.0
London, Ont.	91,770	51,505	39,830	56.1	43.4
Montreal, Que.	924,635	223,365	698,750	24.2	75.6
Oshawa, Ont.	41,445	24,935	16,440	60.2	39.7
Ottawa-Hull, Ont., Que.	225,105	94,105	129,445	41.8	57.5
Québec, Que.	164,600	60,065	103,180	36.5	62.7
Regina, Sask.	49,790	33,310	16,195	66.9	32.5
Saint John, N.B.	34,065	14,780	17,635	43.4	51.8
St. Catharines, Ont.	97,395	67,860	29,205	69.7	30.0
St John's, Nfld.	36,800	18,475	17,690	50.2	48.1
Saskatoon, Sask.	44,800	28,315	16,045	63.2	35.8
Sudbury, Ont.	45,710	26,080	19,030	57.1	41.6
Thunder Bay, Ont.	37,270	26,240	10,735	70.4	28.8
Toronto, Ont.	909,530	361,560	547,435	39.8	60.2
Vancouver, B.C.	407,560	231,915	171,080	56.9	42.0
Victoria, B.C.	81,005	46,995	32,680	58.0	40.3
Windsor, Ont.	80,190	53,705	25,565	67.0	31.9
Winnipeg, Man.	197,305	115,400	81,090	58.5	41.1

AVERAGE WEEKLY EARNINGS, 1961–79

Source and region	Average weekly earnings (dollars)				
	1961	1976	1977	1978	1979
Industry:					
Forestry	79.02	287.36	312.81	326.48	360.29
Mining and milling	95.57	317.13	348.12	376.40	419.39
Manufacturing	81.55	241.19	266.04	285.67	311.19
Durables	88.22	257.46	284.66	305.97	331.44
Nondurables	76.17	225.60	248.39	266.13	291.33
Construction	86.93	331.02	369.88	389.64	422.28
Transportation, communications and other utilities	82.47	262.02	291.14	313.28	341.45
Trade	65.54	176.59	190.96	201.79	218.75
Finance, insurance and real estate	72.82	213.71	229.57	248.43	272.10
Service	57.87	160.49	171.28	108.00	193.26
Province or Territory:					
Newfoundland	71.06	221.63	242.43	248.36	271.64
Prince Edward Island	54.91	170.88	187.73	196.72	209.77
Nova Scotia	63.72	193.21	212.09	223.72	245.33
New Brunswick	63.62	202.56	223.34	232.89	256.49
Quebec	75.67	222.41	244.77	262.89	284.35
Ontario	81.30	228.72	249.46	264.04	285.57
Manitoba	73.66	208.55	227.95	239.71	259.00
Saskatchewan	74.38	214.87	235.61	250.44	275.79
Alberta	80.29	236.89	261.96	276.32	306.79
British Columbia	84.99	259.52	284.13	301.26	327.14
Yukon	—	304.17	351.49	364.93	393.31
Northwest Territories	—	290.97	306.03	310.32	355.85

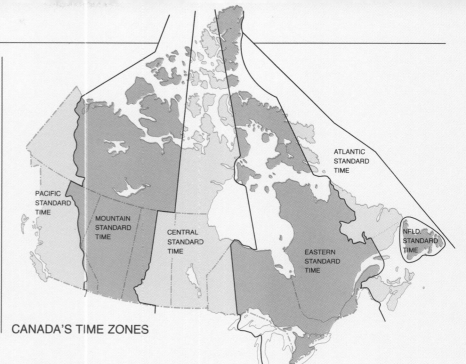

CANADA'S TIME ZONES

PERSONAL EXPENDITURE, 1971–78

Goods and services	Millions of dollars		
	1971	1975	1978
Food, beverages and tobacco	12,148	20,757	27,833
Clothing and footwear	4143	7155	9537
Gross rent, fuel and power	10,582	16,445	24,638
Furniture, furnishings, household equipment and operation	5295	9884	13,078
Medical care and health service	1619	2896	3971
Transportation and communication	8014	14,292	19,652
Recreation, entertainment, education and cultural services	5364	9972	13,844
Personal goods and services	8355	15,062	21,277
Other	96	532	1390
Total	55,616	96,995	135,220

LEISURE: Enjoying free time (percentage of adults involved in activity, Feb. 1978)

Watching TV	Listening to radio	Listening to records or tapes	Reading newspapers	Reading magazines	Reading books	Participation in sports or exercise	Formal instruction	Hobby or craft	Art activity	Music activity
95%	83%	50%	83%	58%	43%	47%	11%	33%	13%	12%

LEISURE: Arts/Culture (percentage of adults involved in activity, Feb. 1978)

Museums	Art galleries	Public libraries	Book-stores	Movies	Popular music performances	Classical music performances	Live theatre
6%	6%	21%	40%	33%	11%	7%	9%

HOUSEHOLDS WITH SELECTED FACILITIES, 1953–78

Year	Refrigerators %	Home freezers %	Washing machines %	Clothes dryers %	Dishwashers %	Sewing machines %	Vacuum cleaners %	Air conditioners %
1953	66.3	2.2	—	—	—	23.4	48.0	—
1961	92.0	13.1	14.2	14.7	1.5	44.8	69.0	1.7
1965	95.8	22.6	23.1	27.4	2.7	52.4	74.9	2.2
1971	98.2	34.0	39.4	43.1	8.6	64.3	82.8	5.3
1975	99.3	41.8	52.1	51.6	15.2	65.4	86.5	12.4
1978	99.4	47.2	59.1	56.0	23.8	—	—	15.3

CRIME

Types of crime	1973 No.	1973 Rate (per 100,000 people)	1977 No.	1977 Rate (per 100,000 people)	1973–77 Rate % change
All crimes of violence:	117,764	533.0	135,745	582.8	9.2
Murder	475	2.1	624	2.6	23.8
Rape	1594	7.2	1886	8.0	11.1
Robbery	13,166	59.6	19,491	83.6	40.1
All property crimes:	883,329	371.6	1,059,688	4544.9	20.5
Break and enter	198,043	896.3	270,659	1160.8	29.5
Theft over $200	63,383	286.9	114,000	488.9	70.4
All other offences under the criminal code:	336,312	1522.	458,587	1968.9	14.9
Prostitution	3573	16.2	2843	12.1	-25.3
Gaming and betting	3011	13.6	3487	14.9	9.6
Total	1,302,938	5897.1	1,654,020	7094.0	20.3

RADIO, TELEVISION AND OTHER BROADCASTING OUTLETS, 1979

Province or Territory	AM	FM	TV	LPRT	SW	NT	Total
Newfoundland	28	28	117	17	1		191
Prince Edward Island	4	1	3				8
Nova Scotia	23	13	46	17	1	1	101
New Brunswick	19	7	27	11	1	1	66
Quebec	92	87	148	43	1	8	379
Ontario	110	116	115	58	1	11	411
Manitoba	20	33	57	6		2	118
Saskatchewan	20	19	80	1		1	121
Alberta	44	39	110	17	1	2	213
British Columbia	79	59	296	78	2	6	520
Yukon Territory	3	1	18	11			33
Northwest Territories	7	13	28	14			62
Total	449	416	1045	273	8	32	2223

LPRT: Low-power relay transmitter. SW: Short wave. NT: Network.

NEWSPAPERS: Number and circulation, Sept. 1978

Province or Territory	AM news-papers	PM news-papers	Total daily news-papers	Total AM circulation	Total PM circulation	Number of Sunday news-papers	Total Sunday circulation
Alberta	2	7	9	78,486	344,706	5	411,448
British Columbia	3	14	17	452,523	556,556	3	418,618
Manitoba	0	8	8	—	271,400	2	267,477
New Brunswick	3	3	6	122,500	127,593	2	84,444
Newfoundland	1	2	3	8,759	41,367	2	58,065
Nova Scotia	2	4	6	129,012	175,944	1	8,638
Ontario	5	44	49	913,716	1,725,370	11	1,816,474
Prince Edward Island	1	2	3	22,300	33,303	–	–
Quebec	5	7	12	601,459	510,469	10	1,222,629
Saskatchewan	0	4	4	—	131,842	–	–
Yukon–Northwest Territories	–	–	–	–	–	–	–
Total	22	95	117	2,328,755	3,918,550	36	4,287,793

LIBRARIES

The provinces govern the operation of public libraries in Canada, defining the services they provide and their means of financial support. Individual municipalities can organize and maintain their own public libraries, or join with others to form regional libraries according to provincial guidelines.

In 1977, Canadians borrowed more than 114 million books from 760 public libraries employing 1690 professional librarians. Total book stocks, including material classified as books, numbered more than 39 million.

LIBRARIES

Province or Territory	Libraries reporting	Book stock	Circulation
Nfld.	4	751,946	2,051,716
P.E.I.	1	173,676	523,349
N.S.	12	944,714	3,367,238
N.B.	6	841,788	2,236,314
Que.	100	6,059,263	13,955,576
Ont.	365	19,713,454	53,547,349
Man.	29	1,425,515	4,422,395
Sask.	10	1,867,051	5,810,347
Alta.	167	3,303,536	9,828,385
B.C.	64	4,301,057	18,662,518
Yukon	1	127,633	128,984
N.W.T.	1	88,290	111,523
CANADA	760	39,577,923	114,648,094

COMMUNICATIONS IN THE HOME

	No. of households	% of households
Television[1]	7,121,000	97.3
Color	5,294,000	72.3
Black & white	3,819,000	52.2
Radio (AM & FM)[2]	7,206,000	98.4
Telephone[3]	7,063,000	96.5
Cable television	3,625,000	49.5
Total Canadian households	7,320,000	100.0

[1]Some households have more than one television.
[2]Includes households with one receiver or more.
[3]Includes households with one telephone or more.

VACATION TRAVEL

The chart below shows how the automobile has dropped in popularity since 1966 as the means of travel for vacationing Canadians. About 73 percent of vacation trips were taken by car in 1966 compared with only 55 percent in 1980. Air travel, however, has jumped in popularity. Today, 30 percent of vacationers travel by plane, compared with only 10 percent in 1966.

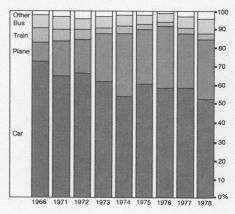

"HELLO MONTRÉAL! VANCOUVER IS SPEAKING"

Although Alexander Graham Bell was born in Scotland and died an American citizen, his life, and the development of the telephone, were closely associated with Canada. It was in his parents' home in Brantford, Ont., in 1874, that Bell first discussed his new invention with his father, and there in 1875 that he wrote the patent specifications for "The Electric Speaking Telephone."

On Aug. 3, 1876, Bell tested his new invention at the Dominion Telegraph office in Mount Pleasant, Ont. In the first transmission between separate buildings, he heard his uncle recite Shakespeare's "To be, or not to be:..." One week later the first long distance call was made—from Brantford to Paris, 13 kilometres away. The Bell Telephone Company was formed and by November 1877 it had four clients. The fifth was Prime Minister Alexander Mackenzie, whose application was predated to make him officially the first subscriber.

The development of a Canadian telephone system was sporadic at best. Rural customers in the early 1900s were even encouraged to erect their own telephone lines. But in 1916, the first Montréal to Vancouver call was placed (partially over American lines) amid much pomp and ceremony. Enthusiastic Vancouver newspapers headlined the story, "Hello Montreal! Vancouver is speaking."

The privately financed TransCanada Telephone System, inaugurated in 1932, allowed voices to traverse the country for the first time without using American facilities. Although most telephone calls are now channeled by microwave or satellite, there are still enough cables and conventional wire lines in use in Canada to circle the Equator 2333 times.

CANADIAN-BORN SPORTS

Canada's long sporting tradition has borrowed much from Indian and European games. Lacrosse, adopted as our national sport in 1867, evolved from an Indian game called *baggataway*. Contests between different tribes involved as many as 400 players, lasted several days and resulted in broken limbs, even death. Settlers began to play a scaled-down, less violent version in the 1840s, and during the last half of the 19th century, it became Canada's most popular sport.

The first organized hockey game was probably played in 1855 at Kingston, Ont., by members of a regiment of the Royal Canadian Rifles, although English troops had played a variation of the game, called shinny, as early as 1783. McGill University students wrote the first official rules about 1880, however, they have been greatly changed since then. A position called rover has been eliminated, for example, and forward passes were legalized in the early 1900s. In 1893, Governor General Lord Stanley presented a cup to Canada's top amateur team. Since 1912, the cup has been awarded to professionals, and since 1926, to the champions of the National Hockey League. The International Ice Hockey Federation, formed by five European countries in 1908, now includes more than 30 nations.

Canoeing and snowshoeing—practical means of transportation invented by native Indians—were turned into sports by early Canadians. Voyageurs took time out from the fur trade to run rapids and race for fun. An annual challenge match on Lake Winnipeg drew as many as 100 canoes to compete in contests that sometimes lasted 40 hours. In the 1870s, canoe clubs were founded in Montréal and Toronto; annual regattas featured singles, doubles and half-mile war canoe races. The sport was made an Olympic event in 1936.

The Montreal Snowshoe Club, founded in 1840, attracted hundreds to torchlight parades, snowball battles and treks to outlying villages. The standard garb was a tuque, blanket coat and sash; the top speed, 11 kilometres an hour.

STANLEY CUP WINNERS PRIOR TO FORMATION OF N.H.L. IN 1917

Season	Champions	Coach
1892-93	Montreal A.A.A.	
1893-94	Montreal A.A.A.	
1894-95	Montreal Victorias	Mike Grant*
1895-96	Winnipeg Victorias (February)	J. C. G. Armytage
1895-96	Montreal Victorias (December, 1896)	Mike Grant*
1896-97	Montreal Victorias	Mike Grant*
1897-98	Montreal Victorias	F. Richardson
1898-99	Montreal Shamrocks	H. J. Trihey*
1899-1900	Montreal Shamrocks	H. J. Trihey*
1900-01	Winnipeg Victorias	D. H. Bain
1901-02	Montreal A.A.A.	C. McKerrow
1902-03	Ottawa Silver Seven	A. T. Smith
1903-04	Ottawa Silver Seven	A. T. Smith
1904-05	Ottawa Silver Seven	A. T. Smith
1905-06	Montreal Wanderers	Cecil Blachford*
1906-07	Kenora Thistles (January)	Tommy Phillips*
1906-07	Montreal Wanderers (March)	Cecil Blachford
1907-08	Montreal Wanderers	Cecil Blachford
1908-09	Ottawa Senators	Bruce Stuart*
1909-10	Montreal Wanderers	Pud Glass*
1910-11	Ottawa Senators	Bruce Stuart*
1911-12	Quebec Bulldogs	C. Nolan
**1912-13	Quebec Bulldogs	Joe Malone*
1913-14	Toronto Blueshirts	Scotty Davidson*
1914-15	Vancouver Millionaires	Frank Patrick
1915-16	Montreal Canadiens	George Kennedy
1916-17	Seattle Metropolitans	Pete Muldoon

***Victoria defeated Quebec in challenge series. No official recognition.*
**In the early years the teams were frequently run by the Captain.*

STANLEY CUP WINNERS

Season	Champions	Coach
1917-18	Toronto Arenas	Dick Carroll
1918-19	No decision	
1919-20	Ottawa Senators	Pete Green
1920-21	Ottawa Senators	Pete Green
1921-22	Toronto St. Pats	Eddie Powers
1922-23	Ottawa Senators	Pete Green
1923-24	Montreal Canadiens	Leo Dandurand
1924-25	Victoria Cougars	Lester Patrick
1925-26	Montreal Maroons	Eddie Gerard
1926-27	Ottawa Senators	Dave Gill
1927-28	New York Rangers	Lester Patrick
1928-29	Boston Bruins	Cy Denneny
1929-30	Montreal Canadiens	Cecil Hart
1930-31	Montreal Canadiens	Cecil Hart
1931-32	Toronto Maple Leafs	Dick Irvin
1932-33	New York Rangers	Lester Patrick
1933-34	Chicago Black Hawks	Tommy Gorman
1934-35	Montreal Maroons	Tommy Gorman
1935-36	Detroit Red Wings	Jack Adams
1936-37	Detroit Red Wings	Jack Adams
1937-38	Chicago Black Hawks	Bill Stewart
1938-39	Boston Bruins	Art Ross
1939-40	New York Rangers	Frank Boucher
1940-41	Boston Bruins	Cooney Weiland
1941-42	Toronto Maple Leafs	Hap Day
1942-43	Detroit Red Wings	Jack Adams
1943-44	Montreal Canadiens	Dick Irvin
1944-45	Toronto Maple Leafs	Hap Day
1945-46	Montreal Canadiens	Dick Irvin
1946-47	Toronto Maple Leafs	Hap Day
1947-48	Toronto Maple Leafs	Hap Day
1948-49	Toronto Maple Leafs	Hap Day
1949-50	Detroit Red Wings	Tommy Ivan
1950-51	Toronto Maple Leafs	Joe Primeau
1951-52	Detroit Red Wings	Tommy Ivan
1952-53	Montreal Canadiens	Dick Irvin
1953-54	Detroit Red Wings	Tommy Ivan
1954-55	Detroit Red Wings	Jimmy Skinner
1955-56	Montreal Canadiens	Toe Blake
1956-57	Montreal Canadiens	Toe Blake
1957-58	Montreal Canadiens	Toe Blake
1958-59	Montreal Canadiens	Toe Blake
1959-60	Montreal Canadiens	Toe Blake
1960-61	Chicago Black Hawks	Rudy Pilous
1961-62	Toronto Maple Leafs	Punch Imlach
1962-63	Toronto Maple Leafs	Punch Imlach
1963-64	Toronto Maple Leafs	Punch Imlach
1964-65	Montreal Canadiens	Toe Blake
1965-66	Montreal Canadiens	Toe Blake
1966-67	Toronto Maple Leafs	Punch Imlach
1967-68	Montreal Canadiens	Toe Blake
1968-69	Montreal Canadiens	Claude Ruel
1969-70	Boston Bruins	Harry Sinden
1970-71	Montreal Canadiens	Al MacNeil
1971-72	Boston Bruins	Tom Johnson
1972-73	Montreal Canadiens	Scotty Bowman
1973-74	Philadelphia Flyers	Fred Shero
1974-75	Philadelphia Flyers	Fred Shero
1975-76	Montreal Canadiens	Scotty Bowman
1976-77	Montreal Canadiens	Scotty Bowman
1977-78	Montreal Canadiens	Scotty Bowman
1978-79	Montreal Canadiens	Scotty Bowman
1979-80	New York Islanders	Al Arbour

THE GREY CUP

1954	Nov. 27	Edmonton	26	Montreal	25
1955	Nov. 26	Edmonton	34	Montreal	19
1956	Nov. 24	Edmonton	50	Montreal	27
1957	Nov. 30	Hamilton	32	Winnipeg	7
1958	Nov. 29	Winnipeg	35	Hamilton	28
1959	Nov. 28	Winnipeg	21	Hamilton	7
1960	Nov. 26	Ottawa	16	Edmonton	6
1961	Dec. 2	Winnipeg	21	Hamilton	14
1962	Dec. 1-2	Winnipeg	28	Hamilton	27
1963	Nov. 30	Hamilton	21	B.C.	10
1964	Nov. 28	B.C.	34	Hamilton	24
1965	Nov. 27	Hamilton	22	Winnipeg	16
1966	Nov. 26	Saskatchewan	29	Ottawa	14
1967	Dec. 2	Hamilton	24	Saskatchewan	1
1968	Nov. 30	Ottawa	24	Calgary	21
1969	Nov. 30	Ottawa	29	Saskatchewan	11
1970	Nov. 28	Montreal	23	Calgary	10
1971	Nov. 28	Calgary	14	Toronto	11
1972	Dec. 3	Hamilton	13	Saskatchewan	10
1973	Nov. 25	Ottawa	22	Edmonton	18
1974	Nov. 24	Montreal	20	Edmonton	7
1975	Nov. 23	Edmonton	9	Montreal	8
1976	Nov. 28	Ottawa	23	Saskatchewan	20
1977	Nov. 27	Montreal	41	Edmonton	6
1978	Nov. 26	Edmonton	20	Montreal	13
1979	Nov. 25	Edmonton	17	Montreal	9

CANADIAN OLYMPIC GOLD MEDALISTS

Summer Games

Athens 1896
No Canadian representation

Paris 1900
3000 m steeplechase, George Orton

St. Louis 1904
56-lb weight, Etienne Desmarteau
Football, Galt Football Club
Golf, George S. Lyon
Lacrosse, Winnipeg Shamrocks

London 1908
200 m, Robert Kerr
Shooting, clay pigeon, W.H. Ewing
Lacrosse, Canadian team

Stockholm 1912
10,000 m walk, George Goulding
Swimming, 400 m, George Ritchie Hodgson
Swimming, 1500 m, George Ritchie Hodgson

Antwerp 1920
110 m hurdles, Earl Thompson
Boxing, welterweight, Albert Schneider

Paris 1924
No gold medal winner

Amsterdam 1928
100 m, Percy Williams
200 m, Percy Williams
400 m relay, women, Canadian team
High jump, women, Ethel Catherwood

Los Angeles 1932
High jump, Duncan McNaughton
Boxing, bantamweight, Horace Gwynne

Berlin 1936
Canoeing, Canadian singles, Francis Amyot

London 1948
No gold medal winner

Helsinki 1952
Shooting, clay pigeon, George Patrick Généreux

Stockholm-Melbourne 1956
Rowing, coxswainless fours, University of British Columbia
Shooting, small-bore rifle, Gerard Ouellette

Rome 1960
No gold medal winner

Tokyo 1964
Rowing, coxswainless pairs, George Hungerford, Roger Charles Jackson

Mexico 1968
Equestrian, prix des nations jumping event, James Day, Jim Elder, Tom Gayford

Munich 1972
No gold medal winner

Montréal 1976
No gold medal winner

Moscow 1980
No Canadian representation

Winter Games

Antwerp 1920
Ice hockey, Winnipeg Falcons

Chamonix 1924
(First Official Winter Games)
Ice hockey, Toronto Granites

Saint-Moritz 1928
Ice hockey, University of Toronto Grads

Lake Placid 1932
Figure skating, men, Montgomery Wilson
Speed skating, women, 500 m, Jean Wilson
Ice hockey, Winnipeg Monarchs

Garmisch-Partenkirchen 1936
No gold medal winner

Saint-Moritz 1948
Figure skating, women, Barbara Ann Scott
Ice hockey, R.C.A.F. Flyers

Oslo 1952
Ice hockey, Edmonton Mercurys

Cortina D'Ampezzo 1956
No gold medal winner

Squaw Valley 1960
Skiing, slalom, women, Anne Heggveit
Figure skating, pairs, Barbara Wagner, Bob Paul

Innsbruck 1964
Bobsled, four-man Canadian team

Grenoble 1968
Skiing, giant slalom, women, Nancy Greene

Sapporo 1972
No gold medal winner

Innsbruck 1976
Skiing, giant slalom, women, Kathy Kreiner

Lake Placid, 1980
No gold medal winner

MUSEUMS (National)

Canadian War Museum, Ottawa. (Artifacts and displays related to Canada's military past)

National Museum of Man, Ottawa. (Art and artifacts in the fields of archaeology, ethnology, physical anthropology, ethnolinguistics, ethnohistory, folklore and the history of Canada)

National Museum of Natural Sciences, Ottawa. (Botany, mineral sciences, vertebrate paleontology, vertebrate zoology and invertebrate zoology)

National Museum of Science and Technology, Ottawa. (Transportation, aviation, agriculture, shipping, industrial technologies, physics and astronomy).

MUSEUMS (Provincial)

British Columbia: British Columbia Provincial Museum, Victoria; Vancouver Centennial Museum, Vancouver.

Yukon and Northwest Territories: Northern Life Museum and National Exhibition Centre, Fort Smith, N.W.T.

Alberta: Provincial Museum of Alberta, Edmonton; Glenbow-Alberta Institute, Calgary.

Saskatchewan: Saskatchewan Museum of Natural History, Regina.

Manitoba: Manitoba Museum of Man and Nature, Winnipeg.

Ontario: Royal Ontario Museum, Toronto; Ontario Science Centre, Toronto.

Quebec: Musée du Québec, Québec; McCord Museum/Musée McCord, Montréal; Musée des Beaux-Arts de Montréal/Montreal Museum of Fine Arts, Montréal.

New Brunswick: New Brunswick Museum, Saint John.

Nova Scotia: Nova Scotia Museum, Halifax.

Prince Edward Island: Confederation Centre Art Gallery and Museum, Charlottetown; Musée Acadien/Acadian Museum, Miscouche.

Newfoundland: Newfoundland Museum, St. John's.

Source: Canadian Museums Association

THE ARTS

Dance Companies (National)

Grands Ballets Canadiens, Les, Montréal (classical ballet)
National Ballet of Canada, Toronto (ballet)
Royal Winnipeg Ballet, Winnipeg (classical ballet/modern ballet)

Dance Companies (by Province)

Alberta:
Alberta Ballet Company, Edmonton (classical ballet/modern ballet)
Alberta Contemporary Dance Theatre, Edmonton (modern dance/experimental dance)

British Columbia:
Anna Wyman Dance Theatre, Vancouver (modern dance)
Fulcrum, Vancouver (experimental dance)
Mountain Dance Theatre, Burnaby (modern dance)
Pacific Ballet Theatre, Vancouver (ballet, classical and modern)
Paula Ross Dancers, Vancouver (modern dance)
Prism Dance Theatre, Vancouver (modern dance)

Manitoba:
Contemporary Dancers, Winnipeg (modern dance)

Ontario:
Ballet Ys of Canada, Toronto (ballet/modern ballet)
Dance Plus Four, Kitchener (modern dance)
Danny Grossman Dance Company, Toronto (modern dance)
Groupe de la Place Royale, Le, Ottawa (modern dance/experimental)
Marijan Bayer City Ballet, The, Toronto (classical ballet/ modern ballet)
Ottawa Dance Theatre, Ottawa (ballet/modern dance/jazz dance)
Toronto Dance Theatre, The, Toronto (modern dance)

Quebec:
Ballets Jazz de Montréal, Les, Montréal (jazz ballet)
Compagnie de Danse Eddy Toussaint, Montréal (contemporary ballet)
Danse-Partout, Aberdeen (modern dance)
Groupe Nouvelle Aire, Montréal (modern ballet)
Sortilèges Troupe Folklorique, Les, Montréal (Quebec folk dance)
Troupe de Danse Pointépiénu, La, Montréal (modern dance)

Saskatchewan:
Pavlychenko Folklorique Ensemble, Saskatoon (Ukrainian/folk/classical ethnic)
Regina Modern Dance Works, Regina (modern dance)

THEATRE

British Columbia:
Arts Club Theatre, Vancouver
Bastion Theatre Company, Victoria
Belfry, The, Victoria
Caravan Stage Company, Armstrong
Citystage, Vancouver
Frederic Wood Theatre, University of B.C., Vancouver
Tamahnous Theatre Workshop Society, Vancouver
Vancouver East Cultural Centre Theatre, Vancouver
Vancouver Playhouse, The, Vancouver
Western Canada Theatre Company, Kamloops

Yukon:
Frantic Follies Theatre, Whitehorse

Alberta:
Citadel Theatre, The, Edmonton
Loose Moose Theatre Company, Calgary
Lunchbox Theatre, Calgary
Northern Light Theatre, Edmonton
Stage West, Edmonton
Theatre Calgary, Calgary
Theatre Network, Edmonton
Theatre 3, Edmonton

Saskatchewan:
Globe Theatre, Regina
Persephone Theatre, Saskatoon
Stage West, Regina
25th Street House Theatre, Saskatoon

Manitoba:
Cercle Molière, Le, Saint-Boniface
Manitoba Theatre Centre, Winnipeg
Manitoba Theatre Workshop, Winnipeg
Neighbourhood Theatre, The, Winnipeg
Rainbow Stage, Winnipeg

Ontario:
Actor's Lab (Théâtre de l'Homme), Hamilton
Black Theatre Canada, Toronto
Centre Stage Theatre, London
Factory Theatre Lab, Toronto
Great Canadian Theatre Company, Ottawa
Hamilton Place Theatre, Hamilton
Magnus Theatre North-West, Thunder Bay
National Arts Centre Theatre, Ottawa
New Theatre, Toronto
O'Keefe Centre, Toronto
Penguin Theatre Company, Ottawa
Phoenix Theatre, Toronto
Press Theatre, St. Catharines
Road Show Theatre Company, The, Guelph

A TRIP ACROSS CANADA, 1912

Completion of the Trans-Canada Highway in 1967 has made cross-country travel safe and enjoyable. It was more difficult in 1912, when Englishman Thomas Wilby attempted the journey. On August 27, the wheels of his spanking new Reo automobile were backed into the Atlantic Ocean near Halifax, and Wilby and his chauffeur F.V. Haney were off.

The trip was a series of mishaps and near-disasters. In Québec, the heavily packed Reo was unable to climb a steep, cobbled street. Haney calmly turned the car around and inched up the hill backwards. Near North Bay, a pair of horses were hitched to the car to pull it from a sandy ditch. Later, the roadless wilderness north of Lake Superior blocked their way. Wilby transported the car to Sudbury by rail, and across Lake Superior by boat.

The Prairies awed Wilby, who wrote, "It was grand and large . . . the real West at last!" In contrast to the flat Prairie tracks, the roads of British Columbia were winding, dangerous trails. While Wilby was driving along the Fraser River at night, the acetylene headlights of the car went out. A young hitchhiker had to lie on the hood of the car dangling an oil lamp to guide the way. Finally, 52 days from Halifax, the wheels of the Reo were edged close to the ocean near Port Alberni on Vancouver Island, and a flask of Atlantic water was emptied into the Pacific.

BALLET IN CANADA

Canada's ballet companies are among the nation's finest arts treasures. The Royal Winnipeg Ballet, often referred to as "Canada's Bolshoi," was the first Commonwealth troupe to earn the title of "royal" in 1953. It was founded as the Winnipeg Ballet Club in 1938 by Gweneth Lloyd, an English ballet teacher, and one of her former pupils, Betty Hey Farrally. Miss Lloyd began to choreograph works that might appeal to people who had never seen a ballet. Among her 21 pieces is *Kilowatt Magic*, a tribute to Manitoba's hydroelectric development.

Over the years the troupe has maintained its blend of classic and experimental productions. For a company of fewer than 30 dancers, the repertoire is surprisingly diverse. There is a saloon western (*Les Whoops-de-doo*), the world's first rock ballet (*Ballet High* performed with the musical group Lighthouse), ballet set to the poetry of Leonard Cohen, a multimedia version of *The Ecstasy of Rita Joe*, and even Agnes de Mille's haunting *Fall River Legend*, which is performed in North America by only one other company, the American Ballet Theater. Among many firsts for the Royal Winnipeg Ballet—the company has mounted 50 original productions—was the troupe's 1977 North American premiere of Argentinian choreographer Oscar Araiz' fantasy, *The Unicorn, the Gorgon and the Manticore*.

The National Ballet of Canada was founded in 1951 in Toronto as the eastern branch of the Royal Winnipeg Ballet. Its repertoire includes classics from Balanchine, de Valois and Ashton, along with more recent works by Bruhn, Neuneier and Nureyev. The troupe's regular tours through Europe and its frequent New York performances have earned it worldwide renown.

Les Grands Ballets Canadiens, a Montréal-based company founded in 1958, performs classics and new works such as the rock ballet *Tommy* set to the music of the British group The Who. The company also established the Académie des Grands Ballets Canadiens as a permanent school to train dancers and choreographers.

Regional groups give ballet national expression. Among them are Les Ballets Jazz and the Compagnie de Danse Eddy Toussaint of Montréal, the Toronto-based Marijan Bayer City Ballet, the Alberta Ballet Company of Edmonton and Vancouver's avant-garde Prism Dance Theatre.

Royal Alexandra Theatre, Toronto
Second City Theatre, Toronto
Shaw Festival Theatre, Niagara-on-the-Lake
Stratford Festival Theatre, Stratford
Sudbury Theatre Centre, Sudbury
Tarragon Theatre, Toronto
Theatre Aquarius, Hamilton
Theatre 5, Kingston
Theatre London, London
Théâtre Passe Muraille, Toronto
Théâtre du P'tit Bonheur, Toronto
Toronto Arts Productions
　(St. Lawrence Centre), Toronto
Toronto Free Theatre, Toronto
Toronto Truck Theatre, Toronto
Toronto Workshop Productions, Toronto
Young People's Theatre, Toronto

Quebec:
Centaur Theatre, Montréal
Compagnie de Quat'Sous, Montréal
Compagnie des Deux Chaises, La, Montréal
Compagnie Jean Duceppe, Montréal
Festival Lennoxville Theatre, Lennoxville
Grand Théâtre de Québec, Québec
Montréal Theatre Lab, Montréal
Patriote, Le, Montréal
Phoenix Theatre, Town of Mount Royal
Piggery Theatre, The, North Hatley
Place des Arts Theatre, Montréal
Rallonge, La, Montréal
Saidye Bronfman Centre Theatre, Montréal
Studio Theatre da Silva, Le, Ste-Sophie-de-Lacorne
Théâtre d'Aujourd'hui, Montréal
Théâtre de la Manufacture, Le, Montréal
Théâtre Denise Pelletier
　(Nouvelle Compagnie Théâtrale), Montréal
Théâtre du Nouveau Monde, Montréal
Théâtre du Rideau Vert, Montréal
Théâtre du Trident, Québec
Théâtre du Vieux Québec, Haute Ville
Théâtre International de Montréal
　(La Poudrière), Montréal
Théâtre National de Mime du Québec, Montréal
Théâtre Populaire du Québec, Montréal

New Brunswick:
Theatre New Brunswick, Fredericton

Théâtre Populaire d'Acadie, Caraquet, N.B.

Nova Scotia:
Mermaid Theatre, Wolfville
Neptune Theatre, Halifax
Portus Productions, Halifax

Prince Edward Island:
Charlottetown Summer Festival Theatre, Charlottetown

Newfoundland:
Arts and Culture Centre Theatre, The, St. John's
Mummers Troupe of Newfoundland, St. John's
Newfoundland Travelling Theatre, St. John's
Rising Tide Theatre, St. John's

ORCHESTRAS

British Columbia:
CBC Vancouver Radio (Chamber) Orchestra, Vancouver
Vancouver Symphony Orchestra, Vancouver
Victoria Symphony Orchestra, Victoria

Alberta:
Calgary Philharmonic, Calgary
Edmonton Symphony Orchestra, Edmonton

Saskatchewan:
Regina Symphony, Regina
Saskatoon Symphony, Saskatoon

Manitoba:
Winnipeg Symphony Orchestra, Winnipeg

Ontario:
Hamilton Philharmonic Orchestra, Hamilton
National Arts Centre Orchestra, Ottawa
Toronto Symphony, Toronto

Quebec:
Montreal Symphony Orchestra, Montreal
L'Orchestre Symphonique de Québec, Québec

Nova Scotia:
Atlantic Symphony Orchestra

Prince Edward Island:
Prince Edward Island Symphony Orchestra,
　Charlottetown

Newfoundland:
St. John's Symphony Orchestra

CANADIAN JOURNALISM: PIONEER PUBLISHING

The first newspaper published in what is now Canada was the *Halifax Gazette*. It was founded by John Bushell, an immigrant from Boston, and the first edition came out on Mar. 23, 1752. Two journalists from Rhode Island and New York began the second English-language newspaper, the *Royal Gazette and Nova Scotia Intelligencer*, in 1783 in what is now Saint John, N.B. Another Bostonian brought out the *Royal American Gazette* in Charlottetown in 1787, while the *Upper Canada Gazette* started in 1793 in Newark, now Niagara-on-the-Lake.

The pioneer newspapers depended, to a large degree, on government business for survival. This provided regular, lucrative work: statutes, orders, proclamations and other official documents were the bread and butter of the infant industry. The early English-language newspapers of the Maritimes and Upper Canada were in fact, if not always in name, King's Printers. But in return, the authorities expected newspapers to be loyal, and did not hesitate to close down critical presses and jail offending proprietors. The idea of a free and critical press was not formulated until the mid-nineteenth century, the period marking the advent of responsible government.

The earliest newspapers were small (the *Halifax Gazette* was only the size of a half page of foolscap) and rarely more than four pages long. They were printed on imported paper using wooden flatbed handpresses with movable type. The only illustrations were the odd clumsy woodcut intended to draw attention to an advertisement for a sale of cows or to the search for a runaway slave or debtor. No attempt was made to produce the kind of eye-catching layouts that modern readers take for granted. The printer—the same man who wrote the news, solicited subscriptions and kept the accounts—simply set his material as it came to hand; the entire first section was often printed in order to reuse limited type for the next.

Apart from government-related material, the pioneer newspapers contained outdated news items copied from British and American publications, literary articles, and local advertisements for such things as "choice butter by the firkin," "New England and West India rum," "sheet cork for nets," and beef at fivepence and sixpence a pound.

The first French-language journals included *La Gazette de Québec* (1764) and *La Gazette du commerce et littéraire* (1778)—later renamed the *Montreal Gazette*, which has survived to this day as Montréal's only English-language daily. Some Quebec papers of the 18th and 19th centuries were published in both English and French; in the case of the *Gazette*, items written in English gradually replaced the French. On the whole, French-language newspapers had a harder time than did the English: they did not enjoy government patronage and addressed themselves to rural readers who were generally less interested in supporting them than was the urban population.

As the country opened up, pioneer newspapers mushroomed in the West. British Columbia's first newspaper was the *Victoria Gazette and Anglo-American*, founded by four Californians in 1858. Later that year the successful *British Colonist* was started by eccentric Amor de Cosmos, who was to become British Columbia's second premier. Winnipeg had the *Nor'Wester* in 1859, and Battleford the *Herald* in 1878. The early western newspapers were very different from eastern journals: an expanding, heterogeneous and literate population provided them with a healthy circulation, while advertising ensured them an income independent of government patronage. A new era had arrived; the papers were beginning to see themselves as critics of government, molders of public opinion and champions of truth.

Economy and Industry

Gross National Product ($ billion)

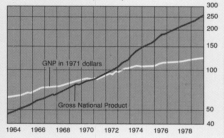

Unemployment (thousands of persons)

Consumer prices (Index 1971 = 100)

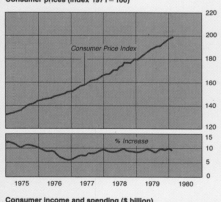

Consumer income and spending ($ billion)

MAJOR ECONOMIC INDICATORS 1978–1980

	1978 ($ million)	Annual percent change	1979 ($ million)	Annual percent change	Forecast 1980 ($ million)	Annual percent change
NATIONAL ACCOUNTS STATISTICS						
Gross National Product	230,407	10.0	260,533	13.1	285,200	9.5
GNP in 1971 dollars	126,127	3.4	129,826	2.9	130,300	0.4
Personal Disposable Income (Personal Income after taxes)	153,954	11.1	172,215	11.9	190,700	10.7
Consumer Expenditure	135,220	10.5	150,831	11.5	167,900	11.3
Consumer Expenditure in 1971 dollars	79,563	3.0	81,399	2.3	82,700	1.6
Corporation Profits (before taxes)	26,069	17.6	34,709	33.1	36,500	5.2
Business Investment (plant, machinery & equipment)	31,262	9.3	37,316	19.4	43,600	16.8
Business Investment in 1971 dollars	17,337	1.0	19,142	10.4	20,400	6.6
House Expenditure	13,358	4.3	13,832	3.5	14,300	3.4
House Expenditure in 1971 dollars	5940	–4.6	5498	–7.4	5100	–7.2
International Transactions Balance	–5345 (deficit)		–5639 (deficit)		–7100 (deficit)	
Exports of Goods and Services	62,296	18.5	76,412	22.7	86,700	13.5
Imports of Goods and Services	67,641	18.1	82,051	21.3	93,800	14.3
OTHER STATISTICS						
Employment (thousands)	9972	3.4	10,369	4.0	10,612	2.3
Unemployment Rate (percent)	8.4	—	7.5	—	8.2	—
Consumer Price Index (1971 = 100)	175.2	9.0	191.2	9.1	210.3	10.0
Industrial Production Index (1971 = 100)	132.4	5.8	137.9	4.2	138.2	0.2
Housing Starts (units)	227,667	–7.3	197,049	–13.4	180,000	–8.7

WEALTH OF THE PROVINCES: Gross Provincial Product, 1978

Province or Territory	Gross Provincial Product	Population	Per Capita GPP
Newfoundland	$2,987.8 million	569,000	$5,250.97
Prince Edward Island	633.7	122,000	5,194.26
Nova Scotia	5,636.1	841,000	6,701.66
New Brunswick	4,396.5	695,000	6,325.90
Quebec	56,180.9	6,283,000	8,941.73
Ontario	89,940.0	8,445,000	10,650.09
Manitoba	9,300.3	1,003,000	9,272.48
Saskatchewan	9,661.5	948,000	10,191.46
Alberta	28,128.9	1,952,000	14,410.30
British Columbia	27,890.7	2,530,000	11,024.00
Yukon and Northwest Territories	705.5	65,000	10,853.85
Total GPP	235,461.9	Total Pop. 23,483,000	Average GPP $10,026.00

Labor Force, 1979

Province or Territory	Labor Force 1979	Employed	Unemployed	Unemployment rate	Participation rate
Newfoundland	207,000	175,000	32,000	15.4	52.7
Prince Edward Island	53,000	47,000	36,000	11.3	59.3
Nova Scotia	352,000	316,000	6000	10.2	56.9
New Brunswick	280,000	249,000	31,000	11.1	55.3
Quebec	2,878,000	2,602,000	277,000	9.6	60.1
Ontario	4,289,000	4,008,000	280,000	6.5	66.6
Manitoba	478,000	453,000	26,000	5.4	63.7
Saskatchewan	433,000	415,000	18,000	4.2	62.6
Alberta	1,015,000	976,000	39,000	3.9	69.4
British Columbia	1,223,000	1,129,000	94,000	7.7	62.7
CANADA	11,207,000	10,369,000	832,000	7.5	63.3

Housing ($ billion)

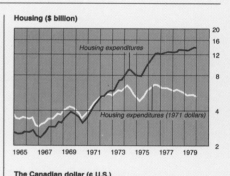

The Canadian dollar (¢ U.S.)

Stock markets (index 1975 = 1000)

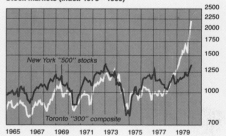

Business investment ($ billion)

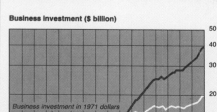

BANKS, 1979

	Nfld.	P.E.I.	N.S.	N.B.	Que.	Ont.	Man.	Sask.	Alta.	B.C.	Yukon	N.W.T.	Can. Total	Outside Can.	Total
Bank of British Columbia									10	35			45	1	46
Bank of Montreal	39	5	34	28	223	492	71	66	132	167	2	3	1262	8	1270
Banque Nationale du Canada	1	2	7	29	755	67	8		3	3			875	8	883
Bank of Nova Scotia	59	10	68	54	95	409	35	47	105	110	1	1	994	83	1077
Canadian Commercial & Industrial Bank				1		1		1	2	1			6	1	7
Canadian Imperial Bank of Commerce	18	9	38	26	214	763	89	110	199	229	6	9	1710	97	1807
Continental Bank of Canada			1		2	5			1	1			10		10
Mercantile Bank of Canada			1	1	2	5	1		2	1			14		14
Northland Bank							1	2	2	1			6		6
Royal Bank of Canada	20	6	84	31	228	587	103	102	148	209	3	3	1524	81	1605
Toronto Dominion Bank	6	2	11	9	98	546	55	49	116	114	2	1	1009	11	1020
Total	143	34	245	178	1617	2875	363	378	720	871	14	17	7455	290	7745

BANKING IN CANADA

Canada has 11 chartered banks (private commercial banks licensed by Parliament), and in the early 1980s they operated more than 7000 branches and offices, including 290 outside the country. Currency and credit are regulated by the central Bank of Canada, which is owned by the federal government. Of the chartered banks' total assets, cash and other liquid assets (such as call loans and government securities) represent approximately 35 percent; short-term business loans, another 35 percent; and agricultural and consumer loans, mortgages and loans to provinces and municipalities, the remaining 30 percent.

CANADA'S LARGEST COMPANIES

Company (head office)	Sales or operating revenue ($ thousand)	% Foreign ownership
General Motors of Canada Ltd. (Oshawa, Ont.)	9,409,838	100
Canadian Pacific Ltd. (Montréal)	8,150,000	35
Ford Motor Co. of Canada (Oakville, Ont.)	7,149,200	89
Imperial Oil Ltd. (Toronto)	6,623,000	71
George Weston Ltd. (Toronto)	5,867,102	—
Bell Canada (Montréal)	5,264,739	4
Alcan Aluminium (Montréal)	5,132,163	61
Massey-Ferguson Ltd. (Toronto)	3,483,424	37
Shell Canada Ltd. (Toronto)	3,436,000	71
Hudson's Bay Co. (Winnipeg)	3,435,209	—
Canadian National Railways (Montréal)	3,294,335	—
Gulf Canada Ltd. (Toronto)	3,007,000	60
Inco Ltd. (Toronto)	2,915,079	38
Canada Packers Inc. (Toronto)	2,711,214	2
Dominion Stores Ltd. (Toronto)	2,663,857	—
Texaco Canada Inc. (Toronto)	2,642,626	91
Simpsons-Sears Ltd. (Toronto)	2,618,213	50
TransCanada PipeLines Ltd. (Calgary)	2,580,972	—
Chrysler Canada Ltd. (Windsor, Ont.)	2,570,160	100
Ontario Hydro (Toronto)	2,568,120	—
Noranda Mines Ltd. (Toronto)	2,484,690	6
Canada Safeway Ltd. (Winnipeg)	2,321,308	100
Provigo Inc. (Montréal)	2,314,407	—
MacMillan Bloedel Ltd. (Vancouver)	2,180,318	4
Steel Co. of Canada (Toronto)	2,091,213	—
Steinberg Inc. (Montréal)	2,082,710	—
Hiram Walker-Consumer's Home Ltd. (Toronto)	1,967,873	—
Canada Development Corp. (Vancouver)	1,965,828	—
Hydro-Quebec (Montréal)	1,956,391	—
Seagram Co. (Montréal)	1,880,881	—

CANADA'S LARGEST UNIONS, 1980

Union	Members
Canadian Union of Public Employees	257,180
United Steelworkers of America	203,000
National Union of Provincial Government Employees	195,754
Public Service Alliance of Canada	155,731
International Union, United Automobile, Aerospace and Agricultural Implement Workers of America	130,000
United Food and Commercial Workers	120,000
International Brotherhood of Teamsters, Chauffeurs, Warehousemen and Helpers of America	91,000
United Brotherhood of Carpenters and Joiners of America	89,010
Quebec Teaching Congress—Centrale de l'enseignement du Québec	81,033
Social Affairs Federation	70,000
International Brotherhood of Electrical Workers	68,637
Service Employees International Union of Canada	65,000
International Association of Machinists and Aerospace Workers	61,500
Canadian Paperworkers Union	61,500
International Woodworkers of America	61,300
Laborer's International Union of North America	51,176

ENERGY: Production and Consumption, 1977

Production	Atlantic	Que.	Ont.	Man.	Sask.	Alta.	B.C., N.W.T., Yukon	Canada
Coal	67,852	—	—	—	79,717	263,898	238,485	649,952
Oil and Liquified Petroleum Gases	29	—	3985	23,211	360,913	2,818,736	97,749	
Natural Gas	86	—	8526	—	56,812	2,405,711	380,091	2,851,226
Electricity	151,579	282,324	209,320	38,020	7181	5206	142,713	836,343
Total	219,546	282,324	221,831	61,231	504,623	5,493,551	859,038	7,642,144
Consumption								
Energy supply industries	43,004	118,617	129,302	21,058	42,481	229,561	81,157	665,180
Transportation	151,240	385,794	561,297	76,136	84,275	193,681	194,729	1,647,152
Domestic and farm	106,496	286,046	343,076	50,313	68,741	121,113	113,511	1,139,296
Commercial	54,565	191,324	309,950	34,406	17,816	126,720	80,388	815,169
Industrial	138,363	401,155	767,318	44,818	68,456	243,604	204,579	1,868,283
Non-energy use (petrochemicals, etc.)	—	19,010	23,878		50	5438	5496	53,872
Losses and adjustments	12,972	854	17,035	1577	7444	33,792	9038	66,121
Total	506,630	1,401,092	2,201,856	228,353	274,375	953,914	688,898	6,255,118

ENERGY CONSUMPTION PER CAPITA (tonnes of oil)

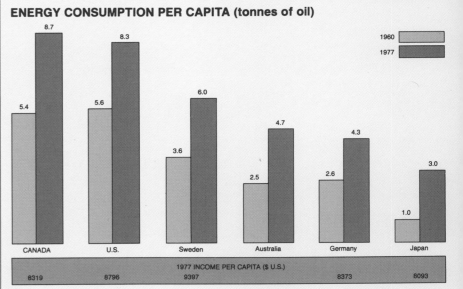

Legend: 1960, 1977

	CANADA	U.S.	Sweden	Australia	Germany	Japan
1960	5.4	5.6	3.6	2.5	2.6	1.0
1977	8.7	8.3	6.0	4.7	4.3	3.0

1977 INCOME PER CAPITA ($ U.S.): 8319, 8796, 9397, 8373, 8093

CANADA'S MINERAL PRODUCTION ($ billion)

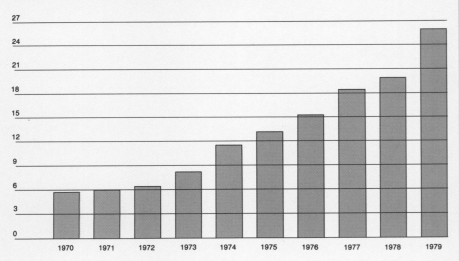

Years: 1970, 1971, 1972, 1973, 1974, 1975, 1976, 1977, 1978, 1979 (scale 0 to 27)

MINING: Mineral production by province, 1968 and 1978

Province or Territory	Rank 1968	1978	1968 $ Million	Percent	1978 $ Million	Percent
Alberta	2	1	1092	23.1	9749	49.6
Ontario	1	2	1356	28.7	2595	13.2
Quebec	3	3	725	15.4	1822	9.3
British Columbia	4	4	389	8.2	1818	9.2
Saskatchewan	5	5	357	7.6	1554	7.9
Newfoundland	6	6	310	6.6	611	3.1
Manitoba	7	7	210	4.4	464	2.4
Northwest Territories	8	8	116	2.4	308	1.6
New Brunswick	9	9	88	1.9	306	1.6
Yukon	11	10	21	0.5	228	1.2
Nova Scotia	10	11	57	1.2	204	1.0
Prince Edward Island	12	12	1	0.02	2	0.01
CANADA			4722		19,661	

MINING: Value of mineral production—selected years, 1945-1978

Year	Metals	Nonmetals	Structural materials	Coal	Crude Petroleum and Natural Gas	Total
1945	$ 316,962,810	$ 39,841,422	$ 48,419,673	$ 67,588,402	$ 25,942,874[1]	$ 498,755,181
1950	617,238,340	94,721,564	132,296,212	110,140,399	91,053,558[1]	1,045,450,073
1955	1,007,839,501	144,920,841	228,232,439	93,579,471	320,738,544	1,795,310,796
1960	1,406,558,061	197,505,783	322,594,308	74,676,240	491,175,589[1]	2,492,509,981
1965	1,907,575,899	327,238,901[1]	434,161,904	75,901,126	969,589,742[2]	3,714,467,572
1970	3,073,344,135	480,537,626[1]	450,446,081	86,067,421	1,631,663,328[2]	5,722,058,591
1975	4,793,853,123	939,180,016[1]	960,336,160	586,423,000	6,057,835,000[2]	13,337,627,299
1976	5,072,755,901	1,162,351,587[1]	1,103,435,203	607,100,000	7,502,012,000[2]	15,447,654,691
1977	5,987,885,986	1,362,468,079[1]	1,249,062,040	609,517,000	9,263,295,000[2]	18,472,528,105
1978p	5,519,569,000	1,553,878,000[1]	1,355,349,000	733,350,000	10,499,193,000[2]	19,661,339,000

p Preliminary. [1] Includes peat. [2] Includes natural gas by-products.

FOREST AREA

Province or Territory	Area (km²)	% of total forest land
Quebec	614,000	17.8
Ontario	570,000	16.7
British Columbia	521,000	15.2
Alberta	341,000	9.8
Newfoundland	338,000	9.8
Northwest Territories	307,000	8.9
Manitoba	257,000	7.5
Yukon Territory	219,000	6.4
Saskatchewan	140,000	4.1
New Brunswick	66,000	1.8
Nova Scotia	41,000	1.2
Prince Edward Island	3000	0.8
CANADA	3,417,000	100.0

FORESTRY: Volume, 1978 (million m³)

Province or Territory	Soft-woods	Hard-woods	Total
Newfoundland	573	47	620
Prince Edward Island	NA	NA	NA
Nova Scotia	151	65	216
New Brunswick	482	185	667
Quebec	1906	856	2762
Ontario	2589	1681	4270
Manitoba	410	163	573
Saskatchewan	274	185	459
Alberta	939	592	1531
British Columbia	7561	205	7766
Yukon	214	39	253
Northwest Territories	103	61	164
CANADA	15,202	4079	19,281

AGRICULTURE

Bar chart, type of farming by percent (0% to 40%), legend: 1966, 1971, 1976

Types of farming: Dairy; Cattle, hogs, sheep; Poultry; Wheat; Other small grains; Other field crops; Fruits and vegetables; Misc. specialty; Mixed

FISHERIES: Catches and value, 1977-78

Region and type	1977 Nominal catches (tonnes)	1977 Marketed value ($ thousand)	1978 Nominal catches (tonnes)	1978 Marketed value ($ thousand)
BY REGION				
Atlantic Coast	1,003,074	750,240	1,153,231	973,054
Pacific Coast	204,350	364,801	198,703	517,557
Freshwater Fisheries	47,289	59,940	47,571	58,910
CANADA	1,254,713	1,174,981	1,399,505	1,549,521
BY PROVINCE—SEA FISHERIES				
Nova Scotia	407,074	315,037	444,869	441,305
New Brunswick	129,117	139,329	151,393	165,866
Prince Edward Island	19,801	28,128	25,660	42,614
Quebec	54,296	43,064	67,350	52,285
Newfoundland	392,786	252,726	463,959	325,004
Atlantic	1,003,074	750,240	1,153,231	973,054
British Columbia	204,350	364,801	198,703	517,557
Sea Fisheries	1,207,424	1,115,041	1,351,934	1,490,611
BY PROVINCE—FRESHWATER FISHERIES				
New Brunswick	2541	298	2280	359
Quebec	703	819	648	979
Ontario	23,529	29,110	25,413	34,322
Manitoba	12,540	19,334	12,830	15,242
Saskatchewan	5214	6936	3748	4521
Alberta	1131	1384	997	1154
Yukon and Northwest Territories	1631	2059	1655	2333
Freshwater Fisheries	47,289	59,940	47,571	58,910

INTERNATIONAL TRADE

The value of exports equals about 17 percent of Canada's Gross National Product (compared to about 4 percent for the United States). Canada's dependence on imports is great, too. The Canadian climate is not suitable for the production of such foods as sugar, coffee and tropical fruits and vegetables. The maintenance of our high material standard of living requires large imports per capita of finished goods ranging from designer jeans to paperback books.

Imports, 1979 ($ thousand)

Live animals	75,419
Food, feed, beverages	4,159,194
Inedible crude materials Including iron ores, crude petroleum, natural gas, coal, aluminum ores, etc.	7,901,083
Inedible fabricated materials Including wood and paper, textiles, chemicals, iron, steel and nonferrous metals	12,058,846
Inedible end products Including industrial machinery, agricultural machinery, transportation equipment, etc.	37,914,059
Special transactions Including unclassifiable imports, shipments of less than $500 each, and goods returned within 5 years	569,082
Total imports	62,677,682

Exports, 1979 ($ thousand)

Live animals	245,634
Food, feed, beverages, tobacco	6,090,952
Inedible crude materials Including iron ores, crude petroleum, natural gas, coal, aluminium ores, etc.	12,549,406
Inedible fabricated materials Including wood and paper, chemicals, iron, steel and nonferrous metals	24,528,786
Inedible end products Including industrial machinery, agricultural machinery, transportation equipment, etc.	21,923,704
Special transactions Including settlers' effects, private donations and gifts, exports for exhibit or competition, exports to Canadian diplomats and forces.	179,836
Total exports	65,518,318

CITIES AND TOWNS WITH POPULATIONS OF 5000 OR MORE

Municipalities within each province vary in name, status and administrative powers:

BOR	Borough
C	City
DM	District municipality
ID	Improvement district
LID	Local improvement district
MD	Municipal district
MUN	Municipality
RM	Rural municipality
TM	Township municipality
T	Town–Ville
V/C	Ville/City
VL	Village

BRITISH COLUMBIA	Type	Pop.
Vancouver	C	410,188
Burnaby	DM	131,870
Surrey	DM	116,497
Richmond	DM	80,034
Saanich	DM	73,383
Delta	DM	64,492
Victoria	C	62,551
Prince George	C	59,929
Kamloops	C	58,311
Coquitlam	DM	55,464
Kelowna	C	51,955
Nanaimo	C	40,336
New Westminster	C	38,393
West Vancouver	DM	37,144
Langley	DM	36,659
North Vancouver	C	31,934
Matsqui	DM	31,178
Maple Ridge	DM	29,462
Chilliwack	DM	28,421
Port Coquitlam	C	23,926
Penticton	C	21,344
Port Alberni	C	19,585
Oak Bay	DM	17,658
Vernon	C	17,546
North Cowichan	DM	15,956
Esquimalt	DM	15,053
Mission	DM	14,997
Prince Rupert	C	14,754
Powell River	DM	13,694
Cranbrook	C	13,510
White Rock	C	12,497
Campbell River	DM	12,072
Kitimat	DM	11,956
Port Moody	C	11,649
Dawson Creek	C	10,528
Terrace	DM	10,251
Langley	C	12,123
Trail	C	9976
Abbotsford	DM	9507
Salmon Arm	DM	9391
Nelson	C	9235
Fort St. John	C	8947
Chilliwack	C	8634
Squamish	DM	8368
Courtenay	C	7733
Quesnel	T	7637
Central Saanich	DM	7413
Kimberley	C	7111
Sidney	T	6732
Summerland	DM	6724
Castlegar	C	6255
Williams Lake	T	6199
Merritt	T	5680
Comox	T	5359
Mackenzie	DM	5338

ALBERTA	Type	Pop.
Calgary	C	469,917
Edmonton	C	461,361
Lethbridge	C	46,752
Strathcona, County No. 20		42,278
Medicine Hat	C	32,811
Red Deer	C	32,184
St. Albert	T	24,129
Parkland, County No. 31		17,762
Grande Prairie	C	17,626
0.44 Rocky View	MD	15,469
Fort McMurray	T	15,424
Red Deer, County No. 23		13,321
090 Sturgeon	MD	12,861
017 I.D.		11,145
Leduc, County No. 25		10,949
Lethbridge, County No. 26		10,262
Camrose	C	10,104
087 Bonnyville	MD	9837
Grande Prairie, County No. 1		9147
031 Foothills	MD	8685
Leduc	T	8576
018 I.D.		8511
Lacombe, County No. 14		8399
Fort Saskatchewan	T	8304
Wetaskiwin, County No. 10		8260
010 I.D.		7811
014 I.D.		7586
Camrose, County No. 22		7344
Spruce Grove	T	6907
Ponoka, County No. 3		6903
Wetaskiwin	C	6754
Hinton	T	6731
Vermilion River, County No. 24		6646
Westlock	MD	6612
Lac Ste. Anne, County No. 28		6586
Brooks	T	6339
Drumheller	C	6154
014 Taber	MD	5909
Kneehill	MD	5830
Newell, County No. 4		5828
Lloydminster (Part)	C	5818
023 I.D.		5765
St. Paul, County No. 19		5443
Athabasca, County No. 12		5406
Taber	T	5296
Barrhead, County No. 11		5148

SASKATCHEWAN	Type	Pop.
Regina	C	149,593
Saskatoon	C	133,750
Moose Jaw	C	32,581
Prince Albert	C	28,631
Swift Current	C	14,264
Yorkton	C	14,119
North Battleford	C	13,158
Weyburn	C	8892
Estevan	C	8847
Corman Park	RM	5625
Melville	C	5149
Melfort	T	5141

MANITOBA	Type	Pop.
Winnipeg	C	560,874
Brandon	C	34,901
Thompson	C	17,291
Portage La Prairie	C	12,555
Selkirk	T	9862
Dauphin	T	9109
Flin Flon (Part)	C	8152
Portage La Prairie	RM	7193
Springfield	RM	6944
Hanover	RM	6931
St. Andrews	RM	6831
The Pas	T	6602
Steinbach	T	5979
Rockwood	RM	5962

ONTARIO	Type	Pop.
Toronto	C	633,318
York, North	BOR	558,398
Scarborough	BOR	387,149
Hamilton	C	312,003
Ottawa	C	304,462
Etobicoke	BOR	297,109
Mississauga	C	250,017
London	C	240,392
Windsor	C	196,526
York	BOR	141,367
Kitchener	C	131,870
St. Catharines	C	123,351
Thunder Bay	C	111,476
Oshawa	C	107,023
York, East	BOR	106,950
Burlington	C	104,314
Brampton	C	103,459
Sudbury	C	97,604
Sault Ste. Marie	C	81,048
Nepean	TM	76,947
Cambridge	C	72,383
Niagara Falls	C	69,423
Oakville	T	68,950
Guelph	C	67,538
Brantford	C	66,950
Peterborough	C	59,683
Gloucester	TM	56,516
Markham	T	56,206
Kingston	C	56,032
Sarnia	C	55,576
North Bay	C	51,639
Waterloo	C	46,623
Cornwall	C	46,121
Welland	C	45,047
Timmins	C	44,747
Chatham	C	38,685
Belleville	C	35,311
Richmond Hill	T	34,716
Halton Hills	T	34,477
Barrie	C	34,389
Newcastle	T	31,928
Stoney Creek	T	30,294
Whitby	T	28,173
Pickering	C	27,879
St. Thomas	C	27,206
Woodstock	C	26,779
Stratford	C	25,657
Newmarket	T	24,795
Kingston	TM	24,737
Orillia	C	24,412
Fort Erie	T	24,031
Flamborough	TM	23,580
Caledon	T	22,434
Ajax	T	20,774
Milton	T	20,756
Port Colborne	C	20,536
Brockville	C	19,903
Vanier	C	19,812
Valley East	T	19,591
Owen Sound	C	19,525
Nanticoke	C	19,489
Dundas	T	19,179
Georgina	TM	18,530
Vaughan	T	17,782
Haldimand	T	16,375
Woolwich	TM	16,238
Rayside–Balfour	T	16,035
Grimsby	T	15,567
Trenton	T	15,465
Sidney	TM	15,318
Delhi	TM	15,209
Thorold	C	14,944
Pembroke	C	14,927
Innisfil	TM	14,839
Lincoln	T	14,460
Essa	TM	14,369
Ancaster	T	14,255
Aurora	T	14,249
Simcoe	T	14,189
King	TM	14,030
Sandwich (West)	TM	13,912
Sarnia	TM	13,775
Goulbourn	TM	13,755
Kirkland Lake	T	13,567
Nickel Centre	T	13,157
Lindsay	T	13,002
Whitchurch–Stouffville	T	12,844
Kapuskasing	T	12,676
Niagara-on-the-Lake	T	12,485
Cumberland	TM	12,377
Orangeville	T	12,021
Scugog	TM	11,851
Dunnville	T	11,642
Midland	T	11,568
Norfolk	TM	11,528
Cobourg	T	11,421
Leamington	T	11,169
Wallaceburg	T	11,132
Huntsville	T	11,123
Collingwood	T	11,114
Uxbridge	TM	10,997
Ernestown	TM	10,935
Gwillimbury, East	TM	10,635
Kenora	T	10,565
Wilmot	T	10,557
Walden	T	10,453
Glandbrook	TM	10,179
Pelham	T	10,071
Pittsburgh	TM	9972
Norwich	TM	9928
Hawkesbury	T	9789
Port Hope	T	9788
Lincoln West	TM	9459
Tillsonburg	T	9404
Fort Frances	T	9325
Smiths Falls	T	9279
Brantford	TM	9137
Mersea	TM	9021
Osgoode	TM	8957
Moore	TM	8952
West Carleton	TM	8904
Elliot Lake	T	8849
Hamilton	TM	8835
Brock	TM	8820
Zorra	TM	8735
Rideau	TM	8677
Renfrew	T	8617
Petawawa	TM	8511
Yarmouth	TM	8430
Bracebridge	T	8428
Maidstone	TM	8396
South–West Oxford	TM	8296
Ingersoll	T	8198
March	TM	8009
Gravenhurst	T	7986
Strathroy	T	7769
Smith	TM	7668
Goderich	T	7385
East Zorra–Tavistock	TM	7208
Chatham	TM	7150
Gosfield South	TM	7144
Elizabethtown	TM	6980
Iroquois Falls	T	6887
Harwich	TM	6868
Dorchester, North	TM	6823
Dryden	T	6799
Blandford–Blenheim	TM	6789
Onaping Falls	T	6776
Paris	T	6713
Tiny	TM	6682
Raleigh	TM	6549
Wellesley	TM	6414
Sturgeon Falls	T	6400
Orillia	TM	6399
Tay	TM	6379
Westminster	TM	6296
Oro	TM	6221
Augusta	TM	6173
Thurlow	TM	6150
Arnprior	T	6111
Murray	TM	6069
Wainfleet	TM	6064
Fergus	T	6001
Espanola	T	5926
London	TM	5923
Pettawawa	VL	5815
Atikokan	TM	5803
Tecumseth	TM	5803
Clarence	TM	5782
Burford	TM	5749
Hanover	T	5691
Charlottenburgh	TM	5686
Perth	T	5675
Caradoc	TM	5671
New Liskeard	T	5601
Essex	T	5577
Amherstburg	T	5566
Deep River	T	5565
Erin	TM	5502
Parry Sound	T	5501
Penetanguishene	T	5460
Tecumseh	T	5326
Vespra	TM	5265
Carleton Place	T	5256
Hearst	T	5195
Listowel	T	5126
Aylmer	T	5125
Gananoque	T	5103
Bradford	T	5080
Port Elgin	T	5069
Dumfries North	TM	5044
Sandwich North	TM	5039
Anderdon	TM	5019

QUEBEC	Type	Pop.
Montréal	V/C	1,080,546
Laval	V/C	246,243
Québec	V/C	177,082
Longueuil	V/C	122,429
Montréal North	C	97,250
St-Léonard	C	78,452
Sherbrooke	C	76,804
Lasalle	C	76,713
Gatineau	V/C	73,479
Ste-Foy	V/C	71,237
St-Laurent	V/C	64,404
Charlesbourg	V/C	63,147
Hull	C	61,039
Jonquière	V/C	60,691
Chicoutimi	V/C	57,737
Beauport	V/C	55,339
Trois-Rivières	V/C	52,518
St-Hubert	V/C	49,706
Lachine	C	41,503
Brossard	T	37,641
St-Hyacinthe	V/C	37,500
Granby	V/C	37,132
Dollard-des-Ormeaux	T	36,837
Anjou	T	36,596
Chateauguay	T	36,329
Pointe-aux-Trembles	C	35,618
Pierrefonds	V/C	35,402
St-Jean	V/C	34,363
Cap-de-la-Madeleine	C	32,126
Sept-Iles	C	30,617
Valleyfield (de Salaberry)	C	29,716
Drummondville	C	29,286
Rimouski	C	27,897
Outremont	V/C	27,089
Repentigny	T	26,698
Pointe-Claire	V/C	25,917
Cote-St-Luc	C	25,721
Aylmer	V/C	25,714
Alma	V/C	25,638
Boucherville	T	25,530
St-Jerome	C	25,175
Shawinigan	C	24,921
Westmount	C	22,153
Victoriaville	T	21,825
St-Bruno-de-Montarville	T	21,272
St-Eustache	T	21,238
Thetford Mines	C	20,784
Mont-Royal	T-V	20,514
Beaconsfield	C	20,417
St-Lambert	V/C	20,318
La Baie	V/C	20,116
Val-d'Or	T	19,915
Sorel	C	19,666
Dorval	C	19,131
Greenfield Park	T	18,430
Joliette	C	18,118
Levis	V/C	17,819
Rouyn	C	17,678
Ste-Therese	V/C	17,479
Gaspé	V/C	16,842
Grand-Mère	V/C	15,999
Beloeil	T	15,913

CITIES AND TOWNS (Continued)

BOR Borough
C City
DM District municipality
ID Improvement district
LID Local improvement district
MD Municipal district
MUN Municipality
RM Rural municipality
TM Township municipality
T Town–Ville
V/C Ville/City
VL Village

Loretteville	C	14,767
Hauterive	T	14,724
Buckingham	V/C	14,328
Mascouche	T	14,266
Sillery	C	13,580
Mirabel	V/C	13,486
Magog	C	13,290
Rivière-du-Loup	C	13,103
Matane	T	12,726
Lauzon	V/C	12,663
Blainville	T	12,517
Montmagny	C	12,326
Tracy	T	12,284
La Tuque	T	12,067
Lachute	C	11,928
Baie Comeau	T	11,911
Cowansville	T	11,902
Chambly	C	11,815
Ancienne Lorette	T	11,694
Terrebonne	T	11,204
Shawinigan Sud	T	11,155
Val Belair	T	10,716
Vanier	T	10,683
Trois Rivières Ouest	T	10,564
Chibougamou	T	10,536
Boisbriand	T	10,132
Noranda	C	9809
Drummondville-Sud	T	9420
Amos	T	4213
La Prairie	T	4173
St-Romuald-d'Etchemin	C	4160
Asbestos	T	9075
Becancour	T	9043
Rock Forest	MUN	9001
Deux-Montagnes	C	8957
Iberville	T	8897
Ste-Julie	T	8666
St-Georges	T	8605
Mont-Laurier	T	8565
Roberval	C	8543
St-Louis-de-Terrebonne	MUN	8479
Dolbeau	T	8451
Port-Cartier	T	8139
Pincourt	T	7892
Mont-St-Hilaire	T	7688
Beauharnois	C	7665
St-Constant	T	7659
Hampstead	T	7562
Kirkland	T	7476
Ascot	MUN	7289
Plessisville	T	7238
Lemoyne	T	7202
Candiac	T	7166
Lachenaie	T	7118
Rosemere	T	7112
Roxboro	T	7106
St-Luc	T	7103
Fleurimont	MUN	6925
St-Antoine	T	6872
Mont-Joli	T	6508
St-Georges-Ouest	T	6478
Farnham	C	6476
Varennes	V/C	6469
Charny	T	6461
Lac-Megantic	T	6457
Coaticook	T	6392
St-Charles-Borromée	MUN	6178
St-Paul-l'Ermite	T	6107
St-Pierre	T	6039
Montréal-Ouest	T	5980
Maniwaki	T	5969
Ste-Anne-des-Monts	T	5945
Arthabaska	T	5907
St-Basile-le-Grand	T	5843
Dorion	T	5843
Notre-Dame-des-Prairies	MUN	5820
Donnacona	T	5800
St-Félix-du-Cap-Rouge	MUN	5716
Windsor	T	5637
Vaudreuil	T	5630
Mistassini	T	5473
Ste-Agathe-des-Monts	T	5435
Lorraine	T	5388
Ste-Anne-des-Plaines	MUN	5283
Ile-Perrot	T	5272
Wendover & Simpson	MUN	5253
Percé	V/C	5198
Malartic	T	5092
Ste-Catherine	T	5036

NEW BRUNSWICK	Type	Pop.
Saint John	C	85,956
Moncton	C	55,934
Fredericton	C	45,248
Bathurst	C	16,301
Riverview	T	14,177
Edmunston	C	12,170
Oromocto	T	10,276
Campbellton	C	9282
Chatham	T	7601
Dieppe	T	7460
Newcastle	T	6423
Grand Falls	T	6223
Sackville	T	5755
Dalhousie	T	5640
St. Stephen	T	5264

NOVA SCOTIA	Type	Pop.
Halifax	C	117,882
Halifax	MUN	95,299
Dartmouth	C	65,341
Cape Breton	MUN	42,969
Kings	MUN	38,091
Sydney	C	30,645
Colchester	MUN	27,524
Lunenburg	MD	22,160
Glace Bay	T	21,836
Pictou	MUN	20,792
Annapolis	MUN	19,610
Inverness	MUN	17,367
Cumberland	MUN	17,076
East Hants	MD	14,042
Truro	T	12,840
West Hants	MD	12,642
Richmond	MUN	12,281
Antigonish	MUN	11,996
New Glasgow	T	10,672
Amherst	T	10,263
Chester	MD	9955
Queens	MUN	9586
New Waterford	T	9223
Digby	MD	9202
Clare	MD	9149
Sydney Mines	T	8965
Yarmouth	MD	8767
Argyle	MD	8618
North Sydney	T	8319
Victoria	MUN	8156
Yarmouth	T	7801
Guysborough	MD	7340
Barrington	MD	7258
Bridgewater	T	6010
Antigonish	T	5442
Stellarton	T	5366
Springhill	T	5220
Shelburne	MD	5094
Kentville	T	5056

PRINCE EDWARD ISLAND	Type	Pop.
Charlottetown	C	17,063
Summerside	T	8592
Sherwood	VL	5602

NEWFOUNDLAND	Type	Pop.
St. John's	C	86,576
Corner Brook	C	25,198
St. John's Area	LID	19,047
Mount Pearl	T	10,193
Conception Bay South	T	9,743
Gander	T	9301
Grand Falls	T	8729
Happy Valley–Goose Bay	T	8075
Windsor	T	6349
Channel–Port aux Basques	T	6187

YUKON TERRITORY	Type	Pop.
Whitehorse	C	13,311

NORTHWEST TERRITORIES	Type	Pop.
Yellowknife	C	8256

KILOMETRE GUIDE

1 KM = 0.6 MI

	BANFF	BRANDON	CALGARY	CHARLOTTETOWN	CHICOUTIMI	DAWSON CREEK	EDMONTON	FLIN FLON	FREDERICTON	GASPÉ	HALIFAX	HAMILTON	JASPER	KENORA	MONCTON	MONTRÉAL	NIAGARA FALLS	OTTAWA	PORT AUX BASQUES	PRINCE ALBERT
BANFF	•	1259	129	5079	4348	1019	428	1362	4706	4823	5121	3631	286	1669	4904	3872	3700	3682	5555	912
BOSTON	4471	3212	4342	999	835	4954	4363	3899	652	1223	921	840	4731	2802	824	546	771	735	1476	3943
BRANDON	1259	•	1130	3864	3090	1741	1151	726	3447	3565	3862	2372	1519	410	3689	2614	2441	2424	4297	731
CALGARY	129	1130	•	4931	4220	890	299	1233	4558	4694	4973	3502	415	1540	4756	3743	3571	3553	5407	784
CHARLOTTETOWN	5079	3864	4931	•	935	5554	4963	4500	373	845	280	1854	5332	3402	175	1199	1860	1389	521	4543
CHICAGO	2905	1646	2776	2577	1846	3388	2797	2334	2203	2321	2618	784	3166	1236	2401	1370	853	1230	3053	2377
CHICOUTIMI	4348	3090	4220	935	•	4831	4241	3777	562	679	977	1083	4609	2680	760	476	1152	666	1411	3821
CINCINNATI	3402	2144	3273	2409	1794	3885	3294	2831	2062	2271	2371	763	3663	1733	2234	1318	734	1218	2886	2874
CLEVELAND	3467	2208	3338	2025	1410	3949	3359	2895	1677	1886	1986	418	3727	1798	1849	933	349	834	2501	2939
DAWSON CREEK	1019	1741	890	5554	4831	•	591	1642	5189	5306	5684	4113	752	2152	5378	4355	4183	4165	6030	1193
DETROIT	3367	2108	3238	2115	1384	3850	3259	2795	1741	1859	2157	322	3627	1698	1939	908	391	768	2591	2839
EDMONTON	428	1151	299	4963	4241	591	•	1051	4598	4715	5013	3523	369	1561	4788	3764	3592	3574	5440	602
FAIRBANKS	3495	4218	3367	8031	7308	2477	3067	4118	7665	7783	8081	6590	3228	4628	7885	6832	6659	6642	8507	3669
FLIN FLON	1362	726	1233	4500	3777	1642	1051	•	4134	4252	4550	3059	1419	1098	4324	3301	3129	3111	4976	449
FREDERICTON	4706	3447	4588	373	562	5189	4598	4134	•	700	415	1440	4966	3037	198	834	1510	1024	850	4178
GASPÉ	4823	3565	4694	845	679	5306	4715	4252	700	•	945	1558	5084	3154	669	951	1627	1141	1321	4295
HALIFAX	5121	3862	4973	280	997	5604	5013	4550	415	945	•	1856	5382	3452	275	1249	1925	1439	576	4593
HAMILTON	3631	2372	3502	1854	1083	4113	3523	3059	1440	1558	1856	•	3891	1962	1630	607	69	467	2282	3103
INDIANAPOLIS	3217	1959	3088	2543	1846	3700	3109	2646	2195	2321	2504	787	3478	1548	2367	1370	853	1230	3019	2689
JASPER	286	1519	415	5332	4609	752	369	1419	4966	5084	5382	3891	•	1930	5156	4133	3961	3943	5808	970
KENORA	1669	410	1540	3402	2680	2152	1561	1098	3037	3154	3452	1962	1930	•	3227	2203	2031	2013	3879	1141
LOS ANGELES	2723	3513	2707	6136	5406	3399	3006	3899	5763	5881	6178	4344	2874	3605	5961	4929	4413	4789	5613	3513
MINNEAPOLIS	2190	932	2062	3058	2335	2673	2082	1619	2692	2810	3108	1447	2451	708	2882	1859	1516	1669	3534	1662
MONCTON	4904	3689	4756	175	760	5378	4788	4324	198	669	275	1630	5156	3227	•	1024	1699	1213	652	4368
MONTREAL	3872	2614	3743	1199	476	4355	3764	3301	834	951	1249	607	4133	2203	1024	•	676	190	1675	3344
NEW YORK	4448	3190	4319	1353	1070	4931	4340	3877	1009	1540	1278	818	4709	2779	1181	613	748	777	1833	3920
NORTH BAY	3314	2055	3185	1757	1035	3796	3206	2742	1392	1510	1807	402	3574	1645	1582	558	472	369	2234	2786
OTTAWA	3682	2424	3553	1389	666	4165	3574	3111	1024	1141	1439	467	3943	3013	1213	190	536	•	1865	3154
PHILADELPHIA	4093	2834	3964	1506	1202	4575	3985	3521	1159	1672	1427	813	4353	2424	1331	745	744	772	1983	3565
PORT AUX BASQUES	5555	4297	5407	521	1411	6030	5440	4976	850	1321	576	2282	5808	3879	652	1675	2351	1865	•	5020
PRINCE ALBERT	912	731	784	4543	3821	1193	602	449	4178	4295	4593	3103	970	1141	4368	3344	3172	3154	5020	•
PRINCE GEORGE	632	1865	761	5678	4955	406	715	1765	5312	5430	5728	4237	346	2276	5502	4479	4307	4289	6154	1316
QUÉBEC	4142	2884	4014	959	206	4625	4035	3571	586	703	982	877	4403	2474	784	270	946	460	1436	3615
REGINA	893	365	764	4178	3455	1376	785	752	3813	3930	4228	2737	1154	776	4002	2979	2807	2789	4654	365
RIVIÈRE-DU-LOUP	4324	3066	4196	755	180	4807	4216	3753	381	499	797	1059	4585	2655	579	452	1128	642	1231	3796
ROCHESTER	3829	2570	3700	1625	1012	4311	3721	3257	1278	1487	1587	200	4089	2160	1450	536	143	436	2102	3301
ROUYN	3154	1896	3026	1843	1120	3637	3046	2583	1477	1595	1893	694	3415	1485	1667	644	763	552	2319	2626
SAINT JOHN	4812	3553	4664	323	649	5295	4704	4241	106	806	309	1547	5073	3143	148	940	1616	1130	800	4284
ST. JOHN'S	6482	5224	6334	1448	2338	6957	6367	5903	1777	2248	1503	3209	6735	4806	1579	2602	3278	2792	927	5947
SAN FRANCISCO	2050	3090	2179	5181	5451	2717	2478	3476	5808	5926	6223	4389	2634	3634	6006	4974	4458	4834	6658	3050
SASKATOON	748	623	620	4435	3713	1118	528	613	4070	4188	4485	2995	896	1033	4260	3236	3064	3046	4912	164
SAULT STE. MARIE	2887	1629	2758	2184	1461	3370	2779	2316	1819	1936	2234	744	3148	1218	2008	985	813	795	2660	2359
SEATTLE	1081	2340	1210	5811	5089	1318	1360	2411	5446	5564	5861	4027	1236	2750	5636	4612	4096	4472	6288	1962
SHERBROOKE	4028	2770	3899	1151	420	4511	3920	3457	777	895	1193	763	4289	2359	975	156	832	346	1627	3500
SUMMERSIDE	5053	3795	4925	63	909	5528	4937	4474	348	819	317	1780	5306	3376	150	1173	1849	1363	584	4517
SYDNEY	5401	4142	5253	367	1257	5876	5285	4822	695	1167	422	2128	5654	3724	497	1521	2197	1711	154	4865
THUNDER BAY	2179	921	2050	2892	2169	2662	2071	1608	2527	2644	2942	1452	2440	510	2717	1693	1521	1503	3368	1651
TORONTO	3563	2305	3434	1738	1015	4046	3455	2992	1373	1490	1788	68	3824	1894	1563	539	137	399	2214	3051
VANCOUVER	929	2187	1057	6000	5277	1202	1244	2290	5634	5752	6050	4559	875	2597	5824	4801	4628	4611	6476	1841
VICTORIA	1033	2292	1162	6104	5382	1307	1349	2395	5739	5856	6154	4664	980	2702	5929	4905	4733	4715	6581	1946
WASHINGTON	4105	2847	3977	1719	1384	4588	3998	3534	1371	1902	1640	832	4366	2437	1543	932	763	1014	2195	3578
WHITEHORSE	2514	3236	2385	7049	6326	1495	2086	3137	6684	6801	7099	5609	2247	3647	6874	5850	5678	5660	7525	2688
WINDSOR	3370	2111	3241	2111	1381	3853	3262	2799	1738	1856	2153	319	3631	1701	1936	904	388	764	2588	2842
WINNIPEG	1465	206	1336	3607	2884	1947	1357	893	3241	3359	3656	2166	1725	204	3431	2408	2235	2218	4083	937
YARMOUTH	4986	3727	4838	497	842	5449	4878	4414	280	980	345	1720	5246	3317	322	1114	1790	1304	840	4458

	PRINCE GEORGE	QUÉBEC	REGINA	RIVIÈRE-DU-LOUP	ROUYN	SAINT JOHN	ST. JOHN'S	SASKATOON	SAULT STE. MARIE	SHERBROOKE	SUMMERSIDE	SYDNEY	THUNDER BAY	TORONTO	VANCOUVER	VICTORIA	WHITEHORSE	WINDSOR	WINNIPEG	YARMOUTH
BANFF	632	4142	893	4324	3154	4812	6482	748	2887	4028	5053	5401	2179	3563	929	1033	2514	3370	1465	4986
BOSTON	5077	629	3578	811	1189	676	2403	3835	1584	423	974	1321	2292	908	5399	5504	6396	1159	2953	571
BRANDON	1865	2884	365	3066	1896	3553	5224	623	1629	2770	3795	4142	921	2305	2187	2292	3236	2111	206	3727
CALGARY	761	4014	764	4196	3026	4664	6334	620	2758	3899	4925	5253	2050	3434	1057	1162	2385	3241	1336	4838
CHARLOTTETOWN	5678	959	4178	755	1843	323	1448	4435	2184	1151	63	367	2892	1738	6000	6104	7049	2111	3607	497
CHICAGO	3512	1640	2012	1822	1444	2309	3980	2269	726	1520	2551	2898	1070	830	3833	3938	4883	465	1440	2483
CHICOUTIMI	4955	206	3455	180	1120	649	2338	3713	1461	420	909	1257	2169	1015	5277	5382	6326	1381	2884	842
CINCINNATI	4009	1590	2509	1770	1436	2086	3813	2766	900	1474	2383	2731	1567	809	4331	4435	5380	444	1938	2021
CLEVELAND	4073	1205	2573	1386	1112	1701	3428	2831	856	1090	1999	2346	1564	486	4395	4500	5444	282	2002	1637
DAWSON CREEK	406	4625	1376	4807	3637	5295	6957	1118	3370	4511	5528	5876	2662	4046	1202	1307	1495	3853	1947	5449
DETROIT	3973	1178	2474	1360	995	1848	3518	2731	566	1064	2089	2437	1286	369	4295	4400	5345	3	1902	2021
EDMONTON	715	4035	785	4216	3046	4704	6367	528	2779	3920	4937	5285	2071	3455	1244	1349	2086	3262	1357	4878
FAIRBANKS	2882	7102	3853	7284	6114	7772	9434	3595	5847	6988	8005	8352	5139	6523	3679	3784	982	6330	4424	7926
FLIN FLON	1765	3571	752	3753	2583	4241	5903	613	2316	3457	4474	4822	1608	2992	2290	2395	3137	2799	893	4414
FREDERICTON	5312	586	3813	381	1477	106	1777	4070	1819	777	348	695	2527	1373	5634	5739	6684	1738	3241	280
GASPÉ	5430	703	3930	499	1595	806	2248	4188	1936	895	819	1167	2644	1490	5752	5856	6801	1856	3359	980
HALIFAX	5728	982	4228	797	1893	309	1503	4485	2234	1193	317	422	2942	1788	6050	6154	7099	2153	3656	345
HAMILTON	4237	877	2737	1059	694	1547	3209	2995	744	763	1780	2128	1452	68	4559	4664	5609	319	2166	1720
INDIANAPOLIS	3824	1640	2324	1822	1456	2219	3946	2581	978	1526	2517	2865	1382	830	4146	4250	5195	465	1753	2155
JASPER	346	4403	1154	4585	3415	5073	6735	896	3148	4289	5306	5654	2440	3824	875	980	2247	3631	1725	5246
KENORA	2276	2474	776	2655	1485	3143	4806	1033	1218	2359	3376	3724	510	1894	2597	2702	3647	1701	204	3317
LOS ANGELES	2993	5200	3148	5382	5003	5869	7540	3405	4286	5086	6111	6458	3756	4390	2313	2211	4894	4025	3401	6043
MINNEAPOLIS	2797	2129	1297	2311	1592	2799	4461	1555	874	2015	3032	3380	560	1493	2812	2710	4168	1128	726	2972
MONCTON	5502	784	4002	579	1667	148	1579	4260	2008	975	150	497	2717	1563	5824	5929	6874	1936	3431	322
MONTREAL	4479	270	2979	452	644	940	2602	3236	985	156	1173	1521	1693	539	4801	4905	5850	904	2408	1114
NEW YORK	5055	864	3555	1041	1257	1033	2760	3813	1561	657	1331	1679	2269	885	5414	5518	6463	1136	2984	929
NORTH BAY	3920	829	2420	1011	291	1498	3161	2678	426	715	1732	2079	1135	335	4242	4347	5279	700	1849	1672
OTTAWA	4289	460	2789	642	552	1130	2792	3046	795	346	1363	1711	1503	399	4611	4715	5660	764	2218	1304
PHILADELPHIA	4699	961	3199	1143	1389	1183	2752	3457	1556	806	1481	1828	2264	880	5021	5126	6070	921	2623	1078
PORT AUX BASQUES	6154	1436	4654	1231	2319	800	927	4912	2660	1627	584	154	3368	2214	6476	6581	7525	2588	4083	840
PRINCE ALBERT	1316	3615	365	3796	2626	4284	5947	164	2359	3500	4517	4865	1651	3051	1841	1946	2688	2842	937	4458
PRINCE GEORGE	•	4749	1500	4931	3761	5419	7081	1242	3481	4635	5652	6000	2786	4170	797	901	1901	3977	2071	5592
QUÉBEC	4749	•	3249	204	914	673	2363	3507	1255	214	933	1281	1963	809	5071	5176	6120	1175	2678	866
REGINA	1500	3249	•	3431	2261	3919	5581	257	1981	3135	4152	4500	1286	2670	1822	1926	2871	2477	571	4104
RIVIÈRE-DU-LOUP	4931	204	3431	•	1096	488	2158	3689	1437	396	729	1077	2145	991	5253	5358	6302	1357	2860	661
ROCHESTER	4435	806	2935	988	893	1302	3029	3193	941	692	1600	1947	1650	266	4757	4862	5807	517	2364	1238
ROUYN	3761	914	2261	1096	•	1584	3246	2519	718	800	1817	2165	975	626	4083	4188	5132	991	1690	1757
SAINT JOHN	5419	673	3919	488	1584	•	1727	4176	1925	864	298	645	2633	1479	5741	5845	6790	1844	3347	174
ST. JOHN'S	7081	2363	5581	2158	3246	1727	•	5839	3587	2554	1511	1081	4295	3141	7403	7775	8452	3515	5010	1783
SAN FRANCISCO	2311	5245	2858	5427	5049	5914	7585	2886	4331	5131	6156	6503	3964	4435	1630	1529	4212	4070	3430	6088
SASKATOON	1242	3507	257	3689	2519	4176	5839	•	2239	3392	4410	4757	1543	2927	1677	1782	2614	2734	829	4350
SAULT STE. MARIE	3481	1255	1981	1437	718	1925	3587	2239	•	1141	2158	2506	708	676	3803	3907	4852	581	1423	2099
SEATTLE	912	4899	1975	5065	4199	5552	7215	1830	3454	4768	5786	6133	3261	4073	232	130	2813	3703	2546	5726
SHERBROOKE	4635	214	3135	396	800	864	2554	3392	1141	•	1125	1473	1849	695	4957	5061	6006	1061	2564	1057
SUMMERSIDE	5652	933	4152	729	1817	298	1511	4410	2158	1125	•	430	2866	1709	5974	6078	7023	2086	3581	472
SYDNEY	6000	1281	4500	1077	2165	645	1081	4757	2506	1473	430	•	3214	2060	6322	6426	7371	2433	3928	702
THUNDER BAY	2786	1963	1286	2145	975	2633	4295	1543	708	1849	2866	3214	•	1384	3108	3212	4157	1289	715	2807
TORONTO	4170	809	2670	991	626	1479	3141	2927	676	695	1709	2060	1384	•	4492	4596	5528	369	2099	1653
VANCOUVER	797	5071	1822	5253	4083	5741	7403	1677	3803	4957	5974	6322	3108	4492	•	105	2697	4299	2232	5914
VICTORIA	901	5176	1926	5358	4188	5845	7775	1782	3907	5061	6078	6426	3212	4596	105	•	2802	4403	2337	6019
WASHINGTON	4712	1178	3212	1360	1576	1395	3122	3454	1394	1048	1693	2041	2271	900	5034	5139	6083	1014	2641	1291
WHITEHORSE	1901	6120	2871	6302	5132	6790	8452	2614	4852	6006	7023	7371	4157	5528	2697	2802	•	5348	3524	6964
WINDSOR	3977	1175	2477	1357	991	1844	3515	2734	581	1061	2086	2433	1289	369	4299	4403	5348	•	1905	2018
WINNIPEG	2071	2678	571	2860	1690	3347	5010	829	1423	2564	3581	3928	715	2099	2232	2337	3524	1905	•	3521
YARMOUTH	5592	866	4104	661	1757	174	1783	4350	2099	1057	472	702	2807	1653	5914	6019	6964	2018	3521	•

Kilometres are calculated along main highways and include ferry distances.

MAPS OF CANADA

With the collaboration of the Surveys and Mapping Branch, Energy, Mines and Resources Canada, the Reader's Digest *Atlas of Canada* offers here a completely new reference series of 48 maps. These maps, and the accompanying index, were originally researched and produced by the Surveys and Mapping Branch, and have been specially adapted for inclusion in the Reader's Digest *Atlas of Canada* by the addition of information and changes in color and scale. The index gives the name, status and position of all populated places recorded in the nation's 1976 census. Selections of physical features as well as roads, railways, and national and provincial parks are included on the maps so that the reader might see more clearly the geographical setting of the populated places. But the maps are not a guide to all Canadian geographical names. For this, a prohibitively large number of maps would be needed.

The authority for the place-names comes from different sources. Each provincial government is responsible for geographical names within its jurisdiction and shares responsibility for names in federal lands with the appropriate federal government department. The authority for adopting, spelling and applying geographical names in the Yukon Territory and the Northwest Territories lies with the federal Minister of Indian and Northern Affairs. Since 1897, when the federal government established the Geographic Board of Canada, there has existed a central national body for the purpose of standardizing geographical naming procedures in Canada, maintaining records of their acceptance and history, and coordinating the work of federal and provincial agencies to ensure acceptance of the principles and procedures for the naming of places and geographical features. This body, now known as the Canadian Permanent Committee on Geographical Names (CPCGN), is composed of provincial and federal representatives. The federal Department of Energy, Mines and Resources provides a Secretariat for the Committee and makes names available upon request through publications such as gazetteers and toponymy studies. Decisions on names made by provincial and territorial

authorities are provided to the Secretariat and subsequently entered into a national toponymic data bank for use in preparing maps, charts, gazetteers, and other documents and publications. Research into the origin and history of geographical names is sponsored by the federal and provincial governments.

An important characteristic of "Maps of Canada" is that it uses geographical names in the language actually approved by the appropriate authorities for the provinces and territories. To preserve the definitive quality of this map section, no translations from one official language to the other have been made. Translations are in everyday use throughout the nation to refer to places and features; but in the absence of official authorization for translations of names, the original authorized forms have been strictly observed. Seas and oceans which are outside the jurisdiction of a particular names authority are identified in both official languages. The names of provinces and territories are also shown in both official languages if there are traditional alternatives in federal statutes.

Our knowledge of the population of Canada and the location of the settlements, villages, towns and cities in which the people live comes almost entirely from national censuses undertaken every five years. This map section uses data collected from the 1976 census. All populated places are shown on the maps and listed in the index, except where such a place had an unapproved name, was unincorporated and had a population of less than fifty persons. However, places with more than fifty persons are included, even though they may not have an approved name and may be unincorporated. The names of unincorporated places given in this part of the book are those available up to 1978.

Incorporated municipalities are shown as they existed in 1976. In general, they are populated places with local government services such as police, transportation, and recreation and health facilities organized by the municipality. The creation of incorporated municipalities is controlled by various provincial and territorial acts; consequently there is no uniform definition of cities, towns and villages. The names of incorporated places appearing in this map section are those authorized by the CPCGN in the census year 1976. In many cases, approved names are available for unincorporated places, and these have been used. Elsewhere, the names as recorded in the census have been used. This means that unapproved names of such settlements as trailer courts and suburban subdivisions

are used, even if they are not widely known and unlikely ever to receive official approval. Since the 1976 census, new municipalities have been created and incorporated by the amalgamation of existing places, but in order to ensure consistency with 1976 census-based information, these later developments have not been shown.

All Indian reserves in Canada are shown as far as the scales of the maps permit. In cases where the smallness and proximity of some reserves presented cartographic difficulties, generalization was required. The population situated in clearly identifiable settlements within the Indian reserves has been mapped and symbolized. Where the population of an Indian reserve is not concentrated, it has not been symbolized on the maps, but the census population figure is given in the index.

Approximately 13,000 physical features, national and large provincial parks are identified and mapped. The sources for this information are the maps of the National Topographic System. Additional information on historic sites and CAA offices has been added by the publisher.

In designing this section of the book, an attempt was made to reduce the number of maps to a minimum. Consequently, the scales of the maps vary depending on the density of named places and features. Rather than increase the number of maps in some localized areas with a high density of approved names, a system of numerical coding has been used with tabulation of the names on the margins or less congested parts of the map. The maps themselves are mosaics of portions of existing topographic maps, redrawn to conform to the style and layout of the atlas. While their accuracy is sufficient for general reference purposes, they should not be used for precise measurements.

Mapping Canada

Early European maps of Canada reflect the difficulty of exploring the remote, rugged New World. The severe climate, treacherous coastline and hostile natives inhibited detailed cartography. But by 1600 the rough outline of Canada had been delineated, however crudely, by its three oceans and the St. Lawrence River. By 1616 Champlain had mapped a recognizable Bay of Fundy and New Brunswick coast, as well as the lower Great Lakes. Fur traders and missionaries provided more knowledge of the geography of eastern Canada.

The mapping of the West, like its exploration, took place in a double line of advance from the Great Lakes and Hudson Bay. The earliest maps were drawn from Indian sources describing travel and trade routes. A 1764 map has the first suggestion—probably from French and Indian reports—of the Rocky Mountains.

More accurate surveys followed. Capt. James Vancouver, in three seasons of charting in the 1790s, placed nearly all of Canada's west coast on the map. Alexander Mackenzie of the North West Company and David Thompson of the Hudson's Bay Company mapped much of Canada's northwest. Surveys by the Royal Navy, begun in 1818, resulted in a clearer picture of the Arctic Coast and, eventually, the true Northwest Passage.

Systematic mapping began in the late 19th century with the advent of photographic surveying. In the early 1900s, the Geological Survey established a topographical division to provide maps for its geologists (a service which, to that time, had been carried out by the geologists themselves). Since then, technology has transformed mapmaking from painstaking ground surveying and copper engraving to satellite photography and computer cartography.

Flat Maps for a Round World

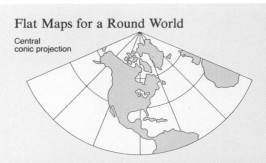

Central conic projection

Reproducing the earth on paper is like trying to flatten an orange peel. No single projection can present an accurate portrait of a globe or even part of a globe. Map projections are therefore constructed to be accurate in selected ways or to reflect a compromise between such features as equal area, conformality (true shape of geographic features) and equidistance. The best projection depends upon the purpose for which the map is used. For navigation, correct directions are important; on road maps, accurate distances are important; and in many thematic maps, correct areas are important.

Central cylindrical projection

Imagine a light shining through a hollow globe, casting shadows of the parallels and meridians. These shadow lines could be captured on a sheet of paper in several ways: as a direct projection onto a plane (azimuthal), or as a projection to a point on a cone (*top*) or cylinder (*above, below*). The lines would be exact only where the paper touched the globe—although these are precise equal-area projections, they result in a distorted view of the earth's surface.

Cylindrical equal-area projection

Canada, because of its size and northerly position, is particularly vulnerable to distortion. In this atlas, the gazetteer maps use a Universal Transverse Mercator projection which preserves the shape and dimension of geographical features. Most of the thematic maps use Lambert's Conformal Conic projection, based on a cone touching along two east-west lines. Meridians and parallels of this projection cross at right angles and are spaced to ensure conformality at every point (useful for areas of greater east-west than north-south extent). The world map on pages 58–59 uses an azimuthal equidistant projection, touching on Ottawa.

The 1550 Desceliers map above represents what was known about the New World 60 years after Columbus' arrival.

Airplanes, Plotters and Painstaking Detail: How Maps Are Made

Most maps of Canada have a common denominator—the topographic map—which provides the basic information for all other maps. Topographic maps represent surface features of the land, usually in various colors, and give their geographic location in terms of latitude, longitude and elevation above sea level.

The first step in making a topographic map is to take a series of aerial photographs of the region to be charted. A special camera, mounted in an airplane flying at a specific speed and height (generally between 4500 and 10,000 metres) takes pictures of the terrain in overlapping, parallel strips so that every portion of land appears twice in the series.

Next, the aerial photographs must be carefully interrelated so that features appear in the proper location relative to each other. Each photo is assigned a grid—a system of horizontal and vertical references by which any feature on the photo can be located by coordinates (much as streets, towns and cities are located on a simple road map). *Aerotriangulation* establishes the latitude, longitude and height above sea level of selected control points. The individual grids of each photo are then compiled by computer into one common grid for the entire area to be mapped.

Information from the composite photograph, or mosaic, is transferred to a map manuscript by *photogrammetry*. A three-dimensional visual model of the area to be mapped is produced in a stereoscopic plotting machine. Two photographs that cover the same area from different angles are combined into one image—the same principle the eyes use in producing a three-dimensional view of the world.

The compiler then traces the required features in the model onto the manuscript. By following a riverbed with a floating mark, the compiler can produce a river line on the sheet beside him.

Using the map manuscript, the draftsman engraves separate negatives from which printing plates for each color are made. Six basic colors are used in topographic mapmaking: black relates to culture; blue indicates water systems and the grid; brown is used for contours; red and orange show road systems; and green, vegetation.

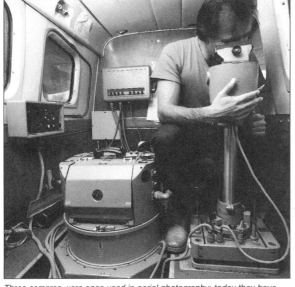

Three cameras were once used in aerial photography; today they have been replaced by an almost distortion-free, single lens guided by means of a navigation sight.

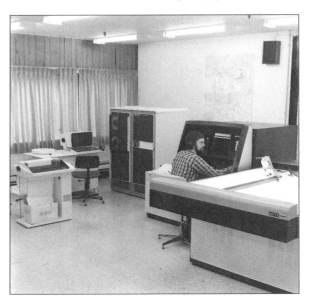

A map manuscript takes form as the operator, viewing two aerial photographs simultaneously, traces the contours and features of the three-dimensional image.

Working over a projection table, a draftsman traces the map manuscript through a sheet of coated plastic, etching and peeling away its coating for every line and color to be printed.

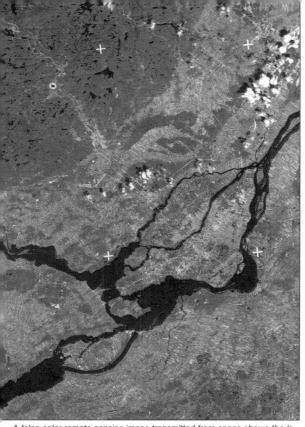

A false-color remote-sensing image transmitted from space shows the Island of Montreal at a scale of 1:1,100,000.

A conventional aerial photograph at a scale of 1:25,000 focuses on Montréal's east end. Parklands, high-density housing and major landmarks such as the ring-shaped Olympic Stadium are recognizable.

How Maps Work for You

Portraits of Canada come in four main types: topographic maps, thematic maps, air photos and remote-sensing images.

Topographic maps, which provide the basic information for most other maps, show a variety of surface features: the elevation and contour of the land, hydrographic (water) patterns, roads, railways, settled areas and boundaries. At a smaller scale and in more generalized form, topographic maps are used in atlases to depict a region's political or physical features. *Cadastral* maps show small areas at a large scale to detail administrative and property boundaries.

Thematic maps illustrate a particular subject or theme, from wheat production to average annual snowfall, population density to national parks. Road and city maps, which provide distances, route names and numbers and tourist information, are a type of thematic map.

Aerial photographs, used in topographic mapmaking, also provide useful cartographic information despite the optical deceptions created by a vertical viewpoint. A series of photos may be combined into a larger *photomosaic* of a region. *Orthophotomaps* are mosaics which have been rectified to correct distortion, and frequently color-enhanced to aid in interpretation. Symbols, boundaries and place names are sometimes superimposed to further transform photos into maps.

Airborne sensors carried in satellites or high-altitude aircraft scan the earth to produce **remote-sensing images,** the latest mapmaking tool. Data from the U.S. Landsat satellites have helped to locate oil and mineral deposits, predict crop yields, monitor land use and forest growth, study water quality, and assess damage due to natural disasters such as tornados and flooding.

By eliminating many extraneous details and adding place names, a map at the same 1:25,000 scale gives a clearer picture of east-end Montreal than the aerial photograph.

Maps Versus Reality: a Matter of Scale

Maps are smaller than the geography they represent; how much so depends on their *scale,* or the size of a map feature as compared to its actual dimensions. Thus a scale of 1:1,000,000 means that a map is one-millionth of reality. Large-scale maps show small areas in great detail; small-scale maps depict large areas in a generalized form.

On a 1:312,500 map of the Island of Montreal (*far right*), neighborhoods and major street names are identifiable, while on a 1:625,000 map (*below*), only highways and major roads are indicated. Although maps, as far as possible, preserve patterns of cultural and physical features, details are sacrificed in this generalization process. Only key towns and cities are located on the small-scale, 1:15,625,000 map below.

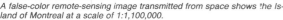

kilometres 1:15 625 000 kilomètres

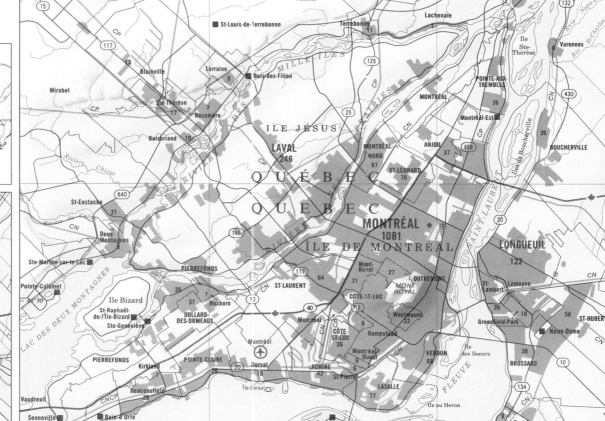

DEFINITIONS

These definitions apply to the status of places as they were at the time of the 1976 Census of Canada. The status and legal extent of some places may have changed since then.

PROVINCE

A major political division of Canada.

TERRITORY

A political area of Canada similar to a province but with fewer administrative powers.

MUNICIPALITIES

Municipality

An area with corporate status which is governed by a Provincial or a Territorial Act. These acts differ from province to province. Moreover, municipalities within each province vary in name, status and administrative powers. Names of municipalities as authorized by the provincial or territorial authority have been accepted by the Canadian Permanent Committee on Geographical Names.

Borough

An amalgamation of one rural municipality with the cities, towns, and villages located within its boundaries. (Boroughs listed in this atlas have changed their status since 1976.)

City, Town, Village

A municipality created and governed according to a Provincial or a Territorial Municipal Act. These acts differ from province to province. Cities and towns exist in all provinces and territories.

Community, Local Improvement District, Rural District

In Newfoundland and Labrador the municipalities incorporated as a Community, a Local Improvement District or a Rural District are established according to the Local Government Act or the Community Councils Act.

District (Municipality)

In British Columbia populated places are incorporated as cities, towns, villages, or districts.

Hamlet

A municipality created and governed by a Territorial Act. Hamlets exist only in the Northwest Territories.

Summer Village

A summer village has the same status as an ordinary village but may have a very small or no permanent population as defined by the census.

NON-MUNICIPALITIES

Unincorporated Place—Name approved

A place with no legally defined boundary and no local government. Census population counts of unincorporated places are only approximate, owing to the empirical choice of boundaries by census representatives.

All unincorporated places which have names approved by the Canadian Permanent Committee on Geographical Names are shown in the atlas. These names do not necessarily correspond to the names published in Statistics Canada bulletins. Some of the places may be known locally by a different name.

Unincorporated Place—Name Not Approved

Although the names have not been approved by the Canadian Permanent Committee on Geographical Names, those unincorporated places having a significant population are shown in the atlas.

Indian Reserve

In general terms an Indian reserve, the legal title to which is vested in Her Majesty the Queen in Right of Canada, is set apart for the use and benefit of an Indian band by an Order-in-Council and is subject to the terms of the Indian Act.

Military Reserves

Military reserves are lands used by the Department of National Defence. The military reserves shown in the atlas are those identified by Statistics Canada in the 1976 Census as being populated.

DIVIDING LINE

The dividing line in the area between Greenland and the Canadian Arctic Islands is a line beyond which neither party to the agreement between the government of the Kingdom of Denmark and the Government of Canada dated December 17, 1978, in exercising its rights under the Convention on the Continental Shelf of April 29, 1958, will extend its sovereign rights for the purpose of exploration and exploitation of the natural resources of the Continental Shelf.

OTHER INFORMATION

Geographical Names

Information on geographical names is available from the Canadian Permanent Committee on Geographical Names or the Toponymy Unit, Surveys and Mapping Branch, Department of Energy, Mines and Resources. Inquiries should be directed to:

Toponymy Unit,
Geographical Services Directorate,
Surveys and Mapping Branch,
Department of Energy, Mines and Resources,
Ottawa, Ontario, Canada.

Published information concerning Canada's geographical names includes the many volumes of the *Gazetteer of Canada* series and the *Répertoire toponymique du Québec*. Information on cost and ordering volumes in the *Gazetteer of Canada* series can be obtained from:

Mail Order Services,
Canadian Government Publishing Centre,
Department of Supply and Services,
Hull, Quebec, Canada,
K1A 0S9

A gazetteer of geographical names of the province of Quebec (*Répertoire toponymique du Québec*) is available from:

L'Éditeur officiel du Québec,
1283, boul. Charest Ouest,
Québec (Quebec),
Canada,
G1N 2C9

A gazetteer of geographical names of the province of Manitoba (*Manitoba Geographical Names 1980–81*) is available from:

Director of Surveys,
Department of Natural Resources,
1007 Century Street,
Winnipeg, Manitoba,
Canada,
R3H 0W4

Maps

The maps of the National Topographic System are published at the following scales: 1:1 000 000, 1:500 000, 1:250 000 1:125 000, 1:50 000, and 1:25 000. Full coverage is shown in map indexes available on request from:

Canada Map Office,
Energy, Mines and Resources Canada,
615, Booth Street,
Ottawa, Ontario,
Canada,
K1A 0E9

Index 1—Eastern Canada
Index 2—Western Canada
Index 3—Northern Canada

These indexes show the position, name, and number of each map in the system and provide complete information on how to obtain them.

Census Population Information

Detailed information on the Census of Canada is contained in publications of Statistics Canada which are listed in *Statistics Canada Catalogue* obtainable from:

Publications Distribution,
Statistics Canada,
Ottawa, Ontario,
Canada,
K1A 0T6

POPULATION 1976

Not Reported in Census

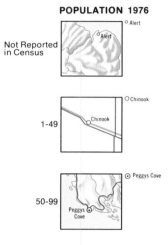

○ Alert

1-49

○ Chinook

50-99

⊙ Peggys Cove

100-399

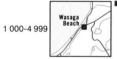

◉ Goodsoil

400-999

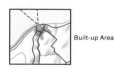

● Ste-Marie-sur-Mer

1 000-4 999

■ Wasaga Beach

5 000 and over

13 Matane

Figure represents actual population in thousands, rounded to the nearest thousand.

Built-up Area

Municipal Area

Rural District, Local Improvement District and Community in Newfoundland

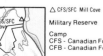

● Fishing Lake 89 A

Indian Reserve

△ CFS/SFC Mill Cove

Military Reserve

Camp
CFS - Canadian Forces Station
CFB - Canadian Forces Base

TRANSPORTATION

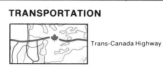

Trans-Canada Highway

Other Roads

Ferry

Railways
CN — Canadian National
CP — Canadian Pacific

International Airport

BOUNDARIES

International

Provincial or Territorial

Territorial District

Undemarcated

Dividing Line — Canada and Greenland

OTHER FEATURES

Rapids Falls, Dam

Spot and Water elevations (metres)

Glaciers

Park: National or Provincial

Park: Provincial

CAA Office

National Historic Park or Site

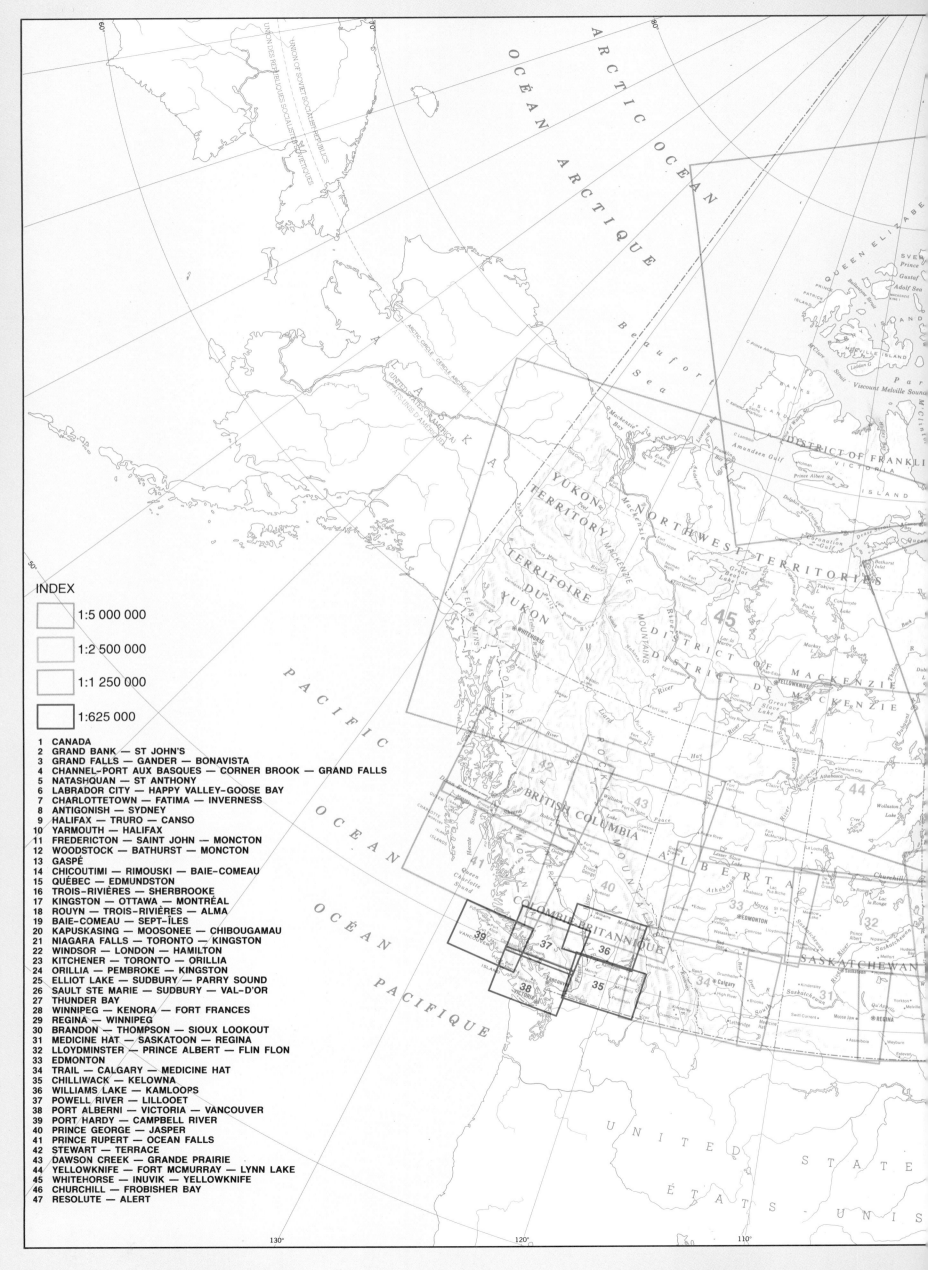

INDEX

☐ 1:5 000 000

☐ 1:2 500 000

☐ 1:1 250 000

☐ 1:625 000

1 CANADA
2 GRAND BANK — ST JOHN'S
3 GRAND FALLS — GANDER — BONAVISTA
4 CHANNEL–PORT AUX BASQUES — CORNER BROOK — GRAND FALLS
5 NATASHQUAN — ST ANTHONY
6 LABRADOR CITY — HAPPY VALLEY–GOOSE BAY
7 CHARLOTTETOWN — FATIMA — INVERNESS
8 ANTIGONISH — SYDNEY
9 HALIFAX — TRURO — CANSO
10 YARMOUTH — HALIFAX
11 FREDERICTON — SAINT JOHN — MONCTON
12 WOODSTOCK — BATHURST — MONCTON
13 GASPÉ
14 CHICOUTIMI — RIMOUSKI — BAIE-COMEAU
15 QUÉBEC — EDMUNDSTON
16 TROIS-RIVIÈRES — SHERBROOKE
17 KINGSTON — OTTAWA — MONTRÉAL
18 ROUYN — TROIS-RIVIÈRES — ALMA
19 BAIE-COMEAU — SEPT-ÎLES
20 KAPUSKASING — MOOSONEE — CHIBOUGAMAU
21 NIAGARA FALLS — TORONTO — KINGSTON
22 WINDSOR — LONDON — HAMILTON
23 KITCHENER — TORONTO — ORILLIA
24 ORILLIA — PEMBROKE — KINGSTON
25 ELLIOT LAKE — SUDBURY — PARRY SOUND
26 SAULT STE MARIE — SUDBURY — VAL-D'OR
27 THUNDER BAY
28 WINNIPEG — KENORA — FORT FRANCES
29 REGINA — WINNIPEG
30 BRANDON — THOMPSON — SIOUX LOOKOUT
31 MEDICINE HAT — SASKATOON — REGINA
32 LLOYDMINSTER — PRINCE ALBERT — FLIN FLON
33 EDMONTON
34 TRAIL — CALGARY — MEDICINE HAT
35 CHILLIWACK — KELOWNA
36 WILLIAMS LAKE — KAMLOOPS
37 POWELL RIVER — LILLOOET
38 PORT ALBERNI — VICTORIA — VANCOUVER
39 PORT HARDY — CAMPBELL RIVER
40 PRINCE GEORGE — JASPER
41 PRINCE RUPERT — OCEAN FALLS
42 STEWART — TERRACE
43 DAWSON CREEK — GRANDE PRAIRIE
44 YELLOWKNIFE — FORT MCMURRAY — LYNN LAKE
45 WHITEHORSE — INUVIK — YELLOWKNIFE
46 CHURCHILL — FROBISHER BAY
47 RESOLUTE — ALERT

82

1 : 15 625 000

ARCTIC OCEAN

OCÉAN ARCTIQUE

PACIFIC OCEAN

OCÉAN PACIFIQUE

UNION OF SOVIET SOCIALIST REPUBLICS

UNION DES RÉPUBLIQUES SOCIALISTES SOVIÉTIQUES

Beaufort Sea

A L A S K A
(UNITED STATES OF AMERICA)
(ÉTATS-UNIS D'AMÉRIQUE)

ARCTIC CIRCLE CERCLE ARCTIQUE

YUKON TERRITORY

TERRITOIRE DU YUKON

⊕ WHITEHORSE

NORTHWEST TERRITORIES

DISTRICT OF FRANKLI
VICTORIA ISLAND

QUEEN ELIZABE
SVER
Prince
Gustaf
Adolf Sea

PARRY ISLAND
MELVILLE ISLAND

Viscount Melville Sound

BANKS ISLAND

Amundsen Gulf

DISTRICT OF MACKENZIE

DISTRICT DE MACKENZIE

⊕ YELLOWKNIFE

Great Bear Lake

Great Slave Lake

BRITISH COLUMBIA

COLOMBIE-BRITANNIQUE

ALBERTA

⊕ EDMONTON

⊕ Calgary

VANCOUVER ISLAND

VANCOUVER

⊕ VICTORIA

QUEEN CHARLOTTE ISLANDS

SASKATCHEWAN

⊕ REGINA

UNITED STATE

ÉTATS-UNIS

84

125 0 125 250 375 500

kilometres **1: 15 625 000** kilomètres

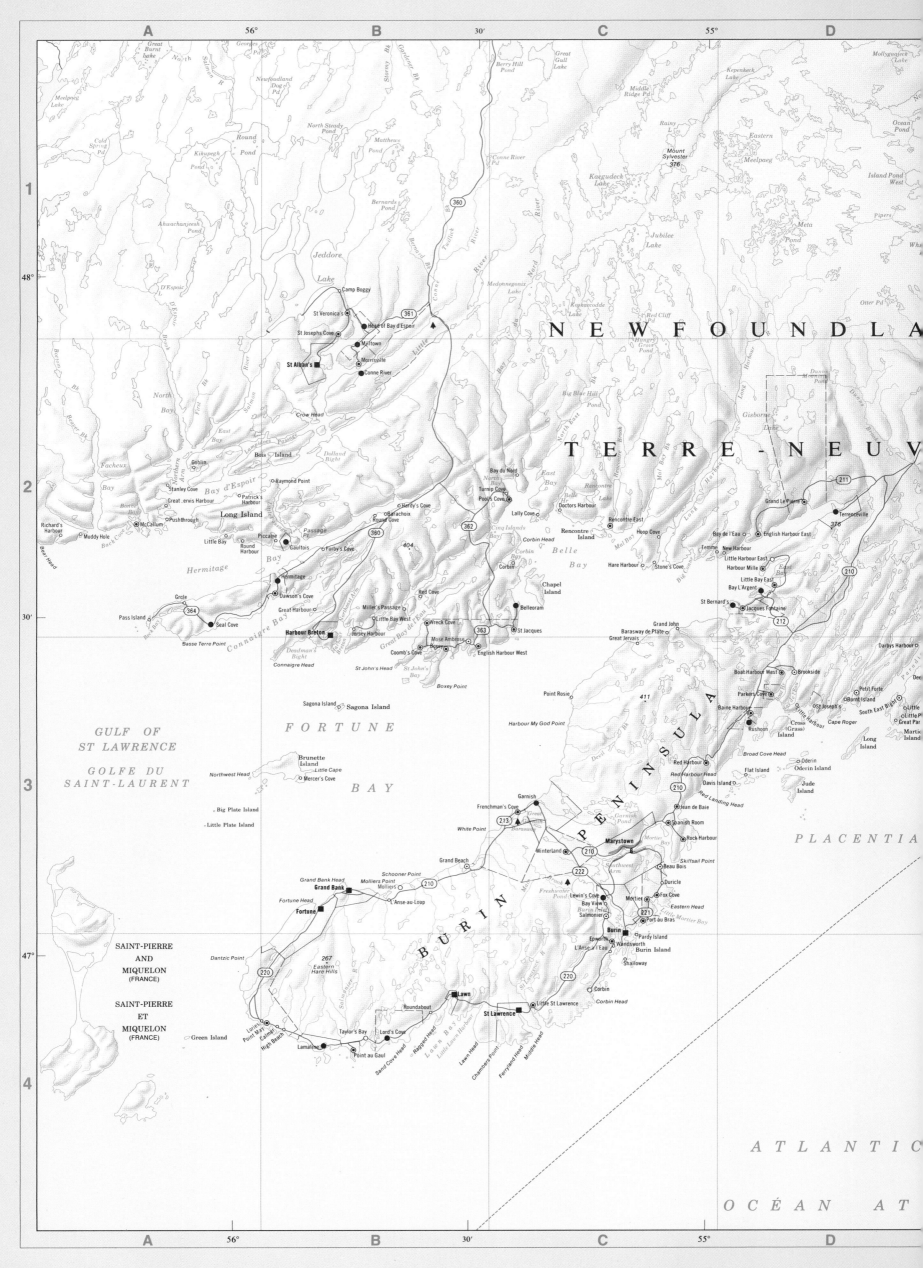

N E W F O U N D L A

T E R R E - N E U V

Great Burnt
Lake

North

Meelpaeg
Lake

Kikupegh
Pond

Cold Spring
Pd

Ahwachanjeesh
Pond

Georges Pd

Newfoundland
Dog Pd

North Steady
Pond

Matthews
Pond

Round
Pond

Bernards
Pond

Stormy Bk

Gardiner Bk

Salmon R

Conne River

Bernard Brook

Taulick R

Conne River Pd

Berry Hill Pond

Great Gull Lake

Middle Ridge Pd

Mount Sylvester
376

Kaegudeck Lake

Koskaecodde Lake

Red Cliff Pd

Hungry Grove Pond

Medonnegonix Lake

Jubilee Lake

Kepenkeck Lake

Eastern Pond

Ocean Pond

Mollyguajeck Lake

Island Pond West

Meta Pond

Pipers

Otter Pd

360

361

1

48°

Jeddore Lake

Camp Boggy

St Veronica's ⊙

Head of Bay d'Espoir ⊙

St Josephs Cove ⊙

Milltown

Morrisville

St Alban's ■

Conne River ⊙

Little R

Bay du Nord River

North East Bay

East Bay

Mol Bay

Lake

Grand Le Pierre ⊙

Terrenceville ■
376

211

Crow Head

North Bay

First Brook

Salmon R

East Bay

Lampidoes Passage

Bois Island

Dolland Bight

Bay du Nord

North Bay

Turnip Cove ⊙

Pool's Cove ⊙

Lally Cove ⊙

Belle Bay

Doctors Harbour ⊙

Rencontre East ⊙

Hoop Cove ⊙

Rencontre Island

Femme ⊙

New Harbour ⊙

Little Harbour East ⊙

Harbour Mille ⊙

Bay de l'Eau ⊙ English Harbour East ⊙

Little Bay East ⊙

Bay L'Argent ⊙

St Bernard's ⊙ ⊙ Jacques Fontaine

210

2

Facheux Bay

D'Espoir

Bay d'Espoir

Goblin ⊙

Stanley Cove ⊙

Great Jervis Harbour ⊙

Patrick's Harbour ⊙

Long Island

Raymond Point ⊙

Hardy's Cove ⊙

Round Cove ⊙

Barachoix ⊙

404

362

Cing Islands Bay

Corbin Head

Corbin Bay

Hare Harbour ⊙

Stone's Cove ⊙

Chapel Island

Grand John

Baraswav de Plate

212

Bonne Bay

Richard's Harbour

McCallum ⊙

Muddy Hole ⊙

Pushthrough ⊙

Little Bay ⊙

Piccaire ⊙

Round Harbour ⊙

Gaultois ⊙

Turby's Cove ⊙

Hermitage

Miller's Passage ⊙

Red Cove ⊙

Belleoram ⊙

St Bernard's

St Jacques

Back Bay

Hermitage Bay

Dawson's Cove ⊙

Great Harbour ⊙

Little Bay West ⊙

Jersey Harbour

Wreck Cove ⊙

Mose Ambrose ⊙

Boxey ⊙

English Harbour West ⊙

363

Great Jervais

St Joseph's ⊙

Burnt Island ⊙

Darbys Harbour ⊙

Petit Forte ⊙

Cape Roger

South East Bight ⊙

Little Pl

Great Par

30'

Grole ⊙

364

Pass Island ⊙

Seal Cove ⊙

Basse Terre Point

Deadman's Bight

Connaigre Head

Harbour Breton ■

Coomb's Cove ⊙

St John's Head

St John's Bay

Boxey Point

Connaigre Bay

Point Rosie

Harbour My God Point

411

P E N I N S U L A

Baine Harbour ⊙

Rushoon ⊙

Cross (Grass) Island

Boat Harbour West ⊙ ⊙ Brookside

Parkers Cove ⊙

Little Harbour

Long Island

Martic

3

G U L F   O F
S T   L A W R E N C E

G O L F E   D U
S A I N T - L A U R E N T

Sagona Island ⊙ Sagona Island

F O R T U N E

B A Y

Brunette Island

Little Cape

Mercer's Cove ⊙

Northwest Head

Big Plate Island

Little Plate Island

Frenchman's Cove ⊙

Garnish ⊙

213

White Point

Great Barasway

Red Harbour ⊙

Red Harbour Head

Davis Island

Jean de Baie ⊙

Spanish Room ⊙

Garnish Pond

Rock Harbour ⊙

Broad Cove Head

Flat Island

Oderin ⊙

Oderin Island

Jude Island

Red Landing Head

P L A C E N T I A

SAINT-PIERRE
AND
MIQUELON
(FRANCE)

SAINT-PIERRE
ET
MIQUELON
(FRANCE)

Grand Bank Head

Grand Bank ■

Fortune Head

Fortune ■

Grand Beach

Schooner Point

Molliers Point
Molliers

210

Anse-au-Loup

B U R I N

Winterland ⊙

210

Marystown ■

Mortier Bay

222

Beau Bois ⊙

Duricle ⊙

Fox Cove ⊙

Lewin's Cove ⊙

Bay View ⊙

Salmonier

Skiffsail Point

Eastern Head

221

Mortier ⊙

Port au Bras ⊙

Pardy Island

47°

Dantzic Point

267

Eastern Hare Hills

220

Lord's ⊙
Point May

Calmar ⊙

High Beach

Lamaline ⊙

Point au Gaul ⊙

Taylor's Bay ⊙

Roundabout

Lord's Cove ⊙

Sand Cove Head

Lawn ■

Little St Lawrence ⊙

St Lawrence ■

Ragged Head

Lawn Bay

Lawn Head

Chambers Point

Ferryland Head

Middle Head

Corbin ⊙

Corbin Head

220

Burin ■

Epworth ⊙

L'Anse à l'Eau ⊙

Wandsworth ⊙

Shalloway

Burin Island

4

A T L A N T I C

O C É A N   A T

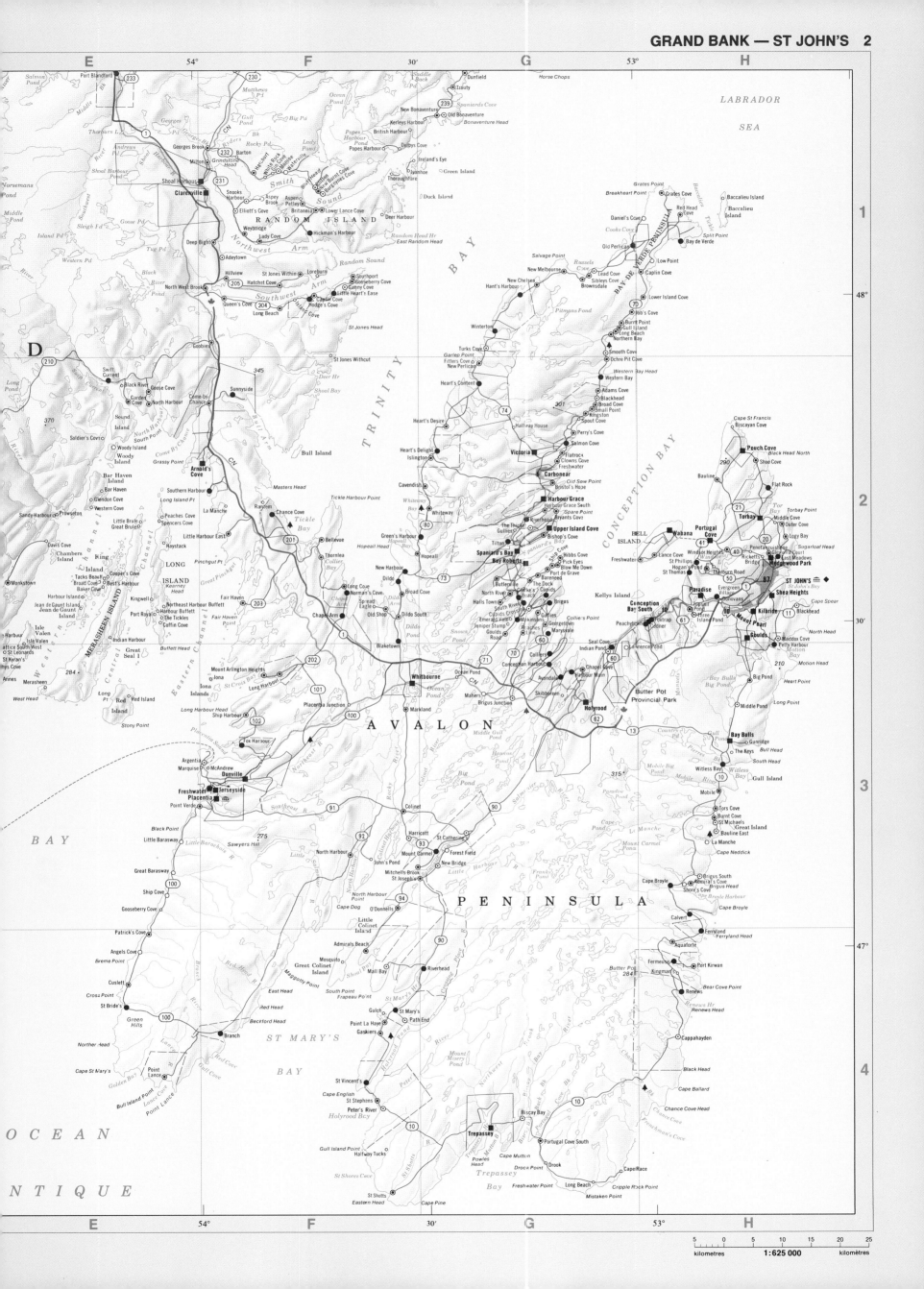

LABRADOR
SEA

TRINITY
BAY

BAY DE VERDE PENINSULA

CONCEPTION BAY

RANDOM ISLAND

AVALON

PENINSULA

ST MARY'S
BAY

BAY

OCEAN

NTIQUE

Port Blandford
Clarenville
Shoal Harbour
Come-by-Chance
Sunnyside
Arnold's Cove
Whitbourne
Holyrood
Placentia
Freshwater
Jerseyside
Dunville
Argentia
Trepassey

Harbour Grace
Carbonear
Victoria
Spaniard's Bay
Bay Roberts
Upper Island Cove
Wabana
Portugal Cove
Torbay
ST JOHN'S
Shea Heights
Kilbride
Mount Pearl
Goulds
Paradise
Conception Bay South
Bay Bulls

5 0   5   10   15   20   25
kilomètres   1:625 000   kilomètres

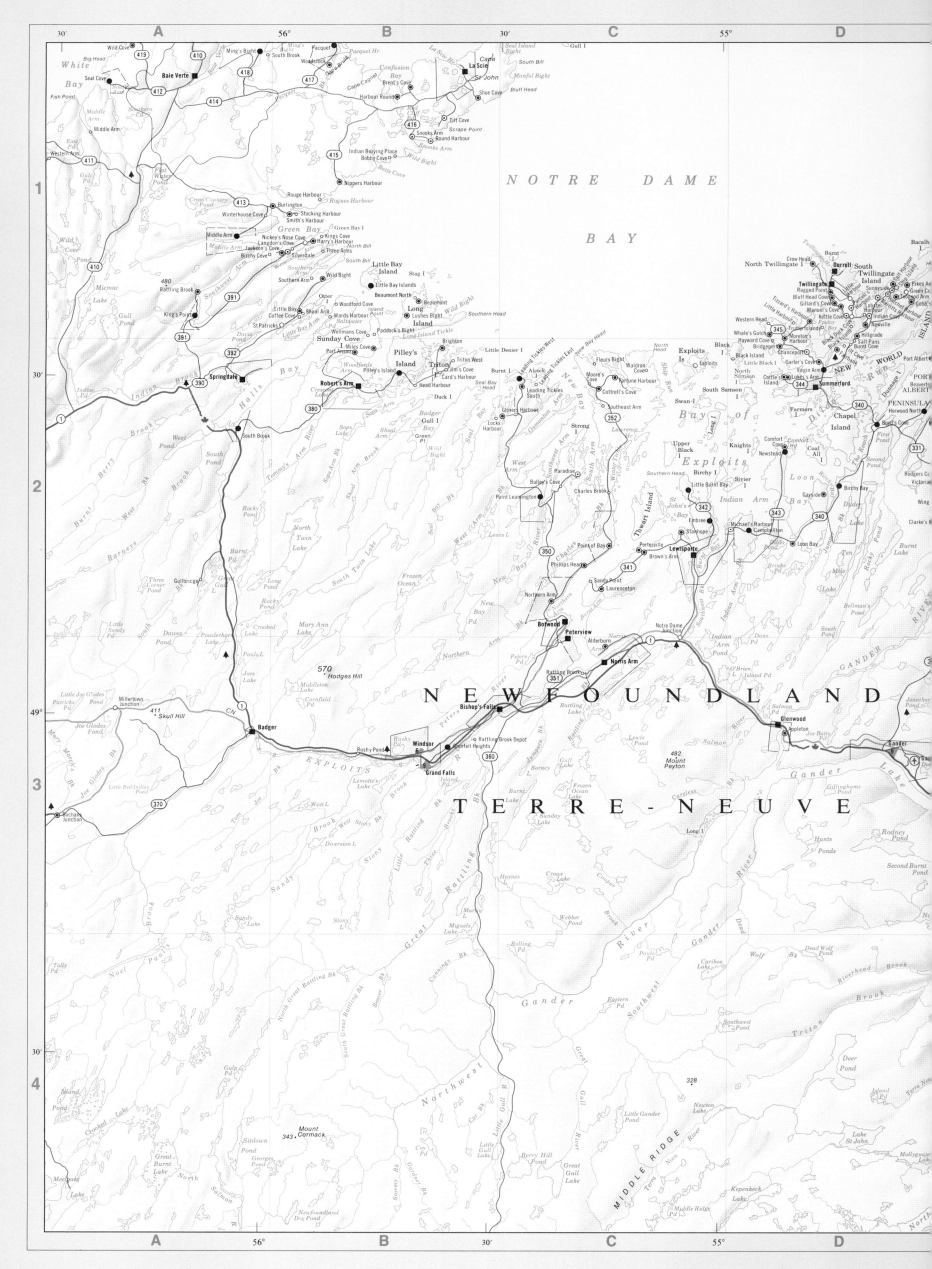

NOTRE DAME BAY

NEW WORLD ISLAND

NEWFOUNDLAND

TERRE-NEUVE

LABRADOR SEA

(ATLANTIC OCEAN)
(OCÉAN ATLANTIQUE)

BONAVISTA

BAY

Trinity
Bay

kilometres   1:625 000   kilometres

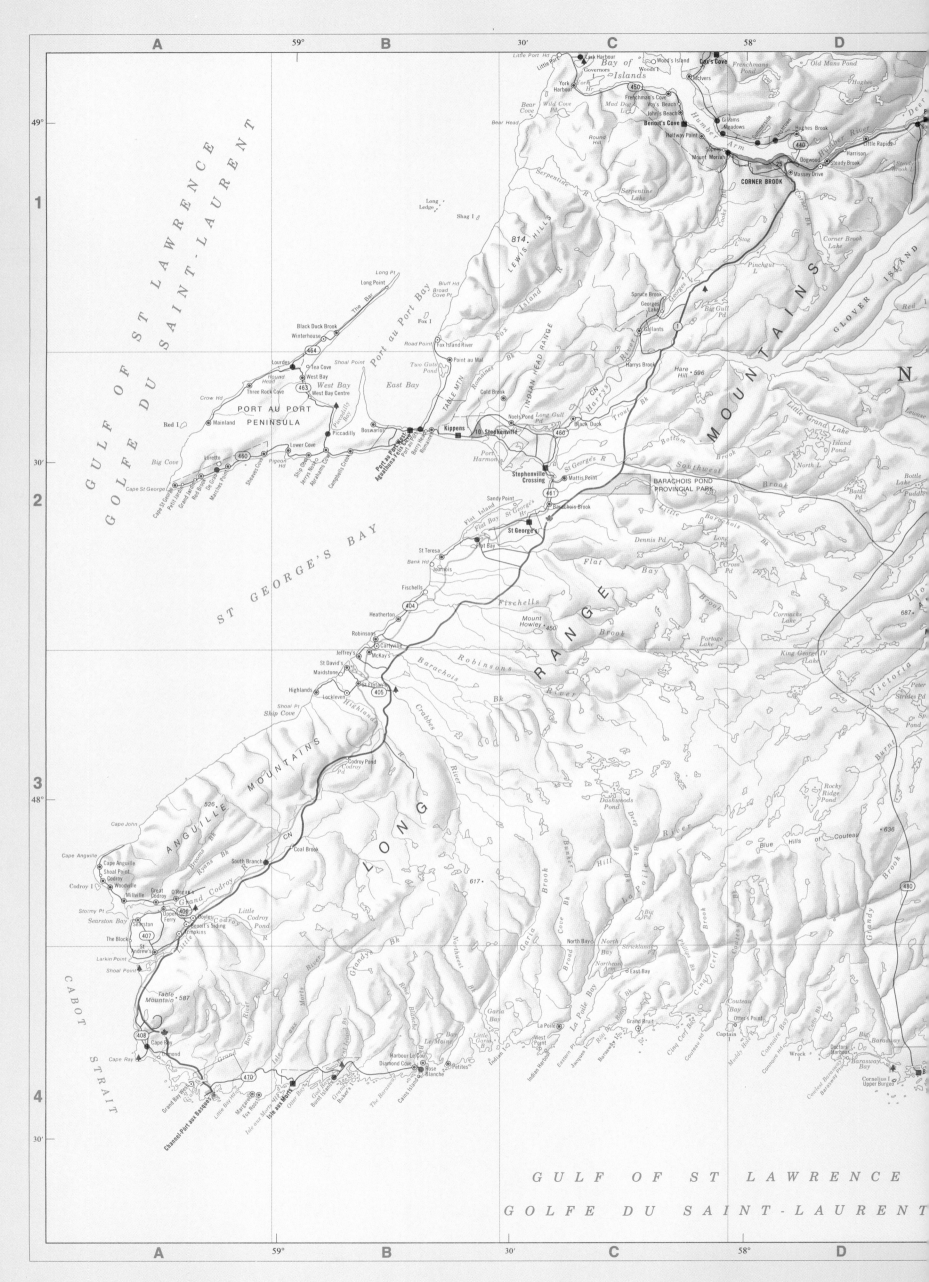

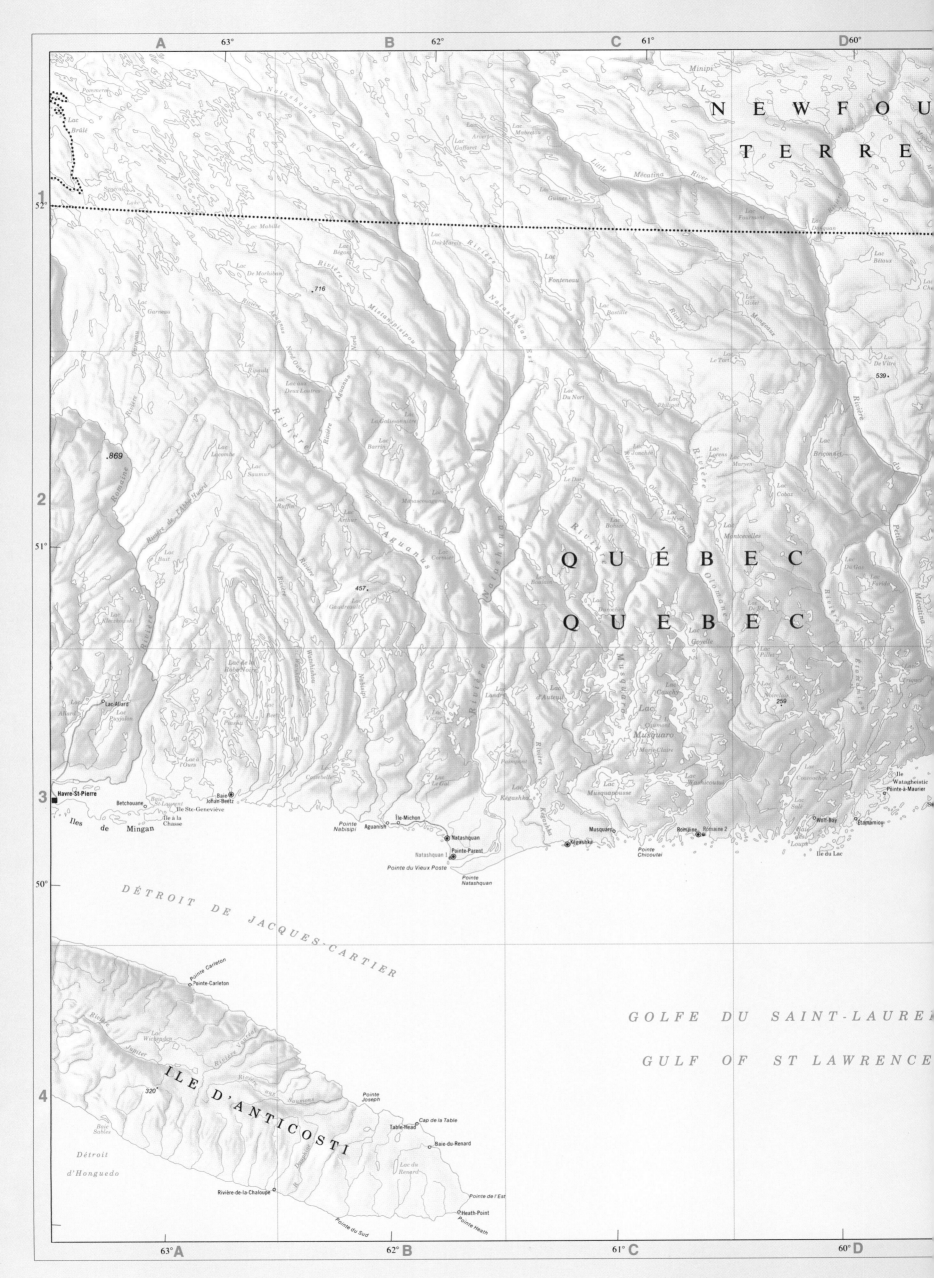

N E W F O U

T E R R E

Minipi

Lac Mabreton

Lac Arvert

Lac Gaffaret

Little Mecatina River

Lac Guines

Lac Fourmont

Lac Duchuan

1

Pommeret L.

Lac Brûlé

Natashquan

Rivière

Blue

Séségal Lake

52°

Lac Mabille

Des Marais

Rivière

Natashquan

Lac Bétaux

Lac Che

Lac Begon

Rivière

Lac De Morhiban

Rivière Nipissis

.716

Mistanipisipou

Natashquan Est

Lac Fonteneau

Lac

Lac Bastille

Rivière

Lac Le Tart

Lac Golet

Monguagu

Lac De Vitré

539.

Lac Garneau

Garneau

Rivière

Rivière Nord Ouest

Rivière Nord

Aguanus

Lac Ripault

Lac aux Deux Loutres

Lac La Galissonnière

Lac Barrin

Rivière

Lac Du Nort

Lac Philpot

Rivière Olomane

Lac Jonchée

Lac Maryen

Lac Larens

Lac Briconnet

Lac

2

Romaine

Rivière de l'Abbé Huard

.869

Lac Locombe

Lac Saumur

Lac Ruffle

Lac Arthur

Aguanus

Lac Masascougama

Lac Cornier

Lac

Le Dart

Rivière

Musquaro

Lac Bohier

Lac Darechi

Rivière Olomane

Lac Cobaz

Lac Montcecolles

Lac De Gas

51°

Lac Klecikoushi

Lac Bait

Rivière

Rivière

457.

Lac Gaudreault

Nabisipi

Lac Boulain

QUÉBEC

QUÉBEC

Lac Goyelle

Lac Pariel

Lac Triquet

Lac de la Robe Noire

Watshishou

Lac Landry

Rivière

Lac Victor

Rivière

Lac d'Auteuil

Musquaro

Lac Cauche

259.

Lac

Lac Coacochou

Île Watagheistic

Pointe-à-Maurier

Lac Allard

Lac Puyjalon

Lac

Pashu

Bec Scies

Lac Le Gal

Lac Pamplona

Lac Guernon

Musquaro

Marie-Claire

Lac Washicoutai

3

Havre-St-Pierre

Betchouane

Baie St-Laurent

Baie Johan-Beetz

Île Ste-Geneviève

Lac Castebelle

Lac Kégashka

Lac Musquapousse

Kégashka

Musquaro

Romaine

Romaine 2

Wolf-Bay

Étamamiou

Îles de Mingan

Île à la Chasse

Pointe Nabisipi

Aguanish

Île-Michon

Natashquan

Natashquan

Pointe-Parent

Kégashka

Pointe Chicoutai

Baie des Loups

Île du Lac

Se

Pointe du Vieux Poste

Pointe Natashquan

50°

D É T R O I T   D E   J A C Q U E S - C A R T I E R

Pointe Carleton

Pointe-Carleton

G O L F E   D U   S A I N T - L A U R E

Rivière

Lac Wickenden

Jupiter

G U L F   O F   S T   L A W R E N C E

4

320.

Î L E   D' A N T I C O S T I

Rivière aux Saumons

Pointe Joseph

Cap de la Table

Baie Sables

Table-Head

Baie-du-Renard

Détroit d'Honguedo

Lac du Renard

Pointe de l'Est

Rivière-de-la-Chaloupe

Pointe du Sud

Heath-Point

Pointe Heath

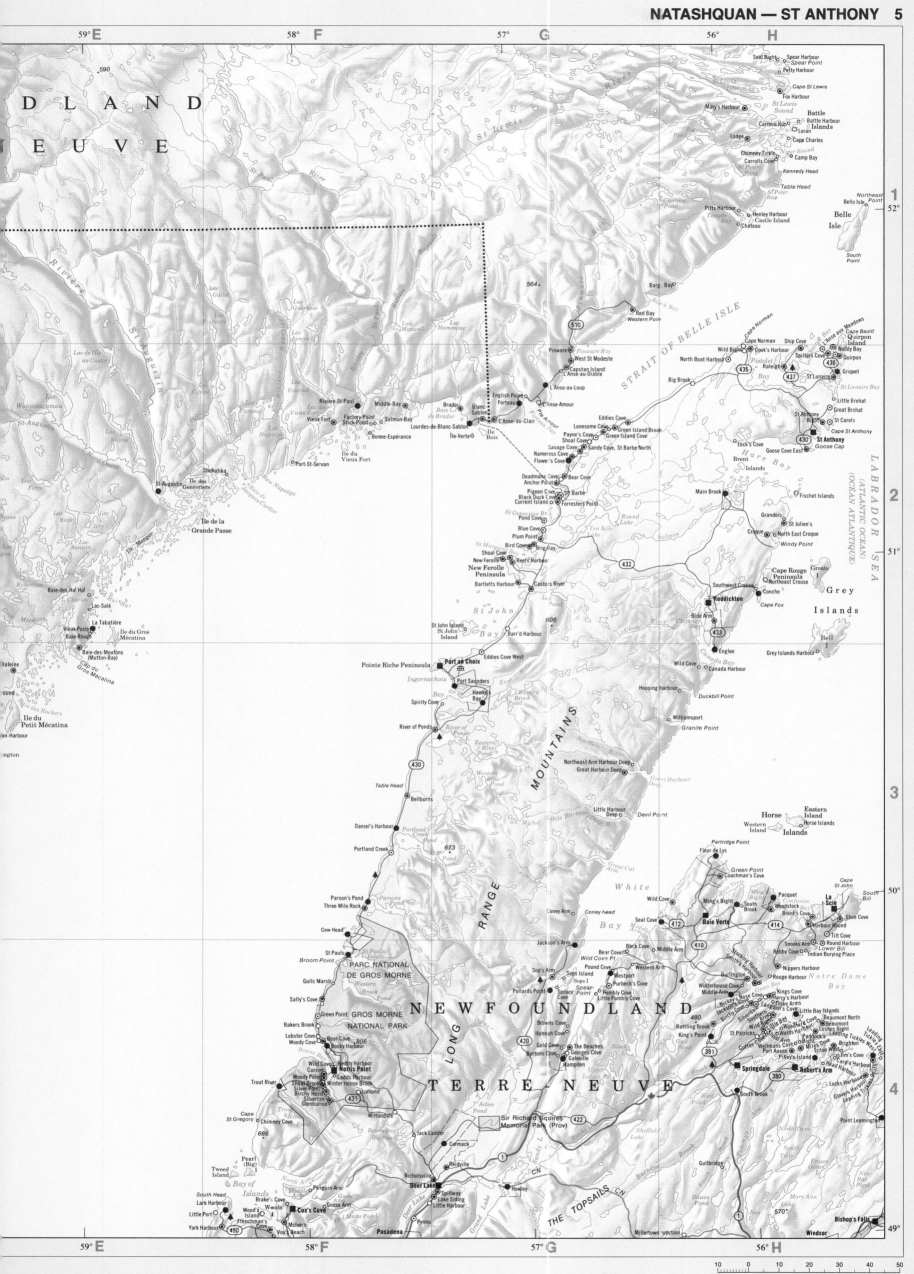

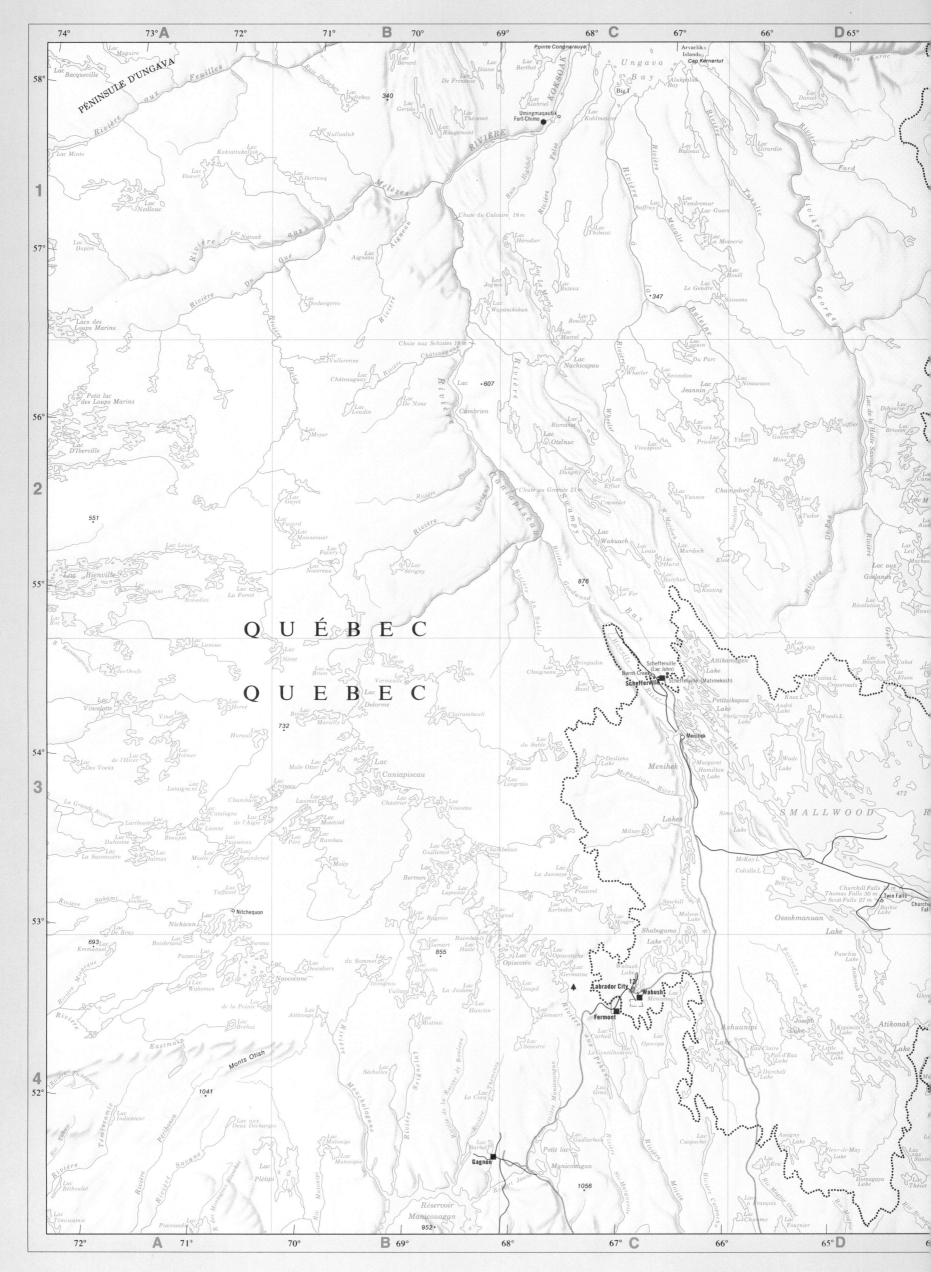

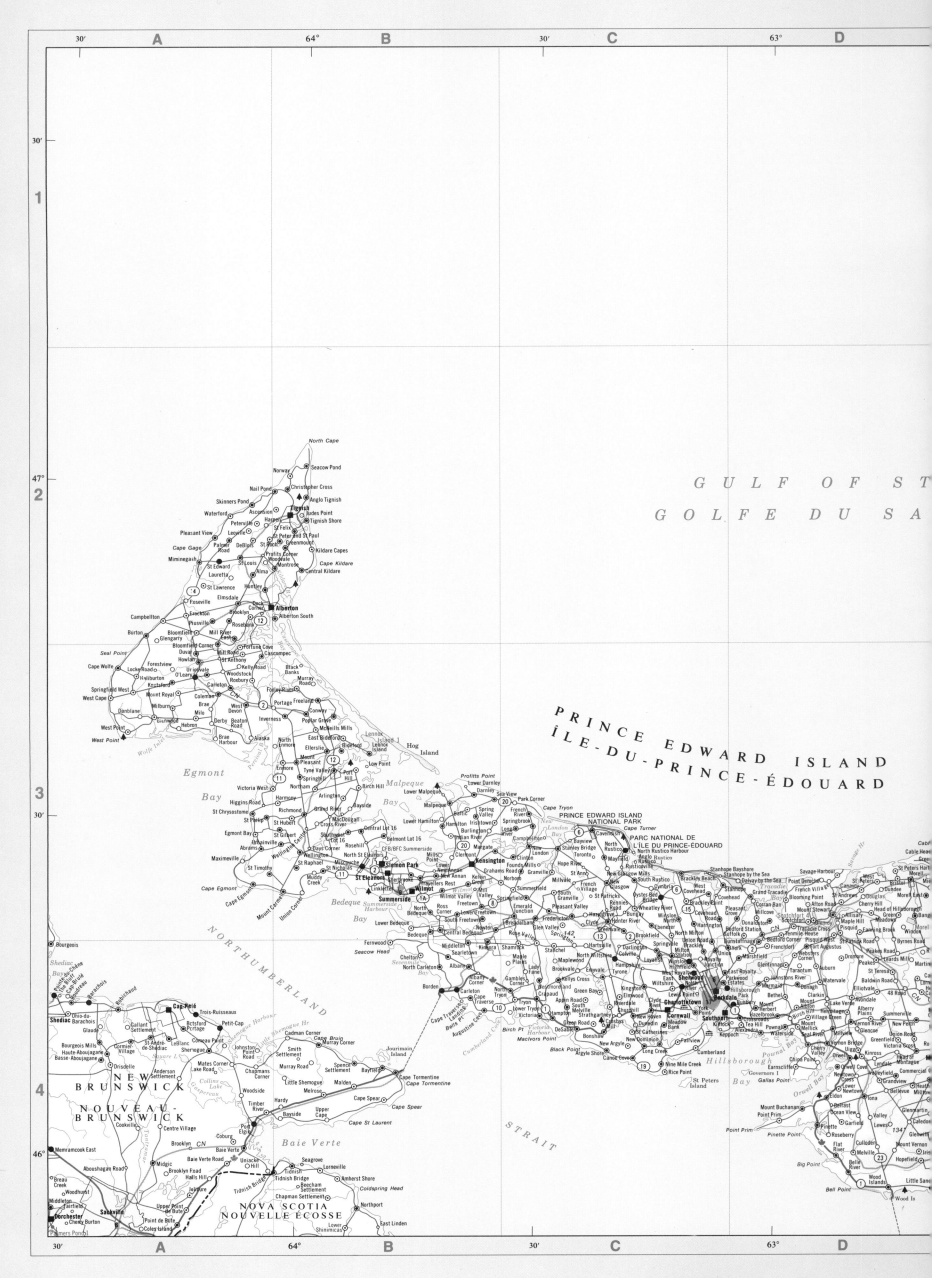

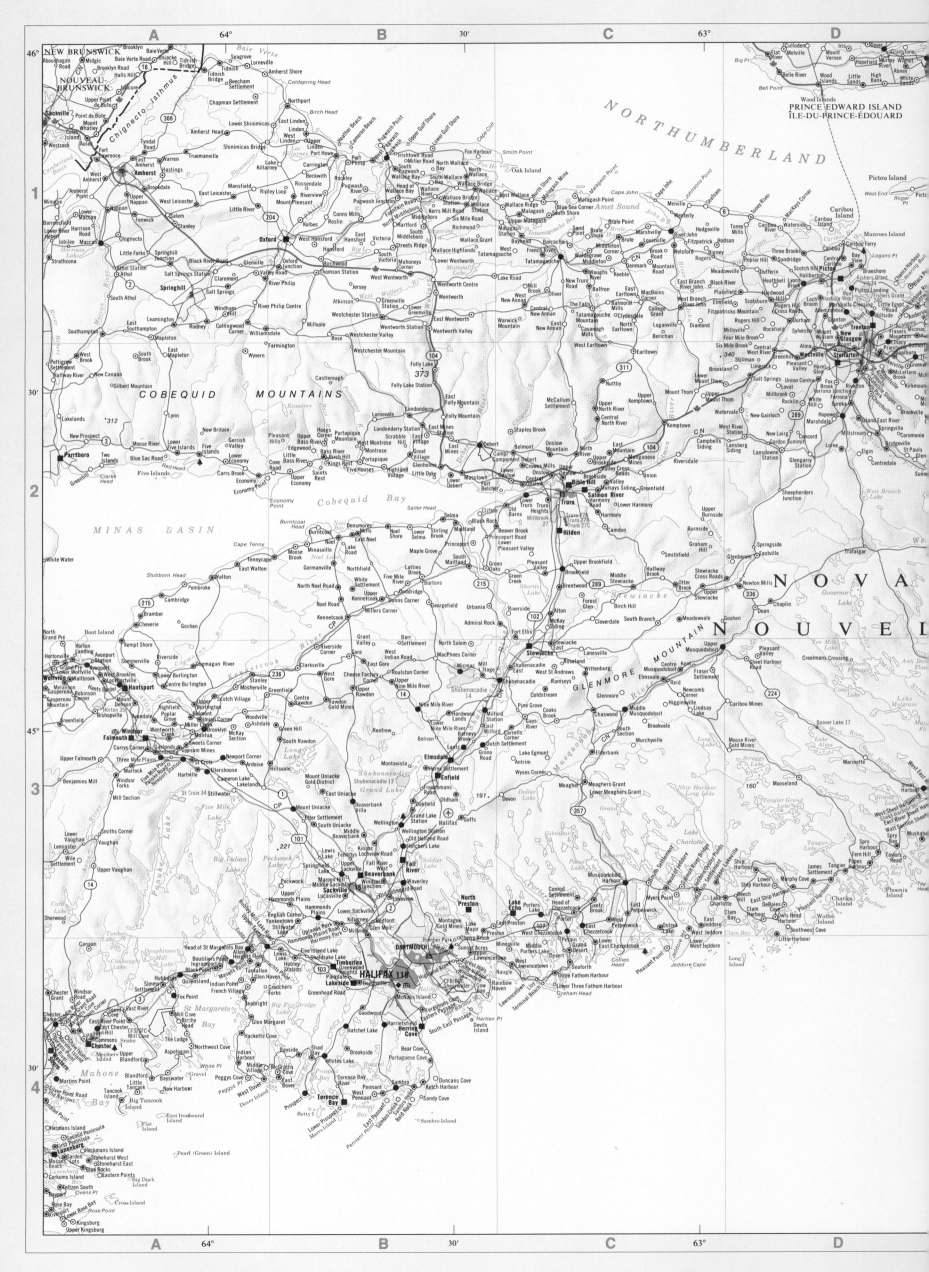

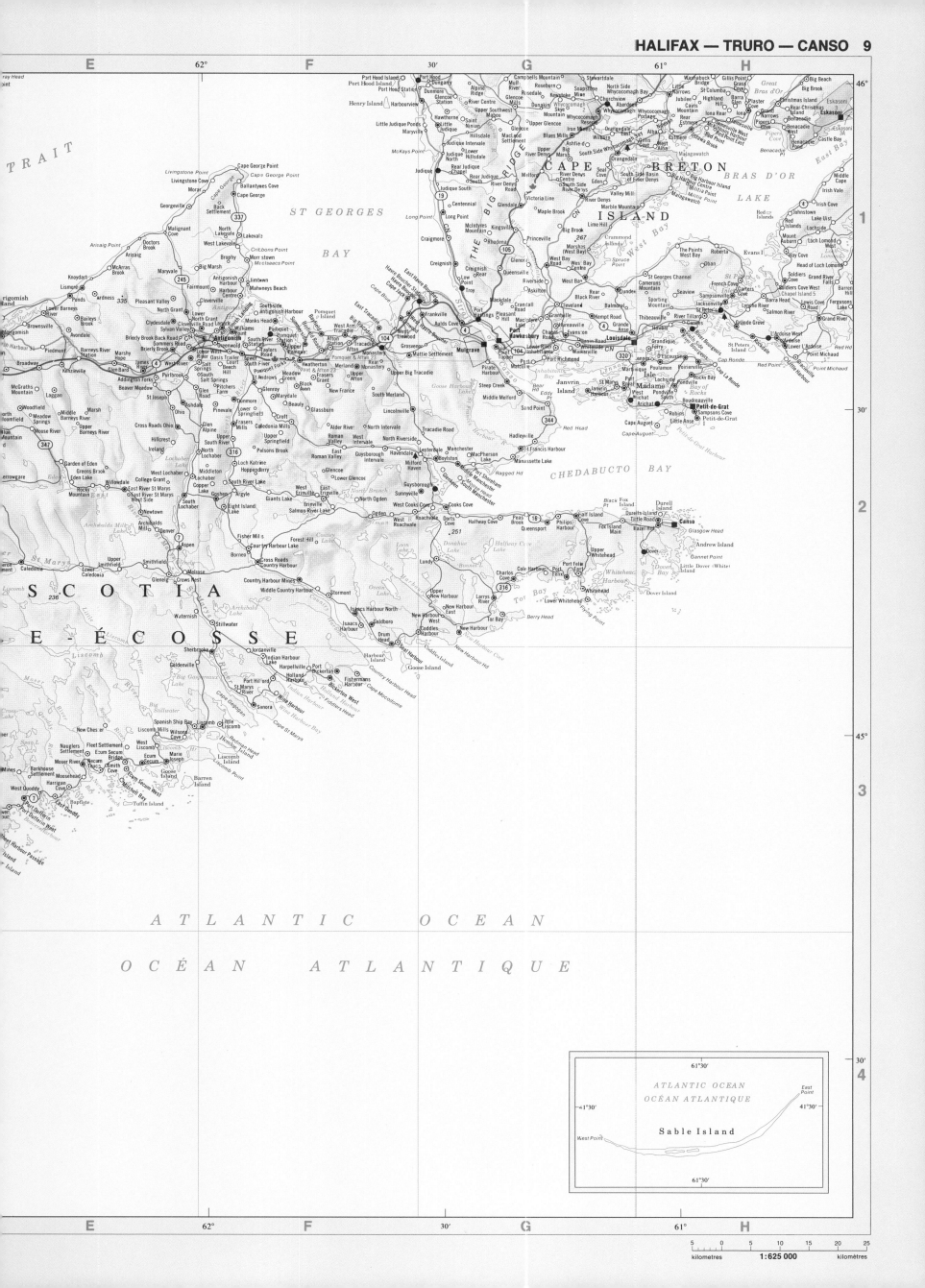

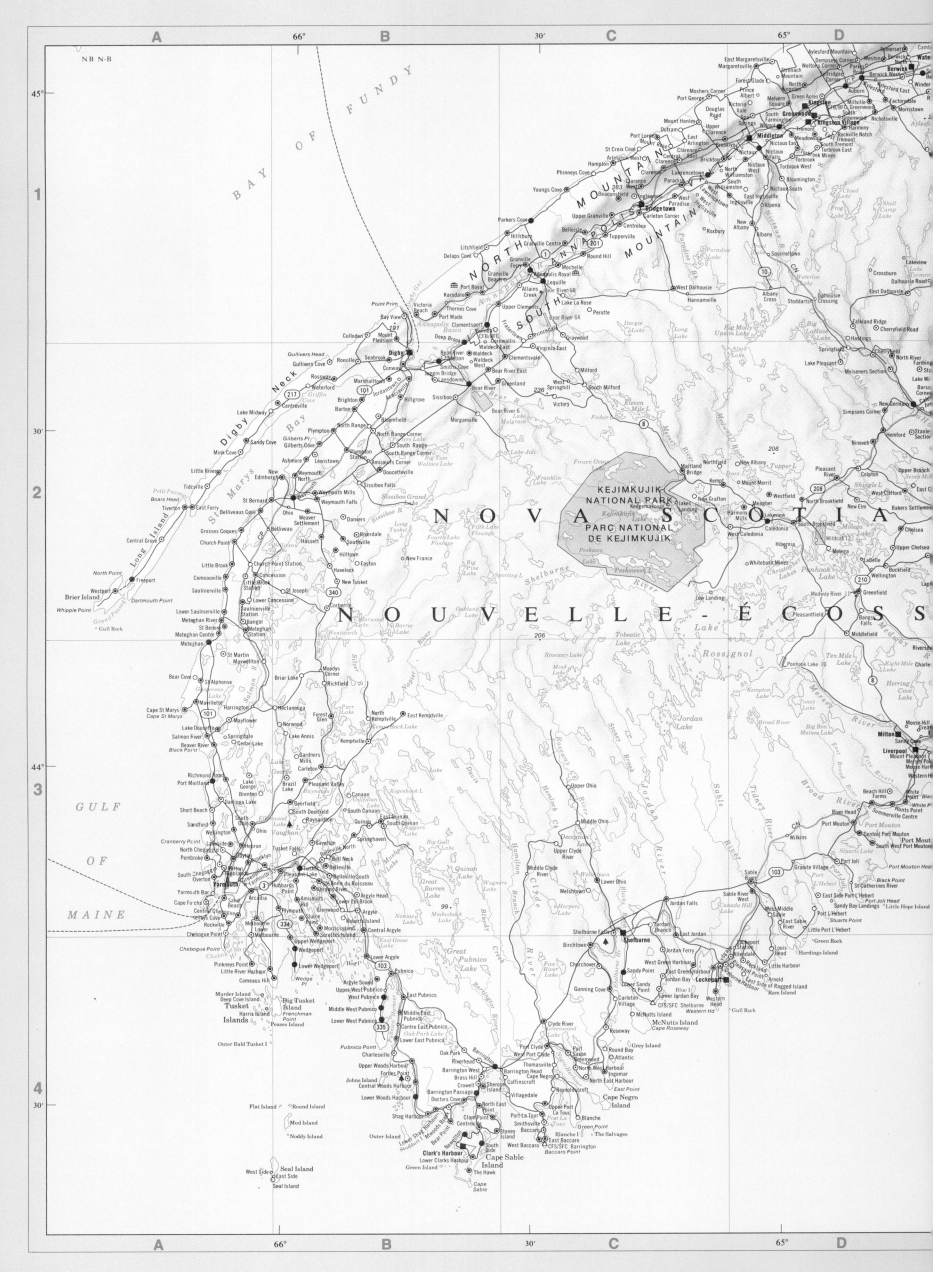

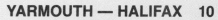

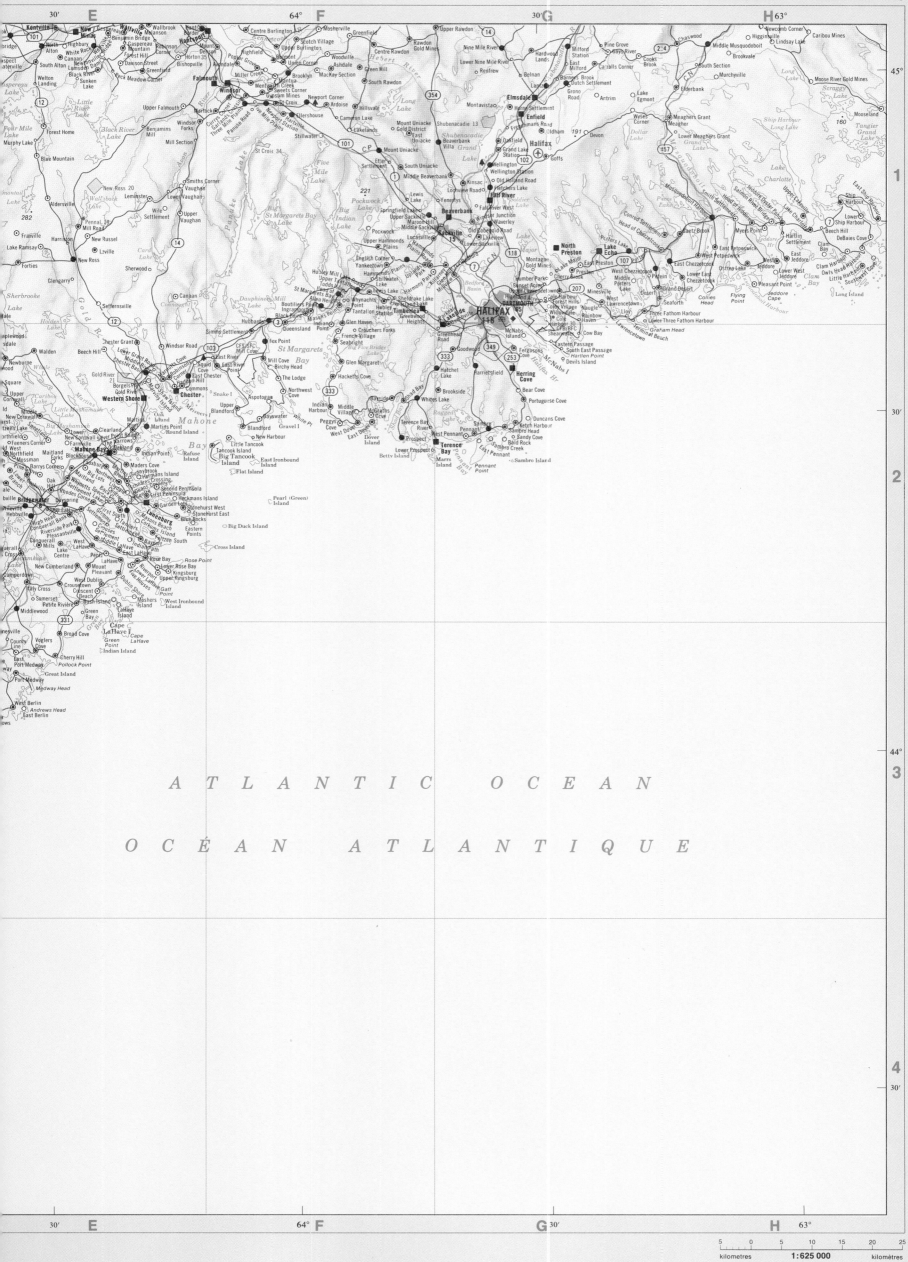

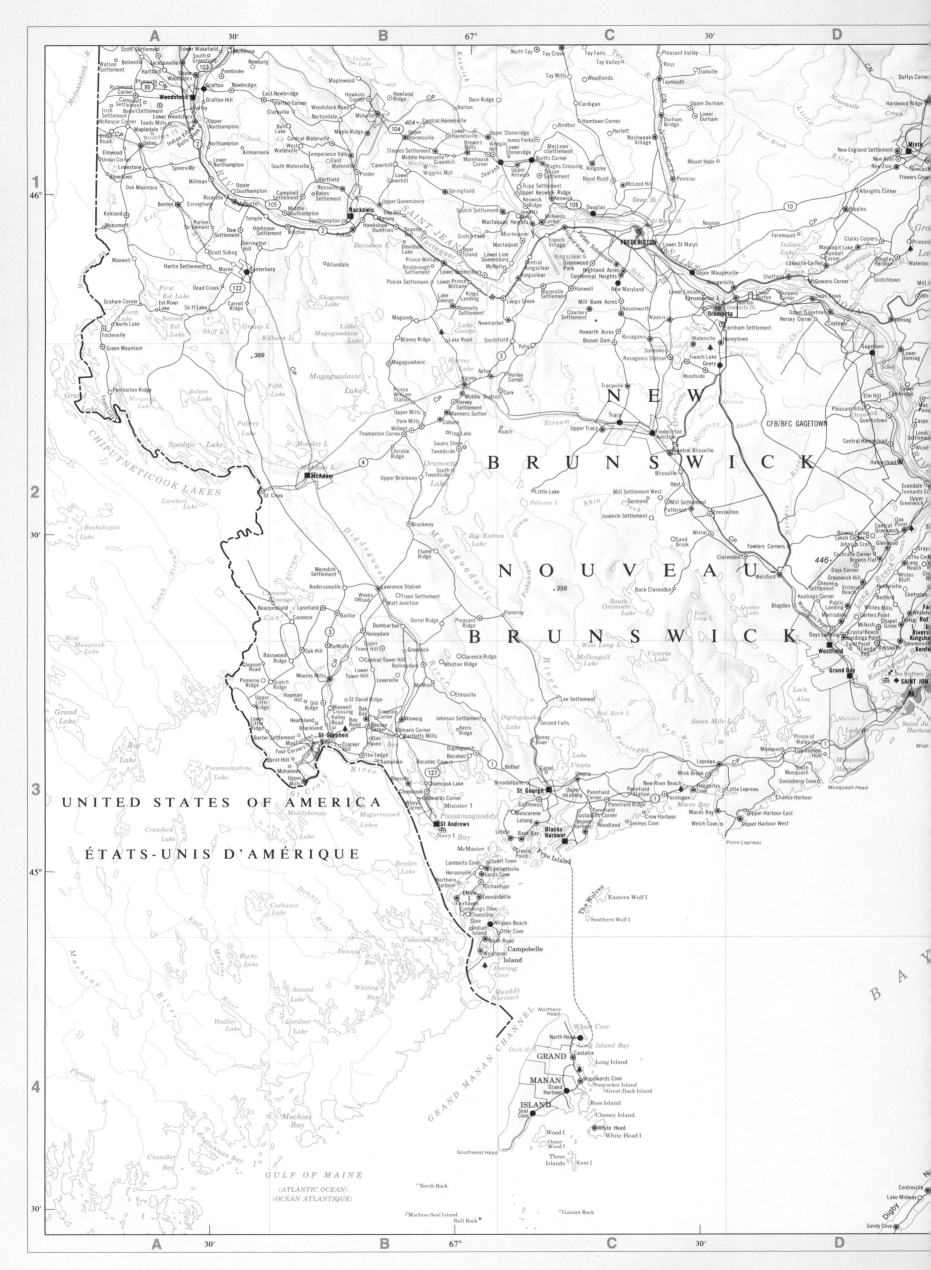

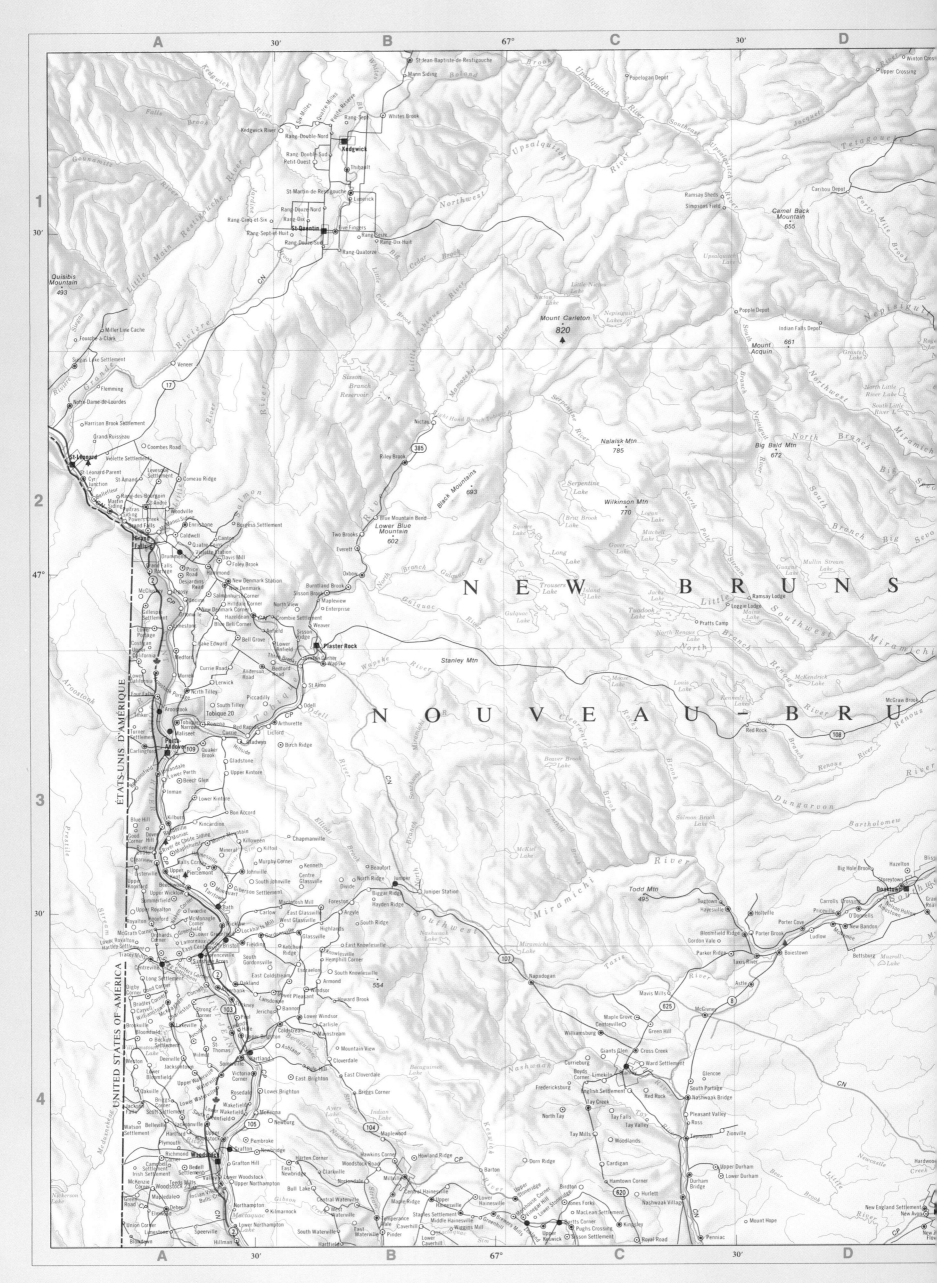

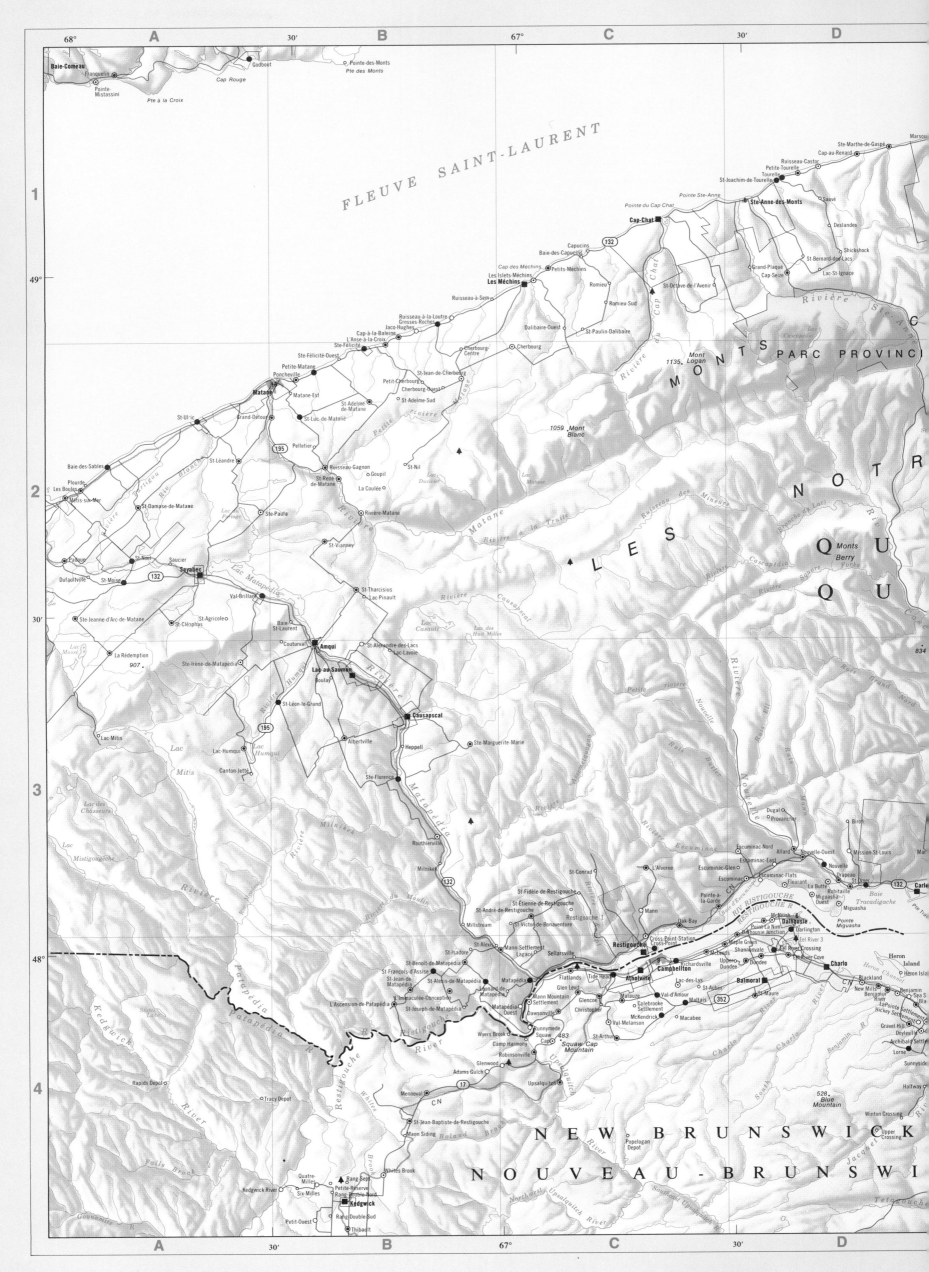

FLEUVE SAINT-LAURENT

Baie-Comeau
Franquelin
Pointe-Mistassini
Pte à la Croix
Godbout
Pointe-des-Monts
Pte des Monts
Cap Rouge

Ste-Marthe-de-Gaspé
Cap-au-Renard
Ruisseau-Castor
Petite-Tourelle
Tourelle
St-Joachim-de-Tourelle
Ste-Anne-des-Monts
Pointe du Cap Chat
Pointe Ste-Anne
Sauvé
Deslandes
Capucins
Cap-Chat
132
Baie-des-Capucins
Cap des Méchins
Petits-Méchins
Les Islets-Méchins
Les Méchins
Ruisseau-à-Sem
Romieu
Romieu-Sud
Cherbourg-Centre
Cherbourg
St-Octave-de-l'Avenir
Grand-Plaqué
Cap-Seize
Lac-St-Ignace
St-Bernard-des-Lacs
Shickshock

Rivière Ste-Amp
PARC PROVINC

Ruisseau-à-la-Loutre
Grosses-Roches
Jaco Hughes
Cap-à-la-Baleine
L'Anse-à-la-Croix
Ste-Félicité
Ste-Félicité-Ouest
Dalibaire-Ouest
St-Paulin-Dalibaire

Petite-Matane
Ponceville
Matane
St-Ulric
Grand-Détour
Matane-Est
St-Adelme-de-Matane
St-Luc-de-Matane
St-Jean-de-Cherbourg
Petit-Cherbourg
Cherbourg-Ouest
St-Adelme-Sud
Mont Logan 1135
MONTS
LES NOTR

Mont Blanc 1059

Baie-des-Sables
Plourde
Les Boules
Métis-sur-Mer
St-Damase-de-Matane
Padoue
St-Noël
Saucier
Dufaultville
St-Moïse
Sayabec
132
195
Pelletier
St-Léandre
Ruisseau-Gagnon
St-René-de-Matane
Goupil
La Coulée
St-Nil
Rivière-Matane
St-Vianney
Lac Dumarie
Lac Matane
QU
QU
Monts Berry Forks

LES

Ste-Jeanne-d'Arc-de-Matane
St-Agricole
St-Cléophas
Val-Brillant
St-Tharcisius
Lac-Pinault
Baie-St-Laurent
834
30'
Lac Masse
La Rédemption
907
Couturval
Amqui
St-Alexandre-des-Lacs
Lac-Lavoie
Ste-Irène-de-Matapédia
Las-au-Saumon
Boulat
St-Léon-le-Grand
Lac Mitis
Lac-Humqui
Lac Humqui
Canton-Jetté
Albertville
Causapscal
Heppell
Ste-Marguerite-Marie
195
Lac des Chasseurs
Lac Mistigougèche
Ste-Florence
Routhierville
Milnikek
132
St-Conrad
L'Alverne
Escuminac-Nord
Allard
Nouvelle-Ouest
Biron
Dugal
Provancher
St-Fidèle-de-Restigouche
St-Étienne-de-Restigouche
St-André-de-Restigouche
Restigouche-J.
Mann
Escuminac-Glen
Escuminac
Escuminac-East
Escuminac-Flats
Fleurant
La Butte
Robitaille
Miguasha-Ouest
Nouvelle
Drapeau
132
Carle

Millstream
St-Victor-de-Bonaventure
Oak-Bay
Pointe-à-la-Garde
CN
Miguasha
Baie Tracadigache
Pte Tra
St-Isadore
St-Alexis
Mann-Settlement
Lagacé
Sellarsville
Restigouche
Cross-Point-Station
Cross-Point
Dalhousie Junction
McNair
Point La Nim
Point La Nim
Darlington
Dalhousie
Pointe Miguasha
48°
St-François-de-Matapédia
St-Jean-de-Matapédia
St-Benoît-de-Matapédia
St-Alexis-de-Matapédia
L'Immaculée-Conception
Matapédia
Flatlands
Tide Head
Glen Levit
Atholville
Campbellton
Richardville
Maple Green
Shannonvale
Upper Dundee
Dundee
Eel River 3
Eel River Crossing
Eel River Cove
Charlo
Heron Island
Heron Island
L'Ascension-de-Patapédia
St-Joseph-de-Matapédia
Léonard-de-Patapédia
Matapédia-Ouest
Dawsonville
Glencoe
Christopher
Val-Melanson
Mann Mountain Settlement
Malaure
McKendrick
Macabee
Colebrooke Settlement
Val-d'Amour
Lac-des-Lys
St-Aubin
Maltais
Balmoral
352
St-Maure
Blackland
New Mills
Benjamin
Sea S
Bla
Runnymede
Squaw Cap
Wyers Brook
Camp Harmony
Robinsonville
Glenwood
Squaw Cap Mountain 483
Val-Melanson
St-Arthur
Benjamin River
Pointe Settlement
Hickey Settlement
Gravel Hill
Doyleville
Archibald Settle
Lorne
Sunnyside
Adams Gulch
Upsalquitch
Menneval
17
Upsalquitch
CN
Blue Mountain 528
Winton Crossing
Halfway
Upper Crossing
St-Jean-Baptiste-de-Restigouche
Maon Siding
Popelogan Depot

NEW BRUNSWICK

NOUVEAU-BRUNSWI

Rapids Depot
Tracy Depot
Kedgwick River
Quatre-Milles
Petite-Réserve
Six-Milles
Rang Sept
Rang Double-Nord
Kedgwick
Petit-Ouest
Rang Double-Sud
Thibadit
Whites Brook

E 30' F 65° G 30' H

1268
Mont
Jacques-Cartier

C-CHOCS

E LA GASPÉSIE

-DAME

B E C
B E C

DÉTROIT
D'HONGUEDO

PARC NATIONAL
DE FORILLON

FORILLON
NATIONAL PARK

Baie de Gaspé

Cap des Rosiers
Anse du Cap
des Rosiers
Cap de
Gaspé

Pointe du Serpent
Pointe au Renard
Pointe Nord-Ouest

GOLFE DU
SAINT-LAURENT

GULF OF
ST LAWRENCE

Baie
de
Malbaie

Pointe Verte

Percé
Rocher Percé
Cap Blanc
Ile de
Bonaventure

BAIE DES CHALEURS

CHALEUR BAY

Miscou Lighthouse
Miscou Plains MacGregors Mal Bay

Miscou
Island

Windsors Mal Bay
Miscou Centre
Wilson Point
Sandy Point Miscou Gully
Niscou Harbour
Little Shippegan
Ile Miscou Harbour
Petite-Rivière-de-l'Ile
Ste-Cécile
Pigeon Hill
Cote-au
Road

Nepisiguit
Bay

Lamèque
Cap-Bateau
St-Raphael-sur-Mer
Ste-Marie-sur-Mer

BATHURST

kilomètres 1:625 000 kilomètres
5 0 5 10 15 20 25

E 30' F 65° G 30' H

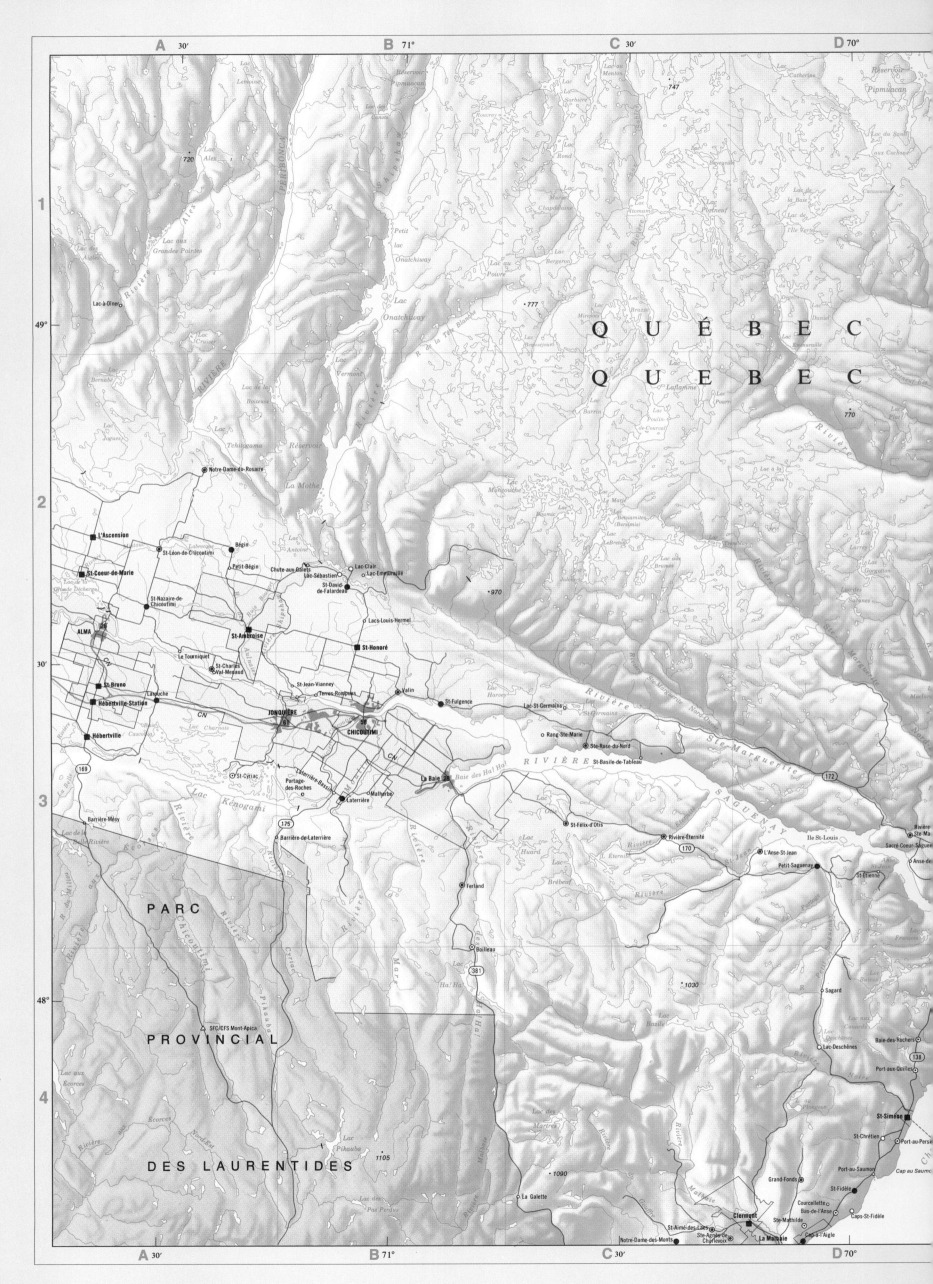

FLEUVE SAINT-LAURENT

LES NOTRE-DAME

NEW BRUNSWICK

NOUVEAU-BRUNSWICK

Péninsule de Manicouagan

Baie-Comeau

Rimouski

Mont-Joli

Rivière-du-Loup

Trois-Pistoles

Les Escoumins

Forestville

1:625 000

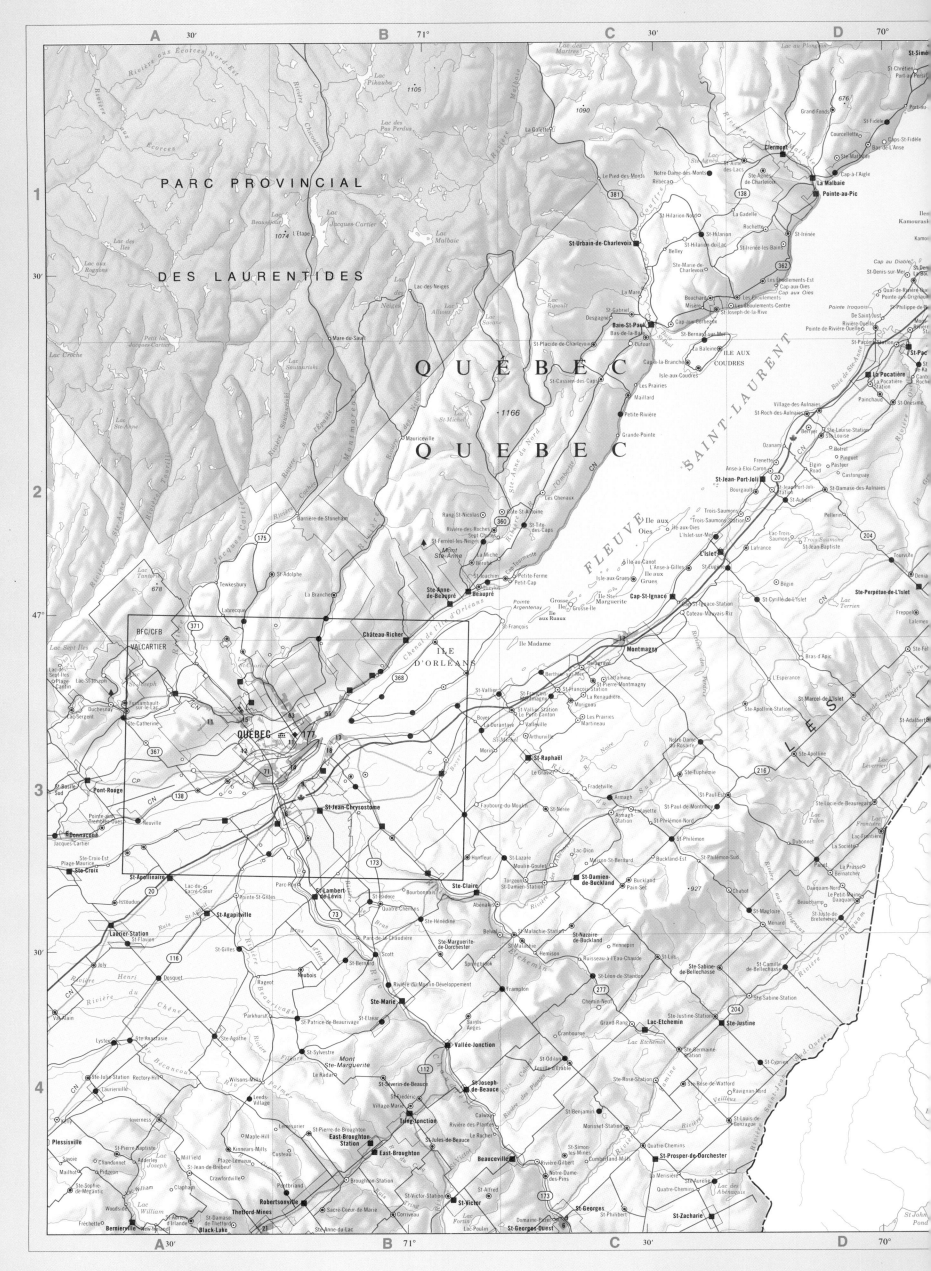

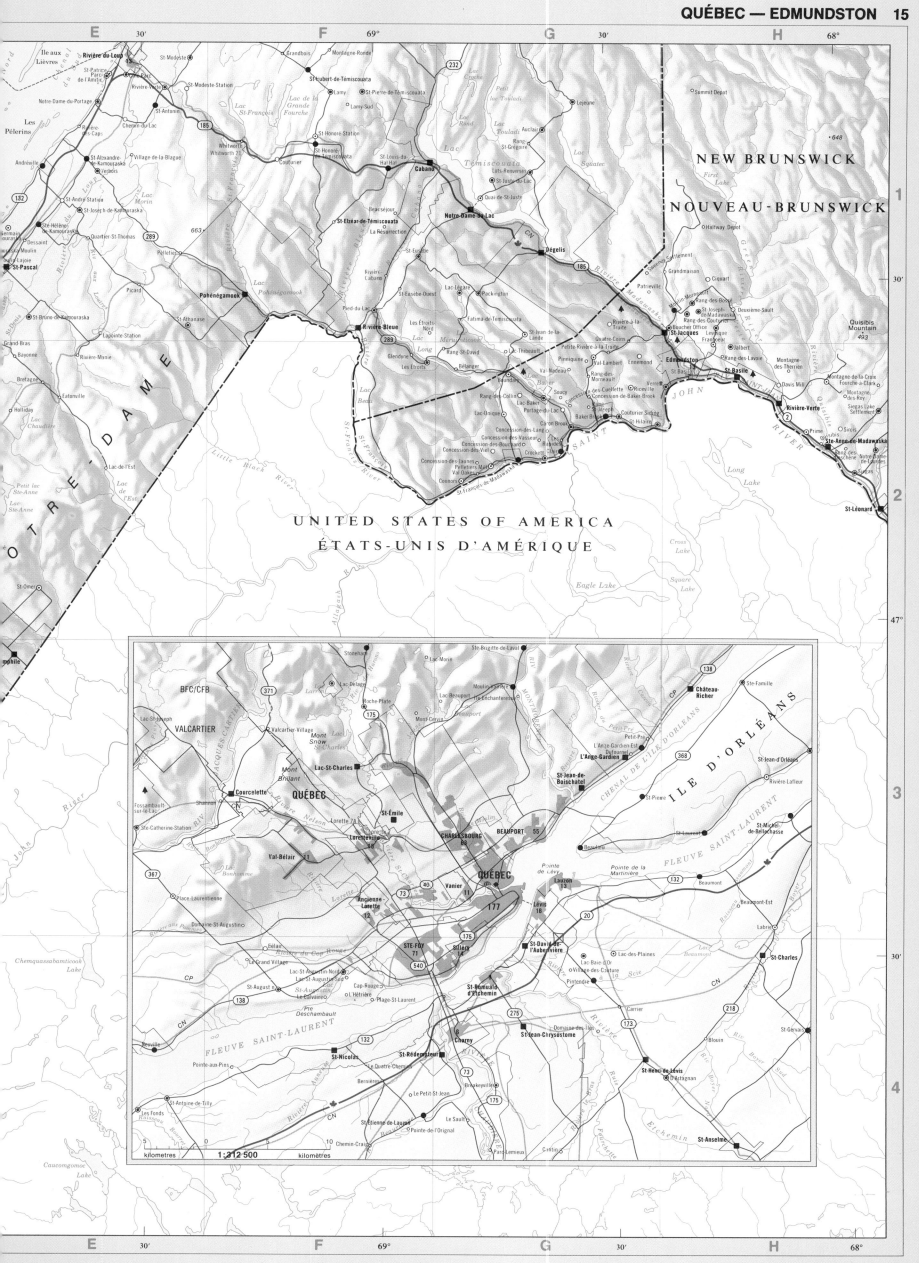

UNITED STATES OF AMERICA
ÉTATS-UNIS D'AMÉRIQUE

NEW BRUNSWICK

NOUVEAU-BRUNSWICK

ILE D'ORLÉANS

1:312 500

1:625 000

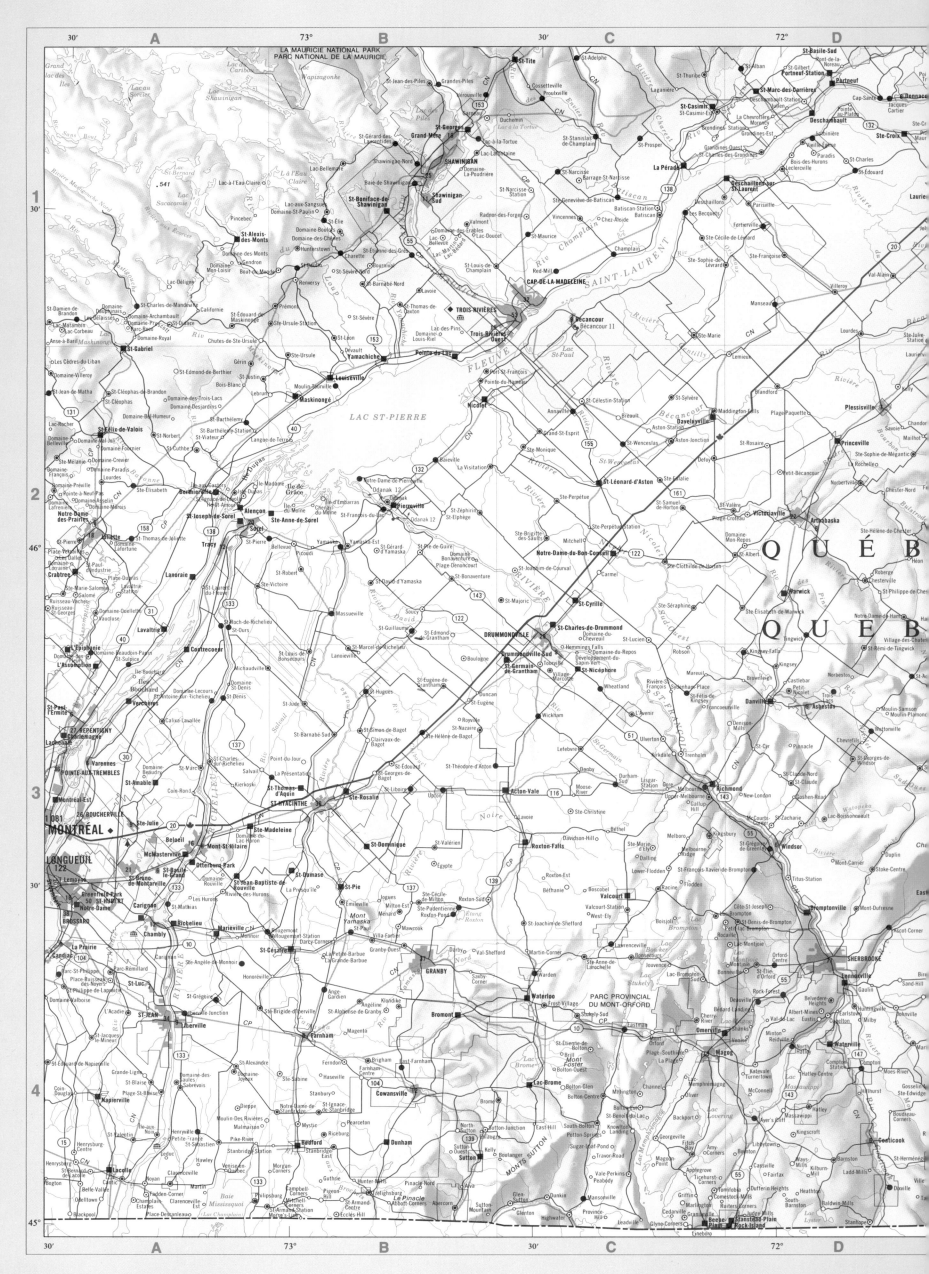

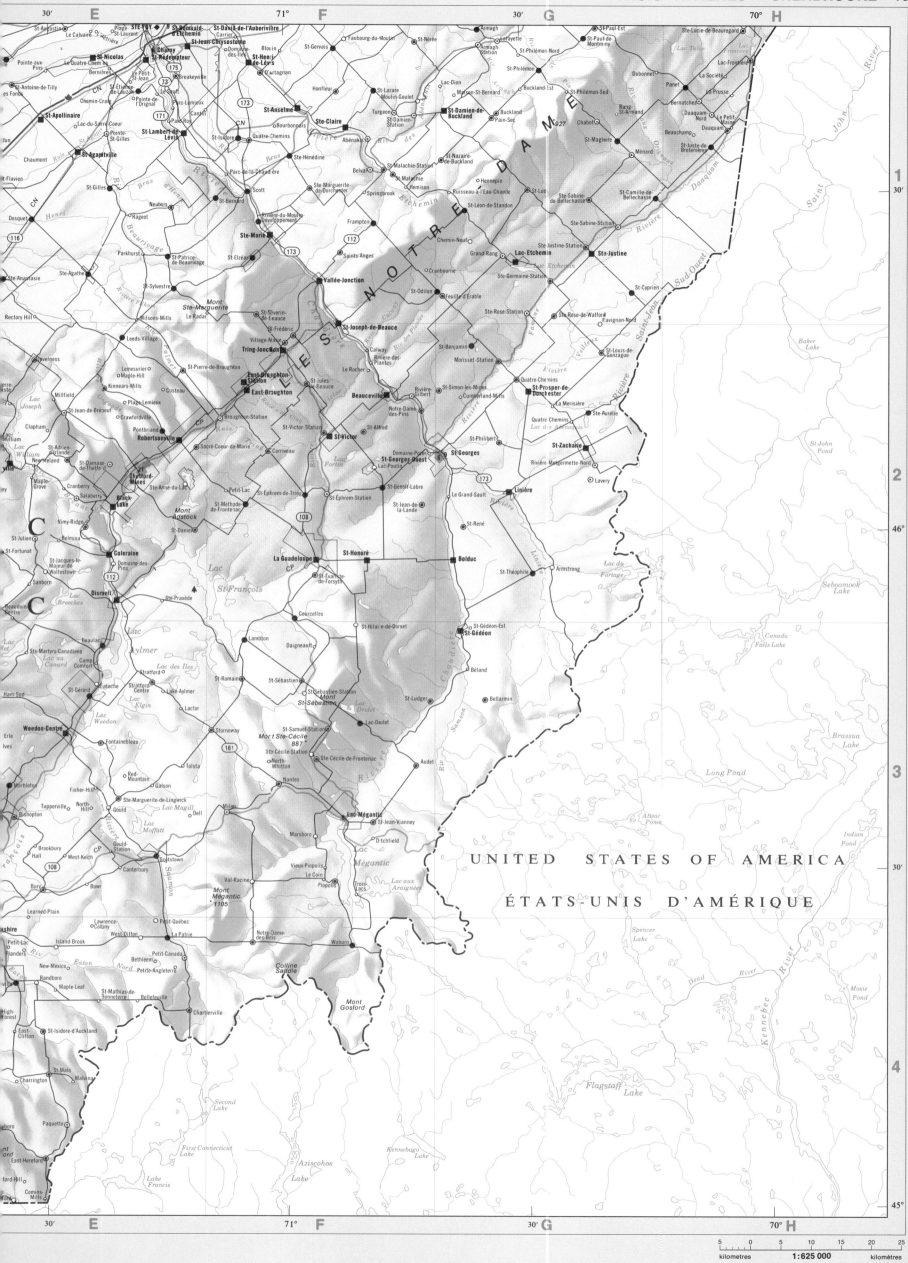

UNITED   STATES   OF   AMERICA

ÉTATS - UNIS   D'AMÉRIQUE

1:312 500

1:312 500

1:625 000

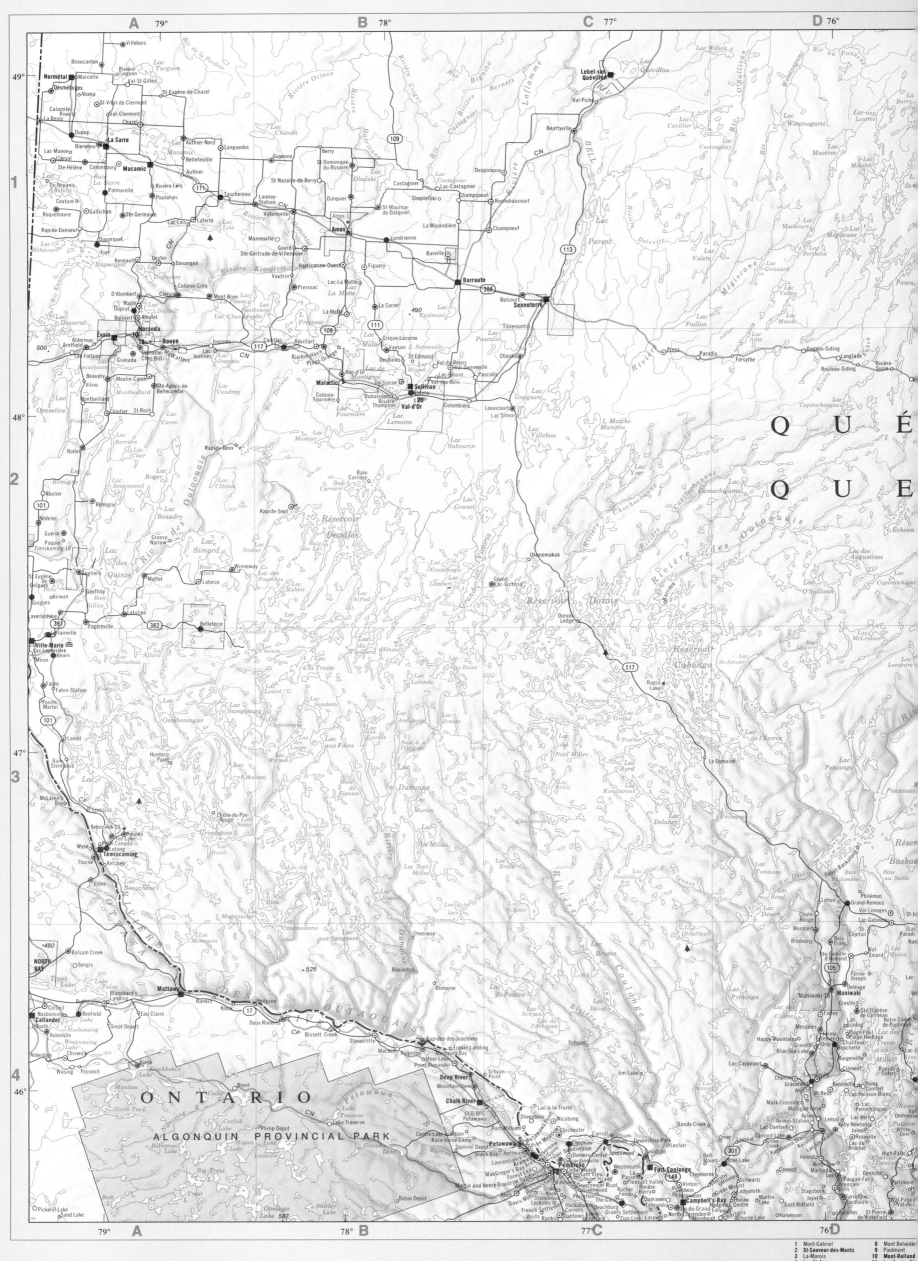

49°

Normétal

Villebois

Beaucanton

Marcotte

Rivière
Lac
Turgeon

Rivière Octave

Rivière de la Perdrix

Lebel-sur-Quévillon

Lac Wilson

Lac Quévillon

Val-Picha

Lac Wetetnagami

La Barry

Desmeloizes
Abana
Calamité
River
La Reine

St-Vital-de-Clermont
Val-Clermont
Chazel

St-Eugène-de-Chazel

Beattyville

CN

Lac
Castonguay

Lac
Maséres

Dupuy
La Sarre
Bienvenu
Macamic

Lac-Mance
Ste-Hélène
Cléval
Colombourg

Authier-Nord
Bellefeuille
Authier
Languedoc

Lac
Chicobi

Despinassy

Rochebaucourt

Lac
Berthelot

Guyenne
Berry

Champdoeur

Champneuf

Île Nepawa
Couture
Roquemaure

Rivière-Loïs
Palmarolle
Ste-Germaine

Tascherau
Launay-Station

Villemontel
St-Nazaire-de-Berry

St-Dominique-
du-Rosaire

Castagnier
Lac-Castagnier
Sheptefski

CN

Lac
Margourt

Lac Valeto

Lac
Mégiscane

Baie
La Sarre

Gallichan

Amos

Dalquier
St-Maurice-
de-Dalquier

La Morandière

Lac
Parent

Lac
Girouard

1

Rapide-Danseur
Duparquet

Laferté

Manneville
Gourd
Ste-Gertrude-de-Villeneuve

Harricanaw-Ouest
Vautrin

Figuery

Landrienne

Barville

113

Lac
Faillon

Lac
Maude

Renault
Destor
Davangus

Colonie-Cinq
Preissac

Lac-La-Motte
La Motte

Barraute

Belcourt
Senneterre

386

D'Alembert
Clérissy

Mont-Brun

La Motte

La Corne

490
Lac
Fiedmont

Tiblemont

Lac
Attic

QUÉ

Waite
Duprat
Boisvert
Aiguebelle

Évain
Noranda
Rouyn

Joannès

Cadillac
Révillard

Crique-Lacorne

L. Senneville

Obaska

Lac
Pascalis

Paradis

Gagnon-Siding
Langlade

2

500°

Arntfield
Lac-Fortune
Granada
Chez-Bill

117

St-Edmond

Val-d'Or

Rivière-Héva
Plage-Orange
Rouleau-Siding

48°

Beaudry
Vilroc
Montbeillard

Moulin-Caron
St-Agnès-de-
Bellecombe

St-Roch

Malartic

Colonie-
Fournière

Dubuissons

Sullivan

Val-d'Or
20

Colombière

Louvicourt
Lac Simon

Lac
Villebon

QUE

Lac
Opasatica

Cloutier

Lac
Vaudray

Lac
Lemoine

Lac
Sabourin

Lac
Échoua

Rollet

Lac
Barrière
Lac
Clair

Rapide-Deux

Lac
Mourier

Lac
Gueguen

Lac
O'Sullivan

Remigny
Roulier

Lac
Beaumesnil

Baie-
Carrière
Baie
Carrière

Lac
Granet

Ukanemakan

Lac
des Augustines

Nédelec
Guérin

Rapide-Sept

Réservoir
Decelles

Lac
Nodier

Baie
des Iles

Lac
Capimitchigama

47°

Timiskaming 19
Paquin

Grassy
Narrow

Lac
des
Quinze

Angliers
Moffet

Winneway

Lac
des Fourches

Lac
Rabbit

Grand
Lac Victoria

Réservoir
Dozois

Dorval
Lodge

117

Réservoir
Cabonga

3

McLaren's
Bay

Hunters'
Point

Laforce
Latulipe

Lac
Simard

Lac
Alfred

Lac
Bay

Rapid
Lake

Le Domaine

Lac
Poulter

Lac
de l'Écorce

Piscatosine

ONTARIO

North Tea L.

ALGONQUIN PROVINCIAL PARK

118

15 St-Calixte-Nord	22 Lac-Echo	29 Domaine-Vilmont	36 Domaine-des-Trois-Lacs	43 Domaine-Racine	50 Pied-de-la-Montagne	57 Lac-Rocher	64 St-Jacques
16 Domaine-du-Joli-Val	23 Les Hauteurs	30 Lac-Lapierre	37 Cordon	44 Ste-Marcell ne-de-Kildare	51 Boscoville	58 Domaine-Val-ioli	65 Ste-Marie-Salomée
17 St-Calixte-de-Kilkenny	24 Lac-Bleu	31 Domaine-Charbonneau	38 St-Jacques-Nord	45 Ste-Ambroise-de-Kildare	52 Lac-des-Français	59 Ste-Mélanie	66 Salomé
18 St-Hippolyte-de-Kilkenny	25 Lac-Connelly	32 Bissonnette	39 Marion	46 Domaine-Lafrenière	53 Dupont	60 Domaine-Paradis	67 Laurence
19 Lac-de-l'Achigan	26 Domaine-Breton	33 Domaine-François	40 Montcalm	47 Domaine-Asselin	54 Domaine-des-Quatre-Hétu	61 Domaine-François	68 Ruisseau-St-Georges
20 Weisbord-Acres	27 Lac-Siesta	34 Ste-Julienne	41 Lac-Clearview	48 Domaine-Prévile	55 Camp-Laclouwhi	62 Place-Versai es	69 Domaine-Beaudoin-Papin
21 Lac-des-Quatorze-Îles	28 Lac-Brien	35 Domaine-Lemenn	42 Achigan-Ouest	49 Domaine-Lafertune	56 Village-des-Geoffroy	63 Domaine-Lorr ine	70 Domaine-des-Fleurs

NEWFOUNDLAND
TERRE-NEUVE

NFLD
T-N

ROULX

B E C
B E C

SEPT-ÎLES

Moisie Salmon Club

Coude-de-la-Rivière-Moisie

De Grasse
Laurent-Val

Seven Islands
Seve n Islands

Moisie
SFC/CF3 Moisie

Baie des Sept Îles

Rivière-Ste-Marguerite-nedes

Baie
Ste-Marguerite

Île Grosse Boule

Pte à la Chasse

Rivière-Brocha

Pointe Ste-Marguerite

Port-Cartier

Pointe Jambon

Détroit de Jacques-Cartier

Magpie

Baie de Mingpie

Mingan

Havre-St-Pierre

Pte Longue

Île Nue de Mingan

Grande Île
Îles de Mingan

Île du Havre

Cap de Rabast

Trois-Ruisseaux

Cap-de Rabast

Baie-Ste-Claire

Pointe de l'Ouest

Pointe-de-l'Ouest

Anse-aux-Fraises

Port-Menier

Île d'Anticosti

Baie-des-Homards

Pointe Sproule

Rivière-Pentecôte

Baie des Homards

Pointe-aux-Anglais

Pointe aux Anglais

GOLFE DU SAINT-LAURENT

GULF OF ST LAWRENCE

Détroit d'Honguedo

Baie-Trinité

Pointe-des-Monts
Pointe des Monts

FLEUVE SAINT-LAURENT

Ste-Anne-des-Monts

Cap-Chat

Les Méchins

Rivière Mont-Louis

Grande-Vallée-des-Monts

Coridarme
St-Yvon
St-Hélier

St-Thomas-de-Cloridorme

Pointe Nord-Ouest

PARC NATIONAL DE FORILLON

Cap des Rosiers

FORILLON NATIONAL PARK

Mont Jacques-Cartier

PARC PROV

NOTRE-DAME

Murdochville

LES   MONTS   DE LA GASPÉSIE   CHIC-CHOCS

Mont Logan

Gaspé

Baie de Gaspé

10   0   10   20   30   40   50
kilomètres   **1 : 1 250 000**   kilomètres

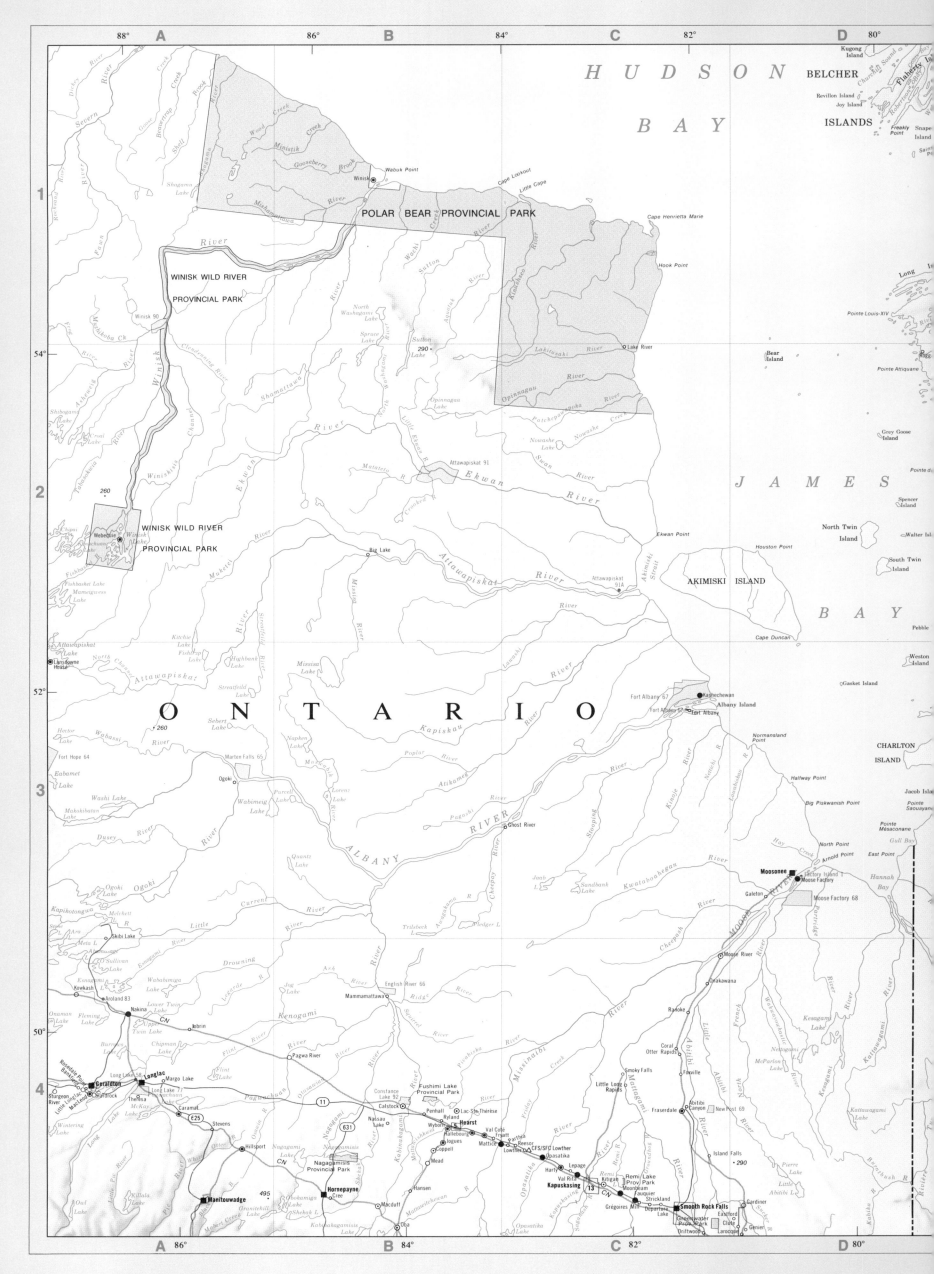

HUDSON

BAY

BELCHER

ISLANDS

POLAR BEAR PROVINCIAL PARK

WINISK WILD RIVER

PROVINCIAL PARK

WINISK WILD RIVER

PROVINCIAL PARK

ONTARIO

JAMES

BAY

AKIMISKI ISLAND

CHARLTON

ISLAND

QUÉBEC

Q U É B E C

E 78°   **F** 76°   **G** 74°   **H** 72°

20   0   20   40   60   80   100

kilomètres   **1 : 2 500 000**   kilomètres

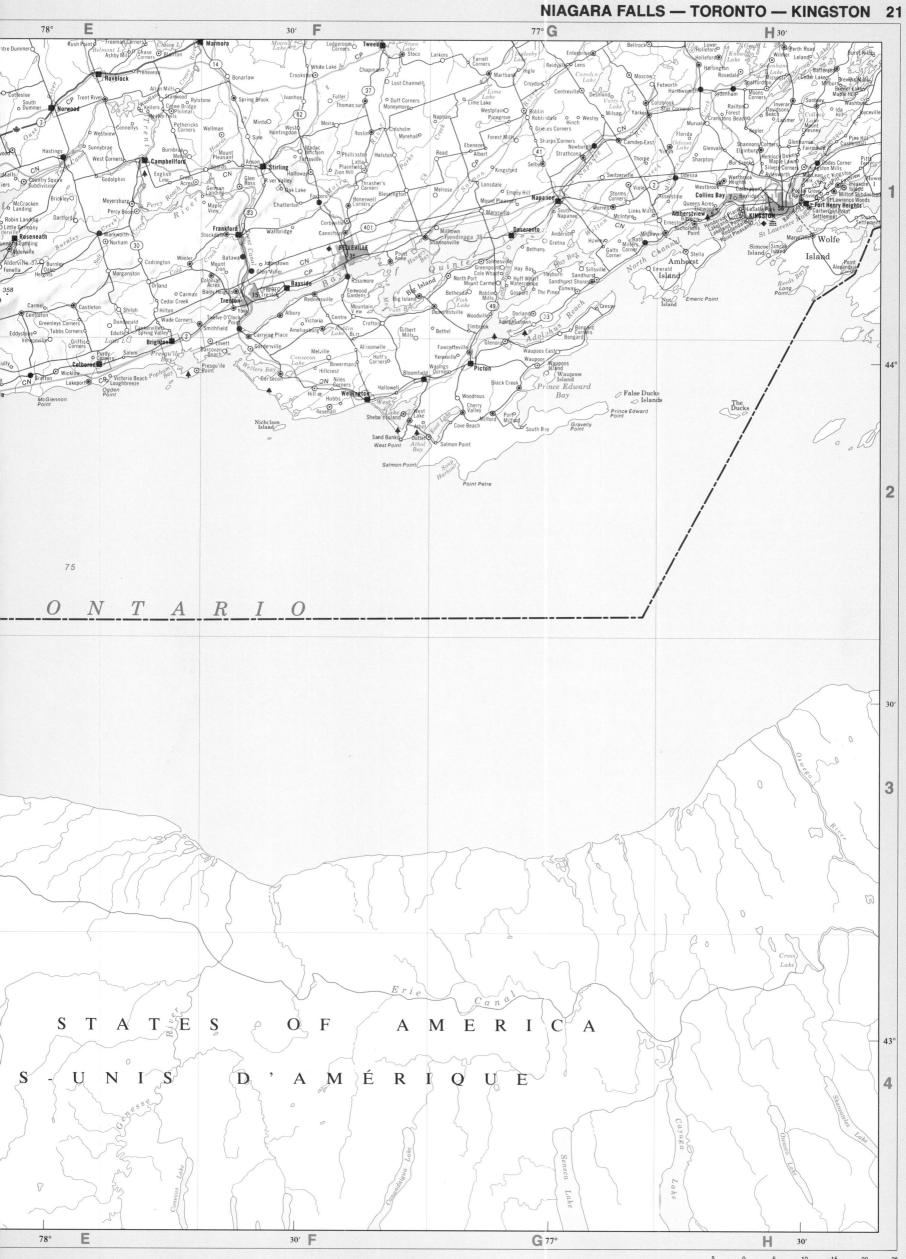

LAKE

HURON

177

UNITED STATES

OF AMERICA

ÉTATS-UNIS

D'AMÉRIQUE

LAKE

ST CLAIR

175

Anchor
Bay

Walpole I
Walpole Island 46

Goose
Lake

Pigeon

Bay

Pelee Passage

POINT PELEE
NATIONAL PARK

PARC NATIONAL DE
LA POINTE PELÉE

Point Pelee

Middle Sister
I

East Sister
I

Pelee
Island

Pelee Island
South

Fish
Pt

Middle I

SARNIA

WINDSOR

CHATHAM

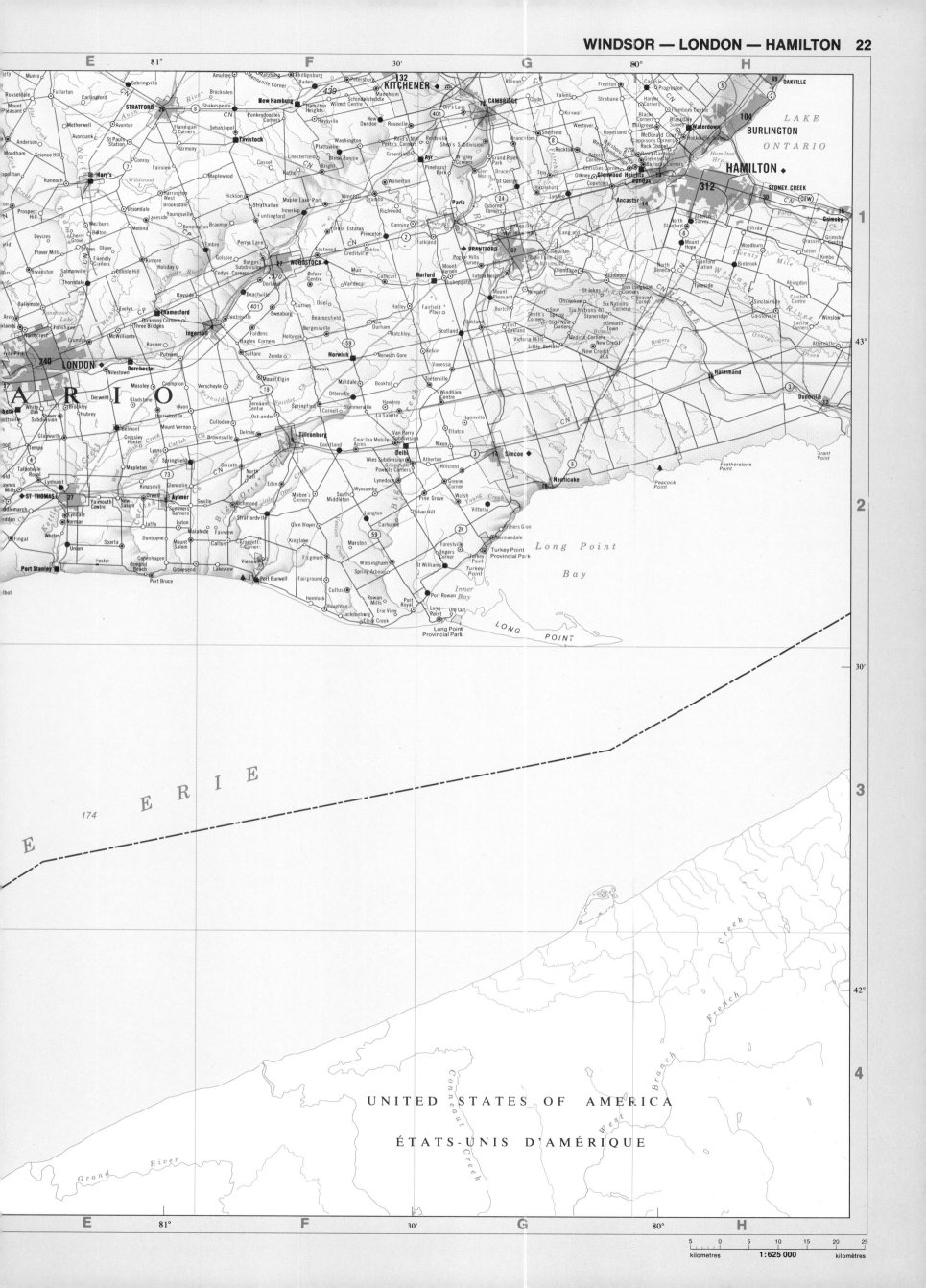

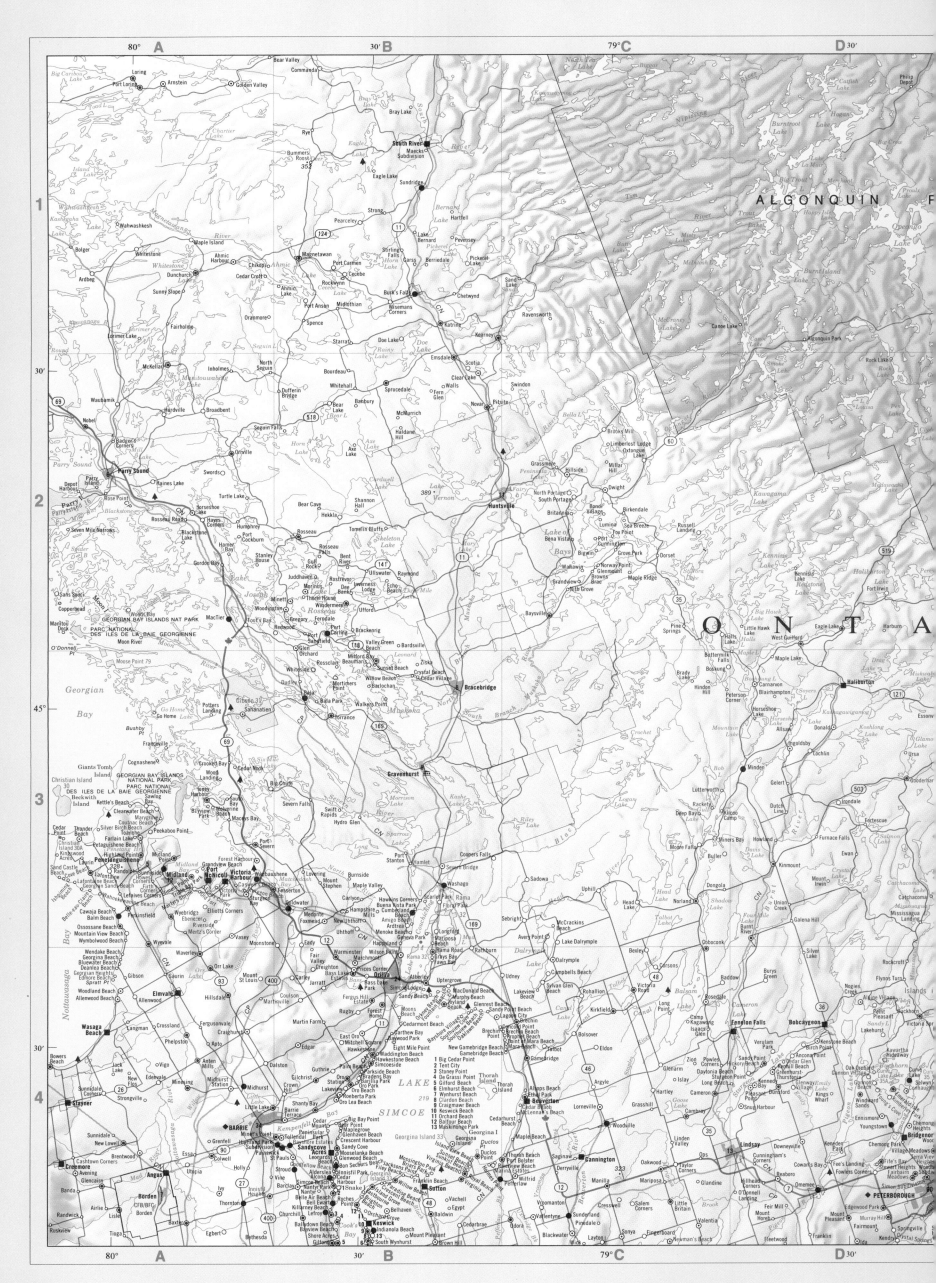

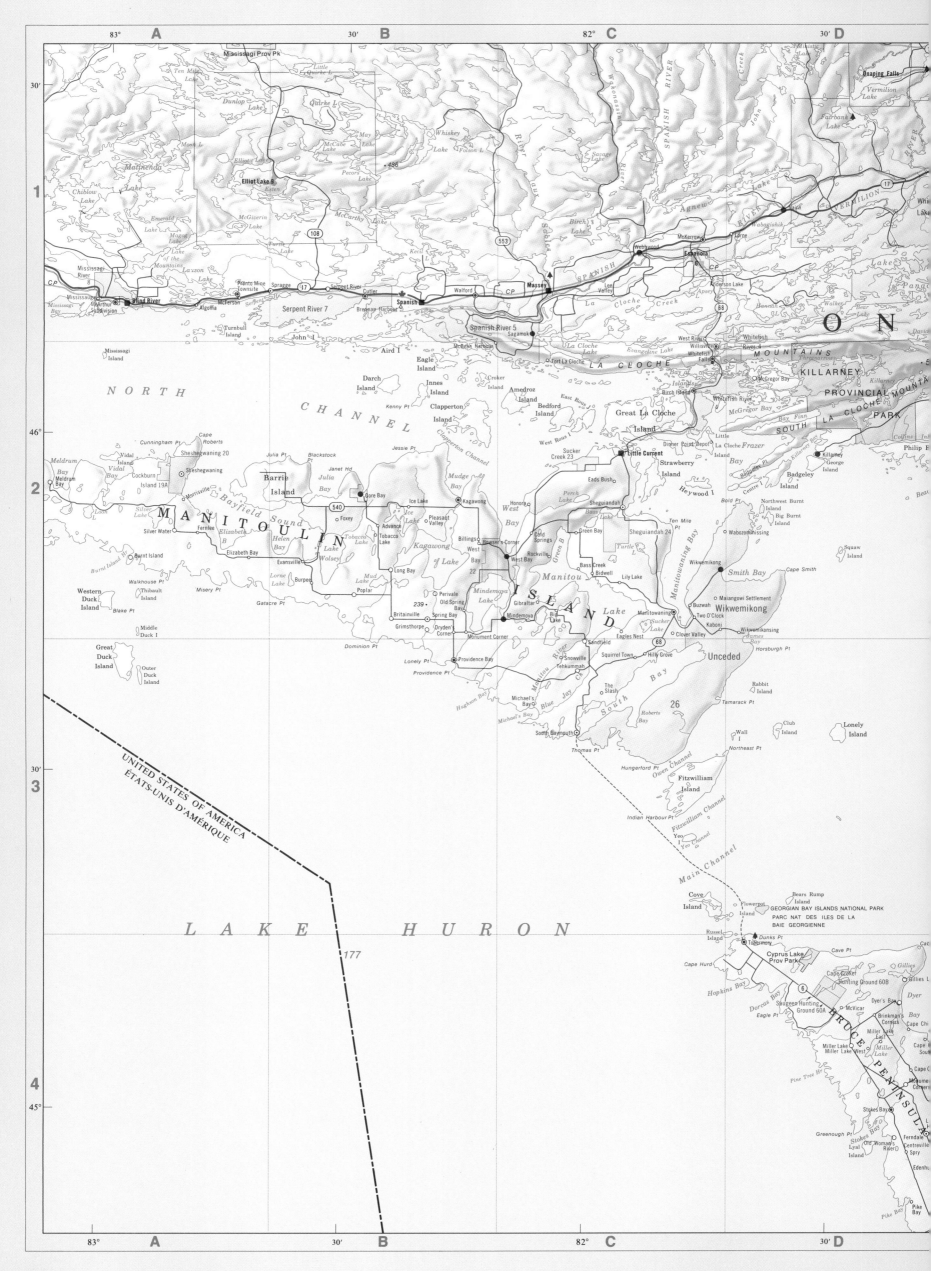

A · · · · · · 83° · · · · · · 30' · · · · · · B · · · · · · 30' · · · · · · 82° · · · · · · C · · · · · · 30' · · · · · · D

1

Mississagi Prov Pk
Ten Mile Lake
Little Quirke L.
Dunlop Lake
Quirke L.
May Lake
Moon L
McCabe Lake
Whiskey Lake
Folson L
Elliot Lake 8
Esten
Pecors Lake
McGiverin Lake
McCarthy Lake
Emerald Lake
Magog Lake
Matinenda Lake
La'zon Lake
Mountains of the La'zon
Chiblou Lake
Turtle Lake
Keel L
Sable Lake
Lake
486
Wakonassin River
Spanish River
Birch's Lake
Agnew Lake
Lorne
Savage Lake
John Creek
Unaping Falls
Vermilion Lake
Fairbank Lake
Killarney
553
108
McKerrow
Webbwood
Espanola
CP
17
Vermilion River
Lake Wabogishik

Mississagi River
CP
Mississauga
McArthur Subdivision
Mississauga Bay
Blind River
Algoma
McFerson
Serpent
Pronto Mine Townsite
Spragge
17
Serpent River
Cutler
Brennan Harbour
Serpent River 7
Walford
CP
Massey
Spanish
Lee Valley
SPANISH
La Cloche Creek
Anderson Lake
Apsey
Bannath
GL
68
Bear Lake
Walker Lake
ON

O N

Turnbull Island
John I
Spanish River 5
Sagamok
McBean Harbour
Whitefish
West River
Willisville
River 4
Whitefish Falls
Mountains
Whitefish River
McGregor Bay
Little La Cloche
KILLARNEY
PROVINCIAL
David
Collins Inlet

46°

Mississagi Island
NORTH
Aird I
Eagle Island
Darch Island
Innes Island
Croker Island
Amedroz Island
Fort La Cloche
U La Cloche Lake
Evangeline Lake
Birch Island
La Cloche
Bay of Islands
Frazer Bay
SOUTH LA CLOCHE
PARK
Philip I

CHANNEL

Kenny Pt
Clapperton Island
Bedford Island
East Rous I
West Rous I
Great La Cloche Island
Little Current
Strawberry Island
Dinner Point Depot
Badgeley Pt
Killarney
George Island
Killarney
Beat

2

Meldrum Bay
Vidal Island
Vidal Bay
Cunningham Pt
Cape Roberts
Sheshegwaning 20
Cockburn Island 19A
Sheshegwaning
Silver Lake
Morrisville
Julia Pt
Blackstock Pt
Janet Hd
Jessie Pt
Clapperton Channel
Mudge Bay
West Bay
Perch Lake
Sucker Creek 23
Honora
Eads Bush
Sheguiandah
Bass Lake
Bold Pt
Ten Mile Lake
Manitouwaning Bay
Northwest Burnt Island
Big Burnt Island
Squaw Island
Wikwemikong

Loon L
Cockburn
Barrie Island
Julia Bay
Gore Bay
Ice Lake
Kagawong
West Bay
Cold Springs
Green B
Green Bay
Sheguiandah 24
Wabozonkissing
Smith Bay
Cape Smith
Meldrum Bay
540
Foxey
Ice Lake
Pleasant Valley
Billings
Bowser's Corner
Rockville
Bass Creek
Turtle L
Heywood I
Centre I
Fernlee
Silver Water
Elizabeth B
Helen Bay
Tobacco Lake
Advance
Tobacco Lake
Kagawong Lake
West Bay 22
West Bay
Bidwell
Lily Lake
Manitou Lake
Manitowaning
Wikwemikong

Burnt Island
Walkhouse Pt
Elizabeth Bay
Evansville
Lake Wolsey
Long Bay
Mud Lake
Mindemoya Lake
Gibraltar
Green B
Two O'Clock
Buzwah
Maiangowi Settlement
Wikwemikonsing
Clover Valley
Western Duck Island
Thibault Island
Burpee
Lorne Lake
Misery Pt
Gatacre Pt
Poplar
239
Perivale
Old Spring Bay
Spring Bay
Mindemoya
Big Lake
Sucker Lake
Kaboni
James Bay

Middle Duck I
Britainville
Dryden's Corner
Monument Corner
Sandfield
Snowville
Squirrel Town
Holly Grove
Horsburgh Pt
Unceded

3

Great Duck Island
Outer Duck Island
Grimsthorpe
Dominion Pt
Lonely Pt
Providence Bay
Providence Pt
Michael's Bay
Blue Jay Ck
Tehkummah
The Slash
Roberts Bay
South Bay
South Baymouth
26
Rabbit Island
Tamarack Pt
Wall I
Club Island
Lonely Island
Northeast Pt

30'

UNITED STATES OF AMERICA
ÉTATS-UNIS D'AMÉRIQUE
Thomas Pt
Hungerford Pt
Owen Channel
Fitzwilliam Island
Main Channel
Indian Harbour Pt
Fitzwilliam Channel
Yeo I
Yeo Channel

L A K E   **H U R O N**
177
Cove Island
Flowerpot I
Bears Rump Island
GEORGIAN BAY ISLANDS NATIONAL PARK
PARC NAT. DES ÎLES DE LA BAIE GEORGIENNE
Russel Island
Dunks Pt
Tobermory
Cape Hurd
Cyprus Lake Prov Park
Cave Pt
Gillies
Hopkins Bay
Cape Hurd
Dorcas Bay
6
Cape Sucker
Hunting Ground 60B
Billies
Dyer
McVicar
Dyer's Bay
Brinkman's Corners
Cape Chi
Eagle Pt
Saugeen Hunting Ground 60A
B R U C E
South
Cape
Maun
Corners

4

45°
Pine Tree Hr
Miller Lake
Miller Lake West
Miller Lake
P E N I N S U L A
Stokes Bay
Ferndale
Centreville
Spry
Edenh
Greenough Pt
Stokes Bay
Lyal I
Old Woman's River I
Pike Bay
Pike Bay

A · · · · · · 83° · · · · · · 30' · · · · · · B · · · · · · 30' · · · · · · 82° · · · · · · C · · · · · · 30' · · · · · · D

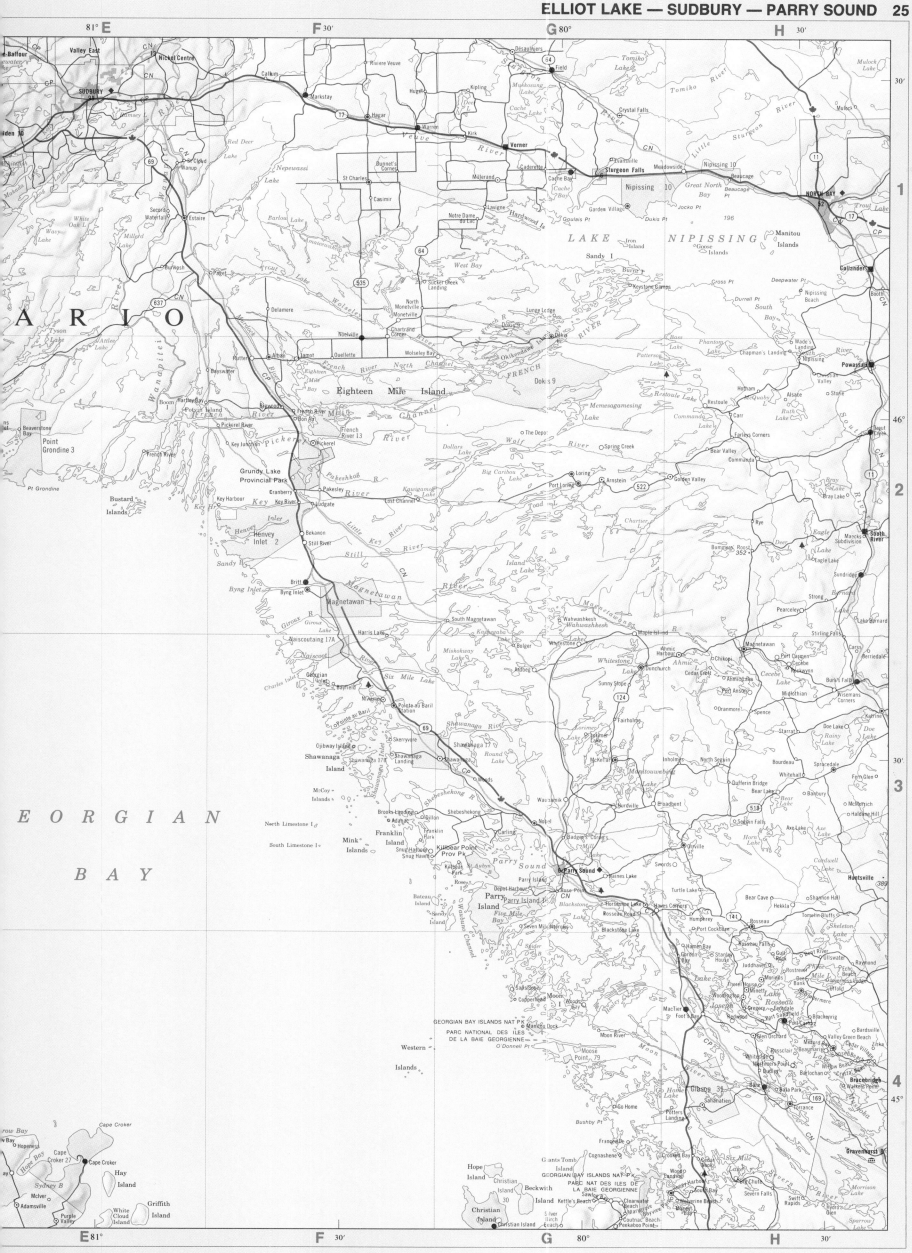

1:625 000

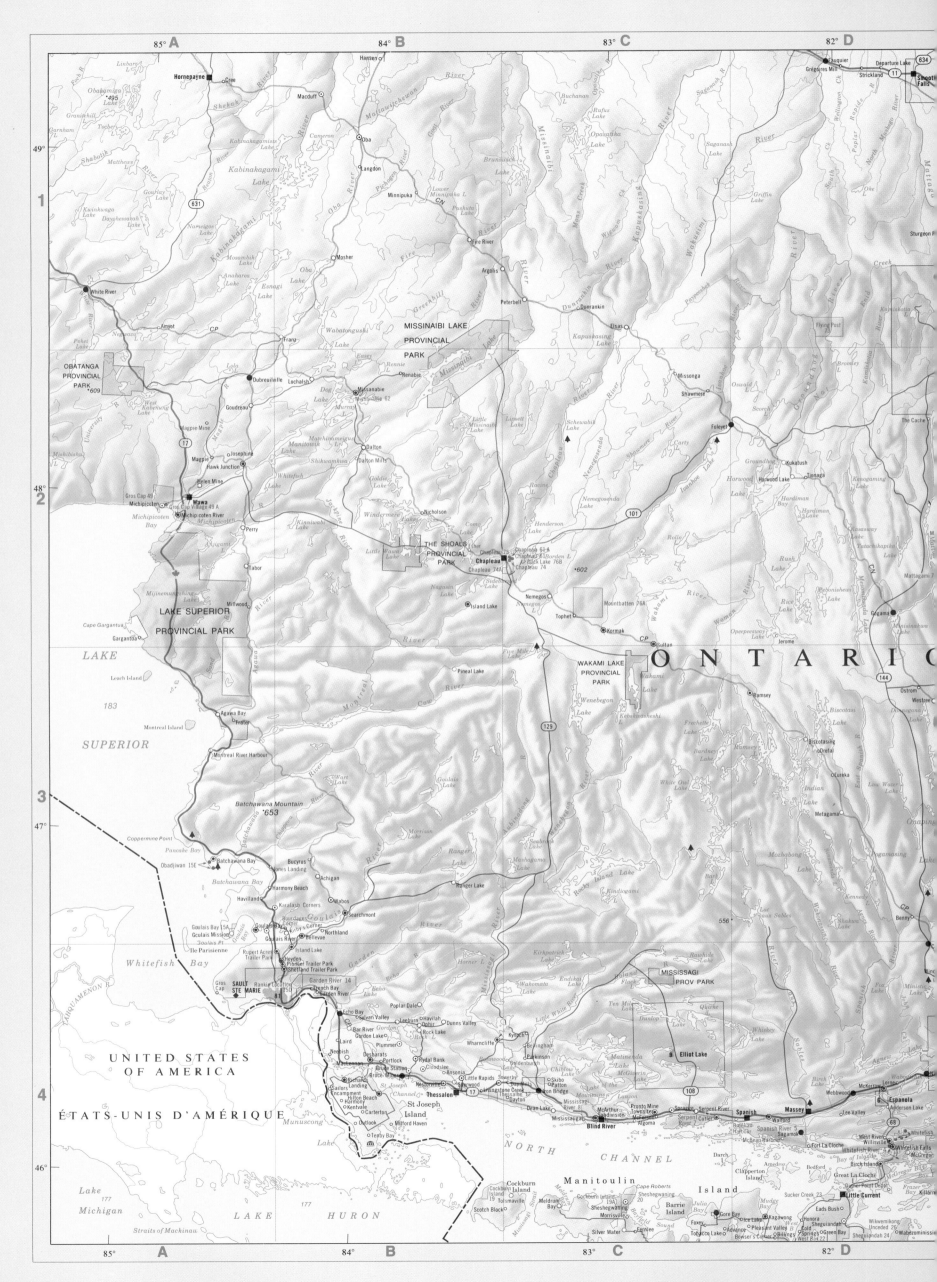

Linbury L.

Horepayne   Cree

Hansen

Obakamiga Lake   *495

Macduff

Shekak River

Granitehill

Tochee

GosHay Lake

Kwinkwaga Lake

Daychessarah Lake

Matthews

Namewigos Lake

631

Kabinakagami Lake

Oba

Langdon

Maltawitchewan River

Buchanan

Grégoires Mill   Strickland   11   634

Cluquier

Smooth Falls

49°

Kabinagami Lake

Minnipuka

Rufus Lake

Lower Minnipuka L.   CN

Pushuta L.

Sagamok River

Mona Creek

Opasatika Lake

Poplar Rapids

Sturgeon L.

White River

Nezuazu

Amyot

CP

Franz

Fire River

Argolis

Greenhill

Peterbell

Dunrankin

Elsas

Kapuskasing Lake

Flying Post

Griffin Lake

Oke

Kinnuskotia Lake

The Cache L.

Obatanga Provincial Park *609

Mosambik Lake

Anaharea Lake

Esnagi Lake

Dubreuilville

Lochalsh

Wabatongushi Lake

Missinaibi Lake Provincial Park

Renabie

Missongo

Shawmere

Schewabik Lake

Foleyet

144

1

Mushibishu

Leach Island

SUPERIOR

183

2

Michipicoten Bay

Gros Cap 49

Gros Cap Village 49 A

Wawa

Michipicoten River

Perry

Tabor

LAKE SUPERIOR PROVINCIAL PARK

Cape Gargantua

Gargantua

Montreal Island

48°

47°

46°

UNITED STATES OF AMERICA

ÉTATS-UNIS D'AMÉRIQUE

Lake Michigan 177

LAKE HURON

177

Manitoulin   Island

SAULT STE MARIE

ONTARIO

3

4

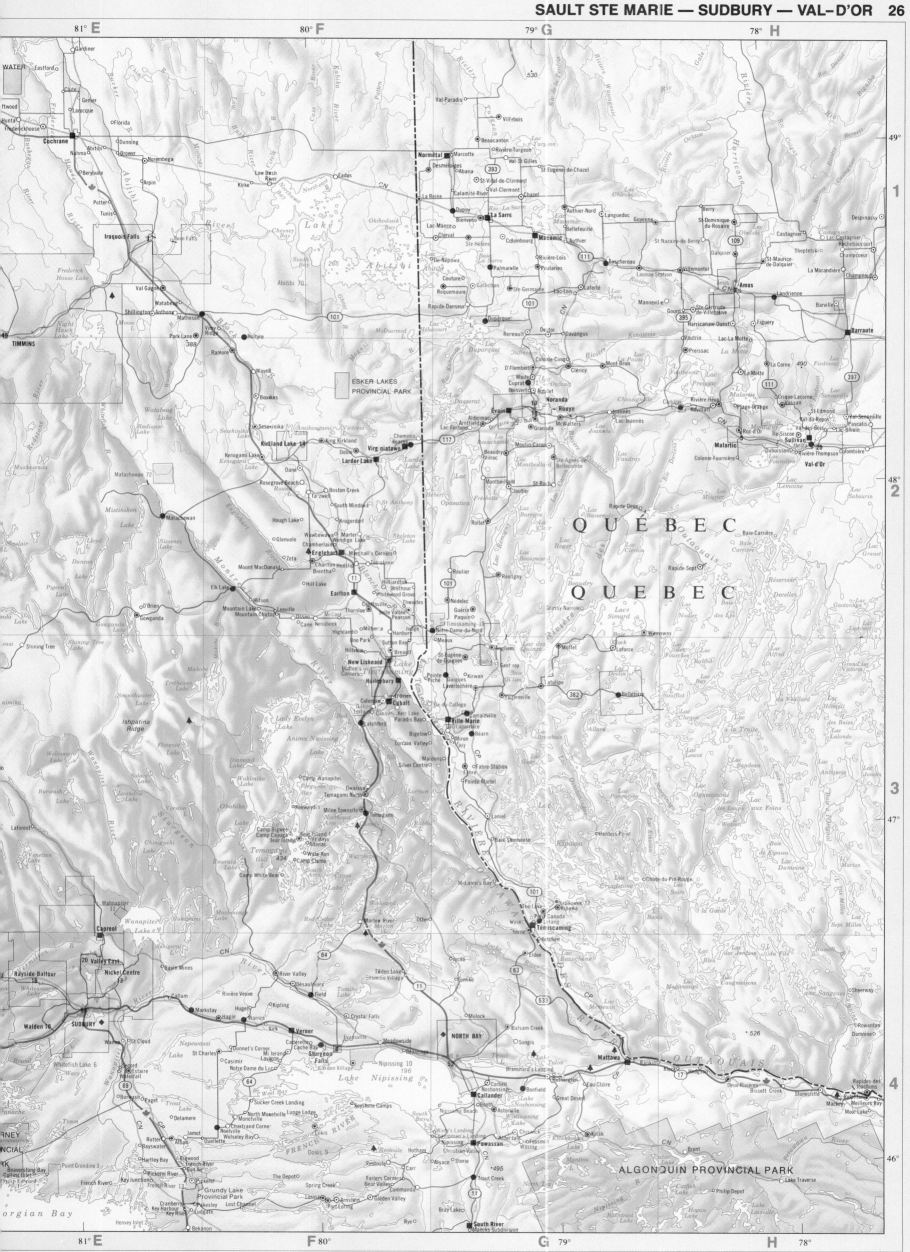

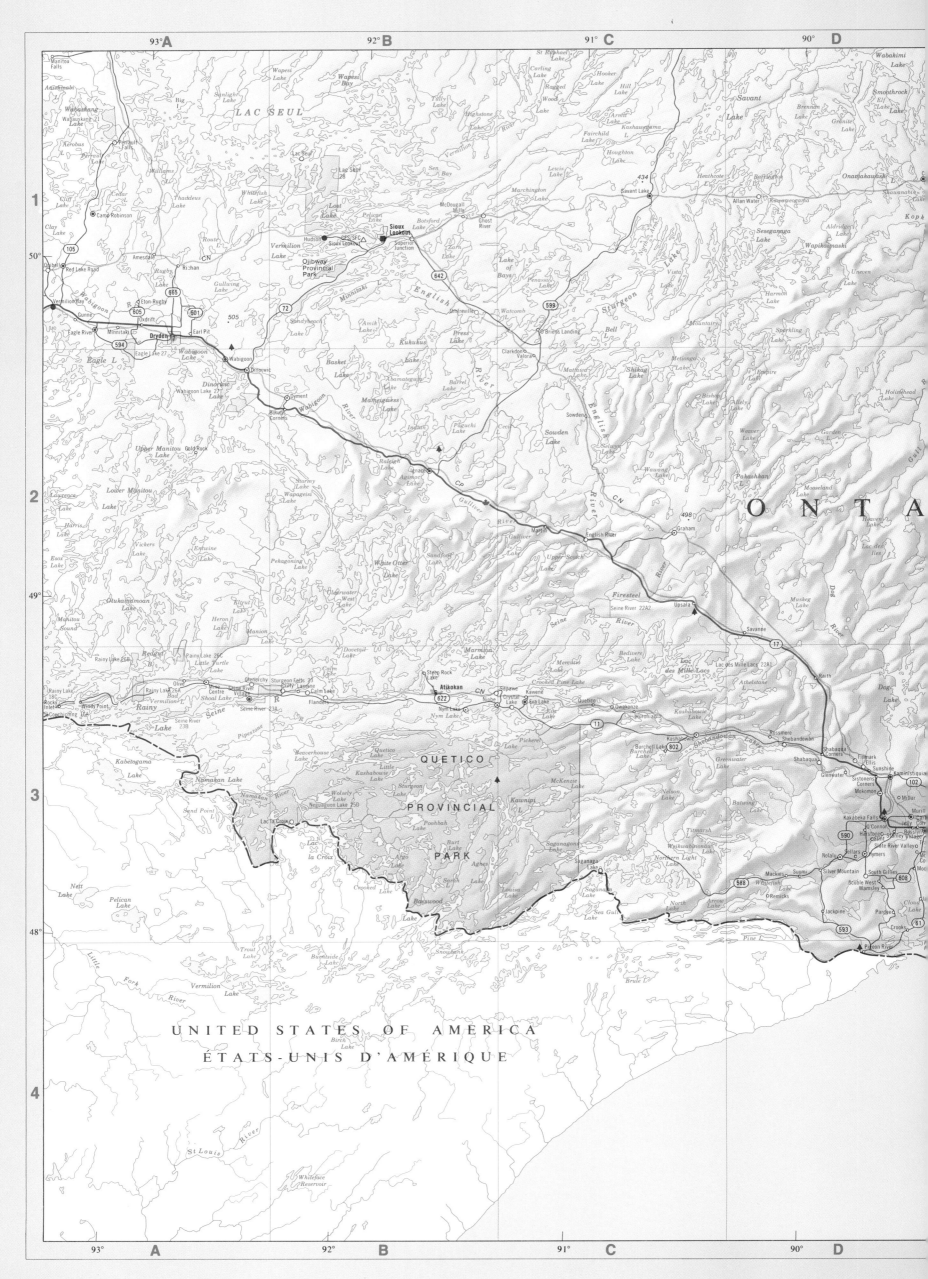

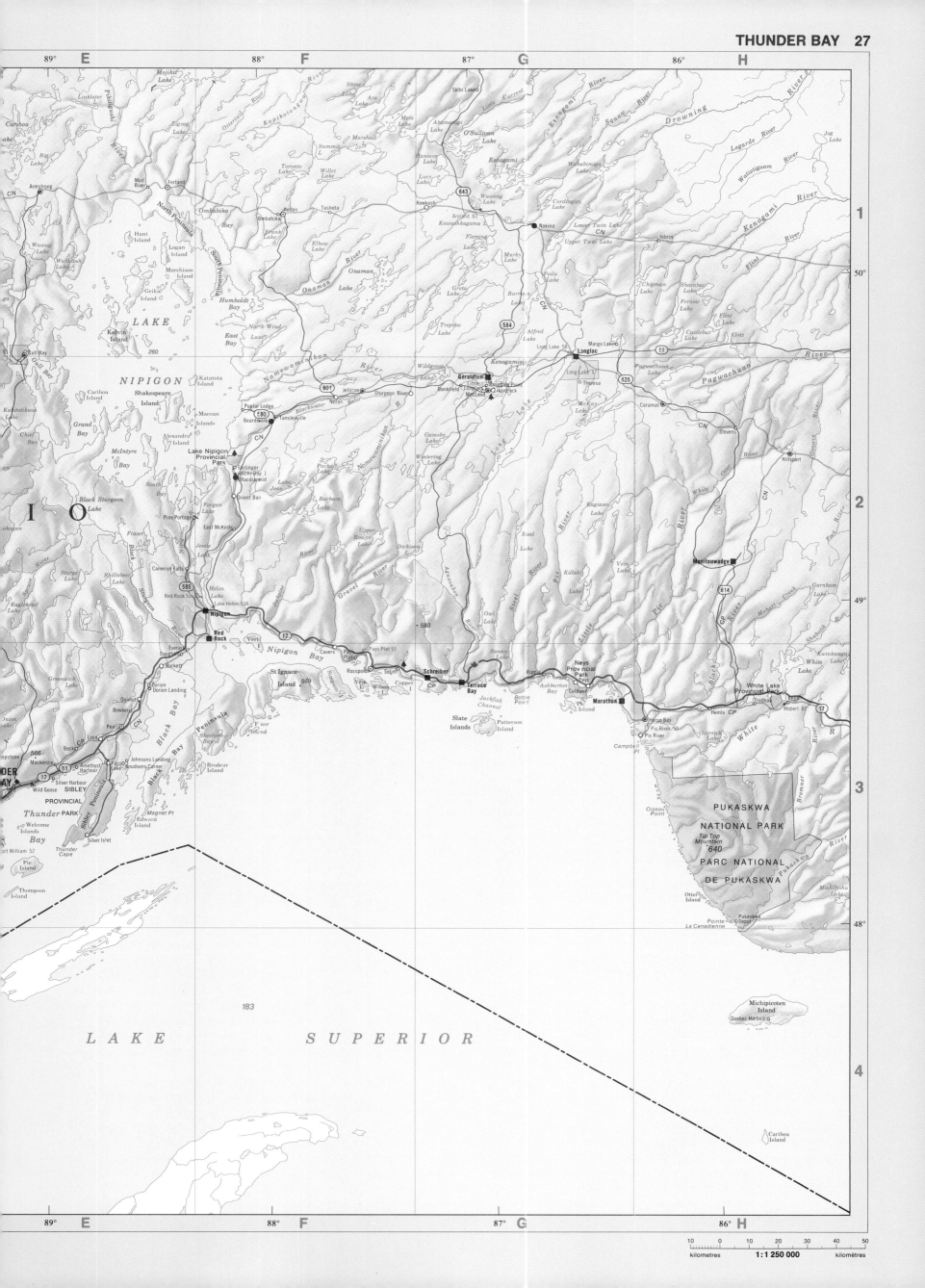

E   88°   F   87°   G   86°   H

89°

1

50°

2

49°

3

48°

4

LAKE   SUPERIOR

E   88°   F   87°   G   86°   H

89°

10   0   10   20   30   40   50
kilometres   1:1 250 000   kilomètres

A   97°   B   30'   C   96°   D   30'

Watery   Creek
                Clandeboye   Lowland
        9   Peguis   Brokenhead   Lac du Bonnet
Cloverdale   Walkleyburg   Allegra
8   Ladywood   Milner Ridge   Dorothy   Bauer   George
Stonewall   Green Oak   CFS/ISFC   Lake   Bay   Lake
Trailer Court   Selkirk 10   Beausejour   WINNIPEG   Pinawa   North
Stonewall   Old England   East Selkirk   Cromwell   Otter Falls   Dorothy   Sailing L.   WHITESHELL
                Little Britain   Bromert   Seven Sisters Falls   Eleanor   Lake   Horseshoe
Stony Mountain   McDonald   Rosdale   Highland   Green Bay   Natalie L.   Lake   Big Whiteshell Lake
    Hillcrest Trailer Park   Lockport   Glen   Tyndall   Sebright   St Ouens   Golden Bay   Betula   Meditation L.
    Blackdale   St Andrews   59   Kirkness   Garson   Beausejour   Seddons Corner   44   Siegs Corner   Betula Lake   309
7   Parkdale   Gonor   Melrose   12   Hazelglen   Molson   River Hills   Scotts Hill   PROVINCIAL
    Emsville   Narol   Cooks Creek   Sapton   Cloverleaf   CP   Moss Spur   White   White L.
1   Gordon   Lilyfield   Riverside   Pine Ridge   Trailer   West   Pine Ridge   Lydiatt   Shelley   Oldenberg   Lake   Cabin L.   Jessica L.   Red Rock Lake
50°   101   Rivercrest   East St Paul   Park   249   Hazelridge   Whitemouth   Scotts Hill   War   307
    Bergen   Middlechurch   Birds Hill   249   Eagle L.   Beauchemin L.
6   CN   Birds Hill Provincial Park   Oakbank   Anola   Elma   44   Moss L.   Mink   PAR
CP   Winnipeg   561   Vivian   Noerse   15   CN   Lewis   South Beach   Turtle L.   Decimal
1   WINNIPEG   Glass   Dugald   Queens Valley   Ste Rita   Stony Hill   Juno   Rennie   307
Assiniboine   River   Deacon   302   Birch
CN   Navin   Meadowvale   Richland   Monominto   Ostenfeld   CN   R.
CN   3   Deacons Corner   Ross   Medika   Boggy
Oak Bluff   Prairie Grove   Ste-Genevieve   Spruce Siding   Franc
        Grande Pointe   Rosewood   506   Hadashville   11   R
La Salle River   Lorette   Seine   River   Dufresne   Prawda   1
    La Salle   Ile des Chênes   1   La Coulée   Richer   McMunn   East Braintree
    Cartier   St Adolphe   Linden   Landmark   Ste Anne   Boggy
Glenlea   Greenland   St Raymond   R
2   New Bothwell   Blumenort   Giroux   MANITOBA   Oak L.   Windy L.   Birch L.
Domain   Niverville   Clear Springs   308
Ste Agathe   Tourond   Randolph   Mitchell   Steinbach   52   La Broquerie   Kerry
Union Point   Otterburne   Kleefeld   Bristol   Friedensfeld   Marchand   St Labre Creek
30'   Silver Plains   Aubigny   Carey   St Pierre   Hochstadt   Rosengard   St Labre
75   23   Grunthal   12   Sarto   Florze
        Dufrost   St Pierre Sud   Jaubert   Trentham   Sandilands
        La Rochelle   Creek   River   Woodridge   Lonesand   Whitemouth Lake
Ste Elizabeth   Barkfield   Pansy   Zhoda   Carrick   Badger
        St Malo   New Rosa   Rosa   Sprague
        59   Carlowrie   River   Sprague Creek   Reed   Ck
Arnaud   Roseau Rapids 2A   Senkiw   Roseau   River   Caliento   Sundown   Menisino   Piney   Vassar   R
Roseau River 2   Green Ridge   Roseau River   Vita   CN   Wampum   South Junction   Sprague
3   Letellier   Dominion City   201   Stuartburn   12   Middlebro
    253   Emerson   Stockport   Woodmore   Gardenton   Arbakka   Somme   Pine Creek
49°   Fredensthal   Ridgeville   Overstoneville   Tolstoi   Sirko
30'

UNITED   STATES   OF

ÉTATS-UNIS   D'AM

A   97°   B   30'   C   96°   D   30'

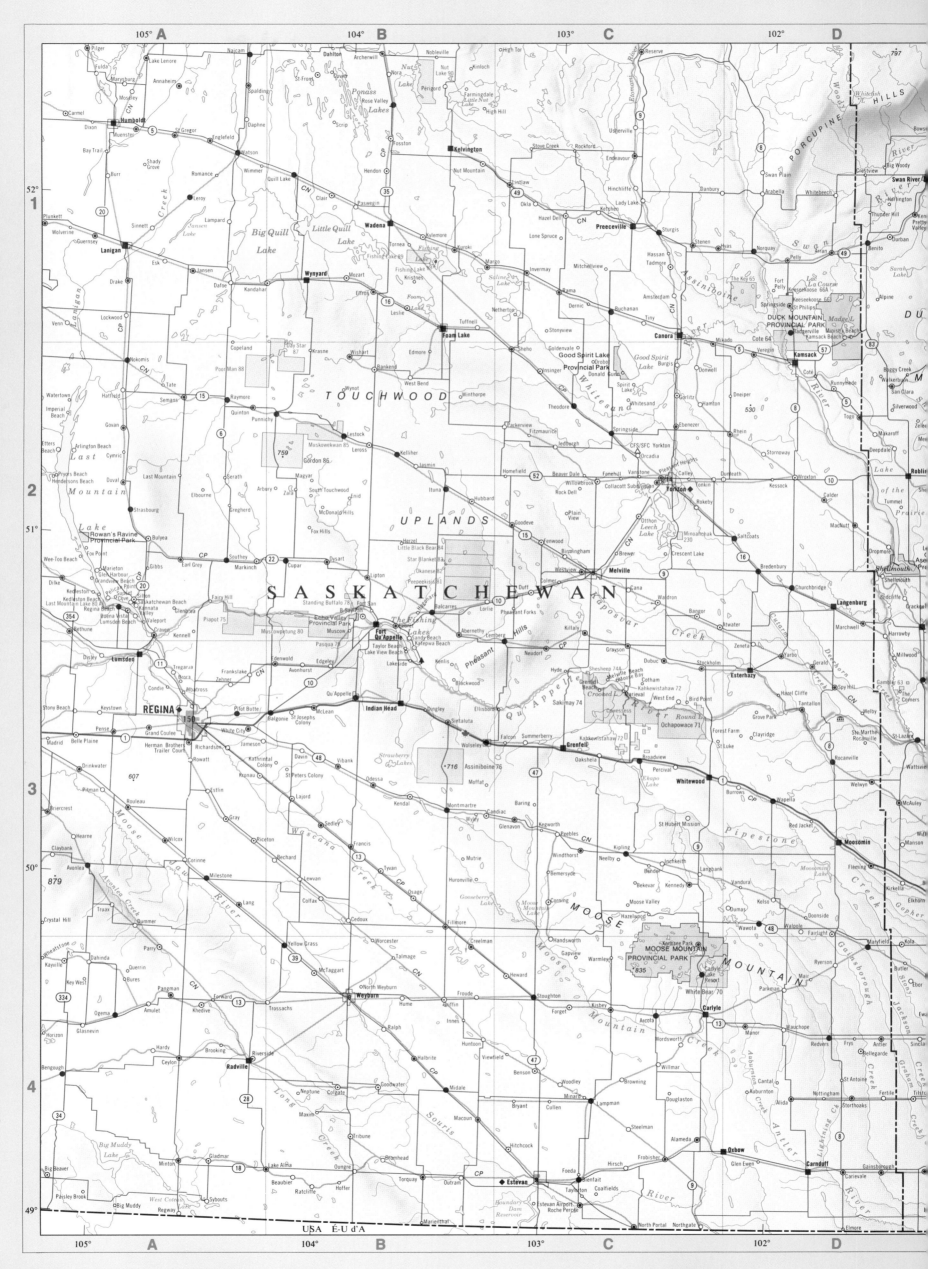

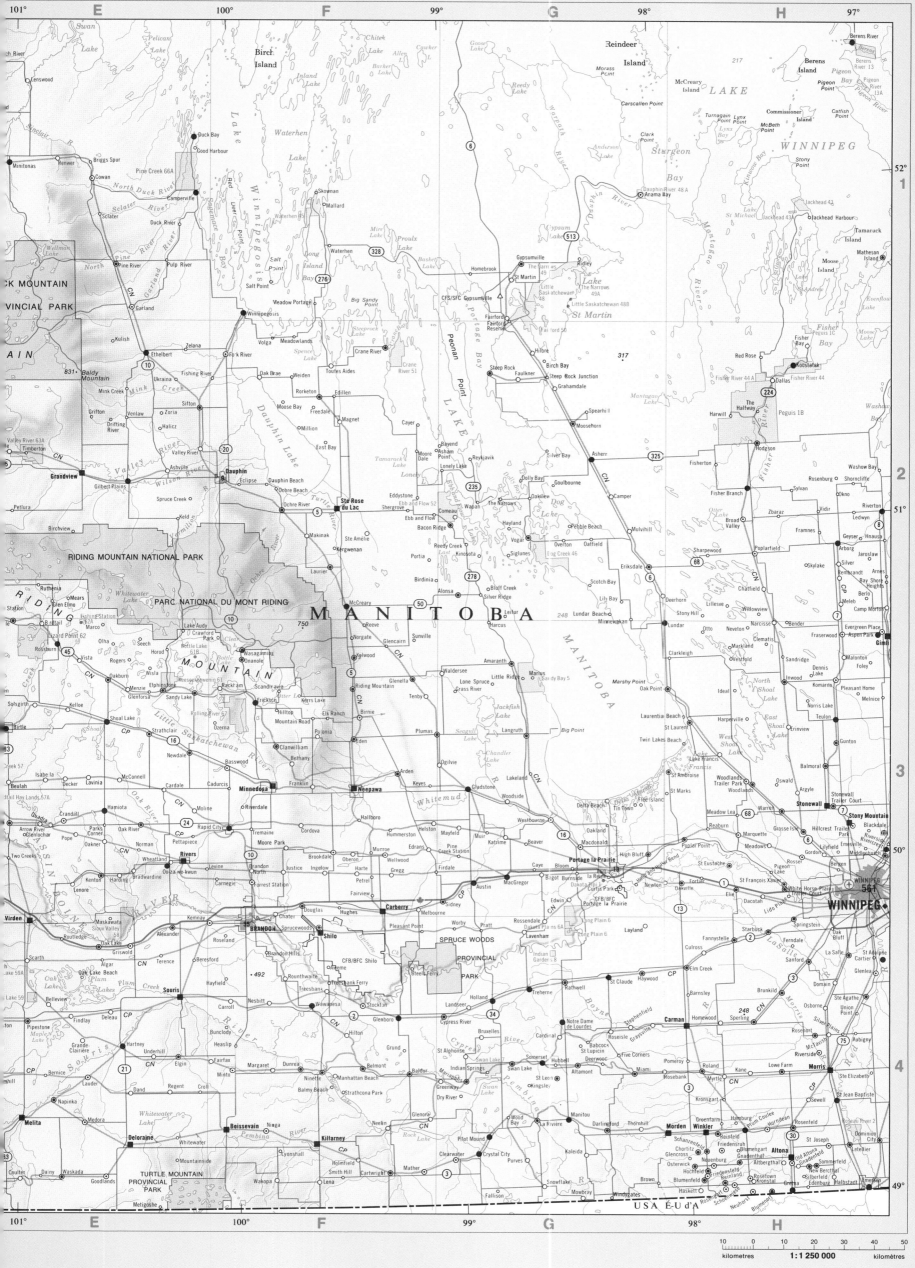

MANITOBA

RIDING MOUNTAIN NATIONAL PARK

PARC NATIONAL DU MONT RIDING

TURTLE MOUNTAIN PROVINCIAL PARK

SPRUCE WOODS PROVINCIAL PARK

WINNIPEG

USA É-U d'A

kilometres   1:1 250 000   kilomètres

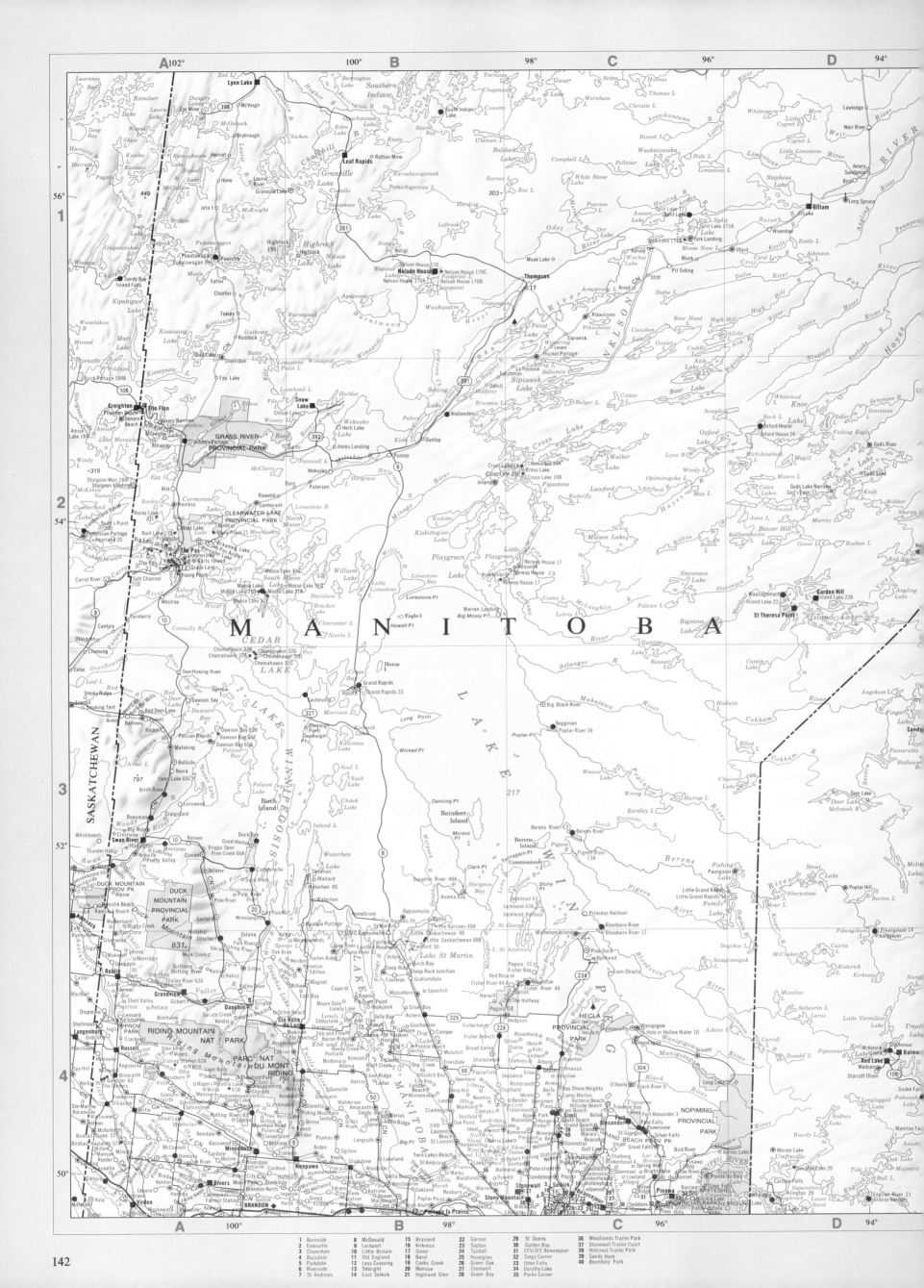

1 Burnside	8 McDonald	15 Brainerd	22 Garson	29 St Ouens	36 Woodlands Trailer Park
2 Emesville	9 Lockport	16 Kirkness	23 Sapton	30 Golden Bay	37 Stonewall Trailer Court
3 Cloverdale	10 Little Britain	17 Gonor	24 Tyndall	31 CFS/SFC Beausejour	38 Hillcrest Trailer Park
4 Rossdale	11 Old England	18 Narol	25 Siegs Corner	32 Siegs Corner	39 Sandy Hook
5 Parkdale	12 Less Crossing	19 Cooks Creek	26 Green Oak	33 Otter Falls	40 Boundary Park
6 Riverside	13 Sebright	20 Melrose	27 Cromwell	34 Dorothy Lake
7 St Andrews	14 East Selkirk	21 Highland Glen	28 Green Bay	35 Parks Corner

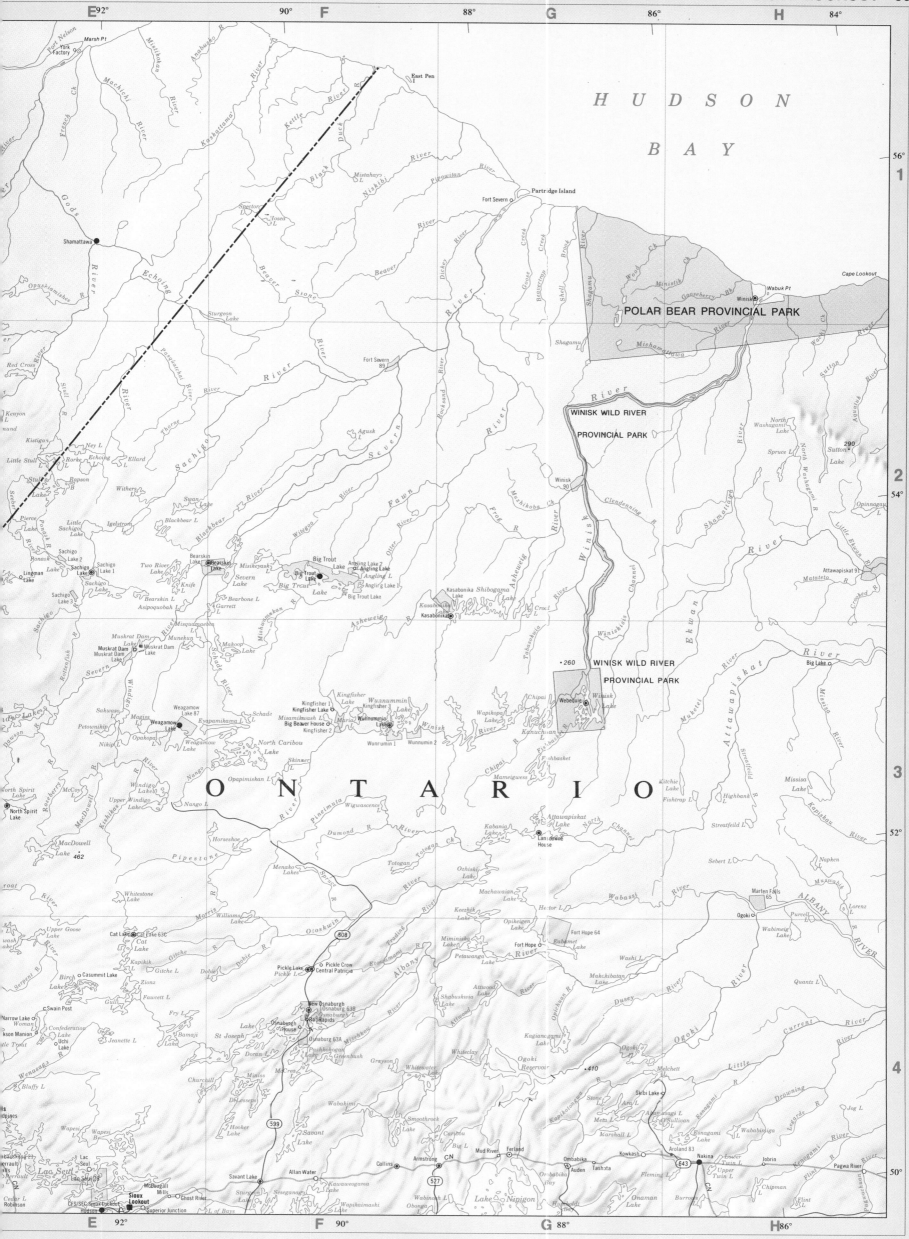

H U D S O N   B A Y

POLAR BEAR PROVINCIAL PARK

WINISK WILD RIVER
PROVINCIAL PARK

WINISK WILD RIVER
PROVINCIAL PARK

O N T A R I O

1 : 2 500 000

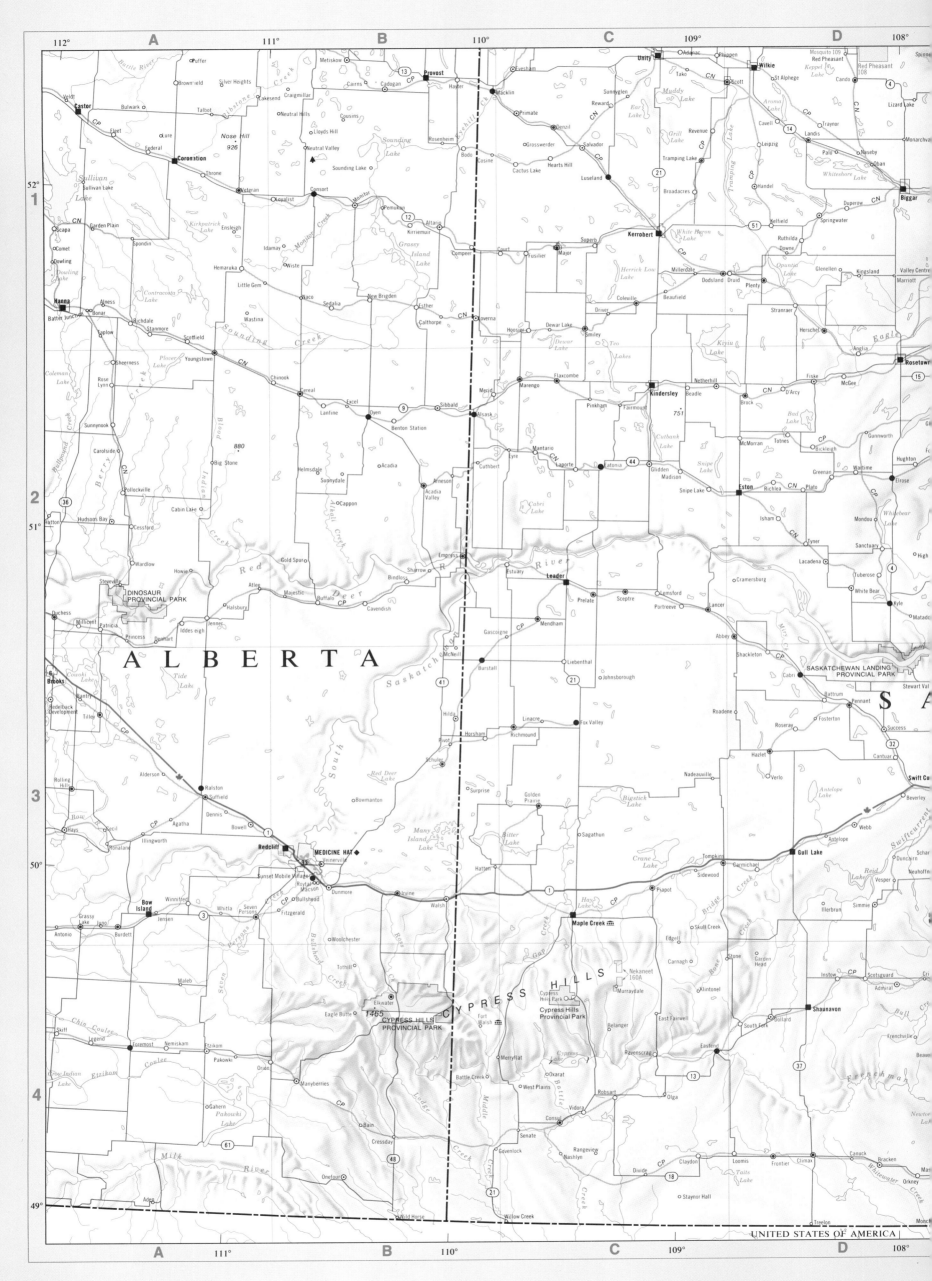

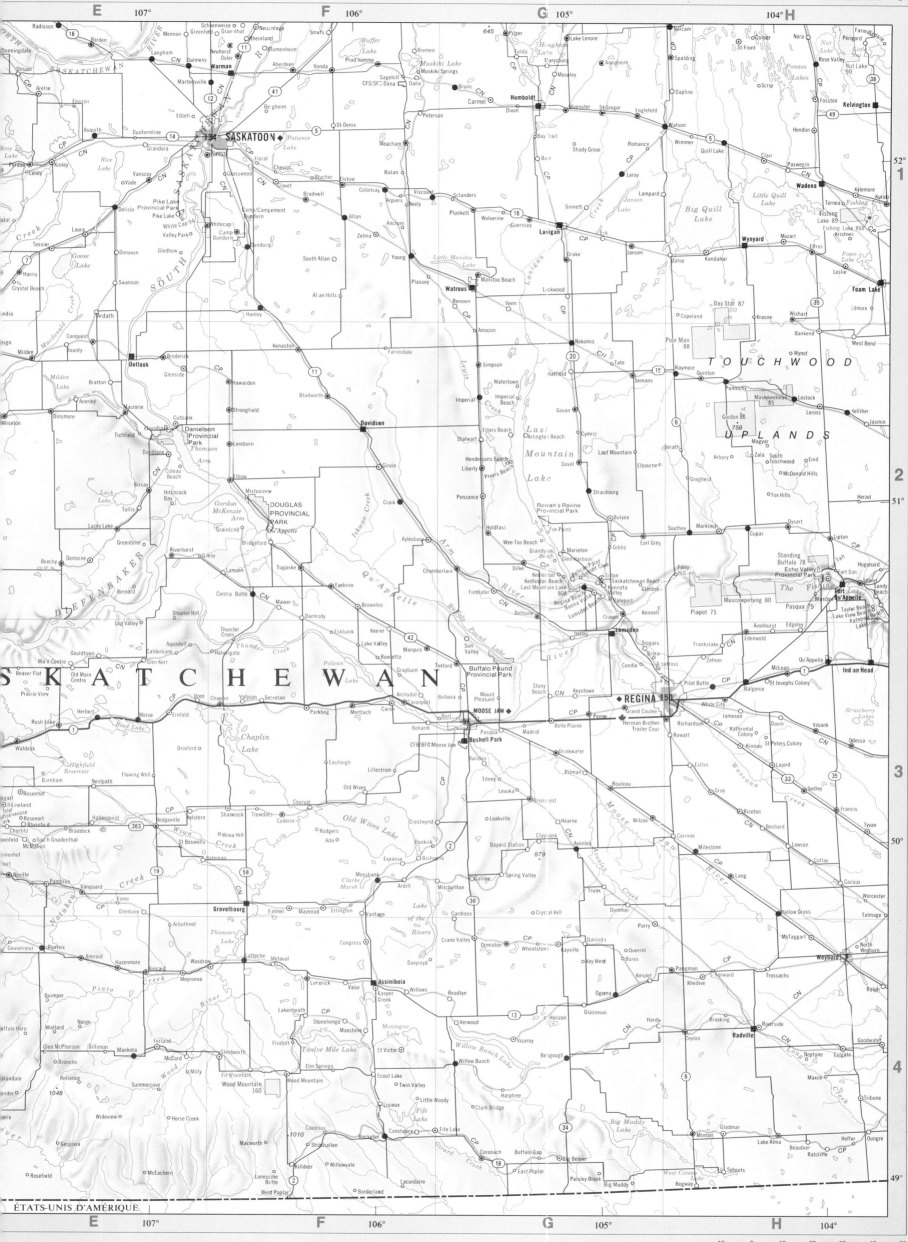

10 0 10 20 30 40 50
kilometres   1:1 250 000   kilomètres

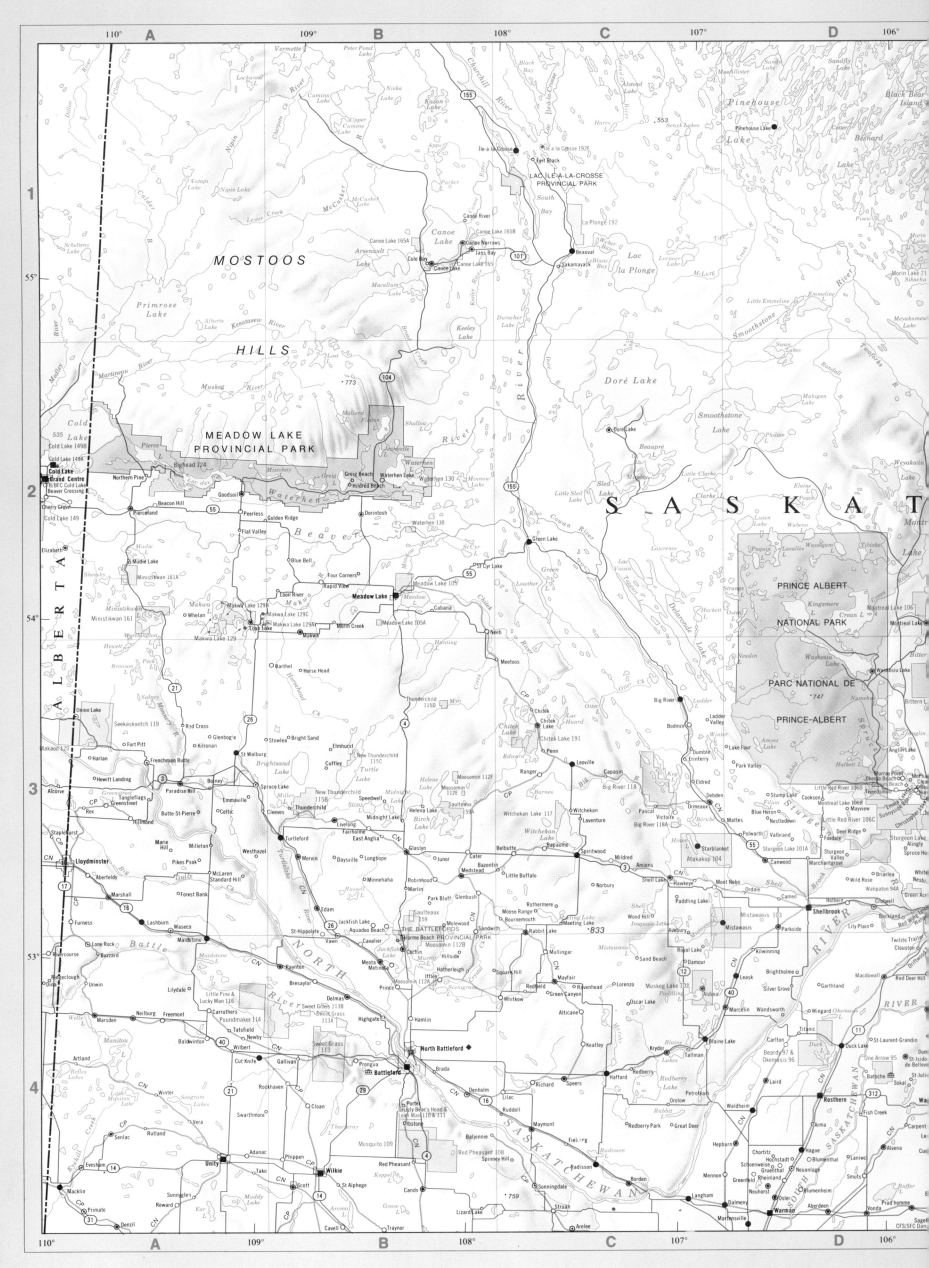

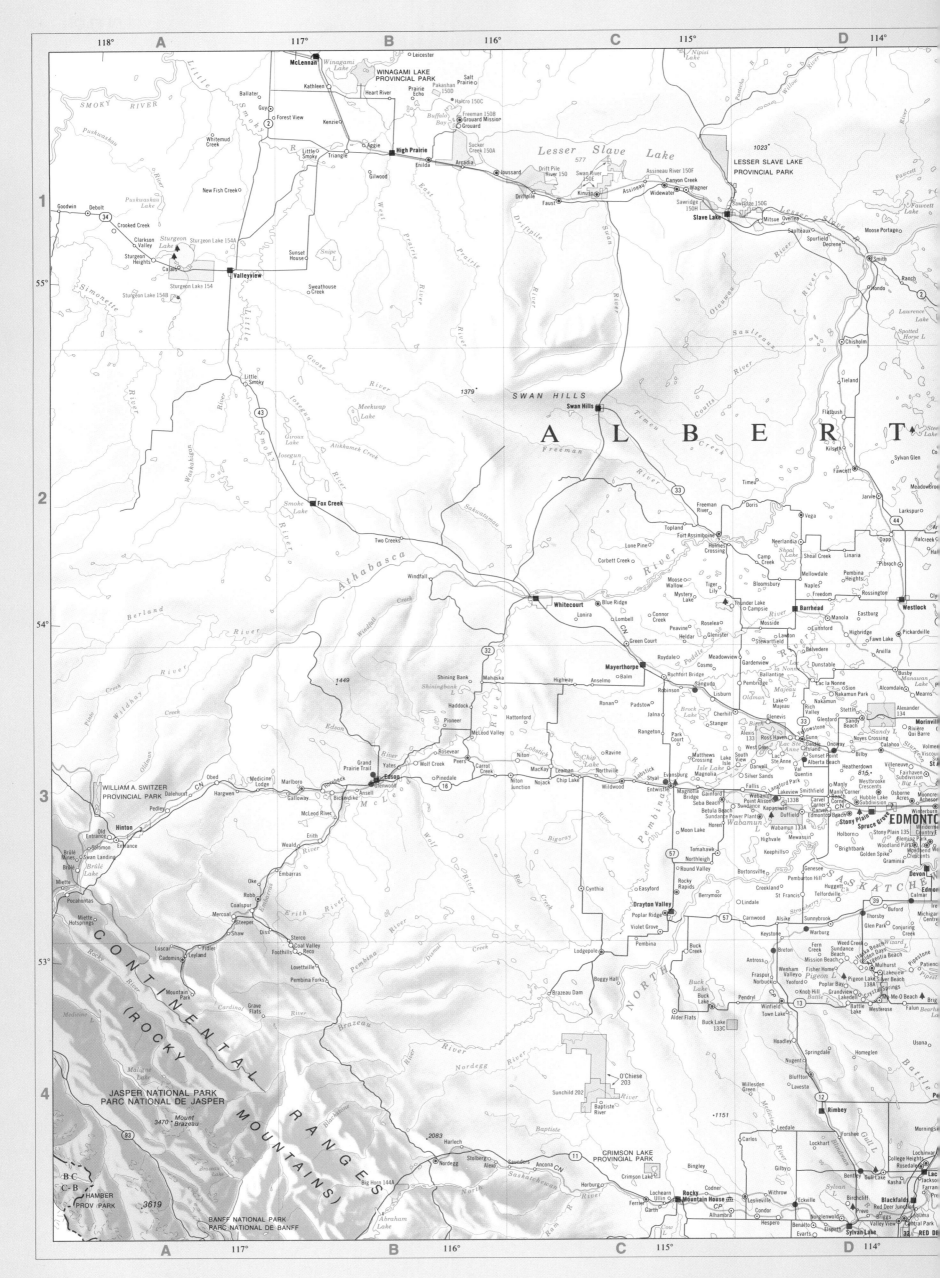

A L B E R T

Lesser Slave Lake

LESSER SLAVE LAKE
PROVINCIAL PARK

WINAGAMI LAKE
PROVINCIAL PARK

McLennan

High Prairie

Valleyview

Slave Lake

Swan Hills

Fox Creek

Whitecourt

Mayerthorpe

Barrhead

Westlock

Edson

Hinton

WILLIAM A. SWITZER
PROVINCIAL PARK

EDMONTON

Spruce Grove
Stony Plain

Devon

Drayton Valley

JASPER NATIONAL PARK
PARC NATIONAL DE JASPER

CONTINENTAL (ROCKY MOUNTAINS) RANGES

Rimbey

CRIMSON LAKE
PROVINCIAL PARK

Rocky
Mountain House

Sylvan Lake

Blackfalds

RED DEER

BANFF NATIONAL PARK
PARC NATIONAL DE BANFF

BC
C-B
CHAMBER
PROV. PARK

SMOKY RIVER

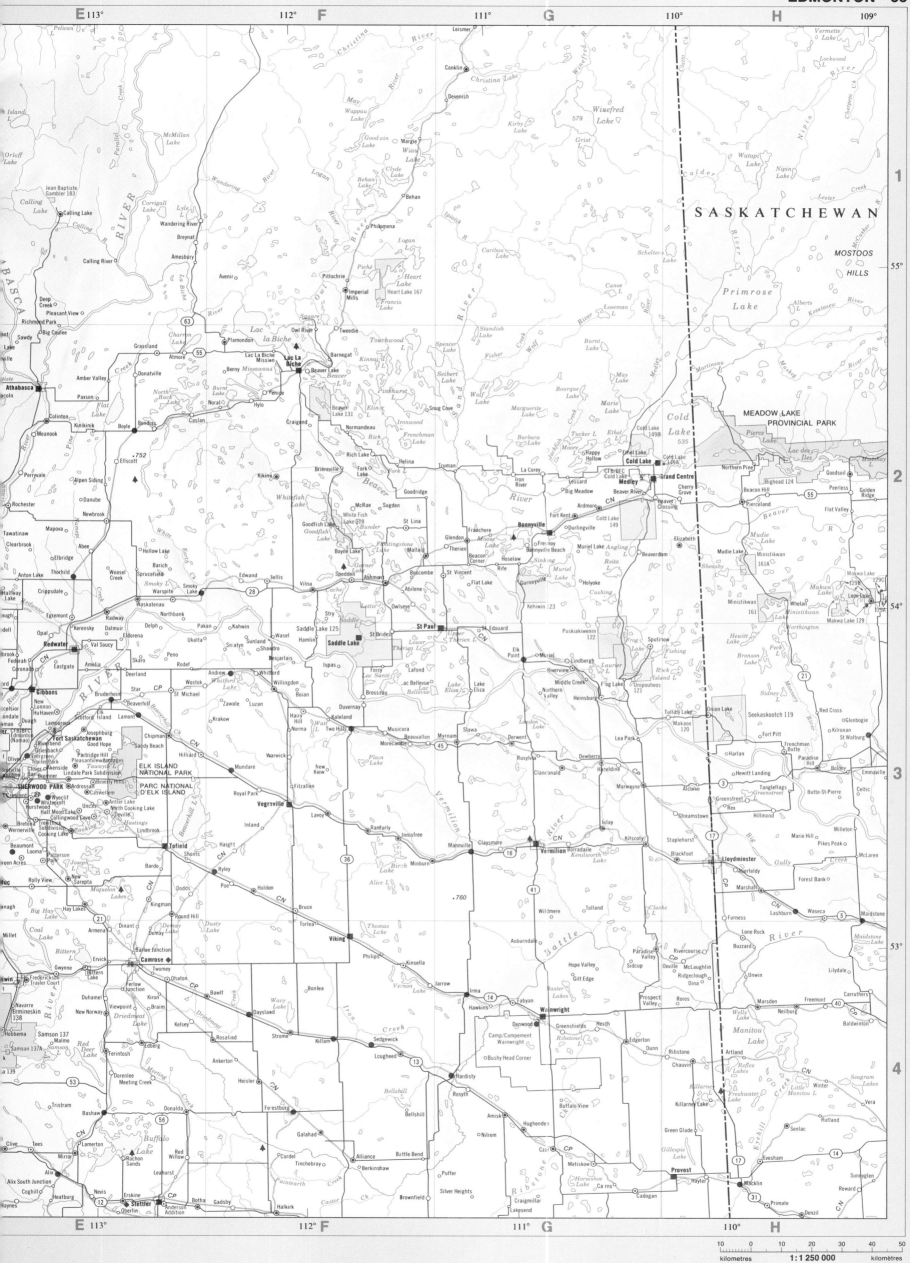

SASKATCHEWAN

MOSTOOS

HILLS

MEADOW LAKE
PROVINCIAL PARK

Primrose
Lake

Cold Lake

ELK ISLAND
NATIONAL PARK

PARC NATIONAL
D'ELK ISLAND

10   0   10   20   30   40   50
kilometres   1:1 250 000   kilometres

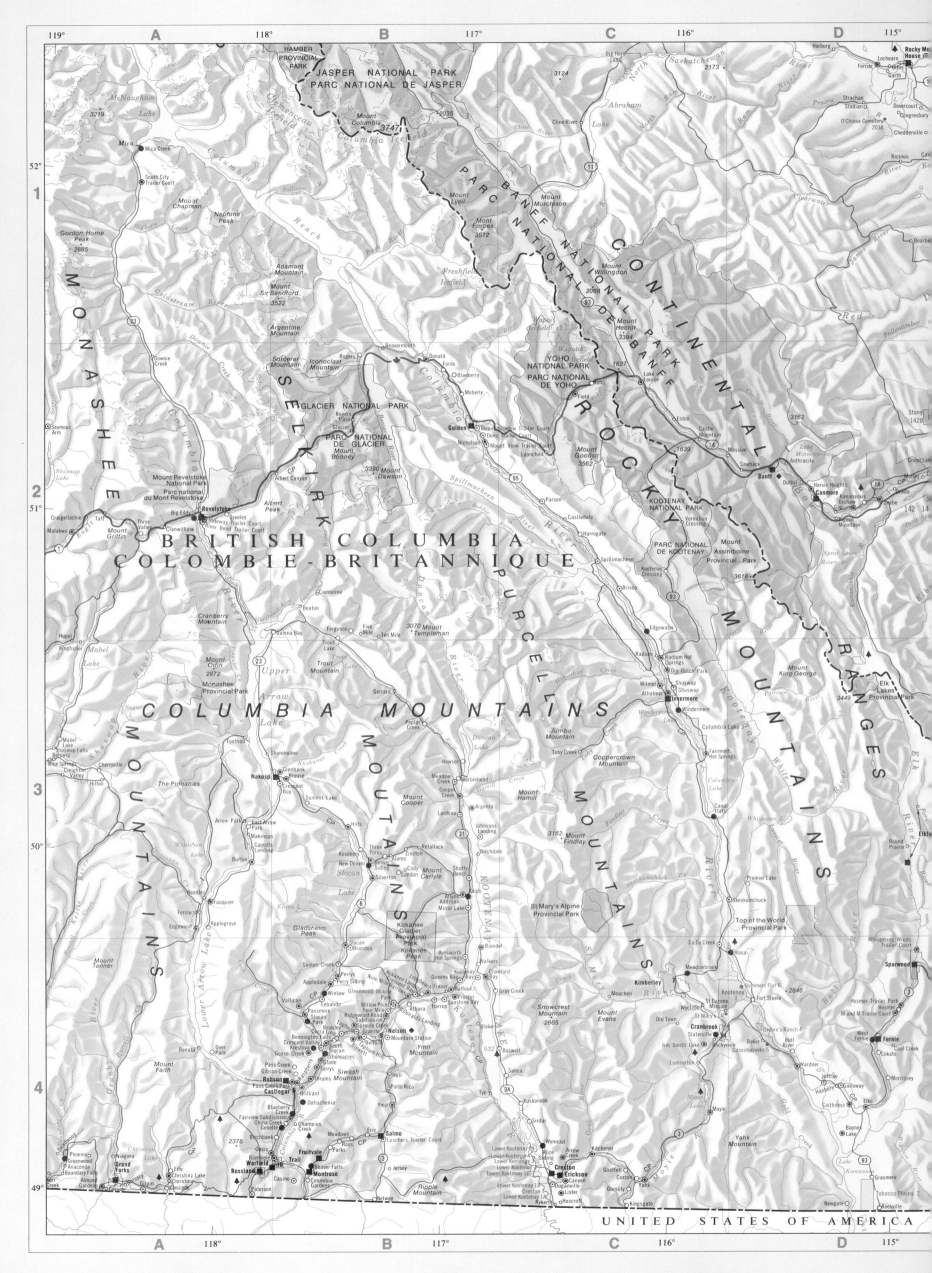

150

ALBERTA

CALGARY

RED DEER

MEDICINE HAT

Sylvan Lake · Blackfalds · Red Deer · Innisfail · Olds · Didsbury · Carstairs · Airdrie · Cochrane · Calgary · Okotoks · Black Diamond · Turner Valley · High River · Nanton · Vulcan · Claresholm · Fort Macleod · Lethbridge · Coaldale · Picture Butte · Pincher Creek · Cardston · Magrath · Raymond · Stirling · Taber · Brooks · Bow Island · Redcliff · Castor · Coronation · Consort · Hanna · Drumheller · Three Hills · Stettler

Dinosaur Provincial Park

Waterton Lakes National Park / Parc National des Lacs Waterton

ÉTATS-UNIS D'AMÉRIQUE

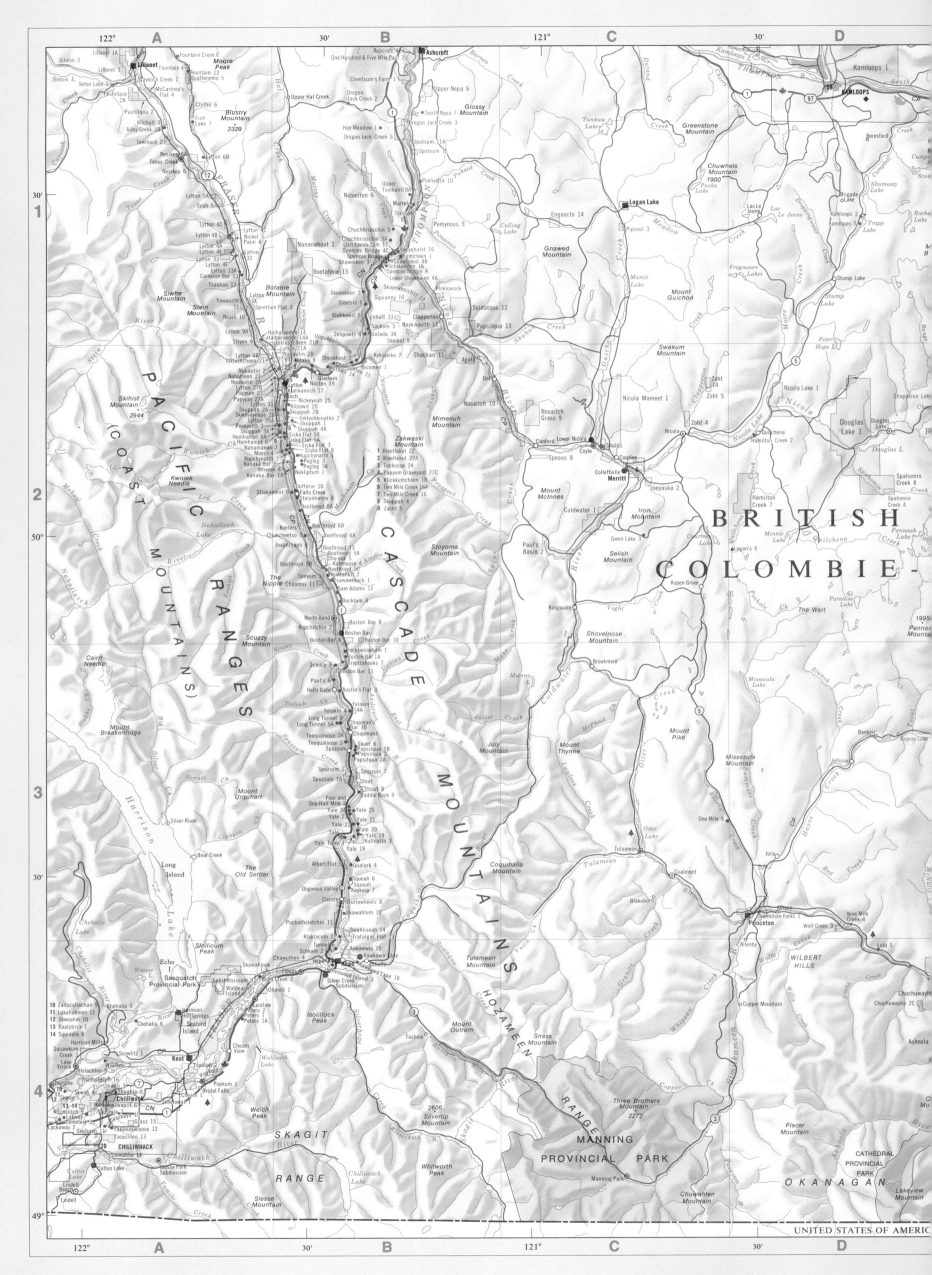

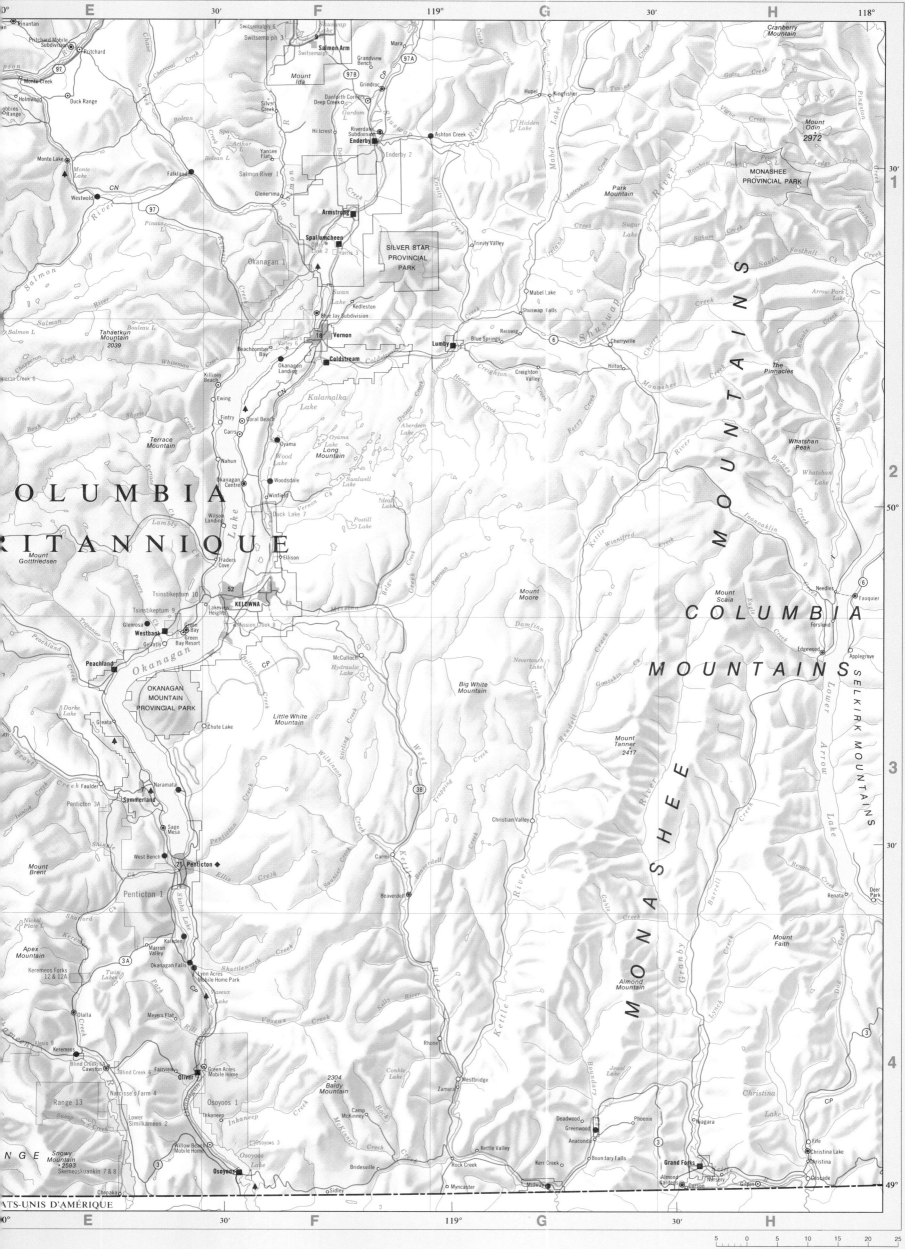

Pinantan
Pritchard Mobile Subdivision
Pritchard
Monte Creek
Holmwood
Duck Range
Robbins Range
97

Chase Creek
Chaperol Hill

Switsemalph 6
Switsemalph 3
Salmon Arm
Switsemalph
Mount Ida
978
Grandview Bench
CP
Grindrod
97A
Mara
Cooke Creek

Hupel
Kingfisher
Mabel Lake
Touix River

Cranberry Mountain
Gates Creek
Vigne Creek

Mount Odin
2972
Peers Ledge
Pingston Creek

MONASHEE PROVINCIAL PARK

Monte Lake
Westwold
CN
Falkland

Monte Lake
Bolean Creek
Salmon River
Pinause L.
97
Bolean L.
Spa L.
Arthur L.
Yankee Flats

Salmon River 1
Glenemma

Hillcrest
Deep Creek
Danforth Corners
Gardom
Riverdale Subdivision
Enderby
Enderby 2
Ashton Creek

Hidden Lake
Park Mountain

Latremouille Creek
Sugar Lake

Sithum Creek
South Fosthall Creek
Arrow Park Lake

Armstrong
Spallumcheen
Otter Lake 2
Harris 3
Okanagan 1

SILVER STAR PROVINCIAL PARK

Trinity Valley
Mabel Lake
Shuswap Falls

Swan Lake
Kedleston
Blue Jay Subdivision
18
Vernon
Coldstream
Priest Valley 6
Beachcomber Bay

Lumby
Blue Springs
Reiswig
Cherryville
6
Hilton

Creighton Valley

The Pinnacles

Killiney Beach
Ewing
Fintry
Coral Beach
Carrs
Oyama
Nahun

Kalamalka Lake
Oyama Lake
Long Mountain
Swalwell Lake
Aberdeen Lake

Duteau Creek
Harris Creek
Bessette Creek

Creighton Creek

Ferry Creek
Monashee Creek

Shuswap River

Whatshan Peak
Whatshan Lake

COLUMBIA
BRITANNIQUE

Terrace Mountain
Okanagan Centre
Woodsdale
Winfield

Wood Lake
Vernon Ck
Postill Lake
Ideal Lake

Duck Lake 7
Wilson Landing

Mount Gottfriedsen

Traders Cove
Ellison

Tsinstikeptum 10
52

Kettle River

Mount Moore
Damfino

Mount Scaia
COLUMBIA

Inonoaklin Creek

Needles
Fauquier
6

Tsinstikeptum 9
KELOWNA
Lakeview Heights
Glenrosa
Green Bay
Westbank
Gellatly
Green Bay Resort

Mission Creek 8

McCulloch
Hydraulic Lake

Nevertouch Lake

MOUNTAINS

Forsland
Edgewood
Applegrove

Peachland
Okanagan
OKANAGAN MOUNTAIN PROVINCIAL PARK

Darke Lake
Greata
Chute Lake

Little White Mountain

Big White Mountain

Mount Tanner
2417

Mount Faith

SELKIRK MOUNTAINS

Lower Arrow Lake

Faulder
Naramata
Summerland
Penticton 3A
Sage Mesa

Wilkinson Creek
Stirling Creek

West Creek

Trepanier Creek
Peachland Creek

Shingle Creek
West Bench
Penticton
2
Penticton 1

Mount Brent

Nickel Plate L.

Apex Mountain
Keremeos Forks 12 & 12A
3A
Marron Valley
Kaleden
Okanagan Falls
Lynn Acres Mobile Home Park
Twin Lakes
Vaseux Lake
Meyers Flat

3B

Tropping Creek
Carmi
Beaverdell

Christian Valley

Kettle River

MONASHEE

Renala Creek

Renata

Deer Park
Renata

Ellis Creek
Shatford Ck

Keremeos
Olalla
Alexis 9

Blind Creek
Cawston
Fairview
Oliver
Green Acres Mobile Home
Narcisse's Farm 4

Baldy Mountain
2304
Camp McKinney

Rhone

Westbridge
Zamora

Jewel Lake
Almond Mountain

Granby River

Burrell Creek

Christina Lake

3

Range 13
Lower Similkameen 2

Inkaneep
Osoyoos 1
Tekaneep
Osoyoos 3

Willow Beach Mobile Home
Osoyoos
Osoyoos Lake

Chepakan

Snowy Mountain
2593
Skemeoskuankin 7 & 8

Bridesville
Sidley

Rock Creek
Kettle Valley
Kerr Creek
Boundary Falls

Conkle Lake
McKinney Creek

Deadwood
Greenwood
Anaconda
Phoenix
Niagara

Almond Gardens
Nursery
Grand Forks
Gilpin

Fife
Christina Lake
Christina
Cascade

Myncaster
Midway
Carson
Boundary Creek

5   0   5   10   15   20   25
kilometres   **1 : 625 000**   kilometres

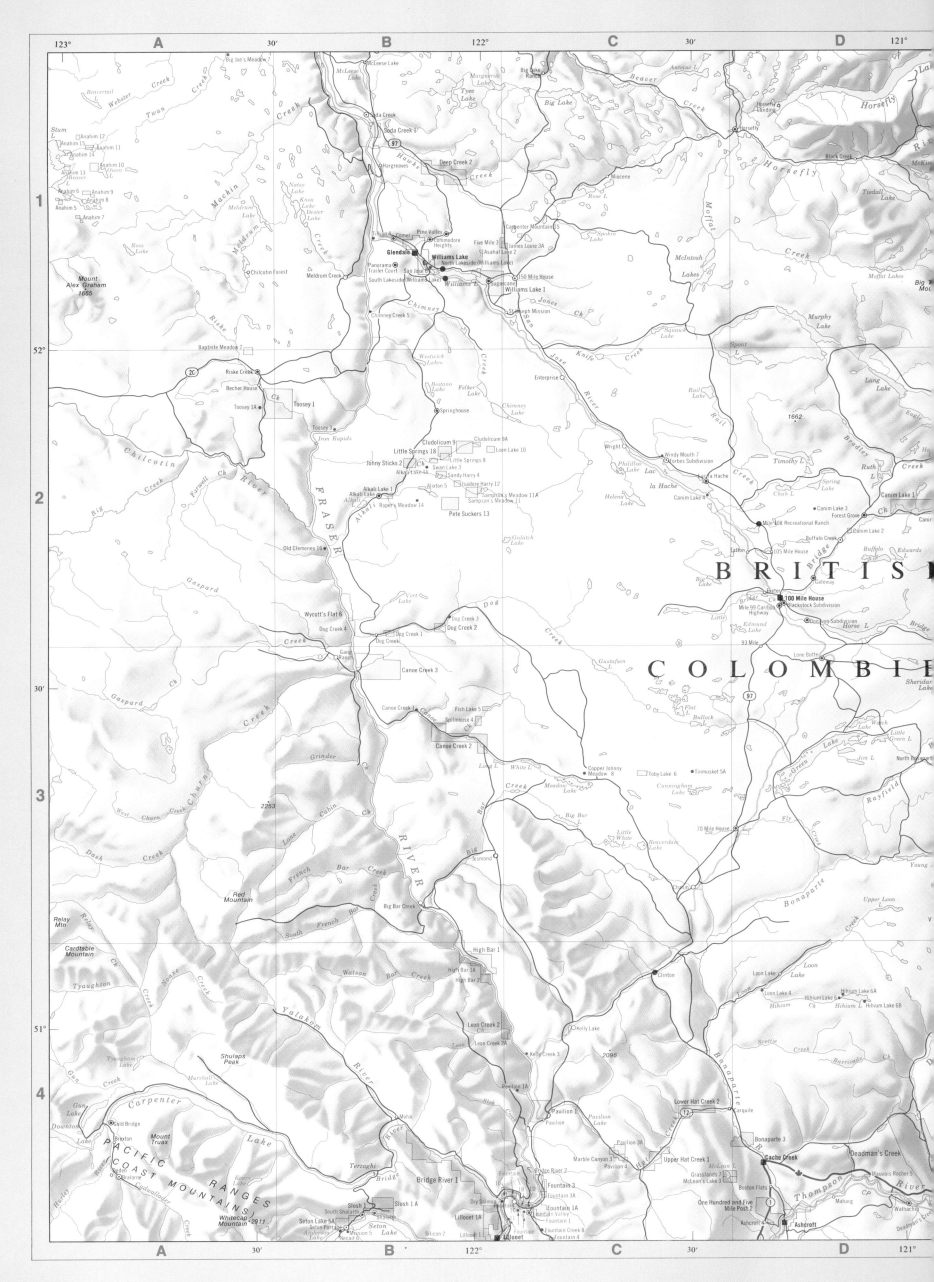

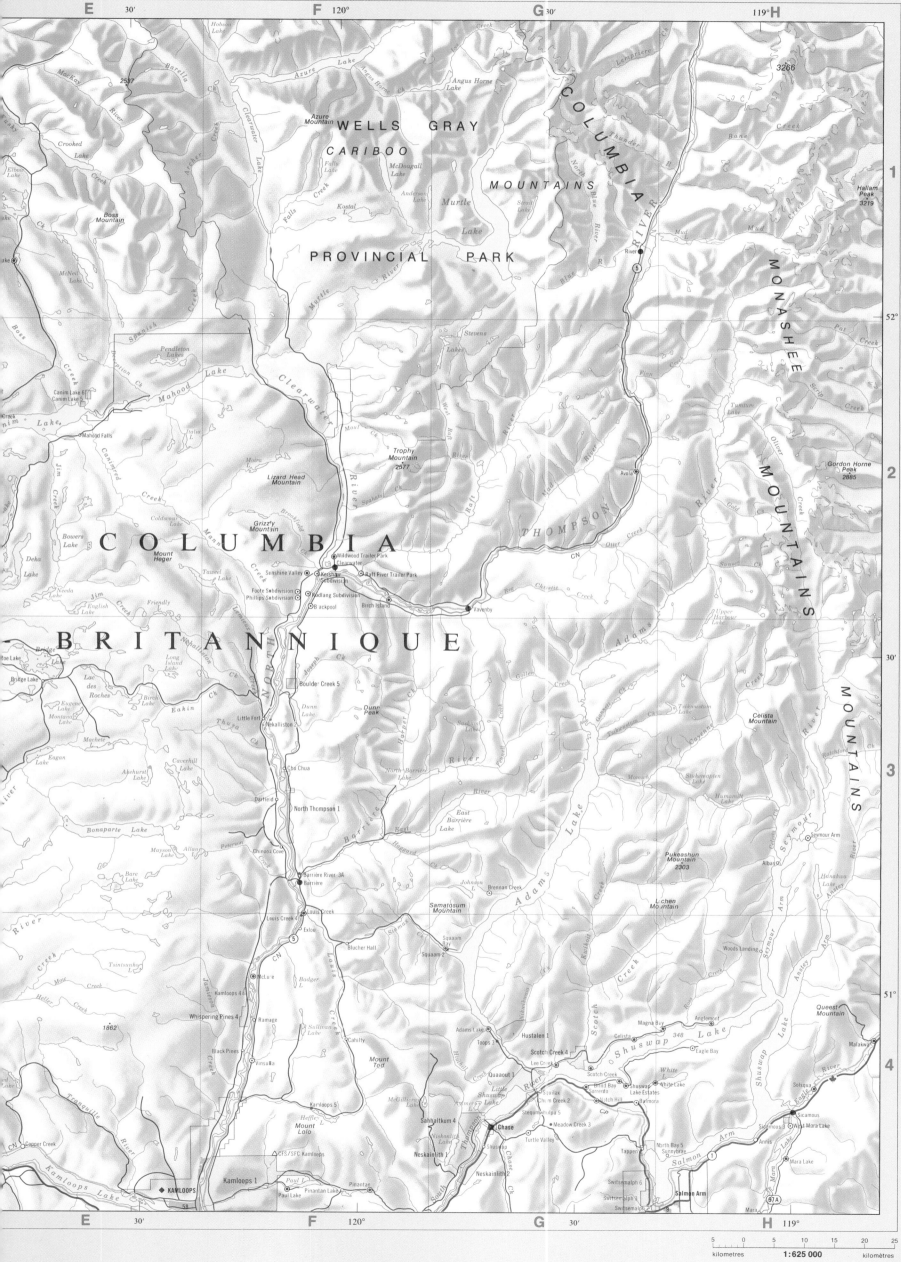

1

52°

2

30'

3

51°

4

5   0   5   10   15   20   25
kilometres   **1:625 000**   kilomètres

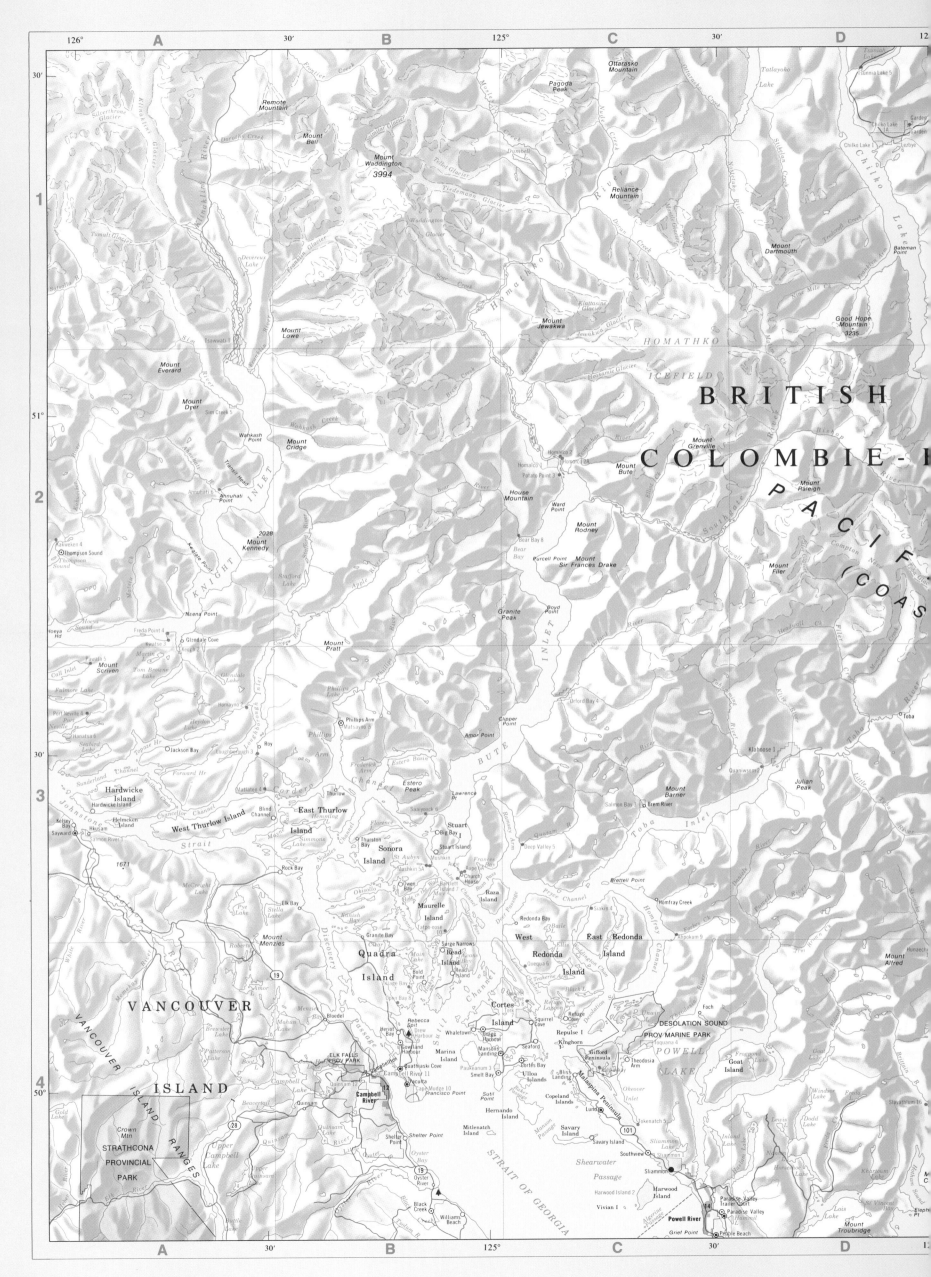

Crown Mountain

Campbell River

Mitlenatch Island

Savary Island

Tokenatch 5

Southview

Sliammon Lake

Inland Lake

Dodd Lake

Lewis Lake

Haslam Lake

Shelter Point
Shelter Point

Quinsam

Quinsam River
Little

Shearwater Passage

Sliammon 1
Sliammon

Harwood Island 2

Harwood Island

Vivian Island

Powell River

Nanton

Powell Lake

Khartoum Lake

Elephant Lake

Upper Campbell Lake

28

Upper Quinsam Lake

Oyster River

Oyster Bay

Black Creek

Williams Beach

Merville

Bates Beach

Algerine Passage

Grief Point
Pebble Beach

Paradise Valley Trailer Court

Mount Troubridge

Mount Vincent

Cape Cockburn

STRATHCONA

Elkhorn Mountain

Donner Lake

Ursus

Mount Washington

Wolf Lake

Headquarters

Grantham

Myrtle Point
Brew Bay

Lang Bay

Saltery Bay

Scotch Fir Point

Hardy I.

1

Matchlee Mountain

Burman

2200
Golden Hinde

Seal Bay Subdivision

Meadowbrook

Little River
CFB BF

Falcon Park
Lazo

Cape Lazo
Cape Lazo

Vananda

Gillies Bay

Billings Bay

Nelson Island

PROVINCIAL PARK

Moyeha Mountain

Moyeha

The Red Pillar

Courtenay
Comox
Comox

Bevan

Puntledge

Royston

Balmoral Beach

Goose Spit 3

TEXADA ISLAND

Cape Cockburn

Saginaw

Pope Landing
Francis Peninsula

Moyeha 23

Big Interior Mountain

Cumberland

19

Union Bay

Buckley Bay

Longbeak Point

Denman Island

Denman Island

Hornby Island

Hornby Island

Stevens Passage

St John Pt

Tribune B

Sabine

Mount Shepherd

Jervis

Vaucroft Point

Upwood Point

Buccaneer Bay

Thormanby Island

30'

Mount Guemes

Oinimitis 14

Fanny Bay

Boyle Point

Sister Islets

Jervis Channel

Lasqueti

Lasqueti I.

Jenkins Island

Young Point

Sangster Island

Herbert Inlet

Peneltle 22

Wahous 20
Wahous 19

Quortsowe 13

Great Central Lake

Doran Lake

Mud Bay

Bowser

Qualicum

Dunsmuir

B R I T I S H   C O

Cypress Bay

Taylor

Dashwood

Qualicum Beach Trailer Park

Ballenas Islands

Bedwell Sound

Onadsith 9

Great Central

Beaver Creek

Qualicum Beach
Qualicum Beach

Parksville

Coombs

4A

Beachcomber

Ballenas Channel

2

Saltaquis 18

Clayoquot Sound

Telsoukis 10

Tranquil Inlet

Kleecot

Klehkoot 2

Cherry Creek

4

Errington

Parksville Trailer Park

Pacific Shore Trailer Court

Secorset Subdivision

West Bay Estates

Dolphin Beach

Winchelsea Islands

Vargas

Cloolthpich

Kakawis 15

Lemmens

Indian Island 30

Thpaya 8

Winche 7

Okeamin 5

Sproat Lake

Sproat Lake

Tsanaheh
Manaknis

Sahara Heights

20

Arrowview Heights

Port Alberni
Alberni

1817
Mount Arrowsmith

Mount Moriarty

Nanoose Bay

Brynmarl

Nanoose Hr

Burden Pt

Lantzville

19

C O L O M B

Meares Island

Opitsat

Clayoquot Island

Clayoqua 6

Two Rivers Arm

Stirling Arm

Cameron Heights

Cous 3

Mount Moriarty

NA

Vargas Island

Tofino

Kootowis 4

Kennedy Lake

Nahmint Lake

China Creek

Mount Hooper

Nanaimo

Nanaimo Lakes

River

Echachis

Esowista Peninsula

Esowista 3

Portland Point

Nahmint

Chuchahacook 4

Kleyklehyus 5

Henderson Lake

Alberni Inlet

Colemen Ck

Mount Grey

Franklin Camp

Mount Whymper

Mount Demers

Cox Point

Wickaninnish Bay

Deekyakus 2

Quinaquilth 4

Elhlateese 2

Uchucklesit Inlet

Green Cove

Parsons Creek

49°

PACIFIC RIM

Quisitis 3
Quisitis Point

Oo-oc'uth 8

Clakamucus 2

Moggie Lake

Macoah 1

Chequis 3

Equis 8

Outs 3

Ahmisa 5

Echoleo

Seeoowa 4

Cowishil 1

Uchuckle

Numukamis 1

Saouk 16

Nutinat

Caycuse

Youbou

Ucluth 6
Ucluelet

Millstream Subdivision

Port Albion

Ittatsoo 1

Tlitatsoo 5A

Chenatha 4

Nettle Island 5

Siebo 6

Ohiahtor Island

Keith Island 7

Kildonan

Numukamis 1

Sarita

Chuchummisape 15

Chuchummisape

Wokitsas 14

Ilctio 12

Nitinat Lake

Lake Cowich

Amphitrite Point

George Fraser Islands

Ittatoo

Dookqua 1

Stuart Bay 6

Dookqua 5

Dodd Island

Benson Island

Effingham Island

Omah 9

Turret

Wouwer Island

Diana

Sachawil 5

Dochsupple 3

Opatseeah 13

Malachan 1

Towincut Mountain
1249

Honeymoon Bay

Cowichan Lake

Mesachie Lake

Kirby Point 6

Haines Island 8

Hamilton Point 7

Keeshan 5

Sachsa 4

Homktan 8

Gordon River

Mount Bolduc

CN

3

Aguila 12

Clutus 11

Kichxa 10

Kechqua

Cape Beale

Masit 13

Dosbah 10

Byres 9

Caycuse River

Edinburgh Mountain

PARC NATIONAL DE PACIFIC RIM

Pachena Point

Tsusquanah 2

Ahuk 1
Iktaksasuk 7

Wyah 1

Whyac 1
Clo-oose

Sarlue 5

Clo-oose 4

Cheewat 4A

Walbran

Mount Modeste

30'

PACIFIC OCEAN

OCÉAN PACIFIQUE

Carmanah Point

Carmanah 6

Collite 4

Pandora Peak

Gordon River

Queesidaquah 2

Pacheena 1

Mount Demers

San Juan

Port San Juan Pt

Port Renfrew

Juan

San Juan River

4

San Juan Point

J U A N   D E   F U C A   S T R A I T

Sombrio Point

San Simon Point

Loss Creek

14

River

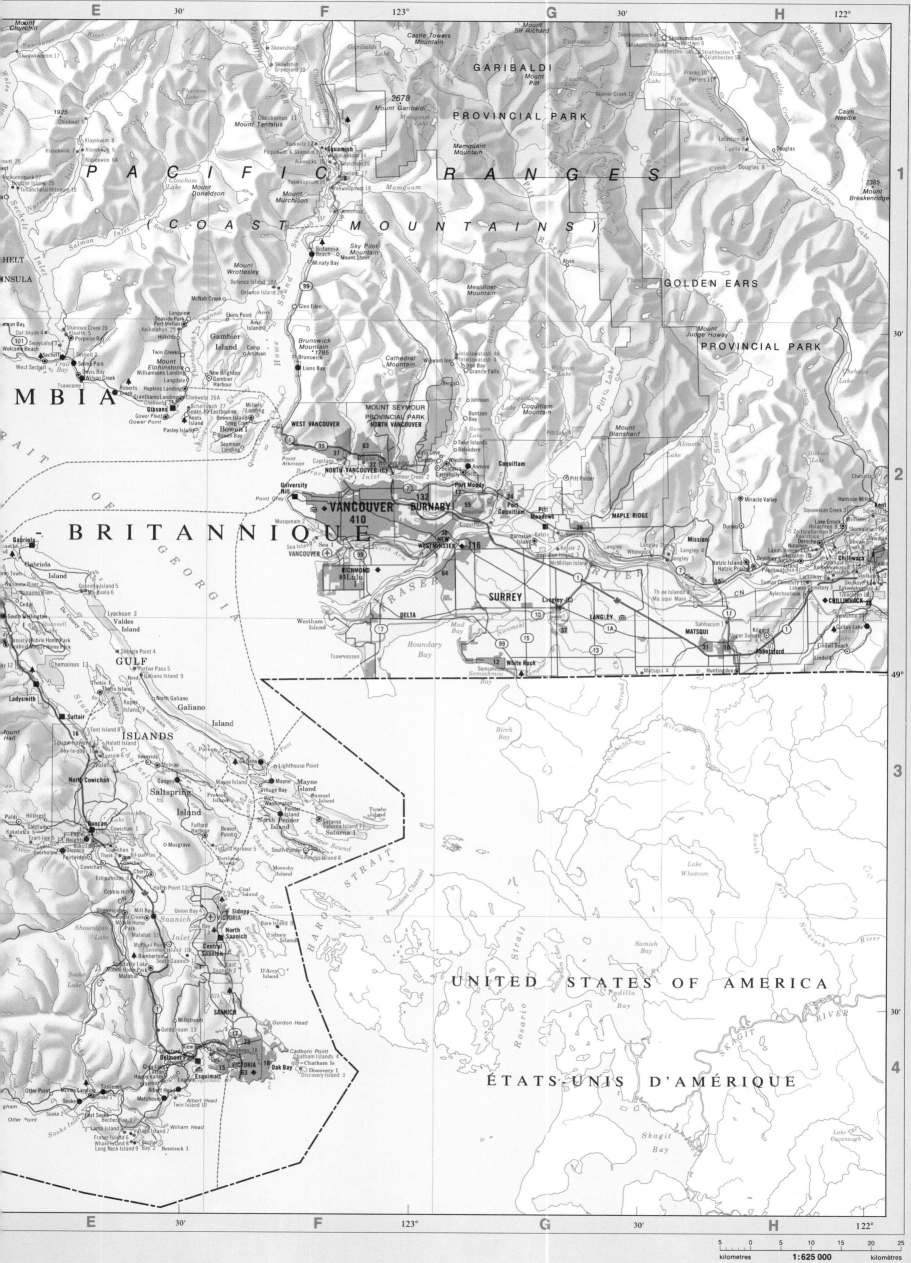

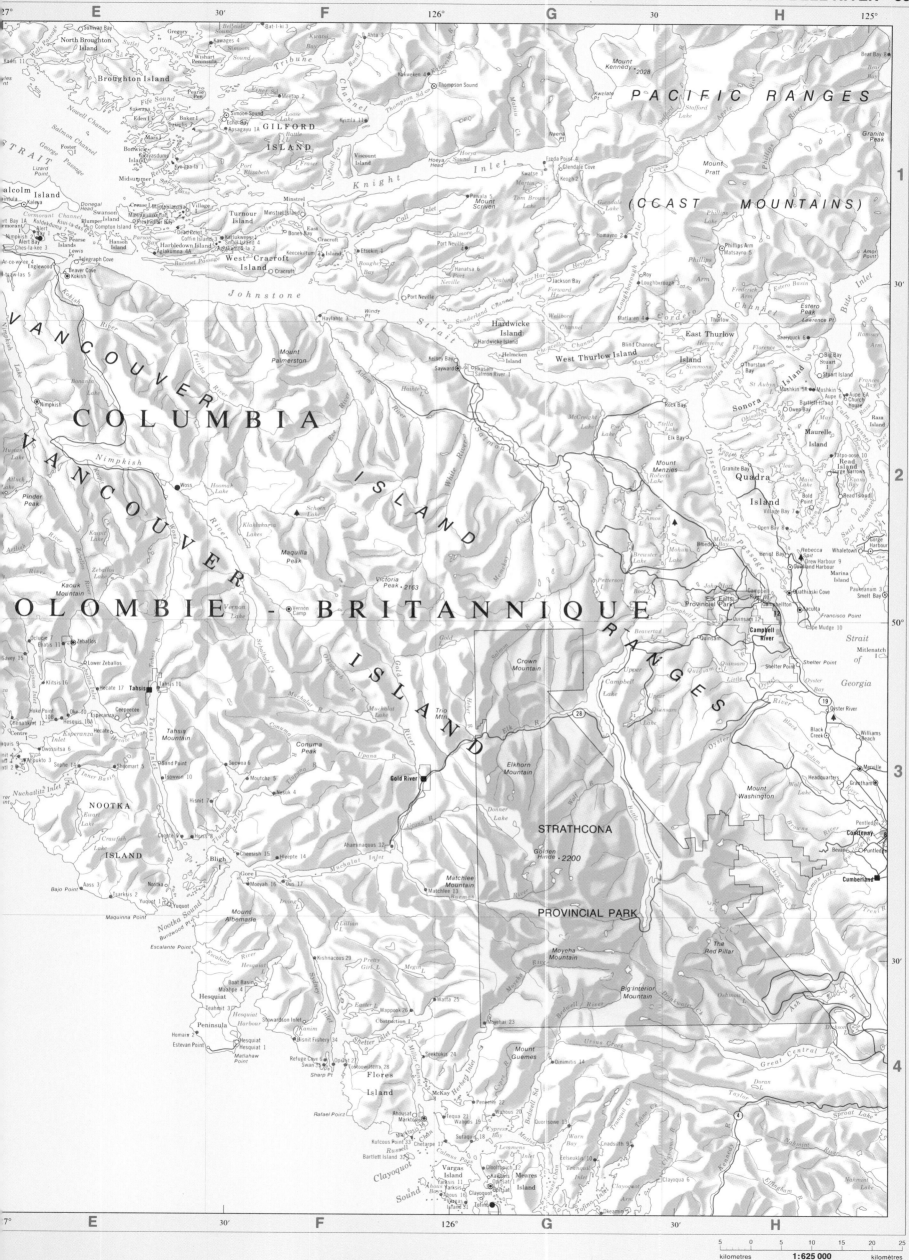

PACIFIC RANGES

(COAST MOUNTAINS)

VANCOUVER

COLUMBIA

VANCOUVER   ISLAND

COLOMBIE - BRITANNIQUE   RANGES

STRATHCONA

PROVINCIAL PARK

NOOTKA

ISLAND

Nootka Sound

Hesquiat

Peninsula

Flores

Island

Clayoquot

Sound

```
5    0    5    10    15    20    25
kilométres      1:625 000      kilométres
```

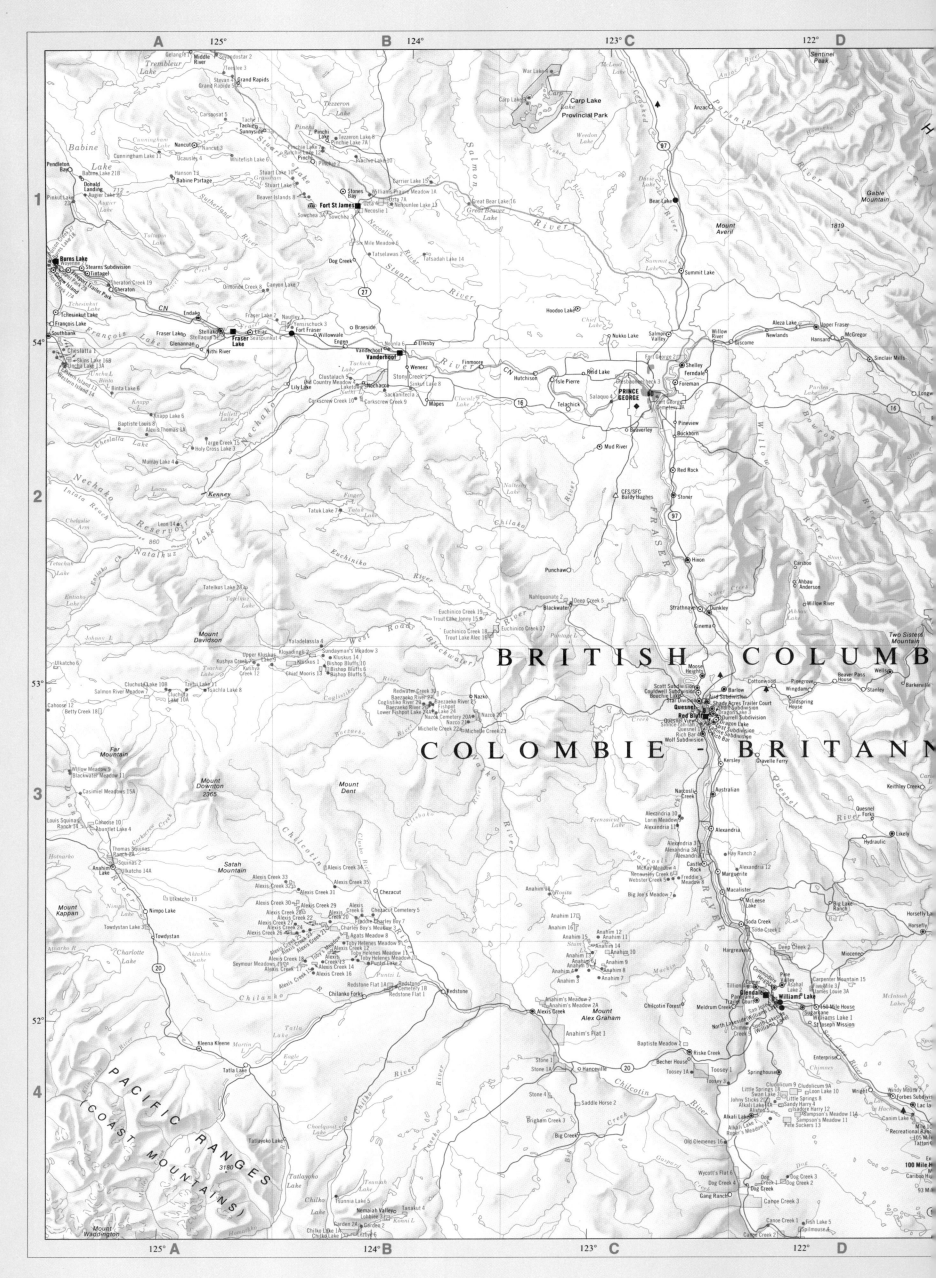

A   125°   B   124°   123°   C   122°   D

1

2

3

4

BRITISH COLUMBIA

COLOMBIE - BRITANNIQUE

Sentinel Peak

Carp Lake Provincial Park

Fort St James

Vanderhoof

PRINCE GEORGE

Burns Lake

Fraser Lake

Quesnel
Red Bluff

Williams Lake

PACIFIC RANGES
(COAST MOUNTAINS)

Mount Waddington

100 Mile House

A   125°   B   124°   123°   C   122°   D

1923 Quintette Mountain

RANGES

ROCKY

2206

Mount May

Mount Sir Alexander 3277

Grande Cache

Redwillow R.

Wapiti

Nose Creek

Belcourt

River

Narraway

River

Kakwa

Sheep Creek

Muskeg River

River

40

Simonette

Berland

Little Smoky

Deep Valley

Washikigan

Smoky

River

River

River

Giroux

Iosegun Lake

43

Little Smoky

Smoke Lake

Fox Creek

ALBERTA

WILLMORE WILDERNESS

PROVINCIAL PARK

M O U N T A I N S

Mount Chown 3331

Oldman Creek

William A Switzer Provincial Park

Dalehurst

Obed

Hargwen

Pedley

16

Galloway

Medicine Lodge

CN

Fraser

Morkill

River

River

McBride

Loos

Crescent Spur

Goat River

North Star Mountain

Quart

River

CARIBOO

PROVINCIAL PARK

COLUMBIA

Robb

Lamming Mills

Eddy

Holmes River

Dunster

Croydon

Mount Robson 3954

MOUNT ROBSON

Mount Robson

Redpass Junction

13

Tête Jaune Cache

Fraser

CONTINENTAL

Snake

Indian

River

River

Snaring

Shale Banks

Miette

Pocahontas

Devona

Snaring

Henry House

Decoigne

1131

Jasper

Jaspe Park Lodge

Geikie

Wynd

Lucerne

CN

Entrance

Old Entrance

Swan Landing

Solomon

Brûlé Mines

Brûlé

Brûlé Lake

Hinton

Miette Hotsprings

JASPER

NATIONAL PARK

Rocky

River

McLeod

Embarras

Oke

Coalspur

Mercoal

Steeper

Shaw

Diss

Luscar

Fidler

Leyland

Cadomin

Mountain Park

Grave Flats

Cardinal River

QUE

2636

Mitchell Lake

MONASHEE

MOUNTAINS

3305 Mount Sir Wilfrid Laurier

Valemount

Cedarside

Canoe River

5

Canoe River

Gosnell

Fraser

River

PROVINCIAL

PARK

R A N G E S

Amethyst Lakes

Mount Edith Cavell 3363

Maligne

Lake

Medicine Lake

PARC NATIONAL

DE JASPER

Mount Brazeau 3470

93

WELLS GRAY

PROVINCIAL PARK

Azure Lake

Angus Horne Lake

Hobson Lake

Clearwater Lake

McDougall

Murtle Lake

Kostal L.

Myrtle Lake

2296

Mount Evans 3300

Fortress L.

Hamber Provincial Park

Chaba River

Brazeau R.

Clemenceau Icefield

Mount Columbia 3747

Columbia Icefield

Banff National Park

Parc national de Banff

Hendrix Lake

Horsefly Lake

Canim Lake 5

Eagle Creek

Canim Lake

Mahood Falls

Mahood Lake

Clearwater

2577 Trophy Mountain

Blue River

Mica

Mica Creek

South City Trailer Court

Mount Chapman

Neptune Peak

Columbia

Lake

SELKIRK

Adamant Mountain

Mount Sir Sandford 3522

23

Gordon Horne Peak 2885

Avola

CN

MOUNTAINS

Argentine Mountain

24

Bridge Lake

Roe Lake

Canim Lake 2

Buffalo Creek

Forest Grove

Deka L.

Bowers

Sheridan Lake

Grizzly Mountain

Sunshine Valley

Kershaw Subdivision

Wildwood Trailer Park

Raft River Trailer Park

Foote Subdivision

Phillips Subdivision

Redlands Subdivision

Blackpool

Birch Island

Vavenby

5

Boulder Creek 5

Little Fort

McAlliston 2

Beavermouth

Downie Creek

Goldstream

Sorcerer Mountain

Iconoclast Mountain

Rogers

Glacier National Park

Parc national de Glacier

Donald

1

Blaeberry

scale:
10   0   10   20   30   40   50
kilometres   kilometres
1 : 1 250 000

DIXON ENTRANCE

Langara I
Yasitkun 21
Cohoe Point 20
Guoyskuit 22
Egeria Bay 19
Tatense 16
Cape Knox
Kiooosta 15
Parry Passage

Klashwun Point
Jalus 14
Yatze 13
Daningay 12
Wiah Point
Meagwan 8
McIntyre Bay
Hiellen 2
Yagan 3a

Virage Sound
Yan 7
Yan 7
Haida
Masset
Saouphten 18

Rose Point

NAIKOON

Frederick Island
Susk 17
Naden 23
Naden 10
Kose 9
Naden Harbour

54°

GRAHAM

PROVINCIAL

1

Tiahn 27
Eden Lake
Ian Lake
Kumdis Island
Sewall

Louis Point
Ain 6
Port Clements
Mayer Lake
Cape Ball

Athlow Bay
Ovun 24
Salipinum 5
Lanas
Mamnin River 25
Juskatla

PARK

Hippa
Shannon Bay

ISLAND

QUEEN

Tlell

QUEEN

Rennell Sound
Kindakun Point
Kano Inlet
Lawn Point

Yakoun Lake
Lawnhill
Skaigha 2

53°

2

Hunter Point
Cartwright Sound
Lagins 5
Queen Charlotte
Black Slate 11
Skidegate 1
Skidegate Mission
Skidegate
Khrana 4
Alliford Bay
Sandspit

CHARLOTTE

Chaatl Island
Chaatl
Beena 3
Kaste 6

CHARLOTTE

Kaisun
Moresby Camp
Aero
Cumshewas 7
Cumshewa Head
Englefield Bay
Hibben
1140
New Clew 10
Skedance 8

Cape Henry
Louise Island

ISLANDS

Sewell Inlet
Selwyn Inlet
Talunkwan I
Thurston Harbour
Laskeek Bay

Tasu Sd
Tasu
Tanu
Tanoo 9

MORESBY
Lockeport
Lyell Island

MOUNTAINS

Juan Perez Sound

Ramsay Island

ISLAND

Burnaby

3

PACIFIC

Gowgaia Bay
Jedway
Carpenter Bay

OCEAN

Nagas Point
Rose Harbour

52°

Ninstints
Kunghit

Island

Kerouard Islands

OCÉAN

PACIFIQUE

4

51°

HECATE STRAIT

Brown Passage
Tugwell Island 21
Shoowahtlans 4
Magantkoon 56
Kasiks River 29
Kasika 22
Kasika 71
Sahli
Tsimpsean 2
Digby Island
Rushton Island 90
Prince Rupert
Wiltimlagon 61
Acagwissawas 63
Kwinitsa 6
Kyex 64
Khyex 8

Hooper Point
Chatham
Sound
Avery Island 92
Port Edward 16
Dashken 23
Haysport
Tyee
Telegraph Point
Alder Creek 70
Temkhaa3

Stephens
Island
Prescott
Island
McInlaw 24
Smith I Osland
Imkusiyan 65
Port Essington
Scuttsap 11
Scuttsap 11A
Khtabda 10

Squaderee 91
Kshaobm 23

Edyel 83
Porcher Island
Hunts Inlet Kennedy
Island
Khada Lake
Alastair 80
Alastair 81
Alastair 82

Gurd
Oona River
Porcher
Island
Kaokmolks 67
1955

Cape George
Goschen
Island
Klapthlon 5A
Klapthlon 5

McCauley
Ketai 28
Keswar 16
Island
Pa-aat 6
Takvas 68

Sand Island 4
Grassy Islet 2
Kitkatla
Dolphin Island 1
Dolphin 1

Kul 18
Bonilla Island

PITT

Kitsemenlagon 19
Kitsemenlagon 19A
Keyarka 17
Island
Tumrairen 15
Red Bluff
Sheganny 14
Parrant

Gil Island 2
Quaal 3A
Quaal
Kitkahta

BANKS

Clewel 13
Toowartz 8
Gribble Island

BRITIS

ISLAND
Koaryet 12
Tsimtack
Turtle Point 12
Kitlawaoo 30
Keecha 11
Fin
Lachkul-jeets 6
Citeyats 1
Kunhunoan 14

COLOMB

Estevan
Group
Caamaño
Gil
Island

Rennison
Island
Lackzuswadda 9
Sound
Gander Island 14
Moore
Islands
Maple Point 5
Kayel 8
Kah

Aristazabal

QUEEN

Island

CHARLOTTE

SOUN

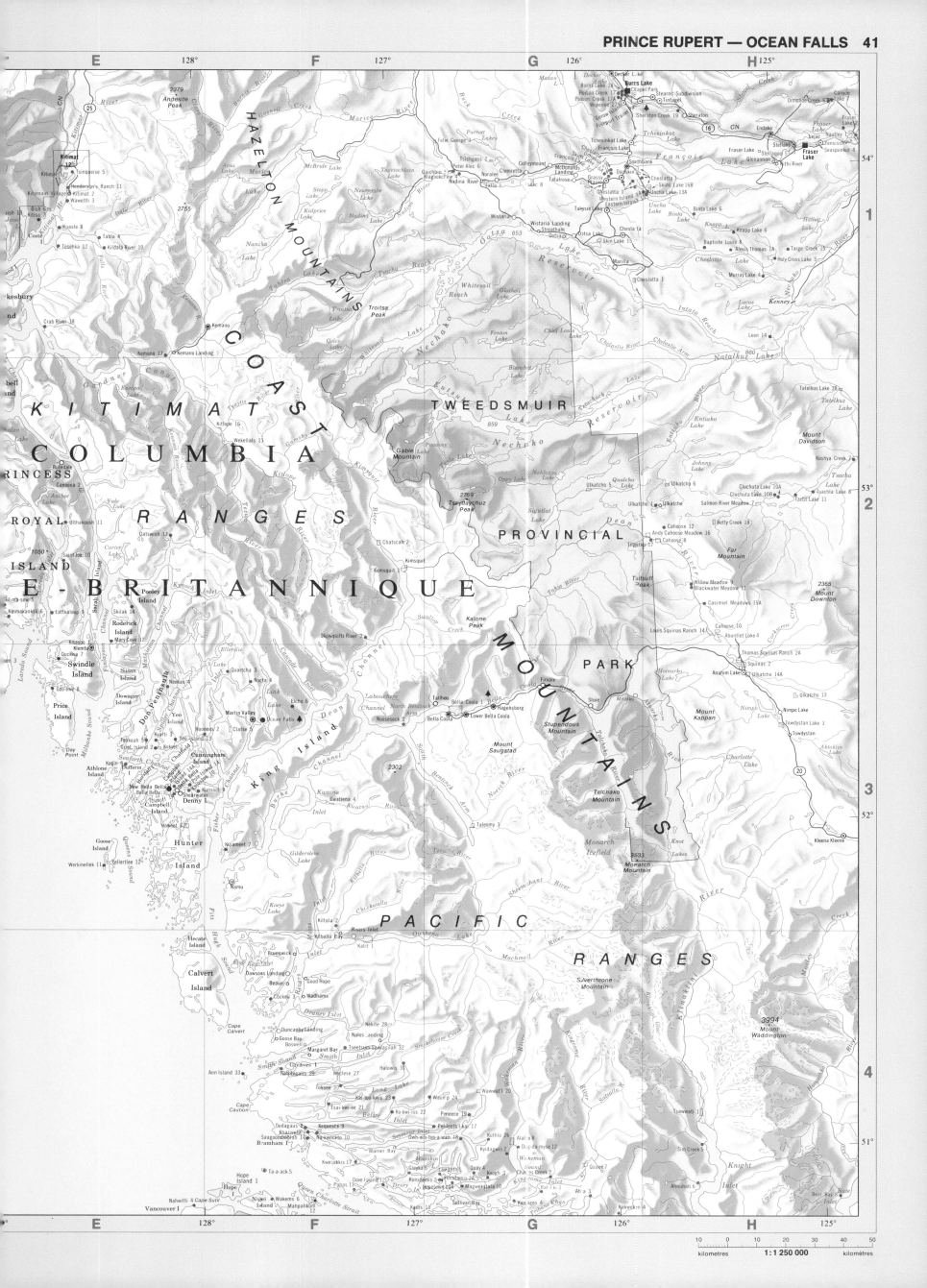

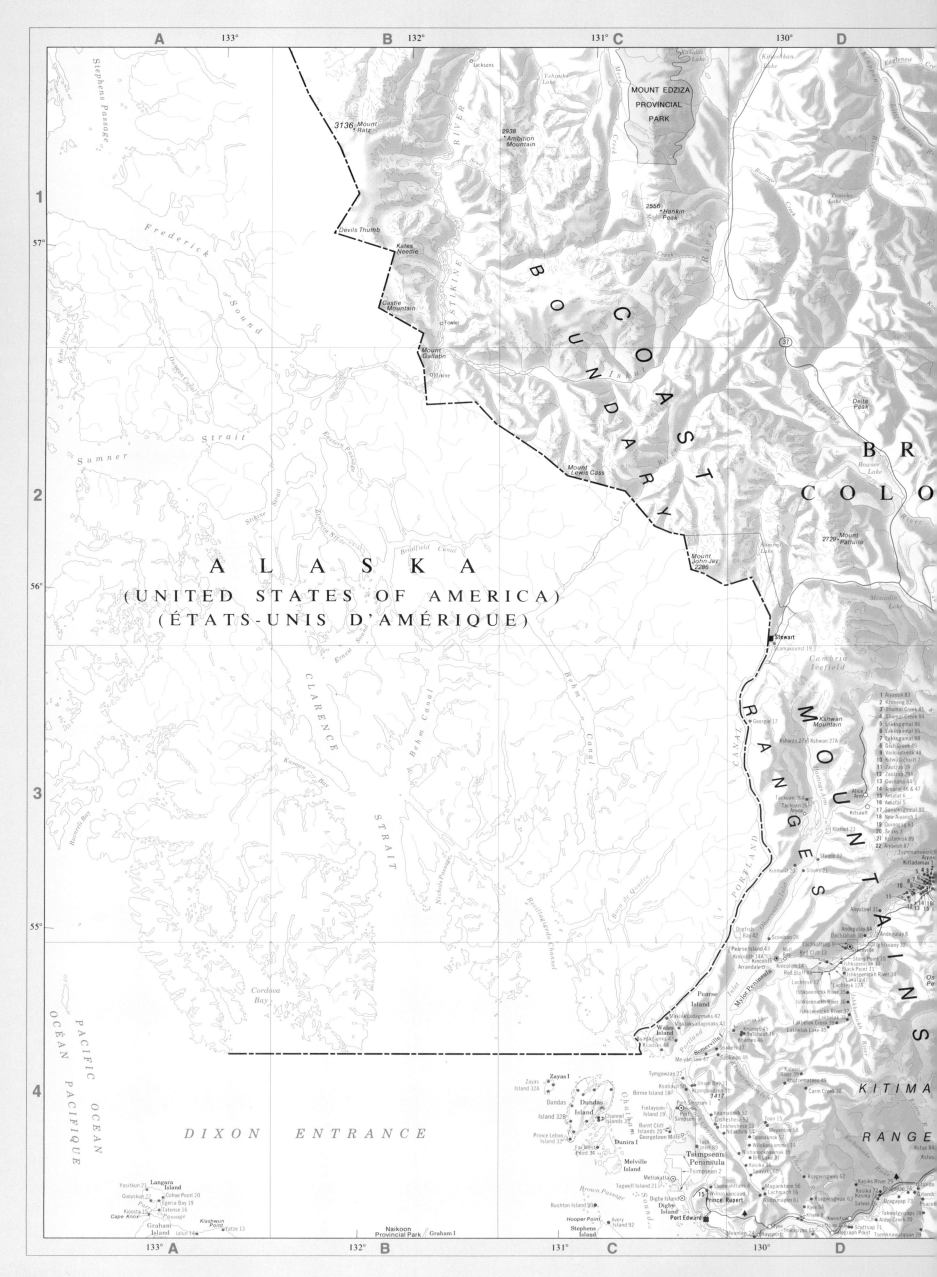

Stephens Passage

Frederick

Sound

Kah Strait

Sumner

Strait

Duncan Canal

Eastern Passage

Zimovia Strait

Stikine Strait

3136 Mount
Ratz

Devils Thumb

Kates
Needle

Castle
Mountain

Fowler

Mount
Gallatin

Stikine

STIKINE

RIVER

2938
Ambition
Mountain

Scud R.

Jacksons

Yehiniko
Lake

Mess Creek

Kinaskan
Lake

MOUNT EDZIZA
PROVINCIAL
PARK

Kitsumkalum
Lake

2556
Hankin
Peak

Little Iskut River

Iskut River

Bowser
Lake

37

Delta
Peak

C O A S T

B O U N D A R Y

B R
C O L O

Mount
Lewis Cass

Unuk River

Leduc River

Mount
John Jay
2286

2729 Mount
Pattullo

Summit
Lake

Mezadin
Lake

Stewart

Bradfield Canal

Ernest Sound

CLARENCE

Kasaan Bay

Behm Canal

Behm Canal

A L A S K A

(UNITED STATES OF AMERICA)

(ÉTATS-UNIS D'AMÉRIQUE)

STRAIT

Nichols Passage

Revillagigedo Channel

Boca de Quadra

Bucareli Bay

Cordova
Bay

PORTLAND CANAL

Observatory Inlet

Bear River

Kamakounst 19.7

Cambria
Icefield

M O U N T A I N S

Kshwan
Mountain

Georgie 17

Kshwan 27B Kshwan 27A

Tackuan 26A
Tackuan 26.
Amyox

Kitsault

Kitsnet 23

Alice
Arm

Khutzeymateen
River

1 Aiyansh 83
2 Kzimeng 82
3 Shumal Creek 81
4 Iskksgamal 86
5 Iskksgamal 85
6 Iakksgamal 88
7 Iakksgamal 88
8 Gish Creek 45
9 Voileadamks 48
10 Kstwilpchisitt 7
11 Zaulzap 29
12 Anilzap 29A
13 Gwinaha 44
14 Amarat 46 & 47
15 Amatal 6
16 Amatal 5
17 Sanalkszamal 80
18 New Aiyansh 1
19 Quinogag 61
20 Scaks 3
21 Kulamnisk 89
22 Aiyansh 87

Tsimpmaweeoncht
Ayan 4
Kitladamax 2

Staqoo 22

Kinmelit 20

Slooks 21

Anyutawl 31

Dogfish
Bay 42

Scowban 26

Andegulay 8A
Dachlabah 30

Lachkaltsap 9

Andegulay 8

lightkeany 32

Pearse Island 43

Kincolith 14A

Kincolith

Arrandale

Kincolith 15
Red Bluff 88

Mill

Kincolith

Red Cliff 13

Greenville

Stony Point 10
Ishkseenickh
Black Point 11
Ishkseenickh River 34
Lakata 12A

Pearse
Island

Lachtesk 12

Ishkseenichka River 35

Ishkseenickh River 36

Ishkseenickh River 37

Lakbelak 12K

Mylor Peninsula

Lakbelak Creek

Lakbelak Lake 46

Makiaksadagmaks 42
Makiaksadagmaks 41

Wales
Island

Sangamaks 43

Kladoks 44

Portland Inlet

Somerville
Island

Kunamaa 15

Khamees 45

Iaf'shaat 16

Khames 46

Me-yan-law 47

Spaksuit 48

Kaiege
River 39

Khutzemateen 49

Tymgowzan 2

Union Bay 51
Ktamgoodzit 53

Carm Creek 38

KITIMA

RANGE

Zayas I.

Zayas
Island 32A

Dundas
Island 19

Dundas
Island 32B

Birnie Island 18C

Dundas
Island

Channel
Islands

Finlayson
Channel 19

Port
Simpson

Port Simpson 1

Burnt Cliff
Georgetown Mills

Khamadees 52
Ensheshese 53
Ensheshese 13

Toon 15

Meyanlin 58

Chatham Sound

Prince Lebeo,
Island 32

Far West
Point 34

Ksabaon 21

Duniira I.

Melville
Island

Tugwell Island 21

Metlakatla

Wilsiakkansumk 3

Nisharockmamak 33
Bill Lake 37
Spaxylit 59

Kasika 36

Wilskaskamm 13

Ksagwisgwas 62

Maganhtoon 56

Tsimpsean
Peninsula

Tsimpsean 2

Lachgach 16
Wildzimagen 61

Kaiaks River 39

Kasiks 72
Kasiks

Kondo

Kitkatla

Brown Passage

Rushton Island 90

Hooper Point

Avery
Island 92

Stephens
Island

Showahtlans 1

Digby Island

Prince Rupert

Kxkx 54

Ksawguesqwas 63

Salvus

Takwalggyapps 78

15 Wilnaskancaund 3
Lachguolach 4

Kwinitsa
River

Alder Creek 70
Kyex 54

Port Edward

Mexjap 24

Kulspai 68

Maxtan 25
Tsenknawalquan 76

Woodcock 71
Scottsap 11

Telegraph Point

Langara
Island

Yasitkun 21

Guoyskut 22

Kioosta 15
Cape Knox

Egeria Bay 19

Cohoe Point 20

Tatense 16

Klashwun
Point

Yatze 13

Graham
Island

Jalun 14

Naikoon
Provincial Park

Graham I.

DIXON ENTRANCE

PACIFIC OCEAN
OCÉAN PACIFIQUE

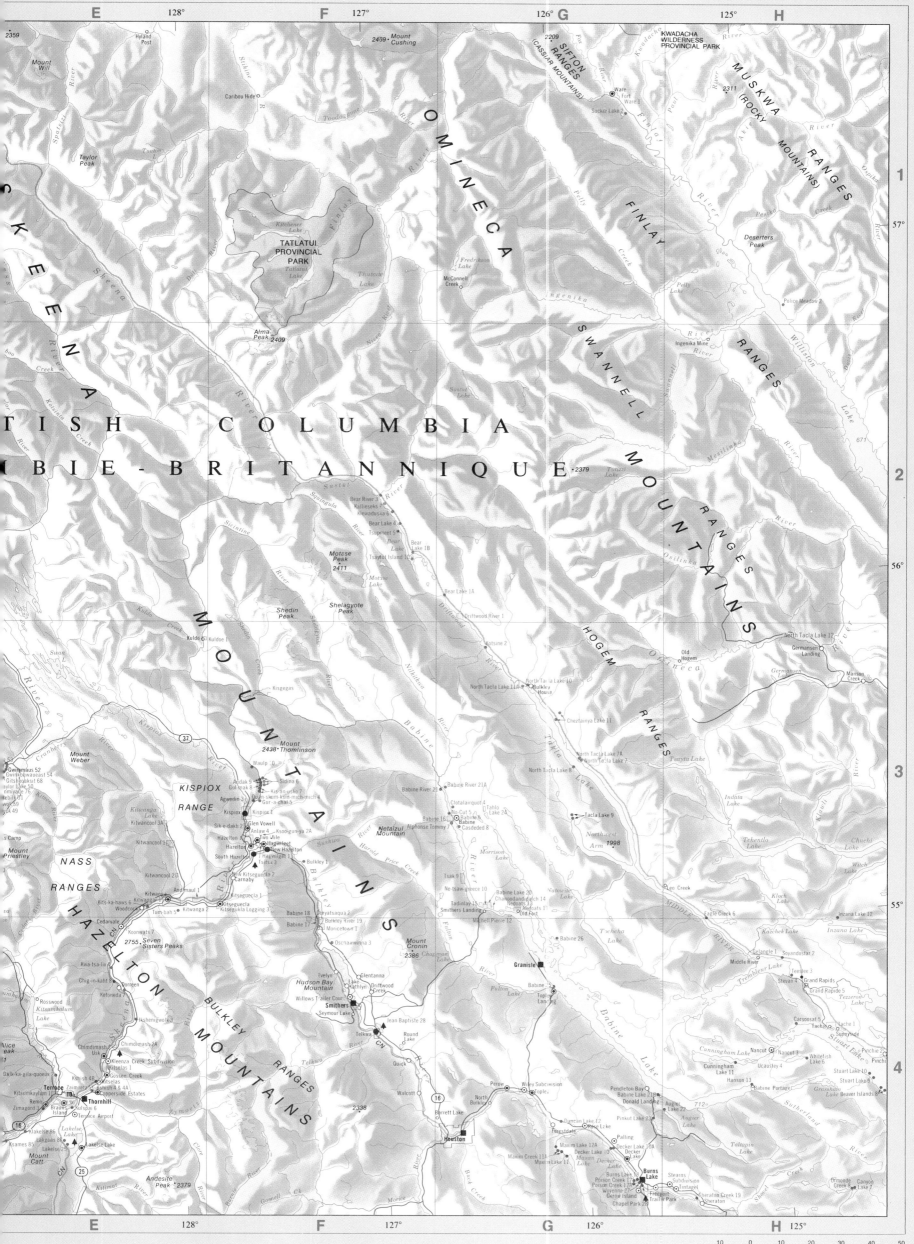

BRITISH COLUMBIA
COLOMBIE-BRITANNIQUE

SKEENA

OMINECA

TATLATUI
PROVINCIAL
PARK

KWADACHA
WILDERNESS
PROVINCIAL PARK

SIFTON
RANGES
(CASSAR MOUNTAINS)

MUSKWA
(ROCKY
MOUNTAINS)
RANGES

FINLAY

SWANNELL
RANGES

M O U N T A I N S

HOGEM
RANGES

OMINECA

KISPIOX
RANGE

NASS
RANGES

HAZELTON

BULKLEY
RANGES

HAZELTON
MOUNTAINS

BULKLEY MOUNTAINS

Mount
Cushing   2459

Taylor
Peak

Mount
Will

Hyland
Post

Caribou Hide

Kitchener
Lake

Alma
Peak 2409

Fredrikson
Lake

McConnell
Creek

Police Meadow 2

Ingenika Mine

Old
Hogem

Germansen
Landing

Manson
Creek

North Tacla Lake 12

2379

Totozi
Lake

Motase
Peak
2411

Bear River 3
Kallieseks 6
Kwadusca 6
Bear Lake 4
Tsaprieet 5
Bear
Lake
Tsaytut Island 1C
Bear Lake 1B

Shedin
Peak

Shelagyote
Peak

Bear Lake 1A

Driftwood River 1

Kotsine 2

Kulde 6 Kuldoe 1

North Tacla Lake 11A
Bulkley
House
North Tacla Lake 10

Cheztainya Lake 11

North Tacla Lake 7A
North Tacla Lake 7
North Tacla Lake 8

Tsuyta Lake

Tacla Lake 9

Northwest
Arm
1998

Indata
Lake

Tchentlo
Lake

Chuchi
Lake

Witch
Lake

Kispiox
Glen Vowell
Anlaw 4
Hazelton
South Hazelton
New Hazelton

Kitseguecla 2
Carnaby
Andimaul 1
Kitwanga
Woodcock
Cedarvale
Kitwancool 20

Mount
Thomlinson 2438

Waulp
Aidak 9
Gitsegukla 6
Sidina 6
Kis-an-usko 7
Kispiox 1

Babine River 23
Babine River 21A

Clotalatrquot 4
Tahlo
Hagwilget 1
Kitseguecla 1
Gitsegukla Logging 3
Kispiox

Netalzul
Mountain

Babine 16
Babine 6
Babine
Casdeded 8
Alphonse Tommy 7

Tsak 9

Morrison
Lake

Leo Creek

Seven
Sisters Peaks
2755

Babine 18
Babine 17
Coyatsaqua 2
Bulkley River 19
Moricetown 1
Oscnawinna 3

Mount
Cronin
2386

Babine Lake 20
Chanoodandidatch 14
Yedoats 1
Medaats 1
Old Fort

Ne-tsaw-greece 10

Natowite
Lake

Tschetta
Lake

Eagle Creek 6

Kaychek Lake

Inzana
Lake

Inzana Lake 12

Mount
Weber

Mount
Priestley

Kitseguecla 2

Hudson Bay
Mountain

Evelyn
Glentanna
Lake
Kathlyn
Willows Trailer Court

Driftwood
Creek

Smithers

Babine 26

Granisle

Middle River

Gelangle 1
Soyandostar 2

Tezzeron
Lake

Tachie

Jessee 3
Stevan 4
Grand Rapids
Grand Rapide 5

Seymour Lake

Telkwa

Jean Baptiste 28
Round
Lake

Babine 5
Topley
Landing

Carsoosat 5
Lache 1
Sunnyside

Rosswood
Kitsumkalum
Lake

Terrace
Thornhill

Kleanza Creek Subdivision
Gossen Creek
Chimdimash 2A

Quick

Perow
Walcott
Topley
Wesley Subdivision

North
Bulkley

Barrett Lake

Houston

Pendleton Bay
Babine Lake 21B
Donald Landing

Cunningham Lake 11
Cunningham Lake

Hanson 13

Nancut
Napcut 3
Whitefish
Lake 6

Ucausley 4

Stuart Lake 10

Andesite
Peak 2379

Maxim Creek 11A
Maxim Lake 11
Maxim Lake 12A

Decker Lake 10
Decker Lake 10A
Decker

Palling

Pinkut Lake 23

Duncan Lake 12

Forestdale

Augier
Lake 22

Beaver Islands 8

Lakelse Lake

Mount
Catt

Burns Lake
Poison Creek
Poison Lake 1
Gerow Island
Chapel Park 21

Stearns
Sutherland
Tintagel

Sheraton
Operation Creek 19

Canyon
Creek 8

Taltapin
Lake

Lakelse Lake

Terrace Airport

10   0   10   20   30   40   50
kilometres   1 : 1 250 000   kilometres

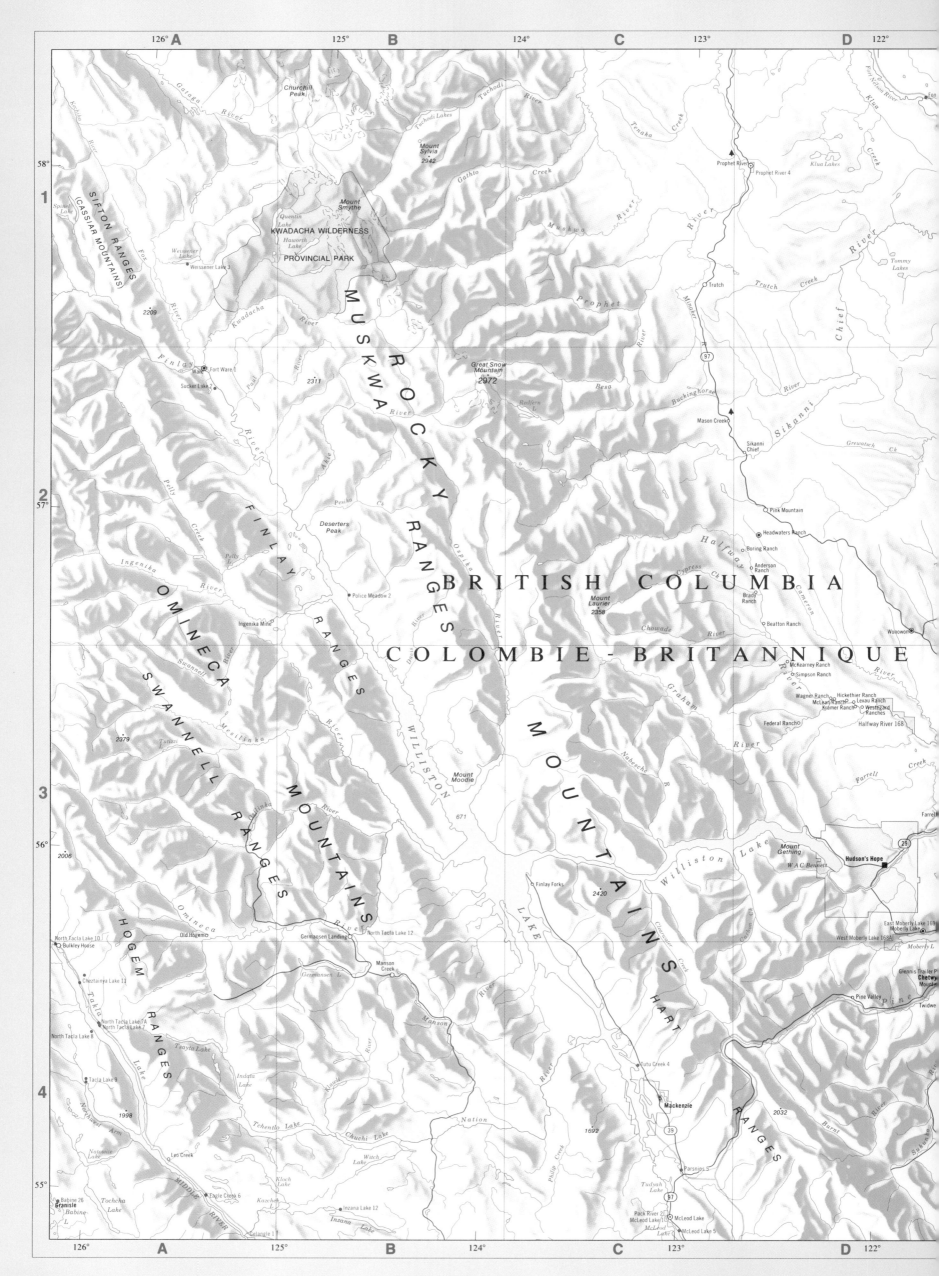

58°

1

Krubla Lake
Spused Lake
SIFTON RANGES
CASSIAR MOUNTAINS

Gataga River
Churchill Peak
Tuchodi Lakes
Tuchodi River
River

Mount Sylvia 2942
Gathto Creek

Mount Smythe
Quentin Lake
KWADACHA WILDERNESS
Haworth Lake
PROVINCIAL PARK

Prophet River
Prophet River 4

Klua Creek
Four Nelson River
Ten
Klua Lakes
Tommy Lakes

Weissener Lake
Weissener Lake 3

Fox River
2209

Finlay River
Kwadacha River

M U S K W A

Muskwa River

Prophet River

Trutch
97
Trutch Creek

Chief River

Fort Ware 1
Watt
Sucker Lake 3

Finlay
R O C K Y

2311

Aksje River
Besa River

Great Snow Mountain 2972
Redfern L.

Minaker River
Buckinghorse River

Sikanni
Mason Creek

Grewatsch Ck.

Sikanni Chief

2

57°

Ingenika River
Pelly Creek

Pelly L.

Peska Ck.
Deserters Peak

R A N G E S

Oospika River

Ospika River

Pink Mountain
Headwaters Ranch
Boring Ranch

Halfway River

O M I N E C A

FINLAY RANGES
Police Meadow 2
Ingenika Mine

Mount Laurier 2358

B R I T I S H   C O L U M B I A

Chowade River

Anderson Ranch
Brady Ranch
Beatton Ranch
Wonowon

SWANNELL RANGES
2379
Tutizzi

Swannell River
Mesilinka River

W I L L I S T O N

C O L O M B I E - B R I T A N N I Q U E

M O U N T A I N S

McKearney Ranch
Simpson Ranch
Wagner Ranch
McLean Ranch
Hickethier Ranch
Kramer Ranch
Lexau Ranch
Westergard Ranches
Federal Ranch
Halfway River 168

3

56°

2006

Omineca River

Osilinka River

Mount Moodie

671

Graham River

Nabesche R.

Farrell Creek

Farrell

Mount Gething
W.A.C. Bennett
Hudson's Hope
29

HOGEM RANGES
North Tacla Lake 10
Bulkley House
Cheztainya Lake 11

Old Hogem
Germansen Landing
North Tacla Lake 12

Manson Creek

Finlay Forks
2420

Williston Lake

L A K E
H A R T

Chowika Creek

East Moberly Lake 169
West Moberly Lake 168A
Moberly L.
Glennis Trailer P.
Chetwynd
Moune

Takla Lake

North Tacla Lake 7A
North Tacla Lake 7
North Tacla Lake 8

Germansen L.

Manson River

Pine Valley

Pine River
Twidwe

4

55°

Tacla Lake 9
1998

Northwest Arm
Natoma Lake

Leo Creek

Tsayta Lake
Indata Lake

Tchentlo Lake
Chuchi Lake

Kloch Lake
Kazchek

Witch Lake

Nation River

M O U N T A I N S

1692

Tutu Creek 4

Mackenzie
39

2032

Burnt River

Sikanni River

Philip Creek

97

Babine 26
Granisle
Babine L.
Tochcha Lake

Tagle Creek 6

Inzana Lake 12
Inzana Lake

Tudyah Lake

Parsnips S.

Middle River

Kuzkwa R.

Gelangie 1

Pack River 2
McLeod Lake 2
McLeod Lake
McLeod Lake 5

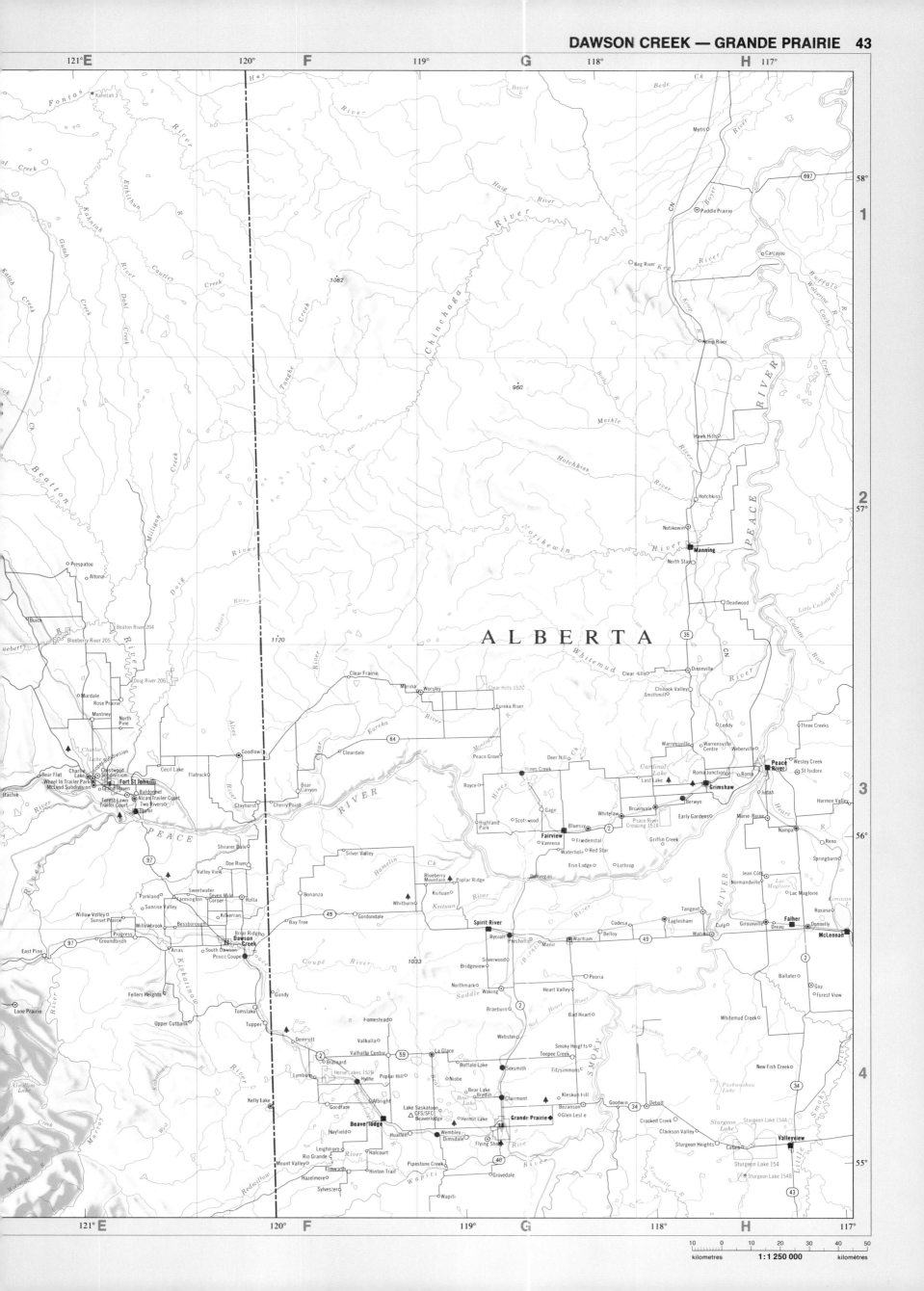

ALBERTA

PEACE RIVER

Fort St John

Dawson Creek

Beaverlodge

Grande Prairie

Peace River

Grimshaw

Fairview

Manning

Spirit River

McLennan

Falher

Valleyview

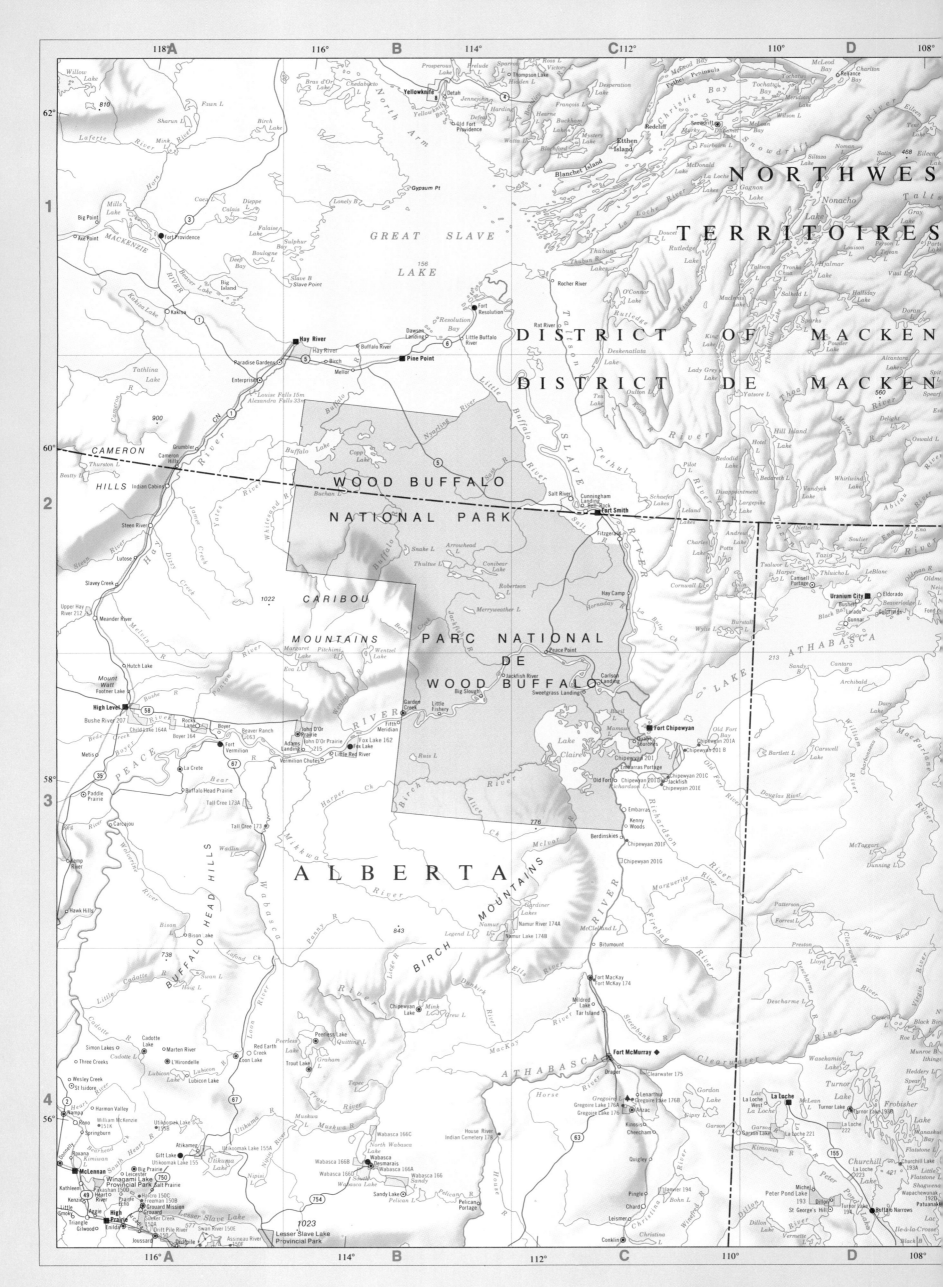

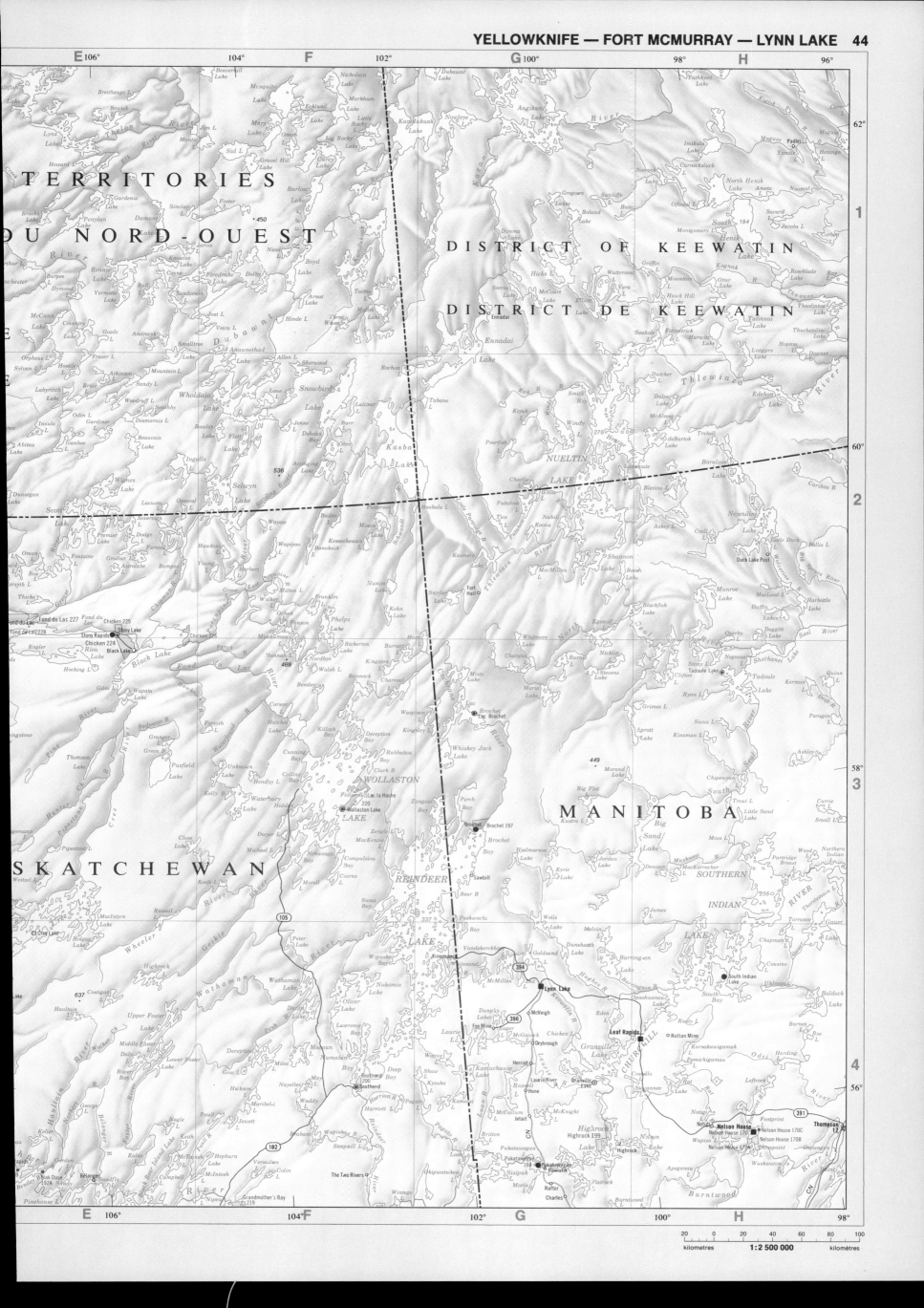

E 106°   104°   F   102°   G 100°   98°   H   96°

TERRITORIES

DU NORD-OUEST

DISTRICT OF KEEWATIN

DISTRICT DE KEEWATIN

NUELTIN LAKE

WOLLASTON LAKE

SASKATCHEWAN

MANITOBA

SOUTHERN INDIAN LAKE

REINDEER LAKE

Lynn Lake

Leaf Rapids

Nelson House

Thompson

E 106°   104° F   102° G   100°   H   98°

20   0   20   40   60   80   100
kilometres   1:2 500 000   kilomètres

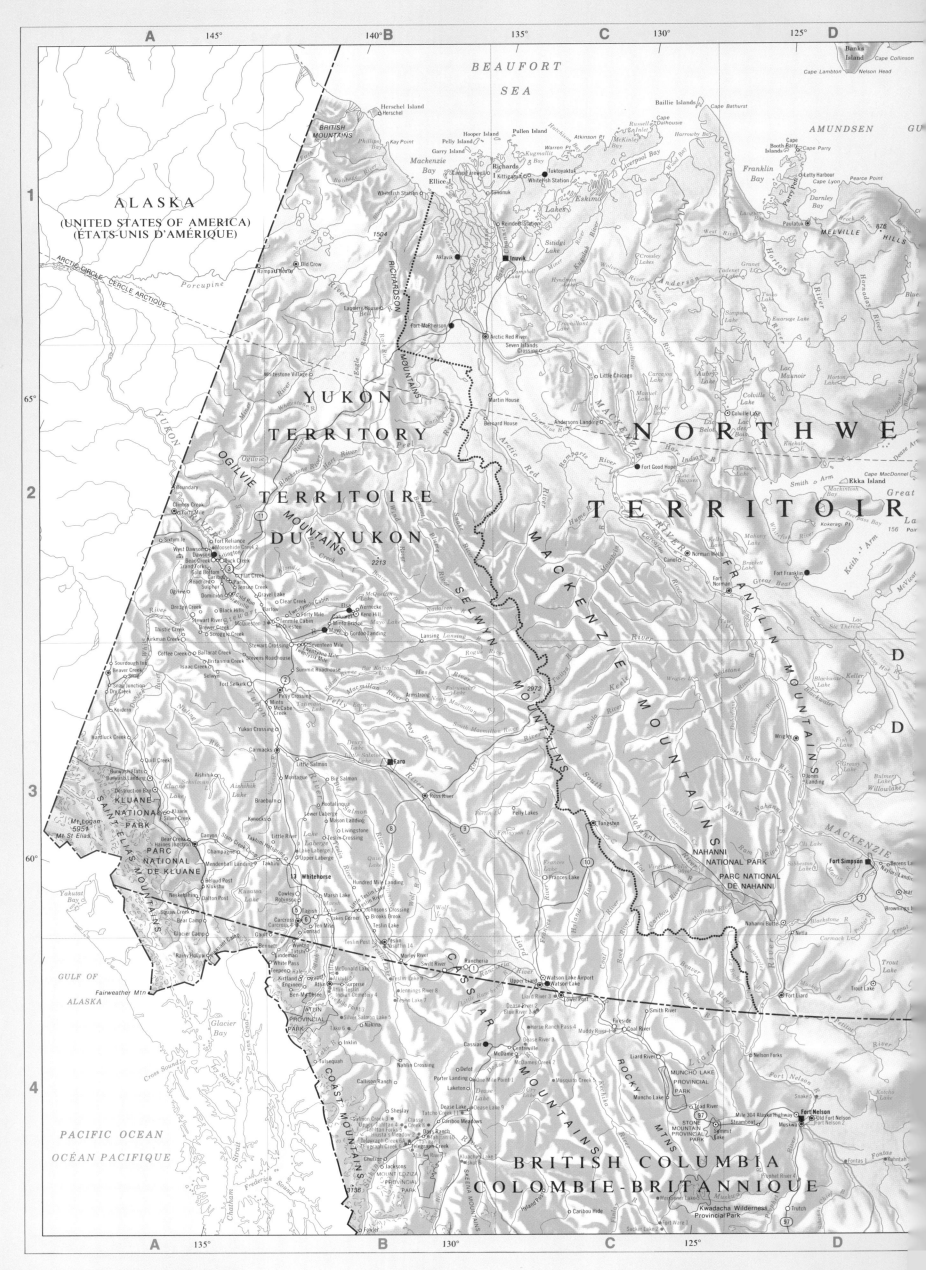

A 145° B 140° 135° C 130° D 125°

BEAUFORT
SEA

Banks
Island
Cape Collinson
Cape Lambton   Nelson Head

AMUNDSEN   GU

ALASKA
(UNITED STATES OF AMERICA)
(ÉTATS-UNIS D'AMÉRIQUE)

1

Herschel Island
Herschel

BRITISH
MOUNTAINS

Phillips Bay
Kay Point

Baillie Islands   Cape Bathurst
Russell   Cape
Inlet   Dalhousie
McKinley Bay   Harrowby Bay   Booth
Islands   Cape Parry
Cape
Parry   Cape
Letty Harbour   Pearce Point
Cape Lyon   Darnley
Bay   Paulatuk   MELVILLE   876
HILLS

Hooper Island   Pullen Island
Garry Island
Mackenzie
Bay   Kugmallit   Toktoyaktuk
Richards   Bay
Whitefish Station   Eskimo
Lakes   Liverpool Bay   Wood Bay   Franklin
Bay

ARCTIC CIRCLE
CERCLE ARCTIQUE

Porcupine

Old Crow
Rampart House

1504

Aklavik   Inuvik

Sitidgi
Lake   Reindeer Station

Campbell Lake   Anderson

65°

Lapierre House
Bell

Whitestone Village

YUKON

TERRITORY

TERRITOIRE

DU YUKON

Fort McPherson

Arctic Red River
Seven Islands
Crossing

Little Chicago

Martin House

Bernard House

Fort Good Hope

NORTHWE

TERRITOIR

Norman Wells
Canol

Fort Franklin

Great Bear

PACIFIC OCEAN
OCÉAN PACIFIQUE

BRITISH COLUMBIA
COLOMBIE-BRITANNIQUE

A 135° B 130° C 125° D

172

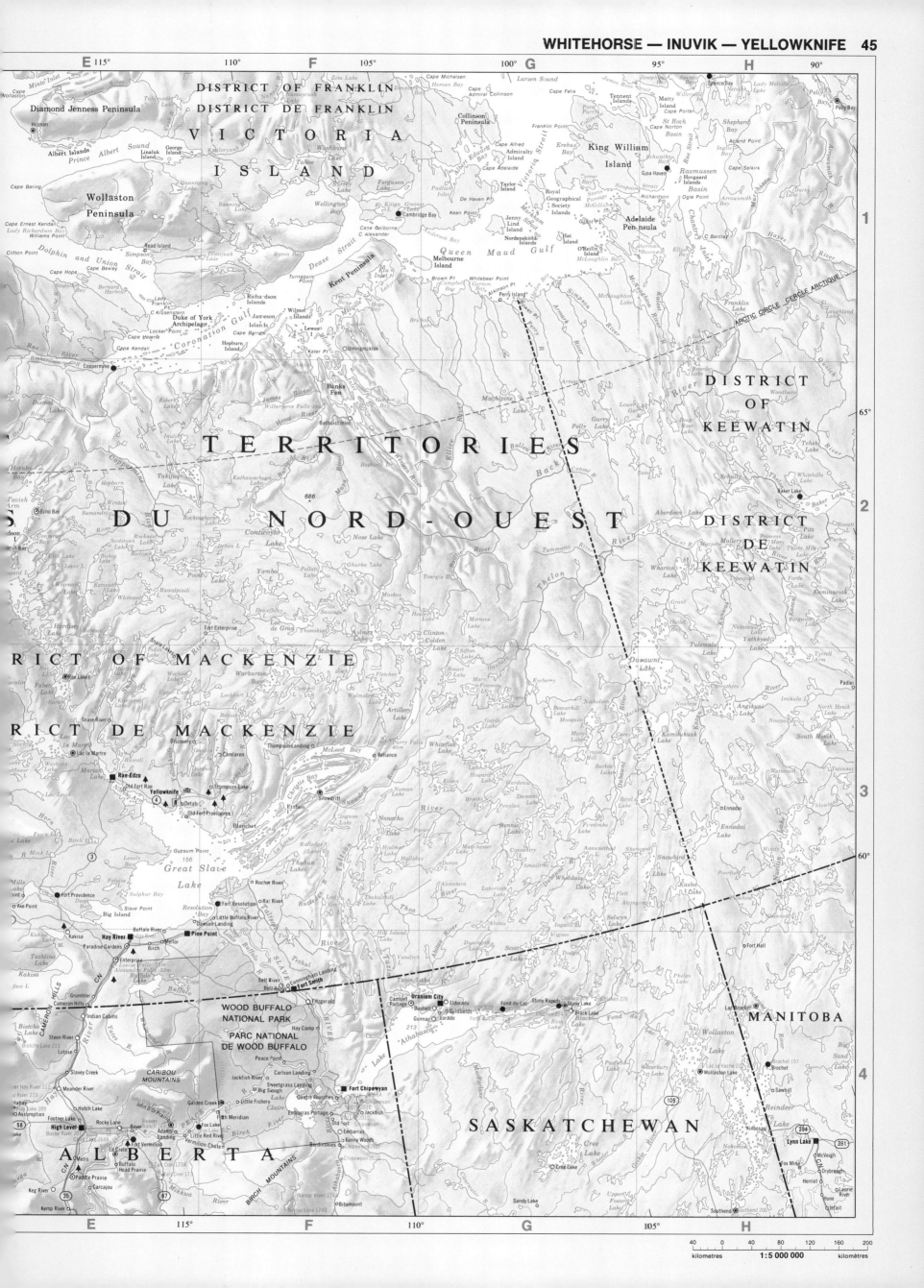

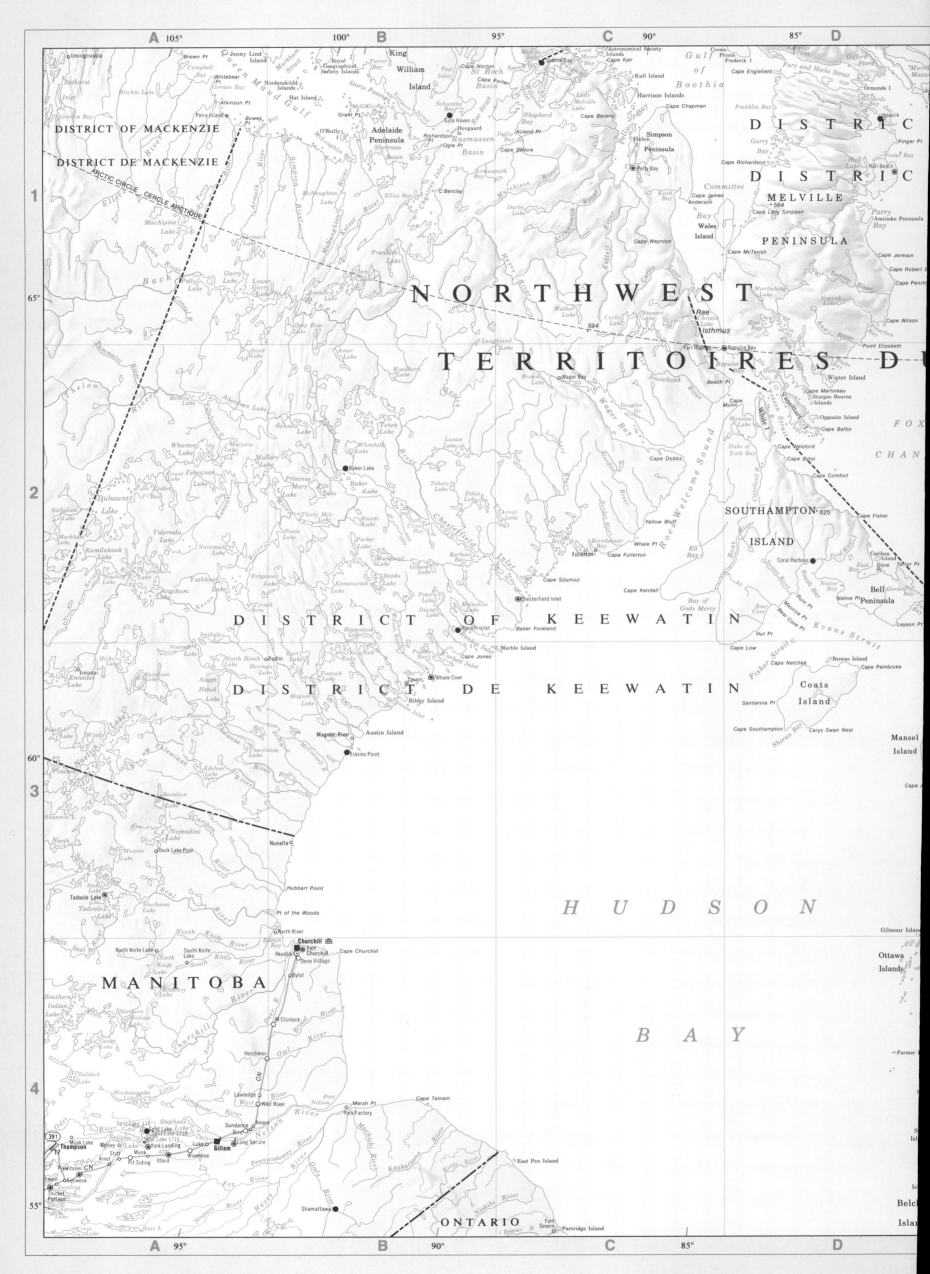

GREENLAND
(DENMARK)
GROENLAND
(DANEMARK)

BARNES
ICE CAP

Cape Raper
Aulitivik Island
Auliiviing Island

Home
Bay

OF FRANKLIN

DE FRANKLIN

BAFFIN

TERRITORIES

NORD-OUEST

ISLAND

Prince
Charles
Island

Air Force
Island

GREAT PLAIN
OF THE
KOUKDJUAK

Fox Peninsula

Cape Dorset

ARCTIC CIRCLE CERCLE ARCTIQUE

AUYUITTUQ NATIONAL PARK
PARC NATIONAL D'AUYUITTUQ

CUMBERLAND
PENINSULA

Pangnirtung

CUMBERLAND Sound

DAVIS STRAIT

Hall Peninsula

Frobisher Bay

Meta Incognita Peninsula

Frobisher Bay

Lake Harbour

HUDSON STRAIT

Edgell Island

Resolution
Island

Resolution Island

LABRADOR
SEA

Charles Island

Ivujivik

Saglouc
Deception

Akulivik

Povungnituk

PÉNINSULE

D'UNGAVA

Cratère du
Nouveau-Québec

Akpatok
Island

UNGAVA

BAY

Button Islands
Gray Strait
Port Burwell
Cape Chidley
Killinek Island

North Aulatsivik Island

TORNGAT MOUNTAINS

MONTS TORNGAT

NEWFOUNDLAND

TERRE-NEUVE

Fort-Chimo

QUÉBEC

QUÉBEC

King George
Islands

Bakers Dozen
Islands

Tukarak
Island

40 0 40 80 120 160 200
kilometres 1:5 000 000 kilomètres

E 80°   Cape Columbia   Good   Cape   Cape   Cape   60° F   Lincoln
Cape Nares   Pt.   Colan   Hecla   Joseph Henry   Sea
Ward Hunt I   Clements   Alert
Cape Discovery   Markham   Cape
Cape Richards   Inlet   Union
M⁰Clintock   Robeson
Cape Bicknor   Milne Fd   Inlet   Channel
Cape Evans   Fort Conger
BRITISH EMPIRE RANGE   Hall
Alert Point   Yelverton   UNITED STATES RANGE   Cape
Bay   Hazen   Baird
Camp   Lake   Basin
Hazen

Phillips Inlet   2604 ·   Franklin I
Barbeau Peak   Judge Daly Promontory

ELLESMERE

Otto   Fiord   Tanquary Camp   C
Fiord   Tanquary   Lawrence

Iceberg   AGASSIZ
Point   Flat   ICE CAP   John
Fosheim   Richardson Bay   Cape Wilkes
ISLAND   Cape
BERG   Eureka   M⁰Clintock   Kane
Mokka   Peninsula   Cape Scoresby B
Fd   Woodward   Cape Louis   Basin
LAND   Stor   ·2072   Princess Marie   Napoleon
RANGE   Bay   Squirel B   Bache   Cape Hawks
Raanes   Strathcona   Bay   Pen
Peninsula   Fiord   Thorvald Pen   Knud Pen   C Sabine   Smith
Buchanan   Dim I   Sound
Ulvingen   Bay   Johan   C Harschel
Hyperite   Peninsula   Baird   Cape
Pt   Inlet   Durnsterville
Svendsen   C Isabella   Codogan In
Pen   Cape Faraday
Bjorne   Baumann   Easter
Peninsula   Hoved I   Island
Fd   Cape Mouat
Bird   ·1493   Smith
Fd   SYDKAP   Bay   Cape Combarmere
ICE CAP   Sorfold
Buckingham   Boull   Clarence Head
Island   Grise Fd   Cape
North   Grise   Cape Norton Shaw
Fram Sd   Fiord
Stennions Pen   Craig   Phillips Point
Cape Storm   Lee Pt   Harbour   Coburg
Cape Vera   Glacier Strait   Island
King Edward Pt   Ward   Lady Ann Strait
Jones Sound   Point
Skruis   Bear Bay   Belcher Pt   Johnson Point
Pt   C Svarten   Cape Parker
·1920   Hide In
Sverdrup   Philpots
DEVON ISLAND   Inlet   Island
TERRITORIES   Cape
Maxwell   Sherard
Bay   Cuming   Cape
Cape   Felfoot   Bundas   Home
William   Pt   Harbour   Cape Warrender
Herschel   Stratton In   Powell In
NORD-OUEST
Prince Leopold I   Lancaster Sound
Cape Clarence   Cape
Port   Crawford
Leopold   Cape York
Elwin   C Charles
Bay   Elwin   Yorke
Jackson   In   BYLOT ISLAND
In   Strathcona   BORDEN   Canada Pt
390   Arctic Bay   Low Point
BRODEUR   Nanisivik   PENINSULA   C Graham
Tikeetawkuk   Moore
PENINSULA   Adams   Pond   Cape Weld
McBean   Sound   Inlet   Cape Macculloch
Bay   Pond Inlet
FRANKLIN   Yeoman   Eclipse   Cape Coutts   Nova Zembla I
FRANKLIN   Sound   Oliver   1963·   Cape Jameson
Moffet   Sou Ed
Eeloojua   Tay   Cape Hunter   Cape Adair
Fitzgerald B   Sound   Paquet
C Kater   Bay   Buchan Gulf   Scott Island
Van Koenig St   Erik   Cape Eglinton
Morin Point   Point
Bernier Bay   BAFFIN   Sillem
Berlinguet   Angmaerjoartuk   Fd   Clyde River
Inlet   Jungersen   River   Clyde Hewett
Bell   Inlet   Inscher B   Conn L   Cape
Bay   Bieler   Aston
Gifford   Erichsen   Nina   Rowley River   Isabella   Cape Raper
Crown Prince   Lake   Bang L   Aulitivik Island
Frederik I   Gifford Fiord   Quartz   Tarmug   Aulitiving Island
Saputing   River   Arm   Henry
Lake   1123·   Kater Pen
Cape Landry   Murray   Kater Pen   Cape Henry Kater
of   Maxwell B   BARNES   Generator
Cape Kjer   Antridge Bay   ICE CAP   Arguyartu Point
Boothia   Koch   Blanchfield   Home
Ormonde I   C Jonsen   Lake   Bay
Melville   Richards B   Ignent   Lake   C Hooper
Iglootik   Gillian   Kekertaluk I   Kangeeak
Astronomical   Melville   Jens   Flint   Point
Society Is   Peninsula   Munk   Bray   L   Manitung   Kivitoo
Island   Island   Ipik   Broughton
Fury and Hecla Strait   Bay   Nudlung   Island
Cape Englefield   Foxe   Baird   Straits   Nettilling Fd   Baffertaluk
Pen   Nanna   Fd
E   90°   F   80°   G   Basin   70°   AUYUITTUQ NATIONAL PARK
Rowley   PARC NATIONAL D'AUYUITTUQ
Island   Dewar
Lakes   H

GREENLAND
(DENMARK)

GROENLAND
(DANEMARK)

BAFFIN

BAY

DAVIS STRAIT

40   0   40   80   120   160   200
kilometres   1:5 000 000   kilomètres

GAZETTEER INDEX

How to Use the Index: The following pages contain an index of the geographical names of Canada shown on the preceding atlas maps. The Index gives the relevant map reference for each of these names, and is divided into two separate sections, each arranged alphabetically.

The first section lists the populated places of Canada depicted on the maps and contains information about their location and status. The second section lists the names of the physical features that are depicted on the maps. Also included in this section are names of international airports, selected national and provincial parks, and large dams.

To locate a geographical name, first determine whether the name is located in the Populated Places or the Physical Features sections of the Index. Search under the alphabetically arranged column of the appropriate section and locate the required name. Note the map number and map reference to the right of the name. The map reference refers to a system of rectangles found on each map sheet, indicated by a series of letters along the top and bottom of each map and numbers along the two sides. Turn to the map identified in the Index by a number and locate the required rectangle. Scan the rectangle and locate the populated place or physical feature for which you are looking. In a few maps where congested detail occurs, the names are numerically coded and listed in a less crowded part of the map sheet.

For example, to find the location of Aspen, a populated place in Newfoundland, turn to the Populated Places section of the Index, find Aspen, and note that the place is located on map 2 in rectangle F1. Turn to map 2, locate rectangle F1, then search the rectangle for Aspen.

ABBREVIATIONS

Name

CFB	Canadian Forces Base
CFS	Canadian Forces Station
Int	International
St	Saint
Ste	Sainte
Sts	Saints
(p)	part
<	within

Status

BOR	Borough
C	City
COMM	Community
DIST	Territorial District
DM	District (Municipality)
HAM	Hamlet
IR	Indian Reserve
LID	Local Improvement District
MIL	Military Reserve
NUP	Unincorporated Place – name not approved
PROV	Province
RD	Rural District
SV	Summer Village
T	Town
TERR	Territory
UP	Unincorporated Place – name approved
VL	Village

Province

Nfld.	Newfoundland
PEI	Prince Edward Island
NS	Nova Scotia
NB	New Brunswick
Que.	Quebec
Ont.	Ontario
Man.	Manitoba
Sask.	Saskatchewan
Alta.	Alberta
BC	British Columbia
YT	Yukon Territory
NWT	Northwest Territories

Name	Status	Province	Map Number	Rectangle
Aspen,	UP	(Nfld.)	2	F1

A

Aass 3, IR (BC) **39 E3**
Abana, UP (Que.) **18 A1**
Abbey, VL (Sask.) **31 D2**
Abbotsford, DM (BC) **38 H3**
Abbott-Corners, UP (Que.) **16 B4**
Abee, UP (Alta.) **33 E2**
Abénakis, UP (Que.) **15 B3**
Aberarder, UP (Ont.) **22 C1**
Abercorn, VL (Que.) **16 B4**
Abercrombie, UP (NS) **9 D1**
Aberdeen, UP (NS) **8 D3**
Aberdeen, UP (Ont.) **17 E1**
Aberdeen, UP (Ont.) **23 D2**
Aberdeen, VL (Sask.) **31 F1**
Aberfeldy, UP (Sask.) **32 A3**
Aberfeldy, UP (Ont.) **22 C2**
Aberfoyle, UP (Ont.) **23 E4**
Abernethy, VL (Sask.) **29 B2**
Abilene, UP (Alta.) **33 F2**
Abingdon, UP (Ont.) **21 A4**
Abitibi, UP (Ont.) **26 E1**
Abitibi 70, IR (Ont.) **26 F1**
Abitibi Canyon, UP (Ont.) **20 C4**
Abney, UP (PEI) **7 E4**
Aboushagan Road, UP (NB) **7 A4**
Abrahams Cove, UP (Nfld.) **4 B2**
Abrams, VL (PEI) **7 A3**
Abrams River, UP (NS) **10 B3**
Abuntlet Lake 4, IR (BC) **40 A3**
Acaciaville, UP (NS) **10 B2**
Academy, UP (NS) **9 D1**
Academy, UP (Alta.) **34 E2**
Acadia, UP (Alta.) **31 B2**
Acadia Valley, UP (Alta.) **31 B2**
Acadie Siding, UP (NB) **12 F3**
Acadieville, UP (NB) **12 F3**
Acheson, UP (Alta.) **33 D3**
Achigan, UP (Ont.) **26 B3**
Achigan-Ouest, NUP (Que.) **18 F4**
Achill, UP (Ont.) **21 A2**
Acme, VL (Alta.) **34 F2**
Acous 1, IR (BC) **39 C2**
Actinolite, UP (Ont.) **24 G4**
Acton, UP (NB) **11 B2**
Actons Corners, UP (Ont.) **17 C2**
Acton-Vale, T (Que.) **16 C3**
Ada, UP (Sask.) **31 F3**
Adams Cove < Small Point – Kingston – Broad Cove – Blackhead – Adams Cove, UP (Nfld.) **2 G2**
Adams Gulch, UP (NB) **13 B4**
Adams Lake, UP (BC) **36 G4**
Adams Landing, UP (Alta.) **44 B3**
Adamsville, UP (NB) **12 F4**
Adamsville, UP (Ont.) **23 C1**
Adanac, UP (Ont.) **26 F3**
Adanac, UP (Ont.) **25 F3**
Adanac, VL (Sask.) **32 A4**
Adderley, UP (Que.) **15 A4**
Addington Forks, UP (NS) **8 B4**
Addison, UP (Ont.) **17 C3**
Adelaide, UP (Ont.) **22 D1**
Aden, UP (Alta.) **34 H4**
Adeytown, UP (Nfld.) **2 F1**
Admaston, UP (Ont.) **17 A1**
Admiral, VL (Sask.) **31 D4**
Admiral Rock, UP (NS) **9 C2**
Admirals Beach, COMM (Nfld.) **2 F4**
Admiral's Cove, UP (Nfld.) **2 H3**
Adolphustown, UP (Ont.) **21 G1**
Advance, UP (Ont.) **25 B2**
Advocate Harbour, UP (NS) **11 G3**
Aerial, UP (Alta.) **34 F2**
Aero, UP (BC) **41 B2**
Aetna, UP (Alta.) **34 F4**
Afton, NUP (NS) **8 B4**
Afton Road, UP (PEI) **7 D3**
Afton Station, UP (NS) **8 B4**
Agate, UP (BC) **35 B2**
Agatha, UP (Alta.) **34 H3**
Agats Meadow 8, IR (BC) **40 B3**
Agawa Bay, UP (Ont.) **26 A3**
Agency 1, IR (Ont.) **28 H4**
Aggie, UP (Alta.) **33 B1**
Aglakumna 4A, IR (BC) **39 E1**
Aglakumna-la 2, IR (BC) **39 F1**
Aguanish, UP (Que.) **5 B3**
Agwedin 3, IR (BC) **42 F3**
Ahahswinis 1, IR (BC) **38 C2**
Ahaminaquus 12, IR (BC) **39 F3**
Ahbau, UP (BC) **40 D2**
Ahmacinnit 3, IR (BC) **39 D3**
Ahmic Harbour, UP (Ont.) **24 A1**
Ahmic Lake, UP (Ont.) **24 B1**
Ahmitsa 5, IR (BC) **38 B3**
Ahnuhati 6, IR (BC) **37 A2**
Ahous 16, IR (BC) **39 G4**
Ahousat, UP (BC) **39 F4**
Ahpokum 9, IR (BC) **37 C3**
Ahpukto 3, IR (BC) **39 E3**
Aita 3, IR (BC) **39 F1**
Ahuk 1, IR (BC) **38 C3**
Ah-we-cha-ol-to 16, IR (BC) **39 C1**
Aikensville, UP (Ont.) **23 E4**
Aikwucks 15, IR (BC) **38 F1**
Aillik, UP (Nfld.) **6 F2**
Ailsa Craig, VL (Ont.) **22 D1**
Ain 6, IR (BC) **41 A1**
Ainslie Glen, UP (NS) **8 D3**
Ainsworth Hot Springs, UP (BC) **34 B4**
Airdrie, T (Alta.) **34 E2**
Aird Subdivision, NUP (BC) **40 C3**
Airlie, UP (Ont.) **23 E2**
Air Ronge, UP (Sask.) **32 E1**
Airy, UP (Ont.) **24 E2**
Aishihik, UP (YT) **45 A3**
Aitchelitch 9, IR (BC) **35 A4**
Aiyansh < Aiyansh 1, UP (BC) **42 D3**
Aiyansh 1, IR (BC) **42 D3**
Aiyansh 83, IR (BC) **42 D3**
Aiyansh 87, IR (BC) **42 D3**
Ajax, T (Ont.) **21 C2**
Akenside, UP (Alta.) **33 E3**
Aklavik, HAM (NWT) **45 B1**
Akudlik, UP (Man.) **46 B4**
Akulivik, UP (Que.) **46 E3**
Alalco 8, IR (BC) **41 G4**
Alameda, T (Sask.) **29 C4**
Alamo, UP (BC) **34 B3**
Alaska, UP (PEI) **7 A3**
Alastair 80, IR (BC) **41 D1**
Alastair 81, IR (BC) **41 D1**
Alastair 82, IR (BC) **41 D1**
Alba, UP (NS) **8 D3**
Alban, UP (Ont.) **25 F2**
Albanel, VL (Que.) **18 H1**
Albany, UP (PEI) **7 B4**
Albany, UP (NS) **10 D1**
Albany Corner, UP (PEI) **7 B4**
Albany Cross, UP (NS) **10 D1**
Albas, UP (BC) **36 H3**
Albatross, UP (Sask.) **31 G3**
Alberni 2, IR (BC) **38 C2**
Alberry Plains, UP (PEI) **7 D4**
Albert, UP (Ont.) **21 G1**
Alberta Beach, SV (Alta.) **33 D3**
Albert Bridge, UP (NS) **8 F3**
Albert Canyon, UP (BC) **34 B2**
Albert Flat 5, IR (BC) **35 B3**
Albert Head, UP (BC) **38 E4**
Albert Mines, UP (NB) **11 G1**
Albert-Mines, UP (Que.) **16 D4**
Alberton, T (PEI) **7 B2**
Alberton South, UP (PEI) **7 B2**
Albertville, UP (Que.) **13 B3**
Albertville, UP (Sask.) **32 E3**
Albion, UP (PEI) **7 E4**
Albion Cross, UP (PEI) **7 E3**
Albright, UP (Alta.) **43 F4**
Albrights Corner, UP (NB) **11 D1**
Albuna, UP (Ont.) **22 B3**
Albury, UP (Ont.) **21 F1**
Alcan Trailer Court, NUP (BC) **43 E3**
Alcida, UP (NB) **12 E1**
Alcomdale, UP (Alta.) **33 D3**
Alcona, UP (Ont.) **21 A1**
Alcove, UP (Que.) **17 C1**
Alcurve, UP (Alta.) **33 H3**
Alder, UP (Ont.) **21 B1**
Alderburn, UP (Nfld.) **3 C3**
Alder Creek 70, IR (BC) **41 D1**
Aldercrest Survey, NUP (Ont.) **21 A3**
Alderdale, UP (Ont.) **18 A4**
Alder Flats, UP (Alta.) **33 C4**
Aldermac, UP (Que.) **18 A2**
Alder Point, UP (NS) **8 E3**
Alder River, UP (NS) **8 B4**
Aldershot, UP (NS) **11 H3**
Alderslea, UP (Ont.) **21 A1**
Alderson, UP (Alta.) **34 H3**
Aldersville, UP (NS) **10 E1**
Aldersyde, UP (Alta.) **34 E3**
Alderville < Alderville 37, UP (Ont.) **21 E1**
Alderville 37, IR (Ont.) **21 E1**
Alderwood, UP (NB) **12 G1**
Aldina < Muskeg Lake 102, UP (Sask.) **32 C4**
Aldouane, UP (NB) **12 G3**
Aldred's Beach, UP (Ont.) **21 C1**
Alençon, UP (Que.) **16 A2**
Alert, UP (NWT) **47 F1**
Alert Bay, VL (BC) **39 E1**
Alert Bay 1, IR (BC) **39 E1**
Alert Bay 1A, IR (BC) **39 E1**
Alexander, UP (Man.) **29 E4**
Alexander 134, IR (Alta.) **83 D3**
Alexandra, UP (PEI) **7 D4**
Alexandria, T (Ont.) **12 E2**
Alexandria, UP (BC) **40 C3**
Alexandria 1, IR (BC) **40 C3**
Alexandria 3, IR (BC) **40 C3**
Alexandria 3A, IR (BC) **40 C3**
Alexandria 10, IR (BC) **40 C3**
Alexandria 11, IR (BC) **40 C3**
Alexandria 12, IR (BC) **40 D3**
Alexandrina, UP (NB) **12 G4**
Alexis 9, IR (BC) **35 E4**
Alexis 133, IR (Alta.) **33 D3**
Alexis Creek, UP (BC) **40 C4**
Alexis Creek 6, IR (BC) **40 B3**
Alexis Creek 12, IR (BC) **40 B4**
Alexis Creek 13, IR (BC) **40 B4**
Alexis Creek 14, IR (BC) **40 B4**
Alexis Creek 15, IR (BC) **40 B4**
Alexis Creek 16, IR (BC) **40 B4**
Alexis Creek 17, IR (BC) **40 B4**
Alexis Creek 18, IR (BC) **40 B4**
Alexis Creek 20, IR (BC) **40 B3**
Alexis Creek 21, IR (BC) **40 B3**
Alexis Creek 22, IR (BC) **40 B3**
Alexis Creek 23, IR (BC) **40 B3**
Alexis Creek 24, IR (BC) **40 B3**
Alexis Creek 25, IR (BC) **40 B3**
Alexis Creek 26, IR (BC) **40 B3**
Alexis Creek 27, IR (BC) **40 B3**
Alexis Creek 28, IR (BC) **40 B3**
Alexis Creek 29, IR (BC) **40 B3**
Alexis Creek 30, IR (BC) **40 B3**
Alexis Creek 31, IR (BC) **40 B3**
Alexis Creek 32, IR (BC) **40 B3**
Alexis Creek 33, IR (BC) **40 B3**
Alexis Creek 34, IR (BC) **40 B3**
Alexis Creek 35, IR (BC) **40 B3**
Alexis Thomas 1A, IR (BC) **40 A2**
Alexo, UP (Alta.) **33 B4**
Aleza Lake, UP (BC) **40 D1**
Alfred, VL (Ont.) **17 E1**
Algar, UP (Man.) **29 E4**
Algoma, UP (Ont.) **25 A1**
Algonquin, UP (Ont.) **17 C3**
Algonquin Park, UP (Ont.) **24 D1**
Algrove, UP (Sask.) **32 F4**
Alhambra, UP (Alta.) **33 C4**
Alice, UP (Ont.) **24 G1**
Alice Arm, UP (BC) **42 D3**
Alice Siding, UP (BC) **34 C4**
Alida, VL (Sask.) **29 D4**
Alingly, UP (Sask.) **32 D3**
Alix, VL (Alta.) **33 E4**
Alix South Junction, UP (Alta.) **33 E4**
Alixton 5, IR (BC) **36 B2**
Alkali Lake < Alkali Lake 1, UP (BC) **36 B2**
Alkali Lake 1, IR (BC) **36 B2**
Alkali Lake 4A, IR (BC) **36 B2**
Alkhili 2, IR (BC) **45 B4**
Allains Creek, UP (NS) **10 C1**
Allainville, UP (NB) **12 F2**
Allan, T (Sask.) **31 F1**
Allan, UP (Ont.) **24 F4**
Allandale, UP (NB) **11 B1**
Allan Hills, UP (Sask.) **31 F1**
Allan Mills, UP (Ont.) **21 E1**
Allan Park, UP (Ont.) **23 C2**
Allans-Corners, UP (Que.) **17 G2**
Allans Corners, UP (Ont.) **24 G1**
Allan Water, UP (Ont.) **27 D1**
Allard, UP (Que.) **13 D3**
Allardville, UP (NB) **12 F1**
Allardville East, UP (NB) **12 F1**
Allegra, UP (Man.) **28 B1**
Allenby, UP (BC) **35 D4**
Allendale, UP (NS) **10 D4**
Allenford, UP (Ont.) **23 C2**
Allen Heights, UP (NS) **9 A4**
Allen Hill, UP (NS) **11 G2**
Allens Addition, NUP (BC) **34 B3**
Allens-Mills, UP (Que.) **18 H3**
Allenwood, UP (Ont.) **23 E2**
Allenwood Beach, UP (Ont.) **23 E2**
Alliance, VL (Alta.) **33 F4**
Alliford Bay, UP (BC) **41 B2**
Allingham, UP (Alta.) **34 F1**
Allisary, UP (PEI) **7 D3**
Allison, UP (NB) **11 G1**
Allison, UP (BC) **35 D3**
Allisonville, UP (Ont.) **21 F2**
Alliston, T (Ont.) **21 A1**
Alliston, UP (PEI) **7 E4**
Allsaw, UP (Ont.) **23 H1**
Alma, UP (Ont.) **23 D3**
Alma, UP (NS) **9 D2**
Alma, UP (PEI) **7 A2**
Alma, C (Que.) **14 A2**
Alma, VL (NB) **11 G2**
Almond Gardens, UP (BC) **35 H4**
Almonte, T (Ont.) **17 B2**
Alness, UP (Alta.) **34 G1**
Alonsa, UP (Man.) **29 G2**
Alpena, UP (NS) **10 D1**
Alpen Siding, UP (Alta.) **33 E2**
Alphonse Tommy 7, IR (BC) **42 G3**
Alpine, UP (Man.) **29 D1**
Alpine Ridge, UP (NS) **8 C3**
Alpine Village, UP (Ont.) **24 D4**
Alsace, UP (Ont.) **25 H2**
Alsask, VL (Sask.) **31 B2**
Alsfeldt, UP (Ont.) **23 C3**
Alsike, UP (Alta.) **33 D3**
Alsops Beach, UP (Ont.) **21 B1**
Altamont, UP (Man.) **29 G4**
Altario, UP (Alta.) **31 B1**
Altbergthal, UP (Man.) **29 H4**
Althorpe, UP (Ont.) **17 A3**
Alticane, UP (Sask.) **32 C4**
Alton, UP (NS) **9 C2**
Altona, T (Man.) **29 H4**
Altona, UP (BC) **43 E2**
Alva, UP (Que.) **16 B4**
Alvanley, UP (Ont.) **23 C2**
Alvena, VL (Sask.) **32 D4**
Alvin, UP (BC) **38 G1**
Alvinston, VL (Ont.) **22 C2**
Amadjuak, UP (NWT) **46 F2**
Amai 15, IR (BC) **39 D2**
Amaral 46 and 47, IR (BC) **42 D3**
Amaranth, UP (Man.) **29 G3**
Amatal 5, IR (BC) **42 D3**
Amatal 6, IR (BC) **42 D3**
Amazon, UP (Sask.) **31 G2**
Amberley, UP (Ont.) **23 B3**
Amber River 211, IR (Alta.) **45 E4**
Amber Valley, UP (Alta.) **33 E2**
Ambleside, UP (Ont.) **23 C3**
Amelia, UP (Alta.) **33 E3**
Ameliasburg, UP (Ont.) **21 F1**
Amery, UP (Man.) **30 D1**
Amesbury, UP (Alta.) **33 E1**
Amesdale, UP (Ont.) **27 A1**
Ames Survey, NUP (Ont.) **23 C1**
Amethyst Harbour, UP (Ont.) **27 E3**
Amherst, T (NS) **9 A1**
Amherstburg, T (Ont.) **22 A4**
Amherst Cove, UP (Nfld.) **3 G4**
Amherst Head, UP (NS) **9 A1**
Amherst Point, UP (NS) **9 A1**
Amherst Pointe, UP (Ont.) **22 A4**
Amherst Shore, UP (NS) **7 B4**
Amherstview, UP (Ont.) **17 A4**
Amiens, UP (Sask.) **32 C3**
Amigo Beach, UP (Ont.) **23 G1**
Amiraults Corner, UP (NS) **10 B2**
Amiraults Hill, UP (NS) **10 B3**
Amisk, VL (Alta.) **33 G4**
Amisk Lake 184, IR (Sask.) **32 G2**
Ammon, UP (NB) **11 G1**
Amos, T (Que.) **18 B1**
Amos 1, IR (Que.) **18 B1**
Amostown, UP (NB) **12 D3**
Amqui, T (Que.) **13 B3**
Amsterdam, UP (Sask.) **29 C1**
Amulet, UP (Que.) **18 A1**
Amulet, UP (Sask.) **31 G4**
Amulree, UP (Ont.) **23 D1**
Amy-Corners, UP (Que.) **16 C4**
Amyot, UP (Ont.) **26 A1**
Anacla 12, IR (BC) **38 B3**
Anaconda, UP (BC) **35 G4**
Anagance, UP (NB) **11 F1**
Anagance Ridge, UP (NB) **11 F1**
Anahim 3, IR (BC) **40 C4**
Anahim 4, IR (BC) **40 C4**
Anahim 5, IR (BC) **36 A1**
Anahim 6, IR (BC) **36 A1**
Anahim 7, IR (BC) **36 A1**
Anahim 8, IR (BC) **36 A1**
Anahim 9, IR (BC) **36 A1**
Anahim 10, IR (BC) **36 A1**
Anahim 11, IR (BC) **36 A1**
Anahim 12, IR (BC) **36 A1**
Anahim 13, IR (BC) **36 A1**
Anahim 14, IR (BC) **36 A1**
Anahim 15, IR (BC) **36 A1**
Anahim 16, IR (BC) **40 C3**
Anahim 17, IR (BC) **40 C3**
Anahim 18, IR (BC) **40 C3**
Anahim Lake, UP (BC) **40 A3**
Anahim's Flat 1, IR (BC) **40 C4**
Anahim's Meadow 2, IR (BC) **40 C4**
Anahim's Meadow 2A, IR (BC) **40 C4**
Analta, UP (Alta.) **33 D2**
Anama Bay < Dauphin River 48A, UP (Man.) **29 G1**
Anastasia, UP (Alta.) **34 F2**
Ancaster, T (Ont.) **22 H1**
Anchor Point, COMM (Nfld.) **5 G2**
Ancienne-Lorette, T (Que.) **15 F3**
Ancona, UP (Alta.) **33 C4**
Ancona Point, UP (Ont.) **23 H2**
Ancrum, UP (Sask.) **31 F1**
Andak 9, IR (BC) **42 F3**
Andegulay 8, IR (BC) **42 D3**
Andegulay 8A, IR (BC) **42 D3**

Anderson, UP (Ont.) 22 E1
Anderson, UP (Que.) 17 G2
Anderson, UP (Ont.) 21 G1
Anderson, UP (BC) 40 D2
Anderson Addition, NUP (Alta.) 34 F1
Anderson Lake, UP (Ont.) 25 C1
Anderson Mountain, UP (NS) 9 D1
Anderson Ranch, UP (BC) 43 D2
Anderson Road, UP (NB) 12 A3
Anderson Settlement, UP (NB) 7 A4
Andersons Landing, UP (NWT) 45 C2
Andersonville, UP (NB) 11 B2
Andimaul 1, IR (BC) 42 E3
Andréville, VL (Que.) 14 E4
Andrew, VL (Alta.) 33 F3
Andrewsville, UP (Ont.) 17 C2
Andy Cahoose Meadow 16, IR (BC) 41 H2
Anerley, UP (Sask.) 31 E2
Aneroid, VL (Sask.) 31 E4
Anfield, UP (NB) 12 A2
Ange-Gardien, VL (Que.) 16 B4
Angéline, UP (Que.) 16 B4
Angels Cove, UP (Nfld.) 2 E4
Anglemont, UP (BC) 36 H4
Anglia, UP (Sask.) 31 D2
Angliers, VL (Que.) 18 A2
Angling Lake < Angling Lake 2, UP (Ont.) 30 F2
Angling Lake 1, IR (Ont.) 30 F2
Angling Lake 2, IR (Ont.) 30 F2
Anglin Lake, UP (Sask.) 32 D3
Anglo Rustico, UP (PEI) 7 C3
Anglo Tignish, UP (PEI) 7 B2
Angus, UP (Ont.) 21 A1
Angusville, UP (Man.) 29 E3
Anjou, T (Que.) 17 H3
Ankerton, UP (Alta.) 33 F4
Anlaw 4, IR (BC) 42 F3
Anmore, UP (BC) 38 G2
Annabelle-Beach < Caughnawaga 14, UP (Que.) 17 G4
Annable Settlement, UP (Ont.) 17 D2
Annaheim, UP (Sask.) 31 G1
Annan, UP (Ont.) 23 D1
Annandale, UP (PEI) 7 E4
Annapolis Royal, T (NS) 10 C1
Annaville, VL (Que.) 16 C2
Annesley, UP (Que.) 17 B1
Annidale, UP (NB) 11 E2
Annis, UP (BC) 36 H4
Ann Island 33, IR (BC) 41 F4
Anokswok 59, IR (BC) 42 E3
Anola, UP (Man.) 28 B1
Anoma Lea, UP (Ont.) 17 C3
Anse-à-Baril, UP (Que.) 16 A1
Anse-à-Eloi-Caron, NUP (Que.) 15 D2
Anse-à-Mercier, UP (Que.) 13 F1
Anse-au-Persil, UP (Que.) 14 E4
Anse-aux-Fraises, UP (Que.) 19 H3
Anse-aux-Gascons, UP (Que.) 13 G3
Anse-Bleue, UP (NB) 13 F4
Anse-de-Roche, UP (Que.) 14 D3
Ansell, UP (Alta.) 33 B3
Anselmo, UP (Alta.) 33 C3
Anse-Pleureuse, UP (Que.) 13 E1
Ansnorveldt, UP (Ont.) 21 A1
Anson, UP (Ont.) 21 F1
Ansonia, UP (Ont.) 26 B4
Anstruther Lake, UP (Ont.) 24 E3
Antelope, UP (Sask.) 31 D3
Anten Mills, UP (Ont.) 23 F2
Anthony, UP (Ont.) 26 E1
Anthracite, UP (Alta.) 34 D2
Antigonish, T (NS) 8 B4
Antigonish Harbour, UP (NS) 8 B4
Antigonish Landing, UP (NS) 8 B4
Antler, VL (Sask.) 29 D4
Antler Lake, NUP (Alta.) 33 E3
Antonio, UP (Alta.) 34 G3
Anton Lake, UP (Alta.) 33 E2
Antrim, UP (Ont.) 17 B1
Antrim, UP (NS) 9 C3
Antross, UP (Alta.) 33 D4
Anvil Island, UP (BC) 38 F2
Anyox, UP (BC) 42 D3
Anyutawl 31, IR (BC) 42 D3
Anzac, UP (Alta.) 44 C4
Anzac, UP (BC) 40 C1
Apohaqui, UP (NB) 11 E2
Appelo, UP (Ont.) 26 E3
Appin, UP (Ont.) 22 D2
Appin Road, UP (PEI) 7 C4
Appledale, UP (BC) 34 B4
Appledore, UP (Ont.) 22 C3
Applegrove, UP (BC) 34 A3
Applegrove, UP (Que.) 16 C4
Apple Hill, UP (Ont.) 17 E2
Apple River, UP (NS) 11 G2
Appleton, LID (Nfld.) 3 D3
Appleton, UP (Ont.) 17 B2
Apsagayu 1A, IR (BC) 39 F1
Apsley, UP (Ont.) 24 E3
Apto, UP (Ont.) 23 F2
Aquadell, UP (Sask.) 31 E3
Aquadeo Beach, UP (Sask.) 32 B3
Aquaforte, COMM (Nfld.) 2 H4
Aquiatulavik Point, UP (NWT) 46 E2
Arabella, UP (Sask.) 29 D1
Arbakka, UP (Man.) 28 B3
Arbeatha Park, UP (Ont.) 17 D4
Arbeau Settlement, UP (NB) 12 E3
Arborfield, T (Sask.) 32 F4
Arborg, VL (Man.) 29 H2
Arbor Vitae, UP (Ont.) 28 G4
Arbury, UP (Sask.) 31 H2
Arbuthnot, UP (Sask.) 31 E4
Arcadia, UP (NS) 10 A3
Arcadia < Sucker Creek 150A, UP (Alta.) 33 B1
Ar-ce-wy-ee 4, IR (BC) 39 E1
Archer, UP (Ont.) 17 D2
Archerwill, VL (Sask.) 29 B1
Archibald Settlement, UP (NB) 13 D4
Archibalds Mill, UP (NS) 9 E2
Archydal, UP (Sask.) 31 F3
Arcola, T (Sask.) 29 C4
Arctic Bay, UP (NWT) 47 E3
Arctic Red River, UP (NWT) 45 B1
Ardath, UP (Sask.) 31 E1
Ardbeg, UP (Ont.) 24 A1
Arden, UP (Man.) 29 F3
Arden, UP (Ont.) 24 G3
Ardendale, UP (Ont.) 24 G3
Ardenode, UP (Alta.) 34 F2
Ardenville, UP (Alta.) 34 F4
Ardill, UP (Sask.) 31 F3
Ardley, UP (Alta.) 34 F1
Ardmore, UP (Alta.) 33 G2
Ardness, UP (NS) 8 A4
Ardoch, UP (Ont.) 24 G3
Ardoise, UP (NS) 9 A3
Ardrossan, UP (Alta.) 33 E3
Ardtrea, UP (Ont.) 23 G1
Arelee, VL (Sask.) 31 E1
Argenta, UP (BC) 34 B3
Argentia, UP (Nfld.) 2 F3
Argentia Beach, SV (Alta.) 33 D4
Argolis, UP (Ont.) 26 C1
Argosy, UP (NB) 12 A2
Argyle, UP (NS) 10 B3
Argyle, UP (NB) 12 B3
Argyle, UP (NS) 9 F2
Argyle, UP (Man.) 29 H3
Argyle, UP (Ont.) 21 C1
Argyle Head, UP (NS) 10 B3
Argyle Shore, UP (PEI) 7 C4
Argyle Sound, UP (NS) 10 B4
Arichat, UP (NS) 8 D4
Arisaig, UP (NS) 8 A4
Ariss, UP (Ont.) 23 E4
Arkell, UP (Ont.) 23 E4
Arklan, UP (Ont.) 17 B2
Arkona, VL (Ont.) 22 C1
Arkwright, UP (Ont.) 23 C2
Arlington, UP (NS) 11 H3
Arlington, UP (PEI) 7 B3
Arlington, UP (YT) 45 A2
Arlington Beach, UP (Sask.) 31 G2
Arlington West, UP (NS) 10 C1
Arlington Woods, UP (Ont.) 17 D4
Arma, UP (Sask.) 32 D4
Armada, UP (Alta.) 34 F3
Armagh, VL (Que.) 15 C3
Armagh-Station, UP (Que.) 15 C3
Armena, UP (Alta.) 33 E4
Armit, UP (Sask.) 32 H4
Armley, UP (Sask.) 32 F4
Armond, UP (NB) 12 B4
Armow, UP (Ont.) 23 B2
Armstrong, C (BC) 35 F1
Armstrong, UP (Ont.) 27 E1
Armstrong, UP (Que.) 16 G2
Armstrong, UP (YT) 45 B3
Armstrong Brook, UP (NB) 13 E4
Armstrong Mills, UP (Ont.) 23 E4
Armstrongs Corners, UP (Ont.) 17 B2
Arnaud, UP (Man.) 28 A3
Arner, UP (Ont.) 22 A4
Arnes, UP (Man.) 30 C4
Arneson, UP (Alta.) 31 B2
Arnold, UP (NS) 10 D4
Arnold's Cove, T (Nfld.) 2 F2
Arnot, UP (Man.) 30 C1
Arnott, UP (Ont.) 23 D2
Arnprior, T (Ont.) 17 B1
Arnstein, UP (Ont.) 24 A1
Arntfield, UP (Que.) 18 A2
Aroland < Aroland 83, UP (Ont.) 27 G1
Aroland 83, IR (Ont.) 27 G1
Aroostook, VL (NB) 12 A3
Aroostook Portage, NUP (NB) 12 A3
Arpiers, UP (Sask.) 31 F1
Arpin, UP (Ont.) 26 E1
Arran, VL (Sask.) 29 D1
Arrandale, UP (BC) 42 D4
Arranvale, UP (Ont.) 23 C2
Arras, UP (BC) 43 E4
Arrow Creek, UP (BC) 34 C4
Arrow Park, UP (BC) 34 A3
Arrow River, UP (Man.) 29 E3
Arrowview Heights, UP (BC) 38 C2
Arrowwood, VL (Alta.) 34 F2
Arseneault, UP (Que.) 7 F1
Arthabaska, T (Que.) 16 D2
Arthur, VL (Ont.) 23 D3
Arthurette, UP (NB) 12 A3
Arthurville, UP (Que.) 15 C3
Artland, UP (Sask.) 32 A4
Artlish 12, IR (BC) 39 D2
Arundel, UP (Que.) 18 E4
Arva, UP (Ont.) 22 E1
Arvilla, UP (Alta.) 33 D3
Asahal Lake 2, IR (BC) 36 B1
Asbestos, T (Que.) 16 D3
Ascension, UP (PEI) 7 B2
Ascot-Corner, UP (Que.) 16 D3
Asham Point, UP (Man.) 29 F2
Ashby Mill, UP (Ont.) 24 E4
Ashcroft, VL (BC) 36 D4
Ashcroft 4, IR (BC) 36 D4
Ashdad, UP (Ont.) 17 A1
Ashdale, UP (NS) 8 B4
Ashdale, UP (NS) 9 A3
Ashdale, UP (Ont.) 17 E4
Ashern, UP (Man.) 29 G2
Ashfield, UP (NS) 8 D4
Ashland, UP (NB) 12 B4
Ashmont, UP (Alta.) 33 F2
Ashmore, UP (NS) 10 B2
Ashnola 10, IR (BC) 35 E4
Ashton, UP (Ont.) 17 B2
Ashton, UP (PEI) 7 E3
Ashton Creek, UP (BC) 35 F1
Ashton Station, UP (Ont.) 17 B2
Ashville, UP (Man.) 29 E2
Askilton, UP (NS) 8 C4
Aspen, UP (NS) 9 E2
Aspen, UP (Nfld.) 2 F1
Aspen Cove, UP (Nfld.) 3 E2
Aspen Grove, UP (BC) 35 C2
Aspen Park, UP (Man.) 30 C4
Aspey Brook, UP (Nfld.) 2 F1
Aspotogan, UP (NS) 9 A4
Aspy Bay, UP (NS) 8 E1
Asquith, T (Sask.) 31 E1
Asselstine, UP (Ont.) 17 A4
Assineau, UP (Alta.) 33 C1
Assineau River 150F, IR (Alta.) 33 C1
Assiniboia, T (Sask.) 31 F4
Assiniboine 76, IR (Sask.) 29 B3
Assumption < Hay Lake 209, UP (Alta.) 45 E4
Astle, UP (NB) 12 D4
Aston-Jonction, VL (Que.) 16 C2
Aston-Station, UP (Que.) 16 C2
Astorville, UP (Ont.) 18 A4
Atakakup 104, IR (Sask.) 32 C3
Atbara, UP (BC) 34 B4
Athabasca, T (Alta.) 33 E2
Athalmer, UP (BC) 34 C3
Athapap, UP (Man.) 32 H2
Athelstan, UP (Que.) 17 F2
Athens, VL (Ont.) 17 C3
Atherley, UP (Ont.) 23 G1
Atherton, UP (Ont.) 22 G2
Athlone, UP (Ont.) 21 A1
Athol, UP (NS) 9 A1
Athol, UP (Ont.) 17 E2
Athol, UP (Ont.) 21 F2
Athol Station, UP (NS) 9 A1
Atholville, VL (NB) 13 C4
Atik, UP (Man.) 32 H2
Atikameg, UP (Alta.) 44 A4
Atikameg Lake, UP (Man.) 30 A2
Atikokan, UP (Ont.) 27 B3
Atironto, UP (Ont.) 17 B2
Atkinson, UP (NS) 9 B1
Atkinson, UP (Ont.) 17 B4
Atlanta, UP (NS) 11 H3
Atlantic, UP (NS) 10 C4
Atlee, UP (Alta.) 31 A2
Atlin, UP (BC) 45 B4
Atlin-Teslin Indian Cemetery 4, IR (BC) 45 B4
Atluck, UP (BC) 39 E2
Atmore, UP (Alta.) 33 E2
Atnarko, UP (BC) 41 G3
Attachie, UP (BC) 43 E3
Attawapiskat < Attawapiskat 91A, UP (Ont.) 20 C2
Attawapiskat 91, IR (Ont.) 20 B2
Attawapiskat 91A, IR (Ont.) 20 C2
Attercliffe, UP (Ont.) 21 A4
Atwater, VL (Sask.) 29 C2
Atwood, UP (Ont.) 23 C4
Atwoods Brook, UP (NS) 10 B4
Aubigny, UP (Man.) 28 A2
Aubrey, UP (Que.) 17 G2
Auburn, UP (NS) 10 D1
Auburn, UP (Ont.) 23 B3
Auburn, UP (PEI) 7 D4
Auburndale, UP (NS) 10 E2
Auburndale, UP (Alta.) 33 G4
Auburnton, UP (Sask.) 29 D4
Auburnville, UP (NB) 12 F2
Auclair, UP (Que.) 14 G4
Auden, UP (Ont.) 27 F1
Audet, UP (Que.) 16 F3
Augier Lake 22, IR (BC) 40 A1
Augsburg, UP (Ont.) 24 G2
Augustine Cove, UP (PEI) 7 B4
Aulac, UP (NB) 11 H1
Aulds Cove, UP (NS) 8 C4
Aupaluk, UP (Que.) 46 F3
Aupe 6, IR (BC) 37 B3
Aupe 6A, IR (BC) 37 B3
Aurigny, UP (Que.) 7 F1
Aurora, T (Ont.) 21 B2
Austin, UP (Man.) 29 G3
Austin's Flat 3, IR (BC) 35 B3
Australian, UP (BC) 40 C3
Authier, UP (Que.) 18 A1
Authier-Nord, UP (Que.) 18 A1
Avataktoo, UP (NWT) 46 F1
Avebury, UP (Sask.) 32 C3
Avening, UP (Ont.) 24 A4
Avenir, UP (Alta.) 33 F1
Avery Island 92, IR (BC) 41 C1
Avery Point, UP (Ont.) 23 G1
Avoca, UP (Que.) 17 E1
Avola, UP (BC) 36 G2
Avon, UP (Ont.) 22 E2
Avon, UP (NB) 11 D1
Avonbank, UP (Ont.) 22 E1
Avondale, T (Nfld.) 2 G3
Avondale, UP (NS) 9 A3
Avondale, UP (NB) 12 A4
Avondale, UP (PEI) 7 D4
Avondale, UP (NS) 8 A4
Avonhurst, UP (Sask.) 31 H3
Avonlea, VL (Sask.) 31 G3
Avonmore, UP (Ont.) 17 E2
Avonport, UP (NS) 9 A3
Avonport Station, UP (NS) 9 A3
Avonry, UP (Ont.) 22 B2
Avonton, UP (Ont.) 22 E1
Aweme, UP (Man.) 29 F4
Axe Lake, UP (Ont.) 24 B2
Axe Point, UP (NWT) 44 A1
Ayer's Cliff, VL (Que.) 16 D4
Aylechootlook 5, IR (BC) 38 H2
Aylen Lake, UP (Ont.) 24 E1
Aylesbury, VL (Sask.) 31 F2
Aylesford, UP (NS) 10 D1
Aylesford East, UP (NS) 10 D1
Aylesford Mountain, UP (NS) 10 D1
Aylesworth, UP (Ont.) 17 A4
Aylmer, T (Ont.) 22 E2
Aylmer, C (Que.) 17 D4
Aylmer-Sound, UP (Que.) 5 E3
Aylsham, VL (Sask.) 32 F3
Aylsworth, UP (Ont.) 28 H4
Aylwin, UP (Que.) 18 D4
Aylwin-Station, UP (Que.) 18 D4
Ayr, UP (Ont.) 22 G1
Ayrness, UP (Que.) 17 G2
Ayton, UP (Ont.) 23 C3
Aywawwis 15, IR (BC) 35 B4
Azure, UP (Alta.) 34 E3

B

Babcock, UP (Man.) 29 G4
Babine < Babine 6, UP (BC) 42 G3
Babine 6, IR (BC) 42 G3
Babine 16, IR (BC) 42 G3
Babine 17, IR (BC) 42 F4
Babine 18, IR (BC) 42 F4
Babine 25, IR (BC) 42 G4
Babine 26, IR (BC) 42 G4
Babine Lake 20, IR (BC) 42 G3
Babine Lake 21B, IR (BC) 40 A1
Babine Portage, UP (BC) 40 A1
Babine River 21, IR (BC) 42 G3
Babine River 21A, IR (BC) 42 G3
Babys Point, UP (Ont.) 22 B2
Baccalieu Island, UP (Nfld.) 2 H1
Baccaro, UP (NS) 10 C4
Back Bay, UP (NB) 11 C3
Back Centre, UP (NS) 10 E2
Back Clarendon, UP (NB) 11 C2
Back Cove, UP (Nfld.) 5 G4
Backport, UP (Que.) 16 C4
Back Settlement, UP (NS) 8 B4
Bacon Ridge, UP (Man.) 29 G2
Baddeck, UP (NS) 8 D3
Baddeck Bay, UP (NS) 7 H4
Baddeck Bridge, UP (NS) 8 D3
Baddow, UP (Ont.) 23 H1
Baden, UP (Ont.) 22 F1
Baden, UP (Man.) 30 A3
Badenoch, UP (Ont.) 23 E4
Badger, T (Nfld.) 3 A3
Badger, UP (Man.) 28 C3
Badger's Corners, UP (Ont.) 24 A2
Badger's Quay – Valleyfield – Pool's Island, RD (Nfld.) 3 F2
Badger's Quay < Badger's Quay – Valleyfield – Pool's Island, UP (Nfld.) 3 F2
Badgerville < Cote 64, UP (Sask.) 29 D1
Bad Heart, UP (Alta.) 43 G4
Badjeros, UP (Ont.) 23 E2
Baezaeko River 25, IR (BC) 40 B3
Baezaeko River 26, IR (BC) 40 B3
Baezaeko River 27, IR (BC) 40 B3
Bagdad, UP (NB) 11 E1
Bagnall, UP (Ont.) 22 B3
Bagot, UP (Man.) 29 G3
Baie-Carrière, UP (Que.) 18 B2
Baie-Comeau, T (Que.) 14 H1
Baie-de-l'Ours, UP (Que.) 18 E4
Baie-des-Bacon, UP (Que.) 14 E3
Baie-des-Brises, UP (Que.) 17 F2
Baie-des-Capucins, UP (Que.) 13 C1
Baie-des-Ha! Ha!, UP (Que.) 5 E2
Baie-de-Shawinigan, VL (Que.) 16 B1
Baie-des-Homards, NUP (Que.) 19 E3
Baie-des-Moutons (Mutton-Bay), UP (Que.) 5 E3
Baie-des-Rochers, UP (Que.) 14 D4
Baie-des-Sables, UP (Que.) 13 A2
Baie du Doré, UP (Ont.) 23 B2
Baie-du-Poste < Mistassini, UP (Que.) 20 G4
Baie-du-Renard, UP (Que.) 5 B4
Baie-d'Urfé, T (Que.) 17 F4
Baie-Johan-Beetz, UP (Que.) 5 A3
Baie-Noire, UP (Que.) 17 D1
Baie-Rouge, UP (Que.) 5 E2
Baie-Ste-Anne, UP (NB) 12 G2
Baie-Ste-Catherine, UP (Que.) 14 E3
Baie-Ste-Claire, UP (Que.) 19 H3
Baie-St-Laurent, UP (Que.) 13 B2
Baie-St-Paul, T (Que.) 15 C1
Baie-Stenhouse, UP (Que.) 18 A3
Baie-Trinité, VL (Que.) 19 E4
Baie Verte, T (Nfld.) 5 H3
Baie Verte, UP (NB) 7 A4
Baie Verte Road, UP (NB) 7 A4
Baieville, VL (Que.) 16 B2
Baildon, UP (Sask.) 31 G3
Baileys Brook, UP (NS) 8 A4
Bailieboro, UP (Ont.) 21 D1
Baillie, UP (NB) 11 B2
Bain, UP (Alta.) 31 B4
Baine Harbour, COMM (Nfld.) 2 D3
Bains Corner, UP (NB) 11 E3
Bainsville, UP (Ont.) 17 F2
Baintree, UP (Alta.) 34 F2
Bairdsville, UP (NB) 12 A3
Baker, UP (BC) 34 D4
Baker Brook, VL (NB) 15 G2
Baker Cove, UP (Nfld.) 2 E2
Baker Lake, UP (NWT) 46 B2
Bakers Brook, UP (Nfld.) 5 F4
Bakers Narrows, UP (Man.) 32 H2
Bakers Settlement, UP (NS) 10 D2
Bala, UP (Ont.) 23 F1
Balaclava, UP (Ont.) 24 G2
Balaclava, UP (Ont.) 23 D1
Bala Park, UP (Ont.) 23 F1
Balcarres, T (Sask.) 29 B2
Balderson, UP (Ont.) 17 B2
Baldonnel, UP (BC) 43 E3
Baldoon, UP (Ont.) 22 B3
Bald Rock, UP (NS) 9 B4
Baldur, UP (Man.) 29 F4
Baldwin, UP (Ont.) 21 B1
Baldwin-Mills, UP (Que.) 16 D4
Baldwin Road, UP (PEI) 7 D4
Baldwins Bridge, UP (Ont.) 17 D2
Baldwinton, UP (Sask.) 32 A4
Baldy Hughes CFS/SFC, MIL (BC) 40 C2
Baleine, UP (NS) 8 F3
Balfour, UP (BC) 34 B4
Balfour Beach, UP (Ont.) 21 B1
Balfron, UP (NS) 9 C1
Balgonie, T (Sask.) 31 H3
Baljennie, UP (Sask.) 32 B4
Ballantine, UP (Alta.) 33 D3
Ballantynes Cove, UP (NS) 8 B4
Balla Philip, UP (NB) 12 G3
Ballarat Creek, UP (YT) 45 A3
Ballater, UP (Alta.) 33 A1
Ballinafad, UP (Ont.) 23 E4
Balls Creek, UP (NS) 8 E3
Ballycanoe, UP (Ont.) 17 C3
Ballycroy, UP (Ont.) 21 A2
Ballydown Beach, UP (Ont.) 21 A1
Ballyduff, UP (Ont.) 21 C1
Ballymote, UP (Ont.) 22 E1
Balm, UP (Alta.) 33 C3
Balm Beach, UP (Ont.) 23 E1
Balmertown, UP (Ont.) 30 D4
Balmoral, UP (Man.) 29 H3
Balmoral, UP (BC) 36 G4
Balmoral, UP (NS) 8 D4
Balmoral, VL (NB) 13 D4
Balmoral Beach, UP (BC) 38 C1
Balmoral Mills, UP (NS) 9 C1
Balmy Beach, UP (Ont.) 23 C1
Balmy Beach, UP (Man.) 29 F4
Balsam Creek, UP (Ont.) 18 A4
Balsam Hill, UP (Ont.) 17 A1
Baltic, UP (PEI) 7 B3
Baltic, UP (PEI) 7 E3
Baltics Corners, UP (Ont.) 17 E1
Baltimore, UP (Ont.) 21 D2
Baltimore, UP (NB) 11 G1
Balvenie, UP (Ont.) 24 G2
Balzac, UP (Alta.) 34 E2
Bamberg, UP (Ont.) 23 D4
Bamberton, UP (BC) 38 E4
Bamfield, UP (BC) 38 B3
Banbury, UP (Ont.) 24 B2
Bancroft, VL (Ont.) 24 E3
Banda, UP (Ont.) 23 E2
Banff, UP (Alta.) 34 D2
Bangor, UP (PEI) 7 D3
Bangor, UP (NS) 10 A2
Bangor, VL (Sask.) 29 C2
Bangs Falls, UP (NS) 10 D2
Bankeir, UP (BC) 35 D3
Bankend, UP (Sask.) 29 B2
Bankfield, UP (Ont.) 27 G2
Banks, UP (Ont.) 23 E2
Banner, UP (Ont.) 22 E1
Bannockburn, UP (Ont.) 24 F4
Bannon, UP (NB) 12 B4
Bantry, UP (Alta.) 34 G3
Bapaume, UP (Sask.) 32 C3
Baptiste, UP (Ont.) 24 E3
Baptiste Louis 8, IR (BC) 40 A2
Baptiste Meadow 2, IR (BC) 36 A2
Baptiste River, UP (Alta.) 33 C4
Baptiste Smith 1A, IR (BC) 37 G4
Baptiste Smith 1B, IR (BC) 37 G4
Barachois, UP (NB) 7 A4
Barachois Brook, UP (Nfld.) 4 C2
Barachoix, UP (Nfld.) 2 B2
Barasway de Plate, UP (Nfld.) 2 C2
Barb, UP (Ont.) 17 F1
Barber's Beach, UP (Ont.) 23 E4
Barclay, UP (Ont.) 21 A1
Barcovan Beach, UP (Ont.) 21 F2
Bar-de-Cocagne, UP (NB) 12 G4
Bardo, UP (Alta.) 33 E3
Bardsville, UP (Ont.) 24 B2
Bare Island 9, IR (BC) 38 F4
Bareneed, UP (Nfld.) 2 G2
Bargain Harbour 24, IR (BC) 38 D1
Barge Bay, UP (Nfld.) 5 H1
Bargrave, UP (Alta.) 34 F2
Bar Haven, UP (Nfld.) 2 E2
Barich, UP (Alta.) 33 E2
Barillia Park, UP (Ont.) 21 B1
Baring, UP (Sask.) 29 C3
Barkerville, UP (BC) 40 D3
Barkfield, UP (Man.) 28 B3
Barkhouse Settlement, UP (NS) 9 E3
Barkmere, T (Que.) 18 F4
Barlee Junction, UP (Alta.) 33 E4
Barlochan, UP (Ont.) 24 B3
Barlow, UP (BC) 40 C3
Barlow, UP (YT) 45 A2
Barnaby River, UP (NB) 12 F3
Barnegat, UP (Alta.) 33 F2
Barnesville, UP (NB) 11 E4
Barnettville, UP (NB) 12 E3
Barneys Brook, UP (NS) 9 B3
Barneys River Station, UP (NS) 8 A4
Barnhart, UP (Ont.) 28 H4
Barnsley, UP (Man.) 29 H4
Barnston, UP (Que.) 16 D4
Barnston Island, UP (BC) 38 G2
Barnston Island 3, IR (BC) 38 G2
Barnwell, UP (Alta.) 34 G4
Barons, VL (Alta.) 34 F3
Barony, UP (NB) 11 B1
Bar Point, UP (Ont.) 22 A4
Barrachois, UP (NS) 9 C1
Barrachois, UP (NS) 8 E3
Barrachois Harbour, UP (NS) 8 E3
Barrage-McLaren, UP (Que.) 18 D4
Barrage-Mistigougèche, UP (Que.) 14 H3
Barrage-Rivière-Rimouski, UP (Que.) 14 G3
Barrage-St-Narcisse, UP (Que.) 16 C1
Barra Glen, UP (NS) 8 D3
Barra Head, UP (NS) 8 D4
Barraute, VL (Que.) 18 B1
Barr'd Harbour, UP (Nfld.) 5 G2
Barr'd Islands < Joe Batt's Arm – Barr'd Islands, UP (Nfld.) 3 E1
Barren Hill, UP (NS) 8 E4
Barrett Chute, UP (Ont.) 17 A2
Barrett Lake, UP (BC) 42 G4
Barrettville, UP (Ont.) 22 A4
Barr Haven, UP (Ont.) 17 E4
Barrhead, T (Alta.) 33 D2
Barrie, C (Ont.) 21 A1
Barrieau, UP (NB) 12 F3
Barriefield, UP (Ont.) 17 A4
Barrier Bay, UP (Man.) 28 D1
Barrière, UP (BC) 36 F3
Barrière, UP (Que.) 18 C2
Barrière-Caribou, UP (Que.) 14 G4
Barrière-de-Laterrière, UP (Que.) 14 B3
Barrière-de-Stoneham, UP (Que.) 15 B2
Barrière-Mésy, UP (Que.) 14 A3
Barrière River 3A, IR (BC) 36 F3
Barrie Terrace, NUP (Ont.) 21 A1
Barrington, UP (NS) 10 B4
Barrington, UP (Que.) 17 H2
Barrington, CFS/SFC, MIL (NS) 10 C4
Barrington Head, UP (NS) 10 C4
Barrington Passage, UP (NS) 10 B4
Barrington West, UP (NS) 10 B4
Bar River, UP (Ont.) 26 B4
Barronsfield, UP (NS) 11 H2
Barrow Bay, UP (Ont.) 23 C1
Barrows, UP (Man.) 30 A3
Barr Settlement, UP (NS) 9 B3
Barry Heights, NUP (Ont.) 21 F1
Barrymere, UP (Ont.) 24 F2
Barry's Bay, VL (Ont.) 24 F2
Barrys Corner, UP (NS) 10 E2
Barryvale, UP (Ont.) 17 A2
Barryville, UP (NB) 12 F2
Barsa Subdivision, NUP (NB) 11 E2
Barss Corner, UP (NS) 10 D2
Barter Settlement, UP (NB) 11 B3
Barthel, UP (Sask.) 32 B3
Bartholomew, UP (NB) 12 E3
Bartibog, UP (NB) 12 F2
Bartibog Bridge, UP (NB) 12 F2
Bartlett Island 7, IR (BC) 37 B3
Bartlett Island 32, IR (BC) 39 F4
Bartletts Harbour, UP (Nfld.) 5 G2
Bartletts Mills, UP (NB) 11 B3
Barton, UP (NS) 10 B2
Barton, UP (Nfld.) 2 F1
Barton, UP (NB) 11 B1
Barstow < Blackfoot 146, UP (Alta.) 34 F2
Barville, T (Que.) 18 B1
Barwick, UP (Ont.) 28 G4
Bas-Caraquet, VL (NB) 13 G4
Bas-de-la-Baie, UP (Que.) 15 C1
Bas-de-l'Anse, UP (Que.) 14 D4
Base Line Road, UP (NS) 11 G3
Bashaw, T (Alta.) 33 E4
Basin Depot, UP (Ont.) 24 F1
Basin Mines, UP (Ont.) 26 E4
Basin Road, UP (NS) 8 D4
Baskin's Beach, UP (Ont.) 17 B1
Bassano, T (Alta.) 34 G2
Bass Creek, UP (Ont.) 25 C2
Basse-Aboujagane, UP (NB) 7 A4
Bassin, UP (Que.) 7 F1
Bass Lake Estates, NUP (Ont.) 23 F1
Bass Lake Park, UP (Ont.) 24 B4
Bass River, UP (NS) 9 B2
Bass River, UP (NB) 12 F3
Bass River Point, UP (NB) 12 G3
Basswood, UP (Man.) 29 F3
Basswood Ridge, UP (NB) 11 B3
Bastarache, UP (NB) 12 G4
Batawa, UP (Ont.) 21 F1
Batchawana Bay, UP (Ont.) 26 A3
Bateman, UP (Sask.) 31 E3
Batemans Mills, UP (NB) 12 G4
Bates Beach, NUP (BC) 38 B1
Bates Settlement, UP (NB) 11 B1
Bateston, UP (NS) 8 F3
Bath, VL (NB) 12 A3
Bath, VL (Ont.) 17 A4
Bathurst, C (NB) 12 E1
Bathurst Inlet, UP (NWT) 45 F2
Bathurst Mines, UP (NB) 12 E1
Batiscan, UP (Que.) 16 C1
Batiscan-Station, UP (Que.) 16 C1
Bat-l-ki 3, IR (BC) 41 G4
Batoche, UP (Que.) 16 E3
Batoche, UP (Sask.) 32 D4
Batteau, UP (Nfld.) 6 H3
Batteaux, UP (Ont.) 23 E2
Batter Junction, UP (Alta.) 34 G1
Battersea, UP (Ont.) 17 B4
Battle Bend, UP (Alta.) 33 F4
Battle Creek, UP (Sask.) 31 B4
Battleford, T (Sask.) 32 B4
Battle Harbour, UP (Nfld.) 5 H1
Battle Heights, UP (Sask.) 32 G3
Battle Lake, UP (Alta.) 33 D4
Battrum, UP (Sask.) 31 D3
Bauline, UP (Nfld.) 2 H2
Bauline East, UP (Nfld.) 2 H3
Bawlf, VL (Alta.) 33 F4
Baxter, UP (Ont.) 21 A1
Baxters Corner, UP (NB) 11 E2
Baxters Corners, UP (Ont.) 17 C2
Baxters Harbour, UP (NS) 11 H3
Bayard, UP (Que.) 18 E4
Bayard Station, UP (Sask.) 31 G3
Bay Bulls, UP (Nfld.) 2 H3
Bay de l'Eau, UP (Nfld.) 2 D2
Bay de Loup, UP (Nfld.) 4 E4
Bay de Verde, T (Nfld.) 2 H1
Bay du Nord, UP (Nfld.) 2 C2
Bay du Vin, UP (NB) 12 F2
Bay du Vin Beach, UP (NB) 12 F2
Bayend, UP (Man.) 29 G2
Bayfield, UP (NS) 8 B4
Bayfield, UP (NB) 7 B4
Bayfield, UP (PEI) 7 E3
Bayfield, UP (Ont.) 25 F3
Bayfield, VL (Ont.) 23 B4
Bayfield Road, UP (NS) 8 B4
Bay Fortune, UP (PEI) 7 E4
Bayhead, UP (NS) 9 C1
Bay L'Argent, T (Nfld.) 2 D2
Baynes Lake, UP (BC) 34 D4
Bayonne, UP (Que.) 15 E2
Bayport, UP (NS) 10 E2
Bayridge, UP (Ont.) 17 A4
Bay Road, UP (NB) 11 B3
Bay Road Valley, UP (NS) 8 E1
Bay Roberts, T (Nfld.) 2 G2
Bay St Lawrence, UP (NS) 8 E1
Bayshore, UP (NB) 12 G1
Bayshore, UP (Ont.) 17 D4
Bayshore Estates, UP (Ont.) 21 A1
Bay Shore Heights, UP (Man.) 30 C4
Bayshore Village, UP (Ont.) 23 G2
Bayside, UP (Ont.) 21 F1
Bayside, UP (NS) 9 B4
Bayside, UP (NB) 11 B3
Bayside, UP (NB) 7 B4
Bayside, UP (PEI) 7 B3
Baysville, UP (Ont.) 24 C2
Bayswater, UP (NS) 9 A4
Bayswater, UP (NB) 11 D3
Bayswater, UP (Ont.) 25 F2
Bay Trail, UP (Sask.) 31 G1
Bay Tree, UP (Alta.) 43 F3
Bay View, UP (NS) 9 D1
Bay View, UP (NB) 11 F2
Bay View, UP (NS) 10 B1
Bayview, UP (PEI) 7 C3
Bayview, UP (Ont.) 17 A4
Bayview, UP (Ont.) 23 D1
Bay View < Lewin's Cove, UP (Nfld.) 2 C3
Bayview Beach, UP (Ont.) 21 A1
Bayview Park, UP (Ont.) 23 F1
Baywood Park, UP (Ont.) 23 G2
Bazentin, UP (Sask.) 32 C3
Beachburg, VL (Ont.) 24 H1
Beachcomber, NUP (BC) 38 D2
Beachcomber Bay, UP (BC) 35 F2
Beach Corner, UP (Alta.) 33 D3
Beach Hill Farms, UP (NS) 10 D3
Beach Meadows, UP (NS) 10 E3
Beach O'Pines, NUP (Ont.) 22 D1
Beach Point, UP (PEI) 7 E4
Beachville, UP (Ont.) 22 F1
Beacon Corner, UP (Alta.) 33 G2
Beacon Heights, UP (Ont.) 17 E4
Beacon Hill, UP (Sask.) 32 A2
Beacon Hill North, UP (Ont.) 17 E4
Beacon Hill South, UP (Ont.) 17 E4
Beaconia, UP (Man.) 30 C4
Beaconsfield, C (Que.) 17 F4
Beaconsfield, UP (NS) 10 C1
Beaconsfield, UP (NB) 11 B2
Beaconsfield, UP (NB) 12 A3
Beaconsfield, UP (Ont.) 22 F1
Beaconwood, UP (Ont.) 17 E4
Beadle, UP (Sask.) 31 C2
Beales Mills, UP (Ont.) 17 C3
Bear Bay 8, IR (BC) 37 C2
Bearberry, UP (Alta.) 34 D1
Bearbrook, UP (Ont.) 17 D1
Bear Camp, UP (BC) 45 A3
Bear Canyon, UP (Alta.) 43 F3
Bear Cave, UP (Ont.) 24 B2
Bear Cove, UP (Nfld.) 5 G2
Bear Cove, UP (NS) 10 A3
Bear Cove, UP (NS) 9 B4
Bear Cove, UP (Nfld.) 5 G4
Bear Cove < Rocky Harbour (COMM), UP (Nfld.) 5 F4
Bear Creek, UP (YT) 45 A2
Bear Creek, UP (BC) 35 A3
Bear Creek, UP (YT) 45 A3
Beardmore, UP (Ont.) 27 F2
Beardy 97 and Okemasis 96, IR (Sask.) 32 D4
Bear Flat, UP (BC) 43 E3
Bear Island, UP (NB) 11 B1
Bear Island < Bear Island 1, UP (Ont.) 26 F3
Bear Island 1, IR (Ont.) 26 F3
Bear Lake, UP (BC) 40 C1
Bear Lake, UP (Ont.) 24 B2
Bear Lake, UP (Alta.) 43 G4
Bear Lake < Bear Lake 4, UP (BC) 42 F2
Bear Lake 1A, IR (BC) 42 G2
Bear Lake 1B, IR (BC) 42 F2
Bear Lake 4, IR (BC) 42 F2
Bear Line, UP (Ont.) 22 B3
Béarn, UP (Que.) 18 A3
Bear Point, UP (NS) 10 B4

Bear Point, UP (Ont.) **21 A1**
Bear River, UP (NS) **10 B2**
Bear River, UP (PEI) **7 E3**
Bear River 3, IR (BC) **42 F2**
Bear River 6, IR (NS) **10 B2**
Bear River 6A, IR (NS) **10 C1**
Bear River 6B, IR (NS) **10 C1**
Bear River East, UP (NS) **10 B2**
Bear River Station, UP (NS) **10 B2**
Bearskin Lake, IR (Ont.) **30 F2**
Bearskin Lake < Bearskin Lake, UP (Ont.) **30 F2**
Bearspaw, UP (Alta.) **34 E2**
Bear Valley, UP (Ont.) **25 H2**
Beasley, UP (BC) **34 B4**
Beaton, UP (BC) **34 B2**
Beaton River 204, IR (BC) **43 E2**
Beaton Road, UP (PEI) **7 A3**
Beatton Ranch, UP (BC) **43 D2**
Beatton River, UP (BC) **43 E2**
Beatty, UP (Ont.) **17 A2**
Beatty, VL (Sask.) **32 E4**
Beattyville, UP (Que.) **18 C1**
Beaubier, UP (Sask.) **31 H4**
Beau Bois, UP (Nfld.) **2 C3**
Beaubois, NUP (NB) **12 F1**
Beaucage < Nipissing 10, UP (Ont.) **25 H1**
Beaucanton, UP (Que.) **18 A1**
Beauceville, T (Que.) **15 C4**
Beauchamp, UP (Que.) **15 D3**
Beaudoin-Centre, UP (Que.) **16 E2**
Beaudry, UP (Que.) **18 A2**
Beaufield, UP (Sask.) **31 C1**
Beaufort, UP (NB) **12 B3**
Beauglen, UP (Que.) **13 E3**
Beauharnois, C (Que.) **17 G2**
Beaulac, UP (Que.) **18 F4**
Beaulac, VL (Que.) **16 E3**
Beaulieu, VL (Que.) **15 G3**
Beauly, UP (NS) **8 B4**
Beaumaris, UP (Ont.) **24 B3**
Beaumont, UP (Que.) **15 H3**
Beaumont, UP (NB) **11 G1**
Beaumont, VL (Alta.) **33 E3**
Beaumont < Lushes Bight - Beaumont - Beaumont North, UP (Nfld.) **3 B1**
Beaumont-Est, UP (Que.) **15 H3**
Beaumont North < Lushes Bight - Beaumont - Beaumont North, UP (Nfld.) **3 B1**
Beauport, C (Que.) **15 H3**
Beaupré, T (Que.) **15 B2**
Beausejour, T (Man.) **28 B1**
Beauséjour, UP (Que.) **15 F1**
Beausejour CFS/SFC, MIL (Man.) **28 C1**
Beauval, UP (Sask.) **32 C1**
Beauvallon, UP (Alta.) **33 F3**
Beaver, UP (Man.) **29 G3**
Beaver, UP (BC) **41 F4**
Beaverbank, UP (NS) **9 B3**
Beaverbank Villa, UP (NS) **9 B3**
Beaver Brook, UP (NS) **9 C2**
Beaver Brook, UP (NB) **11 G2**
Beaver Brook Station, UP (NB) **12 E2**
Beaver Cove, UP (NS) **8 E3**
Beaver Cove, UP (Nfld.) **3 E2**
Beaver Cove, UP (BC) **39 E1**
Beaver Creek, UP (BC) **38 C2**
Beaver Creek, UP (YT) **45 A3**
Beaver Crossing, UP (Alta.) **33 G2**
Beaver-Crossing, UP (Que.) **17 F2**
Beaverdale, UP (Ont.) **23 D2**
Beaver Dale, UP (Sask.) **29 C2**
Beaver Dam, UP (NB) **11 C1**
Beaverdam, UP (Alta.) **33 G2**
Beaverdell, UP (BC) **35 F3**
Beaver Falls, NUP (BC) **34 B4**
Beaver Flat, UP (Sask.) **31 E3**
Beaver Harbour, UP (NB) **11 C3**
Beaver Harbour, UP (NS) **9 E3**
Beaverhill, UP (Alta.) **33 E3**
Beaver Islands 8, IR (BC) **40 B1**
Beaver Lake, UP (Alta.) **33 F2**
Beaver Lake 131, IR (Alta.) **33 F2**
Beaver Lake 17, IR (NS) **9 D3**
Beaverley, UP (BC) **40 C2**
Beaverlodge, T (Alta.) **43 F4**
Beaverlodge, CFS/SFC, MIL (Alta.) **43 F4**
Beaver Meadow, UP (NS) **8 B4**
Beaver Meadow, UP (Ont.) **22 C2**
Beaver Mines, UP (Alta.) **34 E4**
Beavermouth, UP (BC) **34 B2**
Beaver Pass House, UP (BC) **40 D3**
Beaver Point, UP (BC) **38 F3**
Beaver Ranch 163, IR (Alta.) **44 A3**
Beaver River, UP (NS) **10 A3**
Beaver River, UP (Alta.) **33 G2**
Beavers Corner < Six Nations 40, UP (Ont.) **22 G1**
Beaverstone Bay, UP (Ont.) **25 E2**
Beaverton, UP (Ont.) **21 B1**
Beaverton, UP (Nfld.) **3 D2**
Beaver Valley, UP (Sask.) **31 D4**
Beazer, UP (Alta.) **34 F4**
Bécancour, T (Que.) **16 C1**
Bécancour 11, IR (Que.) **16 C1**
Bechard, UP (Sask.) **31 H3**
Becher, UP (Ont.) **22 B2**
Becher Bay 1, IR (BC) **38 E4**
Becher Bay 2, IR (BC) **38 E4**
Becher House, UP (BC) **36 A2**
Beck, UP (Ont.) **27 E3**
Becketts Bridge, UP (Ont.) **21 B4**
Becketts Creek, UP (Ont.) **17 D1**
Becketts Landing, UP (Ont.) **17 C2**
Becketville, UP (NB) **13 E4**
Beckim Settlement, UP (NB) **12 A4**
Beckstead, UP (Ont.) **17 D2**
Beckwith, UP (NS) **9 B1**
Bédard-Landing, UP (Que.) **16 D4**
Beddington, UP (Alta.) **34 E2**
Bedec, UP (NB) **12 G3**
Bedell, UP (Ont.) **17 C2**
Bedell Settlement, UP (NB) **11 A1**
Bedeque, UP (PEI) **7 B3**
Bedford, T (Que.) **16 B4**
Bedford, UP (NS) **9 B3**
Bedford, UP (NB) **11 D2**
Bedford, UP (Ont.) **17 A3**
Bedford Corner, UP (PEI) **7 D4**
Bedford Mills, UP (Ont.) **17 B3**
Bedford Road, UP (NB) **12 A3**
Bedford Station, UP (PEI) **7 D3**
Beebe-Plain, VL (Que.) **16 C4**
Beecham Settlement, UP (NS) **7 B4**
Beech Corners, UP (Ont.) **24 G3**
Beech Glen, UP (NB) **12 A3**
Beech-Grove, UP (Que.) **17 B1**
Beech Hill, UP (NS) **10 E2**
Beech Hill, UP (NB) **11 G1**
Beech Hill, UP (NS) **8 B4**
Beech Hill, UP (NS) **9 D3**
Beechmont, UP (NS) **8 E3**
Beechmont North, UP (NS) **8 E3**
Beechmount, UP (Ont.) **24 E3**
Beechville, UP (NS) **9 B4**
Beechwood, UP (NB) **12 A3**
Beechwood, UP (Ont.) **23 C4**
Beechwood, UP (Ont.) **22 C3**
Beechy, VL (Sask.) **31 E2**
Beersville, UP (NB) **12 F4**
Beeton, VL (Ont.) **21 A1**
Bégin, UP (Que.) **14 A2**
Bégin, UP (Que.) **15 D2**
Behan, UP (Alta.) **33 F1**
Beinn Bhreagh, UP (NS) **7 H4**
Beinn Scalpie, UP (NS) **8 E3**
Beiseker, VL (Alta.) **34 F2**
Bekanon, UP (Ont.) **25 F2**
Bekevar, UP (Sask.) **29 C3**
Bélair, UP (Que.) **15 F4**
Bélair, UP (Man.) **30 C4**
Béland, UP (Que.) **16 G3**
Bélanger, UP (Que.) **15 G2**
Bélanger, UP (Sask.) **44 E4**
Belanger, UP (Sask.) **31 C4**
Belangers Corner, UP (Ont.) **17 A1**
Belbeck, UP (Sask.) **31 G3**
Belbutte, UP (Sask.) **32 C3**
Belcarra, UP (BC) **38 G2**
Belcher Street, UP (NS) **11 H3**
Belcourt, UP (Que.) **18 C1**
Belfast, UP (PEI) **7 D4**
Belfast, UP (Ont.) **23 B3**
Belford, UP (BC) **34 B4**
Belgiumtown, UP (NS) **8 F3**
Belgrave, UP (Ont.) **23 B3**
Belhaven, UP (Ont.) **21 B1**
Bella Bella, UP (BC) **41 E3**
Bella Bella 1, IR (BC) **41 E3**
Bella Coola, UP (BC) **41 G3**
Bella Coola 1, IR (BC) **41 G3**
Bellamys, UP (Ont.) **17 C3**
Bellamys Mill, UP (Ont.) **17 B3**
Bellarmin, UP (Que.) **16 G3**
Bellburns, COMM (Nfld.) **5 F3**
Bellcreft, NUP (Ont.) **22 A4**
Belle Air Beach, UP (Ont.) **21 A1**
Belle Côte, UP (NS) **8 D2**
Belledune, VL (NB) **13 E4**
Belle-eau-Claire Beach, UP (Ont.) **23 E1**
Bellefeuille, UP (Que.) **18 F4**
Bellefeuille, UP (Que.) **16 E4**
Bellefeuille, UP (Que.) **18 A1**
Bellefleur, UP (NB) **12 A2**
Bellefond, UP (NB) **12 E2**
Bellegarde, UP (Sask.) **29 D4**
Belleisle, UP (NS) **10 C1**
Belle Isle, UP (Nfld.) **5 H1**
Belleisle Creek, UP (NB) **11 E2**
Belle-Marche, UP (NS) **8 D2**
Bellecram, T (Nfld.) **2 C2**
Belle Plaine, VL (Sask.) **31 G3**
Belle River, T (Ont.) **22 B3**
Belle River, UP (PEI) **7 D4**
Bellerive-sur-le-Lac, UP (Que.) **18 E4**
Belleterre, T (Que.) **18 A2**
Belle Vallée, UP (Ont.) **26 F2**
Belle-Vallée, NUP (Que.) **16 A4**
Belleview, UP (Man.) **29 E4**
Belleville, C (Ont.) **21 F1**
Belleville, UP (NS) **10 B3**
Belleville, UP (NB) **11 A1**
Belleville North, UP (NS) **10 B3**
Belleville South, UP (NS) **10 B3**
Bellevue, UP (Que.) **18 H1**
Bellevue, UP (Nfld.) **2 F2**
Bellevue, UP (Ont.) **26 B3**
Bellevue, UP (Que.) **16 B2**
Bellevue, UP (PEI) **7 D4**
Bellevue, UP (Que.) **17 G1**
Bellevue, VL (Alta.) **34 E4**
Bell Ewart, UP (Ont.) **21 A1**
Belley, UP (Que.) **15 C1**
Bell-Falls, UP (Que.) **18 E4**
Bell Grove, UP (NB) **12 A2**
Bellheck, UP (Ont.) **24 G4**
Bellin (Payne), UP (Que.) **46 F3**
Bellingham, UP (Ont.) **26 C4**
Bellis, UP (Alta.) **33 F2**
Belliveau, UP (NS) **10 A2**
Belliveaus Cove, UP (NS) **10 A2**
Belliveau Village, UP (NB) **11 G1**
Bell Lake 37, IR (BC) **42 D4**
Bell-Mount, UP (Que.) **18 C4**
Bell Neck, UP (NS) **10 B3**
Belloy, UP (Alta.) **43 G4**
Bell Rapids, UP (Ont.) **24 F2**
Bellrock, UP (Ont.) **17 A3**
Bell Rock, UP (NWT) **44 C2**
Bells Corners, UP (Ont.) **17 D4**
Bells Corners, UP (Ont.) **17 B2**
Bells Crossing, UP (Ont.) **17 C3**
Bellshill, UP (Alta.) **33 F4**
Bellsite, UP (Man.) **30 A3**
Bells Mills, UP (NB) **12 G3**
Bellwood, UP (Ont.) **17 D4**
Bellwood, UP (Ont.) **24 E2**
Belmeade, UP (Ont.) **17 D2**
Belmina, UP (Que.) **16 E2**
Belmont, UP (NS) **9 C2**
Belmont, UP (Man.) **29 F4**
Belmont, UP (NS) **9 A3**
Belmont, VL (Ont.) **22 E2**
Belmont Lot 16, UP (PEI) **7 B3**
Belmont Park, UP (BC) **38 E4**
Belmore, UP (Ont.) **23 C3**
Belnan, UP (NS) **9 B3**
Beloeil, T (Que.) **16 A3**
Beloud Post, UP (YT) **45 A3**
Belton, UP (Ont.) **22 E1**
Belval, UP (Que.) **15 B3**
Belvédère, UP (Que.) **17 G1**
Belvedere, UP (Alta.) **33 D3**
Belvedere, UP (BC) **38 G2**
Belvedere-Heights, UP (Que.) **16 D4**
Belwood, UP (Ont.) **23 D4**
Belyeas Cove, UP (NB) **11 D2**
Bemersyde, UP (Sask.) **29 C3**
Benacadie, UP (NS) **8 E3**
Benacadie Pond, UP (NS) **8 E4**
Benacadie West, UP (NS) **8 E3**
Benalto, UP (Alta.) **33 D4**
Bender, UP (Man.) **29 H3**
Bender, UP (Sask.) **29 C3**
Ben Eoin, UP (NS) **8 E3**
Bengough, T (Sask.) **31 G4**
Benito, VL (Man.) **29 D1**
Benjamin, NUP (NB) **13 D4**
Benjamin Bridge, UP (NS) **11 H3**
Benjamin River, UP (NB) **13 D4**
Benjamins Mill, UP (NS) **9 A3**
Benmiller, UP (Ont.) **23 B3**
Ben-My-Chree, UP (BC) **45 B4**
Bennett, UP (Alta.) **34 E2**
Bennett, UP (BC) **45 B4**
Bennies Corners, UP (Ont.) **17 B2**
Bennington, UP (Ont.) **22 E1**
Bennington Falls, UP (BC) **34 B4**
Benny, UP (Ont.) **26 D3**
Benoit, UP (NB) **12 G1**
Benoit, UP (Ont.) **17 D2**
Benoit's Cove < Halfway Point - Benoit's Cove - John's Beach - Frenchman's Cove, UP (Nfld.) **4 C1**
Benoit's Siding, NUP (Nfld.) **4 A3**
Bensfort Bridge, UP (Ont.) **21 D1**
Bensfort Corners, UP (Ont.) **21 D1**
Bensham, UP (Sask.) **32 F4**
Benson, VL (Sask.) **29 C4**
Benson Corner, UP (NB) **11 B3**
Benson Lake, UP (BC) **39 D2**
Bentinck, UP (Ont.) **23 C2**
Bentley, VL (Alta.) **33 D4**
Benton, COMM (Nfld.) **3 E3**
Benton, UP (NB) **11 A1**
Benton Station, UP (Alta.) **31 B2**
Bentpath, UP (Ont.) **22 C2**
Bent River, UP (Ont.) **24 B2**
Bents, UP (Sask.) **31 E1**
Berdinskies, UP (Alta.) **44 C3**
Berens Landing, UP (NWT) **45 D3**
Berens River < Berens River 13, UP (Man.) **30 C3**
Berens River 13, IR (Man.) **30 C3**
Beresford, UP (Man.) **29 E4**
Beresford, UP (BC) **35 D1**
Beresford, VL (NB) **12 E1**
Bergen, UP (Man.) **28 A1**
Bergen, UP (Alta.) **34 E1**
Bergheim, UP (Sask.) **31 F1**
Bergland, UP (Ont.) **28 F3**
Bergs, UP (BC) **38 G2**
Berichan, UP (NS) **9 C1**
Berkeley, UP (Ont.) **23 D2**
Berkinshaw, UP (Alta.) **33 F4**
Berlett's Corners, UP (Ont.) **23 D4**
Berlo, UP (Man.) **29 H2**
Bernard, UP (Sask.) **31 E2**
Bernard House, UP (NWT) **45 B2**
Bernatchez, UP (Que.) **15 D3**
Bernice, UP (Man.) **29 E2**
Bernic Lake, UP (Man.) **30 C4**
Bernières, UP (Que.) **15 F4**
Bernierville, VL (Que.) **15 A4**
Berny, UP (Alta.) **33 F2**
Berriedale, UP (Ont.) **25 H3**
Berry, UP (Que.) **18 B1**
Berryer, UP (Que.) **15 D2**
Berry Head < Berry Head, Port au Port, UP (Nfld.) **4 B2**
Berry Head, Port au Port, COMM (Nfld.) **4 B2**
Berry Mills, UP (NB) **11 G1**
Berrymoor, UP (Alta.) **33 C3**
Berrys, UP (Ont.) **17 D4**
Berryton, UP (NB) **11 G1**
Berryton, UP (Ont.) **17 B3**
Bersimis 3, IR (Que.) **14 G1**
Berthier-sur-Mer, UP (Que.) **15 C3**
Berthierville, T (Que.) **16 A2**
Bertrand, VL (NB) **12 F1**
Bertwell, UP (Sask.) **32 G4**
Bérubé, UP (Que.) **15 B2**
Bervie, UP (Ont.) **23 B3**
Berwick, T (NS) **10 D1**
Berwick, UP (NB) **11 E2**
Berwick, UP (Ont.) **17 D2**
Berwick North, UP (NS) **10 D1**
Berwick West, UP (NS) **10 D1**
Berwyn, VL (Alta.) **43 H3**
Berylvale, UP (Ont.) **26 E1**
Bessborough, UP (BC) **43 E3**
Bessemer, UP (Ont.) **24 F3**
Best's Harbour, UP (Nfld.) **2 E2**
Bestwick, UP (BC) **35 D1**
Betchouane, UP (Que.) **5 A3**
Béthanie, UP (Que.) **16 C3**
Bethany, UP (Ont.) **21 D1**
Bethany, UP (Man.) **29 F3**
Bethany, UP (Ont.) **21 G1**
Bethel, UP (PEI) **7 D4**
Bethel, UP (Ont.) **17 C3**
Bethel, UP (NB) **11 C3**
Béthel, UP (Que.) **16 C3**
Bethel, UP (Ont.) **21 G1**
Bethesda, UP (Ont.) **21 G1**
Bethesda, UP (Ont.) **21 A1**
Bethléem, UP (Que.) **16 E4**
Bethune, VL (Sask.) **31 G2**
Bethune Bush, UP (Ont.) **17 D2**
Betsiamites < Bersimis 3, UP (Que.) **14 G2**
Bettsburg, UP (NB) **12 D4**
Betty Creek 18, IR (BC) **40 A3**
Betula Beach, SV (Alta.) **33 C3**
Betula Lake, UP (Man.) **28 D1**
Beulah, UP (Man.) **29 E3**
Beulah, UP (NB) **11 D2**
Bevan, UP (BC) **38 B1**
Beveridge Locks, UP (Ont.) **17 B3**
Beverley, UP (Sask.) **31 D3**
Beverley Hills, UP (Ont.) **21 B1**
Beverley Isles, UP (Ont.) **21 B1**
Beverly Hills, NUP (Alta.) **33 E3**
Bewdley, UP (Ont.) **21 D1**
Bexley, UP (Ont.) **24 C4**
Beynon, UP (Alta.) **34 F2**
Bezanson, UP (Alta.) **43 G4**
Bible Hill, UP (NS) **9 C2**
Bic, VL (Que.) **14 G3**
Bickerdike, UP (Alta.) **33 B3**
Bickerton West, UP (NS) **9 F3**
Bickford, UP (Ont.) **22 B2**
Bickleigh, UP (Sask.) **31 D2**
Bide Arm, COMM (Nfld.) **5 H2**
Bideford, UP (PEI) **7 B3**
Bidwell, UP (Ont.) **25 C2**
Bield, UP (Man.) **29 E2**
Bieman's Corners, UP (Ont.) **23 C3**
Biencourt, UP (Que.) **14 G4**
Bienfait, T (Sask.) **29 C4**
Bienvenu, UP (Que.) **18 A1**
Big Baddeck, UP (NS) **8 D3**
Big Bank, UP (NS) **8 E3**
Big Bar Creek, UP (BC) **36 B3**
Big Bay, UP (BC) **37 B3**
Big Bay, UP (Ont.) **23 C1**
Big Bay Point, UP (Ont.) **21 B1**
Big Beach, UP (NS) **8 E3**
Big Beaver, UP (Sask.) **31 G4**
Big Beaver House, UP (Ont.) **30 F3**
Big Black River, UP (Man.) **30 C3**
Big Bras d'Or, UP (NS) **8 E3**
Big Brook, UP (Nfld.) **5 H2**
Big Brook, UP (NS) **8 C4**
Big Brook, UP (NS) **8 E3**
Big Brook, UP (NS) **8 D3**
Big Cedar Point, UP (Ont.) **21 A1**
Big Chute, UP (Ont.) **24 A3**
Big Coulee, UP (Alta.) **33 E2**
Big Cove, UP (NB) **11 E2**
Big Cove < Richibucto 15, UP (NB) **12 G3**
Big Creek, UP (BC) **40 C4**
Big Eddy, UP (BC) **34 A2**
Big Eddy Settlement < The Pas 21E, UP (Man.) **30 A2**
Bigelow, UP (Ont.) **26 F3**
Big Farm, UP (NS) **8 D3**
Big Fork, UP (Ont.) **28 H4**
Biggar, T (Sask.) **31 D1**
Biggar Ridge, UP (NB) **12 B3**
Big Glace Bay, UP (NS) **8 F3**
Big Glen, UP (NS) **8 E4**
Big Glen, UP (NS) **8 C4**
Big Grassy River 35G, IR (Ont.) **28 F3**
Big Harbour, UP (NS) **8 E3**
Big Harbour Centre, UP (NS) **8 D4**
Big Harbour Island, UP (NS) **8 D4**
Bighead 124, IR (Sask.) **32 A2**
Big Hill, UP (NS) **8 E3**
Big Hole, UP (NB) **12 E2**
Big Hole Brook, UP (NB) **12 D3**
Big Hole Tract 8, IR (NB) **12 E2**
Big Horn 144A, IR (Alta.) **33 B4**
Big Intervale, UP (NS) **8 D2**
Big Intervale Cape North, UP (NS) **8 E1**
Big Island, UP (NS) **8 A4**
Big Island, NUP (Ont.) **21 F1**
Big Island 31D, IR (Ont.) **28 F3**
Big Island 31E, IR (Ont.) **28 F3**
Big Island 31F, IR (Ont.) **28 F3**
Big Island 37, IR (Ont.) **28 F3**
Big Island Landing, UP (Man.) **28 E2**
Big Island Mainland 93, IR (Ont.) **28 G3**
Big Joe's Meadow 7, IR (BC) **40 C3**
Big Lake, UP (Ont.) **25 C2**
Big Lake, UP (Ont.) **30 H3**
Big Lake Ranch, UP (BC) **36 C1**
Big Lorraine, UP (NS) **8 F3**
Big Lots, UP (NS) **10 E2**
Big Marsh, UP (NS) **8 D4**
Big Marsh, UP (NS) **8 E3**
Big Meadow, UP (Alta.) **33 G2**
Big Muddy, UP (Sask.) **31 G4**
Bigney, UP (NS) **9 C1**
Big Point, UP (NWT) **44 A1**
Big Pond, UP (Nfld.) **2 H3**
Big Pond, UP (PEI) **7 E3**
Big Pond, NUP (NS) **8 E4**
Big Pond Centre, UP (NS) **8 E4**
Big Prairie, NUP (Alta.) **44 A4**
Big Ridge, UP (NS) **8 F3**
Big Ridge South, UP (NS) **8 F3**
Big River, T (Sask.) **32 C3**
Big River 118, IR (Sask.) **32 C3**
Big River 118A, IR (Sask.) **32 C3**
Big Salmon, UP (YT) **45 B3**
Big Slough, UP (Alta.) **44 B3**
Big Stone, UP (Alta.) **34 H2**
Big Tracadie, UP (NS) **8 C4**
Big Trout Lake, IR (Ont.) **30 F2**
Big Trout Lake < Big Trout Lake, UP (Ont.) **30 F2**
Big Valley, VL (Alta.) **34 F1**
Big Whiteshell Lake, UP (Man.) **28 D1**
Bigwin, UP (Ont.) **24 C2**
Bigwood, UP (Ont.) **25 F2**
Big Woody, UP (Man.) **29 D1**
Bilby, UP (Alta.) **33 D3**
Billimun, UP (Sask.) **31 E4**
Billings, UP (Ont.) **25 B2**
Billings Bay, UP (BC) **38 D1**
Bill Lake 37, IR (BC) **42 D4**
Billtown, UP (NS) **11 H3**
Bilodeau, UP (Que.) **18 H1**
Binbrook, UP (Ont.) **21 A4**
Bindloss, UP (Alta.) **31 B2**
Bingham, NUP (Que.) **17 F1**
Bingley, UP (Alta.) **33 C4**
Binkham, UP (Ont.) **23 E3**
Binscarth, VL (Man.) **29 D3**
Binta Lake 6, IR (BC) **40 A2**
Birch, UP (NWT) **44 B2**
Bircham, UP (Alta.) **34 F2**
Birchbank, UP (BC) **34 B4**
Birch Bay, UP (Man.) **29 G2**
Birchcliff, SV (Alta.) **33 D4**
Birchdale, UP (BC) **34 B3**
Birch Grove, UP (NS) **8 F3**
Birch Hill, UP (PEI) **7 B3**
Birch Hill, UP (NS) **9 C2**
Birch Hill, UP (PEI) **7 D4**
Birch Hill, UP (NS) **9 B2**
Birch Hills, T (Sask.) **32 E4**
Birch Island, UP (BC) **36 F2**
Birch Island < Whitefish River 4, UP (Ont.) **25 C2**
Birch Plain, UP (NS) **8 E2**
Birch Point, UP (Ont.) **23 H2**
Birch Portage 184A, IR (Sask.) **32 G1**
Birch Rapids, UP (Sask.) **32 E1**
Birch Ridge, UP (NB) **12 B3**
Birch Ridge, UP (NB) **12 F4**
Birch River, UP (Man.) **29 E1**
Birchton, UP (Que.) **16 D4**
Birchtown, UP (NS) **10 C4**
Birchview, UP (Man.) **29 E2**
Birchwood, UP (NS) **9 B1**
Birchy Bay, T (Nfld.) **3 D2**
Birchy Cove, UP (Nfld.) **3 G4**
Birchy Cove, UP (Nfld.) **3 A1**
Birchy Head, UP (Nfld.) **5 F4**
Birchy Head, UP (NS) **9 A4**
Bird, UP (Man.) **30 D1**
Bird Cove, UP (Nfld.) **5 G2**
Birdell, UP (Ont.) **23 D2**
Birdinia, UP (Man.) **29 F2**
Bird Point, UP (Sask.) **29 C3**
Bird River, UP (Man.) **30 C4**
Birdsalls, UP (Ont.) **21 E1**
Birds Creek, UP (Ont.) **24 E2**
Birds Hill, UP (Man.) **28 A1**
Birdtail, UP (Man.) **29 E3**
Birdtail Creek 57, IR (Man.) **29 E3**
Birdtail Hay Lands 57A, IR (Man.) **29 E3**
Birdton, UP (NB) **11 C1**
Birge Mills, UP (Ont.) **23 E4**
Birken, UP (BC) **37 G3**
Birkendale, UP (Ont.) **24 C2**
Birmingham, UP (Sask.) **29 C2**
Birnam, UP (Ont.) **22 C1**
Birnie, UP (Man.) **29 F3**
Birnie Island 18, IR (BC) **42 C4**
Biron, UP (Que.) **13 D3**
Birr, UP (Ont.) **22 E1**
Birsay, VL (Sask.) **31 E2**
Birson, UP (Sask.) **32 E3**
Birtle, T (Man.) **29 E3**
Biscayan Cove, UP (Nfld.) **2 H2**
Biscay Bay, COMM (Nfld.) **2 G4**
Biscotasing, UP (Ont.) **26 D3**
Bish 6, IR (BC) **41 E1**
Bishop Bluffs 5, IR (BC) **40 B3**
Bishop Bluffs 6, IR (BC) **40 B3**
Bishop Bluffs 10, IR (BC) **40 B3**
Bishop Corners, UP (Ont.) **24 G3**
Bishopgate, UP (Ont.) **22 G1**
Bishopric, UP (Sask.) **31 F3**
Bishop's Cove, COMM (Nfld.) **2 G2**
Bishop's Falls, T (Nfld.) **3 B3**
Bishops Mills, UP (Ont.) **17 C3**
Bishopton, VL (Que.) **16 E3**
Bishopville, UP (NS) **9 A3**
Bismarck, UP (Ont.) **21 A4**
Bison Lake, UP (Alta.) **44 A3**
Bissett, UP (Man.) **30 C4**
Bissett Creek, UP (Ont.) **18 B4**
Bissonnette, UP (Que.) **18 F4**
Bistcho Lake 213, IR (Alta.) **45 E4**
Bittern Lake, VL (Alta.) **33 E4**
Bittern Lake 218, IR (Sask.) **32 D3**
Bitumount, UP (Alta.) **44 C3**
Bjorkdale, VL (Sask.) **32 F4**
Black Avon, UP (NS) **8 B4**
Black Bank, UP (Ont.) **23 E2**
Black Banks, UP (PEI) **7 B3**
Black Bay, UP (Ont.) **26 H3**
Black Brook, UP (NS) **8 E3**
Blackburn, UP (Ont.) **17 E4**
Blackburn Hamlet, UP (Ont.) **17 E4**
Black Creek, UP (Ont.) **21 G2**
Black Creek, UP (BC) **38 B1**
Black Creek, UP (BC) **36 D1**
Blackdale, UP (Man.) **28 A1**
Blackdale Survey, NUP (Ont.) **21 A3**
Black Diamond, T (Alta.) **34 E2**
Black Donald, UP (Ont.) **24 G2**
Black Duck, UP (Nfld.) **4 C2**
Black Duck Brook, UP (Nfld.) **4 B1**
Black Duck Cove, UP (Nfld.) **5 G2**
Black Duck Cove, UP (Nfld.) **3 D1**
Blacketts Lake, UP (NS) **8 E3**
Blackfalds, VL (Alta.) **33 D4**
Blackfoot, UP (Alta.) **33 H3**
Blackfoot 146, IR (Alta.) **34 F2**
Black Hawk, UP (Ont.) **28 G4**
Blackhead, UP (Nfld.) **2 H2**
Blackhead < Small Point - Kingston - Broad Cove - Blackhead - Adams Cove, UP (Nfld.) **2 G2**
Black Hills, UP (YT) **45 A2**
Blackie, VL (Alta.) **34 F3**
Black Island, UP (Nfld.) **3 D1**
Black Island, UP (Nfld.) **3 D2**
Black-Lake, T (Que.) **16 E2**
Black Lake < Chicken 224, UP (Sask.) **44 E3**
Blackland, UP (NB) **11 B3**
Blackland, NUP (NB) **13 D4**
Black Pines, UP (BC) **36 F4**
Black Point, UP (NS) **9 A4**
Black Point, UP (NB) **13 D4**
Black Point, UP (NS) **9 D1**
Black Point, UP (NS) **8 E1**
Black Point 11, IR (BC) **42 D4**
Black Pond, NUP (PEI) **7 E3**
Blackpool, UP (BC) **36 F2**
Blackpool, UP (Que.) **16 A4**
Black Rapids, UP (Ont.) **17 B3**
Black River, UP (NS) **10 E1**
Black River, UP (NB) **11 E3**
Black River, UP (NB) **12 F2**
Black River, UP (Nfld.) **2 E2**
Black River, UP (NS) **8 C3**
Black River, UP (NS) **9 C1**
Black River, UP (Ont.) **17 E2**
Black River 9, IR (Man.) **30 C4**
Black River Bridge, UP (NB) **12 F2**
Black River Road, UP (NS) **9 A1**
Black Rock, UP (NB) **12 F1**
Black Rock, UP (NS) **8 E3**
Black Rock, UP (NS) **11 G3**
Black Rock, UP (NS) **9 B2**
Black Rock, UP (NS) **11 H2**
Blacks Corners, UP (Ont.) **22 H1**
Blacks Corners, UP (Ont.) **17 B2**
Blacks Corners, UP (Ont.) **23 E3**
Blacks Harbour, VL (NB) **11 C3**
Black Slate 11, IR (BC) **41 B2**
Blackstock, UP (Ont.) **21 C1**
Blackstock Subdivision, NUP (BC) **36 D2**
Blackstone, UP (NS) **8 C3**
Blackstone Lake, UP (Ont.) **24 A2**
Black Tickle, UP (Nfld.) **6 H3**
Blackville, VL (NB) **12 E3**
Blackwater, UP (Ont.) **21 C1**
Blackwater, UP (BC) **40 C2**
Blackwater Meadow 11, IR (BC) **40 A3**
Blackwell, UP (Ont.) **22 B1**
Blackwood, UP (Sask.) **29 B3**
Bladworth, VL (Sask.) **31 F2**
Blaeberry, UP (BC) **34 B2**
Blagdon, UP (NB) **11 D2**
Blaine Lake, T (Sask.) **32 C4**
Blainville, T (Que.) **17 F3**
Blair Court, UP (Ont.) **17 E4**
Blairhampton, UP (Ont.) **24 D3**
Blairmore, T (Alta.) **34 E4**
Blairs Settlement, UP (Ont.) **17 B3**
Blairton, UP (Ont.) **21 E1**
Blake, UP (Ont.) **23 B4**
Blake, UP (BC) **34 B4**
Blakeburn, UP (BC) **35 C3**
Blakeney, UP (Ont.) **17 B2**
Blaketown, UP (Nfld.) **2 G2**
Blanchard Road, UP (NS) **9 E2**
Blanchard Settlement, UP (NB) **12 G1**
Blanchards Hill, UP (Ont.) **17 B3**
Blanchard's Landing, UP (Ont.) **26 G4**
Blanche, UP (NS) **10 C4**
Blanche, UP (Que.) **17 D1**
Blanche-Mills, UP (Que.) **17 D1**
Blanc-Sablon, UP (Que.) **5 G2**
Blandford, UP (Que.) **16 D2**
Blandford, UP (NS) **9 A4**
Blaney Ridge, UP (NB) **11 B1**
Blantyre, UP (Ont.) **23 D2**
Blenheim, T (Ont.) **22 C3**
Blessington, UP (Ont.) **21 F1**
Blewett, UP (BC) **34 B4**
Blezard, UP (Ont.) **21 E1**
Blind Bay, UP (BC) **36 G4**
Blind Channel, UP (BC) **37 A3**
Blind Creek 6, IR (BC) **35 E4**
Blind Creek 6A, IR (BC) **35 E4**
Blind River, T (Ont.) **25 A1**
Blink Bonnie, UP (Ont.) **22 F1**
Blissfield, UP (NB) **12 D3**
Bliss Landing, UP (BC) **37 C4**
Blissville, UP (NB) **11 C2**
Block 14, UP (NB) **12 F3**
Blockhouse, UP (NS) **10 E2**
Bloedel, UP (BC) **37 B4**
Blomidon, UP (NS) **11 H3**
Blood 148, IR (Alta.) **34 F4**
Blood 148A, IR (Alta.) **34 E4**
Bloodvein River < Bloodvein River 12, UP (Man.) **30 C3**
Bloodvein River 12, IR (Man.) **30 C3**
Bloom, UP (Man.) **29 G3**
Bloomfield, UP (Nfld.) **3 F4**
Bloomfield, UP (NB) **11 E2**
Bloomfield, UP (NS) **10 B2**
Bloomfield, UP (NB) **12 A4**
Bloomfield, UP (PEI) **7 A2**
Bloomfield, VL (Ont.) **21 F2**
Bloomfield Corner, UP (PEI) **7 A3**
Bloomfield Ridge, UP (NB) **12 D3**
Bloomfield Ridge, UP (NB) **11 E2**
Bloomingdale, UP (Ont.) **23 D4**
Blooming Point, UP (PEI) **7 D3**
Bloomington, UP (NS) **10 D1**
Bloomington, UP (Ont.) **17 E2**
Bloomsbury, UP (Alta.) **33 D2**
Blossom Park, UP (Ont.) **17 E4**
Blouin, UP (Que.) **15 H4**
Blount, UP (Ont.) **23 E3**
Blowdown, UP (NB) **11 A1**
Blow Me Down, UP (Nfld.) **2 G2**
Blubber Bay, UP (BC) **38 C1**
Blucher, UP (Sask.) **31 F1**
Blucher Hall, UP (BC) **36 F4**
Blue Acres, UP (NS) **9 D2**
Blue Bell, UP (Sask.) **32 B2**
Blue Bell Corner, UP (NB) **12 A2**
Blueberry Creek, UP (BC) **34 B4**
Blueberry Mountain, UP (Alta.) **43 G3**
Blueberry River 205, IR (BC) **43 E2**
Blue Church, UP (Ont.) **17 C3**
Blue Cove, UP (Nfld.) **5 G2**
Blue Heron, UP (Sask.) **32 D3**
Blue Hill, UP (NB) **12 A3**
Blue-Hills, UP (Que.) **18 F4**
Blue Jay, UP (Sask.) **32 F3**
Blue Jay Subdivision, NUP (BC) **35 F1**
Blue Mountain, UP (NS) **8 A4**
Blue Mountain, UP (NS) **10 E1**
Blue Mountain, UP (Ont.) **24 E3**
Blue Mountain Bend, UP (NB) **12 B2**
Blue Mountain Settlement, UP (NB) **12 E1**
Blue Point, NUP (Ont.) **22 C1**
Blue Ridge, UP (Alta.) **33 C2**
Blue River, UP (BC) **36 G1**
Blue River 1, IR (BC) **45 C4**
Blue Rocks, UP (NS) **10 E2**
Blue Sac Road, UP (NS) **9 A2**
Blue Sea Corner, UP (NS) **9 C1**
Blue-Sea-Lake, UP (Que.) **18 D4**
Bluesky, UP (Alta.) **43 G3**
Blues Mills, UP (NS) **8 D3**
Blue Springs, UP (BC) **35 G2**
Bluevale, UP (Ont.) **23 C3**
Bluewater Beach, UP (Ont.) **23 E1**
Bluff Creek, UP (Man.) **29 G2**
Bluff Head Cove, UP (Nfld.) **3 D1**
Bluffton, UP (Alta.) **33 D4**
Blumenfeld, UP (Man.) **29 H4**
Blumengart, UP (Man.) **29 H4**
Blumenheim, UP (Sask.) **31 F1**
Blumenhof, UP (Sask.) **31 E3**
Blumenort, UP (Man.) **28 B2**
Blumenort, UP (Man.) **29 H4**
Blumenort, UP (Sask.) **31 E3**
Blumenthal, UP (Sask.) **32 D4**
Blyth, VL (Ont.) **23 B3**
Blytheswood, UP (Ont.) **22 B3**
Boat Basin, UP (BC) **39 F4**
Boat Harbour West, UP (Nfld.) **2 D3**
Boat Harbour West 37, IR (NS) **9 D1**
Bobby Cove, UP (Nfld.) **3 B1**
Bobcaygeon, VL (Ont.) **24 D4**
Bobs Lake, UP (Ont.) **17 A3**
Bocabec, UP (NB) **11 B3**
Bocabec Cove, UP (NB) **11 B3**
Bodmin, UP (Sask.) **32 C3**
Bodo, UP (Alta.) **31 B1**
Bogart, UP (Ont.) **24 G4**
Boggy Creek, UP (Man.) **29 D2**
Boggy Hall, UP (Alta.) **33 C4**
Bogies Beach, UP (Ont.) **23 B3**
Bognor, UP (Ont.) **23 D2**
Bogton, UP (Que.) **16 A4**
Boharm, UP (Sask.) **31 F3**
Boian, UP (Alta.) **33 F3**
Boiestown, UP (NB) **12 D4**
Boiler Beach, NUP (Ont.) **23 B2**
Boilleau, UP (Que.) **14 B4**
Boilleau, UP (Que.) **18 E4**
Bois-Blanc, UP (NB) **12 F1**
Bois-Blanc, UP (Que.) **16 A2**
Boisbriand, T (Que.) **17 F3**
Boisdale, UP (NS) **8 E3**
Bois-des-Filion, VL (Que.) **17 G3**
Bois-des-Hurons, UP (Que.) **16 D1**
Bois-Franc, UP (Que.) **18 D4**
Bois-Gagnon, UP (NB) **12 F1**
Boishébert, UP (NB) **12 G1**
Boisjoli, UP (Que.) **16 C3**
Boissevain, T (Man.) **29 F4**
Boisvert, UP (Que.) **18 A1**
Boisville, UP (Que.) **7 F1**
Bold Point, UP (BC) **37 B4**
Bolduc, UP (Que.) **16 G2**
Bolger, UP (Ont.) **24 A1**
Bolingbroke, UP (Ont.) **17 A3**
Bolney, UP (Sask.) **32 A3**
Bolsover, UP (Ont.) **23 G2**
Bolton-Centre, UP (Que.) **16 C4**
Bolton-Est, UP (Que.) **16 C4**
Bolton-Glen, UP (Que.) **16 C4**
Bolton-Ouest, UP (Que.) **16 C4**
Bon Accord, UP (NB) **12 A3**
Bon Accord, VL (Alta.) **33 E3**
Bon Air, UP (Ont.) **25 F2**
Bonanza, UP (Alta.) **43 F3**

Bonaparte 3, IR (BC) 36 D4
Bonar, UP (Alta.) 34 G1
Bonarlaw, UP (Ont.) 21 F1
Bonaventure, UP (Que.) 13 F3
Bonaventure-Est, UP (Que.) 13 F4
Bonaventure-Ouest, NUP (Que.) 13 F3
Bonavista, T (Nfld.) 3 G4
Bona Vista, UP (Ont.) 24 C2
Bon-Désir, UP (Que.) 14 E3
Bond Head, UP (Ont.) 21 A1
Bondiss, UP (Alta.) 33 E2
Bondi Village, UP (Ont.) 24 C2
Bon Echo, UP (Ont.) 24 G3
Bones Bay, UP (BC) 39 F1
Bonfield, UP (Ont.) 18 A4
Bongard, UP (Ont.) 21 G1
Bongard Corners, UP (Ont.) 21 G1
Bonlea, UP (Alta.) 33 F4
Bonnechere, UP (Ont.) 24 F1
Bonne-Espérance, UP (Que.) 5 F2
Bonneville, NUP (Que.) 16 D4
Bonney Road, UP (NB) 11 E2
Bonnie Doone, NUP (Ont.) 22 C1
Bonnington Falls, UP (BC) 34 B4
Bonny River, UP (NB) 11 C3
Bonnyville, T (Alta.) 33 G2
Bonnyville Beach, SV (Alta.) 33 G2
Bonsecours, UP (Que.) 16 C4
Bon-Secours, UP (NB) 12 G4
Bon Secours Beach, UP (Ont.) 21 A1
Bonshaw, UP (PEI) 7 C4
Bonville, UP (Ont.) 17 E2
Bookton, UP (Ont.) 22 F2
Boom Road, UP (NB) 12 E2
Bootahnie 15, IR (BC) 35 B1
Booth, UP (Ont.) 25 H1
Boothroyd 5A, IR (BC) 35 B2
Boothroyd 5B, IR (BC) 35 B2
Boothroyd 5C, IR (BC) 35 B2
Boothroyd 6A, IR (BC) 35 B2
Boothroyd 6B, IR (BC) 35 B2
Boothroyd 8A, IR (BC) 35 B2
Boothroyd 13, IR (BC) 35 B2
Boothville, UP (Ont.) 23 D3
Borden, T (PEI) 7 B4
Borden, VL (Sask.) 32 C4
Borden < Borden, CFB/BFC, UP (Ont.) 21 A1
Borden, CFB/BFC, MIL (Ont.) 21 A1
Borden Farm, UP (Ont.) 17 E4
Bordenwood, UP (Ont.) 24 G3
Borderland, UP (Sask.) 31 F4
Borgels Point, UP (NS) 10 E2
Boring Ranch, UP (BC) 43 D2
Borneo, UP (NS) 9 F2
Bornholm, UP (Ont.) 23 C4
Bornish, UP (Ont.) 22 D1
Borradaile, UP (Alta.) 33 G3
Borups Corners, UP (Ont.) 27 B2
Boscobel, UP (Que.) 16 C3
Boscombe, UP (Alta.) 33 F2
Boscoville, UP (Que.) 18 F4
Boskung, UP (Ont.) 24 C3
Boston Bar, UP (BC) 35 B2
Boston Bar 1A, IR (BC) 35 B3
Boston Bar 8, IR (BC) 35 B2
Boston Bar 9, IR (BC) 35 B2
Boston Bar 10, IR (BC) 35 B2
Boston Bar 11, IR (BC) 35 B3
Boston Creek, UP (Ont.) 26 F2
Boston Flats, UP (BC) 36 D4
Boswarlos, UP (Nfld.) 4 B2
Boswell, UP (BC) 34 C4
Boswell, UP (BC) 41 F4
Bosworth, UP (Ont.) 23 D3
Botany, UP (Ont.) 22 C3
Botha, VL (Alta.) 34 G1
Bothwell, T (Ont.) 22 C2
Bothwell, UP (PEI) 7 F3
Bothwell's Corner, UP (Ont.) 23 D2
Botreaux, UP (Que.) 17 G2
Botrel, UP (Que.) 15 D2
Botsford Portage, UP (NB) 7 A4
Bottle Lake 61B, IR (Man.) 29 E3
Bottrel, UP (Alta.) 34 E2
Botwood, T (Nfld.) 3 C2
Bouchard, UP (Que.) 15 C1
Boucher Office, NUP (NB) 15 H2
Boucherville, T (Que.) 17 H3
Bouchette, UP (Que.) 18 D4
Bouchie Lake, UP (BC) 40 C3
Boucks Hill, UP (Ont.) 17 D2
Boudreau, UP (NB) 7 A4
Boudreau-Corners, UP (Que.) 16 D4
Boudreau Road, UP (NB) 12 G1
Boudreau Village, UP (NB) 11 G1
Boudreauville, UP (NS) 8 D4
Boulanger, UP (Que.) 16 C4
Boularderie, UP (NS) 8 E3
Boularderie Centre, UP (NS) 8 E3
Boularderie East, UP (NS) 8 E3
Boularderie West, UP (NS) 8 E3
Boulay, UP (Que.) 13 B3
Boulder Creek 5, IR (BC) 36 F3
Boulder Island 25, IR (BC) 38 E1
Boulogne, UP (Que.) 16 B3
Boulter, UP (Ont.) 24 F2
Boundary, UP (NB) 15 G2
Boundary, UP (YT) 45 A2
Boundary Creek, UP (NB) 11 G1
Boundary Falls, UP (BC) 35 G4
Boundary Park, UP (Man.) 30 C4
Bounty, VL (Sask.) 31 E2
Bourbonnais, UP (Que.) 15 B3
Bourdages, UP (Que.) 13 E3
Bourdages Corner, UP (Ont.) 26 B3
Bourdeau, UP (Ont.) 24 B2
Bourgault, UP (Que.) 15 D2
Bourgeois, UP (NB) 7 A3
Bourgeois Mills, UP (NB) 7 A4
Bourget, UP (Ont.) 17 D1
Bourg-Louis, UP (Que.) 18 H3
Bourkes, UP (Ont.) 26 F2
Bournemouth, UP (Sask.) 32 C3
Bournival, UP (Que.) 16 B1
Bout-du-Monde, UP (Que.) 16 B1
Boutiliers Point, UP (NS) 9 A4
Bow City, UP (Alta.) 34 G3
Bowden, VL (Alta.) 34 E1
Bowell, UP (Alta.) 31 A3
Bowen Bay, UP (BC) 38 F2
Bowen Corner, UP (Ont.) 24 F3
Bowen Island, UP (BC) 38 F2
Bowermans, UP (Ont.) 21 F2
Bowers Beach, NUP (Ont.) 23 E2
Bow Island, T (Alta.) 34 H3
Bowker, UP (Ont.) 27 E3
Bowling Green, UP (Ont.) 23 E3
Bowmanton, UP (Alta.) 31 B3
Bown, UP (Que.) 16 E3
Bowood, UP (Ont.) 22 D1
Bowser, UP (BC) 38 C2
Bowser's Corner, UP (Ont.) 25 B2
Bowsman, VL (Man.) 29 D1
Box Alder, UP (Ont.) 28 H4
Boxey < St Jacques – Coomb's Cove, UP (Nfld.) 2 B3
Boyds, UP (Ont.) 17 B2
Boyds Corner, UP (NB) 12 C4
Boyd's Cove, UP (Nfld.) 3 D2
Boyer, UP (Que.) 15 B3
Boyer, UP (Que.) 18 E4
Boyer, UP (Alta.) 44 A3
Boyer 164, IR (Alta.) 44 A3
Boyle, UP (Ont.) 21 B4
Boyle, VL (Alta.) 33 E2
Boylston, UP (NS) 9 G2
Boyne Lake, UP (Alta.) 33 F2
Boynton, UP (Que.) 16 D4
Bracebridge, T (Ont.) 25 H4
Bracken, VL (Sask.) 31 D4
Brackenrig, UP (Ont.) 24 B2
Brackley, UP (PEI) 7 C4
Brackley Beach, UP (PEI) 7 C3
Brackley Point, UP (PEI) 7 C3
Brada, UP (Sask.) 32 B4
Braddock, UP (Sask.) 31 E3
Bradens Bay, UP (Ont.) 24 B4
Bradford, T (Ont.) 21 A1
Bradford Marsh, NUP (Ont.) 21 A1
Bradley, UP (Ont.) 23 C2
Bradley, UP (Ont.) 22 B2
Bradley Corner, UP (NB) 12 A4
Brador, UP (Que.) 5 G2
Bradshaw, UP (Ont.) 17 A3
Bradshaw, UP (Ont.) 22 B2
Bradwardine, UP (Man.) 29 E3
Bradwell, VL (Sask.) 31 F1
Brady Lake, UP (Ont.) 24 C3
Brady Ranch, UP (BC) 43 D2
Brae, UP (PEI) 7 A3
Braeburn, UP (Alta.) 43 G4
Braeburn, UP (YT) 45 B3
Brae Harbour, UP (PEI) 7 A3
Braemar, UP (Ont.) 22 F1
Braemar Heights, UP (BC) 38 E4
Braeshore, UP (NS) 9 D1
Braeside, UP (BC) 40 B1
Braeside, VL (Ont.) 17 B1
Bragg Creek, UP (Alta.) 34 E2
Braim, UP (Alta.) 33 E4
Brainard, UP (Alta.) 43 F4
Brainerd, UP (Man.) 28 B1
Brake's Cove, UP (Nfld.) 5 F4
Bralorne, UP (BC) 37 G2
Bramber, UP (NS) 9 A2
Brampton, C (Ont.) 21 A2
Brancepeth, UP (Sask.) 32 E4
Branch, COMM (Nfld.) 2 F4
Branch LaHave, UP (NS) 10 E2
Branchton, UP (Ont.) 22 G1
Brandon, C (Man.) 29 F4
Brandon, UP (BC) 34 B4
Brandon Hills, UP (Man.) 29 F4
Brandon North, UP (Man.) 29 F3
Brandy Point, UP (Ont.) 23 C4
Brandywine Falls, UP (BC) 37 F4
Brant, UP (Alta.) 34 F3
Brantford, C (Ont.) 22 G1
Brantville, UP (NB) 12 G1
Bras-d'Apic, UP (Que.) 15 D3
Bras d'Or, UP (NS) 8 E3
Brass Hill, UP (NS) 10 B4
Bratton, UP (Sask.) 31 E2
Brauns Island, NUP (BC) 42 E4
Bray Lake, UP (Ont.) 24 B1
Brazeau Dam, UP (Alta.) 33 C4
Brazil Lake, UP (NS) 10 B3
Breac Brook, UP (NS) 8 E4
Breadalbane, UP (PEI) 7 C3
Breadalbane, UP (Ont.) 17 E1
Breadalbane, UP (NB) 11 C3
Breakeyville, UP (Que.) 15 G4
Breau Creek, UP (NB) 7 A4
Breault, UP (Que.) 16 C2
Breault, NUP (Ont.) 26 C3
Breau Road, UP (NB) 12 F2
Breau-Village, UP (NB) 12 G4
Brébeuf, UP (Que.) 18 E4
Brèche-à-Manon, UP (Que.) 13 H3
Brechin, UP (Ont.) 23 G2
Brechin Beach, UP (Ont.) 23 G2
Brechin Point, UP (Ont.) 23 G2
Breckenridge, UP (Que.) 17 D3
Bredenbury, T (Sask.) 29 D2
Bredin, UP (Alta.) 43 G4
Bremen, UP (Sask.) 31 F1
Bremner, UP (Alta.) 33 E3
Brem River < Salmon Bay 3, UP (BC) 37 C3
Brennan Creek, NUP (BC) 36 G3
Brennan Harbour, UP (Ont.) 25 B1
Brennan-Hills, UP (Que.) 18 D4
Brent, UP (Ont.) 18 A4
Brentha, UP (Ont.) 26 F2
Brenton, UP (NS) 10 A3
Brent's Cove, COMM (Nfld.) 3 B1
Brentwood, UP (NS) 9 C2
Brentwood, UP (Ont.) 21 A1
Brereton Lake, UP (Man.) 28 D1
Bresaylor, UP (Sask.) 32 B4
Breslau, UP (Ont.) 23 D4
Brest, UP (NB) 12 G3
Bretagne, UP (Que.) 15 E2
Bretagneville, UP (NB) 12 G3
Brethour, UP (Ont.) 26 F2
Breton, VL (Alta.) 33 D4
Bretona, UP (Alta.) 33 E3
Breton Cove, UP (NS) 8 E2
Bretville Junction, UP (Alta.) 33 E3
Brew Bay, UP (BC) 38 D1
Brewer, UP (Sask.) 29 C2
Brewer Creek, UP (YT) 45 A2
Brewer Lake, UP (Ont.) 17 B4
Brewers Mills, UP (NB) 11 B1
Brewers Mills, UP (Ont.) 17 B4
Brexton, UP (BC) 37 G2
Breynat, UP (Alta.) 33 E1
Briargreen, UP (Ont.) 17 D4
Briar Lake, UP (NS) 10 B3
Briarlea, UP (Sask.) 32 D3
Briar Ridge, UP (BC) 43 F4
Briars Park, UP (Ont.) 21 B1
Brickley, UP (Ont.) 21 E1
Brickton, UP (NS) 10 C1
Brickyard Road, UP (NS) 8 F3
Bridal Falls, UP (BC) 35 A4
Brideau Settlement, NUP (NB) 12 G1
Bridesville, UP (BC) 35 F4
Bridge End, UP (Ont.) 17 F2
Bridgeford, UP (Sask.) 31 F2
Bridge Lake, UP (BC) 36 E3
Bridgenorth, UP (Ont.) 21 D1
Bridgeport, UP (Nfld.) 3 D2
Bridge River 1, IR (BC) 37 H2
Bridge River 2, IR (BC) 36 C4
Bridgetown, T (NS) 10 C1
Bridgetown, UP (PEI) 7 E4
Bridgetown, UP (Que.) 17 G2
Bridgeview, UP (Alta.) 43 G4
Bridgeville, UP (NS) 9 D2
Bridgewater, T (NS) 10 E2
Briercrest, VL (Sask.) 31 G3
Brièreville, UP (Alta.) 33 F2
Brier Hill, UP (Ont.) 17 B3
Brierly Brook, UP (NS) 8 B4
Brierly Brook Back Road, UP (NS) 8 B4
Brigade Lake, UP (BC) 35 D1
Brig Bay, UP (Nfld.) 5 G2
Brigden, UP (Ont.) 22 B2
Briggs, UP (Alta.) 33 D4
Briggs Corner, UP (NB) 11 E1
Briggs Corner, UP (NB) 12 B4
Briggs Corner, UP (NB) 12 A4
Briggs Spur, UP (Man.) 29 E1
Brigham, UP (Que.) 16 B4
Brigham Creek 3, IR (BC) 40 C4
Bright, UP (Ont.) 22 F1
Brightbank, UP (Alta.) 33 D3
Brightholme, UP (Sask.) 32 D4
Brighton, UP (Nfld.) 3 B2
Brighton, UP (NS) 10 B2
Brighton, VL (Ont.) 21 E2
Brighton Beach, UP (Ont.) 21 B1
Bright Sand, UP (Sask.) 32 B3
Brights Grove, UP (Ont.) 22 C1
Brightside, UP (Ont.) 17 A2
Brightstone, UP (Man.) 30 C4
Brightview, UP (Alta.) 33 D4
Brigus, T (Nfld.) 2 G2
Brigus Junction, UP (Nfld.) 2 G3
Brigus South, UP (Nfld.) 2 H3
Brill, UP (Que.) 16 C4
Brilliant, UP (BC) 34 B4
Brinka, UP (Ont.) 28 F1
Brinkman's Corners, UP (Ont.) 25 D4
Brinsley, UP (Ont.) 22 D1
Brinston, UP (Ont.) 17 D2
Brisbane, UP (Ont.) 23 E3
Brisco, UP (BC) 34 C2
Brise-du-Lac, UP (Que.) 18 F4
Brisson, UP (Ont.) 17 D2
Bristol, UP (PEI) 7 D3
Bristol, UP (Que.) 17 B1
Bristol, UP (Man.) 28 B2
Bristol, VL (NB) 12 A3
Bristol-les-Mines, UP (Que.) 17 B1
Bristol-Ridge, UP (Que.) 17 B1
Bristol's Hope, UP (Nfld.) 2 G2
Britainville, UP (Ont.) 25 B2
Britannia, UP (Nfld.) 2 F1
Britannia, UP (Ont.) 24 C2
Britannia Beach, UP (BC) 38 F1
Britannia Creek, UP (YT) 45 A3
British Harbour, UP (Nfld.) 2 F1
British Settlement, UP (NB) 11 H1
Britt, UP (Ont.) 25 F2
Britton, UP (Ont.) 23 C4
Broadacres, UP (Sask.) 31 C1
Broadbent, UP (Ont.) 24 A2
Broad Cove, UP (NS) 10 E3
Broad Cove, UP (Nfld.) 2 F2
Broad Cove, UP (Nfld.) 2 E2
Broad Cove < Small Point – Kingston – Broad Cove – Blackhead – Adams Cove, UP (Nfld.) 2 G2
Broad Cove Banks, UP (NS) 8 C3
Broad Cove Chapel, UP (NS) 8 C3
Broad Cove Marsh, UP (NS) 8 C3
Broad Valley, UP (Man.) 29 H2
Broadview, T (Sask.) 29 C3
Broadway, UP (NS) 8 A4
Brochet < Brochet 197, UP (Man.) 44 G3
Brochet 197, IR (Man.) 44 G3
Brock, VL (Sask.) 31 D2
Brocket, UP (Alta.) 34 E4
Brock Gardens, UP (Ont.) 22 H1
Brockington, UP (Sask.) 32 E4
Brockley, UP (Ont.) 22 E2
Brocksden, UP (Ont.) 22 F1
Brockton, UP (PEI) 7 A2
Brockville, C (Ont.) 17 C3
Brockway, UP (NB) 11 B2
Broderick, VL (Sask.) 31 E2
Brodeur, UP (Que.) 18 D4
Brodhagen, UP (Ont.) 23 C4
Brodie, UP (Ont.) 17 F1
Brokenhead, UP (Man.) 28 B1
Brokenhead 4, IR (Man.) 30 C4
Brome, VL (Que.) 16 C4
Bromhead, UP (Sask.) 29 B4
Bromley, UP (Ont.) 17 A1
Bromont, T (Que.) 16 B4
Bromptonville, T (Que.) 16 D3
Broncho, UP (Sask.) 31 E4
Bronson, UP (Ont.) 24 F3
Bronson Settlement, UP (NB) 11 E1
Brookbury, UP (Que.) 16 E3
Brookdale, UP (NS) 9 A1
Brookdale, UP (Man.) 29 F3
Brookdale, UP (Que.) 18 E4
Brooke, UP (Ont.) 23 C1
Brooke, UP (Ont.) 17 B3
Brookfield, UP (NS) 9 C2
Brookfield, UP (PEI) 7 C4
Brooking, UP (Sask.) 31 H4
Brookland, UP (NS) 9 D2
Brooklet, UP (Que.) 17 G2
Brooklyn, UP (NS) 10 D3
Brooklyn, UP (NS) 9 A3
Brooklyn, UP (Nfld.) 3 F4
Brooklyn, UP (NS) 10 C1
Brooklyn, UP (NS) 10 A3
Brooklyn, UP (PEI) 7 D4
Brooklyn, UP (PEI) 7 A2
Brooklyn, UP (NB) 7 A4
Brooklyn Corner, UP (NS) 11 G3
Brooklyn Road, UP (NB) 7 A4
Brooklyn Street, UP (NS) 11 G3
Brookmere, UP (BC) 35 C3
Brook Road, UP (NS) 9 C1
Brooks, T (Alta.) 34 G3
Brooks Brook, UP (YT) 45 B3
Brooksby, UP (Sask.) 32 F4
Brooksdale, UP (Ont.) 22 E1
Brookside, UP (NS) 9 B4
Brookside, UP (Nfld.) 2 D3
Brookside, UP (NS) 9 C2
Brookside, UP (Ont.) 21 E2
Brooks Landing, UP (Ont.) 25 F3
Brooks Mill, UP (Ont.) 24 C2
Brookvale, UP (NS) 9 C3
Brookvale, UP (PEI) 7 C4
Brookvale, UP (NB) 11 E1
Brook Village, UP (NS) 8 C3
Brookville, UP (NB) 12 A4
Brookville, UP (NS) 8 A4
Brookville, UP (NS) 11 G2
Brookville, UP (NB) 11 G2
Broomhill, UP (Man.) 29 E4
Brophy, UP (NS) 8 B4
Brora, UP (Sask.) 31 G3
Brossard, T (Que.) 17 H4
Brosseau, UP (Alta.) 33 F3
Brotherston, UP (Ont.) 23 C3
Broughton, UP (NS) 8 F3
Broughton Island, UP (NWT) 46 G1
Broughton-Station, UP (Que.) 15 B4
Brouse, UP (BC) 34 B3
Brouseville, UP (Ont.) 17 D3
Brower, UP (Ont.) 26 E1
Brown, UP (Man.) 29 G4
Brownfield, UP (Alta.) 34 H1
Brown Hill, UP (Ont.) 21 B1
Brown House Corner, UP (Ont.) 17 F2
Browning, UP (Sask.) 29 C4
Brownings Landing, UP (NWT) 45 D3
Brownlee, VL (Sask.) 31 F2
Brownleigh, UP (Que.) 16 D3
Brown's Arm, UP (Nfld.) 3 C2
Browns Brae, UP (Ont.) 24 C2
Brownsburg, VL (Que.) 17 F1
Browns Corner, UP (NB) 11 D2
Browns Cove, UP (Nfld.) 5 G4
Brownsdale, UP (Nfld.) 2 G1
Browns Flat, UP (NB) 11 D2
Brownsville, UP (Ont.) 22 F2
Brownsville, UP (NS) 8 A4
Browns Yard, UP (NB) 12 F3
Brownvale, UP (Alta.) 43 H3
Broxburn, UP (Alta.) 34 F4
Bruce, UP (Alta.) 33 F3
Brucedale, UP (Ont.) 23 E4
Bruce Farm, UP (Ont.) 17 D4
Brucefield, UP (Ont.) 23 B4
Bruce Lake, UP (Ont.) 30 D4
Bruce Mines, T (Ont.) 26 B4
Bruces, UP (Ont.) 22 G1
Bruce Station, UP (Ont.) 26 B4
Bruceton, UP (Ont.) 24 F2
Brudenell, UP (PEI) 7 D4
Brudenell, UP (Ont.) 24 F2
Bruderheim, VL (Alta.) 33 E3
Brule, UP (NS) 9 C1
Brûlé, UP (Alta.) 40 H2
Brûlé Mines, UP (Alta.) 40 H2
Brule Point, UP (NS) 9 C1
Brule Shore, UP (NS) 9 C1
Brumsfield, UP (Ont.) 24 G1
Brunkild, UP (Man.) 29 H4
Brunner, UP (Ont.) 23 C4
Bruno, T (Sask.) 31 G1
Brunswick, UP (Ont.) 21 D1
Brunswick, UP (BC) 38 F2
Brunswick, UP (BC) 41 F4
Brunswick Mines, UP (NB) 12 E1
Brussels, VL (Ont.) 23 C3
Bruxelles, UP (Man.) 29 G4
Bryanston, UP (Ont.) 22 E1
Bryant, UP (Sask.) 29 C4
Bryants Corner, UP (NB) 12 F3
Bryants Cove, UP (Nfld.) 2 G2
Bryenton, UP (NB) 12 E3
Brynmarl, UP (BC) 38 D2
Bryson, VL (Que.) 17 A1
Brysonville, UP (Que.) 17 G2
B-Say-Tah, SV (Sask.) 29 B2
Buccaneer Bay, UP (BC) 38 D2
Buchanan, VL (Sask.) 29 C1
Buchans (p), T (Nfld.) 4 F1
Buchans (p), UP (Nfld.) 4 F1
Buchans Junction, UP (Nfld.) 4 G1
Buck Creek, UP (Alta.) 33 C4
Buckfield, UP (NS) 10 D2
Buckham's Bay, UP (Ont.) 17 B1
Buckhorn, UP (Ont.) 24 D4
Buckhorn, UP (BC) 40 C2
Buckingham, C (Que.) 17 D1
Buck Lake, UP (Alta.) 33 C4
Buck Lake, UP (Ont.) 17 A3
Buck Lake 133C, IR (Alta.) 33 C4
Buckland, UP (Que.) 15 C3
Buckland, UP (Sask.) 32 D3
Buckland-Est, UP (Que.) 15 C3
Bucklaw, UP (NS) 8 D3
Buckley Bay, UP (BC) 38 C2
Buckleys Corner, UP (NS) 11 G3
Buckley Settlement, UP (NB) 11 F1
Bucktum 4, IR (BC) 35 B2
Buckwheat Corner, UP (NS) 8 D3
Buctouche, VL (NB) 12 G3
Buctouche 16, IR (NB) 12 G4
Buctouche Baie, NUP (NB) 12 G3
Bucyrus, UP (Ont.) 26 B3
Budd, UP (Man.) 30 A2
Budd Mills, UP (Ont.) 24 D4
Budd's Point 20D, IR (Sask.) 32 H2
Buena Vista, SV (Sask.) 31 G2
Buena Vista Park, UP (Ont.) 23 G1
Buffalo, UP (Alta.) 31 B2
Buffalo Creek, UP (BC) 36 D2
Buffalo Gap, UP (Sask.) 31 G4
Buffalo Head Prairie, UP (Alta.) 44 A3
Buffalo Horn, UP (Sask.) 31 E4
Buffalo Lake, UP (Alta.) 43 G4
Buffalo Narrows, UP (Sask.) 44 D4
Buffalo Point 36, IR (Man.) 28 E3
Buffalo River, UP (NWT) 44 B1
Buffalo View, UP (Alta.) 33 G4
Buford, UP (Alta.) 33 D3
Bugeaud, UP (Que.) 13 F3
Buick, UP (BC) 43 E2
Bulgers Corners, UP (Ont.) 24 G1
Bulkley 1, IR (BC) 42 F3
Bulkley House, UP (BC) 42 G3
Bulkley River 19, IR (BC) 42 F4
Buller, UP (Ont.) 23 H1
Bulley's Cove, UP (Nfld.) 3 C2
Bullhead, UP (Man.) 30 C4
Bull Lake, UP (NB) 11 B1
Bull Moose Hill, UP (NB) 11 E2
Bullock, UP (Ont.) 24 H2
Bullocks Corners, UP (Ont.) 22 H1
Bullpound, UP (Alta.) 34 G2
Bull River, UP (BC) 34 D4
Bulls Creek, UP (NB) 11 A1
Bullshead, UP (Alta.) 31 B3
Bulwark, UP (Alta.) 34 G1
Bulwer, UP (Que.) 16 D4
Bulyea, VL (Sask.) 31 G2
Bummers Flat 6, IR (BC) 34 D4
Bummers' Roost, UP (Ont.) 25 H2
Bunbury, VL (PEI) 7 D4
Bunclody, UP (Man.) 29 F4
Bunessan, UP (Ont.) 23 D2
Bungay, UP (PEI) 7 C3
Bunker Hill, UP (Ont.) 17 E2
Buntzen Bay, UP (BC) 38 G2
Bunyan, UP (Ont.) 22 B2
Bunyan's Cove, UP (Nfld.) 3 E4
Buoyant, UP (Alta.) 34 F2
Burchell Lake, UP (Ont.) 27 C3
Burchills Flats, UP (NB) 11 E2
Bur Creek, UP (Ont.) 22 G1
Burdett, VL (Alta.) 34 H3
Burditt Lake, UP (Ont.) 28 H4
Bures, UP (Sask.) 31 G4
Burford, UP (Ont.) 22 G1
Burgeo, T (Nfld.) 4 D4
Burgerville, UP (Que.) 18 D4
Burgess Mines, UP (Ont.) 24 F2
Burgess Settlement, UP (NB) 12 A2
Burgess Subdivision, NUP (Ont.) 22 F1
Burgessville, UP (Ont.) 22 F1
Burgis, UP (Sask.) 29 C2
Burgoyne, UP (Ont.) 23 C2
Burgoynes Cove, UP (Nfld.) 2 F1
Burin, T (Nfld.) 2 C3
Burke Settlement, UP (Ont.) 17 A3
Burks-Corners, UP (Que.) 17 D1
Burk's Falls, VL (Ont.) 24 B1
Burleigh Falls, UP (Ont.) 24 E4
Burlington, C (Ont.) 21 A3
Burlington, COMM (Nfld.) 3 B1
Burlington, UP (NS) 11 G3
Burlington, UP (PEI) 7 B3
Burmis, UP (Alta.) 34 E4
Burnaby, DM (BC) 38 F2
Burnaby, UP (Ont.) 21 B4
Burnbank, UP (Man.) 29 D3
Burnbrae, UP (Ont.) 21 E1
Burnet, UP (Que.) 17 D3
Burnham, UP (Sask.) 31 E3
Burnley, UP (Ont.) 21 E1
Burns, UP (Ont.) 23 D4
Burnside, UP (Nfld.) 3 F3
Burnside, UP (NS) 9 C2
Burnside, UP (Ont.) 23 F1
Burnside, UP (Man.) 29 G3
Burns Lake, VL (BC) 42 G4
Burns Lake 18, IR (BC) 42 G4
Burnstown, UP (Ont.) 17 A1
Burnsville, UP (NB) 12 F1
Burnt Church, UP (NB) 12 F2
Burnt Church 14, IR (NB) 12 F2
Burnt Cliff Islands 20, IR (BC) 42 C4
Burntcoat, UP (NS) 9 B2
Burnt Cove, UP (Nfld.) 2 H3
Burnt Cove, UP (Nfld.) 3 D2
Burnt-Creek, UP (Que.) 6 C3
Burnt Hill, UP (NB) 11 B3
Burnt Hills, UP (Ont.) 17 B3
Burnt Island, UP (Ont.) 25 A2
Burnt Island, UP (Nfld.) 2 D3
Burnt Islands, LID (Nfld.) 4 B4
Burntland Brook, UP (NB) 12 B2
Burnt Point, UP (Nfld.) 2 G1
Burnt Point, UP (PEI) 7 E4
Burnt River, UP (Ont.) 23 H1
Burpee, UP (Ont.) 25 B2
Burpees Corner, UP (NB) 11 D1
Burr, UP (Sask.) 31 G1
Burr, UP (Ont.) 21 F1
Burrard Inlet 3, IR (BC) 38 F2
Burridge, UP (Ont.) 17 A3
Burriss, UP (Ont.) 28 H4
Burritts Rapids, UP (Ont.) 17 C2
Burrows, UP (Sask.) 29 D3
Burstall, VL (Sask.) 31 B3
Burt, UP (Sask.) 31 G3
Burtch, UP (Ont.) 22 G1
Burton, UP (NB) 11 D1
Burton, UP (BC) 34 A3
Burton, UP (PEI) 7 A2
Burton, UP (Ont.) 21 C1
Burtons, UP (NS) 9 B2
Burtons Cove < Hampden, UP (Nfld.) 5 G4
Burtonsville, UP (Alta.) 33 D3
Burtts Corner, UP (NB) 11 C1
Burwash, UP (Ont.) 25 E1
Burwash Flats, UP (YT) 45 A3
Burwash Landing, UP (YT) 45 A3
Bury, UP (Que.) 16 E3
Burys Green, UP (Ont.) 23 H1
Busby, UP (Alta.) 33 D3
Bushell, UP (Sask.) 44 D2
Bushell Park < Moose Jaw, CFB/BFC, UP (Sask.) 31 G3
Bushe River 207, IR (Alta.) 44 A3
Bush Glen, UP (Ont.) 17 D2
Bush Island, UP (NS) 10 E2
Bushville, UP (NB) 12 F2
Busy Head Corner, UP (Alta.) 33 G4
Busy Bee Corners, UP (Ont.) 22 A4
Butedale, UP (BC) 41 E2
Butler, UP (Man.) 29 D4
Butlerville, UP (Nfld.) 2 G2
Butte, UP (Alta.) 34 D1
Butte-d'Or, UP (NB) 12 F1
Buttermilk Falls, UP (Ont.) 24 D3
Butternut Bay, UP (Ont.) 17 C3
Butte-St-Pierre, UP (Sask.) 32 A3
Button's Corners, UP (Ont.) 26 F3
Buzwah < Wikwemikong Unceded 26, UP (Ont.) 25 C2
Buzzard, UP (Sask.) 32 A4
Byemoor, UP (Alta.) 34 G1
Bylot, UP (Man.) 46 B4
Byng Inlet, UP (Ont.) 25 F2
Byrnedale, UP (Ont.) 22 B3
Byrnes Road, UP (PEI) 7 D4

C

Cabana, UP (Sask.) 32 B2
Cabano, T (Que.) 15 F1
Cabin Lake, UP (Alta.) 34 H2
Cable Head East, UP (PEI) 7 E3
Cable Head West, UP (PEI) 7 D3
Cabri, T (Sask.) 31 D3
Cache Bay, T (Ont.) 25 G1
Cache Creek, VL (BC) 36 D4
Cacouna 22, IR (Que.) 14 E4
Cacouna-Est, UP (Que.) 14 E4
Cacouna-Station, UP (Que.) 14 E4
Cacouna-Sud, UP (Que.) 14 E4
Cactus Lake, UP (Sask.) 31 C1
Caddy Lake, UP (Man.) 28 E2
Caderette, UP (Ont.) 25 G1
Cadillac, T (Que.) 18 B2
Cadillac, VL (Sask.) 31 E4
Cadman Corner, UP (NB) 7 B4
Cadmus, UP (Ont.) 21 C1
Cadogan, UP (Alta.) 33 G4
Cadomin, UP (Alta.) 33 A4
Cadot, UP (Que.) 18 F4
Cadotte Lake, UP (Alta.) 44 A4
Cadurcis, UP (Man.) 29 F3
Caesarea, UP (Ont.) 21 C1
Cahilty, UP (BC) 36 F4
Cahoose 8, IR (BC) 41 H2
Cahoose 10, IR (BC) 40 A3
Cahoose 12, IR (BC) 41 H2
Cahore, UP (Ont.) 17 D2
Cails Mills, UP (NB) 12 F3
Cains Island, UP (Nfld.) 4 B4
Cains Mountain, UP (NS) 8 D3
Cains Point, UP (NB) 12 F1
Cainsville, UP (Ont.) 22 G1
Caintown, UP (Ont.) 17 C3
Cairngorm, UP (Ont.) 22 D2
Cairns, UP (Alta.) 33 G4
Cairo, UP (Ont.) 22 C2
Caissie-Village, UP (NB) 12 G3
Caistor Centre, UP (Ont.) 21 A4
Caistor Corners, UP (Ont.) 21 A4
Caistorville, UP (Ont.) 21 A4
Caithness, UP (BC) 34 D4
Caithness, UP (NB) 11 C3
Calabogie, UP (Ont.) 17 A2
Calahoo, UP (Alta.) 33 D3
Calais, UP (Alta.) 43 H4
Calamité-River, UP (Que.) 18 A1
Calder, VL (Sask.) 29 D2
Calderbank, UP (Sask.) 31 E3
Calderwood, UP (Ont.) 23 D3
Caldwell, UP (NB) 12 A2
Caldwell, UP (Que.) 17 B1
Caledon, T (Ont.) 23 F3
Caledonia, UP (NS) 10 D2
Caledonia, UP (NS) 9 E2
Caledonia, UP (PEI) 7 D4
Caledonia Front, UP (Ont.) 17 E1
Caledonia Junction, UP (NS) 10 D2
Caledonia Mills, UP (NS) 8 B4
Caledonia Mountain, UP (NB) 11 G1
Caledonia Springs, UP (Ont.) 17 E1
Calgary, C (Alta.) 34 E2
Calhoun, UP (NB) 11 G1
Caliento, UP (Man.) 28 B3
California, UP (Ont.) 17 B3
California, UP (Ont.) 17 A2
Californie, UP (Que.) 16 A1
Calipper Lake, UP (Ont.) 28 G3
Calixa-Lavallée, UP (Que.) 16 A3
Callander, UP (Ont.) 25 H1
Calley, UP (Sask.) 29 C2
Calling Lake, UP (Alta.) 33 E1
Calling River, UP (Alta.) 33 E1
Callison Ranch, UP (BC) 45 B4
Callum, UP (Ont.) 25 F1
Calmar, T (Alta.) 33 D3
Calmer < Point May (COMM), UP (Nfld.) 2 B4
Calm Lake, UP (Ont.) 27 B3
Calstock, UP (Ont.) 20 B4
Calthorpe, UP (Alta.) 31 B1
Calton, UP (Ont.) 22 F2
Calumet, UP (YT) 45 B2
Calumet, VL (Que.) 17 E1
Calvert, UP (Nfld.) 2 H3
Calway, UP (Que.) 15 B4
Camborne, UP (Ont.) 21 D2
Camborne, UP (BC) 34 B2
Cambray, UP (Ont.) 21 C1
Cambria, UP (Alta.) 34 G2
Cambridge, C (Ont.) 23 E4
Cambridge, UP (NS) 10 E1
Cambridge, UP (NS) 9 A2
Cambridge, UP (PEI) 7 E4
Cambridge 32, IR (NS) 10 D1
Cambridge Bay, UP (NWT) 45 F1
Cambridge-Narrows, VL (NB) 11 E1
Camden, UP (NS) 9 C2
Camden East, UP (Ont.) 17 A4
Camel Chute, UP (Ont.) 24 G2
Camelot Beach, UP (Ont.) 21 B4
Cameo, UP (Sask.) 32 D3
Cameron, UP (Ont.) 21 C1
Cameron, UP (Ont.) 21 E1
Cameron Bar 13, IR (BC) 35 A1
Cameron Beach, UP (NS) 9 B1
Cameron Falls, UP (Ont.) 27 E2
Cameron Heights, UP (BC) 38 C2
Cameron Hills, UP (NWT) 44 A2
Cameron Lake, UP (NS) 9 A3
Cameron Settlement, UP (NS) 9 E2
Camerons Mill, UP (NB) 12 F3
Camerons Mountain, UP (NS) 8 D4
Camerons Point, UP (Ont.) 17 F2
Camilla, UP (Ont.) 23 E3
Camlachie, UP (Ont.) 22 C1
Camlaren, UP (NWT) 45 F3
Campania, UP (Ont.) 23 E3
Camp Artaban, UP (BC) 38 F2
Camp Bay, UP (Nfld.) 5 H1
Campbell, UP (Alta.) 33 E3
Campbell-Corners, UP (Que.) 16 B4
Campbellcroft, UP (Ont.) 21 D1
Campbelldale, UP (NS) 8 F4
Campbellford, T (Ont.) 21 E1
Campbell Island < Bella Bella 1, UP (BC) 41 E3
Campbell Maxwell Front, UP (Ont.) 17 B4
Campbell River, DM (BC) 37 B4
Campbell River 11, IR (BC) 37 B4
Campbell's-Bay, VL (Que.) 17 A1
Campbells Beach, UP (Ont.) 23 G1
Campbells Corners, UP (Ont.) 17 C2
Campbells Cove, UP (PEI) 7 E3
Campbells Creek, UP (Nfld.) 4 B2
Campbell Settlement, UP (NB) 11 B1
Campbell Settlement, UP (NB) 11 E2
Campbell Settlement, UP (NB) 11 A1
Campbells Mountain, UP (NS) 8 D3
Campbells Siding, UP (NS) 9 C2
Campbellton, C (NB) 13 C4
Campbellton, T (Nfld.) 3 D2
Campbellton, UP (PEI) 7 A2
Campbellton, UP (PEI) 7 C3
Campbellton, UP (Ont.) 22 D2
Campbellton, UP (BC) 37 B4
Campbellton Road, UP (NS) 8 C3
Campbelltown, UP (Ont.) 21 D1
Campbellvale, NUP (Ont.) 22 D2
Camp Bigwee, UP (Ont.) 26 F3

Camp Boggy, UP (Nfld.) 2 B1
Camp Cayuga, UP (Ont.) 26 F3
Camp Chimo, UP (Ont.) 26 F3
Camp-Comfort, UP (Que.) 16 E3
Camp Creek, UP (Alta.) 33 D2
Camp Dundurn < Dundurn, Camp/Campement, UP (Sask.) 31 F1
Camper, UP (Man.) 29 G2
Camperdown, UP (NS) 10 E2
Camperdown, UP (Ont.) 23 E2
Camperville, UP (Man.) 29 E1
Camp Farewell, UP (NWT) 45 B1
Camp Harmony, UP (NB) 13 C4
Camp Kagawong, UP (Ont.) 23 H2
Camp-Kinkora, UP (Que.) 18 F4
Camp-Laclouwhi, UP (Que.) 18 F4
Camp-Marcel, UP (Que.) 18 F4
Camp McKinney, UP (BC) 35 F4
Camp Morton, UP (Man.) 30 C4
Camp Oconto, UP (Ont.) 17 A3
Camp-Ouareau, UP (Que.) 18 F4
Camp Robinson, UP (Ont.) 27 A1
Campsie, UP (Alta.) 33 D2
Camp Wanapitei, UP (Ont.) 26 F3
Camp Wegesegum, UP (NB) 11 E1
Camp White Bear, UP (Ont.) 26 F3
Camrose, C (Alta.) 33 E4
Camsell Portage, UP (Sask.) 44 D2
Cana, UP (Sask.) 29 C2
Canaan, UP (NS) 10 E1
Canaan, UP (NB) 12 G4
Canaan, UP (NS) 9 A4
Canaan, UP (NS) 10 B3
Canaan, UP (Ont.) 17 D1
Canaan Forks, UP (NB) 11 E1
Canaan Rapids, UP (NB) 11 E1
Canaan Road, UP (NB) 11 F1
Canada Creek, UP (NS) 11 G3
Canada Harbour, UP (Nfld.) 5 H3
Canal, UP (NB) 11 C3
Canal Flats, UP (BC) 34 C3
Canard, UP (NS) 11 H3
Canavoy, UP (PEI) 7 D3
Candiac, T (Que.) 17 H1
Candiac, UP (Sask.) 29 B3
Candle Lake, UP (Sask.) 32 E3
Cando, VL (Sask.) 31 D1
Cane, UP (Ont.) 26 F2
Canford, UP (BC) 35 C2
Canim Lake, UP (BC) 36 D2
Canim Lake 1, IR (BC) 36 D2
Canim Lake 2, IR (BC) 36 D2
Canim Lake 3, IR (BC) 36 D2
Canim Lake 4, IR (BC) 36 C2
Canim Lake 5, IR (BC) 36 E2
Canim Lake 6, IR (BC) 36 E2
Cankerville, UP (Ont.) 21 E1
Canmore, T (Alta.) 34 D2
Cann, UP (Que.) 18 F2
Cannamore, UP (Ont.) 17 D2
Cannell, UP (Alta.) 33 D3
Cannes, UP (NS) 8 D4
Cannifton, UP (Ont.) 21 F1
Canning, UP (NS) 11 H3
Canning, UP (Ont.) 22 F1
Cannings Cove, UP (Nfld.) 3 F4
Cannington, UP (Ont.) 21 C1
Canobie, UP (NB) 12 F1
Canobie South, UP (NB) 12 F1
Canoe Cove, UP (PEI) 7 C4
Canoe Creek 1, IR (BC) 36 B3
Canoe Creek 2, IR (BC) 36 B3
Canoe Creek 3, IR (BC) 36 B3
Canoe Lake, UP (Sask.) 32 B1
Canoe Lake, UP (NS) 8 F4
Canoe Lake, UP (Ont.) 24 D1
Canoe Lake 165, IR (Sask.) 32 B1
Canoe Lake 165A, IR (Sask.) 32 B1
Canoe Lake 165B, IR (Sask.) 32 B1
Canoe Narrows < Canoe Lake 165, UP (Sask.) 32 B1
Canoe River, UP (BC) 40 F3
Canoe River, UP (Sask.) 32 B1
Canol, UP (NWT) 45 C2
Canonto, UP (Ont.) 17 A2
Canoona 2, IR (BC) 41 E2
Canoose, UP (NB) 11 B2
Canopus, UP (Sask.) 31 F4
Canora, T (Sask.) 29 C1
Canso, T (NS) 9 H2
Cantal, UP (Sask.) 29 D4
Canterbury, UP (Que.) 16 E3
Canterbury, VL (NB) 11 A1
Cantic, UP (Que.) 16 A4
Cantin, UP (Que.) 15 G4
Canton, UP (Ont.) 21 D2
Canton, UP (NB) 12 A2
Canton-des-Roches, UP (Que.) 15 D2
Canton-Jetté, UP (Que.) 13 A3
Canton-Pelletier, UP (Que.) 18 H1
Cantuar, UP (Sask.) 31 D3
Cantyre, UP (Sask.) 32 H3
Canuck, UP (Sask.) 31 D4
Canwood, VL (Sask.) 32 D3
Canyon, UP (BC) 34 C4
Canyon, UP (YT) 45 A3
Canyon City, UP (BC) 42 D3
Canyon Creek, UP (Alta.) 33 C1
Canyon Lake 7, IR (BC) 40 A1
Cap-à-la-Baleine, NUP (Que.) 13 B1
Cap-à-la-Branche, UP (Que.) 15 C2
Cap-à-l'Aigle, VL (Que.) 15 D1
Capasin, UP (Sask.) 32 C3
Cap-au-Renard, UP (Que.) 13 D1
Cap-aux-Corbeaux, UP (Que.) 15 C1
Cap-aux-Meules, VL (Que.) 7 F1
Cap-aux-Oies, UP (Que.) 15 D1
Cap-Bateau, UP (NB) 13 H4
Cap-Brulé, UP (NB) 7 A4
Cap-Chat, T (Que.) 13 C1
Cap-de-Cocagne, UP (NB) 12 H4
Cap-de-la-Madeleine, C (Que.) 16 C1
Cap-de-Rabast, UP (Que.) 19 H3
Cap-de-St-Louis, UP (NB) 12 G3
Cap-des-Caissie, UP (NB) 12 H4
Cape Anguille, UP (Nfld.) 4 A3
Cape Auguet, UP (NS) 9 H2
Cape Breton, UP (NB) 11 G1
Cape Broyle, UP (Nfld.) 2 H3
Cape Charles, UP (Nfld.) 5 H1
Cape Chin, UP (Ont.) 25 D4
Cape Chin North, UP (Ont.) 25 D4
Cape Chin South, UP (Ont.) 25 D4
Cape Cove, UP (Nfld.) 3 E1
Cape Croker < Cape Croker 27, UP (Ont.) 23 C1
Cape Croker 27, IR (Ont.) 23 C1
Cape Croker Hunting Ground 60B, IR (Ont.) 25 D4
Cape Dauphin, UP (NS) 8 E3
Cape Dorset, UP (NWT) 46 E2
Cape Dyer, UP (NWT) 46 G1
Cape Egmont, UP (PEI) 7 A3
Cape Enrage, UP (NB) 11 G2
Cape Forchu, UP (NS) 10 A3
Cape Freels, UP (Nfld.) 3 F2
Cape Freels North, UP (Nfld.) 3 F2
Cape George, UP (NS) 8 B4
Cape George Point, UP (NS) 8 B4
Cape-Hopes-Advance, UP (Que.) 46 F3
Cape Jack, UP (NS) 8 C4
Cape John, UP (NS) 9 C1
Cape la Hune, UP (Nfld.) 4 F4
Cape Lazo, NUP (BC) 38 C1
Capelton, UP (Que.) 16 D4
Cape Mudge 10, IR (BC) 37 B4
Cape Negro, UP (NS) 10 C4
Cape Norman, UP (Nfld.) 5 H2
Cape North, UP (NS) 8 E1
Cape Parry, UP (NWT) 45 D1
Cape Race, UP (Nfld.) 2 G4
Cape Ray, UP (Nfld.) 4 A4
Cape St George < Cape St George – Petit Jardin – Grand Jardin – De Grau – Marches Point – Loretto, UP (Nfld.) 4 A2
Cape St George – Petit Jardin – Grand Jardin – De Grau – Marches Point – Loretto, COMM (Nfld.) 4 A2
Cape St Marys, UP (NS) 10 A3
Cape Smith, UP (NWT) 46 E3
Cape Spear, UP (NB) 7 B4
Cape Spencer, UP (NB) 11 E3
Cape Station, UP (NB) 11 G1
Cape Tormentine, UP (NB) 7 B4
Cape Traverse, UP (PEI) 7 B4
Cape Traverse Landing, UP (PEI) 7 B4
Cape Wolfe, UP (PEI) 7 A3
Capilano 5, IR (BC) 38 F2
Caplan, UP (Que.) 13 E3
Caplan-Ouest, UP (Que.) 13 E3
Cap La Ronde, UP (NS) 8 D4
Cap Lemoyne, UP (NS) 8 D2
Caplin Cove, UP (Nfld.) 2 H1
Caplin Cove, UP (Nfld.) 2 F1
Cap-Lumière, UP (NB) 12 G3
Cappahayden < Renews – Cappahayden, UP (Nfld.) 2 H4
Cap-Pelé, VL (NB) 7 A4
Cappon, UP (Alta.) 31 B2
Capreol, T (Ont.) 26 E4
Caprona, UP (Alta.) 34 F1
Cap-Rouge, UP (Que.) 15 F4
Cap-St-Ignace, UP (Que.) 15 C2
Cap-St-Ignace-Station, UP (Que.) 15 C2
Cap-Santé, UP (Que.) 16 D1
Cap-Seize, UP (Que.) 13 D1
Caps-St-Fidèle, UP (Que.) 14 D4
Capstan Island, UP (Nfld.) 5 G2
Capstick, UP (NS) 8 E1
Cap-Tourmente, UP (Que.) 15 C2
Capucins, UP (Que.) 13 C1
Cap-Vert, NUP (Que.) 7 F1
Caradoc, UP (Ont.) 22 D2
Caradoc 42, IR (Ont.) 22 D2
Caramat, UP (Ont.) 27 H2
Caraquet, T (NB) 13 G4
Carberry, T (Man.) 29 F3
Carbon, VL (Alta.) 34 F2
Carbondale, UP (Alta.) 33 E3
Carbondale, NUP (Alta.) 34 E4
Carbonear, T (Nfld.) 2 G2
Carcajou, UP (Alta.) 43 H1
Carcross, UP (YT) 45 B3
Carcross 4, IR (YT) 45 B3
Cardale, UP (Man.) 29 E3
Cardiff, UP (Ont.) 24 E3
Cardiff, UP (Alta.) 33 D3
Cardigan, UP (NB) 11 C1
Cardigan, VL (PEI) 7 D4
Cardigan North, UP (PEI) 7 E4
Cardinal, UP (Man.) 29 G4
Cardinal, VL (Ont.) 17 D3
Cardinal Creek Project, NUP (Ont.) 17 D1
Cardinal Heights, UP (Ont.) 17 E4
Cardross, UP (Sask.) 31 G3
Cardross, UP (PEI) 7 D4
Card's Harbour < Triton – Jim's Cove – Card's Harbour, UP (Nfld.) 3 B2
Cardston, T (Alta.) 34 F4
Cardwell, UP (Ont.) 23 E3
Carey, UP (Man.) 28 A2
Cargill, UP (Ont.) 23 C2
Carholme, UP (Ont.) 22 F2
Cariboo, UP (BC) 40 D2
Cariboo Meadows, UP (BC) 45 B4
Caribou, UP (NS) 9 D1
Caribou, UP (YT) 45 A2
Caribou Depot, UP (NB) 12 D1
Caribou Falls, UP (Ont.) 30 D4
Caribou Ferry, UP (NS) 9 D1
Caribou Hide, UP (BC) 42 F1
Caribou Island, UP (NS) 9 D1
Caribou Marsh, UP (NS) 8 F3
Caribou Marsh 29, IR (NS) 8 F3
Caribou Mines, UP (NS) 9 D3
Caribou River, UP (NS) 9 D1
Caribou Run, UP (Nfld.) 5 H1
Carievale, VL (Sask.) 29 D4
Carignan, T (Que.) 16 A3
Carignan, UP (Que.) 18 G3
Carillon, VL (Que.) 17 F1
Carillon Gardens, NUP (Ont.) 17 F1
Carlea, UP (Sask.) 32 F3
Carleton, T (Que.) 13 D3
Carleton, UP (PEI) 7 B4
Carleton, UP (NS) 10 B3
Carleton, UP (PEI) 7 A3
Carleton Corner, UP (NS) 10 C1
Carleton Place, T (Ont.) 17 B2
Carleton Village, UP (NS) 10 C4
Carley, UP (Ont.) 23 F1
Carleys Corner, UP (Ont.) 17 C3
Carlin, UP (Que.) 17 F1
Carling, UP (Ont.) 25 G3
Carlingford, UP (NB) 12 A3
Carlingford, UP (Ont.) 22 E1
Carlisle, UP (Ont.) 22 H1
Carlisle, UP (Ont.) 22 D1
Carlisle, UP (NB) 12 B4
Carlos, UP (Alta.) 33 D4
Carlow, UP (Ont.) 23 B3
Carlow, UP (NB) 12 A4
Carlowrie, UP (Man.) 28 A3
Carlsbad Springs, UP (Ont.) 17 D1
Carlson Landing, UP (Alta.) 44 C3
Carlsruhe, UP (Ont.) 23 C3
Carlton, UP (Sask.) 32 D4
Carlyle, T (Sask.) 29 C4
Carlyle Lake Resort < White Bear 70, UP (Sask.) 29 C4
Carlyon, UP (Ont.) 23 F1
Carmacks, UP (YT) 45 B3
Carman, T (Man.) 29 H4
Carman, UP (Ont.) 21 E1
Carmanah 6, IR (BC) 38 C4
Carmangay, VL (Alta.) 34 F3
Carmanville, T (Nfld.) 3 E2
Carm Creek 38, IR (BC) 42 D4
Carmel, UP (Sask.) 31 G1
Carmel, UP (Que.) 16 C2
Carmel, UP (Ont.) 21 E1
Carmel, UP (Ont.) 21 D1
Carmi, UP (BC) 35 F3
Carmichael, VL (Sask.) 31 D3
Carmunnock, UP (Ont.) 23 C4
Carnaby, UP (BC) 42 F3
Carnagh, UP (Sask.) 31 C4
Carnarvon, UP (Ont.) 24 D3
Carnduff, T (Sask.) 29 D4
Carnegie, UP (Man.) 29 F3
Carnegie Beach, UP (Ont.) 21 C1
Carnwood, UP (Alta.) 33 D3
Caroline, VL (Alta.) 34 D1
Carolside, UP (Alta.) 34 G2
Caron, UP (Sask.) 31 F3
Caron Brook, UP (NB) 15 G2
Caronport, UP (Sask.) 31 F3
Carp, UP (Ont.) 17 B1
Carpenter, UP (NB) 11 D2
Carpenter, UP (Sask.) 32 D4
Carpenter Mountain 15, IR (BC) 36 C1
Carp Lake 3, IR (BC) 40 C1
Carquile, UP (BC) 36 C4
Carr, UP (Ont.) 25 H2
Carragana, VL (Sask.) 32 G4
Carraholly, UP (BC) 38 G2
Carrick, UP (Man.) 28 C3
Carrier, UP (Que.) 15 G4
Carrier Lake 15, IR (BC) 40 B1
Carrington, UP (NS) 9 B1
Carroll, UP (Man.) 29 F4
Carroll, UP (Que.) 18 C4
Carroll Ridge, UP (NB) 11 A1
Carrolls Corner, UP (NS) 9 C3
Carrolls Cove, UP (Nfld.) 5 H1
Carrolls Crossing, UP (NB) 12 D3
Carrolls Landing, UP (BC) 34 A3
Carrot Creek, UP (Alta.) 33 B3
Carrot River, T (Sask.) 32 F3
Carrot River 27A, IR (Sask.) 32 H3
Carrot River 29A, IR (Sask.) 32 G3
Carrs, UP (BC) 35 F2
Carrs Brook, UP (NS) 9 A2
Carruthers, UP (Sask.) 32 A4
Carrying Place, UP (Ont.) 21 F1
Carseland, UP (Alta.) 34 F2
Carson, UP (BC) 35 H4
Carsonby, UP (Ont.) 17 C2
Carson Grove, UP (Ont.) 17 E4
Carsonville, UP (NB) 11 E1
Carsoosat 5, IR (BC) 40 A1
Carss, UP (Ont.) 24 B1
Carstairs, T (Alta.) 34 E1
Carters Corners, UP (Ont.) 27 D3
Carter's Cove, UP (Nfld.) 3 D2
Carters Cove, UP (NS) 8 D4
Carters Point, UP (NB) 11 D2
Carterton, UP (Ont.) 26 B4
Carthage, UP (Ont.) 23 D4
Carthew Bay, UP (Ont.) 23 G2
Cartier, UP (Ont.) 26 D4
Cartier, UP (Man.) 28 A2
Cartwright, COMM (Nfld.) 6 G3
Cartwright, VL (Man.) 29 F4
Cartwright Point Settlement, NUP (Ont.) 17 A4
Cartyville, UP (Nfld.) 4 B2
Caruso, UP (Alta.) 34 F2
Carvel, UP (Alta.) 33 D3
Carvel Corner, UP (Alta.) 33 D3
Carvell, UP (NB) 12 A4
Carway, UP (Alta.) 34 F4
Cascade, UP (BC) 35 H4
Cascades, UP (Que.) 17 C1
Cascumpec, UP (PEI) 7 A3
Casdeded 8, IR (BC) 42 G3
Case Settlement, UP (NB) 11 E2
Casey, UP (Que.) 18 F2
Cashions Glen, UP (Ont.) 17 E2
Cashtown Corners, UP (Ont.) 23 E2
Casimiel Meadows 15A, IR (BC) 40 A2
Casimir, UP (Ont.) 25 F1
Casino, UP (BC) 34 B4
Caslan, UP (Alta.) 33 E2
Cass Bridge, UP (Ont.) 17 D2
Cassburn, UP (Ont.) 17 E1
Cassel, UP (Ont.) 22 F1
Casselman, VL (Ont.) 17 D2
Cassiar, UP (BC) 45 B4
Cassidy, UP (BC) 38 E3
Cassidy, UP (Ont.) 26 F3
Cassidy Mobile Home Park, NUP (BC) 38 E3
Cassilis, UP (NB) 12 E2
Cassils, UP (Alta.) 34 G3
Cassimayooks 5, IR (BC) 34 D4
Cassville, UP (Que.) 16 D4
Castagnier, UP (Que.) 18 B1
Castalia, UP (NB) 11 C4
Castaway, UP (NB) 12 E4
Castile, UP (Ont.) 24 G2
Castlebar, UP (Que.) 16 D3
Castle Bay, UP (NS) 8 E3
Castledale, UP (BC) 34 C2
Castleford, UP (Ont.) 17 A1
Castlegar, C (BC) 34 B4
Castle Glen Estates, UP (Ont.) 23 E2
Castle Island, SV (Alta.) 33 D3
Castle Mountain, UP (Alta.) 34 C2
Castlereagh, UP (NS) 9 B2
Castle Rock, UP (BC) 40 C3
Castleton, UP (Ont.) 21 E1
Castonguay, UP (Que.) 15 D2
Castor, T (Alta.) 34 G1
Castors River, UP (Nfld.) 5 G2
Casummit Lake, UP (Ont.) 30 E4
Caswellem, NUP (Alta.) 33 E3
Caswell's Beach, UP (Ont.) 23 F1
Catalina, T (Nfld.) 3 G4
Catalone, UP (NS) 8 F3
Catalone Gut, UP (NS) 8 F3
Catalone Road, UP (NS) 8 F3
Catamount, UP (NB) 11 G1
Cataraqui, UP (Ont.) 17 A4
Catchacoma, UP (Ont.) 24 D3
Cater, UP (Sask.) 32 B3
Cathcart, UP (Ont.) 22 F1
Cat Lake < Cat Lake 63C, UP (Ont.) 30 E4
Cat Lake 63C, IR (Ont.) 30 E4
Caughnawaga < Caughnawaga 14, UP (Que.) 17 G4
Caughnawaga 14, IR (Que.) 17 G4
Causapscal, T (Que.) 13 B3
Cavalier, UP (Sask.) 32 B4
Cavan, UP (Ont.) 21 D1
Cavanagh Mills, UP (NS) 9 C1
Cavell, UP (Sask.) 31 D1
Cavendish, UP (Nfld.) 2 G2
Cavendish, UP (PEI) 7 C3
Cavendish, UP (Alta.) 31 B2
Caverhill, UP (NB) 11 B1
Caverlys Landing, UP (Ont.) 24 F3
Cavers, UP (Ont.) 27 F3
Cawaja Beach, UP (Ont.) 23 E1
Cawood, UP (Que.) 18 D4
Cawston, UP (BC) 35 E4
Caycuse, UP (BC) 38 D3
Caye, UP (Man.) 29 G3
Cayer, UP (Man.) 29 F2
Cayilth 5, IR (BC) 39 D2
Cayley, VL (Alta.) 34 E3
Cayoosh Creek 1, IR (BC) 37 H2
Cayuse 6, IR (BC) 39 D2
Cazaville, UP (Que.) 17 F2
Ceba, UP (Sask.) 32 H4
Cecebe, UP (Ont.) 24 B1
Cecil, UP (Sask.) 32 E3
Cecil, UP (Alta.) 34 H3
Cecil Lake, UP (BC) 43 E3
Cedar, UP (BC) 38 E2
Cedar Acres, NUP (Ont.) 17 E4
Cedar Beach, UP (Ont.) 22 A4
Cedar Beach, UP (Ont.) 24 G1
Cedar Beach, UP (Ont.) 21 B1
Cedarbrae, UP (Ont.) 21 B1
Cedar Camp, UP (NB) 11 F2
Cedar Creek, UP (Ont.) 21 E1
Cedar Creek Mobile Home Park, NUP (BC) 38 E4
Cedar Croft, UP (Ont.) 24 A1
Cedardale, UP (Ont.) 17 E4
Cedardale, UP (Ont.) 17 A2
Cedar Glen, UP (Ont.) 24 D4
Cedar Grove, UP (Ont.) 17 E2
Cedar Harbour, UP (Ont.) 21 A1
Cedar Hill, UP (Ont.) 17 B2
Cedarhurst Beach, UP (Ont.) 21 B1
Cedarhurst Park, NUP (Ont.) 22 A4
Cedar Island, NUP (Ont.) 22 A4
Cedar Lake, UP (NS) 10 A3
Cedar Lake, UP (Ont.) 17 B4
Cedarmont Beach, UP (Ont.) 23 G2
Cedar Mount, UP (Ont.) 21 A1
Cedar Nook, UP (Ont.) 23 F1
Cedar Point, UP (Ont.) 23 E1
Cedar Point, UP (Ont.) 22 C1
Cedar Shores, UP (Ont.) 21 C1
Cedarside, UP (BC) 40 F3
Cedar Springs, UP (Ont.) 22 C3
Cedarvale, UP (BC) 42 E4
Cedar Valley, UP (Ont.) 21 D1
Cedar Valley, UP (Ont.) 23 E3
Cedar Village, UP (Ont.) 24 B3
Cedarville, UP (Ont.) 23 D3
Cedarville, UP (Que.) 16 C4
Cedarville, UP (Ont.) 21 A2
Cedoux, UP (Sask.) 29 B3
Ceepeecee, UP (BC) 39 E3
Celista, UP (BC) 36 G4
Celtic, UP (Sask.) 32 A3
Centennial, UP (NS) 8 C4
Centennial Heights, NUP (NB) 11 C1
Central Argyle, UP (NS) 10 B3
Central Bedeque, VL (PEI) 7 B3
Central Blissville, UP (NB) 11 C2
Central Butte, T (Sask.) 31 F2
Central Caribou, UP (NS) 9 D1
Central Chebogue, UP (NS) 10 A3
Central Clarence, UP (NS) 10 C1
Central Greenwich, UP (NB) 11 D2
Central Grove, UP (NS) 10 A2
Central Hainesville, UP (NB) 11 B1
Central Hampstead, UP (NB) 11 D2
Centralia, UP (Ont.) 22 D1
Central Kildare, UP (PEI) 7 B2
Central Kingsclear, UP (NB) 11 C1
Central Lot 16, UP (PEI) 7 B3
Central New Annan, UP (NS) 9 C1
Central North River, UP (NS) 9 C2
Central Norton, UP (NB) 11 E2
Central Onslow, UP (NS) 9 C2
Central Park, NUP (Alta.) 33 D4
Central Patricia, UP (Ont.) 30 F4
Central Port Mouton, UP (NS) 10 D3
Central Saanich, DM (BC) 38 E4
Central Tower Hill, UP (NB) 11 B3
Central Waterville, UP (NB) 11 B1
Central West River, UP (NS) 9 D2
Central Woods Harbour, UP (NS) 10 B4
Centre, UP (NS) 10 E2
Centre, UP (Ont.) 21 F1
Centre-Acadie, UP (NB) 12 F3
Centre Burlington, UP (NS) 9 A3
Centredale, UP (NS) 9 D2
Centre Dummer, UP (Ont.) 21 E1
Centre East Pubnico, UP (NS) 10 B4
Centrefield, UP (Ont.) 17 E1
Centre Glassville, UP (NB) 12 B3
Centre Inn, UP (Ont.) 23 E4
Centre Lake Junction, UP (Ont.) 24 F1
Centrelea, UP (NS) 10 C1
Centre Musquodoboit, UP (NS) 9 C3
Centre Napan, UP (NB) 12 F2
Centre Rawdon, UP (NS) 9 B3
Centre-St-Simon, UP (NB) 12 G1
Centreton, UP (Ont.) 21 E1
Centreton, UP (NB) 11 D2
Centreview, UP (Ont.) 24 F2
Centre Village, UP (NB) 7 A4
Centreville, VL (NB) 12 A4
Centreville, T (Nfld.) 3 F3
Centreville, UP (NS) 11 H3
Centreville, UP (NS) 10 B2
Centreville, UP (Ont.) 22 F1
Centreville, UP (NS) 10 B4
Centreville, UP (NB) 11 E1
Centreville, UP (Ont.) 24 G4
Centreville, UP (NS) 8 C3
Centreville, UP (NB) 12 C4
Centreville, UP (Ont.) 23 D1
Centreville, UP (Ont.) 23 E1
Centreville, UP (BC) 45 C4
Centreville Reserve Mines, UP (NS) 8 F3
Cereal, VL (Alta.) 31 B2
Cessford, UP (Alta.) 34 H2
Ceylon, UP (Ont.) 23 D2
Ceylon, VL (Sask.) 31 H4
Chaatl, UP (BC) 41 A2
Chabot, UP (Que.) 17 E1
Chabot, UP (Que.) 15 D3
Chaffeys Locks, UP (Ont.) 17 B3
Chagoness, UP (Sask.) 32 F4
Chalifoux, UP (Que.) 18 D4
Chalk River, VL (Ont.) 18 B4
Challetkohum 5, IR (BC) 37 G4
Challetkohum 9, IR (BC) 37 G4
Chamberlain, UP (Ont.) 26 F2
Chamberlain, VL (Sask.) 31 G2
Chamberlain Settlement, UP (NB) 12 E1
Chambers Corners, UP (Ont.) 21 B4
Chambers Settlement, UP (NB) 11 F2
Chambly, C (Que.) 16 A3
Chambord, UP (Que.) 18 H1
Chambord-Jonction, UP (Que.) 18 H1
Chambres Corner, UP (NB) 11 E1
Chamcook, UP (NB) 11 B3
Chamcook Lake, UP (NB) 11 B3
Chamiss 7, IR (BC) 39 D2
Chamiss Bay, UP (BC) 39 D2
Champagne, UP (YT) 45 A3
Champcoeur, UP (Que.) 18 B1
Champdoré, UP (NB) 12 G4
Champion, VL (Alta.) 34 F3
Champion Creek, UP (BC) 34 B4
Champlain, UP (NB) 11 B3
Champlain, VL (Que.) 16 C1
Champlain-Estates, NUP (Que.) 16 A4
Champneuf, UP (Que.) 18 C1
Champney's, UP (Nfld.) 3 G4
Champney's Arm < Port Rexton, UP (Nfld.) 3 G4
Champney's West, UP (Nfld.) 3 G4
Chance Cove, T (Nfld.) 2 F2
Chance Harbour, UP (NS) 9 D1
Chance Harbour, UP (NB) 11 D3
Chancellor, UP (Alta.) 34 F2
Chanceport, UP (Nfld.) 3 D2
Chandler, T (Que.) 13 G3
Chandler-Ouest, UP (Que.) 13 G3
Chandonnet, UP (Que.) 15 A4
Chandos Lake, UP (Ont.) 24 E3
Change Islands, T (Nfld.) 3 E1
Channel, UP (Que.) 16 C4
Channel Islands 33, IR (BC) 42 C4
Channel-Port aux Basques, T (Nfld.) 4 A4
Chanoodandidalch 14, IR (BC) 42 G3
Chantelle, UP (Que.) 18 F4
Chantry, UP (Ont.) 17 B3
Chapais, T (Que.) 20 G4
Chapeau, VL (Que.) 18 C4
Chapel Arm, T (Nfld.) 2 F2
Chapel Cove < Harbour Main (COMM), UP (Nfld.) 2 G3
Chapel Grove, UP (NB) 11 D2
Chapel Island 5, IR (NS) 8 D4
Chapel Park 28, IR (BC) 42 G4
Chapel Road, UP (NS) 8 C4
Chapleau, UP (Ont.) 26 C2
Chapleau 61, IR (Ont.) 26 C2
Chapleau 61A, IR (Ont.) 26 C2
Chapleau 74, IR (Ont.) 26 C2
Chapleau 74A, IR (Ont.) 26 C2
Chapleau 75, IR (Ont.) 26 C2
Chaplin, UP (NS) 9 D2
Chaplin, VL (Sask.) 31 F3
Chaplin Island Road, UP (NB) 12 E2
Chapman, UP (Ont.) 21 F1
Chapmans, UP (BC) 35 B3
Chapman's Bar 10, IR (BC) 35 B3
Chapmans Corner, UP (NB) 7 A4
Chapman Settlement, UP (NS) 7 B4
Chapman's Landing, UP (Ont.) 25 H2
Chapmanville, UP (NB) 12 B3
Chapperon Creek 6, IR (BC) 35 E2
Chapperon Lake 5, IR (BC) 35 D2
Chard, UP (Alta.) 44 C4
Charette, UP (Que.) 16 B1
Charing Cross, UP (Ont.) 22 C3
Charlemagne, T (Que.) 17 H3
Charlemont, UP (Ont.) 22 B2
Charles, UP (Man.) 30 A1
Charlesbourg, C (Que.) 15 G3
Charles Brook, UP (Nfld.) 3 C2
Charles Creek 2, IR (BC) 41 G4
Charleston, UP (NS) 10 D3
Charleston, UP (Nfld.) 3 F4
Charleston, UP (Ont.) 17 B3
Charleston, UP (NB) 12 A4
Charlesville, UP (NS) 10 B4
Charleville, UP (Ont.) 17 C3
Charley Boy's Meadow 3, IR (BC) 40 B3
Charlie Lake, UP (BC) 43 E3
Charlo, VL (NB) 13 D4
Charlos Cove, UP (NS) 9 G2
Charlottetown, C (PEI) 7 C4
Charlottetown, UP (Nfld.) 3 E4
Charlottetown, UP (Nfld.) 6 H4
Charlton, T (Ont.) 26 F2
Charny, T (Que.) 15 G3
Charrington, UP (Que.) 16 E4
Charteris, UP (Que.) 17 B1
Charters Settlement, UP (NB) 11 C1
Chartierville, UP (Que.) 16 E4
Chartrand Corner, UP (Ont.) 25 F1
Chase, VL (BC) 36 G4
Chase Corners, UP (Ont.) 21 E1
Chasm, UP (BC) 36 C3
Chaswood, UP (NS) 9 C3
Chateau, UP (Nfld.) 5 H1
Châteauguay, T (Que.) 17 G1
Château-Richer, T (Que.) 15 B3
Chater, UP (Man.) 29 F3
Chatfield, UP (Man.) 29 H2
Chatham, C (Ont.) 22 C3
Chatham, T (NB) 12 F2
Chatham CFB/BFC, MIL (NB) 12 F2
Chatham Head, UP (NB) 12 E2
Chatham Islands 4, IR (BC) 38 F4
Chatscah 2, IR (BC) 41 F2
Chatsworth, VL (Ont.) 23 C2
Chatterton, UP (Ont.) 21 F1
Chaumox 11, IR (BC) 35 B2
Chauvin, VL (Alta.) 33 H4
Chawuthen 4, IR (BC) 35 B4
Chazel, UP (Que.) 18 A1
Cheadle, UP (Alta.) 34 F2
Cheakamus 11, IR (BC) 38 F1
Cheam 1, IR (BC) 35 A4
Cheam View, UP (BC) 35 A4
Chebogue Point, UP (NS) 10 A3
Checkaklis Island 9, IR (BC) 39 D2
Cheddar, UP (Ont.) 24 E3
Chedderville, UP (Alta.) 34 D1
Cheecham, UP (Alta.) 44 C4
Cheeseborough, UP (Ont.) 17 B4
Cheese Factory Corner, UP (NS) 9 B3
Cheesish 15, IR (BC) 39 F3
Cheetsum's Farm 1, IR (BC) 35 B1
Cheewat 4A, IR (BC) 38 C3
Chehalis 5, IR (BC) 35 A4
Chehalis 6, IR (BC) 35 A4
Chekwelp 26, IR (BC) 38 E2
Chekwelp 26A, IR (BC) 38 E2
Chelan, UP (Sask.) 32 G4
Chelmsford, UP (NB) 12 E3
Chelohsin 13, IR (BC) 37 E4
Chelsea, UP (Que.) 17 D3
Chelsea, UP (NS) 10 D2
Chelton, UP (PEI) 7 B4
Chemahawin 32A, IR (Man.) 30 A3
Chemahawin 32B, IR (Man.) 30 A3
Chemahawin 32C, IR (Man.) 30 A3
Chemahawin 32D, IR (Man.) 30 A3
Chemahawin 32G, IR (Man.) 30 A3
Chemainus 13, IR (BC) 38 E3
Chemical Road, UP (NB) 11 G2
Chemin-Craig, UP (Que.) 15 F4
Chemin-des-Buttes, UP (Que.) 7 F1
Chemin-des-Pins, UP (Que.) 17 D3
Chemin-du-Lac, UP (Que.) 14 E4
Chemin-Guay, UP (Que.) 18 F4
Cheminis, UP (Ont.) 26 F2
Chemin-Neuf, UP (Que.) 15 C4
Chemong, UP (Sask.) 32 H3
Chemong Heights, UP (Ont.) 21 D1
Chemong Park, UP (Ont.) 21 D1
Chenahkint 12, IR (BC) 39 E3
Chenail-du-Moine, UP (Que.) 16 B2
Chenatha 4, IR (BC) 38 B3
Chenaux, UP (Ont.) 17 A1
Cheneka < Stony 142,143,144, UP (Alta.) 34 D2
Chénéville, VL (Que.) 18 E4
Cheney, UP (Ont.) 17 D1
Chénier, UP (Que.) 18 D4
Chepstow, UP (Ont.) 23 C2
Chepstow, UP (PEI) 7 E3
Chequis 3, IR (BC) 38 B3
Cherbourg, UP (Que.) 13 C2
Cherbourg-Centre, UP (Que.) 13 B2
Cherbourg-Ouest, UP (Que.) 13 B2
Cherhill, UP (Alta.) 33 D3
Cherry Brook, UP (NS) 9 B4
Cherry Burton, UP (NB) 7 A4
Cherry Creek, UP (BC) 38 C2
Cherryfield, UP (NS) 10 D2
Cherryfield Road, UP (NS) 10 D1
Cherry Grove, UP (Alta.) 33 H2
Cherry Grove, UP (Ont.) 22 E1
Cherry Hill, UP (NS) 10 E3
Cherry Hill, UP (PEI) 7 D3
Cherry Point, UP (Alta.) 43 F3
Cherry Point, NUP (BC) 38 E3
Cherry Ridge, UP (Sask.) 32 F3
Cherry-River, UP (Que.) 16 C4
Cherryvale, UP (NB) 11 F1
Cherry Valley, UP (Ont.) 21 G2
Cherry Valley, UP (PEI) 7 D4
Cherryville, UP (BC) 35 G2
Ches-la-kee 3, IR (BC) 39 E1
Cheslatta, UP (BC) 41 G1
Cheslatta 1, IR (BC) 41 G1
Chesley, T (Ont.) 23 C2
Chester, UP (NS) 10 E2
Chester, UP (NB) 11 G2
Chester, UP (NB) 11 E2
Chester Basin, UP (NS) 10 E2
Chesterfield, UP (Ont.) 22 F1
Chesterfield Inlet, UP (NWT) 46 C2
Chester Grant, UP (NS) 10 E2
Chestermere Lake, UP (Alta.) 34 E2
Chester-Nord, UP (Que.) 16 D2
Chesterville, VL (Ont.) 17 D2
Chesterville, VL (Que.) 16 D2
Chetarpe < Chetarpe 17, UP (BC) 39 G4
Chetarpe 17, IR (BC) 39 G4
Chéticamp, UP (NS) 8 D2
Chéticamp Island, UP (NS) 8 D2
Chetwynd, UP (Ont.) 24 B1
Chetwynd, VL (BC) 43 D4
Cheverie, UP (NS) 9 A2
Chevery, UP (Que.) 5 D3
Cheviot, UP (Sask.) 31 F1
Chevrefils, UP (Que.) 16 D3
Cheyne Settlement, UP (NB) 11 D2
Chezacut, UP (BC) 40 B3
Chezacut Cemetery 5, IR (BC) 40 B3
Chez-Alcide, UP (Que.) 16 C1
Cheztainya Lake 11, IR (BC) 42 G3
Chiasson, UP (NB) 12 G1
Chibougamau, T (Que.) 20 G4
Chichester, UP (Que.) 18 C4
Chicken 224, IR (Sask.) 44 E3
Chicken 225, IR (Sask.) 44 E2
Chicken 226, IR (Sask.) 44 E2
Chickwat 9, IR (BC) 38 E1
Chicoutimi, C (Que.) 14 B3
Chief Mooris 13, IR (BC) 40 B3
Chief's Point 28, IR (Ont.) 23 C1
Chig-in-kaht 8, IR (BC) 42 E4
Chignecto, UP (NS) 9 A1
Chigwell, UP (Alta.) 33 E4
Chikopi, UP (Ont.) 24 A1
Chilanko Forks, UP (BC) 40 B4
Chilcotin Forest, UP (BC) 36 A1
Child Lake 164A, IR (Alta.) 44 A3
Childs Mines, UP (Ont.) 24 F3
Chilhil 6, IR (BC) 35 A1
Chilko Lake 1, IR (BC) 37 D1
Chilko Lake 1A, IR (BC) 37 D1
Chilliwack, C (BC) 35 A4
Chilliwhack, DM (BC) 35 A4
Chimdimash 2, IR (BC) 42 E4
Chimdimash 2A, IR (BC) 42 E4
Chimney Corner, UP (NS) 8 D2
Chimney Cove, UP (Nfld.) 5 F4
Chimney Creek 5, IR (BC) 36 B1
Chimney Tickle, UP (Nfld.) 5 H1
Chin, UP (Alta.) 34 G4
China Creek, UP (BC) 34 B4
China Point, UP (PEI) 7 D4
Chinook, VL (Alta.) 31 B2
Chinook Cove, UP (BC) 36 F3
Chinook Valley, UP (Alta.) 43 H3
Chipewyan 201, IR (Alta.) 44 C3
Chipewyan 201A, IR (Alta.) 44 C3
Chipewyan 201B, IR (Alta.) 44 C3
Chipewyan 201C, IR (Alta.) 44 C3
Chipewyan 201D, IR (Alta.) 44 C3
Chipewyan 201E, IR (Alta.) 44 C3
Chipewyan 201F, IR (Alta.) 44 C3
Chipewyan 201G, IR (Alta.) 44 C3
Chipewyan Lake, UP (Alta.) 44 B4
Chip Lake, UP (Alta.) 33 C3
Chipman, VL (NB) 11 E1
Chipman, VL (Alta.) 33 E3
Chipman Brook, UP (NS) 11 G3
Chipmans Corner, UP (NS) 11 H3

Chippawa Hill < Saugeen 29, UP (Ont.) 23 C2
Chippewa, UP (Ont.) 17 A3
Chiselhurst, UP (Ont.) 23 B4
Chisel Lake, UP (Man.) 30 B2
Chiseuquis 9, IR (BC) 39 E3
Chisholm, UP (Alta.) 33 D1
Chisholm, UP (Ont.) 21 F1
Chiswick, UP (Ont.) 18 A4
Chitek, UP (Sask.) 32 C3
Chitek Lake, UP (Sask.) 32 C3
Chitek Lake 191, IR (Sask.) 32 C3
Choate < Stullawheets 8, UP (BC) 35 B3
Chockpish, UP (NB) 12 G3
Chocolate Cove, UP (NB) 11 B3
Choiceland, VL (Sask.) 32 F3
Chokio < Peigan 147, UP (Alta.) 34 F4
Chopaka, UP (BC) 35 E4
Chortitz, UP (Man.) 29 H4
Chortitz, UP (Sask.) 31 E3
Chortitz, UP (Sask.) 32 D4
Christian Island < Christian Island 30, UP (Ont.) 23 E1
Christian Island 30, IR (Ont.) 23 E1
Christian Island 30A, IR (Ont.) 23 E1
Christian Valley, UP (BC) 35 F3
Christian Valley, UP (Ont.) 25 H2
Christie Beach, UP (Ont.) 23 D1
Christie Lake, UP (Ont.) 17 B3
Christie Ridge, UP (NB) 11 B2
Christies Corner, UP (Ont.) 22 G1
Christieville, UP (Que.) 18 F4
Christina, UP (BC) 35 H4
Christina, UP (Ont.) 22 D2
Christina Lake, UP (BC) 35 H4
Christmas Island, UP (NS) 8 D3
Christopher, UP (NB) 13 C4
Christopher Cross, UP (PEI) 7 B2
Christopher Lake, UP (Sask.) 32 D3
Chuchakacook 4, IR (BC) 38 C3
Chuchhriaschin 5, IR (BC) 35 B1
Chuchhriaschin 5A, IR (BC) 35 B1
Chu Chua, UP (BC) 36 F3
Chuchummisapo 15, IR (BC) 38 C3
Chuchuwayha 2, IR (BC) 35 D4
Chuchuwayha 2C, IR (BC) 35 D4
Chuckchuck 8, IR (BC) 37 F4
Chukcheetso 7, IR (BC) 35 B2
Chum Creek 2, IR (BC) 36 G4
Churchbridge, T (Sask.) 29 D2
Church Hill, UP (NB) 11 F2
Church House, UP (BC) 37 B3
Churchill, UP (Man.) 46 B4
Churchill, UP (Ont.) 21 A1
Churchill, UP (PEI) 7 C4
Churchill Falls, UP (Nfld.) 6 D3
Churchill Heights, UP (Ont.) 17 E2
Churchill Lake 193A, IR (Sask.) 44 D4
Churchover, UP (NS) 10 C4
Church Point, UP (NS) 10 A2
Church Point Station, UP (NS) 10 A2
Church Road, UP (PEI) 7 D3
Churchs Corner, UP (NB) 11 F2
Church Street, UP (NS) 11 H3
Churchview, UP (NS) 8 D3
Churchville, UP (NS) 9 D2
Churchville, UP (Ont.) 22 D2
Chute-à-Blondeau, UP (Ont.) 17 F1
Chute-aux-Galets, UP (Que.) 14 B2
Chute-aux-Outardes, VL (Que.) 14 G1
Chute-des-Passes, UP (Que.) 19 A3
Chute-du-Pin-Rouge, UP (Que.) 18 A3
Chute Lake, UP (BC) 35 F3
Chute-Panet, UP (Que.) 18 H3
Chute-Rouge, UP (Que.) 18 D3
Chute-St-Philippe, UP (Que.) 18 E3
Chutes-de-Ste-Ursule, UP (Que.) 16 A1
Chute-Victoria, UP (Que.) 18 E3
Chutine, UP (BC) 45 B4
Ciné-Parc, NUP (Que.) 14 E4
Cinema, UP (BC) 40 C2
Ciquart, UP (NB) 15 H1
Citeyats 9, IR (BC) 41 D2
City View, UP (Ont.) 17 E4
Clachan, UP (Ont.) 22 D2
Clair, UP (Sask.) 31 H1
Clair, VL (NB) 15 G2
Claire-Fontaine, UP (NB) 12 G3
Clairmont, UP (Alta.) 43 G4
Clairvaux-de-Bagot, UP (Que.) 16 B3
Clairville, UP (NB) 12 F4
Clakamucus 2, IR (BC) 38 A3
Clam Bay, UP (NS) 9 D3
Clam Harbour, UP (NS) 9 D3
Clam Point, UP (NS) 10 B4
Clandeboye, UP (Ont.) 22 D1
Clandeboye, UP (Man.) 28 A1
Clandonald, UP (Alta.) 33 G3
Clanwilliam, UP (Man.) 29 F3
Clanwilliam, UP (BC) 34 A2
Claoose 4, IR (BC) 38 C3
Clapham, UP (Que.) 15 A4
Clapperton, UP (Que.) 13 E3
Clapperton, UP (BC) 35 B1
Clappisons Corners, UP (Ont.) 21 A3
Clarbdon Beach, UP (Ont.) 21 B1
Clare, UP (Ont.) 23 D3
Claremont, UP (NS) 9 A1
Clarence, UP (NS) 10 C1
Clarence, UP (Ont.) 17 D1
Clarence Creek, UP (Ont.) 17 D1
Clarence East, UP (NS) 10 C1
Clarence Ridge, UP (NB) 11 B3
Clarenceville, VL (Que.) 16 A4
Clarenceville-Est, UP (Que.) 16 A4
Clarence West, UP (NS) 10 C1
Clarendon, UP (NB) 11 D2
Clarendon Station, UP (Ont.) 17 A3
Clarenville, T (Nfld.) 2 F1
Claresholm, T (Alta.) 34 F3
Claresholm Airport, NUP (Alta.) 34 F3
Clarina, UP (Ont.) 24 E4
Clark Bridge, UP (Sask.) 31 G4
Clarkdon, UP (Ont.) 27 C2
Clarke's Beach, T (Nfld.) 2 G2
Clarke's Head, UP (Nfld.) 3 D2
Clarkin, UP (PEI) 7 D4
Clarkleigh, UP (Man.) 29 H3
Clark Point, NUP (Ont.) 23 B3
Clarksburg, UP (Ont.) 23 D2
Clarks Church, UP (Ont.) 23 B3
Clarks Corners, UP (NB) 11 D1
Clark's Harbour, T (NS) 10 B4
Clarkson Valley, UP (Alta.) 43 H4
Clarksville, UP (NS) 9 B3
Clarkville, UP (NB) 11 B1
Clashmoor, UP (Sask.) 32 F4
Classy Creek 8, IR (BC) 45 B4
Clatse 5, IR (BC) 41 F3
Clattice Harbour, UP (Nfld.) 2 E2
Clattice South West, UP (Nfld.) 2 E3
Clatux 9, IR (BC) 39 C1
Claverhouse, UP (NS) 8 D3
Clavering, UP (Ont.) 23 C1
Clavet, UP (Sask.) 31 F1
Claybank, UP (Sask.) 31 G3
Clay Bank, UP (Ont.) 17 B1
Claydon, UP (Sask.) 31 C4
Clayhurst, UP (BC) 43 F3
Clayoqua 6, IR (BC) 38 A2
Clayoquot, UP (BC) 39 G4
Clayridge, UP (Sask.) 29 D3
Claysmore, UP (Alta.) 33 G3
Clayton, UP (Ont.) 17 B2
Claytonville, UP (Sask.) 32 E3
Clay Valley, UP (Ont.) 17 B1
Clearbrook, UP (Alta.) 33 E2
Clear Creek, UP (Ont.) 22 F2
Clear Creek, UP (YT) 45 B2
Cleardale, UP (Alta.) 43 F3
Clear Hills, UP (Alta.) 43 H3
Clear Hills 152C, IR (Alta.) 43 G3
Clear Lake, UP (Ont.) 24 B2
Clearland, UP (NS) 10 E2
Clear Prairie, UP (Alta.) 43 F3
Clearsand Beach, UP (Sask.) 32 D3
Clearspring, UP (PEI) 7 E3
Clear Springs, UP (Man.) 28 B2
Clearview, UP (NB) 12 A3
Clearview, UP (Ont.) 17 E4
Clearville, UP (Ont.) 22 D3
Clearwater, UP (BC) 36 F2
Clearwater, UP (Man.) 29 G4
Clearwater 175, IR (Alta.) 44 C4
Clearwater Bay, UP (Ont.) 28 E2
Clearwater Beach, UP (Ont.) 23 F1
Clearwater Lake, UP (Man.) 30 A2
Cleeves, UP (Sask.) 32 A3
Cleho 6, IR (BC) 38 B3
Clematis, UP (Man.) 29 H3
Clemenceau, UP (Sask.) 32 G4
Clément, UP (Que.) 18 D4
Clementsport, UP (NS) 10 B1
Clementsvale, UP (NS) 10 C2
Clemretta, UP (BC) 41 G1
Clemville, UP (Que.) 13 G3
Cléricy, UP (Que.) 18 A1
Clermont, T (Que.) 14 D4
Clermont, UP (PEI) 7 B3
Clerval, UP (Que.) 18 A1
Clesbaoneecheck 3, IR (BC) 40 C2
Cleveland, UP (NS) 8 C4
Clienna 14, IR (BC) 39 C1
Clifford, VL (Ont.) 23 C3
Cliffside Beach, NUP (Ont.) 22 B4
Clifton, UP (NB) 12 F1
Clifton, UP (Nfld.) 2 F1
Clifton, UP (NS) 9 B2
Clifton Royal, UP (NB) 11 D2
Climax, VL (Sask.) 31 D4
Cline River, UP (Alta.) 34 C1
Clinton, T (Ont.) 23 B4
Clinton, UP (PEI) 7 C3
Clinton, VL (BC) 36 C4
Clinton Creek, UP (YT) 45 A2
Clivale, UP (Alta.) 34 G2
Clive, VL (Alta.) 33 E4
Cloan, UP (Sask.) 32 B4
Clontarf, UP (Ont.) 24 G2
Cloolthpich 12, IR (BC) 39 G4
Clo-oose < Claoose 4, UP (BC) 38 C3
Cloridorme, UP (Que.) 13 G1
Cloridorme-Ouest, UP (Que.) 13 G1
Clotalairquot 4, IR (BC) 42 G3
Cloud Bay, UP (Ont.) 27 D3
Cloudslee, UP (Ont.) 26 B4
Clouston, UP (Sask.) 32 D4
Cloutier, UP (Que.) 18 A2
Clova, UP (Que.) 18 E2
Clover Bar, UP (Alta.) 33 E3
Cloverdale, UP (NS) 9 C2
Cloverdale, UP (NB) 12 B4
Cloverdale, UP (Ont.) 17 D2
Cloverdale, UP (Man.) 28 A1
Clover Hill, UP (NB) 11 E2
Cloverleaf, UP (Man.) 28 B1
Clover Valley, UP (Ont.) 23 B3
Clover Valley, UP (Ont.) 25 C2
Cloverville, UP (NS) 8 B4
Cloverville Road, NUP (NS) 8 B4
Clowel 13, IR (BC) 41 D2
Clowns Cove, UP (Nfld.) 2 G2
Cloyne, UP (Ont.) 24 G3
Cluchuta Lake 10A, IR (BC) 40 A3
Cluchuta Lake 10B, IR (BC) 40 A3
Cludolicum 9, IR (BC) 36 B2
Cludolicum 9A, IR (BC) 36 B2
Cluny, VL (Alta.) 34 F2
Clustalach 5, IR (BC) 40 B2
Clute, UP (Ont.) 26 E1
Clutus 11, IR (BC) 38 B3
Clyde, UP (Ont.) 22 G1
Clyde, UP (PEI) 7 C3
Clyde, VL (Alta.) 33 D2
Clyde-Corners, UP (Que.) 17 F2
Clyde Forks, UP (Ont.) 17 A2
Clyde River, UP (PEI) 7 C4
Clyde River, UP (NWT) 47 G4
Clyde River, UP (NS) 10 C4
Clydesdale, UP (NS) 8 B4
Clydesdale, UP (NS) 9 C1
Clydesville, UP (Ont.) 17 B2
Coachman's Cove, COMM (Nfld.) 5 H3
Coady Road, UP (NS) 8 D3
Coal Branch, UP (NB) 12 F4
Coal Brook, UP (Nfld.) 4 B3
Coalburn, UP (NS) 9 D2
Coal Creek, UP (NB) 11 E1
Coal Creek, UP (BC) 34 D4
Coaldale, T (Alta.) 34 G4
Coalfields, UP (Sask.) 29 C4
Coal Harbour, UP (BC) 39 C1
Coalhurst, UP (Alta.) 34 F4
Coalmont, UP (BC) 35 C3
Coal River, UP (BC) 45 C4
Coalspur, UP (Alta.) 33 A3
Coal Valley, UP (Alta.) 33 B4
Coates Mills, UP (NB) 12 G4
Coaticook, T (Que.) 16 D4
Coatsworth Station, UP (Ont.) 22 B3
Cobalt, T (Ont.) 26 F3
Cobble Hill, UP (BC) 38 E3
Cobble Hill, UP (Ont.) 22 E1
Cobb's Arm, UP (Nfld.) 3 D1
Cobden, VL (Ont.) 17 A1
Coboconk, UP (Ont.) 23 H1
Cobourg, T (Ont.) 21 D2
Coburg, UP (NB) 7 A4
Coburn, UP (NB) 11 B2
Cocagne, UP (NB) 12 G4
Cocagne Cove, UP (NB) 12 H4
Cocagne-Nord, UP (NB) 12 G4
Cocagne-Sud, UP (NB) 12 G4
Cochenour, UP (Ont.) 30 D4
Cochin, UP (Sask.) 32 B4
Cochrane, T (Ont.) 26 E1
Cochrane, T (Alta.) 34 E2
Cochrane Corner, UP (NB) 11 D2
Cockburn Island 19, IR (Ont.) 26 B4
Cockburn Island 19A, IR (Ont.) 25 A2
Cockmi 3, IR (BC) 41 F4
Coddles Harbour, UP (NS) 9 F2
Coderre, VL (Sask.) 31 F3
Codesa, UP (Alta.) 43 G3
Codes Corner, UP (Ont.) 17 B4
Codette, VL (Sask.) 32 F3
Codner, UP (Nfld.) 2 H2
Codner, UP (Alta.) 33 C4
Codrington, UP (Ont.) 21 E1
Codroy, UP (Nfld.) 4 A3
Codroy Pond, UP (Nfld.) 4 B3
Cody, UP (BC) 34 B3
Codys, UP (NB) 11 E1
Cody's Corners, UP (Ont.) 22 F1
Coe Hill, UP (Ont.) 24 E3
Coffee Cove, UP (Nfld.) 3 B1
Coffee Creek, UP (YT) 45 A3
Coffin Cove, UP (Nfld.) 2 E2
Coffin Island 3, IR (BC) 39 F1
Coffinscroft, UP (NS) 10 C4
Coghill, UP (Alta.) 33 E4
Coglistiko River 29, IR (BC) 40 B3
Cogmagun River, UP (NS) 9 A3
Cognashene, UP (Ont.) 23 F1
Cognehoe Point 20, IR (BC) 41 A1
Coin-Douglas, UP (Que.) 16 A4
Coin-Lavigne, UP (Que.) 18 F4
Coin-Rond, UP (Que.) 16 A3
Coins Gratton, UP (Ont.) 17 E1
Cokato, UP (BC) 34 D4
Colbeck, UP (Ont.) 23 E3
Colborne, VL (Ont.) 21 E2
Colby Village, UP (NS) 9 B4
Colchester, UP (Ont.) 22 A4
Coldbrook, UP (NS) 10 E1
Cold Brook, UP (Nfld.) 4 C2
Cold Lake, T (Alta.) 33 G2
Cold Lake, UP (Man.) 30 A1
Cold Lake 149, IR (Alta.) 33 G2
Cold Lake 149A, IR (Alta.) 33 H2
Cold Lake 149B, IR (Alta.) 33 G2
Cold Lake, CFB/BFC, MIL (Alta.) 33 G2
Coldspring House, UP (BC) 40 D3
Cold Springs, UP (Ont.) 21 D1
Cold Springs, UP (Ont.) 25 C2
Coldstream, DM (BC) 35 F2
Coldstream, UP (NB) 12 B4
Coldstream, UP (Ont.) 22 D1
Coldstream, UP (NS) 9 C3
Coldwater, VL (Ont.) 23 F1
Coldwater 1, IR (BC) 35 C2
Coldwell, UP (Ont.) 27 G3
Cole Bay, UP (Sask.) 32 B1
Cole Bay 3, IR (BC) 38 E4
Colebrook, UP (Ont.) 17 A4
Colebrooke Settlement, UP (NB) 13 C4
Cole Harbour, UP (NS) 9 G2
Cole Harbour, UP (NS) 9 B4
Cole Harbour 30, IR (NS) 9 B4
Cole Lake, UP (Ont.) 17 A3
Coleman, T (Alta.) 34 E4
Coleman, UP (PEI) 7 A3
Coleman, UP (Ont.) 27 D3
Coleman's Shore, UP (Ont.) 17 B2
Coleraine, UP (Que.) 16 E2
Coleraine, UP (NB) 11 E3
Coles Island, UP (NB) 11 E1
Coles Island, UP (NB) 7 A4
Coleville, VL (Sask.) 31 C1
Cole Wharf, UP (Ont.) 21 G1
Colfax, UP (Sask.) 31 H3
Colgan, UP (Ont.) 21 A2
Colgate, VL (Sask.) 31 H4
Colindale, UP (NS) 8 C3
Colinet, COMM (Nfld.) 2 F3
Colinton, UP (Alta.) 33 E2
Colinville, UP (Ont.) 22 B2
Collacott Subdivision, NUP (Sask.) 29 C2
College Bridge, UP (NB) 11 H1
College Grant, UP (NS) 9 E2
College Grant, UP (NS) 9 C1
College Heights, UP (Alta.) 33 D4
Collette, UP (NB) 12 F3
Collette-Village, UP (NB) 12 G3
Collettville, UP (BC) 35 C2
Colleymount, UP (BC) 41 G1
Collicutt, UP (Alta.) 34 E2
Colliers, T (Nfld.) 2 G3
Collina, UP (NB) 11 E2
Collingwood, T (Ont.) 23 E2
Collingwood Corner, UP (NS) 9 A1
Collingwood Cove, NUP (Alta.) 33 E3
Collins, UP (Ont.) 27 D1
Collins Bay, UP (Ont.) 17 A4
Collins Inlet, UP (Ont.) 25 E2
Colmer, UP (Sask.) 29 C2
Colombier, UP (Que.) 14 F2
Colombière, UP (Que.) 18 B2
Colombourg, UP (Que.) 18 A1
Colonial Acres, NUP (Ont.) 21 F1
Colonie-Cinq, UP (Que.) 18 A1
Colonie-Fournière, UP (Que.) 18 B2
Colonsay, VL (Sask.) 31 F1
Colpitts Settlement, UP (NB) 11 G1
Colpoys Bay, UP (Ont.) 23 C1
Colpton, UP (NS) 10 D2
Colquhoun, UP (Ont.) 17 D2
Columbia Gardens, UP (BC) 34 B4
Columbia Lake 3, IR (BC) 34 C3
Colville, UP (PEI) 7 C4
Colville Lake, UP (NWT) 45 D2
Colwell, UP (Ont.) 21 A1
Colwood, UP (BC) 38 E4
Comber, UP (Ont.) 22 B3
Combermere, UP (Ont.) 24 F2
Comeau, UP (Man.) 29 G2
Comeau Point, UP (NB) 7 A4
Comeau Ridge, UP (NB) 12 A2
Comeau Settlement, NUP (NB) 12 G2
Comeaus Hill, UP (NS) 10 B4
Comeauville, UP (NS) 10 A2
Come-by-Chance, T (Nfld.) 2 F2
Comer, UP (BC) 36 B1
Comestock-Mills, UP (Que.) 16 C4
Comet, UP (Ont.) 22 A4
Comet, UP (Alta.) 34 G1
Comfort Bight, UP (Nfld.) 6 H3
Comfort Cove < Comfort Cove – Newstead, UP (Nfld.) 3 D2
Comfort Cove – Newstead, COMM (Nfld.) 3 D2
Comins-Mills, UP (Que.) 16 E4
Commanda, UP (Ont.) 24 B1
Commercial Cross, UP (PEI) 7 D4
Commodore Heights, NUP (BC) 36 B1
Commons, UP (NS) 10 E2
Comox, T (BC) 38 C1
Comox 1, IR (BC) 38 C1
Comox, CFB/BFC, MIL (BC) 38 C1
Compeer, UP (Alta.) 31 B1
Compton, VL (Que.) 16 D4
Compton Island 6, IR (BC) 39 E1
Compton-Station, UP (Que.) 16 D4
Conception Bay South, T (Nfld.) 2 H2
Conception Harbour, T (Nfld.) 2 G3
Concession, UP (NS) 10 A2
Concession-de-Baker-Brook, UP (NB) 15 G2
Concession-des-Bouchard, UP (NB) 15 G2
Concession-des-Jaunes, UP (NB) 15 G2
Concession-des-Lang, UP (NB) 15 G2
Concession-des-Ouellette, UP (NB) 15 G2
Concession-des-Vasseur, UP (NB) 15 G2
Concession-des-Viel, UP (NB) 15 G2
Conche, COMM (Nfld.) 5 H2
Concord, UP (NS) 9 D2
Concord Point, UP (Ont.) 23 G2
Condie, UP (Sask.) 31 G3
Condor, UP (Alta.) 33 D4
Conestogo, UP (Ont.) 23 D4
Coney Arm, UP (Nfld.) 5 G3
Congresbury, UP (Alta.) 34 D1
Congress, UP (Sask.) 31 F4
Coningsby, UP (Ont.) 23 E3
Conjuring Creek, UP (Alta.) 33 D3
Conklin, UP (Alta.) 33 G1
Conn, UP (Ont.) 23 D3
Connaught, UP (Ont.) 17 D2
Connaught, UP (Ont.) 24 G1
Connaught Heights, NUP (Sask.) 32 E4
Connaught Shore, UP (Ont.) 24 D4
Connell, UP (NB) 12 A4
Connell Creek, UP (Sask.) 32 G3
Connellys, UP (Ont.) 21 E1
Connemara, UP (Alta.) 34 E3
Conne River, LID (Nfld.) 2 B2
Connor, UP (Ont.) 21 A2
Connor Creek, UP (Alta.) 33 C2
Connors, UP (NB) 15 G2
Conns Mills, UP (NS) 9 B1
Conover, UP (Ont.) 23 E2
Conquerall, UP (NS) 10 E2
Conquerall Bank, UP (NS) 10 E2
Conquerall Mills, UP (NS) 10 E2
Conquest, VL (Sask.) 31 E2
Conrad, UP (Alta.) 34 G4
Conrad, UP (YT) 45 B3
Conrich, UP (Alta.) 34 E2
Conrod Settlement, UP (NS) 9 C3
Conroy, UP (Ont.) 22 E1
Consecon, UP (Ont.) 21 F2
Consort, VL (Alta.) 31 B1
Constance, UP (Sask.) 31 F4
Constance Bay, UP (Ont.) 17 B1
Constance Lake 92, IR (Ont.) 20 B4
Constant Creek, UP (Ont.) 24 G2
Consul, VL (Sask.) 31 C4
Contrecoeur, UP (Que.) 16 A3
Convent Glen, UP (Ont.) 17 E3
Conway, UP (NS) 10 B2
Conway, UP (PEI) 7 B3
Conway, UP (Ont.) 21 G1
Cooke's Shore, UP (Ont.) 17 B2
Cooking Lake, UP (Alta.) 33 E3
Cooks Brook, UP (NS) 9 C3
Cooks Cove, UP (NS) 9 G2
Cooks Creek, UP (Man.) 28 B1
Cook's Harbour, LID (Nfld.) 5 H2
Cookshire, T (Que.) 16 E4
Cookson, UP (Sask.) 32 D3
Cookstown, VL (Ont.) 21 A1
Cookville, UP (NS) 10 E2
Cookville, UP (NB) 7 A4
Coolidge, UP (Alta.) 33 D2
Coombe, UP (BC) 38 G2
Coombes Road, UP (NB) 12 A2
Coombs, UP (BC) 38 D2
Coomb's Cove < St Jacques – Coomb's Cove, UP (Nfld.) 2 B3
Cooper, UP (Ont.) 24 F4
Cooper Creek, UP (BC) 34 B3
Cooper's Cove, UP (Nfld.) 2 E2
Coopers Falls, UP (Ont.) 23 G1
Cooper's Trailer Park, UP (Ont.) 21 D1
Cooper Subdivision, NUP (BC) 43 E3
Coopte 9, IR (BC) 39 E3
Copeland, UP (Sask.) 31 H1
Copenhagen, UP (Ont.) 22 E2
Copetown, UP (Ont.) 22 G1
Copp, UP (Ont.) 24 F2
Coppell, UP (Ont.) 20 B4
Copper Creek, UP (BC) 36 E4
Copperhead, UP (Ont.) 21 G2
Copper Johnny Meadow 8, IR (BC) 36 C3
Copperkettle, UP (Ont.) 23 C1
Copper Lake, UP (NS) 9 F2
Coppermine, UP (NWT) 45 E1
Copper Mountain, UP (BC) 35 D4
Copperside Estates, NUP (BC) 42 E4
Coppett, UP (Nfld.) 4 E4
Coppin's Corners, UP (Ont.) 21 B1
Coquitlam, DM (BC) 38 G2
Coquitlam 1, IR (BC) 38 G2
Coquitlam 2, IR (BC) 38 G2
Coral, UP (Ont.) 20 C4
Coral Beach, NUP (BC) 35 F2
Coral Harbour, HAM (NWT) 46 D2
Corbeil, UP (Ont.) 18 A4
Corberrie, UP (NS) 10 B2
Corbett, UP (Ont.) 22 D1
Corbett Creek, UP (Alta.) 33 C2
Corbetton, UP (Ont.) 23 E3
Corbin, UP (Nfld.) 2 C4
Corbin, UP (BC) 34 E4
Corbin, UP (Nfld.) 2 C2
Corbin, UP (Que.) 17 G2
Corbyville, UP (Ont.) 21 F1
Corcoran, UP (Que.) 18 F4
Cordel, UP (Alta.) 33 F4
Cordon, UP (Que.) 18 F4
Cordova, UP (Man.) 29 F3
Cordova Mines, UP (Ont.) 24 F4
Coriander, UP (Sask.) 31 E4
Corinne, UP (Sask.) 31 H3
Corinth, UP (Ont.) 22 F2
Cork, UP (NB) 11 C2
Corkery, UP (Ont.) 17 B2
Corkscrew Creek 9, IR (BC) 40 B2
Corkscrew Creek 10, IR (BC) 40 B2
Corkums Island, UP (NS) 10 E2
Cormac, UP (Ont.) 24 G2
Cormack, COMM (Nfld.) 5 G4
Cormier Cove, UP (NB) 11 G1
Cormier-Village, UP (NB) 7 A4
Cormierville, UP (NB) 12 G4
Cormorant, UP (Man.) 30 A2
Cornell, UP (Ont.) 22 F2
Corner Brook, C (Nfld.) 4 D1
Cornhill, UP (NB) 11 F1
Cornhill East, UP (NB) 11 F1
Corning, UP (Sask.) 29 C3
Cornwall, C (Ont.) 17 E2
Cornwall, VL (PEI) 7 C4
Cornwallis, CFB/BFC, MIL (NS) 10 B1
Cornwall Island < St-Régis Akwesasne 59, UP (Ont.) 17 E2
Coromonie, UP (NS) 9 D2
Coronach, VL (Sask.) 31 G4
Coronado, UP (Alta.) 33 E3
Coronation, T (Alta.) 34 H1
Corra Linn, UP (BC) 34 B4
Corran Ban, UP (PEI) 7 D3
Corraville, UP (PEI) 7 E4
Corriveau, UP (Que.) 15 B4
Corsons, UP (Ont.) 23 H1
Cortes Bay, UP (BC) 37 C4
Corunna, UP (Ont.) 22 B2
Corwhin, UP (Ont.) 23 E4
Coryatsaqua 2, IR (BC) 42 F4
Cosine, UP (Sask.) 31 B1
Cosman Settlement, UP (NB) 11 F1
Cosmo, UP (Alta.) 33 C3
Cossetteville, UP (Que.) 16 C1
Costigan, UP (NB) 12 A2
Cosway, UP (Alta.) 34 F2
Cosy Cove, UP (Ont.) 10 G4
Cosy Cove, UP (BC) 38 G2
Coté, UP (Sask.) 29 D2
Cote 64, IR (Sask.) 29 D1
Coteau Beach, UP (Sask.) 31 E2
Coteau-des-Hêtres, UP (Que.) 17 F1
Coteau-du-Lac, VL (Que.) 17 F2
Coteau-Landing, VL (Que.) 17 F2
Coteau-Mauvais-Riz, UP (Que.) 15 C2
Coteau Road, UP (NB) 13 G4
Côte-d'Or, UP (NB) 12 G4
Côte-Double, UP (Que.) 17 F1
Côte-St-Antoine, UP (Que.) 15 C2
Côte-Ste-Anne, UP (NB) 12 G3
Côte-St-Joseph, UP (Que.) 16 D3
Côte-St-Luc, C (Que.) 17 G4
Côte-St-Paul, NUP (Que.) 17 F1
Côte-St-Pierre, UP (Que.) 18 E4
Cotham, UP (Sask.) 29 C3
Cotieville, UP (Ont.) 24 H2
Cotnam Island, UP (Ont.) 24 G1
Cotswold, UP (Ont.) 23 D3
Cottam, UP (Ont.) 22 A3
Cottesloe, UP (Ont.) 21 E1
Cottle's Island < Cottle's Island – Luke's Arm, UP (Nfld.) 3 D2
Cottle's Island – Luke's Arm, LID (Nfld.) 3 D2
Cottonwood, UP (BC) 40 D3
Cottrell's Cove, UP (Nfld.) 3 C2
Couchiching 16A, IR (Ont.) 28 H4
Coucouache 24A, IR (Que.) 18 G2
Coude-de-la-Rivière-Moisie, UP (Que.) 19 F3
Coughlan, UP (NB) 12 E3
Coughlin, UP (Ont.) 27 E3
Couldwell Subdivision, NUP (BC) 40 C3
Coulson, UP (Ont.) 23 F2
Coulson's Hill, UP (Ont.) 21 A1
Coulter, UP (Man.) 29 E4
Countess, UP (Alta.) 34 G2
Country Harbour Lake, UP (NS) 9 F2
Country Harbour Mines, UP (NS) 9 F2
Country Place, UP (Ont.) 17 E4
Country Squire Subdivision, NUP (Ont.) 21 E1
County Line, UP (NS) 10 E3
Courcelette < Valcartier, BFC/CFB, UP (Que.) 15 F3
Courcelles, UP (Que.) 16 F2
Courcellette, UP (Que.) 14 D4
Court, UP (Sask.) 31 C1
Courtenay, C (BC) 38 B1
Courtland, UP (Ont.) 22 F2
Courtlea Mobile Acres, NUP (Ont.) 22 F2
Courtright, UP (Ont.) 22 B2
Courval, UP (Sask.) 31 F3
Cous 3, IR (BC) 38 C2
Cousins, UP (Alta.) 31 B1
Coutlee, UP (BC) 35 C2
Coutnac Beach, UP (Ont.) 23 F1
Coutts, VL (Alta.) 34 G4
Couttsville, UP (Ont.) 26 F2
Couture, UP (Que.) 18 A1
Couturier, UP (Que.) 14 F4
Couturier Siding, UP (NB) 15 G2
Couturval, UP (Que.) 13 B3
Cove Beach, UP (Ont.) 21 G2
Cove Beach, UP (Ont.) 23 E1
Covedell, UP (NB) 12 G2
Covehead, UP (PEI) 7 C3
Covehead Road, UP (PEI) 7 C3
Coverdale, UP (Ont.) 21 E2
Cove Road, UP (NS) 9 B2
Covey-Hill, UP (Que.) 17 G2
Cowan, UP (Man.) 29 E1
Cowan, UP (Que.) 17 G2
Cowan's Bay, UP (Ont.) 21 D1
Cowans Creek, UP (NB) 12 G1
Cowansville, T (Que.) 16 B4
Cow Bay, UP (NS) 9 B4
Cowessess 73, IR (Sask.) 29 C3
Cow Head, T (Nfld.) 5 F3
Cowichan, UP (BC) 38 E3
Cowichan 1, IR (BC) 38 E3
Cowichan 9, IR (BC) 38 E3
Cowichan Bay, UP (BC) 38 E3
Cowichan Lake, IR (BC) 38 D3
Cowishil 1, IR (BC) 38 B3
Cowley, UP (YT) 45 B3
Cowley, VL (Alta.) 34 E4
Coxby, UP (Sask.) 32 E4
Coxheath, UP (NS) 8 F3
Cox Point, UP (NB) 11 E1
Cox's Cove, COMM (Nfld.) 5 F4
Coxvale, UP (Ont.) 17 A2
Coyle, UP (BC) 35 C2
Coytown, UP (NB) 11 D1
Cozy Corners, UP (Ont.) 28 G3
Crab River 18, IR (BC) 41 E1
Crabtree, VL (Que.) 16 A2
Cracknell, UP (Man.) 29 D2
Cracroft, UP (BC) 39 F1
Craddock, UP (Alta.) 34 G4
Crafts Cove, UP (NB) 11 D2
Craigdhu, UP (Alta.) 34 F2
Craigellachie, UP (BC) 34 A2
Craigend, UP (Alta.) 33 F2
Craig Harbour, UP (NWT) 47 F3
Craig Henry, UP (Ont.) 17 D4
Craighurst, UP (Ont.) 23 F2
Craigleith, UP (Ont.) 23 E2
Craigmawr Beach, UP (Ont.) 21 B1
Craigmillar, UP (Alta.) 33 G4
Craigmont, UP (Ont.) 24 F2
Craigmore, UP (NS) 8 C4
Craigmyle, UP (Alta.) 34 G1
Craigsford, UP (Man.) 29 E1
Craigsholme, UP (Ont.) 23 E3
Craig Shore, UP (Ont.) 17 B2
Craik, T (Sask.) 31 F2
Cramersburg, UP (Sask.) 31 D2
Crammond, UP (Alta.) 34 E1
Crampton, UP (Ont.) 22 E2
Cranberry, UP (Que.) 16 E2
Cranberry, UP (Ont.) 25 F2
Cranberry Portage, UP (Man.) 32 H2
Cranbourne, UP (Que.) 15 C4
Cranbrook, C (BC) 34 C4
Cranbrook, UP (Ont.) 23 C4
Crandall, UP (Man.) 29 E3
Crandall Road, UP (NS) 8 C4
Crane River, UP (Man.) 29 F2
Crane River 51, IR (Man.) 29 F2
Crane Valley, UP (Sask.) 31 G4
Cranford, UP (Alta.) 34 G4
Cranstons Beach, UP (Ont.) 17 A4
Crapaud, VL (PEI) 7 C4
Crathie, UP (Ont.) 22 D1
Craven, VL (Sask.) 31 G2
Crawford, UP (Ont.) 23 C2
Crawford Bay, UP (BC) 34 B4
Crawford Park, UP (Man.) 29 F3
Crawfordville, UP (Que.) 15 A4
Crediton, UP (Ont.) 22 D1
Creditville, UP (Ont.) 22 F1
Cree, UP (Ont.) 26 A1
Creek Bank, UP (Ont.) 23 D4
Creekland, UP (Alta.) 33 D3
Creek Road, UP (NB) 11 F1
Cree Lake, UP (Sask.) 44 E4
Creelman, VL (Sask.) 29 B4
Creelmans Crossing, UP (NS) 9 D3
Creemore, VL (Ont.) 23 E2
Creemorne, UP (Que.) 18 D4
Creighton, T (Sask.) 32 H2
Creighton, UP (Ont.) 23 F1
Creighton Heights, UP (Ont.) 21 D2
Creighton Valley, UP (BC) 35 G2
Creignish, UP (NS) 8 C4
Creignish Rear, UP (NS) 8 C4
Cremona, VL (Alta.) 34 E2
Crescent Bay, UP (BC) 34 B4
Crescent Bay, NUP (BC) 34 B3
Crescent Beach, UP (NS) 10 E2
Crescent Beach, UP (Ont.) 21 B1
Crescent Grove, UP (NS) 7 H4
Crescent Lake, UP (Sask.) 29 C2
Crescent Spur, UP (BC) 40 E2
Crescent Valley, UP (BC) 34 B4
Cresent Harbour, UP (Ont.) 21 A1
Cressday, UP (Alta.) 31 B4
Cressman, UP (Que.) 18 G2
Cresswell, UP (Ont.) 21 C1
Cressy, UP (Ont.) 17 A4
Cresthill, UP (Que.) 18 D4
Creston, T (BC) 34 C4
Creston 1, IR (BC) 34 C4
Crestview, UP (Ont.) 17 E4
Crestview, UP (Man.) 29 D1
Crestwood Subdivision, NUP (BC) 43 E3
Crestwynd, UP (Sask.) 31 G3
Crewe, UP (Ont.) 23 B3
Crewsons Corners, UP (Ont.) 23 E4
Crichton, UP (Sask.) 31 D4
Crieff, UP (Ont.) 23 E4
Crilly, UP (Ont.) 27 B3
Crimson Lake, UP (Alta.) 33 C4
Crinan, UP (Ont.) 22 D2
Crippsdale, UP (Alta.) 33 E2
Crique-Lacorne, UP (Que.) 18 B2
Crocker Hill, UP (NB) 11 B3
Crocketts Corner, UP (NB) 11 F2
Crockett, NUP (NB) 15 G2
Croft, UP (NS) 8 B4
Crofton, UP (Ont.) 21 F1
Croll, UP (Man.) 29 E4
Cromar, UP (Ont.) 22 C2
Cromarty, UP (Ont.) 23 B4
Crombie Settlement, UP (NB) 12 A2
Cromer, UP (Man.) 29 D4
Cromwell, UP (Man.) 28 B1
Crooked Bay, UP (Ont.) 23 F1
Crooked Creek, UP (Alta.) 43 H4
Crooked River, UP (Sask.) 32 F4
Crooks, UP (Ont.) 27 D3
Crookston, UP (Ont.) 21 F1
Croque, UP (Nfld.) 5 H2
Crosby, UP (Ont.) 17 B3
Crosbys Mill, UP (PEI) 7 C4
Crossburn, UP (NS) 10 D1
Cross Creek, UP (NB) 12 C4
Crossfield, VL (Alta.) 34 E2
Crosshill, UP (Ont.) 23 D4
Cross Lake, UP (Ont.) 24 E2
Cross Lake, UP (Man.) 30 C2
Cross Lake 19, IR (Man.) 30 C2
Cross Lake 19A, IR (Man.) 30 C2
Cross Lake 19B, IR (Man.) 30 C2
Cross Lake 19C, IR (Man.) 30 C2
Crossland, UP (Ont.) 23 F2
Crossley Hunter, UP (Ont.) 22 E2
Cross-Point, UP (Que.) 13 C4
Cross Point, UP (NS) 8 E3
Cross-Point-Station, UP (Que.) 13 C4
Cross River, UP (PEI) 7 B3
Crossroads, UP (PEI) 7 D4
Cross Roads Country Harbour, UP (NS) 9 F2
Cross Roads Ohio, UP (NS) 9 E2
Croton, UP (Ont.) 22 C2
Crouchers Forks, UP (NS) 9 A4
Crouses Settlement, UP (NS) 10 E2
Crousetown, UP (NS) 10 E2
Crowchild < Sarcee 145, UP (Alta.) 34 E2
Crowe Bridge, UP (Ont.) 21 E1
Crowell, UP (NS) 10 B4
Crowes Landing, UP (Ont.) 24 E4
Crowes Mills, UP (NS) 9 C2
Crowfoot, UP (Alta.) 34 F2
Crow Harbour, UP (NB) 11 C3
Crow Head, COMM (Nfld.) 3 D1

Crow Lake, UP (Ont.) 17 A3
Crow Lake < Sabaskong Bay 35D, UP (Ont.) 28 G3
Crown Hill, UP (Ont.) 21 A1
Crowsnest, UP (Alta.) 34 E4
Crows Nest, UP (NS) 9 E2
Croydon, UP (Ont.) 21 G1
Croydon, UP (BC) 40 F3
Crozier, UP (Ont.) 28 H4
Cruickshank, UP (Ont.) 23 C1
Crumlin, UP (Ont.) 22 E1
Crutwell, UP (Sask.) 32 D3
Crysler, UP (Ont.) 17 D2
Crystal, UP (Ont.) 17 C3
Crystal Bay, UP (Ont.) 17 D4
Crystal Beach, UP (NB) 11 D2
Crystal Beach, UP (Ont.) 17 D4
Crystal Beach, UP (Ont.) 24 B3
Crystal Beach, UP (Sask.) 31 E1
Crystal Beach, NUP (Ont.) 22 A
Crystal City, VL (Man.) 29 G4
Crystal Falls, UP (Ont.) 25 G1
Crystal Hill, UP (Sask.) 31 G3
Crystal Lake, NUP (Ont.) 27 C3
Crystal Rock, UP (Ont.) 17 D3
Crystal Springs, SV (Alta.) 33 D4
Crystal Springs, UP (Sask.) 32 E4
Crystal Springs, NUP (Ont.) 21 D1
Cudworth, T (Sask.) 32 D4
Cuffley, UP (Sask.) 32 B3
Cul de Sac West, UP (Nfld.) 4 F4
Cullen, UP (Sask.) 29 C4
Cullens-Brook, UP (Que.) 13 F3
Cullite 3, IR (BC) 38 C4
Culloden, UP (Ont.) 22 F2
Culloden, UP (NS) 10 B1
Culloden, UP (PEI) 7 D4
Cull's Harbour, NUP (Nfld.) 3 F4
Culp, UP (Alta.) 43 H3
Culross, UP (Man.) 29 H4
Cultus, UP (Ont.) 22 F2
Cultus Lake, UP (BC) 35 A4
Cumberland, UP (Ont.) 17 D1
Cumberland, UP (PEI) 7 C4
Cumberland, VL (BC) 38 B1
Cumberland 100A, IR (Sask.) 32 E4
Cumberland 20, IR (Sask.) 32 H3
Cumberland Bay, UP (NB) 11 E1
Cumberland Beach, UP (Ont.) 23 G1
Cumberland House, UP (Sask.) 32 H3
Cumberland-Mills, UP (Que.) 15 C4
Cummings Cove, UP (NB) 11 B3
Cumnock, UP (Ont.) 23 D3
Cumshewa < Cumshewas 7, UP (BC) 41 B2
Cumshewas 7, IR (BC) 41 B2
Cunningham Lake 11, IR (BC) 40 A1
Cunningham Landing, UP (NWT) 44 C2
Cunningham's Corners, UP (Ont.) 21 C1
Cupar, T (Sask.) 31 H2
Cupids, T (Nfld.) 2 G2
Cupids Crossing, UP (Nfld.) 2 G2
Curlew, UP (Alta.) 34 F1
Curran, UP (Ont.) 17 E1
Current Island, UP (Nfld.) 5 G2
Currie, UP (NB) 12 A3
Currieburg, UP (NB) 12 C4
Currie Road, UP (NB) 12 A3
Curries, UP (Ont.) 22 F1
Curry Hill, UP (Ont.) 17 F2
Currys Corner, UP (NS) 9 A3
Curryville, UP (NB) 11 G1
Curtis Park < Chatham, CFB/BFC, UP (NB) 12 F2
Curtis Park < Portage la Prairie, CFB/BFC, UP (Man.) 29 G3
Curve Lake < Curve Lake 35, UP (Ont.) 21 D1
Curve Lake 35, IR (Ont.) 21 D1
Curve Lake 35A, IR (Ont.) 21 D1
Curventon, UP (NB) 12 E2
Curzon, UP (BC) 34 C4
Curzon < Woody Point (COMM), UP (Nfld.) 5 F4
Cushendall, UP (Ont.) 17 B4
Cushing, UP (Que.) 17 F1
Cuslett, UP (Nfld.) 2 E4
Custeau, UP (Que.) 15 B4
Cutbank, UP (Sask.) 31 E2
Cuthbert, UP (Sask.) 31 B2
Cut Knife, T (Sask.) 32 A4
Cutler < Serpent River 7, UP (Ont.) 25 B1
Cuvier, UP (Sask.) 32 F4
Cygnet, UP (Alta.) 34 E1
Cymbria, UP (PEI) 7 C3
Cymric, UP (Sask.) 31 G2
Cynthia, UP (Alta.) 33 C3
Cypress Hills Park, UP (Sask.) 31 C4
Cypress River, UP (Man.) 29 G4
Cyr, UP (Que.) 13 E3
Cyr Junction, UP (NB) 12 A2
Cyrville, UP (Ont.) 17 E4
Czar, VL (Alta.) 33 G4

D

Daaquam, UP (Que.) 15 D3
Daaquam-Nord, UP (Que.) 15 D3
Dablon, UP (Que.) 18 H1
Dachlabah 30, IR (BC) 42 D3
Dacotah, UP (Man.) 29 H3
Dacre, UP (Ont.) 24 G2
Dafoe, VL (Sask.) 31 H1
Dahinda, UP (Sask.) 31 G4
Dahlton, UP (Sask.) 32 F4
Daigneault, UP (Que.) 16 F3
Dakiulis 7, IR (BC) 39 E1
Dakota Plains 6A, IR (Man.) 29 G4
Dakota Tipi 1, IR (Man.) 29 G3
Dale, UP (Ont.) 21 D2
Dalehurst, UP (Alta.) 33 A3
D'Alembert, UP (Que.) 18 A1
Dalemead, UP (Alta.) 34 F2
Dalesville, UP (Que.) 17 F1
Dalhousie, T (NB) 13 D3
Dalhousie Crossing, UP (NS) 10 D1
Dalhousie Junction, UP (NB) 13 D4
Dalhousie Lake, UP (Ont.) 17 A2
Dalhousie Mills, UP (Ont.) 17 F2
Dalhousie Road, UP (NS) 10 D1
Dalhousie-Station, UP (Que.) 17 F2
Dalibaire-Ouest, UP (Que.) 13 C1
Dalkeith, UP (Ont.) 17 F1
Dalk-ka-gila-quoeux 2, IR (BC) 42 E4
Dallas, UP (Man.) 29 H2
Dalling, UP (Que.) 16 C3
Dalmeny, UP (Ont.) 17 C2
Dalmeny, VL (Sask.) 31 E1
Dalmuir, UP (Alta.) 33 E3
Dalny, UP (Man.) 29 E4
Dalquier, UP (Que.) 18 B1
Dalroy, UP (Alta.) 34 F2
Dalrymple, UP (Ont.) 23 G1
Dalston, UP (Ont.) 23 F2
Dalton, UP (Ont.) 26 B2
Dalton Mills, UP (Ont.) 26 B2
Dalton Post, UP (YT) 45 A3
Dalum, UP (Alta.) 34 F2
Dalvay by the Sea, UP (PEI) 7 D3
Damascus, UP (Ont.) 23 D3
Damascus, UP (NB) 11 E2
Damour, UP (Sask.) 32 C4
Dana, UP (Sask.) 31 F1
Danal CFS/SFC, MIL (Sask.) 31 F1
Danbury, UP (Sask.) 29 C1
Danby, UP (Que.) 16 C3
Dance, UP (Ont.) 28 H4
Dand, UP (Man.) 29 E4
Dane, UP (Ont.) 26 F2
Danesville, UP (NS) 10 E3
Danford-Lake, UP (Que.) 18 D4
Danforth Corners, NUP (BC) 35 F1
Daniel's Cove, UP (Nfld.) 2 H1
Daniel's Harbour, COMM (Nfld.) 5 F3
Daningay 12, IR (BC) 41 A1
Danis Trailer Court, NUP (Ont.) 27 D3
Danskin, UP (BC) 41 G1
Danube, UP (Alta.) 33 E2
Danvers, UP (NS) 10 B2
Danville, T (Que.) 16 D3
Daphne, UP (Sask.) 31 H1
Dapp, UP (Alta.) 33 D2
Darby, UP (Que.) 16 B4
Darbys Harbour, UP (Nfld.) 2 D3
D'Arcy, UP (BC) 37 G3
D'Arcy, UP (Sask.) 31 D2
Darcy-Corners, UP (Que.) 16 B4
Darfield, UP (BC) 36 F3
Dark Cove < Dark Cove – Middle Brook – Gambo, UP (Nfld.) 3 E3
Dark Cove – Middle Brook – Gambo, RD (Nfld.) 3 E3
Darlingford, UP (Man.) 29 G4
Darlingside, UP (Ont.) 17 C4
Darlings Island, NUP (NB) 11 E2
Darlings Lake, UP (NS) 10 A3
Darlington, UP (NB) 13 D3
Darlington, UP (PEI) 7 C4
Darmody, UP (Sask.) 31 F2
Darnley, UP (PEI) 7 B3
Darrell, UP (Ont.) 22 C3
D'Artagnan, UP (Que.) 15 H4
Dartford, UP (Ont.) 21 E1
Dartmouth, C (NS) 9 B4
Darwell, UP (Alta.) 33 D3
Dashken 22, IR (BC) 41 D1
Dashwood, UP (Ont.) 22 D1
Dashwood, UP (BC) 38 C2
Daulnay, UP (NB) 12 F1
Dauphin, T (Man.) 29 F2
Dauphin Beach, UP (Man.) 29 F2
Dauphin River 48A, IR (Man.) 29 G1
Dauversière, UP (NB) 12 E1
Davangus, UP (Que.) 18 A1
Daveluyville, VL (Que.) 16 C2
Davidson, T (Sask.) 31 F2
Davidson, UP (Que.) 18 C4
Davidson-Hill, UP (Que.) 16 C3
Davidson Lake, UP (NB) 11 B1
Davidsons Beach, UP (Ont.) 17 A4
Davidson's Corners, UP (Ont.) 21 D2
Davin, UP (Sask.) 31 H3
Davis, UP (Sask.) 32 E4
Davis Bay, UP (BC) 38 E2
Davis Cove, UP (Nfld.) 2 E2
Davis Inlet, COMM (Nfld.) 6 F2
Davis Island, UP (Nfld.) 2 D3
Davis Lock, UP (Ont.) 17 B3
Davis Mill, UP (NB) 12 H2
Davis Mill, UP (NB) 15 H2
Davis Mills, UP (Ont.) 24 G1
Davison Street, UP (NS) 10 E1
Davyroyd, UP (Sask.) 31 F4
Dawn Mills, UP (Ont.) 22 C2
Dawn Valley, UP (Ont.) 22 C2
Dawson, C (YT) 45 A2
Dawson Bay, UP (Man.) 30 A3
Dawson Bay 65A, IR (Man.) 30 A3
Dawson Bay 65B, IR (Man.) 30 A3
Dawson Bay 65F, IR (Man.) 30 A3
Dawson Creek, C (BC) 43 F4
Dawson Landing, UP (NWT) 44 B1
Dawson's Cove < Hermitage (COMM), UP (Nfld.) 2 B2
Dawson Settlement, UP (NB) 11 G1
Dawsons Landing, UP (BC) 41 F4
Dawsonville, UP (NB) 13 C4
Day Hill, UP (NB) 11 B1
Day Mills, UP (Ont.) 26 C4
Days Corner, UP (NB) 11 D2
Days Corner, UP (PEI) 7 B3
Daysland, T (Alta.) 33 F4
Days Landing, UP (NB) 11 D2
Dayspring, UP (NS) 10 E2
Days Ranch, UP (BC) 45 B4
Day Star 87, IR (Sask.) 31 H1
Daysville, UP (Sask.) 32 B3
Dayton, UP (NS) 10 A3
Dayton, UP (Ont.) 26 C4
Daytonia Beach, UP (Ont.) 21 C1
Daytown, UP (Ont.) 17 B3
Deacon, UP (Ont.) 24 F1
Deacon, UP (Man.) 28 A1
Deacons Corner, UP (Man.) 28 A1
Dead Creek, UP (NB) 11 A1
Dead Islands, UP (Nfld.) 6 H4
Deadman's Bay, UP (Nfld.) 3 F2
Deadmans Cove, UP (Nfld.) 5 G2
Deadman's Creek, IR (BC) 36 D4
Dead Point 5, IR (BC) 39 E1
Deadwood, UP (Alta.) 43 H2
Deadwood, UP (BC) 35 G4
Dealtown, NUP (Ont.) 22 C3
Dean, UP (NS) 9 D2
Dean Lake, UP (Ont.) 26 C4
Deanlea Beach, UP (Ont.) 23 E1
Deans Corners, UP (NS) 10 E2
Dearlock, UP (Ont.) 28 G4
Dease Lake, UP (BC) 45 B4
Dease Lake 9, IR (BC) 45 B4
Dease River 2, IR (BC) 45 C4
Dease River 3, IR (BC) 45 C4
Deauville, VL (Que.) 16 D4
DeBaies Cove, UP (NS) 9 D3
Debden, VL (Sask.) 32 C3
De Beaujeu, UP (Que.) 17 F1
Debec, UP (NB) 11 A1
Debert, UP (NS) 9 B2
Debert, Camp/Campement, MIL (NS) 9 B2
DeBlois, UP (PEI) 7 A2
Debolt, UP (Alta.) 43 H4
Déception, UP (Que.) 46 E3
Decimal, UP (Man.) 28 D1
Decker, UP (Man.) 29 E3
Decker Hollow, UP (Ont.) 21 D2
Decker Lake, UP (BC) 41 G1
Decker Lake 10, IR (BC) 42 G4
Decker Lake 10A, IR (BC) 42 G4
Decoigne, UP (Alta.) 40 G3
Decrene, UP (Alta.) 33 D1
Dedagaus 8, IR (BC) 41 F4
Dee Bank, UP (Ont.) 24 B2
Deekyakus 2, IR (BC) 38 B3
Deemerton, UP (Ont.) 23 C3
Deena 3, IR (BC) 41 B2
Deep Bay, UP (Nfld.) 3 E1
Deep Bay, UP (Ont.) 23 H1
Deep Bight, UP (Nfld.) 2 F1
Deep Brook, UP (NS) 10 B2
Deep Cove, UP (Nfld.) 2 D3
Deep Cove Island, UP (NS) 10 A4
Deep Creek, UP (Alta.) 33 E1
Deep Creek, UP (BC) 35 F1
Deep Creek 2, IR (BC) 36 B1
Deep Creek 5, IR (BC) 40 C2
Deepdale, UP (NS) 8 C3
Deepdale, UP (Man.) 29 D2
Deep River, T (Ont.) 18 B4
Deep Valley 5, IR (BC) 37 C3
Deer Bay, UP (Ont.) 24 D4
Deerbrook, UP (Ont.) 22 B3
Deerfield, UP (NS) 10 B3
Deer Harbour, UP (Nfld.) 2 F1
Deer Hill, UP (Alta.) 43 G3
Deerholme, UP (BC) 38 E3
Deerhorn, UP (Man.) 29 G2
Deerhurst, UP (Ont.) 21 A1
Deer Island, UP (Nfld.) 4 E4
Deer Lake, T (Nfld.) 5 G4
Deer Lake, UP (Ont.) 24 E3
Deer Lake, UP (Ont.) 30 D3
Deerland, UP (Alta.) 33 E3
Deer Park, UP (BC) 34 A4
Deer Ridge, UP (Sask.) 32 D3
Deerville, UP (NB) 12 A4
Deerwood, UP (Man.) 29 G4
Defence Island 28, IR (BC) 38 F1
Defence Island 28A, IR (BC) 38 F1
Defot, UP (BC) 45 B4
Defoy, UP (Que.) 16 C2
Dégelis, T (Que.) 14 G4
De Grasse, T (Que.) 19 F3
De Grassi Point, UP (Ont.) 21 A1
De Grau < Cape St George – Petit Jardin – Grand Jardin – De Grau – Marches Point – Loretto, UP (Nfld.) 4 A2
DeGros Marsh, UP (PEI) 7 E4
Dejong, UP (Ont.) 22 D1
Delacour, UP (Alta.) 34 E2
Delagrave, NUP (Que.) 15 C3
Delamere, UP (Ont.) 25 F1
Delaps Cove, UP (NS) 10 B1
Delaware, UP (Ont.) 22 D2
Delaware West, UP (Ont.) 22 D2
Del Bonita, UP (Alta.) 34 F4
Delburne, VL (Alta.) 34 F1
Delbys Cove, UP (Nfld.) 2 F1
Deléage, UP (Que.) 18 D4
Deleau, UP (Man.) 29 E4
De Lesseps, UP (Que.) 18 F4
Delhaven, UP (NS) 11 H3
Delhi, UP (Ont.) 22 F2
Delia, VL (Alta.) 34 G1
Delisle, T (Sask.) 31 E1
Dell, UP (Que.) 16 E3
Delmas, UP (Sask.) 32 B4
Delmer, UP (Ont.) 22 F2
Delmont, UP (Que.) 17 F2
Deloraine, T (Man.) 29 E4
Delorme Beach, UP (Sask.) 32 B4
Deloro, VL (Ont.) 24 F4
Delph, UP (Alta.) 33 E3
Delson, T (Que.) 17 H4
Delta, DM (BC) 38 F2
Delta, UP (Ont.) 17 B3
Delta Beach, UP (Man.) 29 G3
Demaine, UP (Sask.) 31 E2
Demay, UP (Alta.) 33 E4
Demers-Centre, UP (Que.) 18 C4
Demmitt, UP (Alta.) 43 F4
Demoiselle Creek, UP (NB) 11 G1
Demorestville, UP (Ont.) 21 G1
Dempseys Corner, UP (NS) 10 D1
Demuth, UP (BC) 35 E3
Denare Beach, UP (Sask.) 32 H2
Denbeigh Point, UP (Man.) 30 B3
Denbigh, UP (Ont.) 24 G2
Dencross, UP (Man.) 30 C4
Dene Village, UP (Man.) 46 B4
Denfield, UP (Ont.) 22 D1
Denhart, UP (Alta.) 34 H2
Denholm, UP (Que.) 18 D4
Denholm, VL (Sask.) 32 B4
Deniau, UP (Que.) 15 D2
Denison-Mills, UP (Que.) 16 D3
Denman Island, UP (BC) 38 C1
Denmark, UP (NS) 9 C1
Dennis, UP (NB) 12 E2
Dennis, UP (Alta.) 31 A3
Dennis Lake, UP (Man.) 29 H3
Densmores Mills, UP (NS) 9 B2
Denver, UP (NS) 9 E2
Denver Siding, NUP (BC) 34 B3
Denwood < Wainwright, Camp/Campement, UP (Alta.) 33 G4
Denzil, VL (Sask.) 31 C1
Departure Lake, UP (Ont.) 26 D1
Dépôt-Baskatong, UP (Que.) 18 D3
Dépôt-des-Loutres, UP (Que.) 20 H4
Depot Harbour, UP (Ont.) 24 A2
Dequen-Nord, UP (Que.) 18 H1
Derby, UP (NB) 12 E3
Derby, UP (PEI) 7 A3
Derby Junction, UP (NB) 12 E2
Dereham Centre, UP (Ont.) 22 F2
Dermid, UP (Ont.) 28 H4
Dernic, UP (Sask.) 29 C1
Deroche, UP (BC) 38 H2
Derrynane, UP (Ont.) 23 D3
Derrys Corner, UP (NB) 11 G2
Derryville, UP (Ont.) 21 B1
Derwent, UP (Ont.) 22 E2
Derwent, VL (Alta.) 33 G3
DeSable, UP (PEI) 7 C4
De Saint-Just, UP (Que.) 15 D1
Désaulniers, UP (Ont.) 25 G1
Desbarats, UP (Ont.) 26 B4
Desbiens, T (Que.) 18 H1
Desboro, UP (Ont.) 23 C2
Deschaillons, VL (Que.) 16 C1
Deschaillons-sur-St-Laurent, VL (Que.) 16 D1
Deschambault, VL (Que.) 16 D1
Deschambault Lake, UP (Sask.) 32 G1
Deschambault-Station, UP (Que.) 16 D1
D'Escousse, UP (NS) 8 D4
Deseronto, T (Ont.) 21 G1
Desert, UP (NS) 9 C4
Desert Lake, UP (Ont.) 17 A3
Desgagné, UP (Que.) 15 C1
Desherbiers, UP (NB) 12 F3
Desjardins Road, UP (NB) 12 A2
Desjardinsville, UP (Que.) 18 C4
Desjarlais, UP (Alta.) 33 F3
Deslandes, UP (Que.) 13 D1
Desmarais, UP (Alta.) 44 B4
Desmaraisville, UP (Que.) 20 F4
Desméloizes, UP (Que.) 26 F1
Desmond, UP (Ont.) 17 A4
Despinassy, UP (Que.) 18 C1
Desprès-Village, UP (NB) 12 G4
Dessaint, UP (Que.) 15 E1
Desserte-du-Lac-d'Argent, UP (Que.) 18 E3
Destor, UP (Que.) 18 A1
Destruction Bay, UP (YT) 45 A3
Detah, UP (NWT) 44 B1
Detlor, UP (Ont.) 24 F3
Deuxième-Sault, UP (NB) 15 H1
Deux-Montagnes, C (Que.) 17 F4
Deux-Rivières, UP (Ont.) 18 B4
Devault, UP (Que.) 16 B2
Développement-du-Sapin-Vert, UP (Que.) 16 C3
Devenish, UP (Alta.) 33 G1
Devereaux, UP (NB) 13 E4
Deville, UP (Alta.) 33 E3
Devils Island, UP (NS) 9 B4
Devine, UP (BC) 37 G3
Devine Corner, UP (NB) 11 E2
Devizes, UP (Ont.) 22 E1
Devlin, UP (Ont.) 28 H4
Devon, T (Alta.) 33 D3
Devon, UP (NS) 9 C3
Devon 30, IR (NB) 11 C1
Devona, UP (Alta.) 40 G2
Devonshire-Park, UP (Que.) 24 H1
Dewar Lake, UP (Sask.) 31 C1
Dewars, UP (Ont.) 17 A1
Dewberry, VL (Alta.) 33 G3
De Winton, UP (Alta.) 34 E2
DeWitts Corners, UP (Ont.) 17 B3
Dewittville, UP (Que.) 17 G2
Dewney, UP (BC) 38 H2
DeWolfe, UP (NB) 11 B3
Dexter, UP (Ont.) 22 E2
Diamond, UP (NS) 9 C1
Diamond City, UP (Alta.) 34 F3
Diamond Cove, UP (Nfld.) 4 B4
Dickie Mountain, UP (NB) 11 E2
Dickson, UP (Alta.) 34 E1
Dicksons Corners, UP (Ont.) 22 E1
Didsbury, T (Alta.) 34 E1
Didyme, UP (Que.) 18 G1
Dieppe, T (NB) 11 G1
Dieppe, NUP (Que.) 16 A4
Digby, T (NS) 10 B2
Digby Corner, UP (NB) 12 A4
Digby Island, UP (BC) 41 C1
Digdeguash, UP (NB) 11 B3
Dignard Settlement, NUP (NB) 12 G1
Dildo, UP (Nfld.) 2 F2
Dildo South, UP (Nfld.) 2 F2
Diligent River, UP (NS) 11 H2
Dilke, VL (Sask.) 31 G2
Dillabough, UP (Sask.) 32 G4
Dillon, UP (Ont.) 25 F3
Dillon < Peter Pond Lake 193, UP (Sask.) 44 D4
Dil-ma-sow 5, IR (BC) 41 E2
Dimock-Creek, UP (Que.) 13 E3
Dimsdale, UP (Alta.) 43 G4
Dina, UP (Alta.) 33 H4
Dinant, UP (Alta.) 33 E4
Dingley, UP (Sask.) 29 B3
Dingwall, UP (NS) 8 E1
Dingwell, UP (PEI) 7 D3
Dingwells Mills, UP (PEI) 7 E3
Dinner Point Depot, UP (Ont.) 25 C2
Dinorwic, UP (Ont.) 27 A2
Dinsmore, VL (Sask.) 31 E2
Dipper Harbour East, UP (NB) 11 D3
Dipper Harbour West, UP (NB) 11 D3
Dipper Rapids 192C, IR (Sask.) 44 E4
Dirleton, UP (Ont.) 17 B1
Discovery, UP (NWT) 45 E3
Discovery Island 3, IR (BC) 38 F4
Disley, VL (Sask.) 31 G3
Disraeli, T (Que.) 16 E2
Diss, UP (Alta.) 33 A3
Ditchfield, UP (Que.) 16 F3
Ditton Park, UP (Sask.) 32 F4
Divide, UP (NB) 12 B3
Divide, UP (Sask.) 31 C4
Dixon, UP (Ont.) 17 E2
Dixon, UP (Sask.) 31 G1
Dixons Corners, UP (Ont.) 17 D2
Dixonville, UP (Alta.) 43 H3
Dixville, VL (Que.) 16 D4
Dneiper, UP (Sask.) 29 D2
Doaktown, VL (NB) 12 D3
Doan, UP (Alta.) 34 E1
Dobbinton, UP (Ont.) 23 C2
Dobie, UP (Ont.) 26 F2
Dobsons Corner, UP (NB) 11 F1
Dochsupple 3, IR (BC) 38 B3
Dock, UP (Que.) 19 G3
Dock Corner, UP (PEI) 7 A2
Dock Cove < St Brendan's (COMM), UP (Nfld.) 3 F3
Doctors Brook, UP (NS) 8 B4
Doctors Cove, UP (NS) 10 B4
Doctors Harbour, UP (Nfld.) 2 C2
Doctors Harbour, UP (Nfld.) 4 D4
Doddridge, UP (NS) 9 B2
Dodds, UP (Alta.) 33 E3
Dodds, UP (Que.) 17 C1
Dodsland, VL (Sask.) 31 C1
Doe Lake, UP (Ont.) 24 B1
Doe River, UP (BC) 43 F3
Dofred Subdivision, NUP (NB) 11 E2
Dog Cove, UP (Nfld.) 4 E4
Dog Creek, UP (BC) 36 B2
Dog Creek, UP (BC) 40 B1
Dog Creek 1, IR (BC) 36 B2
Dog Creek 2, IR (BC) 36 B2
Dog Creek 3, IR (BC) 36 B2
Dog Creek 4, IR (BC) 36 B2
Dog Creek 46, IR (Man.) 29 G2
Dogfish Bay 42, IR (BC) 42 D3
Dogpound, UP (Alta.) 34 E2
Dogwood, UP (Nfld.) 4 D1
Dogwood Valley, UP (BC) 35 B3
Doheny, UP (Que.) 18 H3
Doherty, UP (Que.) 17 B1
Doig River 206, IR (BC) 43 E3
Dokis < Dokis 9, UP (Ont.) 25 G1
Dokis 9, IR (Ont.) 25 G2
Dolbeau, T (Que.) 18 H1
Dollard, VL (Sask.) 31 D4
Dollard-des-Ormeaux, T (Que.) 17 F4
Dolly Bay, UP (Man.) 29 G2
Dolphin Beach, UP (BC) 38 D2
Dolphin Island 1, IR (BC) 41 C1
Domain, UP (Man.) 28 A2
Domaine-Alarie, UP (Que.) 18 F4
Domaine-Archambault, UP (Que.) 16 A1
Domaine-Archambault, UP (Que.) 18 G4
Domaine-Asselin, UP (Que.) 16 A2
Domaine-Bastien, UP (Que.) 18 F4
Domaine-Beaudoin-Papin, NUP (Que.) 16 A3
Domaine-Beaudry, UP (Que.) 16 A3
Domaine-Beauport, UP (Que.) 18 F4
Domaine-Bel-Humeur, UP (Que.) 16 A2
Domaine-Belleville, UP (Que.) 16 A2
Domaine-Bonaventure, UP (Que.) 16 B2
Domaine-Boulots, NUP (Que.) 16 B1
Domaine-Breton, UP (Que.) 18 F4
Domaine-Charbonneau, NUP (Que.) 18 F4
Domaine-Chez-Bill, NUP (Que.) 18 A2
Domaine-Crevier, UP (Que.) 16 A2
Domaine-Dauphinais, UP (Que.) 16 A1
Domaine-de-La Clouterie, UP (Que.) 18 E4
Domaine-de-l'Énergie, UP (Que.) 18 G4
Domaine-de-Provence, UP (Que.) 17 G3
Domaine-des-Bouleaux, UP (Que.) 18 H3
Domaine-des-Chênes, UP (Que.) 16 B1
Domaine-des-Érables, UP (Que.) 16 B1
Domaine-des-Fleurs, NUP (Que.) 16 A3
Domaine-des-Îles, UP (Que.) 15 G4
Domaine-Desjardins, UP (Que.) 16 A2
Domaine-des-Monts, UP (Que.) 16 A1
Domaine-des-Pins, UP (Que.) 16 E2
Domaine-des-Quatre-Hétu, UP (Que.) 18 F4
Domaine-des-Rentiers, UP (Que.) 18 F4
Domaine-des-Saules, UP (Que.) 16 A4
Domaine-des-Trois-Lacs, UP (Que.) 16 A2
Domaine-des-Trois-Lacs, UP (Que.) 18 F4
Domaine-des-Vallées, UP (Que.) 18 F4
Domaine-du-Cap, UP (Que.) 18 F4
Domaine-du-Chevreuil, UP (Que.) 16 C2
Domaine-du-Chevreuil, UP (Que.) 18 H4
Domaine-du-Joli-Val, UP (Que.) 18 F4
Domaine-du-Lac-Huron, UP (Que.) 16 A3
Domaine-du-Repos, UP (Que.) 16 C3
Domaine-Feuille-d'Érable, UP (Que.) 18 F4
Domaine-Fournier, UP (Que.) 16 A2
Domaine-François, UP (Que.) 16 A2
Domaine-François, UP (Que.) 18 F4
Domaine-Gérôme, UP (Que.) 17 G3
Domaine-Joyeux, NUP (Que.) 16 A4
Domaine-Lac-France, UP (Que.) 18 F4
Domaine-Lafortune, UP (Que.) 16 A2
Domaine-Lafrenière, NUP (Que.) 16 A2
Domaine-La Poudrière, UP (Que.) 16 B1
Domaine-Lecours, UP (Que.) 16 A3
Domaine-Lemenn, UP (Que.) 18 F4
Domaine-Levesque, UP (Que.) 18 H1
Domaine-Lorraine, UP (Que.) 16 A2
Domaine-Louis-Riel, UP (Que.) 16 B1
Domaine-Marois, UP (Que.) 16 A2
Domaine-McManiman, UP (Que.) 18 F4
Domaine-Monaco, UP (Que.) 18 F4
Domaine-Mon-Loisir, UP (Que.) 16 A1
Domaine-Mon-Repos, NUP (Que.) 16 D2
Domaine-Ouellet, UP (Que.) 16 A2
Domaine-Paradis, UP (Que.) 16 A2
Domaine-Pozer, UP (Que.) 15 C4
Domaine-Prescott, UP (Que.) 16 A1
Domaine-Préville, NUP (Que.) 16 A2
Domaine-Quintal, UP (Que.) 18 G4
Domaine-Racine, UP (Que.) 18 F4
Domaine-Rouville, UP (Que.) 16 A3
Domaine-Royal, UP (Que.) 16 A1
Domaine-St-Augustin, UP (Que.) 15 F3
Domaine-St-Denis, UP (Que.) 16 A3
Domaine-St-Paulin, UP (Que.) 16 B1
Domaine-Valboise, UP (Que.) 17 H1
Domaine-Val-Joli, UP (Que.) 16 A2
Domaine-Villeroy, UP (Que.) 16 A2
Domaine-Vilmont, UP (Que.) 18 F4
Dome Creek, UP (BC) 40 E2
Dominion, T (NS) 8 F3
Dominion, UP (YT) 45 A2
Dominion City, UP (Man.) 28 A3
Dominionville, UP (Ont.) 17 E2
Domino, UP (Nfld.) 6 H3
Domremy, VL (Sask.) 32 D4
Domville, UP (Ont.) 17 C3
Donagh, UP (PEI) 7 D4
Donald, UP (BC) 34 B2
Donald, UP (Ont.) 24 D3
Donalda, VL (Alta.) 33 E4
Donald Gunn, UP (Sask.) 29 C2
Donald Landing, UP (BC) 40 A1
Donaldson, UP (Ont.) 17 A2
Donaldston, UP (PEI) 7 D3
Donatville, UP (Alta.) 33 E2
Donavon, UP (Sask.) 31 E1
Donavon Subdivision, NUP (BC) 36 D2
Doncaster 17, IR (Que.) 18 F4
Doncrest, UP (Sask.) 32 G4
Donegal, UP (Ont.) 23 C4
Donegal, UP (NB) 11 E1
Donegal, UP (Ont.) 24 G2
Dongola, UP (Ont.) 23 H1
Donkin, UP (NS) 8 F3
Donnacona, T (Que.) 15 A3
Donnelly, VL (Alta.) 43 H3
Donnelly Settlement, UP (NB) 11 B1
Donnely Landing, UP (BC) 38 D1
Donnybrook, UP (Ont.) 23 B3
Donovans, UP (Nfld.) 2 H2
Dons Trailer Court, NUP (BC) 34 B2
Donwell, UP (Sask.) 29 C2
Donwood, UP (Ont.) 21 D1
Doobah 10, IR (BC) 38 C1
Dookqua 5, IR (BC) 38 A3
Dookqua 5A, IR (BC) 38 A3
Doonside, UP (Sask.) 29 D3
Dorchester, UP (Ont.) 22 E2
Dorchester, VL (NB) 11 H1
Dorchester Cape, UP (NB) 11 H1
Dorea, UP (Que.) 17 G2
Doré Bay, UP (Ont.) 24 G1
Doré Lake, UP (Sask.) 32 C2
Dorenlee, UP (Alta.) 33 E4
Dorintosh, UP (Sask.) 32 B2
Dorion, T (Que.) 17 G1
Dorion, UP (Ont.) 27 E3
Dorion Landing, UP (Ont.) 27 E3
Doris, UP (Alta.) 33 D2
Doriston, UP (BC) 38 E1
Dorking, UP (Ont.) 23 D4
Dorland, UP (Ont.) 22 F1
Dorland, UP (Ont.) 21 G1
Dornoch, UP (Ont.) 23 D2
Dorn Ridge, UP (NB) 11 C1
Dorothy, UP (Alta.) 34 G2
Dorothy Lake, UP (Man.) 28 D1
Dorreen, UP (BC) 42 E4
Dorrington Hill, UP (NB) 11 A1
Dorset, UP (Ont.) 24 C2
Dorts Cove, UP (NS) 9 G2
Dorval, C (Que.) 17 G4
Dorval-Lodge, UP (Que.) 18 C2
Dosquet, UP (Que.) 15 A4
Dot, UP (BC) 35 B2
Doucetteville, UP (NS) 10 B2
Douglas, UP (NB) 11 C1
Douglas, UP (Ont.) 24 G2
Douglas, UP (Man.) 29 F3
Douglas, UP (PEI) 7 D3
Douglas, UP (BC) 38 H1
Douglas 8, IR (BC) 38 H1
Douglasfield, UP (NB) 12 F2
Douglas Harbour, UP (NB) 11 D1
Douglas Lake, UP (BC) 35 D2
Douglas Lake 3, IR (BC) 35 D2
Douglas Road, UP (NS) 10 C1
Douglaston, UP (Sask.) 29 C4
Douglastown, VL (NB) 12 F2
Douro, UP (Ont.) 21 D1
Dove Brook, UP (Nfld.) 6 G3
Dove Island 12, IR (BC) 41 F4
Dover, T (Nfld.) 3 F3
Dover, UP (NS) 9 H2
Dover, UP (PEI) 7 D4
Dover, UP (NB) 11 G1
Dover Centre, UP (Ont.) 22 B3
Dovercourt, UP (Alta.) 34 D1
Dover Hill, UP (NB) 12 A3
Dowling, UP (Alta.) 34 G1
Dowling Lake, UP (Alta.) 34 G1
Downe, UP (Sask.) 31 D1
Downeys, UP (Ont.) 23 E4
Downeyville, UP (Ont.) 21 D1
Downie Creek, UP (BC) 34 A2
Dow Settlement, UP (NB) 11 A1
Doyles, UP (Nfld.) 4 A3
Doyles, UP (Ont.) 22 C3
Doyles Brook, UP (NB) 12 E3
Doyleville, UP (NB) 13 D4
Dracon, UP (Ont.) 23 E3
Dragon, UP (Que.) 17 F1
Dragon Lake, NUP (BC) 40 C3
Dragon Lake 3, IR (BC) 40 C3
Drake, VL (Sask.) 31 G1
Drapeau, UP (Que.) 13 D3
Draper, UP (Alta.) 44 C4
Drayton, VL (Ont.) 23 D3
Drayton Valley, T (Alta.) 33 C3
Dreau, UP (Alta.) 43 H3
Dredge Creek, UP (YT) 45 A2
Drefal, UP (Ont.) 26 D3
Dresden, T (Ont.) 22 C2
Drew, UP (Ont.) 23 C3
Drew Harbour 9, IR (BC) 37 B4
Drifting River, UP (Man.) 29 E2
Driftpile, UP (Alta.) 33 C1
Drift Pile River 150, IR (Alta.) 33 C1
Driftwood, UP (Ont.) 26 E1
Driftwood Creek, UP (BC) 42 F4
Driftwood River 1, IR (BC) 42 G2
Driftwood Trailer Court, NUP (Sask.) 32 D3
Drinkwater, VL (Sask.) 31 G3
Driscol Lake, UP (Sask.) 31 D4
Drisdelle, UP (NB) 7 A4
Drisdelle Settlement, UP (NB) 12 F2
Driver, UP (Sask.) 31 C1
Drobot, UP (Sask.) 29 C2
Dromore, UP (PEI) 7 D4
Dromore, UP (Ont.) 23 D3
Drook, UP (Nfld.) 2 G4
Dropmore, UP (Man.) 29 D2
Droxford, UP (Sask.) 31 E3
Druid, UP (Sask.) 31 D1
Drumbo, UP (Ont.) 22 F1
Drum Head, UP (NS) 9 F2
Drumheller, C (Alta.) 34 F2
Drummond, UP (Ont.) 21 D1
Drummond, VL (NB) 12 A2
Drummond Centre, UP (Ont.) 17 B2
Drummondville, C (Que.) 16 C2
Drummondville-Sud, T (Que.) 16 C3
Drurys Cove, UP (NB) 11 E2
Drybrough, UP (Man.) 30 A1
Dry Creek, UP (YT) 45 A3
Dryden, T (Ont.) 27 A1
Dryden, UP (Ont.) 23 C3
Dryden's Corner, UP (Ont.) 25 B2
Dry Gulch Park, NUP (BC) 34 C3
Dry River, UP (Man.) 29 G4
Dry Salmon 7, IR (BC) 36 B4
Drysdale, UP (Ont.) 23 B4
Drywood, UP (Alta.) 34 E4
Duagh, UP (Alta.) 33 E3
Duart, UP (Ont.) 22 D3
Dubee Settlement, UP (NB) 11 F1
Dublin, UP (Ont.) 23 C4
Dublin Shore, UP (NS) 10 E2
Dubonnet, UP (Que.) 15 D3
Dubreuilville, UP (Ont.) 26 A2
Dubuc, VL (Sask.) 29 C3
Dubuisson, UP (Que.) 18 B2
Duchemin, UP (Que.) 16 C1
Duchesnay, UP (Que.) 15 A3
Duchess, VL (Alta.) 34 G2
Duck Bay, UP (Man.) 29 E1
Duck Lake, T (Sask.) 32 D4
Duck Lake 7, IR (BC) 35 F2
Duck Lake 76B, IR (Ont.) 26 C2
Duck Lake Post, UP (Man.) 44 H2
Duck Range, UP (BC) 35 E1
Duck River, UP (Man.) 29 E1
Duclos, UP (Que.) 17 B1
Duclos Point, UP (Ont.) 21 B1
Dudley, UP (Ont.) 24 B3

Dudswell, UP (Que.) **16 E3**
Dufaultville, UP (Que.) **13 A2**
Duff, VL (Sask.) **29 C2**
Duff Corners, UP (Ont.) **21 F1**
Dufferin, UP (NS) **9 D1**
Dufferin, UP (NB) **11 E1**
Dufferin 10, IR (BC) **35 B2**
Dufferin Bridge, UP (Ont.) **24 B2**
Dufferin-Heights, UP (Que.) **16 D4**
Dufferin Mines, UP (NS) **9 E3**
Duffield, UP (Alta.) **33 D3**
Duffys Corner, UP (NB) **11 D1**
Dufour, UP (Que.) **15 C2**
Dufournel, UP (Que.) **15 G3**
Dufourville, UP (NB) **12 G4**
Dufresne, UP (Man.) **28 B2**
Dufrost, UP (Man.) **28 A3**
Dugal, UP (Que.) **13 D3**
Dugald, UP (Man.) **28 B1**
Duganville, NUP (BC) **34 C4**
Dugas, UP (Que.) **18 G4**
Dugas, UP (NB) **13 F4**
Dug-da-myse 12, IR (BC) **41 G4**
Duguayville, UP (NB) **12 F1**
Duguesclin, UP (Que.) **13 H3**
Duhamel, UP (Que.) **18 E4**
Duhamel, UP (Alta.) **33 E4**
Dulcemaine, UP (Ont.) **17 B3**
Dumas, UP (Sask.) **29 D3**
Dumbarton, UP (NB) **11 B2**
Dumblane, UP (Ont.) **23 C2**
Dumble, UP (Sask.) **32 C3**
Dumfries, UP (NB) **11 B1**
Dummer, UP (Sask.) **31 G3**
Dumoine, UP (Que.) **18 B4**
Dumpling Harbour, UP (Nfld.) **6 G3**
Dunakin, UP (NS) **8 C3**
Dunany, UP (Que.) **17 F1**
Dunbar, UP (Ont.) **17 D2**
Dunblane, UP (PEI) **7 A3**
Dunblane, VL (Sask.) **31 E2**
Dunboyne, UP (Ont.) **22 E2**
Duncairn, UP (Sask.) **31 D3**
Duncan, C (BC) **38 E3**
Duncan, UP (Que.) **16 B3**
Duncan, UP (Ont.) **23 D2**
Duncanby Landing, UP (BC) **41 F4**
Duncan Lake 12, IR (BC) **42 G4**
Duncans Cove, UP (NS) **9 B4**
Dunchurch, UP (Ont.) **24 A1**
Duncrief, UP (Ont.) **22 D1**
Dundalk, VL (Ont.) **23 E2**
Dundas, T (Ont.) **22 H1**
Dundas, UP (PEI) **7 E4**
Dundas, UP (NB) **12 G4**
Dundas Harbour, UP (NWT) **47 E3**
Dundas Island 32B, IR (BC) **42 C4**
Dundee, UP (NS) **8 D4**
Dundee, UP (NB) **13 D4**
Dundee, UP (PEI) **7 D3**
Dundee, UP (Que.) **17 F2**
Dundee-Centre, UP (Que.) **17 F2**
Dundela, UP (Ont.) **17 D2**
Dundonald, UP (Ont.) **21 E1**
Dundurn, VL (Sask.) **31 F1**
Dundurn, Camp/Campement, MIL (Sask.) **31 F1**
Dunedin, UP (Ont.) **23 E2**
Dunedin, UP (PEI) **7 C4**
Dune-du-Sud, UP (Que.) **7 F1**
Dunfermline, UP (Sask.) **31 E1**
Dunfield, UP (Nfld.) **3 G4**
Dungannon, UP (Ont.) **23 B3**
Dungarry, UP (NS) **8 C3**
Dunham, T (Que.) **16 B4**
Dunkeld, UP (Ont.) **23 C2**
Dunkerron, UP (Ont.) **21 A1**
Dunkin, UP (Que.) **16 C4**
Dunkirk, UP (Sask.) **31 F3**
Dunkley, UP (BC) **40 C2**
Dunleath, UP (Sask.) **29 C2**
Dunlop, UP (Ont.) **23 B3**
Dunlop, UP (NB) **12 E1**
Dunlop, UP (Man.) **30 B2**
Dunmore, UP (NS) **8 B4**
Dunmore, UP (Alta.) **31 B3**
Dunmore, UP (NS) **8 C3**
Dunn, UP (Alta.) **33 G4**
Dunnet's Corner, UP (Ont.) **25 F1**
Dunnette Landing, UP (Ont.) **21 E1**
Dunning, UP (NS) **9 E2**
Dunnottar, VL (Man.) **30 C4**
Dunns Corner, UP (NS) **9 B2**
Dunns Valley, UP (Ont.) **26 B4**
Dunnville, T (Ont.) **21 A4**
Dunphy, UP (Alta.) **34 F2**
Dunrankin, UP (Ont.) **26 C1**
Dunraven, UP (Que.) **17 A1**
Dunrea, UP (Man.) **29 F4**
Dunrobin, UP (Ont.) **17 B1**
Dunrobin Shore, UP (Ont.) **17 D4**
Dunsford, UP (Ont.) **21 C1**
Dunshalt, UP (Alta.) **34 F2**
Dunsinane, UP (NB) **11 F1**
Dunsmuir, UP (BC) **38 C2**
Dunstable, UP (Alta.) **33 D3**
Dunstaffnage, UP (PEI) **7 D4**
Dunster, UP (BC) **40 F3**
Duntara, COMM (Nfld.) **3 G4**
Duntroon, UP (Ont.) **23 E2**
Dunvegan, UP (NS) **8 C3**
Dunvegan, UP (Ont.) **17 E1**
Dunvegan, UP (Alta.) **43 G3**
Dunville, T (Nfld.) **2 F3**
Duparquet, T (Que.) **18 A1**
Duperow, UP (Sask.) **31 D1**
Duplessis, UP (Que.) **18 G2**
Duplin, UP (Que.) **16 D3**
Dupont, UP (Que.) **18 F4**
Duprat, UP (Que.) **18 A1**
Dupuy, UP (Que.) **18 A1**
Durban, UP (Man.) **29 D1**
Durells Island, UP (NS) **9 H2**
Duret, UP (Que.) **13 F3**
Durham, T (Ont.) **23 D2**
Durham, UP (NS) **9 D1**
Durham Bridge, UP (NB) **11 C1**
Durham-Sud, UP (Que.) **16 C3**
Duricle < Fox Cove – Mortier, UP (Nfld.) **2 C3**
Durieu, UP (BC) **38 H2**
Durlingville, UP (Alta.) **33 G2**
Durrell, T (Nfld.) **3 D1**
Durrell Subdivision, NUP (BC) **40 C3**
Durward, UP (Alta.) **34 E3**
Dutch Brook, UP (NS) **8 F3**
Dutch Line, UP (Ont.) **23 H1**
Dutch Settlement, UP (NS) **9 B3**
Dutch Valley, UP (NB) **11 F2**
Duthil, UP (Alta.) **34 D2**
Duthill, UP (Ont.) **22 B2**
Dutton, VL (Ont.) **22 D2**
Duttona Beach, UP (Ont.) **22 D2**
Duval, VL (Sask.) **31 G2**
Duvar, UP (PEI) **7 A3**
Duvernay, UP (Alta.) **33 F3**
Dwight, UP (Ont.) **24 C2**
Dwyer Hill, UP (Ont.) **17 C2**
Dyce, UP (Man.) **30 B2**
Dyer, UP (Ont.) **17 E2**
Dyer's Bay, UP (Ont.) **25 D4**
Dyment, UP (Ont.) **27 B2**
Dysart, VL (Sask.) **31 H2**
Dzagayap 73, IR (BC) **42 D4**
Dzagayap 74, IR (BC) **42 D4**

E

Eades, UP (Ont.) **26 F1**
Eads Bush, UP (Ont.) **25 C2**
Eady, UP (Ont.) **23 F1**
Eagle, UP (Ont.) **22 D2**
Eagle Bay, UP (BC) **36 H4**
Eagle Butte, UP (Alta.) **31 B4**
Eagle Creek, UP (BC) **36 E2**
Eagle Creek 6, IR (BC) **42 H3**
Eagle Head, UP (NS) **10 E3**
Eagle Heights, UP (BC) **38 E3**
Eagle Hill, UP (Alta.) **34 E1**
Eagle Lake, UP (Ont.) **24 D2**
Eagle Lake, UP (Ont.) **24 B1**
Eagle Lake 27, IR (Ont.) **27 A2**
Eagle River, UP (Ont.) **27 A1**
Eaglesham, VL (Alta.) **43 H3**
Eagles Nest, UP (Ont.) **25 C2**
Eagleson Corners, UP (Ont.) **17 D4**
Earchman, UP (Man.) **30 B2**
Eardley, UP (Que.) **17 B1**
Ear Falls, UP (Ont.) **30 E4**
Earle Wharf, UP (NB) **11 E2**
Earl Grey, VL (Sask.) **31 G2**
Earl Pit, UP (Ont.) **27 A1**
Earls Cove, UP (BC) **38 D1**
Earlstown, UP (Que.) **16 D4**
Earlton, UP (Ont.) **26 F2**
Earltown, UP (NS) **9 C2**
Early Gardens, UP (Alta.) **43 H3**
Earnscliffe, UP (PEI) **7 D4**
Earnscliffe, UP (Ont.) **23 E3**
East Advocate, UP (NS) **11 G3**
East-Aldfield, UP (Que.) **17 B1**
East Amherst, UP (NS) **9 A1**
East Anglia, UP (Sask.) **32 B3**
East-Angus, T (Que.) **16 D3**
East Apple River, UP (NS) **11 G2**
East Arlington, UP (NS) **10 C1**
East Arrow Park, UP (BC) **34 A3**
East Baccaro, UP (NS) **10 C4**
East Bay, UP (NS) **8 E3**
East Bay, UP (Nfld.) **4 C4**
East Bay, UP (Man.) **29 F2**
East Beaver Brook, UP (NB) **12 E2**
East Berlin, UP (NS) **10 E3**
East Bideford, UP (PEI) **7 B3**
Eastbourne, UP (Ont.) **21 B1**
Eastbourne, UP (BC) **38 F2**
East Braintree, UP (Man.) **28 D2**
East Branch, UP (NB) **12 G3**
East Branch River John, UP (NS) **9 C1**
East Brighton, UP (NB) **12 B4**
East Broadway, NUP (NS) **8 F3**
East-Broughton, UP (Que.) **15 B4**
East-Broughton-Station, VL (Que.) **15 B4**
Eastburg, UP (Alta.) **33 D2**
East Centreville, UP (NB) **12 A4**
East Chester, UP (NS) **9 A4**
East Chezzetcook, UP (NS) **9 C3**
East Clifford, UP (NS) **10 D2**
East-Clifton, UP (Que.) **16 E4**
East Cloverdale, UP (NB) **12 B4**
East Coldstream, UP (NB) **12 B4**
East Coleman, NUP (Alta.) **34 E4**
East Collette, UP (NB) **12 F3**
East Coulee, UP (Alta.) **34 G2**
East Dalhousie, UP (NS) **10 D1**
East Dover, UP (NS) **9 B4**
East Earltown, UP (NS) **9 C1**
Eastend, T (Sask.) **31 C4**
East Erinville, UP (NS) **9 F2**
Eastern Island 13, IR (BC) **41 H1**
Eastern Passage, UP (NS) **9 B4**
Eastern Points, UP (NS) **10 E2**
Easterville, UP (Man.) **30 B3**
East Fairwell, UP (Sask.) **31 C4**
East-Farnham, VL (Que.) **16 B4**
East Ferry, UP (NS) **10 A2**
East Folly Mountain, UP (NS) **9 B2**
Eastford, UP (Ont.) **26 E1**
East Fraserville, UP (NS) **11 G2**
East Galloway, UP (NB) **12 G3**
Eastgate, UP (Alta.) **33 E3**
East Glassville, UP (NB) **12 B3**
East Gore, UP (NS) **9 B3**
East Green Harbour, UP (NS) **10 C4**
East Halls Harbour Road, UP (NS) **11 H3**
East Hansford, UP (NS) **9 B1**
East Harrow, UP (Ont.) **22 A4**
East Havre Boucher, UP (NS) **8 C4**
East-Hereford, UP (Que.) **16 E4**
East-Hill, UP (Que.) **16 C4**
East Hungerford, UP (Ont.) **24 G4**
East Inglisville, UP (NS) **10 D1**
East Jeddore, UP (NS) **9 C3**
East Jordan, UP (NS) **10 C3**
East Kemptville, UP (NS) **10 B3**
East Knowlesville, UP (NB) **12 B3**
East Kootenay, UP (Alta.) **34 E4**
East LaHave, UP (NS) **10 E2**
East Lake Ainslie, UP (NS) **8 D3**
East Leicester, UP (NS) **9 A1**
Eastleigh, UP (Sask.) **31 F3**
East Linden, UP (NS) **7 B4**
East Linton, UP (Ont.) **23 C1**
Eastmain, IR (Que.) **20 E3**
Eastman, VL (Que.) **16 C4**
East Mapleton, UP (NS) **9 A2**
East Margaretsville, UP (NS) **10 D1**
East McKirdy, UP (Ont.) **27 F2**
East Meadows, NUP (Nfld.) **2 H2**
East Milford, UP (NS) **9 B3**
East Mines, UP (NS) **9 B2**
East Mines Station, UP (NS) **9 B2**
East Moberly Lake 169, IR (BC) **43 D3**
East Mountain, UP (NS) **9 C2**
East New Annan, UP (NS) **9 C1**
East Newbridge, UP (NB) **11 A1**
East Noel, UP (NS) **9 B2**
East Oakland, UP (Ont.) **22 G1**
Easton, UP (NS) **10 B2**
Eastons Corners, UP (Ont.) **17 C3**
East Oro, UP (Ont.) **23 F2**
East Oxford, UP (Ont.) **17 C2**
East Pennant, UP (NS) **9 B4**
East Petpeswick, UP (NS) **9 C3**
East Pine, UP (BC) **43 E4**
East Point, UP (PEI) **7 F3**
East Poplar, UP (Sask.) **31 G4**
Eastport, T (Nfld.) **3 F4**
East Port Medway, UP (NS) **10 E3**
East Preston, UP (NS) **9 B3**
East Pubnico, UP (NS) **10 B4**
East Quinan, UP (NS) **10 B3**
East Quoddy, UP (NS) **9 E3**
East River, UP (NS) **9 A4**
East River Point, UP (NS) **9 A4**
East River St Marys, UP (NS) **9 E2**
East River St Marys West Side, UP (NS) **9 E2**
East River Sheet Harbour, UP (NS) **9 D3**
East Riverside-Kingshurst, VL (NB) **11 D2**
East Roman Valley UP (NS) **9 F2**
East Royalty, UP (PEI) **7 C4**
East Saanich 2, IR (BC) **38 F4**
East Sable River, UP (NS) **10 D3**
East St Paul, UP (Man.) **28 A1**
East Scotch Settlement, UP (NB) **11 E2**
East Selkirk, UP (Man.) **28 B1**
East Ship Harbour, UP (NS) **9 D3**
East Side, UP (NS) **10 B4**
East Side of Ragged Island, UP (NS) **10 D4**
East Side Port L'Hebert, UP (NS) **10 D3**
East Skye Glen, UP (NS) **8 D3**
East Sooke, UP (BC) **38 E4**
East Southampton, UP (NS) **9 A1**
East Tracadie, UP (NS) **8 C4**
East Tremont, UP (NS) **10 D1**
East Uniacke, UP (NS) **9 B3**
Eastview, UP (Ont.) **17 B4**
East Village, UP (NS) **9 B2**
Eastville, UP (NS) **9 D2**
East Wallace, UP (NS) **9 C1**
East Walton, UP (NS) **9 A2**
East Waterville, UP (NB) **11 B1**
East Wentworth, UP (NS) **9 B1**
East Wiltshire, UP (PEI) **7 C4**
Eastwood, UP (Ont.) **22 F1**
East York, BOR (Ont.) **21 B2**
Easyford, UP (Alta.) **33 C3**
Eaton, UP (Que.) **16 E4**
Eatonia, T (Sask.) **31 C2**
Eatonville, UP (Ont.) **22 C3**
Eatonville, UP (NS) **11 G2**
Eatonville, UP (Que.) **15 E2**
Eau Claire, UP (Ont.) **18 A4**
Ebb and Flow, UP (Man.) **29 F2**
Ebb and Flow 52, IR (Man.) **29 G2**
Ebbs Shore, UP (Ont.) **17 B2**
Ebenezer, UP (PEI) **7 C3**
Ebenezer, UP (Ont.) **17 B4**
Ebenezer, UP (Ont.) **21 G1**
Ebenezer, UP (Ont.) **24 A3**
Ebenezer, VL (Sask.) **29 C2**
Eberts, UP (Ont.) **22 C3**
Ebor, UP (Man.) **29 D4**
Eccles-Hill, UP (Que.) **16 B4**
Echachis 2, IR (BC) **38 A2**
Echo Bay, UP (Ont.) **26 B4**
Echo Bay, UP (BC) **39 F1**
Echo Bay, UP (NWT) **5 E2**
Echo Beach, UP (Ont.) **24 B2**
Eckville, T (Alta.) **33 D4**
Eclipse, UP (Man.) **29 F2**
Economy, UP (NS) **9 A2**
Economy Point, UP (NS) **9 A2**
Ecoole, UP (BC) **38 B3**
Ecum Secum, UP (NS) **9 E3**
Ecum Secum Bridge, UP (NS) **9 E3**
Ecum Secum West, UP (NS) **9 E3**
Edam, VL (Sask.) **32 B3**
Edberg, VL (Alta.) **33 E4**
Eddies Cove, UP (Nfld.) **5 G2**
Eddies Cove West, UP (Nfld.) **5 G3**
Eddy, UP (BC) **40 F2**
Eddystone, UP (Ont.) **21 E1**
Eddystone, UP (Man.) **29 F2**
Eden, UP (Ont.) **22 F2**
Eden, UP (Man.) **29 F3**
Eden, UP (NS) **8 D4**
Edenburg, UP (Man.) **29 H4**
Eden Grove, UP (Ont.) **23 C2**
Edenhurst, UP (Ont.) **25 D4**
Eden Lake, UP (NS) **9 E2**
Eden Mills, UP (Ont.) **23 E4**
Edenvale, UP (Ont.) **21 A1**
Eden Valley 216, IR (Alta.) **34 E3**
Edenwold, VL (Sask.) **31 H3**
Edgar, UP (Ont.) **23 F2**
Edgars, UP (Ont.) **22 A3**
Edge Hill, UP (Ont.) **23 D2**
Edgeley, UP (Sask.) **31 H3**
Edgell, UP (Sask.) **31 C3**
Edgerton, VL (Alta.) **33 G4**
Edgetts Landing, UP (NB) **11 G1**
Edgewater, UP (BC) **34 C2**
Edgewood, UP (BC) **35 H3**
Edgewood, UP (NS) **9 B2**
Edgewood Park, UP (Ont.) **21 D1**
Edillen, UP (Man.) **29 F2**
Edina, UP (Ont.) **17 F1**
Edmonton, C (Alta.) **33 E3**
Edmonton Beach, SV (Alta.) **33 D3**
Edmonton (Namao), CFB/BFC, MIL (Alta.) **33 E3**
Edmore, UP (Sask.) **29 B2**
Edmore Beach, UP (Ont.) **23 E1**
Edmundston, C (NB) **15 H2**
Edrans, UP (Man.) **29 F3**
Edson, T (Alta.) **33 B3**
Edville, UP (Ont.) **21 E1**
Edward, UP (Alta.) **33 F2**
Edwards, UP (Ont.) **17 D2**
Edwards Corner, UP (NB) **11 B3**
Edwards Project, NUP (Ont.) **17 D2**
Edwardsville, UP (NS) **8 F3**
Edwin, UP (Man.) **29 G3**
Edye 93, IR (BC) **41 C1**
Edys Mills, UP (Ont.) **22 C2**
Edzell, UP (Sask.) **31 E1**
Eel Cove, UP (NS) **8 E3**
Eel Ground < Eel Ground 2, UP (NB) **12 E2**
Eel Ground 2, IR (NB) **12 E2**
Eeloojua, UP (NWT) **47 E4**
Eel River 3, IR (NB) **13 D4**
Eel River Bridge, UP (NB) **12 G2**
Eel River Cove, UP (NB) **13 D4**
Eel River Crossing, VL (NB) **13 D4**
Eel River Lake, UP (NB) **11 A1**
Eelseuklis 10, IR (BC) **38 A2**
Eepikitajuk, UP (NWT) **47 E4**
Egan Creek, UP (Ont.) **24 F3**
Eganville, VL (Ont.) **24 G1**
Eganville Station, NUP (Ont.) **24 G2**
Egbert, UP (Ont.) **21 A1**
Egeria Bay 19, IR (BC) **41 A1**
Egerton, UP (NS) **8 A4**
Egerton, UP (Ont.) **23 D3**
Eglington, UP (PEI) **7 E4**
Egmondville, UP (Ont.) **23 B4**
Egmont, UP (BC) **38 E1**
Egmont 26, IR (BC) **38 E1**
Egmont Bay, UP (PEI) **7 A3**
Egremont, UP (Alta.) **33 E2**
Egypt, UP (Ont.) **21 B1**
Égypte, UP (Que.) **16 B3**
Egypt Road, UP (NS) **8 D3**
Ehatis 11, IR (BC) **39 E3**
Ehatisaht < Oke 10, UP (BC) **39 E3**
Eight Island Lake, UP (NS) **9 F2**
Eight Mile Point, UP (Ont.) **23 G2**
Ekfrid, UP (Ont.) **22 D2**
Ekins Point, UP (BC) **38 F1**
Eladesor, UP (Alta.) **34 G2**
Elak Dase 192A, IR (Sask.) **44 E4**
Elba, UP (Ont.) **23 E3**
Elbourne, UP (Sask.) **31 G2**
Elbow, VL (Sask.) **31 F2**
Elbridge, UP (Alta.) **33 E2**
Elcho, UP (Ont.) **21 A4**
Elcho 6, IR (BC) **41 F3**
Eldee, UP (Ont.) **18 A3**
Elder, UP (Ont.) **23 E3**
Elderbank, UP (NS) **9 C3**
Eldersley, UP (Sask.) **32 F4**
Eldon, UP (PEI) **7 D4**
Eldon, UP (Ont.) **23 H2**
Eldon, UP (Alta.) **34 C2**
Eldorado, UP (Ont.) **24 F4**
Eldorado, UP (Sask.) **44 D2**
Eldorena, UP (Alta.) **33 E3**
Eldred, UP (Sask.) **32 C3**
Electric, UP (Ont.) **22 B3**
Elford, UP (Ont.) **22 A4**
Elfrida, UP (Ont.) **21 A3**
Elfros, VL (Sask.) **29 B1**
Elgin, UP (Ont.) **17 B3**
Elgin, UP (NB) **11 F1**
Elgin, UP (Man.) **29 E4**
Elgin, UP (NS) **9 D2**
Elgin, UP (Que.) **17 F2**
Elginburg, UP (Ont.) **17 A4**
Elginfield, UP (Ont.) **22 E1**
Elgin-Road, UP (Que.) **15 D2**
Elhlateese 2, IR (BC) **38 B3**
Elie, UP (Man.) **29 H3**
Elimere Point, UP (Ont.) **23 F1**
Elimville, UP (Ont.) **22 D1**
Elizabeth, NUP (Alta.) **33 H2**
Elizabeth Bay, UP (Ont.) **25 A2**
Elizabeth Park < Ottawa (South/Sud), CFB/BFC, UP (Ont.) **17 E4**
Elizabethville, UP (Ont.) **21 D2**
Elk Bay, UP (BC) **37 B3**
Elkford, VL (BC) **34 D3**
Elk Hill, UP (Sask.) **32 F3**
Elkhorn, VL (Man.) **29 D3**
Elk Island, UP (Alta.) **33 E3**
Elk Lake, UP (Ont.) **26 F2**
Elko, UP (BC) **34 D4**
Elk Point, T (Alta.) **33 G3**
Elk Ranch, UP (Man.) **29 F3**
Elkton, UP (Alta.) **34 E1**
Elkwater, UP (Alta.) **31 B4**
Ellaton, UP (Ont.) **22 G2**
Ellengowan, UP (Ont.) **23 C2**
Ellershouse, UP (NS) **9 A3**
Ellerslie, UP (PEI) **7 B3**
Ellerslie, UP (Alta.) **33 E3**
Ellesby, UP (BC) **40 B1**
Elliot Lake, T (Ont.) **25 B1**
Elliotts Corners, UP (Ont.) **23 F1**
Elliott's Cove, UP (Nfld.) **2 F1**
Elliotvale, UP (PEI) **7 D4**
Ellis, UP (Ont.) **27 D3**
Ellisboro, UP (Sask.) **29 C3**
Ellison, UP (BC) **35 F2**
Elliston, T (Nfld.) **3 G4**
Ellisville, UP (Ont.) **17 B3**
Ellscott, UP (Alta.) **33 E2**
Ellsmere Village, UP (Ont.) **26 F4**
Elm, UP (Ont.) **17 B1**
Elma, UP (Man.) **28 C1**
Elma, UP (Ont.) **17 D2**
Elm Brook, UP (NB) **11 E2**
Elmbrook, UP (Ont.) **21 G1**
Elm Creek, UP (Man.) **29 H4**
Elmdale, UP (Ont.) **22 B4**
Elmfield, UP (NS) **9 D1**
Elmgrove, UP (Ont.) **17 B3**
Elmgrove, UP (Ont.) **21 A1**
Elmhedge, UP (Ont.) **23 D2**
Elm Hill, UP (NB) **11 D2**
Elmhurst, UP (NB) **11 E2**
Elmhurst, UP (Sask.) **32 B3**
Elmhurst Beach, UP (Ont.) **21 B1**
Elmira, UP (Ont.) **23 D4**
Elmira, UP (PEI) **7 F3**
Elmore, UP (Sask.) **29 D4**
Elmsdale, UP (NS) **9 B3**
Elmsdale, UP (PEI) **7 A2**
Elmside, UP (Que.) **17 B1**
Elmsley, UP (Ont.) **17 B2**
Elm Springs, UP (Sask.) **31 F4**
Elmstead, UP (Ont.) **22 A3**
Elmsvale, UP (NS) **9 C3**
Elmsville, UP (NB) **11 B3**
Elmtree, UP (NB) **12 E3**
Elm Tree, UP (Ont.) **24 G3**
Elmvale, VL (Ont.) **23 F1**
Elmwood, UP (Ont.) **23 C2**
Elmwood, UP (PEI) **7 C4**
Elmwood, UP (NS) **10 E2**
Elmwood, UP (NB) **11 A1**
Elmwood, UP (Ont.) **21 H1**
Elmworth, UP (Alta.) **43 F4**
Elnora, VL (Alta.) **34 F1**
Eloida, UP (Ont.) **17 C3**
Elora, VL (Ont.) **23 D4**
Elphin, UP (Ont.) **17 A2**
Elphinstone, UP (Man.) **29 E3**
Elrose, T (Sask.) **31 D2**
Elsa, UP (YT) **45 B2**
Elsas, UP (Ont.) **26 C1**
Elsinore, UP (Ont.) **23 C2**
Elspeth, UP (Alta.) **33 D4**
Elstow, VL (Sask.) **31 F1**
Eltham, UP (Alta.) **34 F3**
Elva, UP (Man.) **29 E4**
Elzevir, UP (Ont.) **24 G4**
Embarras, UP (Alta.) **44 C3**
Embarras, UP (Alta.) **33 A3**
Embarras Portage, UP (Alta.) **44 C3**
Embree, T (Nfld.) **3 C2**
Embro, UP (Ont.) **22 F1**
Embrun, UP (Ont.) **17 D2**
Emerald, UP (Ont.) **21 G1**
Emerald, UP (NS) **8 D3**
Emerald Isle, NUP (Ont.) **21 D1**
Emerald Junction, UP (PEI) **7 C3**
Emerald Vale, UP (Nfld.) **2 G2**
Emerson, T (Man.) **28 A3**
Emerson, UP (NB) **12 F4**
Emery, UP (Ont.) **17 B4**
Emeryville, UP (Ont.) **22 A3**
Émesville, UP (Man.) **28 A1**
Emileville, UP (Que.) **16 B3**
Emily Harbour, UP (Nfld.) **6 G3**
Emma Lake UP (Sask.) **32 D3**
Emmaville, UP (Sask.) **32 A3**
Emo, UP (Ont.) **28 G4**
Empey Hill, UP (Ont.) **21 G1**
Empress, VL (Alta.) **31 B2**
Emsdale, UP (Ont.) **24 B2**
Emyvale, UP (PEI) **7 C4**
Ena Lake, UP (Ont.) **28 F1**
Enchant, UP (Alta.) **34 G3**
Endako, UP (BC) **40 A1**
Endcliffe, UP (Man.) **29 D2**
Endeavour, VL (Sask.) **29 C1**
Enderby, C (BC) **35 F1**
Enderby 2, IR (BC) **35 F1**
Endiang, UP (Alta.) **34 G1**
Enfield, UP (NS) **9 B3**
Engen, UP (BC) **40 B1**
Engineer, UP (BC) **45 B4**
Englee, T (Nfld.) **5 H3**
Englefeld, VL (Sask.) **31 G1**
Englehart, T (Ont.) **26 F2**
Englewood, UP (BC) **39 E1**
English Corner, UP (NS) **9 B3**
English Harbour, UP (Nfld.) **3 G4**
English Harbour East, COMM (Nfld.) **2 D2**
English Harbour West < St Jacques – Coomb's Cove, UP (Nfld.) **2 B3**
English Line, UP (Ont.) **21 E1**
English Point, UP (Nfld.) **5 G2**
English River, UP (Ont.) **27 C2**
English River 21, IR (Ont.) **28 G1**
English River 66, IR (Ont.) **20 B4**
English Settlement, UP (NB) **12 C4**
Englishtown, UP (NS) **8 E3**
Enhalt 11, IR (BC) **35 B1**
Enid, UP (Sask.) **31 H2**
Enilda, UP (Alta.) **33 B1**
Enlaugra, UP (Que.) **16 B4**
Enmore, UP (PEI) **7 B3**
Ennadai, UP (NWT) **44 G1**
Ennemond, UP (NB) **15 G2**
Ennishone, UP (NB) **12 A2**
Enniskillen, UP (NB) **11 C2**
Ennismore, UP (Ont.) **21 D1**
Ennotville, UP (Ont.) **23 E4**
Enon, UP (NS) **8 E4**
Enquocto 14 IR (BC) **35 C1**
Ens, UP (Sask.) **32 D4**
Ensheshese 13, IR (BC) **42 C4**
Ensheshese 53, IR (BC) **42 C4**
Ensign, UP (Alta.) **34 F3**
Ensleigh, UP (Alta.) **34 H1**
Enterprise, UP (Ont.) **17 A3**
Enterprise, UP (NWT) **44 A2**
Enterprise, UP (BC) **36 C2**
Enterprise, UP (NB) **12 B2**
Entice, UP (Alta.) **34 F2**
Entrance, UP (Alta.) **40 H2**
Entrelacs, UP (Que.) **18 F4**
Entwistle, VL (Alta.) **33 C3**
Environ, UP (Sask.) **31 E1**
Epping, UP (Ont.) **23 D2**
Epsom, UP (Ont.) **21 C1**
Epworth, UP (Nfld.) **2 C4**
Equis 8, IR (BC) **38 B3**
Equity, UP (Alta.) **34 F1**
Eramosa, UP (Ont.) **23 E4**
Erbs Cove, UP (NB) **11 E2**
Erb Settlement, UP (NB) **11 E2**
Erickson, UP (BC) **34 C4**
Erickson, VL (Man.) **29 F3**
Erie, UP (BC) **34 B4**
Erieau, VL (Ont.) **22 C3**
Erie Beach, VL (Ont.) **22 C3**
Erie View, UP (Ont.) **22 F2**
Eriksdale, UP (Man.) **29 G2**
Erin, VL (Ont.) **23 E3**
Erinferry, UP (Sask.) **32 C3**
Erin Lodge, UP (Alta.) **43 G3**
Erinsville, UP (Ont.) **24 G4**
Erinview, UP (Man.) **29 H3**
Erinville, UP (NS) **9 F2**
Erith, UP (Alta.) **33 B3**
Erle, UP (Que.) **16 E3**
Ermineskin 138, IR (Alta.) **33 E4**
Ernestown, UP (Ont.) **17 A4**
Ernfold, VL (Sask.) **31 E3**
Errington, UP (BC) **38 D2**
Errol, UP (Ont.) **22 C1**
Erskine, UP (Alta.) **33 E4**
Ervick, UP (Alta.) **33 E4**
Erwood, UP (Sask.) **32 H4**
Escott, UP (Ont.) **17 C3**
Escoumains 25, IR (Que.) **14 E3**
Escuminac, UP (NB) **12 G2**
Escuminac, UP (Que.) **13 D3**
Escuminac-Est, UP (Que.) **13 D3**
Escuminac-Flats, UP (Que.) **13 D3**
Escuminac-Glen, UP (Que.) **13 D3**
Escuminac-Nord, UP (Que.) **13 D3**
Esdraelon, UP (NB) **12 B4**
Esher, UP (Ont.) **26 B2**
Esk, UP (Sask.) **31 G1**
Eskasoni < Eskasoni 3, UP (NS) **8 E3**
Eskasoni 3, IR (NS) **8 E3**
Eskasoni 3A, IR (NS) **8 E3**
Eskbank, UP (Sask.) **31 F3**
Eskdale, UP (Ont.) **23 B2**
Eskimo Point, UP (NWT) **46 B3**
Esme, UP (Sask.) **31 E3**
Esmonde, UP (Ont.) **24 G2**
Esowista 3, IR (BC) **38 A3**
Espanola, T (Ont.) **25 C1**
Esperanza, UP (BC) **39 E3**
Esprit-Saint, UP (Que.) **14 G4**
Esquimalt, DM (BC) **38 F4**
Esquimalt, IR (BC) **38 F4**
Essa, UP (Ont.) **21 A1**
Essex, T (Ont.) **22 A3**
Essonville, UP (Ont.) **24 D3**
Estaire, UP (Ont.) **25 E1**
Estérel, T (Que.) **18 F4**
Esterhazy, T (Sask.) **29 D3**
Estevan, C (Sask.) **29 C4**
Estevan Airport, UP (Sask.) **29 C4**
Estevan Point, UP (BC) **39 F4**
Esther, UP (Alta.) **31 B1**
Estlin, UP (Sask.) **31 H3**
Estmere, UP (NS) **8 D3**
Eston, T (Sask.) **31 D2**
Est-patrolas 4, IR (BC) **38 E3**
Estuary, UP (Sask.) **31 C2**
Étamamiou, UP (Que.) **5 D3**
Étang-des-Caps, UP (Que.) **7 F1**
Étang-du-Nord, UP (Que.) **7 F1**
Ethel, UP (Ont.) **23 C3**
Ethelbert, VL (Man.) **29 E2**
Ethel Lake, UP (Alta.) **33 G2**
Ethel Park, UP (Ont.) **21 B1**
Ethelton, UP (Sask.) **32 E4**
Etobicoke, BOR (Ont.) **21 A2**
Etomami, UP (Sask.) **32 H4**
Etoncourt, NUP (Ont.) **22 C1**
Eton-Rugby, UP (Ont.) **27 A1**
Etsekin 1, IR (BC) **39 F1**
Etters Beach, VL (Sask.) **31 G2**
Etter Settlement, UP (NS) **9 B3**
Ettington, UP (Sask.) **31 F3**
Ettyville, UP (Ont.) **17 D1**
Etzikom, UP (Alta.) **31 A4**
Euchinico Creek 17, IR (BC) **40 B2**
Euchinico Creek 18, IR (BC) **40 B2**
Euchinico Creek 19, IR (BC) **40 B2**
Eugenia, UP (Ont.) **23 D2**
Eureka, UP (NS) **9 D2**
Eureka, UP (Ont.) **26 D3**
Eureka, UP (NWT) **47 E2**
Eureka River, UP (Alta.) **43 G3**
Eustis, UP (Que.) **16 D4**
Évain, VL (Que.) **18 A2**
Eva Lake, NUP (Ont.) **27 C3**
Evandale, UP (NB) **11 D2**
Evangeline, UP (NB) **12 G1**
Evangeline, UP (NB) **12 G4**
Evansburg, VL (Alta.) **33 C3**
Evans Corner, UP (Ont.) **23 F1**
Evanston, UP (NS) **8 C4**
Evansville, UP (Ont.) **25 G1**
Evansville, UP (Ont.) **25 B2**
Evarts, UP (Alta.) **34 E1**
Evelyn, UP (BC) **42 F4**
Evelyn, UP (Ont.) **22 E1**
Everard, UP (Ont.) **27 E3**
Everett, UP (Ont.) **21 A1**
Everett, UP (NB) **12 B2**
Evergreen, UP (Alta.) **34 E1**
Evergreen Place, NUP (Man.) **30 C4**
Evergreen Trailer Park, NUP (Alta.) **33 E3**
Evergreen Village, NUP (Nfld.) **2 H2**
Eversley, UP (Ont.) **21 B2**
Everton, UP (Ont.) **23 E4**
Evesham, VL (Sask.) **32 A4**
Ewan, UP (Ont.) **24 D3**
Ewart, UP (Man.) **29 D4**
Ewing, UP (BC) **35 F2**
Excel, UP (Alta.) **31 B2**
Excelsior, UP (Alta.) **33 E3**
Exeter, T (Ont.) **22 D1**
Exeter, UP (BC) **36 D2**
Exlou, UP (BC) **36 F4**
Exmoor, UP (NB) **12 E2**
Expanse, UP (Sask.) **31 F3**
Exploits, UP (Nfld.) **3 C2**
Exshaw, UP (Alta.) **34 D2**
Extension, UP (BC) **38 D2**
Eyebrow, VL (Sask.) **31 F2**
Eyre, UP (Sask.) **31 C2**
Eyre Corners, UP (Ont.) **17 B3**

F

Fabre, UP (Que.) **18 A3**
Fabre-Station, UP (Que.) **18 A3**
Fabyan, UP (Alta.) **33 G4**
Factorydale, UP (NS) **10 D1**
Factory Island 1, IR (Ont.) **20 D3**
Factory-Point, UP (Que.) **5 F2**
Fadden-Corner, UP (Que.) **16 A4**
Fairbairn Meadows, UP (Ont.) **21 D1**
Fairbank, UP (Nfld.) **3 D2**
Fairbridge, NUP (BC) **38 E3**
Fairfax, UP (Man.) **29 F4**
Fairfax, UP (Que.) **16 D4**
Fairfax, UP (Ont.) **17 B4**
Fairfield, UP (NB) **11 E3**
Fairfield, UP (PEI) **7 F3**
Fairfield, UP (NB) **7 A4**
Fairfield, UP (Ont.) **17 C3**
Fairfield East, UP (Ont.) **17 C3**
Fairfield Heights, UP (Ont.) **17 D4**
Fairfield Plain, UP (Ont.) **22 G1**
Fairford, UP (Man.) **29 G1**
Fairford 50, IR (Man.) **29 G1**
Fairford Reserve, UP (Man.) **30 B4**
Fairground, UP (Ont.) **22 F2**
Fair Harbour, UP (BC) **39 D2**
Fair Haven, UP (Nfld.) **2 F2**
Fairhaven, UP (NB) **11 B3**
Fairhaven Subdivision, NUP (Alta.) **33 D3**
Fairholme, UP (Sask.) **32 B3**
Fairholme, UP (Ont.) **24 A1**
Fairisle, UP (NB) **12 F2**
Fairlight, VL (Sask.) **29 D3**
Fairmont, UP (Ont.) **17 A4**
Fairmont Hot Springs, UP (BC) **34 C3**
Fairmount, UP (NS) **8 B4**
Fairmount, UP (Ont.) **21 D1**
Fairmount, UP (Ont.) **23 D2**
Fairmount, UP (Sask.) **31 C2**
Fairplay, UP (Ont.) **22 A3**
Fairvale, VL (NB) **11 D2**
Fair Valley, UP (Ont.) **23 F1**
Fairview, T (Alta.) **43 G3**
Fairview, UP (PEI) **7 C4**
Fair View, UP (NB) **11 F2**
Fairview, UP (Ont.) **24 G1**
Fairview, UP (Ont.) **22 F2**
Fairview, UP (Ont.) **22 E1**
Fairview, UP (Man.) **29 F3**
Fairview, UP (BC) **35 E4**
Fairview Subdivision, NUP (Alta.) **34 F4**
Fairview Subdivision, NUP (BC) **34 B4**
Fairydell, UP (Alta.) **33 E3**
Fairy Glen, UP (Sask.) **32 F4**
Fairy Hill, UP (Sask.) **31 H2**
Falcon, UP (Sask.) **29 C3**
Falconbridge, UP (Ont.) **22 D2**
Falcon Lake, UP (Man.) **28 D2**

Falcon Park, NUP (BC) 38 C1
Falher, T (Alta.) 43 H3
Falkland, UP (BC) 35 E1
Falkland, UP (Ont.) 22 G1
Falkland Ridge, UP (NS) 10 D1
Fallbrook, UP (Ont.) 17 B2
Fallis, UP (Alta.) 33 D3
Fallison, UP (Man.) 29 G4
Fallowfield, UP (Ont.) 17 D4
Fall River, UP (NS) 9 B3
Fall River West, UP (NS) 9 B3
Falls Creek, UP (BC) 35 B2
Falmouth, UP (NS) 9 A3
Faloma, UP (Man.) 28 E2
Falun, UP (Alta.) 33 D4
Fanning Brook, UP (PEI) 7 D3
Fanny Bay, UP (BC) 38 C2
Fannystelle, UP (Man.) 29 H4
Fanshawe, UP (Ont.) 22 E1
Faraday, UP (Ont.) 24 E3
Farewell, UP (Ont.) 23 D3
Farlain Lake, UP (Ont.) 23 E1
Farlane, UP (Ont.) 28 G1
Farley, UP (Que.) 18 D4
Farleys Corners, UP (Ont.) 25 H2
Farlinger, UP (Ont.) 27 F2
Farmers-Rapids, UP (Que.) 17 D3
Farmingdale, UP (Sask.) 29 B1
Farmington, UP (NS) 10 D2
Farmington, UP (PEI) 7 E3
Farmington, UP (NS) 9 A2
Farmington, UP (Ont.) 23 E3
Farmington, UP (BC) 43 E3
Farm-Point, UP (Que.) 17 C1
Farmville, UP (NS) 10 E2
Farnham, C (Que.) 16 B4
Farnham, UP (Ont.) 23 E4
Farnham-Centre, UP (Que.) 16 B4
Farnham Settlement, NUP (NB) 11 C1
Faro, T (YT) 45 B3
Farquhar, UP (Ont.) 22 E1
Farrant, UP (Alta.) 33 D4
Farrell Corners, UP (Ont.) 21 G1
Farrell Creek, UP (BC) 43 D3
Farrellton, UP (Que.) 17 C1
Farrerdale, UP (Sask.) 31 F2
Farrow, UP (Alta.) 34 F2
Far West Point 34, IR (BC) 42 C4
Fassett, UP (Que.) 17 E1
Fassifern, UP (Ont.) 17 E1
Fatima, UP (Que.) 7 F1
Fatima-de-Témiscouata, UP (Que.) 15 G1
Faubourg-du-Moulin, UP (Que.) 15 B3
Faulder, UP (BC) 35 E3
Faulkner, UP (Man.) 29 G2
Fauquier, UP (Ont.) 26 D1
Fauquier, UP (BC) 35 H2
Faust, UP (Alta.) 33 C1
Fauvel, UP (Que.) 13 F4
Fauxburg, UP (NS) 10 E2
Fawcett, UP (Alta.) 33 D2
Fawcett Hill, UP (NB) 11 F1
Fawcettville, UP (Ont.) 21 G2
Fawn Bay, UP (Ont.) 23 G1
Fawn Lake, UP (Alta.) 33 D2
Fay Lake, UP (Man.) 30 A2
Federal, UP (Alta.) 34 G1
Federal Ranch, UP (BC) 43 D3
Fedorah, UP (Alta.) 33 E3
Feeners Corner, UP (NS) 10 E2
Fee's Landing, UP (Ont.) 21 D1
Feir Mill, UP (Ont.) 21 C1
Felix George 3, IR (BC) 41 G1
Fellers Heights, UP (BC) 43 E4
Felton, UP (Ont.) 17 D2
Feltzen South, UP (NS) 10 E2
Femme, UP (Nfld.) 2 C2
Fenaghvale, UP (Ont.) 17 E1
Fenella, UP (Ont.) 21 E1
Fenelon Falls, VL (Ont.) 23 H2
Fenertys, UP (NS) 9 B3
Fenn, UP (Alta.) 34 F1
Fennell, UP (Ont.) 21 A1
Fenton, UP (Sask.) 32 E4
Fenwick, UP (NS) 9 A1
Fenwood, VL (Sask.) 29 C2
Fenwood Gardens, UP (Ont.) 21 F1
Fergus, T (Ont.) 23 E4
Fergus Hill Estate, UP (Ont.) 23 G2
Ferguslea, UP (Ont.) 17 A1
Ferguson, UP (BC) 34 B2
Ferguson Corners, UP (Ont.) 24 G3
Fergusons Beach, UP (Ont.) 17 A1
Fergusons Cove, UP (NS) 9 B4
Fergusons Falls, UP (Ont.) 17 B2
Fergusons Lake, UP (NS) 8 E4
Fergusonvale, UP (Ont.) 23 F2
Ferintosh, VL (Alta.) 33 E4
Ferland, UP (Que.) 14 B3
Ferland, UP (Ont.) 27 E1
Ferland, VL (Sask.) 31 E4
Ferlow Junction, UP (Alta.) 33 E4
Ferme-Joseph, UP (Que.) 18 D4
Ferme-Lefebvre, UP (Que.) 18 D4
Ferme-Neuve, VL (Que.) 18 E3
Ferme-Rouge, UP (Que.) 18 E4
Fermeuse, COMM (Nfld.) 2 H4
Fermont, T (Que.) 6 C4
Fermoy, UP (Ont.) 17 A3
Fernbank, UP (Ont.) 17 C3
Fernbank, UP (Ont.) 23 D4
Fern Creek, UP (Alta.) 33 D4
Ferndale, UP (Ont.) 23 C1
Ferndale, UP (NB) 11 G2
Ferndale, UP (Ont.) 24 B2
Ferndale, UP (Man.) 29 H4
Ferndale, UP (BC) 40 C2
Ferndell, UP (Ont.) 22 D2
Ferndon, UP (Que.) 16 B4
Fern Glen, UP (Ont.) 24 B2
Fern Hill, UP (NS) 9 D3
Fernhill, UP (Ont.) 22 D1
Fernie, C (BC) 34 D4
Fernlee, UP (Ont.) 25 A2
Fernleigh, UP (Ont.) 24 G3
Fernmount, UP (NB) 11 D1
Fernwood, UP (PEI) 7 B4
Ferrier, UP (Alta.) 33 C4
Ferrona, UP (NS) 9 D2
Ferrona Junction, UP (NS) 9 D2
Ferryland, COMM (Nfld.) 2 H4
Ferry Road, UP (NB) 12 F2
Fertile, UP (Sask.) 29 D4
Fesserton, UP (Ont.) 23 F1
Festubert, UP (Que.) 18 G3
Feudal, UP (Sask.) 31 E1
Feuille-d'Érable, NUP (Que.) 15 C4
Feversham, UP (Ont.) 23 E2
Ficko, UP (Ont.) 17 E4
Fidler, UP (Alta.) 33 A4
Field, UP (Ont.) 25 G1
Field, UP (BC) 34 C2
Fielding, UP (NB) 12 A3
Fielding, UP (Sask.) 32 C4
Fife, UP (BC) 35 H4
Fife Lake, VL (Sask.) 31 G4
Fife's Bay, UP (Ont.) 21 D1
Fifth Meridian, UP (Alta.) 44 B3
Figuery, UP (Que.) 18 B1
Filey Beach, UP (Ont.) 21 B1
Filion, UP (Que.) 18 F4
Fillmore, VL (Sask.) 29 B3
Fincastle, UP (Alta.) 34 G3
Finch, VL (Ont.) 17 D2
Findlater, VL (Sask.) 31 G2
Findlay, UP (Man.) 29 E4
Fingal, UP (Ont.) 22 E2
Fingerboard, UP (Ont.) 21 C1
Finland, UP (Ont.) 28 G4
Finlay Forks, UP (BC) 43 C3
Finlayson Island 19, IR (BC) 42 C4
Finmark, UP (Ont.) 27 D3
Finmoore, UP (BC) 40 B2
Finnegan, UP (Alta.) 34 G2
Fintry, UP (BC) 35 F2
Firdale, UP (Man.) 29 G3
Fire River, UP (Ont.) 26 B1
Fireside, UP (BC) 45 C4
Fir Mountain, UP (Sask.) 31 F4
Fir Ridge, UP (Sask.) 32 E3
First Peninsula, UP (NS) 10 E2
First South, UP (NS) 10 E2
Firth's Corners, UP (Ont.) 23 F1
Firvale, UP (BC) 41 G3
Fischells, UP (Nfld.) 4 B2
Fischot Islands, UP (Nfld.) 5 H2
Fish Creek, UP (Sask.) 32 D4
Fisher, UP (Sask.) 32 E4
Fisher Bay, UP (Man.) 29 H2
Fisher Branch, UP (Man.) 29 H2
Fisher Heights, UP (Ont.) 17 E4
Fisher-Hill, UP (Que.) 16 E3
Fisher Home, UP (Alta.) 33 D4
Fishermans Harbour, UP (NS) 9 F3
Fisher Mills, UP (NS) 9 F2
Fisher River 44, IR (Man.) 29 H2
Fisher River 44A, IR (Man.) 29 H2
Fishers Glen, UP (Ont.) 22 G2
Fishers Grant 24, IR (NS) 9 D1
Fishers Grant 24G, IR (NS) 9 D1
Fisherton, UP (Man.) 29 H2
Fishing Lake 89, IR (Sask.) 29 B1
Fishing Lake 89A, IR (Sask.) 29 B1
Fishing River, UP (Man.) 29 F2
Fishing Ships Harbour, UP (Nfld.) 6 H4
Fishing Station 62A, IR (Man.) 29 E3
Fish Lake 5, IR (BC) 36 B3
Fish Lake 7, IR (BC) 35 A1
Fishpot Lake 24, IR (BC) 40 B3
Fiske, UP (Sask.) 31 D2
Fiskes Corners, UP (Ont.) 17 E1
Fitch-Bay, UP (Que.) 16 C4
Fitters Cove < New Perlican, UP (Nfld.) 2 G2
Fitzallen, UP (Alta.) 33 F3
Fitzgerald, UP (Alta.) 44 C2
Fitzgerald, UP (Alta.) 31 B3
Fitzmaurice, UP (Sask.) 29 C2
Fitzpatrick, UP (Que.) 18 G2
Fitzpatrick, UP (NS) 9 C1
Fitzpatricks Mountain, UP (NS) 9 D1
Fitzroy, UP (Ont.) 17 B1
Fitzroy Harbour, UP (Ont.) 17 B1
Fitzsimmons, UP (Alta.) 43 G4
Five Corners, UP (NB) 11 B3
Five Corners, UP (Ont.) 21 D1
Five Corners, UP (Man.) 29 G4
Five Fathom Hole, UP (NB) 11 D3
Five Fingers, UP (NB) 12 B1
Five Houses, UP (NS) 10 E2
Five Houses, UP (PEI) 7 E3
Five Houses, UP (NS) 9 B2
Five Island Lake, UP (NS) 9 B4
Five Islands, UP (NS) 9 A2
Five Mile, UP (BC) 34 B2
Five Mile 3, IR (BC) 36 B1
Five Mile Plains, UP (NS) 9 A3
Five Mile Point 3, IR (BC) 45 B4
Five Mile River, UP (NS) 9 B2
Five Points, UP (NB) 11 G1
Five Points, UP (NB) 11 F1
Flamboro Centre, UP (Ont.) 21 A3
Flanders, UP (Ont.) 27 B3
Flanders, UP (Que.) 16 E4
Flannigan Corners, UP (Ont.) 22 E1
Flat Bay, UP (Nfld.) 4 B2
Flatbush, UP (Alta.) 33 D2
Flat Creek, UP (YT) 45 A2
Flathead, UP (BC) 34 E4
Flathead, UP (BC) 34 E4
Flat Island, UP (Nfld.) 2 D3
Flat Lake, UP (Alta.) 33 G2
Flatlands, UP (NB) 13 C4
Flat River, UP (PEI) 7 D4
Flat Rock, T (Nfld.) 2 H2
Flatrock, UP (Nfld.) 2 G2
Flatrock, UP (BC) 43 F3
Flat Valley, UP (Sask.) 32 A2
Flaxcombe, VL (Sask.) 31 C2
Flee Island, UP (Man.) 29 G3
Fleet, UP (Alta.) 34 G1
Fleet Settlement, UP (NS) 9 E3
Fleetwood, UP (Ont.) 24 D4
Fleming, T (Sask.) 29 D3
Fleming Park, NUP (Alta.) 33 D3
Flemming, UP (NB) 12 A2
Flesherton, VL (Ont.) 23 D2
Fletcher, UP (Ont.) 22 B3
Fletchers Lake, UP (NS) 9 B3
Flett Springs, UP (Sask.) 32 E4
Fleurant, UP (Que.) 13 D3
Fleur de Lys, LID (Nfld.) 5 H3
Fleuriault, UP (Que.) 14 H3
Fleury Bight, UP (Nfld.) 3 C2
Flin Flon (p), C (Man.) 32 H2
Flin Flon (p), C (Sask.) 32 H2
Flint, UP (Ont.) 27 D3
Flintoft, UP (Sask.) 31 F4
Flinton, UP (Ont.) 24 G3
Flinton Corner, UP (Ont.) 24 G3
Flodden, UP (Que.) 16 C3
Floods, UP (BC) 35 B4
Floradale, UP (Ont.) 23 D4
Floral, UP (Sask.) 31 F1
Floral Park, UP (Ont.) 23 G1
Florence, UP (NS) 8 E3
Florence, UP (Ont.) 22 C2
Florenceville, VL (NB) 12 A4
Florida, UP (Ont.) 17 A4
Florida, UP (Ont.) 26 E1
Florze, UP (Man.) 28 C3
Flower's Cove, LID (Nfld.) 5 G2
Flowers Cove, UP (NB) 11 D1
Flower Station, UP (Ont.) 17 A2
Flowing Well, UP (Sask.) 31 E3
Flume Ridge, UP (NB) 11 B2
Flying Post 73, IR (Ont.) 26 D1
Flying Shot, NUP (Alta.) 43 G4
Flynns Turn, UP (Ont.) 24 D4
Foam Lake, T (Sask.) 29 B1
Foch, UP (BC) 37 C4
Foeda, UP (Sask.) 29 C4
Fogo, T (Nfld.) 3 E1
Foisy, UP (Alta.) 33 F3
Foldens, UP (Ont.) 22 F1
Foley, UP (Man.) 29 H3
Foley Brook, UP (NB) 12 A2
Foleyet, UP (Ont.) 26 C2
Folger, UP (Ont.) 17 A2
Folly Lake, UP (NS) 9 B2
Folly Lake Station, UP (NS) 9 B2
Folly Mountain, UP (NS) 9 B2
Fond-des-Ormes, UP (Que.) 14 G3
Fond-du-Lac < Fond du Lac 227, UP (Sask.) 44 E2
Fond du Lac 227, IR (Sask.) 44 E2
Fond du Lac 228, IR (Sask.) 44 E2
Fond du Lac 229, IR (Sask.) 44 D2
Fonehill, UP (Sask.) 29 C2
Fontaine, UP (NB) 12 G3
Fontainebleau, UP (Que.) 16 E3
Fontas < Fontas 1, UP (BC) 43 D1
Fontas 1, IR (BC) 43 D1
Foot Cape, UP (NS) 8 C3
Foote Subdivision, NUP (BC) 36 F2
Foothills, UP (Alta.) 33 B4
Footner Lake, UP (Alta.) 44 A3
Foot's Bay, UP (Ont.) 24 A2
Forbes Point, UP (NS) 10 B4
Forbes Subdivision, NUP (NB) 11 C1
Forbes Subdivision, NUP (BC) 36 C2
Ford, UP (Nfld.) 6 F2
Ford Bank, UP (NB) 12 G3
Forde, UP (BC) 34 B2
Fords Mills, UP (NB) 12 F3
Fordview, UP (NS) 8 D2
Fordwich, UP (Ont.) 23 C3
Fordyce, UP (Ont.) 23 B3
Foreman, UP (BC) 40 C2
Foremost, VL (Alta.) 34 H4
Forest, T (Ont.) 22 C1
Forest, UP (Ont.) 17 A4
Forest Bank, UP (Sask.) 32 A3
Forestburg, VL (Alta.) 33 F4
Forest City, UP (NB) 11 A2
Forest Corner, UP (NB) 12 F2
Forestdale, UP (BC) 42 G4
Foresters Falls, UP (Ont.) 17 A1
Forest Estates, NUP (Ont.) 22 F1
Forest Farm, UP (Sask.) 29 D3
Forest Field, UP (Nfld.) 2 G3
Forest Gate, UP (Sask.) 32 E3
Forest Glade, UP (NS) 10 D1
Forest Glen, UP (NS) 10 B3
Forest Glen, UP (NS) 9 C2
Forest Glen, UP (NS) 8 D2
Forest Grove, UP (BC) 36 D2
Forest Harbour, NUP (Ont.) 23 F1
Forest Hill, UP (NS) 10 E1
Forest Hill, UP (NB) 11 G1
Forest Hill, UP (PEI) 7 E3
Forest Hill, UP (NS) 9 F2
Forest Hills, UP (NS) 9 B4
Forest Home, UP (Ont.) 23 G2
Forest Home, UP (NS) 10 E1
Forest Lawn Trailer Court, NUP (BC) 43 E3
Forest Lea, UP (Ont.) 24 G1
Forest Mills, UP (Ont.) 21 G1
Foreston, UP (NB) 12 B3
Forestview, UP (PEI) 7 A3
Forest View, UP (Alta.) 33 A1
Forestville, T (Que.) 14 E2
Forestville, UP (Ont.) 22 G2
Forfar, UP (Ont.) 17 B3
Forgan, UP (Sask.) 31 D2
Forget, UP (Ont.) 17 D2
Forget, VL (Sask.) 29 C4
Fork Lake, UP (Alta.) 33 F2
Fork River, UP (Man.) 29 F2
Forks Baddeck, UP (NS) 8 D3
Forks Road, UP (Ont.) 21 B4
Forks Stream, UP (NB) 11 E1
Formosa, UP (Ont.) 23 C3
Forresters Point, UP (Nfld.) 5 G2
Forrest Station, UP (Man.) 29 F3
Forshee, UP (Alta.) 33 D4
Forslund, UP (BC) 35 H3
Forsythe, UP (Que.) 18 D2
Fort à la Corne, UP (Sask.) 32 E3
Fort Albany, UP (Ont.) 20 C3
Fort Albany 67, IR (Ont.) 20 C3
Fort Alexander < Fort Alexander 3, UP (Man.) 30 C4
Fort Alexander 3, IR (Man.) 30 C4
Fort Assiniboine, VL (Alta.) 33 C2
Fort Augustus, UP (PEI) 7 D4
Fort Belcher, UP (NS) 9 C2
Fort Black, UP (Sask.) 32 C1
Fort-Chimo, UP (Que.) 6 C1
Fort Chipewyan, UP (Alta.) 44 C3
Fort Churchill, UP (Man.) 46 B4
Fort Collinson, UP (NWT) 47 B3
Fort Conger, UP (NWT) 47 F1
Fort-Coulonge, VL (Que.) 18 C4
Forteau, COMM (Nfld.) 5 G2
Fort Ellis, UP (NS) 9 C2
Fort Enterprise, UP (NWT) 45 F2
Fort Erie, T (Ont.) 21 C4
Fortescue, UP (Ont.) 24 D3
Fort Frances, T (Ont.) 28 H4
Fort Franklin, HAM (NWT) 45 D2
Fort Fraser, UP (BC) 40 B1
Fort-George, UP (Que.) 20 E2
Fort George 2, IR (BC) 40 C2
Fort George Cemetery 1A, IR (BC) 40 C2
Fort Good Hope, UP (NWT) 45 C2
Fort Hall, UP (Man.) 44 G2
Fort Henry Heights < Kingston, CFB/BFC, UP (Ont.) 17 A4
Fort Hope, UP (NWT) 46 C2
Fort Hope, UP (Ont.) 30 G4
Fort Hope 64, IR (Ont.) 20 A3
Forthton, UP (Ont.) 17 C3
Fortier, UP (Man.) 29 H3
Fortierville, VL (Que.) 16 D1
Forties, UP (NS) 10 E1
Fort Irwin, UP (Ont.) 24 D2
Fort Kent, UP (Alta.) 33 G2
Fort La Cloche, UP (Ont.) 25 C2
Fort la Reine, UP (Man.) 29 G3
Fort Lawrence, UP (NS) 9 A1
Fort Liard, UP (NWT) 45 D4
Fort MacKay, UP (Alta.) 44 C4
Fort MacKay 174, IR (Alta.) 44 C4
Fort Macleod, T (Alta.) 34 F4
Fort McMurray, T (Alta.) 44 C4
Fort McPherson, UP (NWT) 45 B1
Fort Nelson, VL (BC) 45 D4
Fort Nelson 2, IR (BC) 45 D4
Fort Norman, UP (NWT) 45 D2
Fort Pelly, UP (Sask.) 29 D1
Fort Pitt, UP (Sask.) 32 A3
Fort Providence, UP (NWT) 44 A1
Fort Qu'Appelle, T (Sask.) 29 B2
Fort Reliance, UP (YT) 45 A2
Fort Resolution, UP (NWT) 44 B1
Fort Ross, UP (NWT) 47 D4
Fort-Rupert, UP (Que.) 20 E3
Fort Rupert 1, IR (BC) 39 D1
Fort St James, VL (BC) 40 B1
Fort St John, C (BC) 43 E3
Fort San, UP (Sask.) 29 B2
Fort Saskatchewan, T (Alta.) 33 E3
Fort Selkirk, UP (YT) 45 A3
Fort Severn, UP (Ont.) 30 G1
Fort Severn 89, IR (Ont.) 30 F2
Fort Simpson, VL (NWT) 45 D3
Fort Smith, T (NWT) 44 C2
Fort Steele, UP (BC) 34 D4
Fort Stewart, UP (Ont.) 24 F2
Fortune, T (Nfld.) 2 B3
Fortune Bridge, UP (PEI) 7 E3
Fortune Cove, UP (PEI) 7 A3
Fortune Harbour, UP (Nfld.) 3 C2
Fortune Harbour, UP (PEI) 7 E3
Fort Vermilion, UP (Alta.) 44 A3
Fort Walsh, UP (Sask.) 31 B4
Fort Ware 1, IR (BC) 42 G1
Fort-William, UP (Que.) 18 C4
Fort William 52, IR (Ont.) 27 E3
48 Road, UP (PEI) 7 D4
Forty Mile, UP (YT) 45 B2
Forty Mile, UP (YT) 45 A2
Forward, UP (Ont.) 17 D2
Forward, UP (Sask.) 31 H4
Fossambault-sur-le-Lac, T (Que.) 15 A3
Fossmill, UP (Ont.) 18 A4
Fosston, VL (Sask.) 29 B1
Fosterton, UP (Sask.) 31 D3
Fosterville, UP (NB) 11 A1
Fosthall, UP (BC) 34 A3
Founds Mills, UP (PEI) 7 C3
Fountain, UP (BC) 36 C4
Fountain 1, IR (BC) 36 C4
Fountain 1A, IR (BC) 36 C4
Fountain 1B, IR (BC) 36 C4
Fountain 1C, IR (BC) 36 C4
Fountain 1D, IR (BC) 36 C4
Fountain 2, IR (BC) 36 C4
Fountain 3, IR (BC) 36 C4
Fountain 3A, IR (BC) 36 C4
Fountain 4, IR (BC) 36 C4
Fountain 9, IR (BC) 36 C4
Fountain 10, IR (BC) 36 C4
Fountain 11, IR (BC) 36 C4
Fountain 12, IR (BC) 35 A1
Fountain Beach, UP (Ont.) 23 G1
Fountain Creek 8, IR (BC) 36 C4
Fountain Road, UP (NS) 9 B1
Fountain Valley < Fountain 1, UP (BC) 36 C4
Four and One-Half Mile 2, IR (BC) 35 B3
Fourche-à-Clark, UP (NB) 11 A1
Fourchu, UP (NS) 8 E4
Four Corners, UP (NB) 11 B3
Four Corners, UP (Sask.) 32 B2
Four Falls, UP (NB) 12 A3
Four Mile, NUP (BC) 34 B4
Four Mile Brook, UP (NS) 9 D1
Fournier, UP (Ont.) 17 E1
Four Portages 157C, IR (Sask.) 32 E1
Four Roads, UP (NB) 12 G1
Fourth Chute, UP (Ont.) 24 G2
Fourth Line, UP (Ont.) 22 B2
Fowler, UP (BC) 42 B1
Fowlers Corner, UP (NB) 11 E1
Fowlers Corners, UP (Ont.) 21 D1
Fowlers Corners, UP (NB) 11 D2
Fowlies Mill, UP (NB) 12 F2
Foxboro, UP (Ont.) 21 F1
Fox Brook, UP (NS) 9 D2
Fox Corners, UP (Ont.) 24 F4
Fox Cove < Fox Cove – Mortier, UP (Nfld.) 2 C3
Fox Cove – Mortier, RD (Nfld.) 2 C3
Fox Creek, T (Alta.) 33 B2
Foxdale, UP (Sask.) 32 D3
Foxey, UP (Ont.) 25 B2
Foxford, UP (Sask.) 32 E3
Fox Harbour, COMM (Nfld.) 2 F3
Fox Harbour, UP (Nfld.) 5 H1
Fox Harbour, UP (NS) 9 B1
Fox Hill, UP (NB) 11 E2
Fox Hills, UP (Sask.) 31 H2
Fox Island Harbour, UP (Nfld.) 4 E4
Fox Island Main, UP (NS) 9 G2
Fox Island River, UP (Nfld.) 4 B1
Fox Lake < Fox Lake 162, UP (Alta.) 44 B3
Fox Lake 162, IR (Alta.) 44 B3
Foxley River, UP (PEI) 7 B3
Foxmead, UP (Ont.) 23 F1
Fox Mine, UP (Man.) 30 A1
Fox Point, UP (NS) 9 A4
Fox Point, UP (Ont.) 24 C2
Fox Point, UP (Sask.) 31 G2
Fox Point 157D, IR (Sask.) 32 E1
Fox Point 157E, IR (Sask.) 32 E1
Fox River, UP (NS) 11 H2
Fox Roost, UP (Nfld.) 4 A4
Foxtrap, UP (Nfld.) 2 H2
Fox Valley, VL (Sask.) 31 C3
Foxville, UP (Ont.) 20 C4
Foxwarren, UP (Man.) 29 E3
Foymount, UP (Ont.) 24 G2
Fradetville, NUP (Que.) 15 C3
Fralick's Beach, UP (Ont.) 21 C1
Framboise, UP (NS) 8 E4
Framboise Intervale, UP (NS) 8 E4
Framnes, UP (Man.) 29 H2
Frampton, UP (Que.) 15 C4
Frances Lake, UP (YT) 45 C3
Franceville, UP (Ont.) 23 F1
Franchere, UP (Alta.) 33 G2
Francis, T (Sask.) 29 B3
Francis Harbour, UP (Nfld.) 6 H4
Francis Peninsula, NUP (BC) 38 D1
Francoeur, UP (NB) 15 H2
Francoeurville, UP (Que.) 16 C3
François, UP (Nfld.) 4 F4
François Lake, UP (BC) 41 G1
François Lake 7, IR (BC) 41 G1
Franey Corner, UP (NS) 10 D1
Frank, VL (Alta.) 34 E3
Frankford, VL (Ont.) 21 F1
Franklin, UP (Man.) 29 F3
Franklin, UP (Ont.) 21 D1
Franklin, District of/de, DIST (NWT) 1
Franklin Beach, UP (Ont.) 21 B1
Franklin Camp, UP (BC) 38 C3
Franklin-Centre, UP (Que.) 17 G2
Franklin Manor 22, IR (NS) 11 H2
Franklin Park, UP (Ont.) 25 F3
Franklins Corners, UP (Ont.) 17 E1
Franks 10, IR (BC) 37 H4
Frankslake, UP (Sask.) 31 H3
Franktown, UP (Ont.) 17 B2
Frankville, UP (NS) 8 C4
Frankville, UP (Ont.) 17 C3
Franquelin, UP (Que.) 13 A1
Franz, UP (Ont.) 26 B1
Fraser, UP (BC) 34 B4
Fraserdale, UP (Ont.) 20 C4
Fraser Island 6, IR (BC) 38 E4
Fraser Lake, VL (BC) 40 A1
Fraser Lake 2, IR (BC) 40 B1
Fraser-Landing, UP (Que.) 18 B4
Fraser Settlement, UP (NS) 9 C3
Frasers Grant, UP (NS) 8 B4
Frasers Mills, UP (NS) 8 B4
Frasers Mountain, UP (NS) 9 D1
Frasertown, UP (NS) 10 C1
Fraserville, UP (Ont.) 21 D1
Fraserville (Parrsboro Shore), UP (NS) 11 G2
Fraserwood, UP (Man.) 29 H3
Fraspur, UP (Alta.) 33 D4
Frater, UP (Ont.) 26 A3
Fraxville, UP (NS) 10 E1
Fréchette, UP (Que.) 15 A4
Freda Point 4, IR (BC) 39 G1
Freddie Charley Boy 7, IR (BC) 40 B3
Freddie's Meadow 8, IR (BC) 40 C3
Fredensthal, UP (Man.) 28 A3
Frederickhouse, UP (Ont.) 26 E1
Fredericksburg, UP (NB) 12 C4
Fredrickson Trailer Court, NUP (Alta.) 33 E4
Frederickton, UP (Nfld.) 3 E2
Fredericton, C (NB) 11 C1
Fredericton, UP (PEI) 7 C3
Fredericton Junction, VL (NB) 11 C2
Fredericton Road, UP (NB) 11 F1
Freedale, UP (Man.) 29 F2
Freedom, UP (Alta.) 33 D2
Free Grant, UP (NB) 12 E1
Freeland, UP (PEI) 7 B3
Freeland, UP (Ont.) 17 B3
Freelton, UP (Ont.) 22 G1
Freeman 150B, IR (Alta.) 33 B1
Freeman Corners, UP (Ont.) 24 F4
Freeman River, UP (Alta.) 33 C2
Freemont, UP (Sask.) 32 A4
Freeport, UP (NS) 10 A2
Freeport Trailer Park, NUP (BC) 42 G4
Freetown, UP (PEI) 7 B3
Frelighsburg, VL (Que.) 16 B4
Fremo Corners, UP (Ont.) 17 A1
French Bay < Garden River 14, UP (Ont.) 26 B4
French Cove, UP (NS) 8 D4
Frenchfort, UP (PEI) 7 D4
French Hill, UP (Ont.) 17 D1
French Lake, UP (NB) 11 C2
French Line, UP (Ont.) 17 A2
Frenchman Butte, UP (Sask.) 32 A3
Frenchman's Cove, COMM (Nfld.) 2 C3
Frenchman's Cove < Halfway Point – Benoit's Cove – John's Beach – Frenchman's Cove, UP (Nfld.) 4 C1
Frenchmans Island, UP (Nfld.) 6 H3
Frenchmans Road, UP (NS) 9 B3
French Portage, UP (Ont.) 28 F2
French River, UP (PEI) 7 C3
French River, UP (NS) 9 C1
French River, UP (NS) 8 A4
French River, UP (NS) 8 E2
French River, UP (Ont.) 25 F2
French River, UP (Ont.) 25 E2
French River 13, IR (Ont.) 25 F2
French Road, UP (NS) 8 F4
French Settlement, UP (Ont.) 24 G1
Frenchvale, UP (NS) 8 E3
French Village, UP (NB) 11 E2
French Village, UP (NS) 9 A4
French Village, UP (NB) 11 C1
French Village, UP (PEI) 7 D3
French Village, UP (PEI) 7 C3
Frenchville, UP (Sask.) 31 D4
Frenette, UP (Que.) 15 D2
Freppel, UP (Que.) 15 D2
Freshwater, T (Nfld.) 2 F3
Freshwater, UP (Nfld.) 2 G2
Freshwater, UP (Nfld.) 2 H2
Freshwater, UP (Que.) 18 C4
Freshwater Bay, UP (BC) 39 E1
Fresnoy, UP (Alta.) 33 G2
Fridays, UP (Ont.) 26 F3
Friedensfeld, UP (Man.) 29 H4
Friedensfeld, UP (Man.) 28 B2
Friedensruh, UP (Man.) 29 H4
Friedenstal, UP (Alta.) 43 G3
Friendly Corners, UP (Ont.) 22 E1
Fringewood, NUP (Ont.) 17 D4
Froatburn, UP (Ont.) 17 D2
Frobisher, VL (Sask.) 29 C4
Frobisher Bay, VL (NWT) 46 F2
Froggetts Corners, UP (Ont.) 22 F2
Frog Lake, UP (NB) 11 B2
Frog Lake < Unipouheos 121, UP (Alta.) 33 G3
Frogmore, UP (Ont.) 22 F2
Frome, UP (Ont.) 22 E2
Front Centre, UP (NS) 10 E2
Frontier, VL (Sask.) 31 D4
Front Lake, UP (NS) 8 F3
Froomfield, UP (Ont.) 22 B2
Frost-Village, UP (Que.) 16 C4
Froude, UP (Sask.) 29 B4
Fruitvale, VL (BC) 34 B4
Fryatt, UP (Ont.) 20 B4
Frys, UP (Sask.) 29 D4
Fugèreville, UP (Que.) 18 A2
Fulda, UP (Sask.) 31 G1
Fulford Harbour, UP (BC) 38 E3
Fulford Harbour 5, IR (BC) 38 F3
Fullarton, UP (Ont.) 22 E1
Fuller, UP (Ont.) 21 F1
Fullerton, UP (NWT) 46 C2
Fulton, UP (Ont.) 21 A4
Fultons, UP (Ont.) 23 C3
Furby's Cove, UP (Nfld.) 2 B2
Furdale, UP (Sask.) 31 E1
Furman, UP (Alta.) 34 E3
Furnace Falls, UP (Ont.) 23 H1
Furness, UP (Sask.) 32 A3
Fusilier, UP (Sask.) 31 C1

G

Gabarus, UP (NS) 8 F4
Gabarus Lake, UP (NS) 8 F4
Gabriola, UP (BC) 38 E2
Gabriola Island 5, IR (BC) 38 E2
Gadds Harbour, UP (Nfld.) 5 F4
Gadsby, VL (Alta.) 34 G1
Gads Hill, UP (Ont.) 23 C4
Gads Hill Station, UP (Ont.) 23 C4
Gaetz Brook, UP (NS) 9 C3
Gage, UP (Alta.) 43 G3
Gagetown, VL (NB) 11 D2
Gagetown, CFB/BFC, MIL (NB) 11 D2
Gagné, UP (Que.) 13 E3
Gagnon, T (Que.) 19 D1
Gagnon, UP (Ont.) 17 D1
Gagnon-Siding, UP (Que.) 18 D2
Gahern, UP (Alta.) 31 A4
Gaichbin 5, IR (BC) 41 G1
Gainford, UP (Alta.) 33 C3
Gainsborough, VL (Sask.) 29 D4
Galahad, VL (Alta.) 33 F4
Galarneauville, UP (Alta.) 34 G2
Galbraith, UP (Ont.) 17 B2
Galena Bay, UP (BC) 34 B2
Galena Hill, UP (Ont.) 23 H1
Galesburg, UP (Ont.) 21 D1
Galeton, UP (Ont.) 20 D3
Galetta, UP (Ont.) 17 B1
Galeville, UP (Nfld.) 5 G4
Galiano, UP (BC) 38 F3
Galiano Island 9, IR (BC) 38 E3
Galilee, UP (Sask.) 31 G3
Gallagher Ridge, UP (NB) 11 G1
Gallant, UP (Que.) 14 F2
Gallants, COMM (Nfld.) 4 C1
Gallant Settlement, UP (NB) 7 A4
Gallichan, UP (Que.) 18 A1
Gallingertown, UP (Ont.) 17 D2
Gallivan, UP (Sask.) 32 B4
Galloway, UP (BC) 34 D4
Galloway, UP (NB) 12 G4
Galloway, UP (Alta.) 33 B3
Gallup-Hill, UP (Que.) 16 C3
Galson, UP (Que.) 16 E3
Galts Corner, UP (Ont.) 17 A4
Gambier Harbour, UP (BC) 38 F2
Gambler 63, IR (Man.) 29 D3
Gambles Corner, UP (PEI) 7 C4
Gambo < Dark Cove – Middle Brook – Gambo, UP (Nfld.) 3 E3
Gamebridge, UP (Ont.) 23 G2
Gamebridge Beach, UP (Ont.) 23 G2
Gameland, UP (Ont.) 28 F4
Gananoque, T (Ont.) 17 B4
Gander, T (Nfld.) 3 D3
Gander Bay, UP (Nfld.) 3 E2
Gander Bay South, UP (Nfld.) 3 E2
Gander Island 14, IR (BC) 41 D2
Ganges, UP (BC) 38 E3
Gang Ranch, UP (BC) 36 B3
Gannon Beach, UP (Ont.) 21 D1
Gannon Road, UP (NS) 8 E3
Gannon Village, UP (Ont.) 21 D1
Ganny Cove, UP (Nfld.) 2 F1
Gap, UP (Alta.) 34 D2
Gapview, UP (Sask.) 29 C4
Garden 2, IR (BC) 37 D1
Garden 2A, IR (BC) 37 D1
Garden Bay, UP (BC) 38 D1
Garden Cove, UP (Nfld.) 2 E2
Garden Creek, UP (Alta.) 44 B3
Garden Head, UP (Sask.) 31 D4
Garden Hill, UP (Ont.) 21 D1
Garden Hill < Island Lake 22A, UP (Man.) 30 D2
Garden Lots, UP (NS) 10 E2
Garden of Eden, UP (NS) 9 E2
Garden of Eden, UP (Ont.) 17 A1
Garden Plain, UP (Alta.) 34 G1
Garden River < Garden River 14, UP (Ont.) 26 B4
Garden River 14, IR (Ont.) 26 B4
Garden Road, UP (NB) 12 E2
Gardenton, UP (Man.) 28 B3
Gardenview, UP (Alta.) 33 D3
Garden Village < Nipissing 10, UP (Ont.) 25 G1
Gardenville, UP (Ont.) 21 F2
Gardiner, UP (Ont.) 26 E1
Gardiner Mines, UP (NS) 8 F3
Gardner Creek, UP (NB) 11 E3
Gardners Mills, UP (NS) 10 B3
Garfield, UP (PEI) 7 D4
Garfield, UP (Alta.) 34 E1
Gargantua, UP (Ont.) 26 A2
Garibaldi, UP (BC) 37 F4
Garin, UP (Que.) 13 F3
Garland, UP (Man.) 29 E1
Garland, UP (NS) 11 G3
Garlands Crossing, UP (NS) 9 A3
Garneau, UP (Que.) 16 B1
Garnett Settlement, UP (NB) 11 E3
Garnier, UP (Que.) 18 E3
Garnish, T (Nfld.) 2 C3
Garretton, UP (Ont.) 17 C3
Garrick, UP (Sask.) 32 F3
Garrington, UP (Alta.) 34 E1
Garryowen, UP (Ont.) 23 D1
Garson, VL (Man.) 28 B1
Garson Lake, UP (Sask.) 44 C4
Garth, UP (Alta.) 33 C4
Garthland, UP (Sask.) 32 D4
Gartly, UP (Alta.) 34 G1
Gascoigne, UP (Sask.) 31 C2
Gascons, UP (Que.) 13 G3
Gascons-Est, UP (Que.) 13 G3
Gascons-Ouest, UP (Que.) 13 G3
Gaskiers < Gaskiers – Point La Haye, UP (Nfld.) 2 F4
Gaskiers – Point La Haye, COMM (Nfld.) 2 F4
Gaspé, C (Que.) 13 H2
Gaspereau, UP (NS) 10 E1
Gaspereau, UP (NB) 12 G1
Gaspereau Forks, UP (NB) 12 E4
Gaspereau Mountain, UP (NS) 10 E1
Gaspereaux, UP (PEI) 7 E4

Gates, UP (BC) 37 G3
Gateway, UP (BC) 36 D2
Gatine, UP (Alta.) 34 F2
Gatineau, C (Que.) 17 E3
Gaulin, UP (Que.) 16 D4
Gault, UP (BC) 45 B3
Gaultois, T (Nfld.) 2 B2
Gauthier, UP (Que.) 13 G3
Gautreau Village, UP (NB) 11 G1
Gauvin, UP (Que.) 13 D3
Gauvreau, UP (NB) 12 G1
Gavelton, UP (NS) 10 B3
Gayford, UP (Alta.) 34 F2
Gayside, COMM (Nfld.) 3 D2
Gays River, UP (NS) 9 C3
Gaythorne, UP (NB) 12 F1
Gaytons, UP (NB) 11 H1
Gazer Subdivision, NUP (Ont.) 23 E4
Geary, UP (NB) 11 C2
Geikie, UP (Alta.) 40 G3
Gelangle 1, IR (BC) 42 H4
Gelert, UP (Ont.) 23 H1
Gellatly, UP (BC) 35 E3
Gem, UP (Alta.) 34 G2
Gendron, UP (Que.) 16 A1
Genelle, UP (BC) 34 B4
Genesee, UP (Alta.) 33 D3
Geneva, UP (Que.) 17 F1
Geneva Park, UP (Ont.) 23 G1
Genier, UP (Ont.) 20 D4
Geoffroy, UP (Que.) 18 A2
Georgefield, UP (NS) 9 B2
Georges Brook, UP (Nfld.) 2 F1
Georges Cove, UP (Nfld.) 5 G4
Georges Cove, UP (Nfld.) 6 H4
Georges Lake, UP (Nfld.) 4 C1
Georges River, UP (NS) 8 E3
Georgetown, T (PEI) 7 E4
Georgetown, UP (Nfld.) 2 G2
Georgetown Mills, UP (BC) 42 C4
Georgeville, UP (Que.) 16 C4
Georgeville, UP (NS) 8 B4
Georgian Beach, UP (Ont.) 23 D1
Georgian Heights, UP (Ont.) 24 A4
Georgian Inlet, UP (Ont.) 25 F3
Georgian Sands Beach, UP (Ont.) 23 E1
Georgie 17, IR (BC) 42 D3
Georgina Beach, UP (Ont.) 23 E1
Georgina Island < Georgina Island 33, UP (Ont.) 21 B1
Georgina Island 33, IR (Ont.) 21 B1
Gerald, VL (Sask.) 29 D3
Geraldton, T (Ont.) 27 G2
Gergovia, UP (Sask.) 31 E4
Gérin, UP (Que.) 16 A2
Germanicus, UP (Ont.) 24 G1
German Landing, UP (Ont.) 21 F1
Germansen Landing, UP (BC) 42 H3
German Settlement, UP (Ont.) 24 F2
Germantown, UP (NB) 11 G2
Germany, UP (NB) 11 C2
Gerow Island, NUP (BC) 42 G4
Gerrard, UP (BC) 34 B3
Gerrish Valley, UP (NS) 9 A2
Gerrow's Beach, UP (Ont.) 21 C1
Gesto, UP (Ont.) 22 A3
Geyser, UP (Man.) 29 H2
Ghost Lake, VL (Alta.) 34 D2
Ghost Pine Creek, UP (Alta.) 34 F1
Ghost River, UP (Ont.) 27 B1
Ghost River, UP (Ont.) 20 C3
Giants Glen, UP (NB) 12 C4
Giants Lake, UP (NS) 9 F2
Gibbon, UP (NB) 11 E1
Gibbon, UP (NS) 8 F3
Gibbons, VL (Alta.) 33 E3
Gibbs, UP (Sask.) 31 G2
Giberson Settlement, UP (NB) 12 A3
Gibraltar, UP (Ont.) 23 E2
Gibraltar, UP (Ont.) 25 C2
Gibson, UP (Ont.) 23 E1
Gibson 31, IR (Ont.) 23 F1
Gibson Creek, UP (BC) 34 B4
Gibsons, VL (BC) 38 E2
Gift Lake, UP (Alta.) 44 A4
Gignac, UP (Que.) 13 F3
Gilbert Mills, UP (Ont.) 21 F1
Gilbert Mountain, UP (NS) 9 A2
Gilbert Plains, VL (Man.) 29 E2
Gilberts Corner, UP (NB) 12 H4
Gilberts Cove, UP (NS) 10 B2
Gilbertville, UP (Ont.) 22 F2
Gilby, UP (Alta.) 33 D4
Gilchrist, UP (Ont.) 21 A1
Gilchrist Bay, UP (Ont.) 24 E4
Gildale, UP (Ont.) 23 D3
Gilford, UP (Ont.) 21 A1
Gilford Beach, UP (Ont.) 21 A1
Gillam, UP (Man.) 30 D1
Gillams, COMM (Nfld.) 4 C1
Gillard's Cove, UP (Nfld.) 3 D1
Gillespie Settlement, UP (NB) 12 A2
Gillies, UP (Ont.) 26 F3
Gillies Bay, UP (BC) 38 C1
Gillies Corners, UP (Ont.) 17 B2
Gillies Hill, UP (Ont.) 23 C2
Gillies Lake, NUP (Ont.) 25 D4
Gillis Cove, UP (NS) 8 D4
Gillisdale, UP (NS) 8 D3
Gillis Lake, UP (NS) 8 E3
Gill Island 2, IR (BC) 41 D1
Gillis Point, UP (NS) 8 D3
Gillis Point East, UP (NS) 8 D3
Gillson's Point, UP (Ont.) 21 C1
Gilmans Corner, UP (NB) 11 B3
Gilmour, UP (Ont.) 24 F3
Gilpin, UP (BC) 35 H4
Gilroy, UP (Sask.) 31 E2
Gilt Edge, UP (Alta.) 33 G4
Gilwood, UP (Alta.) 33 B1
Gimli, T (Man.) 30 C4
Gin Cove, UP (Nfld.) 2 F1
Girardville, UP (Que.) 18 G1
Giroux, UP (Man.) 28 B2
Girouxville, VL (Alta.) 43 H3
Girvin, VL (Sask.) 31 F2
Giscome, UP (BC) 40 D1
Gish Creek 45, IR (BC) 42 D3
Gitandoiks 75, IR (BC) 42 D4
Gitandoiks 76, IR (BC) 42 D4
Gitquinmiyaue 76, IR (BC) 42 E3
Gitsheoaksit 68, IR (BC) 42 E3
Gjoa Haven, UP (NWT) 45 H1
Glace Bay, T (NS) 8 F3
Glacier, UP (BC) 34 B2
Glacier Camp, UP (BC) 45 A3
Glade, UP (BC) 34 B4
Gladeside, UP (NB) 12 G4
Gladmar, VL (Sask.) 31 H4
Gladstone, T (Man.) 29 G3
Gladstone, UP (Ont.) 22 E2
Gladstone, UP (PEI) 7 E4
Gladstone, NUP (NB) 12 A3
Gladwin, UP (BC) 35 B2
Gladwyn, UP (NB) 12 A3
Gladys, UP (Alta.) 34 E2
Glamis, UP (Sask.) 31 D2
Glammis, UP (Ont.) 23 B2
Glandine, UP (Ont.) 21 C1
Glanford Station, UP (Ont.) 21 A4
Glanmire, UP (Ont.) 24 F3
Glanworth, UP (Ont.) 22 E2
Glascott, UP (Ont.) 23 D2
Glasgow, UP (NS) 8 E3
Glasgow, UP (Ont.) 21 B2
Glasgow Station, UP (Ont.) 17 A1
Glaslyn, VL (Sask.) 32 B3
Glasnevin, UP (Sask.) 31 G4
Glass, UP (Man.) 28 B1
Glassburn, UP (NS) 8 B4
Glassville, UP (NB) 12 B3
Glastonbury, UP (Ont.) 24 G3
Glaude, UP (NB) 7 A4
Glazier Creek 12, IR (BC) 37 G4
Gleason Road, UP (NB) 11 A3
Glebe Farm 40B, IR (Ont.) 22 G1
Gledhow, UP (Sask.) 31 E1
Gleichen, T (Alta.) 34 F2
Glen, UP (Ont.) 23 D2
Glen Alda, UP (Ont.) 24 E3
Glen Allan, UP (Ont.) 23 D4
Glen Alpine, UP (NS) 9 F2
Glen Andrew, UP (Ont.) 17 F1
Glenannan, UP (Ont.) 23 C3
Glenannan, UP (BC) 40 A1
Glenarm, UP (Ont.) 24 C4
Glenavon, VL (Sask.) 29 C3
Glenbain, UP (Sask.) 31 E3
Glenbank, UP (BC) 34 B3
Glen Bard, UP (NS) 8 A4
Glen Becker, UP (Ont.) 17 D2
Glenbervie, UP (NS) 9 D2
Glenbogie, UP (Sask.) 32 A3
Glenboro, VL (Man.) 29 F4
Glenbow, UP (Alta.) 34 E2
Glenbrea, UP (Sask.) 31 G2
Glenbrook, UP (Ont.) 17 E2
Glen Buell, UP (Ont.) 17 C3
Glenburn, UP (Ont.) 17 D1
Glenburnie, UP (Nfld.) 5 F4
Glenburnie, UP (Ont.) 17 A4
Glenbush, UP (Sask.) 32 B3
Glen Cairn, UP (Ont.) 17 D4
Glencairn, UP (Ont.) 23 E2
Glencairn, UP (Man.) 29 F3
Glen Campbellton, UP (NS) 8 C3
Glencoe, UP (NB) 13 C4
Glencoe, UP (NS) 9 D2
Glencoe, UP (NS) 8 C3
Glencoe, UP (PEI) 7 D4
Glencoe, UP (NS) 9 F2
Glencoe, UP (NB) 12 C4
Glencoe, VL (Ont.) 22 D2
Glencoe Mills, UP (NS) 8 C3
Glencoe Station, UP (NS) 8 C3
Glencolin, UP (Ont.) 22 E2
Glencorradale, UP (PEI) 7 E3
Glen Cross, UP (Ont.) 23 E3
Glencross, UP (Man.) 29 H4
Glendale, UP (BC) 36 B1
Glendale, UP (NS) 8 C4
Glendale Beach, UP (Ont.) 22 C1
Glendale Cove, UP (BC) 39 G1
Glendale Subdivision, NUP (Ont.) 17 E2
Glendon, VL (Alta.) 33 G2
Glendon Cove, UP (Nfld.) 2 E2
Glendower, UP (Ont.) 17 A3
Glendyer, UP (NS) 8 C3
Glendyer Station, UP (NS) 8 C3
Glendyne, UP (Que.) 15 F2
Gleneagle, UP (Que.) 17 D3
Glen Eden, UP (BC) 38 F1
Glen Eden, UP (Ont.) 22 A4
Glen Elbe, UP (Ont.) 17 C3
Glenelg, UP (NS) 9 E2
Glenelg Centre, UP (Ont.) 23 D2
Glenella, UP (Man.) 29 F3
Glenellen, UP (Sask.) 31 D1
Glenelm, UP (Que.) 17 F2
Glen Elmo, UP (Man.) 29 E2
Glenemma, UP (BC) 35 F1
Glenevis, UP (Alta.) 33 D3
Glen Ewen, VL (Sask.) 29 D4
Glen Falloch, UP (Ont.) 17 E2
Glenfanning, UP (PEI) 7 E4
Glenfield, UP (Ont.) 24 G2
Glenfinnan, UP (PEI) 7 D4
Glenford, UP (Alta.) 33 D3
Glenforsa, UP (Man.) 29 E3
Glengarry, UP (PEI) 7 A2
Glengarry, UP (NS) 8 C3
Glengarry, UP (NS) 10 E1
Glengarry Station, UP (NS) 9 D2
Glengarry Valley, UP (NS) 8 E4
Glen-gla-ouch 5, IR (BC) 39 C1
Glen Gordon, UP (Ont.) 17 F2
Glen Harbour, UP (Sask.) 31 G2
Glen Haven, UP (NS) 9 A4
Glenhaven Beach, UP (Ont.) 21 A1
Glenholme, UP (NS) 9 B2
Glen Huron, UP (Ont.) 23 E2
Glenister, UP (Alta.) 33 C2
Glenkeen, UP (NS) 9 G2
Glen Kerr, UP (Sask.) 31 E3
Glen Lake, UP (BC) 38 E4
Glenlea, UP (Man.) 28 A2
Glenlee, UP (Ont.) 23 D3
Glen Leslie, UP (Alta.) 43 G4
Glen Levit, UP (NB) 13 C4
Glenlily, UP (BC) 34 C4
Glenlochar, UP (Man.) 29 E3
Glen Margaret, UP (NS) 9 A4
Glenmartin, UP (PEI) 7 D4
Glen McPherson, UP (Sask.) 31 E4
Glen Meyer, UP (Ont.) 22 F2
Glen Miller, UP (Ont.) 21 F1
Glen Moir, UP (NS) 9 B3
Glenmont, UP (NS) 11 H3
Glenmoor, UP (Man.) 30 C4
Glenmore, UP (NS) 9 C3
Glenmore, UP (Ont.) 17 C3
Glen Morris, UP (Ont.) 22 G1
Glen Morris, UP (Ont.) 17 C3
Glen Morrison, UP (NS) 8 E3
Glenmount, UP (Ont.) 24 C2
Glen Nevis, UP (Ont.) 17 F2
Glennis Trailer Park, NUP (BC) 43 D4
Glen Norman, UP (Ont.) 17 F2
Glen Oak, UP (Ont.) 22 D2
Glenora, UP (Ont.) 21 G2
Glenora, UP (Man.) 29 F4
Glenora, UP (NS) 8 C4
Glenora, NUP (BC) 38 E3
Glenora Falls, UP (NS) 8 C3
Glen Orchard, UP (Ont.) 24 B2
Glenorchy, UP (Ont.) 27 A3
Glen Park, UP (Alta.) 33 D3
Glen Rae, UP (Ont.) 22 C2
Glenrest Beach, UP (Ont.) 23 G2
Glen Ridge Terrace, UP (Ont.) 17 E4
Glen Road, UP (NS) 8 B4
Glen Robertson, UP (Ont.) 17 F1
Glenrosa, UP (BC) 35 E3
Glen Ross, UP (Ont.) 21 F1
Glenroy, UP (Ont.) 17 E2
Glenroy, UP (NS) 8 B4
Glenroy < Scotchfort 4, UP (PEI) 7 D3
Glen Sandfield, UP (Ont.) 17 F1
Glenside, VL (Sask.) 31 E2
Glen Smail, UP (Ont.) 17 D3
Glen Stewart, UP (Ont.) 17 D2
Glen-Sutton, UP (Que.) 16 C4
Glentanna, UP (BC) 42 F4
Glen Tay, UP (Ont.) 17 B3
Glenton, UP (Que.) 16 C4
Glen Tosh, UP (NS) 8 E3
Glentworth, VL (Sask.) 31 F4
Glenvale, UP (NB) 11 F1
Glenvale, UP (Ont.) 17 A4
Glenvale, UP (Ont.) 26 F2
Glen Valley, UP (PEI) 7 C3
Glenview, UP (Ont.) 17 B2
Glenvilla Court, NUP (Nfld.) 2 H2
Glenville, UP (NS) 8 C3
Glenville, UP (Ont.) 21 A1
Glenville, UP (NS) 9 A1
Glen Vowell < Sik-e-dakh 2, UP (BC) 42 F3
Glen Walter, UP (Ont.) 17 E2
Glenwater, UP (Ont.) 27 D3
Glenway Village, UP (Ont.) 21 C1
Glenway Village, UP (Ont.) 23 H2
Glenwilliam, UP (PEI) 7 D4
Glenwood, T (Nfld.) 3 D3
Glenwood, UP (NB) 11 D2
Glenwood, UP (PEI) 7 A3
Glenwood, UP (NS) 10 B3
Glenwood, UP (Ont.) 22 B3
Glenwood, UP (NB) 13 C4
Glenwood, UP (NB) 12 F2
Glenwood, VL (Alta.) 34 F4
Glenwood, NUP (Alta.) 33 B3
Glenwood Beach, UP (Ont.) 21 B1
Glenwood Beach, UP (Ont.) 21 A1
Glenwood Heights, NUP (Ont.) 22 H1
Gleyka 6, IR (BC) 41 F4
Glidden, VL (Sask.) 31 C2
Gloucester, UP (Ont.) 17 E4
Gloucester Glen, UP (Ont.) 17 E4
Gloucester Junction, UP (NB) 12 E1
Glovers Harbour, UP (Nfld.) 3 C2
Glovertown, T (Nfld.) 3 E4
Glyne-Corners, UP (Que.) 16 C4
Gnadenfeld, UP (Man.) 29 H4
Gnadenthal, UP (Man.) 29 H4
Goatfell, UP (BC) 34 C4
Goat River, UP (BC) 40 E2
Gobles, UP (Ont.) 22 F1
Goblin, UP (Nfld.) 2 A2
Godbout, VL (Que.) 13 A1
Goderich, T (Ont.) 23 B3
Godfrey, UP (Ont.) 17 A3
Godolphin, UP (Ont.) 21 E1
Gods Lake, UP (Man.) 30 D2
God's Lake 23, IR (Man.) 30 D2
Gods Lake Narrows, UP (Man.) 30 D2
Gods River, UP (Man.) 30 D2
Goffs, UP (NS) 9 B3
Gogama, UP (Ont.) 26 D2
Go Home, UP (Ont.) 23 F1
Golburn, UP (Sask.) 32 F4
Goldboro, UP (NS) 9 F2
Gold Bottom, UP (YT) 45 A2
Gold Bridge, UP (BC) 37 G2
Gold Brook, UP (NS) 8 D3
Gold Cove < Hampden, UP (Nfld.) 5 G4
Golden, T (BC) 34 B2
Golden Bay, UP (Man.) 28 B1
Goldenburgh, UP (Ont.) 26 C4
Golden Days, SV (Alta.) 33 D4
Golden Hill, UP (Ont.) 17 E1
Golden Lake, UP (Ont.) 24 G1
Golden Lake 39, IR (Ont.) 24 G1
Golden Prairie, VL (Sask.) 31 C3
Golden Ridge, UP (Sask.) 32 B2
Golden Spike, UP (Alta.) 33 D3
Goldenvale, UP (Sask.) 29 C2
Golden Valley, UP (Ont.) 24 A1
Goldenville, UP (NS) 9 E3
Goldfield, UP (Ont.) 17 D2
Goldfields, UP (Sask.) 44 D2
Goldpines, UP (Ont.) 30 E4
Gold River, UP (NS) 10 E2
Gold River, VL (BC) 39 F3
Gold River 21, IR (NS) 10 E2
Gold Rock, UP (Ont.) 27 A2
Gold Run, UP (YT) 45 A2
Goldsmith, UP (Ont.) 22 B3
Gold Spur, UP (Alta.) 31 B2
Goldstone, UP (Ont.) 23 D3
Goldstream 13, IR (BC) 38 E4
Goldwin, UP (Que.) 18 C4
Golspie, UP (Ont.) 22 F1
Gondola Point, VL (NB) 11 E2
Gonor, UP (Man.) 28 A1
Goobies, UP (Nfld.) 2 F1
Good Corner, UP (NB) 12 A4
Good Corner, UP (NB) 12 A3
Gooderham, UP (Ont.) 24 D3
Goodeve, VL (Sask.) 29 C2
Goodfare, UP (Alta.) 43 F4
Goodfellow Beach, UP (Ont.) 21 A1
Goodfish Lake < White Fish Lake 128, UP (Alta.) 33 F2
Good Harbour, UP (Man.) 29 E1
Good Hope, UP (Alta.) 33 E3
Good Hope, UP (BC) 41 F4
Goodlands, UP (Man.) 29 E4
Goodlow, UP (BC) 43 F3
Goodridge, UP (Alta.) 33 F2
Goodsoil, VL (Sask.) 32 A2
Goodstown, UP (Ont.) 17 C2
Goodwater, VL (Sask.) 29 B4
Goodwin, UP (Alta.) 43 G4
Goodwin Mill, NUP (NB) 12 E1
Goodwood, UP (Ont.) 21 B2
Goodwood, UP (NS) 9 B4
Goo-ewe 8, IR (BC) 41 E3
Goose Arm, UP (Nfld.) 5 F4
Goose Bay, UP (BC) 41 F4
Gooseberry Cove, UP (Nfld.) 2 F1
Gooseberry Cove, UP (Nfld.) 2 E3
Gooseberry Cove, UP (NB) 11 D3
Gooseberry Island, UP (Nfld.) 3 F3
Goose Cove, UP (Nfld.) 2 E2
Goose Cove, UP (NS) 8 E3
Goose Cove < Goose Cove East, UP (Nfld.) 5 H2
Goose Cove < Trinity (COMM), UP (Nfld.) 3 G4
Goose Cove East, COMM (Nfld.) 5 H2
Goose Creek, NUP (BC) 34 B4
Goose River, UP (PEI) 7 E3
Goose Spit 3, IR (BC) 38 C1
Gordon, UP (Man.) 28 A1
Gordon 86, IR (Sask.) 31 H2
Gordon Bay, UP (Ont.) 24 A2
Gordondale, UP (Alta.) 43 F3
Gordon Lake, UP (Ont.) 26 B4
Gordon Landing, UP (YT) 45 B2
Gordon River, UP (BC) 38 D3
Gordon River 2, IR (BC) 38 D4
Gordon Summit, UP (NS) 9 D2
Gordonsville, UP (NB) 12 A3
Gordon Vale, UP (NB) 12 C3
Gordonville, UP (Que.) 17 F1
Gordonville, UP (Ont.) 23 D3
Gore, UP (NS) 9 B3
Gore, UP (Que.) 16 C3
Gore Bay, T (Ont.) 25 E2
Gores Landing, UP (Ont.) 21 D1
Gorge Harbour, NUP (BC) 37 B4
Goring, UP (Ont.) 23 D2
Gorlitz, UP (Sask.) 29 C2
Gormanville, UP (NS) 9 B2
Gorrie, UP (Ont.) 23 C3
Gorr Subdivision, NUP (Ont.) 18 C4
Goshen, UP (NS) 9 F2
Goshen, UP (NB) 11 F2
Goshen, UP (NS) 9 C2
Goshen, UP (NS) 9 A2
Goshen, UP (NB) 11 E1
Goshen, UP (Ont.) 17 A1
Goshen, UP (Ont.) 23 B4
Goshen-Road, UP (Que.) 16 D3
Gosnell, UP (BC) 40 F3
Gosport, UP (Ont.) 21 G1
Gosselin-Mills, UP (Que.) 16 D4
Gossen Creek, NUP (BC) 42 E4
Gotham, UP (Ont.) 23 C4
Goudalie, UP (NB) 12 G4
Goudreau, UP (Ont.) 26 A2
Goulais Bay, UP (Ont.) 26 A3
Goulais Bay 15A, IR (Ont.) 26 A3
Goulais Mission < Goulais Bay 15A, UP (Ont.) 26 A3
Goulais River, UP (Ont.) 26 A3
Goulbourne, UP (Man.) 29 G2
Gould, UP (Que.) 16 E3
Goulds, T (Nfld.) 2 H2
Goulds Road, UP (Nfld.) 2 G2
Gould-Station, UP (Que.) 16 E3
Gouldtown, UP (Sask.) 31 E3
Goupil, UP (Que.) 13 B2
Gourd, UP (Que.) 18 B1
Gouverneur, UP (Sask.) 31 E4
Govan, T (Sask.) 31 G2
Govenlock, UP (Sask.) 31 B4
Government Landing, UP (Ont.) 28 H4
Government Road, UP (Ont.) 24 G1
Gowanbrae, UP (PEI) 7 E3
Gowanstown, UP (Ont.) 23 C3
Gower Point, NUP (BC) 38 E2
Gowganda, UP (Ont.) 26 E2
Gowland Mountain, UP (NB) 11 F1
Gowland Harbour, NUP (BC) 37 B4
Gracefield, VL (Que.) 18 D4
Grace Lake, UP (Man.) 30 A2
Gracieville, UP (NS) 8 E4
Grady Harbour, UP (Nfld.) 6 H3
Grafton, UP (NB) 11 A1
Grafton, UP (Ont.) 21 E2
Grafton, UP (NS) 11 G3
Grafton, NUP (Alta.) 34 E4
Grafton Hill, UP (NB) 11 A1
Graham, UP (Ont.) 27 C2
Graham Corner, UP (NB) 11 A1
Grahamdale, UP (Man.) 29 G2
Graham Hill, UP (NS) 9 C2
Graham Park, UP (Ont.) 17 D4
Grahams Road, UP (PEI) 7 C3
Grainfield, UP (NB) 12 E3
Grainger, UP (Alta.) 34 F2
Grainland, UP (Sask.) 31 F2
Graminia, UP (Alta.) 33 D3
Gramont, UP (Que.) 18 E4
Granada, UP (Que.) 18 A2
Granby, C (Que.) 16 B4
Granby-Ouest, UP (Que.) 16 B4
Grand Bank, T (Nfld.) 2 B3
Grand Bay, VL (NB) 11 D3
Grand Bay West, UP (Nfld.) 4 A4
Grand Beach, UP (Nfld.) 2 B3
Grand Beach, UP (Man.) 30 C4
Grand Bend, VL (Ont.) 22 D1
Grandbois, UP (Que.) 14 F4
Grand-Bras, UP (Que.) 15 E2
Grand Bruit, UP (Nfld.) 4 C4
Grand-Cascapédia, UP (Que.) 13 E3
Grand Centre, T (Alta.) 33 G2
Grand Coulee, UP (Sask.) 31 G3
Grand Desert, UP (NS) 9 C4
Grand-Détour, UP (Que.) 13 B2
Grande-Aldouane, UP (NB) 12 G3
Grande Anse, UP (NS) 8 D4
Grande-Anse, UP (Que.) 18 G3
Grande-Anse, VL (NB) 13 F4
Grande Cache, T (Alta.) 40 F2
Grande-Clairière, UP (Man.) 29 E4
Grande-Digue, UP (NB) 12 H4
Grande-Entrée, UP (Que.) 7 G1
Grande Greve, UP (NS) 8 D4
Grande-Ligne, UP (Que.) 16 A4
Grande Pointe, UP (Man.) 28 A2
Grande Pointe, UP (Ont.) 22 B3
Grande-Pointe, UP (Que.) 15 C2
Grande Prairie, C (Alta.) 43 G4
Grande-Presqu'île, UP (Que.) 17 E1
Grande-Rivière, T (Que.) 13 H3
Grandes-Bergeronnes, VL (Que.) 14 E3
Grandes-Piles, UP (Que.) 16 B1
Grand Étang, UP (NS) 8 D2
Grande-Vallée, UP (Que.) 13 F1
Grande-Vallée, UP (Que.) 18 F4
Grande-Vallée-des-Monts, UP (Que.) 13 F1
Grand Falls, T (Nfld.) 3 B3
Grand Falls, T (NB) 12 A2
Grand Falls Hill, NUP (NB) 12 A2
Grand Falls Portage, UP (NB) 12 A2
Grand-Fonds, UP (Que.) 14 D4
Grand Forks, C (BC) 35 H4
Grand Forks, UP (YT) 45 A2
Grand Harbour, VL (NB) 11 C4
Grand Haven, UP (BC) 43 E3
Grandique Ferry, UP (NS) 8 D4
Grand Jardin < Cape St George – Petit Jardin – Grand Jardin – De Grau – Marches Point – Loretto, UP (Nfld.) 4 A2
Grand John, UP (Nfld.) 2 C2
Grand-Lac-Neigette, UP (Que.) 14 H3
Grand-Lac-Victoria, UP (Que.) 18 C2
Grand Lake Road, UP (NS) 8 F3
Grand Lake Road, UP (NB) 12 A2
Grand Lake Station, UP (NS) 9 B3
Grand Le Pierre, COMM (Nfld.) 2 D2
Grandmaison, UP (NB) 15 H1
Grand Marais, UP (Man.) 30 C4
Grand-Mère, C (Que.) 16 B1
Grand-Métis, UP (Que.) 14 H2
Grand Mira North, UP (NS) 8 E4
Grand Mira South, UP (NS) 8 E4
Grandmother's Bay 219, IR (Sask.) 32 E1
Grand Narrows, UP (NS) 8 D3
Grandois, UP (Nfld.) 5 H2
Grandora, UP (Sask.) 31 E1
Grand-Pabos, UP (Que.) 13 G3
Grand-Pabos-Ouest, UP (Que.) 13 G3
Grand-Plaqué, UP (Que.) 13 D1
Grand Prairie Trail, NUP (Alta.) 33 B3
Grand Pré, UP (NS) 9 A3
Grand-Rang, NUP (Que.) 15 C4
Grand Rapide 5, IR (BC) 40 A1
Grand Rapids, UP (Man.) 30 B3
Grand Rapids < Grand Rapide 5, UP (BC) 40 A1
Grand Rapids 33, IR (Man.) 30 B3
Grand-Remous, UP (Que.) 18 D3
Grand River, UP (NS) 8 E4
Grand River, UP (PEI) 7 B3
Grand River Falls, UP (NS) 8 E4
Grand River Park, NUP (Ont.) 22 G1
Grand-Ruisseau, UP (Que.) 7 F1
Grand-Ruisseau, UP (NB) 12 A2
Grand-St-Esprit, UP (Que.) 16 C2
Grand Tracadie, UP (PEI) 7 D3
Grand Valley, VL (Ont.) 23 E3
Grandview, SV (Alta.) 33 D4
Grandview, T (Man.) 29 E2
Grandview, UP (PEI) 7 D4
Grandview, UP (Ont.) 24 C2
Grandview Beach, SV (Sask.) 31 G2
Grandview Beach, UP (Ont.) 23 F1
Grandview Bench, UP (BC) 35 F1
Granger, UP (Ont.) 23 E3
Grangeville, UP (NB) 12 F4
Granisle, VL (BC) 42 G4
Granite, UP (BC) 34 B4
Granite Bay, UP (BC) 37 B3
Granite Falls, UP (BC) 38 G2
Granite Hill, UP (NB) 11 B1
Granite Island 4, IR (BC) 39 D2
Granite Lake, UP (Ont.) 28 E2
Granite Village, UP (NS) 10 D3
Graniteville, UP (Que.) 16 C4
Grantham, UP (BC) 38 B1
Grantham, UP (Alta.) 34 G3
Granthams Landing, UP (BC) 38 E2
Grantley, UP (Ont.) 17 D2
Granton, UP (Ont.) 22 E1
Granton, UP (NS) 9 D1
Grants Corners, UP (Ont.) 17 E2
Grants Settlement, UP (NB) 11 E1
Grants Settlement, UP (Ont.) 17 A1
Grant Valley, UP (NS) 9 B3
Grantville, UP (NS) 8 C4
Grantville, NUP (Alta.) 34 F1
Granum, T (Alta.) 34 F3
Granville, UP (PEI) 7 C3
Granville, UP (YT) 45 A2
Granville Beach, UP (NS) 10 C1
Granville Centre, UP (NS) 10 C1
Granville Ferry, UP (NS) 10 C1
Granville Lake, UP (Man.) 30 B1
Graphite, UP (Ont.) 24 E2
Grasmere, UP (BC) 34 D4
Grass 15, IR (BC) 35 A4
Grass Cove, UP (NS) 8 D3
Grasshill, UP (Ont.) 21 C1
Grassie, UP (Ont.) 21 A4
Grassland, UP (Alta.) 33 E2
Grasslands 7, IR (BC) 36 C4
Grassmere, UP (Ont.) 24 C2
Grass Point 13, IR (BC) 39 C1
Grass River, UP (Man.) 29 G3
Grasswood, UP (Sask.) 31 F1
Grassy Island 17, IR (BC) 39 D3
Grassy Islet 2, IR (BC) 41 C1
Grassy Lake, VL (Alta.) 34 G3
Grassy-Narrow, UP (Que.) 18 A2
Grassy Narrows < English River 21, UP (Ont.) 28 G1
Grassy Plains, UP (BC) 41 G1
Grates Cove, UP (Nfld.) 2 H1
Grave Flats, UP (Alta.) 33 A4
Gravel, UP (Que.) 13 E3
Gravelbourg, T (Sask.) 31 F3
Gravel Hill, UP (NB) 13 D4
Gravel Hill, UP (Ont.) 17 E2
Gravel Lake, UP (YT) 45 A2
Gravelle, UP (Que.) 18 D4
Gravelle Ferry, UP (BC) 40 D3
Gravenhurst, T (Ont.) 23 G1
Graveyard 5, IR (BC) 38 G2
Gray, UP (Sask.) 31 H3
Grayburn, UP (Sask.) 31 F3
Gray Creek, UP (BC) 34 B4
Gray Rapids, UP (NB) 12 E3
Grays, UP (Ont.) 22 C2
Grays Bay, UP (Ont.) 23 G1
Grays Mills, UP (NB) 11 D2
Grayson, VL (Sask.) 29 C3
Graysville, UP (Man.) 29 G4
Gray-Valley, UP (Que.) 18 E4
Graywood, UP (NS) 10 C1
Greata, UP (BC) 35 E3
Great Barasway, UP (Nfld.) 2 E3
Great Bear Lake 16, IR (BC) 40 B1
Great Bona, UP (Nfld.) 2 D3
Great Brehat, UP (Nfld.) 5 H2
Great Brule, UP (Nfld.) 2 E2
Great Central, UP (BC) 38 B2
Great Codroy, UP (Nfld.) 4 A3
Great Deer, UP (Sask.) 32 C4
Great Desert, UP (Ont.) 18 A4
Great Falls, UP (Man.) 30 C4
Great Harbour, UP (Nfld.) 2 B2
Great Harbour Deep, COMM (Nfld.) 5 G3
Great Hill, UP (NS) 10 D3
Great Jervais, UP (Nfld.) 2 C3
Great Jervis Harbour, UP (Nfld.) 2 A2
Great Paradise, UP (Nfld.) 2 D3
Great Village, UP (NS) 9 B2
Greece's Point, UP (Que.) 17 F1
Greeley, UP (BC) 34 A2
Greely, UP (Ont.) 17 E4
Green Acres, UP (NS) 10 D1
Green Acres, UP (Ont.) 21 E1
Green Acres, NUP (Ont.) 17 E4
Green Acres, NUP (Sask.) 32 D3
Green Acres, NUP (Alta.) 33 E3
Green Acres Mobile Home, UP (BC) 35 F4
Greenan, UP (Sask.) 31 D2
Greenbank, UP (Ont.) 21 C1
Green Bay, UP (PEI) 7 C4
Green Bay, UP (NS) 10 E2
Green Bay, UP (Ont.) 25 C2
Green Bay, UP (Man.) 28 B1
Green Bay, NUP (BC) 35 E3
Green Bay Resort, NUP (BC) 35 E3
Greenbrier, UP (Sask.) 31 E2
Greenbush, UP (Ont.) 17 C3
Green Canyon, UP (Sask.) 32 C4
Green Corners, UP (Ont.) 24 F3
Green Court, UP (Alta.) 33 C2
Green Cove, UP (Nfld.) 3 D1
Green Cove, UP (BC) 38 B3
Green Creek, UP (NS) 9 C2
Greenfarm, UP (Man.) 29 H4
Greenfeld, UP (Sask.) 31 F1
Greenfield, UP (NS) 10 D2
Greenfield, UP (NS) 9 A3
Greenfield, UP (PEI) 7 D4
Greenfield, UP (NS) 9 A3
Greenfield, UP (NS) 9 C2
Greenfield, UP (NB) 12 A3
Greenfield, UP (Ont.) 17 E2
Greenfield, UP (Ont.) 17 B3
Greenfield, UP (Ont.) 22 F1
Greenfield-Park, T (Que.) 17 H4
Green Glade, UP (Alta.) 33 H4
Green Haven Trailer Park, NUP (Ont.) 22 B2
Greenhead Road, UP (NS) 9 B4
Green Hill, UP (NS) 9 B3
Greenhill, UP (NS) 9 D2
Green Hill, UP (NB) 12 C4
Greenhill, UP (NS) 11 H2
Greenhill, UP (NB) 11 B1
Greenhurst-Thurstonia, UP (Ont.) 24 D4
Green Island Brook, UP (Nfld.) 5 G2
Green Island Cove, UP (Nfld.) 5 G2
Green Lake, UP (Sask.) 32 C2
Green Lake, UP (Ont.) 24 G1
Greenland, UP (NS) 10 B2
Greenland, UP (Man.) 28 B2
Greenlands, UP (Ont.) 17 B1
Green Lane, UP (Ont.) 17 E1
Greenleys Corners, UP (Ont.) 21 E1
Green Meadows, UP (PEI) 7 D3
Greenmount, UP (PEI) 7 B2
Green Mountain, UP (NB) 11 A2
Green Oak, UP (Man.) 28 B1
Green Oaks, UP (NS) 9 B2
Greenock, UP (Ont.) 23 C3
Greenock, UP (NB) 11 B3
Green Park, UP (Ont.) 23 D3
Green Point, UP (Nfld.) 5 F4
Greenpoint, UP (Ont.) 21 G1
Green Ridge, UP (Man.) 28 A3
Green Road, UP (PEI) 7 C4
Green Road, UP (NB) 11 A1
Greens Brook, UP (NS) 9 E2
Greens Corner, UP (Ont.) 22 G2
Green's Harbour, UP (Nfld.) 2 G2
Greenshields, UP (Alta.) 33 G4
Greens Point, UP (NS) 9 D1
Greens Point, UP (NB) 11 C3
Greenspond, T (Nfld.) 3 F3
Greenstreet, UP (Sask.) 32 A3
Greensville, UP (Ont.) 22 H1
Greenvale, UP (PEI) 7 C3
Greenvale, UP (NS) 8 A4
Greenvale, UP (PEI) 7 E3
Green Valley, UP (Ont.) 17 E2
Greenview, UP (Ont.) 24 E2
Greenville, UP (NS) 10 A3
Greenville < Lachkaltsap 9, UP (BC) 42 D4
Greenville Station, UP (NS) 9 B1
Greenwald, UP (Man.) 30 C4
Greenwater Lake, UP (Sask.) 32 G4
Greenway, UP (Ont.) 22 D1
Greenway, UP (Man.) 29 G4
Greenwich, UP (NS) 11 H3
Greenwich, UP (PEI) 7 D3
Greenwich Hill, UP (NB) 11 D2
Greenwold, UP (NS) 8 B4
Greenwood, C (BC) 35 G4
Greenwood, UP (NS) 8 A4
Greenwood, UP (NS) 10 C4
Greenwood, UP (Ont.) 18 C4
Greenwood, NUP (Alta.) 34 E2
Greenwood < Greenwood, CFB/BFC, UP (NS) 10 D1
Greenwood, CFB/BFC, MIL (NS) 10 D1
Greenwood Heights, UP (NS) 9 B4
Greenwood Island 3, IR (BC) 35 B4
Greenwood Mobile Park, NUP (BC) 34 B4
Greenwood Park, NUP (NB) 11 C1
Greer-Mount, UP (Que.) 24 H1
Gregan, UP (NB) 12 F2
Gregg, UP (Man.) 29 F3
Gregg Settlement, UP (NB) 12 A4
Gregherd, UP (Sask.) 31 H2
Gregoire Lake 176, IR (Alta.) 44 C4
Gregoire Lake 176A, IR (Alta.) 44 C4
Gregoire Lake 176B, IR (Alta.) 44 C4
Grégoires Mill, UP (Ont.) 26 D1
Gregory, UP (Ont.) 24 B2
Greig Beach, UP (Sask.) 32 B2
Grenadier Island, UP (Ont.) 17 C4
Grenfell, T (Sask.) 29 C3
Grenfell, UP (Ont.) 21 A1
Grenfell Beach < Sakimay 74, UP (Sask.) 29 C3
Grenfell Glen, UP (Ont.) 17 E4
Grenfell Heights, NUP (Nfld.) 3 B3
Grenville, VL (Que.) 17 E1
Grenville-Bay, UP (Que.) 17 E1
Gresham, UP (Ont.) 23 B2
Gretna, UP (Ont.) 21 G1
Gretna, VL (Man.) 29 H4
Grey Islands Harbour, UP (Nfld.) 5 H3
Grey River, UP (Nfld.) 4 E4
Gribble Island 10, IR (BC) 41 D2
Grief Island 2, IR (BC) 41 E3

Griersville, UP (Ont.) 23 D2
Griesbach, UP (Alta.) 33 E3
Grieves Corners, UP (Ont.) 21 G1
Griffin, UP (Sask.) 29 B4
Griffin, UP (Que.) 16 C4
Griffin Creek, UP (Alta.) 43 H3
Griffis Corners, UP (Ont.) 21 E2
Griffith, UP (Ont.) 24 G2
Grifton, UP (Man.) 29 E2
Grimms Settlement, UP (NS) 10 E2
Grimsby, T (Ont.) 21 A3
Grimsby Centre, UP (Ont.) 21 A4
Grimshaw, T (Alta.) 43 H3
Grimsthorpe, UP (Ont.) 25 B2
Grimston, UP (Ont.) 23 C2
Grindrod, UP (BC) 35 F1
Griquet < St Lunaire - Griquet, UP (Nfld.) 5 H2
Grise Fiord, UP (NWT) 47 E2
Griswold, UP (Man.) 29 E4
Grizzly Bear's Head and Lean Man 110 and 111, IR (Sask.) 32 B4
Grole, UP (Nfld.) 2 A2
Grondines-Est, UP (Que.) 16 D1
Grondines-Ouest, UP (Que.) 16 D1
Grondines-Station, UP (Que.) 16 D1
Gronlid, UP (Sask.) 32 F4
Grono Road, UP (NS) 9 B3
Gros-Cap, UP (Que.) 7 F1
Gros Cap, UP (Ont.) 26 A4
Gros Cap 49, IR (Ont.) 26 A2
Gros Cap Village 49A, IR (Ont.) 26 A2
Grosmont, UP (Alta.) 33 E2
Gros-Morne, UP (Que.) 13 E1
Grosse-Île, UP (Que.) 7 G1
Grosse-Île, UP (Que.) 15 C2
Grosse Isle, UP (Man.) 29 H3
Grosses Coques, UP (NS) 10 A2
Grosses-Roches, UP (Que.) 13 B1
Grosswerder, UP (Sask.) 31 C1
Grosvenor, UP (NS) 8 C4
Grouard, UP (Alta.) 33 B1
Grouard Mission, UP (Alta.) 33 B1
Groundbirch, UP (BC) 43 E4
Grove-Creek, UP (Que.) 18 D4
Grovedale, UP (Alta.) 43 G4
Grove Hill, UP (NB) 11 E2
Grove Park, UP (Ont.) 24 C2
Grove Park, UP (Sask.) 29 D3
Grovesend, UP (Ont.) 22 E2
Groves Point, UP (NS) 8 E3
Groveton, UP (Ont.) 17 C2
Grub Road, UP (NB) 11 G1
Gruenthal, UP (Sask.) 31 F1
Grumbler, UP (NWT) 44 A2
Grund, UP (Man.) 29 F4
Grunthal, UP (Man.) 28 A2
Guaytown, UP (Ont.) 17 E1
Guelph, C (Ont.) 23 E4
Guénette, UP (Que.) 18 E4
Guérin, UP (Que.) 18 A2
Guerin, UP (Ont.) 21 D1
Guernsey, VL (Sask.) 31 G1
Guernsey Cove, UP (PEI) 7 E4
Guigues, UP (Que.) 26 G3
Guilds, UP (Ont.) 22 C3
Guimond-Village, UP (NB) 12 G3
Guinea, UP (NS) 10 B1
Guiney, UP (Ont.) 24 F2
Guises Beach, UP (Sask.) 32 D3
Guité, UP (Que.) 13 E3
Gulada 3A, IR (BC) 35 B1
Gulch < St Mary's (COMM), UP (Nfld.) 2 F4
Gull Bay < Gull River 55, UP (Ont.) 27 E1
Gullbridge, UP (Nfld.) 3 A2
Gull Creek, UP (Ont.) 24 G4
Gull Harbour, UP (Man.) 30 C4
Gullies, UP (Nfld.) 2 G2
Gullies < Tilton, UP (Nfld.) 2 G2
Gull Island, UP (Nfld.) 2 G1
Gullivers Cove, UP (NS) 10 B2
Gull Lake, T (Sask.) 31 D3
Gull Lake, VL (Alta.) 33 D4
Gull Lake, NUP (Man.) 30 C4
Gull River 55, IR (Ont.) 27 E1
Gull Rock, UP (Ont.) 24 B2
Gulls Marsh, UP (Nfld.) 5 F4
Gul-mak 8, IR (BC) 42 F3
Gun-a-chal 5, IR (BC) 42 F3
Gundy, UP (Alta.) 43 F4
Gunn, UP (Alta.) 33 D3
Gunnar, UP (Sask.) 44 D2
Gunne, UP (Ont.) 28 H1
Gunning Cove, UP (NS) 10 C4
Gunnworth, UP (Sask.) 31 D2
Gunridge, UP (Nfld.) 2 H3
Gunter, UP (Ont.) 24 F3
Gunton, UP (Man.) 29 H3
Guoyskun 22, IR (BC) 41 A1
Gurneyville, UP (Alta.) 33 G2
Gustin Grove, UP (Ont.) 22 C1
Guthrie, UP (Ont.) 24 B4
Guthrie, UP (Que.) 16 B4
Guy, UP (Alta.) 33 A1
Guyenne, UP (Que.) 18 B1
Guysborough, UP (NS) 9 G2
Guysborough Intervale, UP (NS) 9 F2
Gwayasdums 1, IR (BC) 39 E1
Gwen Lake 3, IR (BC) 35 C2
Gwimmaus 52, IR (BC) 42 E3
Gwinaha 44, IR (BC) 42 D3
Gwindebilk 51, IR (BC) 42 E3
Gwingag 53, IR (BC) 42 E3
Gwinkbawaueast 54, IR (BC) 42 E3
Gwynne, UP (Alta.) 33 E4
Gypsum Mines, UP (NS) 9 A3
Gypsumville, UP (Man.) 29 G1
Gypsumvillel CFS/SFC, MIL (Man.) 29 G1

H

Habay < Hay Lake 209, UP (Alta.) 45 E4
Habermehl, UP (Ont.) 23 C2
Habitant, UP (NS) 11 H3
Haché Road, UP (NB) 12 G1
Hacheyville, UP (NB) 12 F1
Hackett, UP (Alta.) 34 G1
Hacketts Cove, UP (NS) 9 A4
Hadashville, UP (Man.) 28 C2
Haddo, UP (Ont.) 17 D3
Haddock, UP (Alta.) 33 B3
Haddon Hill, UP (NS) 9 A4
Hadleyville, UP (NS) 9 G2
Hafford, VL (Sask.) 32 C4
Hagar, UP (Ont.) 25 F1
Hagen, UP (Sask.) 32 E4
Hagensborg, UP (BC) 41 G3
Haggertys Cove, UP (NB) 11 C3
Hagles Corners, UP (Ont.) 22 F1
Hague, VL (Sask.) 32 D4
Hagwilget < Hagwilget 1, UP (BC) 42 F3
Hagwilget 1, IR (BC) 42 F3
Haida < Masset 1, UP (BC) 41 B1
Haight, UP (Alta.) 33 F3
Haileybury, T (Ont.) 26 F3
Haina < Khrana 4, UP (BC) 41 B2
Haines Island 8, IR (BC) 38 B3
Haines Junction, UP (YT) 45 A3
Haines Lake, UP (Ont.) 24 A2
Hainsville, UP (Ont.) 17 D2
Hairy Hill, VL (Alta.) 33 F3
Halach, UP (Alta.) 33 D2
Halalt 2, IR (BC) 38 E3
Halalt Island 1, IR (BC) 38 E3
Halbrite, VL (Sask.) 29 B4
Halbstadt, UP (Man.) 29 H4
Halcomb, UP (NB) 12 E2
Halcourt, UP (Alta.) 43 F4
Halcreek, UP (Alta.) 33 D2
Halcro, UP (Sask.) 32 E4
Halcro 150C, IR (Alta.) 33 B1
Haldane Hill, UP (Ont.) 24 B2
Haldimand, T (Ont.) 22 H2
Hale, UP (NB) 12 A4
Hale, UP (BC) 45 B4
Hales Landing, UP (Man.) 30 B2
Haley, UP (Ont.) 17 A1
Haley Station, UP (Ont.) 17 A1
Half Island Cove, UP (NS) 9 G2
Halfmoon Bay, UP (BC) 38 E2
Half Moon Lake, NUP (Alta.) 33 E3
Halfway, UP (NB) 13 D4
Halfway, UP (Ont.) 21 D1
Halfway Brook, UP (NS) 9 C2
Halfway Cove, UP (NS) 9 G2
Halfway Depot, UP (NB) 15 H1
Halfway House, UP (Nfld.) 2 G2
Halfway Lake, UP (Alta.) 33 E2
Halfway Point < Halfway Point - Benoit's Cove - John's Beach - Frenchman's Cove, UP (Nfld.) 4 C1
Halfway Point - Benoit's Cove - John's Beach - Frenchman's Cove, RD (Nfld.) 4 C1
Halfway River, UP (NS) 11 H2
Halfway River 168, IR (BC) 43 D3
Halfway Tucks, UP (Nfld.) 2 F4
Halhalaedan 14, IR (BC) 35 A1
Halhalaeden 14A, IR (BC) 35 A1
Haliburton, UP (Ont.) 24 D3
Haliburton, UP (NS) 9 D1
Haliburton, UP (PEI) 7 A3
Halicz, UP (Man.) 29 E2
Halifax, C (NS) 9 B4
Halkirk, VL (Alta.) 34 G1
Hall, UP (Que.) 16 E3
Hall, UP (BC) 34 B4
Hall Beach, UP (NWT) 5 D1
Hallboro, UP (Man.) 29 F3
Hallebourg, UP (Ont.) 20 B4
Hallecks, UP (Ont.) 17 C3
Hallerton, UP (Que.) 17 H2
Hall Glen, UP (Ont.) 24 E4
Hall Landing, UP (Ont.) 21 D1
Hallonquist, UP (Sask.) 31 E3
Halloway, UP (Ont.) 21 F1
Hallowell, UP (Ont.) 21 F2
Halls Corner, UP (NB) 12 A3
Halls Harbour, UP (NS) 11 G3
Halls Hill, UP (NB) 7 A4
Halls Lake, UP (Ont.) 24 C2
Halls Mills, UP (Ont.) 17 B2
Halls Town, UP (Nfld.) 2 G2
Hallville, UP (Ont.) 17 D2
Halowis 31, IR (BC) 41 F4
Halpenny, UP (Ont.) 17 B2
Halsbury, UP (Alta.) 34 H2
Halstead Beach, UP (Ont.) 21 D1
Halsteads Bay, UP (Ont.) 17 B4
Halston, UP (Ont.) 21 F1
Halton Hills, T (Ont.) 23 F4
Halverson, UP (Que.) 17 B1
Halvorgate, UP (Sask.) 31 F3
Hamburg, UP (Man.) 29 H4
Hamer Bay, UP (Ont.) 24 A2
Hamilton, C (Ont.) 22 H1
Hamilton, UP (PEI) 7 B3
Hamilton Creek 2, IR (BC) 35 D2
Hamilton Creek 7, IR (BC) 35 D2
Hamilton Heights, UP (Ont.) 22 F1
Hamilton Point 7, IR (BC) 38 B3
Hamiltonsfield, UP (Ont.) 24 D1
Hamilton Subdivision, UP (Ont.) 23 E4
Hamiota, VL (Man.) 29 E3
Hamlet, UP (Ont.) 23 G1
Hamlet, UP (Alta.) 34 F2
Hamlin, UP (Sask.) 32 B4
Hamlin, UP (Alta.) 33 F3
Hammertown, UP (Ont.) 21 A2
Hammond, UP (Ont.) 17 D1
Hammond, NUP (NB) 12 A2
Hammonds Plains, UP (NS) 9 B3
Hammonds Plains Road, UP (NS) 9 B3
Hammondvale, UP (NB) 11 F2
Ham-Nord, UP (Que.) 16 D2
Hampden, COMM (Nfld.) 5 G4
Hampden, UP (Ont.) 23 C3
Hampelsfield, UP (Ont.) 24 G1
Hampshire, UP (PEI) 7 C4
Hampshire Mills, UP (Ont.) 23 G1
Hampstead, T (Que.) 17 G4
Hampstead, UP (NB) 11 D2
Hampstead, UP (Ont.) 23 D4
Hampton, UP (PEI) 7 C4
Hampton, UP (NS) 10 C1
Hampton, VL (NB) 11 E2
Ham-Sud, UP (Que.) 16 E3
Hamton, UP (Sask.) 29 C2
Hamtown Corner, UP (NB) 11 C1
Hanatsa 6, IR (BC) 39 G1
Hanbury, UP (Ont.) 26 F2
Hanbury, UP (BC) 34 D4
Hanceville, UP (BC) 40 C4
Handel, VL (Sask.) 31 D1
Handsworth, UP (Sask.) 29 C4
Haneytown, UP (NB) 11 C1
Hanford Brook, UP (NB) 11 E2
Hanley, T (Sask.) 31 F1
Hanna, T (Alta.) 34 G1
Hannah Cove, UP (Nfld.) 5 G4
Hannamville, UP (NS) 10 C1
Hanover, T (Ont.) 23 C2
Hansard, UP (BC) 40 D1
Hansen, UP (Ont.) 26 B1
Hansford, UP (NS) 9 B1
Hanson 13, IR (BC) 40 A1
Hants Border, UP (NS) 9 A3
Hant's Harbour, LID (Nfld.) 2 G1
Hantsport, T (NS) 9 A3
Hanwell, UP (NB) 11 C1
Happy Adventure, COMM (Nfld.) 3 F4
Happy Hollow, UP (Ont.) 17 E1
Happy Hollow, UP (Alta.) 33 G2
Happyland, UP (Ont.) 23 G1
Happy-Mountains, UP (Que.) 18 D4
Happy Valley, UP (Ont.) 21 A2
Happy Valley, UP (BC) 38 E4
Happy Valley - Goose Bay, T (Nfld.) 6 F3
Harbour Breton, T (Nfld.) 2 B2
Harbour Buffett, UP (Nfld.) 2 E2
Harbour Centre, UP (NS) 8 B4
Harbour Grace, T (Nfld.) 2 G2
Harbour Grace South, COMM (Nfld.) 2 G2
Harbour Island, UP (Nfld.) 2 E2
Harbour Le Cou < Rose Blanche - Harbour Le Cou, UP (Nfld.) 4 B4
Harbour Main, COMM (Nfld.) 2 G3
Harbour Main < Harbour Main (COMM), UP (Nfld.) 2 G3
Harbour Mille, UP (Nfld.) 2 D2
Harbour Round, UP (Nfld.) 3 B1
Harbourview, UP (NS) 8 C3
Harbourview, UP (NS) 8 E3
Harbourville, UP (NS) 11 G3
Harburn, UP (Ont.) 24 D2
Harcourt, UP (Nfld.) 2 F1
Harcourt, UP (Ont.) 24 E3
Harcourt, UP (NB) 12 F3
Harcus, UP (Man.) 29 G3
Hardieville, UP (Alta.) 34 F4
Harding, UP (Man.) 29 E3
Hardings Point, UP (NB) 11 D2
Hardingville, UP (NB) 11 E2
Hardisty, T (Alta.) 33 G4
Hardluck Creek, UP (YT) 45 A3
Hardrock, UP (Ont.) 27 G2
Hardwicke, UP (NB) 12 G2
Hardwicke Island, UP (BC) 39 G2
Hardwood Hill, UP (NS) 9 D1
Hardwood Lake, UP (Ont.) 24 F2
Hardwood Lands, UP (NS) 9 B3
Hardwood Ridge, UP (NB) 11 D1
Hardwood Settlement, UP (NB) 12 G2
Hardy, UP (NB) 7 B4
Hardy, VL (Sask.) 31 G4
Hardy's Cove, UP (Nfld.) 2 B2
Hare Bay, T (Nfld.) 3 E3
Hare Harbour, UP (Nfld.) 2 C2
Harewood, UP (NB) 11 F1
Hargrave, UP (Man.) 29 E3
Hargreaves, UP (BC) 36 B1
Hargwen, UP (Alta.) 33 A3
Harkaway, UP (Ont.) 23 D2
Harlan, UP (Sask.) 32 A3
Harlech, UP (Alta.) 33 B4
Harlem, UP (Ont.) 17 B3
Harley, UP (Ont.) 22 F1
Harley Road, UP (NB) 11 E1
Harlington, UP (Man.) 29 D1
Harlock, UP (Ont.) 23 B4
Harlowe, UP (Ont.) 24 G3
Harmattan, UP (Alta.) 34 E1
Harmon Valley, UP (Alta.) 43 H3
Harmony, UP (NS) 9 C2
Harmony, UP (NS) 10 D1
Harmony, UP (PEI) 7 B3
Harmony, UP (Ont.) 22 E1
Harmony, UP (Ont.) 17 D2
Harmony, UP (Ont.) 26 B4
Harmony Beach, UP (Ont.) 26 A3
Harmony Junction, UP (PEI) 7 E3
Harmony Mills, UP (NS) 10 D2
Harmony Park, UP (NS) 9 B3
Harmony Road, UP (NS) 9 C2
Harpellville, UP (NS) 9 F3
Harper, UP (PEI) 7 A2
Harper, UP (Ont.) 17 B2
Harper Corners, UP (Ont.) 22 H1
Harper Settlement, UP (NB) 11 F1
Harperville, UP (Man.) 29 H3
Harptree, UP (Sask.) 31 G4
Harpurhey, NUP (Ont.) 23 B4
Harricanaw-Ouest, UP (Que.) 18 B1
Harricott, UP (Nfld.) 2 F3
Harriets Corners, UP (Ont.) 24 F2
Harrietsfield, UP (NS) 9 B4
Harrietsville, UP (Ont.) 22 E2
Harrigan Cove, UP (NS) 9 E3
Harrington, UP (PEI) 7 C3
Harrington, UP (Que.) 18 E4
Harrington, UP (NS) 10 A3
Harrington-Harbour, UP (Que.) 5 E3
Harrington West, UP (Ont.) 22 E1
Harris, VL (Sask.) 31 E1
Harris 3, IR (BC) 35 F1
Harris Brook Settlement, UP (NB) 12 E2
Harrisburg, UP (Ont.) 22 G1
Harris Hill, UP (Ont.) 28 F4
Harris Island, UP (NS) 10 A4
Harris Lake, UP (Ont.) 25 F2
Harrison, UP (Nfld.) 4 D1
Harrison Brook Settlement, UP (NB) 12 A2
Harrison Hot Springs, VL (BC) 35 A4
Harrison Mills, UP (BC) 35 A4
Harrison Road, UP (NS) 11 H2
Harrisons Corners, UP (Ont.) 17 E2
Harrison Settlement, UP (NS) 11 H2
Harrison Settlement, UP (NB) 11 G1
Harriston, T (Ont.) 23 C3
Harriston, UP (NS) 10 E1
Harrogate, UP (BC) 34 C2
Harrop, UP (BC) 34 B4
Harrow, T (Ont.) 22 A4
Harrowby, UP (Man.) 29 D2
Harrowsmith, UP (Ont.) 17 A4
Harrys Brook, UP (Nfld.) 4 C2
Harry's Harbour, UP (Nfld.) 3 B1
Harstone, UP (Ont.) 27 D3
Harte, UP (Man.) 29 F3
Hartell, UP (Alta.) 34 E3
Harten Corner, UP (NB) 11 B1
Hartfell, UP (Ont.) 24 B1
Hartfield, UP (NB) 11 B1
Hartford, UP (NS) 9 B1
Hartford, UP (NB) 11 A1
Hartington, UP (Ont.) 17 A3
Hartin Settlement, UP (NB) 11 A1
Hartland, T (NB) 12 A4
Hartley, UP (Ont.) 21 C1
Hartley Bay, UP (Ont.) 25 E2
Hartley Bay < Kulkayu (Hartley Bay) 4A, UP (BC) 41 D2
Hartley Settlement, UP (NB) 12 A3
Hartleyville, UP (Alta.) 34 F4
Hartlin Settlement, UP (NS) 9 C3
Hartney, T (Man.) 29 E4
Hartshorn, UP (Alta.) 34 G1
Hartsmere, UP (Ont.) 24 F3
Hartsville, UP (PEI) 7 C4
Hartville, UP (NS) 9 A3
Harty, UP (Ont.) 20 C4
Harvey, UP (NB) 11 A2
Harvey, VL (NB) 11 B2
Harvey Bank, UP (NB) 11 G2
Harvey Settlement, NUP (NB) 11 B2
Harvie Heights, UP (Alta.) 34 D2
Harwich, UP (Ont.) 22 C3
Harwill, UP (Man.) 29 H2
Harwood, UP (Ont.) 21 D1
Harwood Island 2, IR (BC) 38 C1
Harwood Plains, UP (Ont.) 17 D4
Haseville, UP (Que.) 16 B4
Haskett, UP (Man.) 29 H4
Hassan, UP (Sask.) 29 C1
Hassett, UP (NS) 10 B2
Hastings, UP (NS) 9 A1
Hastings, UP (NS) 10 D1
Hastings, VL (Ont.) 21 E1
Hatchet Cove, UP (Nfld.) 2 F1
Hatchet Harbour, UP (Nfld.) 3 D1
Hatchet Lake, UP (NS) 9 B4
Hatchley, UP (Ont.) 22 F1
Hatch Point 12, IR (BC) 38 E3
Hatfield, UP (Sask.) 31 G2
Hatfield Point, UP (NB) 11 E2
Hatherleigh, UP (Sask.) 32 B4
Hatherton, UP (Ont.) 23 E2
Hatley, VL (Que.) 16 D4
Hatley-Centre, UP (Que.) 16 D4
Hatton, UP (Sask.) 31 B3
Hattonford, UP (Alta.) 33 C3
Hatzic Island, NUP (BC) 38 H2
Hatzic Prairie, NUP (BC) 38 H2
Haultain, UP (Ont.) 24 E4
Haute-Aboujagane, UP (NB) 7 A4
Hauterive, T (Que.) 14 G1
Haut-Lamèque, UP (NB) 13 G4
Haut-Paquetville, UP (NB) 12 F1
Haut-St-Antoine, UP (NB) 12 G4
Haut-Ste-Rose, UP (NB) 12 G1
Haut-St-Isidore, UP (NB) 12 F1
Haut-St-Simon, UP (NB) 12 G1
Haut-Shippegan, UP (NB) 12 G1
Havelock, UP (NB) 11 F1
Havelock, UP (NS) 10 B2
Havelock, UP (Que.) 17 G2
Havelock, VL (Ont.) 21 E1
Havendale, UP (NS) 9 F2
Havergal, UP (Ont.) 24 F2
Havilah, UP (Ont.) 26 B4
Havilland, UP (Ont.) 26 A3
Havre-Aubert, UP (Que.) 7 F1
Havre-aux-Maisons, UP (Que.) 7 F1
Havre Boucher, UP (NS) 8 C4
Havre Boucher Station, UP (NS) 8 C4
Havre-St-Pierre, UP (Que.) 19 H3
Hawarden, VL (Sask.) 31 F2
Hawke Harbour, UP (Nfld.) 6 H3
Hawker, UP (NS) 8 D4
Hawkes, UP (Ont.) 17 G1
Hawke's Bay, T (Nfld.) 5 G3
Hawkesbury, T (Ont.) 17 E1
Hawkestone, UP (Ont.) 23 G2
Hawkestone Beach, UP (Ont.) 23 G2
Hawkesville, UP (Ont.) 23 D4
Hawkeye, UP (Sask.) 32 C3
Hawk Hills, UP (Alta.) 43 H2
Hawkins, UP (Alta.) 33 G4
Hawkins Corner, UP (NB) 11 B1
Hawkins Corners, UP (Ont.) 23 G1
Hawk Junction, UP (Ont.) 26 A2
Hawk Lake, UP (Ont.) 28 G2
Hawkshaw, UP (NB) 11 B1
Hawley, UP (Que.) 16 A4
Hawley, UP (Ont.) 17 A4
Hawleys Hill, UP (NS) 8 C3
Hawthorne, UP (NS) 8 C3
Hawtrey, UP (Ont.) 22 F2
Hay Bay, UP (Ont.) 21 G1
Hayburn, UP (Ont.) 21 G1
Hay Camp, UP (Alta.) 44 C2
Hay Cove, UP (NS) 8 E4
Hayden Ridge, UP (NB) 12 B3
Hayes Corners, UP (Ont.) 24 A2
Hayes Corners, UP (Ont.) 17 C3
Hayesland, UP (Ont.) 22 G1
Hayesville, UP (NB) 12 C3
Hayfield, UP (Man.) 29 F4
Hayfield, UP (Alta.) 43 F4
Haylahte 3, IR (BC) 39 F1
Hay Lake 209, IR (Alta.) 45 E4
Hay Lakes, VL (Alta.) 33 E3
Hayland, UP (Man.) 29 G2
Hayman Hill, UP (NB) 11 B3
Hay Meadow 1, IR (BC) 35 B1
Haynes, UP (Alta.) 33 E4
Hay Ranch 2, IR (BC) 40 C3
Hay River, IR (NWT) 44 B1
Hay River, T (NWT) 44 B1
Hays, UP (Alta.) 34 G3
Haysport, UP (BC) 41 D1
Hays River, UP (NS) 8 C3
Hay's Shore, UP (Ont.) 17 B2
Haystack, UP (Nfld.) 2 E2
Haysville, UP (Ont.) 22 F1
Hayter, UP (Alta.) 33 H4
Hayward Cove, UP (Nfld.) 3 D1
Haywards Cove < St Brendan's (COMM), UP (Nfld.) 3 F3
Haywood, UP (Man.) 29 G4
Hazelbrook, UP (PEI) 7 D4
Hazel Cliffe, UP (Sask.) 29 D3
Hazeldale, UP (NS) 8 D3
Hazeldean, UP (NB) 12 A2
Hazeldean, UP (Ont.) 17 D4
Hazel Dell, UP (Sask.) 29 C1
Hazeldine, UP (Alta.) 33 G3
Hazel Glen, UP (NS) 9 D2
Hazelglen, UP (Man.) 28 B1
Hazelgrove, UP (PEI) 7 C3
Hazel Hill, UP (NS) 9 H2
Hazell, UP (Alta.) 34 E4
Hazelmere, UP (Alta.) 43 F4
Hazelridge, UP (Man.) 28 B1
Hazelton, UP (NB) 12 D3
Hazelton, VL (BC) 42 F3
Hazelton 1, IR (BC) 42 F3
Hazelwood, UP (Sask.) 29 C3
Hazen Camp, UP (NWT) 47 F1
Hazenmore, VL (Sask.) 31 E4
Hazlet, VL (Sask.) 31 D3
Hazzards Corners, UP (Ont.) 24 F4
Head Harbour, UP (Nfld.) 3 B2
Head Lake, UP (Ont.) 23 H1
Head of Bay d'Espoir < Milltown - Head of Bay d'Espoir, UP (Nfld.) 2 B1
Head of Cardigan, UP (PEI) 7 D4
Head of Chezzetcook, UP (NS) 9 C3
Head of Hillsborough, UP (PEI) 7 D3
Head of Jeddore, UP (NS) 9 C3
Head of Loch Lomond, UP (NS) 8 E4
Head of Millstream, UP (NB) 11 E1
Head of Montague, UP (PEI) 7 D4
Head of St Margarets Bay, UP (NS) 9 A4
Head of Wallace Bay, UP (NS) 9 B1
Headquarters, UP (BC) 38 B1
Headwaters Ranch, NUP (BC) 43 D2
Healey Falls, UP (Ont.) 21 E1
Hearne, UP (Sask.) 31 G3
Hearst, T (Ont.) 20 B4
Heart Lake, UP (Alta.) 34 G1
Heart Lake 167, IR (Alta.) 33 F1
Heart River, UP (Alta.) 33 B1
Heart's Content, T (Nfld.) 2 G2
Heart's Delight < Heart's Delight - Islington, UP (Nfld.) 2 G2
Heart's Delight - Islington, LID (Nfld.) 2 G2
Heart's Desire, LID (Nfld.) 2 G2
Hearts Desire, UP (Ont.) 17 E4
Hearts Hill, UP (Sask.) 31 C1
Heart Valley, UP (Alta.) 43 G4
Heaslip, UP (Ont.) 26 F2
Heaslip, UP (Man.) 29 F4
Heatburg, UP (Alta.) 33 E4
Heath, UP (Alta.) 33 G4
Heathbell, UP (NS) 9 D1
Heathcote, UP (Ont.) 23 D2
Heather Beach, UP (NS) 9 B1
Heatherdale, UP (PEI) 7 D4
Heatherdown, UP (Alta.) 33 D3
Heatherton, UP (Nfld.) 4 B2
Heatherton, UP (NS) 8 B4
Heathland, UP (NB) 11 B3
Heath-Point, UP (Que.) 5 B4
Heathton, UP (Que.) 16 D4
Hebbs Cross, UP (NS) 10 E2
Hebbville, UP (NS) 10 E2
Hébert, UP (NB) 12 F4
Hébertville, UP (Que.) 14 A3
Hébertville-Station, VL (Que.) 14 A3
Hebron, UP (NS) 10 A3
Hebron, UP (PEI) 7 A3
Hebron, UP (Nfld.) 6 E1
Hecate, UP (BC) 39 E3
Hecate 17, IR (BC) 39 E3
Heckmans Island, UP (NS) 10 E2
Heckston, UP (Ont.) 17 C2
Hecla, UP (Man.) 30 C4
Hectanooga, UP (NS) 10 B3
Hedgeville, UP (NS) 9 C1
Hedley, UP (BC) 35 D4
Heidelberg, UP (Ont.) 23 D4
Heinsburg, UP (Alta.) 33 G3
Heisler, VL (Alta.) 33 F4
Hekkla, UP (Ont.) 24 B2
Heldar, UP (Alta.) 33 C2
Helena Lake, UP (Sask.) 32 B3
Helen Mine, UP (Ont.) 26 A2
Helina, UP (Alta.) 33 F2
Hells Gate, UP (BC) 35 B3
Helmsdale, UP (Alta.) 31 B2
Helmsdale, UP (Alta.) 34 E2
Helston, UP (Man.) 29 F3
Hemaruka, UP (Alta.) 34 H1
Hemford, UP (NS) 10 D2
Hemison, UP (Que.) 15 C4
Hemlo, UP (Ont.) 27 H3
Hemlock, UP (Ont.) 22 F2
Hemlock Corners, UP (Ont.) 17 C3
Hemlock Downs, UP (Ont.) 17 A4
Hemmingford, VL (Que.) 17 H2
Hemmings-Falls, UP (Que.) 16 C3
Hemphill Corner, UP (NB) 12 B4
Hemstock Mills, UP (Ont.) 23 C2
Henday, UP (Alta.) 34 E1
Henderson, UP (Ont.) 24 G3
Henderson Place, UP (Ont.) 17 A4
Hendersons Beach, UP (Sask.) 31 G2
Henderson Settlement, UP (NB) 11 E2
Henderson's Ranch 11, IR (BC) 41 E1
Hendon, UP (Sask.) 29 B1
Hendrick-Développement, NUP (Que.) 17 E3
Hendrix Lake, UP (BC) 36 E1
Henfryn, UP (Ont.) 23 C4
Henley Harbour, UP (Nfld.) 5 H1
Hennepin, UP (Que.) 15 C4
Henribourg, UP (Sask.) 32 E3
Henry House, UP (Alta.) 40 G3
Henrysburg, UP (Que.) 16 A4
Henrysburg-Centre, NUP (Que.) 16 A4
Henrys Corner, UP (Ont.) 17 E1
Henryville, VL (Que.) 16 A4
Hensall, VL (Ont.) 23 B4
Henvey Inlet 2, IR (Ont.) 25 F2
Héon, UP (Que.) 16 D2
Hepburn, VL (Sask.) 32 D4
Heppell, UP (Que.) 13 B3
Hepworth, VL (Ont.) 23 C1
Herbert, T (Sask.) 31 E3
Herbert Corners, UP (Ont.) 17 C2
Herb Lake, UP (Man.) 30 B2
Herchmer, UP (Man.) 46 A4
Herdman, UP (Que.) 17 G2
Hereford, UP (Que.) 16 E4
Hereford-Hill, UP (Que.) 16 E4
Hereward, UP (Ont.) 23 E3
Heriot Bay, UP (BC) 37 B4
Herman Brothers Trailer Court, NUP (Sask.) 31 H3
Hermans Island, UP (NS) 10 E2
Hermanville, UP (PEI) 7 E3
Hermitage, COMM (Nfld.) 2 B2
Hermitage, UP (PEI) 7 D4
Hermitage < Hermitage (COMM), UP (Nfld.) 2 B2
Hermit Lake, UP (Alta.) 43 G4
Heron Bay, UP (Ont.) 27 H3
Heron Island, UP (NB) 13 D4
Hérouxville, UP (Que.) 16 B1
Herring Cove, UP (NS) 9 B4
Herriot, UP (Man.) 30 A1
Herrons Corners, UP (Ont.) 17 C3
Herrons Mills, UP (Ont.) 17 B2
Herronton, UP (Alta.) 34 F3
Herschel, UP (YT) 45 B1
Herschel, VL (Sask.) 31 D1
Hersey Corner, UP (NB) 11 D1
Hersonville, UP (NB) 11 B3
Hervey-Jonction, UP (Que.) 18 H3
Herzel, UP (Sask.) 29 B2
Hesketh, UP (Alta.) 34 F2
Hespero, UP (Alta.) 33 D4
Hesquiat < Hesquiat 1, UP (BC) 39 F4
Hesquiat 1, IR (BC) 39 F4
Hesquis 10A, IR (BC) 39 E3
Hesson, UP (Ont.) 23 D4
Heward, VL (Sask.) 29 C4
Hewitt Landing, UP (Sask.) 32 A3
Heyden, UP (Ont.) 26 B4
Heyworth, UP (Que.) 17 D3
Hiawatha < Hiawatha 36, UP (Ont.) 21 D1
Hiawatha 36, IR (Ont.) 21 D1
Hiawatha Park, UP (Ont.) 17 E3
Hibbard, UP (Que.) 18 F2
Hibbs Cove, UP (Nfld.) 2 G2
Hibernia, UP (NS) 10 D2
Hickethier Ranch, UP (BC) 43 D3
Hickey Settlement, UP (NB) 13 D4
Hickey Settlement, UP (Ont.) 24 E2
Hickman's Harbour, UP (Nfld.) 2 F1
Hickory Beach, UP (Ont.) 23 H2
Hickory Corner, UP (Ont.) 22 D1
Hickson, UP (Ont.) 22 F1
Hicksville, UP (NB) 11 F1
Hideway Trailer Court, NUP (BC) 34 A2
Hiellen 2, IR (BC) 41 B1
Higgins Road, UP (PEI) 7 A3
Higginsville, UP (NS) 9 C3
High Bank, UP (PEI) 7 E4
Highbank, UP (NB) 12 E2
High Bar 1, IR (BC) 36 B4
High Bar 1A, IR (BC) 36 B4
High Bar 2, IR (BC) 36 B4
High Beach < Point May (COMM), UP (Nfld.) 2 B4
High Bluff, UP (Man.) 29 G3
Highbury, UP (NS) 10 E1
High-Falls, UP (Que.) 18 D4
High Falls, UP (Ont.) 17 A2
Highfield, UP (PEI) 7 C4
Highfield, UP (NB) 11 E1
Highfield, UP (NS) 9 A3
High-Forest, UP (Que.) 16 E4
Highgate, UP (Sask.) 32 B4
Highgate, VL (Ont.) 22 D3
High Head, UP (NS) 10 E2
High Hill, UP (Sask.) 29 B1
Highland, UP (Ont.) 26 F2
Highland Acres, UP (NS) 9 B4
Highland Acres, NUP (NB) 11 C1
Highland Beach, UP (Ont.) 21 C1
Highland Glen, UP (Ont.) 22 C1
Highland Glen, UP (Man.) 28 B1
Highland Grove, UP (Ont.) 24 E3
Highland Hill, UP (NS) 8 D3
Highland Park, UP (Alta.) 43 G3
Highland Park Subdivision, NUP (Ont.) 21 A1
Highland Point, UP (Ont.) 23 E1
Highland Ranch, UP (Alta.) 34 F1
Highlands, UP (Nfld.) 4 B3
Highlands, UP (NB) 12 B3
Highland Village, UP (NS) 9 B2
High Level, T (Alta.) 44 A3
High Point, UP (Ont.) 21 C2
High Point, UP (Sask.) 31 D2
High Prairie, T (Alta.) 33 B1
Highridge, UP (Alta.) 33 D2
High River, T (Alta.) 34 E3
Highrock, UP (Man.) 30 B2
Highrock 199, IR (Man.) 30 B1
High Tor, UP (Sask.) 32 G4
Highvale, UP (Alta.) 33 D3
Highwater, UP (Que.) 16 C4
Highway, UP (Alta.) 33 C3
Hihium Lake 6, IR (BC) 36 D4
Hihium Lake 6A, IR (BC) 36 D4
Hihium Lake 6B, IR (BC) 36 D4
Hilbre, UP (Man.) 29 G2
Hilda, UP (Alta.) 31 B3
Hilden, UP (NS) 9 C2
Hildred Beach, UP (Sask.) 32 B2
Hillandale, UP (NB) 12 A3
Hillandale, UP (Sask.) 31 E4
Hillaton, UP (NS) 11 H3
Hillcrest, UP (NS) 9 E2
Hillcrest, UP (Ont.) 17 C3
Hillcrest, UP (Ont.) 21 F2
Hillcrest, UP (Alta.) 34 E4
Hillcrest, UP (BC) 35 F1
Hillcrest, UP (BC) 38 E3
Hillcrest, NUP (Ont.) 22 G2
Hillcrest Mines, UP (Alta.) 34 E4
Hillcrest Trailer Park, NUP (Man.) 28 A1
Hilldale Corner, UP (NB) 12 A2
Hillgrade, UP (Nfld.) 3 D1
Hillgrove, UP (NS) 10 B2
Hillgrove, UP (NB) 11 F1
Hillhead Corners, UP (Ont.) 21 C1
Hillhurst, UP (Que.) 16 D4
Hilliard, UP (Alta.) 33 E3
Hilliardton, UP (Ont.) 26 F2
Hillier, UP (Ont.) 21 F2
Hill Lake, UP (Ont.) 26 F2
Hillman, UP (NB) 11 A1
Hillmond, UP (Sask.) 32 A3
Hills, UP (BC) 34 B3
Hillsboro, UP (NS) 8 C3
Hillsborough, VL (NB) 11 G1
Hillsborough Beach, UP (Ont.) 22 C1
Hillsborough Park, UP (PEI) 7 C4
Hillsburgh, UP (Ont.) 23 E3
Hillsburn, UP (NS) 10 C1
Hillsdale, UP (Ont.) 23 F2
Hillsdale, UP (NB) 11 E2
Hillsdale, UP (NS) 8 C3
Hillsdale Road, UP (NS) 8 E3
Hillsdown, UP (Alta.) 34 F1
Hills Green, UP (Ont.) 23 B4
Hillside, UP (NS) 9 D1
Hillside, UP (NS) 8 F3
Hillside, UP (Ont.) 24 C2
Hillside, UP (NB) 12 A3
Hillside, UP (NB) 11 G2
Hillside, UP (Sask.) 32 B4
Hillside, UP (BC) 38 E2
Hillside Beach, UP (Man.) 30 C4
Hillside Boularderie, UP (NS) 8 E3
Hillside Gardens, NUP (Ont.) 17 C2
Hillsport, UP (Ont.) 27 H2
Hill Spring, VL (Alta.) 34 F4
Hills Road, UP (NS) 8 F3
Hillsvale, UP (NS) 9 B3
Hilltop, UP (Man.) 29 F3
Hilltown, UP (NS) 10 B2
Hillview, UP (Nfld.) 2 F1
Hillview, UP (Ont.) 26 F3
Hilly Grove, UP (Ont.) 25 C3
Hilton, UP (Ont.) 21 E1
Hilton, UP (Man.) 29 F4

Hilton, UP (BC) 35 G2
Hilton Beach, VL (Ont.) 26 B4
Hinch, UP (Ont.) 21 G1
Hinchliffe, UP (Sask.) 29 C1
Hindon Hill, UP (Ont.) 24 C3
Hines Creek, VL (Alta.) 43 G3
Hinton, T (Alta.) 40 H2
Hinton Trail, UP (Alta.) 43 F4
Hippa, UP (BC) 41 A1
Hirsch, UP (Sask.) 29 C4
Hisnit 4, IR (BC) 39 D2
Hisnit 7, IR (BC) 39 F3
Hisnit Fishery 34, IR (BC) 39 F4
Hitchcock, UP (Sask.) 29 C4
Hitchcock Bay, UP (Sask.) 31 E2
Hiusta's Meadow 2, IR (BC) 45 B4
Hixon, UP (BC) 40 C2
Hkusam, UP (BC) 39 G2
Hleepte 14, IR (BC) 39 F3
Hnausa, UP (Man.) 30 C4
Hoadley, UP (Alta.) 33 D4
Hoards, UP (Ont.) 21 F1
Hoasic, UP (Ont.) 17 D2
Hoath Head, UP (Ont.) 23 D2
Hobbema, UP (Alta.) 33 E4
Hochfeld, UP (Man.) 29 H4
Hochstadt, UP (Man.) 28 A2
Hochstadt, UP (Sask.) 32 D4
Hockley, UP (Ont.) 23 E3
Hocquart, UP (Que.) 14 F4
Hodderville, UP (Nfld.) 3 G4
Hodge's Cove, LID (Nfld.) 2 F1
Hodgeville, VL (Sask.) 31 E3
Hodgin, UP (NB) 13 E4
Hodgins, UP (Que.) 17 B1
Hodgson, UP (Man.) 29 H2
Hodgson, UP (Ont.) 18 B4
Hodson, UP (NS) 9 C1
Hoegs Corner, UP (NS) 9 B2
Hoey, UP (Sask.) 32 D4
Hoffer, UP (Sask.) 31 H4
Hoffman, UP (Ont.) 18 C4
Hoffman Corners, UP (Ont.) 22 C3
Hogan's Pond, LID (Nfld.) 2 H2
Hogg, UP (Ont.) 23 C1
Hoiss 8, IR (BC) 39 E3
Hoke Point 10B, IR (BC) 39 E3
Holachten 8, IR (BC) 35 A4
Holbein, UP (Sask.) 32 D3
Holberg, UP (BC) 39 C1
Holberg, CFS/SFC, MIL (BC) 39 C1
Holborn, UP (Alta.) 33 D3
Holbrook, UP (Ont.) 22 F1
Holden, VL (Alta.) 33 F3
Holderville, UP (NB) 11 D2
Holdfast, VL (Sask.) 31 G2
Hole or Hollow Water 10, IR (Man.) 30 C4
Holford, UP (Ont.) 23 D2
Holiday, UP (Ont.) 22 E1
Holiday Harbour, UP (Ont.) 22 B4
Holland, UP (Man.) 29 G4
Holland, UP (Ont.) 17 C4
Holland Centre, UP (Ont.) 23 D2
Holland Harbour, UP (NS) 9 F3
Holland Landing, UP (Ont.) 21 B1
Holland-Mills, UP (Que.) 18 D4
Holleford, UP (Ont.) 17 A3
Hollen, UP (Ont.) 23 D3
Holliday, UP (Que.) 15 E2
Hollow Lake, UP (Alta.) 33 E2
Holly, UP (Ont.) 21 A1
Holly Park, UP (Ont.) 21 A2
Holman, UP (NWT) 47 A4
Holmes Crossing, UP (Alta.) 33 C2
Holmes Point, UP (Ont.) 21 B1
Holmesville, UP (NB) 12 A3
Holmesville, UP (Ont.) 23 B4
Holmfield, UP (Man.) 29 F4
Holmwood, UP (BC) 35 E1
Holstein, UP (Ont.) 23 D3
Holt, UP (Ont.) 21 B1
Holton, UP (Nfld.) 6 G3
Holton-Station, NUP (Que.) 17 G2
Holtville, UP (NB) 12 D3
Holtyre, UP (Ont.) 26 F1
Holy Cross Lake 3, IR (BC) 40 A2
Holyoke, UP (Alta.) 33 G2
Holyrood, T (Nfld.) 2 G3
Holyrood, UP (Ont.) 23 B3
Homais 2, IR (BC) 39 E4
Homalco 1, IR (BC) 37 C2
Homalco 2, IR (BC) 37 C2
Homalco 2A, IR (BC) 37 C2
Homayno 2, IR (BC) 39 G1
Homebrook, UP (Man.) 29 G1
Homefield, UP (Sask.) 29 C2
Homeglen, UP (Alta.) 33 D4
Homestead, UP (Alta.) 43 F4
Homewood, UP (Man.) 29 H4
Homfray Creek, UP (BC) 37 C3
Homitan 8, IR (BC) 38 C3
Hondo, UP (Alta.) 33 D1
Hone, UP (Man.) 30 A1
Honeydale, UP (NB) 11 B2
Honeygables, UP (Ont.) 17 E4
Honey Harbour, UP (Ont.) 23 F1
Honeymoon, UP (Sask.) 32 E3
Honeymoon Bay, UP (BC) 38 D3
Honey's Beach, UP (Ont.) 21 C1
Honeywell Corners, UP (Ont.) 21 F1
Honeywood, UP (Ont.) 23 E2
Honfleur, UP (Que.) 15 B3
Honora, UP (Ont.) 25 C2
Honoréville, UP (Que.) 16 B4
Hood, UP (Ont.) 17 A2
Hoodoo Lake, NUP (BC) 40 C1
Hoonees 2, IR (BC) 41 E3
Hoop and Holler Bend, UP (Man.) 29 G3
Hoop Cove, UP (Nfld.) 2 C2
Hooping Harbour, UP (Nfld.) 5 H3
Hoosier, UP (Sask.) 31 C1
Hootalinqua, UP (YT) 45 B3
Hope, T (BC) 35 B4
Hope 1, IR (BC) 35 B4
Hopeall, UP (Nfld.) 2 G2
Hope Bay, UP (Ont.) 23 C1
Hopedale, COMM (Nfld.) 6 F2
Hopefield, UP (PEI) 7 D4
Hopefield, UP (Ont.) 24 F2
Hope Island 1, IR (BC) 41 F4
Hopeness, UP (Ont.) 25 E4
Hope River, UP (PEI) 7 C3
Hope-Town, UP (Que.) 13 F3
Hopetown, UP (Ont.) 17 B2
Hopetown 10A, IR (BC) 41 G4
Hope Valley, UP (Alta.) 33 G4
Hopeville, UP (Ont.) 23 D3
Hopewell, UP (NS) 9 D2
Hopewell Cape, UP (NB) 11 G1
Hopewell Hill, UP (NB) 11 G2
Hopkins Landing, UP (BC) 38 E2
Hoppenderry, UP (NS) 9 F2
Horburg, UP (Alta.) 33 C4
Horen, UP (Alta.) 33 C3
Horizon, UP (Sask.) 31 G4
Hornbeck, UP (Alta.) 33 B3
Hornby Island, UP (BC) 38 C2
Horndean, UP (Man.) 29 H4
Hornepayne, UP (Ont.) 26 A1
Horne Settlement, UP (NS) 9 B3
Hornes Road, UP (NS) 8 F3
Horning's Mills, UP (Ont.) 23 E2
Horod, UP (Man.) 29 E3
Horse Creek, UP (Sask.) 31 E4
Horsefly, UP (BC) 36 D1
Horsefly Landing, UP (BC) 36 D1
Horse Head, UP (Sask.) 32 B3
Horse Islands, UP (Nfld.) 5 H3
Horse Lakes 152B, IR (Alta.) 43 F4
Horse Ranch Pass 4, IR (BC) 45 C4
Horseshoe Lake, UP (Ont.) 24 A2
Horseshoe Lake, UP (Ont.) 23 H1
Horseshoe Lake, UP (Alta.) 34 E1
Horsham, UP (Sask.) 31 B3
Horton 35, IR (NS) 9 A3
Horton Landing, UP (NS) 9 A3
Hortons Creek, UP (NB) 12 F2
Hortonville, UP (NS) 9 A3
Horwood, UP (Nfld.) 3 D2
Horwood Lake, UP (Ont.) 26 D2
Horwood North, UP (Nfld.) 3 D2
Hoselaw, UP (Alta.) 33 G2
Hosmer, UP (BC) 34 D4
Hosmer Trailer Park, NUP (BC) 34 D4
Hotchkiss, UP (Alta.) 43 H2
Hotham, UP (Ont.) 25 H2
Hough Lake, UP (Ont.) 26 F2
Houghton, UP (Ont.) 22 F2
Houpsitas 6, IR (BC) 39 D2
House River Indian Cemetery 178, IR (Alta.) 44 B4
Houston, DM (BC) 42 G4
Howard, UP (NB) 12 E3
Howard Brook, UP (NB) 12 B4
Howarth Acres, NUP (NB) 11 C1
Howdenvale, UP (Ont.) 23 C1
Howe Bay, UP (PEI) 7 E4
Howeet 8, IR (BC) 41 E3
Howes Corners, UP (Ont.) 23 F1
Howick, VL (Que.) 17 G2
Howie, UP (Alta.) 34 H2
Howie Centre, UP (NS) 8 E3
Howlan, UP (PEI) 7 A3
Howland, UP (Ont.) 23 H1
Howland Ridge, UP (NB) 11 B1
Howley, LID (Nfld.) 5 G4
Howser, UP (BC) 34 B3
Hoyt, UP (NB) 11 C2
Huallen, UP (Alta.) 43 F4
Huard, UP (Que.) 13 F3
Hubbard, UP (NWT) 47 C3
Hubbard, VL (Sask.) 29 B2
Hubbards, UP (NS) 9 A4
Hubbards Point, UP (NS) 10 B3
Hubbell, UP (Man.) 29 G4
Hubble Lake Subdivision, NUP (Alta.) 33 D3
Hubbs, UP (Ont.) 21 F2
Huberdeau, UP (Que.) 18 E4
Hubley Mill Lake Road, UP (NS) 9 B4
Hubley Station, UP (NS) 9 B4
Hubrey, UP (Ont.) 22 E2
Hub-toul 2A, IR (BC) 39 C2
Huckabones Corners, UP (Ont.) 24 G1
Hudson, T (Que.) 17 F1
Hudson, UP (Ont.) 27 B1
Hudson Bay, T (Sask.) 32 H4
Hudsons Bay, NUP (Alta.) 34 G2
Hudson's Hope, DM (BC) 43 D3
Huff's Corners, UP (Ont.) 21 F2
Huffs Corners, UP (Ont.) 22 C2
Huff Wharf, UP (Ont.) 21 G1
Hugel, UP (Ont.) 25 F1
Huggett, UP (Alta.) 33 D3
Hughenden, VL (Alta.) 33 G4
Hughes, UP (Ont.) 24 E2
Hughes, UP (Man.) 29 F3
Hughes Brook, COMM (Nfld.) 4 D1
Hughton, UP (Sask.) 31 D2
Hugonard, UP (Sask.) 29 B2
Hu Haven, NUP (Alta.) 33 E3
Hulbert, UP (Ont.) 17 D2
Hulbert Crescent, NUP (Alta.) 33 E3
Hull, C (Que.) 17 E4
Humber Heights Subdivision, NUP (Ont.) 21 A2
Humber Park, UP (NS) 9 B4
Humboldt, T (Sask.) 31 G1
Hume, UP (Sask.) 29 B4
Humes Rear, UP (NS) 8 D3
Humhampt 6, IR (BC) 35 B2
Humhampt 6A, IR (BC) 35 B2
Hummerston, UP (Man.) 29 F3
Humphrey, UP (Ont.) 24 A2
Humphrey Corner, UP (NB) 11 E1
Hunaechin 11, IR (BC) 37 D4
Hundred Mile Landing, UP (YT) 45 B3
Hungerford, UP (Ont.) 24 G4
Hunta, UP (Ont.) 26 E1
Hunter-Mills, UP (Que.) 16 B4
Hunter River, VL (PEI) 7 C3
Hunters Corner, UP (NB) 12 A4
Hunters Home, UP (NB) 11 E1
Hunters Mountain, UP (NS) 8 D3
Hunters-Point, UP (Que.) 18 A3
Hunterstown, UP (Que.) 16 B1
Huntingdon, T (Que.) 17 G2
Huntingdon, UP (BC) 38 H3
Huntingford, UP (Ont.) 22 F1
Huntington, UP (NS) 8 E3
Huntingville, UP (Que.) 16 D4
Huntley, UP (PEI) 7 A2
Huntley, UP (Ont.) 17 D4
Huntoon, UP (Sask.) 29 B4
Hunts Inlet, UP (BC) 41 C1
Hunts Point, UP (NS) 10 D3
Huntsville, T (Ont.) 24 B2
Hupel, UP (BC) 35 G1
Hurds Lake, UP (Ont.) 17 A1
Hurdville, UP (Ont.) 24 A2
Hureauville, UP (NS) 8 C4
Hurkett, UP (Ont.) 27 E3
Hurlett, UP (NB) 11 C1
Hurley Corner, UP (NB) 11 C2
Hurondale, UP (Ont.) 23 B4
Huron Heights, UP (Ont.) 22 C1
Huronian, UP (Ont.) 27 C3
Huron Park, UP (Ont.) 22 D1
Huron Ridge, UP (Ont.) 23 B2
Huronville, UP (Sask.) 29 B3
Hurstwood, NUP (Alta.) 33 E3
Husavik, UP (Man.) 30 C4
Huscroft, UP (BC) 34 C4
Hussar, VL (Alta.) 34 F2
Hustalen 1, IR (BC) 36 G4
Hutchison, UP (BC) 40 C2
Hutchison's Corners, UP (Ont.) 23 D2
Hutch Lake, UP (Alta.) 44 A3
Hutton, UP (Alta.) 34 G2
Hutton Heights Subdivision, NUP (Ont.) 23 B3
Huxley, UP (Alta.) 34 F1
Hyannas, UP (NS) 8 C3
Hyas, VL (Sask.) 29 C1
Hybla, UP (Ont.) 24 E2
Hybord, UP (Man.) 30 B3
Hyde, UP (Sask.) 29 C3
Hyde Park, UP (Ont.) 22 E1
Hydraulic, UP (BC) 40 D3
Hydro Glen, UP (Ont.) 23 F1
Hyland Post, UP (BC) 45 C4
Hylo, UP (Alta.) 33 F2
Hymers, UP (Ont.) 27 D3
Hyndford, UP (Ont.) 24 G2
Hyndman, UP (Ont.) 17 D2
Hythe, VL (Alta.) 43 F4

I

Iakgwas 69, IR (BC) 41 D1
Iakvas 68, IR (BC) 41 D1
Iakwulgyiyaps 78, IR (BC) 41 D1
Iberville, T (Que.) 16 A4
Iberville-Jonction, UP (Que.) 16 A4
Ibstone < Grizzly Bear's Head and Lean Man 110 and 111, UP (Sask.) 32 B4
Ice Lake, UP (Ont.) 25 B2
Ida, UP (Ont.) 21 D1
Ida Hill, UP (Ont.) 17 B4
Idamay, UP (Alta.) 31 B1
Iddesleigh, UP (Alta.) 34 H2
Ideal, UP (Man.) 29 H3
Iffley, UP (Sask.) 32 B4
Ightkeany 32, IR (BC) 42 D4
Igloolik, HAM (NWT) 46 D1
Iglunga, UP (NWT) 46 F1
Ignace, UP (Ont.) 27 B2
Ikshenigwolk 3, IR (BC) 42 E4
Iktuksasuk 7, IR (BC) 38 C3
Ilclo 12, IR (BC) 38 C3
Ilderton, UP (Ont.) 22 D1
Île-à-la-Crosse, UP (Sask.) 32 C1
Ile a la Crosse 192E, IR (Sask.) 32 C1
Île-au-Canot, UP (Que.) 15 C2
Île-aux-Castors, UP (Que.) 16 A2
Île-aux-Chats, UP (Que.) 17 F1
Île-aux-Noix, UP (Que.) 16 A4
Île-aux-Oies, UP (Que.) 15 C2
Île-Bouchard, UP (Que.) 16 A3
Île-Cadieux, T (Que.) 17 G1
Île-d'Embarras, UP (Que.) 16 B2
Île-d'Entrée, VL (Que.) 7 F1
Ile des Chênes, UP (Man.) 28 A2
Île-Dorval, T (Que.) 17 G4
Île-du-Collège, UP (Que.) 26 F3
Île-du-Grand-Calumet, UP (Que.) 17 A1
Île-du-Moine, UP (Que.) 16 B2
Île-Enchanteresse, UP (Que.) 15 G3
Île-Madame, UP (Que.) 16 A2
Île-Michon, UP (Que.) 5 B3
Île-Népawa, UP (Que.) 26 G1
Île-Perrot, T (Que.) 17 F4
Île-St-Amour, UP (Que.) 16 A2
Île-St-Régis, UP (Que.) 17 E2
Île-Siscoe, UP (Que.) 18 B2
Îles-Ste-Marie, UP (Que.) 5 D3
Îlets-Jérémie, UP (Que.) 14 F2
Île-Verte, UP (Que.) 5 G2
Ilford, UP (Man.) 30 D1
Illerbrun, UP (Sask.) 31 D3
Illingworth, UP (Alta.) 34 H3
Îlots-de-Newport, UP (Que.) 13 G3
Ilthpaya 8, IR (BC) 38 A2
Imkusiyan 65, IR (BC) 41 D1
Imperial, T (Sask.) 31 G2
Imperial Beach, UP (Sask.) 31 G2
Imperial Mills, UP (Alta.) 33 F1
Inchkeith, UP (Sask.) 29 C3
Independent, UP (Nfld.) 6 H3
Indian Bay, COMM (Nfld.) 3 F3
Indian Bay, UP (Man.) 28 E2
Indian Bay < Indian Bay (COMM), UP (Nfld.) 3 F3
Indian Brook, UP (NS) 8 E2
Indian Burying Place, UP (Nfld.) 3 B1
Indian Cabins, UP (Alta.) 44 A2
Indian Cove, UP (Nfld.) 3 D1
Indian Falls Depot, UP (NB) 12 D1
Indian Gardens 8, IR (Man.) 29 G4
Indian Harbour, UP (NS) 9 A4
Indian Harbour, UP (Nfld.) 2 E2
Indian Harbour, UP (Nfld.) 4 C4
Indian Harbour Lake, UP (NS) 9 F3
Indian Head, T (Sask.) 29 B3
Indian Island, UP (NB) 11 B3
Indian Island 28, IR (NB) 12 G3
Indian Island 30, IR (BC) 38 A2
Indian Mountain, UP (NB) 11 G1
Indianola Beach, UP (Ont.) 21 B1
Indian Path, UP (NS) 10 E2
Indian Point, UP (NS) 10 E2
Indian Point, NUP (NS) 9 A4
Indian Point 1, IR (NB) 12 E2
Indian Pond, UP (Nfld.) 2 G3
Indian River, UP (PEI) 7 B3
Indian River, UP (Ont.) 21 D1
Indian Springs < Swan Lake 7, UP (Man.) 29 G4
Indian Tickle, UP (Nfld.) 6 H3
Indian Village < Woodstock 23, UP (NB) 11 A1
Indus, UP (Alta.) 34 E2
Ingelow, UP (Man.) 29 F3
Ingenika Mine, UP (BC) 42 H2
Ingersoll, T (Ont.) 22 F1
Ingle, UP (Ont.) 21 G1
Ingleside, UP (Ont.) 17 E2
Inglewood, NUP (NS) 10 C1
Inglis, UP (Man.) 29 D2
Inglis Falls, UP (Ont.) 23 C2
Inglisville, UP (NS) 10 D1
Ingoldsby, UP (Ont.) 23 H1
Ingolf, UP (Ont.) 28 E2
Ingomar, UP (NS) 10 C4
Ingonish, UP (NS) 8 E2
Ingonish Beach, UP (NS) 8 E2
Ingonish Centre, UP (NS) 8 E2
Ingonish Ferry, UP (NS) 8 E2
Ingramport, UP (NS) 9 A4
Inholmes, UP (Ont.) 24 A2
Inkahtsaph 6, IR (BC) 35 B2
Inkaneep, UP (BC) 35 F4
Inkerman, UP (NB) 12 G1
Inkerman, UP (Ont.) 17 D2
Inkerman Ferry, UP (NB) 12 G1
Inklin, UP (BC) 45 B4
Inkluckcheen 21, IR (BC) 35 B2
Inkluckcheen 21B, IR (BC) 35 B1
Inklyuhkinatko 2, IR (BC) 35 B2
Inkster, UP (Sask.) 32 F3
Inlailawatash 4, IR (BC) 38 G2
Inlailawatash 4A, IR (BC) 38 G2
Inland, UP (Alta.) 33 F3
Inlet, UP (Que.) 18 E4
Inlet Baddeck, UP (NS) 8 D3
Inman, UP (NB) 12 A3
Innerkip, UP (Ont.) 22 F1
Innes, UP (Sask.) 29 B4
Innes Park, UP (Ont.) 17 E4
Innisfail, T (Alta.) 34 E1
Innisfil Heights, UP (Ont.) 21 A1
Innisfil Park, UP (Ont.) 21 A1
Innisfree, VL (Alta.) 33 F3
Innisville, UP (Ont.) 17 B2
Inoucdjouac, UP (Que.) 46 E4
Insinger, VL (Sask.) 29 C2
Instow, UP (Sask.) 31 D4
Intervale, UP (NB) 11 F1
Inuvik, T (NWT) 45 C1
Inverary, UP (Ont.) 17 A4
Inverhaugh, UP (Ont.) 23 D4
Inverhuron, UP (Ont.) 23 B2
Inverlake, UP (Alta.) 34 F2
Invermay, UP (Ont.) 23 C2
Invermay, VL (Sask.) 29 C1
Invermere, VL (BC) 34 C3
Inverness, UP (NS) 8 C3
Inverness, UP (PEI) 7 B3
Inverness, VL (Que.) 15 A4
Inverness Lodge, UP (Ont.) 24 B2
Inverside, UP (NS) 8 C3
Inwood, UP (Ont.) 22 C2
Inwood, UP (Man.) 29 H3
Inzana Lake 12, IR (BC) 42 H3
Ioco, UP (BC) 38 G2
Iona, UP (NS) 8 D3
Iona, UP (PEI) 7 D4
Iona, UP (Ont.) 22 D2
Iona, UP (Nfld.) 2 F3
Iona Rear, UP (NS) 8 D3
Iona Station, UP (Ont.) 22 D2
Ipperwash, Camp/Campement, MIL (Ont.) 22 C1
Ipperwash Beach, UP (Ont.) 22 C1
Ireland, UP (NS) 9 E2
Ireland, UP (Ont.) 24 F2
Ireland's Eye, UP (Nfld.) 2 F1
Irena, UP (Ont.) 17 D2
Ireton, UP (Alta.) 33 D3
Iris, UP (PEI) 7 D4
Irish Cove, UP (NS) 8 E4
Irish Lake, UP (Ont.) 23 D2
Irish Settlement, UP (NB) 11 E2
Irish Settlement, UP (NB) 11 A1
Irishtown, COMM (Nfld.) 4 D1
Irishtown, UP (PEI) 7 B3
Irishtown, NUP (NB) 11 G1
Irishtown Road, UP (NS) 9 B1
Irish Vale, UP (NS) 8 E4
Irma, VL (Alta.) 33 G4
Iron Bay, UP (BC) 38 G2
Iron Bound Cove, UP (NB) 11 E1
Iron Bridge, VL (Ont.) 26 C4
Irondale, UP (Ont.) 24 D3
Iron Mines, UP (NS) 8 D3
Iron River, UP (Alta.) 33 G2
Iron Rock, UP (NS) 9 D2
Ironsides, UP (Ont.) 24 E3
Iron Springs, UP (Alta.) 34 F3
Ironville, UP (NS) 8 E3
Iroquois, VL (Ont.) 17 D3
Iroquois Falls, T (Ont.) 26 E1
Irricana, VL (Alta.) 34 F2
Irvine, T (Alta.) 31 B3
Irvines Landing, UP (BC) 38 D1
Isaac 8, IR (BC) 41 G1
Isaac Creek, UP (YT) 45 A3
Isaacs Glen, UP (Ont.) 23 H2
Isaacs Harbour, UP (NS) 9 F2
Isabella, UP (Man.) 29 E3
Isaccs Harbour North, UP (NS) 9 F2
Isachsen, UP (NWT) 47 D2
Isadore Harry 12, IR (BC) 36 B2
Isaiah Corner, UP (NB) 11 G1
Isham, UP (Sask.) 31 D2
Ishkseenickh 33, IR (BC) 42 D4
Ishkseenickh River 34, IR (BC) 42 D4
Ishkseenickh River 35, IR (BC) 42 D4
Ishkseenickh River 36, IR (BC) 42 D4
Ishkseenickh River 37, IR (BC) 42 D4
Ishpiming Beach, UP (Ont.) 23 E1
Isidore's Ranch 4, IR (BC) 34 D4
Iskut < Iskut 6, UP (BC) 45 B4
Iskut 6, IR (BC) 45 B4
Island 14A, IR (BC) 41 E1
Island-Brook, UP (Que.) 16 E4
Island Cove < Hodge's Cove, UP (Nfld.) 2 F1
Island East River, UP (NS) 9 D2
Island Falls, UP (Ont.) 20 C4
Island Falls, UP (Sask.) 32 G1
Island Grove, UP (Ont.) 21 B1
Island Harbour, UP (Nfld.) 3 E1
Island Harbour, UP (Nfld.) 6 H3
Island Lake, SV (Alta.) 33 E2
Island Lake, UP (Ont.) 26 B2
Island Lake, UP (Ont.) 26 B4
Island Lake 22, IR (Man.) 30 D2
Island Lake 22A, IR (Man.) 30 D2
Island Point, UP (NS) 8 E3
Islands in the Trent Waters 36A, IR (Ont.) 24 D4
Island View, UP (NB) 11 C1
Island View, UP (NS) 8 E3
Island View Beach, UP (Ont.) 21 B1
Islay, UP (Alta.) 33 G3
Islay, UP (Ont.) 21 C1
Isle-aux-Coudres, UP (Que.) 15 C2
Isle-aux-Grues, UP (Que.) 15 C2
Isle aux Morts, LID (Nfld.) 4 B4
Isle-Dupas, UP (Que.) 16 A2
Isle-of-Skye, UP (Que.) 17 F2
Isle Pierre, UP (BC) 40 C2
Isle Valen, UP (Nfld.) 2 E2
Islington < Heart's Delight – Islington, UP (Nfld.) 2 G2
Islington 29, IR (Ont.) 28 E1
Ispas, UP (Alta.) 33 F3
Issoudun, UP (Que.) 15 A3
Italy Cross, UP (NS) 10 E2
Ittaska Beach, SV (Alta.) 33 D4
Ittatsoo 1, IR (BC) 38 A3
Ituna, T (Sask.) 29 B2
Ivan, UP (Ont.) 22 D1
Ivanhoe, UP (Ont.) 21 F1
Ivanhoe, UP (Nfld.) 2 F1
Ives, UP (Que.) 16 E3
Ivry, UP (Que.) 18 F4
Ivry-Nord, UP (Que.) 18 F4
Ivujivik, UP (Que.) 46 E3
Ivy, UP (Ont.) 21 A1
Ivy Lea, UP (Ont.) 17 B4

J

Jackfish, UP (Alta.) 44 C3
Jackfish Lake, UP (Sask.) 32 B3
Jackfish Point 214, IR (Alta.) 45 E4
Jackfish River, UP (Alta.) 44 B3
Jackhead 43, IR (Man.) 29 H1
Jackhead 43A, IR (Man.) 29 H1
Jackhead Harbour, UP (Man.) 29 H1
Jack Ladder, UP (Nfld.) 5 F4
Jack Lake, UP (Ont.) 24 E3
Jack Lake, UP (Ont.) 23 E2
Jackpine, UP (Ont.) 27 D3
Jackson, UP (Ont.) 23 C2
Jackson, UP (Alta.) 33 D4
Jackson Bay, UP (BC) 39 G1
Jacksonburg, UP (Ont.) 22 F2
Jackson Falls, UP (NB) 12 A4
Jackson Manion, UP (Ont.) 30 E4
Jacksons, UP (BC) 42 B1
Jackson's Arm, UP (Nfld.) 5 G4
Jackson's Cove, UP (Nfld.) 3 B1
Jacksons Point, UP (Ont.) 21 B1
Jacksontown, UP (NB) 12 A4
Jacksonville, UP (NB) 11 A1
Jacksonville, UP (NS) 8 D4
Jackville, UP (Alta.) 34 E2
Jaco-Hughes, UP (Que.) 13 B1
Jacola, UP (Que.) 18 B2
Jacques-Cartier, UP (Que.) 15 A3
Jacques Fontaine, COMM (Nfld.) 2 D2
Jacquet River, VL (NB) 13 E4
Jaffa, UP (Ont.) 22 E2
Jaffray, UP (BC) 34 D4
Jailletville, UP (NB) 12 G4
Jakes Corner, UP (YT) 45 B3
Jakes Landing, UP (NS) 10 C2
Jalbert, UP (NB) 15 H2
Jalna, UP (Alta.) 33 C3
Jalun 14, IR (BC) 41 A1
James Louie 3A, IR (BC) 36 C1
Jameson, UP (Sask.) 31 H3
James River, UP (NS) 8 B4
James River Bridge, UP (Alta.) 34 E1
James Settlement, UP (NS) 9 D3
James Smith 100, IR (Sask.) 32 E3
Jamestown, UP (Nfld.) 3 F4
Jamestown, UP (Ont.) 23 C3
Jamesville, UP (NS) 8 D3
Jamesville West, UP (NS) 8 D3
Jamot, UP (Ont.) 25 F2
Janet, UP (Alta.) 34 E2
Janetville, UP (Ont.) 21 C1
Janeville, UP (NB) 12 F1
Jan Lake, UP (Sask.) 32 G1
Janow Corners, UP (Sask.) 32 E3
Jans Bay, UP (Sask.) 32 B1
Jansen, VL (Sask.) 31 G1
Janvier 194, IR (Alta.) 44 C4
Janvrin Harbour, UP (NS) 8 D4
Jardineville, UP (NB) 12 G3
Jarnac, UP (Que.) 18 E4
Jaroslaw, UP (Man.) 29 H2
Jarratt, UP (Ont.) 23 F1
Jarrow, UP (Alta.) 33 F4
Jarvie, UP (Alta.) 33 D2
Jarvis River, UP (Ont.) 27 D3
Jasmin, UP (Sask.) 29 B2
Jasper, UP (Alta.) 40 G3
Jasper, UP (Ont.) 17 C3
Jasper-in-Québec, UP (Que.) 18 F4
Jasper Park Lodge, UP (Alta.) 40 G3
Jean Baptiste 28, IR (BC) 42 F4
Jean Baptiste Gambler 183, IR (Alta.) 33 E1
Jean Côté, UP (Alta.) 43 H3
Jean de Baie, UP (Nfld.) 2 C3
Jean de Gaunt Island, UP (Nfld.) 2 E2
Jean Marie River, UP (NWT) 45 D3
Jeanne-Mance, UP (NB) 12 F1
Jeannettes Creek, UP (Ont.) 22 B3
Jedburgh, VL (Sask.) 29 C2
Jeddore Oyster Ponds, UP (NS) 9 C3
Jedway, UP (BC) 41 C3
Jefferson, UP (NS) 8 E3
Jeffrey, UP (Alta.) 33 E2
Jeffrey's, UP (Nfld.) 4 B3
Jeffries Corner, UP (NB) 11 F2
Jellicoe, UP (Ont.) 27 F2
Jellicoe, UP (BC) 35 D3
Jelly, UP (Ont.) 27 D3
Jellyby, UP (Ont.) 17 C3
Jemseg, UP (NB) 11 D1
Jenner, UP (Alta.) 34 H2
Jennings River 8, IR (BC) 45 B4
Jenpeg, UP (Man.) 30 B2
Jensen, UP (Alta.) 34 H3
Jensen Creek, UP (YT) 45 A2
Jericho, UP (NB) 12 A4
Jericho, UP (Ont.) 22 C1
Jermyn, UP (Ont.) 21 D1
Jerome, UP (Ont.) 26 D2
Jerrys Nose, UP (Nfld.) 4 B2
Jersey, UP (Ont.) 21 B1
Jersey, UP (NS) 9 B1
Jersey, UP (BC) 34 B4
Jersey Cove, UP (NS) 8 E3
Jersey Harbour, UP (Nfld.) 2 B2
Jerseyside, T (Nfld.) 2 F3
Jesmond, UP (BC) 36 B3
Jessopville, UP (Ont.) 23 E3
Jessups Falls, UP (Ont.) 17 D1
Jetait, UP (Man.) 30 A1
Jewellville, UP (Ont.) 24 F2
Jewetts Mills, UP (NB) 11 C1
Jim-Lake, UP (Que.) 18 C4
Jim's Cove < Triton – Jim's Cove – Card's Harbour, UP (Nfld.) 3 B2
Jim Smith Lake, NUP (BC) 34 C4
Jimtown, UP (NS) 8 B4
Joannès, UP (Que.) 18 A2
Jobrin, UP (Ont.) 27 H1
Job's Cove, UP (Nfld.) 2 G1
Jocko, UP (Ont.) 26 G4
Jockvale, UP (Ont.) 17 E4
Joe Batt's Arm < Joe Batt's Arm – Barr'd Islands, UP (Nfld.) 3 E1
Joe Batt's Arm – Barr'd Islands, RD (Nfld.) 3 E1
Joes Lake, UP (Ont.) 17 A2
Joeyaska 2, IR (BC) 35 C2
Joffre, UP (Alta.) 33 E4
Joggin Bridge, UP (NS) 10 B2
Joggins, UP (NS) 11 H2
Jogues, UP (Ont.) 20 B4
Jogues, UP (Que.) 16 B3
John D'Or Prairie < John D'Or Prairie 215, UP (Alta.) 44 B3
John D'Or Prairie 215, IR (Alta.) 44 B3
John's Beach < Halfway Point – Benoit's Cove – John's Beach – Frenchman's Cove, UP (Nfld.) 4 C1
Johnsborough, UP (Sask.) 31 C3
Johnson, UP (Ont.) 23 D1
Johnson, UP (BC) 38 G2
Johnson Addition, NUP (Alta.) 34 G3
Johnson-Beach < Caughnawaga 14, UP (Que.) 17 G4
Johnson Croft, UP (NB) 11 D2
Johnson Mills, UP (NB) 11 H1
Johnsons Crossing, UP (YT) 45 B3
Johnson Settlement, UP (NB) 11 B3
Johnson Settlement, UP (NB) 11 A1
Johnsons Landing, UP (BC) 34 B3
Johnsons Landing, UP (Ont.) 27 E3
John's Pond, UP (Nfld.) 2 F3
Johnston Corners, UP (Ont.) 17 E4
Johnston Point Road, UP (NB) 7 A4
Johnstons River, UP (PEI) 7 D4
Johnstown, UP (Ont.) 17 D3
Johnstown, UP (NS) 8 E4
Johnstown, UP (Ont.) 21 F1
Johnville, UP (NB) 12 A3
Johnville, UP (Que.) 16 D4
Johny Sticks 2, IR (BC) 36 B2
Jolicure, UP (NB) 7 A4
Joliette, C (Que.) 16 A2
Joliffs Brook, UP (NB) 11 E2
Joly, UP (Que.) 15 A4
Jones, UP (Ont.) 28 G1
Jones Falls, UP (Ont.) 17 B3
Jones Forks, UP (NB) 11 C1
Jones Landing, UP (Ont.) 26 A3
Jones Landing, UP (NWT) 45 D3
Jonquière, C (Que.) 14 B3
Jordan Bay, UP (NS) 10 C4
Jordan Branch, UP (NS) 10 C3
Jordan Falls, UP (NS) 10 C3
Jordan Ferry, UP (NS) 10 C4
Jordan Mountain, UP (NB) 11 F1
Jordan River, UP (Sask.) 32 G3
Jordantown, UP (NS) 10 B2
Jordanville, UP (NS) 9 F3
Josephburg, UP (Alta.) 33 E3
Josephine, UP (Ont.) 26 A2
Josephsburg, UP (Ont.) 23 D4
Journois, NUP (PEI) 4 B2
Joussard, UP (Alta.) 33 B1
Joutel, UP (Que.) 20 E4
Jouvence, UP (Que.) 16 C4
Joyceville, UP (Ont.) 17 B4
Joyland Beach, UP (Ont.) 23 G2
Joynt, UP (Que.) 17 B1
Jubilee, UP (NS) 8 D3
Jubilee, UP (NS) 11 H2
Judah, UP (Alta.) 43 H3
Juddhaven, UP (Ont.) 24 B2
Judd's-Mills, UP (Que.) 16 D4
Judes Point, UP (PEI) 7 B2
Judge, UP (Ont.) 26 F2
Judgeville, UP (Ont.) 17 B3
Judique, UP (NS) 8 C4
Judique Intervale, UP (NS) 8 C4
Judique North, UP (NS) 8 C4
Judique South, UP (NS) 8 C4
Judson, UP (Alta.) 34 G4
Jules, UP (Que.) 18 D4
Julien, UP (Que.) 16 D1
Junetown, UP (Ont.) 17 C3
Juniper, UP (NB) 12 B3
Juniper Island, UP (Ont.) 24 E4
Juniper Mountain, UP (NS) 8 E3
Juniper Station, UP (NB) 12 B3
Juniper Stump, UP (Nfld.) 2 G2
Juno, UP (Man.) 28 C1
Juno, UP (Alta.) 34 H3
Junor, UP (Sask.) 32 B3
Jupitagon, UP (Que.) 19 G3
Jura, UP (BC) 35 D3
Jura, UP (Ont.) 22 C1
Juskatla, UP (BC) 41 B1
Justasons Corner, UP (NB) 11 C3
Justice, UP (Man.) 29 F3
Juvenile Settlement, UP (NB) 11 C2

K

Kaboni < Wikwemikong Unceded 26, UP (Ont.) 25 C2
Kadis 11, IR (BC) 39 E1
Kagawong, UP (Ont.) 25 B2
Kahas 7, IR (BC) 41 D2
Kahkaykay 6, IR (BC) 37 C4
Kahkewistahaw 72, IR (Sask.) 29 C3
Kahmoose 4, IR (BC) 35 B2
Kahntah < Kahntah 3, UP (BC) 45 D4
Kahntah 3, IR (BC) 43 E1
Kahwin, UP (Alta.) 33 F3
Kaikalahun 25, IR (BC) 38 E2
Kaisun, UP (BC) 41 A2
Kai-too-kwis 23, IR (BC) 41 F4
Kajustus 10, IR (BC) 41 E3
Kakabeka Falls, UP (Ont.) 27 D3
Kakalatza 6, IR (BC) 38 E3
Kakawis, UP (BC) 39 G4
Kakisa, UP (NWT) 44 A1
Kakweken 4, IR (BC) 39 F1
Kaladar, UP (Ont.) 24 G4
Kaleden, UP (BC) 35 E4
Kaleida, UP (Man.) 29 G4
Kaleland, UP (Alta.) 33 F3
Kaleva, NUP (BC) 39 E1
Kallieseks 7, IR (BC) 42 F2
Kalyna, UP (Sask.) 32 E3
Kamarsuk, UP (Nfld.) 6 E2
Kaministiquia, UP (Ont.) 27 D3
Kamloops, C (BC) 35 D1
Kamloops 1, IR (BC) 36 F4
Kamloops 2, IR (BC) 35 D1
Kamloops 3, IR (BC) 35 D1

Kamloops 4, IR (BC) **36 F4**
Kamloops 5, IR (BC) **36 F4**
Kamloops, CFS/SFC, MIL (BC) **36 F4**
Kamouraska, VL (Qué.) **15 D1**
Kamouraska-Moulin, UP (Qué.) **15 E1**
Kamsack, T (Sask.) **29 D2**
Kamsack Beach, UP (Sask.) **29 D1**
Kanaaupscow, UP (Que.) **20 F2**
Kanaka Bar 1A, IR (BC) **35 B2**
Kanaka Bar 2, IR (BC) **35 B2**
Kananaskis, UP (Alta.) **34 D2**
Kanata, UP (Ont.) **17 D4**
Kanawana, UP (Que.) **18 F4**
Kandahar, UP (Sask.) **31 H1**
Kane, UP (Man.) **29 H4**
Kaneville, UP (NS) **8 F3**
Kannata Valley, VL (Sask.) **31 G2**
Kaoowinch 10, IR (BC) **39 D2**
Kaouk 13, IR (BC) **39 D2**
Kapasiwin, SV (Alta.) **33 D3**
Kapuskasing, T (Ont.) **20 C4**
Karalash Corners, UP (Ont.) **26 B3**
Karlukwees < Karlukwees 1, UP (BC) **39 F1**
Karlukwees 1, IR (BC) **39 F1**
Kars, UP (Ont.) **17 C2**
Kars, UP (NB) **11 E2**
Karsdale, UP (NS) **10 B1**
Kasabonika < Kasabonika Lake, UP (Ont.) **30 G2**
Kasabonika Lake, IR (Ont.) **30 G2**
Kasha, UP (Alta.) **33 D4**
Kashabowie, UP (Ont.) **27 C3**
Kashechewan < Fort Albany 67, UP (Ont.) **20 C3**
Kashittle 9, IR (BC) **39 D2**
Kasika 36, IR (BC) **42 D4**
Kasika 71, IR (BC) **42 D4**
Kasika 72, IR (BC) **42 D4**
Kasiks River 29, IR (BC) **42 D4**
Kasil, UP (Que.) **18 E4**
Kaslo, VL (BC) **34 B3**
Kasper Creek, NUP (Sask.) **31 F4**
Kasshabog Lake, UP (Ont.) **24 E4**
Kaste 6, IR (BC) **41 B2**
Kaszuby, UP (Ont.) **24 F2**
Kateen River 39, IR (BC) **42 D4**
Katepwa Beach, SV (Sask.) **29 B3**
Katevale, UP (Que.) **16 D4**
Kathleen, UP (Alta.) **33 B1**
Kathrintal Colony, UP (Sask.) **31 H3**
Kathryn, UP (Alta.) **34 E2**
Katit 1, IR (BC) **41 F4**
Katrime, UP (Man.) **29 G3**
Katrine, UP (Ont.) **24 B1**
Katzie 1, IR (BC) **38 G2**
Katzie 2, IR (BC) **38 G2**
Kauk Bight, UP (Nfld.) **6 E2**
Kavanagh, UP (Alta.) **33 E3**
Kawages 4, IR (BC) **39 F1**
Kawartha Hideaway, NUP (Ont.) **24 D4**
Kawartha Park, UP (Ont.) **24 E4**
Kawene, UP (Ont.) **27 C3**
Kawkawa Lake, NUP (BC) **35 B4**
Kawkawa Lake 16, IR (BC) **35 B4**
Kayel 8, IR (BC) **41 D2**
Kaykaip 7, IR (BC) **35 B3**
Kayouk 8, IR (BC) **39 D2**
Kay Settlement, UP (NB) **11 F1**
Kayville, UP (Sask.) **31 G4**
Kazabazua, UP (Que.) **18 D4**
Kazabazua-Station, UP (Que.) **18 D4**
Kdad-eesh 4, IR (BC) **41 D2**
Keady, UP (Ont.) **23 C2**
Kearney, T (Ont.) **24 B1**
Kearns, UP (Ont.) **26 F2**
Keatings Corner, UP (NB) **11 D2**
Keatley, UP (Sask.) **32 C4**
Keats Island, UP (BC) **38 E2**
Kebaowek 12, IR (Que.) **18 A3**
Keddys Corner, UP (NS) **11 H3**
Kedgemakooge, UP (NS) **10 C2**
Kedgwick, VL (NB) **12 B1**
Kedgwick River, UP (NB) **12 B1**
Kedleston, UP (Sask.) **31 G2**
Kedleston, UP (BC) **35 F1**
Kedleston Beach, UP (Sask.) **31 G2**
Keeble, UP (NS) **9 C1**
Keecekiltum 2, IR (BC) **39 F1**
Keecha 11, IR (BC) **41 D2**
Keefers, UP (BC) **35 B2**
Keeler, VL (Sask.) **31 F3**
Keelerville, UP (Ont.) **17 B3**
Keels, COMM (Nfld.) **3 G4**
Keenan Siding, UP (NB) **12 E3**
Keenansville, UP (Ont.) **21 A1**
Keene, UP (Ont.) **21 D1**
Keephills, UP (Alta.) **33 D3**
Keeseekoose 66, IR (Sask.) **29 D1**
Keeseekoose 66A, IR (Sask.) **29 D1**
Keeseekoowenin 61, IR (Man.) **29 E3**
Keeshan 9, IR (BC) **38 B3**
Keewatin, T (Ont.) **28 F2**
Keewatin, District of/de, DIST (NWT) **1**
Keewaydin, UP (Ont.) **26 F3**
Kégashka, UP (Que.) **5 C3**
Keg River, UP (Alta.) **43 G1**
Kegworth, UP (Sask.) **29 C3**
Kehiwin 123, IR (Alta.) **33 G2**
Keirsteadville, UP (NB) **11 E2**
Keith, UP (Alta.) **34 E2**
Keith Island 7, IR (BC) **38 B3**
Keithley Creek, UP (BC) **40 D3**
Kekertuk, UP (NWT) **46 G1**
Keld, UP (Man.) **29 E2**
Keldon, UP (Ont.) **23 E3**
Kelfield, VL (Sask.) **31 D1**
Keller Bridge, UP (Ont.) **24 F4**
Kellers, UP (Ont.) **21 E1**
Kelleys Cove, UP (NS) **10 A3**
Kelliher, VL (Sask.) **29 B2**
Kelloe, UP (Man.) **29 E3**
Kelly, UP (Que.) **13 F3**
Kelly, UP (Que.) **15 A4**
Kelly, UP (Que.) **16 B4**
Kelly Creek 3, IR (BC) **36 C4**
Kelly Lake, UP (BC) **43 F4**
Kelly Lake, UP (BC) **36 C4**
Kelly-Newton, UP (Que.) **18 D4**
Kelly Road, UP (PEI) **7 A3**
Kellys Corner, UP (Ont.) **24 G1**
Kellys Cross, UP (PEI) **7 C4**
Kelowna, C (BC) **35 F2**
Kelsey, UP (Alta.) **33 E4**
Kelsey, UP (Man.) **30 C1**
Kelsey Bay, UP (BC) **39 G2**
Kelso, UP (Sask.) **29 D3**
Kelstern, UP (Sask.) **31 E3**
Keltic Lodge, UP (NS) **8 E2**
Kelvin, UP (Ont.) **22 G1**
Kelvin Grove, UP (PEI) **7 B3**
Kelvington, T (Sask.) **29 B1**
Kelwood, UP (Man.) **29 F3**
Kemano, UP (BC) **41 F1**
Kemano 17, IR (BC) **41 E1**
Kemano Landing, UP (BC) **41 E1**
Kemble, UP (Ont.) **23 C1**
Kemnay, UP (Man.) **29 F4**
Kempark, UP (Ont.) **17 E4**
Kemp River, UP (Alta.) **43 H1**
Kempt, UP (NS) **10 C2**
Kempt Head, UP (NS) **8 E3**
Kemptown, UP (NS) **9 C2**
Kempt Road, UP (NS) **8 D4**
Kempt Shore, UP (NS) **9 A3**
Kemptville, T (Ont.) **17 C2**
Kemptville, UP (NS) **10 B3**
Kemsquit 1, IR (BC) **41 F2**
Kenabeek, UP (Ont.) **26 F2**
Kenaston, VL (Sask.) **31 F2**
Kendal, VL (Sask.) **29 B3**
Kendry, UP (Ont.) **21 D1**
Keneden Park, UP (Ont.) **21 D1**
Kenhill Beach, UP (Ont.) **24 D4**
Kenilworth, UP (Ont.) **23 D3**
Kenlis, UP (Sask.) **29 B3**
Kenloch, UP (NS) **8 C3**
Kenmore, UP (Ont.) **17 D2**
Kennaway, UP (Ont.) **24 E2**
Kennedy, VL (Sask.) **29 C3**
Kennedy Bay, UP (Ont.) **21 C1**
Kennell, UP (Sask.) **31 G2**
Kennetcook, UP (NS) **9 B2**
Kenneth, UP (NB) **12 B3**
Kennicott, UP (Ont.) **23 C4**
Kennisis Lake, UP (Ont.) **24 D2**
Kennyville, UP (Que.) **18 D4**
Kenny Woods, UP (Alta.) **44 C3**
Kenogami Lake, UP (Ont.) **26 F2**
Keno Hill, UP (YT) **45 B2**
Kenora, T (Ont.) **28 F2**
Kenora 38B, IR (Ont.) **28 F2**
Kenosee Park, UP (Sask.) **29 C4**
Kensington, T (PEI) **7 B3**
Kensington, UP (Que.) **17 F2**
Kenstone Beach, UP (Ont.) **23 H2**
Kent, DM (BC) **35 A4**
Kent, UP (NS) **9 C3**
Kent Boom, NUP (NB) **12 G4**
Kent Bridge, UP (Ont.) **22 C3**
Kent Centre, UP (Ont.) **22 C3**
Kent Junction, UP (NB) **12 F3**
Kent Lake, UP (NB) **12 F3**
Kenton, UP (Man.) **29 E3**
Kentvale, UP (Ont.) **26 B4**
Kentville, T (NS) **11 H3**
Kenville, UP (Man.) **29 D1**
Kenzie, UP (Alta.) **33 B1**
Kenzieville, UP (NS) **8 A4**
Keogh 2, IR (BC) **39 G1**
Keogh 3, IR (BC) **41 G4**
Keogh 6, IR (BC) **39 D1**
Keoma, UP (Alta.) **34 F2**
Kepler, UP (Ont.) **17 A4**
Keppel, UP (Sask.) **31 E1**
Keppoch, UP (NS) **8 D3**
Keppoch, UP (PEI) **7 C4**
Kequesta 9, IR (BC) **41 F4**
Keremeos, VL (BC) **35 E4**
Keremeos Forks 12 and 12A, IR (BC) **35 E4**
Kerensky, UP (Alta.) **33 E3**
Kergwenan, UP (Man.) **29 F2**
Kerleys Harbour, UP (Nfld.) **3 G4**
Kerr Creek, UP (BC) **35 G4**
Kerr Lake, UP (Ont.) **26 F3**
Kerr Line, UP (Ont.) **17 A1**
Kerrobert, T (Sask.) **31 C1**
Kerrowgare, UP (NS) **9 E2**
Kerrs Lake, UP (Man.) **29 F3**
Kerrs Mill Road, UP (NS) **9 B1**
Kerrs Ridge, UP (NB) **11 B3**
Kerry, UP (Man.) **28 C2**
Kersey, UP (Alta.) **34 E2**
Kershaw Subdivision, NUP (BC) **36 F2**
Kersley, UP (BC) **40 C3**
Kertch, UP (Ont.) **22 C2**
Kerwood, UP (Ont.) **22 D2**
Kessock, UP (Sask.) **29 D2**
Keswar 16, IR (BC) **41 C1**
Keswick, UP (Ont.) **21 B1**
Keswick, UP (NB) **11 C1**
Keswick Beach, UP (Ont.) **21 B1**
Keswick Ridge, UP (NB) **11 C1**
Ketai 28, IR (BC) **41 D1**
Ketchen, UP (Sask.) **29 C1**
Ketchen, UP (Que.) **18 A3**
Ketch Harbour, UP (NS) **9 B4**
Ketchum Ridge, UP (NB) **12 B3**
Ketoneda 7, IR (BC) **42 E4**
Kettleby, UP (Ont.) **21 A2**
Kettle Cove, UP (Nfld.) **3 D1**
Kettle Point < Kettle Point 44, UP (Ont.) **22 C1**
Kettle Point 44, IR (Ont.) **22 C1**
Kettle's Beach, UP (Ont.) **23 E1**
Kettle Valley, UP (BC) **35 G4**
Kevisville, UP (Alta.) **34 E1**
Kew, UP (Alta.) **34 E2**
Keward, UP (Ont.) **23 C2**
Kewstoke, UP (NS) **8 C3**
Keyarka 17, IR (BC) **41 C1**
Keyes, UP (Man.) **29 F3**
Key Harbour, UP (Ont.) **25 F2**
Key Junction, UP (Ont.) **25 F2**
Key River, UP (Ont.) **25 F2**
Keyser, UP (Ont.) **22 D1**
Keystone, UP (Alta.) **33 D3**
Keystone Camps, UP (Ont.) **25 G1**
Keystown, UP (Sask.) **31 G3**
Key West, UP (Sask.) **31 G4**
Khartum, UP (Ont.) **24 G2**
Khazisela 7, IR (BC) **41 F4**
Khedive, VL (Sask.) **31 H4**
Khiva, UP (Ont.) **22 D1**
Khrana 4, IR (BC) **41 B2**
Khtahda 10, IR (BC) **41 D1**
Khutzemateen 49, IR (BC) **42 D4**
Khyex 8, IR (BC) **42 D4**
Kiamika, UP (Que.) **18 E4**
Kichha 10, IR (BC) **38 B3**
Kierkoski, UP (Que.) **16 A3**
Kierstead Mountain, UP (NB) **11 E1**
Kikino, UP (Alta.) **33 F2**
Kilbella Bay, UP (BC) **41 F4**
Kilbride, UP (Nfld.) **2 H2**
Kilburn, UP (NB) **12 A3**
Kilburn-Mill, UP (Que.) **16 D4**
Kilchult 3, IR (BC) **35 A1**
Kilcoo Camp, UP (Ont.) **23 H1**
Kildala Arm < Tahla 4, UP (BC) **41 E1**
Kildala River 10, IR (BC) **41 E1**
Kildare Capes, UP (PEI) **7 B2**
Kildonan, UP (BC) **38 B3**
Kilfoil, UP (NB) **12 A3**
Kilgard < Upper Sumas 6, UP (BC) **38 H3**
Kilgorie, UP (Ont.) **23 E2**
Kilkerran, UP (BC) **43 F3**
Killaloe, UP (Ont.) **24 F1**
Killaloe Station, VL (Ont.) **24 F1**
Killaly, VL (Sask.) **29 C2**
Killam, T (Alta.) **33 F4**
Killams Mills, UP (NB) **11 F1**
Killarney, T (Man.) **29 F4**
Killarney, UP (Ont.) **25 D2**
Killarney, UP (NS) **9 B3**
Killarney Beach, UP (Ont.) **21 A1**
Killarney Lake, UP (Alta.) **33 H4**
Killbear Park, UP (Ont.) **25 G3**
Killdeer, UP (Sask.) **31 F4**
Killean, UP (Ont.) **22 G1**
Killiney Beach, NUP (BC) **35 F2**
Killoween, UP (NB) **12 A3**
Kilmar, UP (Que.) **18 E4**
Kilmarnock, UP (NB) **11 A1**
Kilmarnock, UP (Ont.) **17 C2**
Kilmartin, UP (Ont.) **22 D2**
Kilmaurs, UP (Ont.) **17 B1**
Kilmuir, UP (PEI) **7 D4**
Kil-pah-las 3, IR (BC) **38 E3**
Kilronan, UP (Sask.) **32 A3**
Kilselas < Kshish 4 and 4A, UP (BC) **42 E4**
Kilsyth, UP (Ont.) **23 C2**
Kilsyth, UP (Alta.) **33 D2**
Kiltala 2, IR (BC) **41 F3**
Kiltarlity, UP (NS) **8 D3**
Kiltuish 13, IR (BC) **41 E1**
Kilwinning, UP (Sask.) **32 D4**
Kilworth, UP (Ont.) **22 D2**
Kimball, UP (Alta.) **34 F4**
Kimball, UP (Ont.) **22 B2**
Kimberley, C (BC) **34 C4**
Kimberley, UP (Ont.) **23 D2**
Kimberley Park, UP (Ont.) **21 D1**
Kimbo, UP (Ont.) **21 A4**
Kimsquit, UP (BC) **41 F2**
Kinburn, UP (Ont.) **17 B1**
Kinburn, UP (Ont.) **23 B4**
Kincaid, VL (Sask.) **31 E4**
Kincardine, T (Ont.) **23 B2**
Kincardine, UP (NB) **12 A3**
Kincolith < Kincolith 14, UP (BC) **42 D4**
Kincolith 14, IR (BC) **42 D4**
Kincolith 14A, IR (BC) **42 D4**
Kindersley, T (Sask.) **31 C2**
Kingarf, UP (Ont.) **23 B2**
King City, UP (Ont.) **21 A2**
King Creek, UP (Ont.) **21 A2**
Kingfisher, UP (BC) **35 G1**
Kingfisher 1, IR (Ont.) **30 F3**
Kingfisher 2, IR (Ont.) **30 F3**
Kingfisher 3, IR (Ont.) **30 F3**
Kingfisher Lake < Kingfisher 1, UP (Ont.) **30 F3**
Kinghorn, UP (Ont.) **21 A2**
Kinghurst, UP (Ont.) **23 C2**
King Kirkland, UP (Ont.) **26 F2**
Kinglake, UP (Ont.) **22 F2**
Kingman, UP (Alta.) **33 E3**
Kingman's < Fermeuse, UP (Nfld.) **2 H4**
King Pitt, UP (Ont.) **17 B4**
Kingross, UP (NS) **8 D2**
Kingsboro, UP (PEI) **7 F3**
Kingsbridge, UP (Ont.) **23 B3**
Kingsburg, UP (NS) **10 E2**
Kingsbury, VL (Que.) **16 C3**
Kingsclear, UP (NB) **11 C1**
Kingsclear 6, IR (NB) **11 C1**
Kingscote, UP (Ont.) **23 D3**
King's Cove, COMM (Nfld.) **3 G4**
Kings Cove, UP (Nfld.) **6 H4**
Kings Cove, UP (Nfld.) **3 B1**
Kingscroft, UP (Que.) **16 D4**
Kingscross Estates, UP (Ont.) **21 A2**
Kingsey, UP (Que.) **16 D3**
Kingsey-Falls, VL (Que.) **16 D3**
Kingsford, UP (Ont.) **21 G1**
Kingsgate, UP (BC) **34 C4**
Kings Head, UP (NS) **9 D1**
Kingsland, UP (Sask.) **31 D1**
Kings Landing, UP (NB) **11 B1**
Kingsley, UP (NB) **11 C1**
Kingsley, UP (Man.) **29 G4**
Kingsmere, UP (Que.) **17 D3**
Kingsmill, UP (Ont.) **22 E2**
Kings Mines, UP (NB) **11 E1**
King's Point, COMM (Nfld.) **3 A1**
Kingsport, UP (NS) **11 H3**
Kings Rest, UP (NS) **9 B2**
Kingston, C (Ont.) **17 A4**
Kingston, UP (NS) **10 D1**
Kingston, UP (PEI) **7 C4**
Kingston, UP (NB) **11 E2**
Kingston < Small Point - Kingston - Broad Cove - Blackhead - Adams Cove, UP (Nfld.) **2 G2**
Kingston, CFB/BFC, MIL (Ont.) **17 B4**
Kingston Corner, UP (NB) **11 E2**
Kingston Mills, UP (Ont.) **17 A4**
Kingston Village, UP (NS) **10 D1**
Kingsvale, UP (BC) **35 C2**
Kingsville, T (Ont.) **22 A4**
Kingsville, UP (NS) **8 C4**
Kings Wharf, UP (Ont.) **21 D1**
Kingswood Acres, UP (Ont.) **23 E1**
Kingwell, UP (Nfld.) **2 E2**
Kingwood, UP (Ont.) **23 D4**
Kinhuron, NUP (Ont.) **23 B2**
Kinikinik, UP (Alta.) **33 E2**
Kinistino, T (Sask.) **32 E4**
Kinistino 91, IR (Sask.) **32 F4**
Kinistino 91A, IR (Sask.) **32 F4**
Kinkora, UP (Ont.) **23 C4**
Kinkora, VL (PEI) **7 B4**
Kinley, VL (Sask.) **31 E1**
Kinloch, UP (Sask.) **29 B1**
Kinlock, UP (PEI) **7 D4**
Kinloss, UP (Ont.) **23 B3**
Kinlough, UP (Ont.) **23 B3**
Kinmakanksk 6, IR (BC) **41 E2**
Kinmelit 20, IR (BC) **42 D3**
Kinmount, UP (Ont.) **23 H1**
Kinnaird, UP (Ont.) **22 C1**
Kinnamax 15, IR (BC) **42 D4**
Kinnear Settlement, UP (NB) **11 F1**
Kinnears-Mills, UP (Que.) **15 A4**
Kinoosao, UP (Sask.) **44 G4**
Kinosis, UP (Alta.) **44 C4**
Kinosota, UP (Man.) **29 G2**
Kinross, UP (PEI) **7 D4**
Kinsac, UP (NS) **9 B3**
Kinsella, UP (Alta.) **33 F4**
Kinsmans Corner, UP (NS) **11 G3**
Kintail, UP (Ont.) **23 B3**
Kintore, UP (Ont.) **22 E1**
Kintyre, UP (Ont.) **22 D2**
Kinusisipi, UP (Man.) **30 C2**
Kinuso, VL (Alta.) **33 C1**
Kinyug 57, IR (BC) **42 E3**
Kioosta 15, IR (BC) **41 A1**
Kiosk, UP (Ont.) **18 A4**
Kiowana Beach, UP (Ont.) **23 D1**
Kipabiskau, UP (Sask.) **32 F4**
Kipawa, UP (Que.) **18 A3**
Kipisa, UP (NWT) **46 F2**
Kipling, T (Sask.) **29 C3**
Kipling, UP (Ont.) **25 G1**
Kipp, UP (Alta.) **34 F4**
Kippase 2, IR (BC) **39 D1**
Kippen, UP (Ont.) **23 B4**
Kippens, LID (Nfld.) **4 B2**
Kirby Point 6, IR (BC) **38 B3**
Kirby's Corner, UP (Ont.) **26 B3**
Kirk, UP (Ont.) **25 G1**
Kirkcaldy, UP (Alta.) **34 F3**
Kirk Cove, UP (Ont.) **24 G3**
Kirkdale, UP (Que.) **16 C3**
Kirke, UP (Ont.) **26 F1**
Kirkella, UP (Man.) **29 D3**
Kirkfield, UP (Ont.) **23 H2**
Kirkhill, UP (Ont.) **17 E1**
Kirkhill, UP (NS) **11 H2**
Kirkland, T (Que.) **17 F4**
Kirkland, UP (NB) **11 A1**
Kirkland Lake, T (Ont.) **26 F2**
Kirkman Creek, UP (YT) **45 A2**
Kirkmount, UP (NS) **8 A4**
Kirkness, UP (Man.) **28 A1**
Kirkpatrick, UP (Alta.) **34 F2**
Kirks-Ferry, UP (Que.) **17 D3**
Kirkton, UP (Ont.) **22 E1**
Kirkwall, UP (Ont.) **22 G1**
Kirkwood, UP (NB) **12 E2**
Kiron, UP (Alta.) **33 E4**
Kirriemuir, UP (Alta.) **31 B1**
Kirtland, UP (BC) **45 B4**
Kirwan, UP (Que.) **18 A2**
Kisameet 7, IR (BC) **41 F3**
Kis-an-usko 7, IR (BC) **42 F3**
Kisbey, VL (Sask.) **29 C4**
Kisgegas, IR (BC) **42 F3**
Kishnacous 29, IR (BC) **39 F4**
Kiskissink, UP (Que.) **18 H2**
Kispiox < Kispiox 1, UP (BC) **42 F3**
Kispiox 1, IR (BC) **42 F3**
Kitamaat Village < Kitimat 2, UP (BC) **41 E1**
Kitasoo 1, IR (BC) **41 E3**
Kitchener, C (Ont.) **23 D4**
Kitchener, UP (BC) **34 C4**
Kitigan, UP (Ont.) **20 C4**
Kitimat, DM (BC) **41 E1**
Kitimat 1, IR (BC) **41 E1**
Kitimat 2, IR (BC) **41 E1**
Kitisa 7, IR (BC) **41 E1**
Kitkahta 1, IR (BC) **41 D1**
Kitkatla < Dolphin Island 1, UP (BC) **41 C1**
Kitladamax 1A, IR (BC) **42 D3**
Kitlawaoo 10, IR (BC) **41 D2**
Kitlope 16, IR (BC) **41 F2**
Kitsakie 156B, IR (Sask.) **32 E1**
Kitsault, UP (BC) **42 D3**
Kitscoty, VL (Alta.) **33 G3**
Kitseguecla < Kitseguecla 1, UP (BC) **42 F3**
Kitseguecla 1, IR (BC) **42 F3**
Kitsegukla Logging 3, IR (BC) **42 F3**
Kitselas 1, IR (BC) **42 E4**
Kitsemenlagan 19, IR (BC) **41 D1**
Kitsemenlagan 19A, IR (BC) **41 D1**
Kits-ka-haws 6, IR (BC) **42 D3**
Kitsumkaylum 1, IR (BC) **42 E4**
Kittigazuit, UP (NWT) **45 C1**
Kitwancool 1, IR (BC) **42 E3**
Kitwancool 2, IR (BC) **42 E3**
Kitwancool 3A, IR (BC) **42 E3**
Kitwanga < Kitwangar 1, UP (BC) **42 E3**
Kitwanga 2, IR (BC) **42 E3**
Kitwangar 1, IR (BC) **42 E3**
Kitwilluchsilt 7, IR (BC) **42 D3**
Kitzowit 20, IR (BC) **35 B2**
Kiusta < Kioosta 15, UP (BC) **41 A1**
Kivitoo, UP (NWT) **46 G1**
Klaalth 5, IR (BC) **38 E2**
Klagookchew 4, IR (BC) **41 G1**
Klahkamich 17, IR (BC) **35 B2**
Klahkowit 5, IR (BC) **35 B1**
Klahoose 1, IR (BC) **37 D3**
Klakelse 86, IR (BC) **42 E4**
Klaklacum 12, IR (BC) **35 B3**
Klapthlon 5, IR (BC) **41 D1**
Klapthlon 5A, IR (BC) **41 D1**
Klaskish 3, IR (BC) **39 C2**
Klayekwim 6, IR (BC) **38 E1**
Klayekwim 6A, IR (BC) **38 E1**
Klayekwim 7, IR (BC) **38 E1**
Klayekwim 8, IR (BC) **38 E1**
Kleecoot, UP (BC) **38 C2**
Kleefeld, UP (Man.) **28 A2**
Kleena Kleene, UP (BC) **40 A4**
Kleenza Creek Subdivision, NUP (BC) **42 E4**
Kleetlekut 22, IR (BC) **35 B2**
Kleetlekut 22A, IR (BC) **35 B2**
Klehkoot 2, IR (BC) **38 C3**
Kleindale, UP (BC) **38 D1**
Klemmer Subdivision, NUP (Sask.) **32 F3**
Klemtu < Kitasoo 1, UP (BC) **41 E3**
Kleskun Hill, UP (Alta.) **43 G4**
Klewaduska 6, IR (BC) **42 E4**
Kleykleyhous 5, IR (BC) **38 C3**
Klickkumcheen 18, IR (BC) **35 B2**
Klickseewy 7, IR (BC) **39 D1**
Klie's Beach, NUP (Ont.) **22 A4**
Klintonel, UP (Sask.) **31 C4**
Klitsis 16, IR (BC) **39 E3**
Klock, UP (Ont.) **18 A4**
Kloklowuck 7, IR (BC) **35 B1**
Klondike, NUP (Que.) **16 B4**
Klondyke, UP (Ont.) **22 A4**
Kloyadingli 2, IR (BC) **40 B3**
Kluachon Lake 1, IR (BC) **45 B4**
Kluane, UP (YT) **45 A3**
Klukshu, UP (YT) **45 A3**
Kluskus 1, IR (BC) **40 B3**
Kluskus 14, IR (BC) **40 B3**
Knamadeek 52, IR (BC) **42 C4**
Knames 45, IR (BC) **42 D4**
Knames 46, IR (BC) **42 D4**
Knapp Lake 6, IR (BC) **40 A2**
Kneehill, UP (Alta.) **34 F2**
Knee Hill Valley, UP (Alta.) **34 E1**
Knee Lake 192B, IR (Sask.) **45 E4**
Knights Cove, UP (Nfld.) **3 G4**
Knightville, UP (NB) **11 F1**
Knob Hill, UP (Alta.) **33 D4**
Knokmolks 67, IR (BC) **41 D1**
Knowlesville, UP (NB) **12 B3**
Knowlton-Landing, UP (Que.) **16 C4**
Knoxford, UP (NB) **12 A4**
Knoydart, UP (NS) **8 A4**
Knudsens Corner, UP (Ont.) **27 E3**
Knutsford, UP (PEI) **7 A3**
Koartac, UP (Que.) **46 F3**
Koidern, UP (YT) **45 A3**
Kokanee Landing, UP (BC) **34 B4**
Kokish, UP (BC) **39 E1**
Koksilah, UP (BC) **38 E3**
Ko-kwi-iss 22, IR (BC) **41 F4**
Kokyet 1, IR (BC) **41 E3**
Kola, UP (Man.) **29 D4**
Kolapore, UP (Ont.) **23 E2**
Kolbec, UP (NS) **9 B1**
Komarno, UP (Man.) **29 H3**
Komoka, UP (Ont.) **22 D2**
Koonwats 7, IR (BC) **42 E4**
Kooryet 12, IR (BC) **41 D2**
Koostatak < Fisher River 44, UP (Man.) **29 H2**
Kootenay 1, IR (BC) **34 D4**
Kootenay Bay, UP (BC) **34 B4**
Kootenay Crossing, UP (BC) **34 C2**
Kootowis 4, IR (BC) **38 A2**
Kopchitchin 2, IR (BC) **35 B2**
Koprino 10, IR (BC) **39 C1**
Koqui 6, IR (BC) **41 E3**
Kormak, UP (Ont.) **26 C2**
Kose 9, IR (BC) **41 A1**
Kossuth, UP (Ont.) **23 E4**
Kotsine 2, IR (BC) **42 G3**
Kouchibouguac, UP (NB) **12 G3**
Kowkash, UP (Ont.) **27 G1**
Kowtain 17, IR (BC) **38 F1**
Krakow, UP (Alta.) **33 F3**
Kramer, UP (Ont.) **24 G1**
Kramer Ranch, UP (BC) **43 D3**
Krasne, UP (Sask.) **31 H1**
Krestova, UP (BC) **34 B4**
Kristnes, UP (Sask.) **29 B1**
Kronau, UP (Sask.) **31 H3**
Kronsgart, UP (Man.) **29 H4**
Kronstal, UP (Man.) **29 H4**
Krugerdorf, UP (Ont.) **26 F2**
Krydor, VL (Sask.) **32 C4**
Ksabasn 50, IR (BC) **42 C4**
Ksadagamks 43, IR (BC) **42 C4**
Ksadsks 44, IR (BC) **42 C4**
Ksagwisgwas 62, IR (BC) **42 D4**
Ksagwisgwas 63, IR (BC) **42 D4**
Ksames 85, IR (BC) **42 E4**
Kshaoom 23, IR (BC) **41 D1**
Kshish 4 and 4A, IR (BC) **42 E4**
Kshish 4B, IR (BC) **42 E4**
Kshwan 27, IR (BC) **42 D3**
Kshwan 27A, IR (BC) **42 D3**
Ksilamisk 89, IR (BC) **42 D3**
Ksituan, UP (Alta.) **43 G3**
Ksoo-gun-ya 2A, IR (BC) **42 F3**
Kstus 83, IR (BC) **42 D4**
Kstus 84, IR (BC) **42 D4**
Ksui-la-das 6, IR (BC) **39 E1**
Ktamgaodzen 51, IR (BC) **42 C4**
Ktsinet 23, IR (BC) **42 D3**
Kuaste 8, IR (BC) **41 E1**
Kuhryville, UP (Ont.) **23 C4**
Kukatush, UP (Ont.) **26 D2**
Kukwapa 5, IR (BC) **39 E1**
Kul 18, IR (BC) **41 C1**
Kuldekduma 7, IR (BC) **39 E1**
Kuldo < Kuldoe 1, UP (BC) **42 E3**
Kuldoe 1, IR (BC) **42 E3**
Kulish, UP (Man.) **29 E2**
Kulkayu 4, IR (BC) **41 D2**
Kulkayu (Hartley Bay) 4A, IR (BC) **41 D2**
Kulspai 6, IR (BC) **42 E4**
Kultah 4, IR (BC) **39 D1**
Kumcheen 1, IR (BC) **35 B1**
Kumowdah 3, IR (BC) **41 D1**
Kumpfville, UP (Ont.) **23 D4**
Kung < Kung 11, UP (BC) **41 A1**
Kung 11, IR (BC) **41 A1**
Kunhunoan 13, IR (BC) **41 D2**
Kunsoot 9, IR (BC) **41 E3**
Kunstamis 2, IR (BC) **41 G4**
Kunstamis 2A, IR (BC) **41 G4**
Kupchynalth 1, IR (BC) **35 B2**
Kupchynalth 2, IR (BC) **35 B2**
Kuper Island 7, IR (BC) **38 E3**
Kuroki, UP (Sask.) **29 B1**
Kurtzville, UP (Ont.) **23 C3**
Kushya Creek 7, IR (BC) **40 A3**
Kushya Creek 12, IR (BC) **40 A3**
Kuskonook, UP (BC) **34 C4**
Kutcous Point 33, IR (BC) **39 F4**
Kuthlalth 3, IR (BC) **35 B3**
Kuthlo 26, IR (BC) **41 G4**
Kwatlena 4, IR (BC) **41 F3**
Kwa-tsa-lix 4, IR (BC) **42 E4**
Kwatse 3, IR (BC) **39 G1**
Kwawkwawapilt 6, IR (BC) **35 A4**
Kwetahkis 17, IR (BC) **41 F4**
Kwinamuck 49, IR (BC) **42 E3**
Kwinitsa, UP (BC) **42 D4**
Kyarti 3, IR (BC) **41 E3**
Kyex 64, IR (BC) **42 D4**
Kye-yaa-la 1, IR (BC) **39 E1**
Kyidagwis 2, IR (BC) **41 G4**
Kyimla 11, IR (BC) **39 F1**
Kyikinalko 2, IR (BC) **35 B2**
Kyle, T (Sask.) **31 D2**
Kylemore, UP (Sask.) **29 B1**
Kynoch, UP (Ont.) **26 C4**
Kynocks, UP (YT) **45 B3**
Kytes Hill, UP (NS) **8 F3**
Kyuquot, UP (BC) **39 D2**
Kzimeng 82, IR (BC) **42 D3**

L

La Baie, C (Que.) **14 B3**
La Baleine, UP (Que.) **15 C2**
La Barrière, UP (Que.) **18 F4**
Labelle, UP (Que.) **18 E4**
LaBelle, UP (NS) **10 D2**
Laberge, UP (Que.) **17 G2**
Laberge, UP (Que.) **18 F4**
La Bostonnais, UP (Que.) **18 G2**
Labrador City, LID (Nfld.) **6 C4**
La Branche, UP (Que.) **15 B2**
Labrecque, UP (Que.) **15 A2**
Labrie, UP (Que.) **15 H3**
Labrieville, UP (Que.) **14 E1**
Labrieville-Sud, UP (Que.) **14 F1**
La Broquerie, UP (Man.) **28 B2**
Labuma, UP (Alta.) **33 D4**
La Butte, UP (Que.) **13 D3**
Lac-à-Beauce, UP (Que.) **18 G3**
Lac-à-Belley, UP (Que.) **18 H1**
Lac-à-Dîner, UP (Que.) **14 A1**
Lac-à-Foin, UP (Que.) **18 D4**
Lac-à-la-Croix, UP (Que.) **18 H1**
Lac-à-la-Loutre, UP (Que.) **18 E4**
Lac-à-la-Tortue, UP (Que.) **16 B1**
Lac-à-la-Truite, UP (Que.) **18 C4**
Lac-à-l'Eau-Claire, UP (Que.) **16 A1**
Lacadena, UP (Sask.) **31 D2**
L'Acadie, UP (Que.) **16 A4**
Lac-Allard, UP (Que.) **5 A3**
Lac-Alouette, UP (Que.) **18 F4**
Lac-André, UP (Que.) **18 F4**
Lac-au-Saumon, VL (Que.) **13 B3**
Lac-aux-Brochets, UP (Que.) **18 G3**
Lac-aux-Castors, NUP (Que.) **18 E4**
Lac-aux-Ours, UP (Que.) **18 F4**
Lac-aux-Sables, UP (Que.) **18 H3**
Lac-aux-Sangsues, NUP (Que.) **16 B1**
La Cavée, UP (Que.) **18 H1**
Lac-Bachelor, UP (Que.) **20 F4**
Lac-Baie-d'Or, NUP (Que.) **15 G4**
Lac-Baker, VL (NB) **15 G2**
Lac-Beaudry, UP (Que.) **18 F4**
Lac-Beauport, UP (Que.) **15 G3**
Lac-Bédard, UP (Que.) **16 B1**
Lac-Bélisle, NUP (Que.) **18 E4**
Lac-Bellemare, UP (Que.) **16 B1**
Lac-Bellevue, UP (Que.) **18 E4**
Lac Bellevue, UP (Alta.) **33 F3**
Lac-Bevin, UP (Que.) **18 E4**
Lac-Bitobig, UP (Que.) **18 D4**
Lac-Blanc, UP (Que.) **18 E4**
Lac-Bleu, NUP (Que.) **18 F4**
Lac-Blouin, UP (Que.) **18 B2**
Lac-Boissonneault, UP (Que.) **16 D3**
Lac-Bouchette, VL (Que.) **18 H2**
Lac-Brien, UP (Que.) **18 F4**
Lac-Brière, UP (Que.) **18 F4**
Lac Brochet, UP (Man.) **44 G3**
Lac-Brome, T (Que.) **16 C4**
Lac-Brompton, UP (Que.) **16 C3**
Lac-Brompton-Sud, UP (Que.) **16 C4**
Lac-Brûlé, UP (Que.) **18 F4**
Lac-Cameron, UP (Que.) **20 F4**
Lac-Cameron, UP (Que.) **18 E4**
Lac-Campion, UP (Que.) **18 D4**
Lac-Capri, NUP (Que.) **17 F1**
Lac-Caribou, UP (Que.) **18 F4**
Lac-Carré, VL (Que.) **18 F4**
Lac-Castagnier, UP (Que.) **18 B1**
Lac-Castor, UP (Que.) **18 E4**
Lac-Cayamant, UP (Que.) **18 D4**
Lac-Chanoine, UP (Que.) **18 F4**
Lac-Chapleau, UP (Que.) **18 F4**
Lac-Chapleau, UP (Que.) **18 E4**
Lac-Charlebois, UP (Que.) **18 F4**
Lac-Chat, UP (Que.) **18 G3**
Lac-Clair, UP (Que.) **18 G2**
Lac-Clair, UP (Que.) **18 F4**
Lac-Clair, NUP (Que.) **14 B2**
Lac-Clearview, NUP (Que.) **18 F4**
Lac-Clef, UP (Que.) **18 F4**
Lac-Cloche, UP (Que.) **18 E4**
Lac-Connelly, UP (Que.) **18 F4**
Lac-Corbeau, UP (Que.) **16 A1**
Lac-Cornu, UP (Que.) **18 F4**
Lac-Cristal, UP (Que.) **18 F4**
Lac-Croche, UP (Que.) **18 F4**
Lac-Daigle, UP (Que.) **19 F3**
Lac-Danford, UP (Que.) **18 D4**
Lac-Darey, UP (Que.) **18 G2**
Lac-David, UP (Que.) **18 E3**
Lac-de-l'Achigan, UP (Que.) **18 F4**
Lac-Delage, T (Que.) **15 F3**
Lac-de-la-Montagne-Noire, UP (Que.) **18 F4**
Lac-de-l'Est, UP (Que.) **15 E2**
Lac-Déligny, NUP (Que.) **16 A1**
Lac-de-l'Orignal, UP (Que.) **18 F4**
Lac-des-Aigles, UP (Que.) **14 G4**
Lac-des-Becs-Scie, UP (Que.) **18 F4**
Lac-des-Échos, UP (Que.) **14 G4**
Lac-des-Écorces, VL (Que.) **18 E4**
Lac-Désert, UP (Que.) **18 E4**
Lac-des-Français, UP (Que.) **18 F4**
Lac-Deshênes, UP (Que.) **14 D4**
Lac-des-Îles, UP (Que.) **18 E4**
Lac-des-Loups, UP (Que.) **17 B1**
Lac-des-Lys, UP (NB) **13 C4**
Lac-Desmarais, UP (Que.) **18 E4**
Lac des Mille Lacs 22A1, IR (Ont.) **27 C3**
Lac-des-Neiges, UP (Que.) **15 B1**
Lac-des-Pins, UP (Que.) **18 F4**
Lac-des-Pins, UP (Que.) **16 B1**
Lac-des-Plages, UP (Que.) **18 E4**
Lac-des-Plaines, NUP (Que.) **15 G4**
Lac-des-Quatorze-Îles, UP (Que.) **18 F4**
Lac-des-Seize-Îles, UP (Que.) **18 F4**
Lac-des-Seize-Îles-Sud, UP (Que.) **18 F4**
Lac-des-Sept-Îles, UP (Que.) **15 A3**
Lac-Dion, UP (Que.) **15 C3**
Lac-Doucet, UP (Que.) **16 B1**
Lac-Drolet, UP (Que.) **16 F3**
Lac-du-Bois-Franc, UP (Que.) **18 F4**
Lac du Bonnet, VL (Man.) **28 C1**
Lac-du-Brochet, UP (Que.) **18 D4**
Lac-du-Cerf, UP (Que.) **18 E4**
Lac-du-Chevreuil, UP (Que.) **18 F4**
Lac-Duffy, UP (Que.) **18 F4**
Lac-Duhamel, UP (Que.) **18 E4**
Lac-du-Sacré-Coeur, UP (Que.) **15 A3**
Lac-Écho, UP (Que.) **18 F4**
Lac-Écho, UP (Que.) **18 E4**
Lac-Écho, NUP (Que.) **18 F4**
Lac-Édouard, UP (Que.) **18 H2**
Lac-Emmuraillé, UP (Que.) **14 B2**
Lac-en-Coeur, UP (Que.) **18 F4**
Lac-Équerre, UP (Que.) **18 E4**
Lac-Etchemin, T (Que.) **15 C4**
Lac-Fortune, UP (Que.) **18 A2**
Lac-Français, UP (Que.) **18 F4**
Lac-Frontière, UP (Que.) **15 D3**
Lac-Gagnon, UP (Que.) **18 F4**
Lac-Gatineau, UP (Que.) **18 D4**
Lac-Gauthier, UP (Que.) **18 F4**
Lac-Gélinas, UP (Que.) **18 E4**
Lac-Gémont, UP (Que.) **18 F4**

Lac-Grosleau, UP (Que.) 18 E4
Lac-Guindon, UP (Que.) 18 F4
Lachenaie, T (Que.) 17 H3
La Chevrotière, UP (Que.) 16 D1
Lachine, C (Que.) 17 G4
Lachkaltsap 9, IR (BC) 42 D4
Lachkul-jeets 6, IR (BC) 41 D2
Lachmach 16, IR (BC) 38 H2
Lachtesk 12, IR (BC) 42 D4
Lachtesk 12A, IR (BC) 42 D4
Lac-Humqui, UP (Que.) 13 A3
Lachute, C (Que.) 17 F1
Lac-Joannès, UP (Que.) 18 A2
Lac-Jolicoeur, UP (Que.) 18 F4
Lackaway 2, IR (BC) 38 H2
Lac-Keatley, UP (Que.) 18 E4
Lackzuswadda 9, IR (BC) 41 D2
Lac-Labelle, UP (Que.) 18 E4
Lac La Biche, T (Alta.) 33 F2
Lac La Biche Mission, UP (Alta.) 33 F2
Lac-Labrie, UP (Que.) 19 E3
Lac la Croix, NUP (Ont.) 27 B3
Lac-Lafontaine, NUP (Que.) 16 B1
Lac la Hache, UP (BC) 36 C2
Lac la Hache 220, IR (Sask.) 44 F3
Lac-Lajoie, UP (Que.) 18 F4
Lac la Martre, UP (NWT) 45 E2
Lac-La Motte, UP (Que.) 18 B1
Lac-Lamoureux, UP (Que.) 18 E4
Lac la Nonne, UP (Alta.) 33 D3
Lac-Laperrière, NUP (Que.) 18 A3
Lac-Lapierre, UP (Que.) 18 F4
Lac la Ronge 156, IR (Sask.) 32 E1
Lac-Lasalle, UP (Que.) 18 F4
Lac-Lavoie, UP (Que.) 13 B3
Lac-Légaré, UP (Que.) 15 G1
Lac Le Jeune, UP (BC) 35 D1
Lac-Loïs, UP (Que.) 18 A1
Lac-Long-Nord, UP (Que.) 18 F4
Lac-Long-Sud, UP (Que.) 18 F4
Laclu, UP (Ont.) 28 F2
Lac Magloire, UP (Alta.) 43 H3
Lac-Mance, UP (Que.) 18 A1
Lac-Manitou-Sud, UP (Que.) 18 F4
Lac-Marois, UP (Que.) 18 F4
Lac-Martin, UP (Que.) 16 B1
Lac-Masketsi, UP (Que.) 18 H3
Lac-Maskinongé, UP (Que.) 18 E4
Lac-Matambin, UP (Que.) 16 A1
Lac-McDonald, UP (Que.) 18 E4
Lac-McGregor, UP (Que.) 17 C1
Lac-Meach, UP (Que.) 17 D3
Lac-Mégantic, T (Que.) 16 F3
Lac-Memphrémagog, UP (Que.) 16 C4
Lac-Michaudville, NUP (Que.) 18 E4
Lac-Mitis, UP (Que.) 13 A3
Lac-Montjoie, NUP (Que.) 16 D4
Lac-Moore, UP (Que.) 18 E4
Lac-Morin, UP (Que.) 18 F4
Lac-Morin, UP (Que.) 15 F3
Lac-Noir, UP (Que.) 18 G4
Lacolle, VL (Que.) 16 A4
Lacombe, T (Alta.) 33 D4
La Conception, UP (Que.) 18 E4
La Conception-Station, UP (Que.) 18 E4
Laconia, UP (NS) 10 E2
Lacordaire, UP (Sask.) 31 F4
La Corey, UP (Alta.) 33 G2
La Corne, UP (Que.) 18 B1
La Corniche, UP (Que.) 18 F4
Lacoste, UP (Que.) 18 E4
Lac-Ouareau, UP (Que.) 18 F4
Lac-Ouimet, UP (Que.) 18 E4
Lac-Ouimet, UP (Que.) 18 E4
La Coulée, UP (Que.) 13 B2
La Coulée, UP (Man.) 28 B2
Lac-Paradis, NUP (Que.) 18 D4
Lac-Paré, UP (Que.) 18 F4
Lac-Pauzé, UP (Que.) 18 F4
Lac Pelletier, UP (Sask.) 31 D3
Lac-Pemichangan, UP (Que.) 18 D4
Lac-Pérodeau, UP (Que.) 18 E3
Lac-Pimbina, UP (Que.) 18 F4
Lac-Pinault, UP (Que.) 13 B2
Lac-Poisson-Blanc, UP (Que.) 18 D4
Lac-Poulin, VL (Que.) 16 F2
Lac-Provost, UP (Que.) 18 F4
Lac-Quenouille, UP (Que.) 18 F4
Lac-Quinn, UP (Que.) 18 F4
Lac-Rémi, UP (Que.) 18 E4
La Crete, UP (Alta.) 44 A3
Lac-Rimouski, UP (Que.) 14 H4
La Croche, UP (Que.) 18 G2
Lac-Rocher, UP (Que.) 16 A2
Lacroixville, UP (Que.) 18 D4
Lac-Rouge-Nord, UP (Que.) 18 F4
Lac-Saguay, UP (Que.) 18 E4
Lac-St-Amour, UP (Que.) 18 F4
Lac-St-Augustin-Nord, UP (Que.) 15 F4
Lac-St-Augustin-Sud, UP (Que.) 15 F4
Lac-St-Charles, UP (Que.) 15 F3
Lac-St-Denis < Lac-St-Denis, SFC/CFS, UP (Que.) 18 F4
Lac-St-Denis, SFC/CFS, MIL (Que.) 18 F4
Lac Ste Anne, UP (Alta.) 33 D3
Lac-Ste-Anne, UP (Que.) 19 D3
Lac-Ste-Marie, UP (Que.) 18 D4
Lac-Ste-Thérèse, UP (Ont.) 20 B4
Lac-St-Germains, UP (Que.) 14 C3
Lac-St-Ignace, UP (Que.) 13 D1
Lac-St-Joseph, T (Que.) 15 A3
Lac-St-Paul, UP (Que.) 18 E3
Lac-Salé, UP (Que.) 5 E2
Lac-Scryer, UP (Que.) 18 E4
Lac-Sébastien, UP (Que.) 14 B2
Lac-Sergent, T (Que.) 15 A3
Lac Seul, UP (Ont.) 27 B1
Lac Seul 28, IR (Ont.) 27 B1
Lac-Siesta, UP (Que.) 18 F4
Lac Simon, IR (Que.) 18 C2
Lac-Simon, UP (Que.) 18 E4
Lacs-Louis-Hermel, UP (Que.) 14 B2
Lac-Supérieur, UP (Que.) 18 F4
Lac-Thibeault, UP (Que.) 15 G2
Lactor, UP (Que.) 16 E3
Lac-Tremblant-Nord, UP (Que.) 18 E4
Lac-Trois-Saumons, UP (Que.) 15 D2
Lac-Unique, UP (NB) 15 G2
Lac-Vert, UP (Sask.) 32 F4
Lac-Vert, UP (Que.) 18 D4
Lac-Vert-Nord, UP (Que.) 18 F4
Lac-Vert-Sud, UP (Que.) 18 F4
Lac-Wallace, UP (Que.) 18 F4
Lac-William, UP (Que.) 15 A4
Ladder Valley, UP (Sask.) 32 C3
Ladd-Mills, UP (Que.) 16 D4
Ladle Cove, UP (Nfld.) 3 E2
Ladrière, UP (Que.) 14 F3
La Durantaye, UP (Que.) 15 B3
Lady Bank, UP (Ont.) 23 D2
Lady Cove, UP (Nfld.) 2 F1
Lady Fane, UP (PEI) 7 C4
Lady Lake, UP (Sask.) 29 C1
Ladysmith, T (BC) 38 E3
Ladysmith, UP (Que.) 18 D4
Ladysmith, UP (Ont.) 22 B2
Ladywood, UP (Man.) 28 B1
Lafayette, NUP (Que.) 15 C3
Laferté, UP (Que.) 18 A1
Laflamme, NUP (Que.) 15 C3
Lafleche, T (Sask.) 31 F4
Lafond, UP (Alta.) 33 F3
Lafontaine, UP (Ont.) 23 E1
Lafontaine, VL (Que.) 18 F4
Lafontaine Beach, UP (Ont.) 23 E1
Laforce, UP (Que.) 18 A2
Laforest, UP (Ont.) 26 E3
La Fourche, UP (Que.) 18 F4
Lafrance, UP (Que.) 15 D2
Lagacé, UP (Que.) 13 C4
Lagacéville, UP (NB) 12 F2
La Gadelle, UP (Que.) 15 D1
La Galette, UP (Que.) 14 C4
Laganière, UP (Que.) 16 C1
Laggan, UP (NS) 8 A4
Laggan, UP (Ont.) 17 E1
Lagins 5, IR (BC) 41 B2
La Glace, UP (Alta.) 43 G4
La Glacière, UP (Que.) 18 F4
Lagoon, UP (BC) 38 E4
Lagoon City, UP (Ont.) 23 G2
La Grande-Barbue, UP (Que.) 16 B4
La Grande-Trois, UP (Que.) 20 F2
La Guadeloupe, VL (Que.) 16 F2
La Guerre, UP (Que.) 17 F2
Lahaieville, UP (Alta.) 33 E2
LaHave, UP (NS) 10 E2
LaHave Island, UP (NS) 10 E2
La Hêtrière, UP (NB) 11 G1
Laidlaw, UP (BC) 35 A4
Laird, UP (Ont.) 26 B4
Laird, VL (Sask.) 32 D4
Lajeunesse Bridge, UP (Ont.) 28 F1
Lajord, UP (Sask.) 31 H3
Lakahahmen 11, IR (BC) 38 H2
Lakata 41, IR (BC) 42 D4
Lakbelak 38, IR (BC) 42 D4
Lakbelak Creek 39, IR (BC) 42 D4
Lakbelak Lake 40, IR (BC) 42 D4
Lake, UP (Ont.) 24 E3
Lake Alma, VL (Sask.) 31 H4
Lake Annis, UP (NS) 10 B3
Lake Audy, UP (Man.) 29 E3
Lake-Aylmer, UP (Que.) 16 E3
Lake Bernard, UP (Ont.) 24 B1
Lake Centre, UP (NS) 10 E2
Lake Charles, UP (Ont.) 23 C1
Lake Charlotte, UP (NS) 9 C3
Lake Clear, UP (Ont.) 24 G2
Lake Cowichan, VL (BC) 38 D3
Lake Dalrymple, UP (Ont.) 23 G1
Lakedell, UP (Alta.) 33 D4
Lake Doré, UP (Ont.) 24 G1
Lake Doucette, UP (NS) 10 A3
Lake Echo, UP (NS) 9 C3
Lake Edward, UP (NB) 12 A2
Lake Egmont, UP (NS) 9 C3
Lake Eliza, UP (Alta.) 33 G3
Lake Erie Country Club, UP (Ont.) 22 A4
Lake Errock, UP (BC) 35 A4
Lakefield, UP (Que.) 17 F1
Lakefield, VL (Ont.) 21 D1
Lake Four, UP (Sask.) 32 D3
Lake Francis, UP (Man.) 29 H3
Lake George, UP (NB) 11 B1
Lake George, UP (NS) 10 A3
Lake George, UP (NS) 10 D1
Lake Harbour, UP (NWT) 46 F3
Lake Helen 53A, IR (Ont.) 27 F2
Lake Huron Highland, NUP (Ont.) 23 B2
Lakehurst, UP (Ont.) 24 D4
Lake Isle, UP (Alta.) 33 C3
Lake Kathlyn, UP (BC) 42 F4
Lake Killarney, UP (NS) 9 B1
Lake Laberge 1, IR (YT) 45 B3
Lakeland, UP (Man.) 29 G3
Lakeland Acres, UP (Ont.) 17 A4
Lakeland Point, UP (Ont.) 17 A4
Lakelands, UP (NS) 11 H2
Lakelands, UP (NS) 9 A3
Lake La Rose, UP (NS) 10 C1
Lake Lenore, VL (Sask.) 31 G1
Lakelet, UP (Ont.) 23 C3
Lake Louise, UP (Alta.) 34 C2
Lakelse 25, IR (BC) 42 E4
Lakelse Lake, UP (BC) 42 E4
Lake Majeau, UP (Alta.) 33 D3
Lake Major, UP (NS) 9 B3
Lake Midway, UP (NS) 10 A2
Lakenheath, UP (Sask.) 31 F4
Lake of the Woods 31B, IR (Ont.) 28 E2
Lake of the Woods 31C, IR (Ont.) 28 F3
Lake of the Woods 31G, IR (Ont.) 28 E3
Lake of the Woods 31H, IR (Ont.) 28 F3
Lake of the Woods 34, IR (Ont.) 28 F3
Lake of the Woods 35J, IR (Ont.) 28 F3
Lake of the Woods 37, IR (Ont.) 28 E3
Lake of the Woods 37B, IR (Ont.) 28 F3
Lake Opinicon, UP (Ont.) 17 B3
Lake Park, UP (Ont.) 17 B2
Lake Park, UP (Sask.) 32 E4
Lake Paul, UP (NS) 10 D1
Lake Pleasant, UP (NS) 10 D2
Lakeport, UP (Ont.) 21 E2
Lake Ramsay, UP (NS) 10 E1
Lake River, UP (Ont.) 20 C2
Lake Road, UP (NS) 9 B1
Lake Road, UP (NS) 9 B2
Lake Road, UP (NB) 7 A4
Lake Road, UP (NB) 11 B1
Lake Rosalind, UP (Ont.) 23 C2
Lake St Peter, UP (Ont.) 24 E2
Lake Saskatoon, UP (Alta.) 43 G4
Lakesend, UP (Alta.) 34 H1
Lakeside, UP (NS) 9 B4
Lakeside, UP (NS) 10 A3
Lakeside, UP (Ont.) 22 E1
Lakeside, UP (Sask.) 29 B3
Lakeside Beach, UP (Ont.) 21 C1
Lake Siding, UP (Nfld.) 5 G4
Laketon, UP (NB) 12 F3
Laketon, UP (BC) 45 B4
Laketown 3, IR (BC) 40 B2
Lake Traverse, UP (Ont.) 24 E1
Lake Uist, UP (NS) 8 E4
Lakevale, UP (NS) 8 B4
Lake Valley, UP (Sask.) 31 F3
Lake Verde, UP (PEI) 7 D4
Lakeview, SV (Alta.) 33 D3
Lakeview, UP (NS) 9 B3
Lakeview, UP (Que.) 18 F4
Lakeview, UP (Ont.) 21 B1
Lakeview, UP (Ont.) 22 F2
Lakeview, UP (NS) 10 D1
Lakeview, UP (NS) 10 D2
Lakeview, NUP (Alta.) 33 D4
Lakeview Beach, UP (Ont.) 23 G1
Lake View Beach, UP (Man.) 29 B3
Lakeview Heights, UP (Ont.) 17 E2
Lakeview Heights, UP (BC) 35 F2
Lakeview Park, UP (Ont.) 17 D4
Lakeville, UP (NB) 11 G1
Lakeville, UP (NS) 11 G3
Lakeville, UP (NB) 12 A4
Lakeville, UP (PEI) 7 F3
Lakeville Corner, UP (NB) 11 D1
Lake Wasaw, UP (Ont.) 28 H4
Lake William, UP (NS) 10 D2
Lakewood Beach, UP (Ont.) 22 A4
Lakgeas 87, IR (BC) 41 E1
Lakksgamal 85, IR (BC) 42 D3
Lakksgamal 86, IR (BC) 42 D3
Lakksgamal 88, IR (BC) 42 D3
Lakway Cemetery 3, IR (BC) 38 H2
Lalement, UP (Que.) 15 D2
Lally Cove, UP (Nfld.) 2 C2
La Loche, UP (Sask.) 44 D4
La Loche 221, IR (Sask.) 44 D4
La Loche 222, IR (Sask.) 44 D4
La Loche 223, IR (Sask.) 44 D4
La Loche West, UP (Sask.) 44 D4
L'Alverne, UP (Que.) 13 C3
L'Amable, UP (Ont.) 24 E2
La Macaza, UP (Que.) 18 E4
La Malbaie, T (Que.) 15 D1
Lamaline, T (Nfld.) 2 B4
La Manche, UP (Nfld.) 2 H3
La Manche, UP (Nfld.) 2 F2
La Mare, UP (Que.) 15 C1
La Martine, UP (Que.) 18 H1
Lambert, UP (Ont.) 23 C4
Lamberts Cove, UP (NB) 11 B3
Lambertville, UP (NB) 11 B3
Lambeth, UP (Ont.) 22 E2
Lamb Island 5, IR (BC) 38 E4
Lambton, VL (Que.) 16 F3
Lamèque, VL (NB) 13 G4
Lamèque-Portage, NUP (NB) 13 G4
La Merisière, UP (Que.) 15 C4
Lamerton, UP (Alta.) 33 E4
La Miche, UP (Que.) 15 B2
La Minerve, UP (Que.) 18 E4
Lamlash, UP (Ont.) 23 C2
Lammermoor, UP (Ont.) 17 A2
Lamming Mills, UP (BC) 40 E2
Lamont, T (Alta.) 33 E3
La Montagne, UP (NB) 11 G1
La Morandière, UP (Que.) 18 B1
Lamoreaux Corner, UP (NB) 12 A3
La Motte, UP (Que.) 18 B1
Lamoureux, UP (Alta.) 33 E3
Lampard, UP (Sask.) 31 G1
Lampman, T (Sask.) 29 C4
Lamy, UP (Que.) 14 F4
Lamy-Sud, UP (Que.) 14 F4
Lanark, UP (NS) 8 B4
Lanark, VL (Ont.) 17 B2
Lanas 4, IR (BC) 41 B1
La Nation, UP (Que.) 18 E4
Lancaster, UP (Nfld.) 3 G4
Lancaster, VL (Ont.) 17 F2
Lancaster Park < Edmonton (Namao), CFB/BFC, UP (Alta.) 33 E3
Lance Cove, UP (Nfld.) 2 H2
Lance Cove, UP (Nfld.) 3 G4
Lancer, VL (Sask.) 31 C2
Landerkin, UP (Ont.) 23 D3
Landis, VL (Sask.) 31 D1
Landmark, UP (Man.) 28 B2
Landreville, UP (Que.) 17 G2
Landrienne, UP (Que.) 18 B1
Landry, UP (NB) 12 G1
Landseer, UP (Man.) 29 G4
Lands End, UP (NB) 11 D3
Lanes, UP (Ont.) 23 B3
Lanesville, UP (NS) 9 C3
Lanfine, UP (Alta.) 31 B2
Lang, UP (Ont.) 21 D1
Lang, VL (Sask.) 31 H3
Langbank, UP (Sask.) 29 C3
Lang Bay, UP (BC) 38 D1
Langdale, UP (BC) 38 E3
Langdon, UP (Alta.) 34 E2
Langdon, UP (Ont.) 26 E1
Langdon's Cove, UP (Nfld.) 3 B1
L'Ange-Gardien, UP (Que.) 15 G3
L'Ange-Gardien, UP (Ont.) 17 E1
L'Ange-Gardien-Est, UP (Que.) 15 G3
Langenburg, T (Sask.) 29 D2
Langford, UP (Ont.) 22 G1
Langford, UP (BC) 38 E4
Langford Park, UP (Alta.) 33 D3
Langham, T (Sask.) 31 E1
Langlade, UP (Que.) 18 D2
Langley, C (BC) 38 G2
Langley, DM (BC) 38 G2
Langley 2, IR (BC) 38 H2
Langley 3, IR (BC) 38 H2
Langley 4, IR (BC) 38 H2
Langley 5, IR (BC) 38 G2
Langman, UP (Ont.) 23 E2
Langruth, UP (Man.) 29 G3
Langside, UP (Ont.) 23 B3
Langton, UP (Ont.) 22 F2
Langue-de-Terre, UP (Que.) 16 B2
Languedoc, UP (Que.) 18 A1
Laniel, UP (Que.) 18 A3
Lanigan, T (Sask.) 31 G1
Laniwci, UP (Sask.) 32 D4
L'Annonciation, VL (Que.) 18 E4
Lanoieville, UP (Que.) 16 B3
Lanoraie, UP (Que.) 16 A2
Lansberg Siding, UP (NS) 9 D2
Lansdowne, UP (Ont.) 17 B4
Lansdowne, UP (NS) 10 B2
Lansdowne, UP (NB) 12 A4
Lansdowne House, UP (Ont.) 20 A3
Lansdowne Station, UP (NS) 9 D2
L'Anse-à-Gilles, UP (Que.) 15 C2
L'Anse-à-la-Cabane, UP (Que.) 7 F1
L'Anse-à-la-Croix, UP (Que.) 13 B2
L'Anse-à-l'Eau, UP (Nfld.) 2 C4
L'Anse-Amour, UP (Nfld.) 5 G2
L'Anse-au-Clair, COMM (Nfld.) 5 G2
L'Anse-au-Diable, UP (Nfld.) 5 G2
L'Anse-au-Loup, COMM (Nfld.) 5 G2
L'Anse-au-Loup, UP (Nfld.) 2 B3
L'Anse aux Meadows, UP (Nfld.) 5 H2
L'Anse-McInnes, UP (Que.) 13 G3
L'Anse-St-Jean, UP (Que.) 14 D3
Lansing, UP (YT) 45 B2
Lantier, UP (Que.) 18 F4
Lantz, UP (NS) 9 B3
Lantzville, UP (BC) 38 D2
La Passe, UP (Ont.) 24 H1
La Patrie, VL (Que.) 16 E4
La Pérade, VL (Que.) 16 C1
La Pérouse, UP (Man.) 30 C2
La Petite-Barbue, UP (Que.) 16 B4
Lapierre House, UP (YT) 45 B1
La Plage, UP (Que.) 16 C4
La Plaine, UP (Que.) 18 F4
Lapland, UP (NS) 10 D2
LaPlante, UP (NB) 12 E1
La Plonge 192, IR (Sask.) 32 C1
La Pocatière, T (Que.) 15 D2
La Pocatière-Station, UP (Que.) 15 D2
La Poile, UP (Nfld.) 4 C4
Lapointe, NUP (Ont.) 22 A3
LaPointe Settlement, UP (NB) 13 D4
Lapointe-Station, UP (Que.) 15 E1
Laporte, UP (Sask.) 31 C2
Lappe, UP (Ont.) 27 D3
La Prairie, T (Que.) 17 H4
La Prairie, UP (NS) 8 D2
La Présentation, UP (Que.) 16 B3
La Presqu'île, UP (Que.) 16 B3
La Prusse, UP (Que.) 15 D3
Larawls, UP (Que.) 17 A1
L'Archeveque, UP (NS) 8 E4
Lardeau, UP (BC) 34 B3
Larder Lake, UP (Ont.) 26 F2
L'Ardoise, UP (NS) 8 D4
L'Ardoise West, UP (NS) 8 D4
La Rédemption, UP (Que.) 13 A3
La Reine, VL (Que.) 26 F1
La Renaudière, NUP (Que.) 15 C3
La Renouche, UP (Ont.) 17 F1
La Résurrection, UP (Que.) 15 F1
Largie, UP (Ont.) 22 D2
La Richardière, UP (Que.) 14 E4
La Rivière, UP (Man.) 29 G4
Lark Harbour, COMM (Nfld.) 4 C1
Larkins, UP (Ont.) 21 G1
Larkspur, UP (Alta.) 33 D2
La Rochelle, UP (Man.) 28 A3
La Rochelle, UP (Que.) 16 D2
Larocque, UP (Ont.) 26 E1
La Ronge, VL (Sask.) 32 E1
Larouche, UP (Que.) 14 A3
Larrimac, UP (Que.) 17 D3
Larrys River, UP (NS) 9 G2
L'Artifice, UP (Que.) 17 G2
LaRue Mills, UP (Ont.) 17 C4
La Salette, UP (Ont.) 22 F2
LaSalle, C (Que.) 17 G4
La Salle, UP (Ont.) 22 A3
La Salle, UP (Man.) 28 A2
LaSalle Park, UP (Ont.) 17 A4
La Sarre, T (Que.) 18 A1
Lascelles, UP (Que.) 17 C1
L'Ascension, UP (Que.) 14 A2
L'Ascension, UP (Que.) 18 E4
L'Ascension-de-Patapédia, UP (Que.) 13 B4
La Scie, T (Nfld.) 3 B1
Laseine, UP (Ont.) 27 B3
Lashburn, VL (Sask.) 32 A3
Laskay, UP (Ont.) 21 A2
La Société, UP (Que.) 14 F4
La Société, UP (Que.) 15 D3
Lasqueti, UP (BC) 38 D2
L'Assomption, T (Que.) 16 A3
Lasswade, UP (Ont.) 24 E3
La Station-du-Coteau, VL (Que.) 17 F2
Last Lake, UP (Alta.) 43 H3
Last Mountain, UP (Sask.) 31 G2
Last Mountain Lake 80A, IR (Sask.) 31 G2
La Tabatière, UP (Que.) 5 E2
Latchford, T (Ont.) 26 F3
Latchford Bridge, UP (Ont.) 24 F2
Laterrière, VL (Que.) 14 B3
Laterrière-Bassin, UP (Que.) 14 B3
Lathom, UP (Alta.) 34 G2
Latimer, UP (Ont.) 21 H1
Latour, UP (Que.) 14 F2
La Trappe, UP (Que.) 17 G1
Latta, UP (Ont.) 21 F1
Latties Brook, UP (NS) 9 B2
Lattkaloup 9, IR (BC) 41 E2
Latulipe, UP (Que.) 18 A2
La Tuque, T (Que.) 18 G2
Lauder, UP (Man.) 29 E4
Lauderbach, UP (Ont.) 23 C3
Launay-Station, UP (Que.) 18 B1
Launching Place, UP (PEI) 7 E4
Laura, UP (Sask.) 31 E1
Lauréat, UP (Que.) 18 D4
Laurel, UP (Ont.) 23 E3
Laurel, UP (Que.) 18 F4
Laurel-Station, UP (Que.) 18 F4
Laurence, UP (Que.) 18 G4
Laurenceton, UP (Nfld.) 3 C2
Laurentia Beach, UP (Man.) 29 H3
Laurentian View, UP (Ont.) 24 G1
Laurentides, T (Que.) 18 F4
Laurent-Val, UP (Que.) 19 F3
Lauretta, UP (PEI) 7 A2
Laurier, UP (Man.) 29 F2
Laurie River, UP (Man.) 30 A1
Laurier-Station, VL (Que.) 15 A3
Laurierville, VL (Que.) 15 A4
Laurin, UP (Ont.) 23 E1
Lauriston, UP (Ont.) 23 D2
Lauvergot, UP (NB) 12 F2
Lauzon, C (Que.) 15 G3
Laval, C (Que.) 17 G3
La Vallée, UP (Ont.) 28 H4
Lavallée, NUP (Ont.) 17 D1
Lavaltrie, VL (Que.) 16 A2
Lavaltrie-Station, UP (Que.) 16 A2
Lavant, UP (Ont.) 17 A2
Lavant Station, UP (Ont.) 17 A2
Lavender, UP (Ont.) 23 E2
Lavenham, UP (Man.) 29 G4
L'Avenir, VL (Que.) 16 C3
Laventure, UP (Sask.) 32 C3
Laverlochère, UP (Que.) 18 A2
La Vernière, UP (Que.) 7 F1
Lavery, NUP (Que.) 16 G2
Lavesta, UP (Alta.) 33 D4
La Vigie, UP (Que.) 13 G3
Lavigne, UP (Ont.) 25 G1
Lavillette, UP (NB) 12 F2
Lavinia, UP (Man.) 29 E3
La Visitation, UP (Que.) 16 B2
Lavoie, UP (Que.) 16 B1
Lavoie, UP (Que.) 14 H2
Lavoie, UP (Que.) 16 C3
Lavoy, VL (Alta.) 33 F3
Lawanth 5, IR (BC) 41 G4
Lawledge, UP (Man.) 30 D1
Lawn, T (Nfld.) 2 B4
Lawnhill, UP (BC) 41 B2
Lawrence-Colony, UP (Que.) 16 E4
Lawrence Pond, LID (Nfld.) 2 G3
Lawrence Station, UP (NB) 11 B2
Lawrence Station, UP (Ont.) 22 D2
Lawrencetown, UP (NS) 10 C1
Lawrencetown, UP (NS) 9 C4
Lawrenceville, VL (Que.) 16 C4
Lawson, VL (Sask.) 31 F2
Lawsonburg, UP (Alta.) 34 G2
Lawton, UP (Alta.) 33 D2
Layland, UP (Man.) 29 G4
Layton, UP (Ont.) 21 C1
Lazo < Comox, CFB/BFC, UP (BC) 38 C1
Leacross, UP (Sask.) 32 F4
Leadbury, UP (Ont.) 23 C4
Lead Cove, UP (Nfld.) 2 G1
Leader, T (Sask.) 31 C2
Leading Tickles East < Leading Tickles West (COMM), UP (Nfld.) 3 C2
Leading Tickles South < Leading Tickles West (COMM), UP (Nfld.) 3 C2
Leading Tickles West, COMM (Nfld.) 3 C2
Leading Tickles West < Leading Tickles West (COMM), UP (Nfld.) 3 C2
Leadville, UP (Que.) 16 C4
Leaf Rapids, UP (Man.) 30 B1
Leahurst, UP (Alta.) 33 E4
Leakville, UP (Sask.) 31 G3
Leaman, UP (Alta.) 33 C3
Leamington, T (Ont.) 22 B4
Leamington, UP (NS) 9 A1
Leanchoil, UP (BC) 34 C2
Lea Park, UP (Alta.) 33 G3
Leards Mill, UP (PEI) 7 D4
Learned-Plain, UP (Que.) 16 E3
Leask, VL (Sask.) 32 D4
Leaskdale, UP (Ont.) 21 B1
Leavitt, UP (Alta.) 34 F4
Lebahdo, UP (BC) 34 B4
Lebanon, UP (Ont.) 23 D3
Lebel-sur-Quévillon, T (Que.) 18 C1
LeBlanc, UP (NB) 7 A4
LeBlancville, UP (NB) 12 G4
Le Boom, UP (Que.) 18 H1
Lebret, VL (Sask.) 29 B2
Lebrun, UP (Que.) 16 B2
Le Calvaire, UP (Que.) 15 F4
Leclair, UP (Que.) 18 C4
Leclercville, VL (Que.) 16 D1
Le Coin, UP (Que.) 16 F3
Leddy, UP (Alta.) 43 H3
Le Domaine, UP (Que.) 18 C3
Leduc, T (Alta.) 33 E3
Leduc, UP (Que.) 16 A4
Ledwyn, UP (Man.) 29 H2
Leeburn, UP (Ont.) 26 B4
Leech, UP (NB) 12 G1
Lee Creek, UP (BC) 36 G4
Leedale, UP (Alta.) 33 D4
Leeds, UP (Ont.) 17 B3
Leeds-Village, UP (Que.) 15 A4
Lee River, UP (Man.) 30 C4
Lee's-Corner, UP (Que.) 17 F2
Lee Settlement, UP (NB) 11 C3
Lee Valley, UP (Ont.) 25 C1
Leeville, UP (Ont.) 26 F2
Lefaives Corners, UP (Ont.) 23 E1
Lefaivre, UP (Ont.) 17 E1
Lefebvre, UP (Que.) 16 C3
Lefroy, UP (Ont.) 21 A1
Legal, VL (Alta.) 33 D3
Legend, UP (Alta.) 34 H4
Légerville, UP (NB) 12 G4
Leggatt, UP (Ont.) 23 E3
Legge, UP (Ont.) 17 B4
Le Goulet, UP (NB) 12 G1
Le Grand-Sault, UP (Que.) 16 G2
Le Grand-Village, UP (Que.) 15 F4
Le Gravier, UP (Que.) 15 C3
Lehigh, UP (Alta.) 34 G2
Lehighs Corners, UP (Ont.) 17 C3
Leicester, UP (Alta.) 33 B1
Leifur, UP (Man.) 29 G2
Leighmore, UP (Alta.) 43 F4
Leinan, UP (Sask.) 31 D3
Leipzig, VL (Sask.) 31 D1
Leismer, UP (Alta.) 33 G1
Leitches Creek, UP (NS) 8 E3
Leith, UP (Ont.) 23 C1
Leitrim, UP (Ont.) 17 E4
Lejac < Seaspunkut 4, UP (BC) 40 A1
Lejeune, UP (Que.) 14 G4
Le Lac, UP (NB) 11 H1
Lelachen 6, IR (BC) 38 H1
Leland, UP (Ont.) 21 H1
Le Martinet, UP (Que.) 7 F1
Lemay, UP (Que.) 18 D4
Lemberg, T (Sask.) 29 C3
Lemesurier, UP (Que.) 15 B4
Lemieux, UP (Que.) 16 D2
Lemieux, UP (Ont.) 17 D1
Leminster, UP (NS) 9 A3
Lemon Creek, UP (BC) 34 B4
Lemoyne, T (Que.) 17 H4
Lemsford, UP (Sask.) 31 C2
Lena, UP (Man.) 29 F4
Lenarthur, UP (Alta.) 44 C4
Leney, UP (Sask.) 31 E1
Lennard, UP (Man.) 29 D2
Lennox, UP (NS) 8 D4
Lennox Island < Lennox Island 1, UP (PEI) 7 B3
Lennox Island 1, IR (PEI) 7 B3
Lennoxville, T (Que.) 16 D4
Lenore, UP (Man.) 29 E3
Lens, UP (Ont.) 21 G1
Lens, UP (Sask.) 32 G4
Lenswood, UP (Man.) 29 E1
Lenvale, UP (Sask.) 32 F4
Leo, UP (Alta.) 34 G1
Leo Creek, UP (BC) 42 H3
Leofnard, UP (Sask.) 32 D4
Leon 14, IR (BC) 40 A2
Leonard, UP (Ont.) 17 D1
Léonard-de-Matapédia, UP (Que.) 13 C4
Leonards Beach, UP (Ont.) 21 A1
Leonardville, UP (NB) 11 B3
Leon Creek 2, IR (BC) 36 C4
Leon Creek 2A, IR (BC) 36 C4
Leoville, UP (PEI) 7 A2
Leoville, VL (Sask.) 32 C3
Lepage, UP (Que.) 17 F3
Lepage, UP (Ont.) 20 C4
Le Petit-Canton, UP (Que.) 15 C3
Le Petit-Maine, UP (Que.) 15 D3
Le Petit-St-Jean, UP (Que.) 15 F4
Le Pied-des-Monts, UP (Que.) 15 C1
Lepine, UP (Sask.) 32 E4
L'Épiphanie, T (Que.) 16 A3
Le Pré, UP (Que.) 7 F1
Lepreau, UP (NB) 11 C3
Le Quatre-Chemins, UP (Que.) 15 F4
Lequille, UP (NS) 10 C1
Le Radar, UP (Que.) 15 B4
Le Rocher, UP (Que.) 15 B4
Leross, VL (Sask.) 29 B2
Leroy, T (Sask.) 31 G1
Lerwick, UP (NB) 12 A3
Léry, T (Que.) 17 G1
Lesage, UP (Que.) 18 F4
Le Sault, UP (Que.) 15 G4
Les Becquets, VL (Que.) 16 C1
Les Boules, UP (Que.) 13 A2
Les Caps, UP (Que.) 7 F1
Les Cèdres, VL (Que.) 17 G2
Les Cèdres-du-Liban, UP (Que.) 16 A2
Les Chenaux, UP (Que.) 15 C2
Les Côtes-du-Portage, UP (Que.) 13 E1
Les Dalles, UP (Que.) 16 A2
Les Délaissés, UP (Que.) 16 A1
Les Éboulements, UP (Que.) 15 D1
Les Éboulements-Centre, UP (Que.) 15 D1
Les Éboulements-Est, UP (Que.) 15 D1
Les Escoumins, UP (Que.) 14 E3
Les Étroits, UP (Que.) 15 F2
Les Étroits-Nord, UP (Que.) 15 F1
Les Fonds, UP (Que.) 15 E4
Les Hauteurs, UP (Que.) 18 F4
Les Hauteurs-de-Rimouski, UP (Que.) 14 H3
Les Hurons, UP (Que.) 16 A3
Les Îslets-Méchins, NUP (Que.) 13 C1
Leslie, UP (Que.) 7 G1
Leslie, VL (Sask.) 29 B1
Leslie Park, UP (Ont.) 17 D4
Leslieville, UP (Alta.) 33 D4
Les Méchins, UP (Que.) 13 C1
L'Espérance, UP (Que.) 15 D3
Les Prairies, UP (Que.) 15 C3
Les Prairies, UP (Que.) 15 C2
Les Quatre-Chemins, UP (Que.) 18 F4
Les Rapides, UP (NB) 15 G2
Les Sables, UP (Que.) 18 H1
Lessard, UP (Alta.) 33 G2
Less Crossing, UP (Man.) 28 A1
Lesterdale, UP (NS) 9 G2
Lestock, VL (Sask.) 31 H2
Letang, UP (Que.) 18 A3
Letang, UP (NB) 11 C3
L'Étape, UP (Que.) 15 B1
Letellier, UP (Man.) 28 A3
Letete, UP (NB) 11 C3
Lethbridge, C (Alta.) 34 F4
Lethbridge, UP (Nfld.) 3 F4
Le Tourniquet, UP (Que.) 14 A2
Letterbreen, UP (Ont.) 23 D3
Letterkenny, UP (Ont.) 24 F2
Letts Corners, UP (Ont.) 24 G1
Letty Harbour, UP (NWT) 45 D1
Leven, UP (Man.) 30 C1
Leverville, UP (NB) 11 B3
Levesque, UP (NB) 15 H1
Levesque Settlement, UP (NB) 12 A2
Leville, UP (NS) 10 E1
Levine, UP (Man.) 29 E3
Lévis, C (Que.) 15 G3
Levuka, UP (Sask.) 31 G3
Lewes, UP (PEI) 7 D4
Lewin's Cove, COMM (Nfld.) 2 C3
Lewis, UP (Man.) 28 C1
Lewis Bay West, UP (NS) 8 E4
Lewis Corners, UP (Ont.) 22 D2
Lewis Cove Road, UP (NS) 8 E4
Lewis Lake, UP (NS) 9 B3
Lewis Lake, UP (NS) 9 B3
Lewis Mountain, UP (NB) 11 F1
Lewis Mountain, UP (NS) 8 D3
Lewis Point, UP (PEI) 7 C4
Lewisporte, T (Nfld.) 3 C2
Lewistown, UP (NS) 10 B2
Lewvan, UP (Sask.) 31 H3
Lexau Ranch, UP (BC) 43 D3
Leyland, UP (Alta.) 33 A4
Lezbye 6, IR (BC) 37 D1
L'Hêtrière, UP (Que.) 15 F4
L'Hirondelle, UP (Alta.) 44 A4
Liard River, UP (BC) 45 C4
Liard River 3, IR (BC) 45 C4
Libau, UP (Man.) 30 C4
Libbytown, UP (Que.) 16 D4
Liberty, VL (Sask.) 31 G2
Licford, UP (NB) 12 A3
Lido Plage, UP (Man.) 29 H3
Lidstone, UP (Man.) 29 E1
Liebenthal, UP (Sask.) 31 C3
Lieury, UP (Ont.) 22 D1
Lifford, UP (Ont.) 21 C1
Lighthouse Area, NUP (Ont.) 22 B3
Lighthouse Point, UP (BC) 38 F3
Lightwoods, UP (Sask.) 32 F4
Likely, UP (BC) 40 D3
Lilac, UP (Sask.) 32 C4
Lillestrom, UP (Sask.) 31 F3
Lillesve, UP (Man.) 29 H2
Lillies, UP (Ont.) 17 C3
Lillooet, VL (BC) 37 H2
Lillooet 1, IR (BC) 37 H2
Lillooet 1A, IR (BC) 37 H2
Lily Bay, UP (Man.) 29 G2
Lilydale, UP (NS) 10 E2
Lilydale, UP (Sask.) 32 A4
Lilyfield, UP (Man.) 28 A1
Lily Lake, UP (Ont.) 25 C2
Lily Lake, UP (BC) 40 B2
Lily Oak, UP (Ont.) 23 D2
Lily Plain, UP (Sask.) 32 D3
Limberlost Lodge, UP (Ont.) 24 C2
Lime Hill, UP (NS) 8 D4
Limekiln, UP (NB) 12 C4
Lime Lake, UP (Ont.) 21 G1
Limerick, UP (NB) 12 B1
Limerick, UP (Ont.) 17 D2
Limerick, VL (Sask.) 31 F4
Limerock, UP (NS) 9 D2
Limestone, UP (NB) 12 A2
Limestone, UP (NB) 11 A1
L'Immaculée-Conception, UP (Que.) 13 B4
Limoges, UP (Ont.) 17 D1
Linacre, UP (Sask.) 31 C3
Linacy, UP (NS) 9 D2

Linaria, UP (Alta.) 33 D2
Lincoln, T (Ont.) 21 B3
Lincoln, UP (Alta.) 33 E2
Lincolnville, UP (NS) 8 C4
Lindale, UP (Alta.) 33 D3
Lindale Park Subdivision, NUP (Alta.) 33 E3
Lindbergh, UP (Alta.) 33 G3
Lindbrook, UP (Alta.) 33 E3
Lindell, UP (BC) 35 A4
Lindell Beach, UP (BC) 35 A4
Lindeman, UP (BC) 45 B4
Linden, UP (NS) 9 B1
Linden, UP (Man.) 28 A2
Linden, VL (Alta.) 34 F1
Linden Beach, UP (Ont.) 22 A4
Linden Valley, UP (Ont.) 21 C1
Lindenwood, UP (Ont.) 23 C1
Lindsay, T (Ont.) 21 C1
Lindsay Lake, UP (NS) 9 C3
Lindys, UP (NB) 11 F1
Lineboro, UP (Que.) 16 C4
Lingan, UP (NS) 8 F3
Lingan Road, UP (NS) 8 F3
Lingman Lake, UP (Ont.) 30 E2
Linière, VL (Que.) 16 G2
Linkletter, UP (PEI) 7 B3
Links Mills, UP (Ont.) 17 A4
Lintlaw, VL (Sask.) 29 C1
Linton, UP (Que.) 18 H3
Linton, UP (Ont.) 21 A2
Linton Corner, UP (NB) 12 B3
Linwood, UP (Ont.) 23 D4
Linwood, UP (NS) 8 C4
Lions Bay, VL (BC) 38 F2
Lion's Head, VL (Ont.) 23 C1
Lipton, VL (Sask.) 29 B2
Lisbon, UP (Ont.) 23 D4
Lisburn, UP (Alta.) 33 C3
Liscomb, UP (NS) 9 F3
Liscomb Mills, UP (NS) 9 E3
Lisgar-Station, UP (Que.) 16 C3
Lish-Leesh-Tum 17, IR (BC) 35 B1
Lisieux, UP (Sask.) 31 F4
Lisle, UP (Ont.) 23 E2
L'Islet, T (Que.) 15 C2
L'Islet-sur-Mer, VL (Que.) 15 C2
L'Isle-Verte, VL (Que.) 14 E4
Lismore, UP (NS) 8 A4
Lisson Settlement, UP (NB) 11 F2
Lister, UP (BC) 34 C4
Listerville, UP (NB) 12 A3
Listowel, T (Ont.) 23 C3
Litchfield, UP (NS) 10 B1
Little Anse, UP (NS) 8 D4
Little Barasway, UP (Nfld.) 2 E3
Little Bartibog, UP (NB) 12 F2
Little Bass River, UP (NS) 9 B2
Little Bay, COMM (Nfld.) 3 B1
Little Bay, UP (Nfld.) 2 A2
Little Bay East, UP (Nfld.) 2 D2
Little Bay Islands, COMM (Nfld.) 3 B1
Little Bay West, UP (Nfld.) 2 B2
Little Beach, UP (NB) 11 F2
Little Black Bear 84, IR (Sask.) 29 B2
Little Bona, UP (Nfld.) 2 D3
Little Branch, UP (NB) 12 F2
Little Bras d'Or, UP (NS) 8 E3
Little Bras d'Or South Side, UP (NS) 8 E3
Little Brehat, UP (Nfld.) 5 H2
Little Britain, UP (Ont.) 21 C1
Little Britain, UP (Man.) 28 A1
Little Brook, UP (NS) 10 A2
Little Brook Station, UP (NS) 10 A2
Little Brule, UP (Nfld.) 2 E2
Little Buffalo, UP (Sask.) 32 C3
Little Buffalo < Six Nations 40, UP (Ont.) 22 G1
Little Buffalo River, UP (NWT) 44 B1
Little Burnt Bay, T (Nfld.) 3 C2
Little Canada, UP (Ont.) 30 E4
Little Catalina, T (Nfld.) 3 G4
Little Chicago, UP (NWT) 45 C2
Little Current, T (Ont.) 25 C2
Little Dover, UP (NB) 11 G1
Little Dyke, UP (NS) 9 B2
Little Egypt, UP (Ont.) 23 B3
Little Egypt Road, UP (NS) 9 D1
Little Fishery, UP (Alta.) 44 B3
Little Forks, UP (NS) 9 A1
Little Fort, UP (BC) 36 F3
Little Gaspereau, UP (NB) 12 G1
Little Gem, UP (Alta.) 31 A1
Little Germany, UP (Ont.) 21 E1
Little Germany, UP (Ont.) 23 D2
Little Grand Rapids, UP (Man.) 30 D3
Little Grand Rapids 14, IR (Man.) 30 D3
Little Harbour, UP (NS) 8 A4
Little Harbour, UP (NS) 10 D4
Little Harbour, UP (Nfld.) 3 D1
Little Harbour, UP (PEI) 7 E3
Little Harbour, UP (NS) 8 E4
Little Harbour, UP (Nfld.) 5 F4
Little Harbour, UP (Nfld.) 2 D3
Little Harbour, UP (Nfld.) 3 D1
Little Harbour, NUP (NS) 9 D3
Little Harbour Deep, UP (Nfld.) 5 G3
Little Harbour East, UP (Nfld.) 2 F2
Little Harbour East, UP (Nfld.) 2 D2
Little Harbour Road, UP (NS) 9 D1
Little Hawk Lake, UP (Ont.) 24 D2
Little Heart's Ease, UP (Nfld.) 2 F1
Little Hills 158, IR (Sask.) 32 E1
Little Hills 158A, IR (Sask.) 32 E1
Little Hills 158B, IR (Sask.) 32 E1
Little Judique, UP (NS) 8 C3
Little Judique Ponds, UP (NS) 8 C3
Little Lake, UP (NB) 11 C2
Little Lake, UP (Ont.) 23 E4
Little Lake, NUP (Ont.) 21 A1
Little Lepreau, UP (NB) 11 C3
Little Liscomb, UP (NS) 9 F3
Little Longlac, UP (Ont.) 27 G2
Little Long Rapids, UP (Ont.) 20 C4
Little Lorraine, UP (NS) 8 F3
Little Mabou, UP (NS) 8 C3
Little Narrows, UP (NS) 8 D3
Little Paradise, UP (Nfld.) 2 D3
Little Pine and Lucky Man 116, IR (Sask.) 32 A4
Little Pond, UP (NS) 8 E3
Little Pond, UP (PEI) 7 E4
Little Port, UP (Nfld.) 4 C1
Little Port L'Hebert, UP (NS) 10 D3
Little Pumbly Cove, UP (Nfld.) 5 G4
Little Rapids, UP (Nfld.) 4 D1
Little Rapids, UP (Ont.) 26 B4
Little Red River, UP (Alta.) 44 B3
Little Red River 106C, IR (Sask.) 32 D3
Little Red River 106D, IR (Sask.) 32 D3
Little Ridge, UP (NB) 11 G2
Little Ridge < Sandy Bay 5, UP (Man.) 29 G3
Little River, UP (NS) 10 A2
Little River, UP (NS) 9 A1
Little River, UP (NB) 11 G1
Little River, UP (NS) 8 E2
Little River, UP (BC) 38 C1
Little River, UP (YT) 45 B3
Little River Harbour, UP (NS) 10 A4
Little St Lawrence, UP (Nfld.) 2 C4
Little Salmon, UP (YT) 45 B3
Little Sands, UP (PEI) 7 D4
Little Saskatchewan 48, IR (Man.) 29 G1
Little Saskatchewan 48B, IR (Man.) 29 G1
Little Seldom < Seldom – Little Seldom, UP (Nfld.) 3 E1
Little Shemogue, UP (NB) 7 B4
Little Shippegan, UP (NB) 13 G4
Little Smoky, UP (Alta.) 33 A2
Little Smoky, UP (Alta.) 33 B1
Little Springs 8, IR (BC) 36 B2
Little Springs 18, IR (BC) 36 B2
Little Tancook, UP (NS) 9 A4
Little Teslin Lake, UP (YT) 45 B3
Little Tracadie, UP (NB) 12 G1
Littlewood, UP (Ont.) 22 E2
Little Woody, UP (Sask.) 31 F4
Livelong, UP (Sask.) 32 B3
Liverpool, T (NS) 10 D3
Living Springs, UP (Ont.) 23 E3
Livingstone, UP (YT) 45 B3
Livingstone Cove, UP (NS) 8 B4
Livingstone Creek, UP (Ont.) 26 B4
Lizard Lake, UP (Sask.) 31 D1
Lizard Point 62, IR (Man.) 29 E3
Lloy, UP (NS) 9 C4
Lloyd, UP (Ont.) 17 B2
Lloydminster (p), C (Alta.) 33 H3
Lloydminster (p), C (Sask.) 33 H3
Lloyds Hill, UP (Alta.) 31 B1
Lloydtown, UP (Ont.) 21 A2
L'Oasis, UP (Que.) 18 H3
Lobo, UP (Ont.) 22 D1
Lobster Cove < Rocky Harbour (COMM), UP (Nfld.) 5 F4
Lobster Harbour, UP (Nfld.) 3 D1
Lobstick, UP (Alta.) 33 C3
Lochaber, UP (NS) 9 E2
Lochaber, UP (Que.) 17 D1
Lochaber Mines, UP (NS) 9 E3
Lochalsh, UP (Ont.) 26 B2
Lochalsh, UP (Ont.) 23 B3
Loch Broom, UP (NS) 9 D1
Lochearn, UP (Alta.) 33 C4
Lochiel, UP (Ont.) 17 E1
Lochinvar, UP (Ont.) 17 E1
Lochinvar, UP (Alta.) 33 D4
Loch Katrine, UP (NS) 9 F2
Lochlin, UP (Ont.) 23 H1
Loch Lomond, UP (NS) 8 E4
Loch Lomond, UP (NB) 11 E3
Loch Lomond West, UP (NS) 8 E4
Lochside, UP (NS) 8 E4
Lochside, UP (NS) 8 D4
Lochview Road, UP (NS) 9 B3
Lochwinnoch, UP (Ont.) 17 A1
Lockeport, T (NS) 10 C4
Lockeport, UP (BC) 41 B2
Lockeport Station, UP (NS) 10 D4
Lockerby, UP (Ont.) 23 C2
Locke Road, UP (PEI) 7 A3
Lockhart, UP (Alta.) 33 D4
Lockharts Mill, UP (NB) 12 A3
Lockhartville, UP (NS) 9 A3
Lockleven, UP (Nfld.) 4 B3
Lockport, UP (Man.) 28 A1
Lock's Cove, UP (Nfld.) 5 H2
Locks Cove, UP (Nfld.) 4 G4
Locks Harbour, UP (Nfld.) 3 B2
Locksley, UP (Ont.) 24 G1
Lockstead, UP (NB) 12 E3
Lockston, UP (Nfld.) 3 G4
Lockwood, VL (Sask.) 31 G1
Lodge, UP (Nfld.) 5 H1
Lodgepole, UP (Alta.) 33 C4
Lodgeroom Corners, UP (Ont.) 24 F4
Lodi UP (Ont.) 17 E2
Logan Lake, VL (BC) 35 C1
Logan's 6, IR (BC) 35 D2
Loganville, UP (NS) 9 C1
Loggiecroft, UP (NB) 12 G3
Loggie Lodge, UP (NB) 12 C2
Loggieville, VL (NB) 12 F2
Log Valley, UP (Sask.) 31 E3
Logy Bay, UP (Nfld.) 2 H2
Lohbiee 3, IR (BC) 37 E1
Lokla 4, IR (BC) 37 G3
Lombardy, UP (Ont.) 17 B3
Lombell, UP (Alta.) 33 C2
Lomond, UP (Nfld.) 5 F4
Lomond, VL (Alta.) 34 G3
Loncesborough, UP (Ont.) 23 B3
Loncon, C (Ont.) 22 E2
Loncondery, UP (NS) 9 B2
Loncondery, UP (NB) 11 F2
Loncondery Station, UP (NS) 9 B2
Loncon Settlement, UP (NB) 11 D2
Lone Butte, UP (BC) 36 D3
Lonebutte, UP (Alta.) 34 G2
Lonely Lake, UP (Man.) 29 G2
Lone Pine, UP (Alta.) 33 C2
Lone Prairie, UP (BC) 43 E4
Lone Rock, UP (Sask.) 32 A4
Lonesand, UP (Man.) 28 C3
Lonesome Butte, UP (Sask.) 31 F4
Lonesome Cove, UP (Nfld.) 5 G2
Lone Spruce, UP (Man.) 29 G3
Lone Spruce, UP (Sask.) 29 C1
Long Bay, UP (Ont.) 25 B2
Longbeach, UP (BC) 34 B4
Long Beach, UP (Ont.) 21 B4
Long Beach, UP (Nfld.) 2 F1
Long Beach, UP (Nfld.) 2 G1
Long Beach, UP (NS) 8 F3
Long Beach, UP (Nfld.) 2 G4
Long Beach, UP (Nfld.) 3 F4
Long Beach, UP (Ont.) 21 C1
Longbow Lake, UP (Ont.) 28 F2
Long Cove < Norman's Cove – Long Cove, UP (Nfld.) 2 F2
Long Creek, UP (PEI) 7 C4
Long Creek, UP (NB) 11 E1
Longford, UP (Ont.) 23 G1
Long Harbour < Long Harbour – Mount Arlington Heights, UP (Nfld.) 2 F3
Long Harbour – Mount Arlington Heights, LID (Nfld.) 2 F3
Long Hill, UP (NS) 8 E3
Longhope, UP (Sask.) 32 B3
Long Island Main, UP (NS) 8 E3
Longlac, UP (Ont.) 27 G1
Long Lake, UP (Ont.) 17 A3
Long Lake, UP (Man.) 30 D4
Long Lake 58, IR (Ont.) 27 G1
Long Lake 77, IR (Ont.) 27 G1
Long Neck Island 9, IR (BC) 38 E4
Long Plain 6, IR (Man.) 29 G4
Long Point, UP (Ont.) 22 G2
Long Point, UP (NS) 8 C4
Long Point, UP (NB) 11 E2
Long Point, UP (Nfld.) 4 B1
Long Point, UP (Ont.) 17 B3
Long Point, UP (Ont.) 23 H2
Long Reach, UP (NB) 11 D2
Long River, UP (PEI) 7 C3
Long Sault, UP (Ont.) 17 E2
Longs Creek, UP (NB) 11 C1
Long Settlement, UP (NB) 12 A4
Long Spruce, UP (Man.) 30 D1
Longtinville, UP (Ont.) 17 D2
Long Tunnel 5, IR (BC) 35 B3
Long Tunnel 5A, IR (BC) 35 B3
Longue-Pointe-de-Mingan, UP (Que.) 19 H3
Longueuil, C (Que.) 17 H4
Longview, UP (BC) 38 E1
Longview, VL (Alta.) 34 E3
Longwood, UP (Ont.) 22 D2
Longworth, UP (BC) 40 D2
Loni Beach, UP (Man.) 30 C4
Lonira, UP (Alta.) 33 C2
Lonsdale, UP (Ont.) 21 G1
Looma, UP (Alta.) 33 E3
Loomis, UP (Sask.) 31 D4
Loon, UP (Ont.) 27 E3
Loon Bay, UP (Nfld.) 3 D2
Loon Lake, UP (Alta.) 44 A4
Loon Lake, UP (BC) 36 D4
Loon Lake, VL (Sask.) 32 A2
Loon Lake 4, IR (BC) 36 D4
Loon Lake 10, IR (BC) 36 B2
Loon River, UP (Sask.) 32 B2
Loon Straits, UP (Man.) 30 C4
Loos, UP (BC) 40 E2
Lorado, UP (Sask.) 44 D2
Loran, UP (Nfld.) 5 H1
Loranger, UP (Que.) 18 E4
Lord's Cove, COMM (Nfld.) 2 B4
Lords Cove, UP (NB) 11 B3
Lords Mills, UP (Ont.) 17 C3
Lordsvale, UP (Que.) 17 C1
Loreburn, UP (Nfld.) 2 F1
Loreburn, VL (Sask.) 31 F2
Loree, UP (Ont.) 23 E2
Lorenzo, UP (Sask.) 32 C4
Lorette, UP (Man.) 28 A2
Lorette 7, IR (Que.) 15 F3
Lorette 7A, IR (Que.) 15 F3
Loretteville, C (Que.) 15 F3
Loretto, UP (Ont.) 21 A1
Loretto < Cape St George – Petit Jardin – Grand Jardin – De Grau – Marches Point – Loretto, UP (Nfld.) 4 A2
Lories < Point May (COMM), UP (Nfld.) 2 B4
L'Orignal, VL (Ont.) 17 E1
Lorimer Lake, UP (Ont.) 24 A1
Loring, UP (Ont.) 24 A1
Lorin Meadow 9, IR (BC) 40 C3
Lorlie, UP (Sask.) 29 B2
Lorne, UP (NB) 13 D4
Lorne, UP (NS) 9 D2
Lorne, UP (Ont.) 17 E1
Lorne, UP (Ont.) 23 B2
Lorne, UP (Ont.) 25 D1
Lorne Beach, UP (Ont.) 23 B2
Lornevale, UP (NS) 9 B2
Lorne Valley, UP (PEI) 7 D4
Lorneville, UP (NS) 7 B4
Lorneville, UP (Ont.) 21 C1
Lorrain, UP (Ont.) 26 F3
Lorraine, T (Que.) 17 G3
Lorrain Valley, UP (Ont.) 26 F3
Lorrainville, VL (Que.) 18 A3
Losier Settlement, UP (NB) 12 G1
Lost Channel, UP (Ont.) 21 F1
Lost Channel, UP (Ont.) 25 F2
Lost Nation, UP (Ont.) 24 F2
Lost-River, UP (Que.) 18 F4
Lost River, UP (Sask.) 32 F3
Lotbinière, VL (Que.) 16 D1
Lothian, UP (Ont.) 23 B3
Lothrop, UP (Alta.) 43 G3
Lots-Renversés, UP (Que.) 15 G1
Lotus, UP (Ont.) 21 C1
Loughborough 3, IR (BC) 37 A3
Loughbreeze, UP (Ont.) 21 E2
Lougheed, VL (Alta.) 33 F4
Louisa, UP (Que.) 18 F4
Louisa-Beach, UP (Que.) 18 F4
Louisbourg, T (NS) 8 F3
Louisbourg Road, UP (NS) 8 F3
Louis Bull 138B, IR (Alta.) 33 E4
Louis Creek, UP (BC) 36 F3
Louis Creek 4, IR (BC) 36 F4
Louisdale, UP (NS) 8 D4
Louise, UP (Ont.) 23 C2
Louiseville, T (Que.) 16 B2
Louis Head, UP (NS) 10 D4
Louis Squinas Ranch 14, IR (BC) 40 A3
Louisville, UP (NS) 9 C1
Louisville, UP (Ont.) 22 C3
Lourdes, COMM (Nfld.) 4 B2
Lourdes, UP (Que.) 16 A2
Lourdes, UP (Que.) 16 D1
Lourdes-de-Blanc-Sablon, UP (Que.) 5 G2
Lousana, UP (Alta.) 34 F1
Louvicourt, UP (Que.) 18 C2
Lovat, UP (NS) 9 D2
Lovat, UP (Ont.) 23 C2
Love, VL (Sask.) 32 F3
Lovering, UP (Ont.) 23 F1
Loverna, VL (Sask.) 31 B1
Lovett, UP (Ont.) 21 F2
Lovettville, UP (Alta.) 33 B4
Low, UP (Que.) 18 D4
Low Bush River, UP (Ont.) 26 F1
Lowe Farm, UP (Man.) 29 H4
Lower Anfield, UP (NB) 12 A2
Lower Argyle, UP (NS) 10 B4
Lower Barnaby, UP (NB) 12 E3
Lower Barneys River, UP (NS) 8 A4
Lower Bedeque, UP (PEI) 7 B3
Lower Bella Coola, NUP (BC) 41 G3
Lower Blomidon, UP (NS) 11 H3
Lower Bloomfield, UP (NB) 12 A4
Lower Branch, UP (NS) 10 E2
Lower Brighton, UP (NB) 12 A4
Lower Burlington, UP (NS) 9 A3
Lower Burton, UP (NB) 11 D1
Lower Caledonia, UP (NS) 9 E2
Lower California, UP (NB) 12 A3
Lower Cambridge, UP (NB) 11 D2
Lower Canard, UP (NS) 11 H3
Lower Cape, UP (NB) 11 G1
Lower Caverhill, UP (NB) 11 B1
Lower Chatham Head, UP (NB) 12 F2
Lower Clarks Harbour, UP (NS) 10 B4
Lower Concession, UP (NS) 10 A2
Lower Cove, UP (Nfld.) 4 B2
Lower Cove, UP (NS) 11 H2
Lower Cove, UP (NB) 11 E2
Lower Coverdale, UP (NB) 11 G1
Lower Dacre, UP (Ont.) 24 G2
Lower Darnley, UP (PEI) 7 B3
Lower Debert, UP (NS) 9 B2
Lower Derby, UP (NB) 12 E2
Lower Durham, UP (NB) 11 C1
Lower East Chezzetcook, UP (NS) 9 C4
Lower East Pubnico, UP (NS) 10 B4
Lower Economy, UP (NS) 9 A2
Lower Eel Brook, UP (NS) 10 B3
Lower Fishpot Lake 24A, IR (BC) 40 B3
Lower Five Islands, UP (NS) 9 A2
Lower-Flodden, NUP (Que.) 16 C3
Lower Freetown, UP (PEI) 7 B3
Lower Glencoe, UP (NS) 9 F2
Lower Grant Road, UP (NS) 10 E2
Lower Greenfield, UP (NB) 12 A3
Lower Greenville, UP (NS) 9 B1
Lower Gulf Shore, UP (NS) 9 B1
Lower Hainesville, UP (NB) 11 B1
Lower Hamilton, UP (PEI) 7 B3
Lower Harmony, UP (NS) 9 C2
Lower Hat Creek 2, IR (BC) 36 C4
Lower Hillsdale, UP (NS) 8 C4
Lower Holleford, UP (Ont.) 17 A3
Lower Island Cove, UP (Nfld.) 2 H1
Lower Jemseg, UP (NB) 11 D2
Lower Jordan Bay, UP (NS) 10 C4
Lower Kars, UP (NB) 11 E2
Lower Kingston, UP (NB) 11 E2
Lower Kintore, UP (NB) 12 A3
Lower Kootenay 1A, IR (BC) 34 C4
Lower Kootenay 1B, IR (BC) 34 C4
Lower Kootenay 1C, IR (BC) 34 C4
Lower Kootenay 2, IR (BC) 34 C4
Lower Kootenay 3, IR (BC) 34 C4
Lower Kootenay 4, IR (BC) 34 C4
Lower Kootenay 5, IR (BC) 34 C4
Lower Laberge, UP (YT) 45 B3
Lower LaHave, UP (NS) 10 E2
Lower Lance Cove, UP (Nfld.) 2 F1
Lower Langside, UP (Ont.) 23 B3
Lower L'Ardoise, UP (NS) 8 D4
Lower Lincoln, UP (NB) 11 C1
Lower Line Queensbury, UP (NB) 11 C1
Lower Little Ridge, UP (NB) 11 A3
Lower Maccan, UP (NS) 11 H2
Lower Main River, UP (NB) 12 G3
Lower Malpeque, UP (PEI) 7 B3
Lower Meaghers Grant, UP (NS) 9 C3
Lower Melbourne, UP (NS) 10 A3
Lower Middle River, UP (NS) 8 D3
Lower Millstream, UP (NB) 11 E2
Lower Montague, UP (PEI) 7 E4
Lower Mount Thom, UP (NS) 9 D2
Lower Mount William, NUP (NS) 9 D2
Lower Napan, UP (NB) 12 F2
Lower New Annan, UP (PEI) 7 B3
Lower Newcastle, UP (NB) 12 F2
Lower New Cornwall, UP (NS) 10 E2
Lower Newtown, UP (PEI) 7 D4
Lower Nicola, UP (BC) 35 C2
Lower Nine Mile River, UP (NS) 9 B3
Lower Northampton, UP (NB) 11 A1
Lower North Branch, UP (NS) 10 E2
Lower North Grant, UP (NS) 8 B4
Lower Ohio, UP (NS) 10 C3
Lower Onslow, UP (NS) 9 C2
Lower Perth, UP (NB) 12 A3
Lower Pleasant Valley, UP (NS) 9 C2
Lower Portage, UP (NB) 12 A2
Lower Post, UP (BC) 45 C4
Lower Prince William, UP (NB) 11 B1
Lower Prospect, UP (NS) 9 B4
Lower Queensbury, UP (NB) 11 B1
Lower Ridge, UP (NB) 11 F1
Lower River Hébert, UP (NS) 11 H2
Lower River Inhabitants, UP (NS) 8 C4
Lower Rockport, UP (NB) 11 H2
Lower Rollo Bay, UP (PEI) 7 E3
Lower Rose Bay, UP (NS) 10 E2
Lower Royalton, UP (NB) 12 A3
Lower Sackville, UP (NS) 9 B3
Lower St-Charles, UP (NB) 12 G3
Lower St Esprit, UP (NS) 8 E4
Lower St Marys, UP (NB) 11 C1
Lower Sandy Point, UP (NS) 10 C4
Lower Saulnierville, UP (NS) 10 A2
Lower Selma, UP (NS) 9 B2
Lower Shag Harbour, UP (NS) 10 B4
Lower Shawniken 4A, IR (BC) 35 B1
Lower Shinimicas, UP (NS) 7 B4
Lower Ship Harbour, UP (NS) 9 D3
Lower Similkameen 2, IR (BC) 35 E4
Lower South River, UP (NS) 8 B4
Lower Springfield, UP (NS) 8 B4
Lower Stafford, UP (Ont.) 24 G1
Lower Stoneridge, UP (NB) 11 C1
Lower Three Fathom Harbour, UP (NS) 9 C4
Lower Tower Hill, UP (NB) 11 B3
Lower Truro, UP (NS) 9 C2
Lower Tryon, UP (PEI) 7 C4
Lower Turtle Creek, UP (NB) 11 G1
Lower Vaughan, UP (NS) 9 A3
Lower Wakefield, UP (NB) 12 A4
Lower Washabuck, UP (NS) 8 D3
Lower Waterville, UP (NB) 12 A4
Lower Wedgeport, UP (NS) 10 B4
Lower Wentworth, UP (NS) 9 B1
Lower West Jeddore, UP (NS) 9 C4
Lower West Pubnico, UP (NS) 10 B4
Lower West River, UP (NS) 8 B4
Lower Whitehead, UP (NS) 9 G2
Lower Windsor, UP (NB) 12 B4
Lower Wingham, UP (Ont.) 23 B3
Lower Wolfville, UP (NS) 11 H3
Lower Woods Harbour, UP (NS) 10 B4
Lower Woodstock, UP (NB) 11 A1
Lower Zeballos, UP (BC) 39 E3
Lowland, UP (Man.) 28 B1
Low Landing, UP (NS) 10 C2
Low Point, UP (Nfld.) 2 H1
Low Point, UP (NS) 8 C4
Low Point, UP (PEI) 7 B3
Lowther, UP (Ont.) 20 C4
Lowther, UP (Ont.) 28 E2
Lowther, UP (CFS/SFC, MIL (Ont.) 20 C4
Loyal, UP (Ont.) 23 B3
Loyalist, UP (PEI) 7 C4
Loyalist, UP (Alta.) 31 B1
Lubicon Lake, UP (Alta.) 44 A4
Lucan, VL (Ont.) 22 D1
Lucasville, UP (NS) 9 B3
Lucasville, UP (Ont.) 22 B2
Lucerne, UP (Que.) 40 G3
Luceville, VL (Que.) 14 G2
Lucille, UP (Ont.) 23 E3
Lucknow, VL (Ont.) 23 B3
Lucky Lake, VL (Sask.) 31 E2
Lucyville, UP (Nfld.) 6 G3
Ludgate, UP (Ont.) 25 F2
Ludlow, UP (NB) 12 D3
Lueck Mill, UP (Ont.) 23 C2
Lugar, UP (NB) 12 E1
Luke, UP (Man.) 30 D1
Lukerville, UP (Ont.) 22 A3
Luke's Arm < Cottle's Island – Luke's Arm, UP (Nfld.) 3 D2
Lukseetsissum 9, IR (BC) 35 A4
Lulu 5, IR (BC) 35 D4
Lumberton, UP (BC) 34 C4
Lumby, VL (BC) 35 G2
Lumina, UP (Ont.) 24 C2
Lumley, UP (Ont.) 22 D1
Lumsden, T (Sask.) 31 G3
Lumsden, T (Nfld.) 3 F2
Lumsden Beach, SV (Sask.) 31 G2
Lumsden Dam, UP (NS) 10 E1
Lumsden Road, UP (NB) 12 E2
Lund, UP (BC) 37 C4
Lundar, UP (Man.) 29 G3
Lundar Beach, UP (Man.) 29 G2
Lundbreck, UP (Alta.) 34 E4
Lundy, UP (NS) 9 G2
Lundys Corners, UP (Ont.) 17 A1
Lunenburg, T (NS) 10 E2
Lunenburg, UP (Ont.) 17 E2
Lunge Lodge, UP (Ont.) 25 G1
Lunnford, UP (Alta.) 33 D2
Lure, UP (Alta.) 34 G1
Lurgan, UP (Sask.) 32 F4
Lurgan Beach, UP (Ont.) 23 B3
Luscar, UP (Alta.) 33 A4
Luschers Trailer Court, NUP (BC) 34 B4
Luseland, T (Sask.) 31 C1
Lushes Bight < Lushes Bight – Beaumont – Beaumont North, UP (Nfld.) 3 B1
Lushes Bight – Beaumont – Beaumont North, COMM (Nfld.) 3 B1
Luskville, UP (Que.) 17 B1
Lussier, UP (Que.) 18 F4
Lust Subdivision, UP (BC) 40 C3
Luton, UP (Ont.) 22 E1
Lutose, UP (Alta.) 44 A2
Lutterworth, UP (Ont.) 24 C3
Luxton, UP (BC) 38 E4
Luzan, UP (Alta.) 33 F3
Lyacksun 3, IR (BC) 38 E2
Lyalta, UP (Alta.) 34 F2
Lydgate, UP (NS) 10 C4
Lydiatt, UP (Man.) 28 B1
Lyleton, UP (Man.) 29 D4
Lymburn, UP (Alta.) 43 F4
Lyn, UP (Ont.) 17 C3
Lynch Corner, UP (NB) 11 D2
Lynche River, UP (NS) 8 D4
Lyndale, UP (PEI) 7 D4
Lyndale, NUP (Ont.) 22 E2
Lynden, UP (Ont.) 22 G1
Lyndhurst, UP (Ont.) 17 B3
Lyndon, UP (Alta.) 34 E3
Lynedoch, UP (Ont.) 22 F2
Lynhurst, NUP (Ont.) 22 E2
Lynn, UP (NS) 9 A2
Lynn Acres Mobile Home Park, NUP (BC) 35 E4
Lynnfield, UP (NB) 11 B2
Lynn Lake, UP (Man.) 30 A1
Lynnville, UP (Ont.) 22 G2
Lynwood, NUP (Ont.) 22 C3
Lynwood Village, UP (Ont.) 17 D4
Lyons, UP (Ont.) 22 E2
Lyons Brook, UP (NS) 9 D1
Lyonshall, UP (Man.) 29 F4
Lyster, VL (Que.) 15 A4
Lyttleton, UP (NB) 12 E2
Lytton, UP (Que.) 18 D3
Lytton, VL (BC) 35 B2
Lytton 3A, IR (BC) 35 A1
Lytton 4A, IR (BC) 35 A1
Lytton 4B, IR (BC) 35 A1
Lytton 4C, IR (BC) 35 A1
Lytton 4D, IR (BC) 35 A1
Lytton 4E, IR (BC) 35 A1
Lytton 4F, IR (BC) 35 A1
Lytton 5A, IR (BC) 35 A1
Lytton 6B, IR (BC) 35 A1
Lytton 9B, IR (BC) 35 A2
Lytton 13A, IR (BC) 35 A1
Lytton 21A, IR (BC) 35 B2
Lytton 26A, IR (BC) 35 B2
Lytton 27B, IR (BC) 35 B2
Lytton 31, IR (BC) 35 B2
Lytton 32, IR (BC) 35 A1
Lytton 33, IR (BC) 35 A1

M

Maahpe 4, IR (BC) 39 F4
Mabee's Corners, UP (Ont.) 22 F2
Mabel Lake, UP (BC) 35 G1
Maberly, UP (Ont.) 17 A3
Mabou, UP (NS) 8 C3
Mabou Harbour, UP (NS) 8 C3
Mabou Harbour Mouth, UP (NS) 8 C3
Mabou Mines, UP (NS) 8 C3
Mabou Station, UP (NS) 8 C3
Macabee, UP (NB) 13 C4
Macalister, UP (BC) 40 C3
Macamic, T (Que.) 18 A1
MacAulays Hill, UP (NS) 8 E3
MacBains Corner, UP (NS) 9 C1
Maccan, UP (NS) 11 H2
MacCormicks Corner, UP (NS) 8 C3
Macdiarmid, UP (Ont.) 27 F2
Macdonald, UP (Man.) 29 G3
MacDonald Bay, UP (Ont.) 24 E3
MacDonald Beach, UP (Ont.) 23 G1
MacDonalds Glen, UP (NS) 8 C3
MacDonalds Grove, UP (Ont.) 17 E2
MacDonalds Point, UP (NB) 11 D2
MacDougall, UP (NB) 12 G4
MacDougall, UP (PEI) 7 B3
Macdowall, UP (Sask.) 32 D4
Macduff, UP (Ont.) 26 B1
Maces Bay, UP (NB) 11 C3
Maceys Bay, UP (Ont.) 23 F1
MacGillivrays Bridge, UP (Ont.) 17 E2
MacGregor, VL (Man.) 29 G3
MacGregor's Bay Area, NUP (Ont.) 24 G1
Machta 16, IR (BC) 39 D3
MacIntosh Mill, UP (NB) 12 B3
MacIntyre Lake, UP (NS) 8 C4
MacKay, UP (Alta.) 33 C3
MacKays Corner, UP (NS) 9 D1
Mackdale, UP (NS) 8 C4
Mackenzie, DM (BC) 43 C4
Mackenzie, UP (Ont.) 27 E3
Mackenziel District of/de, DIST (NWT) 1
Mackey, UP (Ont.) 18 B4
Mackies, UP (Ont.) 27 D3
MacKinnons Brook, UP (NS) 8 C3
Macklin, T (Sask.) 31 B1
Macksville, UP (Ont.) 22 D2
Macksville, UP (Ont.) 22 D2
MacLarens Landing, UP (Ont.) 17 B1
MacLean Park, UP (Ont.) 17 A4
MacLean Settlement, UP (NB) 11 C1
MacLennan, UP (Ont.) 26 B4
MacLeod, UP (Ont.) 27 G2
MacLeod Settlement, UP (NS) 8 C3
MacLeods Point, UP (NS) 8 E3
MacNeils Vale, UP (NS) 8 D3
MacNutt, VL (Sask.) 29 D2
Macoah 1, IR (BC) 38 B3
Macoun, VL (Sask.) 29 B4
Macpès, UP (Que.) 14 G3
MacPhees Corner, UP (NS) 9 B3
MacPherson Lake, UP (NS) 9 G2
Macrorie, VL (Sask.) 31 E2
Macson, UP (Alta.) 31 B3
Mactaquac, UP (NB) 11 C1
Mactaquac Heights, NUP (NB) 11 C1
MacTier, UP (Ont.) 24 A2
Macton, UP (Ont.) 23 D4
Macworth, UP (Sask.) 31 F4
Madawaska, UP (Ont.) 24 E2
Madden, UP (Alta.) 34 E2
Maddington-Falls, UP (Que.) 16 C2
Maddox Cove < Petty Harbour – Maddox Cove, UP (Nfld.) 2 H2
Madeira Park, UP (BC) 38 D1
Madeleine-Centre, UP (Que.) 13 F1
Maders Cove, UP (NS) 10 E2
Madison, VL (Sask.) 31 C2
Madoc, VL (Ont.) 24 F4
Madoc Junction, UP (Ont.) 21 F1
Madran, UP (NB) 13 E4
Madrid, UP (Sask.) 31 G3
Madsen, UP (Ont.) 30 D4
Maecks Subdivision, UP (Ont.) 24 B1
Mafeking, UP (Man.) 30 A3
Mafeking, UP (Ont.) 23 B3
Magaguadavic, UP (NB) 11 B2
Maganktoon 56, IR (BC) 42 D4
Magenta, UP (Que.) 16 B4
Magna Bay, UP (BC) 36 H4
Magnet, UP (Man.) 29 F2
Magnetawan, VL (Ont.) 24 B1
Magnetawan 1, IR (Ont.) 25 F2
Magnolia, UP (Alta.) 33 C3
Magnolia Bridge, UP (Alta.) 33 C3
Magog, C (Que.) 16 C4
Magoon-Point, UP (Que.) 16 C4
Magpie, UP (Que.) 19 G3
Magpie, UP (Ont.) 26 A2
Magpie Mine, UP (Ont.) 26 A2
Magrath, T (Alta.) 34 F4
Ma-guala 6, IR (BC) 38 E2
Magundy, UP (NB) 11 B1
Maguse River, UP (NWT) 46 B3
Magwekstala 10, IR (BC) 41 G4
Magyar, UP (Sask.) 31 H2
Maharg, UP (BC) 36 D4
Mahaska, UP (Alta.) 33 B3
Mahatta River, UP (BC) 39 C1
Mahers, UP (Nfld.) 2 G3
Mahmalillikullah 1, IR (BC) 39 E1
Mahone Bay, T (NS) 10 E2
Mahoneys Beach, UP (NS) 8 B4
Mahoneys Corner, UP (NS) 9 B1
Mahood Falls, UP (BC) 36 E2
Mahope 3, IR (BC) 39 C2
Mahpahkum 12, IR (BC) 39 D1
Mah-te-nicht 8, IR (BC) 39 C1
Maiangowi Settlement < Wikwemikong Unceded 26, UP (Ont.) 25 C2
Maidens, UP (Ont.) 26 G3
Maidstone, T (Sask.) 32 A4
Maidstone, UP (Ont.) 22 A3
Maidstone, UP (Nfld.) 4 B3
Mailhot, UP (Que.) 15 A4
Maillard, UP (Que.) 15 C2
Main-à-Dieu, UP (NS) 8 F3
Main Brook, T (Nfld.) 5 H2
Main Centre, UP (Sask.) 31 E3
Mainland, UP (Nfld.) 4 A2
Main Point, UP (Nfld.) 3 D2
Mainstream, UP (NB) 12 B4
Mainsville, UP (Ont.) 17 D3
Mair, UP (Sask.) 29 D4
Mair Mills, UP (Ont.) 23 E2
Maisonnette, UP (NB) 13 G4
Maison-St-Bernard, UP (Que.) 15 C3
Maitland, UP (Ont.) 17 C3
Maitland, UP (NS) 10 E2
Maitland, UP (NS) 9 B2
Maitland Bridge, UP (NS) 10 C2
Maitland Forks, UP (NS) 10 E2
Majestic, UP (Alta.) 31 B2
Major, VL (Sask.) 31 C1
Majorville, UP (Alta.) 34 F3
Maka 8, IR (BC) 35 B2
Makaoo 120 (p), IR (Sask.) 33 H3
Makaoo 120 (p), IR (Alta.) 33 H3
Makaroff, UP (Man.) 29 D2
Makepeace, UP (Alta.) 34 G2
Makinak, UP (Man.) 29 F2
Makinson, UP (BC) 34 A3
Makinsons, UP (Nfld.) 2 G2
Makkovik, COMM (Nfld.) 6 F2
Maklaksadagmaks 41, IR (BC) 42 C4
Maklaksadagmaks 42, IR (BC) 42 C4
Makwa, VL (Sask.) 32 B2
Makwa Lake 129, IR (Sask.) 32 A2
Makwa Lake 129A, IR (Sask.) 32 B2
Makwa Lake 129B, IR (Sask.) 32 A2
Makwa Lake 129C, IR (Sask.) 32 B2
Malachan 11, IR (BC) 38 C3
Malachi, UP (Ont.) 28 E1

Malagash, UP (NS) 9 C1
Malagash Mine, UP (NS) 9 C1
Malagash Point, UP (NS) 9 C1
Malagash Station, UP (NS) 9 C1
Malagawatch, UP (NS) 8 D4
Malagawatch 4, IR (NS) 8 D4
Malahat, UP (BC) 38 E4
Malahat 11, IR (BC) 38 E4
Malahide, UP (Ont.) 22 F2
Malakoff, UP (NB) 11 H1
Malakoff, UP (Ont.) 17 C2
Malakwa, UP (BC) 36 H4
Malartic, T (Que.) 18 B2
Malauze, UP (NB) 13 C4
Malay Falls, UP (NS) 9 E3
Malcolm, UP (Ont.) 23 C2
Malcolm Island 8, IR (BC) 39 D1
Malden, UP (NB) 7 B4
Malden Centre, UP (Ont.) 22 A4
Maleb, UP (Alta.) 34 H4
Malherbe, UP (Alta.) 14 B3
Malibu < Swaywelat 12, UP (BC) 37 E4
Malignant Cove, UP (NS) 8 B4
Maliseet < Tobique 20, UP (NB) 12 A3
Malksope 7, IR (BC) 39 D2
Mallaig, UP (Alta.) 43 H2
Mallard, UP (Man.) 29 F1
Mall Bay, UP (Nfld.) 2 F4
Mallorytown, UP (Ont.) 17 C3
Mallorytown Landing, UP (Ont.) 17 C3
Malmaison, UP (Que.) 16 A4
Malmo, UP (Alta.) 33 E4
Malone, UP (Ont.) 24 F4
Malonton, UP (Man.) 28 H3
Malpeque, UP (PEI) 7 B3
Maltais, UP (NB) 13 C4
Maltempec, UP (NB) 12 G1
Malvina, UP (Que.) 16 E4
Mamalilaculla < Mahmalillikullah 1, UP (BC) 39 E1
Ma-Me-O Beach, SV (Alta.) 33 D4
Mammamattawa, UP (Ont.) 20 B4
Mammin River 25, IR (BC) 41 B1
Manassette Lake, UP (NS) 9 G2
Manche-d'Épée, UP (Que.) 13 F1
Manchester, UP (Ont.) 21 C1
Manchester, UP (NS) 9 G2
Mandaumin, UP (Ont.) 22 C2
Manders, UP (Ont.) 28 G4
Manganese Mines, UP (NS) 9 C2
Manhattan Beach, UP (Man.) 29 F4
Manic-Cinq, UP (Que.) 19 C2
Manigotagan, UP (Man.) 30 C4
Manilla, UP (Ont.) 21 C1
Manion Corners, UP (Ont.) 17 B2
Manir, UP (Alta.) 43 G4
Manitou, UP (Que.) 19 G3
Manitou, VL (Man.) 29 G4
Manitou Beach, SV (Sask.) 31 G1
Manitou Dock, UP (Ont.) 24 A2
Manitou Falls, UP (Ont.) 27 A1
Manitou Rapids 11, IR (Ont.) 28 G4
Manitouwadge, UP (Ont.) 27 H2
Manitowaning, UP (Ont.) 25 C2
Maniwaki, T (Que.) 18 D4
Maniwaki 18, IR (Que.) 18 D4
Mankota, VL (Sask.) 31 E4
Manley, UP (Ont.) 23 C4
Manly, UP (Alta.) 33 D3
Manly Corner, UP (Alta.) 33 D3
Mann, UP (Ont.) 13 C3
Manners Sutton, UP (NB) 11 B2
Manneville, UP (Que.) 18 B1
Mannheim, UP (Ont.) 22 E2
Mannhurst, UP (NB) 11 F1
Manning, T (Alta.) 43 H2
Manning Park, UP (BC) 35 C4
Mann Mountain Settlement, UP (NB) 13 C4
Mann Point, UP (Nfld.) 3 E2
Mann-Settlement, UP (Que.) 13 C4
Mann Siding, UP (NB) 12 B1
Mannville, VL (Alta.) 33 G3
Manola, UP (Alta.) 33 D2
Manomin, UP (Ont.) 28 H4
Manor, VL (Sask.) 29 D4
Manordale, UP (Ont.) 17 E4
Manotick, UP (Ont.) 17 C2
Manotick Station, UP (Ont.) 17 E4
Manouane, UP (Que.) 18 F2
Manouane < Manuan 26, UP (Que.) 18 F3
Manseau, VL (Que.) 16 D1
Mansfield, UP (Ont.) 17 B1
Mansfield, UP (Ont.) 23 E2
Mansfield, UP (Ont.) 17 C2
Mansfield, UP (NS) 9 A1
Manson, UP (Man.) 29 D3
Manson Creek, UP (BC) 42 H3
Mansons Landing, UP (BC) 37 B4
Mansonville, UP (Que.) 16 C4
Mantario, VL (Sask.) 31 C2
Mantua, UP (NS) 9 A3
Manuan 26, IR (Que.) 18 F3
Manuels, UP (NB) 12 G2
Manuel's Cove, UP (Nfld.) 3 D1
Manvers, UP (Ont.) 21 D1
Manyberries, UP (Alta.) 31 B4
Mapes, UP (BC) 40 B2
Maple Beach, UP (Ont.) 21 B1
Maple Creek, T (Sask.) 31 C3
Mapledale, UP (NB) 11 A1
Maple Glen, UP (NB) 12 E2
Maple Green, UP (NB) 13 G4
Maple-Grove, T (Que.) 17 G1
Maple Grove, UP (NB) 12 E2
Maple Grove, UP (Ont.) 17 B4
Maple Grove, UP (Que.) 16 E2
Maplegrove, UP (Que.) 21 A1
Maple Grove, UP (Ont.) 23 E3
Maple Hill, UP (PEI) 7 D3
Maple-Hill, UP (NS) 15 A4
Maple Hill, UP (Ont.) 17 B4
Maple Hill, UP (Ont.) 21 B1
Maple Hill, UP (Ont.) 23 C2
Maplehurst, UP (NB) 12 A3
Maple Island, UP (Ont.) 24 A1
Maple Lake, UP (Ont.) 23 D2
Maple Lake Park, NUP (Ont.) 22 F1
Maple Lawn, UP (Ont.) 17 A4
Maple Leaf, UP (Ont.) 24 E2
Maple-Leaf, UP (Que.) 16 E4
Maplemore, UP (NB) 12 G2
Maple Plains, UP (PEI) 7 C4
Maple Point 11, IR (BC) 41 D2
Maple Ridge, DM (BC) 38 G2

Maple Ridge, UP (NB) 11 B1
Maple Ridge, UP (Ont.) 17 D2
Maple-Ridge, UP (Que.) 17 B1
Maple Ridge, UP (Ont.) 24 C2
Mapleton, UP (NS) 9 A1
Mapleton, UP (Ont.) 22 F2
Mapleton, UP (NB) 11 F1
Maple Valley, UP (Ont.) 23 E2
Maple Valley, UP (Ont.) 23 G1
Mapleview, UP (NB) 12 B2
Maple View, UP (Ont.) 21 F1
Maplewood, UP (NS) 10 E2
Maplewood, UP (NB) 11 B1
Maplewood, UP (Ont.) 22 F1
Maplewood, UP (Que.) 22 C2
Maplewood (PEI) 7 C4
Mapova, UP (Alta.) 33 E2
Maquapit Lake, UP (NB) 11 D1
Maquazneecht Island 17, IR (NB) 39 D1
Mar, UP (Ont.) 25 E4
Mara, UP (BC) 35 F1
Mara Beach, UP (Ont.) 23 G2
Mara Lake, UP (BC) 36 H4
Marathon, UP (Ont.) 27 G3
Marathon, UP (Ont.) 17 B1
Marathon Village, UP (Ont.) 17 B1
Marble Canyon 3, IR (BC) 36 C4
Marblehead, UP (BC) 34 B3
Marble Hill, UP (NS) 8 C3
Marble Mountain, UP (NS) 8 D4
Marble Rock, UP (Ont.) 17 B4
Marbleton, VL (Que.) 16 E3
Marcelin, VL (Sask.) 32 A3
Marcelville, UP (NB) 12 F3
Marchand, UP (Man.) 28 B2
Marchantgrove, UP (Sask.) 32 D3
Marches Point < Cape St George – Petit Jardin – Grand Jardin – De Grau – Marches Point – Loretto, UP (Nfld.) 4 A2
Marchhurst, UP (Ont.) 17 D4
Marchmont, UP (Ont.) 23 F1
Marchwell, UP (Sask.) 29 D2
Marcil, UP (Que.) 17 G1
Marco, UP (Man.) 29 E3
Marconi Towers, UP (NS) 8 F3
Marcotte, UP (Que.) 18 A1
Marden, UP (Ont.) 23 E4
Marean Lake, UP (Sask.) 32 F4
Mare-du-Sault, UP (Que.) 15 B1
Marelan, UP (Que.) 17 F1
Marengo, VL (Sask.) 31 C2
Marentette Beach, UP (Ont.) 22 B4
Mareuil, UP (Que.) 16 C3
Margaree, UP (Nfld.) 4 A4
Margaree, UP (NS) 8 D2
Margaree 25, IR (NS) 8 D3
Margaree Brook, UP (NS) 8 D3
Margaree Centre, UP (NS) 8 D3
Margaree Forks, UP (NS) 8 D3
Margaree Harbour, UP (NS) 8 D2
Margaree Valley, UP (NS) 8 D3
Margaret, UP (Man.) 29 F4
Margaret Bay, UP (BC) 41 F4
Margaretsville, UP (NS) 10 D1
Margate, UP (PEI) 7 B3
Margie, UP (Alta.) 33 F1
Margo, VL (Sask.) 29 B1
Margo Lake, UP (Sask.) 27 G1
Marguerite, UP (BC) 40 C3
Maria, UP (Que.) 13 E3
Maria 2, IR (Que.) 13 E3
Maria-de-Kent, UP (NB) 12 G4
Maria-Ouest, UP (Que.) 13 D3
Mariapolis, UP (Man.) 29 G4
Mariatown, UP (Ont.) 17 E2
Maricourt (Wakeham), UP (Que.) 46 F3
Marie, UP (PEI) 7 D3
Marie Hill, UP (Sask.) 32 A3
Marie Joseph, UP (NS) 9 E3
Marienthal, UP (Sask.) 29 B4
Marie-Reine, UP (Alta.) 43 H3
Marieton, UP (Sask.) 32 A1
Marieval < Cowessess 73, UP (Sask.) 29 C3
Marieville, T (Que.) 16 A3
Marilla, UP (BC) 41 G1
Marina, UP (Alta.) 43 F3
Marina Estates, UP (Ont.) 21 B1
Marinette, UP (NS) 9 D3
Marion, UP (Que.) 18 F4
Marion Bridge, UP (NS) 8 F3
Marion Bridge Road, UP (NS) 8 F3
Marionville, UP (Ont.) 17 D2
Mariposa, UP (Ont.) 21 C1
Mariposa Beach, UP (Ont.) 23 G1
Maritana, UP (Ont.) 17 G2
Marius < Sandy Bay 5, UP (Man.) 29 G3
Markale 14, IR (BC) 39 D2
Mark-Crossing, UP (Que.) 18 D4
Markdale, VL (Ont.) 23 D2
Markerville, UP (Alta.) 34 E1
Markham, T (Ont.) 21 B2
Markhamville, UP (NB) 11 F2
Markinch, UP (Sask.) 31 H2
Markland, UP (Nfld.) 2 F3
Markland, UP (Man.) 29 H3
Markstay, UP (Ont.) 25 C1
Marktosis < Marktosis 15, UP (BC) 39 F4
Marktosis 15, IR (BC) 39 F4
Marlbank, UP (Ont.) 21 G1
Marlboro, UP (Alta.) 33 B3
Marlin, UP (Sask.) 32 B3
Marlington, UP (Que.) 16 C4
Marmion, UP (Ont.) 23 C2
Marmora, VL (Ont.) 24 F4
Marne, UP (NB) 11 A1
Marnoch, UP (Ont.) 23 B3
Maroon Hill, UP (NS) 9 B3
Marquette, UP (Man.) 29 H3
Marquis, VL (Sask.) 31 F3
Marquise, UP (Nfld.) 2 F3
Marriott, UP (Sask.) 31 D1
Marriotts Cove, UP (NS) 10 E2
Marron Valley, UP (NS) 35 E4
Marrtown, UP (NB) 11 E1
Marsboro, UP (Que.) 16 E4
Marsboro Survey, NUP (Ont.) 22 G1
Marsden, VL (Sask.) 32 A4
Marsh, UP (NS) 8 A4
Marshall, VL (Sask.) 32 A3
Marshall Bay, UP (Ont.) 17 B1
Marshall's Corners, UP (Ont.) 26 F2
Marshalltown, UP (NS) 10 B2
Marshalls Crossing, UP (NS) 9 D1
Marshdale, UP (NS) 9 D2
Marshes (West Bay), UP (NS) 8 D4
Marshfield, UP (PEI) 7 D4
Marshfield, UP (Ont.) 22 A4

Marsh Hill, UP (Ont.) 21 B1
Marsh Lake, UP (YT) 45 B3
Marshville, UP (NS) 9 C1
Marshy Hope, UP (NS) 8 A4
Marsoui, VL (Que.) 13 D1
Marston, UP (Que.) 22 E2
Marsville, UP (Ont.) 23 E3
Martel, UP (BC) 35 B1
Martels Corners, UP (Ont.) 17 D1
Marten Falls 65, IR (Ont.) 20 A3
Marten River, UP (Ont.) 26 F3
Marten River, UP (Alta.) 44 A4
Martensville, T (Sask.) 31 F1
Marter, UP (Ont.) 26 F2
Marthaville, UP (Ont.) 22 C2
Martigny, UP (Que.) 17 F1
Martin, UP (Que.) 13 F3
Martin, UP (Que.) 16 A4
Martin, UP (Que.) 27 C2
Martin-Corner, UP (Que.) 16 C4
Martindale, UP (Que.) 18 D4
Martineau, UP (Que.) 15 C3
Martin Farm, UP (Ont.) 23 F2
Martin House, UP (NWT) 44 B3
Martinique, UP (NS) 8 D4
Martin-Lake, UP (Que.) 17 B1
Martins Brook, UP (NS) 10 E2
Martins Corner, UP (Ont.) 17 D1
Martins Corners, UP (Ont.) 17 D1
Martin Siding, UP (NB) 12 A2
Martins Point, UP (NS) 10 E2
Martins River, UP (NS) 10 E2
Martintown, UP (Ont.) 17 E2
Martinvale, UP (PEI) 7 D4
Martin Valley, NUP (BC) 41 F3
Martinville, UP (Que.) 16 D4
Martinville, UP (Que.) 23 F2
Martock, UP (NS) 9 A3
Martyrs Shrine, UP (Ont.) 23 F1
Marvelville, UP (Ont.) 17 D2
Marvins Island, UP (NS) 10 E2
Marwayne, VL (Alta.) 33 G3
Mary Cove 12, IR (BC) 41 E2
Marydale, UP (NS) 8 B4
Maryfield, VL (Sask.) 29 D4
Marygrove, UP (Ont.) 23 F1
Maryhill, UP (Ont.) 23 E4
Maryland, UP (Que.) 17 B1
Mary March, UP (Nfld.) 4 F1
Marysburg, UP (Sask.) 31 G1
Mary's Harbour, COMM (Nfld.) 5 H1
Marystown, T (Nfld.) 2 G3
Marysvale, UP (Nfld.) 2 G2
Marysville, UP (Ont.) 21 H1
Marysville, UP (Ont.) 21 G1
Maryvale, UP (NB) 8 B4
Maryville, UP (NS) 8 C3
Maryville, UP (Sask.) 32 F4
Mascarene, UP (NB) 11 C3
Mascouche, T (Que.) 18 G4
Masefield, UP (Sask.) 31 D4
Masit 13, IR (BC) 38 B3
Maskawata, UP (Man.) 29 E4
Maskinongé, VL (Que.) 16 B2
Maskinonge Park, UP (Ont.) 21 B1
Mason Creek, UP (BC) 43 C2
Mason Landing, UP (YT) 45 B3
Mason Point, UP (NS) 8 C4
Masons Beach, UP (NS) 10 E2
Masons Point, UP (NS) 9 A4
Massanoga, UP (Ont.) 24 G3
Massawippi, UP (Que.) 16 D4
Masset, VL (BC) 41 B1
Massey, T (Ont.) 25 B1
Massey Drive, LID (Nfld.) 4 D1
Massie, UP (Ont.) 23 D2
Massive, UP (Alta.) 34 D2
Masstown, UP (NS) 9 B3
Massueville, VL (Que.) 16 B2
Matachewan, UP (Ont.) 26 E2
Matachewan 72, IR (Ont.) 26 E2
Matador, UP (Sask.) 31 D2
Matagami, T (Que.) 20 E4
Matamec, UP (Que.) 19 F3
Matane, T (Que.) 13 B2
Matapédia, UP (Que.) 13 C4
Matapédia-Ouest, UP (Que.) 13 C4
Matawatchan, UP (Ont.) 24 G2
Matchlee 13, IR (BC) 39 F3
Mates Corner, UP (NB) 7 A4
Mather, UP (Man.) 29 F4
Mathers Corners, UP (Ont.) 21 D1
Matheson, UP (Ont.) 26 D1
Matheson Island, UP (Man.) 30 C4
Matlaten 4, IR (BC) 37 E4
Matsayno 5, IR (BC) 37 B3
Matsqui, DM (BC) 38 H3
Matsqui 4, IR (BC) 38 G3
Matsqui Main 2, IR (BC) 38 H2
Mattagami 71, IR (Ont.) 26 D2
Mattawa, T (Ont.) 18 A4
Mattes, UP (Sask.) 32 C3
Matthews, UP (NB) 12 E2
Matthews Crossing, JP (Alta.) 33 C3
Mattice, UP (Ont.) 20 B4
Mattie Settlement, UP (NS) 8 C4
Mattis Point, UP (Nfld.) 4 C2
Maugerville, UP (NB) 11 D1
Mauriceville, UP (Que.) 15 B2
Mauvais Rocher 5, IR (BC) 36 D4
Mavillette, UP (NS) 10 A3
Mavis Mills, UP (NB) 12 C4
Mawcook, UP (Que.) 16 B3
Mawer, UP (Sask.) 31 F2
Maxim, UP (Ont.) 17 B1
Maxim Creek 11A, IR (BC) 42 G4
Maximeville, UP (PEI) 7 A3
Maxim Lake 11, IR (BC) 42 G4
Maxim Lake 12A, IR (BC) 42 G4
Maxstone, UP (Sask.) 31 F4
Maxville, VL (Ont.) 17 E2
Maxwell, UP (Ont.) 23 D2
Maxwell, UP (NB) 11 A1
Maxwell, UP (NB) 12 E2
Maxwell Crossing, UP (NB) 11 B3
Maxwellton, UP (NS) 8 B4
Maybank, UP (Sask.) 31 F2
Maybee, UP (Ont.) 22 D1
Maycroft, UP (Alta.) 34 E3
Mayerthorpe, T (Alta.) 33 C3
Mayfair, UP (Sask.) 32 C4
Mayfair, UP (Man.) 29 G3
Mayfield, UP (Ont.) 17 D2
Mayfield, UP (NS) 8 C4
Mayfield, UP (PEI) 7 C4
Mayfield, UP (NB) 11 B3

Mayflower, UP (NS) 10 A3
Mayhews Landing, UP (Ont.) 24 F2
Maymont, VL (Sask.) 32 C4
Maynard, UP (Ont.) 17 C2
Mayne, UP (BC) 38 F3
Mayne Corners, UP (Ont.) 23 C3
Mayne Island 6, IR (BC) 38 F3
Maynooth, UP (Ont.) 24 E2
Maynooth Station, UP (Ont.) 24 E2
Mayo, UP (YT) 45 B2
Mayo, UP (Ont.) 24 F2
Mayton, UP (Alta.) 34 E1
Mayview, UP (Sask.) 32 D3
Mazenod, VL (Sask.) 31 F3
Mazeppa, UP (Alta.) 34 E3
Mazerolle Settlement, UP (NB) 11 C1
McAdam, VL (NB) 11 B2
McAdams Lake, UP (NS) 8 E3
McAlpine, UP (Ont.) 17 E1
McAlpine Corners, UP (Ont.) 24 E2
McAndrew, UP (Ont.) 17 D4
McArras Brook, UP (NS) 8 A4
McArthur Subdivision, NUP (Ont.) 25 A1
McArthurs Mills, UP (Ont.) 24 F2
McAuley, UP (Man.) 29 D3
McBean, UP (Que.) 18 D4
McBean Harbour < Spanish River 5, UP (Ont.) 25 B2
McBride, VL (BC) 40 D1
McCabe Creek, UP (YT) 45 B3
McCain Settlement, UP (NB) 11 E2
McCallum, UP (Nfld.) 2 D3
McCallum Settlement, UP (NS) 9 C2
McCann's Shore, UP (Ont.) 17 B2
McCarleys Corners, UP (Ont.) 17 C2
McCartney's Flat 4, IR (BC) 35 A1
McCluskey, UP (Man.) 12 A2
McCluskeys Corners, UP (Ont.) 27 D3
McConnell, UP (Man.) 29 E3
McConnell, UP (Que.) 16 D4
McConnell Creek, UP (BC) 42 G1
McCool, UP (Ont.) 26 F2
McCord, UP (Sask.) 31 E4
McCormick, UP (Ont.) 17 E1
McCourts-Corner, UP (Que.) 16 D3
McCracken Landing, UP (Ont.) 21 E1
McCrackens Landing, UP (Ont.) 24 E4
McCrackins Beach, UP (Ont.) 23 G1
McCrae, UP (Ont.) 24 F3
McCreadyville, UP (NS) 9 E3
McCreary, VL (Man.) 29 F2
McCrearys, UP (Ont.) 17 B2
McCreary's Shore, UP (Ont.) 17 B2
McCrimmon, UP (Ont.) 17 E1
McCulloch, UP (BC) 35 F3
McCulloughs Landing, UP (Ont.) 17 B2
McDame, UP (BC) 45 C4
McDames Creek 2, IR (BC) 45 C4
McDiarmid's Shore, UP (Ont.) 17 B2
McDonald, UP (Man.) 28 A1
McDonald Court, UP (Ont.) 21 A3
McDonald Hills, UP (Sask.) 31 H2
McDonalds Corners, UP (Ont.) 17 A2
McDonalds Landing, UP (BC) 41 G1
McDonalds Landing, UP (BC) 34 B4
McDougall, UP (Ont.) 17 A1
McDougall Mills, UP (Ont.) 27 B1
McDougalls Landing, UP (Man.) 28 E2
McEachern, UP (Sask.) 31 E4
McElhanney, UP (Sask.) 32 A4
McFerson, UP (Sask.) 25 A1
McGary Flats, UP (Ont.) 24 E2
McGaw, UP (Ont.) 23 B3
McGee, UP (Sask.) 31 D2
McGillivray, UP (BC) 37 G3
McGinleys Corner, UP (NB) 11 G1
McGinnis Creek, UP (Ont.) 28 F4
McGivney, UP (NB) 12 C4
McGowans Corner, UP (NB) 11 D1
McGrath, UP (Ont.) 24 G2
McGrath Corner, UP (NB) 12 A3
McGraths Cove, UP (NS) 9 B4
McGraths Mountain, UP (NS) 8 A4
McGraw Brook, UP (NB) 12 B3
McGregor, UP (Ont.) 22 A3
McGregor, UP (BC) 40 D1
McGregor Bay, UP (Ont.) 25 B1
McGregor Brook, UP (NB) 11 E2
McGuire, UP (BC) 37 F4
McGuire, UP (Ont.) 24 G1
McGuire Settlement, UP (Ont.) 24 G4
McIntosh, UP (Ont.) 28 H1
McIntosh, UP (Ont.) 23 C3
McIntosh Mills, UP (Ont.) 17 C3
McIntyre, UP (Ont.) 23 E2
McIntyre, UP (Ont.) 17 A4
McIntyres Mountain, UP (NS) 8 C4
McIver, UP (Ont.) 23 C1
McIvers, COMM (Nfld.) 4 C1
McKague, UP (Sask.) 32 B3
McKay Meadow 4, IR (BC) 40 C3
McKay's, UP (Nfld.) 4 B3
McKay Section, UP (NS) 9 A3
McKay Siding, UP (NS) 9 C2
McKeaghan, UP (NB) 12 A4
McKearney Ranch, UP (BC) 43 D3
McKee, UP (Ont.) 17 B1
McKeens Corner, UP (NB) 11 C1
McKees Mills, UP (NB) 12 G4
McKellar, UP (Ont.) 24 A2
McKenna, UP (NB) 12 A4
McKenzie Corner, UP (NB) 11 A1
McKenzie Island, UP (Ont.) 30 D4
McKenzie Lake, UP (Ont.) 24 E2
McKenzie Subdivision, NUP (Alta.) 34 E1
McKerrow, UP (Ont.) 25 C1
McKinleyville, UP (NB) 12 A4
McKinnons Harbour, UP (NS) 7 H4
McLaren, UP (Sask.) 32 A3
McLaren's Bay, UP (Ont.) 21 C1
McLarens Settlement, UP (Ont.) 17 A1
McLaughlin, UP (Alta.) 33 H4
McLean, UP (Ont.) 17 A3
McLean, VL (Sask.) 31 H3
McLean Ranch, UP (BC) 43 D3
McLean Settlement, UP (NB) 12 G4
McLean's Lake 3, IR (BC) 36 C4
McLean's Trailer Park, NUP (Ont.) 23 E3
McLeese Lake, UP (BC) 36 B1
McLellans Brook, UP (NS) 8 A4
McLellans Mountain, UP (NS) 8 A4
McLennan, T (Alta.) 33 B1
McLennan's Beach, UP (Ont.) 21 B1
McLeod Hill, UP (NB) 11 C1
McLeod Lake, UP (BC) 43 C4
McLeod Lake 1, IR (BC) 43 C4
McLeod Lake 5, IR (BC) 43 C4

McLeod River, UP (Alta.) 33 B3
McLeods, UP (NB) 13 C4
McLeod Subdivision, NUP (Alta.) 43 E3
McLeod Valley, JP (Alta.) 33 B3
McLure, UP (BC) 36 F4
McMahon, UP (Sask.) 31 E3
McManus Siding, UP (NB) 12 A2
McMasterville, T (Que.) 16 A3
McMillan Island 6, IR (BC) 38 G2
McMillans Corners, UP (Ont.) 17 E2
McMinn, UP (NB) 11 B3
McMonagle Corner, UP (NB) 11 H1
McMorran, UP (Sask.) 31 D2
McMunn, UP (Ont.) 28 D2
McMurchy Settlement, UP (Ont.) 23 E2
McMurrich, UP (Ont.) 24 B2
McNab, UP (Alta.) 34 G4
McNab Creek, UP (BC) 38 F1
McNabs Island, UP (NS) 9 B4
McNairn, UP (NB) 12 G4
McNallys, UP (NB) 11 C1
McNamee, UP (NB) 12 D3
McNaughton Shore, UP (Ont.) 17 B2
McNeill, UP (Alta.) 31 B3
McNeills Mills, UP (PEI) 7 B3
McNeish, UP (NB) 13 D3
McNutts Island 49, IR (NS) 10 C4
McPhail Cove, JP (Sask.) 32 C3
McPhail Point, NUP (BC) 38 E4
McPhersons Mills, UP (NS) 8 A4
McQuade, UP (NB) 12 G2
McQuesten, UP (YT) 45 B2
McQuesten 3, IR (YT) 45 B2
McRae, UP (Alta.) 33 F2
McReynolds, UP (Ont.) 17 C3
McRoberts Corner, UP (Ont.) 17 C3
McTaggart, VL (Sask.) 31 H4
McTavish, UP (Man.) 29 H4
McVeigh, UP (Man.) 30 A1
McVicar, UP (Ont.) 25 D4
McWatters, UP (Que.) 18 A2
McWilliams, NUP (Ont.) 22 E1
Meacham, VL (Sask.) 31 F1
Meachen, UP (BC) 34 C4
Mead, UP (Ont.) 20 B4
Meadow, UP (NS) 8 A4
Meadow, UP (NB) 11 G1
Meadow Bank, UP (PEI) 7 C4
Meadow Brook, UP (NS) 11 G1
Meadowbrook, UP (Alta.) 33 D3
Meadowbrook, NUP (BC) 34 C4
Meadowbrook, NUP (BC) 38 B1
Meadow Creek 3, IR (BC) 36 G4
Meadow Green, UP (NS) 8 D3
Meadow Lake, T (Sask.) 32 B2
Meadow Lake 105, IR (Sask.) 32 B2
Meadow Lake 105A, IR (Sask.) 32 B2
Meadowlands, UP (Ont.) 17 E4
Meadowlands, UP (Man.) 29 F3
Meadow Lee, UP (Man.) 29 H3
Meadow Portage, UP (Man.) 28 F1
Meadows, COMM (Nfld.) 4 C1
Meadows, UP (BC) 34 B4
Meadows, UP (Man.) 29 H3
Meadowside, UP (Ont.) 25 H1
Meadow Springs, UP (NS) 8 A4
Meadows Road, UP (NS) 8 E3
Meadowvale, UP (NS) 9 C2
Meadowvale, UP (NS) 10 D1
Meadowvale, UP (Man.) 28 D1
Meadowview, UP (Alta.) 33 D3
Meadowville, UP (NS) 9 D1
Meaford, T (Ont.) 23 D1
Meagher, UP (NS) 9 C3
Meagher, UP (NS) 10 D2
Meaghers Grant, UP (NS) 9 C3
Meagwan 8, IR (BC) 41 B1
Meander River, UP (Alta.) 44 A2
Meanlaw 24, IR (BC) 41 D1
Meanook, UP (Alta.) 33 E2
Mearns, UP (Alta.) 33 D3
Mears, UP (Man.) 29 E2
Meat Cove, UP (NS) 8 E1
Meath Park, VL (Sask.) 32 E3
Meaux, UP (Que.) 26 G3
Mechanic Settlement, UP (NB) 11 F2
Medford, UP (NS) 11 H3
Medford, UP (NB) 12 A2
Medicine Hat, C (Alta.) 31 B3
Medicine Lodge, UP (Alta.) 33 A3
Medika, UP (Man.) 28 C2
Medina, UP (Ont.) 22 E1
Medina Corners < Six Nations 40, UP (Ont.) 22 G1
Medley < Cold Lake, CFB/BFC, UP (Alta.) 33 G2
Medonte, UP (Ont.) 23 F1
Medora, UP (Man.) 29 E4
Medstead, VL (Sask.) 32 B3
Meductic, VL (NB) 11 A1
Medway, UP (NS) 10 E3
Meeting Creek, UP (Alta.) 33 E4
Meeting Lake, UP (Sask.) 32 C3
Meetoos, UP (Sask.) 32 C3
Meetup 2, IR (BC) 39 F1
Meilleurs Bay, UP (Ont.) 18 B4
Meiseners Section, UP (NS) 10 D2
Melançon, UF (Que.) 18 H1
Melancthon, UP (Ont.) 23 E3
Melanson, UF (NS) 9 A4
Melanson Settlement, UP (NB) 11 G1
Melaval, UP (Sask.) 31 F4
Melbourne, UP (Ont.) 22 D2
Melbourne, UP (NS) 10 A3
Melbourne, UP (Man.) 29 F3
Melbourne, UP (Que.) 16 C3
Melbourne-Ridge, UP (Que.) 16 C3
Meldrum Bay, UP (Ont.) 25 A2
Meldrum's Beach, UP (Ont.) 21 C1
Meleb, UP (Man.) 29 H2
Melford, UP (NS) 8 C4
Melfort, T (Sask.) 32 E4
Melita, T (Man.) 29 E4
Mellor, UP (NWT) 44 B2
Mellowdale, UP (Alta.) 33 C3
Melnice, UP (Man.) 30 C4
Melocheville, VL (Que.) 17 G1
Melrose, COMM (Nfld.) 3 G4
Melrose, UP (NB) 7 B4
Melrose, UP (Ont.) 21 G1
Melrose, UP (NS) 9 E2
Melrose, UP (Ont.) 22 D1
Melrose, UP (Man.) 28 D1
Melrose Hill, UP (NS) 9 E2
Melvern Square, UP (NS) 10 D1
Melville, C (Sask.) 29 C2

Melville, UP (PEI) 7 D4
Melville, UP (NS) 9 C1
Melville, UP (Ont.) 21 F2
Melville Beach < Shesheep 74A, UP (Sask.) 29 C3
Melvin, UP (Ont.) 17 D2
Memel Settlement, UP (NB) 11 G1
Memramcook, UP (NB) 11 H1
Memramcook East, UP (NB) 11 H1
Memramcook West, UP (NB) 11 G1
Menaik, UP (Alta.) 33 E4
Ménard, UP (Que.) 15 D3
Ménard, NUP (Que.) 16 B3
Mendenhall Landing, UP (YT) 45 A3
Mendham, VL (Sask.) 31 C2
Menie, UP (Ont.) 21 E1
Menihek, UP (Nfld.) 6 C3
Menisino, UP (Man.) 28 C3
Menneval, UP (NB) 13 B4
Mennon, UP (Sask.) 31 F4
Mennonite Corner, UP (Ont.) 23 D4
Menoke Beach, UP (Ont.) 23 G1
Menzie, UP (Man.) 29 E3
Meota, VL (Sask.) 32 B4
Merasheen, COMM (Nfld.) 2 E3
Mercer's Cove, UP (Nfld.) 2 B3
Mercier-de-Caplan, UP (Que.) 13 E3
Mercier, T (Que.) 17 G2
Mercoal, UP (Alta.) 33 A3
Meredith Settlement, UP (NB) 11 B2
Merid, UP (Sask.) 31 B2
Merigomish, UP (NS) 8 A4
Merigomish Harbour 31, IR (NS) 8 A4
Merivale, UP (Ont.) 17 E4
Merivale Gardens, UP (Ont.) 17 E4
Merland, UP (NS) 8 C4
Merle, UP (Sask.) 32 F4
Merlin, UP (Ont.) 22 C3
Mermaid, UP (PEI) 7 D4
Merrickville, VL (Ont.) 17 C2
Merridale, UP (Man.) 29 D2
Merritt, T (BC) 35 C2
Merritts Harbour, UP (Nfld.) 3 D1
Merryflat, UP (Sask.) 31 B4
Mersey Point, UP (NS) 10 D3
Mertz's Corner, UP (Ont.) 23 F1
Merville, UP (BC) 38 B1
Mervin, VL (Sask.) 32 B3
Mesachie Lake, UP (BC) 38 D3
Meskanaw, UP (Sask.) 32 E4
Messines, UP (Que.) 18 D4
Métabetchouan, T (Que.) 18 H1
Metagama, UP (Ont.) 26 D3
Metcalfe, UP (Ont.) 17 D2
Metchosin, UP (BC) 38 E4
Meteghan, UP (NS) 10 A3
Meteghan Centre, UP (NS) 10 A2
Meteghan River, UP (NS) 10 A2
Meteghan Station, UP (NS) 10 A2
Metigoshe, UP (Man.) 29 E4
Metinota, VL (Sask.) 32 B4
Metis, UP (Alta.) 43 H1
Metiskow, UP (Alta.) 33 G4
Métis-sur-Mer, VL (Que.) 14 H2
Metlakatla < Tsimpsean 2, UP (BC) 42 C4
Metropolitan, UP (Ont.) 22 E1
Metz, UP (Ont.) 23 D3
Mewassin, UP (Alta.) 33 D3
Me-yan-law 47, IR (BC) 42 C4
Meyanlow 58, IR (BC) 42 D4
Meyersburg, UP (Ont.) 21 E1
Meyers Flat, UP (BC) 35 E4
Meyronne, VL (Sask.) 31 E4
Miami, UP (Man.) 29 G4
Miami Beach, UP (Man.) 21 B1
Mica Creek, UP (BC) 34 A1
Michael's Bay, UP (Ont.) 25 C3
Michael's Harbour, UP (Nfld.) 3 D2
Michaudville, UP (Que.) 16 A3
Michel < Peter Pond Lake 193, UP (Sask.) 44 B4
Michelle Creek 22, IR (BC) 40 B3
Michelle Creek 23, IR (BC) 40 B3
Michell Pierre 12, IR (BC) 42 G3
Michichi, UP (Alta.) 34 G1
Michigan Centre, UP (Alta.) 33 D3
Michipicoten, UP (Ont.) 26 A2
Michipicoten River, UP (Ont.) 26 A2
Micksburg, UP (Ont.) 24 G1
Micmac, UP (NS) 8 A4
Micmac < Shubenacadie 14, UP (NS) 9 B3
Micoua, UP (Que.) 19 C3
Midale, T (Sask.) 29 B4
Middle Amherst Cove, UP (Nfld.) 3 G4
Middle Arm, COMM (Nfld.) 3 A1
Middle Arm, UP (Que.) 5 G4
Middle Barneys River, UP (NS) 8 A4
Middle-Bay, UP (Que.) 5 F2
Middle Beaverbank, UP (NS) 9 B3
Middleboro, UP (Man.) 28 D3
Middlebro, UP (Man.) 28 D3
Middle Brook < Dark Cove – Middle Brook – Gambo, UP (Nfld.) 3 E3
Middle Cape, UP (NS) 8 E4
Middlechurch, UP (Man.) 28 D3
Middle Clyde River, UP (NS) 10 C3
Middle Country Harbour, UP (NS) 9 F2
Middle Cove, UP (Nfld.) 2 H2
Middle Creek, UP (Alta.) 33 G3
Middle District, NUP (NB) 11 B2
Middle East Pubnico, UP (NS) 10 B4
Middlefield, UP (NS) 10 D2
Middle Hainesville, UP (NB) 11 B1
Middle LaHave, UP (NS) 10 E3
Middle Lake, VL (Sask.) 32 E4
Middle Manchester, UP (NS) 9 G2
Middlemarch, UP (Ont.) 22 D2
Middle Melford, UP (NS) 8 C4
Middlemiss, UP (Ont.) 22 D2
Middle Musquodoboit, UP (NS) 9 C3
Middle New Cornwall, UP (NS) 10 E2
Middle Ohio, UP (NS) 10 C3
Middle Pereaux, UP (NS) 11 H3
Middle Pond, NUP (Nfld.) 2 H3
Middleport, UP (Ont.) 22 G1
Middle Porters Lake, UP (NS) 9 C4
Middle River, UP (NS) 10 E2
Middle River, UP (NS) 10 E2
Middle River, NUP (NB) 12 E1
Middle River < Gelangle 1, UP (BC) 42 H4
Middle Sackville, UP (NS) 9 B3
Middlesex, UP (NB) 11 G1
Middle Southampton, UP (NB) 11 B1
Middle Stewiacke, UP (NS) 9 C2
Middleton, T (NS) 10 D1
Middleton, UP (PEI) 7 B4
Middleton, UP (NB) 11 H1

Mi

POPULATED PLACES

Middleton, UP (NS) **9 C1**
Middleton, UP (NS) **9 F2**
Middleton Corner, UP (NS) **9 C1**
Middle Village, UP (NS) **9 A4**
Middleville, UP (Ont.) **17 B2**
Middle West Pubnico, UP (NS) **10 B4**
Middlewood, UP (NS) **10 E2**
Midgell, UP (PEI) **7 D3**
Midgic, UP (NB) **7 A4**
Midhurst, UP (Ont.) **21 A1**
Midhurst Station, NUP (Ont.) **21 A1**
Midland, T (Ont.) **23 F1**
Midland, UP (NB) **11 F2**
Midland, UP (NB) **11 E1**
Midland Point, UP (Ont.) **23 F1**
Midlothian, UP (Ont.) **24 B1**
Midnight Lake, UP (Sask.) **32 B3**
Midville Branch, UP (NS) **10 E2**
Midway, UP (NB) **11 G2**
Midway, VL (BC) **35 G4**
Miette, UP (Alta.) **40 H2**
Miette Hotsprings, UP (Alta.) **40 H2**
Miguasha, UP (Que.) **13 D3**
Miguasha-Ouest, UP (Que.) **13 D3**
Mikado, UP (Sask.) **29 C2**
Milan, UP (Que.) **16 F3**
Milberta, UP (Ont.) **26 F2**
Milburn, UP (PEI) **7 A3**
Milburn, UP (PEI) **7 D3**
Milburn, UP (Ont.) **17 B4**
Milby, UP (Que.) **16 D4**
Milden, VL (Sask.) **31 E2**
Mildmay, VL (Ont.) **23 C3**
Mildred, UP (Sask.) **32 C3**
Mildred Lake, UP (Alta.) **44 C4**
Mile 108 Recreational Ranch, NUP (BC) **36 D2**
Mile 304 Alaska Highway, NUP (BC) **45 D4**
Mile 99 Cariboo Highway, NUP (BC) **36 D2**
Miles Cove, COMM (Nfld.) **3 B2**
Milestone, T (Sask.) **31 H3**
Milford, UP (Ont.) **21 G2**
Milford, UP (NS) **10 C2**
Milford Bay, UP (Ont.) **24 B3**
Milford Haven, UP (NS) **9 G2**
Milford Haven, UP (Ont.) **26 B4**
Milford Station, UP (NS) **9 B3**
Militia Point, UP (NS) **8 D4**
Milkish, UP (NB) **11 D2**
Milk River, T (Alta.) **34 G4**
Millar, UP (Ont.) **27 D3**
Millar Hill, UP (Ont.) **24 C2**
Millars Corner, UP (Ont.) **17 A1**
Millars Corners, UP (Ont.) **17 C2**
Millarton, UP (Ont.) **23 B2**
Millarville, UP (Alta.) **34 E2**
Millbank, UP (Ont.) **23 D4**
Millbank, UP (NB) **12 F2**
Mill Bank Acres, NUP (NB) **11 C1**
Mill Bay, UP (BC) **38 E4**
Mill Bay, UP (BC) **42 D4**
Millbridge, UP (Ont.) **24 F3**
Millbrook, UP (NS) **9 D2**
Mill Brook, UP (NS) **9 C1**
Millbrook, VL (Ont.) **21 D1**
Millbrook 27, IR (NS) **9 C2**
Mill Cove, UP (NS) **9 A4**
Millcove, UP (PEI) **7 D3**
Mill Cove, UP (NB) **11 D1**
Mill Cove, CFS/SFC, MIL (NS) **9 A4**
Mill Creek, UP (NS) **8 E3**
Mill Creek, UP (NS) **11 H2**
Milldale, UP (Ont.) **22 F2**
Mille-Isles, UP (Que.) **18 F4**
Millerand, UP (Que.) **7 F1**
Millerand, UP (Ont.) **25 G1**
Miller Creek, UP (NS) **9 A3**
Millerdale, UP (Sask.) **31 C1**
Millerfield, UP (Alta.) **34 G2**
Miller Lake, UP (Ont.) **25 D4**
Miller Lake East, UP (Ont.) **25 D4**
Miller Lake West, UP (Ont.) **25 D4**
Miller Line Cache, UP (NB) **12 A1**
Miller Road, UP (NS) **9 B1**
Millers Corner, UP (NS) **9 B2**
Millers Corner, UP (Ont.) **17 A4**
Millers Landing, UP (BC) **38 F2**
Miller's Passage, UP (Nfld.) **2 B2**
Millerton, UP (NB) **12 E2**
Millertown, COMM (Nfld.) **4 F1**
Millertown Junction, UP (Nfld.) **4 G1**
Millet, VL (Alta.) **33 E4**
Milleton, UP (Sask.) **32 A3**
Millfield, UP (Que.) **15 A4**
Millgrove, UP (Ont.) **22 H1**
Millhaven, UP (Ont.) **17 A4**
Millicent, UP (Alta.) **34 G2**
Millington, UP (Que.) **16 C4**
Million, UP (Man.) **29 F2**
Mill Pond, UP (NS) **8 E3**
Mill River East, UP (PEI) **7 A2**
Mill Road, UP (NS) **10 E1**
Mill Road, UP (PEI) **7 A3**
Mills Corners, UP (Ont.) **17 C2**
Mill Section, UP (NS) **9 A3**
Mill Settlement, UP (NB) **11 C2**
Mill Settlement West, UP (NB) **11 C2**
Mills Point, UP (PEI) **7 B3**
Millstream, UP (NS) **9 D2**
Millstream, UP (Que.) **13 B3**
Millstream, UP (BC) **38 E4**
Millstream Subdivision, NUP (BC) **38 A3**
Millsville, UP (NS) **9 D1**
Milltown, UP (Ont.) **21 G1**
Milltown < Milltown – Head of Bay d'Espoir, UP (Nfld.) **2 B2**
Milltown Cross, UP (PEI) **7 D4**
Milltown – Head of Bay d'Espoir, RD (Nfld.) **2 B1**
Millvale, UP (NS) **9 B1**
Millvale, UP (PEI) **7 C3**
Mill Valley, UP (PEI) **7 B3**
Millview, UP (NS) **9 B3**
Millview, UP (PEI) **7 D4**
Mill Village, UP (NS) **10 E3**
Mill Village, UP (NS) **9 B3**
Millville, UP (NS) **10 D1**
Millville, UP (Nfld.) **4 A3**
Millville, VL (NB) **11 B1**
Millville Boularderie, UP (NS) **8 E3**
Millwater, UP (Man.) **32 H2**
Millwood, UP (Man.) **29 D3**
Millwood, UP (Ont.) **26 A2**
Milly, UP (Sask.) **31 E4**
Milner Ridge, UP (Man.) **28 C1**
Milnerton, UP (Alta.) **34 F1**
Milnes Landing, UP (BC) **38 E4**
Milne Townsite, NUP (Ont.) **26 F3**
Milnikek, UP (Que.) **13 B3**
Milo, UP (PEI) **7 A3**
Milo, VL (Alta.) **34 F3**
Milot, UP (Que.) **18 H1**
Milsap, UP (Ont.) **21 G1**
Milton, T (Ont.) **23 F4**
Milton, UP (NS) **10 D3**
Milton, UP (Nfld.) **2 F1**
Milton-Est, UP (Que.) **16 B3**
Milton Highlands, UP (NS) **10 A3**
Milton Station, UP (PEI) **7 C4**
Milton Subdivision, NUP (Ont.) **17 B4**
Milverton, VL (Ont.) **23 C4**
Miminegash, VL (PEI) **7 A2**
Mimosa, UP (Ont.) **23 E3**
Minahico, UP (Ont.) **28 F3**
Minaki, UP (Ont.) **28 F1**
Minard, UP (Sask.) **29 C4**
Minaret, UP (Alta.) **34 E1**
Minasville, UP (NS) **9 B2**
Minaty Bay, UP (BC) **38 F1**
Minburn, VL (Alta.) **33 F3**
Mindemoya, UP (Ont.) **25 C2**
Minden, UP (Ont.) **23 H1**
Mine Centre, UP (Ont.) **27 A3**
Mineral, UP (NB) **12 A3**
Miners Bay, UP (Ont.) **23 H1**
Minesing, UP (Ont.) **21 A1**
Minesville, UP (NS) **9 C4**
Minet's Point, UP (Ont.) **21 A1**
Minett, UP (Ont.) **24 B2**
Mingan, UP (Que.) **19 H3**
Ming's Bight, COMM (Nfld.) **3 A1**
Miniota, UP (Man.) **29 E3**
Ministik Beach, UP (Sask.) **29 D1**
Ministikwan 161, IR (Sask.) **32 A2**
Ministikwan 161A, IR (Sask.) **32 A2**
Minitonas, VL (Man.) **29 E1**
Mink Brook, UP (NB) **11 C3**
Mink Cove, UP (NS) **10 A2**
Mink Creek, UP (Man.) **29 E2**
Mink Lake, UP (Ont.) **24 G1**
Minnedosa, T (Man.) **29 F3**
Minnehaha, UP (Sask.) **32 B3**
Minnewakan, UP (Man.) **29 G2**
Minniehill, UP (Ont.) **23 D2**
Minnipuka, UP (Ont.) **26 B1**
Minnitaki, UP (Ont.) **27 A1**
Minoahchak 230, IR (Sask.) **29 C2**
Minowukaw Beach, UP (Sask.) **32 E3**
Minstrel Island, UP (BC) **39 F1**
Mintlaw, UP (Alta.) **34 E1**
Minto, UP (Man.) **29 F4**
Minto, UP (Ont.) **21 F1**
Minto, UP (YT) **45 B3**
Minto, VL (NB) **11 D1**
Minto Bridge, UP (YT) **45 B2**
Minton, UP (Que.) **16 D4**
Minton, VL (Sask.) **31 H4**
Minto Park, NUP (Sask.) **32 E4**
Minudie, UP (NS) **11 H2**
Miocene, UP (BC) **36 C1**
Miquelon, UP (Que.) **20 F4**
Mirabel, C (Que.) **17 G1**
Miracle Valley, NUP (BC) **38 H2**
Mira Gut, UP (NS) **8 F3**
Miramichi, UP (NB) **12 F2**
Miramichi, UP (NS) **8 C3**
Mira Road, UP (NS) **8 F3**
Miron, UP (Que.) **26 G3**
Mirond Lake 184E, IR (Sask.) **32 G1**
Mirror, VL (Alta.) **33 E4**
Mirror Lake, UP (BC) **34 B3**
Miscampbell, NUP (Ont.) **28 H4**
Miscou Centre, UP (NB) **13 G4**
Miscouche, VL (PEI) **7 B3**
Miscou Harbour, UP (NB) **13 G4**
Miscou Lighthouse, UP (NB) **13 H4**
Miscou Plains, UP (NB) **13 H4**
Misère, UP (Que.) **15 C1**
Mis-kat-la 14, IR (BC) **41 D1**
Mispec, UP (NB) **11 E3**
Missanabie, UP (Ont.) **26 B2**
Missanabie 62, IR (Ont.) **26 B2**
Missinipe, UP (Sask.) **32 E1**
Mission, DM (BC) **38 H2**
Mission 1, IR (BC) **38 F2**
Mission 5, IR (BC) **37 H2**
Mission Beach, UP (Alta.) **33 D4**
Mission Creek 8, IR (BC) **35 F3**
Mission Island 2, IR (BC) **39 D3**
Mission-St-Louis, UP (Que.) **13 D3**
Mississagi River 8, IR (Ont.) **25 A1**
Mississagua Landing, UP (Ont.) **24 D3**
Mississauga, C (Ont.) **23 F4**
Mississauga, UP (Ont.) **25 A1**
Mississippi Station, UP (Ont.) **17 A2**
Missonga, UP (Ont.) **26 C2**
Missouri, UP (Ont.) **17 A4**
Mistassini, IR (Que.) **20 G4**
Mistassini, T (Que.) **18 H1**
Mistatim, VL (Sask.) **32 G4**
Mistawasis < Mistiwasis 103, UP (Sask.) **32 D3**
Mistawasis 103, IR (Sask.) **32 D3**
Mistusinne, UP (Sask.) **31 F2**
Mitchell, T (Ont.) **23 C4**
Mitchell, UP (Man.) **28 B2**
Mitchell, UP (Que.) **16 C2**
Mitchell Bay, UP (Ont.) **22 B3**
Mitchell Bay, UP (NS) **9 E3**
Mitchell-Corners, UP (Que.) **16 B4**
Mitchells Brook < Mount Carmel – Mitchells Brook – St Catherine's, UP (Nfld.) **2 F3**
Mitchells Corner, UP (NB) **11 G2**
Mitchell Settlement, UP (NB) **13 E4**
Mitchell Square, UP (Ont.) **23 F2**
Mitchellton, UP (Sask.) **31 G3**
Mitchellview, UP (Sask.) **29 C1**
Mitchellville, UP (Ont.) **17 B4**
Mitford, UP (Alta.) **34 E2**
Mitsue, UP (Alta.) **33 D1**
Moak Lake, UP (Man.) **30 C1**
Moberly, UP (BC) **34 B2**
Moberly Lake, UP (BC) **43 D3**
Mobile, UP (Nfld.) **2 H3**
Mobrae Subdivision, NUP (BC) **38 E3**
Mochelle, UP (NS) **10 C1**
Moes-River, UP (Que.) **16 D4**
Moffat, UP (Sask.) **29 B3**
Moffet, UP (Que.) **18 A2**
Moha, UP (BC) **37 H2**
Mohannes, UP (NB) **11 B3**
Mohr Corners, UP (Ont.) **17 B1**
Moira, UP (Ont.) **21 F1**
Moisie, UP (Que.) **19 F3**
Moisie, SFC/CFS, MIL (Que.) **19 F3**
Moisie-Salmon-Club, UP (Que.) **19 F3**
Mokomon, UP (Ont.) **27 D3**
Molanosa, UP (Sask.) **32 E2**
Molega, UP (NS) **10 D2**
Molesworth, UP (Ont.) **23 C3**
Molewood, UP (Sask.) **32 B3**
Moline, UP (Man.) **29 E3**
Molliers, UP (Nfld.) **2 B3**
Molson, UP (Man.) **28 C1**
Moltke, UP (Ont.) **23 C3**
Molus River, UP (NB) **12 F3**
Monarch, UP (Alta.) **34 F3**
Monarchvale, UP (Sask.) **31 D1**
Monastery, UP (NS) **8 C4**
Monchy, UP (Sask.) **31 D4**
Monck, UP (Ont.) **23 D3**
Monck Road, UP (Ont.) **24 E3**
Moncrieff, UP (Ont.) **23 C4**
Moncton, C (NB) **11 G1**
Moncton Road, UP (NB) **11 G1**
Mondou, UP (Sask.) **31 D2**
Monet, UP (Que.) **18 D2**
Monetville, UP (Ont.) **25 F1**
Moneymore, UP (Ont.) **21 F1**
Monitor, UP (Alta.) **31 B1**
Monkland, UP (Ont.) **17 E2**
Monks Head, UP (NS) **8 B4**
Monkstown, UP (Nfld.) **2 E2**
Monkton, UP (Ont.) **23 C4**
Monnoir, UP (Que.) **16 A3**
Mono Centre, UP (Ont.) **23 E3**
Monominto, UP (Man.) **28 B2**
Monquart, UP (NB) **12 A3**
Monroe, UP (Nfld.) **2 F1**
Montagne-de-la-Croix, UP (NB) **15 H2**
Montagne-des-Roy, UP (NB) **15 H2**
Montagne-des-Therrien, UP (NB) **15 H2**
Montagne-Noire, UP (Que.) **18 F4**
Montagne-Ronde, UP (Que.) **14 F4**
Montague, T (PEI) **7 D4**
Montague, UP (Ont.) **21 B4**
Montague, UP (YT) **45 B3**
Montague Gold Mines, UP (NS) **9 B3**
Montana 139, IR (Alta.) **33 E4**
Mont-Apica, SFC/CFS, MIL (Que.) **14 A4**
Montavista, UP (NS) **9 B3**
Montbeillard, UP (Que.) **18 A2**
Mont-Belvédère, UP (Que.) **18 F4**
Mont-Brun, UP (Que.) **18 A1**
Montcalm, UP (Que.) **18 G4**
Mont-Carmel, UP (Que.) **15 D1**
Mont-Carrier, UP (Que.) **16 D3**
Mont-Castor, UP (Que.) **18 F4**
Montcerf, UP (Que.) **18 D4**
Mont-Cervin, UP (Que.) **15 F3**
Mont-Dufresne, UP (Que.) **16 D3**
Monteagle, UP (NB) **11 F1**
Monteagle Valley, UP (Ont.) **24 F2**
Montebello, VL (Que.) **17 E1**
Monte Creek, UP (BC) **35 E1**
Monte Lake, UP (BC) **35 E1**
Montfort, UP (Que.) **18 F4**
Mont-Gabriel, T (Que.) **18 F4**
Montgomery Park, UP (Ont.) **17 B2**
Monticello, UP (PEI) **7 E3**
Monticello, UP (Ont.) **23 E3**
Montigny, UP (Que.) **18 E4**
Montjoie, UP (Que.) **16 D4**
Mont-Joli, T (Que.) **14 H2**
Mont-Laurier, T (Que.) **18 E4**
Mont-Lebel, UP (Que.) **14 G3**
Mont-Louis, UP (Que.) **13 E1**
Montmagny, C (Que.) **15 C3**
Montmartre, VL (Sask.) **29 B3**
Mont Nebo, UP (Sask.) **32 C3**
Montney, UP (BC) **43 E3**
Mont-Orford, UP (Que.) **16 C4**
Montpellier, UP (Que.) **18 E4**
Mont-Plaisant, UP (Que.) **18 H1**
Montréal, C (Que.) **17 G4**
Montréal-Est, T (Que.) **17 H3**
Montreal Lake < Montreal Lake 106, UP (Sask.) **32 D2**
Montreal Lake 106, IR (Sask.) **32 D2**
Montreal Lake 106B, IR (Sask.) **32 D3**
Montréal-Nord, C (Que.) **17 G3**
Montréal-Ouest, T (Que.) **17 G4**
Montreal River Harbour, UP (Ont.) **26 A3**
Mont-Rolland, UP (Que.) **18 F4**
Montrose, UP (PEI) **7 B2**
Montrose, UP (NS) **9 B2**
Montrose, VL (BC) **34 B4**
Mont-Royal, T (Que.) **17 G4**
Mont-St-Hilaire, T (Que.) **16 A3**
Mont-St-Michel, UP (Que.) **18 E3**
Mont-St-Pierre, VL (Que.) **13 E1**
Mont-Tremblant, UP (Que.) **18 E4**
Mont-Tremblant-Village, UP (Que.) **18 E4**
Monument, UP (NB) **11 A1**
Monument Corner, UP (Ont.) **25 B2**
Monument Corners, UP (Ont.) **25 D4**
Moodys Corner, UP (NS) **10 B3**
Moonbeam, UP (Ont.) **20 C4**
Mooncrest, NUP (Alta.) **33 D3**
Moon Lake, UP (Alta.) **33 C3**
Moon River, UP (Ont.) **24 A2**
Moons Beach, UP (Ont.) **23 G2**
Moons Corners, UP (Ont.) **17 A4**
Moonstone, UP (Ont.) **23 F1**
Moore Centre, UP (Ont.) **22 B2**
Moore Dale, UP (Man.) **29 F2**
Moore Falls, UP (Ont.) **23 H1**
Moorefield, UP (Ont.) **23 D3**
Moorefield, UP (NB) **12 F2**
Moore Park, UP (Man.) **29 F3**
Mooresburg, UP (Ont.) **23 C2**
Moores Corners, UP (Ont.) **17 C2**
Moore's Cove, UP (Nfld.) **3 C2**
Moores Harbour, UP (Nfld.) **6 E1**
Moores Lake, UP (Ont.) **17 A1**
Moores Mills, UP (NB) **11 B3**
Mooresville, UP (Ont.) **22 D1**
Mooretown, UP (Ont.) **22 B2**
Moor Lake, UP (Ont.) **18 B4**
Moose Bay, UP (Man.) **29 F2**
Moose Bay, UP (Sask.) **29 C3**
Moose Brook, UP (NS) **9 B2**
Moose Creek, UP (Ont.) **17 E2**
Moose Factory, UP (Ont.) **20 D3**
Moose Factory 68, IR (Ont.) **20 D3**
Moose Harbour, UP (NS) **10 D3**
Moosehead, UP (NS) **9 E3**
Moose Heights, UP (BC) **40 C3**
Moosehide Creek 2, IR (YT) **45 A2**
Moose Hill, UP (NS) **10 D3**
Moose Hill, UP (Ont.) **27 D3**
Moosehorn, UP (Man.) **29 G2**
Moose Jaw, C (Sask.) **31 G3**
Moose Jaw, CFB/BFC, MIL (Sask.) **31 G3**
Moose Lake, UP (Man.) **30 A2**
Moose Lake, UP (Man.) **28 E3**
Moose Lake 31A, IR (Man.) **30 A2**
Moose Lake 31C, IR (Man.) **30 A2**
Moose Lake 31D, IR (Man.) **30 A2**
Moose Lake 31F, IR (Man.) **30 A2**
Moose Lake 31G, IR (Man.) **30 A2**
Mooseland, UP (NS) **9 D3**
Mooselanka Beach, UP (Ont.) **21 A1**
Moose Mountain, UP (NB) **12 A3**
Moose Point 79, IR (Ont.) **24 A3**
Moose Portage, UP (Alta.) **33 D1**
Moose Range, UP (Sask.) **32 F3**
Moose Range, UP (Sask.) **32 C3**
Moose River, UP (Ont.) **20 C4**
Moose River, UP (NS) **8 A4**
Moose River, UP (NS) **9 A2**
Moose-River, UP (Que.) **16 C3**
Moose River Gold Mines, UP (NS) **9 D3**
Moose Valley, UP (Sask.) **29 C3**
Moose Wallow, UP (Alta.) **33 C2**
Moosh 4, IR (BC) **35 B2**
Moosomin, T (Sask.) **29 D3**
Moosomin 112A, IR (Sask.) **32 B4**
Moosomin 112B, IR (Sask.) **32 B3**
Moosomin 112E, IR (Sask.) **32 B3**
Moosomin 112F, IR (Sask.) **32 B3**
Moosonee, UP (Ont.) **20 D3**
Mooyah 16, IR (BC) **39 F3**
Morar, UP (NS) **8 B4**
Moravian 47, IR (Ont.) **22 C2**
Moraviantown, UP (Ont.) **22 C2**
Moray, UP (Ont.) **22 D1**
Morbert 82, IR (Ont.) **27 H3**
Morden, T (Man.) **29 H4**
Morden, UP (NS) **11 G3**
Morecambe, UP (Alta.) **33 F3**
Morehead, UP (Que.) **17 A1**
Morehouse Corner, UP (NB) **11 B1**
Morell, VL (PEI) **7 D3**
Morell East, UP (PEI) **7 D3**
Morency, UP (Que.) **16 D1**
Moresby Camp, UP (BC) **41 B2**
Moreton's Harbour, UP (Nfld.) **3 D1**
Morewood, UP (Ont.) **17 D2**
Morgan-Corners, UP (Que.) **16 B4**
Morgans Point, UP (Ont.) **21 B4**
Morganston, UP (Ont.) **21 E1**
Morganville, UP (NS) **10 B2**
Moricetown 1, IR (BC) **42 F4**
Morien, UP (NS) **8 F3**
Morien Junction, UP (NS) **8 F3**
Morigeau, UP (Que.) **15 C3**
Morin, UP (Que.) **15 B3**
Morin Creek, UP (Sask.) **32 B2**
Morindale, UP (Que.) **18 F4**
Morin-Heights, UP (Que.) **18 F4**
Morin Lake 217, IR (Sask.) **32 D1**
Morinus, UP (Ont.) **24 B2**
Morinville, T (Alta.) **33 D3**
Morisset-Station, UP (Que.) **15 C4**
Morley, UP (Ont.) **23 D1**
Morley < Stony 142, 143, 144, UP (Alta.) **34 D2**
Morley River, UP (YT) **45 B4**
Morningside, UP (Alta.) **33 D4**
Morpeth, UP (Ont.) **22 C3**
Morrell, UP (NB) **12 A3**
Morrell 2, IR (PEI) **7 D3**
Morrin, VL (Alta.) **34 F1**
Morris, T (Man.) **29 H4**
Morrisburg, VL (Ont.) **17 D2**
Morrisdale, UP (NB) **11 D2**
Morrish, UP (Ont.) **21 D2**
Morris Island, UP (NS) **10 B3**
Morrison, UP (Que.) **18 F4**
Morrison Cove, UP (NB) **12 F2**
Morrison Road, UP (NS) **8 F3**
Morrissey, UP (BC) **34 D4**
Morriston, UP (Ont.) **23 E4**
Morristown, UP (NS) **10 D1**
Morristown, UP (NS) **8 B4**
Morrisville, COMM (Nfld.) **2 B2**
Morrisville, UP (Ont.) **25 A2**
Morse, T (Sask.) **31 E3**
Morse's-Line, UP (Que.) **16 B4**
Morson, UP (Ont.) **28 F3**
Morteen 9, IR (BC) **37 H4**
Mortier < Fox Cove – Mortier, UP (Nfld.) **2 C3**
Mortimer, UP (NB) **12 F3**
Mortimers Point, UP (Ont.) **24 B3**
Mortlach, VL (Sask.) **31 F3**
Morton, UP (Ont.) **17 B3**
Morven, UP (Ont.) **17 A4**
Moscow, UP (Ont.) **17 A4**
Mose Ambrose < St Jacques – Coomb's Cove, UP (Nfld.) **2 B3**
Moseley, UP (Sask.) **31 G1**
Moser River, UP (NS) **9 E3**
Moserville, UP (Ont.) **23 C4**
Mosher, UP (Ont.) **26 B1**
Moshers Corner, UP (NS) **10 C1**
Moshers Island, UP (NS) **10 E2**
Mosherville, UP (NS) **9 A3**
Mosquito, UP (Nfld.) **2 F4**
Mosquito 109, IR (Sask.) **32 B4**
Mosquito Creek 5, IR (BC) **45 C4**
Mossbank, T (Sask.) **31 F3**
Moss Glen, UP (NB) **11 D2**
Mosside, UP (Alta.) **33 D2**
Mossington Park, UP (Ont.) **21 B1**
Mossleigh, UP (Alta.) **34 F2**
Mossley, UP (Ont.) **22 E2**
Mossman, UP (NS) **10 E2**
Moss Spur, UP (Man.) **28 C1**
Mossyvale, UP (Sask.) **32 F3**
Motherwell, UP (Ont.) **22 E1**
Motts Mills, UP (Ont.) **17 B3**
Mould Bay, UP (NWT) **47 B2**
Moulin-Caron, UP (Que.) **18 A2**
Moulin-Des Rivières, UP (Que.) **16 A4**
Moulin-Dufour, UP (Que.) **15 E1**
Moulin-Goulet, UP (Que.) **15 C3**
Moulin-Lajoie, UP (Que.) **15 E1**
Moulin-Morneault, UP (NB) **15 H1**
Moulin-Plamondon, UP (Que.) **16 D3**
Moulin-Samson, UP (Que.) **16 D3**
Moulin-Tourville, UP (Que.) **16 B2**
Moulin-Vallière, UP (Que.) **15 G3**
Mound, UP (Alta.) **34 E1**
Mountain, UP (Ont.) **17 D2**
Mountain Chutes, UP (Ont.) **26 F2**
Mountain Front, UP (NS) **11 G3**
Mountain Grove, UP (Ont.) **17 A3**
Mountain House, UP (Alta.) **34 E1**
Mountain Lake, UP (Ont.) **26 F2**
Mountain Park, UP (Alta.) **33 A4**
Mountain Road, UP (NS) **9 C1**
Mountain Road, UP (Man.) **29 F3**
Mountainside, UP (Man.) **29 E4**
Mountain Station, NUP (BC) **34 B4**
Mountain View, UP (Ont.) **18 B4**
Mountain View, UP (Alta.) **34 F4**
Mountain View, UP (Ont.) **21 F1**
Mountain View, UP (NB) **12 B4**
Mountain View, NUP (BC) **43 D4**
Mountain View Beach, UP (Ont.) **23 E1**
Mountain View Heights, NUP (Ont.) **23 E3**
Mountain View Trailer Court, NUP (Alta.) **34 E2**
Mount Albert, UP (Ont.) **21 B1**
Mount Albion, UP (PEI) **7 D4**
Mount Arlington Heights < Long Harbour – Mount Arlington Heights, UP (Nfld.) **2 F3**
Mount Auburn, UP (NS) **8 E4**
Mountbatten 76A, IR (Ont.) **26 C2**
Mount Brydges, UP (Ont.) **22 D2**
Mount Buchanan, UP (PEI) **7 D4**
Mount Carmel, UP (PEI) **7 B3**
Mount Carmel, UP (Ont.) **22 D1**
Mount Carmel, UP (Ont.) **21 G1**
Mount Carmel, UP (Ont.) **22 B4**
Mount Carmel < Mount Carmel – Mitchells Brook – St Catherine's, UP (Nfld.) **2 G3**
Mount Carmel – Mitchells Brook – St Catherine's, RD (Nfld.) **2 G3**
Mount Chesney, UP (Ont.) **21 H1**
Mount Currie, UP (BC) **37 G3**
Mount Currie 1, IR (BC) **37 G3**
Mount Currie 2, IR (BC) **37 G3**
Mount Currie 6, IR (BC) **37 G3**
Mount Currie 7, IR (BC) **37 G3**
Mount Currie 8, IR (BC) **37 G3**
Mount Currie 10, IR (BC) **37 G3**
Mount Denson, UP (NS) **9 A3**
Mount Elgin, UP (Ont.) **22 F2**
Mount Forest, T (Ont.) **23 D3**
Mount Hanley, UP (NS) **10 C1**
Mount Hebron, UP (NB) **11 F1**
Mount Herbert, UP (PEI) **7 D4**
Mount Hope, UP (Ont.) **21 A3**
Mount Hope, UP (PEI) **7 E3**
Mount Hope, UP (NB) **11 C1**
Mount Hope, UP (Ont.) **23 C2**
Mount Horeb, UP (Ont.) **21 C1**
Mount Irwin, UP (Ont.) **24 D3**
Mount Julian, UP (Ont.) **24 E4**
Mount-Loyal, UP (Que.) **18 F4**
Mount MacDonald, UP (Ont.) **26 F2**
Mount-Maple, UP (Que.) **17 F1**
Mount Mellick, UP (PEI) **7 D4**
Mount Merrit, UP (NS) **10 D2**
Mount Middleton, UP (NB) **11 E2**
Mount Moriah, LID (Nfld.) **4 C1**
Mount Pearl, T (Nfld.) **2 H2**
Mount Pisgah, UP (NB) **11 F1**
Mount Pleasant, UP (Ont.) **22 G1**
Mount Pleasant, UP (NS) **10 B1**
Mount Pleasant, UP (PEI) **7 B3**
Mount Pleasant, UP (Ont.) **21 D1**
Mount Pleasant, UP (NS) **9 B1**
Mount Pleasant, UP (NS) **10 E2**
Mount Pleasant, UP (NB) **12 A4**
Mount Pleasant, UP (NS) **10 D3**
Mount Pleasant, UP (Ont.) **21 G1**
Mount Pleasant, UP (Ont.) **21 F1**
Mount Pleasant, UP (Ont.) **21 B1**
Mount Pleasant, UP (Ont.) **22 E1**
Mount Pleasant, UP (Sask.) **31 G3**
Mount Prospect, UP (NB) **11 E2**
Mount Robson, UP (BC) **40 F3**
Mount Rose, UP (NS) **10 C1**
Mount Royal, UP (PEI) **7 A3**
Mount St Louis, UP (Ont.) **23 F1**
Mount St Patrick, UP (Ont.) **17 A1**
Mount Salem, UP (Ont.) **22 E2**
Mountsberg, UP (Ont.) **23 E4**
Mount Shadow Trailer Court, NUP (BC) **34 B3**
Mount Sheer, UP (BC) **38 F1**
Mount Stephen, UP (Ont.) **23 F1**
Mount Stewart, VL (PEI) **7 D3**
Mount Thom, UP (NS) **9 C2**
Mount Uniacke, UP (NS) **9 B3**
Mount Uniacke Gold District, UP (NS) **9 B3**
Mount Valley, UP (Alta.) **43 F4**
Mount Vernon, UP (PEI) **7 D4**
Mount Vernon, UP (Ont.) **22 E2**
Mount Vernon, NUP (Ont.) **22 G1**
Mount View, UP (Ont.) **23 D3**
Mount View Trailer Court, NUP (BC) **34 B2**
Mountville, UP (NS) **9 D2**
Mountville, UP (NB) **11 G1**
Mount Whatley, UP (NB) **11 H1**
Mount William, UP (NS) **9 D1**
Mount Young, UP (NS) **8 C3**
Mount Zion, UP (Ont.) **21 F1**
Mousseauvillle, UP (Que.) **13 E3**
Moutcha 5, IR (BC) **39 F3**
Mowbray, UP (Man.) **29 G4**
Moyehai 23, IR (BC) **39 G4**
Moyie, UP (BC) **34 C4**
Mozart, UP (Sask.) **31 H1**
Mud Bay, UP (BC) **38 C2**
Muddy Bay, UP (Nfld.) **6 G3**
Muddy Creek, UP (PEI) **7 B3**
Muddy Hole, UP (Nfld.) **4 G4**
Muddy River 1, IR (BC) **45 C4**
Mudie Lake, UP (Sask.) **32 A2**
Mud Lake, UP (Nfld.) **6 F3**
Mud River, UP (BC) **40 C2**
Mud River, UP (Ont.) **27 E1**
Muenster, VL (Sask.) **31 G1**
Muir, UP (Ont.) **22 F1**
Muir, UP (Man.) **29 G3**
Muirkirk, UP (Ont.) **22 D3**
Mulgrave, T (NS) **8 C4**
Mulhurst, UP (Alta.) **33 D4**
Mull, UP (Ont.) **22 C3**
Mullifarry, UP (Ont.) **22 D2**
Mulligan-Ferry, UP (Que.) **18 D4**
Mullingar, UP (Sask.) **32 C4**
Mulloys, UP (Ont.) **17 D2**
Mull River, UP (NS) **8 C3**
Mulmur, UP (Ont.) **23 E3**
Mulock, UP (Ont.) **25 H1**
Mulock, UP (Ont.) **23 C2**
Mulvihill, UP (Man.) **29 G2**
Muncey, UP (Ont.) **22 D2**
Muncey 1, IR (Ont.) **22 D2**
Muncho Lake, UP (BC) **45 C4**
Mundare, T (Alta.) **33 F3**
Mundleville, UP (NB) **12 G3**
Muniac, UP (NB) **12 A3**
Munk, UP (Man.) **30 C1**
Munns Road, UP (PEI) **7 F3**
Munro, UP (Ont.) **23 C4**
Munroe, UP (Man.) **29 F3**
Munroes Mills, UP (Ont.) **17 E2**
Munson, VL (Alta.) **34 F1**
Munster, UP (Ont.) **17 C2**
Murchison, UP (Ont.) **24 E2**
Murchyville, UP (NS) **9 C3**
Murdale, UP (BC) **43 E3**
Murdochville, T (Que.) **13 F1**
Muriel, UP (Alta.) **33 G3**
Muriel Lake, UP (Alta.) **33 G2**
Murillo, UP (Ont.) **27 D3**
Murphy Beach, UP (Ont.) **23 G1**
Murphy Corner, UP (NB) **12 A3**
Murphy Corners, UP (Ont.) **24 F3**
Murphy Cove, UP (NS) **9 D3**
Murphy Lake, UP (NS) **10 E1**
Murphys Cove, UP (Nfld.) **2 E3**
Murphy Settlement, UP (NB) **12 G3**
Murray, UP (NS) **8 E3**
Murray Corner, UP (NB) **7 B4**
Murraydale < Nekaneet 160A, UP (Sask.) **31 C4**
Murray Harbour, VL (PEI) **7 E4**
Murray Harbour North, UP (PEI) **7 E4**
Murray Hill, NUP (Ont.) **21 D1**
Murray Lake 4, IR (BC) **40 A2**
Murray Point, UP (Sask.) **32 D3**
Murray River, VL (PEI) **7 E4**
Murray Road, UP (PEI) **7 B3**
Murray Road, UP (NB) **7 B4**
Murray Settlement, UP (NB) **12 F3**
Murrays Siding, UP (NS) **9 C2**
Murrell, UP (Que.) **17 A1**
Murvale, UP (Ont.) **17 A4**
Musclow, UP (Ont.) **24 F2**
Muscow, UP (Sask.) **31 H2**
Muscowpetung 80, IR (Sask.) **31 H2**
Musgrave, UP (BC) **38 E3**
Musgrave Harbour, T (Nfld.) **3 F2**
Musgravetown, T (Nfld.) **3 F4**
Mushaboom, UP (NS) **9 D3**
Mushkin 5, IR (BC) **37 B3**
Mushkin 5A, IR (BC) **37 B3**
Musidora, UP (Alta.) **33 F3**
Muskeegan, UP (Sask.) **32 G4**
Muskeg Lake 102, IR (Sask.) **32 C4**
Muskeg River, UP (Alta.) **40 G2**
Muskeg River 20C, IR (Sask.) **32 G2**
Muskiki Springs, UP (Sask.) **31 F1**
Muskoday 99, IR (Sask.) **32 E4**
Muskowekwan 85, IR (Sask.) **31 H2**
Muskrat Dam < Muskrat Dam Lake, UP (Ont.) **30 E3**
Muskrat Dam Lake, IR (Ont.) **30 E3**
Muskwa, UP (BC) **45 D4**
Musquaro, UP (Que.) **5 C3**
Musquash, UP (NB) **11 D3**
Musqueam 2, IR (BC) **38 F2**
Musquodoboit Harbour, UP (NS) **9 C3**
Musselyville, UP (Que.) **13 E3**
Mutchler, UP (Sask.) **32 G4**
Mutrie, UP (Sask.) **29 B3**
Muttonville, UP (Ont.) **17 D2**
Myers Cave, UP (Ont.) **24 G3**
Myers Point, UP (NS) **9 C3**
Myncaster, UP (BC) **35 G4**
Myrehall, UP (Ont.) **21 F1**
Myrnam, VL (Alta.) **33 G3**
Myrtle, UP (Man.) **29 H4**
Myrtle Point, UP (BC) **38 C1**
Mystery Lake, UP (Alta.) **33 C2**
Mystic, UP (Que.) **16 B4**

N

Nackawic, T (NB) **11 B1**
Nacmine, UP (Alta.) **34 F2**
Naco, UP (Alta.) **31 B1**
Nadeauville, UP (Sask.) **31 C3**
Naden 10, IR (BC) **41 A1**
Naden 23, IR (BC) **41 A1**
Nadina River, UP (BC) **41 G1**
Nahamanak 7, IR (BC) **35 B2**
Nahanni Butte, UP (NWT) **45 D3**
Nahlin Crossing, UP (BC) **45 B4**
Nahlquonate 2, IR (BC) **40 C2**
Nahma, UP (Ont.) **26 E1**
Nahun, UP (BC) **35 F2**
Nahwitti 4, IR (BC) **39 C1**
Naicam, T (Sask.) **32 F4**
Nail Pond, UP (PEI) **7 B2**
Nain, COMM (Nfld.) **6 E2**
Nairn, UP (Ont.) **25 D1**
Nairn, UP (Ont.) **22 D1**
Naiscoutaing 17A, IR (Ont.) **25 F3**
Nakamun, UP (Alta.) **33 D3**
Nakamun Park, SV (Alta.) **33 D3**
Nakina, UP (Ont.) **27 G1**
Nakina, UP (BC) **45 B4**
Nakusp, VL (BC) **34 B3**
Na-kwockto 10, IR (BC) **41 F4**
Nalos Landing, UP (BC) **41 F4**
Namaka, UP (Alta.) **34 F2**
Namao, UP (Alta.) **33 E3**
Nameless Cove, UP (Nfld.) **5 G2**
Nampa, VL (Alta.) **43 H3**
Namu, UP (BC) **41 F3**
Namur, UP (Que.) **18 E4**
Namur Lake 174B, IR (Alta.) **44 B3**
Namur River 174A, IR (Alta.) **44 C3**
Nanaimo, C (BC) **38 D2**
Nanaimo River 2, IR (BC) **38 E2**
Nanaimo River 3, IR (BC) **38 E2**
Nanaimo River 4, IR (BC) **38 E2**
Nanaimo Town 1, IR (BC) **38 E2**
Nananahout 1, IR (BC) **35 B1**
Nancut < Nancut 3, UP (BC) **40 A1**
Nancut 3, IR (BC) **40 A1**
Nanisivik, UP (NWT) **47 E3**
Nanoose, IR (BC) **38 D2**
Nanoose Bay, UP (BC) **38 D2**
Nantel, UP (Que.) **18 F4**
Nantes, UP (Que.) **16 F3**
Nanticoke, C (Ont.) **22 G2**
Nanton, T (Alta.) **34 E3**
Nantyr, UP (Ont.) **21 A1**
Nantyr Park, UP (Ont.) **21 A1**
Naongashing < Naongashing 31A an[d] 35A, UP (Ont.) **28 F3**
Naongashing 31A and 35A, IR (Ont.) **28 F3**
Napadogan, UP (NB) **12 C4**
Napan Bay, UP (NB) **12 F2**
Napanee, T (Ont.) **21 G1**
Napan Trailer Park, NUP (NB) **12 F2**
Naphan, UP (Ont.) **21 G1**
Naphtha, UP (Alta.) **34 E3**

Napier, UP (Ont.) 22 D2
Napierville, VL (Que.) 16 A4
Napinka, VL (Man.) 29 E4
Naples, UP (Alta.) 33 D2
Nappan, UP (NS) 9 A1
Napperton, UP (Ont.) 22 D2
Naramata, UP (BC) 35 E3
Narcisse, UP (Man.) 29 H3
Narcisse's Farm 4, IR (BC) 35 E4
Narcosli Creek, UP (BC) 40 C3
Narol, UP (Man.) 28 A1
Narrow Lake, UP (Ont.) 30 E4
Narrows, UP (Ont.) 17 C4
Narva, UP (Ont.) 23 B2
Naseby, UP (Sask.) 31 D1
Nash Creek, UP (NB) 13 D4
Nashlyn, UP (Sask.) 31 C4
Nashwaak Bridge, UP (NB) 12 C4
Nashwaak Village, UP (NB) 11 C1
Nasonworth, UP (NB) 11 C1
Nassau Lake, UP (Ont.) 20 B4
Nass Camp, UP (BC) 42 E3
Natashquan, UP (Que.) 5 B3
Natashquan 1, IR (Que.) 5 B3
Nathlegalis 29, IR (BC) 41 F4
National Mills, UP (Man.) 30 A3
Nation Valley, UP (Ont.) 17 D2
Naufrage, UP (PEI) 7 E3
Naugle, UP (NS) 9 C4
Nauglers Settlement, UP (NS) 9 E3
Nautley 1, IR (BC) 40 B1
Nauwigewauk, UP (NB) 11 E2
Navan, UP (Ont.) 17 D1
Navarre, UP (Que.) 18 D4
Navarre, UP (Alta.) 33 E4
Navin, UP (Man.) 28 A1
Naykikoulth 13, IR (BC) 35 B1
Naylors Landing, UP (NWT) 45 D3
Nazco 20, IR (BC) 40 B3
Nazco 21, IR (BC) 40 B3
Nazco Cemetery 20A, IR (BC) 40 B3
Nazko, UP (BC) 40 B3
Ndakdolk 54, IR (BC) 42 C4
Neapolis, UP (Alta.) 34 E1
Necait 6, IR (BC) 37 H2
Necausley Creek 6, IR (BC) 40 C3
Nechacco < Laketown 3, UP (BC) 40 B2
Necoslie 1, IR (BC) 40 B1
Necum Teuch, UP (NS) 9 E3
Neddy Harbour < Norris Point, UP (Nfld.) 5 F4
Nédelec, UP (Que.) 18 A4
Nedoats 11, IR (BC) 42 G3
Nedoats 13, IR (BC) 42 G3
Neeb, UP (Sask.) 32 B2
Neebish, UP (Ont.) 26 B4
Needles, UP (BC) 35 H2
Neekas 4, IR (BC) 41 E3
Neelby, UP (Sask.) 29 C3
Neelin, UP (Man.) 29 F4
Neely, UP (Sask.) 31 F1
Neepawa, T (Man.) 29 F3
Neerlandia, UP (Alta.) 33 D2
Negginan < Popular River 16, UP (Man.) 30 C3
Neguac, VL (NB) 12 F2
Neguaguon Lake 25D, IR (Ont.) 27 B3
Nehounlee Lake 13, IR (BC) 40 B1
Neidpath, UP (Sask.) 31 E3
Neigette, UP (Que.) 14 G3
Neilburg, VL (Sask.) 32 A4
Neils Harbour, UP (NS) 8 E1
Nekalliston 2, IR (BC) 36 F3
Nekaneet 160A, IR (Sask.) 31 C4
Nekite 28, IR (BC) 41 F4
Nekliptum 1, IR (BC) 35 B2
Nelson, C (BC) 34 B4
Nelson Forks, UP (BC) 45 D4
Nelson Hollow, UP (NB) 12 D3
Nelson House < Nelson House 170, UP (Man.) 30 B1
Nelson House 170, IR (Man.) 30 B1
Nelson House 170A, IR (Man.) 30 B1
Nelson House 170B, IR (Man.) 30 B1
Nelson House 170C, IR (Man.) 30 B1
Nelson-Miramichi, VL (NB) 12 E2
Nelway, UP (BC) 34 B4
Nemaiah Valley, UP (BC) 37 E1
Nemegos, UP (Ont.) 26 C2
Némiscau, UP (Que.) 20 F3
Nemiskam, UP (Alta.) 34 H4
Nenagh, UP (Ont.) 23 D3
Nephton, UP (Ont.) 24 E4
Neptune, UP (Sask.) 31 H4
Nequatque 1, IR (BC) 37 G3
Nequatque 2, IR (BC) 37 G3
Nequatque 3, IR (BC) 37 G3
Nequatque 3A, IR (BC) 37 G3
Nequatque 4, IR (BC) 37 G3
Nesbitt Heights, NUP (Sask.) 32 D3
Nesbitt, UP (Man.) 29 F4
Nesikep 6, IR (BC) 35 A1
Nesikep 6A, IR (BC) 35 A1
Neskainlith 1, IR (BC) 36 G4
Neskainlith 2, IR (BC) 36 G4
Nesketahin, UP (YT) 45 A3
Nestledown, UP (Sask.) 32 D3
Nestleton, UP (Ont.) 23 H2
Nestleton Station, UP (Ont.) 21 C1
Nestor Falls, UP (Ont.) 28 G3
Nestorville, UP (Ont.) 26 B4
Nestow, UP (Alta.) 33 D2
Nesuch 3, IR (BC) 37 G3
Nesuk 4, IR (BC) 39 F3
Netherhill, VL (Sask.) 31 C2
Netherton, UP (Sask.) 29 C1
Netla, UP (NWT) 45 D3
Netley, UP (Man.) 30 C4
Netook, UP (Alta.) 34 E1
Ne-tsaw-greece 10, IR (BC) 42 G3
Nettle Island 5, IR (BC) 38 B3
Neuanlage, UP (Sask.) 31 F1
Neubois, UP (Que.) 15 B4
Neudorf, VL (Sask.) 29 C3
Neuenburg, UP (Man.) 29 H4
Neuhoffnung, UP (Sask.) 31 D3
Neuhorst, UP (Sask.) 31 F1
Neuhorst, UP (Man.) 29 H4
Neustadt, VL (Ont.) 23 C3
Neutral Hills, UP (Alta.) 31 B1
Neutral Valley, UP (Alta.) 31 B1
Neuville, VL (Que.) 15 A3
Nevada Valley, UP (NS) 8 C3
Neveton, UP (Man.) 29 H3
Neville, VL (Sask.) 31 E3
Nevis, UP (Alta.) 33 E4
New Acadia, UP (PEI) 7 E3
New Aiyansh < New Aiyansh 1, UP (BC) 42 D3
New Aiyansh 1, IR (BC) 42 D3
New Albany, UP (NS) 10 D1
New Albany, UP (NS) 10 D2
New Annan, UP (PEI) 7 B3
New Argyle, UP (PEI) 7 C4
Newark, UP (Ont.) 22 F2
New Avon, UP (NB) 11 D1
Newaygo, UP (Que.) 18 F4
New Bandon, UP (NB) 12 D3
New Bandon, UP (NB) 12 F1
New Bella Bella < Bella Bella 1, UP (BC) 41 E3
New Bercthal, UP (Man.) 29 H4
Newbliss, UP (Ont.) 17 C3
New Bonaventure, UP (Nfld.) 3 G4
Newboro, VL (Ont.) 17 B3
New Boston, UP (NS) 8 F3
New Bothwell, UP (Man.) 28 A2
Newboyne, UP (Ont.) 17 B3
New Bridge, UP (Nfld.) 2 G3
Newbridge, UP (NB) 11 A1
Newbridge, UP (Ont.) 23 C3
New Brigden, UP (Alta.) 31 B1
New Brighton, UP (BC) 38 E2
New Britain, UP (NS) 9 A2
Newbrook, UP (Alta.) 33 E2
Newburg, UP (NB) 11 A1
Newburgh, VL (Ont.) 24 H4
Newburne, UP (NS) 10 E2
New Burnt Cove, UP (Nfld.) 2 F1
Newbury, VL (Ont.) 22 D2
Newby, UP (Sask.) 32 A4
New California, UP (Ont.) 22 A4
New Campbellton, UP (NS) 8 E3
New Canaan, UP (NS) 9 A2
New Canaan, UP (NB) 11 F1
New Canaan, UP (Ont.) 22 A3
New Canada, UP (NS) 10 D2
New-Carlisle, UP (Que.) 13 F4
New-Carlisle-East, UP (Que.) 13 F4
New-Carlisle-West, UP (Que.) 13 F4
New Carlow, UP (Ont.) 24 F2
Newcastle, T (Ont.) 21 C2
Newcastle, T (NB) 12 E2
Newcastle Centre, UP (NB) 11 E1
Newcastle Creek, UP (NB) 11 D1
New Chelsea, UP (Nfld.) 2 G1
New Chester, UP (NS) 9 E3
New Clew < New Clew 10, UP (BC) 41 B2
New Clew 10, IR (BC) 41 B2
Newcomb Corner, UP (NS) 9 C3
Newcombville, UP (NS) 10 E2
New Credit < New Credit 40A, UP (Ont.) 22 G1
New Credit 40A, IR (Ont.) 22 G1
New Cumberland, UP (NS) 10 E2
Newdale, UP (Man.) 29 E3
New Dayton, UP (Alta.) 34 G4
New Denmark, UP (NB) 12 A4
New Denmark Corner, UP (NB) 12 A2
New Denmark Station, UP (NB) 12 A2
New Denver, VL (BC) 34 B3
New Dominion, UP (PEI) 7 C4
New Dominion, UP (NS) 8 E3
New Dublin, UP (Ont.) 17 C3
New Dundee, UP (Ont.) 22 F1
New Durham, UP (Ont.) 22 F2
New Edinburgh, UP (NS) 10 B2
Newellton, UP (NS) 10 B4
New Elm, UP (NS) 10 D2
New England, UP (Sask.) 32 E4
New England Settlement, UP (NB) 11 D1
New-Erin, UP (Que.) 17 F2
New Ferolle, UP (Nfld.) 5 G2
New Fish Creek, UP (Alta.) 33 A1
New Flos, UP (Ont.) 21 A1
Newfoundout, UP (Ont.) 24 G2
New France, UP (NS) 8 B4
New France, UP (NS) 10 B2
New Gairloch, UP (NS) 9 D2
New Gamebridge Beach, UP (Ont.) 23 G2
Newgate, UP (BC) 34 D4
New Germany, UP (NS) 10 D2
New Glasgow, T (NS) 9 D1
New Glasgow, UP (PEI) 7 C3
New Glasgow, UP (Ont.) 22 D3
New-Glasgow, VL (Que.) 18 F4
New Glasgow Mills, UP (PEI) 7 C3
New Glen, UP (NS) 8 D3
New Grafton, UP (NS) 10 C2
New Hamburg, UP (Ont.) 22 F1
New Harbour, UP (Nfld.) 2 F2
New Harbour, UP (NS) 9 G2
New Harbour, UP (Nfld.) 2 D2
New Harbour, UP (Nfld.) 4 F4
New Harbour, UP (NS) 9 A4
New Harbour East, UP (NS) 9 G2
New Harbour West, UP (NS) 9 G2
New Harmony, UP (PEI) 7 E3
New Harris Forks, UP (NS) 8 E3
New Harris Settlement, UP (NS) 8 E3
New Haven, UP (PEI) 7 C4
New Haven, UP (NS) 8 E1
New Hazelton, UP (BC) 42 F3
New Hermon, UP (Ont.) 24 F2
New Horton, UP (NB) 11 G2
Newington, UP (Ont.) 17 E2
New-Ireland, UP (Que.) 16 E2
New Jersey, UP (NB) 12 F2
New Kiew, UP (Alta.) 33 F3
New Kitseguecla 2, IR (BC) 42 F3
New Lairg, UP (NS) 9 D2
Newlands, UP (BC) 40 D1
New Line Road, UP (NB) 11 F2
New Liskeard, T (Ont.) 26 F3
New London, UP (PEI) 7 C3
New-London, UP (Que.) 16 D3
New Lowell, UP (Ont.) 23 E2
New Lunnon, UP (Alta.) 33 E3
Newman's Beach, UP (Ont.) 21 C1
Newmans Cove, UP (Nfld.) 3 G4
Newmanville, UP (Ont.) 17 C2
Newmarket, T (Ont.) 19 B2
Newmarket, UP (NB) 11 C1
New Maryland, UP (NB) 11 C1
New Melbourne, UP (Nfld.) 2 G1
New-Mexico, UP (Que.) 16 E4
New Mills, UP (NB) 13 D4
New Minas, UP (NS) 11 H3
New Norway, VL (Alta.) 33 E4
New Osgoode, UP (Sask.) 32 F4
New Osnaburgh < Osnaburgh 63B, UP (Ont.) 30 F4
New Perlican, LID (Nfld.) 2 G2
New Perth, UP (PEI) 7 D4
Newport, UP (Que.) 13 G3
Newport, UP (PEI) 7 E4
Newport, UP (Ont.) 22 G1
Newport, UP (Nfld.) 3 F3
Newport-Centre, UP (Que.) 13 G3
Newport Corner, UP (NS) 9 A3
Newport-Ouest, UP (Que.) 13 G3
Newport-Point, UP (Que.) 13 G3
Newport Station, UP (NS) 9 A3
New Post 69, IR (Ont.) 20 C4
New Prospect, UP (NS) 9 A2
New Prussia, UP (Ont.) 23 D4
New-Richmond, T (Que.) 13 E3
New River Beach, UP (NB) 11 C3
New Rosa, UP (Man.) 28 A3
New Ross, UP (NS) 10 E1
New Ross 20, IR (NS) 10 E1
New Russel, UP (NS) 10 E1
Newry, UP (Ont.) 23 C4
New Salem, UP (NS) 11 G2
New Sarepta, VL (Alta.) 33 E3
New Sarum, UP (Ont.) 22 E2
New Scotland, UP (NB) 12 G4
New Scotland, UP (Ont.) 21 A2
New Scotland, UP (Ont.) 22 C3
New Songhees 1A, IR (BC) 38 F4
Newstead < Comfort Cove – Newstead, UP (Nfld.) 3 D2
New Thunderchild 115B, IR (Sask.) 32 B3
New Thunderchild 115C, IR (Sask.) 32 B3
Newton, UP (Ont.) 23 C4
Newton, UP (PEI) 7 B3
Newton, UP (Man.) 29 H3
Newton Mills, UP (NS) 9 D2
Newton Robinson, UP (Ont.) 21 A1
Newtonville, UP (NS) 10 E1
Newtown, T (Nfld.) 3 F2
Newtown, UP (NB) 11 F1
Newtown, UP (NS) 9 E2
Newtown Cross, UP (PEI) 7 D4
New Truro Road, UP (NS) 9 C1
New Tusket, UP (NS) 10 B2
New Uhthoff, UP (Ont.) 23 F1
New Victoria, UP (NS) 8 F3
Newville, UP (Nfld.) 3 D1
New Waterford, T (NS) 8 F3
New Westminster, C (BC) 38 G2
New Yarmouth, UP (NS) 11 G2
New Zealand, UP (PEI) 7 E3
New Zion, UP (NB) 11 D1
Neys, UP (Ont.) 27 G3
Nezah, UP (Ont.) 27 F2
Niagara, UP (BC) 35 H4
Niagara Falls, C (Ont.) 21 B4
Niagara-on-the-Lake, T (Ont.) 21 B3
Nicabong, UP (Que.) 18 C4
Nicholas Denys, UP (NB) 12 E1
Nicholson, UP (BC) 34 B2
Nicholson, UP (Ont.) 26 B2
Nicholsons Point, UP (Ont.) 17 A4
Nicholsville, UP (Nfld.) 5 G4
Nicholsville, UP (NS) 10 D1
Nickel Centre, T (Ont.) 25 E1
Nickel Palm 4, IR (BC) 35 A1
Nickel Plate, UP (BC) 35 E4
Nickeyeah 25, IR (BC) 35 B2
Nickey's Nose Cove, UP (Nfld.) 3 B1
Nicoelton 6, IR (BC) 35 B1
Nicola, UP (BC) 35 C2
Nicola Lake 1, IR (BC) 35 D2
Nicola Mameet 1, IR (BC) 35 C2
Nicolet, T (Que.) 16 B2
Nicolston, UP (Ont.) 21 A1
Nicomen, UP (BC) 38 H2
Nicomen 1, IR (BC) 35 B2
Nicomen Island, NUP (BC) 38 H2
Nictau, UP (NB) 12 B2
Nictaux, UP (NS) 10 D1
Nictaux East, UP (NS) 10 D1
Nictaux Falls, UP (NS) 10 D1
Nictaux South, UP (NS) 10 D1
Nictaux West, UP (NS) 10 D1
Nier, UP (Alta.) 34 E2
Nies Beach, UP (Sask.) 32 D3
Nigadoo, VL (NB) 12 E1
Nigadoo North, NUP (NB) 12 E1
Night < Sarcee 145, UP (Alta.) 34 E2
Nightingale, UP (Alta.) 34 F2
Nile, UP (Ont.) 23 B3
Niles Corners, UP (Ont.) 21 F2
Nilestown, UP (Ont.) 22 E2
Nilrem, UP (Alta.) 33 G4
Nimpkish, UP (BC) 39 E2
Nimpkish 2, IR (BC) 39 E1
Nimpo Lake, UP (BC) 40 A3
Ninastoko, UP (Alta.) 34 F4
Nine Mile Creek, UP (PEI) 7 C4
Nine Mile Creek 4, IR (BC) 35 D3
Nine Mile Narrows, NUP (BC) 34 B4
Nine Mile River, UP (NS) 9 B3
Ninette, UP (Man.) 29 F4
93 Mile, UP (BC) 36 D3
Nineveh, UP (NS) 10 D2
Nineveh, UP (NS) 8 D3
Ninga, UP (Man.) 29 F4
Ninstints, UP (BC) 41 B3
Niobe, UP (Alta.) 34 E1
Niobe, UP (Alta.) 43 G4
Niobe, NUP (Ont.) 27 B3
Nipawin, T (Sask.) 32 F3
Nipigon, UP (Ont.) 27 F2
Nipissing, UP (Ont.) 25 H2
Nipissing 10, IR (Ont.) 25 G1
Nipissing Beach, UP (Ont.) 25 H1
Nippers Harbour, COMM (Nfld.) 3 B1
Nisbet, UP (Alta.) 34 E1
Nishanocknawnak 35, IR (BC) 42 D4
Nisku, UP (Alta.) 33 E3
Nisutlin 14, IR (YT) 45 B4
Nitchequon, UP (Que.) 6 A3
Nithburg, UP (Ont.) 23 D4
Nith Grove, UP (Ont.) 24 C2
Nithi River, UP (BC) 40 A2
Nitinat, UP (BC) 38 C3
Niton, UP (Alta.) 33 C3
Niton Junction, UP (Alta.) 33 C3
Nitro, UP (Que.) 17 G2
Niverville, VL (Man.) 28 A2
Niweme, UP (Ont.) 25 F3
Nixon, UP (Ont.) 22 G2
Nixon, UP (NB) 11 G1
Nkaih 10, IR (BC) 35 A1
Nobbs Siding, UP (Ont.) 24 F3
Nobel, UP (Ont.) 24 D2
Nobleford, VL (Alta.) 34 F3
Nobleton, UP (Ont.) 21 A2
Nobleville, UP (Sask.) 32 F4
Nocten 19, IR (BC) 35 B2
No-cut 5, IR (BC) 42 G3
Noddy Bay, UP (Nfld.) 5 H2
Noel, UP (NS) 9 B2
Noel Road, UP (NS) 9 B2
Noel Shore, UP (NS) 9 B2
Noels Pond, UP (Nfld.) 4 C2
Noelville, UP (Ont.) 25 F1
Noggin Cove, UP (Nfld.) 3 E2
Nogies Creek, UP (Ont.) 24 D4
Nohomeen 23, IR (BC) 35 B2
Noinville, UP (NB) 12 F3
Nojack, UP (Alta.) 33 C3
Nokomis, T (Sask.) 31 E2
Nolalu, UP (Ont.) 27 D3
Nolan, UP (Alta.) 34 F4
Nolans Corners, UP (Ont.) 17 C2
Nominingue, UP (Que.) 18 E4
Nooaitch 10, IR (BC) 35 B2
Nooaitch Grass 9, IR (BC) 35 C2
Noonan, UP (NB) 11 C1
Noonla 6, IR (BC) 40 B2
Nooseseck 2, IR (BC) 41 F3
Noota 4, IR (BC) 41 F3
Nootka, UP (BC) 39 E3
Nora, UP (Sask.) 29 B1
Noralee, UP (BC) 41 G1
Noranda, C (Que.) 18 A1
Norbertville, VL (Que.) 16 D2
Norbestos, UP (Que.) 16 D3
Norboro, UP (PEI) 7 C3
Norbuck, UP (Alta.) 33 D4
Norbury, UP (Sask.) 32 C3
Nordegg, UP (Alta.) 33 B4
Nordin, UP (NB) 12 E2
Norembega, UP (Ont.) 26 E1
Norfolk, UP (Alta.) 34 E2
Norgate, UP (Man.) 29 F3
Norge, UP (Sask.) 31 E4
Norglenwold, SV (Alta.) 33 D4
Norham, UP (Ont.) 21 E1
Norland, UP (Ont.) 23 H1
Norma, UP (Alta.) 33 F3
Norman, UP (Ont.) 22 E2
Norman, UP (Man.) 29 E3
Normandale, UP (Ont.) 22 G2
Normandeau, UP (Alta.) 33 F2
Normandie, UP (NB) 12 G3
Normandin, VL (Que.) 18 G1
Normandville, UP (Alta.) 43 H3
Norman's Cove < Norman's Cove – Long Cove, UP (Nfld.) 2 F2
Norman's Cove – Long Cove, RD (Nfld.) 2 F2
Norman Wells, UP (NWT) 45 C2
Normétal, UP (Que.) 18 A1
Norquay, T (Sask.) 29 D1
Norris Arm, T (Nfld.) 3 C3
Norris Lake, UP (Man.) 29 H3
Norris Point, COMM (Nfld.) 5 F4
North Ainslie, UP (NS) 8 D3
North Alton, UP (NS) 10 E1
Northam, UP (PEI) 7 B3
Northampton, UP (NB) 11 A1
North Augusta, UP (Ont.) 17 C3
Northbank, UP (Alta.) 33 E2
North Battleford, C (Sask.) 32 B4
North Bay, C (Ont.) 26 G4
North Bay, UP (Nfld.) 4 C3
North Bay 5, IR (BC) 36 G4
North Bedeque, UP (PEI) 7 B3
North Bend, UP (BC) 35 B2
North Bloomfield, UP (NS) 8 A4
North Boat Harbour, UP (Nfld.) 5 H2
North Bonaparte, UP (BC) 36 D3
North Branch, UP (Ont.) 28 G4
North Branch, UP (Ont.) 17 E2
Northbrook, UP (Ont.) 24 G3
North Brookfield, UP (NS) 10 D2
North Bruce, UP (Ont.) 23 B3
North Bulkley, UP (BC) 42 G4
North Buxton, UP (Ont.) 22 C3
North Cape Highlands, UP (NS) 8 C3
North Carleton, UP (PEI) 7 B4
North Chegoggin, UP (NS) 10 A3
North-Clarendon, UP (Que.) 17 A1
Northcliffe, UP (Alta.) 34 F4
North Cooking Lake, UP (Alta.) 33 E3
Northcote, UP (Ont.) 17 A1
North Cove, UP (Nfld.) 6 H3
North Cowichan, DM (BC) 38 E3
Northcrest, NUP (Ont.) 22 E1
North Earltown, UP (NS) 9 C1
Northeast Arm Harbour Deep, UP (Nfld.) 5 G3
North East Croque, UP (Nfld.) 5 H2
Northeast Crouse, UP (Nfld.) 5 H2
North East Harbour, UP (NS) 10 C4
Northeast Harbour Buffet, UP (Nfld.) 2 E2
Northeast Mabou, UP (NS) 8 C3
North East Margaree, UP (NS) 8 D3
North East Point, UP (NS) 10 B4
North Ekfrid, UP (Ont.) 22 D2
North Enmore, UP (PEI) 7 B3
Northern Arm, LID (Nfld.) 3 C2
Northern Bay, UP (Nfld.) 2 G1
Northern Harbour, UP (NB) 11 B3
Northern Light, UP (Sask.) 32 E4
Northern Pine, UP (Sask.) 32 A2
Northern Valley, UP (Alta.) 33 G3
North Esk Boom, UP (NB) 12 E2
Northfield, UP (NS) 10 C2
Northfield, UP (Ont.) 17 E2
Northfield, UP (NS) 9 E2
Northfield, UP (NS) 10 E2
Northfield Station, UP (Ont.) 17 E2
North Forks, UP (NB) 11 E1
North Fourchu, UP (NS) 8 F4
North Framboise, UP (NS) 8 E4
North Galiano, UP (BC) 38 E3
Northgate, UP (Sask.) 29 C4
North-Georgetown, UP (Que.) 17 G2
North Glanford, UP (Ont.) 21 A3
North Glen, UP (NS) 8 E4
North Gower, UP (Ont.) 17 C2
North Grand Pré, UP (NS) 9 A3
North Grant, UP (NS) 8 B4
North Greville, UP (NS) 11 H2
North Hall, UP (Ont.) 22 F2
North Harbour, UP (Nfld.) 2 E2
North Harbour, UP (Nfld.) 2 F3
North-Hatley, VL (Que.) 16 D4
North Head, VL (NB) 11 C4
North-Hill, UP (Que.) 16 E3
North Intervale, UP (NS) 9 F2
North Kemptville, UP (NS) 10 B3
North Kingston, UP (NS) 10 D1
North Knife Lake, UP (Man.) 46 A4
North Lake, UP (PEI) 7 F3
North Lake, UP (NB) 11 A1
North Lakeside (Williams Lake), NUP (BC) 36 B1
North Lakevale, UP (NS) 8 B4
North Lancaster, UP (Ont.) 17 F2
Northland, UP (Ont.) 26 B3
Northleigh, UP (Alta.) 33 C3
North Lochaber, UP (NS) 9 E2
North-Low, UP (Que.) 18 D4
North Lunenburg, UP (Ont.) 17 E2
Northmark, UP (Alta.) 43 G4
North Medford, UP (NS) 11 H3
North Middleboro, UP (NS) 9 B1
North Milton, UP (PEI) 7 C3
North Monetville, UP (Ont.) 25 F1
North-Nation-Mills, UP (Que.) 17 D1
North Noel Road, UP (NS) 9 B2
North Ogden, UP (NS) 9 F2
North-Onslow, UP (Que.) 17 B1
North Pine, UP (BC) 43 E3
Northport, UP (NS) 7 B4
North Port, UP (Ont.) 21 G1
North Portage, UP (Ont.) 24 C2
North Portal, VL (Sask.) 29 C4
North Preston, UP (NS) 9 B3
North Range, UP (NS) 10 B2
North Range Corner, NUP (NS) 10 B2
North Renous, UP (NB) 12 E3
North Ridge, UP (Ont.) 22 A3
North Ridge, UP (NB) 12 B3
North River, COMM (Nfld.) 2 G2
North River, UP (PEI) 7 C4
North River, UP (NS) 10 D2
North River, UP (NS) 9 C2
North River, UP (Nfld.) 6 G3
North River, UP (Man.) 46 B3
North River Bridge, UP (NS) 8 E3
North River Centre, UP (NS) 8 E3
North Riverside, UP (NS) 9 F2
North Road, UP (NB) 11 B4
North Rogersville, UP (NB) 12 F3
Northrups Corner, UP (NB) 11 E2
North Russell, UP (Ont.) 17 D2
North Rustico, VL (PEI) 7 C3
North Rustico Harbour, UP (PEI) 7 C3
North Saanich, DM (BC) 38 F4
North St Eleanors, UP (PEI) 7 B3
North Salem, UP (NS) 9 B3
Norths Corner, UP (NS) 11 H3
North Seguin, UP (Ont.) 24 A2
North Seneca, UP (Ont.) 22 H1
North Shore, UP (NS) 9 C1
North Shore, UP (NS) 8 E3
Northside, UP (Sask.) 32 D3
Northside East Bay, UP (NS) 8 E3
North Side Whycocomagh Bay, UP (NS) 8 D3
North Spirit Lake, UP (Ont.) 30 E3
North Star, UP (Alta.) 43 H2
North Star, UP (Sask.) 32 E4
North-Sutton, UP (Que.) 16 B4
North Sydney, T (NS) 8 F3
North Tacla Lake 7, IR (BC) 42 G3
North Tacla Lake 7A, IR (BC) 42 G3
North Tacla Lake 8, IR (BC) 42 G3
North Tacla Lake 10, IR (BC) 42 G3
North Tacla Lake 11A, IR (BC) 42 G3
North Tacla Lake 12, IR (BC) 42 H3
North Tay, UP (NB) 12 C4
North Tetagouche, UP (NB) 12 E1
North Thamesville, UP (Ont.) 22 C2
North Thompson 1, IR (BC) 36 F3
North Tilley, UP (NB) 12 A3
North Tryon, UP (PEI) 7 C4
North Valley, UP (Ont.) 17 D2
North Vancouver, C (BC) 38 F2
North Vancouver, DM (BC) 38 F2
North View, UP (NB) 12 B2
Northville, UP (NS) 11 H3
Northville, UP (Ont.) 22 C1
Northville, UP (Alta.) 33 C3
North Wallace, UP (NS) 9 B1
North Wallace Bay, UP (NS) 9 B1
Northway, UP (Sask.) 32 E4
Northwest, UP (NS) 10 E2
Northwest Angle 33B, IR (Ont.) 28 E2
Northwest Angle 34C, IR (Man.) 28 E3
Northwest Angle 34C and 37B, IR (Ont.) 28 E2
Northwest Angle 37C, IR (Man.) 28 E3
North West Arm, UP (NS) 8 E3
Northwest Bay < Rainy Lake 17A, UP (Ont.) 28 H4
North West Brook, UP (Nfld.) 2 F1
Northwest Cove, UP (NS) 9 A4
North West Harbour, UP (NS) 10 C4
Northwest Point, UP (Man.) 28 E2
North West River, LID (Nfld.) 6 F3
North Weyburn, UP (Sask.) 29 B4
North-Whitton, UP (Que.) 16 F3
North Williamston, UP (NS) 10 C1
North Wiltshire, UP (PEI) 7 C4
North Winchester, UP (Ont.) 17 D2
Northwood, UP (Ont.) 22 C3
North Woodslee, UP (Ont.) 22 B3
North Woolwich, UP (Ont.) 23 D4
North York, BOR (Ont.) 21 B2
Norton, VL (NB) 11 E2
Nortondale, UP (NB) 11 B1
Norway, UP (PEI) 7 B2
Norway-Bay, UP (Que.) 17 B1
Norway House, UP (Man.) 30 C2
Norway House 17, IR (Man.) 30 C2
Norway Point, UP (Ont.) 24 C2
Norwich, UP (Ont.) 22 F1
Norwich Gore, UP (Ont.) 22 F1
Norwood, UP (NS) 10 B3
Norwood, VL (Ont.) 21 E1
Nosbonsing, UP (Ont.) 18 A4
Notch Hill, UP (BC) 36 G4
Notigi, UP (Man.) 30 B1
Notikewin, UP (Alta.) 43 H2
Notre-Dame, UP (Que.) 17 H4
Notre-Dame, UP (NB) 12 G4
Notre-Dame-de-Beaulac, UP (Que.) 18 F4
Notre-Dame-de-Ham, UP (Que.) 16 D2
Notre-Dame-de-la-Doré, UP (Que.) 18 G1
Notre-Dame-de-la-Merci, UP (Que.) 18 F4
Notre-Dame-de-la-Paix, UP (Que.) 18 E4
Notre-Dame-de-l'Isle-Verte, UP (Que.) 14 E4
Notre-Dame-de-Lourdes, UP (NB) 12 A2
Notre Dame de Lourdes, VL (Man.) 29 G4
Notre-Dame-de-Montauban, VL (Que.) 18 H3
Notre-Dame-de-Pierreville, UP (Que.) 16 B2
Notre-Dame-de-Pontmain, UP (Que.) 18 D4
Notre-Dame-des-Bois, UP (Que.) 16 F4
Notre-Dame-des-Champs, UP (Ont.) 17 D1
Notre-Dame-des-Érables, UP (NB) 12 F1
Notre-Dame-des-Monts, UP (Que.) 15 C1
Notre-Dame-des-Pins, UP (Que.) 15 C4
Notre-Dame-des-Prairies, UP (Que.) 16 A2
Notre-Dame-de-Stanbridge, UP (Que.) 16 B4
Notre-Dame-du-Bon-Conseil, VL (Que.) 16 C2
Notre-Dame-du-Lac, T (Que.) 15 G1
Notre Dame du Lac, UP (Ont.) 25 G1
Notre-Dame-du-Laus, UP (Que.) 18 D4
Notre-Dame-du-Nord, UP (Que.) 26 G2
Notre-Dame-du-Portage, UP (Que.) 14 E4
Notre-Dame-du-Rosaire, UP (Que.) 15 C3
Notre-Dame-du-Rosaire, UP (Que.) 14 A2
Notre-Dame-du-Sourire, NUP (Que.) 17 G2
Notre Dame Junction, UP (Nfld.) 3 C2
Nottawa, UP (Ont.) 23 E2
Nottingham, UP (Sask.) 29 D4
Nottingham Island, UP (NWT) 46 E3
Nourse, UP (Man.) 28 B1
Nouveau-Comptoir (Wemindji), UP (Que.) 20 E2
Nouvelle, UP (Que.) 13 D3
Nouvelle-Ouest, UP (Que.) 13 D3
Novar, UP (Ont.) 24 B2
Novra, UP (Man.) 30 A3
Noyan, UP (Que.) 16 A4
Noyes Crossing, UP (Alta.) 33 D3
Nuchaquis 2, IR (BC) 38 B3
Nuchatl 1, IR (BC) 39 E3
Nuchatl 2, IR (BC) 39 E3
Nuchatlitz < Nuchatl 1, UP (BC) 39 E3
Nudell Bush, UP (Ont.) 17 D2
Nugent, UP (Alta.) 33 D4
Nukko Lake, UP (BC) 40 C1
Numogate, UP (Ont.) 17 B2
Numukamis 1, IR (BC) 38 B3
Nunalla, UP (Man.) 46 B3
Nunatak, UP (NWT) 46 F1
Nursery, UP (BC) 35 H4
Nutak, UP (Nfld.) 6 E1
Nutimik Lake, UP (Man.) 28 D1
Nut Lake 90, IR (Sask.) 29 B1
Nut Mountain, UP (Sask.) 29 B1
Nuttby, UP (NS) 9 C2
Nuuautin 2, IR (BC) 35 B2
Nuuautin 2A, IR (BC) 35 B2
Nuuautin 2B, IR (BC) 35 B2
Nuwata, UP (NWT) 46 E2
Nyanza, UP (NS) 7 H4
Nym Lake, NUP (Ont.) 27 B3

O

Oakbank, UP (Man.) 28 B1
Oak Bay, DM (BC) 38 F4
Oak Bay, UP (NB) 11 B3
Oak-Bay, UP (Que.) 13 C3
Oak Bluff, UP (Man.) 28 A2
Oak Brae, UP (Man.) 29 F2
Oakburn, UP (Man.) 29 E3
Oakdale, UP (Ont.) 22 C2
Oakdene Point, UP (Ont.) 21 C1
Oakfield, UP (NS) 9 B3
Oakfield, UP (NS) 8 F3
Oak Flats, UP (Ont.) 17 A3
Oakgrove, UP (Ont.) 17 A1
Oak Haven, UP (NB) 11 B3
Oak Heights, UP (Ont.) 21 E1
Oak Hill, UP (NS) 10 E2
Oak Hill, UP (NB) 11 B3
Oak Lake, T (Man.) 29 E4
Oak Lake, UP (Ont.) 24 E4
Oak Lake, UP (Ont.) 21 F1
Oak Lake 59, IR (Man.) 29 E4
Oak Lake 59A, IR (Man.) 29 E4
Oak Lake Beach, UP (Man.) 29 E4
Oakland, UP (NS) 10 E2
Oakland, UP (Ont.) 22 G1
Oakland, UP (NB) 12 A4
Oakland, UP (Ont.) 22 B3
Oakland, UP (Man.) 29 G3
Oaklawn Beach, UP (Ont.) 24 B4
Oak Leaf, UP (Ont.) 17 B3
Oak Mountain, UP (NB) 11 A1
Oakner, UP (Man.) 29 E3
Oak Orchard, UP (Ont.) 24 D4
Oak Park, UP (NS) 10 B4
Oak Point, UP (Man.) 29 H3
Oak Point, UP (NB) 11 D2
Oak Point, UP (NB) 12 F2
Oak River, UP (Man.) 29 E3
Oakshela, UP (Sask.) 29 C3
Oak Valley, UP (Ont.) 17 D2
Oakview, UP (Man.) 29 G2
Oakville, T (Ont.) 22 H1
Oakville, UP (Man.) 29 H3
Oakville, UP (NB) 12 A4
Oakwood, UP (Ont.) 21 C1
Oalthkyim 4, IR (BC) 38 E2
Oasis, UP (BC) 34 B4
Oasis Trailer Court, NUP (NS) 8 B4
Oatfield, UP (Man.) 29 G2
Oatswish 13, IR (BC) 41 E2
Oba, UP (Ont.) 20 B4
Obabikong 35B, IR (Ont.) 28 G3
Obadjiwan 15E, IR (Ont.) 26 A3
Oban, UP (NS) 8 D4
Oban, UP (Sask.) 31 D1
Obaska, UP (Que.) 18 C2
Obed, UP (Alta.) 33 A3
Obedjiwan < Obedjiwan 28, UP (Que.) 18 E1
Obedjiwan 28, IR (Que.) 18 E1
Oberlin, UP (Alta.) 34 F1
Oberon, UP (Man.) 29 F3
O'Brien, UP (Ont.) 26 F3
O'Brien, UP (Ont.) 26 E2
O'Briens Landing, UP (Ont.) 27 C1
Occosh 8, IR (BC) 39 D3
Ocean Falls, UP (BC) 41 F3
Ocean Pond, UP (Nfld.) 2 G3
Ocean View, UP (PEI) 7 D4
Oceanview, UP (NS) 8 F4
Ochapowace 71, IR (Sask.) 29 C3
O'Chiese 203, IR (Alta.) 33 C4
O'Chiese Cemetery 203A, IR (Alta.) 34 D1
Ochre Beach, UP (Man.) 29 F2
Ochre Pit Cove, UP (Nfld.) 2 G2
Ochre River, UP (Man.) 29 F2
Oclucje 7, IR (BC) 39 E3
O'Connor, UP (Ont.) 27 D3
Oconto, UP (Ont.) 17 A3

Odanak < Odanak 12, UP (Que.) 16 B2
Odanak 12, IR (Que.) 16 B2
Odell, UP (NB) 12 B3
Odelltown, UP (Que.) 16 A4
Oderin, UP (Nfld.) 2 D3
Odessa, UP (Ont.) 17 A4
Odessa, VL (Sask.) 29 B3
Odhill, UP (Man.) 30 B2
O'Donnell Landing, UP (Ont.) 21 C1
O'Donnells, UP (Nfld.) 2 F3
O'Donnells, UP (NB) 12 D3
Off Lake Corner, UP (Ont.) 28 G4
Ogden, UP (NS) 9 F2
Ogden, UP (BC) 37 G2
Ogdensburg, UP (Que.) 17 F1
Ogema, T (Sask.) 31 G4
Ogilvie, UP (Man.) 29 G3
Ogilvie, UP (NS) 11 G3
Ogilvie, UP (YT) 45 A2
Ogoki, UP (Ont.) 20 A3
O'Grady Settlement, UP (Ont.) 24 F2
Ohamil 1, IR (BC) 35 A4
O'Hanly < Black River 9, UP (Man.) 30 C4
Ohaton, UP (Alta.) 33 E4
Ohio, UP (NS) 8 B4
Ohio, UP (NS) 10 B2
Ohio, UP (NS) 10 A3
Ohio-du-Barachois, UP (NB) 7 A4
Ohsweken < Six Nations 40, UP (Ont.) 22 G1
Oil City, UP (Ont.) 22 C2
Oil Springs, VL (Ont.) 22 C2
Oinimitis 14, IR (BC) 38 A2
Ojibway Island, UP (Ont.) 25 F3
Oka, UP (Que.) 17 G1
Oka 16, IR (Que.) 17 F1
Okanagan 1, IR (BC) 35 F1
Okanagan Centre, UP (BC) 35 F2
Okanagan Falls, UP (BC) 35 E4
Okanagan Landing, UP (BC) 35 F2
Okanese 82, IR (Sask.) 29 B2
Oka-sur-le-Lac, T (Que.) 17 G1
Oke, UP (Alta.) 33 A3
Oke 10, IR (BC) 39 E3
Okeamin 5, IR (BC) 38 A2
Okema Beach, UP (Sask.) 32 D3
Okla, UP (Sask.) 29 C1
Okno, UP (Man.) 29 H2
Okotoks, T (Alta.) 34 E2
Olalla, UP (BC) 35 E4
Old Altona, UP (Man.) 29 H4
Old Barns, UP (NS) 9 C2
Old Bonaventure, UP (Nfld.) 3 G4
Oldcastle, UP (Ont.) 22 A3
Old-Chelsea, UP (Que.) 17 D3
Old Clemenes 16, IR (BC) 36 B2
Old Cobequid Road, UP (NS) 9 B3
Old Country Meadow 4, IR (BC) 40 B2
Old Crow, UP (YT) 45 B1
Old Cut, UP (Ont.) 22 G2
Oldenberg, UP (Man.) 28 C1
Old England, UP (Man.) 28 A1
Old Entrance, UP (Alta.) 40 H2
Oldfield, UP (Ont.) 22 B3
Old Fort, UP (Ont.) 23 F1
Old Fort, UP (Alta.) 44 C3
Old Fort < Nedoats 11, UP (BC) 42 G3
Old Fort 157B, IR (Sask.) 32 E1
Old Fort Nelson, UP (BC) 45 D4
Old Fort Providence, UP (NWT) 44 B1
Old Fort Rae, UP (NWT) 45 E3
Oldham, UP (NS) 9 B3
Old-Harry, UP (Que.) 7 G1
Old Hogem, UP (BC) 42 H3
Old Holland Road, UP (NS) 9 B3
Old Main Centre, UP (Sask.) 31 E3
Old Perlican, T (Nfld.) 2 G1
Old Ridge, UP (NB) 11 B3
Olds, T (Alta.) 34 E1
Old Shop, UP (Nfld.) 2 F2
Old Spring Bay, UP (Ont.) 25 B2
Old Stittsville, UP (Ont.) 17 D4
Old Town, UP (BC) 34 C4
Old Wives, UP (Sask.) 31 F3
Old Woman's River, NUP (Ont.) 23 C1
O'Leary, VL (PEI) 7 A3
Olga, UP (Sask.) 31 C4
Olha, UP (Man.) 29 E3
Olinda, UP (Ont.) 22 B4
Oliphant, UP (Ont.) 23 C1
Olive, UP (Ont.) 27 A3
Oliver, UP (Ont.) 22 A3
Oliver, UP (NS) 9 C1
Oliver, UP (Que.) 16 C4
Oliver, UP (Ont.) 22 E1
Oliver, UP (Alta.) 33 E3
Oliver, VL (BC) 35 E4
Olivet, UP (Ont.) 23 D3
Olscamps, UP (Que.) 18 G3
Omaktai, UP (Alta.) 34 F4
Ombabika, UP (Ont.) 27 F1
Omemee, VL (Ont.) 21 D1
Omer, UP (Que.) 18 D4
Omerville, VL (Que.) 16 C4
Omineca 1, IR (BC) 41 G1
Omoah 9, IR (BC) 38 B3
Ompah, UP (Ont.) 17 A2
Onadsilth 9, IR (BC) 38 A2
Onakawana, UP (Ont.) 20 C4
Onanole, UP (Man.) 29 F3
Onaping Falls, T (Ont.) 26 E4
One Arrow 95, IR (Sask.) 32 D4
Onefour, UP (Alta.) 31 B4
100 Mile House, VL (BC) 36 D2
105 Mile House, UP (BC) 36 D2
One Hundred and Five Mile Post 2, IR (BC) 36 D4
150 Mile House, UP (BC) 36 C1
Oneida 41, IR (Ont.) 22 D2
O'Neil, UP (NB) 11 G1
O'Neil, UP (Que.) 17 F2
One Man Lake 29, IR (Ont.) 30 D4
One Mile 6, IR (BC) 35 C3
One Mile Point 1, IR (BC) 45 B4
Onion Lake, UP (Sask.) 32 A3
Onondaga, UP (Ont.) 22 G1
Onoway, VL (Alta.) 33 D3
Onslow, UP (NS) 9 C2
Onslow-Corners, UP (Que.) 17 B1
Onslow Mountain, UP (NS) 9 C2
Oolahwan, UP (Que.) 18 F4
Oona River, UP (BC) 41 C1
Oo-oolth 8, IR (BC) 38 A3
Ootischenia, UP (BC) 34 B4
Ootsa, UP (BC) 41 G1
Ootsa Lake, UP (BC) 41 G1
Oo-za-we-kwun, NUP (Man.) 29 E3
Opal, UP (Alta.) 33 E3
Opasatika, UP (Ont.) 20 C4
Opasquia, UP (Ont.) 30 D3
Opatseeah 13, IR (BC) 38 C3
Opemit 4, IR (BC) 39 E3
Open Bay 8, IR (BC) 37 B4
Open Hall, UP (Nfld.) 3 G4
Openit 27, IR (BC) 39 F4
Ophir, UP (Ont.) 26 B4
Opitsat < Opitsat 1, UP (BC) 39 G4
Opitsat 1, IR (BC) 39 G4
Ops, UP (Ont.) 21 C1
Orangedale, UP (NS) 8 D4
Orangedale East, UP (NS) 8 D3
Orange Hill, UP (NB) 11 E2
Orangeville, T (Ont.) 23 E3
Oranmore, UP (Ont.) 24 A1
Orcadia, UP (Sask.) 29 C2
Orchard Beach, UP (Ont.) 21 B1
Orchard Grove, UP (Ont.) 21 B1
Orchards Corner, UP (NB) 12 A3
Orchardside, UP (Ont.) 17 D2
Orchardville, UP (Ont.) 23 D3
Ordale, UP (Sask.) 32 D3
O'Regan's, UP (Nfld.) 4 A3
Oregon, UP (NS) 8 E3
Oregon Jack Creek 2, IR (BC) 35 B1
Oregon Jack Creek 3, IR (BC) 35 B1
Oregon Jack Creek 5, IR (BC) 35 B1
Orford Bay 4, IR (BC) 37 C3
Orford-Centre, NUP (Que.) 16 D4
Oriel, UP (Ont.) 22 F1
Orient, UP (Ont.) 17 D1
Orient Bay, UP (Ont.) 27 F2
Orillia, C (Ont.) 23 G1
Orion, UP (Alta.) 31 A4
Orkney, UP (Sask.) 31 D4
Orkney, NUP (Ont.) 22 G1
Orkney Beach, UP (Ont.) 23 G1
Orland, UP (Ont.) 21 E1
Orleans, UP (Ont.) 17 F3
Orley, UP (Sask.) 32 G4
Orlo UP (Que.) 18 D4
Ormeaux, UP (Sask.) 32 C3
Ormston, UP (Sask.) 31 G4
Ormond, UP (Ont.) 17 D2
Ormond Beach, UP (Ont.) 22 E2
Ormonde Creek 8, IR (BC) 40 A1
Ormsby, UP (Ont.) 24 F3
Ormstown, VL (Que.) 17 G2
Oro Beach, UP (Ont.) 21 B1
Oro Lea Beach, UP (Ont.) 21 A1
Orolow, UP (Sask.) 32 C4
Oromocto, T (NB) 11 C1
Oromocto 26, IR (NB) 11 C1
Oro Park, UP (Ont.) 21 B1
Oro Station, UP (Ont.) 21 B1
Orr Lake, UP (Ont.) 23 F1
Orr's Lake, UP (Ont.) 22 G1
Orrville, UP (Ont.) 24 A2
Orton, UP (Ont.) 23 E3
Orton, UP (Alta.) 34 F4
Ortonville, UP (NB) 12 A2
Orwell, UP (Ont.) 22 E2
Orwell, UP (PEI) 7 D4
Orwell Cove, UP (PEI) 7 D4
Osaca, UP (Ont.) 21 D2
Osage, VL (Sask.) 29 B3
Osborne, UP (Man.) 29 H4
Osborne, UP (Ont.) 22 C2
Osborne Acres, NUP (Alta.) 33 D3
Osborne Corner, UP (NB) 11 G1
Osborne Corners, UP (Ont.) 22 G1
Osborne Harbour, UP (NS) 10 C4
Oscar Lake, UP (Sask.) 32 C4
Osceola, UP (Ont.) 24 G1
Oschawwinna 3, IR (BC) 42 F4
Osgoode, UP (Ont.) 17 C2
Osgoode Gardens, NUP (Ont.) 17 E4
Oshawa, C (Ont.) 21 C2
Oskélanéo, UP (Que.) 18 E2
Osland, UP (BC) 41 C1
Osler, VL (Sask.) 31 F1
Osmond, UP (Nfld.) 4 A4
Osnabruck Centre, UP (Ont.) 17 E2
Osnaburg 63A, IR (Ont.) 30 F4
Osnaburg 63B, IR (Ont.) 30 F4
Osnaburgh House, UP (Ont.) 30 F4
Oso, UP (Ont.) 17 A3
Osoyoos, UL (BC) 35 F4
Osoyoos 1, IR (BC) 35 F4
Osoyoos 3, IR (BC) 35 F4
Osprey Lake, UP (BC) 35 D3
Ospringe, UP (Ont.) 23 E4
Osseo, UP (Ont.) 26 F2
Ossossane Beach, UP (Ont.) 23 E1
Ostenfeld, UP (Man.) 28 B2
Osterwick, UP (Man.) 29 H4
Ostrander, UP (Ont.) 22 F2
Ostrea Lake, UP (NS) 9 C3
Ostrom, UP (Ont.) 26 D3
Oswald, UP (Man.) 29 H3
Othello, UP (BC) 35 B4
Otoreke, UP (Que.) 18 F4
Otosquen, UP (Sask.) 32 H3
O-tsaw-las 5, IR (BC) 39 E1
Ottawa, C (Ont.) 17 E4
Ottawa Brook, UP (NS) 8 D3
Ottawa (South/Sud), CFB/BFC, MIL (Ont.) 17 C2
Otter, UP (Ont.) 26 F3
Otter < Sarcee 145, UP (Alta.) 34 E2
Otter Brook, UP (NS) 9 C2
Otterburne, UP (Man.) 28 A2
Otterburn-Park, T (Que.) 16 A3
Otter Cove, UP (NB) 11 C3
Otter Creek, UP (Ont.) 24 G4
Otter Creek, UP (Ont.) 23 C3
Otter Falls, UP (Man.) 28 D1
Otter-Lake, UP (Que.) 18 D4
Otter Lake 2, IR (BC) 35 F1
Ottermere, UP (Ont.) 28 E1
Otter Point, UP (BC) 38 E4
Otter Rapids, UP (Ont.) 20 C4
Otter's Point, UP (Nfld.) 4 D4
Otterville, UP (Ont.) 22 F2
Otthon, UP (Sask.) 29 C2
Otto, UP (Man.) 29 H3
Ouchton 3, IR (BC) 39 B1
Ouellette, UP (Ont.) 25 F2
Ouiatchouan 5, IR (Que.) 18 H1
Ouimet, UP (Ont.) 27 E3
Oungah, UP (Ont.) 22 B3
Oungre, UP (Sask.) 29 B4
Ououkinsh 5, IR (BC) 39 D2
Ous 17, IR (BC) 39 F3
Oustic, UP (Ont.) 23 E4
Outer Cove, UP (Nfld.) 2 H2
Outlet, UP (Ont.) 21 G2
Outlet, UP (Ont.) 17 B3
Outlook, T (Sask.) 31 E2
Outlook, UP (Ont.) 26 B4
Outram, UP (NS) 10 C1
Outram, UP (Sask.) 29 B4
Outremont, C (Que.) 17 H1
Outs 3, IR (BC) 38 B3
Ouvry, UP (Ont.) 22 C3
Overflowing River, UP (Man.) 30 A3
Overlea, UP (Alta.) 33 D1
Overstoneville, UP (Man.) 28 A3
Overton, UP (NS) 10 A3
Overton, UP (Man.) 29 G2
Owaissa, UP (Ont.) 26 F3
Owakonze, UP (Ont.) 27 C3
Owen Bay, UP (BC) 37 B3
Owenbrook, UP (Ont.) 24 E3
Owendale, UP (Alta.) 34 F4
Owen Sound, C (Ont.) 23 C2
Owh-wis-too-a-wan 18, IR (BC) 41 G4
Owl River, UP (Alta.) 33 F2
Owlseye, UP (Alta.) 33 F2
Owls Head Harbour, UP (NS) 9 D3
Owossitsa 6, IR (BC) 39 E3
Owun 24, IR (BC) 41 A1
Oxarat, UP (Sask.) 31 C4
Oxbow, T (Sask.) 29 D4
Oxbow, UP (NB) 12 B2
Oxdrift, UP (Ont.) 27 A1
Oxenden, UP (Ont.) 23 C1
Oxford, T (NS) 9 B1
Oxford Centre, UP (Ont.) 22 F1
Oxford House < Oxford House 24, UP (Man.) 30 D2
Oxford House 24, IR (Man.) 30 D2
Oxford Junction, UP (NS) 9 B1
Oxford Mills, UP (Ont.) 17 C2
Oxford Station, UP (Ont.) 17 C2
Oxley, UP (Ont.) 22 A4
Oxmead, UP (Ont.) 23 D1
Oxtongue Lake, UP (Ont.) 24 C2
Oxville, UP (Alta.) 33 H4
O-ya-kum-la 11, IR (BC) 39 C1
Oyama, UP (BC) 35 F2
Oyees 9, IR (BC) 38 C3
Oyen, T (Alta.) 31 B2
Oyster Bay 12, IR (BC) 38 E3
Oyster Bed Bridge, UP (PEI) 7 C3
Oyster River, UP (BC) 38 B1
Ozada < Stony 142, 143, 144, UP (Alta.) 34 D2
Ozanam, UP (Que.) 15 D2
Ozerna, UP (Man.) 29 F3

P

Pa-aat 6, IR (BC) 41 D1
Pabineau 11, IR (NB) 12 E1
Pabos-Mills, UP (Que.) 13 G3
Pabos-Nord, UP (Que.) 13 G3
Pa-cat'l-lin-ne 3, IR (BC) 39 C1
Pacheena 1, IR (BC) 38 D4
Pacific Junction, UP (NB) 11 G1
Pacific Shore Trailer Court, NUP (BC) 38 D2
Packington, UP (Que.) 15 G1
Pack River 2, IR (BC) 43 C4
Packs Harbour, UP (Nfld.) 6 G3
Pacquet, COMM (Nfld.) 5 H3
Paddle Prairie, UP (Alta.) 43 H1
Paddling Lake, UP (Sask.) 32 C3
Paddock's Bight, UP (Nfld.) 3 B1
Paddockwood, VL (Sask.) 32 E3
Padlei, UP (NWT) 44 H1
Padloping Island, UP (NWT) 46 G1
Padoue, UP (Que.) 13 A2
Padstow, UP (Alta.) 33 C3
Pageant, UP (Alta.) 34 F3
Paget, UP (Ont.) 25 F1
Pagwa River, UP (Ont.) 20 B4
Pahas 11, IR (BC) 41 F4
Pahonan, UP (Sask.) 32 E4
Painchaud, UP (Que.) 15 D2
Paincourt, UP (Ont.) 22 B3
Painsec, UP (NB) 11 G1
Pain-Sec, UP (Que.) 15 C3
Painsec Junction, UP (NB) 11 G1
Painswick, UP (Ont.) 21 A1
Paisley, VL (Ont.) 23 C2
Paisley Brook, UP (Sask.) 31 G4
Pakan, UP (Alta.) 33 F3
Pakashan 150D, IR (Alta.) 33 B1
Pakenham, UP (Ont.) 17 B1
Pakesley, UP (Ont.) 25 F2
Pakowki, UP (Alta.) 31 A4
Pakwaw Lake < Shoal Lake 28A, UP (Sask.) 32 G3
Paldi, UP (BC) 38 E3
Palling, UP (BC) 42 G4
Palmarolle, UP (Que.) 18 A1
Palm Beach, UP (Ont.) 24 B4
Palmer, VL (Sask.) 31 F3
Palmer Rapids, UP (Ont.) 24 F2
Palmer Road, UP (PEI) 7 A2
Palmers Pond 1, IR (NB) 11 H1
Palmerston, T (Ont.) 23 D3
Palmyra, UP (Ont.) 22 D3
Palo, UP (Sask.) 31 D1
Pambrun, UP (Sask.) 31 E3
Panet, UP (Que.) 15 D3
Pangman, VL (Sask.) 31 H4
Pangnirtung, HAM (NWT) 46 G2
Panmure, UP (Ont.) 17 B2
Panmure Island, UP (PEI) 7 E4
Panorama Trailer Court, NUP (BC) 36 B1
Pansy, UP (Man.) 28 B3
Panuke Road, UP (NS) 9 A3
Papekwatchin 4, IR (BC) 38 H2
Papinachois, UP (Que.) 14 G1
Papineauville, VL (Que.) 17 E1
Papsilqua 2, IR (BC) 35 B3
Papsilqua 2A, IR (BC) 35 B3
Papsilqua 2B, IR (BC) 35 B3
Papsilqua 13, IR (BC) 35 B1
Papyum 27, IR (BC) 35 B2
Papyum 27A, IR (BC) 35 B2
Papyum Graveyard 27C, IR (BC) 35 B2
Paquette, UP (Que.) 16 E4
Paquette, UP (Ont.) 22 A3
Paquetville, VL (NB) 12 F1
Paquin, UP (Que.) 18 A2
Paradis, UP (Que.) 18 C2
Paradis, NUP (Que.) 16 D1
Paradis Bay, UP (Ont.) 26 F3
Paradise, T (Nfld.) 2 H2
Paradise, UP (NS) 10 C1
Paradise, UP (Nfld.) 3 C2
Paradise, UP (Nfld.) 6 F2
Paradise Beach, UP (Ont.) 21 B1
Paradise Gardens, NUP (NWT) 44 A2
Paradise Hill, VL (Sask.) 32 A3
Paradise Point, UP (Nfld.) 6 G3
Paradise River, UP (Nfld.) 6 G3
Paradise Valley, VL (Alta.) 33 G4
Paradise Valley, NUP (BC) 38 C1
Paradise Valley Trailer Court, NUP (BC) 38 C1
Parc-Bleu, UP (Que.) 18 G4
Parc-d'Avignon, UP (Que.) 17 G2
Parc-de-la-Chaudière, UP (Que.) 15 B4
Parc-de-l'Amitié, NUP (Que.) 14 E4
Parc-Lemieux, UP (Que.) 15 G4
Parc-le-Rousson, NUP (Que.) 17 F2
Parc-Lookout, UP (Que.) 18 F4
Parc-Montcalm, UP (Que.) 18 F4
Parc-Rémillard, NUP (Que.) 17 H4
Parc-Roco, UP (Que.) 16 A1
Parc-Roy, UP (Que.) 15 B3
Parc-St-Philippe, NUP (Que.) 17 H4
Pardee, UP (Ont.) 27 D3
Pardy Island, UP (Nfld.) 2 C4
Parent, VL (Que.) 18 E2
Parham, UP (Ont.) 17 A3
Paris, T (Ont.) 22 G1
Paris, UP (YT) 45 A2
Parisville, UP (Que.) 16 D1
Parkbeg, UP (Sask.) 31 F3
Parkbend, UP (Alta.) 34 F4
Park Bluff, UP (Sask.) 32 B3
Park Corner, UP (PEI) 7 C3
Park Court, UP (Alta.) 33 C3
Parkdale, T (PEI) 7 C4
Parkdale, UP (NS) 10 E1
Parkdale, UP (NS) 9 B4
Parkdale, UP (Man.) 28 A1
Parker, UP (Ont.) 23 D3
Parker Ridge, UP (NB) 12 C4
Parker Road, UP (NS) 10 D1
Parkers Corners, UP (Ont.) 17 E1
Parkers Cove, COMM (Nfld.) 2 D3
Parkers Cove, UP (NS) 10 C1
Parkerview, UP (Sask.) 29 C2
Park Head, UP (Ont.) 23 C1
Parkhill, T (Ont.) 22 D1
Parkhurst, UP (Que.) 15 A4
Parkindale, UP (NB) 11 G1
Parkinson, UP (Ont.) 26 C4
Parkland, UP (Alta.) 34 F3
Parkland, UP (BC) 43 E3
Park Lane, NUP (Ont.) 26 E1
Parkman, UP (Sask.) 29 D4
Parks, UP (BC) 34 B4
Parks Corner, UP (Man.) 29 E3
Parkside, VL (Sask.) 32 D3
Parkside Beach, UP (Ont.) 24 B4
Parksville, VL (BC) 38 D2
Park Valley, UP (Sask.) 32 D3
Parkville Trailer Park, NUP (BC) 38 D2
Parkwood Estates, NUP (PEI) 7 C4
Parkwood Hills, UP (Ont.) 17 E4
Parlee Brook, UP (NB) 11 F2
Parleeville, UP (NB) 11 E2
Parrsboro, T (NS) 11 H2
Parry, UP (Sask.) 31 G4
Parry Island < Parry Island 16, UP (Ont.) 24 A2
Parry Island 16, IR (Ont.) 24 A2
Parry Sound, T (Ont.) 24 A2
Parsnips 5, IR (BC) 43 C4
Parson, UP (BC) 34 C2
Parsons Point < Indian Bay (COMM), UP (Nfld.) 3 F3
Parson's Pond, COMM (Nfld.) 5 F3
Parthia, UP (Ont.) 20 C4
Partridge Hill, UP (Alta.) 33 E3
Partridge Valley, UP (NB) 11 E1
Pasadena, T (Nfld.) 4 D1
Pascal, UP (Sask.) 32 C3
Pascalis, UP (Que.) 18 B2
Pascobac, UP (NB) 11 E2
Pashilqua 2, IR (BC) 37 H3
Pashilqua 2A, IR (BC) 37 H3
Pasley Island, UP (BC) 38 E2
Paspébiac, UP (Que.) 13 F4
Paspébiac-Est, UP (Que.) 13 F4
Paspébiac-Ouest, UP (Que.) 13 F4
Pasqua, UP (Sask.) 31 G3
Pasqua 79, IR (Sask.) 29 B2
Pass Creek, UP (BC) 34 B4
Pass Creek Park, NUP (BC) 34 B4
Passekeag, UP (NB) 11 E2
Pass Island, UP (Nfld.) 2 A2
Pass Lake, UP (Ont.) 27 E3
Passmore, UP (BC) 34 B4
Pasteur, UP (Que.) 15 D2
Pas Trail, UP (Sask.) 32 F3
Paswegin, UP (Sask.) 31 H1
Paterson, UP (BC) 34 A4
Paterson, UP (Man.) 30 B2
Path End < St Mary's (COMM), NUP (Nfld.) 2 F4
Pathlow, UP (Sask.) 32 E4
Patience, UP (Alta.) 33 D4
Patricia, UP (Alta.) 34 G2
Patrick's Cove, UP (Nfld.) 2 E4
Patrick's Harbour, UP (Nfld.) 2 A2
Patrickton, UP (Que.) 13 E3
Patrieville, UP (NB) 15 G1
Patterson, UP (NB) 11 C2
Patterson, UP (Que.) 17 C1
Patterson Park, NUP (Alta.) 33 E3
Pattersons Corners, UP (Ont.) 17 C2
Patterson Siding, UP (NB) 12 E2
Patton, UP (Ont.) 26 C4
Patuanak < Wapachewunak 192D, UP (Sask.) 44 D4
Paudash, UP (Ont.) 24 E3
Paudash Lake, UP (Ont.) 24 E3
Paugan-Falls, UP (Que.) 18 D4
Paugh Lake, UP (Ont.) 24 F1
Paukeanum 3, IR (BC) 37 B4
Paulatuk, UP (NWT) 45 D1
Paul Lake, NUP (BC) 36 F4
Paul's 6, IR (BC) 35 B3
Paul's Basin 2, IR (BC) 35 C2
Paungassi, UP (Man.) 30 D3
Pavilion, UP (BC) 36 C4
Pavilion 1, IR (BC) 36 C4
Pavilion 1A, IR (BC) 36 C4
Pavilion 3A, IR (BC) 36 C4
Pavilion 4, IR (BC) 36 C4
Pawala 5, IR (BC) 39 G1
Pawistik, UP (Man.) 30 A1
Paxson, UP (Alta.) 33 E2
Paykulkum 14, IR (BC) 37 E4
Payne, UP (Ont.) 22 B2
Payne's Cove, UP (Nfld.) 5 G2
Paynes Mills, UP (Ont.) 22 E2
Paynton, VL (Sask.) 32 B4
Pays Plat, UP (Ont.) 27 F3
Pays Plat 51, IR (Ont.) 27 F3
Peabody, UP (Que.) 16 C4
Peabody, UP (Ont.) 23 C2
Peace Grove, UP (Alta.) 43 G3
Peace Point, UP (Alta.) 44 C2
Peace River, T (Alta.) 43 H3
Peace River Crossing 151A, IR (Alta.) 43 H3
Peaches Cove, UP (Nfld.) 2 E2
Peachland, DM (BC) 35 E3
Peachytown, NUP (Nfld.) 2 H2
Peacock, UP (Alta.) 34 F3
Peakes, UP (PEI) 7 D4
Peakes Road, UP (PEI) 7 D4
Pearce, UP (Alta.) 34 F4
Pearceley, UP (Ont.) 24 B1
Pearceton, UP (Que.) 16 B4
Pearl, UP (Ont.) 27 E3
Pearl Lake, UP (Ont.) 23 C2
Pearse Island 43, IR (BC) 42 D4
Pearson, UP (Ont.) 26 F2
Pearsonville, UP (NB) 11 E1
Peas Brook, UP (NS) 9 G2
Peavey, UP (Alta.) 33 D3
Peavine, UP (Alta.) 33 C2
Pebble Beach, UP (Man.) 29 G2
Pebble Beach, NUP (BC) 38 C1
Peck Meadow Corner, UP (NS) 10 E1
Pecten, UP (Alta.) 34 E4
Pedley, UP (Alta.) 33 A3
Peebles, UP (Sask.) 29 C3
Peekaboo Point, UP (Ont.) 23 F1
Peel, UP (NB) 12 A4
Peepabun, UP (Ont.) 23 E3
Peepeekisis 81, IR (Sask.) 29 B2
Peerless, UP (Sask.) 32 A2
Peerless Lake, UP (Alta.) 44 B4
Peers, UP (Alta.) 33 B3
Peesane, UP (Sask.) 32 F4
Pefferlaw, UP (Ont.) 21 B1
Peffers, UP (Ont.) 23 C4
Peggys Cove, UP (NS) 9 A4
Pegleg 3, IR (BC) 35 B2
Pegleg 3A, IR (BC) 35 B2
Peguis, UP (Man.) 28 B1
Peguis 1B, IR (Man.) 29 H2
Peguis 1C, IR (Man.) 29 H2
Peigan 147, IR (Alta.) 34 F4
Peigan 147B, IR (Alta.) 34 E4
Pekisko, UP (Alta.) 34 E3
Pelee Island, UP (Ont.) 22 B4
Pelee Island South, UP (Ont.) 22 B4
Pelerin, UP (NB) 12 G4
Pelham, T (Ont.) 21 B4
Pelican Narrows, UP (Sask.) 32 G1
Pelican Narrows 184B, IR (Sask.) 32 G1
Pelican Point, UP (Sask.) 31 G2
Pelican Portage, UP (Alta.) 44 B4
Pelican Rapids, UP (Man.) 30 A3
Pellegrin, UP (Que.) 13 G2
Pellerin, UP (Que.) 15 D2
Pelletier, UP (Que.) 13 B2
Pelletier, UP (Que.) 15 E1
Pelletier Bridge, UP (Ont.) 28 F1
Pelletiers Mill, UP (NB) 15 G2
Pel-looth'l-kai 17, IR (BC) 41 G4
Pelly, VL (Sask.) 29 D1
Pelly Bay, HAM (NWT) 46 C1
Pelly Crossing, UP (YT) 45 B3
Pelly Lakes, UP (YT) 45 C3
Pemberton, VL (BC) 37 G3
Pemberton Meadows, UP (BC) 37 F3
Pemberton Ridge, UP (NB) 11 A2
Pembina, UP (Alta.) 33 C3
Pembina Forks, UP (Alta.) 33 B4
Pembina Heights, UP (Alta.) 33 D2
Pembridge, UP (Alta.) 33 D3
Pembroke, C (Ont.) 18 C4
Pembroke, UP (NS) 10 A3
Pembroke, UP (NS) 9 A2
Pembroke, UP (NB) 11 A1
Pembroke, UP (PEI) 7 E4
Pemburton Hill, UP (Alta.) 33 D3
Pemmican Portage < Cumberland 20, UP (Sask.) 32 H3
Pémonca, UP (Que.) 18 G1
Pemukan, UP (Alta.) 31 B1
Pemynoos 9, IR (BC) 35 B1
Pender Island, UP (BC) 38 F3
Pender Island 8, IR (BC) 38 F3
Pendleton, UP (Ont.) 17 D1
Pendleton Bay, UP (BC) 40 A1
Pendryl, UP (Alta.) 33 D4
Peneece 19, IR (BC) 41 G4
Peneetle 22, IR (BC) 39 G4
Penetanguishene, T (Ont.) 23 F1
Penetanguishene, UP (Nfld.) 2 H2
Pengelly Landing, UP (Ont.) 21 D1
Penguin Arm, UP (Nfld.) 5 F4
Penhall, UP (Ont.) 20 B4
Penhold, VL (Alta.) 34 E1
Penhold, CFB/BFC, MIL (Alta.) 34 E1
Peninsular Park, UP (Ont.) 21 A1
Penn, UP (Sask.) 32 C3
Penn 19, IR (NS) 10 E1
Pennant, VL (Sask.) 31 D3
Pennant, NUP (NS) 9 B4
Pennfield, UP (NB) 11 C3
Pennfield Corner, UP (NB) 11 C3
Pennfield Ridge, UP (NB) 11 C3
Pennfield Station, UP (NB) 11 C3
Penniac, UP (NB) 11 C1
Penny, UP (BC) 40 D2
Peno, UP (Alta.) 33 E3
Penobsquis, UP (NB) 11 F2
Pense, VL (Sask.) 31 G3
Pensons Arm, UP (Nfld.) 6 H4
Penticton, C (BC) 35 E3
Penticton 1, IR (BC) 35 E3
Penticton 3A, IR (BC) 35 E3
Pentledge 2, IR (BC) 38 B1
Pentz, UP (NS) 10 E2
Penville, UP (Ont.) 21 A1
Penzance, VL (Sask.) 31 G2
Peoria, UP (Alta.) 43 G4
Perbeck, UP (Alta.) 34 F1
Percé, C (Que.) 13 H2
Percival, UP (Sask.) 29 C3
Percy Boom, UP (Ont.) 21 E1
Perdue, VL (Sask.) 31 E1
Pereaux, UP (NS) 11 H3
Péribonka, UP (Que.) 18 H1
Périgord, UP (Sask.) 29 B1
Perivale, UP (Ont.) 25 B2
Perkins, UP (Que.) 17 C1
Perkinsfield, UP (Ont.) 23 E1
Perkins-sur-le-Lac, UP (Que.) 17 C1
Perm, UP (Ont.) 23 E2
Perotte, UP (NS) 10 C1
Perow, UP (BC) 42 G4
Perrault, UP (Ont.) 24 G2
Perrault Falls, UP (Ont.) 27 A1
Perrets 11, IR (BC) 37 H4
Perretton, UP (Ont.) 24 G1
Perrins Corners, UP (Ont.) 17 C3
Perry, UP (Ont.) 21 B4
Perry, UP (Ont.) 26 A2
Perryboro, UP (Que.) 16 E4
Perry Island, UP (NWT) 45 G1
Perry Point, UP (NB) 11 E2
Perrys, UP (BC) 34 B4
Perry's Corners, UP (Ont.) 22 F1
Perry's Cove, UP (Nfld.) 2 G2
Perry Settlement, UP (NB) 11 F1
Perry Siding, UP (BC) 34 B4
Perrys Lane, UP (Ont.) 22 F1
Perrytown, UP (Ont.) 21 D2
Perryvale, UP (Alta.) 33 E2
Perth, T (Ont.) 17 B2
Perth-Andover, VL (NB) 12 A3
Perth Road, UP (Ont.) 17 A3
Perthuis, UP (Que.) 18 H3
Petaguishene Beach, UP (Ont.) 23 E1
Petaigan, UP (Sask.) 32 F3
Petain, UP (NS) 9 C4
Petawawa, VL (Ont.) 24 G1
Petawawa, CFB/BFC, MIL (Ont.) 18 C4
Petawawa Point, UP (Ont.) 24 G1
Peter Alec 6, IR (BC) 41 G1
Peterbell, UP (Ont.) 26 C1
Peterborough, C (Ont.) 21 D1
Peter Pond Lake 193, IR (Sask.) 44 D4
Peters 1, IR (BC) 35 A4
Peters 1A, IR (BC) 35 A4
Peters 2, IR (BC) 35 A4
Petersburg, UP (Ont.) 23 D4
Peters Corners, UP (Ont.) 22 G1
Petersfield, UP (Man.) 30 C4
Peters Mills, UP (NB) 12 G3
Peterson, UP (Sask.) 31 F1
Peterson Corner, UP (Ont.) 24 C3
Peter's River < St Vincent's – St Stephens – Peter's River, UP (Nfld.) 2 F4
Peters Road, UP (PEI) 7 E4
Peterview, LID (Nfld.) 3 C2
Peterville, UP (PEI) 7 A2
Pete Suckers 13, IR (BC) 36 B2
Pethericks Corners, UP (Ont.) 21 E1
Petherton, UP (Ont.) 23 D3
Petit-Bécancour, UP (Que.) 16 D2
Petit-Bégin, UP (Que.) 14 A2
Petit-Canada, UP (Que.) 18 A3
Petit-Canada, NUP (Que.) 16 E4
Petit-Cap, UP (NB) 7 A4
Petit-Cap, UP (Que.) 15 C2
Petit-Cherbourg, UP (Que.) 13 B2
Petit-Chertsey, UP (Que.) 18 F4
Petit-Chockpish, UP (NB) 12 G3
Petitcodiac, VL (NB) 11 F1
Petit-de-Grat, UP (NS) 8 D4
Petite-Aldouane, UP (NB) 12 G3
Petite-Allemagne, UP (Que.) 18 E4
Petite-Angleterre, UP (Que.) 16 E4
Petite-Anse, UP (Que.) 13 G1
Petite-Baie, NUP (Que.) 7 F1
Petite-Ferme, UP (Que.) 15 C2
Petite-France, UP (Que.) 17 H2
Petite-France, UP (Que.) 16 A4
Petite-Lamèque, UP (NB) 13 G4
Petite-Matane, UP (Que.) 13 B2
Petite-Presqu'île, UP (Que.) 17 D1
Petite-Réserve, UP (NB) 12 B1
Petite-Rivière, UP (Que.) 15 C2
Petite-Rivière, UP (NS) 10 E2
Petite-Rivière-à-la-Truite, UP (NB) 15 G2
Petite-Rivière-de-l'Île, UP (NB) 13 G4
Petite-Rivière-Est, UP (Que.) 13 H3
Petite-Rivière-Pabos, UP (Que.) 13 G3
Petite-Romaine, UP (Que.) 14 E3
Petites, UP (Nfld.) 4 B4
Petites-Bergeronnes, UP (Que.) 14 E3
Petit Étang, UP (NS) 8 D2
Petite-Tourelle, UP (Que.) 13 D1
Petite-Vallée, UP (Que.) 13 F1
Petit Forte, UP (Nfld.) 2 D3
Petit Jardin < Cape St George – Petit Jardin – Grand Jardin – De Grau – Marches Point – Loretto, UP (Nfld.) 4 A2
Petit-Lac, UP (Que.) 16 F2
Petit-Lac, UP (Que.) 16 E4
Petit-Lac-Brompton, NUP (Que.) 16 D3
Petit-Lac-Long, UP (Que.) 18 F4
Petit-Large, UP (NB) 12 G3
Petit-Nicolet, UP (Que.) 16 D3
Petit-Ouest, UP (NB) 12 B1
Petit-Paquetville, UP (NB) 12 F1
Petit Pokemouche, NUP (NB) 12 G1
Petit-Pré, UP (Que.) 15 G3
Petit-Québec, UP (Que.) 16 E4
Petit-Rocher, VL (NB) 12 E1
Petit-Rocher-Nord, UP (NB) 13 E4
Petit-Rocher-Station, NUP (NB) 12 E1
Petit-Rocher-Sud, UP (NB) 12 E1
Petit-Saguenay, UP (Que.) 14 D3
Petits-Escoumins, UP (Que.) 14 E3
Petits-Méchins, UP (Que.) 13 C1
Petley, UP (Nfld.) 2 F1
Petlura, UP (Man.) 29 E2
Petrel, UP (Man.) 29 F3
Petrie Shore, UP (Ont.) 17 B2
Petrofka, UP (Sask.) 32 C4
Petrolia, T (Ont.) 22 C2
Pettapiece, UP (Man.) 29 E3
Pettigrew Settlement, UP (NS) 11 H2
Petty Harbour, UP (Nfld.) 5 H1
Petty Harbour < Petty Harbour – Maddox Cove, UP (Nfld.) 2 H3
Petty Harbour – Maddox Cove, RD (Nfld.) 2 H3
Petworth, UP (Ont.) 17 A4
Pevensey, UP (Ont.) 24 B1
Peveril, UP (Que.) 17 F2
Phantom Beach, UP (Sask.) 32 H2
Pheasant Forks, UP (Sask.) 29 C2
Phelpston, UP (Ont.) 23 F2
Philémon, UP (Que.) 18 D3
Philip Depot, UP (Ont.) 24 D1
Philips, UP (Alta.) 33 F4
Philipsburg, VL (Que.) 16 A4
Philips Harbour, UP (NS) 9 G2
Philipsville, UP (Ont.) 17 B3
Phillips Arm < Matsayno 5, UP (BC) 37 B3
Phillipsburg, UP (Ont.) 23 D4
Phillips Head, UP (Nfld.) 3 C2
Phillips Subdivision, NUP (BC) 36 F2
Phillipston, UP (Ont.) 21 F1
Phillipstown, UP (NB) 11 E1
Philmar, NUP (Ont.) 21 E1

Philomena, UP (Alta.) 33 F1
Phil's Trailer Court, NUP (Ont.) 17 D1
Phinneys Cove, UP (NS) 10 C1
Phippen, UP (Sask.) 32 B4
Phoenix, UP (BC) 35 G4
Piapot, VL (Sask.) 31 C3
Piapot 75, IR (Sask.) 31 H2
Pibroch, UP (Alta.) 33 D2
Picadilly, UP (NB) 11 F2
Picard, UP (Que.) 15 E1
Piccadilly, UP (Nfld.) 4 B2
Piccadilly, UP (NB) 12 A3
Piccadilly, UP (Ont.) 17 A3
Piccaire, UP (Nfld.) 2 B2
Pickardville, UP (Alta.) 33 D2
Pickerel < French River 13, UP (Ont.) 25 F2
Pickerel Lake, UP (Ont.) 24 B1
Pickerel River, UP (Ont.) 25 F2
Pickering, T (Ont.) 21 B2
Pick Eyes, UP (Nfld.) 2 G2
Pickle Crow, UP (Ont.) 30 F4
Pickle Lake, UP (Ont.) 30 F4
Picnic Grove, UP (Ont.) 17 F2
Picoudi, UP (Que.) 16 B2
Pic River, UP (Ont.) 27 H3
Pic River 50, IR (Ont.) 27 H3
Picton, T (Ont.) 21 G2
Pictou, T (NS) 9 D1
Pictou Island, UP (NS) 9 D1
Pictou Landing, UP (NS) 9 D1
Picture Butte, T (Alta.) 34 F3
Pidgeon, UP (Que.) 15 A4
Pied-de-la-Montagne, UP (Que.) 18 G4
Pied-du-Lac, UP (Que.) 15 F1
Piedmont, UP (Que.) 18 F4
Piedmont, UP (NS) 8 A4
Pierceland, VL (Sask.) 32 A2
Piercemont, UP (NB) 12 A3
Pierces Corners, UP (Ont.) 17 C2
Pierrefonds, C (Que.) 17 F4
Pierreville, VL (Que.) 16 B2
Pierson, UP (Man.) 29 D4
Pigeon Cove, UP (Nfld.) 5 G2
Pigeon Hill, UP (NB) 13 H4
Pigeon-Hill, UP (Que.) 16 B4
Pigeon Lake, UP (Man.) 29 H3
Pigeon Lake 138A, IR (Alta.) 33 D4
Pigeon Mountain, UP (Alta.) 34 D2
Pigeon River, UP (Ont.) 27 D4
Pigeon River 13A, IR (Man.) 30 C3
Pikangikum < Pikangikum 14, UP (Ont.) 30 D4
Pikangikum 14, IR (Ont.) 30 D4
Pike Bay, UP (Ont.) 23 C1
Pike Creek, UP (Ont.) 22 A3
Pike Lake, UP (Sask.) 31 E1
Pike-River, UP (Que.) 16 A4
Pikes Arm, UP (Nfld.) 3 D1
Pikes Peak, UP (Sask.) 32 A3
Pikwitonei, UP (Man.) 30 C1
Pilger, VL (Sask.) 31 G1
Pilley's Island, COMM (Nfld.) 3 B2
Pilot Butte, VL (Sask.) 31 H3
Pilot Mound, VL (Man.) 29 G4
Pinacle-Nord, UP (Que.) 16 B4
Pinantan, NUP (BC) 36 F4
Pinantan Lake, UP (BC) 36 F4
Pinawa, UP (Man.) 28 C1
Pinawa Bay, UP (Man.) 30 C4
Pincebec, UP (Que.) 16 A1
Pinchards Island, UP (Nfld.) 3 F2
Pincher, UP (Alta.) 34 E4
Pincher Creek, T (Alta.) 34 E4
Pinchi < Pinchie 2, UP (BC) 40 B1
Pinchie 2, IR (BC) 40 B1
Pinchie Lake 7, IR (BC) 40 B1
Pinchie Lake 7A, IR (BC) 40 B1
Pinchie Lake 10, IR (BC) 40 B1
Pinchie Lake 12, IR (BC) 40 B1
Pinchi Lake, UP (BC) 40 B1
Pincourt, T (Que.) 17 F4
Pincourt, UP (Que.) 17 G3
Pinder, UP (NB) 11 B1
Pineal Lake, UP (Ont.) 26 B3
Pineau, UP (NB) 12 F3
Pine Beach, UP (Ont.) 23 G2
Pine Bluff, UP (Sask.) 32 E4
Pine Bluff 20Al 20B, IR (Sask.) 32 G2
Pine Creek 66A, IR (Man.) 29 E1
Pine Creek Station, UP (Man.) 29 G3
Pine-Croft, UP (Que.) 18 F4
Pinedale, UP (Ont.) 21 C1
Pinedale, UP (Alta.) 33 B3
Pine Dock, UP (Man.) 30 C4
Pine Falls, UP (Man.) 30 C4
Pine Glen, UP (NB) 11 G1
Pineglen, UP (Ont.) 17 E4
Pineglen Annex, UP (Ont.) 17 E4
Pine Grove, UP (NS) 10 E2
Pinegrove, UP (Ont.) 17 B1
Pine Grove, UP (NS) 9 C3
Pine Grove, UP (Ont.) 17 B4
Pine Grove, UP (Ont.) 17 B2
Pinegrove, UP (Ont.) 21 G1
Pinegrove, UP (BC) 40 D3
Pine Grove, NUP (Ont.) 22 G2
Pine-Hill, UP (Que.) 17 F1
Pine Hill, UP (Ont.) 17 F2
Pine Hill, UP (Ont.) 17 B4
Pinehouse Lake, UP (Sask.) 32 D1
Pinehurst, UP (NS) 10 E2
Pinehurst, UP (Ont.) 22 C3
Pinehurst Park, UP (Ont.) 22 G1
Pine Lake, UP (Alta.) 34 F1
Pine-Lodge, NUP (Que.) 17 B1
Pine Meadows, UP (Ont.) 24 G1
Pine Point, T (NWT) 44 B2
Pine Point, UP (Ont.) 21 C1
Pine Portage, UP (Ont.) 27 E2
Pine Ridge, UP (Man.) 28 B1
Pine Ridge, UP (NB) 12 G3
Pine Ridge Valley Trailer Park, NUP (Man.) 28 A1
Pine River, UP (Man.) 29 E1
Pine River, UP (Ont.) 23 B3
Pine River, UP (Sask.) 44 E4
Pine Springs, UP (Ont.) 24 C2
Pine Tree, UP (NS) 9 D1
Pinette, UP (PEI) 7 D4
Pinevale, UP (NS) 8 B4
Pine Valley, UP (BC) 36 B1
Pine Valley, UP (Ont.) 24 G1
Pine Valley, UP (BC) 43 D4
Pineview, UP (BC) 40 C2
Pineville, UP (NB) 12 E3
Pinewood, UP (Ont.) 28 G4
Piney, UP (Man.) 28 C3
Pingle, UP (Alta.) 44 C4
Pinguet, UP (Que.) 15 D2
Pinkerton, UP (Ont.) 23 C2
Pinkerton, UP (Ont.) 21 A1
Pinkham, UP (Sask.) 31 C2
Pink Mountain, UP (BC) 43 D2
Pinkneys Point, UP (NS) 10 A4
Pinkut Lake 23, IR (BC) 40 A1
Pinnacle, UP (Que.) 16 D3
Pinniquine, UP (NB) 15 G2
Pintendre, UP (Que.) 15 G4
Pinware, UP (Nfld.) 5 G2
Pioneer, UP (Alta.) 33 B3
Pioneer Trailer Park, NUP (Ont.) 26 B4
Piopolis, UP (Que.) 16 F3
Pipers Cove, UP (NS) 8 D3
Pipers Glen, UP (NS) 8 D3
Piperville, UP (Ont.) 17 F4
Pipestone, UP (Man.) 29 E4
Pipestone, UP (Alta.) 33 D4
Pipestone Creek, UP (Alta.) 43 G4
Pipseul 3, IR (BC) 35 C1
Pirate Harbour, UP (NS) 8 C4
Pirmez Creek, UP (Alta.) 34 E2
Pirogue, UP (NB) 12 G3
Pisquid, UP (PEI) 7 D3
Pisquid West, UP (PEI) 7 D3
Pitchers Farm, UP (NS) 8 B4
Pitlochrie, UP (Alta.) 33 F1
Pitman, UP (Sask.) 31 G3
Pit Siding, UP (Man.) 30 C1
Pitsite, UP (Ont.) 24 B2
Pitt Island 27, IR (BC) 41 D1
Pitt Lake 4, IR (BC) 38 G2
Pitt Meadows, DM (BC) 38 G2
Pitt Polder, NUP (BC) 38 G2
Pitts Ferry, UP (Ont.) 17 B4
Pitts Harbour, UP (Nfld.) 5 H1
Pittston, UP (Ont.) 17 D3
Piusville, UP (PEI) 7 A2
Pivot, UP (Alta.) 31 B3
Piyami, UP (Alta.) 34 F3
Place-Desranleau, UP (Que.) 16 A4
Place-Dupras, NUP (Que.) 16 A2
Place-Laurentienne, NUP (Que.) 15 E3
Placentia, T (Nfld.) 2 F3
Placentia Junction, UP (Nfld.) 2 F3
Place-Ruisseau-des-Noyers, NUP (Que.) 16 A4
Place-Versailles, UP (Que.) 16 A2
Plage-Cantin, UP (Que.) 15 A3
Plage-Croteau, NUP (Que.) 16 D2
Plage-Denoncourt, UP (Que.) 16 B2
Plage-Héritage, UP (Que.) 18 D4
Plage-Lemieux, UP (Que.) 15 A4
Plage-Maurice, UP (Que.) 15 A3
Plage-Nando, UP (Que.) 18 H3
Plage-Orange, UP (Que.) 18 B2
Plage-Paquette, UP (Que.) 16 D2
Plage-Paul, UP (Que.) 18 D4
Plage-St-Blaise, NUP (Que.) 16 A4
Plage-St-François, UP (Que.) 17 F2
Plage-St-Laurent, UP (Que.) 15 F4
Plage-Somerville, UP (Que.) 17 F2
Plage-Southière, UP (Que.) 16 C4
Plainfield, UP (NS) 9 D1
Plainfield, UP (Ont.) 21 F1
Plain View, UP (Sask.) 29 C2
Plainville, UP (Ont.) 21 D1
Plaisance, UP (Que.) 17 D1
Plaister Mines, UP (NS) 8 E3
Plamondon, VL (Alta.) 33 F2
Plantagenet, VL (Ont.) 17 E1
Plassey, UP (Sask.) 31 F1
Plaster Cove, UP (NS) 8 D3
Plaster Rock, VL (NB) 12 B2
Plateau, UP (NS) 8 D2
Plate Cove East, COMM (Nfld.) 3 G4
Plate Cove West, COMM (Nfld.) 3 F4
Plato, VL (Sask.) 31 D2
Plattsville, UP (Ont.) 22 F1
Playfairville, UP (Ont.) 17 B2
Pleasant Bay, UP (NS) 8 D1
Pleasant Camp, UP (BC) 45 A4
Pleasant Corners, UP (Ont.) 17 E1
Pleasantdale, NUP (Sask.) 32 F4
Pleasantfield, UP (NS) 10 D2
Pleasant Grove, UP (PEI) 7 D3
Pleasant Harbour, UP (NS) 9 D3
Pleasant Heights, NUP (Sask.) 29 C2
Pleasant Hill, UP (NS) 8 C4
Pleasant Hills, UP (NS) 9 B2
Pleasant Home, UP (Man.) 29 H3
Pleasant Lake, UP (NS) 10 B3
Pleasant Park, UP (Ont.) 22 A3
Pleasant Point, UP (Ont.) 21 C1
Pleasant Point, UP (NS) 9 C4
Pleasant Point, UP (NS) 10 D4
Pleasant Point, UP (Man.) 29 F4
Pleasant Ridge, UP (NB) 12 F3
Pleasant Ridge, UP (NB) 11 B2
Pleasant Ridge, UP (NB) 11 E1
Pleasant River, UP (NS) 10 D2
Pleasant Vale, UP (NB) 11 G1
Pleasant Valley, UP (NS) 9 C2
Pleasant Valley, UP (PEI) 7 C3
Pleasant Valley, UP (NS) 10 B3
Pleasant Valley, UP (NS) 9 D3
Pleasant Valley, UP (NS) 8 B4
Pleasant Valley, UP (NS) 9 D2
Pleasant Valley, UP (NB) 11 C1
Pleasant Valley, UP (Ont.) 17 D2
Pleasant Valley, UP (Ont.) 17 D2
Pleasant Valley, UP (Ont.) 24 H1
Pleasant Valley, UP (Ont.) 25 B2
Pleasant Valley, UP (Sask.) 32 E4
Pleasant View, UP (PEI) 7 A2
Pleasant View, UP (Ont.) 24 G1
Pleasant View, UP (Alta.) 33 E1
Pleasantview Acreages, NUP (Alta.) 33 E3
Pleasant Villa, UP (NB) 11 D2
Pleasantville, UP (NS) 10 E2
Plenty, VL (Sask.) 31 D1
Plessisville, T (Que.) 16 D2
Plevna, UP (Ont.) 24 G3
Plourde, UP (Que.) 13 A2
Plover Mills, UP (Ont.) 22 E1
Plumas, UP (Man.) 29 F3
Plum Coulee, VL (Man.) 29 H4
Plum Hollow, UP (Ont.) 17 B3
Plummer, UP (Ont.) 26 B4
Plum Point, UP (Nfld.) 5 G2
Plumweseep, UP (NB) 11 F2
Plunkett, VL (Sask.) 31 G1
Plymouth, UP (NS) 9 D2
Plymouth, UP (NS) 10 B3
Plymouth, UP (NB) 11 A1
Plymouth Park, UP (NS) 9 D2
Plympton, UP (NS) 10 B2
Plympton Station, UP (NS) 10 B2
Pocahontas, UP (Alta.) 40 H2
Pockwock, UP (NS) 9 B3
Pocologan, UP (NB) 11 C3
Poe, UP (Alta.) 33 F3
Pohénégamook, T (Que.) 15 F1
Point Aconi, UP (NS) 8 E3
Point Alexander, UP (Ont.) 18 B4
Point Alexandria, UP (Ont.) 17 B4
Point Alison, SV (Alta.) 33 D3
Point Anne, UP (Ont.) 21 F1
Point au Gaul, COMM (Nfld.) 2 B4
Point au Mal, UP (Nfld.) 4 B2
Point aux Carr, UP (NB) 12 F2
Point Brule < Chipewyan 201F, UP (Alta.) 44 C3
Point-Comfort, UP (Que.) 18 D4
Point Cross, UP (NS) 8 D2
Point de Bute, UP (NB) 7 A4
Point Deroche, UP (PEI) 7 D3
Point-du-Jour, UP (Que.) 16 B3
Pointe-à-Bouleau, UP (NB) 12 G1
Pointe-à-la-Frégate, UP (Que.) 13 G1
Pointe-à-la-Garde, UP (Que.) 13 C3
Pointe-à-Maurier, UP (Que.) 5 D3
Pointe-à-Neuf-Pas, UP (Que.) 16 A2
Pointe-Alexandre, UP (NB) 13 G4
Pointe au Baril, UP (Ont.) 25 F3
Pointe au Baril Station, UP (Ont.) 25 F3
Pointe-au-Boisvert, UP (Que.) 14 F2
Pointe-au-Bouleau, UP (Que.) 14 E4
Pointe-au-Chêne, UP (Que.) 17 E1
Pointe-au-Père, UP (Que.) 14 G3
Pointe-au-Pic, VL (Que.) 15 D1
Pointe-au-Platon, UP (Que.) 16 D1
Pointe-au-Sable, UP (Que.) 17 F1
Pointe-au-Sable (Pointe-aux-Dorés), NUP (Que.) 17 F1
Pointe-aux-Anglais, UP (Que.) 19 E3
Pointe-aux-Anglais, UP (Que.) 17 F1
Pointe-aux-Loups, UP (Que.) 7 F1
Pointe-aux-Orignaux, UP (Que.) 15 D1
Pointe-aux-Outardes, VL (Que.) 14 G1
Pointe-aux-Pins, UP (Que.) 15 F4
Pointe-aux-Trembles, C (Que.) 17 H3
Pointe-aux-Trembles-Ouest, UP (Que.) 15 A3
Pointe-Basse, UP (Que.) 7 F1
Pointe-Bleue < Ouiatchouan 5, UP (Que.) 18 H1
Pointe-Brûlé, UP (NB) 12 G1
Pointe-Calumet, VL (Que.) 17 F4
Pointe-Canot, UP (NB) 13 G4
Pointe-Carleton, UP (Que.) 5 A4
Pointe-Castagner, UP (Que.) 17 F2
Pointe-Chambord, UP (Que.) 18 H1
Pointe-Claire, C (Que.) 17 F4
Pointe-de-l'Orignal, UP (Que.) 15 F4
Pointe-de-l'Ouest, UP (Que.) 19 H3
Pointe-de-Rivière-Ouelle, UP (Que.) 15 D1
Pointe-des-Cascades, VL (Que.) 17 G1
Pointe-des-Monts, UP (Que.) 13 B1
Pointe du Bois, UP (Man.) 30 C4
Pointe-du-Chêne, UP (NB) 7 A4
Pointe-du-Domaine, UP (Que.) 17 F4
Pointe-du-Hameau, NUP (Que.) 16 B2
Pointe-du-Lac, UP (Que.) 16 B2
Pointe-du-Lac, UP (Que.) 18 H1
Pointe-du-Moulin, T (Que.) 17 G1
Point Edward, UP (NS) 8 E3
Point Edward, VL (Ont.) 22 B1
Pointe-Fortune, UP (Ont.) 17 F1
Pointe-Fortune, VL (Que.) 17 F1
Pointe-Fraser, UP (Que.) 17 F2
Pointe-Lalonde, UP (Que.) 17 F2
Pointe-Lebel, VL (Que.) 14 H1
Pointe-Leblanc, UP (Que.) 17 F2
Pointe-Martel, UP (Que.) 18 A3
Pointe-Mistassini, NUP (Que.) 13 A1
Pointe-Parent, UP (Que.) 5 B3
Pointe-Piché, UP (Que.) 26 F3
Pointe-St-Gilles, UP (Que.) 15 A3
Pointe-St-Méthode, UP (Que.) 18 H1
Pointe-Sapin, UP (NB) 12 G2
Pointe-Sapin-Centre, UP (NB) 12 G2
Pointe-Sauvage, UP (NB) 12 G1
Pointe-Verte, VL (NB) 13 E4
Point Gardiner, UP (NB) 12 F2
Point Grondine 3, IR (Ont.) 25 E2
Point Hill, UP (NS) 11 G3
Point La Haye < Gaskiers – Point La Haye, UP (Nfld.) 2 F4
Point Lance, COMM (Nfld.) 2 E4
Point La Nim, UP (NB) 13 D3
Point Leamington, T (Nfld.) 3 C2
Point May, COMM (Nfld.) 2 B4
Point May < Point May (COMM), UP (Nfld.) 2 B4
Point Michaud, UP (NS) 8 E4
Point of Bay, COMM (Nfld.) 3 C2
Point of Mara Beach, UP (Ont.) 23 G2
Point Pleasant, UP (PEI) 7 E4
Point Pleasant, UP (Ont.) 24 D4
Point Pleasant, UP (Ont.) 21 H1
Point Prim, UP (PEI) 7 D4
Point Rosie, UP (Nfld.) 2 C3
Point Tupper, UP (NS) 8 C4
Point Verde, UP (Nfld.) 2 E3
Poirier, UP (NB) 12 G4
Poirierville, UP (NS) 8 D4
Poison Creek 17, IR (BC) 42 G4
Poison Creek 17A, IR (BC) 42 G4
Poissant, UP (Que.) 18 E3
Poisson-Blanc, UP (Que.) 18 G1
Poitras Siding, UP (NB) 12 A2
Pokemouche, UP (NB) 12 G1
Pokemouche 13, IR (NB) 12 G1
Pokeshaw, UP (NB) 13 F4
Pokesudie, UP (NB) 13 G4
Pokheitsk 10, IR (BC) 35 B1
Pokiok, UP (NB) 11 B1
Pokiok Settlement, UP (NB) 11 B1
Poland, UP (Ont.) 17 A2
Pole Hill, UP (NB) 12 B3
Pole Island 14, IR (BC) 41 E3
Police Meadow 2, IR (BC) 42 H1
Pollards Point, UP (Nfld.) 5 G4
Pollett River, UP (NB) 11 F1
Pollockville, UP (Alta.) 34 G2
Polonia, UP (Man.) 29 F3
Polsons Brook, UP (NS) 9 F2
Poltimore, UP (Que.) 18 D4
Polwarth, UP (Sask.) 32 D3
Pomeroy, UP (NB) 11 C2
Pomeroy, UP (Man.) 29 H4
Pomeroy Ridge, UP (NB) 11 A3
Pomona, UP (Ont.) 23 D2
Pomquet, UP (NS) 8 B4
Pomquet and Afton 23, IR (NS) 8 B4
Pomquet Forks, UP (NS) 8 B4
Pomquet Station, UP (NS) 8 B4
Poncheville, UP (Que.) 13 B2
Pond Cove, UP (Nfld.) 5 G2
Pond Inlet, UP (NWT) 47 F3
Ponds, UP (NS) 8 A4
Pondville, UP (NS) 8 D4
Pondville South, UP (NS) 8 D4
Ponhook Lake 10, IR (NS) 10 D3
Ponoka, T (Alta.) 33 D4
Ponsonby, UP (Ont.) 23 E4
Pontbriand, UP (Que.) 15 B4
Pont-Château, UP (Que.) 17 F1
Pont-de-la-Noreau, UP (Que.) 16 D1
Pont-du-Milieu, UP (NB) 12 G3
Ponteix, T (Sask.) 31 E4
Pontgravé, UP (NB) 12 G1
Pontiac, UP (Que.) 17 B1
Pont-Lafrance, UP (NB) 12 G1
Pont-Landry, UP (NB) 12 G1
Pont-Laval, UP (Que.) 14 F2
Pont-Mousseau, UP (Que.) 18 F4
Ponton, UP (Man.) 30 B2
Pontrilas, UP (Sask.) 32 F3
Pont-Rouge, VL (Que.) 15 A3
Pontypool, UP (Ont.) 21 C1
Poodiac, UP (NB) 11 E2
Pooeyelth 3, IR (BC) 35 B2
Poole, UP (Ont.) 23 C4
Pooles Corner, UP (PEI) 7 D4
Pooles Resort, UP (Ont.) 17 C4
Pool's Cove, COMM (Nfld.) 2 C2
Pool's Island < Badger's Quay – Valleyfield – Pool's Island, UP (Nfld.) 3 F3
Poor Man 88, IR (Sask.) 31 H2
Pope, UP (Man.) 29 E3
Pope Landing, UP (BC) 38 D1
Popelogan Depot, UP (NB) 12 C1
Popes Harbour, UP (NS) 9 D3
Popes Harbour, UP (Nfld.) 2 F1
Popkum, UP (BC) 35 A4
Popkum 1, IR (BC) 35 A4
Poplar, UP (Ont.) 25 B2
Poplar Bay, SV (Alta.) 33 D4
Poplar Creek, UP (BC) 34 B3
Poplar Dale, UP (Ont.) 26 B4
Poplarfield, UP (Man.) 29 H2
Poplar Grove, UP (PEI) 7 B3
Poplar Grove, UP (NS) 9 A3
Poplar Grove, UP (Ont.) 21 H1
Poplar Hill, UP (Ont.) 22 D1
Poplar Hill, UP (Ont.) 30 D3
Poplar Hill, UP (NS) 9 D1
Poplar Hill, UP (Alta.) 43 F4
Poplar Hills Survey, NUP (Ont.) 22 G1
Poplar Lodge, UP (Ont.) 27 F2
Poplar Park, UP (Man.) 30 C4
Poplar Point, UP (Man.) 29 H3
Poplar Point, UP (PEI) 7 E4
Poplar Ridge, UP (Alta.) 43 G3
Poplar Ridge, NUP (Alta.) 33 C3
Poplar River 16, IR (Man.) 30 C3
Popple Depot, UP (NB) 12 D1
Poquiosin and Skamain 13, IR (BC) 38 F1
Porcher Island, UP (BC) 41 C1
Porcupine Plain, T (Sask.) 32 G4
Porpoise Bay, NUP (BC) 38 E2
Portage, UP (NS) 8 E3
Portage, UP (PEI) 7 B3
Portage-de-la-Nation, UP (Que.) 17 E1
Portage-des-Roches, UP (Que.) 14 B3
Portage-du-Cap, UP (Que.) 7 F1
Portage-du-Fort, VL (Que.) 17 A1
Portage-du-Lac, UP (NB) 15 G2
Portage la Prairie, C (Man.) 29 G3
Portage la Prairie, CFB/BFC, MIL (Man.) 29 G3
Portage Vale, UP (NB) 11 F1
Port Alberni, C (BC) 38 C2
Port Albert, UP (Nfld.) 3 D2
Port Albert, UP (Ont.) 23 B3
Port Albion, UP (BC) 38 A3
Port Alice, VL (BC) 39 D2
Port Alma, UP (Ont.) 22 C3
Port Anson, COMM (Nfld.) 3 B2
Port Anson, UP (Ont.) 24 B1
Portapique, UP (NS) 9 B2
Portapique Mountain, UP (NS) 9 B2
Port au Bras, COMM (Nfld.) 2 C3
Port au Choix, T (Nfld.) 5 G3
Port-au-Persil, UP (Que.) 14 D4
Port au Port < Berry Head, Port au Port, UP (Nfld.) 4 B2
Port au Port West – Aguathuna – Felix Cove, T (Nfld.) 4 B2
Port-au-Saumon, UP (Que.) 14 D4
Port-aux-Quilles, UP (Que.) 14 D4
Port Ban, UP (NS) 8 C3
Port Bickerton, UP (NS) 9 F3
Port Blandford, LID (Nfld.) 3 E4
Port Bolster, UP (Ont.) 21 B1
Port Britain, UP (Ont.) 21 D2
Port Bruce, UP (Ont.) 22 E2
Port Burwell, UP (NWT) 46 G3
Port Burwell, VL (Ont.) 22 F2
Port Caledonia, UP (NS) 8 F3
Port Carling, UP (Ont.) 24 B1
Port Carmen, UP (Ont.) 24 B1
Port-Cartier, T (Que.) 19 E3
Port Clements, VL (BC) 41 B1
Port Clyde, UP (NS) 10 C4
Port Cockburn, UP (Ont.) 24 A2
Port Colborne, C (Ont.) 21 B4
Port Coquitlam, C (BC) 38 G2
Port Crewe, UP (Ont.) 22 C3
Port Cunnington, UP (Ont.) 24 C2
Port-Daniel, UP (Que.) 13 G3
Port-Daniel-Centre, UP (Que.) 13 G3
Port-Daniel-Est, UP (Que.) 13 G3
Port-Daniel-Ouest, UP (Que.) 13 G3
Port de Grave, UP (Nfld.) 2 G2
Port Dufferin, UP (NS) 9 E3
Port Dufferin West, UP (NS) 9 E3
Port Edward, VL (BC) 41 C1
Port Elgin, T (Ont.) 23 B2
Port Elgin, VL (NB) 7 A4
Port Elmsley, UP (Ont.) 17 B2
Porten Settlement, UP (NB) 11 A1
Porter, UP (NS) 9 C3
Porter, UP (Sask.) 32 B4
Porter Brook, UP (NB) 12 D3
Porter Cove, UP (NB) 12 D3
Porter Landing, UP (BC) 45 B4
Porter Road, UP (NB) 11 E2
Porter's Hill, UP (Ont.) 23 B4
Porters Lake, UP (NS) 9 C3
Porterville, UP (Nfld.) 3 C2
Port Essington, IR (BC) 41 D1
Port Essington < Port Essington, UP (BC) 41 D1
Port Felix, UP (NS) 9 G2
Port Felix East, UP (NS) 9 G2
Port Franks, UP (Ont.) 22 C1
Port George, UP (NS) 10 C1
Port Glasgow, UP (Ont.) 22 D3
Port Greville, UP (NS) 11 H2
Port Hardy, DM (BC) 39 D1
Port Hastings, UP (NS) 8 C4
Port Hawkesbury, T (NS) 8 C4
Port Hilford, UP (NS) 9 F3
Port Hill, UP (PEI) 7 B3
Port Hood, UP (NS) 8 C3
Port Hood Island, UP (NS) 8 C3
Port Hood Station, UP (NS) 8 C3
Port Hope, T (Ont.) 21 D2
Port Hope Simpson, COMM (Nfld.) 6 H4
Port Howe, UP (NS) 9 B1
Portia, UP (Man.) 29 F2
Portier Pass 5, IR (BC) 38 E3
Port Joli, UP (NS) 10 D3
Port Kirwan, COMM (Nfld.) 2 H4
Port Lambton, UP (Ont.) 22 B2
Portland, UP (Ont.) 17 B3
Portland, UP (Nfld.) 3 F4
Portland Creek, UP (Nfld.) 5 F3
Port La Tour, UP (NS) 10 C4
Port Law, UP (Ont.) 23 D2
Port-Lewis, UP (Que.) 17 F2
Port L'Hebert, UP (NS) 10 D3
Portlock, UP (Ont.) 26 B4
Port Loring, UP (Ont.) 24 A1
Port Lorne, UP (NS) 10 C1
Port Maitland, UP (NS) 10 A3
Port Malcolm, UP (NS) 8 C4
Port McNeill, VL (BC) 39 D1
Port McNicoll, VL (Ont.) 23 F1
Port Medway, UP (NS) 10 E3
Port Mellon, UP (BC) 38 E2
Port-Menier, UP (Que.) 19 H3
Port Metcalf, UP (Ont.) 17 B4
Port Milford, UP (Ont.) 21 G2
Port Moody, C (BC) 38 G2
Port Morien, UP (NS) 8 F3
Port Mouton, UP (NS) 10 D3
Port Nelson, UP (Nfld.) 3 F3
Portneuf, T (Que.) 16 D1
Portneuf-Station, UP (Que.) 16 D1
Portneuf-sur-Mer, UP (Que.) 14 F2
Port Neville, UP (BC) 39 F1
Port Neville 4, IR (BC) 39 G1
Port-Nouveau-Québec, UP (Que.) 46 G4
Porto Rico, UP (BC) 34 B4
Port Perry, UP (Ont.) 21 C1
Port Philip, UP (NS) 9 B1
Port-Pic, UP (Que.) 14 F3
Portree, UP (NS) 8 D2
Portreeve, UP (Sask.) 31 C2
Port Renfrew, UP (BC) 38 D4
Port Rexton, COMM (Nfld.) 3 G4
Port Richmond, UP (NS) 8 C4
Port Rowan, UP (Ont.) 22 G2
Port Royal, UP (NS) 8 D4
Port Royal, UP (NS) 10 B1
Port Royal, UP (Ont.) 22 F2
Port Royal, UP (Nfld.) 2 E2
Port-St-François, UP (Que.) 16 B2
Port-St-Servan, UP (Que.) 5 F2
Port Sandfield, UP (Ont.) 24 B2
Port Saunders, T (Nfld.) 5 G3
Port Saxon, UP (NS) 10 C4
Port Severn, UP (Ont.) 23 F1
Port Shoreham, UP (NS) 9 G2
Port Simpson, UP (BC) 42 C4
Port Simpson 1, IR (BC) 42 C4
Port Stanley, VL (Ont.) 22 E2
Port Stanton, UP (Ont.) 23 G1
Port Talbot, UP (Ont.) 22 E2
Portugal Cove, UP (Nfld.) 2 H2
Portugal Cove South, COMM (Nfld.) 2 G4
Portuguese Cove, UP (NS) 9 B4
Port Union, T (Nfld.) 3 G4
Port View Beach, UP (Ont.) 21 C1
Port Wade, UP (NS) 10 B1
Port Washington, UP (BC) 38 F3
Port Williams, UP (NS) 11 H3
Poste-de-la-Baleine, UP (Que.) 20 E1
Postville, COMM (Nfld.) 6 F3
Potato Point 3, IR (BC) 37 C2
Potato River 156A, IR (Sask.) 32 E1
Pottageville, UP (Ont.) 21 A2
Potter, UP (Ont.) 26 E1
Potters Landing, UP (Ont.) 23 F1
Potton-Springs, UP (Que.) 16 C4
Pouce Coupe, VL (BC) 43 G4
Pouch Cove, T (Nfld.) 2 H2
Poulamon, UP (NS) 8 D4
Poularies, UP (Que.) 18 A1
Pouliot, UP (Que.) 14 F4
Pound Cove < Westport, UP (Nfld.) 5 G4
Poundmaker 114, IR (Sask.) 32 B4
Povungnituk, UP (Que.) 46 E3
Powassan, T (Ont.) 25 H2
Powell, UP (Man.) 30 A3
Powell River, DM (BC) 38 C1
Powells Corners, UP (Ont.) 22 F2
Powerscourt, UP (Que.) 17 F2
Powers Creek, UP (NB) 12 A2
Powerview, VL (Man.) 30 C4
Powles Corners, UP (Ont.) 21 C1
Pownal, UP (PEI) 7 D4
Poyam 9, IR (BC) 37 F4
Pradine Subdivision, NUP (BC) 40 C3
Prairie Echo, UP (Alta.) 33 B1
Prairie Grove, UP (Man.) 28 A2
Prairie River, UP (Sask.) 32 G4
Prairie Siding, UP (Ont.) 22 B3
Prairie View, UP (Sask.) 31 E3
Pratt, UP (Man.) 29 G4
Pratts Camp, UP (NB) 12 C2
Prawda, UP (Man.) 28 D2
Pré-d'en-Haut, UP (NB) 11 G1
Pré-Ste-Marie, UP (Sask.) 32 F4
Precious Corners, UP (Ont.) 21 D2
Preeceville, T (Sask.) 29 C1
Preissac, UP (Que.) 18 B1
Prelate, VL (Sask.) 31 C2
Premier Lake, UP (BC) 34 D3
Prémont, UP (Que.) 16 B1
Preneveau, UP (Ont.) 21 E1
Prentiss, UP (Alta.) 33 D4
Prescott, T (Ont.) 17 C3
Prespatou, UP (BC) 43 E2
Presque, UP (Nfld.) 2 D3
Presqu'ile Point, UP (Ont.) 21 E2
Press, UP (Que.) 18 C2
Preston, UP (NS) 9 B3
Prestonvale, UP (Ont.) 17 B2
Prestville, UP (Alta.) 43 G4
Pretty Valley, UP (Man.) 29 D1
Prevo, UP (Alta.) 33 D4
Prévost, UP (Que.) 18 F4
Price, UP (NB) 11 G1
Price, VL (Que.) 14 H2
Price Road, UP (NB) 12 A2
Prices Corner, UP (Ont.) 23 F1
Prices Corners, UP (Ont.) 23 E3
Price Settlement, UP (NB) 12 F2
Priceville, UP (Ont.) 23 D2
Priceville, UP (NB) 12 D3
Priddis, UP (Alta.) 34 E2
Priest Pond, UP (PEI) 7 E3
Priest's Valley 6, IR (BC) 35 F2
Priestville, UP (NS) 9 D2
Primate, VL (Sask.) 31 C1
Prime, UP (NB) 15 H2
Prime Brook, UP (NS) 8 F3
Primrose, UP (PEI) 7 E4
Primrose, UP (Ont.) 23 E3
Primrose, UP (NB) 11 E2
Prince, UP (Sask.) 32 B4
Prince Albert, C (Sask.) 32 E3
Prince Albert, UP (NS) 10 D1
Prince Albert, UP (Ont.) 21 C1
Princedale, UP (NS) 10 C1
Prince George, C (BC) 40 C2
Prince Leboo Island 32, IR (BC) 42 C4
Prince of Wales, UP (NB) 11 D3
Princeport, UP (NS) 9 B2
Princeport Road, UP (NS) 9 B2
Prince Rupert, C (BC) 41 C1
Princess, UP (Alta.) 34 H2
Princess Harbour, UP (Man.) 30 C3
Princess Park, UP (NB) 11 D1
Princeton, UP (Ont.) 22 F1
Princeton, UP (Nfld.) 3 F4
Princeton, VL (BC) 35 D3
Princeville, T (Que.) 16 D2
Princeville, UP (NS) 8 C4
Prince William, UP (NB) 11 B1
Prince William Station, UP (NB) 11 B2
Pritchard, UP (BC) 35 E1
Pritchard Mobile Subdivision, UP (BC) 35 E1
Procter, UP (BC) 34 B4
Profits Corner, UP (PEI) 7 A2
Progress, UP (BC) 43 E4
Progreston, UP (Ont.) 22 H1
Projet-Saddlebrook, NUP (Que.) 17 F1
Prongua, UP (Sask.) 32 B4
Pronto Mine Townsite, NUP (Ont.) 25 A1
Prophet Beach, UP (Ont.) 23 G2
Prophet River < Prophet River 4, UP (BC) 43 D1
Prophet River 4, IR (BC) 43 D1
Prospect, UP (NS) 9 B4
Prospect, UP (NS) 10 E1
Prospect, UP (Ont.) 17 C2
Prospect, UP (Ont.) 21 C2
Prospect Hill, UP (Ont.) 22 E1
Prospector, UP (Man.) 30 A2
Prospect Valley, UP (Alta.) 33 G4
Prosperity, UP (Ont.) 23 B3
Prosser Brook, UP (NB) 11 G1
Proton Station, UP (Ont.) 23 D2
Proulx, UP (Ont.) 17 E1
Proulxville, UP (Que.) 16 C1
Provancher, UP (Que.) 13 D3
Providence Bay, UP (Ont.) 25 B3
Province-Hill, UP (Que.) 16 C4
Provost, T (Alta.) 33 H4
Prowseton, UP (Nfld.) 2 E2
Prud'homme, VL (Sask.) 31 F1
Pryors Beach, UP (Sask.) 31 G2
Psacelay 77, IR (BC) 41 D1
Public Landing, UP (NB) 11 D2
Pubnico, UP (NS) 10 B4
Puce, UP (Ont.) 22 A3
Puckatholetchin 11, IR (BC) 35 B3
Puffer, UP (Alta.) 33 G4
Pughs Crossing, UP (NB) 11 C1
Pugwash, UP (NS) 9 B1
Pugwash Junction, UP (NS) 9 B1
Pugwash Point, UP (NS) 9 B1
Pugwash River, UP (NS) 9 B1
Pukaskwa Depot, UP (Ont.) 27 H3
Pukatawagan < Pukatawagan 198, UP (Man.) 30 A1
Pukatawagan 198, IR (Man.) 30 A1
Pulcah 15, IR (BC) 39 C1
Pulp River, UP (Man.) 29 E1
Pulteney, UP (Alta.) 34 F3
Pumbly Cove, UP (Nfld.) 5 G4
Punchaw, UP (BC) 40 C2
Punkeydoodles Corners, UP (Ont.) 22 F1
Punnichy, VL (Sask.) 31 H2
Puntledge, UP (BC) 38 B1
Puntzi Lake 2, IR (BC) 40 B4
Purbeck's Cove, UP (Nfld.) 5 G4
Purcell's Harbour, UP (Nfld.) 3 D1
Purdy, UP (Ont.) 24 F2
Purdy Corners, UP (Ont.) 21 E2
Purlbrook, UP (NS) 8 B4
Purple Grove, UP (Ont.) 23 B3
Purple Hill, UP (Ont.) 23 E3
Purple Hill, UP (Ont.) 21 C1
Purple Springs, UP (Alta.) 34 G3
Purple Valley, UP (Ont.) 23 C1
Purtuniq, UP (Que.) 46 F3
Purves, UP (Man.) 29 G4
Pusey, UP (Ont.) 24 E3
Pushthrough, UP (Nfld.) 2 A2
Puskiakiwenin 122, IR (Alta.) 33 G3
Puslinch, UP (Ont.) 23 E4
Putkwa 14, IR (BC) 35 B2
Putnam, UP (Ont.) 22 E1
Pynns, UP (Nfld.) 4 D1

Q

Quaal 3, IR (BC) 41 D1
Quaal 3A, IR (BC) 41 D1
Quaaout 1, IR (BC) 36 G4
Quabbin, UP (Ont.) 17 C3
Quaco Road, UP (NB) 11 E2
Quadeville, UP (Ont.) 24 F2
Quadra, UP (Man.) 29 E3
Quaee 7, IR (BC) 41 G4
Quai-de-Rivière-Ouelle, UP (Que.) 15 D1
Quai-de-St-Juste, UP (Que.) 15 G1
Quaker Brook, UP (NB) 12 A3
Qualark 4, IR (BC) 35 B3
Qualicum, IR (BC) 38 C2
Qualicum Beach, VL (BC) 38 D2
Qualicum Beach Trailer Park, NUP (BC) 38 C2
Qualicum Park, UP (Ont.) 17 D4
Quaniwsom 2, IR (BC) 37 D3

Quan-skum-ksin-mich-mich 4, IR (BC) 42 F3
Qu'Appelle, T (Sask.) 29 B3
Quarindale, UP (Ont.) 23 D4
Quarry St Anns, UP (NS) 8 E3
Quarryville, UP (NB) 12 E3
Quartcha 3, IR (BC) 41 F3
Quartier-St-Thomas, UP (Que.) 15 E1
Quathiaski Cove, UP (BC) 37 B4
Quatlenemo 5, IR (BC) 35 A1
Quatleyo 12, IR (BC) 39 C1
Quatre-Chemins, UP (Que.) 15 C4
Quatre-Chemins, UP (Que.) 15 B3
Quatre-Chemins, UP (Que.) 15 C4
Quatre-Coins, UP (NB) 12 A2
Quatre-Coins, UP (NB) 15 G1
Quatre Fourches, UP (Alta.) 44 C3
Quatre-Milles, UP (NB) 12 B1
Quatsino, UP (BC) 39 C1
Quatsino 18, IR (BC) 39 C1
Quattishe 1, IR (BC) 39 C1
Quay 4, IR (BC) 41 G4
Quckwa 7, IR (BC) 41 E3
Québec, C (Que.) 15 G3
Quebec Harbour, UP (Ont.) 27 H4
Queen Charlotte, UP (BC) 41 B2
Queens Acres, UP (Ont.) 21 H1
Queens Bay, UP (BC) 34 B4
Queensborough, UP (Ont.) 24 F4
Queen's Cove, UP (Nfld.) 2 F1
Queensland, UP (NS) 9 A4
Queens Line, UP (Ont.) 17 A1
Queensport, UP (NS) 9 G2
Queenstown, UP (NB) 11 D2
Queenstown, UP (Alta.) 34 F3
Queens Valley, UP (Man.) 28 B1
Queensville, UP (Ont.) 21 B1
Queensville, UP (NS) 8 C4
Queenswood Heights, UP (Ont.) 17 F3
Queenswood Village, UP (Ont.) 17 F3
Quesidaquah 4, IR (BC) 38 D4
Quequa 6, IR (BC) 37 C4
Querrin, UP (Sask.) 31 G4
Quesnel, T (BC) 40 C3
Quesnel 1, IR (BC) 40 C3
Quesnel Forks, UP (BC) 40 D3
Quesnel View, UP (BC) 40 C3
Quetico, UP (Ont.) 27 C3
Queylus, UP (Que.) 15 B2
Quibell, UP (Ont.) 28 H1
Quick, UP (BC) 42 F4
Quigley, UP (Alta.) 44 C4
Quilchena, UP (BC) 35 D2
Quill Creek, UP (YT) 45 A3
Quill Lake, VL (Sask.) 31 H1
Quimper, UP (Sask.) 31 E4
Quinan, UP (NS) 10 B3
Quinaquilth 4, IR (BC) 38 B3
Quineex 8, IR (BC) 39 C2
Quinn, UP (Ont.) 22 B3
Quinn Settlement, UP (Ont.) 17 B2
Quinogag 61, IR (BC) 42 D3
Quinsam, UP (BC) 37 B4
Quinsam 12, IR (BC) 37 B4
Quinton, VL (Sask.) 31 H2
Quirpon, UP (Nfld.) 5 H2
Quisibis, UP (NB) 15 H2
Quisitis 9, IR (BC) 38 A3
Quispamsis, VL (NB) 11 E2
Quortsowe 13, IR (BC) 38 A2
Quyon, UP (Que.) 17 B1
Quyon Ferry Landing, UP (Ont.) 17 B1

R

Rabbit Lake, VL (Sask.) 32 C3
Race Horse Camp, UP (Ont.) 24 F1
Racine, UP (Que.) 16 C3
Rackety, UP (Ont.) 23 H1
Rackham, UP (Man.) 29 F3
Radford, UP (Que.) 17 A1
Radisson, T (Sask.) 32 C4
Radisson, UP (Que.) 20 E2
Radium, UP (BC) 34 C3
Radium Hot Springs, UP (BC) 34 C3
Radnor, UP (Alta.) 34 E2
Radnor-des-Forges, UP (Que.) 16 C1
Radville, T (Sask.) 31 H4
Radway, VL (Alta.) 33 E2
Rae-Edzo, HAM (NWT) 45 E3
Rae Lakes, UP (NWT) 45 E3
Rafter, UP (Man.) 30 A1
Raft River Trailer Park, NUP (BC) 36 F2
Rageot, UP (Que.) 15 A4
Ragged Point, NUP (Nfld.) 3 D1
Ragged Reef, UP (NS) 11 H2
Raglan, UP (Ont.) 22 C3
Railton, UP (Ont.) 17 A4
Rainbow, UP (Alta.) 34 G2
Rainbow, NUP (Ont.) 22 B1
Rainbow Haven, UP (NS) 9 B4
Rainbow Lake, T (Alta.) 45 E4
Rainier, UP (Alta.) 34 G3
Rainy Hollow, UP (BC) 45 A4
Rainy Lake 17A, IR (Ont.) 28 H4
Rainy Lake 17B, IR (Ont.) 28 H4
Rainy Lake 18C, IR (Ont.) 28 H4
Rainy Lake 26A, IR (Ont.) 27 A3
Rainy Lake 26B, IR (Ont.) 27 A3
Rainy Lake 26C, IR (Ont.) 27 A3
Rainy River, T (Ont.) 28 F4
Raith, UP (Ont.) 27 D3
Raleigh, COMM (Nfld.) 5 H2
Raley, UP (Alta.) 34 F4
Ralls Island, UP (Man.) 30 A2
Ralph, UP (Sask.) 29 B4
Ralston, UP (Alta.) 34 H3
Rama, VL (Sask.) 29 C1
Rama 32, IR (Ont.) 23 G1
Ramage, UP (BC) 36 F4
Rama Road < Rama 32, UP (Ont.) 23 G1
Ramea, T (Nfld.) 4 E4
Rameau, UP (Que.) 13 H2
Ramore, UP (Ont.) 26 F2
Rampart House, UP (YT) 45 A1
Ramsay Lodge, UP (NB) 12 D2
Ramsay Sheds, UP (NB) 12 C1
Ramsayville, UP (Ont.) 17 E4
Ramsey, UP (Ont.) 26 D3
Ramseys, UP (NS) 9 C3
Ranch, UP (Alta.) 33 D1
Rancheria, UP (YT) 45 B4
Randall Corner, UP (NB) 11 D1
Randboro, UP (Que.) 16 E4
Randolph, UP (Ont.) 23 E1
Randolph, UP (Man.) 28 B2
Randwick, UP (Ont.) 23 E2
Ranfurly, UP (Alta.) 33 F3
Rang-Cinq-et-Six, UP (NB) 12 A1
Rang-des-Bossé, UP (NB) 15 H1
Rang-des-Bourgoin, UP (NB) 12 A2
Rang-des-Collin, UP (NB) 15 G2
Rang-des-Couturier, UP (NB) 15 H1
Rang-des-Deschêne, UP (NB) 15 H2
Rang-des-Hamelins, NUP (Que.) 18 G3
Rang-des-Lavoie, UP (NB) 15 H2
Rang-des-Morneault, UP (NB) 15 G2
Rang-Dix, UP (NB) 12 B1
Rang-Dix-Huit, UP (NB) 12 B1
Rang-Double-Nord, UP (NB) 12 B1
Rang-Double-Sud, UP (NB) 12 B1
Rang-Douze-Nord, UP (NB) 12 B1
Rang-Douze-Sud, UP (NB) 12 B1
Range 13, IR (BC) 35 E4
Ranger, UP (Sask.) 32 C3
Ranger Lake, UP (Ont.) 26 B3
Rangeton, UP (Alta.) 33 C3
Rangeview, UP (Sask.) 31 C4
Rang-Quatorze, UP (NB) 12 B1
Rang-St-David, UP (Que.) 15 G2
Rang-Ste-Marie, UP (Que.) 14 C3
Rang-St-Georges, UP (NB) 12 F1
Rang-St-Joseph, UP (NB) 15 G2
Rang-St-Nicolas, UP (Que.) 15 B2
Rang-Seize, UP (NB) 12 B1
Rang-Sept, UP (NB) 12 B1
Rang-Sept-et-Huit, UP (NB) 12 B1
Rankin, UP (Ont.) 24 G1
Rankin, UP (Ont.) 18 A4
Rankin Inlet, HAM (NWT) 46 B2
Rankin Location 15D, IR (Ont.) 26 B4
Rankinville, UP (NS) 8 C3
Rannoch, UP (Ont.) 22 E1
Ranoke, UP (Ont.) 20 C4
Rantem, UP (Nfld.) 2 F2
Rapid City, T (Man.) 29 F3
Rapide-Blanc, UP (Que.) 18 G2
Rapide-Danseur, UP (Que.) 18 A1
Rapide-des-Chiens, UP (Que.) 18 E3
Rapide-des-Pins, UP (Que.) 18 E3
Rapide-Deux, UP (Que.) 18 A2
Rapide-Dufort, UP (Que.) 18 D4
Rapides-des-Joachims, UP (Que.) 18 B4
Rapide-Sept, UP (Que.) 18 B2
Rapid Lake, IR (Que.) 18 C3
Rapids Depot, UP (NB) 13 A4
Rapid Valley, UP (Ont.) 17 B4
Rapid View, UP (Sask.) 32 B2
Raspberry, UP (BC) 34 B4
Ratcliffe, UP (Sask.) 31 H4
Rathburn, UP (Ont.) 23 G1
Ratho, UP (Ont.) 22 F1
Rathwell, UP (Man.) 29 G4
Rathwell's Shore, UP (Ont.) 17 B2
Ratner, UP (Sask.) 32 F3
Rat Portage 38A, IR (Ont.) 28 F2
Rat Rapids, UP (Ont.) 30 F4
Rat River, UP (NWT) 44 F1
Ratter Corner, UP (NB) 11 E2
Rattling Brook, UP (Nfld.) 3 A1
Rattling Brook, UP (Nfld.) 3 C3
Rattling Brook Depot, UP (Nfld.) 3 B3
Ratzburg, UP (Ont.) 23 D4
Raudot, UP (Que.) 14 F4
Raven, UP (Alta.) 34 E1
Ravendale, UP (Sask.) 32 G3
Ravenhead, UP (Sask.) 32 C4
Ravenna, UP (Ont.) 23 D2
Ravenscrag, UP (Sask.) 31 C4
Ravenshoe, UP (Ont.) 21 B1
Ravensview, UP (Ont.) 17 B4
Ravenswood, UP (Ont.) 22 C1
Ravensworth, UP (Ont.) 24 C1
Ravignan-Nord, UP (Que.) 15 D4
Ravine, UP (Alta.) 33 C3
Rawcliffe, UP (Que.) 17 F1
Rawdon, VL (Que.) 18 F4
Rawdon Gold Mines, UP (NS) 9 B3
Rawebb, UP (Man.) 30 A2
Raymond, T (Alta.) 34 G4
Raymond, UP (Ont.) 24 B2
Raymond Point, UP (Nfld.) 2 B2
Raymonds Corners, UP (Ont.) 17 A3
Raymore, T (Sask.) 31 H2
Raynardton, UP (NS) 10 B3
Raysice, UP (Ont.) 22 E1
Raysice-Balfour, T (Ont.) 26 E4
Reaboro, UP (Ont.) 21 C1
Reaburn, UP (Man.) 29 H3
Read, UP (Ont.) 21 G1
Readford, UP (YT) 45 A2
Reading, UP (Ont.) 23 E3
Read Island, UP (BC) 37 B4
Read Island, UP (NWT) 47 B4
Readlyn, UP (Sask.) 31 G4
Rear Ealls Creek, UP (NS) 8 E3
Rear Big Hill, UP (NS) 8 E3
Rear Big Pond, UP (NS) 8 E3
Rear Black River, UP (NS) 8 D4
Rear Boisdale, UP (NS) 8 E3
Rear Christmas Island, UP (NS) 8 E3
Rear Dunvegan, UP (NS) 8 D3
Rear Estmere, UP (NS) 8 D3
Rear Forks, UP (NS) 8 D3
Rear Judique Chapel, UP (NS) 8 C4
Rear Judique South, UP (NS) 8 C4
Rear Little River, UP (NS) 8 E2
Rear Monastery, UP (NS) 8 C4
Rear of East Bay, UP (NS) 8 E3
Rébéca, UP (Que.) 15 C1
Reco, UP (Alta.) 33 B4
Rectory-Hill, UP (Que.) 15 A4
Redan, UP (Ont.) 17 C3
Red Bank, UP (NB) 12 E2
Redbank, UP (NB) 11 E1
Red Bank 4, IR (NB) 12 E2
Red Bank 7, IR (NB) 12 E2
Red Bay, COMM (Nfld.) 5 G1
Red Bay, UP (Ont.) 23 C1
Redberry, UP (Sask.) 32 C4
Redberry Park, UP (Sask.) 32 C4
Red Bluff, UP (BC) 40 C3
Red Bluff 88, IR (BC) 42 D4
Red Brook < Cape St George - Petit Jardin - Grand Jardin - De Grau - Marches Point - Loretto, UP (Nfld.) 4 A2
Redcliff, T (Alta.) 31 B3
Red Cliff, UP (Nfld.) 3 G4
Red Cliff 13, IR (BC) 42 D4
Red Cove, UP (Nfld.) 2 B2
Red Cross, UP (Sask.) 32 A3
Red Deer, C (Alta.) 34 E1
Red Deer Hill, UP (Sask.) 32 D4
Red Deer Junction, UP (Alta.) 33 D4
Red Deer Lake, UP (Man.) 30 A3
Reddendale, UP (Ont.) 17 A4
Redditt, UP (Ont.) 28 F1
Red Earth < Carrot River 29A, UP (Sask.) 32 G3
Red Earth 29, IR (Sask.) 32 G3
Red Earth Creek, UP (Alta.) 44 A4
Redelback Development, NUP (Alta.) 34 G3
Redfield, UP (Sask.) 32 C4
Red Harbour, COMM (Nfld.) 2 C3
Red Head Cove, UP (Nfld.) 2 H1
Red House, UP (PEI) 7 E4
Redickville, UP (Ont.) 23 E2
Red Island, UP (Nfld.) 2 E3
Red Island, UP (Nfld.) 4 E4
Red Islands, UP (NS) 8 D4
Red Jacket, UP (Sask.) 29 D3
Red Lake, UP (Ont.) 30 D4
Red Lake Road, UP (Ont.) 28 H1
Redland, UP (Alta.) 34 F2
Red-Mill, UP (Que.) 16 C1
Redmondville, UP (NB) 12 F2
Red-Mountain, UP (Que.) 16 E3
Rednersville, UP (Ont.) 21 F1
Redonda Bay, UP (BC) 37 C3
Redpass Junction, UP (BC) 40 G3
Red Pheasant, UP (Sask.) 32 B4
Red Pheasant 108, IR (Sask.) 32 B4
Red Point, UP (PEI) 7 E3
Red Point, UP (NS) 8 D3
Red Point, UP (Nfld.) 6 H3
Red Point East, UP (NS) 8 D3
Red Rapids, UP (NB) 12 A3
Red River, UP (NS) 8 D1
Red Rock, UP (Ont.) 27 F2
Red Rock, UP (BC) 40 C2
Red Rock, UP (NB) 12 C4
Red Rock, UP (NB) 12 D3
Red Rock 53, IR (Ont.) 27 E2
Red Rock Lake, UP (Man.) 28 D1
Red Rose, UP (Man.) 29 H2
Red Star, UP (Alta.) 43 G3
Redstone, UP (BC) 40 B4
Redstone Cemetery 1B, IR (BC) 40 B4
Redstone Flat 1, IR (BC) 40 B4
Redstone Flat 1A, IR (BC) 40 B4
Red Sucker Lake, UP (Man.) 30 D2
Redvers, T (Sask.) 29 D4
Redwater, T (Alta.) 33 E3
Redwater Creek 30, IR (BC) 40 B3
Red Willow, UP (Alta.) 33 E4
Red Wing, UP (Ont.) 23 D2
Red Wing Terrace, NUP (Sask.) 32 D3
Redwood, UP (Ont.) 24 B2
Reeces Corners, UP (Ont.) 22 C2
Reeder, UP (Man.) 29 E3
Reed River 36A, IR (Man.) 28 E3
Reeds Point, UP (NB) 11 E2
Reedy Creek, UP (Man.) 29 G2
Reefs Harbour, UP (Nfld.) 5 G2
Rees, UP (NB) 11 E1
Reesor, UP (Ont.) 20 C4
Reeve, UP (Man.) 29 F3
Reevecraig, UP (Ont.) 17 C2
Refuge Cove, UP (BC) 37 C4
Refuge Cove 6, IR (BC) 39 F4
Regan, UP (Ont.) 27 H3
Regent, UP (Man.) 29 E4
Regina, C (Sask.) 31 H3
Regina Beach, VL (Sask.) 31 G2
Regway, UP (Sask.) 31 H4
Reid, UP (NS) 9 C3
Reid Lake, UP (BC) 40 C2
Reid's Corners, UP (Ont.) 23 B3
Reid's Mill, UP (Ont.) 22 G1
Reids Mills, UP (Ont.) 17 C2
Reidsville, UP (Ont.) 22 G1
Reidville, COMM (Nfld.) 5 G4
Reidville, UP (Que.) 16 D4
Reidville, UP (Ont.) 21 G1
Reindeer Station, UP (NWT) 45 C1
Reinfeld, UP (Man.) 29 H4
Reinland, UP (Man.) 29 H4
Reiswig, UP (BC) 35 G2
Relessey, UP (Ont.) 23 E3
Reliance, UP (Sask.) 31 E4
Reliance, UP (NWT) 44 D1
Rembrandt, UP (Man.) 29 H2
Remicks, UP (Ont.) 27 D3
Rémigny, UP (Que.) 18 A2
Remo, NUP (BC) 42 E4
Renabie, UP (Ont.) 26 B2
Renata, UP (BC) 35 H3
Renauds Mills, UP (NB) 12 G4
Rencontre East, COMM (Nfld.) 2 C2
Rencontre West, UP (Nfld.) 4 F4
Reneault, UP (Que.) 18 A1
Renews < Renews - Cappahayden, UP (Nfld.) 2 H4
Renews - Cappahayden, COMM (Nfld.) 2 H4
Renforth, VL (NB) 11 D3
Renfrew, T (Ont.) 17 A1
Renfrew, UP (NS) 9 B3
Rennie, UP (Man.) 28 D1
Rennies Road, UP (PEI) 7 C3
Reno, UP (Alta.) 43 H3
Renous, UP (NB) 12 E3
Renous 12, IR (NB) 12 E3
Renown, UP (Sask.) 31 G1
Renversy, UP (Que.) 16 B1
Renwer, UP (Man.) 29 E1
Renwick, UP (Ont.) 22 B3
Repentigny, T (Que.) 18 G4
Repulse Bay, UP (NWT) 46 D2
Reserve, UP (Sask.) 32 G4
Reserve Mines, UP (NS) 8 F3
Reserve Rows, UP (NS) 8 F3
Resolute, UP (NWT) 47 D3
Resolution Island, UP (NWT) 46 G3
Resource, UP (Sask.) 32 F4
Restigouche < Restigouche 1, UP (Que.) 13 C4
Restigouche 1, IR (Que.) 13 C3
Reston, UP (Man.) 29 E4
Restoule, UP (Ont.) 25 H2
Retallack, UP (BC) 34 B3
Retlaw, UP (Alta.) 34 G3
Revelstoke, C (BC) 34 A2
Revenue, UP (Sask.) 31 C1
Révillart, NUP (Que.) 18 B2
Reward, UP (Sask.) 31 C1
Rex, UP (Sask.) 32 A3
Rexons Cove, UP (Nfld.) 6 H4
Rexton, VL (NB) 12 G3
Reykjavik, UP (Man.) 29 G2
Reynaud, UP (Sask.) 32 E4
Reynoldscroft, UP (NS) 10 C4
Rhein, VL (Sask.) 29 D2
Rheinfeld, UP (Sask.) 31 E3
Rheinland, UP (Sask.) 31 F1
Rhineland, UP (Sask.) 31 E3
Rhodena, UP (NS) 8 C4
Rhodes, UP (Ont.) 22 C3
Rhodes Corner, UP (NS) 10 E2
Rhone, UP (BC) 35 G4
Ribstone, UP (Alta.) 33 H4
Riceburg, UP (Que.) 16 B4
Rice Point, UP (PEI) 7 C4
Riceton, UP (Sask.) 31 H3
Riceville, UP (NB) 15 G2
Riceville, UP (Ont.) 17 E1
Riceville, UP (NB) 11 A1
Richan, UP (Ont.) 27 A1
Richard, VL (Sask.) 32 C4
Richard's Harbour, UP (Nfld.) 2 A2
Richards Landing, UP (Ont.) 26 B4
Richardson, UP (NB) 11 B3
Richardson, UP (Sask.) 31 H3
Richardsville, UP (NB) 13 C4
Richard-Village, UP (NB) 12 F3
Rich Bar, UP (BC) 40 C3
Rich Bar 4, IR (BC) 40 C3
Richdale, UP (Alta.) 34 G1
Riche-en-Bois, UP (Que.) 18 F4
Richelieu, T (Que.) 16 A3
Richer, UP (Man.) 28 B2
Richfield, UP (NS) 10 B3
Rich Hill, UP (Ont.) 21 A2
Richibucto, VL (NB) 12 G3
Richibucto 15, IR (NB) 12 G3
Richibucto-Village, UP (NB) 12 G3
Rich Lake, UP (Alta.) 33 F2
Richland, UP (Man.) 28 B1
Richlea, UP (Sask.) 31 D2
Richmond, DM (BC) 38 F2
Richmond, T (Que.) 16 C3
Richmond, UP (Ont.) 17 C2
Richmond, UP (PEI) 7 B3
Richmond, UP (Ont.) 22 F2
Richmond, UP (NS) 9 B1
Richmond Corner, UP (NB) 11 A1
Richmond Hill, T (Ont.) 21 B2
Richmond Park, UP (Alta.) 33 E1
Richmond Road, UP (NS) 10 A3
Richmound, VL (Sask.) 31 C3
Rich Valley, UP (Alta.) 33 D3
Richwood, UP (Ont.) 22 F1
Ricinus, UP (Alta.) 34 D1
Ricketts Bridge, UP (Nfld.) 2 H2
Rideau Ferry, UP (Ont.) 17 B3
Rideau Glen, UP (Ont.) 17 E4
Ridgeclough, UP (Alta.) 33 H4
Ridgedale, VL (Sask.) 32 F4
Ridgetown, T (Ont.) 22 C3
Ridgeville, UP (Man.) 28 A3
Ridgewood Road Subdivision, NUP (BC) 34 B4
Riding Mountain, UP (Man.) 29 F3
Ridley, UP (Man.) 29 G1
Rife, UP (Alta.) 33 G2
Rigaud, T (Que.) 17 F1
Rigolet, UP (Nfld.) 6 G3
Riley Brook, UP (NB) 12 B2
Riley Creek 1B, IR (BC) 35 A1
Rimbey, T (Alta.) 33 D4
Rimington, UP (Ont.) 24 F4
Rimouski, C (Que.) 14 G3
Rimouski-Est, VL (Que.) 14 G3
Rio Grande, UP (NB) 12 E1
Rio Grande, UP (Alta.) 43 F4
Riondel, UP (BC) 34 B4
Riou, UP (Que.) 14 F4
Ripley, VL (Ont.) 23 B3
Ripley Loop, UP (NS) 9 B1
Ripon, VL (Que.) 18 E4
Ripple, UP (Ont.) 27 G3
Ripples, UP (NB) 11 D1
Riske Creek, UP (BC) 36 A2
Ritchance, UP (Ont.) 17 E1
Ritchie, NUP (NB) 11 B1
Rivard, UP (Que.) 16 D4
Riverbank, UP (NB) 12 A4
Riverbank, UP (NB) 11 E2
Riverbank, UP (Ont.) 23 D3
Riverbend, UP (Alta.) 33 E3
River Bend Trailer Court, NUP (BC) 34 A2
River Bennet, UP (NS) 8 E3
River Bourgeois, UP (NS) 8 D4
River Canard, UP (Ont.) 22 A3
River Centre, UP (NS) 8 C3
Rivercourse, UP (Alta.) 33 H4
Rivercrest, UP (Man.) 28 A1
Riverdale, UP (NS) 10 B2
Riverdale, UP (PEI) 7 C4
Riverdale, UP (Man.) 29 F3
Riverdale Subdivision, NUP (BC) 35 F1
River de Chute, UP (NB) 12 A3
River de Chute Siding, UP (NB) 12 A3
River Denys, UP (NS) 8 D4
River Denys Centre, UP (NS) 8 C4
River Denys Road, UP (NS) 8 C4
River Drive Park, UP (Ont.) 21 B1
Riverfield, UP (Que.) 17 G2
River Glade, UP (NB) 11 F1
Riverhead, COMM (Nfld.) 2 G4
Riverhead, UP (Nfld.) 2 G2
Riverhead, UP (NS) 10 B4
River Head, UP (NS) 10 D3
River Hebert, UP (NS) 11 H2
River Hills, UP (Man.) 28 C1
Riverhurst, VL (Sask.) 31 E2
River John, UP (NS) 9 C1
River Jordan, UP (BC) 38 D4
River of Ponds, COMM (Nfld.) 5 G3
River Philip, UP (NS) 9 A1
River Philip Centre, UP (NS) 9 A1
Riverport, UP (NS) 10 E2
River Ryan, UP (NS) 8 F3
Rivers, T (Man.) 29 E3
Riversdale, UP (Ont.) 23 B3
Riversdale, UP (NS) 9 C2
Riversdale, UP (NS) 10 D3
Riverside, UP (NS) 9 A3
Riverside, UP (Man.) 29 H4
Riverside, UP (NS) 9 C2
Riverside, UP (NS) 8 C4
Riverside, UP (Ont.) 24 A3
Riverside, UP (Ont.) 22 E2
Riverside, UP (Man.) 28 A1
Riverside, NUP (Sask.) 31 H4
Riverside-Albert, VL (NB) 11 G2
Riverside Corner, UP (NS) 9 B3
Riverside Heights, UP (Ont.) 17 D2
Riverside Park, NUP (NS) 10 E2
Riverside Trailer Park, NUP (Ont.) 22 C3
Rivers Inlet, UP (BC) 41 F4
Riverstown, UP (Ont.) 23 D3
River Tillard, UP (NS) 8 D4
Riverton, UP (NS) 9 D2
Riverton, UP (PEI) 7 D4
Riverton, VL (Man.) 30 C4
Rivervale, UP (BC) 34 B4
River Valley, UP (Ont.) 26 F4
River Valley, UP (Ont.) 21 F1
Riverview, T (NB) 11 G1
Riverview, UP (NS) 9 B1
Riverview, UP (Alta.) 33 G3
Riverview, UP (Ont.) 23 E3
River View, UP (NB) 11 F2
Riverview, UP (Ont.) 24 G1
Riverview Beach, UP (Ont.) 21 B1
Riverview Heights, UP (Ont.) 17 C3
Riverview Park, NUP (Alta.) 34 E1
Riverville, UP (NS) 8 C3
Rivière-à-Claude, UP (Que.) 13 E1
Rivière-à-la-Chaloupe, UP (Que.) 19 G3
Rivière-à-la-Truite, UP (NB) 15 G1
Rivière-à-Pierre, UP (Que.) 18 H3
Rivière-au-Portage, UP (NB) 12 G2
Rivière-au-Tonnerre, UP (Que.) 19 G3
Rivière-aux-Graines, UP (Que.) 19 G3
Rivière-aux-Rats, UP (Que.) 18 G3
Rivière-Barry, UP (Que.) 18 C4
Rivière-Beaudette, VL (Que.) 17 F2
Rivière-Bersimis, UP (Que.) 14 G2
Rivière-Bleue, UP (Que.) 15 F1
Rivière-Boisvert, UP (Que.) 20 G4
Rivière-Bonaventure, UP (Que.) 13 F3
Rivière-Brochu, UP (Que.) 19 E3
Rivière-Cabano, UP (Que.) 15 F1
Rivière-Caplan, UP (Que.) 13 E3
Rivière-de-la-Chaloupe, UP (Que.) 5 A4
Rivière-des-Caps, UP (Que.) 14 E4
Rivière-des-Fèves, UP (Que.) 17 G2
Rivière-des-Hurons, UP (Que.) 16 A3
Rivière-des-Plantes, UP (Que.) 15 B4
Rivière-des-Roches, UP (Que.) 15 B2
Rivière-du-Gouffre, UP (Que.) 15 C1
Rivière-du-Loup, C (Que.) 14 E4
Rivière-du-Moulin-Développement, NUP (Que.) 15 B4
Rivière-du-Portage, UP (NB) 12 G1
Rivière-Éperlan, UP (Que.) 14 F2
Rivière-Éternité, UP (Que.) 14 C3
Rivière-Gilbert, UP (Que.) 15 C4
Rivière-Héva, UP (Que.) 18 B2
Rivière-Lafleur, UP (Que.) 15 H3
Rivière-la-Madeleine, UP (Que.) 13 F1
Rivière-Loïs, UP (Que.) 18 A1
Rivière-Manie, UP (Que.) 15 E2
Rivière-Matane, UP (Que.) 13 B2
Rivière-Matawin, UP (Que.) 18 G3
Rivière-Mékinac, UP (Que.) 18 G3
Rivière-Metgermette-Nord, UP (Que.) 16 G2
Rivière-Mont-Louis, UP (Que.) 13 E1
Rivière-Nouvelle, NUP (Que.) 13 F3
Rivière-Ouelle, UP (Que.) 15 D1
Rivière-Ouelle-Station, UP (Que.) 15 D1
Rivière-Paspébiac, UP (Que.) 13 F3
Rivière-Pentecôte, UP (Que.) 19 E3
Rivière-Pigou, UP (Que.) 19 F3
Rivière-Plate, UP (Que.) 14 F4
Rivière-Port-Daniel, UP (Que.) 13 G3
Rivière-Portneuf, UP (Que.) 14 F2
Rivière Qui Barre, UP (Alta.) 33 D3
Rivière-Ste-Marguerite, UP (Que.) 14 D3
Rivière-Ste-Marguerite-en-Bas, UP (Que.) 19 E3
Rivière-St-François, UP (Que.) 16 C3
Rivière-St-Jean, UP (Que.) 19 H3
Rivière-St-Paul, UP (Que.) 5 F2
Rivière-Susie, UP (Que.) 18 D2
Rivière-Thompson, UP (Que.) 18 B2
Rivière-Trois-Pistoles, UP (Que.) 14 F3
Rivière-Turgeon, UP (Que.) 18 A1
Rivière-Verte, UP (Que.) 14 E4
Rivière-Verte, VL (NB) 15 H2
Rivière Veuve, UP (Ont.) 25 F1
Rivington, UP (Que.) 18 E4
Rivulet, UP (NS) 8 D2
Roach, UP (NB) 11 C2
Roaches Line, UP (Nfld.) 2 G2
Roachvale, UP (NS) 9 F2
Roachville, UP (NB) 11 E2
Roadene, UP (Sask.) 31 D3
Robb, UP (Alta.) 33 A3
Robbins Range, UP (BC) 35 E1
Robbtown, UP (Ont.) 23 D3
Roberge, UP (Que.) 16 D2
Roberta, UP (NS) 8 D4
Robert's Arm, T (Nfld.) 3 B2
Roberts Creek, UP (BC) 38 E2
Roberts Island, UP (NS) 10 B3
Robertson, UP (PEI) 7 D4
Robertson's Shore, UP (Ont.) 17 B2
Robertsonville, VL (Que.) 15 B4
Robertsville, UP (Ont.) 17 A2
Robertville, UP (NB) 12 E1
Roberval, C (Que.) 18 H1
Robichaud, UP (NB) 7 A4
Robichaud, UP (Que.) 13 E3
Robichaud Settlement, UP (NB) 12 F2
Robidoux, UP (Que.) 13 E3
Robinhood, UP (Sask.) 32 B3
Robin Landing, UP (Ont.) 21 E1
Robins, UP (NS) 8 D4
Robinson, UP (Alta.) 33 C3
Robinson, UP (YT) 45 B3
Robinson Corner, UP (NS) 9 A3
Robinsons, UP (Nfld.) 4 B2
Robinsons Corner, UP (NS) 10 E2
Robinsonville, UP (NB) 13 C4
Robitaille, UP (Que.) 13 D3
Roblin, T (Man.) 29 D2
Roblin, UP (Ont.) 21 G1
Roblindale, UP (Ont.) 21 G1
Roblin Mills, UP (Ont.) 21 G1
Rob Roy, UP (Ont.) 23 E2
Robsart, VL (Sask.) 31 C4
Robson, UP (BC) 34 B4
Robson, UP (Que.) 16 C3
Rocaille, UP (Que.) 16 C3
Rocanville, T (Sask.) 29 D3
Roc-d'Or, UP (Que.) 18 B2
Rochebaucourt, UP (Que.) 18 C1
Rochefort, UP (Ont.) 24 F2
Roche Percée, VL (Sask.) 29 C4
Roche-Plate, UP (Que.) 15 F3
Rocher Fendu, UP (Ont.) 24 H1
Rocher-Percé, UP (Que.) 18 H1
Rocher River, UP (NWT) 44 C1
Roches Point, UP (Ont.) 21 B1
Rochester, UP (Alta.) 33 E2
Rochette, UP (Que.) 15 D1
Rocheville, UP (NB) 12 F1
Rochfort Bridge, UP (Alta.) 33 C3
Rochon Sands, VL (Alta.) 33 E4
Rock Barra, UP (PEI) 7 E3
Rock Bay, UP (BC) 37 B3
Rockburn, UP (Que.) 17 G2
Rock Chapel, UP (Ont.) 21 A3
Rockcliffe Park, VL (Ont.) 17 E4
Rockcliffe Survey, UP (Ont.) 21 A3
Rock Creek, UP (YT) 45 A2
Rock Creek, UP (BC) 35 G4
Rockcroft, UP (Ont.) 24 D4
Rockdale, UP (NS) 8 D4
Rockdale, UP (Ont.) 17 D1
Rockdale, UP (Ont.) 24 F4
Rock Dell, UP (Sask.) 29 C2
Rock Elm, UP (NS) 8 E3
Rockfield, UP (NS) 9 D1
Rockfield, UP (Ont.) 17 C3
Rockford, UP (Ont.) 23 C2
Rockford, UP (Sask.) 29 C1
Rock-Forest, UP (Que.) 16 D4
Rockglen, T (Sask.) 31 F4
Rock Harbour, UP (Nfld.) 2 C3
Rockhaven, VL (Sask.) 32 B4
Rockhurst, UP (Que.) 17 C1
Rockingham, UP (Ont.) 24 F2
Rock-Island, T (Que.) 16 D4
Rock Lake, UP (Ont.) 26 B4
Rock Lake, UP (Ont.) 24 D2
Rockland, T (Ont.) 17 D1
Rockland, UP (NS) 10 D1
Rockland, UP (NS) 10 D4
Rockley, UP (NS) 9 B1
Rocklin, UP (NS) 9 D2
Rocklyn, UP (Ont.) 23 D2
Rock Mills, UP (Ont.) 23 D2
Rockport, UP (Ont.) 17 C4
Rockport, UP (NB) 11 H2
Rocksprings, UP (Ont.) 17 C3
Rockton, UP (Ont.) 22 G1
Rockville, UP (NS) 10 A3
Rockville, UP (NB) 11 F2
Rockville, UP (Ont.) 25 C2
Rockville Notch, UP (NS) 10 D1
Rockway-Valley, UP (Que.) 18 E4
Rockwood, UP (Ont.) 23 E4
Rockwynn, UP (Ont.) 24 B1
Rocky Bay, UP (NS) 8 D4
Rocky Bay 1, IR (Ont.) 27 F2
Rockyford, VL (Alta.) 34 F2
Rocky Harbour, COMM (Nfld.) 5 F4
Rocky Harbour < Rocky Harbour (COMM), UP (Nfld.) 5 F4
Rocky Inlet, UP (Ont.) 27 A3
Rocky Lake 21L, IR (Man.) 32 H2
Rocky Lane, UP (Alta.) 44 A3
Rocky Mountain, UP (NS) 9 E2
Rocky Mountain House, T (Alta.) 33 C4
Rocky Point, UP (PEI) 7 C4
Rocky Point, UP (Ont.) 17 D4
Rocky Point 3, IR (PEI) 7 C4
Rocky Rapids, UP (Alta.) 33 C3
Rocky Ridge, UP (NS) 8 C3
Rocky Saugeen, UP (Ont.) 23 D2
Rocky View, UP (Alta.) 34 E2
Rockyview, UP (BC) 34 C4
Roddickton, T (Nfld.) 5 H2
Rodef, UP (Alta.) 33 E3
Rodgers, UP (Sask.) 31 F3
Rodgers Cove, UP (Nfld.) 3 D2
Rodney, UP (NS) 9 A1
Rodney, VL (Ont.) 22 D2
Roeberta Park, UP (Ont.) 21 A1
Roebuck, UP (Ont.) 17 C3
Roe Lake, UP (BC) 36 E3
Rogerdale, UP (Que.) 17 F1
Rogers, UP (BC) 34 B2
Rogers, UP (NS) 9 C1
Rogers, UP (Man.) 29 E3
Rogers Hill, UP (NS) 9 D1
Rogers Hill Cross Roads, UP (NS) 9 D1
Rogers Pass, UP (BC) 34 B2
Rogersville, VL (NB) 12 F3
Roggan-River, UP (Que.) 20 D2
Rohallion, UP (Ont.) 23 G1
Rokeby, UP (Sask.) 29 C2
Rokeby, UP (Ont.) 22 C2
Rolag Subdivision, NUP (Alta.) 34 F4
Roland, UP (Man.) 29 H4
Rolla, UP (BC) 43 F3
Rollet, UP (Que.) 18 A2
Rollingdam, UP (NB) 11 B3
Rolling Hills, UP (Alta.) 34 G3
Rolling River 67, IR (Man.) 29 F3
Rollo Bay, UP (PEI) 7 E3
Rolly View, UP (Alta.) 33 E3
Rolphton, UP (Ont.) 18 B4
Roma, UP (Alta.) 43 H3
Romaine, UP (Que.) 5 C3
Romaine 2, IR (Que.) 5 C3
Romaines < Berry Headl Port au Port, UP (Nfld.) 4 B2
Roma Junction, UP (Alta.) 43 H3
Romance, UP (Sask.) 31 G1
Roman Valley, UP (NS) 9 F2
Romieu, UP (Que.) 13 C1
Romieu-Sud, UP (Que.) 13 C1
Ronalane, UP (Alta.) 34 H3
Ronan, UP (Alta.) 33 C3
Rondeau Park, UP (Ont.) 22 C3
Rooney, UP (Que.) 18 D4
Roosville, UP (BC) 34 D4
Root Lake, UP (Man.) 32 H2
Root Lake 231, IR (Man.) 32 H2
Roper's Meadow 14, IR (BC) 36 B2
Roquemaure, UP (Que.) 18 A1
Rorketon, UP (Man.) 29 F2
Roros, UP (Alta.) 33 H4
Rosa, UP (Man.) 28 B3
Rosaireville, UP (NB) 12 F3
Rosalind, VL (Alta.) 33 F4
Rosborough Settlement, UP (NB) 11 B1
Rose, UP (NS) 9 B1
Roseau Rapids 2A, IR (Man.) 28 A3
Roseau River, UP (Man.) 28 B3
Roseau River 2, IR (Man.) 28 A3
Rosebank, UP (PEI) 7 A2
Rosebank, UP (Man.) 29 H4
Rosebank, UP (Ont.) 17 A1
Rose Bay, UP (NS) 10 E2
Roseberry, UP (PEI) 7 D4
Rosebery, UP (BC) 34 B3
Rose Blanche < Rose Blanche - Harbour Le Cou, UP (Nfld.) 4 B4
Rose Blanche - Harbour Le Cou, LID (Nfld.) 4 B4
Rosebud, UP (Alta.) 34 F2
Roseburn, UP (NS) 8 C3
Rosedale, UP (Ont.) 17 A4
Rosedale, UP (Ont.) 23 H1
Rosedale, UP (NB) 12 A4
Rosedale, UP (NS) 8 C3
Rosedale, UP (Ont.) 17 C2

Rosedale, UP (Alta.) 34 F2
Rosedale, NUP (Alta.) 33 D4
Rosedale Point, UP (Ont.) 27 G2
Rosedale Terrace, UP (Ont.) 17 E2
Rosedene, UP (Ont.) 21 B4
Rosefield, UP (Sask.) 31 E4
Rosegrove Beach, UP (Ont.) 26 F2
Rosehall, UP (Ont.) 21 F2
Rose Harbour, UP (BC) 41 C3
Rosehaven, UP (Ont.) 17 D2
Rosehill, UP (PEI) 7 B3
Rose Hill, UP (Ont.) 24 G2
Rose Island, UP (Ont.) 24 E3
Roseisle, UP (Man.) 29 G4
Rose Lake, UP (BC) 42 G4
Roseland, UP (NS) 9 C3
Roseland, UP (Man.) 29 F4
Roselea, UP (Alta.) 33 C2
Rose Lynn, UP (Alta.) 34 G2
Rosemary, VL (Alta.) 34 G2
Rosemère, T (Que.) 17 F3
Rosemont, UP (Ont.) 23 E3
Rosenburg, UP (Man.) 29 H2
Rosendale, UP (Ont.) 23 D4
Roseneath, UP (Ont.) 21 E1
Roseneath, UP (PEI) 7 D4
Rosenfeld, UP (Man.) 29 H4
Rosengard, UP (Man.) 28 B2
Rosengart, UP (Man.) 29 H4
Rosengart, UP (Sask.) 31 E3
Rosenheim, UP (Alta.) 31 B1
Rosenhof, UP (Sask.) 31 E3
Rosenort, UP (Man.) 29 H4
Rosenort, UP (Sask.) 31 E3
Rosenthal, UP (Ont.) 24 F2
Rose Point, UP (Ont.) 24 A2
Rose Prairie, UP (BC) 43 E3
Roseray, UP (Sask.) 31 D3
Rosetown, T (Sask.) 31 D2
Rosetown, UP (Man.) 29 H4
Rosetta, UP (Ont.) 17 B2
Rosevale, UP (NB) 11 G1
Rose Valley, T (Sask.) 29 B1
Rose Valley, UP (PEI) 7 C4
Rosevear, UP (Alta.) 33 B3
Roseville, UP (Ont.) 22 F1
Roseville, UP (Ont.) 21 B1
Roseville, UP (PEI) 7 A2
Roseway, UP (NS) 10 C4
Rosewood, UP (Man.) 28 B2
Roslin, UP (Ont.) 21 F1
Roslin, UP (NS) 9 B1
Ross, UP (BC) 34 B4
Ross, UP (NB) 11 C1
Ross, UP (Man.) 28 B2
Rossburn, VL (Man.) 29 E3
Rossclair, UP (Ont.) 24 B3
Ross Corner, UP (NS) 11 G3
Ross Corner, UP (PEI) 7 B3
Ross Corner, UP (NB) 11 G2
Rossdale, UP (Man.) 28 A1
Rosseau, VL (Ont.) 24 B2
Rosseau Falls, UP (Ont.) 24 B2
Rosseau Road, UP (Ont.) 24 A2
Rossendale, UP (Man.) 29 G4
Rossendale, UP (NS) 9 B1
Rosser, UP (Man.) 29 H3
Ross Ferry, UP (NS) 8 E3
Ross Haven, SV (Alta.) 33 D3
Rossington, UP (Alta.) 33 D2
Rossland, C (BC) 34 A4
Rosslyn Village, UP (Ont.) 27 D3
Rossmere, UP (Ont.) 27 D3
Rossmore, UP (Ont.) 21 F1
Rossmount, UP (Ont.) 21 D2
Rossport, UP (Ont.) 27 F3
Ross River, UP (YT) 45 B3
Rossville, UP (NB) 11 B1
Rossville < Norway House 17, UP (Man.) 30 C2
Rossway, UP (NS) 10 B2
Rosswood, UP (BC) 42 E4
Rosthern, T (Sask.) 32 D4
Rostock, UP (Ont.) 23 C4
Rostrevor, UP (Ont.) 24 B2
Rosyth, UP (Alta.) 33 G4
Rothermere, UP (Sask.) 32 C3
Rothesay, T (NB) 11 D2
Rothsay, UP (Ont.) 23 D3
Rothwell Heights, UP (Ont.) 17 E4
Rothwell Village, UP (Ont.) 17 E4
Rouge Harbour, UP (Nfld.) 3 B1
Rougemont, VL (Que.) 16 A3
Rougemont-Station, NUP (Que.) 16 B3
Rouge-Valley, UP (Que.) 18 E4
Rough Water Road, NUP (NB) 12 E1
Rouleau, T (Sask.) 31 G3
Rouleau-Siding, UP (Que.) 18 D2
Roulier, UP (Que.) 18 A2
Roulston Corner, UP (NS) 9 B3
Roundabout, UP (Nfld.) 2 B4
Round Bay, UP (NS) 10 C4
Round Cove, UP (Nfld.) 2 B2
Round Harbour, UP (Nfld.) 3 B1
Round Harbour, UP (Nfld.) 2 A2
Round Hill, UP (NS) 10 C1
Round Hill, UP (Alta.) 33 E3
Round Island, UP (NS) 8 F3
Round Lake, UP (Ont.) 24 E4
Round Lake, UP (BC) 42 F4
Round Lake Centre, UP (Ont.) 24 F1
Round Prairie, UP (BC) 34 D3
Round Valley, UP (Alta.) 33 C3
Rounthwaite, UP (Man.) 29 F4
Roussillon, UP (Que.) 17 F1
Route 34 Trailer Park, NUP (Ont.) 17 D1
Routhier, UP (Ont.) 17 E1
Routhierville, UP (Que.) 13 B3
Routledge, UP (Man.) 29 E4
Rouyn, C (Que.) 18 A2
Rowan Mills, UP (Ont.) 22 F2
Rowanton, UP (Que.) 18 B4
Rowatt, UP (Sask.) 31 H3
Rowena, UP (NB) 12 A3
Rowena, UP (Ont.) 17 D2
Rowland, UP (Ont.) 24 F2
Rowletta, UP (Sask.) 31 F3
Rowley, UP (Alta.) 34 F1
Rows Corners, UP (Ont.) 17 C3
Roxana, UP (Alta.) 43 H3
Roxboro, T (Que.) 17 F4
Roxbury, UP (PEI) 7 A3
Roxbury, UP (NS) 10 C1
Roxham, UP (Que.) 17 H2
Roxton-Est, UP (Que.) 16 C3
Roxton-Falls, VL (Que.) 16 C3
Roxton-Pond, UP (Que.) 16 B3
Roxton-Sud, UP (Que.) 16 B3
Roxville, UP (NS) 10 B2
Roy, UP (NB) 12 G4
Roy, UP (BC) 37 A3
Royal Beach, UP (Ont.) 21 B1
Royal Lake, UP (Sask.) 32 C4
Royal Park, UP (Alta.) 33 F3
Royal Road, UP (NB) 11 C1
Royalties, UP (Alta.) 34 E3
Royalton, UP (NB) 12 A3
Royalty Junction, UP (PEI) 7 C4
Royce, UP (Alta.) 43 G3
Roydale, UP (Alta.) 33 C3
Royston, UP (BC) 38 C1
Roytal, UP (Alta.) 31 B3
Royville, UP (Que.) 16 B3
Ruarkville, NUP (Alta.) 34 F1
Ruby, UP (Ont.) 24 G1
Ruby Beach, UP (Sask.) 32 H4
Ruby Creek 2, IR (BC) 35 A4
Ruby Mine, UP (Ont.) 24 F2
Ruddell, VL (Sask.) 32 C4
Ruddock, UP (Man.) 30 A1
Rudlang Subdivision, NUP (BC) 36 F2
Ruel, UP (Ont.) 26 D3
Rugby, UP (Ont.) 23 F2
Ruisseau-à-la-Loutre, UP (Que.) 13 B1
Ruisseau-à-l'Eau-Chaude, UP (Que.) 15 C4
Ruisseau-à-Rebours, UP (Que.) 13 E1
Ruisseau-à-Sem, UP (Que.) 13 B1
Ruisseau-Castor, UP (Que.) 13 D1
Ruisseau-des-Anges, UP (Que.) 13 F4
Ruisseau-des-Olives, UP (Que.) 13 E1
Ruisseau-Gagnon, UP (Que.) 13 B2
Ruisseau-Leblanc, UP (Que.) 13 E3
Ruisseau-Noir, UP (Que.) 14 F4
Ruisseau-St-Georges, UP (Que.) 16 A2
Ruisseau-Vacher, UP (Que.) 16 A2
Ruisseau-Vert, UP (Que.) 14 G1
Ruiters-Corners, UP (Que.) 16 C4
Rumsey, VL (Alta.) 34 F1
Runciman, UP (Sask.) 32 F4
Runnymede, UP (Sask.) 29 D2
Runnymede, UP (Que.) 13 C4
Rupert, UP (Que.) 17 C1
Rupert, UP (BC) 45 B4
Rupert Acres Trailer Park, NUP (Ont.) 26 B4
Rusagonis, UP (NB) 11 C1
Rusagonis Station, UP (NB) 11 C2
Ruscom Station, UP (Ont.) 22 B3
Rush Lake, UP (Alta.) 34 F4
Rush Lake, VL (Sask.) 31 E3
Rushoon, COMM (Nfld.) 2 D3
Rush Point, UP (Ont.) 24 E4
Rushton Island 90, IR (BC) 41 C1
Rushy Pond, UP (Nfld.) 3 B3
Ruskview, UP (Ont.) 23 E2
Russeldale, UP (Ont.) 22 E1
Russell, T (Man.) 29 D2
Russell, UP (Ont.) 17 D2
Russell Landing, UP (Ont.) 24 C2
Russellville, UP (NB) 12 F2
Russeltown-Flats, UP (Que.) 17 G2
Rusticoville, UP (PEI) 7 C3
Rusylvia, UP (Alta.) 33 G3
Rutan, UP (Sask.) 31 F1
Ruthenia, UP (Man.) 29 E2
Rutherford, UP (Ont.) 22 C2
Rutherglen, UP (Ont.) 18 A4
Ruthilda, VL (Sask.) 31 D1
Ruthledge, UP (Que.) 17 B1
Ruthven, UP (Ont.) 22 B4
Rutland, UP (Sask.) 32 A4
Ruttan Mine, UP (Man.) 30 B1
Rutter, UP (Ont.) 25 F2
Ryan Farm, UP (Ont.) 17 E4
Ryanville, UP (Que.) 18 D4
Rycroft, VL (Alta.) 43 G4
Rydal Bank, UP (Ont.) 26 B4
Rye, UP (Ont.) 24 B1
Ryerson, UP (Sask.) 29 D4
Rykerts, UP (BC) 34 C4
Ryland, UP (Ont.) 20 B4
Ryley, VL (Alta.) 33 F3
Rylstone, UP (Ont.) 21 E1

S

Saagoombahlah 14, IR (BC) 41 F4
Saaiyouck 6, IR (BC) 37 B3
Saanich, DM (BC) 38 F4
Sabaskong Bay 32C, IR (Ont.) 28 G3
Sabaskong Bay 35C, IR (Ont.) 28 G3
Sabaskong Bay 35D, IR (Ont.) 28 G3
Sabaskong Bay 35F, IR (Ont.) 28 G3
Sabaskong Bay 35H, IR (Ont.) 28 G3
Sabine, UP (Alta.) 34 F1
Sable, UP (Ont.) 22 D1
Sable River, UP (NS) 10 D3
Sable River West, UP (NS) 10 D3
Sabourins Crossing, UP (Ont.) 17 C2
Sabrevois, UP (Que.) 16 A4
Sachawil 5, IR (BC) 38 B3
Sachigo Lake < Sachigo Lake 1, UP (Ont.) 30 E2
Sachigo Lake 1, IR (Ont.) 30 E2
Sachigo Lake 2, IR (Ont.) 30 E2
Sachigo Lake 3, IR (Ont.) 30 E2
Sachsa 4, IR (BC) 38 B3
Sachs Harbour, UP (NWT) 47 A3
Sachteen 2, IR (BC) 37 G4
Sachteen 2A, IR (BC) 37 G4
Sackanitecla 2, IR (BC) 40 B2
Sackum 3, IR (BC) 35 B1
Sackville, T (NB) 11 H1
Sackville, NUP (NS) 9 B3
Sacré-Coeur-de-Marie, UP (Que.) 15 B4
Sacré-Coeur-Saguenay, UP (Que.) 14 D3
Saddle Horse 2, IR (BC) 40 C4
Saddle Lake < Saddle Lake 125, UP (Alta.) 33 F3
Saddle Lake 125, IR (Alta.) 33 F3
Saddle Rock 9, IR (BC) 35 B3
Sadowa, UP (Ont.) 23 G1
Safe Harbour, UP (Nfld.) 3 F3
Sagamok < Spanish River 5, UP (Ont.) 25 C1
Saganaga Lake, UP (Ont.) 27 C3
Sagard, UP (Que.) 14 D4
Sagathun, UP (Sask.) 31 C3
Sagehill, UP (Sask.) 31 F1
Sage Mesa, NUP (BC) 35 E3
Saginaw, UP (Ont.) 21 C1
Saglouc, UP (Que.) 46 E3
Sagona Island, UP (Nfld.) 2 B3
Sahanatien < Gibson 31, UP (Ont.) 23 F1
Sahara Heights, UP (BC) 38 C2
Sahhacum 1, IR (BC) 38 H3
Sahhaltkum 4, IR (BC) 36 G4
Sahtlam, UP (BC) 38 E3
Sailors Encampment, UP (Ont.) 26 B4
St-Adalbert, UP (Que.) 15 D3
St-Adélard, UP (Que.) 13 F3
St-Adelme-de-Matane, UP (Que.) 13 B2
St-Adelme-Sud, UP (Que.) 13 B2
St-Adelphe, UP (Que.) 16 C1
St Adolphe, UP (Man.) 28 A2
St-Adolphe, UP (Que.) 15 B2
St-Adolphe-d'Howard, UP (Que.) 18 F4
St-Adrien, UP (Que.) 16 D3
St-Adrien-d'Irlande, UP (Que.) 15 A4
St-Agapitville, VL (Que.) 15 A3
St Agatha, UP (Ont.) 23 D4
St-Agricole, UP (Que.) 13 A2
St-Aimé-des-Lacs, UP (Que.) 15 D1
St-Alban, VL (Que.) 16 D1
St Alban's, T (Nfld.) 2 B2
St Albert, T (Alta.) 33 D3
St-Albert, UP (Ont.) 17 D2
St-Albert, UP (Que.) 16 D2
St-Alexandre, VL (Que.) 16 A4
St-Alexandre-de-Kamouraska, UP (Que.) 14 E4
St-Alexandre-des-Lacs, UP (Que.) 13 B3
St-Alexis, UP (Que.) 13 B4
St-Alexis, VL (Que.) 18 G4
St-Alexis-de-Matapédia, UP (Que.) 13 B4
St-Alexis-des-Monts, UP (Que.) 16 A1
St-Alfred, UP (Que.) 15 B4
St Almo, UP (NB) 12 B3
St Alphege, UP (Sask.) 31 D1
St-Alphonse, UP (Que.) 18 F4
St Alphonse, UP (NS) 10 A3
St Alphonse, UP (Man.) 29 G4
St-Alphonse-de-Caplan, UP (Que.) 13 E3
St-Alphonse-de-Granby, UP (Que.) 16 B4
St-Amable, UP (Que.) 16 A3
St-Amand, UP (NB) 12 A2
St-Amateur, UP (NB) 12 F1
St Ambroise, UP (Man.) 29 H3
St-Ambroise, VL (Que.) 14 A2
St-Ambroise-de-Kildare, UP (Que.) 18 G4
St-Amédée, UP (Que.) 17 E1
St-Amédée-de-Péribonca, UP (Que.) 18 H1
St-Amour, UP (Ont.) 17 E1
St-Anaclet, UP (Que.) 14 G3
St-André, VL (NB) 12 A2
St-André-Avellin, VL (Que.) 17 D1
St-André-de-Restigouche, UP (Que.) 13 C3
St-André-de-Shédiac, UP (NB) 7 A4
St-André-du-Lac-St-Jean, VL (Que.) 18 H1
St-André-Est, VL (Que.) 17 F1
St-André-Station, UP (Que.) 15 E1
St Andrews, T (NB) 11 B3
St Andrews, UP (Ont.) 17 E2
St Andrew's, UP (Nfld.) 4 A4
St Andrews, UP (NS) 8 B4
St Andrews, UP (PEI) 7 D3
St Andrews, UP (Man.) 28 A1
St Andrews Channel, UP (NS) 8 E3
St-Anicet, UP (Que.) 17 F2
St Ann, UP (PEI) 7 C3
St Annes, UP (Nfld.) 2 E3
St Anns, UP (Ont.) 21 A4
St Anns, UP (NS) 8 E3
St-Anselme, VL (Que.) 15 H4
St Anthony, T (Nfld.) 5 H2
St Anthony, UP (PEI) 7 A3
St Anthony Bight, UP (Nfld.) 5 H2
St-Antoine, T (Que.) 18 F4
St Antoine, UP (Sask.) 29 D4
St-Antoine, VL (NB) 12 G4
St-Antoine-Abbé, UP (Que.) 17 G2
St-Antoine-de-Tilly, UP (Que.) 15 E4
St-Antoine-sur-Richelieu, UP (Que.) 16 A3
St-Antonin, UP (Que.) 14 E4
St-Apollinaire, UP (Que.) 15 A3
St-Armand-Centre, UP (Que.) 16 B4
St-Armand-Station, UP (Que.) 16 A4
St-Arsène, UP (Que.) 14 E4
St-Arthur, UP (NB) 13 C4
St-Athanase, UP (Que.) 15 E1
St-Athanase, UP (NB) 12 F3
St-Aubert, UP (Que.) 15 D2
St-Aubin, UP (NB) 13 C4
St-Augustin, UP (Que.) 5 E2
St-Augustin, UP (Que.) 15 F4
St-Augustin, UP (Que.) 18 H1
St Augustine, UP (Ont.) 23 B3
St Barbe, UP (Nfld.) 5 G2
St-Barnabé-Nord, UP (Que.) 16 B1
St-Barnabé-Sud, UP (Que.) 16 B3
St-Barthélemy, UP (Que.) 16 A2
St-Barthélemy-Station, UP (Que.) 16 A2
St-Basile, VL (NB) 15 H2
St Basile 10, IR (NB) 15 H2
St-Basile-de-Tableau, UP (Que.) 14 C3
St-Basile-le-Grand, T (Que.) 16 A3
St-Basile-Sud, VL (Que.) 18 H3
St Benedict, VL (Sask.) 32 E4
St-Benjamin, UP (Que.) 15 C4
St-Benoît-de-Matapédia, UP (Que.) 13 B4
St-Benoît-du-Lac, UP (Que.) 16 C4
St-Benoît-Labre, UP (Que.) 16 F2
St Benoni, UP (NS) 10 A2
St Bernard, UP (NS) 10 A2
St-Bernard, VL (Que.) 15 B4
St-Bernard-de-Lacolle, UP (Que.) 16 A4
St-Bernard-des-Lacs, UP (Que.) 13 D1
St-Bernardin, UP (Ont.) 17 E1
St Bernard's, COMM (Nfld.) 2 D2
St-Bernard-sur-Mer, UP (Que.) 15 C1
St-Blaise, UP (Que.) 16 A4
St-Bonaventure, UP (Que.) 16 B2
St-Boniface-de-Shawinigan, VL (Que.) 16 B1
St Boswells, UP (Sask.) 31 E3
St Brendan's, COMM (Nfld.) 3 F3
St Brendan's < St Brendan's (COMM), UP (Nfld.) 3 F3
St Bride's, COMM (Nfld.) 2 E4
St Brides, UP (Alta.) 33 F3
St Brieux, VL (Sask.) 32 E4
St-Bruno, VL (Que.) 14 A3
St-Bruno-de-Kamouraska, UP (Que.) 15 E1
St-Bruno-de-Montarville, T (Que.) 16 A3
St-Cajetan, UP (Que.) 18 D4
St-Calixte-de-Kilkenny, UP (Que.) 18 F4
St-Calixte-Nord, UP (Que.) 18 F4
St-Camille, UP (Que.) 16 D3
St-Camille, UP (NB) 12 G2
St-Camille-de-Bellechasse, UP (Que.) 15 D4
St Carols, UP (Nfld.) 5 H2
St-Casimir, VL (Que.) 16 C1
St-Casimir-Est, VL (Que.) 16 C1
St-Cassien-des-Caps, UP (Que.) 15 C2
St Catharines, C (Ont.) 21 B3
St Catherines, UP (PEI) 7 C4
St Catherines, UP (PEI) 7 E3
St Catherine's < Mount Carmel – Mitchells Brook – St Catherine's, UP (Nfld.) 2 G3
St Catherines River, UP (NS) 10 D3
St-Célestin-Station, UP (Que.) 16 C2
St-Césaire, T (Que.) 16 B4
St Chads, UP (Nfld.) 3 F3
St Charles, UP (Ont.) 25 F1
St-Charles, UP (NB) 12 G3
St-Charles, UP (Que.) 14 A3
St Charles, UP (PEI) 7 E3
St-Charles, VL (Que.) 15 H4
St-Charles, NUP (Que.) 18 H3
St-Charles-de-Drummond, UP (Que.) 16 C2
St-Charles-de-Mandeville, UP (Que.) 16 A1
St-Charles-de-Montcalm, UP (Que.) 18 F4
St-Charles-des-Grondines, VL (Que.) 16 D1
St-Charles-Garnier, UP (Que.) 14 H3
St-Charles-Nord, UP (NB) 12 G3
St-Charles-sur-Richelieu, VL (Que.) 16 A3
St-Chrétien, UP (Que.) 14 D4
St Christopher, UP (Ont.) 21 C1
St Chrysostome, UP (PEI) 7 A3
St-Chrysostome, VL (Que.) 17 G2
St Clair Beach, VL (Ont.) 22 A3
St Claire Gardens, UP (Ont.) 17 E4
St-Claude, UP (Que.) 16 D3
St Claude, VL (Man.) 29 G4
St-Claude-Nord, UP (Que.) 16 D3
St-Clément, UP (Que.) 14 F4
St Clements, UP (Ont.) 23 D4
St-Cléophas, UP (Que.) 13 A2
St-Cléophas, UP (Que.) 16 A2
St-Cléophas-de-Brandon, UP (Que.) 16 A2
St-Clet, UP (Que.) 17 F1
St Cloud, UP (Ont.) 25 E1
St-Coeur-de-Marie, VL (Que.) 14 A2
St-Colomban, UP (Que.) 17 F1
St Columba, UP (NS) 8 D3
St Columban, UP (Ont.) 23 B4
St-Côme, UP (Que.) 18 F4
St-Conrad, UP (Que.) 13 C3
St-Constant, T (Que.) 17 G4
St Croix, UP (NS) 9 A3
St Croix, UP (NB) 11 A2
St Croix 34, IR (NS) 9 A3
St Croix Cove, UP (NS) 10 C1
St-Cuthbert, UP (Que.) 16 A2
St-Cyprien, UP (Que.) 14 F4
St-Cyprien, UP (Que.) 15 D4
St-Cyr, UP (Que.) 16 D3
St-Cyriac, UP (Que.) 14 A3
St-Cyrille, UP (NB) 12 G4
St-Cyrille, VL (Que.) 16 C2
St-Cyrille-de-L'Islet, UP (Que.) 15 D2
St Cyr Lake, UP (Sask.) 32 B2
St-Damase, VL (Que.) 16 B3
St-Damase-de-Matane, UP (Que.) 13 A2
St-Damase-des-Aulnaies, UP (Que.) 15 D2
St-Damase-de-Thetford, NUP (Que.) 15 A4
St-Damien, UP (NB) 12 G4
St-Damien-de-Brandon, UP (Que.) 16 A1
St-Damien-de-Buckland, UP (Que.) 15 C3
St-Damien-Station, UP (Que.) 15 C3
St-Daniel, UP (Que.) 16 E2
St-David, UP (NB) 12 G4
St-David-de-Falardeau, UP (Que.) 14 B2
St-David-de-l'Auberivière, T (Que.) 15 G4
St-David-d'Yamaska, UP (Que.) 16 B2
St David Ridge, UP (NB) 11 B3
St David's, UP (Nfld.) 4 B3
St Davids, UP (Ont.) 17 F1
St-Denis, UP (Sask.) 31 F1
St-Denis, VL (Que.) 16 A3
St-Denis-de-Brompton, UP (Que.) 16 D3
St-Denis-de-la-Bouteillerie, UP (Que.) 15 D1
St-Denis-sur-Mer, UP (Que.) 15 D1
St-Didace, UP (Que.) 16 A1
St-Dominique, UP (Que.) 17 F1
St-Dominique, VL (Que.) 16 B3
St-Dominique-du-Rosaire, UP (Que.) 18 B1
St-Donat-de-Montcalm, UP (Que.) 18 F4
St-Donat-de-Rimouski, UP (Que.) 14 H3
Ste-Adélaïde-de-Pabos, UP (Que.) 13 G3
Ste-Adèle, T (Que.) 18 F4
Ste Agathe, UP (Man.) 28 A2
Ste-Agathe, VL (Que.) 15 A4
Ste-Agathe-des-Monts, T (Que.) 18 F4
Ste-Agathe-Sud, VL (Que.) 18 F4
Ste-Agnès-de-Bellecombe, UP (Que.) 18 A2
Ste-Agnès-de-Charlevoix, UP (Que.) 15 D1
Ste-Agnès-de-Dundee, UP (Que.) 17 F2
Ste Amélie, UP (Man.) 29 F2
Ste-Anastasie, UP (Que.) 15 A4
Ste-Angèle-de-Mérici, VL (Que.) 14 H2
Ste-Angèle-de-Monnoir, UP (Que.) 16 A4
Ste-Angélique, UP (Que.) 18 H3
Ste-Anne, UP (NB) 12 E1
Ste Anne, VL (Man.) 28 B2
Ste-Anne-de-Beaupré, T (Que.) 15 B2
Ste-Anne-de-Bellevue, T (Que.) 17 F4
Ste-Anne-de-Kent, UP (NB) 12 G3
Ste-Anne-de-Larochelle, UP (Que.) 16 C4
Ste-Anne-de-Madawaska, VL (NB) 15 H2
Ste-Anne-de-Prescott, UP (Ont.) 17 F1
Ste-Anne-des-Monts, T (Que.) 13 D1
Ste-Anne-de-Sorel, UP (Que.) 16 B2
Ste-Anne-des-Plaines, UP (Que.) 18 F4
Ste-Anne-du-Lac, VL (Que.) 18 E3
Ste-Anne-du-Lac, VL (Que.) 16 E2
Ste Anne du Ruisseau, UP (NS) 10 B3
Ste-Apolline, UP (Que.) 15 D3
Ste-Apolline-Station, UP (Que.) 15 D3
Ste-Aurélie, UP (Que.) 15 C4
Ste-Barbe, UP (Que.) 17 F2
Ste-Béatrix, UP (Que.) 18 G4
Ste-Blandine, UP (Que.) 14 G3
Ste-Brigide-d'Iberville, UP (Que.) 16 A4
Ste-Brigitte-de-Laval, UP (Que.) 15 G3
Ste-Brigitte-des-Saults, UP (Que.) 16 C2
Ste-Catherine, T (Que.) 17 G4
Ste-Catherine, UP (Que.) 15 A3
Ste-Catherine-Station, UP (Que.) 15 E3
Ste-Cécile, UP (NB) 13 G4
Ste-Cécile-de-Frontenac, UP (Que.) 16 F3
Ste-Cécile-de-Lévrard, UP (Que.) 16 C1
Ste-Cécile-de-Masham, UP (Que.) 17 B1
Ste-Cécile-de-Milton, UP (Que.) 16 B3
Ste-Cécile-Station, UP (Que.) 16 F3
Ste-Christine, UP (Que.) 18 H3
Ste-Christine, UP (Que.) 16 C3
Ste-Claire, UP (Que.) 15 B3
Ste-Claire-de-Bonaventure, UP (Que.) 13 E3
Ste-Clothilde-de-Horton, VL (Que.) 16 C2
Ste-Clotilde-de-Châteauguay, UP (Que.) 17 G2
Ste-Croix, VL (Que.) 15 A3
Ste-Croix-Est, UP (Que.) 15 A3
St-Edmond, UP (Que.) 18 B2
St-Edmond-de-Berthier, UP (Que.) 16 A2
St-Edmond-de-Grantham, UP (Que.) 16 B2
St-Edmond-de-Pabos, UP (Que.) 13 G3
St-Edmond-les-Plaines, UP (Que.) 18 G1
St-Édouard, UP (Que.) 16 D1
St-Édouard, UP (Que.) 16 B3
St Edouard, UP (Alta.) 33 G3
St-Édouard-de-Kent, UP (NB) 12 G3
St-Édouard-de-Maskinongé, UP (Que.) 16 A1
St-Édouard-de-Napierville, UP (Que.) 16 A4
St Edward, UP (PEI) 7 A2
Ste-Edwidge, UP (Que.) 16 D4
Ste-Élisabeth, UP (Que.) 16 A2
Ste-Élisabeth-de-Proulx, UP (Que.) 18 H1
Ste-Élisabeth-de-Warwick, UP (Que.) 16 D2
Ste Elizabeth, UP (Man.) 28 A3
Ste-Émélie-de-l'Énergie, UP (Que.) 18 F4
Ste-Eulalie, UP (Que.) 16 C2
Ste-Euphémie, UP (Que.) 15 C3
Ste-Famille, UP (Que.) 15 H3
Ste-Famille-d'Aumond, UP (Que.) 18 D4
Ste-Félicité, UP (Que.) 15 D3
Ste-Félicité, VL (Que.) 13 B2
Ste-Félicité-Ouest, UP (Que.) 13 B2
Ste-Flavie, UP (Que.) 14 H2
Ste-Florence, UP (Que.) 13 B3
Ste-Foy, C (Que.) 15 F4
Ste-Françoise, UP (Que.) 14 F3
Ste-Françoise, UP (Que.) 16 D1
Ste-Geneviève, T (Que.) 17 F4
Ste-Geneviève, UP (Man.) 28 B2
Ste-Geneviève-de-Batiscan, UP (Que.) 16 C1
Ste-Germaine, UP (Que.) 18 A1
Ste-Germaine-Station, UP (Que.) 15 C4
Ste-Gertrude-de-Villeneuve, UP (Que.) 18 B1
Ste-Hedwidge-de-Roberval, UP (Que.) 18 H1
Ste-Hélène, UP (Que.) 18 A1
Ste-Hélène-de-Bagot, VL (Que.) 16 B3
Ste-Hélène-de-Chester, UP (Que.) 16 D2
Ste-Hélène-de-Kamouraska, UP (Que.) 15 E1
Ste-Hélène-de-la-Croix, UP (Que.) 13 F4
Ste-Hénédine, UP (Que.) 15 B3
Ste-Irène-de-Matapédia, UP (Que.) 13 A3
Ste-Jeanne-d'Arc, VL (Que.) 18 H1
Ste-Jeanne-d'Arc-de-Matane, UP (Que.) 13 A2
Ste-Julie, T (Que.) 16 A3
Ste-Julienne, UP (Que.) 18 F4
Ste-Julie-Station, UP (Que.) 15 A4
Ste-Justine, UP (Que.) 15 C4
Ste-Justine-de-Newton, UP (Que.) 17 F1
Ste-Justine-Station, UP (Que.) 15 C4
Ste-Justine-Station, UP (Que.) 17 F1
St Eleanors, VL (PEI) 7 B3
St-Élie, UP (Que.) 16 B1
St-Élie-d'Orford, UP (Que.) 16 D4
St Elmo, UP (Ont.) 17 E2
St-Éloi, UP (Que.) 14 F4
St-Éloi-Station, UP (Que.) 14 F4
Ste-Louise, UP (Que.) 15 D2
Ste-Louise, UP (NB) 12 E1
Ste-Louise-Station, UP (Que.) 15 D2
St-Elphège, UP (Que.) 16 B2
Ste-Luce, UP (Que.) 14 G2
Ste-Lucie-de-Beauregard, UP (Que.) 15 D3
Ste-Lucie-de-Doncaster, UP (Que.) 18 F4
St-Elzéar, VL (Que.) 15 B4
St-Elzéar-de-Bonaventure, UP (Que.) 13 F3
St-Elzéar-de-Témiscouata, UP (Que.) 15 F1
Ste-Madeleine, VL (Que.) 16 A3
Ste-Marcelline-de-Kildare, UP (Que.) 18 G4
Ste-Marguerite, UP (Que.) 18 F4
Ste-Marguerite-de-Dorchester, UP (Que.) 15 B4
Ste-Marguerite-de-Lingwick, UP (Que.) 16 E3
Ste-Marguerite-Marie, UP (Que.) 13 B3
Ste-Marie, T (Que.) 15 B4
Ste-Marie, VL (Que.) 16 C1
Ste-Marie-de-Charlevoix, UP (Que.) 15 C1
Ste-Marie-de-Kent, UP (NB) 12 G4
Ste-Marie-d'Ely, UP (Que.) 16 C3
Ste-Marie-Salomée, UP (Que.) 16 A2
Ste-Marie-sur-Mer, UP (NB) 13 G4
Ste-Marthe, VL (Que.) 17 F1
Ste-Marthe-de-Gaspé, UP (Que.) 13 D1
Ste-Marthe-Rocanville, UP (Sask.) 29 D3
Ste-Marthe-sur-le-Lac, T (Que.) 17 F4
Ste-Martine, UP (Que.) 17 G2
Ste-Mathilde, UP (Que.) 14 D4
Ste-Mélanie, UP (Que.) 16 A2
St-Émile, VL (Que.) 15 F3
St-Émile-de-Suffolk, UP (Que.) 18 E4
Ste-Monique, UP (Que.) 18 H1
Ste-Monique, VL (Que.) 16 C2
Ste-Paula, UP (Que.) 13 A2
Ste-Perpétue, UP (Que.) 16 C2
Ste-Perpétue-de-l'Islet, UP (Que.) 15 D2
Ste-Perpétue-Station, UP (Que.) 16 C2
St-Éphrem-de-Tring, VL (Que.) 16 F2
St-Éphrem-Station, UP (Que.) 16 F2
St-Épiphane, UP (Que.) 14 E4
Ste-Praxède, UP (Que.) 16 E2
Ste-Pudentienne, VL (Que.) 16 B3
Ste-Rita, UP (Que.) 14 F4
Ste Rita, UP (Man.) 28 C1
Ste-Rosalie, VL (Que.) 16 B3
Ste-Rose-de-Prescott, UP (Ont.) 17 E1
Ste-Rose-de-Watford, UP (Que.) 15 C4
Ste Rose du Lac, VL (Man.) 29 F2
Ste-Rose-du-Nord, UP (Que.) 14 C3
Ste-Rose-Gloucester, UP (NB) 12 G1
Ste-Rose-Station, UP (Que.) 15 C4
Ste-Rosette, UP (NB) 12 E1
Ste-Sabine, UP (Que.) 16 B4
Ste-Sabine-de-Bellechasse, UP (Que.) 15 C4
Ste-Sabine-Station, UP (Que.) 15 D4
Ste-Séraphine, UP (Que.) 16 C2
Ste-Sophie, UP (Que.) 18 F4
Ste-Sophie-de-Lévrard, UP (Que.) 16 C1
Ste-Sophie-de-Mégantic, UP (Que.) 15 A4
St-Esprit, UP (Que.) 18 F4
St Esprit, UP (NS) 8 E4
Ste-Thècle, VL (Que.) 18 H3
Ste-Thérèse, C (Que.) 17 F3
Ste-Thérèse-de-Gaspé, UP (Que.) 13 H3
Ste-Thérèse-de-Gatineau, UP (Que.) 18 D4
St-Étienne, UP (Que.) 14 D3
St-Étienne-de-Beauharnois, UP (Que.) 17 G2
St-Étienne-de-Bolton, UP (Que.) 16 C4
St-Étienne-de-Lauzon, UP (Que.) 15 F4
St-Étienne-de-Restigouche, UP (Que.) 13 C3
St-Étienne-des-Grès, UP (Que.) 16 B1
St-Eugène, UP (Que.) 15 C2
St-Eugène, UP (Ont.) 17 F1
St-Eugène, UP (Que.) 18 H1
St-Eugène, UP (Que.) 16 B3
St-Eugène-de-Chazel, UP (Que.) 18 A1
St-Eugène-de-Grantham, UP (Que.) 16 B3
St-Eugène-de-Guigues, UP (Que.) 18 A2
St Eugene Mission, UP (BC) 34 C4
Ste-Ursule, UP (Que.) 16 B2
Ste-Ursule-Station, UP (Que.) 16 B1
St-Eusèbe, UP (Que.) 15 F1
St-Eusèbe-Ouest, UP (Que.) 15 F1
St-Eustache, T (Que.) 17 F4
St Eustache, UP (Man.) 29 H3
St-Évariste-de-Forsyth, UP (Que.) 16 F2
Ste-Véronique, UP (Que.) 18 E4
Ste-Victoire, UP (Que.) 16 A2
St-Fabien, UP (Que.) 14 F3
St-Fabien, UP (NB) 12 G4
St-Fabien-sur-Mer, UP (Que.) 14 F3
St-Faustin, UP (Que.) 18 F4
St-Félicien, T (Que.) 18 H1
St Felix, UP (PEI) 7 B2
St-Félix-de-Kingsey, UP (Que.) 16 C3
St-Félix-de-Valois, VL (Que.) 16 A2
St-Félix-d'Otis, UP (Que.) 14 C3
St-Ferréol-les-Neiges, UP (Que.) 15 B2
St-Fidèle, UP (Que.) 14 D4
St-Fidèle-de-Restigouche, UP (Que.) 13 C3
Saintfield, UP (Ont.) 21 C1
St Fintan's, UP (Nfld.) 4 B3
St-Flavien, VL (Que.) 15 A4
St-Fortunat, UP (Que.) 16 E2
St Francis, UP (Alta.) 33 D3
St Francis Harbour, UP (NS) 9 G2
St-François, UP (Que.) 15 C2
St-François-d'Assise, UP (Que.) 13 B4
St-François-de-Kent, UP (NB) 12 G4
St-François-de-Madawaska, VL (NB) 15 G2
St-François-de-Masham, UP (Que.) 17 B1
St-François-de-Sales, UP (Que.) 18 H1
St-François-du-Lac, VL (Que.) 16 B2
St-François-Montmagny, UP (Que.) 15 C3
St-François-Station, UP (Que.) 15 C3
St François Xavier, UP (Man.) 29 H3
St-François-Xavier-de-Brompton, UP (Que.) 16 D3
St-François-Xavier-de-Viger, UP (Que.) 14 F4
St-Frédéric, UP (Que.) 15 B4
St-Front, UP (Sask.) 32 F4
St-Fulgence, UP (Que.) 14 B3
St-Gabriel, T (Que.) 16 A2
St-Gabriel, NUP (Que.) 15 C1
St-Gabriel-de-Gaspé, UP (Que.) 13 G2
St-Gabriel-de-Kamouraska, UP (Que.) 15 D2
St-Gabriel-de-Kent, UP (NB) 12 G3
St-Gabriel-de-Rimouski, UP (Que.) 14 H3
St-Gédéon, UP (Que.) 18 H1
St-Gédéon, VL (Que.) 16 G3
St-Gédéon-Est, UP (Que.) 16 G3
St-Gédéon-Station, UP (Que.) 18 H1
St-Gédéon-sur-le-Lac, UP (Que.) 18 H1
St George, T (NB) 11 C3
St George, UP (Ont.) 22 G1
St-Georges, T (Que.) 16 G2
St George's, T (Nfld.) 4 C2
St Georges, UP (Man.) 30 C4
St Georges, UP (PEI) 7 E4
St-Georges, VL (Que.) 16 B1
St Georges Channel, UP (NS) 8 D4
St-Georges-de-Bagot, UP (Que.) 16 B3
St-Georges-de-Cacouna, VL (Que.) 14 E4
St-Georges-de-Windsor, VL (Que.) 16 D3
St George's Hill, UP (Sask.) 44 D4
St-Georges-Ouest, T (Que.) 16 G2
St-Gérard, VL (Que.) 16 E3
St-Gérard-des-Laurentides, UP (Que.) 16 B1
St-Gérard-d'Yamaska, UP (Que.) 16 B2
St-Germain-de-Grantham, VL (Que.) 16 C3
St-Germain-de-Kamouraska, UP (Que.) 15 E1
St-Gervais, UP (Que.) 15 H4
St Gilbert, UP (PEI) 7 B3
St-Gilbert, UP (Que.) 16 D1
St-Gilles, UP (Que.) 15 A4
St-Godefroi, UP (Que.) 13 F3
St-Grégoire, UP (NB) 12 G4
St-Grégoire, VL (Que.) 16 A4
St-Grégoire-de-Greenlay, VL (Que.) 16 D3
St Gregor, VL (Sask.) 31 G1
St-Guillaume, VL (Que.) 16 B2
St-Guillaume-Nord, UP (Que.) 18 F3
St-Guy, UP (Que.) 14 F4
St Helens, UP (Ont.) 23 B3
St-Hélier, UP (Que.) 13 G1
St-Henri-de-Lévis, UP (Que.) 15 G4
St-Henri-de-Taillon, UP (Que.) 18 H1
St-Herménégilde, VL (Que.) 16 D4

St-Hilaire, VL (NB) **15 G2**
St-Hilaire-de-Dorset, UP (Que.) **16 F3**
St-Hilarion, UP (Que.) **15 C1**
St-Hilarion-du-Lac, UP (Que.) **15 C1**
St-Hilarion-Nord, UP (Que.) **15 C1**
St Hippolyte, UP (Sask.) **32 B3**
St-Hippolyte-de-Kilkenny, UP (Que.) **18 F4**
St-Honoré, UP (Que.) **14 B2**
St-Honoré, UP (Que.) **16 F2**
St-Honoré-de-Témiscouata, UP (Que.) **14 F4**
St-Honoré-Station, UP (Que.) **14 F4**
St Hubert, UP (PEI) **7 B3**
St-Hubert, C (Que.) **17 H4**
St-Hubert-de-Témiscouata, UP (Que.) **14 F4**
St Hubert Mission, UP (Sask.) **29 C3**
St-Hugues, VL (Que.) **16 B3**
St-Hyacinthe, C (Que.) **16 B3**
St-Ignace, UP (NB) **12 F3**
St-Ignace-de-Loyola, UP (Que.) **16 A2**
St-Ignace-de-Stanbridge, UP (Que.) **16 B4**
St-Ignace-du-Lac, UP (Que.) **18 F3**
St-Irénée, UP (NB) **12 G1**
St-Irénée, UP (Que.) **15 D1**
St-Irénée-les-Bains, UP (Que.) **15 D1**
St-Isadore, UP (Que.) **13 B4**
St-Isidore, UP (Que.) **17 G2**
St Isidore, UP (NB) **12 F1**
St Isidore, UP (Alta.) **43 H3**
St-Isidore, VL (Que.) **15 B3**
St-Isidore-d'Auckland, UP (Que.) **16 E4**
St-Isidore-de-Bellevue, UP (Sask.) **32 D4**
St-Isidore-de-Gaspé, UP (Que.) **13 H3**
St Isidore de Prescott, VL (Ont.) **17 E1**
St-Isidore-Jonction, UP (Que.) **17 G1**
St Ives, UP (Ont.) **22 E1**
St Jacobs, UP (Ont.) **23 D4**
St-Jacques, VL (Que.) **18 G4**
St-Jacques, VL (NB) **15 H1**
St Jacques < St Jacques – Coomb's Cove, UP (Nfld.) **2 C2**
St Jacques – Coomb's Cove, LID (Nfld.) **2 C2**
St-Jacques-le-Majeur-de-Wolfestown, UP (Que.) **16 E2**
St-Jacques-le-Mineur, UP (Que.) **16 A4**
St-Jacques-Nord, UP (Que.) **18 G4**
St-Jean, C (Que.) **16 A4**
St Jean Baptiste, UP (Man.) **29 H4**
St-Jean-Baptiste, UP (Que.) **15 D2**
St-Jean-Baptiste-de-Restigouche, UP (NB) **12 B1**
St-Jean-Baptiste-de-Rouville, UP (Que.) **16 A3**
St-Jean-Chrysostome, T (Que.) **15 B3**
St-Jean-de-Boischatel, VL (Que.) **15 G3**
St-Jean-de-Brébeuf, UP (Que.) **15 A4**
St-Jean-de-Cherbourg, UP (Que.) **13 B2**
St-Jean-de-Dieu, UP (Que.) **14 F4**
St-Jean-de-la-Lande, UP (Que.) **16 F2**
St-Jean-de-la-Lande, UP (Que.) **15 G1**
St-Jean-de-Matapédia, UP (Que.) **13 B4**
St-Jean-de-Matha, UP (Que.) **16 A2**
St-Jean-des-Piles, UP (Que.) **16 B1**
St-Jean-d'Orléans, UP (Que.) **15 H3**
St-Jean-Port-Joli, UP (Que.) **15 D2**
St-Jean-Port-Joli-Station, UP (Que.) **15 D2**
St-Jean-sur-Lac, UP (Que.) **18 D4**
St-Jean-Vianney, UP (Que.) **16 F3**
St-Jean-Vianney, VL (Que.) **14 B3**
St-Jérôme, C (Que.) **17 G1**
St-Joachim, UP (Que.) **15 B2**
St Joachim, UP (Ont.) **22 B3**
St-Joachim-de-Courval, UP (Que.) **16 C2**
St-Joachim-de-Shefford, UP (Que.) **16 C3**
St-Joachim-de-Tourelle, UP (Que.) **13 D1**
Saint Joe 10, IR (BC) **41 E2**
St-Jogues, UP (Que.) **13 F3**
St-Jogues-Sud, UP (Que.) **13 F3**
Saint John, C (NB) **11 D3**
St John Island, UP (Nfld.) **5 G2**
St John's, C (Nfld.) **2 H2**
St Johns < Six Nations 40, UP (Ont.) **22 G1**
St Jones Within, UP (Nfld.) **2 F1**
St Jones Without, UP (Nfld.) **2 F1**
St Joseph, UP (NS) **8 B4**
St Joseph, UP (Man.) **29 H4**
St Joseph, UP (NS) **10 B2**
St-Joseph, UP (NB) **12 F3**
St Joseph, UP (Ont.) **22 D1**
St-Joseph, VL (NB) **11 G1**
St-Joseph-de-Beauce, T (Que.) **15 B4**
St-Joseph-de-Kamouraska, UP (Que.) **15 E1**
St-Joseph-de-Kent, UP (NB) **12 G4**
St-Joseph-de-la-Rive, VL (Que.) **15 C1**
St-Joseph-de-Lepage, UP (Que.) **14 H2**
St-Joseph-de-Madawaska, UP (NB) **15 H1**
St-Joseph-de-Matapédia, UP (Que.) **13 B4**
St-Joseph-de-Mékinac, UP (Que.) **18 G3**
St-Joseph-de-Sorel, T (Que.) **16 A2**
St-Joseph-du-Lac, UP (Que.) **17 G1**
St Joseph du Moine, UP (NS) **8 D2**
St Joseph Mission, UP (BC) **36 C1**
St Joseph's, COMM (Nfld.) **2 G3**
St Joseph's, COMM (Nfld.) **2 D3**
St Josephs Colony, UP (Sask.) **31 H3**
St Josephs Cove, UP (Nfld.) **2 B1**
St-Jovite, VL (Que.) **18 E4**
St-Jude, UP (Que.) **16 B3**
St-Jules-de-Beauce, UP (Que.) **15 B4**
St-Jules-de-Cascapédia, UP (Que.) **13 E3**
St-Julien, UP (Que.) **16 E2**
St-Julien, UP (Sask.) **32 D4**
St Julien's, UP (Nfld.) **5 H2**
St-Juste-de-Bretenières, UP (Que.) **15 D3**
St-Juste-du-Lac, UP (Que.) **15 G1**
St-Justin, UP (Que.) **16 A2**
St Kyran's, UP (Nfld.) **2 E3**
St Labre, UP (Man.) **28 C3**
St-Lambert, C (Que.) **17 H4**
St-Lambert-de-Lévis, UP (Que.) **15 B3**
St-Laurent, UP (Que.) **15 H3**
St-Laurent, UP (NB) **12 E1**
St Laurent, UP (Man.) **29 H3**
St-Laurent, C (Que.) **17 G4**
St-Laurent-du-Fleuve, UP (Que.) **16 A2**
St-Laurent-Grandin, UP (Sask.) **32 D4**
St Lawrence, T (Nfld.) **2 C4**
St Lawrence, UP (PEI) **7 A2**
St Lawrence Woods, UP (Ont.) **17 B4**
St-Lazare, UP (Que.) **15 C3**
St-Lazare, UP (Que.) **17 F1**
St-Lazare, UP (NB) **12 G4**
St-Lazare, VL (Man.) **29 D3**
St-Lazare-de-Vaudreuil, UP (Que.) **17 F1**
St-Léandre, UP (Que.) **13 A2**
St-Léolin, UP (NB) **12 F1**
St-Léon, UP (Que.) **16 B1**
St Leon, UP (Man.) **29 G4**
St-Léonard, C (Que.) **17 G3**
St-Léonard, T (NB) **12 A2**
St-Léonard-d'Aston, VL (Que.) **16 C2**
St-Léonard-de-Portneuf, UP (Que.) **18 H3**
St-Léonard-Parent, UP (NB) **12 A2**
St Leonards, UP (Nfld.) **2 E3**
St-Léon-de-Chicoutimi, UP (Que.) **14 A2**
St-Léon-de-Standon, UP (Que.) **15 C4**
St-Léon-le-Grand, UP (Que.) **13 B3**
St-Liboire, VL (Que.) **16 B3**
St-Liguori, UP (Que.) **18 G4**
St Lina, UP (Alta.) **33 F2**
St Louis, VL (Sask.) **32 D4**
St Louis, VL (PEI) **7 A2**
St-Louis-de-Bonsecours, UP (Que.) **16 B3**
St-Louis-de-Champlain, UP (Que.) **16 B1**
St-Louis-de-Gonzague, UP (Que.) **17 G2**
St-Louis-de-Gonzague, UP (Que.) **15 D4**
St-Louis-de-Kent, VL (NB) **12 G3**
St-Louis-de-Masham, UP (Que.) **17 B1**
St-Louis-de-Terrebonne, UP (Que.) **17 G3**
St-Louis-du-Ha! Ha!, UP (Que.) **15 F1**
St-Luc, T (Que.) **16 A4**
St-Luc, UP (Que.) **15 C4**
St-Luc, UP (NB) **12 F3**
St-Luc-de-Laval, UP (Que.) **14 F2**
St-Luc-de-Matane, UP (Que.) **13 B2**
St-Lucien, UP (Que.) **16 C2**
St-Ludger, VL (Que.) **16 F3**
St Luke, UP (Sask.) **29 C3**
St Lunaire < St Lunaire – Griquet, UP (Nfld.) **5 H2**
St Lunaire – Griquet, COMM (Nfld.) **5 H2**
St Lupicin, UP (Man.) **29 G4**
St-Magloire, UP (Que.) **15 D3**
St-Majoric, UP (Que.) **16 C2**
St-Malachie, UP (Que.) **15 C4**
St-Malachie-d'Ormstown, UP (Que.) **17 G2**
St-Malachie-Station, UP (Que.) **15 C3**
St Malo, UP (Man.) **28 A3**
St-Malo, UP (Que.) **16 E4**
St-Marc, UP (Que.) **16 A3**
St-Marc-des-Carrières, VL (Que.) **16 D1**
St-Marcel, UP (NB) **12 H4**
St-Marcel-de-l'Islet, UP (Que.) **15 D3**
St-Marcel-de-Richelieu, UP (Que.) **16 B3**
St-Marcellin, UP (Que.) **14 G3**
St Margarets, UP (NB) **12 F2**
St Margarets, UP (PEI) **7 E3**
St Margarets, CFS/SFC, MIL (NB) **12 F2**
St Margaret Village, UP (NS) **8 E1**
St Marks, UP (Man.) **29 H3**
St Martin, UP (NS) **10 A3**
St Martin, UP (Man.) **29 G1**
St-Martin-de-Kent, UP (NB) **12 G4**
St-Martin-de-Restigouche, UP (NB) **12 B1**
St Martins, VL (NB) **11 E3**
St Mary's, COMM (Nfld.) **2 F4**
St Mary's, T (Ont.) **22 E1**
St Marys, UP (NS) **8 D4**
St Mary's < St Mary's (COMM), UP (Nfld.) **2 F4**
St Mary's 1A, IR (BC) **34 C4**
St Mary's 24, IR (NB) **11 C1**
St Marys River, UP (NS) **9 F3**
St Marys Road, UP (PEI) **7 E4**
St-Mathias, UP (Que.) **16 A3**
St-Mathias-de-Bonneterre, UP (Que.) **16 E4**
St-Mathieu, UP (Que.) **14 F3**
St-Mathieu-de-Laprairie, UP (Que.) **17 H2**
St-Maure, UP (NB) **13 D4**
St-Maurice, UP (Que.) **16 C1**
St-Maurice, UP (NB) **12 G3**
St-Maurice-de-Dalquier, UP (Que.) **18 B1**
St-Médard, UP (Que.) **14 F4**
St-Méthode, UP (Que.) **18 H1**
St-Méthode-de-Frontenac, UP (Que.) **16 F2**
St Michael, UP (Alta.) **33 E3**
St Michaels, UP (Nfld.) **2 H3**
St-Michel-de-Bellechasse, UP (Que.) **15 H3**
St-Michel-de-Napierville, UP (Que.) **17 H2**
St-Michel-des-Saints, UP (Que.) **18 F3**
St-Michel-de-Wentworth, UP (Que.) **18 F4**
St-Modeste, UP (Que.) **14 E4**
St-Modeste-Station, UP (Que.) **14 E4**
St-Moïse, UP (Que.) **13 A2**
St-Narcisse, UP (Que.) **16 C1**
St-Narcisse-de-Rimouski, UP (Que.) **14 G3**
St-Narcisse-Station, NUP (Que.) **16 C1**
St-Nazaire, UP (Que.) **16 B3**
St-Nazaire-de-Berry, UP (Que.) **18 B1**
St-Nazaire-de-Buckland, UP (Que.) **15 C3**
St-Nazaire-de-Chicoutimi, UP (Que.) **14 A2**
St-Nérée, UP (Que.) **15 C3**
St-Nicéphore, UP (Que.) **16 C3**
St Nicholas, UP (PEI) **7 B3**
St-Nicolas, T (Que.) **15 F4**
St-Nicolas-Est, UP (Que.) **18 F4**
St-Nicolas-Ouest, UP (Que.) **18 F1**
St-Nil, UP (Que.) **13 B2**
St Ninian, UP (NS) **8 C3**
St-Noël, VL (Que.) **13 A2**
St-Norbert, UP (Que.) **16 A2**
St-Norbert, UP (NB) **12 G3**
St-Octave, UP (Que.) **14 H2**
St-Octave-de-l'Avenir, UP (Que.) **13 C1**
St-Odilon, UP (Que.) **15 C4**
St Ola, UP (Ont.) **24 F3**
St-Olivier, UP (NB) **12 G3**
St-Omer, UP (Que.) **13 D3**
St-Omer, UP (Que.) **15 E2**
St-Onésime, UP (Que.) **15 D2**
St-Onge, UP (Ont.) **17 D2**
St Ouens, UP (Man.) **28 B1**
St-Ours, T (Que.) **16 A2**
St-Pacôme, VL (Que.) **15 D2**
St-Pacôme-Station, UP (Que.) **15 D2**
St-Pamphile, T (Que.) **15 E3**
St-Pascal, T (Que.) **15 E1**
St-Pascal, UP (Ont.) **17 D1**
St-Patrice, UP (Que.) **14 E4**
St-Patrice-de-Beaurivage, VL (Que.) **15 B4**
St Patrick Road, UP (PEI) **7 D4**
St Patricks, UP (Nfld.) **3 B1**
St Patricks, UP (PEI) **7 C3**
St Patricks Channel, UP (NS) **8 D3**
St Paul, T (Alta.) **33 G3**
St-Paul, UP (Que.) **16 B3**
St-Paul, UP (NB) **12 G4**
St-Paul-de-la-Croix, UP (Que.) **14 F4**
St-Paul-de-Montminy, UP (Que.) **15 C3**
St-Paul-d'Industrie, UP (Que.) **16 A2**
St-Paul-du-Nord, UP (Que.) **14 F2**
St-Paul-Est, UP (Que.) **15 C3**
St-Paulin, VL (Que.) **16 B1**
St-Paulin-Dalibaire, UP (Que.) **13 C1**
St-Paul-l'Ermite, T (Que.) **16 A3**
St Pauls, COMM (Nfld.) **5 F4**
St Pauls, UP (Ont.) **21 A1**
St Pauls, UP (NS) **9 D2**
St Pauls Station, UP (Ont.) **22 E1**
St Peter and St Paul, UP (PEI) **7 A2**
St Peter's, UP (NS) **8 D4**
St Peters, VL (PEI) **7 E3**
St Peters Colony, UP (Sask.) **31 H3**
St Peters Fishing Station 1A, IR (Man.) **30 C4**
St Peters Harbour, UP (PEI) **7 D3**
St-Philémon, UP (Que.) **15 C3**
St-Philémon-Nord, UP (Que.) **15 C3**
St-Philémon-Sud, UP (Que.) **15 C3**
St-Philibert, UP (Que.) **15 C4**
St Philip, UP (PEI) **7 A3**
St-Philippe, UP (NB) **11 G1**
St-Philippe-d'Argenteuil, UP (Que.) **17 F1**
St-Philippe-de-Chester, UP (Que.) **16 D2**
St-Philippe-de-Laprairie, UP (Que.) **16 A4**
St-Philippe-de-Néri, UP (Que.) **15 D1**
St Philips, UP (Sask.) **29 D1**
St Phillips, UP (Nfld.) **2 H2**
St-Pie, VL (Que.) **16 B3**
St-Pie-de-Guire, UP (Que.) **16 B2**
St-Pierre, T (Que.) **17 G4**
St-Pierre, UP (Que.) **16 A2**
St-Pierre, UP (Que.) **15 G3**
St-Pierre, UP (Que.) **17 G2**
St Pierre, VL (Man.) **28 A2**
St-Pierre, VL (Que.) **16 A2**
St-Pierre-Baptiste, UP (Que.) **15 A4**
St-Pierre-de-Broughton, UP (Que.) **15 B4**
St-Pierre-de-Kent, UP (NB) **12 G3**
St-Pierre-de-Témiscouata, UP (Que.) **14 F4**
St-Pierre-de-Wakefield, UP (Que.) **17 C1**
St-Pierre-Montmagny, UP (Que.) **15 C3**
St Pierre Sud, UP (Man.) **28 A2**
St-Placide, VL (Que.) **17 F1**
St-Placide-de-Charlevoix, UP (Que.) **15 C2**
St-Polycarpe, VL (Que.) **17 F2**
St-Pons, UP (NB) **12 G1**
St-Prime, VL (Que.) **18 H1**
St-Prosper, UP (Que.) **16 C1**
St-Prosper-de-Dorchester, UP (Que.) **15 C4**
St-Quentin, VL (NB) **12 B1**
St Raphael, UP (PEI) **7 B3**
St-Raphaël, VL (Que.) **15 C3**
St-Raphaël-de-l'Île-Bizard, UP (Que.) **17 G1**
St Raphaels, UP (Ont.) **17 E2**
St-Raphaël-sur-Mer, UP (NB) **13 G4**
St-Raymond, T (Que.) **18 H3**
St Raymond, UP (Man.) **28 B2**
St-Rédempteur, UP (Que.) **17 F1**
St-Rédempteur, VL (Que.) **15 G4**
St-Régis, UP (Que.) **17 E2**
St-Régis Akwesasne 15, IR (Que.) **17 F2**
St-Régis Akwesasne 59, IR (Ont.) **17 E2**
St-Rémi, T (Que.) **17 H2**
St-Rémi-de-Tingwick, UP (Que.) **16 D3**
St-René, UP (Que.) **16 G2**
St-René-de-Matane, UP (Que.) **13 B2**
St-Robert, UP (Que.) **16 B2**
St Roch, UP (PEI) **7 B2**
St-Roch, UP (Que.) **18 A2**
St-Roch-de-l'Achigan, UP (Que.) **18 G4**
St-Roch-de-Mékinac, UP (Que.) **18 G3**
St-Roch-de-Richelieu, UP (Que.) **16 A2**
St-Roch-des-Aulnaies, UP (Que.) **15 D2**
St-Romain, UP (Que.) **16 F3**
St-Romuald-d'Etchemin, C (Que.) **15 G4**
St-Rosaire, UP (Que.) **16 D2**
St Rose, UP (NS) **8 D3**
St-Samuel-de-Horton, UP (Que.) **16 C2**
St-Samuel-Station, UP (Que.) **16 F3**
Saints-Anges, UP (Que.) **15 B4**
St-Sauveur, UP (NB) **12 F1**
St-Sauveur-des-Monts, VL (Que.) **18 F4**
St-Sébastien, UP (Que.) **16 F4**
St-Sébastien, UP (Que.) **16 A4**
St-Sébastien-Station, UP (Que.) **16 F3**
St-Sévère, UP (Que.) **16 B1**
St-Sévère-Nord, UP (Que.) **16 B1**
St-Séverin-de-Beauce, UP (Que.) **15 B4**
St Shotts, COMM (Nfld.) **2 F4**
St-Siméon, VL (Que.) **14 D4**
St-Siméon-de-Bonaventure, UP (Que.) **13 E3**
St-Siméon-Est, UP (Que.) **13 E3**
St-Siméon-Ouest, UP (Que.) **13 E3**
St-Simon-de-Bagot, UP (Que.) **16 B3**
St-Simon-de-Rimouski, UP (Que.) **14 F3**
St-Simon-les-Mines, UP (Que.) **15 C4**
St-Simon-sur-Mer, UP (Que.) **14 F3**
St-Sixte, UP (Que.) **17 D1**
Sts-Martyrs-Canadiens, UP (Que.) **16 E3**
St-Sosime, UP (NB) **12 F4**
Sts Rest, UP (NS) **9 B2**
St-Stanislas, UP (Que.) **18 H1**
St-Stanislas-de-Champlain, UP (Que.) **16 C1**
St-Stanislas-de-Kostka, UP (Que.) **17 F2**
St Stephen, T (NB) **11 B3**
St Stephens < St Vincent's – St Stephens – Peter's River, UP (Nfld.) **2 F4**
St-Sulpice, UP (Que.) **16 A3**
St-Sylvère, VL (Que.) **16 C2**
St-Sylvestre, VL (Que.) **15 B4**
St-Télesphore, UP (Que.) **17 F2**
St Teresa, UP (Nfld.) **4 B2**
St Teresa, UP (PEI) **7 D4**
St-Tharcisius, UP (Que.) **13 B2**
St-Théodore, UP (Que.) **18 F4**
St-Théodore-d'Acton, UP (Que.) **16 B3**
St-Théophile, UP (Que.) **16 G2**
St Theresa Point < Island Lake 22, UP (Man.) **30 D2**
St Thomas, C (Ont.) **22 E2**
St Thomas, UP (Nfld.) **2 H2**
St Thomas, UP (NB) **12 A4**
St-Thomas-d'Aquin, UP (Que.) **16 B3**
St-Thomas-de-Caxton, UP (Que.) **16 B1**
St-Thomas-de-Cloridorme, UP (Que.) **13 G1**
St-Thomas-de-Joliette, UP (Que.) **16 A2**
St-Thomas-de-Kent, UP (NB) **12 G4**
St-Thuribe, UP (Que.) **16 C1**
St-Timothée, VL (Que.) **17 G2**
St Timothy, UP (PEI) **7 A3**
St-Tite, T (Que.) **16 C1**
St-Tite-des-Caps, UP (Que.) **15 C2**
St-Ubalde, UP (Que.) **18 H3**
St-Ulric, VL (Que.) **13 A2**
St-Urbain-de-Charlevoix, UP (Que.) **15 C1**
St-Urbain-de-Châteauguay, UP (Que.) **17 G2**
St-Valentin, UP (Que.) **16 A4**
St-Valère, UP (Que.) **16 D2**
St-Valérien, UP (Que.) **16 B3**
St-Valérien-de-Rimouski, UP (Que.) **14 G3**
St-Vallier, VL (Que.) **15 B3**
St-Vallier-Station, UP (Que.) **15 C3**
St Veronica's, UP (Nfld.) **2 B1**
St-Vianney, UP (Que.) **13 B2**
St-Viateur, UP (Que.) **16 A2**
St-Victor, VL (Que.) **15 B4**
St Victor, VL (Sask.) **31 F4**
St-Victor-de-Bonaventure, UP (Que.) **13 C3**
St-Victor-Station, UP (Que.) **15 B4**
St Vincent, UP (Alta.) **33 G2**
St Vincent < St Vincent's – St Stephens – Peter's River, UP (Nfld.) **2 F4**
St Vincent's – St Stephens – Peter's River, LID (Nfld.) **2 F4**
St-Vital-de-Clermont, UP (Que.) **18 A1**
St Walburg, T (Sask.) **32 A3**
St-Wenceslas, VL (Que.) **16 C2**
St-Wilfrid, UP (NB) **12 F2**
St Williams, UP (Ont.) **22 G2**
St-Yvon, UP (Que.) **13 G1**
St-Zacharie, UP (Que.) **16 D3**
St-Zacharie, VL (Que.) **15 C4**
St-Zénon, UP (Que.) **18 F3**
St-Zéphirin, UP (Que.) **16 B2**
St-Zotique, VL (Que.) **17 F2**
Sakamayack, UP (Sask.) **32 C1**
Sakami, UP (Que.) **20 F2**
Sakimay 74, IR (Sask.) **29 C3**
Salaberry, UP (Que.) **16 E2**
Salaberry-de-Valleyfield, C (Que.) **17 F2**
Salaquo 4, IR (BC) **40 C2**
Salem, UP (Ont.) **23 D4**
Salem, UP (NB) **11 G1**
Salem, UP (NS) **9 A1**
Salem, UP (NB) **11 F1**
Salem, UP (Ont.) **17 A3**
Salem, UP (Ont.) **21 E2**
Salem, UP (Ont.) **23 E3**
Salem, UP (Ont.) **23 C2**
Salem, UP (Ont.) **23 C3**
Salem Corners, UP (Ont.) **21 C1**
Salem Road, UP (NS) **8 E4**
Salford, UP (Ont.) **22 F1**
Salina, UP (NB) **11 E2**
Salisbury, VL (NB) **11 F1**
Sallahlus 20, IR (BC) **38 D1**
Sallahlus 20A, IR (BC) **38 D1**
Sally's Cove, COMM (Nfld.) **5 F4**
Salmo, VL (BC) **34 B4**
Salmon Arm, DM (BC) **35 F1**
Salmon-Bay, UP (Que.) **5 F2**
Salmon Bay 3, IR (BC) **37 C3**
Salmon Beach, UP (NB) **12 F1**
Salmon Cove, T (Nfld.) **2 G2**
Salmon Creek, UP (NB) **11 E1**
Salmon Creek, UP (NB) **11 E1**
Salmon Creek 3, IR (BC) **45 B4**
Salmonhurst Corner, UP (NB) **12 A2**
Salmonier, UP (Nfld.) **2 C3**
Salmon Lake 7, IR (BC) **35 E2**
Salmon Point, UP (Ont.) **21 G2**
Salmon River, UP (NS) **9 C2**
Salmon River, UP (NS) **10 A3**
Salmon River, UP (NB) **11 F2**
Salmon River, UP (NS) **8 D4**
Salmon River 1, IR (BC) **35 F1**
Salmon River 1, IR (BC) **39 G2**
Salmon River Bridge, UP (NS) **9 C3**
Salmon River Lake, UP (NS) **9 F2**
Salmon River Meadow 7, IR (BC) **40 A3**
Salmon River Road, UP (NS) **8 E4**
Salmon Valley, UP (BC) **40 C1**
Salmonville, UP (Ont.) **22 E1**
Salomé, UP (Que.) **16 A2**
Saltair, UP (BC) **38 E3**
Salt Channel 21D, IR (Man.) **30 A2**
Saltcoats, T (Sask.) **29 D2**
Saltery Bay, UP (BC) **38 D1**
Saltford, UP (Ont.) **23 B3**
Salt Harbour, UP (Nfld.) **3 D1**
Salt Pans, UP (Nfld.) **3 D2**
Salt Point, UP (Man.) **29 F1**
Salt Prairie, UP (Alta.) **33 B1**
Salt River, UP (NWT) **44 C2**
Salt Springs, UP (NS) **9 D2**
Salt Springs, UP (NS) **9 A1**
Salt Springs, UP (NS) **8 B4**
Salt Springs, UP (NB) **11 E2**
Salt Springs Station, UP (NS) **9 A1**
Salvador, VL (Sask.) **31 C1**
Salvage, LID (Nfld.) **3 F3**
Salvail, UP (Que.) **16 A3**
Salvus 26, IR (BC) **42 D4**
Sam Adams 12, IR (BC) **35 B2**
Samahquam 1, IR (BC) **37 G4**
Sambro, UP (NS) **9 B4**
Sambro Creek, UP (NS) **9 B4**
Sambro Head, UP (NS) **9 B4**
Samburg, UP (Sask.) **32 E3**
Sammit Lake, UP (BC) **45 C4**
Samp Hill, UP (NB) **11 F1**
Sampsons Cove, UP (NS) **8 D4**
Sampson's Meadow 11, IR (BC) **36 B2**
Sampson's Meadow 11A, IR (BC) **36 B2**
Sampsonville, UP (NS) **8 D4**
Samson 137, IR (Alta.) **33 E4**
Samson 137A, IR (Alta.) **33 E4**
Sanborn, UP (Que.) **16 E2**
Sanca, UP (BC) **34 C4**
San Clara, UP (Man.) **29 D2**
Sanctuary, UP (Sask.) **31 D2**
Sand Banks, UP (Ont.) **21 F2**
Sand-Bay, UP (Que.) **17 A1**
Sand Bay Corner, UP (Ont.) **17 B3**
Sand Beach, UP (NS) **10 A3**
Sand Beach, UP (Sask.) **32 C4**
Sand Brook, UP (NB) **11 C2**
Sand Castle Beach, UP (Ont.) **23 E1**
Sandfield, UP (NS) **8 E3**
Sandfield, UP (Ont.) **25 C3**
Sandfield Mills, UP (Ont.) **17 E2**
Sandford, UP (NS) **10 A3**
Sandford, UP (Ont.) **21 B1**
Sandford, UP (Que.) **18 H2**
Sand-Hill, UP (Que.) **16 D4**
Sandhurst, UP (Ont.) **21 G1**
Sandhurst Shores, UP (Ont.) **21 G1**
Sandilands, UP (Man.) **28 C3**
Sand Island 4, IR (BC) **41 C1**
Sandison, UP (Ont.) **22 C3**
Sand Lake, UP (NS) **8 F3**
Sand Lake, UP (Ont.) **24 C1**
Sandon, UP (BC) **34 B3**
Sandown, UP (Ont.) **17 E1**
Sand Point, UP (NS) **9 C1**
Sand Point, UP (Ont.) **17 B1**
Sand Point, UP (NB) **11 D3**
Sand Point, UP (BC) **39 E3**
Sand Point, NUP (NS) **8 C4**
Sandridge, UP (Man.) **29 H3**
Sandringham, COMM (Nfld.) **3 F4**
Sandringham, UP (Ont.) **17 E2**
Sand River, UP (NS) **11 G2**
Sandspit, UP (BC) **41 B2**
Sandtown, UP (Ont.) **17 D2**
Sandwith, UP (Sask.) **32 B3**
Sandy Bay, UP (Sask.) **32 G1**
Sandy Bay 5, IR (Man.) **29 G3**
Sandy Bay Landings, UP (NS) **10 D3**
Sandy Beach, SV (Alta.) **33 D3**
Sandy Beach, SV (Sask.) **29 B2**
Sandy Beach, UP (Ont.) **17 B1**
Sandy Beach, UP (Ont.) **23 G1**
Sandy Beach, UP (Alta.) **33 E3**
Sandy Cove, COMM (Nfld.) **3 F4**
Sandy Cove, UP (Ont.) **21 A1**
Sandy Cove, UP (NS) **10 A2**
Sandy Cove, UP (NS) **9 B4**
Sandy Cove, UP (NS) **10 D3**
Sandy Cove, St Barbe North, COMM (Nfld.) **5 G2**
Sandycove Acres, NUP (Ont.) **21 A1**
Sandy-Creek, UP (Que.) **18 C4**
Sandy Harbour, UP (Nfld.) **2 E2**
Sandy Harry 4, IR (BC) **36 B2**
Sandy Hill, UP (Ont.) **17 E1**
Sandy Hook, UP (Nfld.) **6 H4**
Sandy Hook, UP (Ont.) **17 B1**
Sandy Hook, UP (Man.) **30 C4**
Sandy Lake, UP (Man.) **29 E3**
Sandy Lake, UP (Alta.) **44 B4**
Sandy Lake, UP (Sask.) **44 E4**
Sandy Lake < Sandy Lake 88, UP (Ont.) **30 D3**
Sandy Lake 88, IR (Ont.) **30 E3**
Sandy Narrows < Sandy Narrows 184C, UP (Sask.) **32 G1**
Sandy Narrows 184C, IR (Sask.) **32 G1**
Sandy Point, UP (NS) **10 C4**
Sandy Point, UP (Ont.) **23 H2**
Sandy Point, UP (Nfld.) **3 C2**
Sandy Point, UP (Nfld.) **4 C2**
Sandy Point Beach, UP (Ont.) **24 B4**
Sanford, UP (Man.) **29 H4**
Sangaree, UP (NS) **8 F3**
Sangudo, VL (Alta.) **33 C3**
Sanikiluaq, HAM (NWT) **46 E4**
San Jose 6, IR (BC) **36 B1**
Sanklksgamal 80, IR (BC) **42 D3**
Sanmaur, UP (Que.) **18 F2**
Sans Souci, UP (Ont.) **24 A2**
Saouchten 18, IR (BC) **41 B1**
Saouk 16, IR (BC) **38 C3**
Sapawe, UP (Ont.) **27 B3**
Sapin-Court, UP (NB) **12 F3**
Sapton, UP (Man.) **28 B1**
Saratoga, UP (Ont.) **23 B3**
Sarawak, UP (Ont.) **23 C1**
Sarcee 145, IR (Alta.) **34 E2**
Sarita, UP (BC) **38 B3**
Sarnia, C (Ont.) **22 B2**
Sarnia 45, IR (Ont.) **22 B2**
Sarque 5, IR (BC) **38 C3**
Sarsfield, UP (Ont.) **17 D1**
Sarto, UP (Man.) **28 B3**
Saseenos, UP (BC) **38 E4**
Saskatchewan Beach, SV (Sask.) **31 G2**
Saskatoon, C (Sask.) **31 F1**
Satellite Slopes, UP (NS) **9 D2**
Satunquin 5, IR (BC) **41 B1**
Saturna, UP (BC) **38 F3**
Saturna Island 7, IR (BC) **38 F3**
Sauble Beach, UP (Ont.) **23 C1**
Sauble Beach North, UP (Ont.) **23 C1**
Sauble Beach South < Saugeen 29, UP (Ont.) **23 C1**
Sauble Falls, UP (Ont.) **23 C1**
Saucier, UP (Que.) **13 A2**
Saugeen 29, IR (Ont.) **23 C2**
Saugeen Hunting Ground 60A, IR (Ont.) **25 D4**
Saughanaught 22, IR (BC) **38 D1**
Saulnierville, UP (NS) **10 A2**
Saulnierville Station, UP (NS) **10 A2**
Sault-au-Mouton, VL (Que.) **14 F2**
Saulteaux, UP (Alta.) **33 D1**
Saulteaux 159, IR (Sask.) **32 B3**
Saulteaux 159A, IR (Sask.) **32 B3**
Sault Ste Marie, C (Ont.) **26 A4**
Sault-St-Lin, UP (Que.) **18 F4**
Saumarez, UP (NB) **12 G1**
Saunders, UP (Alta.) **33 C4**
Saurin, UP (Ont.) **23 F1**
Sauvé, UP (Que.) **13 D1**
Savage Cove, UP (Nfld.) **5 G2**
Savage Harbour, UP (PEI) **7 D3**
Savanne, UP (Ont.) **27 D2**
Savant Lake, UP (Ont.) **27 C1**
Savary Island, UP (BC) **37 C4**
Savey 15, IR (BC) **39 E3**
Savoie, UP (Que.) **15 A4**
Savona, UP (BC) **36 E4**
Savoy Landing, UP (NB) **12 G1**
Sawback, UP (Alta.) **34 D2**
Sawbill, UP (Man.) **44 G3**
Sawdy, UP (Alta.) **33 E2**
Sawlog Bay, UP (Ont.) **23 F1**
Sawmill Bay, UP (NWT) **45 E2**
Sawquamain 19A, IR (BC) **38 D1**
Sawridge 150G, IR (Alta.) **33 D1**
Sawridge 150H, IR (Alta.) **33 C1**
Sawyerville, VL (Que.) **16 E4**
Saxby-Corner, UP (Que.) **16 B4**
Sayabec, VL (Que.) **13 A2**
Say-la-quas 10, IR (BC) **38 E3**
Sayward, VL (BC) **39 G2**
Scamakounst 19, IR (BC) **42 D2**
Scandia, UP (Alta.) **34 G3**
Scandinavia, UP (Man.) **29 F3**
Scanterbury < Brokenhead 4, UP (Man.) **30 C4**
Scapa, UP (Alta.) **34 G1**
Scarborough, BOR (Ont.) **21 B2**
Scarlet Park, UP (Ont.) **23 G1**
Scarsdale, UP (NS) **10 E2**
Scarth, UP (Man.) **29 E4**
Scatarie Island, UP (NS) **8 G3**
Scaucy 5, IR (BC) **35 B3**
Sceptre, VL (Sask.) **31 C2**
Schaltuuch 27, IR (BC) **38 E2**
Schantzenfeld, UP (Sask.) **31 E3**
Schanzenfeld, UP (Man.) **29 H4**
Schefferville (Lac John), IR (Que.) **6 C3**
Schefferville (Matimekosh), IR (Que.) **6 C3**
Schefferville, T (Que.) **6 C3**
Schelowat 1, IR (BC) **35 A4**
Schikaelton 16, IR (BC) **35 B1**
Schindelsteddle, UP (Ont.) **22 F1**
Schist Lake, UP (Man.) **32 H2**
Schkam 2, IR (BC) **35 B4**
Schnares Crossing, UP (NS) **10 E2**
Schoenfeld, UP (Sask.) **31 E3**
Schoenweise, UP (Sask.) **31 F1**
Schoenwiese, UP (Man.) **29 H4**
Schoenwiese, UP (Sask.) **31 E3**
Schomberg, UP (Ont.) **21 A2**
Schomberg Heights, UP (Ont.) **23 F3**
Schooner Pond, UP (NS) **8 F3**
Schreiber, UP (Ont.) **27 G3**
Schuler, UP (Alta.) **31 B3**
Schutt, UP (Ont.) **24 F2**
Schwartz, UP (Que.) **18 D4**
Schyan, UP (Que.) **18 C4**
Schyan-Point, UP (Que.) **18 C4**
Science Hill, UP (Ont.) **22 E1**
Sclanders, UP (Sask.) **31 G1**
Sclater, UP (Man.) **29 E1**
Scoble West, UP (Ont.) **27 D3**
Scollard, UP (Alta.) **34 F1**
Scone, UP (Ont.) **23 C2**
Scotch Bay, UP (Man.) **29 G2**
Scotch Block, UP (Ont.) **26 C4**
Scotch Bush, UP (Ont.) **24 E2**
Scotch Bush, UP (Ont.) **24 G2**
Scotch Corners, UP (Ont.) **17 B2**
Scotch Creek, UP (BC) **36 G4**
Scotch Creek 4, IR (BC) **36 G4**
Scotchfort, UP (PEI) **7 D3**
Scotchfort 4, IR (PEI) **7 D3**
Scotch Hill, UP (NS) **8 D2**
Scotch Hill, UP (NS) **9 D1**
Scotch Lake, UP (NS) **8 E3**
Scotch Lake, UP (NB) **11 B1**
Scotch Line, UP (Ont.) **17 B3**
Scotch Point, UP (Ont.) **17 B3**
Scotch Ridge, UP (NB) **11 B3**
Scotch-Road, UP (Que.) **17 E1**
Scotch Settlement, UP (NB) **11 C1**
Scotch Settlement, UP (NB) **12 G4**
Scotch Settlement, UP (Ont.) **17 B4**
Scotch Settlement < Saugeen 29, UP (Ont.) **23 C2**
Scotchtown, UP (NS) **8 F3**
Scotchtown, UP (NB) **11 D1**
Scotch Village, UP (NS) **9 A3**
Scotfield, UP (Alta.) **34 H1**
Scotford, UP (Alta.) **33 E3**
Scotia, UP (Ont.) **24 B2**
Scotland, UP (Ont.) **22 G1**
Scots Bay, UP (NS) **11 H3**
Scots Bay Road, UP (NS) **11 H3**
Scotsburn, UP (NS) **9 D1**
Scotsguard, UP (Sask.) **31 D4**
Scotstown, T (Que.) **16 E3**
Scotsville, UP (NS) **8 D3**
Scotswood, UP (Alta.) **43 G3**
Scott, T (Sask.) **31 D1**
Scott, UP (Que.) **15 B4**
Scott Road, UP (NB) **11 F1**
Scott Settlement, UP (Ont.) **24 E2**
Scott Settlement, UP (Ont.) **24 E3**
Scott Settlement, NUP (NB) **11 A1**
Scotts Hill, UP (Man.) **28 C1**
Scott Siding, UP (NB) **11 A1**
Scotts Landing, UP (Ont.) **24 E3**
Scott Subdivision, NUP (BC) **40 C3**
Scottsville, UP (Ont.) **22 E2**
Scoudouc, UP (NB) **11 G1**
Scout Lake, UP (Sask.) **31 F4**
Scovil, UP (NB) **11 D2**
Scowban 28, IR (BC) **42 D3**
Scowlitz 1, IR (BC) **35 A4**
Scrabble Hill, UP (NS) **9 B2**
Scroggie Creek, UP (YT) **45 A2**
Scudder, UP (Ont.) **22 B4**
Scugog, UP (Ont.) **21 C1**
Scugog 34, IR (Ont.) **21 C1**
Scugog Centre, UP (Ont.) **21 C1**
Scugog Point, UP (Ont.) **21 C1**
Scuttsap 11, IR (BC) **41 D1**
Scuttsap 11A, IR (BC) **41 D1**
Seabird Island, IR (BC) **35 A4**
Seabird Mobile Home Park, NUP (BC) **38 E3**
Sea Breeze, UP (Ont.) **24 C2**
Seabright, UP (NS) **9 A4**
Seabrook, UP (NS) **10 B2**
Seacliffe, UP (Ont.) **22 B4**
Seacow Pond, UP (PEI) **7 B2**
Seacrest Subdivision, NUP (BC) **38 D2**
Seafoam, UP (NS) **9 C1**
Seaford, UP (BC) **37 C4**
Seaforth, T (Ont.) **23 B4**
Seaforth, UP (NS) **9 C4**
Seagrave, UP (Ont.) **21 C1**
Seagrove, UP (NS) **7 B4**
Seah 5, IR (BC) **35 A1**
Seaichem 16, IR (BC) **38 F1**
Sea Island 3, IR (BC) **38 F2**
Seaks 3, IR (BC) **42 D3**
Seaks 60, IR (BC) **42 E3**
Seal Bay Subdivision, NUP (BC) **38 C1**
Seal Bight, UP (Nfld.) **5 H1**
Seal Cove, COMM (Nfld.) **2 A2**
Seal Cove, LID (Nfld.) **3 A1**
Seal Cove, UP (Nfld.) **2 G3**
Seal Cove, UP (NS) **8 D4**
Seal Cove, VL (NB) **11 C4**
Seal Harbour, UP (NS) **9 F2**
Seal Island, UP (NS) **10 B4**
Seal Islands Harbour, UP (Nfld.) **6 H3**
Seal River, UP (PEI) **7 E4**
Seal River, UP (PEI) **7 D4**
Searchmont, UP (Ont.) **26 B3**
Searletown, UP (PEI) **7 B4**
Searston, UP (Nfld.) **4 A3**
Searsville, UP (NB) **11 E2**
Sea Side, UP (NB) **13 D4**

Seaside Park, UP (BC) **38 E2**
Seaspunkut 4, IR (BC) **40 A1**
Sea View, UP (PEI) **7 B3**
Seaview, UP (NS) **8 D4**
Seba Beach, SV (Alta.) **33 C3**
Sebastopol, UP (Ont.) **22 F1**
Sebright, UP (Ont.) **23 G1**
Sebright, UP (Man.) **28 B1**
Sebringville, UP (Ont.) **22 E1**
Sechelt, VL (BC) **38 E2**
Seckerton, UP (Ont.) **22 B2**
Second Falls, UP (NB) **11 C3**
Second North River, UP (NB) **11 F1**
Second Peninsula, UP (NS) **10 E2**
Secord, UP (Ont.) **25 E1**
Secretan, UP (Sask.) **31 F3**
Secret Cove, UP (BC) **38 D1**
Sedalia, UP (Alta.) **31 B1**
Seddons Corner, UP (Man.) **28 C1**
Sedgewick, T (Alta.) **33 F4**
Sedley, VL (Sask.) **31 H3**
Seebe, UP (Alta.) **34 D2**
Seech, UP (Man.) **29 E3**
Seekaskootch 119, IR (Sask.) **32 A3**
Seektukis 24, IR (BC) **39 F4**
Seeley, UP (Ont.) **17 C3**
Seeleys Bay, UP (Ont.) **17 B3**
Seeleys Cove, UP (NB) **11 C3**
Seffernsville, UP (NS) **10 E1**
Seguin Falls, UP (Ont.) **24 B2**
Seine River 22A2, IR (Ont.) **27 C2**
Seine River 23A, IR (Ont.) **27 A3**
Seine River 23B, IR (Ont.) **27 A3**
Seine River Village < Seine River 23A, UP (Ont.) **27 A3**
Sekaleton 21, IR (BC) **38 D1**
Sekaleton 21A, IR (BC) **38 D1**
Selby, UP (Ont.) **21 G1**
Seldom < Seldom – Little Seldom, UP (Nfld.) **3 E1**
Seldom – Little Seldom, RD (Nfld.) **3 E1**
Selfridge Corner, UP (NS) **10 D1**
Selim, UP (Ont.) **27 F3**
Selkirk, T (Man.) **28 A1**
Selkirk, UP (PEI) **7 E3**
Sellars, UP (Ont.) **27 D3**
Sellarsville, UP (Que.) **13 C4**
Selma, UP (NS) **9 B2**
Selma Park, UP (BC) **38 E2**
Selton, UP (Ont.) **17 B4**
Selton, UP (Ont.) **22 C3**
Selwyn, UP (Ont.) **21 D1**
Selwyn, UP (YT) **45 A3**
Semach 2, IR (BC) **39 B1**
Semans, VL (Sask.) **31 G2**
Semiahmoo, IR (BC) **38 G3**
Semiwagan Ridge, UP (NB) **12 E3**
Senanus Island 10, IR (BC) **38 E4**
Senate, UP (Sask.) **31 C4**
Senecal, UP (Ont.) **17 E1**
Senkiw, UP (Man.) **28 A3**
Senlac, VL (Sask.) **32 A4**
Senneterre, T (Que.) **18 C1**
Senneville, VL (Que.) **17 F4**
Sentinel, UP (Alta.) **34 E4**
Seouls Corners, UP (Ont.) **17 A3**
Separation Point, UP (Nfld.) **6 G3**
Sept-Chutes, UP (Que.) **15 B2**
Sept-Îles, C (Que.) **19 F3**
Serath, UP (Sask.) **31 H2**
Serpent River, UP (Ont.) **25 B1**
Serpent River 7, IR (Ont.) **25 B1**
Sesekinika, UP (Ont.) **26 F2**
Seshelt 2, IR (BC) **38 E2**
Seton Lake 5, IR (BC) **37 H2**
Seton Lake 5A, IR (BC) **37 H2**
Seton Portage, UP (BC) **37 H2**
Seven Islands 27, IR (Que.) **19 F3**
Seven Islands 27A, IR (Que.) **19 F3**
Seven Islands Crossing, UP (NWT) **45 C2**
Seven Mile Corner, UP (BC) **43 F3**
Seven Mile Narrows, UP (Ont.) **24 A2**
Seven Persons, UP (Alta.) **31 A3**
Seven Sisters Falls, UP (Man.) **28 C1**
Seventeen Mile, UP (YT) **45 B3**
70 Mile House, UP (BC) **36 D3**
Severn Bridge, UP (Ont.) **23 G1**
Severn Falls, UP (Ont.) **23 F1**
Seville, UP (Ont.) **22 F2**
Sevogle, UP (NB) **12 E2**
Sewall, UP (BC) **41 B1**
Sewell, UP (Man.) **29 H4**
Sewell Inlet, UP (BC) **41 B2**
Sexsmith, VL (Alta.) **43 G4**
Seymour Arm, UP (BC) **36 H3**
Seymour Beach, NUP (Ont.) **22 A4**
Seymour Creek 2, IR (BC) **38 F2**
Seymour Lake, UP (BC) **42 F4**
Seymour Landing, UP (BC) **38 F2**
Seymour Meadows 19, IR (BC) **40 B4**
Seymourville, UP (Man.) **30 C4**
Shabaqua, UP (Ont.) **27 D3**
Shabaqua Corners, UP (Ont.) **27 D3**
Shackan 11, IR (BC) **35 B2**
Shackleton, VL (Sask.) **31 D3**
Shad Bay, UP (NS) **9 B4**
Shady Acres Trailer Court, NUP (BC) **40 C3**
Shady Grove, UP (Sask.) **31 G1**
Shady Nook, UP (Ont.) **24 G1**
Shag Harbour, UP (NS) **10 B4**
Shakespeare, UP (Ont.) **22 F1**
Shalalth < Slosh 1, UP (BC) **37 H2**
Shale Banks, UP (Alta.) **40 G2**
Shalloway, UP (Nfld.) **2 C4**
Shalloway Cove < St Brendan's (COMM), UP (Nfld.) **3 F3**
Shallow Lake, VL (Ont.) **23 C1**
Shamattawa, UP (Man.) **30 E1**
Shamblers Cove, UP (Nfld.) **3 F3**
Shames, UP (BC) **42 E4**
Shampers, UP (NB) **11 D2**
Shamrock, UP (PEI) **7 C4**
Shamrock, UP (Ont.) **17 A1**
Shamrock, VL (Sask.) **31 F3**
Shandro, UP (Alta.) **33 F3**
Shands, UP (Ont.) **23 E3**
Shanes, UP (Ont.) **17 B3**
Shanick, UP (Ont.) **24 F4**
Shanklin, UP (NB) **11 E2**
Shanks, UP (Que.) **16 D4**
Shanly, UP (Ont.) **17 D2**
Shannon, UP (NB) **11 E2**
Shannon, UP (Que.) **15 F3**
Shannon Bay, UP (BC) **41 A1**
Shannon Creek 28, IR (BC) **38 E2**
Shannon Hall, UP (Ont.) **24 B2**
Shannons Corners, UP (Ont.) **17 A4**
Shannonvale, UP (NB) **13 D4**
Shannonville, UP (Ont.) **21 F1**
Shanty Bay, UP (Ont.) **21 A1**
Shantz, UP (Alta.) **34 E1**
Sharbot Lake, UP (Ont.) **17 A3**
Sharon, UP (Ont.) **21 B1**
Sharon, UP (Ont.) **22 E2**
Sharpewood, UP (Man.) **29 H2**
Sharples, UP (Alta.) **34 F2**
Sharps Corners, UP (Ont.) **21 G1**
Sharpton, UP (Ont.) **17 A4**
Sharrow, UP (Alta.) **31 B2**
Shaughnessy, UP (Alta.) **34 F3**
Shaunavon, T (Sask.) **31 D4**
Shaver Subdivision, NUP (Ont.) **22 E2**
Shaw, UP (Alta.) **33 A3**
Shawanaga < Shawanaga 17, UP (Ont.) **25 G3**
Shawanaga 17, IR (Ont.) **25 G3**
Shawanaga 17B, IR (Ont.) **25 F3**
Shawanaga Landing < Shawanaga 17B, UP (Ont.) **25 F3**
Shawbridge, UP (Que.) **18 F4**
Shaw Brook, UP (NB) **12 G4**
Shawinigan, C (Que.) **16 B1**
Shawinigan-Nord, UP (Que.) **16 B1**
Shawinigan-Sud, T (Que.) **16 B1**
Shaw Island, UP (NS) **10 E2**
Shawmere, UP (Ont.) **26 C2**
Shawnigan, UP (BC) **38 E3**
Shawniken 3, IR (BC) **35 B1**
Shawniken 4B, IR (BC) **35 B1**
Shawville, VL (Que.) **17 A1**
Sheahan Estates, UP (Ont.) **17 D4**
Shea Heights, UP (Nfld.) **2 H2**
Shearer Dale, UP (BC) **43 F3**
Shearwater, UP (BC) **41 E3**
Shearwater, CFB/BFC, MIL (NS) **9 B4**
Sheaton, UP (Ont.) **17 C3**
Sheaves Cove < Cape St George – Petit Jardin – Grand Jardin – De Grau – Marches Point – Loretto, UP (Nfld.) **4 A2**
Shebandowan, UP (Ont.) **27 D3**
Sheba's Island, NUP (Ont.) **21 F2**
Shebeshekong, UP (Ont.) **25 G3**
Shedden, UP (Ont.) **22 E2**
Shediac, T (NB) **12 H4**
Shediac Bridge, UP (NB) **12 H4**
Shediac Cape, UP (NB) **12 H4**
Shediac Ridge, UP (NB) **12 F3**
Shediac River, UP (NB) **12 G4**
Sheenboro, UP (Que.) **18 C4**
Sheepherders Junction, UP (NS) **9 D2**
Sheerness, UP (Alta.) **34 G2**
Sheerway, UP (Que.) **18 B4**
Sheet Harbour, UP (NS) **9 D3**
Sheet Harbour 36, IR (NS) **9 D3**
Sheet Harbour Passage, UP (NS) **9 E3**
Sheet Harbour Road, UP (NS) **9 D3**
Sheffield, UP (Ont.) **22 G1**
Sheffield, UP (NB) **11 D1**
Sheffield Mills, UP (NS) **11 H3**
Sheganny 14, IR (BC) **41 D2**
Sheguiandah, UP (Ont.) **25 C2**
Sheguiandah 24, IR (Ont.) **25 C2**
Sheho, VL (Sask.) **29 C2**
Sheila, UP (NB) **12 G1**
Shekatika, UP (Que.) **5 F2**
Shelburne, T (NS) **10 C3**
Shelburne, VL (Ont.) **23 E3**
Shelburne, CFS/SFC, MIL (NS) **10 C4**
Shelburne Falls, NUP (NS) **10 C3**
Sheldon, UP (Ont.) **23 E3**
Sheldon Corners, UP (Ont.) **17 B3**
Sheldrake, UP (Que.) **19 G3**
Sheldrake Lake, UP (NS) **9 B4**
Shellbrook, T (Sask.) **32 D3**
Shelley, UP (BC) **40 C2**
Shelley, UP (Man.) **28 C1**
Shell Island 3, IR (BC) **39 D1**
Shell Lake, VL (Sask.) **32 C3**
Shellmouth, UP (Man.) **29 D2**
Shell Valley, UP (Man.) **29 D2**
Shelter Point, UP (BC) **37 B4**
Shemogue, UP (NB) **7 A4**
Shenston, UP (Ont.) **28 G4**
Shenstone, UP (NB) **11 G1**
Shepard, UP (Alta.) **34 E2**
Shepody, UP (NB) **11 G2**
Sheppardton, UP (Ont.) **23 B3**
Shep's Subdivision, NUP (Ont.) **22 G1**
Sheptetski, UP (Que.) **18 B1**
Sheraton, UP (BC) **40 A1**
Sheraton Creek 19, IR (BC) **40 A1**
Sherbrooke, C (Que.) **16 D4**
Sherbrooke, UP (NS) **9 F3**
Sherbrooke, UP (PEI) **7 B3**
Shergrove, UP (Man.) **29 F2**
Sherose Island, UP (NS) **10 B4**
Sherridon, UP (Man.) **30 A1**
Sherrington, UP (Que.) **17 H2**
Sherwood, UP (Ont.) **26 B4**
Sherwood, UP (NS) **9 A3**
Sherwood, VL (PEI) **7 C4**
Sherwood Park, UP (Alta.) **33 E3**
Sherwood Springs, UP (Ont.) **17 C3**
Sherwood Village, UP (Ont.) **22 B2**
Sheshep 74A, IR (Sask.) **29 C3**
Sheshegwaning < Sheshegwaning 20, UP (Ont.) **25 A2**
Sheshegwaning 20, IR (Ont.) **25 A2**
Sheslay, UP (BC) **45 B4**
Shetland, UP (Ont.) **22 C2**
Shetland Trailer Park, NUP (Ont.) **26 B4**
Shevlin, UP (Man.) **29 D2**
Shickshock, UP (Que.) **13 D1**
Shields Crossing, UP (Ont.) **24 G1**
Shigawake, UP (Que.) **13 F3**
Shigawake-Est, UP (Que.) **13 F3**
Shillington, UP (Ont.) **26 E1**
Shilo < Shilo, CFB/BFC, UP (Man.) **29 F4**
Shilo, CFB/BFC, MIL (Man.) **29 F4**
Shiloh, UP (Ont.) **21 E1**
Shiloh, UP (Ont.) **23 E3**
Shingle Point 4, IR (BC) **38 E3**
Shinimicas Bridge, UP (NS) **9 A1**
Shining Bank, UP (Alta.) **33 B3**
Shining Tree, UP (Ont.) **26 E3**
Shinnickburn, UP (NB) **12 E3**
Ship Cove, UP (Nfld.) **4 B2**
Ship Cove, UP (Nfld.) **5 F4**
Ship Cove, UP (Nfld.) **2 G2**
Ship Cove, UP (Nfld.) **2 E3**
Ship Harbour, UP (Nfld.) **2 F3**
Ship Harbour, UP (NS) **9 D3**
Ship Island, UP (Nfld.) **3 D1**
Shipka, UP (Ont.) **22 D1**
Shipman, UP (Sask.) **32 E3**
Shippegan, T (NB) **12 G1**
Shippegan Portage, UP (NB) **12 G1**
Shirley, UP (Ont.) **21 C1**
Shirley, UP (BC) **38 E4**
Shirleys Bay, UP (Ont.) **17 D4**
Shoal Arm, UP (Nfld.) **3 B1**
Shoal Bay, UP (Nfld.) **3 E1**
Shoal Brook, UP (Nfld.) **5 F4**
Shoal Cove, UP (Nfld.) **5 G2**
Shoal Cove, UP (Nfld.) **5 G2**
Shoal Creek, UP (Alta.) **33 D2**
Shoal Harbour, T (Nfld.) **2 F1**
Shoal Lake, VL (Man.) **29 E3**
Shoal Lake < Shoal Lake 39A, UP (Ont.) **28 E2**
Shoal Lake 28A, IR (Sask.) **32 G3**
Shoal Lake 31J, IR (Ont.) **28 E2**
Shoal Lake 34B1, IR (Ont.) **28 E2**
Shoal Lake 34B2, IR (Ont.) **28 E2**
Shoal Lake 37A (p), IR (Ont.) **28 E2**
Shoal Lake 37A (p), IR (Man.) **28 E2**
Shoal Lake 39 (p), IR (Man.) **28 E2**
Shoal Lake 39 (p), IR (Ont.) **28 E2**
Shoal Lake 39A (p), IR (Ont.) **28 E2**
Shoal Lake 39A (p), IR (Man.) **28 E2**
Shoal Lake 40 (p), IR (Ont.) **28 E2**
Shoal Lake 40 (p), IR (Man.) **28 E2**
Shoal Point, UP (Nfld.) **4 A3**
Shoe Cove, UP (Nfld.) **2 H2**
Shoe Cove, UP (Nfld.) **3 B1**
Shonts, UP (Alta.) **33 E3**
Shoomart 5, IR (BC) **39 E3**
Sho-ook 5, IR (BC) **35 B2**
Shooter Hill, UP (Sask.) **31 E2**
Shoowahtlans 4, IR (BC) **41 C1**
Shoreacres, UP (BC) **34 B4**
Shore Acres, UP (Ont.) **21 A1**
Shoreholme, UP (BC) **34 A3**
Shore's Cove, UP (Nfld.) **2 H3**
Shorncliffe, UP (Man.) **29 H2**
Short Beach, UP (NS) **10 A3**
Shortdale, UP (Man.) **29 E2**
Short Subdivision, NUP (BC) **40 C3**
Shoskhost 7, IR (BC) **35 B2**
Shouldice, UP (Alta.) **34 F2**
Shouldice, UP (Ont.) **23 C1**
Shrewsbury, UP (Ont.) **22 C3**
Shrewsbury, UP (Que.) **18 F4**
Shrigley, UP (Ont.) **23 E2**
Shrypttahooks 7, IR (BC) **35 B3**
Shubenacadie, UP (NS) **9 C3**
Shubenacadie 13, IR (NS) **9 B3**
Shubenacadie 14, IR (NS) **9 B3**
Shubenacadie East, UP (NS) **9 C3**
Shulie, UP (NS) **11 H2**
Shulus < Nicola Mameet 1, UP (BC) **35 C2**
Shumal Creek 81, IR (BC) **42 D3**
Shumal Creek 84, IR (BC) **42 D3**
Shunacadie, UP (NS) **8 E3**
Shunnon Bay, UP (BC) **41 A2**
Shuouchten 15, IR (BC) **35 B2**
Shuswap, IR (BC) **34 C3**
Shuswap, UP (BC) **36 G4**
Shuswap < Shuswap, UP (BC) **34 C3**
Shuswap Falls, UP (BC) **35 G1**
Shuswap Lake Estates, NUP (BC) **36 G4**
Shutty Bench, UP (BC) **34 B3**
Siakin 4, IR (BC) **37 C3**
Sibbald, UP (Alta.) **31 B2**
Siberia, UP (Ont.) **24 F2**
Sibleys Cove, UP (Nfld.) **2 G1**
Sicamous, UP (BC) **36 H4**
Sicamous 3, IR (BC) **36 H4**
Sidcup, UP (Alta.) **33 G4**
Sidewood, UP (Sask.) **31 C3**
Sidina 6, IR (BC) **42 F3**
Sidley, UP (BC) **35 F4**
Sidney, T (BC) **38 F3**
Sidney, UP (Man.) **29 G3**
Siegas, UP (NB) **15 H2**
Siegas Lake Settlement, UP (NB) **12 A2**
Siegs Corner, UP (Man.) **28 C1**
Sienna, UP (Que.) **18 E4**
Sifton, UP (Man.) **29 E2**
Sight Point, UP (NS) **8 C3**
Siglunes, UP (Man.) **29 G2**
Signet, UP (Ont.) **23 D3**
Sikanni Chief, UP (BC) **43 D2**
Sik-e-dakh 2, IR (BC) **42 F3**
Silas, UP (Sask.) **32 G4**
Silberfeld, UP (Man.) **29 H4**
Silcote, UP (Ont.) **23 D1**
Silicon 2, IR (BC) **37 H2**
Sillery, C (Que.) **15 G4**
Sillikers, UP (NB) **12 E2**
Sillsville, UP (Ont.) **21 G1**
Siloam, UP (Ont.) **21 B1**
Silton, VL (Sask.) **31 G2**
Silver, UP (Man.) **29 H2**
Silver Bay, UP (Man.) **29 G2**
Silver Beach, SV (Alta.) **33 D4**
Silver Birch Beach, UP (Ont.) **23 E1**
Silver Centre, UP (Ont.) **26 F3**
Silver Corners, UP (Ont.) **23 C4**
Silver-Creek, UP (Que.) **17 D1**
Silver Creek, UP (BC) **35 F1**
Silver Creek, UP (YT) **45 A3**
Silver Creek Subdivision, NUP (BC) **35 B4**
Silverdale, UP (Nfld.) **3 B1**
Silverdale, UP (Ont.) **21 B4**
Silver Falls, UP (Man.) **30 C4**
Silver Fox Island, UP (Nfld.) **3 F3**
Silver Grove, UP (Sask.) **32 D4**
Silver Harbour, UP (Ont.) **27 E3**
Silver Heights, UP (Alta.) **34 H1**
Silver Hill, UP (Ont.) **22 F2**
Silver Islet, UP (Ont.) **27 E3**
Silver Lake, UP (Ont.) **24 G2**
Silver Lake, UP (Ont.) **23 H1**
Silver Mine, UP (NS) **8 E4**
Silver Mountain, UP (Ont.) **27 D3**
Silver Park, UP (Sask.) **32 F4**
Silver Plains, UP (Man.) **28 A2**
Silver Point, UP (Nfld.) **5 F4**
Silver Point Road, UP (NS) **10 E2**
Silver Ridge, UP (Man.) **29 G2**
Silver River, UP (BC) **35 A3**
Silver Salmon Lake 5, IR (BC) **45 B4**
Silver Sands, SV (Alta.) **33 D3**
Silvers Corners, UP (Ont.) **17 A4**
Silverton, UP (Nfld.) **5 F4**
Silverton, VL (BC) **34 B3**
Silverton Station, UP (Man.) **29 E2**
Silver Valley, UP (Alta.) **43 F3**
Silver Water, UP (Ont.) **25 A2**
Silverwood, UP (Man.) **29 D2**
Silverwood, UP (Alta.) **43 G4**
Simcoe, T (Ont.) **22 G2**
Simcoe Beach, UP (Ont.) **21 A1**
Simcoe Island, UP (Ont.) **17 A4**
Simcoe Lodge, UP (Ont.) **23 G1**
Simcoeside, UP (Ont.) **23 G2**
Sim Creek 5, IR (BC) **37 A2**
Simmie, UP (Sask.) **31 D3**
Simms Settlement, UP (NS) **9 A4**
Simonds, UP (NB) **12 A4**
Simonet, UP (Que.) **18 H1**
Simon Lakes, UP (Alta.) **44 A4**
Simon Subdivision, NUP (Ont.) **21 D1**
Simons Valley, UP (Alta.) **34 E2**
Simoom Sound, NUP (BC) **39 F1**
Simpson, VL (Sask.) **31 G2**
Simpson Corner, UP (NB) **11 B3**
Simpson Corners, UP (Ont.) **23 E3**
Simpson Ranch, UP (BC) **43 D3**
Simpsons Corner, UP (NS) **10 D2**
Simpsons Field, UP (NB) **12 C1**
Sinclair, UP (Man.) **29 D4**
Sinclair Mills, UP (BC) **40 D2**
Sinclair Shore, UP (Ont.) **17 B2**
Sinclairville, UP (Ont.) **21 A4**
Sine, UP (Ont.) **21 F1**
Singer, UP (Que.) **18 E4**
Singhampton, UP (Ont.) **23 E2**
Sinkut Lake 8, IR (BC) **40 B2**
Sinnce-tah-lah 2, IR (BC) **40 C3**
Sinnett, UP (Sask.) **31 G1**
Sintaluta, T (Sask.) **29 B3**
Sion, UP (Alta.) **33 D3**
Sioux Lookout, T (Ont.) **27 B1**
Sioux Lookout, CFS/SFC, MIL (Ont.) **27 B1**
Sioux Narrows, UP (Ont.) **28 G2**
Sioux Valley 58, IR (Man.) **29 E4**
Sipiwesk, UP (Man.) **30 C1**
Sirdar, UP (BC) **34 C4**
Sirko, UP (Man.) **28 C3**
Siska Flat 3, IR (BC) **35 B2**
Siska Flat 5A, IR (BC) **35 B2**
Siska Flat 5B, IR (BC) **35 B2**
Siska Flat 8, IR (BC) **35 B2**
Sissiboo, NUP (NS) **10 B2**
Sissiboo Falls, UP (NS) **10 B2**
Sisson Brook, UP (NB) **12 B2**
Sisson Ridge, UP (NB) **12 B2**
Sisson Settlement, UP (NB) **11 C1**
Sistonens Corners, UP (Ont.) **27 D3**
Six Mile Brook, UP (NS) **9 D1**
Six Mile Meadow 6, IR (BC) **40 B1**
Six Mile Road, UP (NS) **9 B1**
Six-Milles, UP (NB) **12 B1**
Six Nations 40, IR (Ont.) **22 G1**
Six Nations Corner < Six Nations 40, UP (Ont.) **22 G1**
Six Roads, UP (NB) **12 G1**
Sixtymile, UP (YT) **45 A2**
Sixty Nine Corners < Six Nations 40, UP (Ont.) **22 G1**
Skaigha 2, IR (BC) **41 B2**
Skaro, UP (Alta.) **33 E3**
Skawahlook 1, IR (BC) **35 A4**
Skawahlum 10, IR (BC) **35 B3**
Skaynaneichst 12, IR (BC) **35 B1**
Skedance 8, IR (BC) **41 B2**
Skedans < Skedance 8, UP (BC) **41 B2**
Skeikut 9, IR (BC) **35 B1**
Skemeoskuankin 7 and 8, IR (BC) **35 E4**
Skerryvore, UP (Ont.) **25 F3**
Skhpowtz 4, IR (BC) **35 B1**
Skibbereen < Harbour Main (COMM), UP (Nfld.) **2 G3**
Skibi Lake, UP (Ont.) **27 G1**
Skibo, UP (Ont.) **26 C4**
Skidegate, UP (BC) **41 B2**
Skidegate 1, IR (BC) **41 B2**
Skidegate Mission < Skidegate 1, UP (BC) **41 B2**
Skiff, UP (Alta.) **34 G4**
Skiff Lake, UP (NB) **11 A1**
Skilak 14, IR (BC) **41 E2**
Skin Lake 15, IR (BC) **41 G1**
Skinners Pond, UP (PEI) **7 A2**
Skins Lake 16A, IR (BC) **41 G1**
Skins Lake 16B, IR (BC) **41 H1**
Skipness, UP (Ont.) **23 C2**
Skir Dhu, UP (NS) **8 E2**
Sklahhesten 5, IR (BC) **37 H4**
Sklahhesten 5A, IR (BC) **37 H4**
Sklahhesten 5B, IR (BC) **37 H4**
Skookumchuck, UP (BC) **34 D3**
Skookumchuck < Skookumchuck 4, UP (BC) **38 G1**
Skookumchuck 4, IR (BC) **37 H4**
Skookumchuck 4A, IR (BC) **37 H4**
Skookumchuck 27, IR (BC) **38 E1**
Skoonkoon 2, IR (BC) **35 B1**
Skowishin 7, IR (BC) **37 F4**
Skowishin Graveyard 10, IR (BC) **37 F4**
Skownan, UP (Man.) **29 F1**
Skowquiltz River 3, IR (BC) **41 F2**
Skuet 6, IR (BC) **35 B3**
Skulkayn 10, IR (BC) **35 A4**
Skulkayn 11, IR (BC) **35 A4**
Skull Creek, UP (Sask.) **31 C3**
Skumalasph 16, IR (BC) **35 A4**
Skuppah 1, IR (BC) **35 B2**
Skuppah 2A, IR (BC) **35 B2**
Skuppah 2B, IR (BC) **35 B2**
Skuppah 3A, IR (BC) **35 B2**
Skuppah 4, IR (BC) **35 B2**
Skuppah 4A, IR (BC) **35 B2**
Skutz 7, IR (BC) **38 E3**
Skutz 8, IR (BC) **38 D3**
Skwahla 2, IR (BC) **35 A4**
Skwah 4, IR (BC) **35 A4**
Skwali 3, IR (BC) **35 A4**
Skwawkweehm 17, IR (BC) **37 E4**
Skway 5, IR (BC) **38 H2**
Skwayaynope 26, IR (BC) **35 B2**
Skweahm 10, IR (BC) **38 H2**
Skye, UP (Ont.) **17 E1**
Skye Glen, UP (NS) **8 D3**
Skye Mountain, UP (NS) **8 D3**
Skylake, UP (Man.) **29 H2**
Skyline, UP (Ont.) **17 E4**
Slabtown, UP (Ont.) **24 G1**
Slabtown, UP (Ont.) **23 C4**
Slade, UP (Ont.) **23 B2**
Slate Falls, UP (Ont.) **24 G2**
Slate River Valley, UP (Ont.) **27 D3**
Slaterville, NUP (BC) **34 C4**
Slave Falls, UP (Man.) **28 D1**
Slave Lake, T (Alta.) **33 C1**
Slavey Creek, UP (Alta.) **44 A2**
Slawa, UP (Alta.) **33 G3**
Slayathlum 16, IR (BC) **37 D4**
Sleeman, UP (Ont.) **28 F4**
Sleetsis 6, IR (BC) **35 B1**
Slemon Park < Summerside, CFB/BFC, UP (PEI) **7 B3**
Slesse Park Subdivision, NUP (BC) **35 A4**
Sliammon < Sliammon 1, UP (BC) **38 C1**
Sliammon 1, IR (BC) **38 C1**
Slocan, VL (BC) **34 B4**
Slocan Park, UP (BC) **34 B4**
Slooks 21, IR (BC) **42 D3**
Slosh 1, IR (BC) **37 H2**
Slosh 1A, IR (BC) **37 H2**
Sluice Point, UP (NS) **10 B3**
Small Island 4, IR (BC) **39 F1**
Small Point < Small Point – Kingston – Broad Cove – Blackhead – Adams Cove, UP (Nfld.) **2 G2**
Small Point – Kingston – Broad Cove – Blackhead – Adams Cove, LID (Nfld.) **2 G2**
Smeaton, VL (Sask.) **32 E3**
Smelt Bay, NUP (BC) **37 B4**
Smelt Brook, UP (NS) **8 E1**
Smeshalin 18, IR (BC) **38 D1**
Smiley, VL (Sask.) **31 C1**
Smith, UP (Alta.) **33 D1**
Smith Corner, UP (NB) **11 E2**
Smith Cove, UP (NS) **9 E3**
Smithdale, UP (Ont.) **23 E2**
Smithers, T (BC) **42 F4**
Smithers Landing, UP (BC) **42 G3**
Smithfield, UP (Ont.) **21 F1**
Smithfield, UP (NB) **11 C1**
Smithfield, UP (NS) **9 E2**
Smithfield, UP (NS) **9 C2**
Smithfield, UP (Alta.) **33 D3**
Smith Hill, UP (Man.) **29 F4**
Smithmill, UP (Alta.) **43 H3**
Smith River, UP (BC) **45 C4**
Smiths Corner, UP (NS) **9 A3**
Smiths Corner, UP (NB) **12 F3**
Smith's Corners < Six Nations 40, UP (Ont.) **22 G1**
Smiths Cove, UP (NS) **10 B2**
Smiths Creek, UP (NB) **11 F2**
Smiths Crossing, UP (NB) **12 E3**
Smith Settlement, UP (NS) **9 C3**
Smith Settlement, UP (NB) **7 B4**
Smiths Falls, T (Ont.) **17 B2**
Smith's Harbour, UP (Nfld.) **3 B1**
Smithsville, UP (NS) **10 C4**
Smithtown, UP (NB) **11 E2**
Smithville, UP (Ont.) **21 A4**
Smithville, UP (NS) **8 C3**
Smokey, UP (Nfld.) **6 G3**
Smoking Tent, UP (Sask.) **32 H4**
Smoky Burn, UP (Sask.) **32 G3**
Smoky Falls, UP (Ont.) **20 C4**
Smoky Heights, UP (Alta.) **43 G4**
Smoky Lake, T (Alta.) **33 E2**
Smoky Ridge, UP (Sask.) **32 H4**
Smooth Cove, UP (Nfld.) **2 G1**
Smooth Rock Falls, T (Ont.) **26 D1**
Smooth Town < Six Nations 40, UP (Ont.) **22 G1**
Smuts, UP (Sask.) **31 F1**
Snack Cove, UP (Nfld.) **6 H3**
Snag, UP (YT) **45 A3**
Snag Junction, UP (YT) **45 A3**
Snake 5, IR (BC) **45 D4**
Snake Falls, UP (Ont.) **30 D4**
Snake River < Snake 5, UP (BC) **45 D4**
Snare Lakes, UP (NWT) **45 E3**
Snare River, UP (NWT) **45 E3**
Snaring, UP (Alta.) **40 G3**
Sniatyn, UP (Alta.) **33 F3**
Snider Mountain, UP (NB) **11 E1**
Snipe Lake, UP (Sask.) **31 C2**
Snooks Arm, UP (Nfld.) **3 B1**
Snooks Harbour, UP (Nfld.) **2 F1**
Snowball, UP (Ont.) **21 A2**
Snowden, UP (Sask.) **32 E3**
Snowdons Corners, UP (Ont.) **17 C3**
Snowdrift, UP (NWT) **44 C1**
Snowflake, UP (Man.) **29 G4**
Snow Lake, UP (Man.) **30 B2**
Snow Road Station, UP (Ont.) **17 A2**
Snowville, UP (Ont.) **25 C3**
Snug Cove, UP (Alta.) **33 F2**
Snug Cove, UP (BC) **38 F2**
Snug Harbour, UP (Ont.) **21 C1**
Snug Harbour, UP (Ont.) **25 F3**
Snug Harbour, UP (Nfld.) **6 H4**
Snug Haven, UP (Ont.) **25 F3**
Soapstone Mine, UP (NS) **8 D3**
Sober Island, UP (NS) **9 E3**
Soda Creek, UP (BC) **36 B1**
Soda Creek 1, IR (BC) **36 B1**
Sointula, UP (BC) **39 E1**
Sokal, UP (Sask.) **32 D4**
Soldatquo 12, IR (BC) **35 B1**
Soldiers Cove, UP (NS) **8 E4**
Soldier's Cove, UP (Nfld.) **2 E2**
Soldiers Cove West, UP (NS) **8 D4**
Solmesville, UP (Ont.) **21 G1**
Solomon, UP (Alta.) **40 H2**
Solsgirth, UP (Man.) **29 E3**
Solsqua, NUP (BC) **36 H4**
Sombra, UP (Ont.) **22 B2**
Somerset, UP (NS) **10 D1**
Somerset, UP (NS) **10 E2**
Somerset, VL (Man.) **29 G4**
Somerville, UP (NB) **12 A4**
Somme, UP (Sask.) **32 G4**
Somme, UP (Man.) **28 C3**
Sommerfeld, UP (Man.) **29 H4**
Sommers Road, NUP (NS) **8 B4**
Songis, UP (Ont.) **18 A4**
Sonningdale, UP (Sask.) **32 C4**
Sonora, UP (NS) **9 F3**
Sonya, UP (Ont.) **21 C1**
Sooke, UP (BC) **38 E4**
Sooke 1, IR (BC) **38 E4**
Sooke 2, IR (BC) **38 E4**
Soowahlie 14, IR (BC) **35 A4**
Sopers < Mount Moriah, UP (Nfld.) **4 C1**
Soperton, UP (Ont.) **17 B3**
Sophe 14, IR (BC) **39 E3**
Sop's Arm, UP (Nfld.) **5 G4**
Sops Island, UP (Nfld.) **5 G4**
Sorel, C (Que.) **16 A2**
Sormany, UP (NB) **12 E1**
Sorrel Ridge, UP (NB) **11 B2**
Sorrento, UP (BC) **36 G4**
Soucy, UP (Que.) **16 B2**
Soucy, UP (NB) **15 G2**
Sounding Lake, UP (Alta.) **31 B1**
Sourdough Inn, UP (YT) **45 A3**
Souris, T (Man.) **29 E4**
Souris, T (PEI) **7 E3**
Souris Line Road, UP (PEI) **7 E3**
Souris River, UP (PEI) **7 E3**
Souris West, UP (PEI) **7 E3**
Sour Spring < Six Nations 40, UP (Ont.) **22 G1**
South Allan, UP (Sask.) **31 F1**
South Alton, UP (NS) **10 E1**
Southampton, T (Ont.) **23 B2**
Southampton, UP (NS) **9 A1**
Southampton, UP (NB) **11 B1**
Southampton, UP (PEI) **7 E3**
South Athol, UP (NS) **9 A1**
South Augusta, UP (Ont.) **17 C3**
Southbank, UP (BC) **41 G1**
South Bar, UP (NS) **8 F3**
South-Barnston, UP (Que.) **16 D4**
South Bay, UP (Ont.) **21 G2**
South Bay, UP (Ont.) **23 F1**
South Baymouth, UP (Ont.) **25 C3**
South Beach, UP (Man.) **30 C4**
South Beach, UP (Ont.) **24 E4**
South Beach, UP (Man.) **28 D1**
South Berwick, UP (NS) **10 D1**
South-Bolton, UP (Que.) **16 C4**
South Branch, UP (Nfld.) **4 A3**
South Branch, UP (NB) **12 G3**
South Branch, UP (NS) **9 C2**
South Branch, UP (NB) **11 F2**
South Branch, UP (Ont.) **17 C3**
South Brook, COMM (Nfld.) **4 D1**
South Brook, T (Nfld.) **3 A2**
South Brook, UP (NS) **9 A2**
South Brook, UP (Nfld.) **3 A1**
South Brookfield, UP (NS) **10 D2**
South Buxton, UP (Ont.) **22 C3**
South Canaan, UP (NS) **10 B3**
South Cape Highlands, UP (NS) **8 C3**
South Chegoggin, UP (NS) **10 A3**
South City Trailer Court, NUP (BC) **34 A1**
South Cove, UP (NS) **8 D3**
South Dawson, UP (BC) **43 F4**
South Deerfield, UP (NS) **10 B3**
South Dummer, UP (Ont.) **21 E1**
Southeast Arm, UP (Nfld.) **3 C2**
South East Bight, UP (Nfld.) **2 D3**
South East Passage, UP (NS) **9 B4**
Southend < Southend 200, UP (Sask.) **44 F4**
Southend 200, IR (Sask.) **44 F4**
Southern Arm, UP (Nfld.) **3 B1**
Southern Bay, UP (Nfld.) **3 A3**
Southern Harbour, T (Nfld.) **2 F2**
South Esk, UP (NB) **12 E2**
Southesk, UP (Alta.) **34 G3**
Southey, VL (Sask.) **31 H2**
South Farmington, UP (NS) **10 D1**
Southfield, UP (NB) **11 E2**
South Fork, UP (Sask.) **31 D4**
South Freetown, UP (PEI) **7 B3**
Southgate, UP (Ont.) **22 E1**
South Gillies, UP (Ont.) **27 D3**
South Gloucester, UP (Ont.) **17 E4**
South Gnadenthal, UP (Sask.) **31 E3**
South Gordonsville, UP (NB) **12 A4**
South Gower, UP (Ont.) **17 C2**
South Granville, UP (PEI) **7 C3**
South Greenfield, UP (NB) **11 A1**
South Greenwood, UP (NS) **10 D1**
South Harbour, UP (NS) **8 E1**
South Haven, UP (NS) **8 E3**
South Hazelton, UP (BC) **42 G3**
South Indian Lake, UP (Man.) **30 B1**
South Ingonish Harbour, UP (NS) **8 E2**
South Johnville, UP (NB) **12 A3**
South Junction, UP (Man.) **28 D3**
South Knife Lake, UP (Man.) **46 A4**
South Knowlesville, UP (NB) **12 B4**
South Kouchibouguac, UP (NB) **12 G3**
South Lake, UP (PEI) **7 F3**
South Lake Ainslie, UP (NS) **8 D3**
South Lakeside (Williams Lake), NUP (BC) **36 B1**
South Lancaster, UP (Ont.) **17 F2**
South Lochaber, UP (NS) **9 E2**
South Magnetawan, UP (Ont.) **25 G2**
South Maitland, UP (NS) **9 B2**
South Manchester, UP (NS) **9 G2**
South March, UP (Ont.) **17 D4**
South Melville, UP (PEI) **7 C4**
South Merland, UP (NS) **8 C4**
South Middleboro, UP (NS) **9 B1**
South Middleton, UP (Ont.) **22 F2**
South Milford, UP (NS) **10 C2**
South Mindoka, UP (Ont.) **26 F2**
South Monaghan, UP (Ont.) **21 D1**
South Mountain, UP (Ont.) **17 D2**
South Musquash, UP (NB) **11 D3**
South Napanee, UP (Ont.) **21 G1**
South Nepa 7, IR (BC) **35 B1**
South Ohio, UP (NS) **10 A3**
South Pender, UP (BC) **38 F3**
Southport, UP (Nfld.) **2 F1**
Southport, VL (PEI) **7 C4**
South Portage, UP (NB) **12 C4**
South Portage, UP (Ont.) **24 C2**
South Port Morien, UP (NS) **8 F3**
South Pugwash, UP (NS) **9 B1**
South Quinan, UP (NS) **10 B3**
South Range, UP (NS) **10 B2**
South Range Corner, UP (NS) **10 B2**
South Rawdon, UP (NS) **9 B3**
South Ridge, UP (NB) **12 B3**
South River, T (Nfld.) **2 G2**
South River, UP (NB) **12 G1**
South River, VL (Ont.) **24 B1**
South River Lake, UP (NS) **9 F2**
South River Station, UP (NS) **8 B4**
South Rustico, UP (PEI) **7 C3**
South Saanich 1, IR (BC) **38 E4**
South St-Norbert, UP (NB) **12 G4**
South Salt Springs, UP (NS) **8 B4**
South Scots Bay, UP (NS) **11 H3**
South Section, UP (NS) **9 C3**
South Shalalth, UP (BC) **37 H2**
South Shore, UP (NS) **9 C1**
South Side, UP (NS) **10 B4**
Southside Antigonish Harbour, UP (NS) **8 B4**
South Side Basin of River Denys, UP (NS) **8 D4**
South Side of Baddeck River, UP (NS) **8 D3**
South Side of Boularderie, UP (NS) **8 E3**
South Side River Bourgeois, UP (NS) **8 D4**
South Side River Denys, UP (NS) **8 C4**
South Side Whycocomagh Bay, UP (NS) **8 D3**
South Slocan, UP (BC) **34 B4**
South Star, UP (Sask.) **32 F4**
South Tetagouche, UP (NB) **12 E1**

South Tilley, UP (NB) **12 A3**
South Touchwood, UP (Sask.) **31 H2**
South Tremont, UP (NS) **10 D1**
South Tweedside, UP (NB) **11 B2**
South Uniacke, UP (NS) **9 B3**
South Victoria, UP (NS) **9 B1**
South View, SV (Alta.) **33 D3**
Southview, NUP (BC) **38 C1**
Southview Beach, UP (Ont.) **23 G2**
Southview Cove, UP (Ont.) **23 G2**
Southville, UP (NS) **10 B2**
South Wallace Bay, UP (NS) **9 B1**
South Waterville, UP (NS) **10 E1**
South Waterville, UP (NB) **11 B1**
South Wellington, UP (BC) **38 E2**
South West Arm, UP (Nfld.) **3 F3**
Southwest Cove, UP (NS) **9 D3**
Southwest Crouse < Conche, UP (Nfld.) **5 H2**
Southwest Lot 16, UP (PEI) **7 B3**
Southwest Mabou, UP (NS) **8 C3**
South West Margaree, UP (NS) **8 D3**
South West Port Mouton, UP (NS) **10 D3**
Southwest Ridge, UP (NS) **8 C3**
South Wilberforce, UP (Ont.) **24 E3**
South Williamston, UP (NS) **10 C1**
Southwold, UP (Ont.) **22 E2**
South Woodslee, UP (Ont.) **22 B3**
South Wynhurst, UP (Ont.) **21 B1**
Sovereign, VL (Sask.) **31 E2**
Sowchea 3, IR (BC) **40 B1**
Sowchea 3A, IR (BC) **40 B1**
Sowden, UP (Ont.) **27 C2**
Sowerby, UP (Ont.) **26 B4**
Soyandostar 2, IR (BC) **42 H4**
Spaffordton, UP (Ont.) **17 A4**
Spahomin Creek 4, IR (BC) **35 D2**
Spahomin Creek 8, IR (BC) **35 D2**
Spakels 17, IR (BC) **42 C4**
Spalding, VL (Sask.) **31 H1**
Spallumcheen, DM (BC) **35 F1**
Spanaknok 57, IR (BC) **42 D4**
Spaniard's Bay, T (Nfld.) **2 G2**
Spanish, UP (Ont.) **25 B1**
Spanish River 5, IR (Ont.) **25 B1**
Spanish Room, UP (Nfld.) **2 C3**
Spanish Ship Bay, UP (NS) **9 E3**
Sparkle City, UP (Ont.) **17 C3**
Sparta, UP (Ont.) **22 E2**
Sparwood, DM (BC) **34 D4**
Spa Springs, UP (NS) **10 D1**
Spatsum 11, IR (BC) **35 B1**
Spatsum 11A, IR (BC) **35 B1**
Spayaks 60, IR (BC) **42 D4**
Spear Harbour, UP (Nfld.) **5 H1**
Spearhill, UP (Man.) **29 G2**
Spectacle Lake Mobile Home Park, NUP (BC) **38 E4**
Spectacle Lakes, UP (NS) **10 E2**
Spedden, UP (Alta.) **33 F2**
Speedside, UP (Ont.) **23 E4**
Speedwell, UP (Sask.) **32 B3**
Speers, VL (Sask.) **32 C4**
Speerville, UP (NB) **11 A1**
Spence, UP (Ont.) **24 B1**
Spence Bay, UP (NWT) **46 C1**
Spencers Cove, UP (Nfld.) **2 E2**
Spencers Island, UP (NS) **11 G2**
Spencerville, UP (Ont.) **17 C3**
Spences Bridge, UP (BC) **35 B1**
Spences Bridge 4, IR (BC) **35 B1**
Spences Bridge 4C, IR (BC) **35 B1**
Spence Settlement, UP (NB) **7 B4**
Speous 8, IR (BC) **35 C2**
Sperling, UP (Man.) **29 H4**
Speyum 3, IR (BC) **35 B2**
Spillars Cove, UP (Nfld.) **5 H2**
Spillars Cove, UP (Nfld.) **3 G4**
Spillimacheen, UP (BC) **34 C2**
Spillway, NUP (Nfld.) **5 G4**
Spilmouse 4, IR (BC) **36 B3**
Spinney Hill, UP (Sask.) **32 C4**
Spintlum Flat 3, IR (BC) **35 A1**
Spirit Lake, UP (Sask.) **29 C2**
Spirit River, T (Alta.) **43 G3**
Spiritwood, T (Sask.) **32 C3**
Spirity Cove, UP (Nfld.) **5 G3**
Split Lake < Split Lake 171, UP (Man.) **30 C1**
Split Lake 171, IR (Man.) **30 C1**
Split Lake 171A, IR (Man.) **30 C1**
Split Lake 171B, IR (Man.) **30 C1**
Spokwan 48, IR (BC) **42 C4**
Spondin, UP (Alta.) **34 G1**
Sporting Mountain, UP (NS) **8 D4**
Spotswood, UP (Ont.) **18 C4**
Spotted Island, UP (Nfld.) **6 H3**
Spout Cove, UP (Nfld.) **2 G2**
Spragge, UP (Ont.) **25 B1**
Sprague, UP (Man.) **28 D3**
Spread Eagle, UP (Nfld.) **2 F2**
Spring Arbour, UP (Ont.) **22 F2**
Springbank, UP (Ont.) **22 D1**
Spring Bay, UP (Ont.) **25 B2**
Spring Brook, UP (Ont.) **21 F1**
Springbrook, UP (PEI) **7 C3**
Spring Brook, UP (NB) **12 G3**
Springbrook, UP (Que.) **15 B4**
Springburn, UP (Alta.) **43 H3**
Spring Coulee, UP (Alta.) **34 F4**
Spring Creek, UP (Ont.) **25 G2**
Springdale, T (Nfld.) **3 A2**
Springdale, UP (NB) **11 F2**
Springdale, UP (NS) **10 A3**
Springdale, UP (Alta.) **33 D4**
Springfeld, UP (Sask.) **31 E3**
Springfield, UP (NB) **11 E2**
Springfield, UP (NB) **11 B1**
Springfield, UP (PEI) **7 C3**
Springfield, UP (Ont.) **17 B4**
Springfield, UP (NS) **10 D2**
Springfield, UP (NB) **11 A1**
Springfield, UP (Ont.) **22 D2**
Springfield, VL (Ont.) **22 E2**
Springfield Lake, UP (NS) **9 B3**
Springfield Settlement, UP (NB) **12 F1**
Springfield West, UP (PEI) **7 A3**
Springford, UP (Ont.) **22 F2**
Spring Garden, NUP (NB) **11 G1**
Springhaven, UP (NS) **10 B3**
Springhill, T (NS) **9 A1**
Springhill, UP (PEI) **7 B3**
Springhill, UP (NB) **11 F1**
Spring Hill, UP (Ont.) **17 D2**
Springhill Junction, UP (NS) **9 A1**
Springhouse, UP (BC) **36 G4**
Springmount, UP (Ont.) **23 C2**
Spring Point, UP (Alta.) **34 E4**
Springridge, UP (Alta.) **34 F4**
Springside, UP (NS) **9 D2**
Springside, VL (Sask.) **29 C2**
Springside < Keeseekoose 66, UP (Sask.) **29 D1**
Springstein, UP (Man.) **29 H4**
Springton, UP (PEI) **7 C4**
Springtown, UP (Ont.) **17 A1**
Springvale, UP (PEI) **7 C4**
Springvale, UP (Ont.) **22 C1**
Spring Valley, UP (Ont.) **17 C3**
Spring Valley, UP (PEI) **7 B3**
Spring Valley, UP (Ont.) **21 E1**
Spring Valley, VL (Sask.) **31 G3**
Springville, UP (NS) **9 D2**
Springville, UP (Ont.) **21 D1**
Springwater, VL (Sask.) **31 D1**
Springwater Lakes, UP (Ont.) **23 E3**
Spring Well, UP (Man.) **30 C4**
Sproat Lake, UP (BC) **38 C2**
Sproule Creek, NUP (BC) **34 B4**
Spruce Brook, UP (NB) **12 F1**
Spruce Brook, UP (Nfld.) **4 C1**
Spruce Creek, UP (Man.) **29 E2**
Sprucedale, UP (Ont.) **24 B2**
Sprucefield, UP (Alta.) **33 E2**
Spruce Green, UP (Ont.) **23 D3**
Spruce Grove, T (Alta.) **33 D3**
Spruce Hedge, UP (Ont.) **17 A1**
Spruce Home, UP (Sask.) **32 D3**
Spruce Lake, VL (Sask.) **32 A3**
Spruce Siding, UP (Man.) **28 C2**
Spruce View, UP (Alta.) **34 E1**
Sprucewoods, UP (Man.) **29 F4**
Sprucy Cove, UP (Nfld.) **5 G4**
Spry, UP (Ont.) **23 C1**
Spry Bay, UP (NS) **9 D3**
Spry Harbour, UP (NS) **9 D3**
Spurfield, UP (Alta.) **33 D1**
Spurinow, UP (Alta.) **33 G3**
Spuzzum, UP (BC) **35 B3**
Spuzzum 1, IR (BC) **35 B3**
Spuzzum 1A, IR (BC) **35 B3**
Spuzzum 7, IR (BC) **35 B3**
Spy Hill, VL (Sask.) **29 D3**
Squaam 2, IR (BC) **36 G4**
Squaam Bay, NUP (BC) **36 G4**
Squaderee 91, IR (BC) **41 C1**
Squamish, DM (BC) **38 F1**
Square Hill, UP (Sask.) **32 B4**
Square Islands, UP (Nfld.) **6 H4**
Squatec, UP (Que.) **14 G4**
Squaw Cap, UP (NB) **13 C4**
Squaw Creek, UP (BC) **45 A3**
Squaw-hay-one 11, IR (BC) **38 E3**
Squawkum Creek 3, IR (BC) **35 A4**
Squaw Rapids, UP (Sask.) **32 G3**
Squeah, UP (BC) **35 B3**
Squeah 6, IR (BC) **35 B3**
Squiaala 7, IR (BC) **35 A4**
Squiaala 8, IR (BC) **35 A4**
Squianny 10, IR (BC) **35 B1**
Squid Cove, UP (NS) **10 E2**
Squilax, UP (BC) **36 G4**
Squinas 2, IR (BC) **40 A3**
Squire, UP (Ont.) **23 C2**
Squirrel Cove, UP (BC) **37 C4**
Squirrel Cove 8, IR (BC) **37 C4**
Squirrel Depot, UP (Ont.) **24 F1**
Squirreltown, UP (NS) **10 D1**
Squirrel Town, UP (Ont.) **25 C3**
Stadacona, UP (Que.) **18 H2**
Stadian, UP (Alta.) **34 D1**
Staffa, UP (Ont.) **23 B4**
Stag Harbour, UP (Nfld.) **3 E1**
Stagsburn, UP (Que.) **18 D4**
Staiyahanny 8, IR (BC) **35 B2**
Stalwart, UP (Sask.) **31 G2**
Stampville, UP (Ont.) **17 D3**
Stanbridge-Est, UP (Que.) **16 B4**
Stanbridge-Station, UP (Que.) **16 B4**
Stanburne, UP (NS) **10 D2**
Stanbury, UP (Que.) **16 B4**
Stanchel, UP (PEI) **7 C4**
Standard, VL (Alta.) **34 F2**
Standard Hill, UP (Sask.) **32 A3**
Standing Buffalo 78, IR (Sask.) **31 H2**
Stand Off, UP (Alta.) **34 F4**
Stanger, UP (Alta.) **33 C3**
Stanhope, UP (Nfld.) **3 C2**
Stanhope, UP (PEI) **7 C3**
Stanhope, UP (Que.) **16 D4**
Stanhope Bayshore, UP (PEI) **7 C3**
Stanhope by the Sea, UP (PEI) **7 C3**
Stanley, UP (NS) **9 A3**
Stanley, UP (NS) **9 A1**
Stanley, UP (BC) **40 D3**
Stanley, UP (Ont.) **27 D3**
Stanley, VL (NB) **12 C4**
Stanley 157, IR (Sask.) **32 E1**
Stanley 157A, IR (Sask.) **32 F1**
Stanley Bridge, UP (PEI) **7 C3**
Stanley Corners, UP (Ont.) **17 C2**
Stanley Cove, UP (Nfld.) **2 A2**
Stanley House, UP (Ont.) **24 A2**
Stanley Mission, UP (Sask.) **32 E1**
Stanley Section, UP (NS) **10 D2**
Stanleyville, UP (Ont.) **17 B3**
Stanleyville, UP (Sask.) **32 E3**
Stanmore, UP (Alta.) **34 H1**
Stanstead-Plain, VL (Que.) **16 D4**
Stanton, UP (Ont.) **23 E3**
Stanwood, UP (Ont.) **21 E1**
Stapledon, UP (Ont.) **17 C2**
Staplehurst, UP (Alta.) **33 H3**
Staples, UP (Ont.) **22 B3**
Staples Brook, UP (NS) **9 C2**
Staples Settlement, UP (NB) **11 B1**
Staqoo 22, IR (BC) **42 D3**
Star, UP (Alta.) **33 E3**
Starblanket < Atakakup 104, UP (Sask.) **32 C3**
Star Blanket 83, IR (Sask.) **29 B2**
Starbuck, UP (Man.) **29 H4**
Star City, T (Sask.) **32 F4**
Star Corners, UP (Ont.) **17 A4**
Stardale, UP (Ont.) **17 F1**
Star Division, NUP (BC) **40 C3**
Starks-Corners, UP (Que.) **17 A1**
Star Lake, UP (Man.) **28 E2**
Starlight < Sarcee 145, UP (Alta.) **34 E2**
Starrat, UP (Ont.) **24 B1**
Starratt-Olsen, UP (Ont.) **30 D4**
Starr's Beach, UP (Ont.) **21 C1**
Starrs Point, UP (NS) **11 H3**
Starrview Acres, UP (Ont.) **23 E3**
Stauffer, UP (Alta.) **34 E1**
Stavely, T (Alta.) **34 F3**
Stawamus 24, IR (BC) **38 F1**
Stayner, T (Ont.) **23 E2**
Staynerville, UP (Que.) **17 F1**
Staynor Hall, UP (Sask.) **31 C4**
Stead, UP (Man.) **30 C4**
Steady Brook, COMM (Nfld.) **4 D1**
Steamboat, UP (BC) **45 D4**
Steam Mill Village, UP (NS) **11 H3**
Stearns Subdivision, NUP (BC) **40 A1**
Steel, UP (Que.) **17 B1**
Steelman, UP (Sask.) **29 C4**
Steels Ferry, UP (Man.) **29 F4**
Steen, UP (Sask.) **32 F4**
Steenburg Lake, UP (Ont.) **24 F3**
Steen River, UP (Alta.) **44 A2**
Steep Creek, UP (NS) **8 C4**
Steeper, UP (Alta.) **33 A3**
Steep Rock, UP (Man.) **29 G2**
Steep Rock Junction, UP (Man.) **29 G2**
Steep Rock Lake, UP (Ont.) **27 B3**
Steevescote, UP (NB) **11 G1**
Steeves Mills, UP (NB) **11 G1**
Steeves Mountain, UP (NB) **11 G1**
Steeves Settlement, UP (NB) **11 F1**
Steinbach, T (Man.) **28 B2**
Stella, UP (Ont.) **17 A4**
Stellako < Stellaquo 5, UP (BC) **40 A1**
Stellaquo 5, IR (BC) **40 A1**
Stellarton, T (NS) **9 D2**
Stenen, VL (Sask.) **29 C1**
Stephenfield, UP (Man.) **29 G4**
Stephenville, T (Nfld.) **4 B2**
Stephenville Crossing, T (Nfld.) **4 C2**
Stepstone, UP (Ont.) **27 E3**
Stequmwhulpa 5, IR (BC) **36 G4**
Sterco, UP (Alta.) **33 B3**
Stettin, UP (Alta.) **33 D3**
Stettler, T (Alta.) **34 F1**
Stevan 4, IR (BC) **40 A1**
Stevens, UP (Ont.) **27 H2**
Stevenson, UP (Ont.) **22 B3**
Stevens Roadhouse, UP (YT) **45 A3**
Steveville, UP (Alta.) **34 G2**
Stewardson Inlet, UP (BC) **39 F4**
Stewart, DM (BC) **42 D2**
Stewart, UP (Alta.) **34 F4**
Stewart Crossing, UP (YT) **45 B3**
Stewartdale, UP (NS) **8 D3**
Stewart Farm, UP (Ont.) **17 E4**
Stewartfield, UP (Alta.) **33 D2**
Stewart Hall, UP (Ont.) **21 D1**
Stewart Heights, UP (Ont.) **21 D1**
Stewarton, UP (NB) **11 E2**
Stewart River, UP (YT) **45 A2**
Stewarts Glen, UP (Ont.) **17 E1**
Stewart Valley, VL (Sask.) **31 D3**
Stewartville, UP (Ont.) **17 A1**
Stewiacke, T (NS) **9 C3**
Stewiacke Cross Roads, UP (NS) **9 D2**
Stewiacke East, UP (NS) **9 C3**
Stickney, UP (NB) **12 A4**
Stick-Point, UP (Que.) **5 F2**
Stikine, UP (BC) **42 B2**
Stikine River 7, IR (BC) **45 B4**
Stillman, UP (NS) **9 D2**
Still River, UP (Ont.) **25 F2**
Stillwater, UP (BC) **38 D1**
Stillwater, UP (NS) **9 F2**
Stillwater, UP (NS) **9 A3**
Stillwater Lake, UP (NS) **9 B3**
Stirling, UP (NS) **8 E4**
Stirling, VL (Ont.) **21 F1**
Stirling, VL (Alta.) **34 G4**
Stirling Brook, UP (NS) **9 B2**
Stirling Falls, UP (Ont.) **24 B1**
Stirlingville, UP (Alta.) **34 E1**
Stirton, UP (Ont.) **23 D3**
Stitt, UP (Man.) **30 C1**
Stittsville, UP (Ont.) **17 D4**
Stlakament 9, IR (BC) **35 B2**
Stobart, UP (Alta.) **34 F2**
Stock Cove, UP (Nfld.) **3 G4**
Stockdale, UP (Ont.) **21 F1**
Stockholm, VL (Sask.) **29 C3**
Stocking Harbour, UP (Nfld.) **3 B1**
Stockport, UP (Man.) **28 A3**
Stockton, UP (Man.) **29 F4**
Stoco, UP (Ont.) **21 F1**
Stoddarts, UP (NS) **10 D1**
Stoke-Centre, UP (Que.) **16 D3**
Stokes Bay, UP (Ont.) **23 B1**
Stolberg, UP (Alta.) **33 B4**
Stone, UP (Sask.) **31 C4**
Stone 1, IR (BC) **40 C4**
Stone 1A, IR (BC) **40 C4**
Stone 4, IR (BC) **40 C4**
Stonebrook, UP (Ont.) **18 C4**
Stonecliffe, UP (Ont.) **18 B4**
Stonefield, UP (Que.) **17 F1**
Stoneham, UP (Que.) **15 F3**
Stonehaven, UP (NB) **12 F1**
Stonehenge, UP (Sask.) **31 F4**
Stonehenge Project, NUP (Ont.) **17 E4**
Stonehurst East, UP (NS) **10 E2**
Stonehurst West, UP (NS) **10 E2**
Stonelaw, UP (Alta.) **34 G1**
Stoner, UP (BC) **40 C2**
Stoneridge < Six Nations 40, UP (Ont.) **22 G1**
Stones Bay, NUP (BC) **40 B1**
Stones Corners, UP (Ont.) **17 C3**
Stone's Cove, UP (Nfld.) **2 C2**
Stonewall, T (Man.) **28 A1**
Stonewall Trailer Court, NUP (Man.) **28 A1**
Stoney Creek, T (Ont.) **21 A3**
Stoney Creek, UP (NB) **11 G1**
Stoney Island, UP (NS) **10 B4**
Stoney Point, UP (Ont.) **22 B3**
Stoney Point, UP (Ont.) **21 A1**
Stony 142, 143, 144, IR (Alta.) **34 D2**
Stony 142B, IR (Alta.) **34 D2**
Stony Beach, UP (Sask.) **31 G3**
Stony Creek 1, IR (BC) **40 B2**
Stony Creek Camp, UP (YT) **45 A3**
Stony Hill, UP (Man.) **28 C1**
Stony Hill, UP (Man.) **29 H2**
Stony Lake < Chicken 224, NUP (Sask.) **44 E2**
Stony Mountain, UP (Man.) **28 A1**
Stony Plain, T (Alta.) **33 D3**
Stony Plain 135, IR (Alta.) **33 D3**
Stony Point 10, IR (BC) **42 D4**
Stony Point 21, IR (Man.) **30 A2**
Stony Rapids, UP (Sask.) **44 E2**
Stonyridge, UP (Ont.) **24 E4**
Stonyview, UP (Sask.) **29 C1**
Stonywood, UP (Ont.) **23 D3**
Storeytown, UP (NB) **12 D3**
Storie, UP (Ont.) **25 H2**
Storkson's Corner, UP (Ont.) **28 F4**
Stormont, UP (NS) **9 F2**
Storms Corners, UP (Ont.) **17 A4**
Stornoway, UP (Que.) **16 F3**
Stornoway, VL (Sask.) **29 D2**
Storthoaks, VL (Sask.) **29 D4**
Stoughton, T (Sask.) **29 C4**
Stout, UP (BC) **35 B3**
Stout 8, IR (BC) **35 B3**
Stove Creek, UP (Sask.) **29 C1**
Stowe, UP (Alta.) **34 F4**
Stowlea, UP (Sask.) **32 A3**
Strabane, UP (Ont.) **22 G1**
Strachan, UP (Alta.) **34 D1**
Straders Hill, UP (Ont.) **17 D2**
Straffordville, UP (Ont.) **22 F2**
Strange, UP (Ont.) **21 A2**
Strangmuir, UP (Alta.) **34 F2**
Stranraer, UP (Sask.) **31 D1**
Strasbourg, T (Sask.) **31 G2**
Stratford, C (Ont.) **22 E1**
Stratford, UP (Que.) **16 E3**
Stratford-Centre, UP (Que.) **16 E3**
Strathadam, UP (NB) **12 E2**
Strathallan, UP (Ont.) **22 F1**
Strathallen, UP (Sask.) **31 F4**
Strathavon, UP (Ont.) **23 D2**
Strathburn, UP (Ont.) **22 D2**
Strathclair, UP (Man.) **29 E3**
Strathcona, UP (NS) **11 H2**
Strathcona, UP (Ont.) **21 G1**
Strathcona, UP (PEI) **7 E4**
Strathcona Park, UP (Man.) **29 F4**
Strathgartney, UP (PEI) **7 C4**
Strathlorne, UP (NS) **8 C3**
Strathlorne Station, UP (NS) **8 C3**
Strathmore, T (Alta.) **34 F2**
Strathmore, UP (Ont.) **17 E2**
Strathnairn, UP (Ont.) **23 D2**
Strathnaver, UP (BC) **40 C2**
Strathroy, T (Ont.) **22 D2**
Stratton, UP (Ont.) **28 G4**
Streamstown, UP (Alta.) **33 H3**
Streatham, UP (BC) **41 G1**
Streets Ridge, UP (NS) **9 B1**
Strickland, UP (Ont.) **26 D1**
Strome, VL (Alta.) **33 F4**
Stronach Mountain, UP (NS) **10 D1**
Strong, UP (Ont.) **24 B1**
Strong Corner, UP (NB) **12 A4**
Strongfield, VL (Sask.) **31 F2**
Strong Pine, UP (Sask.) **32 E3**
Strongville, UP (Ont.) **21 A1**
Stroud, UP (Ont.) **21 A1**
Struan, UP (Sask.) **31 E1**
Stry, UP (Alta.) **33 F2**
Stryen 9, IR (BC) **35 A1**
Stuart Bay 6, IR (BC) **38 A3**
Stuartburn, UP (Man.) **28 B3**
Stuart Island, UP (BC) **37 B3**
Stuart Lake 9, IR (BC) **40 B1**
Stuart Lake 10, IR (BC) **40 B1**
Stuart Town, UP (NB) **11 B3**
Stuie, UP (BC) **41 G3**
Stukely-Sud, VL (Que.) **16 C4**
Stullawheets 8, IR (BC) **35 B3**
Stump Lake, UP (BC) **35 D1**
Stump Lake, UP (Sask.) **32 D3**
Sturgeon, UP (PEI) **7 E4**
Sturgeon Bay, UP (Ont.) **23 F1**
Sturgeon Beach, UP (Ont.) **23 F1**
Sturgeon Falls, T (Ont.) **25 G1**
Sturgeon Falls, UP (Ont.) **26 D1**
Sturgeon Falls 23, IR (Ont.) **27 B3**
Sturgeon Heights, UP (Alta.) **43 H4**
Sturgeon Lake 101, IR (Sask.) **32 D3**
Sturgeon Lake 101A, IR (Sask.) **32 D3**
Sturgeon Lake 154, IR (Alta.) **43 H4**
Sturgeon Lake 154A, IR (Alta.) **43 H4**
Sturgeon Lake 154B, IR (Alta.) **43 H4**
Sturgeon Landing < Sturgeon Weir 184F, UP (Sask.) **32 H2**
Sturgeon Point, VL (Ont.) **21 C1**
Sturgeon River, UP (Ont.) **27 F2**
Sturgeon Valley, UP (Sask.) **32 D3**
Sturgeon Weir 184F, IR (Sask.) **32 H2**
Sturgis, T (Sask.) **29 C1**
Styal, UP (Alta.) **33 C3**
Stymiest Road, UP (NB) **12 F2**
Suahbin 19, IR (BC) **38 D1**
Success, VL (Sask.) **31 D3**
Sucker Creek 150A, IR (Alta.) **33 B1**
Sucker Creek 23, IR (Ont.) **25 C2**
Sucker Creek Landing, UP (Ont.) **25 F1**
Sucker Lake 2, IR (BC) **42 G1**
Sucker River 156C, IR (Sask.) **32 E1**
Sucwoa 6, IR (BC) **39 F3**
Sudbury, C (Ont.) **25 E1**
Suffield, UP (Alta.) **34 H3**
Suffolk, UP (PEI) **7 D3**
Sugar Bush Estates, NUP (Ont.) **17 C3**
Sugarcane < Williams Lake 1, UP (BC) **36 B1**
Sugar Island 37A, IR (Ont.) **21 D1**
Sugar Loaf, UP (NS) **8 E1**
Sugar-Loaf-Pond, UP (Que.) **16 C4**
Sugden, UP (Alta.) **33 F2**
Sullivan, UP (Que.) **18 B2**
Sullivan Bay, UP (BC) **39 E1**
Sullivan Lake, UP (Alta.) **34 G1**
Sulphide, UP (Ont.) **24 G4**
Sulphur, UP (YT) **45 A2**
Sultan, UP (Ont.) **26 C2**
Sumas Cemetery 12, IR (BC) **38 H2**
Summerberry, UP (Sask.) **29 C3**
Summercove, UP (Sask.) **31 E4**
Summerfield, UP (NB) **12 A3**
Summerfield, UP (PEI) **7 C3**
Summerfield, UP (NB) **11 E1**
Summerford, T (Nfld.) **3 D2**
Summerhill, UP (Ont.) **23 B4**
Summerland, DM (BC) **35 E3**
Summers Corners, UP (Ont.) **22 E2**
Summerside, COMM (Nfld.) **4 D1**
Summerside, T (PEI) **7 B3**
Summerside, UP (NS) **8 B4**
Summerside, CFB/BFC, MIL (PEI) **7 B3**
Summerstown, UP (Ont.) **17 F2**
Summerstown Station, UP (Ont.) **17 E2**
Summerview, UP (Alta.) **34 E4**
Summerville, UP (Nfld.) **3 F4**
Summerville, UP (NS) **9 A3**
Summerville, UP (PEI) **7 D4**
Summerville, UP (NB) **11 D3**
Summerville, UP (Ont.) **22 F2**
Summerville Centre, UP (NS) **10 D3**
Summit Depot, UP (NB) **14 G4**
Summit Lake, UP (BC) **40 C1**
Summit Lake, UP (BC) **34 B3**
Summit Lake, UP (BC) **45 C4**
Summit Roadhouse, UP (YT) **45 B3**
Sunbury, UP (Ont.) **17 B4**
Sunchild 202, IR (Alta.) **33 C4**
Sundance, UP (Man.) **30 D1**
Sundance, UP (Alta.) **33 D3**
Sundance Beach, SV (Alta.) **33 D4**
Sundance Power Plant, NUP (Alta.) **33 D3**
Sundayman's Meadow 3, IR (BC) **40 B3**
Sunderland, UP (Ont.) **21 B1**
Sundown, UP (Man.) **28 C3**
Sundre, T (Alta.) **34 E1**
Sundridge, UP (NS) **9 D1**
Sundridge, VL (Ont.) **24 B1**
Sunken Lake, UP (NS) **10 E1**
Sunkist Beach, UP (Ont.) **21 B1**
Sunland, UP (Alta.) **33 F3**
Sunnidale, UP (Ont.) **23 E2**
Sunnidale Corners, UP (Ont.) **23 E2**
Sunnybrae, UP (NS) **9 D2**
Sunnybrae, UP (Ont.) **21 E1**
Sunnybrae, UP (BC) **36 H4**
Sunnybrook, UP (Alta.) **33 D3**
Sunnybrook, UP (NS) **10 E2**
Sunny Corner, UP (NB) **12 E2**
Sunnydale, UP (Alta.) **31 B2**
Sunnyglen, UP (Sask.) **31 C1**
Sunnynook, UP (Alta.) **34 G2**
Sunnyside, T (Nfld.) **2 F2**
Sunnyside, UP (Ont.) **23 F1**
Sunnyside, UP (NB) **13 D4**
Sunnyside, UP (Nfld.) **3 D1**
Sunnyside < Tache 1, UP (BC) **40 A1**
Sunnyside Beach, UP (Sask.) **32 D3**
Sunnyslope, UP (Alta.) **34 F1**
Sunny Slope, UP (Ont.) **24 A1**
Sunnyville, UP (NS) **9 G2**
Sunpoke, UP (NB) **11 C2**
Sunrise, UP (NS) **8 E1**
Sunrise Beach, UP (Ont.) **21 C1**
Sunrise Valley, UP (BC) **43 E3**
Sunset Acres, UP (NS) **9 B4**
Sunset Beach, UP (Ont.) **21 B1**
Sunset Beach, UP (Ont.) **24 B3**
Sunset Beach, UP (Ont.) **23 B3**
Sunset Beach, UP (Ont.) **22 A4**
Sunset Cove, UP (Sask.) **31 G2**
Sunset House, UP (Alta.) **33 B1**
Sunset Mobile Village, NUP (Alta.) **31 B3**
Sunset Point, SV (Alta.) **33 D3**
Sunset Prairie, UP (BC) **43 E3**
Sunset View, UP (Ont.) **21 C1**
Sunshine, UP (Ont.) **23 B3**
Sunshine, UP (Ont.) **27 D3**
Sunshine Acres, NUP (NB) **12 A4**
Sunshine Bay, UP (BC) **34 B4**
Sunshine Valley, NUP (BC) **36 F2**
Sun Valley, UP (Sask.) **31 G3**
Sunville, UP (Man.) **29 F3**
Suomi, UP (Ont.) **27 D3**
Superb, UP (Sask.) **31 C1**
Superior Junction, UP (Ont.) **27 B1**
Suquash, UP (BC) **39 D1**
Surettes Island, UP (NS) **10 B3**
Surge Narrows, UP (BC) **37 B4**
Surprise, UP (Sask.) **31 B3**
Surprise, UP (BC) **45 B4**
Surrey, DM (BC) **38 G2**
Susk 17, IR (BC) **40 A1**
Sussex, T (NB) **11 F2**
Sussex Corner, VL (NB) **11 F2**
Sutaquis 18, IR (BC) **39 G4**
Sutherlands River, UP (NS) **8 A4**
Sutorville, UP (Ont.) **22 C2**
Sutton, T (Que.) **16 B4**
Sutton, UP (Ont.) **21 B1**
Sutton Bay, UP (Ont.) **26 F3**
Sutton-Junction, UP (Que.) **16 B4**
Sutton-Mountain, UP (Que.) **16 B4**
Sutton-Ouest, UP (Que.) **16 B4**
Swahliseah 14, IR (BC) **35 B3**
Swain Post, UP (Ont.) **30 E4**
Swalwell, UP (Alta.) **34 F1**
Swan 35, IR (BC) **39 F4**
Swan Creek, UP (NB) **11 D1**
Swan Crossing, UP (Ont.) **17 C2**
Swan Hills, T (Alta.) **33 C2**
Swan Lake, UP (Man.) **29 G4**
Swan Lake 3, IR (BC) **36 B2**
Swan Lake 7, IR (Man.) **29 G4**
Swan Lake 29, IR (Ont.) **28 E1**
Swan Lake 65C, IR (Man.) **30 A3**
Swan Landing, UP (Alta.) **40 H2**
Swan Plain, UP (Sask.) **29 D1**
Swan River, T (Man.) **29 D1**
Swan River 150E, IR (Alta.) **33 C1**
Swanson, UP (Sask.) **31 E1**
Swans Shore, UP (NB) **11 B2**
Swarthmore, UP (Sask.) **32 A4**
Swaycalse 3, IR (BC) **38 E2**
Swaywelat 12, IR (BC) **37 E4**
Swaywelat 12A, IR (BC) **37 E4**
Sweaburg, UP (Ont.) **22 F1**
Sweathouse Creek, UP (Alta.) **33 B1**
Sweeney Settlement, UP (NB) **15 G1**
Sweeneyville, UP (NB) **12 G4**
Sweet Bay, UP (Nfld.) **3 F4**
Sweeteen 3, IR (BC) **37 G4**
Sweet Grass 113, IR (Sask.) **32 B4**
Sweet Grass 113A, IR (Sask.) **32 B4**
Sweet Grass 113B, IR (Sask.) **32 B4**
Sweetgrass Landing, UP (Alta.) **44 C3**
Sweetland, UP (NS) **10 E2**
Sweets Corner, UP (NS) **9 A3**
Sweets Corners, UP (Ont.) **17 B3**
Sweetwater, UP (BC) **43 E3**
Swift Current, C (Sask.) **31 D3**
Swift Current, UP (Nfld.) **2 E2**
Swift Rapids, UP (Ont.) **23 F1**
Swift River, UP (YT) **45 B4**
Swindon, UP (Ont.) **24 C2**
Swinton Park, UP (Ont.) **23 D2**
Switsemalph 3, IR (BC) **35 F1**
Switsemalph 6, IR (BC) **36 G4**
Switsemalph 7, IR (BC) **35 F1**
Switzerville, UP (Ont.) **17 A4**
Swords, UP (Ont.) **24 B2**
Sybouts, UP (Sask.) **31 H4**
Sydenham, UP (Ont.) **17 A4**
Sydenham-Place, UP (Que.) **16 C3**
Sydney, C (NS) **8 F3**
Sydney 28A, IR (NS) **8 F3**
Sydney 28B, IR (NS) **8 F3**
Sydney, CFS/SFC, MIL (NS) **8 F3**
Sydney Forks, UP (NS) **8 E3**
Sydney Mines, T (NS) **8 F3**
Sydney River, UP (NS) **8 F3**
Sykeston, UP (Ont.) **22 B2**
Sylvan, UP (Ont.) **22 D1**
Sylvan, UP (Man.) **29 H2**
Sylvan Glen, UP (Alta.) **33 D2**
Sylvan Glen Beach, UP (Ont.) **23 G1**
Sylvania, UP (Sask.) **32 F4**
Sylvan Lake, T (Alta.) **33 D4**
Sylvan Valley, UP (NS) **8 B4**
Sylvan Valley, UP (Ont.) **26 B4**
Sylvester, UP (NS) **9 D1**
Sylvester, UP (Alta.) **43 F4**
Synton, UP (NB) **11 G1**

T

Ta-a-ack 5, IR (BC) **41 F4**
Taber, T (Alta.) **34 G3**
Table-Head, UP (Que.) **5 B4**
Tabor, UP (Ont.) **26 A2**
Tabusintac, UP (NB) **12 G2**
Tabusintac 9, IR (NB) **12 F1**
Taché, UP (Que.) **15 E2**
Tache 1, IR (BC) **40 A1**
Tachie < Tache 1, UP (BC) **40 A1**
Tacks Beach, UP (Nfld.) **2 E2**
Tackuan 26, IR (BC) **42 D3**
Tackuan 26A, IR (BC) **42 D3**
Tacla Lake 9, IR (BC) **42 G3**
Tadinlay 15, IR (BC) **42 G3**
Tadmore, UP (Sask.) **29 C1**
Tadoule Lake, UP (Man.) **46 A3**
Tadoussac, VL (Que.) **14 E3**
Taft, UP (BC) **34 A2**
Taghum, UP (BC) **34 B4**
Taghum Hill, NUP (BC) **34 B4**
Tagish, UP (YT) **45 B3**
Tahla 4, IR (BC) **41 E1**
Tahlo Lake 24, IR (BC) **42 G3**
Tahltan < Tahltan 1, UP (BC) **45 B4**
Tahltan 1, IR (BC) **45 B4**
Tahltan 10, IR (BC) **45 B4**
Tahltan Forks 5, IR (BC) **45 B4**
Tahsis, VL (BC) **39 E3**
Tahsis 11, IR (BC) **39 E3**
Tahsish 11, IR (BC) **39 D2**
Taits Beach, UP (Ont.) **21 D1**
Takhini, UP (YT) **45 B3**
Takhini Hotspring, UP (YT) **45 B3**
Takipy, UP (Man.) **30 A1**
Takla Landing < North Tacla Lake 7, UP (BC) **42 G3**
Tako, UP (Sask.) **31 C1**
Taku 6, IR (BC) **45 B4**
Takysie Lake, UP (BC) **41 G1**
Talahaat 16, IR (BC) **42 D4**
Talbot, UP (Ont.) **23 G2**
Talbot, UP (Alta.) **34 H1**
Talbotville Royal, UP (Ont.) **22 E2**
Taleomy 3, IR (BC) **41 G3**
Tall Cree 173, IR (Alta.) **44 A3**
Tall Cree 173A, IR (Alta.) **44 A3**
Tallheo, UP (BC) **41 G3**
Tallman, UP (Sask.) **32 C4**
Talmage, UP (Sask.) **29 B4**
Tamworth, UP (Ont.) **24 G4**
Tanakut 4, IR (BC) **37 E1**
Tancook Island, UP (NS) **9 A4**
Tancredia, UP (Que.) **17 A1**
Tangent, UP (Alta.) **43 H3**
Tangier, UP (NS) **9 D3**
Tangleflags, UP (Sask.) **32 A3**
Tanglewood, UP (Ont.) **17 E4**
Tanguay, UP (Que.) **16 D4**
Tankeah 5, IR (BC) **41 E3**
Tanners Settlement, UP (NS) **10 E2**
Tanoo 9, IR (BC) **41 B2**
Tanquary Camp, UP (NWT) **47 E1**
Tansleyville, UP (Ont.) **27 F2**
Tantallon, UP (NS) **9 A4**
Tantallon, VL (Sask.) **29 D3**
Tanu < Tanoo 9, UP (BC) **41 B2**
Tapley, UP (Ont.) **21 D1**
Taplow, UP (Alta.) **34 G1**
Tappen < North Bay 5, UP (BC) **36 G4**
Tara, VL (Ont.) **23 C2**
Tarantum, UP (PEI) **7 D4**
Tarbert, UP (Ont.) **23 E3**
Tarbot, UP (NS) **8 E3**
Tarbotvale, UP (NS) **8 E3**
Targe Creek 15, IR (BC) **40 A2**
Targettville, UP (NB) **12 G3**
Tar Island, UP (Alta.) **44 C4**
Tarnopol, UP (Sask.) **32 E4**
Tarrtown, UP (NB) **12 A3**
Tarrys, UP (BC) **34 B4**
Tartan, UP (Ont.) **23 D3**
Tarzwell, UP (Ont.) **26 F2**
Taschereau, UP (Que.) **18 A1**
Tashme, UP (BC) **35 B4**
Tashota, UP (Ont.) **27 F1**
Tasiujaq, UP (Que.) **46 F4**
Tasu, UP (BC) **41 B2**
Ta Ta Creek, UP (BC) **34 C4**
Tatalrose, UP (BC) **41 G1**
Tatamagouche, UP (NS) **9 C1**
Tatamagouche Mountain, UP (NS) **9 C1**
Tatcho Creek 11, IR (BC) **45 B4**
Tatchu 13, IR (BC) **39 D3**
Tatchu 13A, IR (BC) **39 D3**
Tate, UP (Sask.) **31 G2**
Tate Corners, UP (Ont.) **22 D2**
Tatehurst, UP (Que.) **17 G2**
Tatelkus Lake 28, IR (BC) **40 A2**
Tatense 16, IR (BC) **41 A1**
Tatla 1, IR (BC) **41 G1**
Tatla Lake, UP (BC) **40 A4**
Tatlayoko Lake, UP (BC) **40 B4**
Tatlock, UP (Ont.) **17 A2**
Tatpo-oose 10, IR (BC) **37 B3**
Tatsadah Lake 14, IR (BC) **40 B1**
Tatselawas 2, IR (BC) **40 B1**
Tatsfield, UP (Sask.) **32 A4**
Tatton, UP (BC) **36 D2**
Tatuk Lake 7, IR (BC) **40 B2**
Tavani, UP (NWT) **46 B3**
Tavistock, UP (Ont.) **22 F1**
Tawatinaw, UP (Alta.) **33 E2**
Taxis River, UP (NB) **12 D4**
Tay Creek, UP (NB) **12 C4**
Tay Falls, UP (NB) **12 C4**
Taylor, UP (Ont.) **17 B4**
Taylor, VL (BC) **43 E3**
Taylor Beach, UP (Sask.) **29 B3**
Taylor Corners, UP (Ont.) **21 C1**
Taylor Lake 50, IR (BC) **42 E3**
Taylor's Bay, UP (Nfld.) **2 B4**
Taylors Head, UP (NS) **9 D3**
Taylorside, UP (Sask.) **32 E4**
Taylors Road, UP (NS) **8 B4**
Taylorton, UP (Sask.) **29 C4**
Taylor Village, UP (NB) **11 H1**
Taylorville, UP (Alta.) **34 F4**
Tay Mills, UP (NB) **12 C1**
Taymouth, UP (NB) **11 C1**
Tayside, UP (Ont.) **17 E2**

Tay Valley, UP (NB) **11 C1**
Tchahchelailthtenum 10, IR (BC) **38 E1**
Tchesinkut Lake, UP (BC) **41 G1**
Tcimotf 1A, IR (BC) **41 E3**
Tea Cove, UP (Nfld.) **4 B2**
Teahans Corner, UP (NB) **11 G2**
Tea Hill, UP (PEI) **7 D4**
Teahmit 3, IR (BC) **39 F4**
Tecumseh, T (Ont.) **22 A3**
Teeds Mills, UP (NB) **11 A1**
Teepee, UP (BC) **45 B4**
Teepee Creek, UP (Alta.) **43 G4**
Teequaloose 3, IR (BC) **35 B3**
Teequaloose 3A, IR (BC) **35 B3**
Tees, UP (Alta.) **33 E4**
Teeslee 3, IR (BC) **40 A1**
Teeswater, VL (Ont.) **23 C3**
Teeta 7, IR (BC) **39 D2**
Teeterville, UP (Ont.) **22 G2**
Tehkummah, UP (Ont.) **25 C3**
Telachick, UP (BC) **40 C2**
Telegraph Cove, UP (BC) **39 E1**
Telegraph Creek, UP (BC) **45 B4**
Telegraph Creek 6, IR (BC) **45 B4**
Telegraph Creek 6A, IR (BC) **45 B4**
Telegraph Point, UP (BC) **42 D4**
Telford, UP (NS) **8 A4**
Telford, UP (Man.) **28 D1**
Telfordville, UP (Alta.) **33 D3**
Telkwa, VL (BC) **42 F4**
Telly Road Crossing, UP (NB) **12 E2**
Temagami, UP (Ont.) **26 F3**
Temagami North, NUP (Ont.) **26 F3**
Témiscaming, T (Que.) **18 A3**
Temperance Vale, UP (NB) **11 B1**
Temperanceville, UP (Ont.) **21 B2**
Tempest, UP (Alta.) **34 G4**
Temple, UP (NB) **11 A1**
Temple Hill, UP (Ont.) **23 D2**
Tempo, UP (Ont.) **22 E2**
Tenaga, UP (Que.) **17 D3**
Tenby, UP (Man.) **29 F3**
Tenby Bay, UP (Ont.) **26 B4**
Ten Mile, UP (BC) **34 B2**
Ten Mile, UP (YT) **45 B3**
Tenmile Cabin, UP (YT) **45 B2**
Tenmile House, UP (PEI) **7 D3**
Tennants Cove, UP (NB) **11 D2**
Tennessee, UP (Que.) **17 F4**
Tennessee < Caughnawaga 14, UP (Que.) **17 G4**
Tennion, UP (Alta.) **34 G3**
Tennycape, UP (NS) **9 B2**
Tennyson, UP (Ont.) **17 B2**
Tent City, UP (Ont.) **21 A1**
10th Line Shore, UP (Ont.) **17 B2**
Tent Island 8, IR (BC) **38 E3**
Tequa 21, IR (BC) **39 G4**
Terence, UP (Man.) **29 E4**
Terence Bay, UP (NS) **9 B4**
Terence Bay River, UP (NS) **9 B4**
Terminal Beach, UP (NS) **9 C4**
Terminus, UP (Ont.) **22 B2**
Terrace, DM (BC) **42 E4**
Terrace Airport, NUP (BC) **42 E4**
Terrace Bay, UP (Ont.) **27 G3**
Terrains de l'Évêque, UP (NB) **12 G4**
Terra Nova, COMM (Nfld.) **3 E4**
Terra Nova, UP (Ont.) **23 E2**
Terra Nova, UP (NS) **8 E4**
Terrasse-Bigras, UP (Que.) **17 F1**
Terrasse-Raymond, UP (Que.) **17 F1**
Terrasse-Robillard, UP (Que.) **17 F1**
Terrasse-Vaudreuil, UP (Que.) **17 F4**
Terra View Heights, UP (Ont.) **21 D1**
Terrebonne, T (Que.) **17 G3**
Terrenceville, T (Nfld.) **2 D2**
Terre Noire, UP (NS) **8 D2**
Terres-Rompues, UP (Que.) **14 B3**
Territoire du Yukon, TERR **1**
Territoires du Nord-Ouest, TERR **1**
Teslin, UP (YT) **45 B4**
Teslin Crossing, UP (YT) **45 B3**
Teslin Lake, UP (YT) **45 B3**
Teslin Lake 7, IR (BC) **45 B4**
Teslin Lake 9, IR (BC) **45 B4**
Teslin Post 13, IR (YT) **45 B4**
Teslin River, UP (YT) **45 B3**
Tesseralik, UP (NWT) **46 G2**
Tessier, VL (Sask.) **31 E1**
Tête-à-la-Baleine, UP (Que.) **5 E3**
Tête Jaune Cache, UP (BC) **40 F3**
Teulon, VL (Man.) **29 H3**
Teviotdale, UP (Ont.) **23 D3**
Tewkesbury, UP (Que.) **15 A2**
Texas, UP (Que.) **17 G4**
Texas Creek, NUP (BC) **35 A1**
Tezzeron Lake 8, IR (BC) **40 B1**
Thalberg, UP (Man.) **30 C4**
Thamesford, UP (Ont.) **22 E1**
Thames Road, UP (Ont.) **22 D1**
Thamesville, VL (Ont.) **22 C2**
Thaxted, UP (Sask.) **32 F4**
The Beaches, UP (Nfld.) **5 G4**
The Block, UP (Nfld.) **4 A3**
The Bluff, UP (NB) **7 A4**
The Boyne, UP (Ont.) **17 D2**
The Broads, UP (Nfld.) **2 G2**
The Brothers 18, IR (NB) **11 D3**
The Bush, UP (Ont.) **17 B3**
The Cache, UP (Ont.) **26 D2**
The Cedars, UP (NB) **11 D2**
The Corners, UP (Man.) **29 D3**
The Dalles 38C, IR (Ont.) **28 F1**
The Depot, UP (Ont.) **25 G2**
Thedford, VL (Ont.) **22 C1**
The Dock, UP (Nfld.) **2 G2**
The Falls, UP (NS) **9 C1**
The Glades, UP (NB) **11 F1**
The Glen, UP (Ont.) **24 G1**
The Gorge, UP (NB) **11 G1**
The Grant, UP (NB) **11 E2**
The Gully, UP (Ont.) **21 E2**
The Halfway < Peguis 18, UP (Man.) **29 H2**
The Hawk, UP (NS) **10 B4**
Theik 2, IR (BC) **38 E3**
The Island, UP (Ont.) **17 C3**
The Key 65, IR (Sask.) **29 D1**
The Keys, UP (Nfld.) **2 H3**
The Ledge, UP (NB) **11 B3**
The Lodge, UP (NS) **9 A4**
The Lookoff, UP (NS) **11 H3**
The Lots, UP (NB) **12 E3**
The Maples, UP (Ont.) **23 E3**
The Narrows, UP (NS) **10 E2**
The Narrows, UP (Man.) **29 G2**
The Narrows 49, IR (Man.) **29 G1**
The Narrows 49A, IR (Man.) **29 G1**
The Ninth, UP (Ont.) **17 D2**
Theodore, VL (Sask.) **29 C2**
Theodosia Arm, UP (BC) **37 C4**
The Pas, T (Man.) **30 A2**
The Pas 21A, IR (Man.) **30 A2**
The Pas 21B, IR (Man.) **30 A2**
The Pas 21C, IR (Man.) **30 A2**
The Pas 21D, IR (Man.) **30 A2**
The Pas 21E, IR (Man.) **30 A2**
The Pas 21F, IR (Man.) **30 A2**
The Pas 21G, IR (Man.) **30 A2**
The Pas 21I, IR (Man.) **30 A2**
The Pas 21J, IR (Man.) **30 A2**
The Pas 21K, IR (Man.) **30 A2**
The Pas 21N, IR (Man.) **30 A2**
The Pas 21P, IR (Man.) **30 A2**
The Pas Airport, UP (Man.) **30 A2**
The Pines, UP (Ont.) **21 G1**
The Points West Bay, UP (NS) **8 D4**
The Range, UP (NB) **11 E1**
Theresa, UP (Ont.) **27 G2**
The Ridge, UP (NB) **11 E1**
The Ridge, UP (Ont.) **24 E3**
Therien, UP (Alta.) **33 G2**
The Rollway, UP (Ont.) **17 D1**
The Sixth, UP (Ont.) **17 D2**
The Slash, UP (Ont.) **25 C3**
Thessalon, T (Ont.) **26 B4**
Thessalon 12, IR (Ont.) **26 B4**
The Tannery, UP (Ont.) **17 B2**
Thetford-Mines, C (Que.) **16 E2**
The Thicket, UP (Nfld.) **2 G2**
The Tickles, UP (Nfld.) **2 E2**
Thetis Island, UP (BC) **38 E3**
The Two Rivers, UP (Sask.) **44 F4**
The Willows, UP (NB) **12 F2**
Thibault, UP (NB) **12 B1**
Thibeauville, UP (NS) **8 D4**
Thicket Portage, UP (Man.) **30 C1**
Thistle, UP (Ont.) **23 D2**
Thistle Creek, UP (YT) **45 A2**
Thivierge, UP (Que.) **13 F3**
Thomas, UP (Que.) **18 H3**
Thomasburg, UP (Ont.) **21 F1**
Thomas Point 5, IR (BC) **39 D1**
Thomas Point 5A, IR (BC) **39 D1**
Thomas Squinas Ranch 2A, IR (BC) **40 A3**
Thomaston Corner, UP (NB) **11 B2**
Thomasville, UP (NS) **10 C4**
Thom Bay, UP (NWT) **47 D4**
Thompson, C (Man.) **30 C1**
Thompson Corner, UP (NB) **11 E1**
Thompson Hill, UP (Ont.) **17 A1**
Thompson Lake, UP (NWT) **44 B1**
Thompson Landing, UP (NWT) **45 F3**
Thompson Sound, UP (BC) **39 F1**
Thompsonville, UP (Ont.) **21 A1**
Thomson Station, UP (NS) **9 B1**
Thomstown, UP (Ont.) **21 D1**
Thorah Beach, UP (Ont.) **21 B1**
Thorah Island, UP (Ont.) **21 B1**
Thorburn, UP (NS) **8 A4**
Thorburn Road, UP (Nfld.) **2 H2**
Thorel House, UP (Ont.) **24 B2**
Thorhild, VL (Alta.) **33 E2**
Thornbury, T (Ont.) **23 D2**
Thornby, UP (Que.) **18 C4**
Thorncliffe, UP (Ont.) **22 C2**
Thorndale, UP (Ont.) **22 E1**
Thorne, UP (Ont.) **18 A3**
Thorne-Centre, UP (Que.) **17 B1**
Thorne-Lake, UP (Que.) **17 B1**
Thornes Cove, UP (NS) **10 B1**
Thornetown, UP (NB) **11 E1**
Thornhill, UP (BC) **42 E4**
Thornhill, UP (Man.) **29 G4**
Thornlea, UP (Nfld.) **2 F2**
Thornloe, VL (Ont.) **26 F2**
Thornton, UP (Ont.) **21 A1**
Thornyhurst, UP (Ont.) **22 B2**
Thorold, C (Ont.) **21 B4**
Thoroughfare, UP (Nfld.) **2 F1**
Thorpe, UP (Ont.) **17 A4**
Thorsby, VL (Alta.) **33 D3**
Thrasher's Corners, UP (Ont.) **21 F1**
Three Arms, UP (Nfld.) **3 B1**
Three Bridges, UP (Ont.) **22 E1**
Three Brooks, UP (NS) **9 D1**
Three Brooks, UP (NB) **12 B3**
Three Creeks, UP (Alta.) **43 H3**
Three Fathom Harbour, UP (NS) **9 C4**
Three Forks, UP (BC) **34 B3**
Three Hills, T (Alta.) **34 F1**
Three Island Pond, NUP (Nfld.) **2 H2**
Three Islands 3, IR (BC) **38 H2**
Three Mile Plains, UP (NS) **9 A3**
Three Mile Rock, NUP (Nfld.) **5 F3**
Three Rock Cove, UP (Nfld.) **4 A2**
Three Valley, UP (BC) **34 A2**
Throne, UP (Alta.) **34 H1**
Throoptown, UP (Ont.) **17 C3**
Thrums, UP (BC) **34 B4**
Thunder Bay, C (Ont.) **27 E3**
Thunder Beach, UP (Ont.) **23 E1**
Thunderchild < New Thunderchild 115B, UP (Sask.) **32 B3**
Thunderchild 115D, IR (Sask.) **32 B3**
Thunder Creek, UP (Sask.) **31 F3**
Thunder Hill, UP (Man.) **29 D1**
Thunder Lake, UP (Alta.) **33 C2**
Thurlow, UP (BC) **37 B3**
Thurso, T (Que.) **17 D1**
Thurston Bay, UP (BC) **37 B3**
Thurston Harbour, UP (BC) **41 B2**
Thwaites, UP (Ont.) **26 F2**
Tiahn 27, IR (BC) **41 A1**
Tiblemont, UP (Que.) **18 C1**
Ticehurst-Corners, UP (Que.) **16 C4**
Tichborne, UP (Ont.) **17 A3**
Tichfield, UP (Sask.) **31 E2**
Tickle Cove, UP (Nfld.) **3 G4**
Ticouapé, UP (Que.) **18 H1**
Tiddville, UP (NS) **10 A2**
Tide Head, VL (NB) **13 C4**
Tidnish, UP (NS) **7 B4**
Tidnish Bridge, UP (NS) **7 B4**
Tidnish Bridge, UP (NB) **7 A4**
Tieland, UP (Alta.) **33 D2**
Tiger Lily, UP (Alta.) **33 C2**
Tignish, VL (PEI) **7 B2**
Tignish Shore, UP (PEI) **7 B2**
Tikeetawkut, UP (NWT) **47 E4**
Tilbury, T (Ont.) **22 B3**
Tilden Lake, UP (Ont.) **26 F4**
Tilgatko 17, IR (BC) **41 H2**
Tilley, UP (Ont.) **17 B3**
Tilley, VL (Alta.) **34 G3**
Tilley Road, UP (NB) **12 F1**
Tillion 4, IR (BC) **36 B1**
Tillsonburg, T (Ont.) **22 F2**
Tilney, UP (Sask.) **31 G3**
Tilston, UP (Man.) **29 D4**
Tilt Cove, COMM (Nfld.) **3 B1**
Tilt Cove, UP (Nfld.) **3 D2**
Tilting, COMM (Nfld.) **3 E1**
Tilton, LID (Nfld.) **2 G2**
Timber Bay, UP (Sask.) **32 E2**
Timberlea, UP (NS) **9 B4**
Timber River, UP (NB) **7 A4**
Timberton < Valley River 63A, UP (Man.) **29 E2**
Timeu, UP (Alta.) **33 D2**
Timiskaming 19, IR (Que.) **26 G2**
Timmins, C (Ont.) **26 E2**
Tims Harbour, UP (Nfld.) **3 E2**
Tincap, UP (Ont.) **17 C3**
Tinchebray, UP (Alta.) **33 F4**
Tingwick, UP (Que.) **16 D2**
Tinker, UP (NB) **12 A3**
Tinmusket 5A, IR (BC) **36 C3**
Tintagel, UP (BC) **40 A1**
Tin Town, UP (Man.) **29 G3**
Tiny, UP (Sask.) **29 C1**
Tioga, UP (Ont.) **23 E2**
Tionaga, UP (Ont.) **26 D2**
Tipella 7, IR (BC) **38 H1**
Tisdale, T (Sask.) **32 F4**
Titanic, UP (Sask.) **32 D4**
Tittle Road, UP (NS) **9 H2**
Titus-Station, NUP (Que.) **16 D3**
Titusville, UP (NB) **11 E2**
Tiverton, UP (NS) **10 A2**
Tiverton, VL (Ont.) **23 B2**
Tizzard's Harbour, UP (Nfld.) **3 D1**
Tlell, UP (BC) **41 B1**
Toad River, UP (BC) **45 C4**
Toanche, UP (Ont.) **23 E1**
Toba, UP (BC) **37 D3**
Tobacco Lake, UP (Ont.) **25 B2**
Tobacco Plains 2, IR (BC) **34 D4**
Tobermory, UP (Ont.) **25 D4**
Tobin Lake, SV (Sask.) **32 F3**
Tobique 20, IR (NB) **12 A3**
Tobique Narrows, UP (NB) **12 A3**
Toby Creek, UP (BC) **34 C3**
Toby Helenes Meadow 9, IR (BC) **40 B4**
Toby Helenes Meadow 10, IR (BC) **40 B4**
Toby Helenes Meadow 11, IR (BC) **40 B4**
Toby Lake 6, IR (BC) **36 C3**
Toby's Meadow 4, IR (BC) **40 B3**
Tod Creek, UP (Alta.) **34 E4**
Todds Island, UP (NS) **9 A4**
Tofield, T (Alta.) **33 E3**
Tofino, VL (BC) **38 A2**
Togo, VL (Sask.) **29 D2**
Toh-quo-eugh 2, IR (BC) **39 C1**
Toimela, UP (Ont.) **27 D3**
Tokenatch 5, IR (BC) **37 C4**
Toksee 30, IR (BC) **41 F4**
Toledo, UP (Ont.) **17 B3**
Tolland, UP (Alta.) **33 G3**
Tollendal, UP (Ont.) **21 A1**
Tolman, UP (Alta.) **34 F1**
Tolmie, UP (Ont.) **23 C1**
Tolmies Corners, UP (Ont.) **17 E2**
Tolsmaville, UP (Ont.) **26 C4**
Tolsta, UP (Que.) **16 E3**
Tolstoi, UP (Man.) **28 B3**
Tomahawk, UP (Alta.) **33 C3**
Tomelin Bluffs, UP (Ont.) **24 B2**
Tomifobia, UP (Que.) **16 C4**
Tomiko, UP (Ont.) **26 G4**
Tomkinsville, UP (NS) **8 F3**
Tom Longboat Corners < Six Nations 40, UP (Ont.) **22 G1**
Tompkins, UP (Nfld.) **4 A3**
Tompkins, VL (Sask.) **31 C3**
Tomslake, UP (BC) **43 F4**
Tomstown, UP (Ont.) **26 F2**
Toney Mills, UP (NS) **9 D1**
Toney River, UP (NS) **9 D1**
Toniata, UP (Man.) **28 E2**
Tonkin, UP (Sask.) **29 C2**
Toogood Arm, UP (Nfld.) **3 D1**
Toon 15, IR (BC) **42 D4**
Toops 3, IR (BC) **36 G4**
Toosey 1, IR (BC) **36 B2**
Toosey 1A, IR (BC) **36 A2**
Toosey 3, IR (BC) **36 B2**
Tootoowiltena 28, IR (BC) **39 F4**
Toowartz 8, IR (BC) **41 D2**
Topcliff, UP (Ont.) **23 D2**
Tophet < Mountbatten 76A, UP (Ont.) **26 C2**
Topland, UP (Alta.) **33 C2**
Topley, UP (BC) **42 G4**
Topley Landing, UP (BC) **42 G4**
Topping, UP (Ont.) **23 C4**
Topsail Pond, NUP (Nfld.) **2 H2**
Toquana 4, IR (BC) **37 C4**
Torbay, T (Nfld.) **2 H2**
Tor Bay, UP (NS) **9 G2**
Torbrook, UP (NS) **10 D1**
Torbrook East, UP (NS) **10 D1**
Torbrook Mines, UP (NS) **10 D1**
Torbrook West, UP (NS) **10 D1**
Torch River, UP (Sask.) **32 F3**
Tork 7, IR (BC) **37 C4**
Torlea, UP (Alta.) **33 F4**
Tornea, UP (Sask.) **29 B1**
Toronto, C (Ont.) **21 B2**
Toronto, UP (PEI) **7 C3**
Torquay, VL (Sask.) **29 B4**
Torrance, UP (Ont.) **23 F1**
Torrington, VL (Alta.) **34 F1**
Tors Cove, UP (Nfld.) **2 H3**
Tory Hill, UP (Ont.) **24 E3**
Tosehka 12, IR (BC) **41 E1**
Toslow, UP (Nfld.) **2 E3**
Tothill, UP (Alta.) **31 B4**
Totnes, UP (Sask.) **31 D2**
Tottenham, VL (Ont.) **21 A2**
Tourelle, UP (Que.) **13 D1**
Tourond, UP (Man.) **28 A2**
Tourville, UP (Que.) **15 D2**
Tourville, NUP (Que.) **16 C3**
Toutes Aides, UP (Man.) **29 F2**
Towdystan, UP (BC) **40 A3**
Towdystan Lake 3, IR (BC) **40 A3**
Towinock 2, IR (BC) **35 A1**
Town Lake, UP (Alta.) **33 D4**
Toyes Hill, UP (Ont.) **17 D2**
Tracadie, T (NB) **12 G1**
Tracadie, UP (NS) **8 C4**
Tracadie Beach, UP (NB) **12 G1**
Tracadie Cross, UP (PEI) **7 D3**
Tracadie Road, UP (NS) **9 G2**
Tracey Mills, UP (NB) **12 A4**
Tracy, T (Que.) **16 A2**
Tracy, VL (NB) **11 C2**
Tracy Depot, UP (NB) **13 A4**
Tracyville, UP (NB) **11 C2**
Traders Cove, UP (BC) **35 F2**
Trafalgar, UP (NS) **9 D2**
Trafalgar Flat 13, IR (BC) **35 B3**
Trail, C (BC) **34 B4**
Tralee, UP (Ont.) **23 D4**
Tramore, UP (Ont.) **24 F1**
Tramping Lake, VL (Sask.) **31 C1**
Tranquility, UP (Ont.) **22 G1**
Transfiguration, UP (Que.) **14 F4**
Travellers Rest, UP (PEI) **7 B3**
Travers, UP (Alta.) **34 G3**
Traverse Bay, UP (Man.) **30 C4**
Traverston, UP (Ont.) **23 D2**
Travor-Road, UP (Que.) **16 C4**
Traynor, UP (Sask.) **31 D1**
Traytown, COMM (Nfld.) **3 F4**
Treadwell, UP (Ont.) **17 E1**
Treasure Island, NUP (Ont.) **17 B4**
Trecastle, UP (Ont.) **23 D3**
Treelon, UP (Sask.) **31 D4**
Treesbank, UP (Man.) **29 F4**
Treesbank Ferry, UP (Man.) **29 F4**
Trefoil, UP (Alta.) **34 G2**
Tregarva, UP (Sask.) **31 G3**
Treherne, VL (Man.) **29 G4**
Tremaine, UP (Man.) **29 F3**
Tremblay, UP (NB) **12 E1**
Tremont, UP (NS) **10 D1**
Trenche, UP (Que.) **18 G2**
Trend Village, UP (Ont.) **17 D4**
Trenholm, UP (Que.) **16 C3**
Trentham, UP (Man.) **28 B2**
Trenton, T (Ont.) **21 F1**
Trenton, T (NS) **9 D1**
Trenton, CFB/BFC, MIL (Ont.) **21 F1**
Trent River, UP (Ont.) **21 E1**
Trepassey, T (Nfld.) **2 G4**
Trevelyan, UP (Ont.) **17 C3**
Trevithick Subdivision, NUP (Alta.) **33 E3**
Trewdale, UP (Sask.) **31 F3**
Triangle, UP (Alta.) **33 B1**
Triangle, UP (Nfld.) **6 H4**
Tribune, VL (Sask.) **29 B4**
Tring-Jonction, VL (Que.) **15 B4**
Trinité-des-Monts, UP (Que.) **14 G3**
Trinity, COMM (Nfld.) **3 G4**
Trinity, LID (Nfld.) **3 F3**
Trinity < Trinity (COMM), UP (Nfld.) **3 G4**
Trinity East, UP (Nfld.) **3 G4**
Trinity Valley, UP (BC) **35 G1**
Triple Bay Park, UP (Ont.) **23 F1**
Tripp Settlement, UP (NB) **11 C1**
Tristram, UP (Alta.) **33 E4**
Triton – Jim's Cove – Card's Harbour, RD (Nfld.) **3 B2**
Triton West < Triton – Jim's Cove – Card's Harbour, UP (Nfld.) **3 B2**
Trochu, T (Alta.) **34 F1**
Trois-Lacs, UP (Que.) **16 D3**
Trois-Lacs, UP (Que.) **16 F3**
Trois-Pistoles, T (Que.) **14 F3**
Trois-Rivières, C (Que.) **16 C1**
Trois-Rivières-Ouest, T (Que.) **16 B1**
Trois-Ruisseaux, UP (NB) **7 A4**
Trois-Ruisseaux, UP (Que.) **19 H3**
Trois-Saumons, UP (Que.) **15 D2**
Trois-Saumons-Station, UP (Que.) **15 D2**
Trossachs, UP (Sask.) **31 H4**
Trottier, UP (Que.) **16 D2**
Trout Brook, UP (NB) **12 E2**
Trout Brook, UP (NS) **9 B4**
Trout Creek, T (Ont.) **25 H2**
Trout Lake, UP (Alta.) **44 B4**
Trout Lake, UP (NWT) **45 D4**
Trout Lake, UP (BC) **34 B2**
Trout Lake Alec 16, IR (BC) **40 B2**
Trout Lake Jonny 15, IR (BC) **40 B2**
Trout River, COMM (Nfld.) **5 F4**
Trout-River, UP (Que.) **17 F2**
Trout Stream, UP (NB) **12 G1**
Trouty, UP (Nfld.) **3 G4**
Trowbridge, UP (Ont.) **23 C3**
Troy, UP (NS) **8 C4**
Troy, UP (Ont.) **22 G1**
Troy, UP (Ont.) **22 C3**
Truax, UP (Sask.) **31 G3**
Trudeau, UP (Ont.) **27 H3**
Trudel, UP (NB) **12 F1**
Truemanville, UP (NS) **9 A1**
Truman, UP (Alta.) **33 G2**
Trump Islands, UP (Nfld.) **3 D1**
Truro, T (NS) **9 C2**
Truro 27A, IR (NS) **9 C2**
Truro 27B, IR (NS) **9 C2**
Truro 27C, IR (NS) **9 C2**
Truro Heights, UP (NS) **9 C2**
Trutch, UP (BC) **43 C1**
Tryon, UP (PEI) **7 C4**
Tryon Settlement, UP (NB) **11 B2**
Tsachla Lake 8, IR (BC) **40 A3**
Tsahaheh 1, IR (BC) **38 C2**
Tsai-kwi-ee 21, IR (BC) **41 F4**
Tsak 9, IR (BC) **42 G3**
Tsarksis 2, IR (BC) **39 E3**
Tsaukan 12, IR (BC) **35 A1**
Tsawawmuck 1, IR (BC) **35 B2**
Tsawcome 1, IR (BC) **38 E2**
Tsawwassen, IR (BC) **38 F3**
Tsawwati 1, IR (BC) **37 A1**
Tsaytut Island 1C, IR (BC) **42 F2**
Tseatah 2, IR (BC) **35 A4**
Tseetsum-Sawlasilah 32, IR (BC) **41 F4**
Tsemknawalqan 79, IR (BC) **41 D1**
Tseoowa 4, IR (BC) **38 B3**
Tsichgass 2, IR (BC) **41 G1**
Tsimlairen 15, IR (BC) **41 D1**
Tsimmanweenclist 2, IR (BC) **42 D3**
Tsimpsean 2, IR (BC) **42 C4**
Tsimtack 7, IR (BC) **41 D2**
Tsinkahtl 8, IR (BC) **35 B1**
Tsinquiese 5, IR (BC) **41 E1**
Tsinstikeptum 9, IR (BC) **35 E3**
Tsinstikeptum 10, IR (BC) **35 E2**
Tsintahktl 2, IR (BC) **35 B2**
Tsitsk 3, IR (BC) **42 F3**
Tsooahdie 15, IR (BC) **37 E4**
Tsowwin 10, IR (BC) **39 E3**
Tsulquate 4, IR (BC) **39 D1**
Tsunnia Lake 5, IR (BC) **37 D1**
Tsupmeet 5, IR (BC) **42 F2**
Tsuquanah 2, IR (BC) **38 C3**
Tsussie 6, IR (BC) **38 E3**
Tubbs Corners, UP (Ont.) **21 E1**
Tuberose, UP (Sask.) **31 D2**
Tuck Inlet 89, IR (BC) **42 C4**
Tuckkwiowhum 1, IR (BC) **35 B3**
Tuckozap 24, IR (BC) **35 B2**
Tudor, UP (Alta.) **34 F2**
Tuffnell, UP (Sask.) **29 B1**
Tuftsville, UP (Ont.) **21 F1**
Tugaske, VL (Sask.) **31 F2**
Tugtown, UP (NB) **12 C3**
Tugwell Island 21, IR (BC) **42 C4**
Tuktoyaktuk, HAM (NWT) **45 C1**
Tulameen, UP (BC) **35 C3**
Tulliby Lake, UP (Alta.) **33 H3**
Tullis, UP (Sask.) **31 E2**
Tullochgorum, UP (Que.) **17 G2**
Tulsequah, UP (BC) **45 B4**
Tum-bah 5, IR (BC) **42 E3**
Tummel, UP (Ont.) **29 D2**
Tungsten, UP (NWT) **45 C3**
Tunis, UP (Ont.) **26 E1**
Tunnel 6, IR (BC) **35 B4**
Tununuk, UP (NWT) **45 B1**
Tupper, UP (BC) **43 F4**
Tupperville, UP (Ont.) **22 C2**
Tupperville, UP (NS) **10 C1**
Tupperville, UP (Que.) **16 E3**
Turgeon, UP (Que.) **15 C3**
Turin, UP (Alta.) **34 G3**
Turin, UP (Ont.) **22 C3**
Turkey Point, UP (Ont.) **22 G2**
Turks Cove, UP (Nfld.) **2 G1**
Turnberry, UP (Man.) **30 A2**
Turners, UP (Ont.) **23 C2**
Turner's Bight, UP (Nfld.) **6 G3**
Turner Settlement, UP (NB) **12 A3**
Turnertown, UP (Que.) **16 D4**
Turner Valley, VL (Alta.) **34 E3**
Turnerville, UP (Ont.) **22 C3**
Turnip Cove < Pool's Cove (COMM), UP (Nfld.) **2 C2**
Turnor Lake, UP (Sask.) **44 D4**
Turnor Lake 193B, IR (Sask.) **44 D4**
Turnor Lake 194, IR (Sask.) **44 D4**
Turriff, UP (Ont.) **24 F3**
Turtle Creek, UP (NB) **11 G1**
Turtleford, VL (Sask.) **32 B3**
Turtle Lake, UP (Ont.) **24 A2**
Turtle Point 12, IR (BC) **41 D2**
Turtle Valley, UP (BC) **36 G4**
Tusket, UP (NS) **10 B3**
Tusket Falls, UP (NS) **10 B3**
Tutela Heights, NUP (Ont.) **22 G1**
Tutshi, UP (BC) **45 B4**
Tuttle, UP (Alta.) **34 E1**
Tutu Creek 4, IR (BC) **43 C4**
Tuxford, VL (Sask.) **31 G3**
Tway, UP (Sask.) **32 E4**
Tweed, VL (Ont.) **24 G4**
Tweedie, UP (Alta.) **33 F2**
Tweedie, UP (NB) **12 A3**
Tweedie Brook, UP (NB) **12 F3**
Tweedside, UP (NB) **11 B2**
Tweedsmuir, UP (Sask.) **32 D3**
Twelve O'Clock Point, UP (Ont.) **21 F1**
Twentymile Cabin, UP (YT) **45 B2**
Twentyone Mile, UP (YT) **45 B3**
Twentysix Mile, UP (YT) **45 B3**
Twidwell Bend, UP (BC) **43 D4**
Twilite Trailer Court, NUP (Sask.) **32 D3**
Twillingate, T (Nfld.) **3 D1**
Twin Butte, UP (Alta.) **34 E4**
Twin City, UP (Ont.) **27 D3**
Twin Creeks, UP (BC) **38 E2**
Twin Elm, UP (Ont.) **17 C2**
Twin Falls, UP (Nfld.) **6 D3**
Twin Falls, UP (Ont.) **26 E1**
Twining, UP (Alta.) **34 F1**
Twin Island 10, IR (BC) **38 E4**
Twin Islands, UP (BC) **38 G2**
Twin Lakes Beach, UP (Man.) **29 H3**
Twin Rock Valley, UP (NS) **8 D3**
Twin Valley, UP (Sask.) **31 F4**
Two Brooks, UP (NB) **12 B2**
Two Creeks, UP (Man.) **29 E3**
Two Creeks, UP (Alta.) **33 B2**
Two Guns < Sarcee 145, UP (Alta.) **34 E2**
Two Hills, T (Alta.) **33 F3**
Two Islands, UP (NS) **9 A2**
Twomey, UP (Alta.) **33 E4**
Two Mile, UP (BC) **42 F3**
Two Mile Creek 16, IR (BC) **35 B2**
Two Mile Creek 16A, IR (BC) **35 B2**
Two O'Clock < Wikwemikong Unceded 26, UP (Ont.) **25 C2**
Two Rivers, UP (NS) **11 H2**
Two Rivers, UP (BC) **43 E3**
Twoyghalst 16, IR (BC) **35 B1**
Tye, UP (BC) **34 B4**
Tyee, UP (BC) **41 D1**
Tyendinaga 38, IR (Ont.) **21 G1**
Tymgowzan 12, IR (BC) **42 C4**
Tyndall, UP (Man.) **28 B1**
Tyndal Road, UP (NS) **9 A1**
Tynemouth Creek, UP (NB) **11 E3**
Tyner, UP (Sask.) **31 D2**
Tyneside, UP (Ont.) **21 A4**
Tyne Valley, VL (PEI) **7 B3**
Tyotown, UP (Ont.) **17 E2**
Tyrconnell, UP (Ont.) **22 D2**
Tyrone, UP (PEI) **7 C4**
Tyvan, UP (Sask.) **29 B3**
Tzart-lam 5, IR (BC) **38 E3**
Tzeachten 13, IR (BC) **35 A4**
Tzetzi Lake 11, IR (BC) **40 A3**

U

Ucausley 4, IR (BC) **40 A1**
Uchi Lake, UP (Ont.) **30 E4**
Ucluelet, VL (BC) **38 A3**
Ucluth 6, IR (BC) **38 A3**
Udney, UP (Ont.) **23 G1**
Udora, UP (Ont.) **21 B1**
Ufford, UP (Ont.) **24 B2**
Uhthoff, UP (Ont.) **23 F1**
Uigg, UP (PEI) **7 D4**
Ukalta, UP (Alta.) **33 E3**
Ukraina, UP (Man.) **29 E2**
Ukunemask, UP (Que.) **18 C2**
Ulchen, UP (Que.) **17 G2**
Ulkatcho, UP (BC) **41 H2**
Ulkatcho 1, IR (BC) **41 H2**
Ulkatcho 5, IR (BC) **41 G2**
Ulkatcho 6, IR (BC) **41 H2**
Ulkatcho 13, IR (BC) **40 A3**
Ulkatcho 14A, IR (BC) **40 A3**
Ullin, UP (Alta.) **33 C4**
Ullswater, UP (Ont.) **24 B2**
Ulthakoush 11, IR (BC) **41 E2**
Ulverton, UP (Que.) **16 C3**
Umfreville, UP (Ont.) **27 B1**
Umingmaktok, UP (NWT) **45 F1**
Umingmaqautik, UP (Que.) **6 C1**
Umpherville, UP (Man.) **30 A2**
Uncas, UP (Alta.) **33 E3**
Uncha Lake 13A, IR (BC) **41 H1**
Underhill, UP (Man.) **29 E4**
Underwood, UP (Ont.) **23 B2**
Undine, UP (NB) **12 A2**
Ungardlek, UP (Nfld.) **6 E2**
Ungers Corner, UP (Ont.) **22 G2**
Uniacke Hill, UP (NB) **7 A4**
Union, UP (Ont.) **22 E2**
Union, UP (NS) **9 C2**
Union, UP (Ont.) **17 B4**
Union, UP (Ont.) **22 B4**
Union, NUP (PEI) **7 C4**
Union Bay, UP (BC) **38 C1**
Union Bay 4, IR (BC) **38 E3**
Union Bay 31, IR (BC) **42 C4**
Union Centre, UP (NS) **9 D2**
Union Corner, UP (NS) **9 A3**
Union Corner, UP (PEI) **7 B3**
Union Corner, UP (NB) **11 A1**
Union Creek, UP (Ont.) **23 H1**
Uniondale, UP (Ont.) **22 E1**
Union Hall, UP (Ont.) **17 B2**
Union Point, UP (Man.) **28 A2**
Union Road, UP (PEI) **7 C4**
Union Road, UP (PEI) **7 D4**
Union Settlement, UP (NB) **11 E1**
Union Square, UP (NS) **10 E2**
Unionvale, UP (PEI) **7 A3**
Unipouheos 121, IR (Alta.) **33 G3**
Unity, T (Sask.) **32 A4**
University Hill, UP (BC) **38 F2**
Uno, UP (Man.) **29 E3**
Uno Park, UP (Ont.) **26 F3**
Unpukpulquatum 8, IR (BC) **35 B2**
Unwin, UP (Sask.) **32 A4**
Upham, UP (NB) **11 E2**
Uphill, UP (Ont.) **23 H1**
Uplands, UP (Ont.) **22 E1**
Uplands Park, UP (NS) **9 B3**
Upper Afton, UP (NS) **8 B4**
Upper Amherst Cove, UP (Nfld.) **3 G4**
Upper Barnaby, UP (NB) **12 E3**
Upper Barneys River, UP (NS) **8 A4**
Upper Bass River, UP (NS) **9 B2**
Upper Belleisle, UP (NB) **11 E2**
Upper Big Tracadie, UP (NS) **8 C4**
Upper Blackville, UP (NB) **12 E3**
Upper Blackville Bridge, UP (NB) **12 E3**
Upper Blandford, UP (NS) **9 A4**
Upper Branch, UP (NS) **10 D2**
Upper Brighton, UP (NB) **12 A4**
Upper Brockway, UP (NB) **11 B2**
Upper Brookfield, UP (NS) **9 C2**
Upper Brookside, UP (NS) **9 C2**
Upper Buctouche, UP (NB) **12 G4**
Upper Burgeo, UP (Nfld.) **4 D4**
Upper Burlington, UP (NS) **9 A3**
Upper Burnside, UP (NS) **9 C2**
Upper California, UP (NB) **12 A3**
Upper Canada Village, UP (Ont.) **17 D2**
Upper Canard, UP (NS) **11 H3**
Upper Cape, UP (NB) **7 B4**
Upper Chelsea, UP (NS) **10 D2**
Upper Clarence, UP (NS) **10 C1**
Upper Clements, UP (NS) **10 C1**
Upper Clyde River, UP (NS) **10 C3**
Upper Coverdale, UP (NB) **11 G1**
Upper Crossing, UP (NB) **12 D1**
Upper Cutbank, UP (BC) **43 E4**
Upper Derby, UP (NB) **12 E3**
Upper Dorchester, UP (NB) **11 H1**
Upper Dundee, UP (NB) **13 D4**
Upper Durham, UP (NB) **11 C1**
Upper Dyke Village, UP (NS) **11 H3**
Upper Economy, UP (NS) **9 B2**
Upper Falmouth, UP (NS) **9 A3**
Upper Ferry, UP (Nfld.) **4 A3**
Upper Fraser, UP (BC) **40 D1**
Upper Gagetown, UP (NB) **11 D1**
Upper Gaspereau, UP (NB) **12 E4**
Upper Glencoe, UP (NS) **8 C3**
Upper Golden Grove, UP (NB) **11 E2**
Upper Goshen, UP (NB) **11 F2**
Upper Grand Mira, UP (NS) **8 E4**
Upper Granville, UP (NS) **10 C1**
Upper Greenwich, UP (NB) **11 D2**
Upper Gulf Shore, UP (NS) **9 B1**
Upper Hainesville, UP (NB) **11 B1**
Upper Hammonds Plains, UP (NS) **9 B3**
Upper Hat Creek, UP (BC) **35 B1**
Upper Hat Creek 1, IR (BC) **36 C4**
Upper Hay River 212, IR (Alta.) **44 A2**
Upper Island Cove, T (Nfld.) **2 G2**
Upper Kempt Head, UP (NS) **8 E3**
Upper Kemptown, UP (NS) **9 C2**
Upper Kennetcook, UP (NS) **9 B2**
Upper Kent, UP (NB) **12 A3**
Upper Keswick, UP (NB) **11 C1**
Upper Keswick Ridge, NUP (NB) **11 C1**
Upper Kingsburg, UP (NS) **10 E2**
Upper Kintore, UP (NB) **12 A3**
Upper Kluskus Lake 9, IR (BC) **40 A3**
Upper Knoxford, UP (NB) **12 A3**
Upper Laberge, UP (YT) **45 B3**
Upper LaHave, UP (NS) **10 E2**
Upper Lakeville, UP (NS) **9 C3**
Upper Lawrencetown, UP (NS) **9 B4**
Upper Leitches Creek, UP (NS) **8 E3**
Upper Letang, UP (NB) **11 C3**
Upper Liard, UP (YT) **45 C4**
Upper Linden, UP (NS) **9 B1**
Upper Little Ridge, UP (NB) **11 A3**
Upper Loch Lomond, UP (NB) **11 E2**
Upper Malagash, UP (NS) **9 C1**
Upper Margaree, UP (NS) **8 D3**
Upper Maugerville, UP (NB) **11 C1**
Upper-Melbourne, UP (Que.) **16 C3**
Upper Middle River, UP (NS) **8 D3**
Upper Mills, UP (NB) **11 B3**
Upper Mills, UP (NB) **11 B2**
Upper Mount Thom, UP (NS) **9 C2**
Upper Musquodoboit, UP (NS) **9 C3**
Upper Napan, UP (NB) **12 F2**
Upper Nappan, UP (NS) **9 A1**
Upper Nelson, NUP (NB) **12 E3**
Upper Nepa 6, IR (BC) **35 B1**
Upper New Cornwall, UP (NS) **10 E2**
Upper New Harbour, UP (NS) **9 G2**
Upper New Horton, UP (NB) **11 G2**
Upper Nine Mile River, UP (NS) **9 B3**
Upper Northampton, UP (NB) **11 A1**
Upper Northfield, UP (NS) **10 E2**
Upper North River, UP (NS) **9 C2**
Upper North Sydney, UP (NS) **8 E3**
Upper Ohio, UP (NS) **10 C3**
Upper Onslow, UP (NS) **9 C2**
Upper Pereaux, UP (NS) **11 H3**

Up
POPULATED PLACES

Upper Point de Bute, UP (NB) 7 A4
Upper Pokemouche, UP (NB) 12 G1
Upper Pomquet, UP (NS) 8 B4
Upper Port La Tour, UP (NS) 10 C4
Upper Queensbury, UP (NB) 11 B1
Upper Rawdon, UP (NS) 9 B3
Upper Rexton, UP (NB) 12 G3
Upper Ridge, UP (NB) 11 F1
Upper River Denys, UP (NS) 8 C4
Upper Rockport, UP (NB) 11 H2
Upper Royalton, UP (NB) 12 A3
Upper Sackville, UP (NS) 9 B3
Upper St-Maurice, UP (NB) 12 G3
Upper Salt Springs, UP (NB) 11 E2
Upper Sheila, UP (NB) 12 G1
Upper Smithfield, UP (NS) 9 E2
Upper Southampton, UP (NB) 11 A1
Upper South River, UP (NS) 9 F2
Upper Southwest Mabou, UP (NS) 8 C3
Upper Springfield, UP (NS) 9 F2
Upper Stewiacke, UP (NS) 9 C2
Upper Stoneridge, UP (NB) 11 B1
Upper Sumas 6, IR (BC) 38 H3
Upper Tahltan 4, IR (BC) 45 B4
Upper Tantallon, UP (NS) 9 A4
Upper Tilley Road, UP (NB) 12 F1
Upperton, UP (NB) 11 E2
Upper Tower Hill, UP (NB) 11 B3
Upper Tracy, UP (NB) 11 C2
Upper Tsinkahtl 8A, IR (BC) 35 B1
Upper Vaughan, UP (NS) 9 A3
Upper Wards Creek, UP (NB) 11 F2
Upper Washabuck, UP (NS) 8 D3
Upper Waterville, UP (NB) 12 A4
Upper Wedgeport, UP (NS) 10 B4
Upper West Pubnico, UP (NS) 10 B4
Upper Whitehead, UP (NS) 9 G2
Upper Wicklow, UP (NB) 12 A3
Upper Woods Harbour, UP (NS) 10 B4
Upper Woodstock, UP (NB) 11 A1
Upsala, UP (Ont.) 27 C2
Upsalquitch, UP (NB) 13 C4
Upsowis 6, IR (BC) 39 D2
Uptergrove, UP (Ont.) 23 G1
Upton, UP (PEI) 7 E3
Upton, VL (Que.) 16 B3
Uranium City, UP (Sask.) 44 D2
Urbainville, UP (PEI) 7 B3
Urbania, UP (NS) 9 B2
Uren, UP (Sask.) 31 E3
Urney, UP (NB) 11 F2
Ursa, UP (Ont.) 24 D3
Usherville, UP (Sask.) 29 C1
Usk, UP (BC) 42 E4
Usona, UP (Alta.) 33 D4
Usualuk, UP (NWT) 46 F1
Utica, UP (Ont.) 21 C1
Utikoomak Lake 155, IR (Alta.) 44 A4
Utikoomak Lake 155A, IR (Alta.) 44 A4
Utikoomak Lake 155B, IR (Alta.) 44 A4
Utopia, UP (NB) 11 C3
Utopia, UP (Ont.) 21 A1
Uttoxeter, UP (Ont.) 22 C1
Uxbridge, UP (Ont.) 21 B1
Uzta 4, IR (BC) 40 B1
Uzta 7A, IR (BC) 40 B1

V

Vachell, UP (Ont.) 21 B1
Vade, UP (Sask.) 31 E1
Val-Alain, UP (Que.) 15 A4
Val-Barrette, VL (Que.) 18 E4
Val-Bélair, T (Que.) 15 F3
Valbrand, UP (Sask.) 32 D3
Val-Brillant, VL (Que.) 13 A2
Valcartier, BFC/CFB, MIL (Que.) 15 A2
Valcartier-Village, UP (Que.) 15 F3
Val-Clermont, UP (Que.) 18 A1
Val-Comeau, UP (NB) 12 G1
Val Coté, UP (Ont.) 20 B4
Valcourt, T (Que.) 16 C3
Valcourt-Station, NUP (Que.) 16 C3
Val-d'Amour, UP (NB) 13 C4
Val-David, VL (Que.) 18 F4
Val-des-Bois, UP (Que.) 18 D4
Val-des-Bois, UP (Que.) 18 B2
Val-des-Lacs, UP (Que.) 18 F4
Val-d'Or, T (Que.) 18 B2
Valdor, UP (Que.) 17 D1
Val-Doucet, UP (NB) 12 F1
Val-du-Lac, UP (Que.) 16 D4
Val-du-Lac, UP (Que.) 17 C1
Val-du-Repos, UP (Que.) 18 B2
Val-Émard, UP (Que.) 18 D4
Valemount, VL (BC) 40 F3
Valencay, UP (Que.) 17 D1
Valens, UP (Ont.) 22 G1
Valentia, UP (Ont.) 21 C1
Vale-Perkins, UP (Que.) 16 C4
Valeport, UP (Sask.) 31 G2
Valetta, UP (Ont.) 22 B3
Val Gagné, UP (Ont.) 26 E1
Valhalla, UP (Alta.) 43 F4
Valhalla Centre, UP (Alta.) 43 F4
Valin, UP (Que.) 14 B3
Val-Jalbert, UP (Que.) 18 H1
Valjean, UP (Sask.) 31 F3
Val-Lambert, UP (NB) 15 G2
Vallée-Jonction, VL (Que.) 15 B4
Vallentyne, UP (Ont.) 21 B1
Valleville, UP (Que.) 15 C3
Valley, UP (NS) 9 C2
Valley, UP (PEI) 7 D4
Valley, UP (NB) 11 A1
Valley Centre, UP (Sask.) 31 D1
Valley Cross Roads, UP (NS) 9 C2
Valley East, T (Ont.) 26 E4
Valleyfield, UP (PEI) 7 D4
Valleyfield < Badger's Quay – Valleyfield – Pool's Island, UP (Nfld.) 3 F2
Valley Green Beach, UP (Ont.) 24 B3
Valley Mills, UP (NS) 8 D4
Valley Park, UP (Sask.) 31 E1
Valley River, UP (Man.) 29 E2
Valley River 63A, IR (Man.) 29 E2
Valley Road, UP (NS) 9 A1
Valley Road, UP (NB) 11 B3
Valleys Corners, UP (Ont.) 17 E2
Valleyview, T (Alta.) 33 A1
Valley View, UP (BC) 43 F3
Valley View, NUP (Alta.) 33 D4
Vallican, UP (BC) 34 B4
Val-Limoges, UP (Que.) 18 D3
Val Marie, VL (Sask.) 31 E4
Val-Melanson, UP (NB) 13 C4
Val-Menaud, UP (Que.) 14 A3
Val-Michaud, UP (NB) 12 E1
Valmont, UP (Que.) 16 B1
Val-Morin, UP (Que.) 18 F4
Val-Morin-Station, UP (Que.) 18 F4
Val-Nadeau, UP (NB) 15 G2
Val Oakes, UP (NB) 15 G2
Val-Ombreuse, UP (Que.) 18 D4
Valor, UP (Sask.) 31 F4
Valora, UP (Ont.) 27 C2
Val-Paquin, UP (Que.) 17 C1
Val-Paradis, UP (Que.) 26 G1
Valparaiso, VL (Sask.) 32 F4
Val-Piché, UP (Que.) 18 C1
Val Quentin, SV (Alta.) 33 D3
Val-Racine, UP (Que.) 16 F3
Val Rita, UP (Ont.) 20 C4
Val-St-Gilles, UP (Que.) 18 A1
Val-St-Tropez, UP (Que.) 18 G4
Val-Senneville, UP (Que.) 18 B2
Val-Shefford, UP (Que.) 16 B4
Val Soucy, UP (Alta.) 33 E3
Val-Viger, UP (Que.) 18 E3
Van Allens, UP (Ont.) 17 C2
Vananda, UP (BC) 38 C1
Vanastra, UP (Ont.) 23 B4
Vanbrugh, UP (Ont.) 24 G2
Van-Bruyssel, UP (Que.) 18 H2
Van Camp, UP (Ont.) 17 D2
Vancouver, C (BC) 38 F2
Vandecar, UP (Ont.) 22 F1
Vandeleur, UP (Ont.) 23 D2
Vanderhoof, VL (BC) 40 B2
Vandry, UP (Que.) 18 G2
Vandura, UP (Sask.) 29 D3
Vanessa, UP (Ont.) 22 G2
Vanguard, VL (Sask.) 31 E3
Van Horne, UP (Ont.) 22 C3
Vanier, C (Ont.) 17 E4
Vanier, T (Que.) 15 G3
Vankleek Hill, T (Ont.) 17 E1
Vankleek Hill Station, UP (Ont.) 17 E1
Vanneck, UP (Ont.) 22 D1
Van Parry Subdivision, NUP (Ont.) 22 F2
Vanrena, UP (Alta.) 43 G3
Vanscoy, VL (Sask.) 31 E1
Vansickle, UP (Ont.) 24 E4
Vanstone, UP (Sask.) 29 C2
Vantage, UP (Sask.) 31 F3
Vardy, UP (Ont.) 24 F2
Varennes, C (Que.) 17 H3
Vargas Island 31, IR (BC) 39 G4
Varna, UP (Ont.) 23 B4
Varney, UP (Ont.) 23 D3
Vars, UP (Ont.) 17 D1
Vasey, UP (Ont.) 23 F1
Vassan, UP (Que.) 18 B2
Vassar, UP (Man.) 28 C3
Vaucluse, UP (Que.) 16 A2
Vaucroft Beach, UP (BC) 38 D2
Vaudreuil, T (Que.) 17 G1
Vaudreuil-sur-le-Lac, VL (Que.) 17 G1
Vaughan, T (Ont.) 21 A2
Vaughan, UP (NS) 9 A3
Vaughan, UP (Ont.) 21 A4
Vautour, UP (NB) 12 F3
Vautrin, UP (Que.) 18 B1
Vauxhall, T (Alta.) 34 G3
Vavenby, UP (BC) 36 G3
Vawn, VL (Sask.) 32 B4
Vega, UP (Alta.) 33 D2
Vegreville, T (Alta.) 33 F3
Veillardville, UP (Sask.) 32 G4
Veinerville, NUP (Alta.) 31 B3
Veldt, UP (Alta.) 34 G1
Vendée, UP (Que.) 18 E4
Veneer, UP (NB) 12 A2
Venice, UP (Alta.) 33 F2
Venise, UP (Que.) 16 D4
Venise-en-Québec, UP (Que.) 16 A4
Venison Islands, UP (Nfld.) 6 H4
Venlaw, UP (Man.) 29 E2
Venn, UP (Sask.) 31 G1
Vennachar, UP (Ont.) 24 G3
Vennachar Junction, UP (Ont.) 24 G2
Venosta, UP (Que.) 18 D4
Ventnor, UP (Ont.) 17 D2
Ventry, UP (Ont.) 23 D3
Vera, UP (Sask.) 32 A4
Verbois, UP (Que.) 15 E1
Verchères, VL (Que.) 16 A3
Verdun, C (Que.) 17 H1
Verdun, UP (Ont.) 23 B3
Veregin, VL (Sask.) 29 D2
Vereker, UP (Ont.) 22 A4
Verlo, UP (Sask.) 31 D3
Vermilion, T (Alta.) 33 G3
Vermilion Bay, UP (Ont.) 28 H1
Vermilion Chutes, UP (Alta.) 44 B3
Vermilion Crossing, UP (BC) 34 C2
Vermilion Forks 1, IR (BC) 35 D3
Verndale, UP (Sask.) 32 E4
Verner, UP (Ont.) 25 G1
Vernet, UP (Que.) 18 E4
Vernon, C (BC) 35 F2
Vernon, UP (Ont.) 17 D2
Vernon Bridge, UP (PEI) 7 D4
Vernon Camp, UP (BC) 39 F2
Vernon River, UP (PEI) 7 D4
Vernonville, UP (Ont.) 21 E2
Verona, UP (Ont.) 17 A3
Verrett, UP (NB) 15 H2
Verschoyle, UP (Ont.) 22 F2
Verte-Vallée, UP (Que.) 17 F1
Verulam Park, UP (Ont.) 23 H2
Verwood, UP (Sask.) 31 G4
Vesper, UP (Sask.) 31 D3
Vesta, UP (Ont.) 23 C2
Vestfold, UP (Man.) 29 H3
Vesuvius, UP (BC) 38 E3
Veteran, VL (Alta.) 34 H1
Vianney, UP (Que.) 16 E2
Vibank, VL (Sask.) 31 H3
Viceroy, VL (Sask.) 31 G4
Vickers, UP (Ont.) 23 C2
Victoire, UP (Sask.) 32 C3
Victor, UP (Alta.) 34 G1
Victoria, C (BC) 38 F4
Victoria, T (Nfld.) 2 G2
Victoria, UP (NS) 9 B1
Victoria, UP (NB) 12 F2
Victoria, UP (Ont.) 21 F1
Victoria, VL (PEI) 7 C4
Victoria Beach, UP (NS) 10 B1
Victoria Beach, UP (Man.) 30 C4
Victoria Beach, UP (NB) 11 D2
Victoria Beach, UP (Ont.) 21 E2
Victoria Bridge, UP (NS) 8 E4
Victoria Corner, UP (NB) 12 A4
Victoria Corners, UP (Ont.) 21 B1
Victoria Corners, UP (Ont.) 23 D2
Victoria Cove, UP (Nfld.) 3 D2
Victoria Cross, UP (PEI) 7 D4
Victoria Harbour, UP (NS) 11 G3
Victoria Harbour, VL (Ont.) 23 F1
Victoria Line, UP (NS) 8 C4
Victoria Mills, UP (Ont.) 22 G1
Victoria Mines, UP (NS) 8 F3
Victoria Park, UP (Ont.) 23 F1
Victoria Road, UP (Ont.) 23 H1
Victoria Road, UP (NS) 8 C3
Victoria Springs, UP (Ont.) 24 D4
Victoria Vale, UP (NS) 10 D1
Victoriaville, T (Que.) 16 D2
Victoria West, UP (PEI) 7 A3
Victory, UP (NS) 10 C2
Victory Hill, UP (Ont.) 17 E4
Vidette, UP (BC) 36 D3
Vidir, UP (Man.) 29 H2
Vidora, UP (Sask.) 31 C4
Vieille-Église, UP (Que.) 16 D1
Vienna, VL (Ont.) 22 F2
Vieux-Comptoir, UP (Que.) 20 E3
Vieux-Fort, UP (Que.) 5 F2
Vieux-Fort, UP (Que.) 26 G3
Vieux-Piopolis, UP (Que.) 16 F3
Vieux-Poste, UP (Que.) 5 E2
Viewfield, UP (Sask.) 29 C4
Viewlake, UP (Ont.) 21 C1
Viewmount, UP (NS) 11 G3
Viewpoint, UP (Alta.) 33 E4
View Royal, UP (BC) 38 F4
Vigneau, UP (Que.) 7 F1
Vigo, UP (Ont.) 23 F2
Viking, T (Alta.) 33 F4
Villa-Fortier, NUP (Que.) 16 B4
Village Bay, UP (BC) 38 F3
Village Bay 7, IR (BC) 37 B4
Villagedale, UP (NS) 10 C4
Village-de-la-Blague, UP (Que.) 14 E4
Village-des-Arsenault, UP (NB) 12 G3
Village-des-Aulnaies, UP (Que.) 15 D2
Village-des-Belliveau, UP (NB) 12 G4
Village-des-Chutes, UP (Que.) 16 D2
Village-des-Cormier, UP (NB) 12 G4
Village-des-Couture, UP (Que.) 15 G4
Village-des-Geoffroy, UP (Que.) 18 G4
Village-des-Léger, UP (NB) 12 F4
Village-des-Poirier, UP (NB) 13 F4
Village Green, UP (PEI) 7 D4
Village Island 1, IR (BC) 39 D3
Village Island 7, IR (BC) 38 E4
Village-Lafontaine, UP (Que.) 18 F4
Village-la-Prairie, UP (NB) 12 G3
Village-Marcotte, UP (Que.) 16 C3
Village-Marie, NUP (Que.) 15 B4
Village Meadows, NUP (Ont.) 21 D1
Village-Pikogan < Amos 1, UP (Que.) 18 B1
Village-St-Augustin, UP (NB) 12 F4
Village-Ste-Croix, UP (NB) 12 G3
Village-Saint-Irénée, UP (NB) 12 G3
Village-St-Jean, UP (NB) 12 F3
Village-St-Laurent, UP (NB) 12 F2
Village-St-Paul, UP (NB) 13 F4
Village-St-Pierre, UP (NB) 12 F3
Village-sur-le-Lac, UP (Que.) 17 G1
Villebois, UP (Que.) 18 A1
Ville-Marie, T (Que.) 26 G3
Villemontel, UP (Que.) 18 B1
Villeneuve, UP (Alta.) 33 D3
Villeroy, UP (Que.) 16 D1
Villette, UP (Que.) 16 D4
Villiers, UP (Ont.) 21 E1
Vilna, VL (Alta.) 33 F2
Vilroc, UP (Que.) 18 A2
Vimy, UP (Alta.) 33 D2
Vimy-Ridge, UP (Que.) 16 E2
Vimy Ridge, UP (Ont.) 26 F1
Vincennes, UP (Que.) 16 C1
Vine, UP (Ont.) 21 A1
Vinegar Hill, UP (NB) 11 E2
Vinegar Hill, UP (Ont.) 17 D2
Vinegar Hill, NUP (NB) 11 B1
Vinette, UP (Ont.) 17 D1
Vinoy, UP (Que.) 18 E4
Vinsulla, UP (BC) 36 F4
Vinton, UP (Que.) 18 C4
Violet, UP (Ont.) 17 A4
Violet Grove, UP (Alta.) 33 C3
Violet Hill, UP (Ont.) 23 E3
Violette Settlement, UP (NB) 12 A2
Violette Station, UP (NB) 12 A2
Virden, T (Man.) 29 E4
Virgin Arm, UP (Nfld.) 3 D2
Virginia, UP (Ont.) 21 B1
Virginia Beach, UP (Ont.) 21 B1
Virginia East, UP (NS) 10 C2
Virginiatown, UP (Ont.) 26 F2
Viscount, VL (Sask.) 31 F1
Viscount Estate Subdivision, NUP (Alta.) 33 D3
Vista, UP (Man.) 29 E3
Vita, UP (Man.) 28 B3
Vittoria, UP (Ont.) 22 G2
Vivian, UP (Man.) 28 B1
Vogar, UP (Man.) 29 G2
Voglers Cove, UP (NS) 10 E3
Voilnadamtk 48, IR (BC) 42 D3
Volga, UP (Man.) 29 F2
Volmer, UP (Alta.) 33 D3
Vonda, T (Sask.) 31 F1
Vosburg, UP (Ont.) 22 C3
Voydon Acres, UP (Ont.) 17 B1
Voy's Beach < Halfway Point – Benoit's Cove – John's Beach – Frenchman's Cove, UP (Nfld.) 4 C1
Vroomanton, UP (Ont.) 21 B1
Vulcan, T (Alta.) 34 F3
Vyner, UP (Ont.) 22 C1

W

Waasagomach < Island Lake 22, UP (Man.) 30 D2
Waasis, UP (NB) 11 C1
Waba, UP (Ont.) 17 B1
Wabamun, UP (Alta.) 33 D3
Wabamun 133A, IR (Alta.) 33 D3
Wabamun 133B, IR (Alta.) 33 D3
Wabana, T (Nfld.) 2 H2
Wabasca, UP (Alta.) 44 B4
Wabasca 166, IR (Alta.) 44 B4
Wabasca 166A, IR (Alta.) 44 B4
Wabasca 166B, IR (Alta.) 44 B4
Wabasca 166C, IR (Alta.) 44 B4
Wabasca 166D, IR (Alta.) 44 B4
Wabash, UP (Ont.) 22 C2
Wabassee, UP (Que.) 18 D4
Wabauskang 21, IR (Ont.) 27 A1
Wabigoon, UP (Ont.) 27 A2
Wabigoon Lake 27, IR (Ont.) 27 A2
Wabi-Kon, UP (Ont.) 26 F3
Wabos, UP (Ont.) 26 B3
Wabowden, UP (Man.) 30 B2
Wabozominissing < Wikwemikong Unceded 26, UP (Ont.) 25 D2
Wabush, LID (Nfld.) 6 C4
Waco, UP (Que.) 19 F1
Waddens Cove, UP (NS) 8 F3
Waddington Beach, UP (Ont.) 23 G2
Wade, UP (Ont.) 28 F1
Wade Corners, UP (Ont.) 21 E1
Wadena, T (Sask.) 29 B1
Wade's Landing, UP (Ont.) 25 H2
Wadhams, UP (BC) 41 F4
Wadin Bay, UP (Sask.) 32 E1
Wagarville, UP (Ont.) 17 A3
Wager Bay, UP (NWT) 46 C2
Wagmatcook 1, IR (NS) 8 D3
Wagner, UP (Alta.) 33 C1
Wagner Ranch, UP (BC) 43 D3
Wagram, UP (Ont.) 23 D3
Wahawin, UP (Ont.) 24 C2
Wahleach Island 2, IR (BC) 35 A4
Wahnapitei 11, IR (Ont.) 26 E3
Wahnekewaning Beach, UP (Ont.) 23 E1
Wahous 19, IR (BC) 39 G4
Wahous 20, IR (BC) 39 G4
Wahpaton 94A, IR (Sask.) 32 D3
Wahpaton 94B, IR (Sask.) 32 D3
Wahwashkesh, UP (Ont.) 24 A1
Wainfleet, UP (Ont.) 21 B4
Wainwright, T (Alta.) 33 G4
Wainwright, Camp/Campement, MIL (Alta.) 33 G4
Waite, UP (Que.) 18 A1
Waitville, UP (Sask.) 32 E4
Waiwakum 14, IR (BC) 38 F1
Wakaw, T (Sask.) 32 D4
Wakaw Lake, SV (Sask.) 32 E4
Wakefield, UP (NB) 12 A4
Wakefield, UP (Que.) 17 C1
Wakem Corner, UP (NB) 12 A3
Wakems 6, IR (BC) 41 F4
Wakopa, UP (Man.) 29 F4
Walcott, UP (BC) 42 F4
Waldeck, UP (NS) 10 B2
Waldeck, VL (Sask.) 31 E3
Waldeck East, UP (NS) 10 B2
Waldeck West, UP (NS) 10 B2
Waldegrave, UP (NS) 9 C1
Waldemar, UP (Ont.) 23 E3
Walden, T (Ont.) 25 E1
Walden, UP (NS) 10 E2
Walden Place, NUP (Ont.) 22 C1
Waldersee, UP (Man.) 29 G3
Waldheim, T (Sask.) 32 D4
Waldron, VL (Sask.) 29 C2
Waldron Cove, UP (Nfld.) 3 C2
Walford, UP (Ont.) 25 B1
Walhachin, UP (BC) 36 D4
Walkerburn, UP (Man.) 29 D2
Walkers, UP (Ont.) 22 D2
Walkers, UP (BC) 34 B4
Walker Settlement, UP (NB) 11 F2
Walkers Point, UP (Ont.) 23 G1
Walkerton, T (Ont.) 23 C3
Walkerville, UP (NS) 8 D4
Walkerville, NUP (NS) 9 D2
Walker Woods, NUP (Ont.) 22 C1
Walkleyburg, UP (Man.) 28 B1
Wallace, UP (NS) 9 B1
Wallace, UP (Ont.) 23 D3
Wallace, UP (Ont.) 24 E2
Wallace Bay, UP (NS) 9 B1
Wallace Bridge, UP (NS) 9 B1
Wallace Bridge Station, UP (NS) 9 B1
Wallaceburg, T (Ont.) 22 B2
Wallace Grant, UP (NS) 9 B1
Wallace Highlands, UP (NS) 9 B1
Wallace Point, UP (Ont.) 21 D1
Wallace Ridge, UP (NS) 9 C1
Wallace River, UP (NS) 9 B1
Wallace Station, NUP (NS) 9 B1
Wallacetown, UP (Ont.) 22 D2
Wallard, UP (Sask.) 31 E4
Wallbridge, UP (Ont.) 21 F1
Wallbrook, UP (NS) 9 A3
Wallenstein, UP (Ont.) 23 D4
Walls, UP (Ont.) 24 B2
Wallwort, UP (Sask.) 32 F4
Walnut, UP (Ont.) 22 C2
Walpole, UP (Sask.) 29 D3
Walpole Island < Walpole Island 46, UP (Ont.) 22 B2
Walpole Island 46, IR (Ont.) 22 B2
Walsh, UP (Ont.) 22 G2
Walsh, UP (Alta.) 31 B3
Walsingham, UP (Ont.) 22 F2
Walters Falls, UP (Ont.) 23 D2
Waltham-Station, UP (Que.) 18 C4
Walton, UP (NS) 9 A2
Walton, UP (Ont.) 23 C4
Waltons Lake, UP (NB) 11 D2
Wampum, UP (Man.) 28 C3
Wamsley, UP (Ont.) 27 D3
Wandering River, UP (Alta.) 33 E1
Wandsworth, UP (Nfld.) 2 C4
Wandsworth, UP (Sask.) 32 D4
Wanham, VL (Alta.) 43 G4
Wanipogow < Hole or Hollow Water 10, UP (Man.) 30 C4
Wanless, UP (Man.) 32 H2
Wanstead, UP (Ont.) 22 C2
Wanup, UP (Ont.) 25 E1
Wapachewunak 192D, IR (Sask.) 44 D4
Wapah, UP (Man.) 29 G2
Wapella, T (Sask.) 29 D3
Wapiti, UP (Alta.) 43 G4
Wappook 26, IR (BC) 39 F4
Wapske, UP (NB) 12 B3
Warburg, VL (Alta.) 33 D3
Warburton, UP (Ont.) 17 B3
Ward Corner, UP (NB) 12 G4
Warden, UP (Alta.) 34 F1
Warden, VL (Que.) 16 C4
Wardlow, UP (Alta.) 34 H2
Wardner, UP (BC) 34 D4
Wards Brook, UP (NS) 11 H2
Wards Creek, UP (NB) 11 F2
Ward Settlement, UP (NB) 12 C4
Wards Harbour, UP (Nfld.) 3 B1
Wardsville, VL (Ont.) 22 D2
Ware < Fort Ware 1, UP (BC) 42 G1
Wareham, LID (Nfld.) 3 F3
Wareham, UP (Ont.) 23 E2
Warfield, VL (BC) 34 B4
Warina, UP (Ont.) 17 E2
Warings Corner, UP (Ont.) 21 G2
Warkworth, UP (Ont.) 21 E1
War Lake 4, IR (Man.) 40 C1
Warman, T (Sask.) 31 F1
Warminster, UP (Ont.) 23 F1
Warmley, UP (Sask.) 29 C4
Warner, VL (Alta.) 34 G4
Warner Bay, UP (BC) 41 F4
Warren, UP (Ont.) 25 F1
Warren, UP (Man.) 29 H3
Warren, UP (NS) 9 A1
Warren Landing, UP (Man.) 30 B2
Warrensville, UP (Alta.) 43 H3
Warrensville Centre, UP (Alta.) 43 H3
Warsaw, UP (Ont.) 21 D1
Warspite, VL (Alta.) 33 E2
Wartburg, UP (Ont.) 23 C4
Wartime, UP (Sask.) 31 D2
Warwick, T (Que.) 16 D2
Warwick, UP (Ont.) 22 C1
Warwick, UP (Alta.) 33 F3
Warwick Mountain, UP (NS) 9 C1
Warwick Settlement, UP (NB) 12 E3
Wasa, UP (BC) 34 D4
Wasaga Beach, T (Ont.) 23 E2
Wasagaming, UP (Man.) 29 F3
Waseca, VL (Sask.) 32 A3
Wasel, UP (Alta.) 33 F3
Washabuck Bridge, UP (NS) 8 D3
Washabuck Centre, UP (NS) 8 D3
Washademoak, UP (NB) 11 E1
Washago, UP (Ont.) 23 G1
Washburn, UP (Ont.) 17 B4
Washburns Corners, UP (Ont.) 17 B3
Washington, UP (Ont.) 22 F1
Washow Bay, UP (Man.) 30 C4
Wasing, UP (Ont.) 18 A4
Waskada, VL (Man.) 29 E4
Waskatenau, VL (Alta.) 33 E2
Waskesiu Lake, UP (Sask.) 32 D3
Wastina, UP (Alta.) 34 H1
Waswanipi, IR (Que.) 20 F4
Watabeag, UP (Ont.) 26 E1
Waterborough, UP (NB) 11 D1
Watercombe, UP (Ont.) 21 G1
Waterdown, UP (Ont.) 21 A3
Waterfall, UP (Ont.) 25 E1
Waterford, UP (NB) 11 F2
Waterford, UP (PEI) 7 A2
Waterford, UP (NS) 10 B2
Waterhen, UP (Man.) 29 F1
Waterhen 130, IR (Sask.) 32 B2
Waterhen 45, IR (Man.) 29 F1
Waterhen Lake, UP (Sask.) 32 B2
Waterhole, UP (Alta.) 43 G3
Waterloo, C (Ont.) 23 D4
Waterloo, T (Que.) 16 C4
Waterloo, UP (NS) 10 D2
Waterloo Corner, UP (NB) 11 E2
Waternish, UP (NS) 9 E2
Waterside, UP (PEI) 7 D4
Waterside, UP (NB) 11 G2
Waterside, UP (NS) 9 D1
Waterton, UP (Ont.) 17 C4
Waterton Park, UP (Alta.) 34 E4
Watertown, UP (Sask.) 31 G2
Watervale, UP (NS) 9 D2
Watervale, UP (PEI) 7 D4
Water Valley, UP (Alta.) 34 E2
Waterville, T (Que.) 16 C4
Waterville, UP (NS) 10 D1
Waterville, UP (NB) 11 C2
Waterville, UP (NB) 12 A4
Waterville, UP (Nfld.) 2 F1
Watford, UP (NS) 10 D2
Watford, VL (Ont.) 22 C2
Watino, UP (Alta.) 43 H4
Watrous, T (Sask.) 31 G1
Watson, T (Sask.) 31 G1
Watson Lake, UP (YT) 45 C4
Watson Lake Airport, NUP (YT) 45 C4
Watsons Corners, UP (Ont.) 17 A2
Watson Settlement, UP (NB) 11 A1
Watta 25, IR (BC) 39 G4
Watterson Corners, UP (Ont.) 17 C2
Watt Junction, UP (NB) 11 B2
Watts, UP (Alta.) 34 G1
Watt Section Sheet Harbour, UP (NS) 9 D3
Wattsview, UP (Man.) 29 D3
Waubamik, UP (Ont.) 24 A2
Waubaushene, UP (Ont.) 23 F1
Waubuno, UP (Ont.) 22 B2
Wauchope, UP (Sask.) 29 D4
Waudby, UP (Ont.) 23 D2
Waugh, UP (Alta.) 33 E2
Waughs River, UP (NS) 9 C1
Waulp 10, IR (BC) 42 F3
Waump 24, IR (BC) 41 G4
Waupoos, UP (Ont.) 21 G2
Waupoos East, UP (Ont.) 21 G2
Waupoos Island, UP (Ont.) 21 G2
Wavell, UP (Ont.) 26 F2
Waverley, UP (NS) 9 B3
Waverley, UP (Ont.) 23 F1
Wawa, UP (Ont.) 26 A2
Wawanesa, VL (Man.) 29 F4
Wawbewawa, UP (Ont.) 26 F2
Waweig, UP (NB) 11 B3
Wawelth 3, IR (BC) 41 E1
Wawota, T (Sask.) 29 D3
Wawwat'l 20, IR (BC) 41 G4
Waybrook, UP (Alta.) 33 E3
Wayerton, UP (NB) 12 E2
Wayne, UP (Alta.) 34 F2
Ways-Mills, UP (Que.) 16 D4
Weagamow Lake < Weagamow Lake 87, UP (Ont.) 30 E3
Weagamow Lake 87, IR (Ont.) 30 E3
Weald, UP (Alta.) 33 B3
Weasel Creek, UP (Alta.) 33 E2
Weaver, UP (NB) 12 B2
Weaver Settlement, UP (NS) 10 B2
Weaver Siding, UP (NB) 12 E3
Webb, VL (Sask.) 31 D3
Webbwood, T (Ont.) 25 C1
Webequie, UP (Ont.) 20 A2
Weberville, UP (Alta.) 43 H3
Webster, UP (Alta.) 43 G4
Webster Creek 5, IR (BC) 40 C3
Websters Corner, UP (PEI) 7 D4
Websters Corner, UP (NS) 9 D2
Websterville, NUP (Ont.) 23 E2
Wedgeport, UP (NS) 10 B4
Wedgewood Park, LID (Nfld.) 2 H2
Weed Creek, UP (Alta.) 33 D4
Weedon-Centre, VL (Que.) 16 E3
Weekes, VL (Sask.) 32 G4
Weeks Road, UP (NB) 11 B2
Weeteeam 3, IR (BC) 41 E3
Wee-Too Beach, UP (Sask.) 31 G2
Weiden, UP (Man.) 29 F2
Weidmann, UP (Ont.) 22 C2
Weir, UP (Que.) 18 F4
Weirdale, VL (Sask.) 32 E3
Weir River, UP (Man.) 30 D1
Weirstead, UP (Que.) 17 B1
Weisbord-Acres, UP (Que.) 18 F4
Weissenburg, UP (Ont.) 23 E4
Weissener Lake 3, IR (BC) 43 A1
Wekellals 15, IR (BC) 41 F2
Wekusko, UP (Man.) 30 B2
Welbeck, UP (Ont.) 23 C2
Welby, UP (Sask.) 29 D3
Welch Cove, UP (NB) 11 C3
Welcome, UP (Ont.) 21 D2
Welcome Beach, UP (BC) 38 E2
Weldfield, UP (NB) 12 F2
Weldon, UP (NB) 11 G1
Weldon, VL (Sask.) 32 E4
Welland, C (Ont.) 21 B4
Wellandport, UP (Ont.) 21 B4
Wellburn, UP (Ont.) 22 E1
Wellesley, UP (Ont.) 23 D4
Welling, UP (Alta.) 34 F4
Wellington, UP (NS) 9 B3
Wellington, UP (NS) 10 A3
Wellington, UP (NS) 10 D2
Wellington, VL (Ont.) 21 F2
Wellington, VL (PEI) 7 B3
Wellington Centre, UP (PEI) 7 B3
Wellington Station, UP (NS) 9 B3
Wellman, UP (Ont.) 21 F1
Wellmans Cove, UP (Nfld.) 3 B1
Wells, UP (BC) 40 D3
Wells, UP (NB) 11 E2
Wellwood, UP (Man.) 29 F3
Welsford, UP (NB) 11 D2
Welsford, UP (NS) 11 G3
Welsford, UP (NS) 9 C1
Welshpool, UP (NB) 11 B4
Welshtown, UP (NS) 10 C3
Welton Landing, UP (NS) 10 E1
Weltons Corner, UP (NS) 10 D1
Welwyn, VL (Sask.) 29 D3
Wembley, VL (Alta.) 43 G4
Wemyss, UP (Ont.) 17 B3
Wendake Beach, UP (Ont.) 23 E1
Wendigo Lake, UP (Ont.) 26 F2
Wendover, UP (Ont.) 17 D1
Weneez, UP (BC) 40 B2
Wenham Valley, UP (Alta.) 33 D4
Wentworth, UP (NS) 9 B1
Wentworth Centre, UP (NS) 9 B1
Wentworth Creek, UP (NS) 9 A3
Wentworth Station, UP (NS) 9 B1
Wentworth Valley, UP (NS) 9 B1
Wentzells Lake, UP (NS) 10 E2
Werkinellek 11, IR (BC) 41 E3
Wernecke, UP (YT) 45 B2
Werner Lake, UP (Ont.) 30 D4
Wernerville, NUP (Alta.) 33 E3
Weslemkoon, UP (Ont.) 24 F3
Wesley, UP (Ont.) 21 G1
Wesley, UP (Ont.) 23 D3
Wesley Creek, UP (Alta.) 43 H3
Wesleyville, T (Nfld.) 3 F2
Wesleyville, UP (Ont.) 21 D2
West Advocate, UP (NS) 11 G3
West Alba, UP (NS) 8 D4
West Amherst, UP (NS) 9 A1
West Apple River, UP (NS) 11 G2
West Arichat, UP (NS) 8 D4
West Arm Tracadie, NUP (NS) 8 B4
West Baccaro, UP (NS) 10 C4
Westbank, UP (BC) 35 E3
West Bay, UP (Nfld.) 6 G3
West Bay, UP (NS) 8 D4
West Bay, UP (Nfld.) 4 B2
West Bay, UP (NS) 11 H2
West Bay < West Bay 22, UP (Ont.) 25 C2
West Bay 22, IR (Ont.) 25 B2
West Bay Centre, UP (NS) 8 D4
West Bay Centre, UP (Nfld.) 4 B2
West Bay Estates, NUP (BC) 38 D2
West Bay Road, UP (NS) 8 C4
West Beach, UP (NB) 11 E3
West Becher, UP (Ont.) 22 B2
West Bench, UP (BC) 35 E3
West Bend, VL (Sask.) 29 B2
West Berlin, UP (NS) 10 E3
West Black Rock Road, UP (NS) 11 G3
Westbourne, UP (Man.) 29 G3
West Branch, UP (NB) 12 G3
West Branch River John, UP (NS) 9 C1
Westbridge, UP (BC) 35 G4
Westbrook, UP (Ont.) 17 A4
West Brook, UP (NS) 9 A2
Westbrooke Crescents, NUP (Alta.) 33 D3
Westbrook Heights, UP (Ont.) 17 A4
West Brooklyn, UP (NS) 9 A3
West Caledonia, UP (NS) 10 D2
West Cape, UP (PEI) 7 A3
Westchester Mountain, UP (NS) 9 B2
Westchester Station, UP (NS) 9 B1
Westchester Valley, UP (NS) 9 B1
West Chezzetcook, UP (NS) 9 C3
Westcliffe Estates, UP (Ont.) 17 D4
West Clifford, UP (NS) 10 D2
Westcock, UP (NB) 11 H1
West Collette, UP (NB) 12 F3
West Cooks Cove, UP (NS) 9 G2
West Corners, UP (Ont.) 21 E1
Westcott, UP (Alta.) 34 E1
West Cove, SV (Alta.) 33 D3
West Covehead, UP (PEI) 7 C3
West Dalhousie, UP (NS) 10 C1
West Dawson, UP (YT) 45 A2
West Devon, UP (PEI) 7 A3
West-Ditton, UP (Que.) 16 E4
West Dover, UP (NS) 9 A4
West Dublin, UP (NS) 10 E2
West Earltown, UP (NS) 9 C2
West East River, UP (NS) 9 D3
Westegard Ranches, UP (BC) 43 D3
West-Ely, UP (Que.) 16 C3
West End, UP (Sask.) 29 C3
Westerdale, UP (Alta.) 34 E1
West Erinville, UP (NS) 9 F2
Westerly, UP (NS) 9 C1
Western Arm, UP (Nfld.) 5 G4
Western Bay, UP (Nfld.) 2 G2
Western Cove, UP (Nfld.) 2 E2
Western Head, UP (NS) 10 C4
Western Head, UP (NS) 10 D3
Western Head, UP (Nfld.) 3 D1
Western Island 14, IR (BC) 41 G1
Western Monarch, UP (Alta.) 34 G2
Western Shore, UP (NS) 10 E2

Westerose, UP (Alta.) **33 D4**
West Essa, UP (Ont.) **21 A1**
West Fernie, NUP (BC) **34 D4**
Westfield, UP (NS) **10 D2**
Westfield, UP (Ont.) **23 B3**
Westfield, VL (NB) **11 D3**
West Flamborough, UP (Ont.) **22 G1**
Westford, UP (Ont.) **23 B3**
West Franklin, UP (Ont.) **21 B1**
West Galloway, UP (NB) **12 G3**
Westgate, UP (Man.) **30 A3**
West Glassville, UP (NB) **12 B3**
West Glenmont, UP (NS) **11 H3**
West Gore, UP (NS) **9 B3**
West Green Harbour, UP (NS) **10 C4**
West Guilford, UP (Ont.) **24 D2**
West Halls Harbour Road, UP (NS) **11 G3**
West Hansford, UP (NS) **9 B1**
West Havre Boucher, UP (NS) **8 C4**
West Hawk Lake, UP (Man.) **28 E2**
Westhazel, UP (Sask.) **32 A3**
West Huntingdon, UP (Ont.) **21 F1**
West Indian Road, UP (NS) **9 B3**
West Inglisville, UP (NS) **10 C1**
West Intervale, UP (NS) **9 F2**
West Jeddore, UP (NS) **9 C3**
West-Keith, UP (Que.) **16 E3**
West LaHave, UP (NS) **10 E2**
West Lake, UP (Ont.) **21 F2**
West Lake Ainslie, UP (NS) **8 D3**
West Lakevale, UP (NS) **8 B4**
West Lawrencetown, UP (NS) **9 C4**
West Lawrencetown, UP (NS) **10 C1**
West Leicester, UP (NS) **9 A1**
West Linden, UP (NS) **9 B1**
West Linwood, UP (NS) **8 C4**
West Liscomb, UP (NS) **9 E3**
West Lochaber, UP (NS) **9 E2**
Westlock, T (Alta.) **33 D2**
West Lorne, VL (Ont.) **22 D2**
West Mabou Harbour, UP (NS) **8 C3**
West Mara Lake, NUP (BC) **36 H4**
West McGillivray, UP (Ont.) **22 D1**
Westmeath, UP (Ont.) **18 C4**
West Middle River, UP (NS) **8 D3**
West Middle Sable, UP (NS) **10 D3**
Westminster, UP (Ont.) **17 E1**
West Moberly Lake 168A, IR (BC) **43 D3**
West Montrose, UP (Ont.) **23 D4**
West Montrose, UP (NS) **9 B2**
Westmoreland, UP (PEI) **7 C4**
Westmount, C (Que.) **17 G4**
Westmount, UP (NS) **8 F3**
West New Annan, UP (NS) **9 C1**
West Northfield, UP (NS) **10 E2**
Weston, UP (NS) **10 D1**
Weston, UP (NB) **12 A4**
West Osgoode, UP (Ont.) **17 C2**
Westover, UP (Ont.) **22 G1**
West Paradise, UP (NS) **10 C1**
West Pennant, UP (NS) **9 B4**
West Petpeswick, UP (NS) **9 C3**
West Pine Ridge, UP (Man.) **28 A1**
Westplain, UP (Ont.) **21 G1**
West Plains, UP (Sask.) **31 C4**
West Point, UP (PEI) **7 A3**
West Point, UP (Nfld.) **4 C4**
West Poplar, UP (Sask.) **31 F4**
Westport, COMM (Nfld.) **5 G4**
Westport, UP (NS) **10 A2**
Westport, VL (Ont.) **17 B3**
West Port Clyde, UP (NS) **10 C4**
West Pubnico, UP (NS) **10 B4**
West Pugwash, UP (NS) **9 B1**
West Quaco, UP (NB) **11 E3**
West Quoddy, UP (NS) **9 E3**
Westray, UP (Man.) **30 A2**
Westree, UP (Ont.) **26 D3**
West River, UP (NS) **8 B4**
West River, UP (NB) **11 G2**
West River, UP (Ont.) **25 C1**
West River Station, UP (NS) **9 D2**
West Roachvale, UP (NS) **9 F2**
West Royalty, UP (PEI) **7 C4**
West St Andrews, UP (NS) **9 C3**
West St Modeste, COMM (Nfld.) **5 G2**
West St Peters, UP (PEI) **7 D3**
West Scotch Settlement, UP (NB) **11 E2**
West Sechelt, NUP (BC) **38 E2**
West Sheet Harbour, UP (NS) **9 D3**
West Side, UP (NS) **10 A4**
West Springhill, UP (NS) **10 C2**
West Tarbot, UP (NS) **8 E3**
West Tatamagouche, UP (NS) **9 C1**
West Vancouver, DM (BC) **38 F2**
Westview, UP (Sask.) **29 C2**
Westview, UP (Ont.) **21 E1**
Westville, T (NS) **9 D2**
Westward Ho, UP (Alta.) **34 E1**
West Waterville, UP (NB) **11 B1**
West Wentworth, UP (NS) **9 B1**
Westwold, UP (BC) **35 E1**
Westwood, UP (Ont.) **17 B1**
Westwood, UP (Ont.) **21 E1**
Wetaskiwin, C (Alta.) **33 E4**
Wexford, UP (Ont.) **17 D3**
Weybridge, UP (Nfld.) **2 F1**
Weyburn, C (Sask.) **31 H4**
Weymont < Weymontachi 23, UP (Que.) **18 F2**
Weymontachi 23, IR (Que.) **18 F2**
Weymouth, UP (NS) **10 B2**
Weymouth Falls, UP (NS) **10 B2**
Weymouth Mills, UP (NS) **10 B2**
Weymouth North, UP (NS) **10 B2**
Whale Cove, UP (NWT) **46 B3**
Whale Island 8, IR (BC) **38 E4**
Whalen Corners, UP (Ont.) **22 E1**
Whale's Gulch, UP (Nfld.) **3 D1**
Whaletown, UP (BC) **37 B4**
Wharncliffe, UP (Ont.) **26 B4**
Wharton, UP (NS) **11 H2**
Wheatland, UP (Que.) **16 C3**
Wheatland, UP (Man.) **29 E3**
Wheatley, VL (Ont.) **22 B4**
Wheatley River, UP (PEI) **7 C3**
Wheaton Settlement, UP (NB) **11 F1**
Wheatstone, UP (Sask.) **31 G4**
Wheel In Trailer Park, NUP (BC) **43 E3**
Whelan, UP (Sask.) **32 A2**
Whim Road, UP (PEI) **7 E4**
Whiskey Gap, UP (Alta.) **34 F4**
Whispering Pines 4, IR (BC) **36 F4**
Whispering Winds Trailer Court, NUP (BC) **34 D4**
Whistler, VL (BC) **37 F4**
Whitbourne, T (Nfld.) **2 F3**
Whitburn, UP (Alta.) **43 F3**
Whitby, T (Ont.) **21 C2**
Whitchurch-Stouffville, T (Ont.) **21 B2**
White Bear, UP (Sask.) **31 D2**
White Bear 70, IR (Sask.) **29 C4**
Whitebeech, UP (Sask.) **29 D1**
Whitebread, UP (Ont.) **22 B2**
Whiteburn Mines, UP (NS) **10 D2**
Whitecap < White Cap 94, UP (Sask.) **31 E1**
White Cap 94, IR (Sask.) **31 E1**
Whitechurch, UP (Ont.) **23 B3**
White City, VL (Sask.) **31 H3**
Whitecourt, T (Alta.) **33 C2**
Whitecroft, UP (Alta.) **33 E3**
White-Deer, UP (Que.) **18 D4**
Whitedog < Islington 29, UP (Ont.) **28 E1**
White Elk < Sarcee 145, UP (Alta.) **34 E2**
Whitefish Bay < Whitefish Bay 32A, UP (Ont.) **28 G2**
Whitefish Bay 32A, IR (Ont.) **28 G2**
Whitefish Bay 33A, IR (Ont.) **28 G3**
Whitefish Bay 34A, IR (Ont.) **28 G2**
Whitefish Falls, UP (Ont.) **25 C2**
Whitefish Lake 6, IR (Ont.) **25 D1**
Whitefish Lake 6, IR (BC) **40 A1**
Whitefish River 4, IR (Ont.) **25 C2**
Whitefish Station, UP (NWT) **45 B1**
Whitefish Station, UP (YT) **45 B1**
White Fish Lake 128, IR (Alta.) **33 F2**
White Fox, VL (Sask.) **32 F3**
Whitehall, UP (Ont.) **24 B2**
White Head, UP (NB) **11 C4**
Whitehead, UP (NB) **11 D2**
Whitehead, UP (NS) **9 G2**
White Hill, UP (NS) **9 D2**
Whitehorse, C (YT) **45 B3**
White Horse Plain Trailer Court, NUP (Man.) **29 H3**
White Lake, UP (Ont.) **17 A1**
White Lake, UP (Man.) **28 D1**
White Lake, UP (Ont.) **21 F1**
White Lake, NUP (BC) **36 G4**
Whitelaw, UP (Alta.) **43 G3**
Whitemouth, UP (Man.) **28 C1**
Whitemud Creek, UP (Alta.) **33 A1**
White Oak, UP (Ont.) **22 E2**
White Pass, UP (BC) **45 B4**
White Point, UP (NS) **10 D3**
White Point, UP (NS) **8 E1**
White Rapids, UP (NB) **12 E3**
White River, UP (Ont.) **26 A1**
White Rock, C (BC) **38 G3**
White Rock, UP (NS) **10 E1**
White Rock, UP (Nfld.) **2 F1**
Whites, UP (Que.) **17 F2**
Whites, UP (Ont.) **22 E2**
Whitesand, UP (Sask.) **29 C2**
White Sands, UP (PEI) **7 E4**
Whites Bluff, UP (NB) **11 D2**
Whites Brook, UP (NB) **12 B1**
Whites Corner, UP (NS) **11 G3**
Whites Cove, UP (NB) **11 D1**
White Settlement, UP (NS) **9 B2**
Whiteside, UP (NS) **8 D4**
Whiteside, UP (Ont.) **24 B3**
Whites Lake, UP (NS) **9 B4**
Whites Mills, UP (NB) **11 D2**
Whites Mountain, UP (NB) **11 F1**
White Spruce < Yorkton, CFS/SFC, UP (Sask.) **29 C2**
Whites Settlement, UP (NB) **12 G4**
White Star, UP (Sask.) **32 D3**
Whitestone, UP (Ont.) **24 A1**
Whitestone Village, UP (YT) **45 B2**
White Water, UP (NS) **11 H3**
Whitewater, UP (Man.) **29 E4**
Whiteway, COMM (Nfld.) **2 G2**
Whitewood, T (Sask.) **29 C3**
Whitewood Grove, UP (Ont.) **26 F2**
Whitfield, UP (Ont.) **23 E2**
Whitford, UP (Alta.) **33 F3**
Whitkow, UP (Sask.) **32 C4**
Whitla, UP (Alta.) **31 A3**
Whitney, UP (Ont.) **24 E2**
Whitney, UP (NB) **12 E2**
Whitney, UP (Alta.) **34 F3**
Whittier Ridge, UP (NB) **11 B3**
Whittington, UP (Ont.) **23 E3**
Whittome, UP (Sask.) **32 F4**
Whitworth, UP (Que.) **14 E4**
Whitworth 21, IR (Que.) **14 F4**
Whonnock 1, IR (BC) **38 G2**
Whyac < Wyah 3, UP (BC) **38 C3**
Whycocomagh, UP (NS) **8 D3**
Whycocomagh 2, IR (NS) **8 D3**
Whycocomagh Portage, UP (NS) **8 D3**
Whycocomagh Reserve < Whycocomagh 2, UP (NS) **8 D3**
Whyeek 4, IR (BC) **35 B2**
Whynachts Point, UP (NS) **9 A4**
Whynotts Settlement, UP (NS) **10 E2**
Wiarton, T (Ont.) **23 C1**
Wick, UP (Ont.) **21 C1**
Wickham, UP (Que.) **16 C3**
Wickham, UP (NB) **11 D2**
Wicklow, UP (NB) **12 A3**
Wicklow, UP (Ont.) **21 E2**
Wideview, UP (Sask.) **31 E4**
Widewater, UP (Alta.) **33 C1**
Wies Subdivision, NUP (Ont.) **22 F2**
Wiggins Mill, UP (NB) **11 B1**
Wights Corners, UP (Ont.) **17 C3**
Wigle, UP (Ont.) **22 B4**
Wigwam-Beach < Caughnawaga 14, UP (Que.) **17 G4**
Wigwam Inn, UP (BC) **38 G2**
Wikwemikong < Wikwemikong Unceded 26, UP (Ont.) **25 C2**
Wikwemikong Unceded 26, IR (Ont.) **25 C3**
Wikwemikonsing < Wikwemikong Unceded 26, UP (Ont.) **25 D2**
Wilberforce, UP (Ont.) **24 E3**
Wilbert, UP (Sask.) **32 A4**
Wilburn, UP (NS) **8 D3**
Wilcox, VL (Sask.) **31 G3**
Wilcox Lake, UP (Ont.) **23 D2**
Wild Bight, COMM (Nfld.) **3 B1**
Wild Bight, UP (Nfld.) **5 H2**
Wildcat, UP (Alta.) **34 E2**
Wildcat 12, IR (NS) **10 D2**
Wild Cove, UP (Nfld.) **3 A1**
Wild Cove, UP (Nfld.) **5 H3**
Wild Cove < Norris Point, UP (Nfld.) **5 F4**
Wild Goose, UP (Ont.) **27 E3**
Wild Horse, UP (Alta.) **31 B4**
Wildmere, UP (Alta.) **33 G3**
Wild Rose, UP (Sask.) **32 D3**
Wildwood, VL (Alta.) **33 C3**
Wildwood Trailer Park, NUP (BC) **36 F2**
Wile Settlement, UP (NS) **9 A3**
Wileville, UP (NS) **10 E2**
Wileys Corner, UP (NB) **11 B3**
Wiley Subdivision, NUP (BC) **42 G4**
Wilfrid, UP (Ont.) **21 B1**
Wilhelm, NUP (Ont.) **22 B4**
Wilkesport, UP (Ont.) **22 B2**
Wilkie, T (Sask.) **32 B4**
Wilkins, UP (NS) **10 D3**
Wilkinson, UP (Ont.) **17 A3**
Willard Lake, UP (Ont.) **28 G1**
Willen, UP (Man.) **29 D3**
Willesden Green, UP (Alta.) **33 D4**
Willetsholme, UP (Ont.) **17 B4**
William McKenzie 151K, IR (Alta.) **44 A4**
Williams 2, IR (BC) **35 A4**
Williams Beach, UP (BC) **38 B1**
Williamsburg, UP (Ont.) **17 D2**
Williamsburg, UP (NB) **12 C4**
Williamsdale, UP (NS) **9 A1**
Williamsford, UP (Ont.) **23 D2**
Williams Harbour, UP (Nfld.) **6 H4**
Williams Lake, T (BC) **36 B1**
Williams Lake 1, IR (BC) **36 B1**
Williamsons Landing, UP (BC) **38 E2**
Williams Point, UP (NS) **8 B4**
Williams Point, UP (Ont.) **21 C1**
Williamsport, UP (Nfld.) **5 H3**
Williams Prairie Meadow 1A, IR (BC) **40 B1**
Williamstown, UP (Ont.) **17 E2**
Williamstown, UP (NB) **12 A4**
Williamstown, UP (NB) **12 E2**
Willingdon, VL (Alta.) **33 F3**
Williscroft, UP (Ont.) **23 C2**
Willisville, UP (Ont.) **25 C2**
Willmar, UP (Sask.) **29 C4**
Willowbank, UP (Ont.) **17 B4**
Willow Bay, UP (Ont.) **21 B4**
Willow Beach, UP (Ont.) **21 B1**
Willow Beach, UP (Ont.) **22 A4**
Willow Beach, UP (Ont.) **24 B3**
Willow Beach Mobile Home, NUP (BC) **35 F4**
Willowbrook, UP (BC) **43 E3**
Willowbrook, VL (Sask.) **29 C2**
Willow Bunch, T (Sask.) **31 G4**
Willow Creek, UP (Sask.) **31 C4**
Willow Creek, UP (Alta.) **34 G2**
Willowdale, UP (NS) **9 E2**
Willowdale, UP (NS) **9 B4**
Willow Drive, NUP (Alta.) **34 E4**
Willow Grove, UP (NB) **11 E3**
Willow Grove, UP (Ont.) **23 C4**
Willow Meadow 9, IR (BC) **40 A3**
Willowood, UP (Ont.) **22 A4**
Willow Point, UP (BC) **34 B4**
Willow River, UP (BC) **40 D2**
Willow River, UP (BC) **40 C1**
Willows, UP (Sask.) **31 F4**
Willows Trailer Court, NUP (BC) **42 F4**
Willowvale, UP (Sask.) **31 F4**
Willowvale, UP (BC) **40 B1**
Willow Valley, UP (BC) **43 E3**
Willowview, UP (Man.) **29 H2**
Wilmer, UP (BC) **34 C3**
Wilmer, UP (Ont.) **17 A3**
Wilmot, UP (NS) **10 D1**
Wilmot, UP (NB) **12 A4**
Wilmot, UP (NB) **11 B2**
Wilmot, UP (PEI) **7 E4**
Wilmot, VL (PEI) **7 B3**
Wilmot Centre, UP (Ont.) **22 F1**
Wilmot Valley, UP (PEI) **7 B3**
Wilnaskancaud 3, IR (BC) **41 C1**
Wilno, UP (Ont.) **24 F2**
Wilskaskammel 14, IR (BC) **42 D4**
Wilson, UP (Ont.) **24 G2**
Wilson, UP (Ont.) **26 F2**
Wilson, UP (Alta.) **34 G4**
Wilson Creek, UP (BC) **38 E2**
Wilson Landing, UP (BC) **35 F2**
Wilson Point, UP (Ont.) **23 G1**
Wilson Point, UP (NB) **13 H4**
Wilsons Beach, UP (NB) **11 B3**
Wilsons Cove, UP (NS) **9 E3**
Wilsons-Mills, UP (Que.) **15 A4**
Wilsonvale, UP (Que.) **17 F2**
Wilsonwood, NUP (Ont.) **22 C3**
Wilstead, UP (Ont.) **17 B4**
Wilton, UP (Ont.) **17 A4**
Wiltondale, UP (Nfld.) **5 F4**
Wiltsetown, UP (Ont.) **17 C3**
Wiltshire Park, UP (Ont.) **22 B1**
Wimborne, UP (Alta.) **34 F1**
Wimmer, UP (Sask.) **31 H1**
Winch, UP (BC) **35 B2**
Winche 7, IR (BC) **38 B2**
Winchelsea, UP (Ont.) **22 D1**
Winchester, VL (Ont.) **17 D2**
Winchester Springs, UP (Ont.) **17 D2**
Windermere, UP (BC) **34 C3**
Windermere, UP (Ont.) **24 B2**
Windermere, UP (NS) **10 D1**
Windermere Country Estates, NUP (Alta.) **33 D3**
Windfall, UP (Ont.) **22 F1**
Windfall, UP (Ont.) **22 B3**
Windfall, UP (Alta.) **33 B2**
Windham Centre, UP (Ont.) **22 G2**
Windham Hill, UP (NS) **9 A1**
Windigo, UP (Que.) **18 G2**
Windon, UP (PEI) **7 D3**
Windsor, C (Ont.) **22 A3**
Windsor, T (Nfld.) **3 B3**
Windsor, T (Que.) **16 D3**
Windsor, T (NS) **9 A3**
Windsor, UP (NB) **12 B4**
Windsor Forks, UP (NS) **9 A3**
Windsor Heights, UP (Nfld.) **2 H2**
Windsor Junction, UP (NS) **9 B3**
Windsor Park Village, UP (Ont.) **17 E4**
Windsor Road, UP (NS) **10 E2**
Windthorst, VL (Sask.) **29 C3**
Windward Sands, NUP (Ont.) **21 D1**
Windygates, UP (Man.) **29 G4**
Windy Lake, UP (Ont.) **26 D4**
Windy Mouth 7, IR (BC) **36 C2**
Windy Point, UP (Ont.) **27 A3**
Wine Harbour, UP (NS) **9 F3**
Wine River, UP (NB) **12 F3**
Winfield, UP (Alta.) **33 D4**
Winfield, UP (Ont.) **23 D4**
Winfield, UP (BC) **35 F2**
Wingard, UP (Sask.) **32 D4**
Wingdam, UP (BC) **40 D3**
Winger, UP (Ont.) **21 B4**
Wingham, T (Ont.) **23 C3**
Wingle, UP (Ont.) **24 F2**
Wings Point, UP (Nfld.) **3 D2**
Winisk, UP (Ont.) **20 B1**
Winisk 90, IR (Ont.) **20 A1**
Winkler, T (Man.) **29 H4**
Winlaw, UP (BC) **34 B4**
Winneway, UP (Que.) **18 A2**
Winnifred, UP (Alta.) **34 H3**
Winnipeg, C (Man.) **28 A1**
Winnipeg Beach, T (Man.) **30 C4**
Winnipegosis, VL (Man.) **29 F1**
Winsloe, UP (PEI) **7 C4**
Winsloe North, UP (PEI) **7 C3**
Winslow, UP (Ont.) **21 A4**
Winston, UP (NB) **12 F2**
Winter, UP (Sask.) **32 A4**
Winterbourne, UP (Ont.) **23 D4**
Winter Brook, UP (Nfld.) **3 F4**
Winterburn, UP (Alta.) **33 D3**
Winter Harbour, UP (BC) **39 C1**
Winterhouse, UP (Nfld.) **4 B1**
Winter House Brook < Woody Point (COMM), UP (Nfld.) **5 F4**
Winterhouse Cove, UP (Nfld.) **3 A1**
Winterland, COMM (Nfld.) **2 C3**
Winterton, T (Nfld.) **2 G1**
Winthorpe, UP (Sask.) **29 B2**
Winthrop, UP (Ont.) **23 B4**
Winton, UP (Sask.) **32 E4**
Winton Crossing, UP (NB) **12 D1**
Wirral, UP (NB) **11 C2**
Wisbeach, UP (Ont.) **22 D1**
Wisemans Corners, UP (Ont.) **24 B1**
Wiseton, VL (Sask.) **31 E2**
Wishart, VL (Sask.) **31 H1**
Wishart Point, UP (NB) **12 G1**
Wisla, UP (Man.) **29 E3**
Wistaria, UP (BC) **41 G1**
Wiste, UP (Alta.) **31 B1**
Wisteria Landing, UP (BC) **41 G1**
Witchekan, UP (Sask.) **32 C3**
Witchekan Lake 117, IR (Sask.) **32 C3**
Withrow, UP (Alta.) **33 D4**
Witless Bay, UP (Nfld.) **2 H3**
Wittenburg, UP (NS) **9 C3**
Wivenhoe, UP (Man.) **30 D1**
Wiwa Hill, UP (Sask.) **31 F3**
Woburn, UP (Que.) **16 F4**
Wodehouse, UP (Ont.) **23 D2**
Woermke, UP (Ont.) **24 G2**
Woito, UP (Ont.) **24 G1**
Woking, UP (Alta.) **43 G4**
Wokitsas 14, IR (BC) **38 C3**
Wolf < Sarcee 145, UP (Alta.) **34 E2**
Wolf-Bay, UP (Que.) **5 D3**
Wolf Creek, UP (Alta.) **33 B3**
Wolf Creek 3, IR (BC) **35 D3**
Wolfe, UP (Ont.) **24 G2**
Wolfes Landing, UP (NS) **8 F4**
Wolford Chapel, UP (Ont.) **17 C3**
Wolf Subdivision, NUP (BC) **40 C3**
Wolftown, UP (Ont.) **24 G1**
Wolfville, T (NS) **11 H3**
Wolfville Ridge, UP (NS) **11 H3**
Wollaston Lake, UP (Sask.) **44 F3**
Wolseley, T (Sask.) **29 B3**
Wolseley, UP (Ont.) **23 C1**
Wolseley Bay, UP (Ont.) **25 F2**
Wolverine, UP (Sask.) **31 G1**
Wolverine Beach, UP (Ont.) **23 F1**
Wolverton, UP (Ont.) **22 F1**
Wonowon, UP (BC) **43 D2**
Wood Bay, UP (Man.) **29 G4**
Woodbend, UP (Alta.) **33 D3**
Woodbend Crescents, NUP (Alta.) **33 D3**
Woodbine, UP (NS) **8 E3**
Woodboro Subdivision, NUP (Ont.) **21 D1**
Woodbridge, UP (Ont.) **17 B1**
Woodburn, UP (Ont.) **21 A4**
Woodburn, UP (NS) **9 D1**
Woodburn, UP (Ont.) **17 B4**
Woodcock, UP (BC) **42 E3**
Woodfield, UP (NS) **8 A4**
Woodford, UP (Ont.) **23 D1**
Woodford Cove, UP (Nfld.) **3 B1**
Woodgreen, UP (Ont.) **22 D2**
Woodham, UP (Ont.) **22 E1**
Woodhaven, UP (BC) **38 G2**
Wood Hill, UP (Sask.) **32 C3**
Woodhouse, UP (Alta.) **34 F3**
Woodhurst, UP (NB) **7 A4**
Woodington, UP (Ont.) **24 B2**
Wood Islands, UP (PEI) **7 D4**
Woodland, UP (NB) **11 C3**
Woodland, UP (Ont.) **21 E1**
Woodland Acres, NUP (Ont.) **21 D1**
Woodland Beach, UP (Ont.) **23 E1**
Wood Landing, UP (Ont.) **23 F1**
Woodland Park, NUP (Alta.) **33 D3**
Woodlands, UP (Man.) **29 H3**
Woodlands, UP (NB) **11 C1**
Woodlands Trailer Park, NUP (Man.) **29 H3**
Woodlawn, UP (Ont.) **17 B1**
Woodley, UP (Sask.) **29 C4**
Woodmans Point, UP (NB) **11 D2**
Woodmore, UP (Man.) **28 A3**
Wood Mountain, VL (Sask.) **31 F4**
Wood Mountain 160, IR (Sask.) **31 F4**
Woodnorth, UP (Man.) **29 E4**
Woodpecker Hall, UP (NB) **11 E2**
Wood Point, UP (NB) **11 H1**
Woodridge, UP (Man.) **28 C3**
Woodridge, UP (Ont.) **17 C3**
Woodridge, UP (Ont.) **17 B1**
Woodrous, UP (Ont.) **21 G2**
Woodrow, VL (Sask.) **31 F4**
Woods, UP (Ont.) **25 G3**
Woods Bay, NUP (Ont.) **24 A2**
Woodsdale, UP (BC) **35 F2**
Woodside, UP (NS) **11 H3**
Woodside, UP (NB) **11 C2**
Woodside, UP (NB) **7 A4**
Woodside, UP (Man.) **29 G3**
Woodside, UP (Que.) **15 A4**
Woodside, UP (Ont.) **23 E3**
Wood's Island, COMM (Nfld.) **5 F4**
Woods Landing, UP (BC) **36 H4**
Woodstock, C (Ont.) **22 F1**
Woodstock, COMM (Nfld.) **3 B1**
Woodstock, T (NB) **11 A1**
Woodstock, UP (PEI) **7 A3**
Woodstock 23, IR (NB) **11 A1**
Woodstock Road, UP (NB) **11 B1**
Woodvale, UP (PEI) **7 A2**
Woodvale, UP (Ont.) **17 E4**
Woodview, UP (Ont.) **21 D1**
Woodview, UP (Ont.) **24 E4**
Woodville, UP (NS) **11 G3**
Woodville, UP (Nfld.) **4 A3**
Woodville, UP (NS) **9 A3**
Woodville, UP (NB) **12 A2**
Woodville, UP (Ont.) **21 B1**
Woodville, VL (Ont.) **21 C1**
Woodville Mills, UP (PEI) **7 E4**
Woodwards Cove, UP (NB) **11 C4**
Woody Cove < Rocky Harbour (COMM), UP (Nfld.) **5 F4**
Woody Island, COMM (Nfld.) **2 E2**
Woody Lake 184D, IR (Sask.) **32 G1**
Woody Point, COMM (Nfld.) **5 F4**
Woody Point < Woody Point (COMM), UP (Nfld.) **5 F4**
Woolchester, UP (Alta.) **31 B3**
Wooler, UP (Ont.) **21 E1**
Woolford, UP (Alta.) **34 F4**
Worby, UP (Man.) **29 G4**
Worcester, UP (Sask.) **29 B4**
Wordsworth, UP (Sask.) **29 C4**
Worsley, UP (Alta.) **43 G3**
Woss, UP (BC) **39 E2**
Wostok, UP (Alta.) **33 E3**
Wottonville, VL (Que.) **16 D3**
Woyenne 27, IR (BC) **42 G4**
Wreck Cove, UP (NS) **8 E2**
Wreck Cove < St Jacques – Coomb's Cove, UP (Nfld.) **2 B2**
Wrentham, UP (Alta.) **34 G4**
Wright, UP (BC) **36 C2**
Wright, UP (Que.) **18 D4**
Wrightmans Corners, UP (Ont.) **22 D1**
Wrigley, UP (NWT) **45 D3**
Wrigley Corners, UP (Ont.) **22 G1**
Wroxeter, UP (Ont.) **23 C3**
Wroxton, VL (Sask.) **29 D2**
Wudzimagon 61, IR (BC) **42 D4**
Wunnumin 1, IR (Ont.) **30 F3**
Wunnumin 2, IR (Ont.) **30 F3**
Wunnummin Lake < Wunnumin 1, UP (Ont.) **30 F3**
Wya 7, IR (BC) **38 A3**
Wyah 3, IR (BC) **38 C3**
Wyandot, UP (Ont.) **23 D3**
Wyborn, UP (Ont.) **20 B4**
Wyclese 27, IR (BC) **41 F4**
Wycliffe, UP (BC) **34 C4**
Wycott's Flat 6, IR (BC) **36 B2**
Wyebridge, UP (Ont.) **23 F1**
Wyeclif, UP (Alta.) **33 E3**
Wyecombe, UP (Ont.) **22 F2**
Wyers Brook, UP (NB) **13 C4**
Wyevale, UP (Ont.) **23 F1**
Wyley, UP (Sask.) **29 B3**
Wyman, UP (Que.) **17 B1**
Wymark, UP (Sask.) **31 E3**
Wymbolwood Beach, UP (Ont.) **23 E1**
Wynd, UP (Alta.) **40 G3**
Wyndham Hills, UP (Ont.) **22 G1**
Wynhurst Beach, UP (Ont.) **21 B1**
Wynndel, UP (BC) **34 C4**
Wynot, UP (Sask.) **31 H2**
Wynton, UP (BC) **45 B4**
Wynyard, T (Sask.) **31 H1**
Wyoming, VL (Ont.) **22 C2**
Wyse, UP (Ont.) **18 A3**
Wyses Corner, UP (NS) **9 C3**
Wyvern, UP (NS) **9 A2**

Y

Yaalstrick 1, IR (BC) **38 H2**
Yaculta < Cape Madge 10, UP (BC) **37 B4**
Yagan 3, IR (BC) **41 B1**
Yahk, UP (BC) **34 C4**
Yakats 5, IR (BC) **39 D2**
Yaku < Kioosta 15, UP (BC) **41 A1**
Yakweakwioose 12, IR (BC) **35 A4**
Yaladelassla 4, IR (BC) **40 B2**
Yale, UP (BC) **35 B3**
Yale 18, IR (BC) **35 B3**
Yale 19, IR (BC) **35 B3**
Yale 20, IR (BC) **35 B3**
Yale 21, IR (BC) **35 B3**
Yale 22, IR (BC) **35 B3**
Yale 23, IR (BC) **35 B3**
Yale 24, IR (BC) **35 B3**
Yale 25, IR (BC) **35 B3**
Yale Town 1, IR (BC) **35 B3**
Yamachiche, VL (Que.) **16 B2**
Yamaska, VL (Que.) **16 B2**
Yamaska-Est, VL (Que.) **16 B2**
Yan < Yan 7, UP (BC) **41 B1**
Yan 7, IR (BC) **41 B1**
Yankee Flats, UP (BC) **35 F1**
Yankee Line, UP (NS) **8 D3**
Yankeetown, UP (NS) **9 B3**
Yarbo, VL (Sask.) **29 D3**
Yarker, UP (Ont.) **17 A4**
Yarksis < Yarksis 11, UP (BC) **39 G4**
Yarksis 11, IR (BC) **39 G4**
Yarm, UP (Que.) **17 B1**
Yarmouth, T (NS) **10 A3**
Yarmouth 33, IR (NS) **10 A3**
Yarmouth Bar, UP (NS) **10 A3**
Yarmouth Centre, UP (Ont.) **22 E2**
Yasitkun 21, IR (BC) **41 A1**
Yates, UP (Alta.) **33 B3**
Yatton, UP (Ont.) **23 D4**
Yatze 13, IR (BC) **41 A1**
Yawaucht 11, IR (BC) **35 A1**
Yekwaupsum 18, IR (BC) **38 F1**
Yekwaupsum 19, IR (BC) **38 F1**
Yelakin 4, IR (BC) **35 B3**
Yelakin 4A, IR (BC) **35 B3**
Yellertlee 12, IR (BC) **41 E3**
Yellow Creek, VL (Sask.) **32 E4**
Yellow Girl Bay 32B, IR (Ont.) **28 G2**
Yellow Grass, T (Sask.) **31 H3**
Yellowknife, C (NWT) **44 B1**
Yellowstone, SV (Alta.) **33 D3**
Yelverton, UP (Ont.) **21 C1**
Yensischuck 3, IR (BC) **40 B1**
Yeoford, UP (Alta.) **33 D4**
Yeo Island 13, IR (BC) **41 E3**
Yeovil, UP (Ont.) **23 D3**
Yerexville, UP (Ont.) **21 G2**
Ymir, UP (BC) **34 B4**
Yoho, UP (NB) **11 C2**
Yoho, UP (BC) **34 C2**
Yonge Mills, UP (Ont.) **17 C3**
Yookwitz 12, IR (BC) **38 F1**
York, BOR (Ont.) **21 B2**
York, UP (PEI) **7 D4**
York, NUP (Ont.) **21 F1**
Yorke Settlement, UP (NS) **11 H2**
York Factory, UP (Man.) **30 E1**
York Harbour, COMM (Nfld.) **4 C1**
York Landing, UP (Man.) **30 C1**
York Mills, UP (NB) **11 B2**
York Point, UP (PEI) **7 C4**
Yorkton, C (Sask.) **29 C2**
Yorkton, CFS/SFC, MIL (Sask.) **29 C2**
Youbou, UP (BC) **38 D3**
Young, VL (Sask.) **31 F1**
Young Point, UP (Man.) **30 A2**
Young Ridge, UP (NB) **12 F3**
Youngs Cove, UP (NS) **10 C1**
Youngs Cove, UP (NB) **11 E1**
Young's Cove, UP (Ont.) **21 D1**
Youngs Cove Road, UP (NB) **11 E1**
Youngs Harbour, UP (Ont.) **21 B1**
Youngs Point, UP (Ont.) **24 E4**
Youngstown, VL (Alta.) **34 H1**
Youngstown, NUP (Ont.) **21 D1**
Youngsville, UP (Ont.) **22 E1**
Yreka, UP (BC) **39 D1**
Yukon Crossing, UP (YT) **45 B3**
Yuquot < Yuquot 1, UP (BC) **39 E3**
Yuquot 1, IR (BC) **39 E3**

Z

Zacht 5, IR (BC) **35 B2**
Zadow, UP (Ont.) **24 G1**
Zaimoetz 5, IR (BC) **42 E4**
Zaitscullachan 9, IR (BC) **38 H2**
Zala, UP (Sask.) **31 H2**
Zama Lake 210, IR (Alta.) **45 E4**
Zamora, UP (BC) **35 G4**
Zaulzap 29, IR (BC) **42 D3**
Zaulzap 29A, IR (BC) **42 D3**
Zawale, UP (Alta.) **33 F3**
Zayas Island 32A, IR (BC) **42 C4**
Zbaraz, UP (Man.) **29 H2**
Zealand, UP (NB) **11 C1**
Zealand, UP (Ont.) **17 A3**
Zealandia, T (Sask.) **31 E1**
Zeballos, VL (BC) **39 E3**
Zehner, UP (Sask.) **31 H3**
Zelana, UP (Man.) **29 E2**
Zelena, UP (Man.) **29 D2**
Zelma, VL (Sask.) **31 F1**
Zenda, UP (Ont.) **22 F1**
Zeneta, UP (Sask.) **29 D3**
Zenon Park, VL (Sask.) **32 F4**
Zephyr, UP (Ont.) **21 B1**
Zeta, UP (Ont.) **26 F2**
Zhoda, UP (Man.) **28 B3**
Zimagord 3, IR (BC) **42 E4**
Zincton, UP (BC) **34 B3**
Zion, UP (Ont.) **21 D2**
Zion, UP (Ont.) **21 D1**
Zion, UP (Ont.) **23 H2**
Zion, UP (Ont.) **23 D2**
Zion, UP (Ont.) **23 C1**
Zion, UP (Ont.) **23 B3**
Zion Hill, UP (Ont.) **21 F1**
Zion Line, UP (Ont.) **17 A1**
Zionville, UP (NB) **11 C1**
Ziska, UP (Ont.) **24 B3**
Zoht 4, IR (BC) **35 C2**
Zoht 5, IR (BC) **35 C2**
Zoht 14, IR (BC) **35 C2**
Zoria, UP (Man.) **29 E2**
Zuber Corners, UP (Ont.) **23 D4**
Zurich, VL (Ont.) **23 B4**

PHYSICAL FEATURES

Bicknor, Cape, (NWT) **47 E1**
Bic, Rivière du, (Que.) **14 G3**
Biddison Lake, (Ont.) **28 H3**
Bieler Lake, (NWT) **47 G4**
Bienville, Lac, (Que.) **20 G1**
Big Bald Mountain, (NB) **12 D2**
Big Barasway, (Nfld.) **4 D4**
Big Bar Creek, (BC) **36 B3**
Big Bar Lake, (BC) **36 C3**
Big Basin, The, (NS) **8 D4**
Big Bay, (Nfld.) **6 F2**
Big Bear Cove Pond, (Nfld.) **3 E3**
Big Bight *(bay)*, (Nfld.) **6 G2**
Big Blue Hill Pond, (Nfld.) **2 C2**
Big Bon Mature Lake, (NS) **10 D3**
Big Burnt Island, (Ont.) **25 D2**
Big Canyon Lake, (Ont.) **28 H1**
Big Caribou Lake, (Ont.) **25 G2**
Big Caribou River, (NS) **9 D1**
Big Cedar Brook, (NB) **12 B1**
Big Cedar Lake, (Ont.) **24 E4**
Big Clear Lake, (Ont.) **24 G3**
Big Conne *(cove)* (Nfld.) **2 C2**
Big Cove, (Nfld.) **4 A2**
Big Creek, (Ont.) **22 B3**
Big Creek, (Ont.) **22 G1**
Big Creek, (Ont.) **22 F2**
Big Creek, (BC) **36 A2**
Big Crow Lake, (Ont.) **24 D1**
Big Duck Island, (NS) **10 F2**
Big Five Bridge Lake, (NS) **10 F2**
Big Flat Lake, (Man.) **44 G3**
Big Forks Stream, (NB) **12 E4**
Biggar, Lac, (Que.) **20 F3**
Biggar Lake, (Ont.) **24 C1**
Biggars Lake, (NS) **10 B3**
Big Gaspereaux Lake, (NS) **9 E3**
Big Grassy River, (Ont.) **28 G3**
Biggs Point, (NWT) **47 B3**
Big Gull Lake, (NS) **10 B3**
Big Gull Lake, (Ont.) **24 G3**
Big Gull Pond, (Nfld.) **4 C1**
Big Gully Creek, (Alta./Sask.) **32 A3**
Big Harbour Island, (NS) **8 D4**
Big Hawk Lake, (Ont.) **24 D2**
Big Hay Lake, (Alta.) **33 E3**
Big Head, (Nfld.) **3 A1**
Bighead River, (Ont.) **23 D2**
Bighorn Creek, (BC) **34 A1**
Big Indian Lake, (NS) **10 F1**
Big Interior Mountain, (BC) **39 G4**
Big Island, (NWT) **6 C1**
Big Island, (Nfld.) **6 E1**
Big Island, (Ont.) **21 F1**
Big Island, (Ont.) **27 A1**
Big Island, (Ont.) **28 F3**
Big Island, (NWT) **44 A1**
Big Island, (NWT) **46 F3**
Big Kalzas Lake, (YT) **45 B3**
Big Kedron Lake, (NB) **11 B2**
Big LaHave Lake, (NS) **10 D1**
Big Lake, (NS) **9 B1**
Big Lake, (Ont.) **27 E1**
Big Lake, (Alta.) **33 D3**
Big Lake, (BC) **36 C1**
Big Lake, (BC) **36 C2**
Big Liscomb Lake, (NS) **9 E2**
Big Merigomish Island, (NS) **9 E1**
Big Molly Upsim Lake, (NS) **10 D1**
Big Mossy Point, (Man.) **30 B2**
Big Muddy Lake, (Sask.) **31 G4**
Big Mushamush Lake, (NS) **10 E2**
Bigniba, Rivière, (Que.) **20 E4**
Bigoray River, (Alta.) **33 C3**
Bigot, Lac, (Que.) **19 F2**
Big Otter Creek, (Ont.) **22 F2**
Big Pine Lake, (NS) **10 B2**
Big Piskwanish Point, (Ont.) **20 D3**
Big Plate Island, (Nfld.) **2 A3**
Big Point, (PEI) **7 D4**
Big Point, (Man.) **29 G3**
Big Pond, (Nfld.) **2 F1**
Big Pond, (Nfld.) **2 G3**
Big Pond, (Nfld.) **3 F4**
Big Pond, (Nfld.) **4 C3**
Big Pond, (Nfld.) **5 H1**
Big Quill Lake, (Sask.) **29 A1**
Big Rideau Lake, (Ont.) **17 B3**
Big Ridge, The, (NS) **9 G1**
Big River, (Nfld.) **6 F3**
Big River, (Sask.) **32 C3**
Big River, (NWT) **47 A3**
Big Rocky Lake, (NWT) **44 F1**
Big St Margarets Bay Lake, (NS) **10 F1**
Big Salmon River, (NB) **11 F2**
Big Salmon River, (YT) **45 B3**
Big Sand Lake, (Man.) **44 H3**
Big Sandy Lake, (Sask.) **32 F2**
Big Sandy Point, (Man.) **29 F1**
Bigsby Island, (Ont.) **28 F3**
Bigsby Point, (Ont.) **28 F3**
Big Sevogle River, (NB) **12 E2**
Big Silver Creek, (BC) **35 A3**
Big Spruce River, (Man.) **44 H2**
Bigstick Lake, (Sask.) **31 C3**
Big Stillwater, (NS) **9 E3**
Bigstone Bay, (Ont.) **28 F2**
Bigstone Lake, (Man.) **30 C2**
Bigstone Lake, (Sask.) **32 G2**
Bigstone River, (Man.) **30 D2**
Big Tancook Island, (NS) **10 F2**
Big Timothy Mountain, (BC) **36 D1**
Big Tom Wallace Lake, (NS) **10 B2**
Big Tracadie River, (NB) **12 F1**
Big Tracadie River Gully, (NB) **12 G1**
Big Traverse Bay, (Man./Ont.) **28 E3**
Big Trout Lake, (Ont.) **24 D1**
Big Trout Lake, (Ont.) **30 F2**
Big Tusket Island, (NS) **10 B4**
Big White Mountain, (BC) **35 G3**
Big Whiteshell Lake, (Man.) **28 D1**
Billygoat Creek, (BC) **37 G4**
Binta Lake, (BC) **41 H1**
Birchbark Lake, (Sask.) **32 E3**
Birch Head, (NS) **9 B1**
Birch Island, (Man.) **30 A3**
Birch Lake, (Ont.) **25 C1**
Birch Lake, (Man.) **28 D2**
Birch Lake, (Ont.) **30 E4**
Birch Lake, (Sask.) **32 B3**
Birch Lake, (Man.) **32 H3**
Birch Lake, (Alta.) **33 D3**
Birch Lake, (Alta.) **33 F3**
Birch Lake, (BC) **36 E3**
Birch Lake, (NWT) **44 A1**
Birch Mountains, (Alta.) **44 B3**
Birch Point, (PEI) **7 C4**
Birch River, (Man.) **28 D2**
Birch River, (Alta.) **44 B3**
Birchy Bay, (Nfld.) **3 D2**
Birchy Island, (Nfld.) **3 C2**
Birchy Lake, (Nfld.) **5 G4**
Bird Fiord, (NWT) **47 E2**
Bird Islands, (NS) **8 E2**
Birds Hill Provincial Park, (Man.) **28 A1**
Birdtail Creek, (Man.) **29 E3**
Birkenhead Lake, (BC) **37 G3**
Birkenhead Lake Provincial Park, (BC) **37 G3**
Birkenhead River, (BC) **37 G3**
Biscay Bay, (Nfld.) **2 G4**
Biscay Bay River, (Nfld.) **2 G4**
Biscotasi Lake, (Ont.) **26 D3**
Bishop Lake, (Ont.) **27 C2**
Bishop Lake, (NWT) **45 E2**
Bishop River, (BC) **37 D2**
Bison Lake, (Alta.) **44 A3**
Bisset Creek, (Sask.) **32 E3**
Bissett Lake, (Man.) **30 C1**
Bissett Lake, (NWT) **46 B2**
Bistcho Lake, (Alta.) **45 E4**
Bitter Lake, (Sask.) **31 C3**
Bittern Lake, (Sask.) **32 D3**
Bittern Lake, (Alta.) **33 E4**
Bizard, Ile, (Que.) **17 F4**
Bjarni, Lac, (Que.) **6 D2**
Bjork Lake, (Sask.) **32 G4**
Bjorne Peninsula, (NWT) **47 E2**
Blachford Lake, (NWT) **44 C1**
Black Bay, (Nfld.) **5 G1**
Black Bay, (Ont.) **27 E3**
Black Bay, (Sask.) **32 C1**
Black Bay, (Sask.) **44 D2**
Black Bay Peninsula, (Ont.) **27 E3**
Black Bear bay, (Nfld.) **6 H3**
Black Bear Island Lake, (Sask.) **32 D1**
Blackbear Lake, (Ont.) **30 E2**
Black Bear River, (Nfld.) **6 H3**
Blackbear River, (Ont.) **30 E2**
Black Birch Lake, (Sask.) **44 D4**
Black Brook, (NS) **8 E2**
Black Brook Cove, (NS) **8 E2**
Black Creek, (Ont.) **22 C2**
Black Creek, (Ont.) **22 G2**
Black Creek, (Ont.) **23 C4**
Black Creek, (BC) **39 H3**
Black Creek, (BC) **43 E2**
Black Donald Lake, (Ont.) **24 G2**
Black Duck River, (Man./Ont.) **30 F1**
Blacketts Lake, (NS) **8 E3**
Blackfish Lake, (Man.) **44 H2**
Black Head, (Nfld.) **2 H4**
Black Head, (Nfld.) **3 G4**
Blackhead Bay, (Nfld.) **3 G4**
Black Head North, (Nfld.) **2 H2**
Black Island, (Nfld.) **3 C2**
Black Island, (Nfld.) **6 G3**
Black Lake, (Nfld.) **5 G4**
Black Lake, (Ont.) **17 B3**
Black Lake, (Ont.) **28 G2**
Black Lake, (BC) **37 C4**
Black Lake, (Sask.) **44 E3**
Black Mountains, (NB) **12 B2**
Black Point, (Nfld.) **2 E3**
Black Point, (Nfld.) **4 G4**
Black Point, (PEI) **7 C4**
Black Point, (NS) **8 E4**
Black Point, (NS) **9 G2**
Black Point, (NS) **10 A3**
Black Point, (NS) **10 D3**
Black Point, (NS) **10 D3**
Black Point, (Ont.) **28 F3**
Black River, (NB) **11 E3**
Black River, (NB) **12 F2**
Black River, (Ont.) **23 G2**
Black River, (Ont.) **24 C3**
Black River, (Ont.) **24 F3**
Black River, (Ont.) **26 F1**
Black River, (Ont.) **27 H3**
Black River, (Man.) **30 C4**
Black River Lake, (NS) **11 H3**
Black River Pond, (Nfld.) **2 E1**
Blackrock Point, (NS) **8 F4**
Black Rock Point, (Nfld.) **46 G3**
Blacks Brook, (NS) **10 C3**
Blacks Point, (Ont.) **23 B4**
Blackstock Point, (Ont.) **25 B2**
Blackstone Lake, (Ont.) **25 B3**
Blackstone River, (Alta.) **33 B4**
Blackstone River, (YT) **45 B2**
Blackstone River, (NWT) **45 D3**
Black Sturgeon Lake, (Ont.) **27 E2**
Black Sturgeon Lakes, (Ont.) **28 F1**
Black Sturgeon River, (Ont.) **27 E3**
Blackwater Lake, (NWT) **45 D3**
Blackwater River, (Ont.) **27 F2**
Blackwater River, (NWT) **45 D3**
Blaeberry River, (BC) **34 B2**
Blaine Lakes, (Sask.) **32 C4**
Blake Bay, (NWT) **46 D2**
Blake Point, (Ont.) **25 A2**
Blakiston, Mount, (Alta.) **34 E4**
Blanc, Cap, (Que.) **13 H2**
Blanche, Baie, (Que.) **14 F2**
Blanche Island, (NS) **10 C4**
Blanche, Lac la, (Que.) **17 D1**
Blanche River, (Ont.) **26 F2**
Blanche, Rivière, (Que.) **13 A2**
Blanche, Rivière, (Que.) **17 E3**
Blanchet Island, (NWT) **44 C1**
Blanchet, Lac, (Que.) **13 G1**
Blanchet Lake, (BC) **41 G2**
Blanchfield Lake, (NWT) **46 E1**
Blanc, Lac, (Que.) **18 G2**
Blanc, Mont, (Que.) **13 C2**
Blanshard, Mount, (BC) **38 G2**
Blessington Creek, (Ont.) **21 F1**
Bleue, Rivière, (Que.) **15 F1**
Bleuets, Rivière aux, (Que.) **18 E2**
Bleu, Lac, (Que.) **18 B3**
Blevins Lake, (Man.) **44 H2**
Bligh Island, (BC) **39 F3**
Blind Bay, (Ont.) **28 H2**
Blind Bay, (BC) **38 D1**
Blindfold Lake, (Ont.) **28 G2**
Blindman River, (Alta.) **33 D4**
Blizzard Pond, (Nfld.) **4 F2**
Blomidon, Cape, (NS) **11 H3**
Blood Indian Creek, (Alta.) **34 H2**
Bloodsucker Lake, (Sask.) **32 G3**
Bloodvein River, (Man./Ont.) **30 C4**
Bloody Creek, (NS) **10 B3**
Bloody Reach, (Nfld.) **3 F3**
Bloody River, (NWT) **45 D2**
Blouin, Lac, (Que.) **18 B2**
Blow River, (YT) **45 B1**
Blueberry River, (BC) **43 E3**
Blue, Cape, (NS) **9 F1**
Blue Gull Pond, (Nfld.) **3 F4**
Blue Hills of Couteau, (Nfld.) **4 D3**
Blue Island, (NS) **10 C4**
Blue Jay Creek, (Ont.) **25 C3**
Blue Lake, (Ont.) **28 H1**
Blue Mountain, (NB) **13 D4**
Bluenose Lake, (NWT) **45 D1**
Blue Point, (Ont.) **22 C1**
Blue River, (BC) **36 G1**
Bluff, Cape, (Nfld.) **6 H4**
Bluff Head, (Nfld.) **2 F1**
Bluff Head, (Nfld.) **3 C1**
Bluff Head, (Nfld.) **4 B1**
Bluff Head Cove, (Nfld.) **6 G3**
Bluffpoint Lake, (Ont.) **28 H3**
Bluffy Lake, (Ont.) **30 E4**
Blunden Point, (BC) **38 D2**
Blunt Peninsula, (NWT) **46 G2**
Blustry Mountain, (BC) **35 A1**
Boars Head, (NS) **10 A2**
Boas River, (NWT) **46 D2**
Boat Harbour, (Nfld.) **2 D3**
Boat Lake, (Ont.) **23 C1**
Boatswain Bay, (NWT) **20 E3**
Bobbie Burns Creek, (BC) **34 B2**
Boobys Pond, (Nfld.) **4 F2**
Boo Lake, (Ont.) **24 C3**
Boos Lake, (Ont.) **17 A3**
Boeste, Lac, (Que.) **19 E1**
Boffin Lake, (Ont.) **28 H4**
Boggy River, (Man.) **28 D2**
Bog Lake, (Sask.) **32 H3**
Bog River, (Man.) **28 C1**
Bohier, Lac, (Que.) **5 C2**
Bohn Lake, (Alta.) **44 C4**
Boisbriand, Lac, (Que.) **20 H2**
Bois Brûlé, Cap du, (Que.) **13 H2**
Bois, Ile, (Que.) **5 G2**
Bois Island, (Nfld.) **2 B2**
Bois, Lac des, (Ont.) **28 F2**
see Woods, Lake of the
Bois, Lac des, (NWT) **45 D2**
Bois Long, Lac du, (Que.) **19 C2**
Boisvert, Pointe au, (Que.) **2**
Boisvert, Rivière, (Que.) **20 G4**
Boitano Lake, (BC) **36 B2**
Boiteuse, Lac de la, (Que.) **14 A2**
Boivin, Lac, (Que.) **19 B1**
Boland Brook, (NB) **13 B4**
Boland Lake, (NWT) **44 G1**
Boland River, (Ont.) **26 C4**
Bold Point, (Ont.) **25 D2**
Bolduc, Mount, (BC) **38 D3**
Bolean Creek, (BC) **35 E1**
Bolean Lake, (BC) **35 F1**
Bolton Creek, (Ont.) **17 A2**
Bolton Lake, (NB) **11 A2**
Bolton Lake, (Man.) **30 C2**
Bolton River, (Man.) **30 C2**
Bompas Lake, (Sask.) **44 E2**
Bonanza Lake, (BC) **39 E2**
Bonaparte Lake, (BC) **36 E3**
Bonaparte River, (BC) **36 D3**
Bonaparte River, (BC) **36 C4**
Bonaventure Head, (Nfld.) **2 G1**
Bonaventure, Ile de, (Que.) **13 H2**
Bonaventure, Ouest, Rivière, (Que.) **13 E2**
Bonaventure, Pointe, (Que.) **13 E4**
Bonaventure, Rivière, (Que.) **13 F2**
Bonavista Bay, (Nfld.) **3 G3**
Bonavista, Cape, (Nfld.) **3 G3**
Bon-Désir, Cap de, (Que.) **14 E3**
Bond Sound, (BC) **39 F1**
Bon Echo Provincial Park, (Ont.) **24 G3**
Bone Creek, (Sask.) **31 C4**
Bone Creek, (BC) **36 H1**
Bonell Creek, (BC) **38 D2**
Bonhomme, Lac, (Que.) **15 F3**
Bonhomme, Ruisseau, (Que.) **15 F3**
Bonilla Island, (BC) **41 C2**
Bonne Bay, (Nfld.) **4 G4**
Bonne Bay, (Nfld.) **5 F4**
Bonne Bay Big Pond, (Nfld.) **5 F4**
Bonnechere River, (Ont.) **24 F1**
Bonnet, Lac du, (Man.) **30 C4**
Bonnet Lake, (NS) **9 G2**
Bonnet Plume River, (YT) **45 B2**
Bonny River, (NB) **11 C3**
Bonokoski Lake, (Sask.) **44 F2**
Bonwick Island, (BC) **39 E1**
Boom Island, (NS) **8 D4**
Boom Island, (Ont.) **25 E2**
Booney, Mount, (BC) **34 B2**
Boothia Peninsula, (NWT) **47 D4**
Booth Islands, (NWT) **45 D1**
Booth, Lac, (Que.) **26 G3**
Booth Lake, (Ont.) **24 E1**
Booth Lake, (Man.) **44 G2**
Boot Island, (NS) **9 A2**
Boot Lake, (BC) **39 G2**
Borden Island, (NWT) **47 C2**
Borden Lake, (Ont.) **26 C2**
Borden Peninsula, (NWT) **47 F3**
Borden River, (NWT) **46 C2**
Border Ranges, (BC) **34 E4**
Borney Lake, (Nfld.) **3 C3**
Borup Fiord, (NWT) **47 E1**
Boshkung Lake, (Ont.) **24 C3**
Bosk Lake, (BC) **36 E1**
Boss Creek, (BC) **36 E2**
Boss Mountain, (BC) **36 E1**
Boston Creek, (Ont.) **22 G1**
Bostonnais, Rivière, (Que.) **18 H2**
Botanie Creek, (BC) **35 B1**
Botanie Mountain, (BC) **35 B1**
Botanist Lake, (Ont.) **28 G1**
Botha River, (Alta.) **43 G2**
Botsford Lake, (Ont.) **27 B1**
Bottle Lake, (Nfld.) **4 D2**
Bottle Lake, (Man.) **29 F3**
Bottle Point, (Ont.) **27 G3**
Bottom Brook, (Nfld.) **4 C2**
Bottom Brook, (Nfld.) **4 G3**
Bouchard, Iles, (Que.) **16 A3**
Boucher, Lac, (Que.) **5 D2**
Boucher Lake, (Sask.) **32 E4**
Boucher Point, (Ont.) **23 D1**
Boucher, Rivière, (Que.) **14 F1**
Boucherville, Iles de, (Que.) **17 H3**
Boucherville, Port de, (NWT) **46 E3**
Bouchette Point, (Ont.) **21 D2**
Bouchier, Lac, (Que.) **20 E4**
Boudart, Lac, (Que.) **19 E1**
Bouffard, Lac, (Que.) **19 D2**
Boughey Bay, (BC) **39 F1**
Boughton Bay, (PEI) **7 E4**
Boughton Island, (PEI) **7 E4**
Boughton River, (PEI) **7 E4**
Boulain, Lac, (Que.) **5 C2**
Bouleau Lake, (BC) **35 E2**
Bouleau, Monts du, (Alta.) **44 B3**
see Birch Mountains
Bouleau, Rivière au, (Que.) **19 G3**
Boullé, Lac, (Que.) **6 C1**
Boulogne Lake, (NWT) **44 A1**
Boundary Bay, (BC) **38 F3**
Boundary Creek, (BC) **35 G4**
Boundary Dam Reservoir, (Sask.) **29 C4**
Boundary Ranges, (BC) **42 C2**
Bounty, Cape, (NWT) **47 C3**
Bourbon, Rivière, (Que.) **16 D2**
Bourdel, Lac, (Que.) **46 F4**
Bourdon, Lac, (Que.) **6 D3**
Bourget, Ruisseau, (Que.) **14 A2**
Bourne, Cape, (NWT) **47 E1**
Bourque Lake, (Alta.) **33 G2**
Boutin, Rivière, (Que.) **20 F1**
Bowden Lake, (Ont.) **28 H1**
Bowen Island, (BC) **38 F2**
Bowers Lake, (BC) **36 E2**
Bowes Point, (NWT) **45 G1**
Bowker, Lac, (Que.) **16 C4**
Bowman Bay, (NWT) **46 E2**
Bowman Head, (NS) **8 B4**
Bowmanville Creek, (Ont.) **21 C2**
Bow River, (Sask.) **32 E2**
Bow River, (Alta.) **34 D2**
Bowron Lake, (BC) **40 D2**
Bowron Lake Provincial Park, (BC) **40 E2**
Bowron River, (BC) **40 D2**
Bowser Lake, (BC) **42 D2**
Boxey Point, (Nfld.) **2 B3**
Box Lake, (Sask.) **44 E2**
Boyd, Lac, (Que.) **20 F2**
Boyd Lake, (NWT) **44 F1**
Boyd Point, (BC) **37 E2**
Boyer Nord, Rivière, (Que.) **15 H4**
Boyer River, (Alta.) **43 H1**
Boyer, Rivière, (Que.) **15 B3**
Boyer Sud, Rivière, (Que.) **15 H4**
Boyle Drain, (Ont.) **22 B3**
Boyle Point, (BC) **38 C2**
Boyles Point, (BC) **39 E1**
Boyne River, (Ont.) **23 E2**
Boyne River, (Man.) **29 G4**
Brabant Lake, (Sask.) **44 F4**
Bracebridge Inlet, (NWT) **47 D3**
Bracken Lake, (Man.) **30 B2**
Brackett Lake, (NWT) **45 D2**
Bradley Creek, (BC) **36 D2**
Brador, Baie de, (Que.) **5 G2**
Bragg's Island, (Nfld.) **3 F3**
Bramham Island, (BC) **41 F4**
Branch River, (Nfld.) **2 E4**
Brandy Head, (Nfld.) **4 F4**
Bras d'Or Lake, (NS) **8 D4**
Bras d'Or Lake, (NWT) **44 B1**
Bras, Rivière le, (Que.) **15 B3**
Brass Coupé, Lac du, (Que.) **20 F4**
Bray Island, (NWT) **46 E1**
Bray Lake, (Ont.) **24 B1**
Brazeau Lake, (Alta.) **40 H3**
Brazeau, Mount, (Alta.) **40 H3**
Brazeau River, (Alta.) **33 B4**
Brazza, Lac, (Que.) **14 C1**
Breakenridge, Mount, (BC) **35 A3**
Breakheart Point, (Nfld.) **2 G1**
Brébeuf, Lac, (Que.) **14 C3**
Breeches, Lac, (Que.) **16 E2**
Bréhat, Lac, (Que.) **6 A4**
Bréhat, Lac, (Que.) **20 H2**
Breithaupt Lake, (NWT) **44 E1**
Breme Point, (Nfld.) **2 E4**
Bremner River, (Ont.) **27 H3**
Brem River, (BC) **37 C3**
Brennan Lake, (Ont.) **27 D1**
Brentford Bay, (NWT) **47 D4**
Brent Islands, (Nfld.) **5 H2**
Brent, Mount, (BC) **35 E3**
Brereton Lake, (Man.) **28 D1**
Brésolles, Lac, (Que.) **20 H1**
Breton, Cape, (NS) **8 G3**
Brettell Point, (BC) **37 C3**
Brevoort Island, (NWT) **46 G2**
Brew Creek, (BC) **37 B2**
Brewster Lake, (BC) **39 G2**
Brichta Lake, (NWT) **45 G1**
Briçonnet, Lac, (Que.) **5 D2**
Bridgar, Lac, (Que.) **20 F2**
Bridge Creek, (Sask.) **31 C3**
Bridge Creek, (BC) **36 D2**
Bridge Glacier, (BC) **37 E2**
Bridge Lake, (BC) **36 E3**
Bridge River, (BC) **37 F2**
Bridport Inlet, (NWT) **47 C3**
Brier Island, (NS) **10 A2**
Briggs, Cape, (NWT) **47 D2**
Brig Harbour Island, (Nfld.) **6 G3**
Brightsand Lake, (Sask.) **32 B3**
Brigus Head, (Nfld.) **2 H3**
Brillant, Mont, (Que.) **15 F3**
Bringadin, Lac, (Que.) **6 C3**
Brinks Pond, (Nfld.) **3 D2**
Brion, Ile, (Que.) **7 G1**
Brion, Lac, (Que.) **6 B3**
Brisay, Lac, (Que.) **6 B3**
Brisebois, Lac, (Que.) **26 G3**
Brisson, Lac, (Que.) **6 D2**
Britannia Bay, (Ont.) **17 D4**
British Empire Range, (NWT) **47 E1**
Brittain River, (BC) **37 D4**
Britt Brook Lake, (NB) **12 C2**
Britton Lake, (Man.) **30 A1**
Brizley Stream, (NB) **11 C2**
Broadback, Rivière, (Que.) **20 F4**
Broad Cove, (Nfld.) **3 G4**
Broad Cove Brook, (Nfld.) **4 C3**
Broad Cove Head, (Nfld.) **2 D3**
Broad Cove Point, (Nfld.) **4 B1**
Broad Creek, (Sask.) **32 B1**
Broad Island, (Nfld.) **3 F3**
Broad River, (NS) **10 D3**
Broad River, (Man.) **46 B4**
Broad River Lake, (NS) **10 D3**
Brochet Bay, (Man.) **44 G3**
Brochet, Lac, (Man.) **44 G3**
Brochet, Lac au, (Que.) **19 C4**
Brochets, Rivière aux, (Que.) **16 B4**
Brock Island, (NWT) **47 C2**
Brock Lake, (Alta.) **33 C3**
Brock River, (NWT) **45 D1**
Brock, Rivière, (Que.) **20 G4**
Brodeur Island, (Ont.) **27 F3**
Brodeur Peninsula, (NWT) **47 E4**
Brodtkorb, Lac, (Que.) **18 C4**
Brokenhead River, (Man.) **28 B1**
Brome, Lac, (Que.) **16 C4**
Bromley Lake, (Ont.) **26 D2**
Bromley Lake, (NWT) **46 B3**
Brompton, Lac, (Que.) **16 C4**
Bronson Lake, (Sask.) **33 H3**
Bronte Creek, (Ont.) **21 A3**
Brooch, Lac, (Que.) **19 D2**
Brookfield Creek, (BC) **36 F2**
Brooks Bay, (Ont.) **28 H3**
Brooks Bay, (BC) **39 C2**
Brooks Lake, (Ont.) **28 H3**
Brooks Lake, (NWT) **44 E1**
Brooks Peninsula, (BC) **39 C2**
Broomclose Head, (Nfld.) **3 F3**
Broom Point, (Nfld.) **5 F4**
Brooms Brook, (Nfld.) **4 A3**
Broughton Island, (BC) **39 E1**
Broughton Island, (NWT) **46 G1**
Broughton Strait, (BC) **39 D1**
Brown Creek, (Ont.) **22 C2**
Browne Bay, (NWT) **47 D3**
Browne Island, (NWT) **47 D3**
Brownell Lake, (Sask.) **32 F1**
Brown Inlet, (NWT) **46 F2**
Brown Lake, (NWT) **46 C2**
Brown Passage, (BC) **42 C4**
Brown Point, (NWT) **45 G1**
Browns River, (BC) **38 B1**
Broyle, Cape, (Nfld.) **2 H3**
Bruce, Lac, (Que.) **18 C3**
Bruce Lake, (Ont.) **30 E4**
Bruce Peninsula, (Ont.) **25 D4**
Bruin, Cape, (NB) **7 B4**
Brulé, Cape, (Nfld.) **3 B1**
Brûlée, Pointe, (NS) **8 D4**
Brule Harbour, (NS) **9 C1**
Brûlé, Lac, (Que.) **18 C3**
Brûlé, Lac, (Que.) **19 D2**
Brûlé, Lac, (Que.) **19 D4**
Brûlé Lake, (Nfld.) **6 D4**
Brule Lake, (Ont.) **24 G3**
Brûlé Lake, (Alta.) **40 H2**
Brûlé Lake, (NWT) **44 E2**
Brumes, Lac aux, (Que.) **14 C2**
Bruneau Lake, (Man.) **30 B2**
Brune, Lac, (Que.) **20 D4**
Brunette Island, (Nfld.) **2 B3**
Brunswick Lake, (Ont.) **26 C1**
Brunswick Mountain, (BC) **38 F2**
Bryson, Lac, (Que.) **18 C4**
Buade, Lac, (Que.) **18 F1**
Buchanan Bay, (NWT) **47 F2**
Buchanan Lake, (Ont.) **26 C1**
Buchan Bay, (NWT) **45 F1**
Buchan Gulf, (NWT) **47 G4**
Buchan Lake, (Alta./NWT) **44 B2**
Buchans Island, (Nfld.) **4 F1**
Buchans Lake, (Nfld.) **4 F1**
Buchholz Channel, (BC) **39 C1**
Buck Creek, (BC) **42 G4**
Buckham Lake, (NWT) **44 C1**
Buckhorn Lake, (Ont.) **24 D4**
Buckingham Island, (NWT) **47 E2**
Buckinghorse River, (BC) **43 C2**
Buck Lake, (Ont.) **17 B3**
Buck Lake, (Alta.) **33 C4**
Buckshot Lake, (Ont.) **24 G3**
Buctouche, Baie de, (NE) **12 G3**
Buctouche, Dune de, (NB) **12 G3**
Buctouche River, (NB) **12 G4**
Bueil, Lac, (Que.) **20 G3**
Buerger Point, (NWT) **46 G3**
Buet, Rivière, (Que.) **46 F3**
Buffalo Bay, (Man.) **28 E3**
Buffalo Bay, (Alta.) **33 B1**
Buffalo Head Hills, (Alta.) **44 A3**
Buffalo Lake, (Alta.) **33 E4**
Buffalo Lake, (BC) **36 D2**
Buffalo Lake, (NWT) **44 B2**
Buffalo Pound Lake, (Sask.) **31 G2**
Buffalo Pound Provincial Park, (Sask.) **31 G3**
Buffalo River, (Alta.) **43 H1**
Buffalo River, (Alta./NWT) **44 B2**
Buffer Lake, (Sask.) **32 D4**
Buffett Head, (Nfld.) **2 E3**
Bugaboo Creek, (BC) **34 C2**
Buit, Lac, (Que.) **5 A2**
Bujeault, Rivière, (Que.) **5 F1**
Bukken Fiord, (NWT) **47 D1**
Bulger Lake, (Man.) **30 C2**
Bulkley Ranges, (BC) **42 F4**
Bulkley River, (BC) **42 F3**
Bull Arm, (Nfld.) **2 F2**
Bull Creek, (NB) **11 A1**
Bull Creek, (Sask.) **31 D4**
Bullen River, (NWT) **45 G2**
Bull Head, (Nfld.) **2 H3**
Bull Island, (Nfld.) **2 F2**
Bull Island Point, (Nfld.) **2 E4**
Bull Lake, (NWT) **44 E1**
Bullmoose Creek, (BC) **43 E4**
Bullock Lake, (BC) **36 C3**
Bullpound Creek, (Alta.) **34 G2**
Bull River, (BC) **34 D4**
Bull Rock, (NB) **11 B4**
Bullshead Creek, (Alta.) **31 B4**
Bulman, Mount, (BC) **35 D1**
Bulmer Lake, (NWT) **45 D3**
Bulstrode, Rivière, (Que.) **16 D2**
Bulyea River, (Sask.) **44 E2**
Bunde Fiord, (NWT) **47 D1**
Bunder Lake, (Alta.) **33 F2**
Bunker Hill Brook, (Nfld.) **4 C3**
Bunsby Islands, (BC) **39 D2**
Buntzen Lake, (BC) **38 G2**
Burchell Lake, (Ont.) **27 C3**
Burditt Lake, (Ont.) **28 H3**
Burdwood Point, (BC) **39 E4**
Burgeo Islands, (Nfld.) **4 D4**
Burgoyne Bay, (NWT) **46 F3**
Burin Inlet, (Nfld.) **2 C3**
Burin Island, (Nfld.) **2 C4**
Burin Peninsula, (Nfld.) **2 C3**
Burke Channel, (BC) **41 F3**
Burman River, (BC) **39 G3**
Burnaby Island, (BC) **41 B3**
Burnett Bay, (NWT) **47 A3**
Burnett Lake, (Sask.) **44 F3**
Burnett Point, (NWT) **47 C3**
Burney, Cape, (NWT) **47 F3**
Burnie Lake, (Man.) **44 G3**
Burnie River, (BC) **42 F4**
Burnley Creek, (Ont.) **21 E1**
Burnside River, (NWT) **45 F2**
Burns Lake, (Ont.) **24 G2**
Burnt Arm, (Nfld.) **3 C2**
Burnt Bay, (Nfld.) **3 C2**
Burnt Berry Brook, (Nfld.) **3 A2**
Burntbush River, (Ont.) **20 D4**
Burntcoat Head, (NS) **9 B2**
Burnthill Brook, (NB) **12 C3**
Burnt Island, (Nfld.) **3 D1**
Burnt Island, (Nfld.) **3 C2**
Burnt Island, (Nfld.) **3 F3**
Burnt Island, (Ont.) **25 G1**
Burnt Island Brook, (Nfld.) **4 B4**
Burnt Island Harbour, (Ont.) **25 A2**
Burnt Island Lake, (Ont.) **24 D1**
Burnt Lake, (Nfld.) **3 D2**
Burnt Lake, (Nfld.) **3 C3**
Burnt Lake, (Alta.) **33 F2**
Burnt Lake, (Alta.) **33 G2**
Burntout Brook, (Sask.) **32 F4**
Burnt Pond, (Nfld.) **3 A2**
Burnt Pond, (Nfld.) **4 E3**
Burnt Pond River, (Nfld.) **4 D3**
Burnt River, (Ont.) **24 D3**
Burnt River, (BC) **43 D4**
Burntroot Lake, (Ont.) **24 D1**
Burntwood Lake, (Man.) **30 B1**
Burntwood River, (Man.) **30 B1**
Burpee Lake, (NWT) **44 E1**
Burrage Creek, (BC) **42 D1**
Burrard Inlet, (BC) **38 F2**
Burrell Creek, (BC) **35 H3**
Burrows Lake, (Ont.) **27 G1**
Burstall Lake, (Alta.) **44 D2**
Burt Lake, (Ont.) **27 B3**
Burton, Lac, (Que.) **20 E1**
Burwash Bay, (NWT) **46 F2**
Burwash Lake, (Ont.) **26 E3**
Bushby Point, (Ont.) **23 E1**
Bushe River, (Alta.) **44 A3**
Buskegau River, (Ont.) **26 E1**
Bussy, Lac, (Que.) **19 A1**
Bustard Islands, (Ont.) **25 E2**
Bute Inlet, (BC) **37 B3**
Bute, Mount, (BC) **37 C2**
Buteux, Lac, (Que.) **6 C1**
Buteux, Lac, (Que.) **14 D4**
Butler, Ruisseau, (Que.) **13 C3**
Butnau River, (Man.) **30 D1**
Butterfly Lake, (Man.) **30 C2**
Butter Pot *(hill)*, (Nfld.) **2 G4**
Butter Pot Provincial Park, (Nfld.) **2 G3**
Butt Lake, (Ont.) **24 C1**
Buttle Lake, (BC) **39 G3**
Button Bay, (NWT) **46 B4**
Button Islands, (NWT) **46 G3**
Butts Pond, (Nfld.) **3 E3**
Byam Channel, (NWT) **47 C3**
Byam Martin, Cape, (NWT) **47 F3**
Byam Martin Channel, (NWT) **47 C2**
Byam Martin Island, (NWT) **47 C3**
Bylot, Cape, (NWT) **46 D2**
Bylot Island, (NWT) **47 F3**
Bylot, Lac, (Que.) **46 E3**
Byng Inlet, (Ont.) **25 F2**
Byrd, Lac, (Que.) **18 C3**
Byron Bay, (Nfld.) **6 G3**
Byron Bay, (NWT) **45 F1**

C

Caamaño Sound, (BC) **41 D2**
Cabano, Rivière, (Que.) **15 F1**
Cabin Lake, (Man.) **28 D1**
Cabituquimats, Lac, (Que.) **19 C4**
Cable Head, (PEI) **7 D3**
Cabonga, Réservoir, (Que.) **18 C3**
Cabot Head, (Ont.) **25 D4**
Cabot Islands, (Nfld.) **3 G2**
Cabot, Lac, (Que.) **6 D3**
Cabot Lake, (Nfld.) **6 E2**
Cabot Strait, (NS/Nfld.) **8 E1**
Cabri Lake, (Sask.) **31 C2**
Cacaoni, Lac, (Que.) **19 F2**
Cacaoui, Lac, (Que.) **19 E2**
Cache Bay, (Ont.) **25 G1**
Cache Creek, (Alta.) **43 H1**
Cachée, Rivière, (Que.) **15 B2**
Cache Lake, (Ont.) **25 G1**
Cache Lake, (Alta.) **33 F2**
Cachisca, Lac, (Que.) **20 G4**
Cacuscanus, Lac, (Que.) **14 D1**
Cadboro Point, (BC) **38 F4**
Caddy Lake, (Man.) **28 E2**
Cadogan Inlet, (NWT) **47 F2**
Cadotte River, (Alta.) **43 H2**
Cadwallader Creek, (BC) **37 G2**
Caen Lake, (NWT) **44 A1**
Cagnet, Cape, (Nfld.) **3 B1**
Cailleteau, Lac, (Que.) **19 E1**
Caillet, Rivière, (Que.) **20 E2**
Cains River, (NB) **12 E3**
Cairn Needle *(mountain)*, (BC) **35 A3**
Cairns Lake, (Ont.) **30 D4**
Cairns Lake, (Sask.) **44 F3**
Cairo, Cape, (NWT) **47 D2**
Calabogie Lake, (Ont.) **17 A2**
Calais Lake, (NWT) **44 A1**
Calcaire, Chute du, (Que.) **6 B1**
Calder Lake, (Ont.) **28 H3**
Calder, Mount, (BC) **37 D4**
Calder River, (Sask./Alta.) **32 A1**
Calder River, (NWT) **45 E2**
Calgary Int Airport/Aéroport, (Alta.) **34 E2**
Caliper Lake, (Ont.) **28 G3**
Callaghan Creek, (BC) **37 F4**
Callaghan Lake, (BC) **37 F4**
Callaghan, Mount, (BC) **37 F4**
Calling Lake, (Alta.) **33 E1**
Calling Lake, (BC) **35 C1**
Calling River, (Alta.) **33 E1**
Call Inlet, (BC) **39 F1**
Calm Channel, (BC) **37 B3**
Calm Lake, (Ont.) **27 B3**
Calmus Passage, (BC) **39 G4**
Calvert, Cape, (BC) **41 F4**
Calvert Island, (BC) **41 E4**
Calves Nose *(point)*, (Nfld.) **3 G4**
Calway, Ruisseau, (Que.) **16 F1**
Camachigama, Lac, (Que.) **18 D2**
Cambria Icefield, (BC) **42 D3**
Cambridge Fiord, (NWT) **47 G4**
Cambrien, Lac, (Que.) **6 B2**
Camden Lake, (Ont.) **24 H4**
Camel Back Mountain, (NB) **12 D1**
Cameron Hills, (Alta./NWT) **44 A2**
Cameron Island, (NWT) **47 C2**
Cameron Lake, (Ont.) **24 D4**
Cameron Lake, (Ont.) **26 B1**
Cameron Lake, (Ont.) **28 H3**
Cameron Lake, (BC) **38 C2**
Cameron River, (BC) **38 C2**
Cameron River, (BC) **43 D2**
Cameron River, (NWT) **44 A2**
Camousitchouane, Lac, (Que.) **20 F3**
Campania Island, (BC) **41 D2**
Campbell Bay, (NWT) **45 G1**
Campbell Creek, (BC) **35 D1**
Campbell Island, (BC) **41 E3**
Campbell Lake, (Man.) **30 C1**
Campbell Lake, (BC) **35 D1**
Campbell Lake, (BC) **37 B4**
Campbell Lake, (Sask.) **44 E4**
Campbell Lake, (NWT) **45 C1**
Campbell Lake, (NWT) **45 G3**
Campbell Point, (Ont.) **27 H3**
Campbell River, (BC) **38 G3**
Campobello Island, (NB) **11 C4**
Camsell Bay, (NWT) **46 F1**
Camsell Lake, (NWT) **45 F3**
Camsell River, (NWT) **45 E2**
Canaan River, (NB) **11 E1**
Canada Bay, (Nfld.) **5 H3**
Canada Hill Lake, (NS) **10 C3**
Canada Point, (NWT) **47 F3**
Canadienne, Pointe La, (Ont.) **27 H3**
Canal Bay, (Ont.) **28 H2**
Canal Lake, (Ont.) **23 G2**
Cananée, Lac, (Que.) **19 E2**
Canard, Lac au, (Que.) **16 E3**
Canard River, (Ont.) **22 A3**
Canards, Lac aux, (Que.) **14 D4**
Candle Lake, (Sask.) **32 E3**
Caniapiscau, Lac, (Que.) **6 B3**
Caniapiscau, Rivière, (Que.) **6 C2**
Canimina, Lac, (Que.) **18 C3**
Canim Lake, (BC) **36 E2**
Canimred Creek, (BC) **36 E2**
Cannings Brook, (Nfld.) **3 B4**
Cann Island, (Nfld.) **3 E1**
Canoe Creek, (BC) **36 B3**
Canoe Lake, (Ont.) **17 A3**
Canoe Lake, (Ont.) **24 D1**
Canoe Lake, (Sask.) **32 B1**
Canoe Lake, (Alta.) **33 G1**
Canoe Reach, (BC) **40 G3**
Canoe River, (Sask.) **32 B1**
Canoe River, (BC) **40 F3**
Cañon Fiord, (NWT) **47 E1**
Canonto Lake, (Ont.) **24 H3**
Canoose Flowage, (NB) **11 B2**
Canoose Stream, (NB) **11 B2**
Canotaicane, Lac, (Que.) **20 G3**
Canots, Lac des, (Que.) **14 B1**
Canso, Strait of, (NS) **9 G1**
Cantara Bay, (Sask.) **44 D3**
Cantin Lake, (Man.) **30 D3**
Canyon Lake, (Ont.) **28 H1**
Caopacho, Lac, (Que.) **19 F1**
Caopacho, Rivière, (Que.) **19 F1**
Caopatina, Lac, (Que.) **20 G4**
Caotibi, Lac, (Que.) **19 E2**
Capaotigamau, Lac, (Que.) **19 D3**
Cap aux Meules, Ile du, (Que.) **7 F1**
Cap Chat, Pointe du, (Que.) **13 C1**
Cap Chat, Rivière du, (Que.) **13 C1**
Cap des Rosiers, Anse du, (Que.) **13 H2**
Cape Breton Highlands National Park, (NS) **8 D2**
see also Hautes terres du Cap-Breton, Parc national des
Cape Breton Island, (NS) **8 F3**
Cape Broyle Harbour, (Nfld.) **2 H3**
Cape Cove, (Nfld.) **3 E1**
Cape George Point, (NS) **9 F1**
Cape Hope Islands, (NWT) **20 E3**
Cape Kildare, (PEI) **7 B2**
Cape LaHave Island, (NS) **10 E3**
Cape MacDonnel, (NWT) **45 D2**
Cape Negro Island, (NS) **10 C4**
Cape Pond, (Nfld.) **2 G3**
Cape Sable Island, (NS) **10 B4**
Cape Scott Provincial Park, (BC) **39 C1**
Capilano River, (BC) **38 F2**
Capimitchigama, Lac, (Que.) **18 D2**
Capitachouane, Lac, (Que.) **18 D2**
Capitachouane, Rivière, (Que.) **18 C2**
Caplin Bay, (Nfld.) **6 H3**
Cap Rouge, Rivière du, (Que.) **15 F4**
Capstan, Cape, (NS) **11 G2**
Captain Island, (Nfld.) **4 D4**
Caraquet, Baie de, (NB) **13 G4**
Caraquet Island, (NB) **13 G4**
Caraquet, Rivière, (NB) **12 F1**
Carbon Creek, (BC) **43 D3**
Carcajou Lake, (NWT) **45 C2**
Carcajou River, (NWT) **45 C2**
Cardigan Bay, (PEI) **7 E4**
Cardigan Strait, (NWT) **47 E2**
Cardinal Lake, (Alta.) **43 H3**
Cardinal River, (Alta.) **33 A4**
Card Lake, (NS) **10 E1**
Cardtable Mountain, (BC) **37 F2**
Cardwell Lake, (Ont.) **24 B2**
Careen Lake, (Sask.) **44 D4**
Careless Brook, (Nfld.) **3 C3**
Carey Lake, (NWT) **44 F1**
Cargenholm, Cape, (NWT) **47 G4**
Carheil, Lac, (Que.) **6 C4**
Cariboo Lake, (BC) **40 D3**
Cariboo Mountains, (BC) **40 E2**
Caribou Harbour, (NS) **9 D1**
Caribou Island, (NS) **9 D1**
Caribou Island, (Ont.) **27 E2**
Caribou Island, (Ont.) **27 H4**
Caribou Island, (NWT) **46 D2**
Caribou, Lac
see Reindeer Lake
Caribou, Lac du, (Que.) **16 A1**
Caribou Lake, (Nfld.) **3 C4**
Caribou Lake, (NS) **10 E2**
Caribou Lake, (Ont.) **27 E1**
Caribou Lake, (Alta.) **33 G1**
Caribou Mountains, (Alta.) **44 B2**
Caribou River, (YT) **45 B2**
Caribou River, (NWT) **45 C3**
Caribou River, (Man.) **46 A3**
Carl Bay, (Ont.) **28 E2**

Carleton, Mount, (NB) 12 C1
Carleton, Pointe, (Que.) 5 A4
Carling Lake, (Ont.) 27 B1
Carlyle, Mount, (BC) 34 B3
Carmanah Creek, (BC) 38 C3
Carmanah Point, (BC) 38 C3
Carmanville Arm, (Nfld.) 3 E2
Carnecksluck Lake, (NWT) 44 H1
Carnwath River, (NWT) 45 C1
Caron, Lac, (Que.) 19 D2
Caron, Lac, (Que.) 26 G2
Carpenter Bay, (BC) 41 C3
Carpenter Lake, (BC) 37 G2
Carp Lake, (BC) 40 C1
Carp, River, (Ont.) 17 D4
Carrière, Baie, (Que.) 18 B2
Carrière, Lac, (Que.) 18 C3
Carr Lake, (NWT) 46 B3
Carroll Lake, (Man./Ont.) 30 D4
Carroll Lake, (Sask.) 32 F1
Carrot River, (Sask.) 32 G3
Carruthers Lake, (NWT) 45 H3
Carscallen Point, (Man.) 29 G1
Carstens Lake, (Ont.) 28 F3
Carswell Lake, (Sask.) 44 D3
Carter Basin, (Nfld.) 6 F3
Carteret, Lac, (Que.) 19 C3
Carter Lake, (BC) 41 E2
Cartier Lake, (Sask.) 32 F1
Cartwright Sound, (BC) 41 A2
Carty Lake, (Ont.) 26 C2
Carys Swan Nest, (NWT) 46 D3
Casault, Lac, (Que.) 13 B2
Cascade Inlet, (BC) 41 F3
Cascade Mountains, (BC) 35 B3
Cascade River, (Alta.) 34 D2
Cascapédia (Branche du Lac), Rivière, (Que.) 13 D2
Cascapédia, Lac, (Que.) 13 D1
Cascapédia, Rivière, (Que.) 13 D2
Cascapédia, Baie de, (Que.) 13 E3
Cascouia, Baie, (Que.) 14 A3
Cascumpec Bay, (PEI) 7 B3
Case River, (Ont.) 26 F1
Cassels Lake, (Ont.) 26 F3
Cassette, Lac de la, (Que.) 14 E2
Cassiar Mountains, (BC) 45 B4
Castagnier, Lac, (Que.) 18 B1
Castagnier, Rivière, (Que.) 18 B1
Castel Bay, (NWT) 47 B3
Castelnau, Lac, (Que.) 14 H1
Castignon, Lac, (Que.) 46 G4
Castlebar Lake, (Ont.) 27 H1
Castle Cove, (Nfld.) 3 G4
Castle Creek, (BC) 40 E3
Castle Island, (Nfld.) 5 H1
Castle Island, (NWT) 20 E1
Castle Mountain, (BC) 42 B1
Castle River, (Alta.) 34 E4
Castle Towers Mountain, (BC) 37 F4
Castonguay, Lac, (Que.) 18 D1
Castor Creek, (Alta.) 33 F4
Castor River, (Ont.) 17 D2
Castor, Rivière du, (Que.) 20 E2
Catala Island, (BC) 39 D3
Catalina Harbour, (Nfld.) 3 G4
Catalogne, Lac, (Que.) 6 A3
Cataraqui River, (Ont.) 17 A4
Cat Arm River, (Nfld.) 5 G3
Catastrophe Lake, (Ont.) 28 F1
Cat Bay, (Nfld.) 3 E3
Cat Brook, (Nfld.) 3 B4
Catchacoma Lake, (Ont.) 24 D3
Catfish Creek, (Ont.) 22 E2
Catfish Lake, (Ont.) 24 D1
Catfish Point, (Man.) 29 H1
Cathedral Mountain, (BC) 38 F2
Cathedral Provincial Park, (BC) 35 D4
Catherine, Lac, (Que.) 14 D1
Cat Lake, (Ont.) 30 E4
Catt, Mount, (BC) 42 E4
Cauchon Lake, (Man.) 30 C1
Cauchy, Lac, (Que.) 5 C3
Caugnawana, Lac, (Que.) 18 B4
Caumont, Lac, (Que.) 5 C3
Cauouatstacau, Rivière, (Que.) 20 G3
Causapscal, Rivière, (Que.) 13 C2
Caution, Cape, (BC) 41 F4
Cautley Creek, (BC) 43 E1
Cavan Creek, (Ont.) 21 D1
Cave Point, (Ont.) 25 D4
Caverhill Lake, (BC) 36 E3
Caviar Lake, (Ont.) 28 G3
Cawachagamite, Lac, (Que.) 20 G3
Cawker Lake, (Man.) 29 F1
Caycuse River, (BC) 38 C3
Cayenne Creek, (BC) 36 H3
Cayley, Mount, (BC) 37 F4
Cayoosh Creek, (BC) 37 H3
Cazeau, Rivière, (Que.) 15 G3
Cecebe Lake, (Ont.) 24 B1
Cecil Lake, (Ont.) 27 C2
Cedar Lake, (Ont.) 18 A4
Cedar Lake, (Ont.) 27 A1
Cedar Lake, (Man.) 30 A2
Cedar River, (Ont.) 30 E4
Cedar River, (BC) 42 E4
Cedartree Lake, (Ont.) 28 G3
Cedarwood Lake, (NS) 10 B2
Cèdres, Lac aux, (Que.) 14 E2
Cèdres, Lac aux, (Que.) 18 D4
Cèdres, Lac aux, (Que.) 19 E1
Cèdres, Lac des
see Cedar Lake
Cèdres, Rivière des, (Que.) 14 E2
Celista Creek, (BC) 36 H3
Celista Mountain, (BC) 36 H3
Centennial Lake, (Ont.) 24 G2
Central Channel, (Nfld.) 2 E3
Centre Island, (Ont.) 25 D2
Centre Island, (BC) 39 E3
Cerf, Lac du, (Que.) 18 E4
Chaatl Island, (BC) 41 A2
Chaboullié, Lac, (Que.) 20 E3
Chachukew Lake, (Sask.) 32 G1
Chaigneau, Lac, (Que.) 6 C3
Chain Lakes, (Alta.) 34 G1
Chain Pond, (Nfld.) 3 E4
Chaleur Bay, (Nfld.) 4 F4
Chaleur Bay, (NB) 13 F4
see also Chaleurs, Baie des
Chaleur Harbour, (Nfld.) 4 F4
Chaleurs, Baie des (NB/Que.) 13 F4
see also Chaleur Bay (NB)
Chambeaux, Lac, (Que.) 6 B3
Chambers Island, (Nfld.) 2 E2
Chambers Point, (Nfld.) 2 B4
Chambure, Lac, (Que.) 6 A3
Chamburne, Lac, (Que.) 20 H2
Chamouchouane, Rivière, (Que.) 18 G1
Champdoré, Lac, (Que.) 6 D2
Champlain, Lac, (Que.) 16 A4
Champlain, Rivière, (Que.) 16 C1
Chance Cove, (Nfld.) 2 H4
Chance Cove Brook, (Nfld.) 2 G4
Chance Cove Head, (Nfld.) 2 H4
Chance Head, (Nfld.) 3 F4
Chancellor Channel, (BC) 39 G2
Chandindu River, (YT) 45 A2
Chandler Lake, (Man.) 29 G3
Chandler Reach, (Nfld.) 3 F4
Chandos Lake, (Ont.) 24 E3
Change Islands, (Nfld.) 3 E1
Chantrey Inlet, (NWT) 45 H1
Chapel Arm, (Nfld.) 2 F2
Chapel Island, (Nfld.) 2 C2
Chapel Island, (Nfld.) 3 D2
Chapiteau, Lac, (Que.) 6 E2
Chapleau River, (Ont.) 26 C2
Chaplin Lake, (Sask.) 31 F3
Chapman, Cape, (NWT) 46 C1
Chapman Creek, (BC) 38 E2
Chapman Lake, (BC) 42 G4
Chapman Lake, (Man.) 44 H4
Chapman, Mount, (BC) 34 A1
Chapman, Pic, (Que.) 16 D3
Chapperon Creek, (BC) 35 E2
Chapperon Lake, (BC) 35 D2
Charbonneau River, (Sask.) 44 D3
Charcoal Creek, (BC) 35 E1
Charcoal Lake, (Sask.) 44 F3
Chardon, Lac du, (Que.) 19 C4
Charest, Rivière, (Que.) 16 C1
Charland, Lac, (Que.) 18 F3
Charles Bay, (NWT) 46 E3
Charles Brook, (Nfld.) 3 C2
Charles Dickens Point, (NWT) 47 D4
Charles Inlet, (Ont.) 25 F3
Charles Island, (NS) 9 D3
Charles Island, (NWT) 46 E3
Charles, Lac, (Que.) 5 E2
Charles Lake, (Alta.) 44 C2
Charleston Lake, (Ont.) 17 C3
Charles Yorke, Cape, (NWT) 47 E3
Charlie Lake, (BC) 43 E3
Charlie Lake, (Man./NWT) 44 G2
Charlo River, (NB) 13 D4
Charlotte, Lake, (NS) 9 C3
Charlotte Lake, (BC) 41 H3
Charlton Bay, (NWT) 44 D1
Charlton Island, (NWT) 20 D3
Charnois, Lac, (Que.) 14 A3
Charron Lake, (Man.) 30 D3
Charron Lake, (Alta.) 33 E2
Chartier Lake, (Ont.) 25 G2
Chase Creek, (BC) 36 G4
Chasse, Ile à la, (Que.) 5 A3
Chasse, Pointe à la, (Que.) 19 F3
Chasseurs, Lac des, (Que.) 13 A3
Chassignolle, Lac, (Que.) 26 G2
Chastrier, Lac, (Que.) 6 B3
Châteauguay, Lac, (Que.) 6 B2
Châteauguay, Rivière, (Que.) 6 B2
Châteauguay, Rivière, (Que.) 17 G2
Chateau Pond, (Nfld.) 5 H1
Châteauvert, Lac, (Que.) 18 F2
Châtelain, Lac, (Que.) 46 F3
Chatfield Island, (BC) 41 E3
Chatham Islands, (BC) 38 F4
Chatham Sound, (BC) 42 C4
Chatwin Lake, (Man.) 44 G3
Chaudière, Lac, (Que.) 15 E2
Chaudière, Rivière, (Que.) 16 F1
Chauvreulx, Rivière, (Que.) 20 F2
Chavannes, Lac, (Que.) 18 C3
Chavigny, Lac, (Que.) 46 E4
Cheakamus Lake, (BC) 37 F4
Cheakamus River, (BC) 37 F4
Chebogue Harbour, (NS) 10 A4
Chebogue Point, (NS) 10 A4
Checleset Bay, (BC) 39 C2
Chedabucto Bay, (NS) 9 G2
Chedabucto Lake, (NWT) 44 B1
Chepash River, (Ont.) 20 C3
Cheepay River, (Ont.) 20 B3
Cheeseman Lake, (Ont.) 27 E2
Chef, Rivière du, (Que.) 20 G4
Chehalis Lake, (BC) 35 A3
Chehalis River, (BC) 35 A4
Chelaslie Arm, (BC) 41 H2
Chelaslie River, (BC) 41 G2
Chelsea, Ruisseau, (Que.) 17 D3
Chemainus River, (BC) 38 D3
Chemong Lake, (Ont.) 24 D4
Chêne, Rivière du, (Que.) 16 D1
Chêne, Rivière du, (Que.) 17 F4
Cheney Island, (NB) 11 C4
Chenil, Lac, (Que.) 5 D1
Chenon, Lac, (Que.) 18 B3
Chensagi, Lac, (Que.) 20 F4
Cherpeta Creek, (Sask.) 32 B1
Cherry Creek, (BC) 35 C1
Cherry Creek, (BC) 35 G2
Cheslatta Lake, (BC) 40 A2
Chesley Lake, (Ont.) 23 C2
Chesney Bay, (Ont.) 26 F1
Chesterfield Inlet, (NWT) 46 B2
Chéticamp Harbour, (NS) 8 D2
Chéticamp Island, (NS) 8 D2
Chéticamp Lake, (NS) 8 E2
Chéticamp River, (NS) 8 D2
Chiblow Lake, (Ont.) 25 A1
Chibouet, Rivière, (Que.) 16 B3
Chibougamau, Lac, (Que.) 20 G4
Chibougamau, Rivière, (Que.) 20 G4
Chic-Chocs, Monts, (Que.) 13 E1
Chicken Lake, (Sask.) 32 H1
Chicken Lake, (Man.) 44 G4
Chicobi, Lac, (Que.) 26 G1
Chicomo, Lac, (Que.) 19 F1
Chicot, Rivière, (Que.) 16 A2
Chicot, Rivière, (Que.) 17 F3
Chicoutai, Pointe, (Que.) 5 C3
Chicoutimi, Rivière, (Que.) 14 A3
Chidley, Cape, (NWT) 46 G3
Chidliak Bay, (NWT) 46 G2
Chief Bay, (Ont.) 27 E2
Chief Lake, (BC) 40 C1
Chief Louis Lake, (BC) 41 G2
Chiefs Point, (Ont.) 23 C1
Chienne, Lac à la, (Que.) 18 G3
Chiens, Rivière aux, (Que.) 17 F3
Chiganois River, (NS) 9 C2
Chignecto Bay, (NB/NS) 11 G2
Chignecto, Cape, (NS) 11 G3
Chignecto Isthmus, (NS) 9 A1
Chigoubiche, Lac, (Que.) 18 F1
Chilako River, (BC) 40 C2
Chilanko River, (BC) 40 A4
Chilcotin River, (BC) 40 B3
Childs Lake, (Man.) 29 E1
Chilko Lake, (BC) 37 D1
Chilko River, (BC) 40 B4
Chilliwack Lake, (BC) 35 B4
Chilliwack River, (BC) 35 A4
Chimney Bay, (Nfld.) 5 H2
Chimney Creek, (BC) 36 B1
Chimney Lake, (BC) 36 C2
China Creek, (BC) 38 C2
Chin, Cape, (Ont.) 25 D4
Chinchaga River, (Alta./BC) 43 G1
Chin Coulee, (Alta.) 34 H4
Chiniguchi Lake, (Ont.) 26 E3
Chin Lakes, (Alta.) 34 G4
Chin River, (Ont.) 26 E1
Chipai Lake, (Ont.) 30 G3
Chipai River, (Ont.) 30 G3
Chipewyan Lake, (Man.) 44 H3
Chip Lake, (Alta.) 33 C3
Chipman Creek, (BC) 38 E3
Chipman Lake, (Ont.) 27 H1
Chipman River, (Sask.) 44 E2
Chippewa River, (Ont.) 26 B3
Chiputneticook Lakes, (NB) 11 A2
Chitek Lake, (Man.) 29 F1
Chitek Lake, (Sask.) 32 C3
Chitek River, (Sask.) 32 B2
Chochocouane, Rivière, (Que.) 18 C2
Choelquoit Lake, (BC) 40 B4
Chorkbak Inlet, (NWT) 46 E2
Chowade River, (BC) 43 C2
Chown, Mount, (Alta.) 40 F2
Christensen Point, (BC) 39 B1
Christian Island, (Ont.) 23 E1
Christie Bay, (NWT) 44 C1
Christie Lake, (Ont.) 17 B3
Christie Lake, (Man.) 30 C1
Christie Lake, (NWT) 46 C1
Christina Lake, (Alta.) 33 G1
Christina Lake, (BC) 35 H4
Christina River, (Alta.) 44 C4
Christopher Lakes, (NS) 10 D2
Chub Lake, (BC) 36 D2
Chuchi Lake, (BC) 43 B4
Chuckwalla River, (BC) 41 F4
Chukotat, Rivière, (Que.) 46 E3
Chukuni River, (Ont.) 30 D4
Churchill, Cape, (Man.) 46 B4
Churchill Falls, (Nfld.) 6 D3
Churchill Lake, (Ont.) 30 E4
Churchill Lake, (Sask.) 44 D4
Churchill, Mount, (BC) 37 E4
Churchill Peak, (BC) 43 B1
Churchill River, (Nfld.) 6 E4
Churchill River, (Man./Sask.) 46 A4
Churchill Sound, (NWT) 20 D1
Chuwanten Mountain, (BC) 35 C4
Chuwhels Mountain, (BC) 35 C1
Cinconsine, Lac, (Que.) 18 G3
Cinq Cerf Bay, (Nfld.) 4 C4
Cinq Cerf Brook, (Nfld.) 4 C4
Cinq Islands Bay, (Nfld.) 2 C2
Cinq, Rivière du, (Que.) 16 F2
Circle River, (Ont.) 26 F1
Clairambault, Lac, (Que.) 6 B3
Claire, Lake, (Alta.) 44 C3
Clair, Lac, (Que.) 26 G2
Clam Bay, (NS) 9 D3
Clapperton Channel, (Ont.) 25 B2
Clapperton Creek, (BC) 35 C2
Clapperton Island, (Ont.) 25 B2
Clarence, Cape, (NWT) 47 E3
Clarence Head, (NWT) 47 F2
Clarendon, Cape, (NWT) 47 C3
Clark Bay, (Sask.) 44 F3
Clarke Head, (NS) 9 A2
Clarke Lake, (Sask.) 32 C2
Clarke Lake, (Alta.) 33 G3
Clarke Marsh, (Sask.) 31 F3
Clarke River, (NWT) 45 G3
Clark Fiord, (NWT) 47 G4
Clarkie, Lac, (Que.) 20 F3
Clark, Point, (Ont.) 23 B3
Clark Point, (Man.) 29 G1
Clatto Creek, (Sask.) 32 A1
Claude, Rivière à, (Que.) 13 E1
Clay Lake, (Ont.) 28 H1
Clayoquot Arm, (BC) 38 A2
Clayoquot River, (BC) 39 H4
Clayoquot Sound, (BC) 39 F4
Clayton Lake, (Ont.) 17 B2
Clear Bay, (Man.) 30 B3
Clear, Lake, (Ont.) 24 G2
Clear Lake, (Ont.) 24 E4
Clear Lake, (Man.) 29 F3
Clear Lake, (BC) 37 B4
Clear River, (Alta.) 43 F3
Clearsand Lake, (Sask.) 32 E3
Clearwater Brook, (NB) 12 C3
Clearwater Creek, (BC) 43 C3
Clearwater Creek, (NWT) 45 C3
Clearwater Lake
see also Eau Claire, Lac à l'
Clearwater Lake, (Man.) 30 A2
Clearwater Lake, (Man.) 30 B2
Clearwater Lake, (BC) 36 F1
Clearwater Lake Provincial Park, (Man.) 30 A2
Clearwater River, (Alta.) 34 D1
Clearwater River, (BC) 36 F2
Clearwater River, (Alta./Sask.) 44 C4
Clearwater West Lake, (Ont.) 27 B2
Clements Markham Inlet, (NWT) 47 F1
Clendenning Creek, (BC) 37 E3
Clendenning River, (Ont.) 30 G2
Clephane Bay, (NWT) 46 G1
Clérion, Lac, (Que.) 26 G2
Clerke Point, (BC) 39 C2
Cleveland River, (NWT) 46 D2
Cliff, Cape, (NS) 9 B1
Cliff Island, (Ont.) 28 F2
Cliff Lake, (Ont.) 28 H1
Clifton Lake, (Man.) 44 H3
Clifton Point, (NWT) 45 E1
Cli Lake, (NWT) 45 D3
Cline River, (Alta.) 34 C1
Clinton-Colden Lake, (NWT) 45 G2
Clinton Point, (NWT) 45 D1
Clio Channel, (BC) 39 F1
Clipper Point, (BC) 37 C3
Clisbako River, (BC) 40 B3
Clive Lake, (NWT) 45 E3
Clode Sound, (Nfld.) 3 E4
Clore River, (BC) 42 E4
Close Lake, (Sask.) 44 E3
Cloud Lake, (NS) 10 D1
Cloud Lake, (Ont.) 27 D3
Cloud River, (Nfld.) 5 G2
Clowhom Lake, (BC) 38 E1
Club Island, (Ont.) 25 D3
Clucluz Lake, (BC) 40 B2
Clusko River, (BC) 40 B3
Clutewe River, (BC) 39 D1
Clut Lake, (NWT) 45 E2
Clutterbuck Head, (NWT) 46 G3
Clydegale Lake, (Ont.) 24 D2
Clyde Inlet, (NWT) 47 G4
Clyde Lake, (Alta.) 33 F1
Clyde River, (NS) 10 C3
Clyde River, (Ont.) 17 A2
Coacoachou, Lac, (Que.) 5 D3
Coal All Island, (Nfld.) 3 D2
Coal Branch River, (NB) 12 F4
Coal Creek, (NB) 12 E4
Coal Harbour Point, (Nfld.) 3 F2
Coal Island, (BC) 38 F3
Coal Lake, (Alta.) 33 E4
Coal River, (BC/YT) 45 C4
Coast Mountains, (BC) 41 E2
Coast Point, (NWT) 47 A4
Coast, Rivière, (Que.) 20 F1
Coaticook, Rivière, (Que.) 16 D4
Coats Bay, (NWT) 20 D1
Coats Island, (NWT) 46 D3
Cobaz, Lac, (Que.) 5 D2
Cobble Lake, (Ont.) 28 H1
Cobequid Bay, (NS) 9 B2
Cobequid Mountains, (NS) 9 A2
Cobham River, (Man./Ont.) 30 D3
Coburg Island, (NWT) 47 F3
Cocagne Harbour, (NB) 12 H4
Cocagne Island, (NB) 12 H4
Cocagne River, (NB) 12 G4
Cochrane River, (Man./Sask.) 44 G3
Cockburn, Cape, (BC) 38 D1
Cockburn, Cape, (NWT) 47 D3
Cockburn Island, (Ont.) 26 C4
Cockram Strait, (NWT) 46 E1
Coddles Island, (NS) 9 G3
Cod Island, (Nfld.) 6 E1
Codroy Island, (Nfld.) 4 A3
Codroy Pond, (Nfld.) 4 B3
Cody Creek, (Ont.) 17 B2
Cogburn Creek, (BC) 35 A3
Coglistiko River, (BC) 40 B3
Cogmagun River, (NS) 9 A3
Coiffier, Lac, (Que.) 6 D2
Coigny, Rivière, (Que.) 26 H1
Colan, Cape, (NWT) 47 F1
Colborne, Cape, (NWT) 45 F1
Cold Creek, (Ont.) 21 E1
Cold Lake, (Alta./Sask.) 33 H2
Coldscaur Lake, (BC) 36 E2
Coldspring Head, (NS) 9 B1
Cold Spring Pond, (Nfld.) 4 G3
Coldstream Creek, (BC) 35 F2
Coldwater River, (BC) 35 C3
Coleman Creek, (BC) 38 C3
Coleman Island, (Nfld.) 3 F2
Coleman Lake, (Alta.) 34 G2
Colen Lakes, (Man.) 30 D2
Coles Lake, (BC) 41 F2
Colin Archer Peninsula, (NWT) 47 E3
Colinet Harbour, (Nfld.) 2 F3
Colinet River, (Nfld.) 2 G3
Colin Lake, (Alta.) 44 C2
Colin Lake, (Sask.) 44 F4
Collas, Lac, (Que.) 19 H2
Collier Bay, (Nfld.) 2 F2
Colliers Point, (Nfld.) 2 G2
Collies Head, (NS) 9 C4
Collingwood Channel, (BC) 38 E2
Collins Bay, (Sask.) 44 F3
Collins Creek, (Ont.) 17 A4
Collins Inlet, (Ont.) 25 D2
Collins Lake, (NB) 7 A4
Collins Lake, (Ont.) 17 B4
Collinson, Cape, (NWT) 47 A3
Collinson Inlet, (NWT) 45 G1
Collinson Peninsula, (NWT) 47 C4
Colombier, Cap, (Que.) 14 F2
Colombines, Les (*reef*), (Que.) 7 G1
Colonna Lake, (Ont.) 28 G1
Colpoys Bay, (Ont.) 23 C1
Columbia, Cape, (NWT) 47 E1
Columbia Icefield, (Alta./BC) 34 B1
Columbia Lake, (BC) 34 C3
Columbia, Mount, (Alta./BC) 34 B1
Columbia Mountains, (BC) 40 E2
Columbia Reach, (BC) 40 H4
Columbia River, (BC) 34 A2
Colville Bay, (PEI) 7 E3
Colville Lake, (Nfld.) 6 D3
Colville Lake, (NWT) 45 D2
Combermere Cape, (NWT) 47 F2
Come By Chance, (Nfld.) 2 E2
Comencho, Lac, (Que.) 20 F4
Comfort, Cape, (NWT) 46 D2
Comfort Head, (Nfld.) 3 D2
Comité, Baie
see Committee Bay
Comma Island, (Nfld.) 6 F2
Commanda Lake, (Ont.) 25 H2
Commerell Point, (BC) 39 B1
Commissaires, Lac des, (Que.) 18 H2
Commissioner Island, (Man.) 29 H1
Committee Bay, (NWT) 46 C1
Commodore, Cape, (Ont.) 23 C1
Como Lake, (NS) 9 D3
Como Lake, (Ont.) 26 B2
Comox Lake, (BC) 38 B1
Compton Névé, (BC) 37 D2
Compulsion Bay, (Sask.) 44 F3
Conception Bay, (Nfld.) 2 G2
Coney Head, (Nfld.) 5 G3
Confederation Lake, (Ont.) 30 E4
Confusion Bay, (Nfld.) 3 B1
Congnarauya, Pointe, (Que.) 46 G4
Conibear Lake, (Alta.) 44 B2
Coningham Bay, (NWT) 47 D4
Conjuror Bay, (NWT) 45 E2
Conkle Lake, (BC) 35 F4
Connaigre Bay, (Nfld.) 2 A3
Connaigre Head, (Nfld.) 2 B3
Connaught Lake, (NS) 10 E1
Connecting Point, (Nfld.) 3 F4
Conne River, (Nfld.) 2 B1
Conne River Pond, (Nfld.) 2 C1
Conn Lake, (NWT) 47 G4
Connoire Bay, (Nfld.) 4 D4
Connoire Head, (Nfld.) 4 D4
Connolly Bay, (Man.) 30 A2
Conn, Rivière, (Que.) 20 E3
Conroy Creek, (BC) 43 C2
Consecon Lake, (Ont.) 21 F2
Constance Lake, (Ont.) 17 D4
Constant Lake, (Ont.) 24 G2
Consul River, (NWT) 45 G2
Content Reach, (Nfld.) 3 F3
Continental Ranges, (Alta./BC) 34 C1
Contracosta Lake, (Alta.) 34 G1
Contwoyto Lake, (NWT) 45 F2
Conuma Peak, (BC) 39 F3
Conuma River, (BC) 39 F3
Cook Cape, (BC) 39 C2
Cooke Creek, (BC) 35 G1
Cooking Lake, (Alta.) 33 E3
Cook's Bay, (Ont.) 23 F2
Cooks Brook, (Nfld.) 4 C1
Cooks Cove, (Nfld.) 2 G1
Cooks Creek, (Man.) 28 B1
Cooper Brook, (Nfld.) 3 C3
Cooper, Mount, (BC) 34 B3
Cooper Reach, (BC) 37 B2
Copeau River, (Sask.) 32 G4
Copeland Islands, (BC) 37 C4
Copes Bay, (NWT) 47 F2
Copper Creek, (BC) 35 C4
Coppercrown Mountain, (BC) 34 C3
Copper Island, (Nfld.) 3 E2
Copper Island, (Ont.) 27 F3
Coppermine Point, (Ont.) 26 A3
Coppermine River, (NWT) 45 E2
Coppett Harbour, (Nfld.) 4 E4
Copp Lake, (NWT) 44 B2
Coquihalla Mountain, (BC) 35 C3
Coquihalla River, (BC) 35 B3
Coquitlam Lake, (BC) 38 G2
Coquitlam Mountain, (BC) 38 G2
Coquitlam River, (BC) 38 G2
Corbett Inlet, (NWT) 46 B3
Corbett Lake, (NWT) 44 H1
Corbière, Lac, (Que.) 19 F1
Corbin Bay, (Nfld.) 2 C2
Corbin Head, (Nfld.) 2 C2
Corbin Head, (Nfld.) 2 C4
Corbold Creek, (BC) 38 G1
Cordero Channel, (BC) 37 B3
Cordingley Lake, (Ont.) 27 G1
Cordova Channel, (BC) 38 F3
Corkscrew Island, (Ont.) 28 F2
Corkscrew River, (BC) 40 A3
Cormack Lake, (NWT) 45 D4
Cormack, Mount, (Nfld.) 4 H2
Cormacks Lake, (Nfld.) 4 D2
Cormier, Lac, (Que.) 5 B2
Cormorant Channel, (BC) 39 E1
Cormorant Island, (BC) 39 E1
Cormorant Lake, (Man.) 30 A2
Corneille Lake, (Sask.) 32 G1
Corneille, Rivière de la, (Que.) 18 C3
Cornelius Grinnell Bay, (NWT) 46 G2
Cornelius Island, (Nfld.) 4 D4
Corner Brook, (Nfld.) 4 D1
Corner Brook Lake, (Nfld.) 4 D1
Cornfield Pond, (Nfld.) 3 B3
Corn Lake, (Ont.) 28 F1
Cornwallis Island, (NWT) 47 D3
Cornwall Island, (NWT) 47 D2
Cornwall Lake, (Alta.) 44 C2
Coronation Gulf, (NWT) 45 F1
Corps Mort, Le (*island*), (Que.) 7 E1
Corrigall Lake, (Alta.) 33 E1
Corson Lake, (Sask.) 44 F3
Cortes Island, (BC) 37 C4
Corvette, Lac de la, (Que.) 20 G2
Corvette, Rivière de la, (Que.) 20 G2
Cory Bay, (NWT) 46 E2
Cossette, Lac, (Que.) 14 G3
Costebelle, Lac, (Que.) 5 B3
Coste Island, (BC) 41 E1
Costello Lake, (Man.) 44 H4
Costes Lake, (Man.) 30 C2
Costigan Lake, (Nfld.) 4 E2
Costigan Lake, (Sask.) 44 E4
Costley Lake, (NS) 9 F2
Côtière, Chaîne
see Coast Mountains
Cottel Island, (Nfld.) 3 F3
Cottel Reach, (Nfld.) 3 F3
Cotter Lake, (Sask.) 32 D1
Cotton Lake, (Man.) 30 C2
Couchiching, Lake, (Ont.) 24 B3
Coucou, Rivière du, (Que.) 18 E2
Coudres, Ile aux, (Que.) 15 C2
Coulonge, Rivière, (Que.) 18 C4
Country Harbour, (NS) 9 F2
Country Harbour Head, (NS) 9 F3
Country Pond, (Nfld.) 2 H3
Courageous Lake, (NWT) 45 F3
Couronnement, Golfe du
see Coronation Gulf
Courtney Lake, (BC) 35 C2
Courtois, Lac, (Que.) 19 A1
Cousins Lake, (Man.) 44 H4
Couteau Bay, (Nfld.) 4 D4
Couteau Brook, (Nfld.) 4 D3
Couteau Head, (Nfld.) 4 C4
Coutts, Cape, (NWT) 47 F4
Coutts Inlet, (NWT) 47 F4
Coutts River, (Alta.) 33 C2
Couture, Lac, (Que.) 46 E3
Cove Island, (Ont.) 25 C3
Coventry Lake, (NWT) 44 E1
Cowan River, (Sask.) 32 C2
Cow Head, (Nfld.) 3 F3
Cowichan Bay, (BC) 38 E3
Cowichan Lake, (BC) 38 D3
Cowichan River, (BC) 38 D3
Cow Lake, (Alta.) 34 D1
Cowlest Barasway, (Nfld.) 4 D4
Cowoki Lake, (Alta.) 34 G3
Cow River, (Ont.) 26 B3
Coxipi, Lac, (Que.) 5 F2
Coxipi, Rivière, (Que.) 5 E2
Cox Island, (BC) 39 B1
Cox Point, (BC) 38 A2
Coyne Lake, (NWT) 44 E1
Coy Pond, (Nfld.) 3 B4
Crabbes River, (Nfld.) 4 B3
Crabclaw Lake, (Ont.) 28 H1
Crammond Island, (NS) 8 D4
Cramolet, Lac, (Que.) 6 C2
Crampe, Lac de la, (Que.) 18 G1
Cranberry Lake, (NB) 12 E4
Cranberry Lake, (Ont.) 17 C3
Cranberry Mountain, (BC) 35 H1
Cranberry Point, (NS) 10 A3
Cranberry River, (BC) 42 E3
Crane Bay, (Man.) 29 F2
Crane Lake, (Sask.) 31 C3
Cran, Rivière du, (Que.) 18 G1
Crater Mountain, (BC) 35 D4
Crauford, Cape, (NWT) 47 E3
Craven, Lac, (Que.) 20 F2
Crawfish Lake, (BC) 39 E3
Crean Lake, (Sask.) 32 D2
Crean River, (Sask.) 32 D2
Crease Island, (BC) 39 E1
Credit River, (Ont.) 23 F4
Cree Lake, (Sask.) 44 E3
Cree River, (Sask.) 44 E3
Creighton Creek, (BC) 35 G2
Crépeau, Lac, (Que.) 6 B3
Crescent Bay, (BC) 38 C1
Crescent Island, (NWT) 47 D2
Crescent Lake, (Nfld.) 3 B2
Creswell Bay, (NWT) 47 D4
Cribbons Point, (NS) 9 F1
Cridge, Mount, (BC) 37 B2
Crimson Lake Provincial Park, (Alta.) 33 C4
Cripple Rock Point, (Nfld.) 2 G4
Cris, Lac des
see Cree Lake
Criss Creek, (BC) 36 E4
Croal Lake, (Ont.) 30 G2
Croche, Lac, (Que.) 15 A2
Croche, Lac, (Que.) 15 G1
Croche, Rivière, (Que.) 18 G2
Crochet Lake, (Ont.) 24 C3
Crocker Lake, (NB) 12 E3
Croix, Lac à la, (Que.) 19 B2
Croix, Lac à la, (Que.) 14 D2
Croix, Lac la, (Ont.) 27 B3
Croker Bay, (NWT) 47 E3
Croker, Cape, (Ont.) 23 C1
Croker Island, (Ont.) 25 B2
Croker River, (NWT) 45 D1
Croll Lake, (Man.) 44 G4
Cronin, Mount, (BC) 42 F4
Crooked Creek, (NB) 11 G2
Crooked Lake, (Nfld.) 3 A2
Crooked Lake, (Nfld.) 4 G2
Crooked Lake, (Ont.) 27 B3
Crooked Lake, (Sask.) 29 C3
Crooked Lake, (BC) 36 E1
Crooked Lake, (NWT) 47 D4
Crooked Pine Lake, (Ont.) 27 C3
Crooked River, (Nfld.) 6 F3
Crooked River, (Ont.) 20 B2
Crooked River, (BC) 40 C1
Crooks Inlet, (NWT) 46 F2
Crosby Lake, (Ont.) 17 A3
Cross Bay, (Man.) 30 B3
Cross Bay, (NWT) 46 B2
Cross Country Pond, (Nfld.) 3 A1
Crossfield Creek, (Alta.) 34 E2
Cross (Grass) Island, (Nfld.) 2 D3
Crossing Place River, (Nfld.) 2 G4
Cross Island, (Nfld.) 6 F2
Cross Island, (NS) 10 F2
Cross Lake, (NS) 9 E3
Cross Lake, (Ont.) 26 F3
Cross Lake, (Man.) 30 C2
Cross Lake, (Sask.) 32 H2
Crossley Lakes, (NWT) 45 C1
Cross Point, (Nfld.) 2 F2
Cross Point, (Ont.) 25 H1
Cross Pond, (Nfld.) 4 G2
Cross River, (Alta.) 34 D2
Crossroads Lake, (Nfld.) 6 D3
Crossroute Lake, (Ont.) 28 H3
Crotch Lake, (Ont.) 24 H3
Crowduck Lake, (Man.) 28 E1
Crowduck Lake, (Ont.) 28 E2
Crowe Lake, (Nfld.) 3 C3
Crowe Lake, (Ont.) 24 F4
Crowe River, (Ont.) 24 E3
Crowfoot Creek, (Alta.) 34 F2
Crow Head, (Nfld.) 2 B2
Crow Head, (Nfld.) 4 A2
Crow Indian Lake, (Alta.) 34 G4
Crow Lake, (Ont.) 17 A3
Crow Lake, (Man.) 32 H1
Crown Mountain, (BC) 39 G3
Crown Prince Frederik Island, (NWT) 47 E4
Crow River, (BC/YT) 45 C4
Crowsnest Mountain, (Alta.) 34 E4
Crozier Channel, (NWT) 47 B2
Cruickshank River, (BC) 38 B1
Cruiser, Lac, (Que.) 14 A1
Crusoe Lake, (Ont.) 28 G2
Cry Lake, (BC/YT) 45 C4
Crystal Creek, (Sask.) 32 B4
Crystal Lake, (Ont.) 24 D3
Cuckold Head, (Nfld.) 3 G4
Cuddle Lake, (Man.) 30 C1
Culbute, Chenal de la, (Que.) 24 G1
Culloden Lake, (Ont.) 28 F1
Cultus Lake, (BC) 35 A4
Cumberland Basin, (NB/NS) 11 H2
Cumberland Bay, (NB) 11 E1
Cumberland Cove, (PEI) 7 B4
Cumberland Lake, (Sask.) 32 G2
Cumberland Peninsula, (NWT) 46 G1
Cumberland Sound, (NWT) 46 G2
Cuming Inlet, (NWT) 47 E3
Cumins Lake, (Sask.) 32 B1
Cumshewa Head, (BC) 41 B2
Cumshewa Inlet, (BC) 41 B2
Cunning Bay, (Sask.) 44 F3
Cunningham Inlet, (NWT) 47 D3
Cunningham Island, (BC) 41 E3
Cunningham Lake, (BC) 36 C3
Cunningham Lake, (BC) 42 H4
Cunningham Point, (Ont.) 25 A2
Currie Lake, (Man.) 44 H3
Curtis Lake, (NWT) 46 C1
Curtis River, (NWT) 46 C1
Cushing Lake, (Alta.) 33 G2
Cushing, Mount, (BC) 42 F1
Cusson, Pointe, (Que.) 46 E3
Cutarm Creek, (Sask.) 29 D2
Cutbank Lake, (Sask.) 31 C2
Cutbank River, (Alta.) 40 G1
Cut Beaver Lake, (Sask.) 32 G3
Cutler Head, (Nfld.) 3 F4
Cutts Brook, (Nfld.) 4 D4
Cuvillier, Lac, (Que.) 18 C1
Cyclops, Cape, (NWT) 47 B3
Cygnet Lake, (Ont.) 28 E1
Cygnet Lake, (Man.) 30 D1
Cypre River, (BC) 39 G4
Cypress Bay, (BC) 39 G4
Cypress Creek, (BC) 43 C2
Cypress Hills, (Alta./Sask.) 31 B4
Cypress Hills Provincial Park, (Alta.) 31 B4
Cypress Hills Provincial Park, (Sask.) 31 C4
Cypress Lake, (Sask.) 31 C4
Cypress River, (Man.) 29 G4
Cyprus Lake Provincial Park, (Ont.) 25 D4
Cyriac, Rivière, (Que.) 14 B4
Cyril Lake, (Man.) 30 D1
Cyril River, (Man.) 30 D1
Cyrus Field Bay, (NWT) 46 G2

D

Daaquam, Rivière, (Que.) 15 D4
Dafoe Lake, (Man.) 30 C1
Dafoe River, (Man.) 30 D1
Daggitt Lake, (Man.) 44 H2
Dahadinni River, (NWT) 45 D3
Dahl Creek, (BC) 43 E1
D'Ailleboust, Lac, (Que.) 19 A4
Dala River, (BC) 41 E1
Dalgleish, Mount, (BC) 37 E2
Dalhousie, Cape, (NWT) 45 C1
Dalhousie Lake, (Ont.) 17 A2
Dalmas, Lac, (Que.) 20 H2
Dalpe Lake, (NWT) 44 H2
Dalrymple Lake, (Ont.) 24 C3
Daly Bay, (NWT) 46 C2
Daly Lake, (Sask.) 44 E4
Damant Lake, (NWT) 44 E1
Damfino Creek, (BC) 35 G3
Damnable Bay, (Nfld.) 3 F3
Dana, Lac, (Que.) 20 E4
Danby Island, (NWT) 20 D3
Dancing Point, (Man.) 30 B3
Dandurand, Lac, (Que.) 18 E2
Daniel-Johnson Barrage/Dam, (Que.) 19 C2
Daniel, Lac, (Que.) 6 D1
Daniel, Lac, (Que.) 14 D1
Daniel Moore Bay, (NWT) 45 F1
Daniel, Rivière, (Que.) 26 H1
Daniels Lake, (Ont.) 28 G1
Danielson Provincial Park, (Sask.) 31 E2
Daniels River, (BC) 37 D3
Danish Strait, (NWT) 47 D2
Dans Pond, (Nfld.) 3 D2
Dantzic Point, (Nfld.) 2 A4
Darby Lake, (NWT) 46 C1
Darch Island, (Ont.) 25 B2
D'Arcy Island, (BC) 38 F4
Dargie Lake, (NS) 10 C1
Darke Lake, (BC) 35 E3
Dark Harbour, (NB) 11 C4
Darlens, Rivière, (Que.) 18 B2
Darlings Lake, (NB) 11 E2
Darnley Bay, (NWT) 45 D1
Dartmouth, Mount, (BC) 37 D1
Dartmouth Point, (NS) 10 A2
Dartmouth, Rivière, (Que.) 13 G1
Dash Creek, (BC) 37 G1
Dash Lake, (Ont.) 28 H3
Dashwoods Pond, (Nfld.) 4 C3
Dasserat, Lac, (Que.) 26 G2
Dauphin, Cape, (NS) 8 E3
Dauphinees Mill Lake, (NS) 10 F1
Dauphine, Rivière, (Que.) 5 B4
Dauphin Lake, (Man.) 29 F2
Dauphin River, (Man.) 29 G1
David Lake, (Ont.) 25 D2
David, Rivière, (Que.) 16 B2
Davidson Lake, (NB) 11 B1
Davidson Lake, (Man.) 30 B2
Davidson, Mount, (BC) 40 A2
Davie Lake, (BC) 40 C1
Davin Lake, (Sask.) 44 F4
Davis Lake, (Ont.) 24 D3
Davis Pond, (Nfld.) 3 A1
Davis River, (NS) 10 B3
Davis River, (BC) 43 B3
Davis Strait, (NWT) 46 H1
Davy Lake, (Sask.) 44 D3
Dawes Pond, (Nfld.) 3 A2
Dawson Bay, (Man.) 30 A3
Dawson Inlet, (NWT) 46 B3
Dawson Island, (Ont.) 28 F3
Dawson, Mount, (BC) 34 B2
Dawson River, (Ont.) 30 E3
Dayohessarah Lake, (Ont.) 26 A1
Day Point, (BC) 41 E3
Deacon Lake, (Ont.) 28 F1
Deadhorse Lake, (Alta.) 34 F2
Deadman River, (BC) 36 D4
Deadman's Bay, (Nfld.) 3 F2
Deadman's Bight, (Nfld.) 2 B3
Deadman's Brook, (Nfld.) 3 F2
Deadman's Point, (Nfld.) 3 F2
Deadmans Pond, (Nfld.) 3 D3
Deadman's Pond, (Nfld.) 3 F2
Dead Wolf Brook, (Nfld.) 3 D4
Dead Wolf Pond, (Nfld.) 3 D4
Dean Channel, (BC) 41 F3
Dean Lake, (NS) 10 D2
Dean River, (BC) 41 G2
Deans Dundas Bay, (NWT) 47 B3
Dease Arm, (NWT) 45 D2
Dease Lake, (BC) 45 B4
Dease River, (BC) 45 C4
Dease River, (NWT) 45 E2
Dease Strait, (NWT) 45 F1
deBartok Lake, (NWT) 44 H2
Debert River, (NS) 9 B2
De Bray, Lac, (Que.) 20 H2
Decelles, Lac, (Que.) 18 F2
Deception Bay, (Sask.) 44 F3
Deception Bay, (NWT) 46 E3
Deception Creek, (BC) 36 E2
Deception Lake, (NS) 10 C3
Deception Lake, (Ont.) 28 E2
Deception Lake, (Sask.) 44 F4
Dechêne, Lac, (Que.) 19 D2
Decker Lake, (BC) 42 G4
De Courcy Group, (BC) 38 E2
Deep Bay, (Ont.) 28 F3
Deep Bay, (NWT) 44 A1

)eep Bay, (Sask.) 44 F4
)eep Brook, (Nfld.) 4 C3
)eep Creek, (BC) 35 F1
)eep Inlet, (Nfld.) 6 F2
)eep Rose Lake, (NWT) 46 B1
)eep Valley Creek, (Alta.) 40 H1
)eepwater Point, (Ont.) 25 H1
)eer Bay, (Ont.) 24 E4
)eer Bay, (NWT) 47 D2
)eer Creek, (Ont.) 23 C2
)eer Harbour, (Nfld.) 2 F2
)eerhorn Creek, (Man./Sask.) 29 D3
)eer Island, (Nfld.) 3 F3
)eer Island, (Nfld.) 3 F4
)eer Island, (NB) 11 B3
)eer Island, (BC) 39 D1
)eer Lake, (Nfld.) 4 D1
)eer Lake, (Ont.) 24 B1
)eer Lake, (Ont.) 24 E3
)eer Lake, (Ont.) 25 G1
)eer Lake, (Ont.) 30 D3
)eer Passage, (BC) 37 C3
)eerpass Bay, (NWT) 45 D2
)eerPond, (Nfld.) 3 D4
)eer River, (Man.) 46 B4
)efeat Lake, (NWT) 44 B1
)e Freneuse, Lac, (Que.) 6 B1
)égelis, Lac du, (Que.) 14 D1
)e Haven Point, (NWT) 45 G1
)ehoux Bay, (NWT) 44 F2
)eka Lake, (BC) 36 E2
)e la Beche Bay, (NWT) 47 D3
)e La Blache, Lac, (Que.) 19 C3
)elahey, Lac, (Que.) 18 C3
)elaney Lake, (Ont.) 28 G1
)elano Lake, (Ont.) 28 H2
)e La Noue, Lac, (Que.) 6 B2
)elaronde Lake, (Sask.) 32 C2
)elay, Rivière, (Que.) 6 B2
)eLesseps Lake, (Ont.) 30 F4
)elestre, Rivière, (Que.) 18 C1
elight Lake, (NWT) 44 D2
e Lionne, Lac, (Que.) 6 A3
elisle River, (Ont.) 17 E2
see also Delisle, Rivière (Que.)
elisle, Rivière, (Que.) 17 F2
see also Delisle River (Ont.)
elorme, Lac, (Que.) 6 B3
elta Marsh, (Man.) 29 G3
elta Peak, (BC) 42 D2
emay Lake, (Alta.) 33 E4
emers, Lac, (Que.) 19 E2
emers, Mount, (BC) 38 D4
e Morhiban, Lac, (Que.) 5 A1
enbeigh Point, (Man.) 30 B3
enbigh Island, (Nfld.) 6 H4
enison Lake, (Man.) 44 H3
enman Island, (BC) 38 C1
enmark Bay, (NWT) 47 C4
enmark Lake, (Ont.) 28 H2
ennis Pond, (Nfld.) 4 C2
enny Island, (BC) 41 E3
ent, Mount, (BC) 40 B3
enys Basin, (NS) 8 D4
enys, Lac, (Que.) 20 F1
enys, River, (NS) 8 D4
enys, Rivière, (Que.) 20 F1
e Pas, Rivière, (Que.) 6 D2
epot Point, (NWT) 47 E2
e Ré, Lac, (Que.) 5 D2
e Rozière Bay, (NWT) 46 F3
e Salis Bay, (NWT) 47 A3
es Antons, Lac, (Que.) 20 G2
esbarats Strait, (NWT) 47 C2
esbergères, Lac, (Que.) 6 B1
esceliers, Lac, (Que.) 6 B4
eschambault Lake, (Sask.) 32 F1
eschambault, Point, (Que.) 15 F4
escharme Lake, (Sask.) 44 D4
escharme River, (Sask.) 44 D4
eschênes, Lac, (Que./Ont.) 14 D4
eschênes, Lac, (Que.) 17 D4
eserters Group, (BC) 39 D1
eserters Peak, (BC) 43 B2
ésert, Lac, (Que.) 18 D3
esert Lake, (Ont.) 17 A3
ésert, Rivière, (Que.) 18 D3
eskenatlata Lake, (NWT) 44 C1
esliens Lake, (Nfld.) 6 C3
esmarais Lake, (NWT) 44 E2
es Marets, Lac, (Que.) 5 B1
esolation Sound, (BC) 37 C4
esolation Sound Provincial Marine Park, (BC) 37 C4
espair, Lake, (Ont.) 28 H4
esperation Lake, (NWT) 44 C1
espins, Pointe, (Que.) 46 E4
Espoir Brook, (Nfld.) 4 G3
Espoir Lake, (Nfld.) 4 G3
esteffany Lake, (NWT) 45 F2
ester Lake, (BC) 36 B1
es Voeux, Lac, (Que.) 20 G2
etention Harbour, (NWT) 45 F1
etroit River, (Ont.) 22 A3
e Troyes, Rivière, (Que.) 20 F1
eux Décharges, Lac aux, (Que.) 19 B1
eux Loutres, Lac aux, (Que.) 5 B2
eux Montagnes, Lac des, (Que.) 17 G1
evenyns, Lac, (Que.) 18 F3
evereux Lake, (BC) 37 A1
evil Bay, (Nfld.) 4 F4
evil Brook, (Nfld.) 2 C3
evil Creek, (Man.) 28 B1
evil Lake, (Ont.) 17 A3
evil Lake, (Sask.) 32 E1
evil Point, (Nfld.) 5 G3
evils Thumb *(mountain)*, (BC) 42 B1
Vitré, Lac, (Que.) 5 D2
ewlin, Lac, (Que.) 26 G3
ewon Island, (NWT) 47 E3
ewar Lake, (Sask.) 31 C1
ewar Lakes, (NWT) 46 F1
ewey Point, (Ont.) 23 B4
exterity Fiord, (NWT) 47 G4
able, Cap au, (Que.) 15 D1
able, Cape, (Nfld.) 6 H4
able, Lac au, (Que.) 13 F1
able, Rivière du, (Que.) 18 F4
amond Jenness Peninsula, (NWT) 47 B4
amond Lake, (Ont.) 26 F3
ana Bay, (NWT) 46 F3
ana Island, (BC) 38 B3
ana, Lac, (Que.) 6 B1
ana Lake, (NWT) 46 B2
D'Iberville, Lac, (Que.) 20 G1
Dickey Lake, (Ont.) 24 F3
Dickey River, (Ont.) 30 G1
Dickison Lake, (Ont.) 27 F2
Dickson Lake, (Ont.) 24 E1
Dickson Lake, (BC) 38 B2
Dickson Lake, (BC) 38 H2
Dickson Peak, (BC) 37 F2
Diefenbaker, Lake, (Sask.) 31 E2
Dieppe Lake, (NWT) 44 A1
Dieu, Lac de
see Gods Lake
Dieu, Rivière de
see Gods River
Digby Gut, (NS) 10 B1
Digby Island, (BC) 42 C4
Digby Neck *(peninsula)*, (NS) 10 A2
Digdeguash Lake, (NB) 11 C3
Digdeguash River, (NB) 11 B2
Digges Islands, (NWT) 46 E3
Digges Sound, (NWT) 46 E3
Dihourse, Lac, (Que.) 6 D2
Dildo Arm, (Nfld.) 2 F2
Dildo Pond, (Nfld.) 2 F2
Dildo Pond, (Nfld.) 3 D2
Dildo Run *(passage)*, (Nfld.) 3 D2
Dillon Lake, (Sask.) 44 D4
Dillon Point, (BC) 39 D1
Dillon River, (Alta./Sask.) 44 D4
Dimma Lake, (NWT) 44 G1
Dingman Creek, (Ont.) 22 E2
Dinorwic Lake, (Ont.) 27 A2
Dinosaur Provincial Park, (Alta.) 34 H2
Dionne, Lac, (Que.) 19 D4
Dipper Lake, (Sask.) 44 E4
Direct Lake, (Ont.) 28 G1
Disappointment Lake, (Nfld.) 6 E3
Disappointment Lake, (NWT) 44 C2
Discovery, Cape, (NWT) 47 E1
Discovery Island, (BC) 38 F4
Discovery Passage, (BC) 37 B4
Dismal Creek, (Alta.) 33 B4
Dismal Lakes, (NWT) 45 E2
Disraeli Fiord, (NWT) 47 E1
Dissimieux, Lac, (Que.) 19 B3
Diversion Lake, (Nfld.) 3 B3
Dix Milles, Lac, (Que.) 18 B3
Dix Milles, Lac des, (Que.) 18 E2
Dixon Entrance, (BC) 42 A4
Dixon Island, (NWT) 47 D4
Dizzy Creek, (Alta.) 44 A2
Dobbin Bay, (NWT) 47 F1
Dobbs, Cape, (NWT) 46 C2
Dobie Lake, (Ont.) 30 F4
Dobie River, (Ont.) 30 F4
Doda, Lac, (Que.) 20 F4
Dodd Creek, (Ont.) 22 E2
Dodd Island, (BC) 38 B3
Dodd Lake, (BC) 37 D4
Dodge Lake, (Sask.) 44 E2
Dodier, Lac, (Que.) 19 C4
Doe Lake, (Ont.) 24 B1
Dog Bay, (Nfld.) 3 D2
Dog Bay Islands, (Nfld.) 3 E2
Dog Bay Point, (Nfld.) 3 E2
Dog, Cape, (Nfld.) 2 F3
Dog Creek, (BC) 35 H4
Dog Creek, (BC) 36 B2
Doghide River, (Sask.) 32 F4
Dog Island, (Nfld.) 6 F2
Dog Islands, (Nfld.) 6 G3
Dog Lake, (Ont.) 26 B2
Dog Lake, (Ont.) 27 D3
Dog Lake, (Man.) 29 G2
Dogpaw Lake, (Ont.) 28 G2
Dogpound Creek, (Alta.) 34 E2
Dog River, (Ont.) 27 D2
Dogskin Lake, (Man./Ont.) 30 D4
Dogskin River, (Man.) 30 D3
Dogtooth Lake, (Ont.) 28 G2
Doig River, (Alta./BC) 43 E2
Dolbel, Lac, (Que.) 19 G1
Dolby Lake, (NWT) 44 F1
Dolland Bight, (Nfld.) 2 B2
Dolland Brook, (Nfld.) 4 F3
Dolland Pond, (Nfld.) 4 G3
Dollard, Lac, (Que.) 19 F2
Dollar Lake, (NS) 9 C3
Dollars Lake, (Ont.) 25 G2
Dolly Bay, (Man.) 29 G2
Dolphin and Union Strait, (NWT) 45 E1
Dolphin Island, (BC) 41 C1
Dolu, Lac, (Que.) 6 B3
Domagaya Lake, (Nfld.) 19 G1
Dominion, Cape, (NWT) 46 E2
Dominion Lake, (Nfld.) 6 E4
Dominion Point, (Ont.) 25 B3
Donahue Lake, (NS) 9 G2
Donald Lake, (Ont.) 30 D4
Donaldson, Mount, (BC) 38 E1
Donegal Head, (BC) 39 E1
Donjek River, (YT) 45 A3
Donnegana Lake, (Ont.) 26 D3
Donnor Lake, (BC) 39 G3
Don Peninsula, (BC) 41 E3
Donquan, Lac, (Nfld.) 5 D1
Doolittle, Lac, (Que.) 18 C3
Doran Creek, (BC) 37 C1
Doran Lake, (Ont.) 30 F4
Doran Lake, (BC) 38 B2
Doran Lake, (NWT) 44 D1
Dorcas Bay, (Ont.) 25 D4
Dorchester Bay, (NWT) 46 E2
Dorchester, Cape, (NWT) 46 E2
Doré, Baie du, (Ont.) 23 B2
Doré, Lake, (Ont.) 24 G1
Doré Lake, (Sask.) 32 C2
Doré River, (Sask.) 32 C2
Dorés, Lac aux, (Que.) 20 G4
Dorothy Creek, (BC) 37 A1
Dorothy Lake, (Man.) 28 D1
Dorothy Lake, (BC) 37 E1
Double Island, (Nfld.) 6 G3
Double, Lac, (Que.) 19 B2
Double Mer *(inlet)*, (Nfld.) 6 G3
Doucet Lake, (NWT) 44 C1
Doughfig Point, (Nfld.) 3 G4
Douglas Channel, (BC) 41 D2
Douglas Creek, (BC) 38 H1
Douglas Harbour, (NWT) 46 C2
Douglas Harbour, (NWT) 46 F3
Douglas Lake, (BC) 35 D2
Douglas Point, (Ont.) 23 B2
Douglas Provincial Park, (Sask.) 31 F2
Douglas River, (Alta./Sask.) 44 D3
Doumic, Lac, (Que.) 14 C2
Dover Bay, (NS) 9 H2
Dover Island, (NS) 9 H2
Dover Island, (NS) 10 F2
Dovetail Lake, (Ont.) 27 B3
Dowager Island, (BC) 41 E3
Dowling Lake, (Alta.) 34 G1
Downer Lake, (NWT) 44 H1
Downie Creek, (BC) 34 A2
Downton Creek, (BC) 37 H3
Downton Lake, (BC) 37 G2
Downton, Mount, (BC) 40 A3
Doyle Island, (BC) 39 D1
Dozois, Réservoir, (Que.) 18 C2
Drag Lake, (Ont.) 24 D3
Drake Bay, (NWT) 47 D3
Drake Island, (BC) 39 C1
Draney Inlet, (BC) 41 F4
Drew Passage, (BC) 37 B3
Drewry Lake, (BC) 36 E2
Driedmeat Creek, (Alta.) 33 E4
Driedmeat Lake, (Alta.) 33 E4
Driftpile River, (Alta.) 33 C1
Drift River, (Man.) 44 H3
Driftwood Lake, (Man.) 30 A2
Driftwood River, (BC) 42 G2
Drinkwater Creek, (BC) 39 H4
Drolet, Lac, (Que.) 16 F3
Drook Point, (Nfld.) 2 G4
Droppingwater Creek, (BC) 35 D1
Drowning River, (Ont.) 20 A4
Drunken Harbour, (Nfld.) 6 F2
Drury Inlet, (BC) 41 F4
Drury Lake, (YT) 45 B3
Dryberry Lake, (Ont.) 28 G2
Dry Pond, (Nfld.) 4 E3
Dubawnt Lake, (NWT) 45 H3
Dubawnt River, (NWT) 44 F1
Duckbill Point, (Nfld.) 5 H3
Duck Island, (Nfld.) 2 G1
Duck Island, (Nfld.) 3 D1
Duck Island, (Nfld.) 3 B2
Duck Island, (Nfld.) 3 F2
Duck Island, (Ont.) 20 E1
Duck Lake, (Ont.) 28 E1
Duck Lake, (Man.) 30 B2
Duck Lake, (Sask.) 32 D4
Duck Mountain, (Man./Sask.) 29 D2
Duck Mountain Provincial Park, (Sask.) 29 D1
Duck Mountain Provincial Park, (Man.) 29 E1
Ducks, The *(islands)*, (Ont.) 21 H2
Duclos Point, (Ont.) 23 G2
Duder Lake, (Nfld.) 3 D2
Dufault, Lac, (Que.) 26 G2
Dufferin, Cap, (Que.) 46 E4
Dufferin Island, (BC) 41 E3
Duffey Lake, (BC) 37 H3
Duffin Lakes, (Man.) 44 H2
Dufreboy, Lac, (Que.) 6 B1
Dufreboy, Ruisseau, (Que.) 6 B1
Dufresne, Lac, (Que.) 19 F2
Dufresnoy, Lac, (Que.) 26 G2
Dufrost, Pointe, (Que.) 46 E3
Du Gas, Lac, (Que.) 5 D2
Du Glas, Lac, (Que.) 20 F3
Dugré, Lac, (Que.) 18 E2
Du Gué, Rivière, (Que.) 6 A1
Duhamel Lake, (NWT) 44 C1
Duhesme, Lac, (Que.) 20 H2
Duke of York Archipelago, (NWT) 45 E1
Duke of York Bay, (NWT) 46 D2
Dukis Point, (Ont.) 25 G1
Dumbell Lake, (Nfld.) 6 D4
Dumbell Lake, (BC) 37 C1
Dummer Lake, (Ont.) 24 E4
Dumoine, Lac, (Que.) 18 B3
Dumoine, Rivière, (Que.) 18 B4
Dumond River, (Ont.) 30 F3
Dumont, Lac, (Que.) 18 C4
Duncan, Cape, (NWT) 20 D2
Duncan, Lac, (Que.) 20 E2
Duncan Lake, (Ont.) 26 E2
Duncan Lake, (BC) 34 B3
Duncan Lake, (NWT) 45 E3
Duncan River, (BC) 34 B2
Dundas, Cape, (NWT) 47 D3
Dundas Island, (BC) 42 C4
Dundas Island, (NWT) 47 D3
Dundas Peninsula, (NWT) 47 C3
Dungarvon River, (NB) 12 D3
Dungeness, Cape, (NWT) 47 D3
Dunira Island, (BC) 42 C4
Dunkirk River, (Alta.) 44 B4
Dunks Point, (Ont.) 25 D4
Dunlop Lake, (Ont.) 25 A1
Dunnage Island, (Nfld.) 3 D2
Dunning Lake, (Sask.) 44 D3
Dunn Lake, (BC) 36 F3
Dunn Peak, (BC) 36 F3
Dunns Brook, (Nfld.) 2 D2
Dunns Mountain Pond, (Nfld.) 2 D2
Du Nort, Lac, (Que.) 5 C2
Dunphy, Lac, (Que.) 6 C2
Dunphy Lakes, (Man.) 44 G4
Dunphy's Pond, (Nfld.) 3 E4
Dunrankin River, (Ont.) 26 C1
Dunsheath Lake, (Man.) 44 G4
Dunsterville, Cape, (NWT) 47 F2
Dunvegan Lake, (NWT) 44 E2
Du Parc, Lac, (Que.) 6 C2
Duparquet, Lac, (Que.) 26 G2
Dupas, Ile, (Que.) 16 A2
Dupire, Lac, (Que.) 6 A1
Durand Creek, (BC) 35 C1
Durban Island, (NWT) 46 G1
Durell Island, (NS) 9 H2
Durocher, Lac, (Que.) 5 C2
Durocher Lake, (Sask.) 32 C1
Durrell Point, (Ont.) 25 H1
Dusey River, (Ont.) 30 G4
Dusterlo, Lac, (Que.) 6 B4
Dusty Lake, (Alta.) 33 F4
Du Tast, Lac, (Que.) 20 E3
Dutcher Lake, (NWT) 44 H2
Duteau Creek, (BC) 35 F2
Duti River, (BC) 42 E1
Duval Island, (BC) 39 D1
Duval, Lac, (Que.) 18 C4
Duval Lake, (Man.) 32 H1
Duvert, Lac, (Que.) 6 A1
Duvivier, Lac, (Que.) 13 B2
Duxbury, Lac, (Que.) 20 E3
Dwyer Lake, (Sask.) 44 F3
Dyer Bay, (Ont.) 25 D4
Dyer Bay, (NWT) 47 B2
Dyer, Cape, (NWT) 46 G1
Dyer, Mount, (BC) 37 A2
Dyke Lake, (Nfld.) 6 C3
Dymond Lake, (NWT) 44 E1

E

Eabamet Lake, (Ont.) 30 G4
Eagan Lake, (BC) 36 E3
Eager Lake, (Man.) 44 G4
Eagle Creek, (Sask.) 31 D1
Eagle Creek, (BC) 35 H2
Eagle Creek, (BC) 36 D2
Eaglehead Lake, (Ont.) 27 E2
Eagle Island, (Ont.) 25 B2
Eagle Island, (Man.) 30 B2
Eagle Lake, (Ont.) 24 B1
Eagle Lake, (Ont.) 24 H3
Eagle Lake, (Ont.) 28 H2
Eagle Lake, (Alta.) 34 F2
Eagle Lake, (BC) 40 B4
Eaglenest Creek, (BC) 42 D1
Eaglenest Lake, (Man./Ont.) 30 C4
Eagle Point, (Ont.) 25 D4
Eagle River, (Nfld.) 6 G4
Eagle River, (BC) 36 H4
Eagle River, (YT) 45 B2
Eakin Creek, (BC) 36 E3
Eardley Lake, (Man.) 30 C3
Ear Lake, (Sask.) 31 C1
Earl Island, (Nfld.) 6 G3
Earn Lake, (YT) 45 B3
Easey Lake, (Ont.) 26 B2
East Anderson River, (BC) 35 B3
East Arm, (Nfld.) 6 G3
East Barrière Lake, (BC) 36 G3
East Bay, (Nfld.) 2 A2
East Bay, (Nfld.) 2 C2
East Bay, (Nfld.) 2 D2
East Bay, (Nfld.) 4 B2
East Bay, (NS) 8 E4
East Bay, (Ont.) 27 F1
East Bay, (NWT) 46 D2
East Bay Hills, (NS) 8 E4
East Branch Indian Brook, (NS) 8 E2
East Branch Sabbies River, (NB) 12 E3
East Broad River, (NS) 10 D3
East Catfish Creek, (Ont.) 22 E2
East Channel, (NWT) 45 C1
East Cracroft Island, (BC) 39 F1
East Cross Creek, (Ont.) 21 C1
East End *(point)*, (NS) 9 D1
Easter Island, (NWT) 47 F2
Easter Lake, (BC) 39 F4
Eastern Arm, (Nfld.) 3 E2
Eastern Blue Pond, (Nfld.) 5 G3
Eastern Channel, (Nfld.) 2 E3
Eastern Hare Hills, (Nfld.) 2 B4
Eastern Head, (Nfld.) 2 C3
Eastern Head, (Nfld.) 2 F4
Eastern Indian Island, (Nfld.) 3 E2
Eastern Island, (Nfld.) 5 H3
Eastern Meelpaeg, (Nfld.) 2 D1
Eastern Peninsula, (Ont.) 28 F2
Eastern Point, (Nfld.) 4 C4
Eastern Pond, (Nfld.) 3 C4
Eastern Wolf Island, (NB) 11 C3
East Goose Lake, (NS) 10 B4
East Head, (Nfld.) 2 F4
East Head, (NB) 11 E3
East Humber River, (Ont.) 23 F3
East Ironbound Island, (NS) 10 F2
East Lake, (Ont.) 21 G2
East Long Lake, (NB) 11 C2
Eastmain, Rivière, (Que.) 20 F3
East Pen Island, (NWT) 30 F1
East Point, (Nfld.) 3 F4
East Point, (Nfld.) 4 E4
East Point, (PEI) 7 F3
East Point, (NS) 9 H4
East Point, (NS) 10 C4
East Point, (Ont.) 20 D3
East Pond, (Nfld.) 3 A1
East Porcupine River, (Sask.) 44 F2
Eastport Bay, (Nfld.) 3 F4
East Prairie River, (Alta.) 33 B1
East Random Head, (Nfld.) 2 F1
East Redonda Island, (BC) 37 C3
East River, (Nfld.) 5 G3
East River, (Ont.) 24 C2
East River, (BC) 36 F3
East River of Pictou, (NS) 9 D2
East River St Marys, (NS) 9 E2
East Rous Island, (Ont.) 25 C2
East Shoal Lake, (Man.) 29 H3
East Sister Island, (Ont.) 22 A4
East Spanish River, (Ont.) 26 D3
East Thurlow Island, (BC) 37 B3
East Trout Lake, (Sask.) 32 E2
Eaton Nord, Rivière, (Que.) 16 E4
Eaton, Rivière, (Que.) 16 E4
Eau, Bay de l', (Nfld.) 2 D3
Eau-Claire, Lac à l', (Que.) 6 D4
Eau Claire, Lac à l', (Que.) 16 B1
Eau Claire, Lac à l', (Que.) 20 F1
Eau Froide, Lac à l', (Que.) 20 H3
Eau Jaune, Lac à l', (Que.) 20 G4
Eaux Mortes, Lac des, (Que.) 14 H3
Ebb And Flow Lake, (Man.) 29 G2
Echoing Lake, (Ont.) 30 E2
Echoing River, (Man./Ont.) 30 E1
Echo Island, (BC) 35 A4
Écho, Lac, (Que.) 18 E4
Echo Lake, (Ont.) 26 B4
Echo Lake, (Man.) 28 D1
Echo Lake, (Sask.) 32 H4
Echo River, (Ont.) 26 B4
Échouani, Lac, (Que.) 18 D2
Echo Valley Provincial Park, (Sask.) 29 B2
Ecklund Lake, (NWT) 44 F1
Eclipse Harbour, (Nfld.) 46 G3
Eclipse Pond, (Nfld.) 4 F1
Eclipse Sound, (NWT) 47 F4
Economy Lake, (NS) 9 B2
Economy Point, (NS) 9 B2
Écorce, Lac de l', (Que.) 18 D3
Écorces, Lac aux, (Que.) 14 A4
Écorces, Lac aux, (Que.) 18 B3
Écorces Nord-Est, Rivière aux, (Que.) 14 A4
Écorces, Rivière aux, (Que.) 14 A3
Écorces, Rivière aux, (Que.) 16 A1
Ecstall River, (BC) 41 D1
Écueils, Pointe aux, (Que.) 46 E4
Ecum Secum River, (NS) 9 E3
Eddy Point, (NS) 9 G2
Edehon Lake, (NWT) 44 H2
Eden Bay, (NWT) 47 C2
Eden, Cape, (NWT) 47 D3
Eden Island, (BC) 39 E1
Eden Lake, (NS) 9 E2
Eden Lake, (BC) 41 A1
Eden Lake, (Man.) 44 G4
Edgell Island, (NWT) 46 G3
Edinburgh Mountain, (BC) 38 D4
Edith Cavell, Mount, (Alta.) 40 G3
Edmond Creek, (BC) 37 D2
Edmonton Int Airport/Aéroport, (Alta.) 33 D3
Edmund Lake, (Man.) 30 E2
Edmund Lake, (BC) 36 D2
Edmund Walker Island, (NWT) 47 D2
Édouard, Lac, (Que.) 18 H2
Edson River, (Alta.) 33 B3
Edward Island, (Ont.) 27 E3
Edward Lake, (Sask.) 32 C3
Edwards Lake, (BC) 36 D2
Eel River, (NB) 11 A1
Eels Creek, (Ont.) 24 E3
Eels Lake, (Ont.) 24 E3
Effiat, Lac, (Que.) 6 C2
Effingham Inlet, (BC) 38 B3
Effingham Island, (BC) 38 B3
Effingham Lake, (Ont.) 24 F3
Effingham River, (BC) 38 B2
Egenolf Lake, (Man.) 44 G2
Egg Lake, (Sask.) 32 E1
Egg Lake, (Man.) 32 H2
Egg Lake, (Sask.) 32 H3
Eglinton, Cape, (NWT) 47 G4
Eglinton Fiord, (NWT) 47 G4
Eglinton Island, (NWT) 47 B2
Egmont Bay, (PEI) 7 A3
Egmont, Cape, (PEI) 7 A3
Eighteen Mile Bay, (Ont.) 25 F2
Eighteen Mile Island, (Ont.) 25 F2
Eighteen Mile River, (Ont.) 23 B3
Eight Mile Lake, (NS) 10 D3
Eileen Lake, (NWT) 44 D1
Eileen River, (NWT) 44 D1
Ekalugad Fiord, (NWT) 46 F1
Ekapo Lake, (Sask.) 29 C3
Ekka Island, (NWT) 45 D2
Ekouane, Rivière
see Ekwan River
Ekwan Point, (Ont.) 20 C2
Ekwan River, (Ont.) 20 B2
Elaho River, (BC) 37 E3
Elaine Lake, (Sask.) 32 D2
Elbow Lake, (Ont.) 27 F1
Elbow Lake, (Man.) 30 A2
Elbow Lake, (BC) 36 E1
Elbow River, (Alta.) 34 D2
Eldorado Bay, (Ont.) 28 H2
Eldred River, (BC) 37 D4
Eldridge Bay, (NWT) 47 C2
Eleanor Lake, (Man.) 28 D1
Elephant Lake, (Ont.) 24 E2
Elephant Point, (BC) 38 D1
Eleven Mile Lake, (NS) 10 C2
Elf Lake, (Ont.) 27 D1
Elgin, Lac, (Que.) 16 E3
Elinor Lake, (Alta.) 33 F2
Elizabeth Bay, (Ont.) 25 A2
Elizabeth Harbour, (NWT) 47 E4
Elizabeth, Lac, (Que.) 20 F1
Elizabeth, Point, (NWT) 46 D2
Elizabeth, Port, (BC) 39 F1
Eliza, Lake, (Alta.) 33 G3
Eliza, Port, (BC) 39 E3
Elk Falls Provincial Park, (BC) 37 B4
Elkhorn Mountain, (BC) 39 G3
Elk Island National Park, (Alta.) 33 E3
see also Elk Island, Parc national d'
Elk Island, Parc national d', (Alta.) 33 E3
see also Elk Island National Park
Elk Lake, (BC) 38 F4
Elk Lakes Provincial Park, (BC) 34 D3
Elk River, (BC) 34 D3
Elk River, (BC) 39 G3
Elk River, (NWT) 44 E1
Ellard Lake, (Ont.) 30 E2
Ell Bay, (NWT) 46 C2
Ellef Ringnes Island, (NWT) 47 D2
Ellenwood Lake, (NS) 10 B3
Ellerslie Lake, (BC) 41 F3
Ellesmere Island, (NWT) 47 E1
Ellice Island, (NWT) 45 B1
Ellice River, (NWT) 45 G2
Elliot Bay, (NWT) 45 H1
Elliot Creek, (BC) 37 C2
Elliot Lake, (Ont.) 25 A1
Elliot Lake, (Man.) 30 D3
Elliott Brook, (NB) 12 B3
Elliott Lake, (NWT) 44 G1
Ellis, Baie, (Que.) 19 H3
Ellis Creek, (BC) 35 F3
Ellis Lake, (BC) 37 C4
Ell, Lac, (Que.) 20 F2
Ell, Ruisseau, (Que.) 13 D3
Ells River, (Alta.) 44 C4
Elmer, Lac, (Que.) 20 E3
Eloida, Lake, (Ont.) 17 C3
Elphinstone, Mount, (BC) 38 E2
Elsie, Lac, (Que.) 6 D2
Elsie Lake, (BC) 38 B2
Elson, Lac, (Que.) 6 D3
Elton Lake, (BC) 37 H4
Eltrut Lake, (Ont.) 27 A2
Elu Inlet, (NWT) 45 F1
Elwin Bay, (NWT) 47 E3
Elwin Inlet, (NWT) 47 E3
Embarras, Lac, (Que.) 18 D3
Embarras River, (Alta.) 33 A3
Embury Lake, (Man.) 32 H2
Emerald Isle, (NWT) 47 C2
Emerald Lake, (Ont.) 25 A1
Emerald Lake, (Ont.) 26 F3
Emeric Point, (Ont.) 21 H1
Emile River, (NWT) 45 E3
Emily Creek, (Ont.) 24 D4
Emily Lake, (Ont.) 24 D4
Emma Fiord, (NWT) 47 E1
Emmanuel, Lac, (Que.) 20 H2
Emm Bay, (Ont.) 28 G3
Emmeline Lake, (Sask.) 32 D1
Emmuraillé, Lac, (Que.) 14 D1
Empire-Britannique, Chaîne
see British Empire Range
Empire Lake, (Ont.) 27 D2
Ena Lake, (Ont.) 28 F1
Ena Lake, (Sask.) 44 D2
Ena River, (NWT/Sask.) 44 D2
Endikai Lake, (Ont.) 26 C4
Engemann Lake, (Sask.) 44 E3
Englefield Bay, (BC) 41 A2
Englefield, Cape, (NWT) 46 D1
Englehart River, (Ont.) 26 F2
Engler Lake, (Sask.) 44 E3
English, Cape, (Nfld.) 2 F4
English Lake, (BC) 36 E2
Englishman River, (BC) 38 D2
English River, (Ont.) 27 B1
Enic Creek, (Ont.) 26 D1
Ennadai Lake, (NWT) 44 G1
Enragé, Cap, (Que.) 14 G3
Entrée, Ile d', (Que.) 7 F1
Entwine Lake, (Ont.) 27 A2
Envies, Rivière des, (Que.) 16 C1
Épaule, Rivière à l', (Que.) 15 B2
Éphrem, Lac, (Que.) 14 E2
Epinette Creek, (Man.) 29 F4
Equesis Creek, (BC) 35 F1
Era Island, (NWT) 46 E1
Eramosa River, (Ont.) 23 E4
Erebus Bay, (NWT) 45 G1
Ericksen Lake, (NWT) 47 F4
Erickson Lake, (Sask.) 32 G2
Éric, Lac, (Que.) 19 F1
Erie, Lake, (Ont.) 22 E3
Erik Point, (NWT) 47 G4
Erith River, (Alta.) 33 B3
Ernest Kendall, Cape, (NWT) 47 A4
Erskine Inlet, (NWT) 47 D3
Escalante Point, (BC) 39 E4
Escalante River, (BC) 39 F4
Escalier, Réservoir l', (Que.) 18 D4
Esclaves, Rivière des
see Slave River
Escoumins, Baie des, (Que.) 14 E3
Escoumins, Rivière des, (Que.) 14 E3
Escuminac Baie d', (Que.) 13 D3
Escuminac, Point, (NB) 12 G2
Escuminac, Rivière, (Que.) 13 C3
Esker Lakes Provincial Park, (Ont.) 26 F2
Eskimo Lakes, (NWT) 45 C1
Esk Lake, (NWT) 44 D2
Esnagami Lake, (Ont.) 27 G1
Esnagami River, (Ont.) 27 G1
Esnagi Lake, (Ont.) 26 A1
Esnault, Lac, (Que.) 19 H2
Esowista Peninsula, (BC) 38 A2
Esox Lake, (Ont.) 27 A2
Esperanza Inlet, (BC) 39 E3
Espinosa Inlet, (BC) 39 E3
Espoir, Bay d', (Nfld.) 2 A2
Espoir, Cap d', (Que.) 13 H3
Esquimalt Harbour, (BC) 38 F4
Esten Lake, (Ont.) 25 B1
Estero Basin, (BC) 37 B3
Estero Peak, (BC) 37 B3
Estevan Group *(islands)*, (BC) 41 D2
Estevan Sound, (BC) 41 D2
Est, Ile de l', (Que.) 7 G1
Est, Lac de l', (Que.) 15 E2
Est, Pointe de l', (Que.) 5 B4
Est, Pointe de l', (Que.) 7 G1
Etagaulet Bay, (Nfld.) 6 G3
Etagaulet Point, (Nfld.) 6 G3
Étamamiou, Rivière, (Que.) 5 D3
États-Unis, Chaîne
see United States Range
Etawney Lake, (Man.) 46 A4
Etchemin, Lac, (Que.) 16 G1
Etchemin, Rivière, (Que.) 15 C4
Éternité, Lac, (Que.) 14 C3
Éternité, Rivière, (Que.) 14 C3
Ethel Lake, (Alta.) 33 G2
Ethelma Lake, (Ont.) 28 G2
Étienniche, Lac, (Que.) 19 A4
Etna Lake, (NWT) 45 D3
Etomami River, (Sask.) 32 G4
Etowamami River, (Ont.) 30 F4
Etthen Island, (NWT) 44 C1
Etthithun River, (BC) 43 E1
Etzikom Coulee, (Alta.) 34 G4
Euchiniko River, (BC) 40 B2
Eudistes, Lac des, (Que.) 19 G3
Eugene Lake, (BC) 36 E3
Eugenia Lake, (Ont.) 23 D2
Euras Lake, (Sask.) 44 E4
Eureka River, (Alta.) 43 F3
Eureka Sound, (NWT) 47 E2
Europa Lake, (BC) 41 E2
Eusuk Lake, (BC) 41 G2
Eva Lake, (Ont.) 27 C3
Eva Lake, (Alta.) 44 B3
Evangeline Lake, (Ont.) 25 C2
Evans, Cape, (NWT) 47 E1
Evans Island, (NS) 8 D4
Evans, Lac, (Que.) 20 E4
Evans Lake, (BC) 34 B3
Evans, Mount, (BC) 34 C4
Evans, Mount, (Alta.) 40 G3
Evans Point, (Ont.) 22 H2
Evans Strait, (NWT) 46 D2
Evenflow Lake, (Man.) 29 H1
Evening Lake, (Ont.) 28 H1
Everard, Mount, (BC) 37 A2
Eve River, (BC) 39 F2
Evrariege Lake, (NWT) 45 D1
Ewart Creek, (BC) 35 E4
Ewart Lake, (BC) 39 E3
Ewing Lake, (Alta.) 34 F1
Exchamsiks River, (BC) 42 D4
Exeter Bay, (NWT) 46 G1
Exeter Sound, (NWT) 46 G1
Exmouth Lake, (NWT) 45 E2
Exploits, Bay of, (Nfld.) 3 C2
Exploits Islands, (Nfld.) 3 C2
Exploits River, (Nfld.) 3 B3
Exstew River, (BC) 42 D4
Eyapamikama Lake, (Ont.) 30 F3
Eyeberry Lake, (NWT) 45 G3
Eyehill Creek, (Alta./Sask.) 31 B1
Eyre, Cape, (NWT) 47 D4
Eyrie Lake, (Man.) 44 G3

F

Faber Lake, (NWT) 45 E3
Facheux Bay, (Nfld.) 4 G4
Faillon, Lac, (Que.) 18 C1
Fair and False Bay, (Nfld.) 3 F3
Fairbairn Lake, (NWT) 44 C1
Fairbank Lake, (Ont.) 25 D1
Fairchild Creek, (Ont.) 22 G1
Fairchild Lake, (Ont.) 27 C1
Fair Haven Point, (Nfld.) 2 F2
Fair Islands, (Nfld.) 3 F3
Fair Ness *(point)*, (NWT) 46 F2
Fairweather Lake, (YT) 45 B3
Fairy Lake, (Ont.) 24 C2
Faith, Mount, (BC) 35 H4
Falaise, Lac, (Que.) 6 C3
Falaise Lake, (NWT) 44 A1
Falcon Island, (Ont.) 28 F2
Falcon Lake, (Man.) 28 E2
Falcon River, (Man.) 28 E2
Falk Lake, (BC) 37 E4
Fallentimber Creek, (Alta.) 34 D1
Fallis Lake, (Man.) 44 H2
Falls Brook, (NB) 13 A4
Falls Creek, (BC) 36 F1
Falls Lake, (BC) 36 F1
Falls River, (BC) 37 E2
Falls River, (BC) 41 E1
False Cape, (Nfld.) 6 G3
False Ducks Islands, (Ont.) 21 G2
False Head, (BC) 39 D1
Falsen Island, (NWT) 47 C4
False, Rivière, (Que.) 6 C1
Family Lake, (Man.) 30 C3
Famine, Rivière, (Que.) 16 G2
Fanshawe Lake, (Ont.) 22 E1
Fansher Creek, (Ont.) 22 C2
Fanson Lake, (Sask.) 44 F2
Faraday, Cape, (NWT) 47 F2
Faraud Lake, (Sask.) 44 E2
Farewell Lake, (Man.) 30 B2
Faribault, Lac, (Que.) 46 F4
Faride, Lac, (Que.) 5 D2
Farmer Island, (NWT) 46 D4
Farmers Island, (Nfld.) 3 D2
Far Mountain, (BC) 41 H2
Farquhar Lake, (Ont.) 24 E3
Farrant Island, (BC) 41 D2
Farrell Creek, (BC) 43 D3
Farrell Lake, (Alta.) 34 G1
Farrington, Cape, (NWT) 46 G2
Farwell Creek, (BC) 36 A2
Father, Lac, (Que.) 20 F4
Favard, Lac, (Que.) 6 B2
Favery, Lac, (Que.) 6 B2
Favourable Lake, (Ont.) 30 D3
Fawcett Lake, (Ont.) 30 E4
Fawcett Lake, (Alta.) 33 D1
Fawcett River, (Alta.) 33 D1
Fawn Lake, (NWT) 44 A1
Fawn River, (Ont.) 30 F2
Fay Islands, (NWT) 47 D2
Fearney Point, (BC) 38 D1
Featherstone Point, (Ont.) 22 H2
Fehet Lake, (NWT) 46 B2
Feist Lake, (Ont.) 28 G2
Felix, Cape, (NWT) 45 G1
Felker Lake, (BC) 36 B2
Fellfoot Point, (NWT) 47 E3
Fennell Creek, (BC) 36 G3
Fenton Lake, (BC) 41 G2
Ferguson Bay, (Ont.) 26 F3
Ferguson Creek, (Man.) 30 B2
Ferguson Lake, (NWT) 45 F1
Ferguson Lake, (NWT) 46 B2
Fernow Lake, (Ont.) 27 H1
Ferrer Point, (BC) 39 E3
Ferru, Lac, (Que.) 5 E2
Ferry Creek, (BC) 35 G2
Ferryland Head, (Nfld.) 2 C4
Ferryland Head, (Nfld.) 2 H4
Ferry, Rivière, (Que.) 15 G3
Feuilles, Lac aux, (Que.) 46 F4
Feuilles, Rivière aux, (Que.) 46 F4
Fiddlers Head, (NS) 9 F3
Fidler Bay, (Sask.) 44 F3
Fiedmont, Lac, (Que.) 18 B1
Fife Lake, (Sask.) 31 F4
Fife Sound, (BC) 39 E1
Fifth Depot Lake, (Ont.) 24 H4
Fifth Lake, (NB) 11 B2
Fifth Lake Flowage, (NS) 10 B2
Fifty Mile Point, (Ont.) 21 A3
File Axe, Lac, (Que.) 20 G4
File Lake, (Man.) 30 A2
Filer Creek, (BC) 37 D2
Filer Glacier, (BC) 37 D2
File River, (Man.) 30 A2
Filer, Mount, (BC) 37 D2
Filion Lake, (Sask.) 32 D3
Filkars, Rivière, (Que.) 16 E1
Fils, Lac du, (Que.) 18 B3
Findlay Creek, (BC) 34 C3
Findlay Group *(islands)*, (NWT) 47 C2
Findlay, Mount, (BC) 34 C3
Finger Lake, (Ont.) 30 D3
Finger Lake, (BC) 40 B2
Fin Island, (BC) 41 D2
Finlay Point, (NS) 8 C3
Finlay Ranges, (BC) 43 A2
Finlay River, (BC) 43 A2
Finlayson Channel, (BC) 41 E3
Finlayson Lake, (YT) 45 C3
Finn Creek, (BC) 36 G2
Finnie Bay, (NWT) 46 E2
Firebag Island, (Ont.) 28 H1
Firebag River, (Alta.) 44 C3
Fire Creek, (BC) 37 F1
Fire Creek, (BC) 38 H1
Firedrake Lake, (NWT) 44 F1
Fire, Lac, (Que.) 20 G2
Fire Lake, (BC) 38 H1
Fire River, (Ont.) 26 B1
Firesteel River, (Ont.) 27 C2
Fir River, (Sask.) 32 G4
First Brook, (Nfld.) 4 G3
First Burnt Pond, (Nfld.) 3 E3
First Double Pond, (Nfld.) 3 F2
First Eel Lake, (NB) 11 A1
First Lake, (NB) 15 H1
First Pond, (Nfld.) 3 D2
First Pond, (Nfld.) 3 E3
Firth River, (YT) 45 B1
Fischells Brook, (Nfld.) 4 C2
Fishbasket Lake, (Ont.) 30 G3
Fishbasket River, (Ont.) 30 G3
Fish Cove Point, (Nfld.) 6 G3
Fish Creek, (Ont.) 22 E1
Fish Creek, (Alta.) 34 E2
Fish Egg Inlet, (BC) 41 F4
Fishem Lake, (BC) 37 E1
Fisher Bay, (Man.) 29 H2

Fisher Bay, (NWT) 46 F3
Fisher, Cape, (NWT) 46 D2
Fisher, Cape, (NWT) 47 C3
Fisher Channel, (BC) 41 F3
Fisher Creek, (Alta.) 33 G2
Fisher Lake, (NS) 10 C2
Fisher Lake, (Man.) 28 D1
Fisher Lake, (Ont.) 28 H2
Fisherman River, (BC) 39 B1
Fisher River, (Man.) 29 H2
Fisher Strait, (NWT) 46 D3
Fishing Eagle Lake, (Man.) 30 D2
Fishing Islands, (Ont.) 23 B3
Fishing Lake, (Sask.) 29 B1
Fishing Lake, (Man.) 30 C3
Fishing Lake, (Alta.) 33 H3
Fishing Lakes, The, (Sask.) 29 B2
Fish Lake, (Ont.) 21 G1
Fish Lake, (NS) 45 D3
Fish Point, (Nfld.) 3 A1
Fish Point, 22 B4
Fishtail Lake, (Ont.) 24 E2
Fishtrap Lake, (Ont.) 20 A3
Fitzgerald Bay, (NWT) 47 E4
Fitz Hugh Sound, (BC) 41 F4
Fitzpatrick Lake, (NWT) 44 H1
Fitzwilliam Channel, (Ont.) 25 C3
Fitzwilliam Island, (Ont.) 25 C3
Fitzwilliam Owen Island, (NWT) 47 C2
Fitzwilliam Strait, (NWT) 47 B2
Five Islands, (NS) 9 A2
Five Mile Bay, (Ont.) 25 G3
Five Mile Lake, (NS) 10 F1
Five Mile Lake, (NS) 26 C3
Five River Lake, (NS) 10 C4
Five Rivers, (NS) 10 D3
Flack Lake, (Ont.) 26 D4
Flagler Bay, (NWT) 47 E2
Flaherty Island, (NWT) 20 D1
Flamand, Lac, (Que.) 18 G2
Flanagan River, (Ont.) 30 E3
Flat Bay, (Nfld.) 4 B2
Flat Bay Brook, (Nfld.) 4 C2
Flat Creek, (Ont.) 22 E1
Flathead River, (BC) 34 E4
Flat Island, (Nfld.) 4 B3
Flat Island, (NS) 10 A4
Flat Island, (NS) 10 F2
Flat Lake, (Alta.) 33 E2
Flat Lake, (BC) 36 G3
Flat River, (NWT) 45 C3
Flatrock Lake, (Man.) 30 A1
Flatstone Lake, (Man.) 29 H3
Flat Sound, (NWT) 47 E1
Flat Water Pond, (Nfld.) 3 A1
Flèche, Lac à, (Que.) 19 D3
Fleet Lake, (Ont.) 28 H1
Fleet River, (BC) 39 B3
Fleming Creek, (Ont.) 22 D3
Fleming Island, (BC) 38 B3
Fleming Lake, (Ont.) 27 E1
Fletcher Lake, (Sask.) 32 F1
Fletcher Lake, (NWT) 47 F3
Flett Lake, (NWT) 44 F2
Fleur-de-May, Lac, (Nfld.) 19 G1
Flint Lake, (Ont.) 27 H1
Flint Lake, (Ont.) 28 G3
Flint Lake, (NWT) 46 E1
Flint River, (Ont.) 27 H1
Floatingstone Lake, (Alta.) 33 F2
Florence Lake, (Ont.) 26 D4
Florence Lake, (BC) 37 B3
Florencia Bay, (BC) 38 A3
Flores Island, (BC) 39 F4
Flotten Lake, (Sask.) 32 B2
Flowerpot Island, (Ont.) 25 D3
Flowers Bay, (Nfld.) 6 F1
Flowers Island, (Nfld.) 3 G2
Flowers Point, (Nfld.) 3 G4
Fluke Lake, (Ont.) 28 H1
Fluor Island, (Ont.) 27 F3
Fly Creek, (BC) 36 D3
Flying Point, (NS) 9 G2
Flying Post, (NS) 10 N1
Flyway Lake, (NWT) 46 E1
Foam Lake, (Sask.) 29 B1
Foch Lake, (BC) 41 D1
Foch River, (BC) 26 A1
Fogo, Cape, (Nfld.) 3 E1
Fogo Island, (Nfld.) 3 E1
Foin, Rivière au
see Hay River
Foins, Lac aux, (Que.) 18 B3
Foley Island, (NWT) 46 E1
Folson Lake, (Ont.) 26 D1
Fond du Lac, (Sask.) 44 E2
Fond du Lac River, (Sask.) 44 F3
Fontaine, Lac, (Sask.) 44 E2
Fontaine, Lac, (Que.) 19 D2
Fontas River, (BC) 43 D1
Fontbonne, Lac, (Que.) 26 H2
Fontenac, Lac, (Que.) 5 C1
Footprint Lake, (Ont.) 28 H4
Footprint Lake, (Man.) 30 B1
Footprint River, (Man.) 44 H4
Forbes, Lac, (Que.) 18 F4
Forbes Lake, (Man.) 30 N1
Forbes, Mount, (Alta.) 34 B1
Forchu Head, (NS) 8 F4
Forde Lake, (NWT) 46 B2
Fording River, (BC) 34 D3
Ford River, (NWT) 46 D2
Ford Rivière, (Que.) 6 D1
Forgan Lake, (Ont.) 27 E2
Forgotten Lake, (Ont.) 28 F1
Forillon National Park, (Que.) 13 H2
see also Forillon, Parc national de
Forillon, Parc national de, (Que.) 13 H2
see also Forillon National Park
Forked Pond, (Nfld.) 3 E2
Fork Lake, (Alta.) 33 F2
Forks Stream, (NB) 11 E1
Formosa Creek, (Ont.) 23 C3
Forrest, Lac, (Que.) 5 A1
Forrest Lake, (Sask.) 44 D3
Forsyth Lake, (Sask.) 44 E2
Forsyth Lake, (Sask.) 44 F4
Forteau Bay, (Nfld.) 5 G2
Fortin, Lac, (Que.) 16 F2
Fortin, Lac, (Que.) 19 D2
Fortin, Lac, (YT) 45 B3
Fort Nelson River, (BC) 43 D1
Fortress Lake, (BC) 40 H3

Fortune Bay, (Nfld.) 2 B3
Fortune Channel, (BC) 39 G4
Fortune Head, (Nfld.) 2 B3
Fortune Lake, (Ont.) 24 G2
Forty Mile Brook, (NB) 12 D1
Forty Mile Creek, (Ont.) 21 A3
Forward Harbour, (BC) 39 B1
Forward Inlet, (BC) 39 C1
Fosheim Peninsula, (NWT) 47 E1
Foster Bay, (NWT) 46 D1
Foster Island, (BC) 39 B1
Foster Lake, (NWT) 44 F1
Foster, Mont, (Que.) 16 C4
Foster River, (Sask.) 44 E4
Fosthall Creek, (BC) 35 H1
Fouquet, Lac, (Que.) 19 E1
Fourches, Lac aux, (Que.) 18 B2
Fourchu Bay, (NS) 8 F4
Four Mile Lake, (NS) 11 G3
Four Mile Lake, (Ont.) 24 D3
Four Mile Pond, (Nfld.) 3 E2
Fourmont, Lac, (Nfld.) 5 D1
Fourneau, Pointe à, (Que.) 17 F4
Fournel, Lac, (Que.) 5 F2
Fournière, Lac, (Que.) 18 D2
Fournier, Lac, (Que.) 19 G1
Fourth Lake Flowage, (NS) 10 B2
Fox, Cape, (Nfld.) 5 H2
Foxe Basin, (NWT) 46 E1
Foxe Channel, (NWT) 46 D2
Fox Harbour, (NS) 9 B1
Fox Island, (Nfld.) 4 B1
Fox Island, (NS) 9 G2
Fox Island, (NB) 12 G2
Fox Island River, (Nfld.) 4 C1
Fox Lake, (Ont.) 26 D4
Fox Lake, (Ont.) 28 E1
Fox Peninsula, (NWT) 46 E2
Fox River, (NS) 11 H2
Fox River, (Man.) 30 D1
Fox River, (BC) 43 A1
Fox Pond, (Nfld.) 3 E3
Fram Sound, (NWT) 47 E3
Framboise Cove, (NS) 8 E4
Frances Bay, (BC) 37 B3
Frances Lake, (Man.) 28 D2
Frances Lake, (YT) 45 C3
Frances River, (YT) 45 C3
Franchère, Lac, (Que.) 18 E3
Franchetot, Lac, (Que.) 19 F2
Francis Lake, (Ont.) 23 C1
Francis Lake, (Man.) 30 A1
Francis₁ Lake, (Man.) 29 H3
Francis Lake, (Alta.) 33 F1
François Bay, (Nfld.) 4 F4
François, Lac, (Que.) 14 D3
François, Lacs à, (Que.) 19 D4
François Lake, (BC) 41 H1
François Lake, (NWT) 44 C1
Frank Lake, (Ont.) 27 F1
Frank Lake, (Alta.) 34 E3
Franklin Bay, (NWT) 45 D1
Franklin Bay, (NWT) 46 D1
Franklin Glacier, (BC) 37 B1
Franklin Island, (Ont.) 25 F3
Franklin Lake, (NS) 10 C2
Franklin Lake, (Sask.) 44 F2
Franklin Lake, (NWT) 46 B1
Franklin Mountains, (NWT) 45 D2
Franklin Point, (NWT) 45 G1
Franklin River, (BC) 37 A2
Franklin Strait, (NWT) 47 D4
Franklyn Arm, (BC) 37 D1
Franks Pond, (Nfld.) 2 G3
Franquelin, Lac, (Que.) 19 D4
Frapeau Point, (Nfld.) 2 F4
Fraser Island, (NWT) 46 E2
Fraser Lake, (Nfld.) 6 E3
Fraser Lake, (BC) 39 F1
Fraser Lake, (BC) 40 A1
Fraser Lake, (NWT) 44 E2
Fraser River, (Nfld.) 6 E2
Fraser River, (BC) 35 A4
Fraser River, (BC) 40 G2
Fraye, Lac, (Que.) 19 B3
Frazer Bay, (Ont.) 25 D2
Frazer Lake, (Ont.) 27 E2
Freakly Point, (NWT) 20 D1
Fréchette, Lac, (Que.) 26 C3
Fréchette, Rivière, (Que.) 19 G1
Freda Creek, (BC) 37 D4
Freda Lake, (BC) 37 D4
Frederick Arm, (BC) 37 B3
Frederick House Lake, (Ont.) 26 E1
Frederick House River, (Ont.) 26 E1
Frederick Island, (BC) 41 A1
Frederiksen Point, (BC) 39 B1
Fredrikson Lake, (BC) 42 G1
Freels, Cape, (Nfld.) 3 F2
Freeman River, (Alta.) 33 D4
Frégate, Lac, (Que.) 20 F2
Freil Lake, (BC) 37 D4
French Bar Creek, (BC) 36 B3
French Creek, (Man.) 30 N1
French Creek, (NB) 11 D1
French Lake, (NB) 11 C2
Frenchman Lake, (Alta.) 33 F2
Frenchman Point, (NS) 10 B4
Frenchman Point, (Ont.) 23 C1
Frenchman River, (Sask.) 31 D4
Frenchman's Bay, (Ont.) 21 B2
Frenchman's Cove, (Nfld.) 2 H4
Frenchmans Pond, (Nfld.) 4 D1
French River, (Ont.) 25 G2
French River Main Channel, (Ont.) 25 F2
French River North Channel, (Ont.) 25 F2
Freshfield Icefield, (Alta.) 34 B1
Freshwater Bay, (Nfld.) 3 E3
Freshwater Lake, (Alta./Sask.) 33 H4
Freshwater Lake, (NWT) 46 F2
Freshwater Pond, (Nfld.) 2 G4
Freshwater Pond, (Nfld.) 2 C3
Fressel, Lac, (Que.) 20 F1
Freuchen Bay, (NWT) 46 D1
Friday Lake, (Nfld.) 3 F2
Friday Creek, (Ont.) 20 C4
Friday Lake, (Ont.) 28 E3
Friendly Lake, (BC) 36 E2
Frobisher Bay, (NWT) 46 G2

Frobisher Lake, (Sask.) 44 D4
Frog Lake, (NS) 11 G4
Frog Lake, (Alta.) 33 G3
Frogmoore Lakes, (Sask.) 35 D1
Frogpond Lake, (BC) 37 D4
Frog River, (Ont.) 30 G2
Froid, Ruisseau, (Que.) 18 E4
Fromenteau, Lac, (Que.) 13 G2
Fromenteau, Lac, (Que.) 20 G3
Frontier Creek, (BC) 37 B1
Frontière, Lac, (Que.) 15 D3
Frotet, Lac, (Que.) 20 G4
Frozen Ocean Lake, (Nfld.) 3 B2
Frozen Ocean Lake, (Nfld.) 3 C3
Frozen Ocean Lake, (NS) 10 C2
Frozen Strait, (NWT) 46 D2
Frye Island, (NB) 11 C3
Fry Lake, (Ont.) 30 E4
Fullerton, Cape, (NWT) 46 C2
Fulmore Lake, (BC) 39 B1
Fulton Lake, (BC) 42 G4
Fulton River, (BC) 42 G4
Fundy, Bay of, (NB/NS) 10 B1
Fundy National Park, (NB) 11 F2
see also Fundy, Parc national de, (NB) 11 F2
see also Fundy National Park
Funk Island, (Nfld.) 3 G1
Fury And Hecla Strait, (NWT) 47 A4
Fury Point, (NWT) 47 A4
Fushimi Lake Provincial Park, (Ont.) 20 B4

G

Gabarus Bay, (NS) 8 F4
Gabarus, Cape, (NS) 8 F4
Gabarus Lake, (NS) 8 F4
Gable Creek, (BC) 35 G3
Gable Mountain, (BC) 40 D1
Gable Mountain, (BC) 41 F2
Gabriel, Lac, (Que.) 6 C1
Gabriel, Lac, (Que.) 20 G4
Gabriel Strait, (NWT) 46 G3
Gabriola Island, (BC) 38 E2
Gaffaret, Lac, (Nfld.) 5 B1
Gaff Point, (NS) 10 E2
Gage, Cape, (PEI) 7 A2
Gage, Cape, (PEI) 12 H3
Gagnon, Lac, (Que.) 18 E4
Gagnon Lake, (NWT) 44 D1
Gaillarbois, Lac, (Que.) 19 E1
Gaillard, Lac, (Que.) 19 C3
Gainsborough Creek, (Man./Sask.) 29 D4
Galeairy Lake, (Ont.) 24 D2
Gale, Rivière, (Que.) 26 H1
Galiano Island, (BC) 38 E2
Gallas Point, (PEI) 7 D4
Gallatin, Mount, (BC) 42 B2
Galles, Îles de
see Wales Island
Gallet, Lac, (Que.) 5 F1
Galt Creek, (Ont.) 22 G1
Gamart, Lac, (Que.) 6 B4
Gambier Island, (BC) 38 F2
Gambier Lake, (BC) 41 D2
Gambo Pond, (Nfld.) 3 E4
Gammon River, (Man./Ont.) 30 D4
Gamsby Creek, (BC) 27 G2
Gamsby River, (BC) 41 F2
Gananoque Lake, (Ont.) 17 B3
Gananoque River, (Ont.) 17 B4
Ganaraska River, (Ont.) 21 D2
Gander Bay, (Nfld.) 3 E2
Gander Int Airport/Aéroport, (Nfld.) 3 D3
Gander Island, (Nfld.) 3 D3
Gander Lake, (Nfld.) 3 D3
Gander River, (Nfld.) 3 D3
Gannet Point, (NS) 9 H2
Gannet Rock, (NB) 11 C4
Gannett Creek, (BC) 36 G3
Gaotanaga, Lac, (Que.) 18 B2
Gap Creek, (Sask.) 31 C4
Gar, Lac de la, (Que.) 18 B3
Garde Lake, (NWT) 45 G3
Gardenia Lake, (NWT) 44 E1
Garden Lake, (Ont.) 27 D2
Garden Lake, (Ont.) 26 B4
Gardiner Dam/Barrage, (Sask.) 31 E2
Gardiner Lake, (NWT) 44 E2
Gardiner Lakes, (Alta.) 44 C3
Gardner Brook, (Nfld.) 3 B4
Gardner Canal, (BC) 41 E2
Gardner Creek, (NB) 11 E3
Gardom Lake, (BC) 35 F1
Garemand, Lac, (Que.) 19 E2
Gargantua, Cape, (Ont.) 26 A2
Garia Bay, (Nfld.) 4 B4
Garia Brook, (Nfld.) 4 C3
Garibaldi Lake, (BC) 37 F4
Garibaldi, Mount, (BC) 37 F4
Garibaldi Provincial Park, (BC) 37 F4
Garin, Rivière, (Que.) 13 F3
Garland River, (Man.) 29 E1
Garlep Point, (Nfld.) 2 G4
Garneau, Lac, (Que.) 5 A1
Garneau, Rivière, (Que.) 5 A1
Garner Lake, (Alta.) 33 F2
Garnet Bay, (NWT) 46 E2
Garnham Lake, (Ont.) 27 H2
Garnier Bay, (NWT) 47 E3
Garnish Pond, (Nfld.) 2 B3
Garrett Island, (NWT) 47 F3
Garrett Lake, (Ont.) 30 F2
Garry Bay, (NWT) 46 D1
Garry, Cape, (NWT) 47 D4
Garry Island, (NWT) 45 D1
Garry Lake, (NWT) 45 G2
Garry, Loch, (Ont.) 17 E2
Garson Lake, (Alta./Sask.) 44 C4
Garson River, (Sask.) 44 D4
Gary, Lac, (NWT) 46 D1
Gascons, Lac, (NB) 12 C1
Gasket Island, (NWT) 20 D3
Gaspard Creek, (BC) 36 A2
Gasparin, Lac, (Que.) 20 G2
Gaspé, Cap de, (Que.) 13 H2
Gaspé, Havre de, (Que.) 13 H2
Gaspereau Lake, (NS) 10 A3
Gaspereau River, (NB) 7 A4
Gaspereau River, (NS) 11 H3

Gaspereau River, (NB) 12 E4
Gaspésie, Parc provincial de la, (Que.) 13 E2
Gatacre Point, (Ont.) 25 B2
Gataga River, (BC) 43 A1
Gates Creek, (BC) 35 H1
Gateshead Island, (NWT) 47 C4
Gathto Creek, (BC) 43 B1
Gatineau, Parc de la, (Que.) 17 C1
see also Gatineau Park
Gatineau Park, (Que.) 17 C1
see also Gatineau Parc de la
Gatineau, Rivière, (Que.) 17 C1
Gaudreault, Lac, (Que.) 5 B2
Gauer Lake, (Man.) 44 H3
Gauer River, (Man.) 44 H4
Gayot, Lac, (Que.) 6 B2
Gegogan, Cape, (NS) 9 F1
Geikie Island, (Ont.) 27 E1
Geikie River, (Sask.) 44 F4
Generator Lake, (NWT) 46 F1
Genévriers, Île des, (Que.) 6 D2
Gensart, Lac, (Que.) 6 C2
Gentilly, Rivière, (Que.) 16 C2
George, Cape, (NS) 9 F1
George, Cape, (NS) 9 B3
George Fraser Islands, (BC) 38 A3
George Island, (Nfld.) 6 G3
George Island, (Ont.) 25 D2
George Island, (NWT) 47 B4
George, Lake, (NS) 10 B3
George, Lake, (NS) 11 H1
George, Lake, (Man.) 28 D1
George Passage, (BC) 39 C1
George, Lake, (BC) 39 C1
George, Lake, (Sask.) 44 E4
George Richards, Cape, (NWT) 47 C2
George Rivière, (Que.) 6 D1
George, Rivière, (Que.) 6 D2
Georges Brook, (Nfld.) 2 F1
Georges Lake, (Nfld.) 4 C1
Georges Pond, (Nfld.) 2 E1
Georges Pond, (Nfld.) 4 H2
Georgian Bay, (Ont.) 25 D3
Georgian Bay Islands National Park, (Ont.) 25 D3
see also Îles de la baie Georgienne, Parc national des
Georgia, Strait of, (BC) 38 E2
Georgienne, Baie
see Georgian Bay
Georgina Island, (Ont.) 23 G2
Gerald Island, (BC) 38 D2
Gerido, Lac, (Que.) 6 B1
Germaine, Lac, (Que.) 6 C4
Germansen Lake, (BC) 43 B4
Gernon Bay, (NWT) 45 G1
Gerrard, Lac, (Que.) 5 C2
Gething, Mount, (BC) 43 D3
Ghost, Lake, (BC) 40 E3
Ghostpine Creek, (Alta.) 34 F1
Ghost River, (Ont.) 45 F2
Ghurka Lake, (NWT) 45 F1
Ghyvelde Lake, (Nfld.) 6 D4
Giants Causeway (point), (NWT) 47 B2
Giants Tomb Island, (Ont.) 23 E1
Gibbs Point, (NWT) 47 G4
Gibi Lake, (Ont.) 28 G2
Gibraltar Island, (BC) 38 B3
Gibraltar Lake, (NS) 9 C3
Gibraltar Point, (Ont.) 21 B2
Gibson Bay, (NWT) 46 E1
Gibson Creek, (NB) 11 A1
Gibson Lake, (NWT) 46 B2
Giddie Point, (NWT) 47 B2
Gidley Point, (Ont.) 23 E1
Giffard, Lac, (Que.) 20 F3
Gifford Fiord, (NWT) 47 F4
Gifford Peninsula, (NWT) 37 C4
Gifford Point, (NWT) 47 F3
Gifford River, (NWT) 47 F4
Gilbert, Lac, (Que.) 6 H4
Gilbert River, (Nfld.) 6 H4
Gilberts Point, (NS) 10 B2
Gildersleve Lake, (BC) 41 F3
Giles Lake, (Sask.) 44 E3
Gilford Island, (BC) 39 F1
Gil Island, (BC) 41 D2
Gillespie Lake, (Alta.) 33 H4
Gillfillan Lake, (NS) 10 B3
Gillies, Baie, (Que.) 26 G3
Gillies Lake, (Ont.) 25 D4
Gillinghams Pond, (Nfld.) 3 D3
Gilmour Island, (NWT) 20 D3
Gipouloux, Rivière, (Que.) 20 G3
Gipsy Lake, (Alta.) 44 C4
Girard Creek, (Sask.) 31 G4
Girardin, Lac, (Que.) 6 D1
Girouard, Lac, (Que.) 14 F2
Girouard, Lac, (Que.) 18 D1
Girouard Lake, (Man.) 32 H1
Giroux Lake, (Ont.) 25 F2
Giroux, Lac, (Alta.) 33 B2
Giroux River, (Ont.) 25 F2
Gisborne Lake, (Nfld.) 2 D2
Gitche Lake, (Ont.) 30 E4
Gitche River, (Ont.) 24 G1
Glacier Fiord, (NWT) 47 E2
Glacier National Park, (BC) 34 B2
see also Glacier, Parc national du, (BC) 34 B2
see also Glacier National Park
Glacier Strait, (NWT) 47 F3
Gladsheim Peak, (BC) 34 B2
Glamor Lake, (Ont.) 24 D3
Glasgow Head, (NS) 9 H2
Glatheli Lake, (BC) 41 G2
Glendale Lake, (Nfld.) 3 A3
Glenelg Lake, (NS) 9 F4
Glenmore Mountain, (NS) 9 C3
Glennie Lake, (Sask.) 32 F1
Glide Brook, (Nfld.) 4 E1
Glide Lake, (Nfld.) 4 E1
Glossy Mountain, (BC) 35 H1
Glover Island, (Nfld.) 4 D3
Gnawed Mountain, (BC) 35 C1
Goat Island, (BC) 37 D4
Goat Lake, (BC) 37 D4
Goat River, (BC) 26 B1
Goat River, (BC) 34 C4
Goat River, (BC) 40 E2
Goatskin Creek, (BC) 35 G3
God Bay, (Nfld.) 6 H4
Godbout Est, Rivière, (Que.) 19 D3
Godbout, Rivière, (Que.) 19 D2
Gods, Cape, (Man.) 30 D2
Gods Mercy, Bay of, (NWT) 46 C2

Gods River, (Man.) 30 E1
Goéland, Lac au, (Que.) 19 A3
Goéland, Lac au, (Que.) 20 F4
Goélands, Lac aux, (Que.) 6 D2
Gohere Bay, (Ont.) 28 G3
Go Home Lake, (Ont.) 25 H4
Goisard, Lac, (Que.) 19 A3
Gold Creek, (BC) 34 D4
Gold Creek, (BC) 36 D4
Golden Bay, (Nfld.) 2 E4
Golden Ears Provincial Park, (BC) 38 G1
Golden Hinde, (BC) 39 G3
Golden Lake, (Ont.) 24 F1
Golden Lake, (Ont.) 28 H1
Goldie Lake, (Ont.) 26 B2
Gold Lake, (BC) 39 G3
Gold River, (BC) 39 G3
Gold River, (NS) 10 E2
Goldsand Lake, (Man.) 44 G4
Goldsmith Channel, (NWT) 47 C3
Goldstream River, (BC) 34 A1
Goleta Channel, (BC) 39 C1
Golet, Lac, (Que.) 5 D1
Gollen Creek, (BC) 36 G3
Gollfish Lake, (Alta.) 33 F2
Good Friday Bay, (NWT) 47 D2
Good Hope Mountain, (BC) 37 D1
Good Point, (NWT) 47 H1
Goodsir Inlet, (NWT) 47 D3
Goodsir, Mount, (BC) 34 C2
Good Spirit Lake, (Sask.) 29 C2
Good Spirit Lake Provincial Park, (Sask.) 29 C2
Goodwin Lake, (Alta.) 33 F1
Goodwood, Rivière, (Que.) 6 C2
Goose Arm, (Nfld.) 5 F4
Goose Bay, (Nfld.) 3 F4
Goose Bay, (Nfld.) 6 H4
Gooseberry Brook, (Ont.) 20 B1
Gooseberry Lake, (Sask.) 29 B3
Goose Creek, (Ont.) 30 E1
Goose Fiord, (NWT) 47 E2
Goose Harbour Lake, (NS) 9 G2
Goosehunting Creek, (Sask.) 32 E4
Goose Island, (NS) 9 B3
Goose Island, (BC) 41 E3
Goose Islands, (Ont.) 25 H1
Goose, Lac, (Que.) 20 G2
Goose, Lac, (Que.) 22 B3
Goose Lake, (Ont.) 24 C4
Goose Lake, (Man.) 29 G1
Goose Lake, (Man.) 30 D2
Goose Lake, (Ont.) 30 E4
Goose Lake, (Sask.) 31 E1
Goose Lake, (Sask.) 32 B4
Goose Lake, (Man.) 32 H2
Goose Lake, (Man./Sask.) 44 G2
Goose Pond, (Nfld.) 4 D3
Goose Pond, (Nfld.) 5 F4
Goose River, (Nfld.) 6 E3
Goose River, (Alta.) 33 B2
Gopher Creek, (Man./Sask.) 29 D3
Gorden Bay, (NWT) 46 D2
Gordon Bay, (NWT) 45 F2
Gordon Head, (BC) 38 F4
Gordon Horne Peak, (BC) 36 H2
Gordon Lake, (Ont.) 26 B4
Gordon Lake, (Ont.) 28 H1
Gordon Lake, (Alta.) 44 C4
Gordon Lake, (NWT) 45 F3
Gordon McKenzie Arm, (Sask.) 31 F2
Gordon River, (BC) 38 D3
Gordon River, (NWT) 46 D2
Gore Bay, (NWT) 46 D2
Gore Island, (BC) 39 F3
Gore Point, (NWT) 46 D2
Gorgotton, Lac, (Que.) 14 D2
Goschen Island, (BC) 41 C2
Gosford, Mont, (Que.) 16 F4
Gosnell Creek, (BC) 41 F1
Gott Creek, (BC) 37 H3
Gottfriedsen, Mount, (BC) 35 E2
Gott Peak, (BC) 37 G2
Gouffre, Rivière du, (Que.) 15 C1
Gough Lake, (Alta.) 34 F1
Gouin, Lac, (Que.) 19 B4
Gouin, Réservoir, (Que.) 18 E1
Goulais, Lac, (Que.) 26 A3
Goulais Lake, (Ont.) 26 B3
Goulais Point, (Ont.) 26 A3
Goulais River, (Ont.) 26 B3
Goulden Lake, (Sask.) 32 F2
Gould Lake, (Ont.) 23 C1
Gould Lake, (Ont.) 24 H2
Goulet Lake, (Man.) 30 C1
Gounamitz River, (NB) 12 A1
Goupil, Lac, (Que.) 6 C4
Gourlay Lake, (Ont.) 26 A1
Govan Lake, (Sask.) 44 E3
Gover Lake, (NB) 12 C2
Governor Lake, (NS) 9 D2
Governors Island, (Nfld.) 4 C1
Governors Island, (PEI) 7 D4
Gowan Creek, (BC) 37 H4
Gowan River, (BC) 30 D1
Gower Point, (BC) 38 E2
Gowgaia Bay, (BC) 41 B3
Gowganda Lake, (Ont.) 26 C2
Gow Lake, (Sask.) 44 F4
Goyeau, Pointe, (Que.) 6 C3
Goyelle, Lac, (Que.) 5 C2
Gozdz Lake, (NWT) 44 E1
Grâce, Île de la, (Que.) 16 B2
Grace Lake, (NS) 7 F1
Grady Island, (Nfld.) 6 H3
Graham Creek, (Man./Sask.) 29 D4
Graham Head, (NS) 9 C4
Graham Island, (BC) 41 A1
Graham Island, (NWT) 47 E2
Graham Lake, (Ont.) 17 C3
Graham Lake, (Alta.) 44 B4
Graham Moore Bay, (NWT) 47 D3
Graham Moore, Cape, (NWT) 47 F3
Graham River, (BC) 43 C3
Granby River, (BC) 35 H4
Grand Bank Head, (Nfld.) 2 B3
Grand Bay, (Nfld.) 4 A4
Grand Bay River, (Nfld.) 4 A4
Grand Beach Provincial Park, (Man.) 30 C3
Grand Calumet, Île du, (Que.) 24 H1

Grand Codroy River, (Nfld.) 4 A3
Grand Détour, Lac du, (Que.) 19 B3
Grande Baie, (Que.) 19 B2
Grande Décharge, Lac de la, (Que.) 14 E2
Grande Entrée, Harve de la, (Que.) 7 G1
Grande Entrée, Île de, (Que.) 7 G1
Grande, Île, (Que.) 19 H3
Grande Passe, Île de la, (Que.) 5 F2
Grande Pointe, Lac, (Que.) 20 F2
Grande Rivière, (Que.) 12 A2
Grande Rivière, (Que.) 13 G2
Grande rivière de la Baleine, (Que.) 20 F1
Grande rivière de l'Ours
see Great Bear River
Grande Rivière Noire, (Que.) 15 D3
Grande Rivière Ouest, (Que.) 13 G2
Grandes Pointes, Lac aux, (Que.) 14 A1
Grandin, Lac, (NWT) 45 E3
Grand Lac, (Que.) 17 C1
Grand, Lac, (Que.) 18 C3
Grand Lac Bostonnais, (Que.) 18 H2
Grand lac de l'Ours
see Great Bear Lake
Grand lac des Esclaves
see Great Slave Lake
Grand Lac des Îles, (Que.) 16 A1
Grand Lac des Rapides, (Que.) 19 F3
Grand lac du Nord, (Que.) 19 E2
Grand lac Germain, (Que.) 19 E2
Grand lac Touladi, (Que.) 13 C1
Grand lac Victoria, (Que.) 18 B2
Grand Lake, (Nfld.) 4 F3
Grand Lake, (NS) 9 D3
Grand Lake, (NB) 11 A1
Grand Lake, (NB) 11 D1
Grand Lake, (Ont.) 24 E1
Grand Lake, (NWT) 45 H2
Grand Manan Channel, (NB) 11 B4
Grand Manan Island, (NB) 11 C4
Grandmesnil, Lac, (Que.) 19 E2
Grand Nord, Ruisseau, (Que.) 13 D3
Grand Pabos, Baie du, (Que.) 13 G3
Grand Pabos, Rivière du, (Que.) 13 G3
Grand Passage, (NS) 8 E4
Grand River, (Ont.) 22 G1
Grandy Brook, (Nfld.) 4 D3
Grandys Brook, (Nfld.) 4 B4
Grandy Sound, (Nfld.) 4 F3
Granet, Lac, (Que.) 18 B2
Granet Lake, (NWT) 45 D1
Granger Lake, (Sask.) 44 E3
Granite, Cape, (NWT) 47 D3
Granite, Chute au, (Que.) 6 B2
Granite Creek, (BC) 35 C4
Granitehill Lake, (Ont.) 26 A1
Granite Lake, (Nfld.) 4 D3
Granite Lake, (Sask.) 32 G1
Granite Peak, (BC) 37 C2
Granite, Point, (Nfld.) 5 H3
Grant Lake, (NWT) 45 H2
Grant Point, (Ont.) 22 H2
Grant Point, (NWT) 45 G1
Grants Lake, (NB) 12 D2
Grant-Suttie Bay, (NWT) 46 E1
Granville Lake, (Man.) 44 G4
Gras, Lac de, (NWT) 45 F2
Grass River, (Man.) 30 B1
Grass River Provincial Park, (Man.) 30 A2
Grassy Island Lake, (Alta.) 31 B1
Grassy Lake, (NS) 11 A1
Grassy Narrows Lake, (Ont.) 28 G1
Grassy Point, (Nfld.) 2 H1
Grates Point, (Nfld.) 2 H1
Gravel Hill Lake, (NWT) 44 F1
Gravel Island, (NS) 10 F2
Gravell Point, (NWT) 46 E1
Gravelly Point, (Ont.) 27 F2
Gravel River, (Ont.) 27 F2
Graves Strait, (NWT) 46 G3
Gray Lake, (NWT) 46 D1
Grays Bay, (NWT) 45 F2
Grayson River, (Ont.) 30 F4
Gray Strait, (NWT) 46 G3
Grease River, (Sask.) 44 D3
Greasy Lake, (NS) 10 B3
Great Barren Lake, (NS) 10 B3
Great Bay de l'Eau, (Nfld.) 2 B3
Great Bear Lake, (NWT) 45 D2
Great Bear River, (NWT) 45 D2
Great Beaver Lake, (BC) 43 B3
Great Black Island, (Nfld.) 3 F3
Great Bras d'Or, (NS) 8 F3
Great Burnt Lake, (Nfld.) 4 G2
Great Cat Arm, (Nfld.) 5 G3
Great Central Lake, (BC) 38 B2
Great Chance Harbour, (Nfld.) 3 F4
Great Colinet, (Nfld.) 2 F4
Great Duck Island, (NB) 11 C4
Great Duck Island, (Ont.) 25 A3
Great Garnish Barasway, (Nfld.) 2 B3
Great Gull Lake, (Nfld.) 3 A2
Great Gull River, (Nfld.) 3 C4
Great Harbour Deep, (Nfld.) 5 G3
Great Island, (Nfld.) 2 H3
Great Island, (Nfld.) 4 A4
Great Island, (NS) 10 E3
Great La Cloche Island, (Ont.) 25 C2
Great North, (Nfld.) 25 H1
Great Pinchgut, (Nfld.) 2 F2
Great Plain of the Koukdjuak, (NWT) 46 F2
Great Pubnico Lake, (NS) 10 B4
Great Rattling Brook, (Nfld.) 3 B3
Great Seal Island, (Nfld.) 2 E3
Great Slave Lake, (NWT) 44 B1

Great Snow Mountain, (BC) 43 B2
Great Whale River
see Grande rivière de la Baleine
Greaves Island, (BC) 41 F4
Greely Fiord, (NWT) 47 E1
Green Bay, (Nfld.) 3 G4
Green Bay, (NS) 10 E2
Green Bay, (Que.) 25 C2
Green Bay, (Sask.) 44 E3
Green Bay Island, (Nfld.) 3 B1
Greenbush Lake, (Ont.) 30 F4
Greenbush River, (Sask.) 32 G4
Greenhill River, (NB) 26 B1
Green Hills, (Nfld.) 2 A4
Green Island, (Nfld.) 2 G1
Green Island, (Nfld.) 3 E2
Green Island, (NS) 10 B4
Green Lake, (Sask.) 32 C4
Green Lake, (BC) 36 C3
Green Lake, (BC) 37 F4
Greenough Point, (Ont.) 25 D4
Green Point, (Nfld.) 3 B2
Green Point, (Nfld.) 5 H3
Green Point, (NS) 10 C4
Green River, (NB) 15 H1
see also Verte, Rivière
Green River, (BC) 37 G3
Green Rock, (NS) 10 D4
Green's Creek, (Ont.) 17 E4
Greenspond Island, (Nfld.) 3 F3
Greenstone Mountain, (BC) 35 C1
Greenstreet Lake, (Sask.) 32 A3
Greenwater Lake, (Ont.) 27 C3
Greenwater Lake, (Sask.) 32 G4
Greenwater Lake Provincial Park, (Sask.) 32 G4
Greenwater Provincial Park, (Ont.) 26 E1
Greenway Sound, (BC) 39 E1
Greenwich Lake, (Ont.) 27 E3
Greenwood Lake, (NS) 10 C4
Gregoire Lake, (Alta.) 44 C4
Gregory Island, (BC) 39 E1
Greig Lake, (Sask.) 32 B2
Greiner Lake, (NWT) 47 C4
Grenadier Islands, (Ont.) 17 C4
Grenville Bay, (NS) 11 G2
Grenville Channel, (BC) 41 D1
Grenville, Mount, (BC) 37 C2
Greta Lake, (Ont.) 27 G1
Grewatsch Creek, (BC) 43 D2
Grew Lake, (Alta.) 44 B4
Grey Goose Island, (NWT) 20 D2
Grey Island, (NS) 10 F2
Grey Islands, (Nfld.) 5 H1
Grey, Mount, (BC) 38 C3
Grey River, (Nfld.) 4 F3
Grey River Point, (Nfld.) 4 E3
Grey River Rocks, (Nfld.) 4 E3
Griault, Rivière, (Que.) 20 F2
Gribbell Island, (BC) 41 C1
Grief Point, (BC) 38 C1
Griffin Cove, (NS) 10 B2
Griffin Inlet, (NWT) 47 C3
Griffin Lake, (BC) 34 A2
Griffin, Mount, (BC) 34 A2
Griffith Island, (Ont.) 23 D1
Griffith Island, (NWT) 47 D3
Griffon, Lac au, (Que.) 19 C1
Grill Lake, (Sask.) 31 C1
Grimes Lake, (Man.) 44 H3
Grinder Creek, (BC) 36 B3
Grindstone Head, (Nfld.) 2 F1
Grindstone Island, (NB) 11 G2
Grindstone Island, (Que.) 26 G3
Grindstone Point, (NB) 13 F4
Grinnell, Cape, (NWT) 47 E3
Grinnell Peninsula, (NWT) 47 D2
Grippen Lake, (Ont.) 17 B3
Grise Fiord, (NWT) 47 F3
Grist Lake, (Alta.) 33 G1
Grizzly Mountain, (BC) 36 F2
Groais Island, (Nfld.) 5 H2
Grollier Lake, (NWT) 44 E2
Grondine, Point, (Ont.) 25 E2
Gros Cacouna, Île de, (Que.) 14 E4
Gros Mécatina, Cap du, (Que.) 5 E3
Gros Mécatina, Île du, (Que.) 5 E2
Gros Mécatina, Rivière du, (Que.) 5 F4
Gros Morne National Park, (Nfld.)
see also Gros Morne, Parc national de
Gros Morne, Parc national de, (Nfld.) 5 F4
see also Gros Morne National Park
Grosse Boule, Île, (Que.) 19 F3
Grosse Île, (Que.) 7 G1
Grosse Île, (Que.) 15 C2
Groswater Bay, (Nfld.) 6 G3
Grouard Lake, (NWT) 45 E2
Groulx, Les monts, (Que.) 19 F1
Groundhog Creek, (BC) 37 F1
Groundhog Lake, (Ont.) 26 D2
Groundhog River, (Ont.) 26 D2
Grove Lake, (Sask.) 44 F2
Grues, Île aux, (Que.) 15 C2
Grundy Lake Provincial Park, (Ont.) 25 F2
Guagus Lake, (NB) 12 D2
Guay, Lac, (Que.) 26 G3
Guéguen, Lac, (Que.) 18 C2
Guéneveau, Lac, (Que.) 46 F4
Guérard, Lac, (Que.) 6 D2
Guernesé, Lac, (Que.) 5 F1
Guers, Lac, (Que.) 6 C1
Guichon Creek, (BC) 35 D3
Guichon, Mount, (BC) 35 C1
Guillaume-Delisle, Lac, (Que.) 46 E4
Guillemard Bay, (NWT) 47 D4
Guillemot, Lac, (Que.) 6 B3
Guinecourt, Lac, (Que.) 19 C2
Guines, Lac, (Nfld.) 5 G1
Gulatch Lake, (BC) 36 C2
Gulch Cape, (NB) 46 H3
Gulch Cove, (Nfld.) 2 F3
Gulch Island, (Nfld.) 2 F3
Gulf Islands, (BC) 38 E3
Gulf of Boothia, (NWT) 47 E4

Gull Bay, (NWT) 20 D3
Gull Bay, (Ont.) 27 E2
Gull Cove, (Nfld.) 2 E4
Gull Creek, (Sask.) 32 E3
Gull Island, (Nfld.) 2 H3
Gull Island, (Nfld.) 3 C1
Gull Island, (Nfld.) 3 B2
Gull Island, (NWT) 20 E3
Gull Island Point, (Nfld.) 2 F4
Gulliver Lake, (Ont.) 27 C2
Gulliver River, (Ont.) 27 B2
Gullivers Head, (NS) 10 B2
Gull Lake, (Nfld.) 3 C3
Gull Lake, (Nfld.) 6 F4
Gull Lake, (Ont.) 24 C3
Gull Lake, (Ont.) 26 F3
Gull Lake, (Ont.) 30 E4
Gull Lake, (Alta.) 33 D4
Gull Pond, (Nfld.) 2 H3
Gull Pond, (Nfld.) 3 A1
Gull Pond, (Nfld.) 3 A1
Gull Pond, (Nfld.) 3 F2
Gull Pond, (Nfld.) 3 E3
Gull Pond, (Nfld.) 3 E4
Gull Pond, (Nfld.) 3 F4
Gull River, (Ont.) 27 D2
Gull Rock, (NS) 10 A2
Gull Rock, (NS) 10 D4
Gullrock Lake, (Ont.) 30 D4
Gullwing Lake, (Ont.) 27 A1
Gulp Pond, (Nfld.) 4 G2
Gulquac Lake, (NB) 12 C2
Gulquac River, (NB) 12 B2
Gun Creek, (BC) 37 F2
Gundy Lake, (Ont.) 28 E2
Gunisao Lake, (Man.) 30 C3
Gunisao River, (Man.) 30 C2
Gun Lake, (Ont.) 28 F1
Gun Lake, (BC) 37 G2
Gurd Island, (BC) 41 C1
Gustafsen Lake, (BC) 36 C3
Gutah Creek, (BC) 43 E1
Guthrie Lake, (Man.) 30 A1
Guyer, Lac, (Que.) 20 F2
Guyon Island, (NS) 8 F4
Gwillim Lake, (BC) 43 E4
Gypsum Lake, (Man.) 29 G1
Gypsum Point, (NWT) 44 B1
Gyrfalcon Islands, (NWT) 46 G4

H

Haakon Fiord, (NWT) 47 D2
Hache, Lac la, (BC) 36 C2
Hackett Lake, (Sask.) 32 C2
Hadley Bay, (NWT) 47 C4
Haggard Creek, (BC) 36 F3
Haggerty Creek, (Ont.) 22 C2
Hague Creek, (Sask.) 32 F2
Ha! Ha!, Baie des, (Que.) 5 E2
Ha! Ha!, Baie des, (Que.) 14 B3
Ha! Ha!, Lac, (Que.) 14 B4
Ha! Ha!, Rivière des, (Que.) 14 B4
Haig Lake, (Alta.) 44 A4
Haig, Mount, (Alta./BC) 34 E4
Haig River, (Alta.) 43 G1
Haig-Thomas Island, (NWT) 47 D2
Haihte Lake, (BC) 39 F2
Haldane River, (NWT) 45 D2
Haldimand, Cap, (Que.) 13 H2
Hale Lake, (Man.) 30 C1
Haley Lake, (Ont.) 17 B2
Halfway Cove Lake, (NS) 9 G2
Halfway Inlet, (Ont.) 28 H4
Halfway Lake, (Man.) 30 B2
Halfway Point, (Ont.) 20 D3
Halfway Pond, (Nfld.) 3 G4
Halfway River, (NS) 11 H2
Halfway River, (Man.) 30 B2
Halfway River, (BC) 43 C2
Haliburton Lake, (Ont.) 24 D2
Halifax Harbour, (NS) 9 B4
Halifax Int Airport/Aéroport, (NS) 9 B3
Halkett Lake, (Sask.) 32 D3
Hallam Peak, (BC) 36 H1
Hall Basin, (NWT) 47 F1
Hallett Lake, (BC) 40 A2
Halliday Lake, (NWT) 44 D1
Hall Lake, (NWT) 46 D1
Hall, Mount, (BC) 38 E3
Hall Peninsula, (NWT) 46 G2
Hall, Rivière, (Que.) 13 F3
Halls Bay, (Nfld.) 3 A2
Halls Lake, (Ont.) 24 D2
Hamber Provincial Park, (BC) 40 H3
Hamelin Creek, (Alta.) 43 F3
Hamill Creek, (BC) 34 C3
Hamill, Mount, (BC) 34 C3
Hamilton Branch, (NS) 10 C3
Hamilton Harbour, (Ont.) 22 H1
Hamilton Inlet, (Nfld.) 6 G3
Hamilton Sound, (Nfld.) 3 E2
Hammil Lake, (BC) 38 D1
Hammond River, (NB) 11 E2
Hammone, Lac, (Que.) 5 G1
Hanbury River, (NWT) 45 G3
Hanctin, Lac, (Que.) 6 B4
Handhills Lake, (Alta.) 34 G2
Hankin Peak, (BC) 42 C1
Hannah Bay, (NWT) 20 D3
Hannah Lake, (Ont.) 25 D1
Hannah Lake, (Sask.) 44 F3
Hanover Lake, (Ont.) 27 G1
Hansen Lagoon, (BC) 39 B1
Hansine Lake, (NWT) 46 D2
Hanson Island, (BC) 39 E1
Hanson Lake, (Sask.) 32 G2
Hansteen Lake, (NWT) 47 D4
Hantzsch River, (NWT) 46 F1
Happotiyik Lake, (NWT) 46 B2
Happy Isle Lake, (Ont.) 24 D1
Hara Lake, (Sask.) 44 F2
Harbledown Island, (BC) 39 E1
Harbottle Lake, (Man.) 44 H2
Harbour Breton, (Nfld.) 2 B3
Harbour Fiord, (NWT) 47 E2
Harbour Island, (NS) 9 F3
Harbour My God Point, (Nfld.) 2 C3
Hardiman Bay, (Ont.) 26 D2
Hardiman Lake, (Ont.) 26 D2
Hardinge Bay, (NWT) 47 F2
Harding Lake, (Man.) 30 B1
Harding Lake, (NWT) 44 B1
Harding Point, (NWT) 47 D3
Harding River, (NWT) 45 E1
Hardings Island, (NS) 10 D4
Hardisty Lake, (NWT) 45 E2
Hardwicke Island, (BC) 39 G2
Hardwood Islands, (Ont.) 25 G1
Hardy Bay, (BC) 39 D1
Hardy Bay, (NWT) 47 B3
Hardy Creek, (Ont.) 22 D2
Hardy Island, (BC) 38 D1
Hare Bay, (Nfld.) 3 E1
Hare Bay, (Nfld.) 4 G4
Hare Bay, (Nfld.) 5 H2
Hare Bay Head, (Nfld.) 3 E1
Hare Fiord, (NWT) 47 E1
Hare Hill, (Nfld.) 2 C3
Hare Hill, (Nfld.) 4 C2
Hare Indian River, (NWT) 45 C2
Hare Island, (Nfld.) 3 E1
Hares Islands, (Nfld.) 6 F2
Hargrave Lake, (Man.) 30 B2
Hargrave River, (Man.) 30 B2
Harkin Bay, (NWT) 46 E2
Harmon Lake, (Ont.) 27 D1
Harmon, Port, (Nfld.) 4 B2
Harmony Lake, (NS) 10 C2
Harold Price Creek, (BC) 42 F3
Haro Strait, (BC) 38 F4
Harper Creek, (BC) 36 F3
Harper Creek, (Alta.) 44 B3
Harper Lake, (Sask.) 32 E3
Harper Lake, (Sask.) 44 D2
Harpers Lake, (NS) 10 C3
Harp Lake, (Nfld.) 6 E2
Harpoon Brook, (Nfld.) 4 F2
Harpoon Hill, (Nfld.) 4 F2
Harricana, Rivière, (Que.) 20 E4
Harrington, Iles, (Que.) 5 E3
Harriott Lake, (Sask.) 44 F4
Harriott River, (Sask.) 44 F4
Harris Creek, (BC) 35 G2
Harris Creek, (BC) 38 D3
Harris Lake, (Ont.) 27 A2
Harrison, Cape, (Nfld.) 6 G2
Harrison Islands, (NWT) 46 C1
Harrison Lake, (NS) 11 H2
Harrison Lake, (BC) 35 A3
Harrison River, (BC) 35 A4
Harrop Lake, (Man.) 30 C3
Harrowby Bay, (NWT) 45 C1
Harry Lake, (Sask.) 32 C1
Harrys River, (Nfld.) 4 C2
Hart Jaune, Rivière, (Que.) 19 D1
Hartlen Point, (NS) 9 B4
Hart Ranges, (BC) 40 E1
Hart Ranges, (BC) 43 C4
Hart River, (YT) 45 B2
Harvey, Lac, (Que.) 14 B3
Harwood Island, (BC) 38 C1
Hasbala Lake, (Man./Sask.) 44 G2
Haslam Creek, (BC) 38 D3
Haslam Lake, (BC) 37 D4
Hassel Sound, (NWT) 47 D2
Hasté, Lac, (Que.) 6 B4
Hastings Arm, (BC) 42 D3
Hastings Lake, (Alta.) 33 E3
Haswell Point, (NWT) 47 A3
Hatchet Lake, (Sask.) 44 F3
Hat Creek, (BC) 36 C4
Hathaway Creek, (BC) 39 C1
Hathaway Lake, (BC) 36 E2
Hat Island, (NWT) 45 G1
Hatton Headland, (NWT) 46 G3
Haughton, Cape, (NWT) 47 D4
Haultain Lake, (Sask.) 44 E4
Haultain River, (Sask.) 44 E4
Haute, Isle, (NS) 11 G3
Hautes terres du Cap-Breton, Parc national des, (NS) 8 D2
see also Cape Breton Highlands National Park
Havik Lake, (Ont.) 28 G1
Havre Aubert, Ile du (Amherst), (Que.) 7 F1
Havre aux Maisons, Ile du, (Que.) 7 F1
Havre, Ile du, (Que.) 19 H3
Hawcos Pond, (Nfld.) 2 G3
Hawkcliff Lake, (Ont.) 28 H2
Hawke Bay, (Nfld.) 6 H3
Hawke River, (Nfld.) 6 H4
Hawkesbury Island, (BC) 41 E2
Hawkes Point, (NWT) 47 C3
Hawk Hill Lake, (NWT) 44 H1
Hawkins Lake, (BC) 36 D2
Hawkins Lake, (Sask.) 44 F2
Hawk Lake, (Ont.) 28 G2
Hawkrock River, (Sask.) 44 E3
Hawks, Cape, (NWT) 47 F2
Hawks Creek, (BC) 36 B1
Haworth Lake, (BC) 43 B1
Hay Bay, (Ont.) 21 G1
Hay, Cape, (NWT) 47 B3
Hay, Cape, (NWT) 47 F3
Hay Creek, (Ont.) 20 D3
Hayes Creek, (BC) 35 D3
Hayes River, (Man.) 30 D1
Hayes River, (NWT) 46 C1
Hay Island, (Ont.) 23 C1
Hay Island, (Ont.) 28 F2
Hay Islands, (NWT) 47 D3
Hay Lake, (Ont.) 24 E2
Hay Lake, (Sask.) 31 C3
Haylmore Creek, (BC) 37 G3
Haynes Lake, (Nfld.) 3 C3
Hay Point, (NWT) 47 B3
Hay River, (Alta./BC) 45 E4
Hayter Peninsula, (Ont.) 28 G2
Hazel Creek, (Man.) 28 C1
Hazelton Mountains, (BC) 42 E4
Hazen, Lake, (NWT) 47 F1
Hazen Strait, (NWT) 47 C2
Head Lake, (Ont.) 24 C3
Head River, (Ont.) 24 C3
Headwall Creek, (BC) 37 D2
Heakamie Glacier, (BC) 37 C2
Healey Lake, (Ont.) 25 G4
Healey Lake, (NWT) 45 G2
Hearne Bay, (NWT) 44 G2
Hearne, Cape, (NWT) 45 E1
Hearne Lake, (NWT) 44 C1
Hearne Point, (NWT) 47 C3
Heart Lake, (Man.) 28 D1
Heart Lake, (Alta.) 33 F1
Heart Point, (Nfld.) 2 H3
Heart River, (Alta.) 43 H3
Heater Point, (BC) 39 C2
Heathcote Lake, (Ont.) 27 C1
Heath, Pointe, (Que.) 5 B4
Heaven Lake, (Ont.) 27 D2
Hebb Lake, (NS) 10 E2
Hébécourt, Lac, (Que.) 26 G1
Heber River, (BC) 39 G3
Hébert, Lac, (Que.) 20 F4
Hébert, Lac, (Que.) 26 F2
Hébert River, (NB) 11 H2
Hebron Fiord, (Nfld.) 6 E1
Hecate Channel, (BC) 39 E3
Hecate Island, (BC) 41 E4
Hecate Strait, (BC) 41 C2
Hecla and Griper Bay, (NWT) 47 C2
Hecla, Cape, (NWT) 47 F1
Hecla Provincial Park, (Man.) 30 C4
Hector Lake, (Ont.) 28 H3
Hector Lake, (Ont.) 30 G3
Hector, Mount, (Alta.) 34 C1
Heddery Creek, (Sask.) 44 D4
Heddery Lake, (Sask.) 44 D4
Hedley Creek, (BC) 35 D4
Heffley Lake, (BC) 36 F4
Heger, Mount, (BC) 36 E2
Helena Island, (NWT) 47 D2
Helena Lake, (BC) 36 C2
Helen Bay, (Ont.) 25 B2
Helene Lake, (Sask.) 32 B3
Helen Island, (NWT) 46 C1
Helen Lake, (Ont.) 27 F2
Helldiver Lake, (Sask.) 32 H3
Heller Creek, (BC) 36 E4
Hell Gate, (NWT) 47 E2
Helmcken Island, (BC) 39 G2
Helmer Lake, (Sask.) 44 D3
Hemlock Creek, (NS) 10 C3
Hemloe Island, (NS) 9 F3
Hemming Lake, (BC) 37 B3
Hemphill, Cape, (NWT) 47 C2
Hénault, Lac, (Que.) 18 B3
Henday Lake, (Sask.) 44 F3
Henderson Lake, (Ont.) 26 C2
Henderson Lake, (BC) 38 B2
Hendriksen Strait, (NWT) 47 D2
Heninga Lake, (NWT) 44 H1
Henrietta Island, (Nfld.) 6 G3
Henrietta Marie, Cape, (Ont.) 20 C1
Henri, Rivière, (Que.) 16 E1
Henry, Cape, (BC) 41 A2
Henry Island, (NS) 8 C3
Henry Kater, Cape, (NWT) 47 H4
Henry Kater Peninsula, (NWT) 47 H4
Henvey Inlet, (Ont.) 25 F2
Hepburn Island, (NWT) 45 F1
Hepburn Lake, (Sask.) 44 F4
Hepburn Lake, (NWT) 45 E2
Herbert Inlet, (BC) 39 G4
Herbert Lake, (Sask.) 44 F2
Herbert River, (NS) 9 B3
Herblet Lake, (Man.) 30 B2
Hereford, Mont, (Que.) 16 E4
Heritage Lake, (Sask.) 32 E3
Herman Lake, (Sask.) 32 F2
Hermitage Bay, (Nfld.) 2 A2
Hernando Island, (BC) 37 C4
Hérodier, Lac, (Que.) 6 C1
Heron Channel, (NB) 13 D4
Heron, Ile au, (Que.) 17 G4
Heron Island, (NB) 13 D4
Heron Lake, (Ont.) 27 A2
Herrick Creek, (BC) 40 E1
Herrick Lake, (Ont.) 27 H3
Herrick Low Lake, (Sask.) 31 C1
Herring Cove, (NB) 11 C4
Herring Cove Lake, (NS) 10 D3
Herring Head, (Nfld.) 3 D1
Herschel, Cape, (NWT) 47 F2
Herschel Island, (YT) 45 B1
Hervé, Lac, (Que.) 6 A3
Hesquiat Harbour, (BC) 39 F4
Hesquiat Lake, (BC) 39 F4
Hesquiat Peninsula, (BC) 39 F4
Hess River, (YT) 45 B3
Hewett, Cape, (NWT) 47 H4
Hewitt Lake, (Sask.) 33 H3
Heydon Lake, (BC) 39 G1
Heywood Island, (Ont.) 25 C2
Hibben Island, (BC) 41 B2
Hickory Creek, (Ont.) 22 C1
Hicks Lake, (NWT) 44 G1
Hickson Lake, (Sask.) 44 F4
Hidden Bay, (Sask.) 44 F3
Hidden Lake, (BC) 35 G1
Hidden Lake, (NWT) 44 C1
Highbank Lake, (Ont.) 20 A3
High Capes, (NS) 8 E1
Highfall, Ruisseau, (Que.) 6 C1
Highfield Reservoir, (Sask.) 31 E3
High Hill Lake, (Man.) 30 C1
High Hill River, (Man.) 30 D1
High Lake, (Man./Ont.) 28 E2
Highlands River, (Nfld.) 4 B3
Highrock Lake, (Man.) 30 B1
Highrock Lake, (Sask.) 44 E4
Highstone Lake, (Ont.) 27 B1
Highwind Lake, (Ont.) 28 G2
Highwood River, (Alta.) 34 D3
Hihium Creek, (BC) 36 D4
Hihium Lake, (BC) 36 D4
Hill Island Lake, (NWT) 44 D2
Hill Lake, (Ont.) 27 C1
Hill Lake, (Ont.) 28 H3
Hillock Lake, (Ont.) 28 G2
Hillsborough Bay, (PEI) 7 D4
Hills, Lake of the, (Nfld.) 4 E2
Hinde Lake, (NWT) 44 F1
Hinds Brook, (Nfld.) 4 E1
Hinds Lake, (Nfld.) 4 E1
Hines Creek, (Alta.) 43 G3
Hines Lake, (Sask.) 32 C3
Hiuihill Creek, (BC) 36 G4
Hiver, Lac de l', (Que.) 20 H2
Hives Lake, (Sask.) 32 E1
Hjalmar Lake, (NWT) 44 D1
Hjalmarson Lake, (Man.) 44 G3
Hoards Creek, (Ont.) 24 F4
Hoare Bay, (NWT) 46 G1
Hobiton Lake, (BC) 38 C3
Hobson Lake, (BC) 40 E3
Hocking Lake, (Sask.) 44 E3
Hodges Hill, (Nfld.) 3 B3
Hoeya Head, (BC) 39 G1
Hoeya Sound, (BC) 39 G1
Hogan Lake, (Ont.) 24 D1
Hogem Ranges, (BC) 42 G3
Hog Island, (PEI) 7 B3
Hog Island, (NS) 10 B4
Hohoae Island, (BC) 39 D2
Holberg Inlet, (BC) 39 C1
Holden Lake, (NS) 10 E1
Hole in the Wall *(channel)*, (BC) 37 B3
Holgar Lake, (Sask.) 44 E4
Holinshead Lake, (Ont.) 27 D2
Holland Harbour, (NS) 9 F3
Holland River, (Ont.) 23 F3
Holmer, Lac, (Que.) 20 H2
Holmes Lake, (Man.) 30 C1
Holmes River, (BC) 40 F2
Holton Island, (Nfld.) 6 G3
Holyrood Bay, (Nfld.) 2 F4
Holyrood Pond, (Nfld.) 2 F4
Homan Bay, (NWT) 47 C4
Homards, Baie des, (Que.) 19 E3
Homathko Icefield, (BC) 37 C1
Homathko River, (BC) 37 C1
Home Bay, (NWT) 46 F1
Home, Cape, (NWT) 47 E3
Home Pond, (Nfld.) 3 E3
Homfray Channel, (BC) 37 C3
Hominka River, (BC) 40 D1
Hone River, (NWT) 46 F2
Honguedo, Détroit d', (Que.) 19 H4
Hood River, (NWT) 45 F2
Hooker Lake, (Ont.) 27 C1
Hook Point, (Ont.) 20 C1
Hoole River, (YT) 45 B3
Hoomak Lake, (BC) 39 F2
Hooper, Cape, (NWT) 46 F1
Hooper Inlet, (NWT) 46 D1
Hooper Island, (NWT) 45 B1
Hooper, Mount, (BC) 38 C3
Hooper Point, (BC) 41 C1
Hopeall Bay, (Nfld.) 2 F2
Hopeall Head, (Nfld.) 2 F2
Hope Bay, (Ont.) 23 C1
Hope Bay, (NWT) 45 F1
Hope, Cape, (NWT) 45 E1
Hope Island, (Ont.) 23 E1
Hope Island, (BC) 41 F4
Hope Lake, (Ont.) 28 H2
Hopes Advance Bay, (NWT) 46 F3
Hopes Advance, Cap, (Que.) 46 F3
Hopewell Islands, (NWT) 46 E4
Hopkins Bay, (Ont.) 25 D4
Hopton Lake, (NWT) 44 H1
Hornaday River, (Alta.) 44 C2
Hornaday River, (NWT) 45 D1
Hornby Bay, (NWT) 45 E2
Hornby Island, (BC) 38 C1
Horne Lake, (BC) 38 C2
Hornell Lake, (NWT) 45 E3
Horner Lake, (Ont.) 26 B4
Hornet Creek, (BC) 35 A3
Horn Lake, (Ont.) 24 B1
Horn Lake, (Ont.) 24 B2
Horn River, (NWT) 45 E3
Horsburgh Point, (Ont.) 25 D3
Horse Chops *(head)*, (Nfld.) 3 G4
Horsefly Lake, (BC) 36 D1
Horsefly Lake, (BC) 40 E3
Horsefly Lake Reservoir, (Alta.) 34 G4
Horsefly River, (BC) 36 D1
Horsehead Creek, (Sask.) 32 B3
Horse Island, (Man.) 30 B3
Horse Islands, (Nfld.) 5 H3
Horse Lake, (BC) 36 D2
Horse River, (Alta.) 44 C4
Horseshoe Lake, (Ont.) 24 D3
Horseshoe Lake, (Man.) 28 D1
Horseshoe Lake, (Ont.) 30 F3
Horseshoe Lake, (Alta.) 33 G4
Horseshoe Lake, (BC) 37 D4
Horsethief Creek, (BC) 34 C3
Horsfall Island, (BC) 41 E3
Horton Lake, (NWT) 45 D2
Horton River, (NWT) 45 D1
Horwood Lake, (Ont.) 26 D2
Hosea Lake, (Ont.) 30 F1
Hoskyn Channel, (BC) 37 B4
Hospital Pond, (Nfld.) 4 F2
Hostile Lake, (NWT) 44 E2
Hotchkiss River, (Alta.) 43 G2
Hotel Lake, (NWT) 44 D2
Hotham Sound, (BC) 37 D4
Hotnarko Lake, (BC) 41 H3
Hottah Lake, (NWT) 45 E2
Houël, Lac, (Que.) 6 D1
Houghton Lake, (Ont.) 27 C1
Houghton Lake, (Sask.) 32 E4
House Mountain, (BC) 37 C2
House River, (Alta.) 44 B4
Houston Point, (NWT) 20 D2
Hoved Island, (NWT) 47 E2
Hovgaard Islands, (NWT) 45 H1
Howard Creek, (Sask.) 32 E3
Howard Lake, (NWT) 44 E1
Howe Bay, (PEI) 7 E4
Howe Island, (Ont.) 17 B4
Howell Point, (Man.) 30 B2
Howells River, (Nfld.) 6 C3
Howe Point, (PEI) 7 E4
Howe Sound, (BC) 38 F2
Howley, Mount, (Nfld.) 4 C2
Hozameen Range, (BC) 35 C4
Huard, Lac, (Que.) 14 C3
Huard, Lac, (Sask.) 32 C3
Huaskin Lake, (BC) 41 G4
Hubbart Point, (Man.) 46 B3
Huddersfield, Lac, (Que.) 24 H1
Hudson Bay, (NWT) 46 C3
Hudson Bay Mountain, (BC) 42 F4
Hudson Strait, (NWT) 46 F3
Hudwin Lake, (Man.) 30 C3
Hughes Lake, (Nfld.) 4 D1
Hughes River, (Man.) 44 G4
Hughson Bay, (Ont.) 25 B3
Huit Milles, Lac des, (Que.) 13 B2
Humamilt Lake, (BC) 36 H3
Humber Arm, (Nfld.) 4 C1
Humber Bay, (Ont.) 21 B2
Humber River, (Nfld.) 4 D1
Humber River, (Ont.) 23 F3
Humboldt Bay, (Ont.) 27 F1
Hume River, (NWT) 45 C2
Humphries Head, (NWT) 47 B2
Humqui, Lac, (Que.) 13 A3
Humqui, Rivière, (Que.) 13 B3
Hunaechin Creek, (BC) 37 E3
Hunakwa Lake, (BC) 36 H3
Hungerford Point, (Ont.) 25 C3
Hungry Bay, (Ont.) 21 F1
Hungry Grove Pond, (Nfld.) 2 C2
Hungry Hill, (Nfld.) 4 F1
Hunter Bay, (Sask.) 44 E3
Hunter, Cape, (NWT) 47 G4
Hunter Creek, (Sask.) 44 E3
Hunter Island, (BC) 41 E3
Hunter Point, (BC) 41 A2
Huntingdon Island, (Nfld.) 6 G3
Hunting Lake, (Sask.) 32 B3
Hunting River, (Man.) 30 C1
Hunt Island, (Ont.) 27 E1
Hunt Lake, (Sask.) 32 E1
Hunt River, (Nfld.) 6 F2
Hunts Ponds, (Nfld.) 3 D3
Hurault, Lac, (Que.) 6 A3
Hurd, Cape, (Ont.) 25 C4
Hurds Lake, (Ont.) 17 A1
Hurley River, (BC) 37 F2
Hurloc Head, (Nfld.) 3 F4
Huron, Lac, (Que.) 14 H3
Huron, Lake, (Ont.) 25 B3
Huron, Lake, (Ont.) 26 B4
Hurons, Rivière des, (Que.) 15 F3
Hurst Island, (BC) 39 D1
Hurst, Lac, (Que.) 6 C2
Hurwitz Lake, (NWT) 44 H1
Hustan Lake, (BC) 39 E2
Hutchison Bay, (NWT) 45 C1
Hut Point, (NWT) 46 D2
Hutte Sauvage, Lac de la, (Que.) 6 D2
Hyde Inlet, (NWT) 47 F3
Hyde Lake, (NWT) 46 B3
Hydraulic Lake, (BC) 35 F3
Hyland River, (YT) 45 C3
Hyndman Lake, (NWT) 45 C1
Hyperite Point, (NWT) 47 E2

I

Ian Calder Lake, (NWT) 46 B1
Ian Lake, (BC) 41 A1
Ibbett Bay, (NWT) 47 B2
Iceberg Point, (NWT) 47 E1
Ice Lake, (Ont.) 25 B2
Icewall Creek, (BC) 37 D2
Iconoclast Mountain, (BC) 34 B2
Ida, Mount, (BC) 35 F1
Ideal Lake, (BC) 35 F2
Igelstrom Lake, (Ont.) 30 E2
Iglosiatik Island, (Nfld.) 6 F2
Iglusuaktalialuk Island, (Nfld.) 6 E1
Ignace, Rivière, (Que.) 18 C3
Ignerit Point, (NWT) 46 E1
Ikirtuuq, Lac, (Que.) 6 B1
Ikpik Bay, (NWT) 46 E1
Île-à-la-Crosse, Lac, (Sask.) 32 C1
Île au Castor, Lac de l', (Que.) 5 E2
Île d'Orléans, Chenal de l', (Que.) 15 B2
Ile du Prince-Édouard, Parc national de l', (PEI) 7 C3
see also Prince Edward Island National Park
Îles, Baie des
see Islands, Bay of
Iles de la baie Georgienne, Parc national des, (Ont.) 25 D3
see also Georgian Bay Islands National Park
Îles, Lac aux
see Island Lake
Îles, Lac des, (Que.) 15 A1
Îles, Lac des, (Que.) 16 E3
Iles, Lac des, (Que.) 18 D4
Iles, Lac des, (Ont.) 27 D2
Îles, Lac des, (Sask.) 32 A2
Île Verte, Lac de l', (Que.) 14 D1
Illuvertalik Island, (Nfld.) 6 E1
Iluikoyak Island, (Nfld.) 6 F2
Imikula Lake, (NWT) 44 H1
Imperial Eagle Channel, (BC) 38 B3
Incomappleux River, (BC) 34 B2
Indata Lake, (BC) 43 A4
Indian Arm, (Nfld.) 3 D2
Indian Arm, (Nfld.) 3 F4
Indian Arm, (BC) 38 G2
Indian Arm Brook, (Nfld.) 3 C2
Indian Arm Pond, (Nfld.) 3 C3
Indian Bay, (Nfld.) 3 F3
Indian Bay, (NS) 8 F3
Indian Bay, (Man./Ont.) 28 E2
Indian Bay Big Pond, (Nfld.) 3 E3
Indian Bay Pond, (Nfld.) 3 E3
Indian Brook, (Nfld.) 3 A1
Indian Brook, (NS) 8 E2
Indian Creek, (Ont.) 17 B2
Indian Harbour, (NS) 9 F3
Indian Harbour Point, (Ont.) 25 C3
Indian Head Range, (Nfld.) 4 C2
Indian Island, (Nfld.) 4 C4
Indian Island, (NS) 10 E3
Indian Lake, (NB) 11 D1
Indian Lake, (NB) 12 B4
Indian Lake, (Ont.) 26 D3
Indian Lake, (Ont.) 27 B2
Indian Lake, (Ont.) 28 G1
Indian Pond, (Nfld.) 3 A2
Indian River, (Ont.) 17 B2
Indian River, (Ont.) 21 D1
Indian River, (Ont.) 24 F1
Indian River, (BC) 38 F1
Indicateur, Lac, (Que.) 19 A1
Indin Lake, (NWT) 45 E3
Ingalls Lake, (NWT) 44 E2
Ingenika River, (BC) 42 G2
Inglesby Lake, (Ont.) 24 G4
Inglis Bay, (NWT) 46 C1
Ingonish Island, (NS) 8 E2
Ingonish River, (NS) 8 E2
Ingornachoix Bay, (Nfld.) 5 F3
Ingray Lake, (NWT) 45 E3
Inhabitants Bay, (NS) 9 G2
Inhabitants, River, (NS) 8 C4
Inkaneep Creek, (BC) 35 F4
Inland Lake, (Man.) 29 F1
Inland Lake, (BC) 37 C4
Inner Basin, (BC) 39 E3
Inner Bay, (Ont.) 22 G2
Inner Gooseberry Islands, (Nfld.) 3 F3
Inner Pond, (Nfld.) 5 G3
Innes Island, (Ont.) 25 B2
Innetalling Island, (NWT) 20 E1
Innuksuac, Rivière, (Que.) 46 E4
Inonoaklin Creek, (BC) 35 H2
Insula Lake, (NWT) 44 E2
Intrepid Inlet, (NWT) 47 B2
Inugsuin Fiord, (NWT) 47 G4
Inuktorfik Lake, (NWT) 47 F4
Inulik Lake, (NWT) 45 E2
Investigator Point, (NWT) 47 B3
Invincible Point, (NWT) 47 C2
Inzana Lake, (BC) 43 B4
Iona Islands, (Nfld.) 2 F3
Iosegun Lake, (Alta.) 33 B2
Iosegun River, (Alta.) 33 B2
Ipatik River, (Alta.) 33 G1
Ireland Creek, (BC) 35 G1
Irish Lake, (Ont.) 17 C3
Irish River, (NB) 11 E2
Ironbound Islands, (Nfld.) 6 G2
Iron Creek, (Alta.) 33 F4
Iron Island, (Ont.) 25 G1
Iron Mountain, (BC) 35 C2
Iron Rapids, (BC) 36 B2
Ironwood Lake, (Alta.) 33 F2
Iroquois Lake, (Sask.) 32 C3
Iroquois, Pointe, (Que.) 15 D1
Iroquois River, (NWT) 45 C1
Irvine Inlet, (NWT) 46 F2
Irving Lake, (BC) 39 F3
Isaac Lake, (Ont.) 23 C1
Isaac Lake, (BC) 40 E2
Isabella Bay, (NWT) 47 H4
Isabella, Cape, (NWT) 47 F2
Isachsen, Cape, (NWT) 47 D2
Isachsen Peninsula, (NWT) 47 D2
Isbister River, (Man.) 30 D3
Ishkheenickh River, (BC) 42 D4
Ishpatina Ridge, (Ont.) 26 E3
Isidore, Lac, (Que.) 14 E1
Isinglass Lake, (Ont.) 28 H3
Isintok Creek, (BC) 35 E3
Iskut River, (BC) 42 C2
Iskwao Creek, (Sask.) 31 F2
Island Lake, (NB) 12 C2
Island Lake, (NB) 12 E2
Island Lake, (Ont.) 25 G2
Island Lake, (Ont.) 28 F2
Island Lake, (Man.) 30 D2
Island Point, (Nfld.) 3 B1
Island Pond, (Nfld.) 2 E1
Island Pond, (Nfld.) 3 B3
Island Pond, (Nfld.) 3 D3
Island Pond, (Nfld.) 3 D4
Island Pond, (Nfld.) 3 E2
Island Pond, (Nfld.) 4 D2
Island Pond, (Nfld.) 4 G2
Island Pond West, (Nfld.) 2 D1
Islands, Bay of, (Nfld.) 5 F4
Islands, Bay of, (Nfld.) 6 F2
Islands, Bay of, (Ont.) 25 C2
Isle aux Morts Harbour, (Nfld.) 4 A4
Isle aux Morts River, (Nfld.) 4 B4
Isle Lake, (Alta.) 33 C3
Isolillock Peak, (BC) 35 B4
Isortoq River, (NWT) 47 F4
Isthmus Bay, (Ont.) 25 D4
Isurtuq River, (NWT) 46 F1
Italia Lake, (BC) 36 E2
Itchen Lake, (NWT) 45 F2
Ithingo Lake, (Sask.) 44 D4
Itirbilung Fiord, (NWT) 47 H4
Itomamis, Lac, (Que.) 6 B4
Itomamo, Lac, (Que.) 14 C1
Ivanhoe Lake, (Ont.) 26 C2
Ivanhoe Lake, (NWT) 44 E2
Ivanhoe River, (Ont.) 26 C2
Ivry, Lac, (Que.) 5 E2

J

Jaab Lake, (Ont.) 20 C3
Jack, Cape, (NS) 8 C4
Jackfish Channel, (Ont.) 27 G3
Jackfish Creek, (Alta.) 33 G2
Jackfish Lake, (Ont.) 28 H4
Jackfish Lake, (Man.) 29 G3
Jackfish Lake, (Sask.) 32 B4
Jackfish River, (Alta.) 44 B2
Jack Lake, (Ont.) 24 E3
Jackman Sound, (NWT) 46 G3
Jackpine River, (Ont.) 26 B2
Jackpine River, (Ont.) 27 F2
Jack's Island, (Nfld.) 3 D1
Jacks Lake, (NB) 12 C2
Jackson Creek, (Man./Sask.) 29 D4
Jackson Inlet, (NWT) 47 E3
Jacob Island, (NWT) 20 D3
Jacobs Lake, (NWT) 44 H1
Jacques-Cartier, Baie de, (Que.) 5 F2
Jacques-Cartier, Détroit de, (Que.) 5 A3
Jacques-Cartier, Lac, (Que.) 15 B1
Jacques-Cartier, Mont, (Que.) 13 E1
Jacques-Cartier, Rivière, (Que.) 15 A2
Jacques Island, (Nfld.) 4 C4
Jacques, Lac à, (NWT) 45 C2
Jacquet River, (NB) 13 D4
Jadel Lake, (Man./Ont.) 28 E1
Jalobert, Lac, (Que.) 14 C2
Jambon, Pointe, (Que.) 19 E3
James Anderson, Cape, (NWT) 46 C1
James Bay, (NWT) 20 D2
James Bay, (Ont.) 25 D2
James Creek, (Alta.) 44 A2
James Lake, (Man.) 44 H3
Jameson, Cape, (NWT) 47 G4
Jameson Islands, (NWT) 45 F1
James River, (Alta.) 34 D1
James River, (NWT) 45 F2
James Ross, Cape, (NWT) 47 B3
James Ross Strait, (NWT) 45 G1
Jamieson Creek, (BC) 36 F4
Jamyn, Lac, (Que.) 5 F1
Janet Head, (Ont.) 25 B2
Jan Lake, (Sask.) 32 G1
Jannière, Lac, (Que.) 6 D3
Jansen Lake, (Sask.) 31 G1
Janvrin Island, (NS) 9 G2
Jardine Brook, (NB) 12 A1
Jardins, Lac des, (Que.) 18 B3
Jarvis Lake, (Ont.) 24 F4
Jarvis Lake, (NWT) 44 F1
Jasper National Park, (Alta.) 40 H3
see also Jasper, Parc national de
Jasper, Parc national de, (Alta.) 40 H3
see also Jasper National Park
Jaune, Rivière, (Que.) 15 F3
Jean de Gaunt Island, (Nfld.) 2 E2
Jeanette Bay, (Nfld.) 6 G3
Jeanette Lake, (Ont.) 30 E4
Jean, Lake, (Ont.) 27 F2
Jeannette Lake, (Sask.) 32 B2
Jeannettes Creek, (Ont.) 22 B3
Jeannin, Lac, (Que.) 6 C2
Jeannotte, Rivière, (Que.) 18 H2
Jean Péré, Lac, (Que.) 18 C3
Jeddore Harbour, (NS) 9 C3
Jeddore Head, (NS) 9 C4
Jeddore Lake, (Nfld.) 2 B1
Jedediah Island, (BC) 38 D2
Jenkins Island, (BC) 38 D2
Jennejohn Lake, (NWT) 44 B1
Jenne Lake, (NWT) 44 F2
Jenness Island, (NWT) 47 C2
Jenny Lind Island, (NWT) 45 G1
Jensen, Cape, (NWT) 46 E1
Jens Munk Island, (NWT) 46 D1
Jermain, Cape, (NWT) 46 D1
Jervis Inlet, (BC) 37 E4
Jervis Island, (BC) 38 D2
Jesse Lake, (BC) 41 E1
Jessica Lake, (Man.) 28 D1
Jessie Lake, (Ont.) 27 F2
Jessie Point, (Ont.) 25 B2
Jésus, Ile, (Que.) 17 F3
Jewakwa Glacier, (BC) 37 C1
Jewakwa, Mount, (BC) 37 C1
Jewakwa River, (BC) 37 C2
Jewel Lake, (BC) 35 G4
Jewett Lake, (Sask.) 44 F4
Jim Brown Creek, (BC) 37 D3
Jim Creek, (BC) 36 E2
Jim Lake, (BC) 36 D3
Jim Lake, (NWT) 44 F1
Joannès, Lac, (Que.) 26 G2
Jocko Point, (Ont.) 25 H1
Jocko River, (Ont.) 26 G4
Jock River, (Ont.) 17 C2
Joe Batt's Arm, (Nfld.) 3 E1
Joe Batt's Point, (Nfld.) 3 E1
Joe Batts Pond, (Nfld.) 3 D3
Joe Glodes Brook, (Nfld.) 4 G1
Joe Glodes Pond, (Nfld.) 4 G1
Joes Lake, (Nfld.) 3 A3
Joffre Creek, (BC) 37 G3
Jog Lake, (Ont.) 27 B1
Jogues, Lac, (Que.) 6 B1
Jogues, Lac, (Que.) 14 A2
Johan Peninsula, (NWT) 47 F2
John Bay, (NS) 9 C1
John, Cape, (Nfld.) 4 A3
John, Cape, (NS) 9 C1
John Creek, (Ont.) 25 D1
John Dyer, Cape, (NWT) 47 D3
John Halket Island, (NWT) 47 C4
John Hart Lake, (BC) 37 B4
John Island, (Ont.) 25 B1
John Jay, Mount, (BC) 42 C2
Johnny Hoe River, (NWT) 45 D3
John Richardson Bay, (NWT) 47 F1
John, River, (NS) 9 C1
Johns Island, (NS) 10 B4
Johnson Island, (NWT) 46 E4
Johnson Lake, (BC) 36 G3
Johnson Point, (NWT) 47 F3
Johnson River, (NWT) 45 D3
Johnsons Point, (NS) 9 C1
Johnstone Strait, (BC) 39 F1
Joint Lake, (Man.) 30 D2
Joir, Rivière, (Nfld.) 5 D1
Jolicoeur, Rivière, (Que.) 20 E3
Joli, Lac, (NS) 10 C2
Joli, Port, (NS) 10 D3
Jolliet, Lacs, (Que.) 20 F3
Jolly Lake, (NWT) 45 F3
Jonathans Pond, (Nfld.) 3 D3
Joncas, Lac, (Que.) 18 B3
Jonchée, Lac, (Que.) 5 C2
Jones, Cape, (NWT) 46 B3
Jones Creek, (BC) 36 C1
Jones Sound, (NWT) 47 E3
Jordan Lake, (NS) 10 C3
Jordan Lake, (Man.) 44 G3
Jordan River, (NS) 10 C3
Jordan River, (Sask.) 32 F4
Jordan River, (BC) 38 D4
Joseph Creek, (BC) 36 F3
Joseph Henry, Cape, (NWT) 47 F1
Josephine Bay, (NWT) 45 H1
Joseph, Lac, (Nfld.) 6 D4
Joseph, Lac, (Que.) 16 E2
Joseph, Lake, (Ont.) 24 A2
Joseph Lake, (Alta.) 33 E3
Joseph, Pointe, (Que.) 5 B4
Joseph, Rivière, (Que.) 19 F2
Jost Lake, (NWT) 44 F1
Joubert Creek, (Man.) 28 A2
Joubert, Lac, (Que.) 20 H2
Jourimain Island, (NB) 7 B4
Joy Bay, (NWT) 46 F3
Joy Island, (NWT) 20 D1
Juan de Fuca Strait, (BC) 38 D4
Juan Perez Sound, (BC) 41 B3
Jubilee Lake, (Nfld.) 2 C1
Jude Island, (Nfld.) 2 D3
Judge Daly Promontory, (NWT) 47 F1
Judge Howay, Mount, (BC) 38 H2
Juet, Lac, (Que.) 46 E3
Jugeborg Fiord, (NWT) 47 E1
Juillet, Lac, (Que.) 6 D3
Julia Bay, (Ont.) 25 E2
Julian, Lac, (Que.) 20 E2
Julian Peak, (BC) 37 D3
Julia Point, (Ont.) 25 B2
Juliet Creek, (BC) 35 B3
July Mountain, (BC) 35 B3
Jumbo Mountain, (BC) 34 C3
Jump Creek, (BC) 38 D3
Jumper Brook, (Nfld.) 3 D2
Jumpers Brook, (Nfld.) 3 C3
Jumping Lake, (Sask.) 32 E4
Jumpingpound Creek, (Alta.) 34 D2
Junction Bay, (NWT) 46 D2
Jungersen River, (NWT) 47 F4
Jupiter, Rivière, (Que.) 5 A4

K

Kabania Lake, (Ont.) 30 G3
Kabika River, (Ont.) 26 F1
Kabinakagami Lake, (Ont.) 26 A1
Kabinakagami River, (Ont.) 20 B4
Kabinakagamis Lake, (Ont.) 26 A1
Kabitotikwia Lake, (Ont.) 27 E2
Kachiyaskunusi, Lac, (Que.) 20 G1
Kaegudeck Lake, (Nfld.) 2 C1
Kagawong Lake, (Ont.) 25 B2
Kagianagami Lake, (Ont.) 30 G4
Kagiano Lake, (Ont.) 27 G2
Kagloryuak River, (NWT) 47 B4

Kagungatak Island, (Nfld.) 6 F2
Kahntah River, (BC) 43 E1
Kaiashkons Lake, (Ont.) 28 H3
Kains Lake, (BC) 39 C1
Kaipit Creek, (BC) 39 E2
Kaipit Lake, (BC) 39 E2
Kaipokok Bay, (Nfld.) 6 F3
Kaipokok River, (Nfld.) 6 F3
Kairolik Fiord, (NWT) 46 G2
Kakagi Lake, (Ont.) 28 G3
Kakiattukallak, Lac, (Que.) 6 A1
Kakiddi Lake, (BC) 42 C1
Kakinagimak Lake, (Sask.) 32 G1
Kakisa Lake, (NWT) 44 A1
Kakwa River, (Alta.) 40 F1
Kakweiken River, (BC) 37 A2
Kalamalka Lake, (BC) 35 F2
Kaleet River, (NWT) 45 H1
Kalliecahoolie Lake, (Man.) 30 D2
Kalone Peak, (BC) 41 G3
Kalzas River, (YT) 45 B3
Kamaniskeg Lake, (Ont.) 24 F2
Kamatsi Lake, (Sask.) 44 G4
Kamilukuak Lake, (NWT) 44 F1
Kamilukuak River, (NWT) 44 F1
Kaminak Lake, (NWT) 46 B3
Kaminuriak Lake, (NWT) 46 B2
Kamiskotia Lake, (Ont.) 26 D1
Kamiskotia River, (Ont.) 26 D2
Kamloops Lake, (BC) 36 E4
Kamouraska, Iles de, (Que.) 15 D1
Kamouraska, Rivière, (Que.) 15 E1
Kamuchawie Lake, (Man./Sask.) 44 G4
Kanaaupscow, Rivière, (Que.) 20 F1
Kanairiktok Bay, (Nfld.) 6 F2
Kanairiktok River, (Nfld.) 6 E3
Kananaskis River, (Alta.) 34 D2
Kanasuta, Rivière, (Que.) 26 G2
Kane Basin, (NWT) 47 F1
Kangeeak Point, (NWT) 46 G1
Kangilo Fiord, (NWT) 46 F1
Kangok Fiord, (NWT) 46 F1
Kanim Lake, (BC) 39 F4
Kanish Bay, (BC) 37 B3
Kano Inlet, (BC) 41 A2
Kanuchuan Lake, (Ont.) 30 G3
Kaouk Mountain, (BC) 39 E2
Kaouk River, (BC) 39 E2
Kapesakosi Lake, (Ont.) 28 H2
Kapikik Lake, (Ont.) 30 E4
Kapikotongwa River, (Ont.) 27 F1
Kapiskau River, (Ont.) 20 B3
Kaposvar Creek, (Sask.) 29 C2
Kappan, Mount, (BC) 41 H3
Kapuskasing Lake, (Ont.) 26 C2
Kapuskasing River, (Ont.) 26 C1
Karloske River, (Man.) 30 D1
Karsakuwigamak Lake, (Man.) 44 H4
Kasabonika Lake, (Ont.) 30 G2
Kasasway Lake, (Ont.) 26 D2
Kasba Lake, (NWT) 44 F2
Kashabowie Lake, (Ont.) 27 C3
Kashagawigamog Lake, (Ont.) 24 D3
Kashawegama Lake, (Ont.) 27 C1
Kashegaba Lake, (Ont.) 25 G2
Kashe Lake, (Ont.) 24 B3
Kashutl Inlet, (BC) 39 D2
Kashwakamak Lake, (Ont.) 24 G3
Kaskattama River, (Man.) 30 F1
Kasmere Lake, (Man.) 44 G2
Kasshabog Lake, (Ont.) 24 E4
Katah Creek, (BC) 43 E1
Katamiagamak Lake, (Ont.) 28 H3
Katatota Island, (Ont.) 27 F2
Katchewanooka Lake, (Ont.) 24 E4
Kate Harbour, (Nfld.) 3 F4
Kater, Cape, (NWT) 47 E4
Kater Point, (NWT) 45 F1
Kates Needle *(mountain)*, (BC) 42 B1
Kathawachaga Lake, (NWT) 45 F2
Kathleen Lake, (BC) 39 D2
Kathleen, Mount, (BC) 35 E3
Katimik Lake, (Man.) 30 B3
Kattaktoc, Cap, (Que.) 46 G3
Kattawagami Lake, (Ont.) 20 D4
Kattawagami River, (Ont.) 20 D4
Kaumajet Mountains, (Nfld.) 6 E1
Kauwinch River, (BC) 39 D2
Kawagama Lake, (Ont.) 24 D2
Kawashkagama Lake, (Ont.) 27 G1
Kawawaymog Lake, (Ont.) 24 C1
Kawaweogama Lake, (Ont.) 27 D1
Kawigamog Lake, (Ont.) 25 F2
Kawinaw Lake, (Man.) 30 B3
Kawnipi Lake, (Ont.) 27 C3
Kaye, Cape, (NWT) 47 E4
Kay Point, (YT) 45 B1
Kazan Lake, (Sask.) 32 B1
Kazan River, (NWT) 44 G1
Kazchek Lake, (BC) 43 A4
Kean Point, (NWT) 45 G1
Kearney Head, (Nfld.) 2 E2
Keary Lake, (BC) 37 G2
Keating, Lac, (Que.) 6 C2
Keats Island, (BC) 38 E2
Kebskwasheshi Lake, (Ont.) 26 C3
Kechika River, (BC) 45 C4
Kecil Lake, (Ont.) 25 B1
Kedgwick, Lac, (Que.) 14 H3
Kedgwick River, (NB) 13 A4
see also Kedgwick, Rivière (Que.)
Kedgwick, Rivière, (Que.) 14 H4
see also Kedgwick River (NB)
Keefe Lake, (Sask.) 44 F3
Keeha Bay, (BC) 38 B3
Keele River, (NWT) 45 C3
Keeley Lake, (Sask.) 32 B1
Keeley River, (Sask.) 32 B1
Keeper River, (Ont.) 30 D3
Keep Lake, (Sask.) 32 H1
Keewatin River, (Man.) 44 G4
Keezhik Lake, (Ont.) 30 G3
Kégashka, Lac, (Que.) 5 C3
Kégashka, Rivière, (Que.) 5 C3
Kegeshook Lake, (NS) 10 B3
Keg Lake, (Sask.) 32 C3
Keg Lake, (Sask.) 32 F1
Keglo Bay, (NWT) 46 G3
Keg River, (Alta.) 43 H1
Keith Arm, (NWT) 45 D2
Keith Bay, (NWT) 46 C1
Keith Lake, (Sask.) 44 E4
Kejimkujik Lake, (NS) 10 C2
Kejimkujik National Park, (NS) 10 C2
see also Kejimkujik, Parc national de
Kejimkujik, Parc national de, (NS) 10 C2
see also Kejimkujik National Park
Kekek, Rivière, (Que.) 18 D2
Kekertaluk Island, (NWT) 46 F1
Keller Lake, (Sask.) 44 E4
Keller Lake, (NWT) 45 D3
Kellett, Cape, (NWT) 47 A3
Kellett River, (NWT) 46 C1
Kellett River, (NWT) 47 A3
Kellett Strait, (NWT) 47 B2
Kelly Bay, (Sask.) 44 F3
Kelly Lake, (Ont.) 25 E1
Kelly Lake, (NWT) 45 C2
Kelly River, (BC) 35 F4
Kellys Island, (Nfld.) 2 G2
Kelsey Creek, (Sask.) 32 F3
Kelsey Lake, (Man.) 30 A2
Keltie Inlet, (NWT) 46 F2
Kelvin Island, (Ont.) 27 E1
Kemano River, (BC) 41 E2
Kempenfelt Bay, (Ont.) 23 F2
Kemp River, (Alta.) 43 H1
Kemps Point, (NS) 8 E4
Kempt Back Lake, (NS) 10 B3
Kempt Head, (NS) 8 E3
Kempt, Lac, (Que.) 18 F3
Kempton Lake, (NS) 10 D3
Kempt, Rivière, (Que.) 13 C3
Kenamu River, (Nfld.) 6 F4
Kendall, Cape, (NWT) 45 E1
Kendall, Cape, (NWT) 46 C2
Kenemich River, (Nfld.) 6 F3
Kenilworth Lake, (Alta.) 33 G3
Kennebecasis Bay, (NB) 11 D3
Kennebecasis River, (NB) 11 E2
Kennebec Lake, (Ont.) 24 G3
Kennedy Channel, (NWT) 47 F1
Kennedy Head, (Nfld.) 5 H1
Kennedy Island, (BC) 41 C1
Kennedy Lake, (Ont.) 26 D3
Kennedy Lake, (Sask.) 32 G3
Kennedy Lake, (BC) 38 A3
Kennedy Lakes, (NB) 12 D3
Kennedy, Mount, (BC) 37 A2
Kennedy River, (BC) 38 B2
Kennetcook River, (NS) 9 A3
Kenney Dam/Barrage, (BC) 40 A2
Kennisis Lake, (Ont.) 24 D2
Kenny Point, (Ont.) 25 B2
Kénogami, Lac, (Que.) 14 A3
Kenogami Lake, (Ont.) 26 F2
Kenogaming Lake, (Ont.) 26 D2
Kenogami River, (Ont.) 20 B4
Kenogamisis Lake, (Ont.) 27 G2
Kenogamissi Lake, (Ont.) 26 D2
Kent Bay, (NWT) 47 D4
Kent Island, (NB) 11 C4
Kent Peninsula, (NWT) 45 F1
Kenyon Lake, (Man.) 30 E2
Keogh Lake, (BC) 39 D1
Keogh River, (BC) 39 D1
Kepenkeck Lake, (Nfld.) 2 D1
Kepimits Lake, (Nfld.) 6 D4
Keppel Lake, (Sask.) 32 B4
Kerbodot, Lac, (Que.) 6 C3
Keremeos Creek, (BC) 35 E4
Kergus, Lac, (Que.) 14 E2
Kerman Lake, (Man.) 44 H3
Kerrertut, Cap, (Que.) 6 C1
Kerouard Islands, (BC) 41 C3
Kerrs Point, (NS) 8 D1
Kesagami Lake, (Ont.) 20 D4
Kesagami River, (Ont.) 20 D4
Kesatasew River, (Sask.) 32 A1
Keseechewun Lake, (Sask.) 44 F2
Keswick River, (NB) 11 B1
Kettle Creek, (Ont.) 22 E2
Kettle Lake, (Man.) 30 D1
Kettle Point, (Ont.) 22 C1
Kettle River, (Man.) 30 D1
Kettle River, (Man.) 30 F1
Kettle River, (BC) 35 G4
Kettlestone Bay, (NWT) 46 E3
Key Harbour, (Ont.) 25 E2
Key River, (Ont.) 25 F2
Keys Lake, (Ont.) 28 G1
Khartoum Lake, (BC) 37 D4
Khtada Lake, (BC) 41 D1
Khuex River, (BC) 42 D4
Khutzeymateen Inlet, (BC) 42 C4
Kiamika, Réservoir, (Que.) 18 E3
Kidprice Lake, (BC) 41 F1
Kiglapait, Cape, (Nfld.) 6 F1
Kiglapait Mountains, (Nfld.) 6 E1
Kikendatch, Baie, (Que.) 18 F1
Kikerk Lake, (NWT) 45 E2
Kikiktaksoak Island, (Nfld.) 6 E1
Kikkertakgoak Islands, (Nfld.) 6 F2
Kikkertarjote Island, (Nfld.) 6 E1
Kikkertavak Island, (Nfld.) 6 G2
Kikkertoksoak Island, (NWT) 46 G3
Kikupegh Pond, (Nfld.) 4 G3
Kikwissi, Lac, (Que.) 26 G3
Kilbella River, (BC) 41 F4
Kilburn Lake, (NB) 11 B1
Kildare River, (PEI) 7 B2
Kilekale Lake, (NWT) 45 D2
Kilian Island, (NWT) 47 C3
Killala Lake, (Ont.) 27 G2
Killarney Bay, (Ont.) 25 D2
Killarney, Lac, (NS) 9 B1
Killarney Lake, (Ont.) 25 D2
Killarney Lake, (Alta.) 33 H4
Killarney Provincial Park, (Ont.) 25 D2
Killbear Point Provincial Park, (Ont.) 25 G3
Killinek Island, (Nfld./NWT) 46 G3
Killock Bay, (Sask.) 44 F3
Kilvert Lake, (Ont.) 28 G2
Kimiwan Lake, (Alta.) 43 H3
Kimowin River, (Sask.) 44 D4
Kimsquit River, (BC) 41 F2
Kinashkan Lake, (BC) 42 D1
Kindakun Point, (BC) 41 A2
Kindiogami Lake, (Ont.) 26 C3
King Charles Cape, (NWT) 46 E2
King Christian Island, (NWT) 47 D2
Kingcome Inlet, (BC) 41 G4
Kingcome River, (BC) 41 G4
King Edward Point, (NWT) 47 E3
Kingfisher Creek, (BC) 35 G1
Kingfisher Lake, (Ont.) 30 F3
King George Islands, (NWT) 46 E4
King George IV Lake, (Nfld.) 4 D3
King George, Mount, (BC) 34 D3
Kinghorn Island, (BC) 37 C4
King Island, (Nfld.) 2 E2
King Island, (BC) 41 F3
King Lake, (NWT) 44 C1
Kinglet, Lac, (Que.) 20 F1
Kingnait Fiord, (NWT) 46 G1
King Point, (NWT) 47 C3
Kingscote Lake, (Ont.) 24 E2
Kings Harbour Brook, (Nfld.) 4 E4
Kingsley Lake, (Man./Sask.) 44 G3
Kingsmere Lake, (Sask.) 32 D2
Kingston Lake, (Sask.) 44 F3
Kinguk Lake, (NWT) 46 E2
Kingurutik Lake, (Nfld.) 6 E2
Kingurutik River, (Nfld.) 6 E1
King William Island, (NWT) 45 G1
Kinnaird Lake, (Alta.) 33 F2
Kinnear River, (NB) 12 H4
Kinniwabi Lake, (Ont.) 26 B2
Kinoje River, (Ont.) 20 C3
Kinojévis, Rivière, (Que.) 26 G1
Kinonge, Rivière, (Que.) 17 E1
Kinskuch River, (BC) 42 D3
Kinsman Lake, (Man.) 44 H3
Kinushseo River, (Ont.) 20 C1
Kinwow Bay, (Man.) 29 H1
Kioshkokwi Lake, (Ont.) 26 G4
Kipahigan Lake, (Man./Sask.) 32 H1
Kipawa, Baie de, (Que.) 18 B3
Kipawa, Lac, (Que.) 26 G3
Kippen Cove, (Nfld.) 3 E1
Kirby Lake, (Alta.) 33 G1
Kirkness Lake, (Ont.) 30 D4
Kirkpatrick Lake, (Ont.) 26 C4
Kirkpatrick Lake, (Alta.) 34 H1
Kishikas River, (Ont.) 30 E3
Kishkutena Lake, (Ont.) 28 G3
Kiskatinaw River, (BC) 43 E4
Kiski Lake, (Man.) 30 B2
Kiskittogisu Lake, (Man.) 30 B2
Kiskitto Lake, (Man.) 30 B2
Kispiox Range, (BC) 42 E3
Kispiox River, (BC) 42 E3
Kisseynew Lake, (Man.) 32 H1
Kississing Lake, (Man.) 32 H1
Kississing River, (Man.) 30 A1
Kistigan Lake, (Man.) 30 E2
Kitako Lake, (Sask.) 32 F4
Kitchener, Cape, (Nfld.) 6 G2
Kitchener Lake, (BC) 42 F1
Kitchie Lake, (Ont.) 20 A2
Kitchigama, Rivière, (Que.) 20 E4
Kiteen River, (BC) 42 E3
Kitiga Lake, (NWT) 45 F1
Kitimat Harbour, (BC) 41 E1
Kitimat Ranges, (BC) 41 E1
Kitimat River, (BC) 41 E1
Kitlope River, (BC) 41 F2
Kitsumkalum Lake, (BC) 42 E4
Kitsumkalum River, (BC) 42 E4
Kitwanga Lake, (BC) 42 E3
Kiyiu Lake, (Sask.) 31 C1
Kiyuk Lake, (NWT) 44 G2
Kjer, Cape, (NWT) 46 C1
Klaklakama Lakes, (BC) 39 F2
Klanawa River, (BC) 38 C3
Klappan River, (BC) 42 D1
Klashwun Point, (BC) 41 A1
Klaskino Inlet, (BC) 39 C2
Klaskish Inlet, (BC) 39 C2
Klaskish River, (BC) 39 C2
Klattasine Glacier, (BC) 37 C1
Klawli River, (BC) 43 B4
Kleczkowski, Lac, (Que.) 5 A2
Klesilkwa River, (BC) 35 B4
Klinaklini Glacier, (BC) 37 A1
Klinaklini River, (BC) 37 A1
Klite River, (BC) 37 D3
Kloch Lake, (BC) 43 B4
Klock, Baie, (Que.) 26 G3
Klondike River, (YT) 45 B2
Klotz, Lac, (Que.) 46 F3
Klotz Lake, (Ont.) 27 H1
Klua Creek, (BC) 43 D1
Klua Lakes, (BC) 43 D1
Kluane Lake, (YT) 45 A3
Kluane National Park, (YT) 45 A3
see also Kluane, Parc national de
Kluane, Parc national de, (YT) 45 A3
see also Kluane National Park
Knapp Lake, (BC) 41 H1
Kneehills Creek, (Alta.) 34 F1
Knee Lake, (Man.) 30 D2
Knee Lake, (Sask.) 44 E4
Kneeland Bay, (NWT) 46 F2
Knickerbocker Inlet, (Ont.) 28 F2
Knife Creek, (BC) 36 C2
Knife Lake, (Man.) 30 D2
Knife Lake, (Ont.) 30 E2
Knight Inlet, (BC) 39 F1
Knights Island, (Nfld.) 3 D2
Knob Hill, (BC) 39 C1
Knot Lakes, (BC) 41 H3
Knowles Lake, (NWT) 44 E1
Knowlton Lake, (Ont.) 17 A3
Knox, Cape, (BC) 41 A1
Knox Lake, (Nfld.) 6 D3
Knox Lake, (BC) 36 B1
Knud Peninsula, (NWT) 47 F2
Koch Creek, (BC) 34 A4
Koch Island, (NWT) 46 E1
Koeye Lake, (BC) 41 F4
Kogaluc, Rivière, (Que.) 46 E4
Kogaluk Bay, (NWT) 46 E4
Kogaluk River, (Nfld.) 6 E2
Kognak River, (NWT) 44 H1
Kogtok River, (NWT) 44 H1
Kohlmeister, Lac, (Que.) 6 C1
Kohn Lake, (Sask.) 44 F2
Kokanee Glacier Provincial Park, (BC) 34 B3
Kokanee Peak, (BC) 34 B4
Kokeragi Point, (NWT) 45 D2
Kokish River, (BC) 39 E1
Koksoak, Rivière, (Que.) 6 C1
Kondiaronk, Lac, (Que.) 18 C3
Konigus Creek, (BC) 42 D1
Konni Lake, (BC) 37 E1
Konth River, (NWT) 44 C2
Koocanusa, Lake, (BC) 34 D4
Kookipi Creek, (BC) 35 A2
Koona Lake, (Man.) 44 G2
Kootenay Lake, (BC) 34 B3
Kootenay National Park, (BC) 34 C2
see also Kootenay, Parc national de
Kootenay, Parc national de, (BC) 34 C2
see also Kootenay National Park
Kootenay River, (BC) 34 D3
Kopka River, (Ont.) 27 D1
Koprino Harbour, (BC) 39 C1
Korak Bay, (NWT) 46 E3
Koroc, Rivière, (Que.) 46 G4
Koshlong Lake, (Ont.) 24 D3
Koskaecodde Lake, (Nfld.) 2 C1
Kostal Lake, (BC) 36 F1
Kotaneelee River, (NWT) 45 D4
Kotcho Lake, (BC) 45 D4
Kotsinta Creek, (BC) 42 E2
Kouchibouguac Bay, (NB) 12 G3
Kouchibouguacis River, (NB) 12 F3
Kouchibouguac River, (NB) 12 F3
Koukdjuak River, (NWT) 46 F1
Kovic, Rivière, (Que.) 46 E3
Kovik Bay, (NWT) 46 E3
Kowesas River, (BC) 41 E2
Krusenstern, Cape, (NWT) 45 E1
Krusenstern Lake, (NWT) 47 D4
Kshwan Mountain, (BC) 42 D3
Ksituan River, (Alta.) 43 G3
Kugaluk River, (NWT) 45 C1
Kugmallit Bay, (NWT) 45 C1
Kugong Island, (NWT) 46 D4
Kukagami Lake, (Ont.) 26 E3
Kukamaw, Lac, (Que.) 20 G2
Kukukus Lake, (Ont.) 27 B1
Kuldo Creek, (BC) 42 E2
Kull Island, (NWT) 46 C1
Kumdis Island, (BC) 41 B1
Kumlein Fiord, (NWT) 46 G2
Kunakun Point, (BC) 41 A2
Kunghit Island, (BC) 41 C3
Kunwak River, (NWT) 46 A2
Kuper Island, (BC) 38 E3
Kusawa Lake, (YT) 45 A3
Kushog Lake, (Ont.) 28 G2
Kuskanax Creek, (BC) 34 B3
Kustra Lake, (Man.) 44 G3
Kuujjua River, (NWT) 47 B4
Kuuk River, (NWT) 47 B4
Kwadacha River, (BC) 43 A1
Kwadacha Wilderness Provincial Park, (BC) 43 B1
Kwalate Point, (BC) 37 A2
Kwataboahegan River, (Ont.) 20 C3
Kwatna Inlet, (BC) 41 F3
Kwatna River, (BC) 41 F3
Kwatsi Bay, (BC) 39 F1
Kwejinne Lake, (NWT) 45 E3
Kwikoit Creek, (BC) 36 G4
Kwinkwaga Lake, (Ont.) 26 A1
Kwoiek Creek, (BC) 35 A2
Kwoiek Needle *(mountain)*, (BC) 35 A2
Kyaska Lake, (Sask.) 44 G4
Kynoch Inlet, (BC) 41 E3
Kyuquot Channel, (BC) 39 D3
Kyuquot Sound, (BC) 39 D2

L

La Belle Rivière, (Que.) 14 A3
Laberge, Lake, (YT) 45 B3
La Biche River, (Alta.) 33 E1
La Biche River, (YT) 45 D4
Labouchere Channel, (BC) 41 F3
Labouchere Passage, (BC) 39 D1
La Bouille, Lac, (Que.) 19 C1
Labrador Sea, (Nfld.) 5 H2
Labrecque, Lac, (Que.) 14 A2
La Butte Creek, (Alta.) 44 C2
Labyrinth Bay, (Ont.) 28 E2
Labyrinth Bay, (NWT) 45 F1
Labyrinth Lake, (NWT) 44 E2
L'Acadie, Rivière, (Que.) 17 H1
Lac Île-à-la-Crosse Provincial Park, (Sask.) 32 C1
Lac, Ile du, (Que.) 5 D3
Lac la Ronge Provincial Park, (Sask.) 32 E1
La Cloche Creek, (Ont.) 25 C1
La Cloche Lake, (Ont.) 25 C2
La Cloche Mountains, (Ont.) 25 C2
Lacombe, Lac, (Que.) 5 A2
La Course, Lac, (Sask.) 29 D1
Lacroix, Lac, (Que.) 18 E1
Lacs Waterton, Parc national des, (BC) 34 E4
see also Watertoon Lakes National Park
Lacusta Lake, (NWT) 44 E2
Ladder Lake, (Sask.) 32 C3
Laderoute Lake, (NWT) 44 G2
Ladle Point, (Nfld.) 3 E2
Lady Ann Strait, (NWT) 47 F3
Lady Evelyn Lake, (Ont.) 26 F3
Lady Franklin Bay, (NWT) 47 F1
Lady Franklin Island, (NWT) 46 G2
Lady Franklin Point, (NWT) 45 E1
Lady Grey Lake, (NWT) 44 C2
Lady Melville Lake, (NWT) 45 H1
Lady Pond, (Nfld.) 2 F1
Lady Richardson Bay, (NWT) 47 A4
Lady Simpson, Cape, (NWT) 46 D1
Laferte River, (NWT) 44 A1
Laflamme, Lac, (Que.) 14 C1
Laflamme, Rivière, (Que.) 18 C1
Lafond Creek, (Alta.) 44 A4
La Forest, Lac, (Que.) 6 A2
Laforge, Rivière, (Que.) 20 G2
La Galissonnière, Lac, (Que.) 5 B2
La Grande Rivière, (Que.) 15 D2
La Grande Rivière, (Que.) 20 F2
LaHave, Cape, (NS) 10 E3
LaHave River, (NS) 10 D2
La Hune Bay, (Nfld.) 4 D4
La Hune, Cape, (Nfld.) 4 F4
La Jannaye, Lac, (Que.) 6 C3
La Justone, Lac, (Que.) 6 B4
Lake Gillian, (NWT) 46 E1
Lakelse Lake, (BC) 42 E4
Lakeman Island, (Nfld.) 3 F3
Lake Nipigon Provincial Park, (Ont.) 27 F2
Lake Stream, (NB) 12 F4
Lake Stream Lake, (NB) 12 F4
Lake Superior Provincial Park, (Ont.) 26 A2
Lakeview Mountain, (BC) 35 D4
Lakitusaki River, (Ont.) 20 C2
Laliberté, Rivière, (Que.) 14 F1
La Loche, Lac, (Sask.) 44 D4
La Loche Lakes, (NWT) 44 C1
La Loche River, (NWT) 44 C1
La Loche River, (Sask.) 44 D4
Lalonde, Lac, (Que.) 18 B3
La Manche River, (Nfld.) 2 H3
La Mauricie National Park, (Que.) 18 G3
see also Mauricie, Parc national de la
Lambert Channel, (BC) 38 C2
Lambert, Lac, (Que.) 18 B2
Lambly Creek, (BC) 35 E2
Lambton, Cape, (NWT) 47 A3
Lamèque, Ile, (NB) 13 G4
La Moinerie, Lac, (Que.) 6 C1
La Mothe, Réservoir, (Que.) 14 B2
La Motte, Lac, (Que.) 26 H2
Lampidoes Passage, (Nfld.) 2 B2
La Muir, Lake, (Ont.) 24 D1
Lancaster Sound, (NWT) 47 E3
Lance Cove, (Nfld.) 2 E4
Lance, Point, (Nfld.) 2 E4
Lance River, (Nfld.) 2 E4
Landing Lake, (Man.) 30 C2
Landon Lake, (Alta.) 33 G3
Landry, Cape, (NWT) 47 E4
Landryac, (Que.) 5 B3
Landry Lake, (Man.) 30 A2
Lands End *(point)*, (NWT) 47 B2
Lanezi Lake, (BC) 40 E3
Langara Island, (BC) 41 A1
Lang Lake, (BC) 36 D2
Langton Bay, (NWT) 45 D1
Langton Lake, (Ont.) 28 H1
Lanigan Creek, (Sask.) 31 G1
Lansdowne Lake, (Sask.) 44 E3
Lansing River, (YT) 45 B2
Lanz Island, (BC) 39 A1
La Pause, Lac, (Que.) 26 G2
Lapeyrère, Lac, (Que.) 18 H3
La Poile Bay, (Nfld.) 4 C4
La Poile River, (Nfld.) 4 C3
Lapointe, Lac, (Que.) 6 B3
La Potherie, Lac, (Que.) 46 F4
Larch River
see Mélèzes, Rivière aux
Lardeau River, (BC) 34 B3
Larder Lake, (Ont.) 26 F2
Laredo Channel, (BC) 41 D3
Laredo Inlet, (BC) 41 E3
Laredo Sound, (BC) 41 E3
L'Argent, Cape, (Nfld.) 3 G4
Largepike Lake, (NWT) 44 D2
Laribosière, Lac, (Que.) 20 H2
Larive, Lac, (Que.) 18 B3
Larkin Point, (Nfld.) 4 A4
Larocque, Lac, (Que.) 19 C1
Larrey, Lac, (Que.) 14 D2
Larron, Lac, (Que.) 15 F3
Larsen Sound, (NWT) 47 D4
Larus Lake, (Ont.) 30 D4
La Salle, Lac, (Que.) 18 H3
La Salle, Lac, (Que.) 20 G2
La Salle River, (Man.) 29 H4
La Sarre, Baie, (Que.) 26 G1
La Sarre, Rivière, (Que.) 26 G1
La Savonnière, Lac, (Que.) 20 G2
La Scie Harbour, (Nfld.) 3 B1
Laskeek Bay, (BC) 41 B2
La Sorbière, Lac, (Que.) 14 C1
Lasqueti Island, (BC) 38 D2
L'Assomption, Rivière, (Que.) 16 A2
Last Lake, (Man.) 29 G2
Lastman Lake, (BC) 37 E1
Last Mountain Lake, (Sask.) 31 G2
Lataignant, Lac, (Que.) 6 A3
Latewhos Creek, (BC) 35 G1
Latimer Lake, (NWT) 44 F2
Latornell River, (Alta.) 40 G1
La Tourette, Rivière, (Que.) 19 B3
La Tour, Port, (NS) 10 C4
La Trêve, Lac, (Que.) 20 F4
Laughland Lake, (NWT) 46 C1
Laumet, Lac, (Que.) 6 B3
Launching Point, (PEI) 7 E4
Laundrie Lake, (Ont.) 26 E3
Laurentides, Parc provincial des, (Que.) 15 A1
Laurie Lake, (Man./Sask.) 44 G4
Laurie River, (Man.) 44 G4
Laurier Lake, (Alta.) 33 G3
Laurier, Mount, (BC) 43 C2
Lauzon Lake, (Ont.) 25 A1
Lava Lake, (BC) 42 E3
Laval, Baie, (Que.) 14 F2
Laval, Lac, (Que.) 14 F1
Lavallée Lake, (Sask.) 32 D2
La Vallée River, (Ont.) 28 H4
Laval, Rivière, (Que.) 14 F2
Lavieille, Lake, (Ont.) 24 E1
Lawabiskau River, (Ont.) 20 D3
Lawashi River, (Ont.) 20 C3
Lawford Lake, (Man.) 30 C2
Lawford River, (Man.) 30 C2
Lawless Creek, (BC) 35 C3
Lawn Bay, (Nfld.) 2 B4
Lawn Head, (Nfld.) 2 B4
Lawn Point, (BC) 39 C2
Lawn Point, (BC) 41 B2
Lawrence Bay, (Sask.) 44 F4
Lawrence, Cape, (NWT) 47 F1
Lawrence Harbour, (Nfld.) 3 C2
Lawrence Lake, (Ont.) 28 H3
Lawrence Lake, (Sask.) 32 C2
Lawrence Lake, (Alta.) 33 D1
Lawrence Point, (BC) 37 B3
Lazo, Cape, (BC) 38 C1
Leach Bay, (NWT) 46 F2
Leach Island, (Ont.) 26 A3
Leaf Lake, (Sask.) 32 H4
Leaf River
see Feuilles, Rivière aux
Leather River, (Sask.) 32 F4
Leavitt Bay, (Sask.) 44 E4
Le Barbier, Lac, (Que.) 19 C4
LeBlanc Bay, (Sask.) 32 C1
LeBlanc Lake, (Sask.) 44 D2
LeBreton, Lac, (Que.) 14 C2
Lebrix Lake, (Man.) 30 C2
Le Cocq, Lac, (Que.) 19 D1
Lecointre, Lac, (Que.) 18 D3
Ledge Creek, (BC) 35 H1
Le Doré, Lac, (Que.) 5 C2
Leech Lake, (Sask.) 29 C2
Lee Creek, (Alta.) 34 F4
Lee Point, (NWT) 47 E2
Le Fer, Lac, (Que.) 6 B3
Leftrook Lake, (Man.) 30 B1
Le Gal, Lac, (Que.) 5 B3
Legarde River, (Ont.) 27 H1
Le Gardeur, Lac, (Que.) 20 F3
Legaré, Lac, (Que.) 18 F3
Legend Lake, (Alta.) 44 B3
Le Gendre, Lac, (Que.) 6 C1
Le Gentilhomme, Lac, (Que.) 6 C4
Leggat Lake, (Ont.) 17 A3
Legoff, Lac, (Que.) 20 F3
Leg Pond, (Nfld.) 5 G2
Leif, Lac, (Que.) 6 D2
Leith, Point, (NWT) 45 D2
Le Jeune, Lac, (BC) 35 D1
Leland Lakes, (Alta./NWT) 44 C2
Le Mare Lake, (BC) 39 C2
Le Marié, Lac, (Que.) 14 C2
Lemay, Lac, (Que.) 19 D2
Lemieux Creek, (BC) 36 F3
Lemieux Islands, (NWT) 46 G2
Lemmens Inlet, (BC) 39 G4
Le Moine, Bay, (Nfld.) 4 B4
Le Moine, Cap, (NS) 8 D2
Lemoine, Lac, (Que.) 14 A1
Lemoine, Lac, (Que.) 18 B2
Lemotte's Lake, (Nfld.) 3 B3
Le Moyne, Lac, (Que.) 6 C1
Lempriere Creek, (BC) 36 G1
Lennox Passage, (NS) 9 G2
Lenore Lake, (Sask.) 32 E4
L'enôtre, Lac, (Que.) 18 D3
Leonard Lake, (Ont.) 24 B3
Leonard Lake, (Sask.) 32 H2
Leon Creek, (BC) 36 B4
Leopold Island, (NWT) 46 G2
Leopold M'Clintock, Cape, (NWT) 47 C2
Lepreau, Point, (NB) 11 D3
Lepreau River, (NB) 11 C3
Le Rageois, Lac, (Que.) 6 B3
Le Roy, Lac, (Que.) 46 E4
Les Appalaches *(mountains)*, (Que.) 1
Lescot, Lac, (Que.) 18 B3
Lesdiguières, Lac, (Que.) 46 E3
Les Laurentides *(mountains)*, (Que.) 1
Leslie, Lac, (Que.) 24 H1
Lessard, Lac, (Que.) 14 F1
Lesser Slave Lake, (Alta.) 33 C1
Lesser Slave Lake Provincial Park, (Alta.) 33 D1
Lesser Slave River, (Alta.) 33 D1
Lestage, Rivière, (Que.) 46 F3
Lester Creek, (Sask.) 32 A1
Lesueur, Lac, (Que.) 18 E3
Le Tort, Lac, (Que.) 5 C2
Levasseur, Lac, (Que.) 18 F1
Lever Lake, (NWT) 45 E2
Leverrier, Lac, (Que.) 15 D3
Levis, Lac, (NWT) 45 E3
Lévy, Pointe de, (Que.) 15 G3
Lewaseechjeech Brook, (Nfld.) 4 D2
Lewes Island, (NWT) 45 F1
Lewis Cass, Mount, (BC) 42 C2
Lewis Channel, (BC) 37 C4
Lewis Creek, (Sask.) 31 G2
Lewis Head, (Nfld.) 3 F3
Lewis Hills, (Nfld.) 4 C1
Lewis Island, (Nfld.) 3 F3
Lewis Lake, (Nfld.) 3 B2
Lewis Lake, (Ont.) 27 C1
Lewis Lake, (BC) 37 D4
Lewis Point, (BC) 39 E1
Lewis Pond, (Nfld.) 3 C3
Leyson Point, (NWT) 46 D2
LG2 Barrage/Dam, (Que.) 20 E2
L'Hebert, Port, (NS) 10 D3
Liard River, (BC) 45 C4
Lichen Mountain, (BC) 36 H3
Lichteneger, Lac, (Que.) 20 F3
Liddon Gulf, (NWT) 47 C3
Liege River, (Alta.) 44 B4
Lièvre, Rivière du, (Que.) 18 E3
Lièvres, Ile aux, (Que.) 14 E4
Li Fiord, (NWT) 47 D1
Lighthouse Point, (NS) 8 F4
Lighthouse Point, (Ont.) 22 B4
Lightning Creek, (Sask.) 29 D4
Lillian Lake, (BC) 39 F4
Lillooet Glacier, (BC) 37 E2
Lillooet Lake, (BC) 37 G3
Lillooet River, (BC) 37 F3
Lime Lake, (Ont.) 24 G4
Limerick Lake, (Ont.) 24 F3
Limestone Bay, (Man.) 30 B2
Limestone Lake, (Man.) 30 C1
Limestone Lake, (Sask.) 32 G2
Limestone Point, (Man.) 30 B2
Limestone Point Lake, (Man.) 30 A2
Limestone River, (Man.) 30 D1
Linaluk Island, (NWT) 47 B4
Linbarr Lake, (Ont.) 26 A1
Lindstrom Lake, (Sask.) 32 F1
Lingan Bay, (NS) 8 F3
Lingham Lake, (Ont.) 24 F3
Linière, Rivière, (Que.) 16 G2
Link Lake, (BC) 41 F3
Linklater Lake, (Ont.) 27 E1
Lions Den *(bay)*, (Nfld.) 3 F4
Liot Point, (NWT) 47 A3
Lippy Point, (BC) 39 B1
Lipsett Lake, (Ont.) 26 C2
Liscomb Harbour, (NS) 9 E3
Liscomb Island, (NS) 9 F3
Liscomb Point, (NS) 9 F3
Liscomb River, (NS) 9 E3
Listen Lake, (Sask.) 32 D2
Little Abitibi Lake, (Ont.) 20 D4
Little Abitibi River, (Ont.) 20 D4
Little Ausable River, (Ont.) 22 D1
Little Barachois Brook, (Nfld.) 4 C2
Little Barachois River, (Nfld.) 2 F3
Little Bay, (Nfld.) 4 F4
Little Bay Arm, (Nfld.) 3 B1
Little Bay Head, (Nfld.) 4 A4
Little Bay Island, (Nfld.) 3 B1
Little Bear Creek, (Ont.) 22 B3
Little Bear Lake, (Sask.) 32 E2
Little Black Island, (Nfld.) 3 D2
Little Bow River, (Alta.) 34 F3
Little Bridge Creek, (Sask.) 32 F3
Little Bridge Creek, (BC) 36 C2
Little Buffalo River, (NWT) 44 C2
Little Cadotte River, (Alta.) 43 H2
Little Cape, (Nfld.) 2 B3
Little Cape, (Ont.) 20 C1
Little Cedar Brook, (NB) 12 B1
Little Churchill River, (Man.) 30 C1
Little Clarke Lake, (Sask.) 32 C2
Little Clay Lake, (Ont.) 28 H1
Little Codroy Pond, (Nfld.) 4 A3
Little Codroy River, (Nfld.) 4 A3
Little Colinet Island, (Nfld.) 2 F3
Little Cornwallis Island, (NWT) 47 D3
Little Creek, (Ont.) 21 G1
Little Current River, (Ont.) 27 G1
Little Cygnet Lake, (Man.) 30 D1
Little Denier Island, (Nfld.) 3 B2
Little Denier Island, (Nfld.) 3 F4
Little Dover (White) Island, (NS) 9 H2
Little Duck Lake, (Man.) 44 H2
Little Ekwan River, (Ont.) 20 B2
Little Emmeline Lake, (Sask.) 32 D1
Little Fish Lake, (Alta.) 34 G2
Little Flatstone Lake, (Sask.) 44 D4
Little Fogo Islands, (Nfld.) 3 E1
Little Forks Stream, (NB) 12 F4
Little French River, (Ont.) 25 G1
Little Gander Pond, (Nfld.) 3 C4
Little Garia Bay, (Nfld.) 4 B4
Little Grand Lake, (Nfld.) 4 D2
Little Green Lake, (BC) 36 D3
Little Gull Lake, (Nfld.) 3 B4
Little Gull River, (Nfld.) 3 C4
Little Harbour Deep River, (Nfld.) 5 G3
Little Harbour River, (Nfld.) 2 G3
Little Hope Island, (NS) 10 D3
Little Joe Glodes Pond, (Nfld.) 4 G1
Little Kashabowie Lake, (Ont.) 27 B3
Little Key River, (Ont.) 25 F2
Little Klappan River, (BC) 42 D1
Little La Cloche Island, (Ont.) 25 C2
Little Lake, (Ont.) 21 E2
Little Lake, (Ont.) 23 F2
Little Lawn Harbour, (Nfld.) 2 B4
Little Limestone Lake, (Man.) 30 D1
Little Limestone Lake, (Man.) 30 B2
Little Liscomb River, (NS) 9 E2
Little Magaguadavic Lake, (NB) 11 B1
Little Main Restigouche River, (NB) 12 A1
Little Maitland River, (Ont.) 23 C3
Little Manitou Lake, (Sask.) 31 G1
Little Manitou Lake, (Sask.) 32 A4
Little Mecatina River, (Nfld.) 5 C1
see also Petit Mécatina, Rivière du (Que.)
Little Missinaibi Lake, (Ont.) 26 B2
Little Mortier Bay, (Nfld.) 2 C3
Little Mushamush Lake, (NS) 10 E2
Little Nictau Lake, (NB) 12 C1
Little Nut Lake, (Sask.) 29 B1
Little Ocean Pond, (Nfld.) 3 E2
Little Otter Creek, (Ont.) 22 F2
Little Oyster River, (BC) 37 B4
Little Partridge River, (Man./NWT) 44 G2
Little Passage, (Nfld.) 2 B2
Little Pic River, (Ont.) 27 G2
Little Plate Island, (Nfld.) 2 A3
Little Playgreen Lake, (Man.) 30 B2
Little Point, (NWT) 47 C3
Little Port Head, (Nfld.) 4 C1
Little Quill Lake, (Sask.) 29 B1
Little Quirke Lake, (Ont.) 25 B1
Little Rancheria River, (BC) 45 B4
Little Rattling Brook, (Nfld.) 3 B3
Little Red Deer River, (Alta.) 34 E1
Little Red Indian Pond, (Nfld.) 4 G1
Little River, (Nfld.) 2 B2
Little River, (NB) 11 D1
Little River, (NB) 12 A2
Little River, (NB) 12 E1
Little River Lake, (NS) 11 H3
Little Rocky Lake, (NWT) 44 F1
Little Sachigo Lake, (Ont.) 30 E2
Little Salmonier River, (Nfld.) 2 F3
Little Salmon Lake, (YT) 45 B3
Little Salmon River, (NB) 11 F2
Little Sand Lake, (Man.) 44 H3
Little Sandy Pond, (Nfld.) 3 A2
Little Saskatchewan River, (Man.) 29 E3
Little Shemogue Harbour, (NB) 7 A4
Little Shuswap Lake, (BC) 36 G4
Little Sled Lake, (Sask.) 32 C2
Little Smoky River, (Alta.) 33 A1
Little Southwest Miramichi River, (NB) 12 D2
Littles Point, (Ont.) 22 A4
Little Stull Lake, (Man.) 30 E2
Little Sturgeon River, (Ont.) 25 H1
Little Toba River, (BC) 37 D3
Little Tobique River, (NB) 12 B1
Little Traverse Bay, (Ont.) 28 F3
Little Trout Lake, (Ont.) 30 E4
Little Turtle Lake, (Ont.) 27 A3
Little Vermilion Lake, (Ont.) 30 D4
Little Wawa Lake, (Ont.) 26 B2
Little Whale River
see Petite rivière de la Baleine
Little White Lake, (BC) 36 C3
Little White Mountain, (BC) 35 F3
Little White River, (Ont.) 26 C4
Little Whiteshell Lake, (Man.) 28 D1
Little Yoho Brook, (NB) 11 C2
Livain, Lac a, (NB) 12 G2
Livernois, Rivière, (Que.) 18 G3
Liverpool Bay, (NWT) 45 C1
Liverpool, Cape, (NWT) 47 F3
Livingstone Lake, (Sask.) 44 E3
Livingstone Point, (NS) 9 F1
Lizard Head Mountain, (BC) 36 F2
Lizard Point, (BC) 39 E1
Lizzie Lake, (BC) 37 H4
Lloyd Lake, (Ont.) 26 E2
Lloyd Lake, (Sask.) 44 D4
Lloyds Lake, (Nfld.) 4 E2
Lloyds River, (Nfld.) 4 D2
Lobstick Bay, (Ont.) 28 G2
Lobstick River, (Alta.) 33 C3
Lochaber Lake, (NS) 9 E2
Locke Bay, (Ont.) 28 F1
Locker Point, (NWT) 45 E1
Lockers Bay, (Nfld.) 3 F3
Lockers Flat Island, (Nfld.) 3 F3
Lockers Reach, (Nfld.) 3 F3

Mimenuh Mountain, (BC) 35 B2
Miminiska Lake, (Ont.) 30 G4
Minago River, (Man.) 30 B2
Minaker River, (BC) 43 C1
Mina, Lac, (Que.) 6 D2
Minamkeak Lake, (NS) 10 E2
Minas Basin, (NS) 9 A2
Minas Channel, (NS) 11 G3
Mindemoya Lake, (Ont.) 25 B2
Mine, Lac, (Que.) 19 G2
Minerai, Pointe au, (Que.) 19 G3
Miner River, (NWT) 45 C1
Miner River, (YT) 45 A2
Mines, Bassin des
see Minas Basin
Mineurs, Ruisseau des, (Que.) 13 C2
Mingan, Chenal de, (Que.) 19 H3
Mingan, Iles de, (Que.) 19 H3
Mingan, Rivière, (Que.) 19 H2
Mingo Lake, (NWT) 46 F2
Mingré, Lac, (Que.) 6 C3
Ming's Bight, (Nfld.) 5 H3
Minipi Lake, (Nfld.) 5 C1
Minipi River, (Nfld.) 6 F4
Minisinakwa Lake, (Ont.) 26 D2
Miniss Lake, (Ont.) 30 F4
Minister Island, (NB) 11 B3
Ministic Lake, (Ont.) 25 D1
Ministik Creek, (Ont.) 20 B1
Ministikwan Lake, (Sask.) 32 A2
Mink Creek, (Ont.) 24 E2
Mink Creek, (Man.) 29 E2
Mink Islands, (Ont.) 25 F3
Mink Lake, (NS) 10 C3
Mink Lake, (Ont.) 24 G1
Mink Lake, (NWT) 44 A1
Mink Lake, (Alta.) 44 B4
Minnewanka, Lake, (Alta.) 34 D2
Minnie Lake, (BC) 35 D2
Minnitaki Lake, (Ont.) 27 B1
Minnow Lake, (Sask.) 32 B2
Minstrel Island, (BC) 39 F1
Minto Head, (NWT) 47 C3
Minto Inlet, (NWT) 47 B4
Minto, Lac, (Que.) 46 E4
Miquelon Lakes, (Alta.) 33 E3
Mira Bay, (NS) 8 F3
Mirage Bay, (NWT) 46 F1
Miramichi Bay, (NB) 12 G2
Miramichi Inner Bay, (NB) 12 F2
Miramichi Lake, (NB) 12 C3
Miramichi River, (NB) 12 F2
Mira River, (NS) 8 E3
Mirasty Lake, (Sask.) 32 C2
Mire Lake, (Man.) 29 F1
Mirepoix, Lac, (Que.) 14 C1
Mirond Lake, (Sask.) 32 G1
Mirror River, (Sask.) 44 D3
Miry Creek, (Sask.) 31 D2
Misamikwash Lake, (Ont.) 30 F3
Misasque, Rivière, (Que.) 20 H2
Misaw Lake, (Sask.) 44 F2
Miscou Gully, (NB) 13 H4
Miscou Harbour, (NB) 13 H4
Miscou Island, (NB) 13 H4
Misehkow River, (Ont.) 30 F4
Misekumaw Lake, (Sask.) 44 F2
Misèle, Lac, (Que.) 6 A3
Misèle, Lac, (Que.) 20 H2
Miséricorde, Baie de la
see Gods Mercy, Bay of
Misery Point, (Ont.) 25 A2
Mishamattawa River, (Ont.) 30 G2
Mishibishu Lake, (Ont.) 27 H3
Mishwamakan River, (Ont.) 30 F2
Misikeyask Lake, (Ont.) 30 F2
Misikokway Lake, (Ont.) 25 G3
Miskwabi Lake, (Ont.) 24 D3
Mispec Point, (NB) 11 D3
Mispec River, (NB) 11 E3
Misquamaebin Lake, (Ont.) 30 E3
Missawawi Lake, (Alta.) 33 F2
Missezula Lake, (BC) 35 D3
Missezula Mountain, (BC) 35 D3
Missi Island, (Sask.) 32 H2
Missi Lake, (Sask.) 44 F4
Missinaibi Lake, (Ont.) 26 B2
Missinaibi Lake Provincial Park, (Ont.) 26 B1
Missinaibi River, (Ont.) 26 C1
Mission Creek, (BC) 35 F2
Mission Group (islands), (BC) 39 D3
Missionnaire, Lac du, (Que.) 18 H3
Missipuskiow River, (Sask.) 32 F3
Missisa Lake, (Ont.) 20 B3
Missisa River, (Ont.) 20 B2
Missisicabi, Rivière, (Que.) 20 E4
Mississagagon Lake, (Ont.) 24 G3
Mississagi Bay, (Ont.) 25 A1
Mississagi Island, (Ont.) 25 A2
Mississagi Provincial Park, (Ont.) 26 C4
Mississagi River, (Ont.) 26 B4
Mississagi Strait, (Ont.) 26 C4
Mississagua Lake, (Ont.) 24 D3
Mississagua River, (Ont.) 24 D4
Mississippi Lake, (Ont.) 17 B2
Mississippi, River, (Ont.) 17 B2
Missisquoi, Baie, (Que.) 16 A4
Mistachagagane, Lac, (Que.) 19 D2
Mistahayo Lake, (Ont.) 30 F1
Mistaken Point, (Nfld.) 2 G4
Mistango River, (Ont.) 26 E1
Mistanipisipou, Rivière, (Que.) 5 B1
Mistaouac, Lac, (Que.) 20 E4
Mistaouac, Rivière, (Que.) 20 E4
Mistassibi Nord-Est, Rivière, (Que.) 20 H4
Mistassibi, Rivière, (Que.) 20 H4
Mistassini, Lac, (Que.) 20 G3
Mistassini, Rivière, (Que.) 18 H1
Mistawasis Creek, (Sask.) 32 C3
Mistawasis Lake, (Sask.) 32 C4
Mistigougèche, Lac, (Que.) 14 H3
Mistikokan River, (Man.) 30 E1
Mistinibi, Lac, (Que.) 6 D2
Mistinic, Lac, (Que.) 6 B4
Mistinikon Lake, (Ont.) 26 E2
Mistinippi Lake, (Nfld.) 6 F3
Mistohay Lake, (Sask.) 32 B2
Mistouc, Riviere, (Que.) 14 A2
Misty Lake, (Ont.) 24 C1
Misty Lake, (Man.) 44 G3
Mitchell Bay, (Ont.) 22 B3
Mitchell Lake, (NB) 12 C2
Mitchell Lake, (BC) 40 E3
Mitchell Point, (Ont.) 22 B3
Mitchinamécus, Réservoir, (Que.) 18 E3
Mitchinamécus, Rivière, (Que.) 18 E2
Mitis, Baie, (Que.) 14 H2
Mitishto River, (Man.) 30 B2
Mitis, Lac, (Que.) 13 A3
Mitis, Pointe, (Que.) 14 H2
Mitis, Rivière, (Que.) 14 H3
Mitlenatch Island, (BC) 37 B4
Moar Bay, (NWT) 20 E2
Moar Lake, (Man./Ont.) 30 D3
Moberley River, (BC) 43 E3
Moberly Lake, (BC) 43 D4
Mobert Creek, (Ont.) 27 H2
Mobile Big Pond, (Nfld.) 2 H3
Mobile River, (Nfld.) 2 H3
Moccasin Pond, (Nfld.) 3 E2
Mocodome, Cape, (NS) 9 F3
Modeste, Mount, (BC) 38 D4
Modsley Lake, (NB) 11 B2
Moe, Rivière, (Que.) 16 D4
Moffat Creek, (BC) 36 C1
Moffat Lakes, (BC) 36 D1
Moffatt, Lac, (Que.) 16 E3
Moffet Inlet, (NWT) 47 E4
Mohun Lake, (BC) 37 A4
Moira Lake, (Ont.) 24 F4
Moira Lake, (BC) 36 F2
Moira River, (Ont.) 21 F1
Moisie, Baie de, (Que.) 19 F3
Moisie, Rivière, (Que.) 19 F1
Mojikit Lake, (Ont.) 27 E1
Moketas Island, (BC) 39 D2
Mokka Fiord, (NWT) 47 E2
Molanosa Lake, (Sask.) 32 E2
Molega Lake, (NS) 10 D2
Mollet, Lac, (Que.) 20 G1
Molliers Point, (Nfld.) 2 B3
Mollyguajeck Lake, (Nfld.) 3 D4
Molson Lake, (Nfld.) 6 C3
Molson Lake, (Man.) 30 C2
Molson River, (Man.) 30 C2
Momich Lake, (BC) 36 G3
Monarch Icefield, (BC) 41 G3
Monarch Mountain, (BC) 41 G4
Monashee Creek, (BC) 35 H2
Monashee Provincial Park, (BC) 35 H1
Moncouche, Lac, (Que.) 14 C2
Mondonac, Lac, (Que.) 18 F3
Money Point, (NS) 8 E1
Monger, Ile, (Que.) 5 E2
Mongus Lake, (Ont.) 28 H3
Monitor Creek, (Alta.) 31 B1
Monkman Pass, (BC) 40 E1
Monks Head, (NS) 8 B4
Monmouth Mountain, (BC) 37 E2
Monnery River, (Sask.) 32 A3
Monquart Stream, (NB) 12 A3
Mons Creek, (Ont.) 22 C1
Montagne du Pin, Lac de la, (Que.) 20 F2
Montagnes Blanches, Rivière des, (Que.) 19 B2
Montagnes, Lac des, (Que.) 20 F3
Montagneuse River, (Alta.) 43 G3
Montague Lake, (Sask.) 31 F4
Montana Lake, (BC) 36 E3
Montauban, Lac, (Que.) 18 H3
Montbeillard, Lac, (Que.) 26 G2
Montcevelles, Lac, (Que.) 5 C2
Monte Lake, (BC) 35 E1
Montgomery Lake, (NWT) 44 H1
Montigny, Lac de, (Que.) 18 B2
Montjoie, Lac, (Que.) 16 D4
Montjoie, Lac, (Que.) 18 E3
Mont-Louis, Rivière de, (Que.) 13 E1
Montmorency, Rivière, (Que.) 15 B2
Mont-Orford, Parc provincial du, (Que.) 16 C4
Montréal (Dorval) Int Airport/ Aéroport, (Que.) G
Montreal Island, (Ont.) 26 A3
Montreal Lake, (Sask.) 32 D2
Montréal (Mirabel) Int Airport/ Aéroport, (Que.) G
Montreal River, (Ont.) 26 B3
Montreal River, (Ont.) 26 F2
Montreal River, (Sask.) 32 D1
Mont Revelstoke, Parc national du, (BC) 34 A2
see also Mount Revelstoke National Park
Mont Riding, Parc national du, (Man.) 29 E2
see also Riding Mountain National Park
Montrose Creek, (BC) 37 D3
Monts, Pointe des, (Que.) 19 E4
Mont Tremblant, Parc provincial du, (Que.) 18 F4
Montviel, Lac, (Que.) 6 B3
Monument Bay, (Ont.) 28 E2
Monument Brook, (NB) 11 A1
Moodie Island, (NWT) 46 G2
Moodie, Mount, (BC) 43 C3
Moon Island, (Ont.) 25 G4
Moon Lake, (Ont.) 25 A1
Moon River, (Ont.) 25 G4
Moore Bay, (NWT) 47 C2
Moore Creek, (BC) 35 D1
Moore Islands, (BC) 41 D3
Moore Lake, (Ont.) 24 E2
Moore Lake, (Alta.) 33 G2
Moore, Mount, (BC) 35 G2
Moore Peak, (BC) 35 A1
Moore Point, (Ont.) 21 C2
Moose Head, (NS) 9 G2
Moosehorn Creek, (NB) 11 E2
Moose Island, (Man.) 29 H1
Moose Jaw River, (Sask.) 31 G3
Moose Lake, (NB) 12 C3
Moose Lake, (Ont.) 26 E1
Moose Lake, (Man.) 28 D3
Moose Lake, (Man.) 29 H2
Moose Lake, (Man.) 30 B2
Moose Lake, (Alta.) 33 G2
Mooseland Lake, (Ont.) 27 D2
Moose Mountain, (Sask.) 29 C3
Moose Mountain Creek, (Sask.) 29 C4
Moose Mountain Lake, (Sask.) 29 C3
Moose Mountain Provincial Park, (Sask.) 29 C4
Moose Nose Lake, (Man.) 30 C1
Moose River, (Ont.) 20 D3
Moosomin Lake, (Sask.) 29 D3
Moraine Lake, (NWT) 45 G2
Morand Lake, (Man.) 44 G3
Morass Point, (Man.) 29 G1
More Creek, (BC) 42 C1
Morell Lake, (Sask.) 44 F3
Moresby Island, (BC) 38 F3
Moresby Island, (BC) 41 B3
Morgan Arm, (Nfld.) 4 G4
Morgan Brook, (Nfld.) 4 G3
Morgans Point, (Ont.) 21 B4
Moriarty, Mount, (BC) 38 C2
Morice Lake, (BC) 41 F1
Morice River, (BC) 41 F1
Morien Bay, (NS) 8 F3
Morin, Lac, (Que.) 15 E1
Morin Lake, (Sask.) 32 D1
Morin Lake, (Man.) 32 H1
Morin Point, (NWT) 47 E4
Morkill River, (BC) 40 E2
Morris Channel, (Nfld.) 3 F3
Morris Island, (Nfld.) 3 F3
Morrison Lake, (Ont.) 24 B3
Morrison Lake, (Ont.) 26 B3
Morrison Lake, (Man.) 30 B3
Morrison Lake, (BC) 42 G3
Morris River, (Man.) 29 H4
Morris River, (Ont.) 30 F3
Morrogh Creek, (Ont.) 22 D2
Morse, Pointe du, (Que.) 20 D2
Mortier Bay, (Nfld.) 2 C3
Mosambik Lake, (Ont.) 26 A1
Moser River, (NS) 9 E3
Moses Inlet, (BC) 41 F4
Mosher River, (NB) 11 E2
Mosley Creek, (BC) 37 B1
Mosquito Bay, (NWT) 46 E3
Mosquito Creek, (Alta.) 34 E3
Mosquito Lake, (NWT) 44 F1
Moss Lake, (Man.) 28 D2
Moss Lake, (Man.) 44 H3
Mossy River, (Man.) 30 A4
Mossy River, (Sask.) 32 F2
Mostoos Hills, (Sask.) 32 A1
Motase Lake, (BC) 42 F2
Motase Peak, (BC) 42 F2
Motion Bay, (Nfld.) 2 H3
Motion Head, (Nfld.) 2 H3
Mouat, Cape, (NWT) 47 F2
Mouchalagane, Rivière, (Que.) 6 B4
Moul Creek, (BC) 36 F2
Moulin, Rivière, (Que.) 13 B3
Moulin, Rivière du, (Que.) 14 B3
Moulin, Ruisseau du, (Que.) 15 G3
Moulton Bay, (Ont.) 21 B4
Mountain Lake, (Ont.) 23 C1
Mountain Lake, (Ont.) 23 D1
Mountain Lake, (Ont.) 24 D3
Mountain Lake, (Sask.) 32 F1
Mountain Lake, (NWT) 44 H1
Mountain Lake, (NWT) 44 E2
Mountain River, (NWT) 45 C2
Mountains, Lake of the, (Ont.) 25 A1
Mountains, Lake of the, (BC) 39 C1
Mountairy Lake, (Ont.) 27 C1
Mount Assiniboine Provincial Park, (BC) 34 D2
Mount Carmel Pond, (Nfld.) 2 G3
Mount Edziza Provincial Park, (BC) 42 C1
Mount Guemes, (BC) 39 G4
Mount Misery Pond, (Nfld.) 2 G4
Mount Revelstoke National Park, (BC) 34 A2
see also Mont Revelstoke, Parc national du
Mount Robson Provincial Park, (BC) 40 G3
Mount Seymour Provincial Park, (BC) 38 F2
Mount Washington, (BC) 39 H3
Mourier, Lac, (Que.) 18 B2
Mourier, Ruisseau, (Que.) 13 F2
Mousseau (Harrington), Lac, (Que.) 17 D3
Mouton, Port, (NS) 10 D3
Moüy, Lac, (Que.) 6 B3
Mow Creek, (BC) 36 E4
Mowhokam Creek, (BC) 35 B2
Moyeha Mountain, (BC) 39 G4
Moyeha River, (BC) 39 G4
Moyen, Lac, (Que.) 6 D2
Moyer, Lac, (Que.) 6 B2
Moyie Lake, (BC) 34 C4
Moyie River, (BC) 34 C4
Mozhabong Lake, (Ont.) 26 D3
Mucalic, Rivière, (Que.) 6 C1
Muchalat Inlet, (BC) 39 F3
Muchalat Lake, (BC) 39 F3
Muchalat River, (BC) 39 F3
Muckaboo Creek, (BC) 42 E2
Mud Bay, (BC) 38 G3
Mud Creek, (BC) 36 H1
Muddy Hole Bay, (Nfld.) 4 D4
Muddy Lake, (Sask.) 31 C1
Muddy Point, (Nfld.) 3 F2
Mudge Bay, (Ont.) 25 B2
Mudge, Cape, (NWT) 47 C3
Mudie Lake, (Sask.) 32 A2
Mud Island, (NS) 10 B4
Mudjatik River, (Sask.) 44 D4
Mud Lake, (Ont.) 24 B3
Mud Lake, (Ont.) 25 B2
Mud Lake, (BC) 36 H1
Mud Turtle Lake, (Man.) 28 D1
Mugford, Cape, (Nfld.) 6 E1
Muir Creek, (BC) 38 E4
Muketei River, (Ont.) 30 H3
Mukutawa River, (Man.) 30 C3
Mulcuish Lake, (NS) 8 F4
Mule, Lac la, (Que.) 19 F1
Mulgrave, Lake, (NS) 9 D3
Mulgrave, Lake, (NS) 10 C2
Mulligan Bay, (Nfld.) 6 F3
Mulligan River, (Nfld.) 6 F3
Mullin Stream Lake, (NB) 12 D2
Mulock Lake, (Ont.) 25 H1
Muncho Lake Provincial Park, (BC) 45 C4
Mundy Harbour, (NWT) 47 E4
Munekun Lake, (Ont.) 30 E3
Munn, Cape, (NWT) 46 D2
Munroe Bay, (Sask.) 44 D4
Munroe Lake, (Man.) 44 H2
Munroes Island, (NS) 9 D1
Munro Lake, (Man.) 30 D2
Munuscong Lake, (Ont.) 26 B4
Murchison Island, (Ont.) 27 E1
Murchison, Mount, (Alta.) 34 C1
Murchison, Mount, (BC) 38 F1
Murchison River, (NWT) 46 C1
Murder Island, (NS) 10 A4
Murdoch, Lac, (Que.) 6 C2
Murdoch, Rivière, (Que.) 6 C2
Murdock River, (Ont.) 25 F1
Mureau, Lac, (Que.) 20 F1
Muriel Lake, (Alta.) 33 G2
Murky Lake, (Ont.) 27 G1
Murky Lake, (NWT) 44 C1
Murphy Lake, (BC) 36 D1
Murray Bay, (NWT) 47 D4
Murray, Cape, (NWT) 47 C2
Murray Creek, (BC) 35 B1
Murray Harbour, (PEI) 7 E4
Murray Head, (PEI) 7 E4
Murray Inlet, (NWT) 47 C3
Murray Lake, (Ont.) 26 B2
Murray Lake, (Man.) 30 D2
Murray Lake, (Sask.) 32 B4
Murray Lake, (BC) 35 C3
Murray Maxwell Bay, (NWT) 46 D1
Murray Mountain, (NS) 8 E3
Murray River, (BC) 43 E4
Murtle Lake, (BC) 36 G1
Murtle River, (BC) 36 F1
Musclow Lake, (Ont.) 30 D4
Muscote Bay, (Ont.) 21 F1
Mushaboom Harbour, (NS) 9 D3
Mushpauk Lake, (NS) 10 B3
Muskasenda Lake, (Ont.) 26 E2
Muskeg Bay, (Ont.) 28 H2
Muskeg Bay, (Man.) 28 E3
Muskeg Lake, (Ont.) 27 D2
Muskeg River, (Sask.) 32 A2
Muskeg River, (BC) 40 C1
Muskeg River, (Alta.) 40 G2
Muskeg River, (NWT) 45 D4
Muskiki Lake, (Sask.) 31 F1
Musk Lake, (Man./Ont.) 28 E1
Muskoka, Lake, (Ont.) 24 B3
Muskosung Lake, (Ont.) 25 G1
Muskox Fiord, (NWT) 47 E2
Muskox Lake, (NWT) 45 F2
Muskrat Dam Lake, (Ont.) 30 E3
Muskrat Falls, (Nfld.) 6 F4
Muskrat Lake, (Ont.) 24 G1
Muskwa Lake, (Alta.) 44 B4
Muskwa Ranges, (BC) 43 B2
Muskwa River, (BC) 43 B1
Muskwa River, (Alta.) 44 B4
Muskwesi River, (Man.) 44 H3
Musquanousse, Lac, (Que.) 5 C3
Musquaro, Lac, (Que.) 5 C3
Musquaro, Rivière, (Que.) 5 C3
Musquash Harbour, (NB) 11 D3
Musquash Head, (NB) 11 D3
Musquash Lake, (NB) 11 A2
Musquodoboit Harbour, (NS) 10 H1
Musquodoboit River, (NS) 9 C3
Muswabik River, (Ont.) 20 B3
Mutton Bay, (Nfld.) 2 G4
Mutton, Cape, (Nfld.) 2 G4
Muzhikoba Creek, (Ont.) 30 G2
Muzroll Brook, (NB) 12 D3
Muzroll Lake, (NB) 12 D4
Mylor Peninsula, (BC) 42 D4
Myo Creek, (Sask.) 32 B3
Myre Lake, (Man.) 30 D1
Mystery Lake, (NWT) 44 C1

N

Nabakwasi Lake, (Ont.) 26 E3
Nabesche River, (BC) 43 C3
Nabisipi, Pointe, (Que.) 5 B3
Nabisipi, Rivière, (Que.) 5 B3
Nachicapau, Lac, (Que.) 6 C2
Nachvak Fiord, (Nfld.) 46 H3
Nackawic Stream, (NB) 12 B4
Nadaleen River, (YT) 45 B2
Naden Harbour, (BC) 41 A1
Nadila Creek, (BC) 37 F1
Nadina Lake, (BC) 41 F1
Nadina River, (BC) 41 F1
Naena Point, (BC) 39 G1
Nagagami Lake, (Ont.) 20 B4
Nagagami River, (Ont.) 20 B4
Nagagamisis Lake, (Ont.) 20 B4
Nagagamisis Provincial Park, (Ont.) 20 B3
Nagasin Lake, (Ont.) 26 B2
Nagle Lake, (Sask.) 44 E4
Naguak Lake, (NWT) 46 D1
Nahanni National Park, (NWT) 45 C3
see also Nahanni, Parc national de
Nahanni, Parc national de, (NWT) 45 C3
see also Nahanni, National Park
Nahatlatch Lake, (BC) 35 A2
Nahatlatch River, (BC) 35 A2
Nahili Lake, (Man.) 44 G2
Nahlouza Lake, (BC) 41 G2
Nahmint Lake, (BC) 38 B2
Nahmint River, (BC) 38 B2
Nahwitti Lake, (BC) 39 C1
Nahwitti River, (BC) 39 C1
Naikoon Provincial Park, (BC) 41 B1
Nain Bay, (Nfld.) 6 E2
Naiscoot River, (Ont.) 25 F3
Nalaisk Mountain, (NB) 12 C2
Naltesby Lake, (BC) 40 C2
Namakan Lake, (Ont.) 27 A3
Namakan River, (Ont.) 27 A3
Namaycush Lake, (NWT) 47 C4
Namego Lake, (Ont.) 28 F1
Nameigos Lake, (Ont.) 26 A1
Namekus Lake, (Sask.) 32 D3
Nameless Lake, (Sask.) 44 D4
Namepi Creek, (Alta.) 33 E2
Namewaminikan River, (Ont.) 27 F2
Namew Lake, (Man./Sask.) 32 H2
Namur Lake, (Alta.) 44 B3
Nanaimo Lakes, (BC) 38 D3
Nanaimo River, (BC) 38 D3
Nango Lake, (Ont.) 30 E3
Nango River, (Ont.) 30 E3
Nanika Lake, (BC) 41 F1
Nanook River, (NWT) 47 C4
Nanoose Harbour, (BC) 38 D2
Nansen Sound, (NWT) 47 E1
Nantais, Lac, (Que.) 46 F3
Nanticoke Creek, (Ont.) 22 G2
Nanton Lake, (BC) 37 D4
Nantucket Island, (NB) 11 C4
Naococane, Lac, (Que.) 6 B4
Naosap Lake, (Sask.) 32 H1
Napaktok (Black Duck) Bay, (Nfld.) 6 E1
Napanee River, (Ont.) 21 G1
Napatalik Island, (Nfld.) 6 F2
Napetipi, Baie, (Que.) 5 F2
Napetipi, Lac, (Que.) 5 F2
Napetipi, Rivière, (Que.) 5 F1
Napier River, (NS) 10 B3
Napken Lake, (Ont.) 20 B3
Nappan River, (NS) 9 A1
Narcosli Creek, (BC) 40 C3
Nares, Cape, (NWT) 47 B2
Nares, Cape, (NWT) 47 E1
Narpaing Fiord, (NWT) 46 F1
Narraway River, (Alta./BC) 40 E1
Narrows Inlet, (BC) 38 E1
Narrows The (channel), (Nfld.) 6 G3
Nashwaak Lake, (NB) 12 B3
Nashwaak River, (NB) 11 C1
Naskaupi River, (Nfld.) 6 E3
Nasparti Inlet, (BC) 39 C2
Nass Ranges, (BC) 42 E3
Nass River, (BC) 42 D2
Nastapoca, Rivière, (Que.) 46 E4
Nastapoka Islands, (NWT) 46 E4
Natalie Lake, (Man.) 28 C1
Natalkuz Lake, (BC) 40 A2
Natashquan Est, Rivière, (Que.) 5 C1
Natashquan, Pointe, (Que.) 5 B3
Natashquan River, (Nfld.) 5 B1
see also Natashquan, Rivière (Que.)
Natashquan, Rivière, (Que.) 5 B2
see also Natashquan River (Nfld.)
Nataweuse Lake, (Sask.) 32 F1
Nathorst, Cape, (NWT) 47 D2
Nation River, (BC) 43 B4
Natipi, Lac, (Que.) 19 A1
Native Bay, (NWT) 46 D2
Native Point, (NWT) 46 D2
Natkusiak Peninsula, (NWT) 47 C3
Natla River, (NWT) 45 C3
Natowite Lake, (BC) 42 G3
Nat River, (Ont.) 26 D2
Natsy Lake, (BC) 36 B1
Natuak, Lac, (Que.) 6 A1
Nauja Bay, (NWT) 46 E1
Naver Creek, (BC) 40 C2
Navy Board Inlet, (NWT) 47 F3
Navy Island, (NB) 11 B3
Nayelles Lake, (Sask.) 44 F4
Nazko River, (BC) 40 B3
Neagle Lake, (Sask.) 32 G2
Neakongut Bay, (NWT) 46 E3
Nechako Reservoir, (BC) 40 A2
Nechako River, (BC) 40 A2
Neck Point, (BC) 38 D2
Necoslie River, (BC) 40 B1
Necum Teuch Bay, (NS) 9 E3
Neddick, Cape, (Nfld.) 2 H3
Nedlouc, Lac, (Que.) 6 A1
Nedlukseak Fiord, (NWT) 46 F1
Needa Lake, (BC) 36 E2
Neely Lake, (Sask.) 32 G4
Neergaard Lake, (NWT) 47 F4
Negassa Lake, (Man.) 44 H3
Negro Harbour, (NS) 10 C4
Neguac Bay, (NB) 12 G2
Neguac Beach, (NB) 12 G2
Negwazu Lake, (Ont.) 26 A1
Nehalliston Creek, (BC) 36 E3
Neiges, Lac des, (Que.) 15 B1
Neiges, Rivière des, (Que.) 15 B2
Neigette, Lac, (Que.) 14 H3
Neigette, Rivière, (Que.) 14 H3
Neiman Lake, (Sask.) 44 D2
Nejanilini Lake, (Man.) 44 H2
Nekweaga Bay, (Sask.) 44 F3
Nelson Head, (NWT) 47 A3
Nelson Island, (BC) 38 D1
Nelson Lake, (Ont.) 27 C3
Nelson Lake, (Man.) 30 B1
Nelson Lake, (Man.) 44 H4
Nelson, Port, (Man.) 30 E1
Nelson River, (Man.) 30 C1
Nelson, Rivière, (Que.) 15 F3
Nemegosenda Lake, (Ont.) 26 C2
Nemegosenda River, (Ont.) 26 C2
Nemegos Lake, (Ont.) 26 C2
Nemeiben Lake, (Sask.) 32 E1
Némiscachingue, Lac, (Que.) 18 F2
Némiscau, Lac, (Que.) 20 F3
Némiscau, Rivière, (Que.) 20 F3
Nepewassi Lake, (Ont.) 25 F1
Nepisiguit Bay, (NB) 13 E4
Nepisiguit Lakes, (NB) 12 C1
Nepisiguit River, (NB) 12 D1
Neptune, Lac, (Que.) 20 G2
Neptune Peak, (BC) 34 A1
Nerepis River, (NB) 11 D2
Néret, Lac, (Que.) 6 B3
Neroutsos Inlet, (BC) 39 D1
Nesslin Lake, (Sask.) 32 D3
Nestaocano, Rivière, (Que.) 20 G4
Netalzul Mountain, (BC) 42 F3
Netchek, Cape, (NWT) 46 D3
Netsilik Lake, (NWT) 45 H1
Nettell Lake, (Sask.) 44 D2
Nettichi River, (Ont.) 20 C3
Nettiling Lake, (NWT) 46 F1
Nettilling Fiord, (NWT) 46 F2
Nettle Island, (BC) 38 B3
Nettogami Lake, (Ont.) 20 D4
Neuf Milles, Lac des, (Que.) 18 C3
Nevers Brook, (NB) 11 F1
Nevertouch Lake, (BC) 35 G3
Neville, Port, (BC) 39 G1
Nevins Lake, (Sask.) 44 D2
New Bay, (Nfld.) 3 C2
New Bay Head, (Nfld.) 3 C2
New Bay Pond, (Nfld.) 3 B2
New Bay River, (Nfld.) 3 C2
Newboro Lake, (Ont.) 17 B3
Newcastle Creek, (NB) 12 D4
Newcastle Island, (BC) 38 E2
Newcombe Lake, (BC) 41 F1
Newell, Lake, (Alta.) 34 G3
Newell Sound, (NWT) 46 F2
Newfoundland Dog Pond, (Nfld.) 4 H2
New Harbour Cove, (NS) 9 G2
New Harbour Head, (NS) 9 G3
New Harbour River, (NS) 9 F2
New London Bay, (PEI) 7 C3
Newman Sound, (Nfld.) 3 F4
Newport, Pointe de, (Que.) 13 G3
New Quebec Crater
see Nouveau-Québec, Cratère du
New River, (NB) 11 C3
Newton Fiord, (NWT) 46 G2
Newton Lake, (Nfld.) 3 C4
Newton Lake, (Sask.) 31 D4
New World Island, (Nfld.) 3 D2
Ney Lake, (Ont.) 30 E2
Neys Provincial Park, (Ont.) 27 G3
Niagara Creek, (BC) 40 E3
Niagara River, (Ont.) 21 B4
Nias Point, (NWT) 47 C3
Nicabau, Lac, (Que.) 20 G4
Nicette, Lac, (Que.) 14 E2
Nichicun, Lac, (Que.) 6 A3
Nichols Creek, (BC) 37 F2
Nicholson Island, (Ont.) 21 F2
Nicholson Lake, (NWT) 44 F1
Nickel Plate Lake, (BC) 35 E4
Nicklin Lake, (Man.) 44 G3
Nickoll Passage, (BC) 39 F1
Nick Power Cove, (Nfld.) 4 F4
Nicoamen River, (BC) 35 B2
Nicobi, Lac, (Que.) 20 F4
Nicola Lake, (BC) 35 D2
Nicola River, (BC) 35 D2
Nicolet, Lac, (Que.) 16 E3
Nicolet, Rivière, (Que.) 16 D3
Nicolet Sud-Ouest, Rivière, (Que.) 16 D3
Nicol Lake, (NWT) 44 F1
Nicomekl River, (BC) 38 G3
Nicomen Island, (BC) 38 H2
Nictau Lake, (NB) 12 C1
Nictaux River, (NS) 10 D1
Nigadoo River, (NB) 13 E4
Nigei Island, (BC) 39 C1
Niger Sound, (Nfld.) 5 H1
Night Hawk Lake, (Ont.) 26 E1
Nikip Lake, (Ont.) 30 E3
Nikwikwaia Creek, (BC) 36 G4
Nilgaut, Lac, (Que.) 18 C3
Nilkitkwa River, (BC) 42 F3
Nimpkish Lake, (BC) 39 E2
Nimpkish River, (BC) 39 E2
Nimpo Lake, (BC) 40 A3
Nina Bang Lake, (NWT) 47 F4
Ninawawe, Lac, (Que.) 6 D2
Nine Mile Creek, (BC) 37 D1
Nipawin Provincial Park, (Sask.) 32 E2
Nipekamew Lake, (Sask.) 32 E2
Nipekamew River, (Sask.) 32 E2
Nipew Lake, (Sask.) 32 E1
Nipigon Bay, (Ont.) 27 F3
Nipigon, Lake, (Ont.) 27 E2
Nipigon River, (Ont.) 27 E2
Nipi, Lac, (Que.) 14 F1
Nipin Lake, (Sask.) 32 A1
Nipin River, (Sask.) 32 A1
Nipi, Rivière, (Que.) 14 G1
Nipishish Lake, (Nfld.) 6 F3
Nipisi Lake, (Alta.) 44 A4
Nipisi River, (Alta.) 44 A4
Nipissing, Lake, (Ont.) 25 H1
Nipissing River, (Ont.) 24 C1
Nipissis, Lac, (Que.) 19 F2
Nipissis, Rivière, (Que.) 19 F2
Nipisso, Lac, (Que.) 19 F2
Nipisso, Rivière, (Que.) 19 F2
Nipple, The (mountain), (BC) 35 B2
Niska Lake, (Sask.) 32 B1
Niskibi River, (Ont.) 30 F1
Niskonlith Lake, (BC) 36 G4
Nisling River, (YT) 45 A3
Nistowiak Lake, (Sask.) 32 F1
Nisutlin River, (YT) 45 B3
Niteal Creek, (BC) 43 E1
Nith River, (Ont.) 22 F1
Nitinat Lake, (BC) 38 C3
Nitinat River, (BC) 38 C3
Niven River, (BC) 42 F2
Noaxe Creek, (BC) 37 G2
Nodales Channel, (BC) 37 B3
Noddy Island, (NS) 10 B4
Nodier, Lac, (Que.) 18 B2
Noeick River, (BC) 41 G3
Noel Bay, (NS) 9 B2
Noel Creek, (BC) 37 G2
Noel Lake, (NS) 9 B2
Noel Paul's Brook, (Nfld.) 4 F2
Noggin Cove, (Nfld.) 3 E2
Noice Peninsula, (NWT) 47 D2
Noirclair, Lac, (Que.) 5 D3
Noire, Rivière, (Que.) 14 D4
Noire, Rivière, (Que.) 15 C3
Noire, Rivière, (Que.) 16 B3
Noire, Rivière, (Que.) 18 C4
Noir, Lac, (Que.) 13 B3
Noisy River, (Ont.) 23 E2
Nokomis Lake, (Sask.) 44 F4
Noman Lake, (NWT) 44 D1
Nominingue, Lac, (Que.) 18 E4
Nonacho Lake, (NWT) 44 D1
Nonias Lake, (NS) 10 B3
Nonne, Lac la, (Alta.) 33 D3
Noomut River, (NWT) 44 H1
Noonan Stream, (NB) 11 D1
Nootka Island, (BC) 39 E3
Nootka Sound, (BC) 39 E4
Nopiming Provincial Park, (Man.) 30 C4
Nora Lake, (Man.) 28 E1
Norbert River, (Sask.) 44 E4
Norcan Lake, (Ont.) 24 H2
Nordbye Lake, (Sask.) 44 F3
Nord, Chenal du, (Que.) 14 D4
Nordegg River, (Alta.) 33 B4
Nordenskiöld Islands, (NWT) 45 G1
Nordenskiold River, (YT) 45 B3
Nord-Est, Lac du, (Que.) 19 E2
Nord-Ouest, Bassin du, (Que.) 13 H2
Nord-Ouest, Pointe, (Que.) 13 H1
Nord, Rivière du, (Que.) 17 G1
Norfolk Inlet, (NWT) 47 E2
Norman, Cape, (Nfld.) 5 H1
Normandin, Rivière, (Que.) 20 G4
Normand, Lac, (Que.) 18 G3
Normansland Point, (Ont.) 20 D3
Norris Arm, (Nfld.) 3 C3
Norrish Creek, (BC) 38 H2
Norris Lake, (Man.) 30 B2
Norsemans Pond, (Nfld.) 2 E1
North Arm, (Nfld.) 5 F4
North Arm, (Ont.) 27 C1
North Arm, (BC) 38 F2
North Arm, (NWT) 44 B1
North Arm, (NWT) 47 F4
North Aspy River, (NS) 8 E1
North Aulatsivik Island, (Nfld.) 46 G3
North Barrière Lake, (BC) 36 F3
North Bay, (Nfld.) 2 C2
North Bay, (Nfld.) 4 C3
North Bay, (Ont.) 22 B4
North Bay, (NWT) 46 F3
North Bay Ingonish, (NS) 8 E2
North Bentinck Arm, (BC) 41 F3
North Bill (point), (Nfld.) 3 B1
North Bill (point), (Nfld.) 3 F2
North Blue River, (BC) 36 G1
North Branch Big Sevogle River, (NB) 12 D2
North Branch Gulquac River, (NB) 12 B2
North Branch Lake, (NS) 9 F2
North Branch Muskoka River, (Ont.) 24 B2
North Branch Renous River, (NB) 12 D3
North Branch Southwest Miramichi River, (NB) 12 B3
North Branch Tomogonops River, (NB) 12 E2
North Broughton Island, (BC) 39 E1
North Buck Lake, (Alta.) 33 E2
North Cape, (PEI) 7 B1
North, Cape, (NS) 8 E1
North Caribou Lake, (Ont.) 30 F3
North Castor River, (Ont.) 17 E4
North Channel, (Ont.) 21 G1
North Channel, (Ont.) 25 A2
North Channel, (Ont.) 30 G3
North Driftwood River, (Ont.) 26 E1
North Duck River, (Man.) 29 E1
Northeast Arm, (Nfld.) 2 B2
Northeast Arm, (Nfld.) 3 F4
Northeast Arm, (Nfld.) 4 C4
Northeast Arm, (Nfld.) 4 F4
Northeast Arm, (NB) 11 E1
Northeast Arm, (Ont.) 26 F3
Northeast Arm, (BC) 34 A2
Northeast Bay, (Ont.) 26 F1
North East Brook, (Nfld.) 2 C2
Northeast Margaree River, (NS) 8 D2
Northeast Point, (Nfld.) 5 H1
Northeast Point, (NS) 8 F1
Northeast Point, (Ont.) 25 D3
Northeast River, (Nfld.) 2 F3
North End (point), (Nfld.) 3 E1
Norther Head, (Nfld.) 2 E4
Northern Arm, (Nfld.) 3 C2
Northern Arm, (Nfld.) 4 G4
Northern Arm Brook, (Nfld.) 3 B3
Northern Head, (NS) 8 F3
Northern Head, (NB) 11 C4
Northern Indian Lake, (Man.) 46 A4
Northern Light Lake, (Ont.) 27 C3
Northern Peninsula, (Ont.) 28 F2
Norther Point, (Nfld.) 3 G4
North Etomami River, (Man.) 30 C3
North French River, (Ont.) 20 D4
North Great Rattling Brook, (Nfld.) 3 B4
North Harbour, (Nfld.) 2 E2
North Harbour, (Nfld.) 2 F3
North Harbour, (NS) 8 E1
North Harbour Point, (Nfld.) 2 F3
North Head, (Nfld.) 2 H2
North Head, (Nfld.) 3 C2
North Head, (Nfld.) 3 G4
North Head, (Nfld.) 6 H3
North Henik Lake, (NWT) 44 H1
North Island, (Ont.) 28 F3
North Kent Island, (NWT) 47 E2
North Knife Lake, (Man.) 46 A4
North Knife River, (Man.) 46 A3
North Lake, (Nfld.) 4 D2
North Lake, (NB) 11 A1
North Lake, (Ont.) 27 C3
North Limestone Island, (Ont.) 25 F3
North Little River Lake, (NB) 12 D2
North Macmillan River, (YT) 45 B3
North Milk River, (Alta.) 34 F4
North Moose Lake, (Man.) 30 B2
North Mountain, (NS) 8 D4
North Mountain, (NS) 10 C1
North Muskego River, (Ont.) 26 D1
North Nahanni River, (NWT) 45 D3
North Pender Island, (BC) 38 F3
North Penetangore River, (Ont.) 23 B2
North Peninsula, (Ont.) 27 E1
North Pine River, (Man.) 29 E1
North Point, (NS) 10 A2
North Point, (Ont.) 20 D3
North Pole Stream, (NB) 12 C2
North Pond, (Nfld.) 3 D3
North Pond, (Nfld.) 3 F2
North Ram River, (Alta.) 34 C1
North Renous Lake, (NB) 12 C2
North River, (Nfld.) 6 E1
North River, (Nfld.) 6 G3
North River, (NS) 8 E3
North River, (NS) 9 C2
North River, (NB) 11 F1
North River, (Ont.) 24 B3
North Rock, (NB) 11 B4
North Sailing Lake, (Man.) 28 D1
North Salmon River, (Nfld.) 4 G2
North Samson Island, (Nfld.) 3 D2
North Saskatchewan River, (Sask./Alta.) 33 D3
North Saugeen River, (Ont.) 23 C2
North Scot Lake, (Ont.) 28 E1
North Seal River, (Man.) 46 A3
North Shoal Lake, (Man.) 29 H3
North Spicer Island, (NWT) 46 E1
North Spirit Lake, (Ont.) 30 E3
North Stag Islands, (Nfld.) 6 G3
North Star Mountain, (BC) 40 E2
North Steady Pond, (Nfld.) 2 B1
North Sydenham River, (Ont.) 22 B2
North Tea Lake, (Ont.) 24 C1
North Thames River, (Ont.) 22 E1
North Thompson River, (BC) 36 F3
North Twillingate Island, (Nfld.) 3 D1
North Twin Island, (NWT) 20 D2
North Twin Lake, (Nfld.) 3 B2
Northumberland Strait, (NS) 9 C1
North Wabasca Lake, (Alta.) 44 B4
North Washagami Lake, (Ont.) 20 B1

North Washagami River, (Ont.) 20 B2
Northwest Arm, (Nfld.) 3 E3
Northwest Arm, (Nfld.) 3 F4
Northwest Arm, (Nfld.) 4 F4
North West Arm, (NS) 8 E3
Northwest Arm, (BC) 42 G3
Northwest Bay, (Ont.) 26 F1
Northwest Bay, (Ont.) 28 H4
Northwest Bay, (BC) 38 D2
Northwest Brook, (Nfld.) 2 G4
Northwest Brook, (Nfld.) 3 E3
Northwest Brook, (Nfld.) 4 C3
Northwest Brook, (Nfld.) 4 B4
Northwest Burnt Island, (Ont.) 25 D2
Northwest, Cape, (NWT) 47 D1
Northwest (First) Pond, (Nfld.) 3 F3
Northwest Gander River, (Nfld.) 3 C4
Northwest Head, (Nfld.) 2 A3
Northwest Island, (Nfld.) 4 E4
Northwest Millstream, (NB) 12 E2
Northwest Miramichi River, (NB) 12 D2
Northwest Pond, (Nfld.) 3 F4
Northwest River, (Nfld.) 3 D4
Northwest Upsalquitch River, (NB) 12 C1
North Wind Lake, (Ont.) 27 F1
Norton, Cape, (NWT) 45 H1
Norton Shaw, Cape, (NWT) 47 F2
Norvégienne, Baie
see Norwegian Bay
Norway Bay, (NWT) 47 C4
Norway Island, (NWT) 47 A3
Norway Lake, (Ont.) 17 A1
Norwegian Bay, (NWT) 47 E2
Nosbonsing, Lake, (Ont.) 26 G4
Nose Creek, (Alta.) 40 F1
Nose Hill, (Alta.) 34 H1
Nose Lake, (NWT) 45 F2
Nostetuko River, (BC) 37 D1
Notakwanon River, (Nfld.) 6 E2
Notawassi, Lac, (Que.) 18 E3
Notigi Lake, (Man.) 30 B1
Notikewin River, (Alta.) 43 G2
Notre Dame Bay, (Nfld.) 3 C1
Notre-Dame, Les *(mountains)*, (Que.) 13 D3
Notre-Dame, Ruisseau, (Que.) 17 H3
Nottawasaga Bay, (Ont.) 23 E1
Nottawasaga River, (Ont.) 23 F2
Nottaway, Rivière, (Que.) 20 E4
Nottingham Island, (NWT) 46 E2
Notukeu Creek, (Sask.) 31 E3
Nouël, Lac, (Que.) 19 G2
Noueux, Ruisseau, (Que.) 17 E3
Nouveau, Lac, (Que.) 6 B3
Nouveau-Québec, Cratère du, (Que.) 46 F3
Nouvel, Lacs, (Que.) 19 C3
Nouvelle-France, Cap de, (Que.) 46 F3
Nouvelle, Rivière, (Que.) 13 D3
Nouvelle-Zemble, Ile
see Nova Zembla Island
Nova Zembla Island, (NWT) 47 G4
Novereau, Lac, (Que.) 6 B2
Nowashe Creek, (Ont.) 20 C2
Nowashe Lake, (Ont.) 20 C2
Nowell Channel, (BC) 39 E1
Nowleye Lake, (NWT) 44 G1
Nowyak Lake, (NWT) 44 H1
Noyrot, Lac, (Que.) 5 E2
Nuchatlitz Inlet, (BC) 39 E3
Nude Creek, (BC) 37 C1
Nudlung Fiord, (NWT) 46 F1
Nue de Mingan, Ile, (Que.) 19 H3
Nueltin Lake, (Man./NWT) 44 G2
Nulki Lake, (BC) 40 B2
Nulluaiuk, Lac, (Que.) 6 B1
Nuluarniavik, Lac, (Que.) 46 E4
Numabin Bay, (Sask.) 44 F4
Numao Lake, (Man.) 28 D1
Numas Islands, (BC) 39 D1
Nunaksaluk Island, (Nfld.) 6 F2
Nungesser Lake, (Ont.) 30 D4
Nunim Lake, (Sask.) 44 F2
Nunn Lake, (Sask.) 32 F1
Nutarawit Lake, (NWT) 46 A2
Nut Island, (Ont.) 21 H1
Nut Lake, (Sask.) 29 B1
Nuvuk Islands, (NWT) 46 E3
Nyanza Bay, (NS) 8 D3
Nyarling River, (NWT) 44 B2
Nyel, Lac, (Que.) 5 C2
Nym Lake, (Ont.) 27 B3

O

Oak Bay, (NB) 11 B3
Oak Island, (NS) 9 C1
Oak Island, (NS) 10 E2
Oak Lake, (Ont.) 24 E4
Oak Lake, (Man.) 28 C2
Oak Lake, (Man.) 29 E4
Oak Lake, (Ont.) 30 D4
Oakland Lake, (NS) 10 B2
Oak Park Lake, (NS) 10 B4
Oak River, (Man.) 29 E3
Oakville Creek, (Ont.) 21 A3
Obabika Lake, (Ont.) 26 F3
Obabikon Lake, (Ont.) 28 G3
Obakamiga Lake, (Ont.) 26 A1
Oba Lake, (Ont.) 26 B1
Obalski, Lac, (Que.) 26 H1
Obamsca, Lac, (Que.) 20 E4
Obamsca, Rivière, (Que.) 20 E4
Oba River, (Ont.) 26 B1
Obatanga Provincial Park, (Ont.) 26 A2
Obatogamau, Lac, (Que.) 20 G4
Obatogamau, Rivière, (Que.) 20 G4
Obonga Lake, (Ont.) 27 E1
Obre Lake, (NWT) 44 F2
O'Brien Lake, (Nfld.) 3 D3
Observatory Inlet, (BC) 42 D3
Obstruction Island, (BC) 39 F4
Ocean Lake, (NS) 9 F2
Ocean Pond, (Nfld.) 2 D1
Ocean Pond, (Nfld.) 2 G3
Ocean Pond, (Nfld.) 3 E2
Ocean Pond, (Nfld.) 3 F4
Ochak Lake, (Sask.) 44 F2
Ochre River, (Man.) 29 F2
O'Connell Lake, (BC) 39 C2
O'Connor Lake, (NWT) 44 C1
Octave, Rivière, (Que.) 26 H1
Odei River, (Man.) 30 C1
O'Dell Lake, (Ont.) 28 F3
Odell River, (NB) 12 B3
Oderin Island, (Nfld.) 2 D3
Odessa Lake, (Ont.) 21 H1
Odin Lake, (NWT) 44 E2
Odin, Mount, (BC) 35 H1
O'Donnell Point, (Ont.) 25 G4
Oeufs, Lac des, (Que.) 20 G1
Offer Gooseberry Island, (Nfld.) 3 F3
Offer Wadham Island, (Nfld.) 3 F1
Off Lake, (Ont.) 28 G4
Oftedal Lake, (NWT) 44 H1
Ogascanane, Lac, (Que.) 18 B3
Ogden Bay, (NWT) 45 G1
Ogden Channel, (BC) 41 C1
Ogden Point, (Ont.) 21 E2
Ogilvie Mountains, (YT) 45 A2
Ogilvie River, (YT) 45 A2
Ogle Point, (NWT) 45 H1
Ogoki Lake, (Ont.) 30 G4
Ogoki Reservoir, (Ont.) 30 G4
Ogoki River, (Ont.) 30 H4
Ohio River, (NS) 8 B4
Ohio River, (NS) 10 D2
Oies, Cap aux, (Que.) 15 D1
Oies, Ile aux, (Que.) 15 C2
Oiseau Point, (Ont.) 27 H3
Oiseau River, (Man./Ont.) 30 C4
Oiseaux, Rochers aux, (Que.) 7 H1
Ojibway Provincial Park, (Ont.) 27 B1
Okak Bay, (Nfld.) 6 E1
Okak Islands, (Nfld.) 6 E1
Okanagan Lake, (BC) 35 E3
Okanagan Mountain Provincial Park, (BC) 35 E3
Okanagan Range, (BC) 35 D4
Okanagan River, (BC) 35 F4
Okaopéo, Lac, (Que.) 19 C3
Okawakenda Lake, (Ont.) 26 E2
Oke Lake, (Ont.) 26 D1
Okemasis Lake, (Sask.) 32 D4
Okeover Inlet, (BC) 37 C4
Okikendawt Island, (Ont.) 25 G2
Okikodosik Bay, (Ont.) 26 F1
Okipwatsikew Lake, (Sask.) 32 G1
Okisollo Channel, (BC) 37 B3
Okoa Bay, (NWT) 46 F1
Oktwanch River, (BC) 39 F3
Old Crow River, (YT) 45 B1
Old Factory Bay, (NWT) 20 E3
Old Fort Bay, (Alta.) 44 C3
Old Fort River, (Alta.) 44 C3
Oldman Creek, (Alta.) 33 A3
Oldman Lake, (Alta.) 33 D3
Oldman Lake, (Sask.) 44 D2
Oldman River, (Alta.) 34 F3
Oldman River, (Sask.) 44 D2
Old Mans Pond, (Nfld.) 4 D1
Old Settler, The *(mountain)*, (BC) 35 A3
Old Sow Point, (Nfld.) 2 G2
Old Tabusintac Gully, (NB) 12 G2
Old Tracadie Gully, (NB) 12 G1
Old Wives Lake, (Sask.) 31 F3
O'Leary Lake, (Sask.) 32 H2
Olga, Lac, (Que.) 20 E4
Oliver Creek, (BC) 36 H2
Oliver Lake, (Sask.) 44 F4
Oliver Sound, (NWT) 47 F4
Olomane Ouest, Rivière, (Que.) 5 C2
Olomane, Rivière, (Que.) 5 C2
Oman Lake, (NWT) 44 F1
Oman Lake, (Sask.) 44 E2
Omarolluk Sound, (NWT) 20 E1
Ombabika Bay, (Ont.) 27 F1
Ombrette, Rivière l', (Que.) 15 C2
Omineca Mountains, (BC) 42 G1
Omineca River, (BC) 43 A3
Ominuk, Lac, (Que.) 20 D1
Ommanney Bay, (NWT) 47 D3
Onamakawash Lake, (Ont.) 27 D1
Onaman Lake, (Ont.) 27 F1
Onaman River, (Ont.) 27 F1
Onaping Lake, (Ont.) 26 D3
Onaping River, (Ont.) 26 E3
Onatchiway, Lac, (Que.) 14 B1
Onion Lake, (Ont.) 27 E3
Onistagane, Lac, (Que.) 19 A2
Ontaratue River, (NWT) 45 C2
Ontario, Lake, (Ont.) 21 E2
Ootsa Lake, (BC) 41 G1
Opachuanau Lake, (Man.) 44 H4
Opakopa Lake, (Ont.) 30 E3
Opapimiskan Lake, (Ont.) 30 F3
Opasatica, Lac, (Que.) 26 G2
Opasatika Lake, (Ont.) 26 C1
Opasatika River, (Ont.) 20 C4
Opasquia Lake, (Ont.) 30 D3
Opataca, Lac, (Que.) 20 G4
Opataouaga, Lac, (Que.) 20 F4
Opawica, Lac, (Que.) 20 F4
Opawica, Rivière, (Que.) 20 F4
Opeepeesway Lake, (Ont.) 26 D2
Opémisca, Lac, (Que.) 20 F4
Open Bay, (Nfld.) 6 H3
Opeongo Lake, (Ont.) 24 D1
Opescal Lake, (NWT/Sask.) 44 E2
Opichuan River, (Ont.) 30 G4
Opikeigen Lake, (Ont.) 30 G4
Opikinimika Lake, (Ont.) 26 E3
Opiminegoka Lake, (Man.) 30 C2
Opinaca, Lac, (Que.) 20 F3
Opinaca, Rivière, (Que.) 20 F2
Opingiviksuak Island, (Nfld.) 6 E1
Opinicon Lake, (Ont.) 17 B3
Opinnagau Lake, (Ont.) 20 B2
Opinnagau River, (Ont.) 20 C2
Opiscotéo, Lac, (Que.) 6 C4
Opiscotiche, Lac, (Que.) 6 C4
Opitoune, Lac, (Que.) 19 B2
Opocopa, Lac, (Que.) 6 C4
Opposite Island, (NWT) 46 D2
Oppy Lake, (BC) 41 G2
Opuntia Lake, (Sask.) 31 D1
Opuskiamishes River, (Sask./Man.) 30 E1
Or, Cape d', (NS) 11 G3
Orchard Point, (BC) 39 C2
O'Reilly Island, (NWT) 45 G1
Orford River, (BC) 37 C2
Orient, Pointe, (Que.) 14 F2
Orignal, Baie à l', (Que.) 18 B3
Orignaux, Rivière aux, (Que.) 16 D1
Orléans Ile d', (Que.) 15 B3
Orloff Lake, (Alta.) 33 E1
Ormonde Island, (NWT) 46 D1
Oromocto Island, (NB) 11 C1
Oromocto Lake, (NB) 11 B2
Oromocto River, (NB) 11 C2
Orpheus Lake, (NWT) 44 E2
Orr Lake, (Ont.) 23 F1
Orr Lake, (Man.) 30 C1
Orsogna, Lac, (Que.) 5 E2
Ortona, Lac, (Que.) 5 E2
Orton Island, (Nfld.) 6 F1
Orwell Bay, (PEI) 7 D4
Osawin River, (Ont.) 27 H2
Osborn, Cape, (NWT) 47 E3
Osborn River, (Alta./BC) 43 F2
Oscar Peak, (BC) 42 D4
Osgoode, Rivière, (Que.) 16 E2
Oshinow Lake, (BC) 39 H4
Osilinka River, (BC) 43 B3
Oskélanéo, Lac, (Que.) 18 E2
Osmonton Arm, (Nfld.) 3 C2
Osnaburgh Lake, (Ont.) 30 F4
Osoyoos Lake, (BC) 35 F4
Ospika River, (BC) 43 B2
Ospry Lake, (Ont.) 23 C1
Ospwagan Lake, (Man.) 30 B1
Ossant, Lac, (Que.) 20 G1
Ossokmanuan Lake, (Nfld.) 6 D3
Ostaboningue, Lac, (Que.) 26 G3
Osten Lake, (Sask.) 32 D2
O'Sullivan, Lac, (Que.) 18 D2
O'Sullivan Lake, (Ont.) 27 G1
O'Sullivan, Rivière, (Que.) 18 D1
Oswald Lake, (Ont.) 26 D2
Oswald Lake, (NWT) 44 D4
Oswego Creek, (Ont.) 21 A4
Otakus Lake, (Ont.) 28 G2
Otasawian River, (Ont.) 20 B4
Otauwau River, (Alta.) 33 C1
Otelnuc, Lac, (Que.) 6 C2
Otherside River, (Sask.) 44 D3
Otish, Monts, (Que.) 6 A4
Otis, Lac, (Que.) 14 C3
Otnabog Lake, (NB) 11 D2
Otonabee River, (Ont.) 21 D1
Otoskwin River, (Ont.) 30 F4
Ottarasko Creek, (BC) 37 C1
Ottarasko Mountain, (BC) 37 C1
Ottawa Int Airport/Aéroport, (Ont.) 17 E4
Ottawa Islands, (NWT) 46 D4
Ottawa River, (Ont.) 17 A1
see also Outaouais, Rivière des (Que.)
Otter Bay, (Nfld.) 4 B4
Otter Creek, (Sask.) 32 C3
Otter Creek, (BC) 35 C3
Otter Island, (Nfld.) 3 B1
Otter Island, (Ont.) 27 G3
Otter Lake, (Nfld.) 6 F3
Otter Lake, (Ont.) 17 B3
Otter Lake, (Man.) 29 H2
Otter Lake, (Man.) 29 F3
Otter Lake, (Sask.) 32 C3
Otter Lake, (Sask.) 32 E1
Otter Lake, (Alta.) 33 D1
Otter Lake, (BC) 35 C3
Otter Lake, (NWT) 44 H1
Otter Point, (BC) 38 E4
Otter Pond, (Nfld.) 2 D1
Otter River, (Ont.) 30 F2
Otterskin Lake, (Ont.) 28 H3
Ottertail Lake, (Ont.) 28 H3
Ottertail River, (Ont.) 27 F1
Otto Fiord, (NWT) 47 E1
Otty Lake, (Ont.) 17 B3
Otukamamoan Lake, (Ont.) 27 A2
Ouagama, Lac, (Que.) 20 E4
Ouasiemsca, Rivière, (Que.) 20 H4
Ouelle, Rivière, (Que.) 15 D2
Ouescapis, Lac, (Que.) 20 E4
Ouest, Pointe de l', (Que.) 13 G3
Ouest, Pointe de l', (Que.) 19 G3
Oulton Lake, (NWT) 44 C2
Ououkinsh Inlet, (BC) 39 D2
Ours, Lac à l', (Que.) 5 A3
Ours, Rivière aux, (Que.) 14 E2
Ouse River, (Ont.) 21 E1
Outaouais, Rivières des, (Que.) 17 E1
see also Ottawa River (Ont.)
Outardes, Baie aux, (Que.) 14 G1
Outardes Quatre, Réservoir, (Que.) 19 C3
Outardes, Rivière aux, (Que.) 19 D4
Outardes-Trois Barrage/Dam, (Que.) 19 C4
Outer Bald Tusket Island, (NS) 10 A4
Outer Cat Island, (Nfld.) 3 F2
Outer Duck Island, (Ont.) 25 A3
Outer Island, (NS) 10 B4
Outer Wood Island, (NB) 11 C4
Outlet Bay, (NWT) 45 H2
Outram, Mount, (BC) 35 B4
Ovens Point, (NS) 9 A4
Overby Lake, (Man.) 44 H2
Overflow Bay, (Man.) 30 A3
Overflowing River, (Man./Sask.) 32 H3
Overlord Mountain, (BC) 37 G4
Owen Channel, (Ont.) 25 C3
Owen Lake, (BC) 36 A1
Owen Sound, (Ont.) 23 C1
Owikeno Lake, (BC) 41 G4
Owl Lake, (Ont.) 27 G2
Owl River, (Alta.) 33 F1
Owl River, (Man.) 46 B4
Oxford Lake, (Man.) 30 C2
Oxtongue River, (Ont.) 24 C2
Oyama Lake, (BC) 35 F2
Oyster Bay, (BC) 39 H3
Oyster River, (BC) 39 H3
Ozhiski Lake, (Ont.) 30 G3

P

Paces Lake, (NS) 9 C3
Pachena Bay, (BC) 38 B3
Pachena Point, (BC) 38 B3
Pachena River, (BC) 38 B3
Pacific Ocean 1
see also Pacifique, Océan
Pacific Ranges, (BC) 37 D2
Pacific Rim National Park, (BC) 38 B3
see also Pacific Rim, Parc national de
Pacific Rim, Parc national de, (BC) 38 C4
see also Pacific Rim National Park
Pacifique, Océan 1
see also Pacific Ocean
Pacquet Brook, (Nfld.) 3 B1
Pacquet Harbour, (Nfld.) 3 B1
Paddle River, (Alta.) 33 C3
Paddling Lake, (Sask.) 32 C4
Padille Pond, (Nfld.) 4 D2
Padle Fiord, (NWT) 46 G1
Padliak Inlet, (NWT) 45 G1
Padliak Inlet, (NWT) 47 C4
Padloping Island, (NWT) 46 G1
Pagashi River, (Ont.) 20 B3
Pagato Lake, (Sask.) 44 G4
Pagato River, (Sask.) 44 G4
Pagoda Peak, (BC) 37 C1
Paguchi Lake, (Ont.) 27 B2
Pagwachuan Lake, (Ont.) 27 H2
Pagwachuan River, (Ont.) 27 H2
Paimpont, Lac, (Que.) 5 C3
Painteарth Creek, (Alta.) 33 F4
Painted Rock Island, (Ont.) 28 F3
Paint Lake, (Man.) 30 C1
Paix, Rivière de la
see Peace River
Pakashkan Lake, (Ont.) 27 D2
Pakeshkag River, (Ont.) 25 F2
Pakowki Lake, (Alta.) 31 A4
Pakwa Lake, (Man.) 30 B2
Pakwash Lake, (Ont.) 30 D4
Palairet, Lac, (Que.) 19 A2
Palfrey Lake, (NB) 11 A2
Palliser River, (BC) 34 D3
Palmer, Rivière, (Que.) 16 E2
Palmerston, Cape, (BC) 39 B1
Palmerston, Cape, (NWT) 47 D4
Palmerston Lake, (Ont.) 24 H3
Palmerston, Mount, (BC) 39 F2
Pamburn, Lac, (Que.) 19 B1
Pamemen, Lac, (Que.) 20 G2
Pamialic Bay, (Nfld.) 6 G3
Pamigamachi, Lac, (Que.) 20 E2
Panache, Lake, (Ont.) 25 D1
Panache, Rivière au, (Que.) 18 D1
Pancake Bay, (Ont.) 26 A3
Panchia Lake, (Nfld.) 6 D4
Pandora Island, (NWT) 47 D4
Pandora Peak, (BC) 38 C4
Pangnikto Lake, (NWT) 46 C1
Pangnirtung Fiord, (NWT) 46 G1
Panmure Island, (PEI) 7 E4
Panny River, (Alta.) 44 B3
Panorama Lake, (Ont.) 28 G3
Pantage Lake, (BC) 40 C2
Panuke Lake, (NS) 10 F1
Papikwan River, (Sask.) 32 G3
Papinachois, Rivière de, (Que.) 14 F1
Papineau, Lac, (Que.) 18 E4
Papineau Lake, (Ont.) 24 E2
Paquet Bay, (NWT) 47 F4
Paquin Lake, (Sask.) 32 D2
Paradise Brook, (NS) 10 C1
Paradise Lake, (NS) 10 C1
Paradise Lake, (BC) 35 D2
Paradise River, (Nfld.) 2 D2
Paradise River, (Nfld.) 6 G4
Paradise Sound, (Nfld.) 2 D3
Paradis, Lac, (Que.) 14 E3
Paradis, Lac, (Que.) 19 C2
Paragon Lake, (Man.) 44 H3
Parallel Creek, (Alta.) 33 E1
Paramé, Lac, (Que.) 5 F2
Parent, Lac, (Que.) 18 C1
Parisienne, Ile, (Ont.) 26 A4
Parker, Cape, (NWT) 47 F3
Parker Island, (BC) 38 F3
Parker Lake, (Sask.) 32 B1
Parker Lake, (NWT) 46 B2
Parkhill Creek, (Ont.) 22 D1
Parkins, Cape, (BC) 39 C2
Park Lake, (Sask.) 32 F1
Park Mountain, (BC) 35 G1
Park Rill *(creek)*, (BC) 35 E4
Parks Creek, (Ont.) 21 F1
Parks Lake, (Ont.) 27 F2
Parr Lake, (NS) 10 B3
Parrott Lakes, (BC) 41 G1
Parry Bay, (NWT) 45 F1
Parry Bay, (NWT) 46 D1
Parry, Cape, (NWT) 45 D1
Parry Falls, (NWT) 45 F3
Parry Island, (Ont.) 25 G3
Parry Islands, (NWT) 47 C2
Parry Passage, (BC) 41 A1
Parry Peninsula, (NWT) 45 D1
Parry, Port, (NWT) 45 G1
Parry Sound, (Ont.) 25 G3
Parsnip River, (BC) 40 D1
Parson Bay, (BC) 39 E1
Parsons Creek, (BC) 38 C3
Parsons Pond, (Nfld.) 3 E4
Parsons Pond, (Nfld.) 5 F3
Partridge Bay, (Nfld.) 6 H3
Partridge Breast Lake, (Man.) 44 H3
Partridge Creek, (Ont.) 24 F3
Partridge Island, (Ont.) 30 G1
Partridge Point, (Nfld.) 5 H3
Partridge River, (Ont.) 20 D3
Pasayten River, (BC) 35 D4
Pascagama, Lac, (Que.) 18 D1
Pascagama, Rivière, (Que.) 18 E1
Pascalis, Lac, (Que.) 18 C2
Pas d'Eau, Lac, (Nfld.) 6 D4
Pasfield Lake, (Sask.) 44 E3
Pashkokogan Lake, (Ont.) 30 F4
Paska Lake, (BC) 35 C1
Paskwachi Bay, (Man./Sask.) 44 G3
Pasley Bay, (NWT) 47 D4
Paspébiac, Baie de, (Que.) 13 F4
Paspébiac, Pointe de, (Que.) 13 F4
Pas Perdus, Lac des, (Que.) 14 B4
Pasquatchai River, (Man./Ont.) 30 E2
Pasquia Hills, (Sask.) 32 G3
Pasquia River, (Sask./Man.) 32 H3
Passage Point, (Nfld.) 2 B2
Passamaquoddy Bay, (NB) 11 B3
Passe, La *(channel)*, (Que.) 7 F1
Pastecho River, (Alta.) 33 D1
Pasteur, Lac, (Que.) 19 E3
Patamisk, Lac, (Que.) 6 A4
Patamisk, Lac, (Que.) 20 H2
Patapédia River, (NB) 13 A4
see also Patapédia, Rivière (Que.)
Patapédia , Rivière, (Que.) 13 A4
see also Patapédia River (NB)
Patchepawapoka River, (Ont.) 20 C2
Pat Creek, (BC) 36 H2
Patewagia, Ruisseau, (Que.) 13 G2
Patience Lake, (Sask.) 31 F1
Patrick Point, (Ont.) 22 D2
Patricks Pond, (Nfld.) 4 G1
Patten River, (Ont.) 26 F1
Patterson Island, (Ont.) 27 G3
Patterson Lake, (Ont.) 17 A2
Patterson Lake, (Ont.) 25 G2
Patterson Lake, (BC) 39 G2
Patterson Lake, (Sask.) 44 D3
Patterson Lake, (Sask.) 44 F2
Pattullo, Mount, (BC) 42 D2
Patukami, Lac, (Que.) 20 F2
Paudash Lake, (Ont.) 24 E3
Paugh Lake, (Ont.) 24 F1
Paul Creek, (BC) 35 D4
Paul Island, (Nfld.) 6 F2
Paul, Lac à, (Que.) 19 A3
Paul Lake, (BC) 36 F4
Paull Lake, (Sask.) 44 F4
Paull River, (Sask.) 44 F4
Paul River, (BC) 43 A2
Pauls Lake, (Nfld.) 3 A3
Pauls Pond, (Nfld.) 3 C4
Pavilion Lake, (BC) 36 C4
Payne Bay, (NWT) 46 F3
Payne, Lac, (Que.) 46 E4
Payne River, (Ont.) 17 D2
Paypeeshek River, (Ont.) 26 C1
Peace River, (Alta./BC) 43 H2
Peachland Creek, (BC) 35 E3
Peacock Point, (Ont.) 22 H2
Pearce Point, (NWT) 45 D1
Pearkes, Mount, (BC) 37 E4
Pearl (Big) Island, (Nfld.) 5 F4
Pearl (Green) Island, (NS) 10 F2
Pearse Island, (BC) 42 C4
Pearse Islands, (BC) 39 E1
Pearse Peninsula, (BC) 39 E1
Pearson Creek, (BC) 35 G2
Pearson Lake, (Man.) 30 C1
Peary Channel, (NWT) 47 D2
Pease Lake, (Sask.) 32 D2
Peases Island, (NS) 10 B4
Pebble Creek, (BC) 37 F2
Pebble Island, (NWT) 20 D2
Pebonishewi Lake, (Ont.) 26 D2
Peche Island, (Ont.) 22 A3
Pêche, Lac la, (Que.) 17 B1
Pêche, Rivière la, (Que.) 20 E3
Peckford Island, (Nfld.) 3 F2
Peck Lake, (Sask.) 32 A3
Peck Lake, (Sask.) 33 H3
Pecors Lake, (Ont.) 25 B1
Pecten Harbour, (NWT) 46 E3
Pedder Point, (NWT) 47 B2
Peel Inlet, (NWT) 46 B1
Peel Island, (BC) 39 D1
Peel Point, (NWT) 47 B3
Peel River, (YT) 45 B2
Peel Sound, (NWT) 47 D3
Peerless Lake, (Alta.) 44 B4
Pefferlaw Brook, (Ont.) 23 G2
Peggys Point, (NS) 9 A4
Pekagoning Lake, (Ont.) 27 B2
Pékans, Rivière aux, (Que.) 6 C4
Pelee Island, (Ont.) 22 B4
Pelee Passage, (Ont.) 22 B4
Pelee, Point, (Ont.) 22 B4
Pèlerins, Les *(islands)*, (Que.) 14 E4
Pelican Bay, (Man.) 30 A3
Pélican Lac, (Que.) 46 F3
Pelican Lake, (Ont.) 27 B1
Pelican Lake, (Man.) 29 F4
Pelican Lake, (Man.) 30 C2
Pelican Lake, (Man.) 30 A3
Pelican Lake, (Sask.) 31 F3
Pelican Lake, (Sask.) 32 G1
Pelican Lake, (Alta.) 44 B4
Pelicanpouch Lake, (Ont.) 28 E1
Pelican River, (Alta.) 44 B4
Pellatt Lake, (NWT) 45 F2
Pelletier Lake, (Man.) 30 C1
Pell Inlet, (NWT) 47 D3
Pelly Bay, (NWT) 46 C1
Pelly Creek, (BC) 43 A2
Pelly Island, (NWT) 45 B1
Pelly Lake, (BC) 43 A2
Pelly River, (YT) 45 B3
Peltoma Lake, (NB) 11 C2
Pembina River, (Man.) 29 F4
Pembina River, (Alta.) 33 C3
Pembroke, Cape, (NWT) 46 D3
Pembroke Lake, (NS) 8 D2
Pembroke River, (NS) 9 C2
Pemichangan, Lac, (Que.) 18 D4
Pemichigamau Lake, (Man.) 44 H4
Pemmican Point, (NWT) 47 A3
Penassi Lake, (Ont.) 27 C1
Pendleton Lakes, (BC) 36 E2
Pendrell Sound, (BC) 37 C3
Penetang Harbour, (Ont.) 23 E1
Penetangore River, (Ont.) 23 B2
Penguin Islands, (Nfld.) 3 F2
Penguin Islands, (Nfld.) 4 F4
Peninsula Lake, (Ont.) 24 C2
Pen Lake, (Ont.) 24 D2
Pennant Bay, (NS) 10 G2
Pennant Point, (NS) 10 G2
Pennask Lake, (BC) 35 D2
Pennask Mountain, (BC) 35 D2
Pennycutaway River, (Man.) 30 D1
Penny Ice Cap, (NWT) 46 F1
Penny Strait, (NWT) 47 D2
Penrhyn, Cape, (NWT) 46 D1
Pentecôte, Lac, (Que.) 19 E3
Pentecôte, Rivière, (Que.) 19 E3
Penticton Creek, (BC) 35 F3
Penylan Lake, (NWT) 44 E1
Penzance Lake, (NWT) 44 E2
Peonan Creek, (Sask.) 32 E4
Peonan Point, (Man.) 29 G2
Pepaw River, (Sask.) 32 H4
Percé, Rocher, (Que.) 13 H2
Perch Bay, (Man.) 44 G3
Perches, Lac des, (Que.) 14 E2
Perch Lake, (Ont.) 25 C2
Perch Lake, (Ont.) 28 F1
Perch River, (Sask.) 44 F3
Percival Bay, (PEI) 7 A3
Percy Lake, (Ont.) 24 D2
Percy Reach, (Ont.) 21 E1
Perdix, Rivière des, (Que.) 15 C3
Perdrix, Rivière de la, (Que.) 26 G1
Perdu, Lac, (Que.) 19 B2
Péré, Lac, (Que.) 6 B3
Péré, Lac, (Que.) 20 H2
Péribonca, Lac, (Que.) 19 A3
Péribonca, Rivière, (Que.) 14 B1
Péribonca, Rivière, (Que.) 19 A1
Péribonca, Rivière, (Que.) 20 H3
Perrault Lake, (Ont.) 27 A1
Perrot, Ile, (Que.) 17 F4
Perry River, (BC) 34 A2
Perry River, (NWT) 45 G1
Person Lake, (NWT) 44 D1
Pesika Creek, (BC) 43 B2
Peskawa Lake, (NS) 10 C2
Peskowesk Lake, (NS) 10 C2
Petawaga, Lac, (Que.) 18 D3
Petawanga Lake, (Ont.) 30 G4
Petawawa River, (Ont.) 18 B4
Peter Hope Lake, (BC) 35 D1
Peter Lake, (Sask.) 44 F4
Peter Lake, (NWT) 46 B2
Peterlong Lake, (Ont.) 26 E2
Peter Pond Lake, (Sask.) 44 D4
Peter Richards, Cape, (NWT) 47 A3
Peters, Lac, (Que.) 46 F3
Peters Lake, (BC) 35 H1
Peterson Creek, (BC) 36 F3
Peters Point, (NWT) 46 G3
Peters Pond, (Nfld.) 3 C3
Peter's River, (Nfld.) 2 F4
Peters River, (Nfld.) 3 B3
Peter Strides Pond, (Nfld.) 4 D3
Pethei Peninsula, (NWT) 44 C1
Petitcodiac River, (NB) 11 G1
Petit-de-Grat Harbour, (NS) 9 H2
Petit-de-Grat Island, (NS) 9 H2
Petite Nation, Rivière de la, (Que.) 17 D1
Petite rivière Blanche, (Que.) 17 E3
Petite rivière Cascapédia, (Que.) 13 E3
Petite rivière Cascapédia Est, (Que.) 13 E2
Petite rivière Cascapédia Ouest, (Que.) 13 E2
Petite rivière de la Baleine, (Que.) 20 F1
Petite rivière Manicouagan, (Que.) 6 C4
Petite rivière Manouane, (Que.) 19 A3
Petite rivière Matane, (Que.) 13 B2
Petite rivière Nouvelle, (Que.) 13 C3
Petite rivière Port-Daniel, (Que.) 13 F3
Petite rivière Rimouski, (Que.) 14 G3
Petit lac Caotibi, (Que.) 19 E2
Petit lac des Esclaves
see also Lesser Slave Lake
Petit lac des Loups Marins, (Que.) 20 G1
Petit lac du Nord, (Que.) 19 E2
Petit lac Jacques-Cartier, (Que.) 15 A1
Petit lac Joseph, (Nfld.) 6 D4
Petit lac Manicouagan, (Que.) 19 D1
Petit lac Onatchiway, (Que.) 14 B1
Petit lac Opinaca, (Que.) 20 F3
Petit lac Ste-Anne, (Que.) 15 E2
Petit lac Touladi, (Que.) 15 G1
Petit Mécatina, Ile du, (Que.) 5 E3
Petit Mécatina, Rivière du, (Que.) 5 D2
see also Little Mécatina River (Nfld.)
Petitot River, (BC/NWT) 45 D4
Petit Pabos, Rivière du, (Que.) 13 G3
Petit Passage, (NS) 10 A2
Petit-Pré, Rivière du, (Que.) 15 G3
Petit Saguenay, Rivibre, (Que.) 14 D4
Petitsikapau Lake, (Nfld.) 6 C3
Petownikip Lake, (Ont.) 30 E3
Petrel Channel, (BC) 41 D1
Petre, Point, (Ont.) 21 G2
Peuplier, Rivière du, (Que.) 20 E2
Peyton, Mount, (Nfld.) 3 C3
Phantom Lake, (Ont.) 25 H2
Phantom Lake, (BC) 38 E1
Pheasant Hills, (Sask.) 29 B3
Phelan Lake, (Sask.) 32 H1
Phelps Lake, (Sask.) 44 F2
Phililloo Lake, (BC) 36 C2
Philion Lake, (Sask.) 32 D2
Philip Creek, (BC) 43 C4
Philip Edward Island, (Ont.) 25 D2
Philipot, Lac, (Que.) 5 C2
Philippe, Lac, (Que.) 17 C1
Philip, River, (NS) 9 B1
Phillips Arm, (BC) 37 B3
Phillips Bay, (YT) 45 B1
Phillips Brook, (Nfld.) 4 C4
Phillips, Cape, (NWT) 47 D3
Phillips Inlet, (NWT) 47 E1
Phillips Lake, (BC) 37 B3
Phillips Point, (NWT) 47 F3
Phillips River, (BC) 37 B2
Philomène, Baie, (Que.) 18 D3
Philpots Island, (NWT) 47 F3
Phoenix Island, (NS) 9 D3
Phoque, Rivière au, (Que.) 20 E1
Piacouadie, Lac, (Que.) 19 A2
Piacouadie, Lac, (Que.) 20 H3
Piagochioui, Rivière, (Que.) 20 E2
Piashti, Lac, (Que.) 5 A3
Picanoc, Rivière, (Que.) 18 D4
Piccadilly Bay, (Nfld.) 4 B2
Piché Lake, (Alta.) 33 F1
Pichogen River, (Ont.) 26 B1
Pic Island, (Ont.) 27 G3
Pickerel Lake, (Ont.) 24 B1
Pickerel Lake, (Ont.) 27 C3
Pickerel Lake, (Ont.) 28 E2
Pickerel River, (Ont.) 25 F2
Pickle Lake, (Ont.) 30 F4
Pic River, (Ont.) 27 G2
Pictou Harbour, (NS) 9 D1
Pictou Island, (NS) 9 D1
Pie Island, (Ont.) 27 E3
Pierce Lake, (Man./Ont.) 30 E2
Pierce Lake, (Sask.) 32 A2
Pierre Lake, (Ont.) 20 D4
Pierre, Rivière à, (Que.) 18 H3
Pierres Brook, (Nfld.) 2 H3
Pierres, Lac, (Que.) 19 G1
Pierron, Lac, (Que.) 18 F3
Piers Island, (BC) 38 F3
Pigeon Bay, (Ont.) 22 B4
Pigeon Bay, (Man.) 29 H1
Pigeon Head, (Nfld.) 4 B2
Pigeon Island, (Nfld.) 3 E1
Pigeon Lake (Ont.) 24 D4
Pigeon Lake (Ont.) 26 E2
Pigeon Lake (Alta.) 33 D4
Pigeon Point, (Man.) 29 H1
Pigeon River, (Ont.) 21 C1
Pigeon River, (Man.) 30 C3
Pikangikum Lake, (Ont.) 30 D4
Pikauba, Lac, (Que.) 14 B4
Pikauba, Rivière, (Que.) 14 A4
Pike Bay, (Ont.) 23 B1
Pike Lake, (Ont.) 17 B3
Pike Lake Provincial Park, (Sask.) 31 E1
Pike, Mount, (BC) 35 C3
Pikitigushi River, (Ont.) 27 E1
Pikwitonei Lake, (Man.) 30 C1
Piles, Lac des, (Que.) 16 B1
Piling Bay, (NWT) 46 E1
Pillet, Lac, (Que.) 5 D3
Pilley's Island, (Nfld.) 3 B2
Pilley's Tickle, (Nfld.) 3 B2
Pilot Lake, (NWT) 44 C2
Pimainus Creek, (BC) 35 B1
Pim Island, (NWT) 47 F2
Pinacle, Le *(mountain)*, (Que.) 16 B4
Pinaus Lake, (BC) 35 E1
Pinawa Channel, (Man.) 28 C1
Pinchard's Bight, (Nfld.) 3 F2
Pinchards Island, (Nfld.) 3 F2
Pinchgut Lake, (Nfld.) 4 D1
Pinchgut Point, (Nfld.) 2 F2
Pinchi Lake, (BC) 40 B1
Pinder Peak, (BC) 39 E2
Pine, Cape, (Nfld.) 2 G4
Pine Creek, (Man.) 28 C3
Pine Creek, (Man.) 30 C2
Pine Creek, (Alta.) 33 E2
Pinehouse Lake, (Sask.) 32 D1
Pinehurst Lake, (Alta.) 33 F2
Pineimuta River, (Ont.) 30 F3
Pine Lake, (Ont.) 24 G3
Pine Lake, (Alta.) 34 F1
Pine Point, (Ont.) 27 D4
Pine River, (Ont.) 23 A3
Pine River, (Ont.) 23 E2
Pine River, (BC) 43 D4
Pine River, (Sask.) 44 E3
Pinery Provincial Park, (Ont.) 22 C1
Pine Tree Harbour, (Ont.) 25 D4
Pinette Point, (PEI) 7 D4
Pinewood River, (Ont.) 28 G4
Pinger Point, (NWT) 46 D1
Pingston Creek, (BC) 35 H1
Pink River, (Sask.) 44 F4
Pinnacles, The *(Peaks)*, (BC) 35 H2
Pin, Rivière du, (Que.) 16 G1
Pins, Pointe aux, (Ont.) 22 C3
Pins, Rivière aux, (Que.) 15 E3
Pins, Rivière des, (Que.) 16 D2
Pinto Creek, (Sask.) 31 E4
Pinto Creek, (Alta.) 40 F1
Pinto Creek, (Alta.) 40 H2
Pinus Lake (Ont.) 28 G3
Pinware Bay, (Nfld.) 5 G2
Pinware River, (Nfld.) 5 G1
Pipers Cove, (NS) 8 D3
Pipers Hole River, (Nfld.) 2 D1
Pipestem Inlet, (BC) 38 B3
Pipestone Bay, (Ont.) 30 D4
Pipestone Creek, (Man./Sask.) 29 D3
Pipestone Creek, (Alta.) 33 D4
Pipestone Lake, (Ont.) 28 H3
Pipestone Lake, (Man.) 30 C2
Pipestone Lake, (Sask.) 44 E3
Pipestone River, (Ont.) 27 A3
Pipestone River, (Ont.) 30 E3
Pipestone River, (Sask.) 44 E3
Pipichicau, Rivière, (Que.) 19 C1
Pipmuacan, Réservoir, (Que.) 14 B1
Pipmuacan, Réservoir, (Que.) 19 B3
Pipowitan River, (Ont.) 30 G1
Piraube, Lac, (Que.) 19 A2
Pisew Lake, (Sask.) 32 D1
Piskahegan Stream, (NB) 11 C2
Pistol Bay, (NWT) 46 B3
Pistolet Bay, (Nfld.) 5 G1
Pitchimi Lake, (Alta.) 44 B2
Pitmans Pond, (Nfld.) 2 G1
Pitt Island, (BC) 41 D2
Pitt Lake, (BC) 38 G2
Pitt, Mount, (BC) 37 G4
Pitt River, (BC) 38 G1
Pitt Sound Island, (Nfld.) 3 F3
Pitt Sound Reach, (Nfld.) 3 F3
Pitts Pond, (Nfld.) 3 E4
Pitz Lake, (NWT) 46 B2
Pivabiska River, (Ont.) 20 B4
Piwei River, (Sask.) 32 G4
Placentia Bay, (Nfld.) 2 D3
Placentia Sound, (Nfld.) 2 F3
Placer Mountain, (BC) 35 D4
Plain Lake, (Alta.) 33 F3
Plaisance, Baie de
see Placentia Bay
Plaisance, Baie de, (Que.) 7 F1
Planinshek Lake, (Sask.) 32 F1
Plantes, Rivière des, (Que.) 16 F2
Plat, Lac, (Que.) 14 D2
Playgreen Lake, (Man.) 30 B2
Pleasant Bay, (NS) 8 D1
Pledger Lake, (Ont.) 20 B3
Plétipi, Lac, (Que.) 19 B1
Pleureuse Pointe, (Que.) 13 E1
Plonge, Lac la, (Sask.) 32 C1
Plongeon, Lac au, (Que.) 14 D4
Plover Lake, (Alta.) 34 H2
Pluie, Lac de la
see Rainy Lake
Plum Creek, (Man.) 29 E4
Plume, Lacs à la
see Big Quill Lake
Plum Lakes, (Man.) 29 E4
Plumper Islands, (BC) 39 E1
Plumper Sound, (BC) 38 F3
Plum Point, (Ont.) 22 D2
Pocket Knife Lake, (Nfld.) 6 F3
Pockwock Lake, (NS) 10 F1
Pocologan River, (NB) 11 C3
Pogamasing Lake, (Ont.) 26 D3

Pohénégamook, Lac, (Que.) 15 F1
Poilu Lake, (Ont.) 27 G1
Poincaré, Lac, (Que.) 5 F1
Point Atkinson, (BC) 38 F2
Pointe, Lac de la, (Que.) 6 A4
Pointe Pelée, Parc national de la, (Ont.) 22 B4
see also Point Pelee National Park
Pointer Lake, (Sask.) 32 F1
Point Grey, (BC) 38 F2
Point Lake, (NWT) 45 E2
Point Pelee National Park, (Ont.) 22 B4
see also Pointe Pelée, Parc national de la
Point Wolfe River, (NB) 11 F2
Poisson Blanc, Réservoir du, (Que.) 18 D4
Poissons, Rivière aux, (Nfld.) 6 D4
Poivre, Lac au, (Que.) 14 B1
Pokei Lake, (Ont.) 26 A1
Pokemouche Gully, (NB) 12 G1
Pokemouche River, (NB) 12 F1
Pokesudie Island, (NB) 13 G4
Polar Bear Provincial Park, (Ont.) 20 B1
Polette, Lac, (Que.) 14 E3
Pollett River, (NB) 11 F1
Pollock Point, (NS) 10 E3
Polonais, Lac des, (Que.) 18 E3
Polynia Islands, (NWT) 47 C2
Pommerel Lake, (Nfld.) 5 A1
Pommeroy, Lac, (Que.) 26 G3
Pommes, Rivière aux, (Que.) 15 E3
Pomquet Island, (NS) 9 F1
Ponask Lake, (Ont.) 30 E2
Ponask River, (Ont.) 30 E2
Ponass Lakes, (Sask.) 29 B1
Poncheville, Lac, (Que.) 20 F4
Pond Inlet, (NWT) 47 F3
Pondosy Lake, (BC) 41 G2
Ponds, Island of, (Nfld.) 6 H3
Ponhook Lake, (NS) 10 D2
Pons, Rivière, (Que.) 6 B2
Pontapique River, (NS) 9 B2
Pontax, Rivière, (Que.) 20 E3
Pontchartrain, Promontoire, (Que.) 46 E3
Ponton River, (Alta.) 44 A3
Poohbah Lake, (Ont.) 27 B3
Poole Point, (NWT) 46 E1
Pooley Island, (BC) 41 E3
Pool's Harbour, (Nfld.) 3 F3
Poorfish Lake, (NWT) 44 G2
Popes Harbour Pond, (Nfld.) 2 F1
Popham Bay, (Ont.) 21 E2
Popham Bay, (NWT) 46 G2
Popham Point, (Ont.) 25 E2
Poplar Island, (Ont.) 28 F3
Poplar Point, (Man.) 30 C3
Poplar Rapids, (Ont.) 26 D1
Poplar River, (Ont.) 20 B3
Poplar River, (Man.) 30 C3
Poplar River, (NWT) 45 D3
Porcher Island, (BC) 41 C1
Porcupine Bay, (Nfld.) 6 H3
Porcupine, Cape, (Nfld.) 6 G3
Porcupine Hills, (Man./Sask.) 32 H4
Porcupine River, (Sask.) 44 F2
Porcupine River, (YT) 45 A1
Porcus Lake, (Ont.) 28 G2
Porée, Lac, (Que.) 6 B3
Pork Island, (Nfld.) 3 F3
Portage, Baie du, (Que.) 19 A2
Portage Bay, (Ont.) 28 H2
Portage Bay, (Man.) 29 G2
Portage Gully, (NB) 12 G2
Portage Island, (NB) 12 F2
Portage, Lac du, (Que.) 13 A2
Portage, Lac du, (Que.) 16 G2
Portage Lake, (Nfld.) 4 C2
Portage Lake, (Nfld.) 4 E2
Portage, Rivière du, (Que.) 14 D3
Port Alberni Harbour, (BC) 38 C3
Port Albert Peninsula, (Nfld.) 3 D2
Port au Port Bay, (Nfld.) 4 B1
Port au Port Peninsula, (Nfld.) 4 B2
Port-Daniel, Baie de, (Que.) 13 G3
Port-Daniel Nord, Rivière, (Que.) 13 G3
Porter, Cape, (NWT) 45 H1
Porter Lake, (NWT) 44 D1
Porter Lake, (Sask.) 44 E4
Porters Lake, (NS) 9 C3
Porters Lake, (NS) 10 B2
Port Hood Island, (NS) 8 C3
Port Joli Head, (NS) 10 D3
Portland Canal, (BC) 42 D3
Portland Creek Pond, (Nfld.) 5 F3
Portland Inlet, (BC) 42 C4
Portland Island, (BC) 38 F3
Portland Point, (BC) 38 A3
Port Leopold, (NWT) 47 E3
Port Mouton Head, (NS) 10 D3
Port Mouton Island, (NS) 10 D3
Portneuf Est, Rivière, (Que.) 14 D2
Portneuf, Lac, (Que.) 14 C1
Portneuf, Rivière, (Que.) 14 E2
Portugal Cove Brook, (Nfld.) 2 G4
Poshkokagan Lake, (Ont.) 27 E2
Poste, Baie du, (Que.) 20 G4
Postill Lake, (BC) 35 F2
Potato Lake, (Sask.) 32 H3
Pothier Lake, (Man.) 32 H2
Pothole Creek, (BC) 35 D2
Potter Island, (NWT) 46 G3
Pottles Bay, (Nfld.) 6 G3
Potts Lake, (Alta.) 44 C2
Potvin Island, (Ont.) 25 E2
Pouce Coupé River, (Alta./BC) 43 F4
Poulin-de-Courval, Lac, (Que.) 14 C2
Poulter, Lac, (Que.) 18 C3
Pourri, Lac, (Que.) 14 C2
Pouterel, Lac, (Que.) 6 C3
Poutrincourt, Lac, (Que.) 18 F1
Poutrincourt, Lac, (Que.) 20 G4
Povungnituk Bay, (NWT) 46 E3
Povungnituk, Lac de, (Que.) 46 E3
Povungnituk, Rivière de, (Que.) 46 E3
Powderhorn Lake, (Nfld.) 3 A2
Powder Lake, (NWT) 44 D1
Powell Inlet, (NWT) 47 E3
Powell Lake, (BC) 37 C4
Powell River, (BC) 37 D3
Power Hill Pond, (Nfld.) 3 F2
Powers Creek, (BC) 35 E2
Powles Head, (Nfld.) 2 G4
Pownal Bay, (PEI) 7 D4
Prairie River, (Alta.) 34 D1
Prairies, Lac des, (Que.) 19 B2
Prairies, Lake of the, (Man./Sask.) 29 D2
Prairies, Rivière des, (Que.) 17 G3
Praslin, Lac, (Que.) 19 B3
Pratt, Mount, (BC) 37 B3
Preissac, Lac, (Que.) 26 H2
Prelude Lake, (NWT) 44 B1
Premier Lake, (Sask.) 44 E2
Prescott Island, (BC) 41 C1
Prescott Island, (NWT) 47 D3
Presqu'ile Bay, (Ont.) 21 E2
Press Lake, (Ont.) 27 B1
Pressure Point, (NWT) 47 D3
Preston Lake, (Sask.) 44 D3
Pretty Girl Lake, (BC) 39 F4
Pretty River, (Ont.) 23 E2
Prévert, Lac, (Que) 19 E4
Prevost Island, (BC) 38 F3
Priam Lake, (Ont.) 28 H3
Price Island, (BC) 41 E3
Pricket Point, (NWT) 46 E2
Priestley, Mount, (BC) 42 E3
Primeau Lake, (Sask.) 44 E4
Prim, Point, (PEI) 7 D4
Prim, Point, (NS) 10 B1
Primrose Lake, (Sask.) 32 A1
Prince Albert National Park, (Sask.) 32 D2
see also Prince-Albert, Parc national de
Prince-Albert, Parc national de, (Sask.) 32 D3
see also Prince Albert National Park
Prince Albert Peninsula, (NWT) 47 B3
Prince Albert Sound, (NWT) 47 B4
Prince Alfred Bay, (NWT) 47 D3
Prince Alfred, Cape, (NWT) 47 A2
Prince Charles Island, (NWT) 46 E1
Prince-de-Galles, Cap du, (Que.) 46 F3
Prince-de-Galles, Détroit de
see Prince of Wales Strait
Prince-de-Galles, Île
see Prince of Wales Island
Prince Edward Bay, (Ont.) 21 G2
Prince Edward Island National Park, (PEI) 7 C3
see also Île du Prince-Edouard, Parc national de l'
Prince Edward Point, (Ont.) 21 G2
Prince Gustaf Adolf Sea, (NWT) 47 C2
Prince Leopold Island, (NWT) 47 E3
Prince of Wales Island, (NWT) 47 D3
Prince of Wales Reach, (BC) 37 E4
Prince of Wales Strait, (NWT) 47 B3
Prince Patrick Island, (NWT) 47 B2
Prince Regent Inlet, (NWT) 47 E4
Princess Louisa Inlet, (BC) 37 E4
Princess Margaret Range, (NWT) 47 E2
Princess Marie Bay, (NWT) 47 F2
Princess Mary Lake, (NWT) 46 B2
Princess Royal Island, (BC) 41 E2
Princess Royal Reach, (BC) 37 E4
Principe Channel, (BC) 41 D2
Privert, Lac, (Que.) 6 C2
Profitts Point, (PEI) 7 B3
Prophet River, (BC) 43 C1
Prospect Bay, (NS) 9 B4
Prospect Creek, (BC) 35 B2
Prosperous Lake, (NWT) 44 B1
Proulx Lake, (Ont.) 24 D1
Proulx Lake, (Man.) 29 F1
Providence, Cape, (NWT) 47 C3
Providence Point, (Ont.) 25 B3
Pryce Channel, (BC) 37 C3
Ptarmigan Fiord, (NWT) 46 G2
Ptolemy, Mount, (Alta./BC) 34 E4
Pubnico Harbour, (NS) 10 B4
Pubnico Point, (NS) 10 B4
Puddle Pond, (Nfld.) 4 D2
Pugwash River, (NS) 9 B1
Pukaist Creek, (BC) 35 B1
Pukaskwa National Park, (Ont.) 27 H3
see also Pukaskwa, Parc national de
Pukaskwa, Parc national de, (Ont.) 27 H3
see also Pukaskwa National Park
Pukaskwa River, (Ont.) 27 H3
Pukatawagan Lake, (Man.) 30 A1
Pukeashun Mountain, (BC) 36 H3
Pullen Island, (NWT) 45 C1
Puntledge River, (BC) 38 B1
Puntzi Lake, (BC) 40 B4
Purcell Lake, (Ont.) 20 B3
Purcell Mountains, (BC) 34 C2
Purcell Point, (BC) 37 C2
Purchase Bay, (NWT) 47 B2
Purden Lake, (BC) 40 D2
Puskuta Lake, (Ont.) 26 B1
Puskwakau River, (Sask.) 32 F2
Puskwaskau Lake, (Alta.) 33 A1
Puskwaskau River, (Alta.) 33 A1
Puslinch Lake, (Ont.) 23 E4
Pusticamica, Lac, (Que.) 20 F4
Putahow Lake, (Man.) 44 G2
Putahow River, (Man./NWT) 44 G2
Putnam Island, (NWT) 46 E2
Puyjalon, Lac, (Que.) 5 A3
Pye Lake, (BC) 39 G2
Pythonga, Lac, (Que.) 18 D4

Q

Qilalugalik, Lac, (Que.) 46 E4
Quaco Bay, (NB) 11 E3
Quaco Head, (NB) 11 E3
Quadra Island, (BC) 37 B4
Quaker Hat (island), (Nfld.) 6 G3
Qualcho Lake, (BC) 41 G4
Qualicum River, (BC) 38 C2
Qualluviartuuq, Lac, (Que.) 46 E3
Quamichan Lake, (BC) 38 E3
Quantz Lake, (Ont.) 20 B3
Qu'Appelle Dam/Barrage, (Sask.) 31 F2
Qu'Appelle River, (Man./Sask.) 29 C3
Quartz Lake, (NWT) 47 F4
Quatam River, (BC) 37 C3
Quatse Lake, (BC) 39 C1
Quatsino Sound, (BC) 39 C1
Queen, Cape, (NWT) 46 E2
Queen Charlotte Channel, (BC) 38 F2
Queen Charlotte Islands, (BC) 41 B2
Queen Charlotte Mountains, (BC) 41 A1
Queen Charlotte Sound, (BC) 41 D4
Queen Charlotte Strait, (BC) 39 D1
Queen Elizabeth Foreland, (NWT) 46 G3
Queen Elizabeth Islands, (NWT/NWT) 47 D1
Queen Maud Gulf, (NWT) 45 G1
Queens Channel, (NWT) 47 D3
Queens Lake, (NB) 11 D2
Queens Reach, (BC) 37 E4
Queens Sound, (BC) 41 E3
Quest Mountain, (BC) 36 H4
Quennell Lake, (BC) 38 E3
Quénonisca, Lac, (Que.) 20 F4
Quentin Lake, (BC) 43 B1
Quesnel Lake, (BC) 40 E3
Quesnel River, (BC) 40 D3
Quetico Lake, (Ont.) 27 B3
Quetico Provincial Park, (Ont.) 27 B3
Quévillon, Lac, (Que.) 18 C1
Quiddy River, (NB) 11 F2
Quiet Lake, (YT) 45 B3
Quilchena Creek, (BC) 35 D2
Quinan Lake, (NS) 10 B3
Quinn, Lac, (Que.) 18 D4
Quinn Lake, (Man.) 44 H3
Quinn Pond, (Nfld.) 4 F2
Quinsam Lake, (BC) 39 H3
Quinsam River, (BC) 39 H3
Quinte, Bay of, (Ont.) 21 F1
Quintette Mountain, (BC) 40 E1
Quinze, Lac des, (Que.) 26 G3
Quirke Lake, (Ont.) 25 B1
Quirpon Island, (Nfld.) 5 H1
Quisibis Mountain, (NB) 12 A1
Quisibis, Rivière, (NB) 15 H2
Quisitis Point, (BC) 38 A3
Quitting Lake, (Alta.) 44 B4
Quoddy Narrows, (NB) 11 C4
Quoddy River, (NS) 9 E3
Quoich River, (NWT) 46 B2
Quunnguq Lake, (NWT) 47 B4
Quyon, Rivière, (Que.) 17 B1

R

Raanes Peninsula, (NWT) 47 E2
Rabast, Cap de, (Que.) 19 H3
Rabbabou Bay, (Sask.) 44 F3
Rabbit Creek, (Sask.) 32 D3
Rabbit Island, (Ont.) 25 D3
Rabbit, Lac, (Que.) 18 B2
Rabbit Lake, (Ont.) 26 F3
Rabbit Lake, (Sask.) 32 C4
Rabbitskin River, (NWT) 45 D3
Raby Head, (Ont.) 21 C2
Raccourci, Lac du, (Que.) 14 F1
Racine de Bouleau, Rivière de la, (Que.) 6 B4
Racine Lake, (Ont.) 26 C2
Radisson Lake, (Ont.) 26 E2
Radisson Lake, (Sask.) 32 C4
Radisson, Pointe, (Que.) 46 F3
Radstock Bay, (NWT) 47 E3
Rae Creek, (YT) 45 B2
Rae Isthmus, (NWT) 46 C1
Rae Lake, (NWT) 45 E3
Rae River, (NWT) 45 E1
Rae Strait, (NWT) 45 H1
Rafael Point, (BC) 39 F4
Raft Cove, (BC) 39 B1
Raft River, (BC) 36 G2
Rafuse Island, (NS) 10 E2
Ragged Harbour, (Nfld.) 3 E2
Ragged Harbour River, (Nfld.) 3 E2
Ragged Head, (Nfld.) 2 B4
Ragged Head, (NS) 9 G2
Ragged Islands, (Nfld.) 6 G2
Ragged Lake, (NS) 10 G2
Ragged Point, (Nfld.) 3 E2
Ragged Point, (NS) 11 H2
Ragged Wood Lake, (Ont.) 27 C1
Rail Creek, (BC) 36 C2
Rail Lake, (BC) 36 C2
Raimbault, Lac, (Que.) 6 B4
Rainbow Creek, (BC) 35 H1
Rainbow Mountain, (BC) 37 F4
Rainy Lake, (Nfld.) 2 C1
Rainy Lake, (Nfld.) 4 E1
Rainy Lake, (Ont.) 24 B1
Rainy Lake, (Ont.) 27 A4
Rainy River, (Ont.) 28 G4
Raisin River, (Ont.) 17 E2
Raleigh Lake, (Ont.) 27 B2
Raleigh, Mount, (BC) 37 D2
Ralleau, Lac, (Que.) 6 C1
Ramah Bay, (Nfld.) 46 H3
Rambau, Lac, (Que.) 6 B3
Ramea Islands, (Nfld.) 4 E4
Ramea Southeast Rocks, (Nfld.) 4 E4
Ram Island, (NS) 10 D4
Ramparts River, (NWT) 45 C2
Ram River, (Alta.) 34 D1
Ram River, (NWT) 45 D3
Ramsay Arm, (BC) 37 C3
Ramsay Island, (NWT) 47 A3
Ramsey Lake, (Ont.) 25 E1
Ramsey Lake, (Ont.) 26 D3
Ramusio, Lac, (Que.) 6 D3
Rancheria River, (YT) 45 B4
Ranch Lake, (Sask.) 32 E4
Randall River, (Sask.) 32 D2
Random Head Harbour, (Nfld.) 2 F1
Random Island, (Nfld.) 2 F1
Random Sound, (Nfld.) 2 F1
Range Creek, (BC) 35 D1
Ranger Lake, (Ont.) 26 B3
Rankin Inlet, (NWT) 46 B2
Raper, Cape, (NWT) 47 H4
Rapides, Lac des, (Que.) 19 F3
Rapson Bay, (Ont.) 30 E2
Rasmussen Basin, (NWT) 45 H1
Ratchford Creek, (BC) 36 H3
Rat Creek, (Alta.) 33 C3
Rathouse Bay, (Ont.) 30 D3
Rat Lake, (Man.) 30 B1
Rat Lake, (Man.) 30 D2
Rat Portage Bay, (Ont.) 28 F2
Rat River, (Man.) 28 A3
Rat River, (Man.) 30 B1
Rats, Rivière aux, (Que.) 18 G3
Rats, Rivière aux, (Que.) 20 H4
Rattling Brook, (Nfld.) 3 C3
Rattling Lake, (Nfld.) 3 C3
Ratz, Mount, (BC) 42 B1
Raude, Lac, (Que.) 6 D2
Raush River, (BC) 40 F3
Raven River, (Alta.) 34 D1
Rawalpindi Lake, (NWT) 45 E2
Rawhide Lake, (Ont.) 26 C4
Ray, Cape, (Nfld.) 4 A4
Rayfield River, (BC) 36 D3
Ray Lake, (NWT) 46 A3
Raynards Lake, (NS) 10 B3
Raynor Group, (BC) 39 D1
Raza Island, (BC) 37 B3
Raza Passage, (BC) 37 B3
Reach, The (channel), (Nfld.) 3 D2
Reader Lake, (Man.) 32 H2
Read Head, (NS) 9 G2
Read Island, (BC) 37 B4
Rebecca Spit, (BC) 37 B4
Rebesca Lake, (NWT) 45 E2
Reboul, Rivière, (Que.) 13 F3
Recluse, Lac, (Que.) 19 F2
Redberry Lake, (Sask.) 32 C4
Red Bluff Lake, (BC) 41 D2
Red Cedar Lake, (Ont.) 26 F3
Redcliff Island, (NWT) 44 C1
Red Cliff Pond, (Nfld.) 2 C1
Red Cliff Pond, (Nfld.) 3 B1
Red Cove, (Nfld.) 2 F4
Red Creek, (BC) 35 D3
Red Cross Lake, (Man.) 30 E2
Red Deer Creek, (BC) 40 E1
Red Deer Lake, (Ont.) 25 F1
Red Deer Lake, (Ont.) 28 G1
Red Deer Lake, (Alta.) 31 B3
Red Deer Lake, (Man.) 32 H4
Red Deer Lake, (Alta.) 33 E4
Red Deer point (penninsula), (Man.) 29 F1
Red Deer River, (Alta.) 31 B2
Red Deer River, (Man./Sask.) 32 G4
Redding Creek, (BC) 34 C4
Red Earth Creek, (Sask.) 32 G3
Redfern Lake, (BC) 43 C2
Redgut Bay, (Ont.) 27 A3
Red Harbour Head, (Nfld.) 2 C3
Red Head, (Nfld.) 2 F4
Red Head, (NS) 8 E4
Red Head, (NS) 9 A2
Red Head, (NS) 9 G2
Red Head River, (Nfld.) 2 F4
Redhorse Lake, (Ont.) 24 H2
Red Indian Brook, (Nfld.) 4 D1
Red Indian Lake, (Nfld.) 4 F1
Red Island, (Nfld.) 2 E3
Red Island, (Nfld.) 4 A2
Red Islands, (NS) 8 D4
Red Lake, (Ont.) 30 D4
Red Lake, (BC) 36 E4
Red Landing Head, (Nfld.) 2 C3
Redman Head, (NS) 9 F3
Red Mountain, (BC) 37 G1
Red Pillar, The (mountain), (BC) 38 B2
Red Point, (NS) 9 H2
Red River, (NS) 8 D1
Red River, (Man.) 28 A1
Red River, (NWT) 44 G2
Red River Floodway, (Man.) 28 A2
Red Rock Lake, (NB) 11 C3
Redrock Lake, (NWT) 45 E2
Red Rock Point, (Nfld.) 6 G3
Redstone Lake, (Ont.) 24 D2
Redstone River, (Ont.) 26 E2
Redstone River, (NWT) 45 C3
Red Sucker Lake, (Man.) 30 D2
Red Sucker River, (Man./Ont.) 30 D2
Redwater River, (Alta.) 33 E2
Redwillow Creek, (Sask.) 32 G3
Redwillow River, (Alta./BC) 43 F4
Red Wine River, (Nfld.) 6 E3
Reed Lake, (Man.) 30 A2
Reed Lake, (Sask.) 31 E3
Reed River, (Man.) 28 D3
Reeds Bay, (Ont.) 21 H1
Reedy Lake, (Man.) 29 G1
Reflex Lakes, (Alta./Sask.) 33 H4
Refuge Lagoon, (BC) 37 C4
Reg Christie Creek, (BC) 36 G2
Regina Bay, (Ont.) 28 G2
Reid Island, (BC) 38 E3
Reid Lake, (Sask.) 31 D3
Reindeer Island, (Man.) 30 B3
Reindeer Lake, (Man./Sask.) 44 G3
Reindeer River, (Sask.) 44 F4
Reine-Charlotte, Bassin
see Queen Charlotte Sound
Reine-Charlotte, Détroit de la
see Queen Charlotte Strait
Reine-Charlotte, Îles
see Queen Charlotte Islands
Reine-Elisabeth, Îles
see Queen Elizabeth Islands
Reita Lake, (Alta.) 33 G2
Relay Creek, (BC) 37 G1
Relay Mountain, (BC) 37 F1
Reliance Mountain, (BC) 37 C1
Rémigny, Lac, (Que.) 26 G2
Remi Lake, (Ont.) 20 C4
Remi Lake Provincial Park, (Ont.) 20 C4
Remi River, (Ont.) 20 C4
Remote Mountain, (BC) 37 B1
Renard, Lac à, (Que.) 19 G2
Renard, Lac du, (Que.) 5 B4
Renard, Pointe au, (Que.) 13 H1
Renards, Point aux, (NB) 12 H4
Renata Creek, (BC) 35 H3
Rencontre Bay, (Nfld.) 4 F4
Rencontre Brook, (Nfld.) 2 C2
Rencontre Island, (Nfld.) 2 C2
Rencontre Lake, (Nfld.) 2 C2
Rendell Creek, (BC) 35 G3
Renews Harbour, (Nfld.) 2 H4
Renews Head, (Nfld.) 2 H4
Rennell Sound, (BC) 41 A2
Rennie Lake, (Ont.) 26 B2
Rennie Lake, (NWT) 44 E1
Rennie River, (Man.) 28 D1
Rennison Island, (BC) 41 D2
Renouard, Lac, (Que.) 19 C4
Renous River, (NB) 12 D3
Repulse Bay, (NWT) 46 D2
Repulse Island, (BC) 37 C4
Resolution Bay, (NWT) 44 B1
Resolution Island, (NWT) 46 G3
Résolution, Lac, (Que.) 6 D2
Restigouche River, (NB) 13 B4
see also Ristigouche, Rivière (Que.)
Restless Bay, (BC) 39 C2
Restoule Lake, (Ont.) 25 G2
Retreat Passage, (BC) 39 E1
Revillon Island, (NWT) 20 D1
Reynolds Creek, (Ont.) 22 F2
Rib Lake, (Ont.) 26 F3
Ribstone Creek, (Alta.) 33 G4
Ribstone Lake, (Alta.) 33 G4
Rice Lake, (Ont.) 21 D1
Rice Lake, (Ont.) 26 D2
Rice Lake, (Ont.) 28 E1
Rice Lake, (Sask.) 31 E1
Richard Collinson, Cape, (NWT) 47 C4
Richard Collinson Inlet, (NWT) 47 B3
Richards Bay, (NWT) 46 D1
Richards, Cape, (NWT) 47 E1
Richards Island, (Nfld.) 3 F4
Richards Island, (NWT) 45 B1
Richards Lake, (Sask.) 44 E3
Richardson, Cape, (NWT) 46 D1
Richardson Island, (NWT) 45 E2
Richardson Islands, (NWT) 45 F1
Richardson Lake, (Alta.) 44 C3
Richardson Mountains, (YT) 45 B1
Richardson Point, (NWT) 45 H1
Richardson River, (Alta./Sask.) 44 C3
Richardson River, (NWT) 45 E2
Rich, Cape, (Ont.) 23 D1
Richelieu, Rivière, (Que.) 16 A3
Richibucto Cape, (NB) 12 G3
Richibucto Harbour, (NB) 12 G3
Richibucto River, (NB) 12 F3
Rich Lake, (Alta.) 33 F2
Richmond Gulf
see Guillaume-Delisle, Lac
Ricketts, Cape, (NWT) 47 E3
Rideau Canal, (Ont.) 17 B3
Rideau River, (Ont.) 17 C2
Ridge River, (Ont.) 20 B4
Riding Mountain, (Man.) 29 E2
Riding Mountain National Park, (Man.) 29 E2
see also Mont Riding, Parc national du
Rigaud River, (Ont.) 17 F1
see also Rigaud, Rivière (Que.)
Rigaud, Rivière, (Que.) 17 F1
see also Rigaud River (Ont.)
Right Hand Branch Tobique River, (NB) 12 B2
Riley Lake, (Ont.) 24 C3
Rimouski, Rivière, (Que.) 14 G3
Riou Lake, (Sask.) 44 E3
Rioulx Creek, (BC) 35 H2
Ripault, Lac, (Que.) 5 A2
Ripault, Lac, (Que.) 15 C1
Ripple Mountain, (BC) 34 B4
Riske Creek, (BC) 36 A1
Ristigouche, Rivière, (Que.) 13 B4
see also Restigouche River (NB)
Rivedoux, Lac, (Que.) 14 D3
Riverhead Brook, (Nfld.) 3 D4
River of Ponds Lake, (Nfld.) 5 G3
Rivers Inlet, (BC) 41 F4
Rivers, Lake of the, (Sask.) 31 F3
Rivière à Pierre, Baie de la, (Que.) 13 E1
Road Point, (Nfld.) 4 B1
Roaring Bull Point, (NS) 9 D1
Roaring River, (Man.) 29 D1
Robe Noire, Lac de la, (Que.) 5 A3
Robert Brown, Cape, (NWT) 46 D1
Robert, Lac, (Que.) 20 G4
Robert Peel Inlet, (NWT) 46 F2
Roberts Bay, (Ont.) 25 C3
Roberts, Cape, (Ont.) 25 A2
Roberts Lac, (Que.) 46 F3
Roberts Lake, (BC) 39 G2
Robertson Bay, (NWT) 20 D1
Robertson, Lac, (Que.) 5 E2
Robertson Lake, (Alta.) 44 B2
Robertson Point, (NWT) 47 C3
Robertson River, (BC) 38 D3
Robeson Channel, (NWT) 47 F1
Robilliard Island, (NWT) 47 A3
Robinhood Bay, (Nfld.) 3 G4
Robinson Sound, (NWT) 46 G2
Robinsons River, (Nfld.) 4 B3
Roblin Lake, (Ont.) 21 F1
Robson, Mount, (BC) 40 F3
Roche Lake, (BC) 35 D1
Rocher Bay, (NB) 11 G2
Rocher, Lac, (Que.) 20 F4
Rochers, Baie des, (Que.) 5 E3
Rochers, Rivière aux, (Que.) 19 E3
Roches, Lac des, (BC) 36 E3
Rocheuses, Montagnes
see Rocky Mountains
Rochon Lake, (Man.) 30 D2
Rochon Lake, (NWT) 44 F2
Rock Creek, (BC) 35 F4
Rockinghorse Lake, (NWT) 45 F2
Rock Island Lake, (Alta.) 33 E1
Rock Island Lake, (Alta.) 33 H3
Rock Lake, (Ont.) 24 D2
Rock Lake, (Ont.) 26 B4
Rock Lake, (Man.) 29 F4
Rocknest Lake, (NWT) 45 E2
Rock River, (YT) 45 B1
Rock River, (YT) 45 C4
Rocksand River, (Ont.) 30 G2
Rocks, Bay of, (NS) 9 H2
Rockwell Stream, (NB) 11 D2
Rocky Bay, (Nfld.) 3 E2
Rocky Bay, (Nfld.) 6 H3
Rocky Brook, (NB) 12 C3
Rocky Cove, (Nfld.) 6 G3
Rocky Island Lake, (Ont.) 26 C3
Rocky Lake, (Man.) 32 H2
Rocky Mountains, (BC) 1
see also
Rocky Mountains, (Alta.) 1
Rocky Point, (Nfld.) 3 E2
Rocky Pond, (Nfld.) 2 F1
Rocky Pond, (Nfld.) 3 A2
Rocky Pond, (Nfld.) 3 B2
Rocky Pond, (Nfld.) 3 D2
Rocky Ridge, (Nfld.) 4 C3
Rocky Ridge Pond, (Nfld.) 3 F2
Rocky Ridge Pond, (Nfld.) 4 D3
Rocky River, (Nfld.) 2 F3
Rocky River, (Alta.) 40 H3
Rocky Saugeen River, (Ont.) 23 D2
Rodayer, Lac, (Que.) 20 E4
Roderick Island, (BC) 41 E3
Roderick Lake, (Ont.) 30 D4
Rodeross Lake, (Nfld.) 4 F2
Rodney, Mount, (BC) 37 C2
Rodney Pond, (Nfld.) 3 D3
Roe Lake, (Man.) 30 C1
Roe Lake, (Sask.) 44 D4
Roes Welcome Sound, (NWT) 46 C2
Roger, Cape, (Nfld.) 2 D3
Roger Creek, (BC) 37 G4
Roger, Lac, (Que.) 26 G2
Roger Lake, (NB) 12 D1
Roger Lake, (BC) 36 D2
Roger Point, (NS) 9 D1
Rogers Creek, (Ont.) 22 H1
Rogers Head, (NB) 11 E3
Rogerson Lake, (Nfld.) 4 F2
Rogers Point, (Nfld.) 3 E1
Roggan, Lac, (Que.) 20 E2
Roggan, Rivière, (Que.) 20 E2
Rognons, Lac aux, (Que.) 15 A1
Rogue River, (YT) 45 B3
Rogues Harbour, (Nfld.) 3 B1
Rohault, Lac, (Que.) 20 G4
Roi-George, Iles
see King George Islands
Roi-Guillaume, Ile
see King William Island
Rolling Cove, (Nfld.) 3 G4
Rolling Pond, (Nfld.) 3 C4
Rollo Bay, (PEI) 7 E3
Rollo Lake, (Ont.) 26 C2
Romaine, Lac, (Que.) 14 E3
Romaine, Rivière, (Que.) 19 H3
Romaines Brook, (Nfld.) 4 B2
Romanet, Lac, (Que.) 6 C2
Ronayne, Mount, (BC) 37 G3
Rondeau Harbour, (Ont.) 22 C3
Rondeau Provincial Park, (Ont.) 22 D3
Ronde, Cap, (NS) 9 H1
Rond, Lac, (Que.) 14 C1
Rond, Lac, (Que.) 15 G1
Rond, Lac, (Que.) 18 D3
Rond, Lac, (Que.) 19 E2
Ronge, Lac la, (Sask.) 32 E1
Root Lake, (Man.) 32 H2
Root River, (NWT) 45 D3
Roper Bay, (Sask.) 44 E4
Rorey Lake, (NWT) 45 C2
Rorke Lake, (Man./Ont.) 30 E2
Roscoe Inlet, (BC) 41 F3
Roscoe River, (NWT) 45 D1
Roseau River, (Man.) 28 B3
Roseberry River, (Ont.) 30 E3
Roseblade Lake, (NWT) 44 H1
Rose Blanche Brook, (Nfld.) 4 B4
Rosebud River, (Alta.) 34 E2
Rosée, Lac, (Que.) 2
Rose Island, (Ont.) 25 G3
Rose Lake, (BC) 36 C1
Rose Point, (NS) 10 E2
Rose Point, (BC) 41 B1
Roseway, Cape, (NS) 10 C4
Roseway Lake, (NS) 10 C3
Roseway River, (NS) 10 C3
Rosiers, Cap des, (Que.) 13 H2
Rosiers, Rivière aux, (Que.) 14 G1
Rosita Lake, (BC) 40 C3
Ross Bay, (NWT) 46 D1
Ross Creek, (Alta.) 31 B3
Ross Creek, (BC) 36 H4
Rosseau, Lake, (Ont.) 24 B2
Rosse, Cape, (NWT) 47 D3
Rossignol, Lac, (Que.) 20 G2
Rossignol, Lake, (NS) 10 C3
Ross Island, (NB) 11 C4
Ross Lake, (Sask.) 32 C2
Ross Lake, (BC) 36 A1
Ross Lake, (NWT) 44 C1
Ross Point, (NWT) 47 C3
Ross River, (YT) 45 B3
Rôti Bay, (Nfld.) 4 C4
Rôti Brook, (Nfld.) 4 C4
Rottenfish River, (Ont.) 30 E3
Rouge, Cap, (Que.) 13 A1
Rouge, Cape, (Nfld.) 6 G3
Rougemont, Lac, (Que.) 6 B1
Rouge River, (Ont.) 21 B2
Rouge, Rivière
see Red River
Rouge, Rivière, (Que.) 17 E1
Rouge, Rivière, (Que.) 18 E3
Rouget, Lac, (Que.) 20 G2
Roughrock Lake, (Ont.) 28 E1
Roundeyed, Lac, (Que.) 6 A3
Round Head, (Nfld.) 3 E1
Round Head (mountain), (Nfld.) 4 B2
Round Hill, (Nfld.) 4 C1
Round Island, (NS) 10 B4
Round Island, (NS) 10 E2
Round Lake, (Nfld.) 5 G2
Round Lake, (Ont.) 24 F1
Round Lake, (Ont.) 24 E4
Round Lake, (Ont.) 25 G3
Round Lake, (Ont.) 26 F2
Round Lake, (Sask.) 29 C3
Round Pond, (Nfld.) 2 A1
Route Lake, (Ont.) 27 A1
Rouvray, Lac, (Que.) 14 B1
Rowan Lake, (Ont.) 28 H3
Rowan's Ravine Provincial Park, (Sask.) 31 G2
Rowdy Lake, (Ont.) 30 D4
Rowley Island, (NWT) 46 E1
Rowley Lake, (NWT) 44 F2
Rowley River, (NWT) 47 F4
Roxton, Étang, (Que.) 16 B3
Royal Geographical Society Islands, (NWT) 45 G1
Royal, Mont, (Que.) 17 G4
Royal Oak Creek, (Ont.) 23 B3
Royal Society Fiord, (NWT) 47 G4
Roy Island, (NS) 8 A4
Roy, Lac, (Que.) 18 E1
Roy, Lac, (Que.) 19 B3
Roz, Lac, (Que.) 20 G1
Ruaux, Ile aux, (Que.) 15 C2
Ruby Lake, (BC) 38 D1
Ruffin, Lac, (Que.) 5 B2
Rufus Lake, (Ont.) 26 C1
Rugby Lake, (Ont.) 27 A1
Ruin Point, (NWT) 46 D2
Ruis Lake, (Alta.) 44 B3
Rupert Bay, (NWT) 20 E3
Rupert Inlet, (BC) 39 D1
Rupert, Rivière de, (Que.) 20 F3
Ruscom River, (Ont.) 22 B3
Rush Lake, (Ont.) 26 D2
Rushy Pond, (Nfld.) 3 B3
Russel Island, (Ont.) 25 C3
Russell, Cape, (BC) 39 B1
Russell, Cape, (NWT) 47 B2
Russell Channel, (BC) 39 F4
Russell Creek, (Sask.) 31 E3
Russell Inlet, (NWT) 45 C1
Russell Island, (NWT) 47 D3
Russell, Lac, (Que.) 18 B3
Russell Lake, (Sask.) 32 B3
Russell Lake, (Sask.) 44 E3
Russell Lake, (Man.) 44 G4
Russell Lake, (NWT) 45 E3
Russell Point, (NWT) 47 B3
Russell Pond, (Nfld.) 3 E3
Russels Cove, (Nfld.) 2 G1
Russick Lake, (Man.) 32 H1
Rustico Island, (PEI) 7 C3
Rusty Lake, (Man.) 44 H4
Rutherford Creek, (BC) 37 F3
Ruth Lake, (Ont.) 25 H2
Ruth Lake, (BC) 36 D2
Rutledge Lake, (NWT) 44 C1
Rutledge River, (NWT) 44 C1
Ruzé, Lac, (Que.) 5 E2
Ryan Lake, (Man.) 44 H3
Ryan River, (BC) 37 F3
Ryans Bay, (Nfld.) 46 H3
Ryans Brook, (Nfld.) 4 A3
Ryders Brook, (Nfld.) 2 F1

S

Saanich Inlet, (BC) 38 E4
Sabaskong Bay, (Ont.) 28 G3
Sabaskong Peninsula, (Ont.) 28 G3
Sabaskosing Bay, (Ont.) 28 F3
Sabbies River, (NB) 12 E3
Sabine Bay, (NWT) 47 C3
Sabine, Cape, (NWT) 47 F2
Sabine Channel, (BC) 38 D1
Sabine Peninsula, (NWT) 47 C2
Sable, Baie au, (Que.) 18 D3
Sable, Cape, (NS) 10 B4
Sable Island, (NS) 9 H4
Sable Islands, (Ont.) 28 F4
Sable, Lac du, (Que.) 6 C3
Sable River, (NS) 10 C3
Sable, Rivière du, (Que.) 6 C2
Sables, Baie, (Que.) 5 A4
Sables, Lac aux, (Ont.) 26 D3
Sables, Lac des, (Que.) 14 E3
Sables, Réservoir des, (Que.) 18 D4
Sables, River aux, (Ont.) 25 C1
Sables, Rivière aux, (Que.) 14 C1
Sabomin Lake, (Man.) 30 C2
Sabourin, Lac, (Que.) 18 B2
Sabourin Lake, (Ont.) 30 D4
Sacacomie, Lac, (Que.) 16 A1
Sachigo Lake, (Ont.) 30 E2
Sachigo River, (Ont.) 30 E2
Sacred Bay, (Nfld.) 5 H2
Saddle Back Pond, (Nfld.) 3 G4
Saddle (Burnt) River, (Alta.) 43 G4
Saddle, Colline, (Que.) 16 F4
Saddle Lake, (Man.) 28 D1
Saddle Lake, (Alta.) 33 F2
Sadler Lake, (Sask.) 32 F1
Saffray, Lac, (Que.) 6 C1
Saganaga Lake, (Ont.) 27 C3
Saganagons Lake, (Ont.) 27 C3
Saganash Lake, (Ont.) 26 C1
Saganash River, (Ont.) 26 C1
Sagawitchewan River, (Man./Ont.) 30 D2
Sagemace Bay, (Man.) 29 F1
Saglek Bay, (Nfld.) 6 E1
Sagona Island, (Nfld.) 2 B3
Saguenay, Rivière, (Que.) 14 D3
Sailing Lake, (Man.) 28 D1
Saindon, Lacs, (Que.) 20 G1
Sainsbury Point, (NWT) 20 D1
St-Agapit, Ruisseau, (Que.) 15 A3
St-Amour, Lac, (Que.) 18 D3
St Andrew, Lake, (Man.) 29 H1
St Andrews Channel, (NS) 8 E3
St Anns Bay, (NS) 8 E3
St Anns Harbour, (NS) 8 E3
St Anthony, Cape, (Nfld.) 5 H2
St Anthony Lake, (Ont.) 26 F2
St Aubyn Bay, (Ont.) 25 G3
St Aubyn Lake, (BC) 37 B3
St-Augustin, Lac, (Que.) 15 F4
St-Augustin Nord-Ouest, Rivière, (Que.) 5 E2
St-Augustin, Rivière, (Que.) 5 E2
St-Barnabé, Ile, (Que.) 14 G3
St-Bernard, Ile, (Que.) 17 G4
St-Bernard, Lac, (Que.) 16 A1
St-Charles, Lac, (Que.) 15 A3
St-Charles, Pointe, (Que.) 19 F3
St-Charles, Rivière, (NB) 12 G3
St-Charles, Rivière, (Que.) 15 F3
St-Charles, Rivière, (Que.) 17 H3
St Clair, Lake, (Ont.) 22 B3
St Clair River, (Ont.) 22 B2
St Croix Bay, (Nfld.) 2 F3
St Croix Cove, (NS) 11 F3
St Croix River, (NB) 11 B3
St-Cyr, Lac, (Que.) 18 D1
St Cyr Lake, (Sask.) 32 B2
St-Cyr, Rivière, (Que.) 18 E1
St David, Cape, (NWT) 46 G2
St-Denis, Rivière, (Que.) 15 E1
Ste-Agnès, Lac, (Que.) 15 C1
Ste-Anne, Baie, (NB) 12 G2
Ste-Anne, Baie de, (Que.) 15 D2
Ste-Anne du Nord, Rivière, (Que.) 15 C2
Ste-Anne, Lac, (Que.) 13 D2
Ste-Anne, Lac, (Que.) 15 A2
Ste-Anne, Lac, (Que.) 15 E2

Ste-Anne, Lac, (Que.) 19 D3
Ste Anne, Lac, (Alta.) 33 D3
Ste-Anne, Mont, (Que.) 15 B2
Ste-Anne, Pointe, (Que.) 13 C1
Ste-Anne, Rivière, (Que.) 13 D1
Ste-Anne, Rivière, (Que.) 15 A2
Ste-Cécile, Mont, (Que.) 16 F3
Ste-Cécile, Lac
see St Clair, Lake
Ste-Geneviève, Ile, (Que.) 5 A3
Saint Elias Mountains, (BC/YT) 45 A3
Ste-Maire, Iles, (Que.) 5 D3
Ste-Marguerite, Baie, (Que.) 19 E3
Ste-Marguerite, Ile, (Que.) 15 C2
Ste-Marguerite, Mont, (Que.) 16 F1
Ste-Marguerite Nord-Est, Rivière, (Que.) 14 D3
Ste-Marguerite Nord-Ouest, Rivière, (Que.) 14 C3
Ste-Marguerite, Pointe, (Que.) 19 E3
Ste-Marguerite, Rivière, (Que.) 14 D3
Ste-Marguerite, Rivière, (Que.) 19 E2
St Esprit Island, (NS) 8 E4
St Esprit Lake, (NS) 8 E4
Ste-Thérèse, Ile, (Que.) 17 H3
Ste Thérèse, Lac, (NWT) 45 D2
Saint-Fond, Rivière, (Que.) 46 F3
St Francis, Cape, (Nfld.) 2 H2
St Francis Harbour River, (NS) 9 G2
St Francis, Lake, (Ont.) 17 F2
see also St-François, Lac (Que.)
St-Francis River, (NB/Que.) 15 F2
see also St-François, Rivière (Que./NB)
St-François, Lac, (Que.) 15 F1
St-François, Lac, (Que.) 16 F2
St-François, Lac, (Que.) 17 F2
see also St Francis Lake (Ont.)
St-François, Rivière, (NB/Que.) 15 F1
see also St-Francis River (NB)
St-François, Rivière, (Que.) 16 C3
St Genervieve Bay, (Nfld.) 5 G2
St George, Cape, (Nfld.) 4 A2
St George, Lake, (Man.) 29 H1
St George's Bay, (Nfld.) 4 B2
St Georges Bay, (NS) 9 F1
St George's Harbour, (Nfld.) 4 C2
St George's River, (Nfld.) 4 C2
St-Germain, Rivière, (Que.) 16 C3
St-Germains, Lac, (Que.) 14 C3
St Gregory, Cape, (Nfld.) 5 F4
St Ignace Island, (Ont.) 27 F3
Saint-Jacques, Lac, (Que.) 19 A4
St-Jean, Anse, (Que.) 14 D3
St-Jean, Lac, (Que.) 14 F4
Saint-Jean, Lac, (Que.) 18 H1
Saint-Jean Nord-Est, Rivière, (Que.) 19 H2
Saint-Jean, Rivière, (NB) 11 B1
see also Saint John River
St-Jean, Rivière, (Que.) 13 G2
St-Jean, Rivière, (Que.) 14 D3
Saint-Jean, Rivière, (Que.) 19 H2
Saint-Jean Sud-Ouest, Rivière, (Que.) 16 H1
St John Bay, (Nfld.) 5 G2
St John, Cape, (Nfld.) 3 B1
Saint John Harbour, (NB) 11 D3
St John Island, (Nfld.) 5 G2
St John, Lake, (Nfld.) 3 D4
St John Point, (BC) 38 C2
Saint John River, (NB) 11 D1
see also Saint-Jean, Rivière
St John's Bay, (Nfld.) 2 B3
St John's Bay, (Nfld.) 2 H2
St John's Bay, (Nfld.) 3 C2
St John's Head, (Nfld.) 2 B3
St Jones Head, (Nfld.) 2 F1
St Joseph Channel, (Ont.) 26 B4
St Joseph Island, (Ont.) 26 B4
St-Joseph, Lac, (Que.) 15 A3
St Joseph, Lake, (Ont.) 30 F4
St Labre Creek, (Man.) 28 C2
St-Lambert, Rivière, (Que.) 17 H4
St-Laurent, Baie, (Que.) 5 A3
St Laurent, Cape, (NB) 7 B4
Saint-Laurent, Fleuve 6
see also St Lawrence River
Saint-Laurent, Golfe du 6
see also St Lawrence, Gulf of
St Lawrence, Bay, (NS) 8 E1
St Lawrence, Cape, (NS) 8 E1
St Lawrence, Gulf of 6
see also Saint-Laurent, Golfe du
St Lawrence River 6
see also Saint-Laurent, Fleuve
St Lawrence River, (Nfld.) 2 C4
St Lewis, Cape, (Nfld.) 5 H1
St Lewis Inlet, (Nfld.) 5 H1
St Lewis River, (Nfld.) 5 G1
St Lewis Sound, (Nfld.) 5 H1
St-Louis, Baie de, (NB) 12 G3
St-Louis, Ile, (Que.) 14 D3
St-Louis, Lac, (Que.) 17 F4
St Lunaire Bay, (Nfld.) 5 H2
St Margaret Bay, (Nfld.) 5 G2
St Margarets Bay, (NS) 10 F2
St Martin, Lake, (Man.) 29 G1
St Mary Reservoir, (Alta.) 34 F4
St Mary River, (BC) 34 C4
St Mary River, (Alta.) 34 F4
St Mary's Alpine Provincial Park, (BC) 34 C3
St Mary's Bay, (Nfld.) 2 F4
St Marys Bay, (PEI) 7 E4
St Marys Bay, (NS) 10 A2
St Mary's, Cape, (Nfld.) 2 E4
St Marys, Cape, (NS) 9 F3
St Marys, Cape, (NS) 10 A3
St Mary's Harbour, (Nfld.) 2 F4
St Marys River, (NS) 9 F2
St-Mathieu, Lac, (Que.) 14 F3
St-Maurice, Rivière, (Que.) 18 F2
St Michael, Lake, (Man.) 29 H1
St Michaels Bay, (Nfld.) 6 H4
St-Michel, Lac, (Que.) 15 B2
St-Michel, Lac, (Que.) 15 C3
St Nora Lake, (Ont.) 24 C2
St-Onge, Lac, (Que.) 14 E3
St-Pancrace, Pointe, (Que.) 14 H1
St-Patrice, Lac, (Que.) 18 B4
St Patricks Channel, (NS) 8 D3
St-Paul, Baie, (Que.) 15 C1
St Paul Island, (NS) 8 F1
St-Paul, Lac, (Que.) 16 C2
St-Paul, Rivière, (Nfld./Que.) 5 F1
St Pauls Inlet, (Nfld.) 5 F4
St Peter Bay, (Nfld.) 5 H1
St Peters Bay, (PEI) 7 E3
St Peters Bay, (NS) 8 D4
St Peters Inlet, (NS) 8 D4
St Peters Island, (PEI) 7 C4
St Peters Pond, (Nfld.) 5 H1
St-Pierre, Lac, (Que.) 16 B2
Saint-Pierre, Lac, (Que.) 19 D3
St Raphael Lake, (Ont.) 27 B1
St-Sébastien, Mont, (Que.) 16 F3
St Shores Cove, (Nfld.) 2 F4
St Shotts River, (Nfld.) 2 F4
St-Victor, Rivière, (Que.) 16 F2
St Vincent Bay, (BC) 38 D1
St-Wenceslas, Rivière, (Que.) 16 C2
Sakami, Lac, (Que.) 20 F2
Sakami, Rivière, (Que.) 20 G2
Sakinaw Lake, (BC) 38 D1
Sakwaso Lake, (Ont.) 30 E3
Sakwatamau River, (Alta.) 33 B2
Salamandre, Lac, (Que.) 20 F4
Salé, Lac, (Que.) 5 D3
Saline Lake, (Sask.) 29 C1
Salisbury Island, (NWT) 46 E2
Salkeld Lake, (NWT) 44 D1
Salmon Arm, (BC) 36 H4
Salmon Brook Lake, (NB) 12 C3
Salmon Channel, (BC) 39 E1
Salmon Cove Pond, (Nfld.) 3 G4
Salmonier Arm, (Nfld.) 2 G3
Salmonier River, (Nfld.) 2 B4
Salmonier River, (Nfld.) 2 G3
Salmon Inlet, (BC) 38 E1
Salmon Lake, (Ont.) 24 D3
Salmon Lake, (BC) 35 E2
Salmon Point, (Ont.) 21 F2
Salmon Pond, (Nfld.) 3 D3
Salmon Pond, (Nfld.) 3 E4
Salmon River, (Nfld.) 2 A2
Salmon River, (Nfld.) 3 C3
Salmon River, (Nfld.) 5 H2
Salmon River, (NS) 8 E1
Salmon River, (NS) 8 E4
Salmon River, (NS) 9 C2
Salmon River, (NS) 9 F2
Salmon River, (NS) 10 A3
Salmon River, (NB) 12 A2
Salmon River, (NB) 12 E4
Salmon River, (Ont.) 21 G1
Salmon River, (BC) 35 E1
Salmon River, (BC) 39 G2
Salmon River, (BC) 40 B1
Salmontail Lake, (NS) 10 E1
Salone, Lac, (Que.) 18 F3
Salt Creek, (Ont.) 21 E1
Salter Head, (NS) 9 B2
Salters Brook, (NS) 10 D2
Salt Point, (Man.) 29 F1
Salt River, (Alta./NWT) 44 C2
Saltspring Island, (BC) 38 E3
Saltwater Pond, (Nfld.) 3 B1
Salvage Point, (Nfld.) 2 G1
Salvages, The *(rock & ledges)*, (NS) 10 C4
Salvail, Rivière, (Que.) 16 A3
Samandré Lake, (NWT) 45 E2
Samaqua, Rivière, (Que.) 20 H4
Samatosum Mountain, (BC) 36 G3
Sambro Island, (NS) 10 G2
Sam Ford Fiord, (NWT) 47 G4
Samson (Flat) Islands, (Nfld.) 3 F3
Samson Lake, (Alta.) 33 E4
Samson, Rivière, (Que.) 16 G3
Samuel Island, (BC) 38 F3
Sandbank Lake, (Ont.) 20 C3
Sand Bay, (NWT) 47 D2
Sand Brook, (NB) 11 C2
Sand Cove, (NS) 11 G2
Sand Cove Head, (Nfld.) 2 B4
Sandeau, Lac, (Que.) 18 B3
Sanderson Lake, (NWT) 44 E1
Sandfly Lake, (Sask.) 32 D1
Sandford Lake, (Ont.) 27 B2
Sand Hill Cove, (Nfld.) 6 H3
Sandhill Creek, (Sask.) 32 F3
Sand Hill River, (Nfld.) 6 H3
Sand Lake, (NS) 8 F3
Sand Lake, (Ont.) 17 B3
Sand Lake, (Ont.) 24 C1
Sand Lake, (Ont.) 28 F1
Sand Lake, (NWT) 46 A2
Sand Point Lake, (Ont.) 27 A3
Sand River, (Ont.) 26 A3
Sand River, (Man.) 28 C3
Sand River, (Alta.) 33 G2
Sandusk Creek, (Ont.) 22 G2
Sandwich Bay, (Nfld.) 6 G3
Sandy Bay, (Ont.) 25 F2
Sandy Bay, (Sask.) 44 D3
Sandybeach Lake, (Ont.) 27 B1
Sandy Brook, (Nfld.) 3 B3
Sandy Cove, (Nfld.) 3 F4
Sandy Harbour River, (Nfld.) 2 E2
Sandy Island, (Ont.) 25 G1
Sandy Island, (Ont.) 25 G3
Sandy Lake, (Nfld.) 5 G4
Sandy Lake, (Ont.) 24 D4
Sandy Lake, (Ont.) 30 G3
Sandy Lake, (Sask.) 32 D1
Sandy Lake, (Alta.) 33 D3
Sandy Lake, (Alta.) 44 B4
Sandy Lake, (NWT) 44 E2
Sandy Lake, (Sask.) 44 E4
Sandy Point, (NB) 13 H4
Sango Bay, (Nfld.) 6 F2
Sangster Island, (BC) 38 D2
Sangsues, Lac aux, (Que.) 18 B4
San Josef Bay, (BC) 39 B1
San Josef River, (BC) 39 B1
San Jose River, (BC) 36 C2
San Juan Point, (BC) 38 C4
San Juan, Port, (BC) 38 C4
San Juan River, (BC) 38 D4
Sans Bout, Rivière, (Que.) 16 A1
San Simon Point, (BC) 38 D4
Santein, Lac, (Que.) 5 E2
Santé, Lac, (Alta.) 33 F3
Santianna Point, (NWT) 46 D3
Santoy Lake, (Ont.) 27 G3
Saouayane, Pointe, (Que.) 20 D3
Saputing Lake, (NWT) 47 E4
Sarah, Cape, (NWT) 46 G2
Sarah Island, (BC) 41 E3
Sarah Lake, (Ont.) 27 B3
Sarah Lake, (Man.) 29 D1
Sarah Lake, (NWT) 45 E3
Sargent Point, (NWT) 47 D3
Sarita River, (BC) 38 C3
Sartine Island, (BC) 39 A1
Sasaginnigak Lake, (Man.) 30 C4
Saseginaga, Lac, (Que.) 26 H3
Saskatchewan Landing Provincial Park, (Sask.) 31 D3
Saskatchewan River, (Man./Sask.) 32 F3
Saskoba Lake, (Man./Sask.) 32 H2
Saskum Lake, (BC) 36 G3
Sasquatch Provincial Park, (BC) 35 A4
Sass River, (NWT) 44 B2
Satah Mountain, (BC) 40 A3
Satellite Bay, (NWT) 47 B2
Satin Lake, (NWT) 44 D1
Satsalla River, (BC) 41 G4
Saturna Island, (BC) 38 F3
Sauble River, (Ont.) 23 C1
Saubosq, Lac, (Que.) 19 G1
Saugeen River, (Ont.) 23 C2
Saugstad, Mount, (BC) 41 G3
Sault au Mouton, Rivière du, (Que.) 14 E2
Sault aux Cochons, Lac du, (Que.) 14 D1
Sault aux Cochons, Rivière du, (Que.) 14 E1
Saulteaux River, (Alta.) 33 D1
Saumon, Cap au, (Que.) 14 D4
Saumon, Rivière, (Que.) 16 E3
Saumons, Rivière aux, (Que.) 5 A4
Saumons, Rivière aux, (Que.) 18 G1
Saumur, Lac, (Que.) 5 A2
Saunders Lake, (Ont.) 20 G1
Saunders Lake, (Sask.) 32 G2
Sauniat, Lac, (Que.) 14 E2
Saunier Creek, (BC) 35 F3
Sautasuriski, Rivière, (Que.) 15 B2
Sautauriski, Lac, (Que.) 15 B2
Sauterelles, Lac aux, (Que.) 19 H1
Sauvage, Lac du, (NWT) 45 F2
Sauvage, Pointe, (Que.) 14 E3
Sauvolles, Lac, (Que.) 20 G2
Savage Harbour, (PEI) 7 D3
Savage Lake, (Ont.) 25 C1
Savalette, Rivière, (Que.) 6 D2
Savane, Lac, (Que.) 15 B1
Savane, Rivière, (Que.) 20 H3
Savanes, Lac des, (Que.) 14 D2
Savant Lake, (Ont.) 27 D1
Savard Lake, (NWT) 44 H1
Savary Island, (BC) 37 C4
Savignon, Lac, (Que.) 20 E1
Sawbill Lake, (Nfld.) 6 C3
Sawyer Bay, (NWT) 47 E2
Sawyers Hill, (Nfld.) 2 F3
Scaia, Mount, (BC) 35 H2
Scar Creek, (BC) 37 B1
Scarth River, (Sask.) 32 F2
Scatarie Island, (NS) 8 G3
Scenic Lake, (Ont.) 28 G1
Scentgrass Lake, (Sask.) 32 B4
Schade Lake, (Ont.) 30 F3
Schade River, (Ont.) 30 F3
Schaefer Lakes, (NWT) 44 C2
Scheltens Lake, (Alta.) 33 G1
Schewabik Lake, (Ont.) 26 C2
Schistes, Chute aux, (Que.) 6 B2
Schistose Lake, (Ont.) 28 H3
Schoen Lake, (BC) 39 F2
Schooner Harbour, (NWT) 46 E2
Schooner Point, (Nfld.) 2 B3
Schultz Lake, (Ont.) 28 H1
Schultz Lake, (NWT) 46 B2
Schwandt River, (NWT/Sask.) 44 F2
Schwatka Bay, (NWT) 45 H1
Schyan, Lac, (Que.) 18 C4
Scie, Rivière à la, (Que.) 15 G4
Scimitar Glacier, (BC) 37 B1
Sclater River, (Man.) 29 E1
Scorch Lake, (Ont.) 26 D2
Scoresby Bay, (NWT) 47 F1
Scoresby, Cape, (NWT) 47 D4
Scot Bay, (Ont.) 28 E1
Scotch Creek, (BC) 36 G4
Scotch Fir Point, (BC) 38 D1
Scotia Lake, (Ont.) 26 E3
Scot River, (Ont.) 28 E1
Scots Bay, (NS) 11 H3
Scotstoun Lake, (NWT) 45 E2
Scott Bay, (NWT) 47 D3
Scott, Cape, (BC) 39 B1
Scott Channel, (BC) 39 B1
Scott Falls, (Nfld.) 6 D3
Scottie Creek, (BC) 36 D4
Scott Island, (NWT) 47 G4
Scott Islands, (BC) 39 A1
Scott Lake, (NWT/Sask.) 44 E2
Scraggy Lake, (NS) 9 D3
Scrape Point, (Nfld.) 3 B1
Scrip Creek, (BC) 36 H2
Scriven, Mount, (BC) 39 G1
Scud River, (BC) 42 B1
Scugog, Lake, (Ont.) 21 C1
Scugog River, (Ont.) 21 C1
Scuitto Lake, (BC) 35 D1
Scuzzy Creek, (BC) 35 B3
Scuzzy Mountain, (BC) 35 A2
Seabird Lake, (BC) 39 G1
Seabrook Lake, (Ont.) 26 C3
Seacow Head, (PEI) 7 B4
Seaforth Channel, (BC) 41 E3
Seager Wheeler Lake, (Sask.) 32 F2
Seagram Lakes, (Sask.) 32 A4
Seagull Lake, (Man.) 29 G3
Seahole Lake, (NWT) 44 H1
Seahorse Lake, (Nfld.) 19 F1
Seahorse Point, (NWT) 46 D2
Sea Island, (BC) 38 F2
Seal Bay, (Nfld.) 3 B2
Seal Bay Brook, (Nfld.) 3 B2
Seal Bay Head, (Nfld.) 3 B2
Seal Brook, (Nfld.) 4 D4
Seal Island, (NS) 10 B4
Seal Island Bight, (Nfld.) 3 C1
Seal Lake, (Nfld.) 6 E3
Seal Point, (PEI) 7 A4
Seal River, (Man.) 46 A3
Searston Bay, (Nfld.) 4 B3
Sebalhall Creek, (BC) 39 F3
Sebaskachu Bay, (Nfld.) 6 F3
Sebaskachu River, (Nfld.) 6 F3
Sebert Lake, (Ont.) 20 A3
Séchelles, Lac, (Que.) 6 B4
Sechelt Creek, (BC) 38 E1
Sechelt Inlet, (BC) 38 E1
Sechelt Peninsula, (BC) 38 E1
Sèche, Pointe, (Que.) 13 G1
Second Burnt Pond, (Nfld.) 3 D3
Second Cranberry Lake, (Man.) 32 H2
Second Double Pond, (Nfld.) 3 E2
Second Eel Lake, (NB) 11 A1
Secondon, Lac, (Que.) 6 C2
Second Pond, (Nfld.) 3 D2
Seeber Lake, (Ont.) 30 E2
Seeber River, (Man./Ont.) 30 E2
Segise Lake, (Ont.) 28 H1
Seguin Lake, (Ont.) 24 A1
Seibert Lake, (Alta.) 33 G2
Seignelay, Rivière, (Que.) 19 C1
Seine River, (Man.) 28 B2
Sekulmun Lake, (YT) 45 A3
Selish Mountain, (BC) 35 C2
Selkirk, Cape, (NWT) 45 H1
Selkirk, Cape, (NWT) 46 C1
Selkirk Mountains, (BC) 34 B2
Seller Lake, (Man.) 30 D2
Seloam Lake, (NS) 9 D2
Selwyn Inlet, (BC) 41 B2
Selwyn Lake, (Ont.) 27 C2
Selwyn Lake, (NWT/Sask.) 44 F2
Selwyn Mountains, (NWT/YT) 45 B2
Semiahmoo Bay, (BC) 38 G3
Semiwagan River, (NB) 12 E3
Semmens Lake, (Man.) 30 D2
Semmens River, (Man.) 30 D2
Semple Lake, (Man.) 30 C2
Sen Bay, (Ont.) 27 B1
Senécal Lake, (Nfld.) 5 A1
Sénescoupé, Rivière, (Que.) 14 F4
Senneville, Lac, (Que.) 18 B2
Sentinel Peak, (BC) 40 D1
Senyk Lakes, (Sask.) 32 C1
Separation Lake, (Ont.) 30 D4
Sept Îles, Baie des, (Que.) 19 F3
Sept Îles, Lac, (Que.) 15 A3
Sept Îles, Lac des, (Que.) 13 G3
Sept Milles, Lac, (Que.) 18 B3
Sept Milles, Lac de, (Que.) 19 B2
Sequart Lake, (Nfld.) 6 D4
Sérigny, Lac, (Que.) 6 B2
Sérigny, Rivière, (Que.) 6 B2
Serpent Harbour, (Ont.) 25 B1
Serpentine Lake, (Nfld.) 4 C1
Serpentine Lake, (NB) 12 C2
Serpentine River, (Nfld.) 4 C1
Serpentine River, (NB) 12 C2
Serpent, Lac du, (Que.) 19 A3
Serpent, Pointe du, (Que.) 13 H1
Serpent River, (Ont.) 30 E4
Serpent, Rivière au, (Que.) 19 A3
Seseganaga Lake, (Ont.) 27 D1
Sesekinika Lake, (Ont.) 26 F2
Seton Lake, (BC) 37 H2
Settee Lake, (Man.) 30 C1
Setting Lake, (Man.) 30 B2
Seul, Lac, (Ont.) 27 B1
Seven Islands Bay, (Nfld.) 46 H3
Sevenmile Bay, (PEI) 7 B4
Seven Mile Lake, (NS) 10 D2
Seven Mile Lake, (NB) 11 C3
Seven Persons Creek, (Alta.) 31 A3
Seven Sisters Peaks, (BC) 42 E4
Severn Lake, (Ont.) 30 F2
Severn River, (Ont.) 24 B3
Severn River, (Ont.) 30 G1
Sevestre, Lac, (Que.) 6 C4
Seymour Arm, (BC) 36 H4
Seymour Inlet, (BC) 41 F4
Seymour River, (BC) 36 H3
Seymour River, (BC) 38 F2
Sgurra Bhreac *(hill)*, (NS) 8 E3
Shabogamo Lake, (Nfld.) 6 C3
Shabotik River, (Ont.) 26 A1
Shabuskwia Lake, (Ont.) 30 G4
Shacabac Lake, (Ont.) 27 H1
Shad Bay, (NS) 10 F2
Shadow Lake, (Ont.) 24 C3
Shagamu Lake, (Ont.) 30 G2
Shagamu River, (Ont.) 30 G1
Shag, Ile, (Que.) 7 F1
Shag Island, (Nfld.) 4 B1
Shag Islands, (Nfld.) 3 F3
Shagwenaw Lake, (Sask.) 44 D4
Shakan Creek, (BC) 35 B2
Shakespeare Island, (Ont.) 27 E2
Shakwa Lake, (Ont.) 26 D3
Shaler Mountains, (NWT) 47 B4
Shalloway Brook, (Nfld.) 3 F2
Shallow Lake, (Sask.) 32 B2
Shamattawa River, (Ont.) 20 B2
Shammis Island, (Ont.) 28 F2
Shanadithit Brook, (Nfld.) 4 E1
Shand Creek, (Sask.) 32 G4
Shanks Lake, (Alta.) 34 G4
Shannon Lake, (Man.) 44 G2
Shapio Lake, (Nfld.) 6 F3
Sharbot Lake, (Ont.) 17 A3
Sharp, Cape, (PEI) 7 E4
Sharp, Cape, (NS) 11 H2
Sharpe Lake, (Man.) 30 D2
Sharpes Creek, (Ont.) 23 B3
Sharp Point, (BC) 39 F4
Sharpstone Lake, (Ont.) 30 D3
Sharun Lake, (NWT) 44 A1
Shatford Creek, (BC) 35 E4
Shawanabis Lake, (Ont.) 27 D1
Shawanaga Inlet, (Ont.) 25 F3
Shawanaga Island, (Ont.) 25 F3
Shawanaga River, (Ont.) 25 G3
Shawinigan, Lac, (Que.) 16 A1
Shawinigan, Rivière, (Que.) 16 B1
Shaw Lake, (Sask.) 44 D4
Shawmere River, (Ont.) 26 C2
Shawnigan Lake, (BC) 38 E4
Shearwater Passage, (BC) 37 C4
Sheasby Lake, (Sask.) 32 A2
Shebandowan Lakes, (Ont.) 27 C3
Shebeshekong River, (Ont.) 25 G3
Shediac Bay, (NB) 12 H4
Shediac Island, (NB) 12 H4
Shediac River, (NB) 12 G4
Shedin Creek, (BC) 42 F3
Shedin Peak, (BC) 42 F2
Sheemahant River, (BC) 41 G4
Sheep Creek, (Alta.) 40 F2
Sheep Lake, (Man.) 28 E1
Sheep River, (Alta.) 34 E3
Sheet Harbour, (NS) 9 D3
Sheffield Lake, (Nfld.) 5 G4
Shekak Lake, (Ont.) 20 B4
Shekak River, (Ont.) 20 B4
Shelagyote Peak, (BC) 42 F2
Shelagyote River, (BC) 42 F3
Shelburne Harbour, (NS) 10 C4
Shelburne River, (NS) 10 C2
Sheldrake, Rivière, (Que.) 19 G3
Shell Brook, (Ont.) 30 G1
Shell Brook, (Sask.) 32 D3
Shell Camp Lake, (NS) 11 G4
Shell Lake, (Sask.) 32 C3
Shell River, (Man.) 29 D2
Shelter Inlet, (BC) 39 F4
Shelter Point, (BC) 37 B4
Shemogue Harbour, (NB) 7 A4
Shepherd Bay, (NWT) 45 H1
Shepherd, Mount, (BC) 38 D1
Shepody Bay, (NB) 11 G2
Sherard Bay, (NWT) 47 C2
Sherard, Cape, (NWT) 47 F3
Sherard Head, (NWT) 47 D3
Sherard Osborn Island, (NWT) 47 D2
Sherard Osborn Point, (NWT) 47 C4
Sherbrooke Lake, (NS) 10 E1
Sherbrooke River, (NS) 10 D1
Sheridan Lake, (BC) 36 D3
Sheridan Point, (Ont.) 22 B4
Sheringham Point, (BC) 38 E4
Sherman Basin, (NWT) 45 H1
Sherwood Lake, (NWT) 44 F2
Sherwood River, (Ont.) 24 F1
Shesheeb Bay, (Ont.) 27 F3
Shethanei Lake, (Man.) 44 H3
Shethanei Lake, (Man.) 46 A3
Shibogama Lake, (Ont.) 30 G2
Shikag Lake, (Ont.) 27 C2
Shikwamkwa Lake, (Ont.) 26 B2
Shillabeer Lake, (Ont.) 27 E2
Shin Creek, (BC) 40 D1
Shingle Creek, (BC) 35 E3
Shingle Lake, (NS) 10 D2
Shingwak Lake, (Ont.) 28 H3
Shinimicas River, (NS) 9 A1
Shiningbank Lake, (Alta.) 33 B3
Shining Tree Lake, (Ont.) 26 E3
Ship Cove, (Nfld.) 4 B3
Ship Harbour, (NS) 9 D3
Ship Harbour Long Lake, (NS) 9 C3
Shipiskan Lake, (Nfld.) 6 E3
Ship Island, (Nfld.) 3 F3
Shippegan, Baie de, (NB) 13 G4
Shippegan Gully, (NB) 13 G4
Ship Run, (Nfld.) 3 C2
Shipshaw, Rivière, (Que.) 14 B1
Shirley Lake, (Ont.) 24 E1
Shoal Arm, (Nfld.) 3 B2
Shoal Arm Brook, (Nfld.) 3 B2
Shoal Bay, (Nfld.) 2 F2
Shoal Bay, (Nfld.) 2 F4
Shoal Bay, (Nfld.) 3 E1
Shoal Bay, (Nfld.) 3 E2
Shoal Harbour Pond, (Nfld.) 2 E1
Shoal Harbour River, (Nfld.) 2 E1
Shoal Lake, (Ont.) 27 A3
Shoal Lake, (Man./Ont.) 28 E2
Shoal Lake, (Man.) 29 E3
Shoal Lake, (Alta.) 33 D2
Shoal Point, (Nfld.) 4 B2
Shoal Point, (Nfld.) 4 B3
Shoal Point, (Nfld.) 4 A4
Shoe Cove Point, (Nfld.) 3 F3
Shogomoc Lake, (NB) 11 B1
Shoran Bay, (NWT) 46 D3
Shorts Creek, (BC) 35 E2
Shortts Lake, (NS) 9 C2
Shovel Creek, (BC) 40 A1
Shovelnose Mountain, (BC) 35 C2
Shubenacadie Grand Lake, (NS) 9 B3
Shubenacadie River, (NS) 9 B3
Shugba Bay, (NWT) 46 E2
Shukbuk Bay, (NWT) 46 E2
Shulaps Peak, (BC) 37 G2
Shulie River, (NS) 11 G2
Shumway Lake, (BC) 35 D1
Shushartie River, (BC) 39 C1
Shuswap Lake, (BC) 36 G4
Shuswap River, (BC) 35 F1
Shuttleworth Creek, (BC) 35 F4
Sibbeston Lake, (NWT) 45 D3
Sibley Peninsula, (Ont.) 27 E3
Sibley Provincial Park, (Ont.) 27 E3
Sicintine River, (BC) 42 F2
Sideburned Lake, (Ont.) 26 B2
Side Saddle Lake, (Man.) 28 E1
Sid Lake, (NWT) 44 F1
Sidney Channel, (BC) 38 F4
Sidney Island, (BC) 38 F4
Sidney Lake, (Sask.) 32 A3
Sidney Webb Point, (NWT) 47 C4
Siegas, Rivière, (NB) 12 A1
Siffleur River, (Alta.) 34 C1
Sifton Lake, (NWT) 45 G3
Sifton Ranges, (BC) 43 A1
Sigutlat Lake, (BC) 41 G2
Sikachu Lake, (Sask.) 32 D1
Sikanni Chief River, (BC) 43 D2
Sillem Island, (NWT) 47 G4
Silsby Lake, (Man.) 30 D1
Siltaza Lake, (NWT) 44 D1
Silumiut, Cape, (NWT) 46 C2
Silver Fox Island, (Nfld.) 3 F3
Silverhope Creek, (BC) 35 B4
Silver Lake, (Ont.) 17 A3
Silver Lake, (Ont.) 25 E3
Silver Lake, (Ont.) 28 G1
Silver River, (NS) 10 B3
Silver Star Provincial Park, (BC) 35 F1
Silverthrone Glacier, (BC) 37 A1
Silverthrone Mountain, (BC) 41 G4
Silvertip Mountain, (BC) 35 B4
Silvy, Lac, (Que.) 20 F1
Simard, Lac, (Que.) 19 E3
Simard, Lac, (Que.) 26 G2
Simcoe Island, (Ont.) 17 A4
Simcoe, Lake, (Ont.) 23 G2
Similkameen River, (BC) 35 D4
Simmons Lake, (BC) 37 B3
Simmons Peninsula, (NWT) 47 E2
Simonette River, (Alta.) 33 A1
Simonhouse Lake, (Man.) 32 H2
Simon, Lac, (Que.) 18 E4
Simoom Sound, (BC) 39 F1
Simpson Bay, (NWT) 47 B4
Simpson Island, (Ont.) 27 F3
Simpson Lake, (NWT) 45 D1
Simpson Peninsula, (NWT) 46 C1
Simpson River, (NWT) 45 G1
Simpson Strait, (NWT) 45 G1
Sim River, (BC) 37 A1
Sims Creek, (BC) 37 E3
Sims Lake, (Nfld.) 6 D3
Sinaminda Lake, (Ont.) 26 D3
Sincennes, Lac, (Que.) 18 F2
Sinclair Lake, (Ont.) 26 E2
Sinclair Lake, (NWT) 44 E1
Sinclair River, (Man.) 29 E1
Singer Point, (NWT) 46 G3
Sinking Lake, (Alta.) 33 G2
Sinmax Creek, (BC) 36 F4
Sioux Lake, (Man.) 44 H3
Sipiwesk Lake, (Man.) 30 C2
Sir Alexander, Mount, (BC) 40 E2
Sir Frances Drake, Mount, (BC) 37 C2
Sir Richard, Mount, (BC) 37 G4
Sir Sandford, Mount, (BC) 34 B1
Sir Wilfrid Laurier, Mount, (BC) 40 F3
Sisib Lake, (Man.) 30 B3
Sisipuk Lake, (Man./Sask.) 30 A1
Sisseney Lake, (Ont.) 26 E2
Sissiboo Grand Lake, (NS) 10 B2
Sissiboo River, (NS) 10 B2
Sisson Branch Reservoir, (NB) 12 B2
Sister Islets, (BC) 38 D2
Sitdown Pond, (Nfld.) 4 H2
Sitidgi Lake, (NWT) 45 C1
Sitkum Creek, (BC) 35 H1
Siugak Brook, (Nfld.) 6 E1
SivierIsland, (Nfld.) 3 D2
Siwash Creek, (BC) 35 D3
Siwash Mountain, (BC) 34 B4
Siwhe Mountain, (BC) 35 A1
Six Mile Lake, (Ont.) 24 A3
Skaare Fiord, (NWT) 47 E2
Skagit Range, (BC) 35 B4
Skagit River, (BC) 35 B4
Skaha Lake, (BC) 35 E3
Skeena Mountains, (BC) 42 E1
Skeena River, (BC) 42 E1
Skeleton Lake, (Ont.) 24 B2
Skeleton Lake, (Ont.) 26 F2
Skene Bay, (NWT) 47 C3
Skidegate Inlet, (BC) 41 B2
Skiff Island, (Ont.) 28 F3
Skiff Lake, (NB) 11 A1
Skiffsail Point, (Nfld.) 2 C3
Skihist Mountain, (BC) 35 A2
Skinner Lake, (Ont.) 30 F3
Skookumchuck Creek, (BC) 34 C3
Skootamatta Lake, (Ont.) 24 G3
Skootamatta River, (Ont.) 24 G3
Skraeling Point, (NWT) 47 E2
Skrugar Point, (NWT) 47 D2
Skruis Point, (NWT) 47 E3
Skuhun Creek, (BC) 35 C1
Skull Hill, (Nfld.) 3 A3
Skwawka River, (BC) 37 D3
Skye River, (NS) 8 D3
Sky Lake, (Ont.) 23 C1
Sky Pilot Mountain, (BC) 38 F1
Slate Islands, (Ont.) 27 G3
Slave Bay, (NWT) 44 B1
Slave Point, (NWT) 44 B1
Slave River, (Alta./NWT) 44 C2
Sled Creek, (NWT) 44 E1
Sled Lake, (Sask.) 32 C2
Sleeper Islands, (NWT) 46 D4
Sleigh Pond, (Nfld.) 2 E1
Slemon Lake, (NWT) 45 E3
Slesse Creek, (BC) 35 A4
Slesse Mountain, (BC) 35 A4
Slimamon Lake, (BC) 37 C4
Slidre Fiord, (NWT) 47 E2
Slim Creek, (BC) 37 F2
Slim Creek, (BC) 40 D2
Sloan River, (NWT) 45 E2
Slocan Lake, (BC) 34 B3
Slok Creek, (BC) 36 B4
Slollicum Peak, (BC) 35 A4
Sloquet Creek, (BC) 38 H1
Small Island, (Nfld.) 3 F1
Small Lake, (Man.) 44 H3
Smalltree Lake, (NWT) 44 E1
Smallwood Reservoir, (Nfld.) 6 D3
Smart Lake, (NWT) 45 G3
Smith Arm, (NWT) 45 D2
Smith Bay, (Ont.) 25 D2
Smith Bay, (NWT) 44 G2
Smith Bay, (NWT) 47 D3
Smith Bay, (NWT) 47 F2
Smith, Cape, (Ont.) 25 D2
Smith Creek, (BC) 35 D4
Smith Inlet, (BC) 41 F4
Smith Island, (BC) 41 C1
Smith Island, (NWT) 46 E3
Smith Point, (NS) 9 C1
Smith Pond, (Nfld.) 3 F2
Smith Sound, (Nfld.) 2 F1
Smith Sound, (BC) 41 F4
Smith Sound, (NWT) 47 F2
Smokehouse Creek, (BC) 41 G4
Smoke Lake, (Ont.) 24 D2
Smoke Lake, (Alta.) 33 B2
Smokey, Cape, (NS) 8 E2
Smoky Lake, (Alta.) 33 E2
Smoky River, (Alta.) 43 G4
Smoothrock Lake, (Ont.) 27 D1
Smoothstone Lake, (Sask.) 32 C2
Smoothstone River, (Sask.) 32 D1
Smoothwater Lake, (Ont.) 26 E3
Smyth, Cape, (NWT) 47 B3
Smythe, Mount, (BC) 43 B1
Snake Bay, (Ont.) 28 F3
Snake Creek, (Ont.) 23 C2
Snake Indian River, (Alta.) 40 G2
Snake Island, (NS) 10 F2
Snake Island, (Ont.) 23 F2
Snake Lake, (Alta.) 44 B2
Snake River, (YT) 45 B2
Snape Island, (NWT) 20 D1
Snare Lake, (Sask.) 44 D3
Snare River, (Sask.) 44 E3
Snare River, (NWT) 45 E3
Snaring River, (Alta.) 40 G3
Snass Mountain, (BC) 35 C4
Snegamook Lake, (Nfld.) 6 E3
Snelgrove Lake, (Nfld.) 6 D3
Snipe Lake, (Sask.) 31 C2
Snipe Lake, (Alta.) 33 B1
Snook Lake, (Ont.) 28 F1
Snooks Arm, (Nfld.) 3 B1
Snowbank River, (NWT) 46 C2
Snowbird Lake, (NWT) 44 F2
Snowcap Creek, (BC) 38 G1
Snowcap Lake, (BC) 37 G4
Snowcrest Mountain, (BC) 34 C4
Snowdrift River, (NWT) 44 D1
Snow, Mont, (Que.) 15 F3
Snowshoe Bay, (Man.) 28 E2
Snowshoe Pond, (Nfld.) 4 F2
Snows Pond, (Nfld.) 2 G2
Snowy Mountain, (BC) 35 E4
Snyder Lake, (Man.) 44 G2
Sober Island, (NS) 9 E3
Soeurs, Ile des, (Que.) 17 H4
Soissons, Lac, (Que.) 6 C1
Sokatisewin Lake, (Sask.) 32 G1
Solace Lake, (Ont.) 26 E3
Soldier Lake, (NS) 9 B3
Somass River, (BC) 38 C2
Sombrio Point, (BC) 38 D4
Somerset Island, (NWT) 46 D3
Somerville Island, (BC) 42 C4
Sommet, Lac du, (Que.) 6 B4
Sonora Island, (BC) 37 B3
Sooke Inlet, (BC) 38 E4
Sooke Lake, (BC) 38 E4
Sooke River, (BC) 38 E4
Soo River, (BC) 37 F4
Sops Arm, (Nfld.) 3 B2
Sops Arm Brook, (Nfld.) 3 B2
Sops Island, (Nfld.) 5 G4
Sops Lake, (Nfld.) 3 B2
Sorcerer Mountain, (BC) 34 B2
Sorcier, Lac au, (Que.) 16 A1
Soscumica, Lac, (Que.) 20 E4
Soufflets River, (Nfld.) 5 G3
Soufflot, Lac, (Que.) 26 H3
Soulier Lake, (Sask.) 44 D2
Soulis Pond, (Nfld.) 3 E3
Soul Lake, (Man.) 30 B3
Sounding Creek, (Alta.) 31 A1
Sounding Lake, (Alta.) 31 B1
Sound Island, (Nfld.) 2 E2
Soup Harbour, (Ont.) 21 G2
Sourd, Lac du, (Que.) 18 E4
Souris River, (Man./Sask.) 29 B4
Southampton, Cape, (NWT) 46 D3
Southampton Island, (NWT) 46 D2
South Arm, (Nfld.) 3 C2
South Arm, (Ont.) 26 F3
South Aulatsivik Island, (Nfld.) 6 F2
South Bay, (Ont.) 22 B4
South Bay, (Ont.) 25 C3
South Bay, (Ont.) 25 H1
South Bay, (Ont.) 26 F1
South Bay, (Ont.) 27 E2
South Bay, (Sask.) 32 C1
South Bay, (Man.) 44 H4
South Bay, (NWT) 46 D2
South Bay Ingonish, (NS) 8 E2
South Bentinck Arm, (BC) 41 G3
South Bill *(point)*, (Nfld.) 3 B1
South Bill *(point)*, (Nfld.) 3 C1
South Branch Big Sevogle River, (NB) 12 D2
South Branch Kedgwick River, (NB) 14 H4
South Branch Muskoka River, (Ont.) 24 C3
South Branch Nepisiguit River, (NB) 12 D2
South Branch Renous River, (NB) 12 D3
South Brook, (Nfld.) 3 A2
Southby Lake, (NWT) 44 E2
South Cape Fiord, (NWT) 47 E2
South Charlo River, (NB) 13 D4
South Creek, (Ont.) 26 D1
South Cross Lake, (Man.) 28 E1
Southeast Arm, (Nfld.) 4 F4
Southeast Arm, (Sask.) 32 G2
Southeast River, (Nfld.) 2 F3
Southeast Upsalquitch River, (NB) 12 C1
South End *(point)*, (Nfld.) 3 E1
Southern Arm, (Nfld.) 3 A1
Southern Arm, (Nfld.) 3 B1
Southern Bay, (Nfld.) 3 F4
Southern Head, (Nfld.) 3 B1
Southern Head, (Nfld.) 3 C2
Southern Head, (Nfld.) 3 G4
Southern Indian Lake, (Man.) 44 H3
Southern Pond, (Nfld.) 3 A1
Southern Pond, (Nfld.) 3 E3
Southern Wolf Island, (NB) 11 C3
South Fosthall Creek, (BC) 35 H1
South French Bar Creek, (BC) 36 B3
Southgate River, (BC) 37 C2
South Great Rattling Brook, (Nfld.) 3 B4
South Green Island, (Nfld.) 6 G3
South Harbour, (NS) 8 E1
South Head, (Nfld.) 2 H3
South Head, (Nfld.) 3 G4
South Head, (Nfld.) 5 F4
South Head, (NS) 8 G3
South Heart River, (Alta.) 44 A4
South Henik Lake, (NWT) 44 H1
South Knife River, (Man.) 46 A4
South La Cloche Mountains, (Ont.) 25 D2
South Lake, (Ont.) 17 B4
South Limestone Island, (Ont.) 25 F3
South Little River Lake, (NB) 12 D2
South Macmillan River, (YT) 45 B3
South Maitland River, (Ont.) 23 B4
South Moose Lake, (Man.) 30 A2
South Mountain, (NS) 10 C1
South Nahanni River, (NWT) 45 C3
South Nanaimo River, (BC) 38 D3
South Nation River, (Ont.) 17 D2
South Oromocto Lake, (NB) 11 C2
South Pender Island, (BC) 38 F3
South Peninsula, (Ont.) 27 F1
South Point, (Nfld.) 2 E2
South Point, (Nfld.) 2 F4
South Point, (Nfld.) 5 H1
South Pond, (Nfld.) 3 A2
South Pond, (Nfld.) 3 D2
South River, (NS) 9 F2
South River, (Ont.) 25 H2
South Samson Island, (Nfld.) 3 D2
South Saskatchewan River, (Alta./Sask.) 31 E1
South Saugeen River, (Ont.) 23 C3
South Scot Lake, (Ont.) 28 E1
South Seal River, (Man.) 44 H3
South Spicer Island, (NWT) 46 E1
South Stag Island, (Nfld.) 6 G3
South Thompson River, (BC) 36 G4

South Tweedsmuir Island, (NWT) 46 E1
South Twillingate Island, (Nfld.) 3 D1
South Twin Island, (NWT) 20 D2
South Twin Lake, (Nfld.) 3 B2
South Wabasca Lake, (Alta.) 44 B4
Southwest Arm, (Nfld.) 2 C3
Southwest Arm, (Nfld.) 2 F1
Southwest Arm, (Nfld.) 3 A1
Southwest Arm, (Nfld.) 3 C2
Southwest Arm, (Nfld.) 3 F4
Southwest Brook, (Nfld.) 3 C2
Southwest Brook, (Nfld.) 4 C2
Southwest, Cape, (NWT) 47 E2
Southwest Gander River, (Nfld.) 3 C4
Southwest Head, (NB) 11 B4
Southwest Mabou River, (NS) 9 G1
Southwest Margaree River, (NS) 8 D3
Southwest Miramichi River, (NB) 12 C3
Southwest Point, (NS) 8 F1
Southwest Pond, (Nfld.) 3 D4
Southwest Pond, (Nfld.) 3 E3
Southwest River, (Nfld.) 2 E1
South Wolf Island, (Nfld.) 6 H3
Sovereign Lake, (Sask.) 44 E2
Sowaqua Creek, (BC) 35 B4
Sowden Lake, (Ont.) 27 C2
Soyers Lake, (Ont.) 24 D3
Spahats Creek, (BC) 36 F2
Spahomin Creek, (BC) 35 D2
Spa Lake, (BC) 35 F1
Spaniard's Bay, (Nfld.) 2 G2
Spaniards Cove, (Nfld.) 3 G4
Spanish Creek, (BC) 36 E2
Spanish River, (Ont.) 25 C1
Sparbo, Cape, (NWT) 47 E3
Spare Point, (Nfld.) 2 G2
Sparkling Lake, (Ont.) 27 D1
Sparks Lake, (NWT) 44 D1
Spar Lake, (NS) 9 E3
Sparrow Lake, (Ont.) 24 B3
Sparrow Lake, (NWT) 44 B1
Spatsizi River, (BC) 42 E1
Spear, Cape, (Nfld.) 2 H2
Spear, Cape, (NB) 7 B4
Spearfish Lake, (NWT) 44 D2
Spear Lake, (Sask.) 44 D4
Spear Point, (Nfld.) 5 H1
Spear Point, (Nfld.) 5 G4
Spector Lake, (Man.) 30 F1
Spednic Lake, (NB) 11 A2
Speed River, (Ont.) 23 E4
Spence Bay, (NWT) 46 C1
Spence Lake, (Man.) 29 F2
Spencer, Cape, (NB) 11 E3
Spencer, Cape, (NS) 11 G3
Spencer Island, (NWT) 20 D2
Spencer Lake, (Alta.) 33 G2
Sphene Lake, (Ont.) 28 H3
Spider Bay, (Ont.) 25 G4
Spiller Channel, (BC) 41 E3
Spillmacheen River, (BC) 34 B2
Spinel Lake, (BC) 43 A1
Spitfire Lake, (NWT) 44 D2
Spittler Creek, (Ont.) 22 F2
Spius Creek, (BC) 35 B2
Splatt Bay, (Ont.) 21 A4
Split, Cape, (NS) 11 H3
Split Island, (NWT) 46 D4
Split Lake, (Man.) 30 C1
Split Point, (Nfld.) 2 H1
Splitrock Bay, (Ont.) 28 G3
Splitrock Island, (Ont.) 28 F3
Splitrock River, (Ont.) 28 G3
Spokin Lake, (BC) 36 C1
Sporting Lake, (NS) 10 C2
Spotted Horse Lake, (Alta.) 33 D1
Spotted Island, (Nfld.) 6 H3
Spout Lake, (BC) 36 D1
Sprague Creek, (Man.) 28 D3
Spratt Point, (Ont.) 23 E1
Spray Lakes Reservoir, (Alta.) 34 D2
Spring Lake, (BC) 36 D2
Spring Passage, (BC) 39 E1
Sproat Lake, (BC) 38 B2
Sprott Lake, (Man.) 44 H3
Sproule Peninsula, (NWT) 47 C2
Sproule, Pointe, (Que.) 19 E3
Spruce Island, (Man.) 30 A3
Spruce Lake, (Ont.) 20 B1
Spruce Point, (NS) 8 D4
Spruce Pond, (Nfld.) 4 D3
Spruce River, (Ont.) 27 E2
Spruce River, (Ont.) 30 F3
Spruce River, (Sask.) 32 D3
Spruce Woods Provincial Park, (Man.) 29 G4
Spry Bay, (NS) 9 D3
Spry, Cape, (PEI) 7 E4
Spuzzum Creek, (BC) 35 B3
Squally Channel, (BC) 41 D2
Squally Point, (NS) 11 G2
Squamish Harbour, (BC) 38 F1
Squamish River, (BC) 38 F1
Square Forks, Rivière, (Que.) 13 D2
Square Island, (Nfld.) 6 H4
Square Lake, (NB) 7 H4
Square Lake, (NB) 12 C2
Square Lake, (Alta.) 33 F1
Square Pond, (Nfld.) 3 E3
Squatec, Lac, (Que.) 15 G1
Squaw Cap Mountain, (NB) 13 C4
Squaw Island, (Ont.) 25 D2
Squawk Lake, (BC) 36 C1
Squaw Lake, (Ont.) 28 E2
Squaw River, (Ont.) 27 G1
Squingula River, (BC) 42 F2
Squirrel Island, (Ont.) 22 B2
Squirrel River, (Ont.) 20 B4
Stafford Lake, (BC) 37 B2
Stafford River, (BC) 37 B2
Stag Island, (Nfld.) 3 B1
Stag Island, (NWT) 20 E3
Stag Lake, (Nfld.) 4 D1
Stallworthy, Cape, (NWT) 47 D1
Stamp River, (BC) 38 B2
Standish Lake, (Alta.) 33 G2
Stang, Cape, (NWT) 47 C4
Stanjikoming Bay, (Ont.) 28 H4
Stanley Mountain, (NB) 12 B3
Stanley Smith Glacier, (BC) 37 E2
Stanwell-Fletcher Lake, (NWT) 47 D4
Staples River, (Ont.) 24 C4
Stapylton Bay, (NWT) 45 E1
Star Lake, (Nfld.) 4 E2
Starnes Fiord, (NWT) 47 E2
States Lake, (NB) 13 A4
Statlu Creek, (BC) 38 H2
Stave Lake, (BC) 38 H2
Stave River, (BC) 38 G1
Stawamus River, (BC) 38 F1
Steady Brook Lake, (Nfld.) 4 D1
Steele Lake, (Alta.) 33 D2
Steel Lake, (Ont.) 27 G2
Steel River, (Ont.) 27 H2
Steen River, (Alta.) 44 A2
Steensby Inlet, (NWT) 47 F4
Steepbank River, (Alta.) 44 C4
Steephill Lake, (Sask.) 44 F4
Steeprock Lake, (Man.) 29 F2
Steeprock River, (Man.) 30 A3
Stefansson Island, (NWT) 47 C3
Stein Lake, (BC) 37 H4
Stein Mountain, (BC) 35 A1
Stein River, (BC) 35 A2
Stella Lake, (BC) 37 A3
Stephen Lake, (Ont.) 28 G3
Stephens Island, (BC) 41 C1
Stephens Lake, (Man.) 30 D1
Stephensons Pond, (Nfld.) 4 E3
Stepp Lake, (BC) 41 F1
Sterns Lake, (NWT) 44 G1
Stevens Bay, (Ont.) 28 G3
Stevens Head, (NWT) 47 B2
Stevens Lake, (Man.) 44 G3
Stevens Lakes, (BC) 36 G2
Stevenson Lake, (Man.) 30 C2
Stevenson River, (Man.) 30 C2
Stevens Passage, (BC) 38 C1
Stewart Lake, (NWT) 46 C1
Stewart River, (YT) 45 A2
Stewiake River, (NS) 9 C2
Stikelan Creek, (BC) 37 D1
Stikine River, (BC) 42 B1
Still River, (Ont.) 25 F2
Stirling Arm, (BC) 38 B2
Stirling Creek, (BC) 35 F3
Stobart Creek, (BC) 37 G1
Stoco Lake, (Ont.) 24 G4
Stoddart Island, (NS) 10 B4
Stoke, Rivière, (Que.) 16 D3
Stokes Bay, (Ont.) 25 D4
Stokke Creek, (BC) 35 A3
Stone Lake, (Ont.) 27 F1
Stone Mountain Provincial Park, (BC) 45 C4
Stoney Arm, (Nfld.) 6 H3
Stoney Brook, (NS) 10 C3
Stoney Creek, (Ont.) 22 H2
Stoney Point, (Ont.) 22 B3
Stony Brook, (Nfld.) 3 B3
Stony Creek, (Man.) 28 E3
Stony Creek, (Man./Sask.) 29 D4
Stony Island, (Nfld.) 6 H4
Stony Lake, (Nfld.) 3 B3
Stony Lake, (Ont.) 24 E4
Stony Lake, (Sask.) 32 B3
Stony Lake, (BC) 40 D2
Stony Lake, (Man.) 44 H3
Stony Point, (Nfld.) 2 E3
Stony Point, (Man.) 29 H1
Stony, Pointe, (Que.) 46 G4
Stooping River, (Ont.) 20 C3
Stor Island, (NWT) 47 E2
Storis Passage, (NWT) 45 G1
Storkerson Bay, (NWT) 47 A3
Storkerson Peninsula, (NWT) 47 C3
Storm, Cape, (NWT) 47 E3
Storm, Lac, (Que.) 20 F4
Stormy Brook, (Nfld.) 3 B4
Stormy Lake, (Ont.) 27 B2
Stormy Point, (Nfld.) 4 A3
Stout Lake, (Ont.) 30 D3
Stoyoma Mountain, (BC) 35 B2
Straight Lake, (Ont.) 28 H2
Strait Lake, (BC) 36 G1
Straits Bay, (NWT) 46 E1
Stranby River, (BC) 39 B1
Strand Bay, (NWT) 47 D2
Strange Lake, (Sask.) 32 D2
Strathcona Fiord, (NWT) 47 E2
Strathcona Islands, (NWT) 46 F2
Strathcona Provincial Park, (BC) 39 G3
Strathcona Sound, (NWT) 47 E3
Stratton Inlet, (NWT) 47 E3
Strawberry, Cape, (Nfld.) 6 G2
Strawberry Creek, (Alta.) 33 D3
Strawberry Island, (Ont.) 25 C2
Strawberry Lakes, (Sask.) 29 B3
Straw Lake, (Ont.) 28 H3
Streatfeild Lake, (Ont.) 20 A3
Streatfeild River, (Ont.) 20 A2
Strickland Pond, (Nfld.) 4 C4
Striding River, (NWT/Sask.) 44 F2
Strong Island, (Nfld.) 3 C2
Strutton Islands, (NWT) 20 E3
Stuart Channel, (BC) 38 E3
Stuart Island, (BC) 37 B3
Stuart Lake, (BC) 40 B1
Stuart River, (BC) 40 B1
Stuarts Lake, (NS) 10 D3
Stuarts Point, (NS) 10 D3
Stubborn Head, (NS) 9 A2
Stukely, Lac, (Que.) 16 C4
Stukemapten Lake, (BC) 36 H3
Stull Lake, (Man./Ont.) 30 E2
Stull River, (Man./Ont.) 30 E2
Stum Lake, (BC) 36 A1
Stump Lake, (BC) 35 D1
Stupart River, (Man.) 30 D1
Stupendous Mountain, (BC) 41 G3
Sturge Lake, (Ont.) 27 E2
Sturgeon Bay, (Man.) 29 H1
Sturgeon Creek, (Ont.) 28 G4
Sturgeon Lake, (Ont.) 24 D4
Sturgeon Lake, (Ont.) 27 C1
Sturgeon Lake, (Ont.) 27 B3
Sturgeon Lake, (Ont.) 30 E1
Sturgeon Lake, (Alta.) 33 A1
Sturgeon River, (Ont.) 23 F1
Sturgeon River, (Ont.) 25 G1
Sturgeon River, (Ont.) 30 D4
Sturgeon River, (Sask.) 32 D3
Sturgeon River, (Alta.) 33 D3
Sturgeon-weir River, (Sask.) 32 G2
Sturges Bourne Islands, (NWT) 46 D2
Styx River, (Ont.) 23 C2
Success Point, (NWT) 47 C2
Sucker Lake, (Ont.) 25 C2
Sucker River, (Ont.) 26 E1
Sucker, Ruisseau, (Que.) 20 E1
Sud, Chenal du, (Que.) 14 E4
Sud des Indiens, Lac
see Southern Indian Lake
Sud-Ouest, Bassin du, (Que.) 13 G2
Sud-Ouest, Cap du, (Que.) 7 F1
Sud-Ouest, Rivière du, (Que.) 14 F3
Sud, Pointe du, (Que.) 5 B4
Sud, Rivière du, (Que.) 15 C3
Sugar Lake, (BC) 35 G1
Sugarloaf Head, (Nfld.) 2 H2
Sugarloaf Mountain, (NS) 8 D2
Suggi Lake, (Sask.) 32 G2
Sugluk Inlet, (NWT) 46 E3
Sukunka River, (BC) 43 D4
Sullivan Lake, (Alta.) 34 G1
Sullivan Lake, (BC) 36 F4
Sullivan River, (BC) 34 B1
Sulphur Bay, (NWT) 44 B1
Sulphurous Lake, (BC) 36 E2
Sulphur River, (Alta.) 40 G2
Sumallo River, (BC) 35 B4
Sumas River, (BC) 38 H2
Summers Creek, (BC) 35 D3
Summerside Harbour, (PEI) 7 B3
Summit Lake, (Ont.) 27 F1
Summit Lake, (BC) 40 C1
Summit Lake, (BC) 42 D2
Sunday Cove Island, (Nfld.) 3 B1
Sunday Lake, (Nfld.) 3 C3
Sunderland Channel, (BC) 39 G1
Sunlight Lake, (Ont.) 27 A1
Sunset Creek, (BC) 36 H2
Superior, Lake, (Ont.) 27 F4
Sureau, Lac, (Que.) 6 A4
Surf Inlet, (BC) 41 E2
Surprise, Lac, (Que.) 20 G4
Surrey Lake, (NWT) 47 C4
Susan Island, (BC) 41 E3
Susap Creek, (BC) 35 E4
Suskwa River, (BC) 42 F3
Sustut Lake, (BC) 42 G2
Sustut River, (BC) 42 F2
Sutcliffe Lake, (NWT) 44 G1
Sutherland River, (BC) 40 A1
Sutil, Cape, (BC) 39 C1
Sutil Channel, (BC) 37 B4
Sutil Point, (BC) 37 B4
Sutlej Channel, (BC) 39 E1
Sutton Lake, (Ont.) 20 B1
Sutton, Monts, (Que.) 16 C4
Sutton River, (Ont.) 20 B1
Sutton River, (NWT) 46 D2
Suwannee Lake, (Man.) 44 H4
Svarten, Cape, (NWT) 47 E3
Svendsen Peninsula, (NWT) 47 E2
Sverdrup, Cape, (NWT) 47 C4
Sverdrup Channel, (NWT) 47 D1
Sverdrup Inlet, (NWT) 47 E3
Sverdrup Islands, (NWT) 47 D2
Sverre Cape, (NWT) 47 D2
Swakum Mountain, (BC) 35 C2
Swale Island, (Nfld.) 3 F4
Swale Tickle, (Nfld.) 3 F4
Swallop Creek, (BC) 41 G3
Swalwell Lake, (BC) 35 F2
Swampy Bay, Rivière, (Que.) 6 C2
Swan Bay, (Sask.) 44 F3
Swan Creek, (NB) 11 D2
Swan Hills, (Alta.) 33 C2
Swan Island, (Nfld.) 3 C2
Swan Lake, (Ont.) 28 E1
Swan Lake, (Man.) 29 G4
Swan Lake, (Man.) 30 A3
Swan Lake, (Ont.) 30 E2
Swan Lake, (BC) 35 F1
Swan Lake, (BC) 42 E3
Swan Lake, (Alta.) 44 A4
Swan Lakes, (Sask.) 32 D2
Swannell Ranges, (BC) 42 G2
Swannell River, (BC) 43 A3
Swan River, (Ont.) 20 C2
Swan River, (Man./Sask.) 29 D1
Swan River, (Alta.) 33 C1
Swanson Channel, (BC) 38 F3
Swanson Island, (BC) 39 E1
Sweet Bay, (Nfld.) 3 F4
Swift Current, (Nfld.) 2 E2
Swiftcurrent Creek, (Sask.) 31 D3
Swinburne, Cape, (NWT) 47 D4
Swindle Island, (BC) 41 E3
Sydenham Lake, (Ont.) 17 A4
Sydenham River, (Ont.) 22 C2
Sydenham River, (Ont.) 23 C2
Sydkap Ice Cap, (NWT) 47 E2
Sydney Bay, (Ont.) 23 C1
Sydney Harbour, (NS) 8 F3
Sydney Inlet, (BC) 39 F4
Sydney Lake, (Ont.) 30 D4
Sylvan Lake, (Alta.) 34 E1
Sylvan Lake, (NWT) 44 E2
Sylvester, Mount, (Nfld.) 2 C1
Sylvia Grinnell Lake, (NWT) 46 F2
Sylvia, Mount, (BC) 43 B1

T

Tabane Lake, (NWT) 44 G2
Tabasokwia River, (Ont.) 30 G2
Table Bay, (Nfld.) 6 H3
Table, Cap de la, (Que.) 5 B4
Table Head, (Nfld.) 5 H1
Table Head, (Nfld.) 5 F3
Table Head, (NS) 8 E3
Table Island, (NWT) 47 D2
Table Mountain, (Nfld.) 4 B2
Table Mountain, (Nfld.) 4 A4
Tabusintac Bay, (NB) 12 G1
Tabusintac River, (NB) 12 F1
Taché, Lac, (Que.) 14 G3
Taché, Lac, (NWT) 45 D3
Tachick Lake, (BC) 40 B2
Tadenet Lake, (NWT) 45 D1
Tadoule Lake, (Man.) 44 H3
Tadpole Lake, (Ont.) 28 H2
Taffanel, Lac, (Que.) 6 A3
Tagetochlain Lake, (BC) 41 F1
Taggart Lake, (Sask.) 32 C2
Tagiguak Lake, (Nfld.) 6 E2
Tagish Lake, (BC/YT) 45 B4
Tahaetkun Mountain, (BC) 35 E2
Tahiryuak Lake, (NWT) 47 B4
Tahoe Lake, (NWT) 47 B4
Tahsis Inlet, (BC) 39 E3
Tahsis Mountain, (BC) 39 E3
Tahsis River, (BC) 39 E3
Tahtsa Lake, (BC) 41 F1
Tahtsa Reach, (BC) 41 F1
Tahumming River, (BC) 37 C3
Taignoagny Lake, (Nfld.) 19 G1
Tait Lake, (Man.) 32 H1
Taitna Lake, (NWT) 44 F1
Taits Lake, (Sask.) 31 C4
Takia River, (BC) 41 G3
Takijuq Lake, (NWT) 45 E2
Takla Lake, (BC) 42 G3
Taku River, (BC) 45 B4
Takwa, Rivière, (Que.) 20 H3
Talbot Creek, (Ont.) 22 D2
Talbot Inlet, (NWT) 47 F2
Talbot Lake, (Ont.) 24 C3
Talbot Lake, (Man.) 30 B2
Talbot River, (Ont.) 24 C4
Talchako Mountain, (BC) 41 G3
Talchako River, (BC) 41 G3
Tally Pond, (Nfld.) 4 G2
Talon, Lac, (Que.) 15 D3
Talon, Lake, (Ont.) 26 G4
Taltapin Lake, (BC) 42 H4
Taltson Lake, (NWT) 44 D1
Taltson River, (NWT) 44 C1
Talunkwan Island, (BC) 41 B2
Tamarack Island, (Man.) 29 H1
Tamarack Lake, (Man.) 29 F2
Tamarack Point, (Ont.) 25 D3
Tamihi Creek, (BC) 35 A4
Tammarvi River, (NWT) 45 G2
Tangamoug Lake, (Ont.) 24 E3
Tanghe Creek, (Alta.) 43 F2
Tangier Grand Lake, (NS) 9 D3
Tangier Harbour, (NS) 9 D3
Tangier Lake, (NS) 9 D3
Tanner, Mount, (BC) 35 G3
Tanquary Fiord, (NWT) 47 E1
Tantalus, Mount, (BC) 38 F1
Tantarie, Lac, (Que.) 15 A2
Tantramar River, (NB) 7 A4
Taoti, Rivière, (Que.) 19 F1
Tapani, Lac, (Que.) 18 E3
Tariujaq Arm, (NWT) 47 F4
Tartigou, Rivière, (Que.) 13 A2
Taseko Lakes, (BC) 37 E1
Taseko Mountain, (BC) 37 E1
Taseko River, (BC) 37 E1
Tasiaalujjuaq, Lac, (Que.) 46 F4
Tasiataq, Lac, (Que.) 46 F4
Tasmania Islands, (NWT) 47 D4
Tassialouc, Lac, (Que.) 46 F4
Tassijuak Lake, (NWT) 47 B4
Tasu Sound, (BC) 41 B2
Tatachikapika Lake, (Ont.) 26 D2
Tatamagouche Bay, (NS) 9 C1
Tatchu Point, (BC) 39 D3
Tate Lake, (NWT) 45 D2
Tatelkuz Lake, (BC) 40 A2
Tathlina Lake, (NWT) 44 A2
Tatinnai Lake, (NWT) 44 H1
Tatla Lake, (BC) 40 B4
Tatlatui Lake, (BC) 42 F1
Tatlatui Provincial Park, (BC) 42 F1
Tatlayoko Lake, (BC) 37 D1
Tatlmain Lake, (YT) 45 B3
Tatlow, Mount, (BC) 37 E1
Tatnam, Cape, (Man.) 46 B4
Tatuk Lake, (BC) 40 B2
Taureau, Réservoir, (Que.) 18 F3
Taverner Bay, (NWT) 46 F1
Tawatinaw River, (Alta.) 33 E2
Tawayik Lake, (Alta.) 33 E3
Taweel Lake, (BC) 36 F2
Taxis River, (NB) 12 C4
Taylor Island, (NWT) 45 G1
Taylor Lake, (Ont.) 17 B2
Taylor Peak, (BC) 42 E1
Taylor River, (BC) 38 B2
Taylor River, (BC) 42 E2
Taylors Head, (NS) 9 D3
Tay River, (NB) 12 C4
Tay River, (YT) 45 B3
Tay Sound, (NWT) 47 F4
Tazin Lake, (Sask.) 44 D2
Tazin River, (NWT/Sask.) 44 D2
Tchaikazan River, (BC) 37 E1
Tchentlo Lake, (BC) 43 A4
Tchesinkut Lake, (BC) 41 H1
Tchitogama, Lac, (Que.) 14 A2
Teagues Lake, (NB) 12 F1
Teakerne Arm, (BC) 37 C4
Teaquahan River, (BC) 37 C2
Tebesjuak Lake, (NWT) 46 A2
Teeswater River, (Ont.) 23 C2
Teggau Lake, (Ont.) 28 H2
Tehek Lake, (NWT) 46 B2
Tehery Lake, (NWT) 46 B2
Tejean Lake, (NWT) 44 D1
Telkwa River, (BC) 42 F4
Tellot Glacier, (BC) 37 B1
Temagami, Lake, (Ont.) 26 F3
Témiscamie, Lac, (Que.) 20 H3
Témiscamie, Rivière, (Que.) 19 A1
Témiscamie, Rivière, (Que.) 20 H3
Témiscamingue, Lac, (Que.) 26 F3
see also Timiskaming, Lake (Ont.)
Témiscouata, Lac, (Que.) 15 G1
Temple Bay, (Nfld.) 5 H1
Templeman, Mount, (BC) 34 B2
Tenaka Creek, (BC) 43 C1
Ten Mile Lake, (Nfld.) 3 D2
Ten Mile Lake, (Nfld.) 5 G2
Ten Mile Lake, (NS) 9 D3
Ten Mile Lake, (NS) 10 D3
Ten Mile Lake, (Ont.) 25 A1
Ten Mile Point, (Ont.) 25 C2
Ten Mile Pond, (Nfld.) 3 E3
Tennent Islands, (NWT) 45 G1
Tenny, Cape, (NS) 9 A2
Tenquille Creek, (BC) 37 G3
Tent Lake, (NWT) 44 D1
Teo Lakes, (Sask.) 31 C1
Tepee Lake, (Alta.) 44 B4
Terrace Creek, (BC) 35 E2
Terrace Mountain, (BC) 35 E2
Terra Nova Lake, (Nfld.) 3 E4
Terra Nova National Park, (Nfld.) 3 F4
see also Terra Nova, Parc national de
Terra Nova North River, (Nfld.) 3 D4
Terra Nova, Parc national de, (Nfld.) 3 F4
see also Terra Nova National Park
Terra Nova River, (Nfld.) 3 C4
Terra Nova River, (Nfld.) 3 E4
Terrien, Lac, (Que.) 15 D2
Terror Bay, (NWT) 45 G1
Terror Point, (NWT) 46 D2
Terzaghi Dam/Barrage, (BC) 37 H2
Tésécau, Lac, (Que.) 20 F3
Tesla Lake, (BC) 41 G2
Teslin Lake, (BC/YT) 45 B4
Teslin River, (YT) 45 B3
Tessier, Lac, (Que.) 18 E2
Tessik Lake, (NWT) 46 E2
Testu, Lac, (Que.) 6 C2
Tetachuck Lake, (BC) 41 G2
Tetagouche River, (NB) 12 D1
Tête Blanche, Rivière de la, (Que.) 14 B1
Tête, Lac de la, (Que.) 18 E1
Tétépisca, Lac, (Que.) 19 C2
Tethul River, (NWT) 44 C2
Tetu Lake, (Ont.) 28 E1
Texada Island, (BC) 38 D1
Texas Creek, (BC) 35 A1
Tezwa River, (BC) 41 F2
Tezzeron Lake, (BC) 40 B1
Thackeray Lake, (Sask.) 32 B4
Thaddeus Lake, (Ont.) 27 A1
Thames River, (Ont.) 22 C3
Thaolintoa Lake, (NWT) 44 H1
The Battlefords Provincial Park, (Sask.) 32 B4
Thekulthili Lake, (NWT) 44 D1
Thelon River, (NWT) 44 E1
Thémines, Rivière, (Que.) 19 D1
Théodat, Lac, (Que.) 20 F3
Theodosia River, (BC) 37 C4
The Shoals Provincial Park, (Ont.) 26 B2
Thesiger Bay, (NWT) 47 A3
Thetis Island, (BC) 38 E3
Thévenet, Lac, (Que.) 6 B1
Thévet, Lac, (Que.) 19 H1
Thibault Island, (Ont.) 25 A2
Thibaut, Lac, (Que.) 6 C1
Thiboult Bay, (NWT) 47 E4
Thicke Lake, (Sask.) 44 E2
Thicksons Point, (Ont.) 21 C2
Thirty Mile Lake, (NWT) 46 B2
Thlewiaza River, (NWT) 46 A3
Thluicho Lake, (Sask.) 44 D2
Thoa River, (NWT) 44 D2
Thomas Falls, (Nfld.) 6 D3
Thomas Hubbard, Cape, (NWT) 47 D1
Thomas Lake, (Man.) 30 C1
Thomas Lake, (Alta.) 33 F4
Thomas Lake, (BC) 38 G1
Thomas Lee Inlet, (NWT) 47 E3
Thomas Point, (Ont.) 25 C3
Thomas River, (Nfld.) 6 E3
Thom Bay, (NWT) 47 E4
Thomlinson, Mount, (BC) 42 F3
Thompson Harbour, (NWT) 46 E3
Thompson Island, (Ont.) 27 E3
Thompson River, (BC) 35 B1
Thompson Sound, (BC) 39 F1
Thomsen River, (NWT) 47 B3
Thomson Arm, (Sask.) 31 E2
Thomson Lake, (Sask.) 31 F4
Thomson Lake, (Sask.) 44 E3
Thonokied Lake, (NWT) 45 F2
Thorah Island, (Ont.) 23 G2
Thorburn Lake, (Nfld.) 2 E1
Thormanby Islands, (BC) 38 D2
Thornbrough Channel, (BC) 38 E2
Thorne, Lac, (Que.) 17 B1
Thorne River, (Ont.) 30 E2
Thorstein, Cape, (NWT) 47 D2
Thorsteinson Lake, (Man.) 44 H3
Thorvald Peninsula, (NWT) 47 F2
Thousand Islands, (Ont.) 17 B4
Three Brooks, (Nfld.) 3 B3
Three Brothers Mountain, (BC) 35 C4
Three Corner Pond, (Nfld.) 3 A2
Threehills Creek, (Alta.) 34 F1
Three Islands, (NB) 11 C4
Three Mile Lake, (Ont.) 24 B2
Threenarrows Lake, (Ont.) 25 D2
Threepoint Creek, (Alta.) 34 E2
Threepoint Lake, (Man.) 30 B1
Three Wives Lake, (NWT) 44 F1
Throat River, (Ont.) 30 E3
Thubun Lakes, (NWT) 44 C1
Thubun River, (NWT) 44 C1
Thuchonilini Lake, (NWT) 44 H1
Thultue Lake, (Alta.) 44 B2
Thunder Bay, (Ont.) 27 E3
Thunder Bay, (BC) 38 D1
Thunder Cape, (Ont.) 27 E3
Thunder Creek, (Sask.) 31 F3
Thunder River, (BC) 36 G1
Thurston Lake, (Alta.) 44 A2
Thutade Lake, (BC) 42 F1
Thuya Creek, (BC) 36 E3
Thwart Island, (Nfld.) 3 C2
Thynne, Mount, (BC) 35 C3
Tibiska Lake, (Sask.) 32 D2
Tice Lake, (Man.) 44 G2
Tichégami, Rivière, (Que.) 20 G3
Tickle Bay, (Nfld.) 2 F2
Tickle Harbour Point, (Nfld.) 2 F2
Tide Lake, (Ont.) 30 D4
Tide Lake, (Alta.) 34 H3
Tidney River, (NS) 10 D3
Tidnish River, (NS) 9 A1
Tiedemann Glacier, (BC) 37 B1
Tikkoatokak Bay, (Nfld.) 6 E2
Tilly, Lac, (Que.) 20 G2
Timber Lake, (NS) 9 A3
Timeu Creek, (Alta.) 33 C2
Timiskaming, Lake, (Ont.) 26 F3
see also Témiscamingue, Lac (Que.)
Timothy Lake, (BC) 36 D2
Tim River, (Ont.) 24 C1
Tingin Fiord, (NWT) 47 H4
Tinniswood, Mount, (BC) 37 E3
Tippo River, (Sask.) 32 D1
Tip Top Mountain, (Ont.) 27 H3
Tisdall Lake, (BC) 36 D1
Titmarsh Lake, (Ont.) 27 C3
Tlupana Inlet, (BC) 39 F3
Tlupana River, (BC) 39 F3
Toad Lake, (Ont.) 25 G2
Tobacco Lake, (Ont.) 25 B2
Toba Glacier, (BC) 37 D2
Toba Inlet, (BC) 37 C3
Toba River, (BC) 37 D3
Tobeatic Lake, (NS) 10 C2
Tobin Lake, (Sask.) 32 F3
Tobique River, (NB) 12 B3
Toby Creek, (BC) 34 C3
Tochatwi Bay, (NWT) 44 D1
Tochatwi Lake, (NWT) 44 D1
Tochcha Lake, (BC) 42 G4
Tocheri Lake, (Ont.) 26 A1
Todd, Mount, (BC) 38 E4
Todd Mountain, (NB) 12 C3
Tod Lake, (Man.) 44 G4
Tod, Mount, (BC) 36 F4
Tofino Creek, (BC) 39 G4
Tofino Inlet, (BC) 38 A2
Tomasine, Lac, (Que.) 18 D3
Tom Browne Lake, (BC) 39 G1
Tomiko Lake, (Ont.) 25 G1
Tomiko River, (Ont.) 25 H1
Tom Joe Brook, (Nfld.) 3 A3
Tom Luscombe Brook, (Nfld.) 6 G3
Tom, Mount, (BC) 37 F1
Tommy Lakes, (BC) 43 D1
Tommy's Arm River, (Nfld.) 3 B2
Toney Lake, (NS) 10 D3
Tonnerre, Pointe au, (Que.) 19 G3
Toodoggone River, (BC) 42 F1
Toothpick Lake, (Ont.) 28 G1
Tootyak Lake, (NWT) 46 B3
Topascom Lake, (Sask.) 32 G1
Topaze Harbour, (BC) 39 G1
Topknot Point, (BC) 39 B1
Top of the World Provincial Park, (BC) 34 D3
Top Pond, (Nfld.) 4 E3
Topsails, The (*bluff*), (Nfld.) 4 F1
Toquart Bay, (BC) 38 B3
Toquart Lake, (BC) 38 B2
Tor Bay, (Nfld.) 2 H2
Tor Bay, (NS) 9 G2
Torbay Point, (Nfld.) 2 H2
Torch Lake, (Sask.) 32 E3
Torch River, (Sask.) 32 E3
Tormentine, Cape, (NB) 7 B4
Torment, Lake, (NS) 10 D1
Tornado Mountain, (Alta./BC) 34 E3
Torngat, Monts, (Que.) 46 H4
see also Torngat Mountains (Nfld.)
Torngat Mountains, (Nfld.) 46 G3
see also Torngat, Monts (Que.)
Toronto Int Airport/Aéroport, (Ont.) 23 F4
Toronto Island, (Ont.) 21 B2
Toronto Lake, (Ont.) 27 F1
Torpy River, (BC) 40 D2
Torrance Lake, (Man.) 44 H3
Tortue, Lac, (Que.) 19 G2
Tortue, Lac à la, (Que.) 16 C1
Tortue, Rivière, (Que.) 19 G2
Totogan Creek, (Ont.) 30 F3
Totogan Lake, (Ont.) 30 F3
Touak Fiord, (NWT) 46 G2
Touchwood Lake, (Man.) 30 D2
Touchwood Lake, (Alta.) 33 F2
Touchwood Uplands, (Sask.) 29 B2
Touladi, Lac, (Que.) 15 G1
Touladi, Rivière, (Que.) 14 G4
Toulnustouc Nord-Est, Rivière, (Que.) 19 E2
Toulnustouc, Rivière, (Que.) 19 D3
Tourbis, Lac, (Que.) 18 F3
Tourgis Lake, (NWT) 45 G2
Tourilli, Rivière, (Que.) 15 A2
Touzel, Lac, (Que.) 19 G3
Towincut Mountain, (BC) 38 D3
Tracadie, Baie de, (NB) 12 G1
Tracadie Bay, (PEI) 7 D3
Tracadie River, (NS) 9 F1
Tracadigache, Baie, (Que.) 13 D3
Tracadigache, Pointe, (Que.) 13 D3
Tracy, Pointe de, (Que.) 46 F3
Trade Lake, (Sask.) 32 F1
Trading River, (Ont.) 30 F4
Trail Bay, (BC) 38 E2
Train Lake, (Sask.) 44 E2
Trainor Lake, (NWT) 45 D4
Tramping Lake, (Sask.) 31 D1
Tranquil Creek, (BC) 39 G4
Tranquil Inlet, (BC) 39 G4
Tranquille River, (BC) 36 E4
Transit Head, (BC) 37 A2
Transition (Kennedy) Bay, (NWT) 47 D4
Trapping Creek, (BC) 35 G3
Trapp Lake, (BC) 35 D1
Travaillant Lake, (NWT) 45 C1
Traverse Bay, (Man.) 30 C4
Traverse Brook, (Nfld.) 3 E3
Traverse, Lac, (Ont.) 18 B4
Traverspine River, (Nfld.) 6 F4
Travers Reservoir, (Alta.) 34 F3
Trebell Lake, (NWT) 44 D2
Tredcroft Creek, (BC) 37 D1
Tree River, (NWT) 45 F2
Tremblant, Mont, (Que.) 18 F4
Tremblay, Lac, (Que.) 14 C2
Tremblay, Lac, (Que.) 14 E2
Tremblay Sound, (NWT) 47 F4
Trembleur Lake, (BC) 42 H4
Trenche, Rivière, (Que.) 18 G2
Trent Canal, (Ont.) 21 D1
Trente et un Milles, Lac des, (Que.) 18 D4
Trent River, (Ont.) 21 E1
Trent River, (BC) 38 B1
Trépanier Creek, (BC) 35 E3
Trepassey Bay, (Nfld.) 2 G4
Trepassey Harbour, (Nfld.) 2 G4
Treptow Lake, (Ont.) 27 G1
Tretheway Creek, (BC) 38 H1
Trethewey Lake, (Ont.) 26 E3
Trevor Channel, (BC) 38 B3
Triangle Island, (BC) 39 A1
Tribune Bay, (BC) 38 C2
Tribune Channel, (BC) 39 F1
Trilsbeck Lake, (Ont.) 20 B3
Trincomali Channel, (BC) 38 E3
Tring, Ruisseau, (Que.) 16 F2
Trinité, Baie de la
see Trinité Bay
Trinité, Rivière de la, (Que.) 19 E4
Trinity Bay, (Nfld.) 2 F2
Trinity Bay, (Nfld.) 3 F3
Trinity Creek, (BC) 35 G1
Trinity Harbour, (Nfld.) 3 G4
Trinity Pond, (Nfld.) 3 G4
Trio Mountain, (BC) 39 G3
Triquet, Lac, (Que.) 5 D3
Triton Brook, (Nfld.) 3 D4
Triton Island, (Nfld.) 3 B2
Trodely Island, (NWT) 20 D3
Troilus, Lac, (Que.) 20 G3
Trois Pistoles, Rivière des, (Que.) 14 F4
Trois Saumons, Lac, (Que.) 15 D2
Troitsa Lake, (BC) 41 F2
Troitsa Peak, (BC) 41 F2
Tromso Fiord, (NWT) 47 G4
Tronka Chua Lake, (NWT) 44 D1
Trophy Mountain, (BC) 36 F2
Troubridge, Mount, (BC) 38 D1
Trousers Lake, (NB) 12 C2
Trout Brook, (Nfld.) 4 C2
Trout Creek, (BC) 35 E3
Trout Lake, (NS) 10 D1
Trout Lake, (Ont.) 24 D1
Trout Lake, (Ont.) 24 F2
Trout Lake, (Ont.) 25 F1
Trout Lake, (Ont.) 25 H1
Trout Lake, (Ont.) 30 D4
Trout Lake, (Sask.) 32 E1
Trout Lake, (BC) 34 B3
Trout Lake, (Man.) 44 H3
Trout Lake, (NWT) 45 D4
Trout Mountain, (BC) 34 B3
Trout River, (Alta.) 44 B4
Trout River, (NWT) 45 D3
Troyes, Lac, (Que.) 18 F3
Truax, Mount, (BC) 37 G2
Truchon, Ruisseau à, (Que.) 14 E1
Truite, Lac à la, (Que.) 18 B3
Truite, Rivière à la, (Que.) 13 C2
Truro Island, (NWT) 47 D3
Trutch Creek, (BC) 43 D1
Tryon, Cape, (PEI) 7 C3
Tsable River, (BC) 38 B1
Tsacha Lake, (BC) 40 A3
Tsalwor Lake, (Sask.) 44 D2
Tsaydaychuz Peak, (BC) 41 G2
Tsayta Lake, (BC) 42 H3
Tsaytis River, (BC) 41 F2
Tsikwustum Creek, (BC) 36 G3
Tsikwustum Lake, (BC) 36 H3
Tsileuh Creek, (BC) 35 B3
Tsimpsean Peninsula, (BC) 42 C4
Tsintsunko Lake, (BC) 36 E4
Tsitika River, (BC) 39 E2
Tsitsutl Peak, (BC) 41 G3
Tsoko Lake, (NWT) 45 D1
Tsolum River, (BC) 38 B1
Tsuius Creek, (BC) 35 G1
Tsu Lake, (NWT) 44 C2
Tsulquate River, (BC) 39 C1
Tsuniah Lake, (BC) 37 D1
Tsusiat Lake, (BC) 38 C3
Tuadook Lake, (NB) 12 C2
Tuaton Lake, (BC) 42 E1
Tuber Lake, (Man.) 28 E1
Tuchialic Bay, (Nfld.) 6 G3
Tuchodi Lakes, (BC) 43 B1
Tuchodi River, (BC) 43 B1
Tucker Lake, (Alta.) 33 G2
Tudor, Lac, (Que.) 6 D2
Tudyah Lake, (BC) 43 C4
Tuffin Island, (NS) 9 E3
Tug Pond, (Nfld.) 2 E1
Tugwell Creek, (BC) 38 E4
Tukarak Island, (NWT) 20 E1
Tulabi Lake, (Sask.) 32 G2
Tulameen Mountain, (BC) 35 B4
Tulameen River, (BC) 35 C3
Tulemalu Lake, (NWT) 45 H2
Tully Lake, (Ont.) 27 B1
Tumbledown Dick Island, (Nfld.) 6 G3
Tumbler Island, (Nfld.) 3 F3
Tumbo Island, (BC) 38 F3
Tumeka Lake, (BC) 42 D1
Tumtum Lake, (BC) 36 H2
Tumult Glacier, (BC) 37 A1
Tunago Lake, (NWT) 45 D2
Tunkwa Lake, (BC) 35 C1
Tunulic, Rivière, (Que.) 6 D1
Tunungayualok Island, (Nfld.) 6 F2
Tupper Lake, (NS) 10 D2
Turgeon, Lac, (Que.) 26 G1
Turgeon, Rivière, (Que.) 26 G1
Turkey Point, (Ont.) 22 G2
Turkey Point Provincial Park, (Ont.) 22 G2
Turks Cove, (Nfld.) 4 E4
Turnagain Point, (Man.) 29 H1
Turnagain Point, (NWT) 45 F1
Turnavik Islands, (Nfld.) 6 F2
Turnbull Island, (Ont.) 25 A1
Turner, Cape, (PEI) 7 C3
Turnor Lake, (Sask.) 44 D4
Turnour Island, (BC) 39 F1
Turret Island, (BC) 38 B3
Turtle Lake, (Ont.) 25 B1
Turtle Lake, (Ont.) 25 C2
Turtle Lake, (Man.) 28 D1
Turtle Lake, (Sask.) 32 B3
Turtlelake River, (Sask.) 32 B3
Turtle Mountain Provincial Park, (Man.) 29 E4
Turtle River, (Man.) 29 F2
Tusket Islands, (NS) 10 A4
Tutizzi Lake, (BC) 42 G2
Tuwasus Creek, (BC) 37 G4
Tuzcha Lake, (BC) 37 E1
Twaal Creek, (BC) 35 B1
Twan Creek, (BC) 36 A1
Tweed Island, (Nfld.) 5 F4
Tweedsmuir Provincial Park, (BC) 41 G2
Twelve Mile Lake, (Sask.) 31 F4
Twelve Mile Stream, (NS) 9 D3
Twenty Mile Creek, (Ont.) 21 A4
Twigge Lake, (Sask.) 32 G2
Twillick Brook, (Nfld.) 2 B1
Twillingate Harbour, (Nfld.) 3 D1
Twin Lakes, (BC) 35 E4
Twitya River, (NWT) 45 C3
Twoforks River, (Sask.) 32 D2
Two Guts Pond, (Nfld.) 4 B2
Two River Lake, (Ont.) 30 E2
Two Rivers Arm, (BC) 38 B2
Two Sisters Mountain, (BC) 40 D2
Tyaughton Creek, (BC) 37 F2
Tyaughton Lake, (BC) 37 G2
Tyee Lake, (BC) 36 B1
Tyrrell Arm, (NWT) 46 A2
Tyrrell Lake, (Sask.) 32 H1
Tyrrell Lake, (NWT) 45 G3
Tyson Lake, (Ont.) 25 E1
Tzartus Island, (BC) 38 B3
Tzenzaicut Lake, (BC) 40 C3
Tzeo River, (BC) 41 G3
Tzoonie River, (BC) 38 E1

PICTURE CREDITS

The abbreviations used here are these:

IBC   Image Bank of Canada
ROM   Royal Ontario Museum
PAC   Public Archives of Canada
WNB   Webster Collection of Pictorial Canadiana,
       New Brunswick Museum

Credits are left to right, top to bottom, with
supplementary information as needed.

6–7 Globe at National Museum of Science &
Technology © Rand McNally & Company,
R.L. 80-GP-21/photo by John Evans.

9 Crespi-Madrid; Crombie McNeil; Geological
Survey of Canada, G.S.C. 202872-G.

10 Courtesy of the Field Museum of Natural
History; Chicago (3).

11 Susanne M. Swibold; National Museum of
Man, National Museums of Canada.

12 From the *Reader's Digest Complete Atlas of the
British Isles*; Smithsonian Institute #72-5994.

13 Harold V. Green; from "Field Guide to Snow
Crystals" by Edward R. Lachapelle, University of
Washington Press (2).

15 *Weather-Making Oceans* courtesy National
Geographical Mapping Division, Surveys &
Mapping Branch, Energy, Mines & Resources
Canada.

16 *Length of High Summer* courtesy Canadian
Climate Centre, Atmospheric Environment
Services, Environment Canada; *Hours of Bright
Sunshine* courtesy John Wiley & Sons Canada Ltd.

17 *Montreal in March* from Oke (1978);
"Boundary Layer Climates" Methuen, London.

18 *Length of Snow Cover Season* courtesy
Canadian Climate Centre, Atmospheric
Environment Services, Environment Canada;
(bottom 3) *Snow Accumulation* from Oke (1978);
"Boundary Layer Climates" Methuen, London.

19 Robert J. Cheng, Atmospheric Sciences
Research Center, State University of New York at
Albany (3); Atmospheric Environment Services;
Robert J. Cheng, Atmospheric Sciences Research
Center, State University of New York at Albany;
from "Clouds, Rain & Rainmaking" by
B.J. Mason, Cambridge University Press/photo
by U. Makaya; National Hydrology Research
Institute (3); © Dave Timewell/Image Finders;
Patrick Morrow; Gary Corbett.

22 BM 2683–Brian Milne/Valan Naturefotos;
Mark K. Peck; Leonard Lee Rue III; R.N. Smith;
(bottom) Mary Ferguson; Harold V. Green.

23 Norman R. Lightfoot; Leonard Lee Rue III;
Maxime St-Amour; Leonard Lee Rue III;
Edgar T. Jones.

24 Doris Mowry; Cynthia Chalk; Mary Ferguson.

25 (Bottom left) Doris Mowry; (top right)
Barbara K. Deans; MT 654–Mark Tomalty/Valan
Naturefotos.

26 Richard Wright; © Jack Fields/Photo
Researchers; Susanne M. Swibold; Menno Fieguth;
© Bill Brooks/Bruce Coleman Inc.

27 (Top) Rick Filler; Paul von Baich.

28 ROM (2); courtesy Glenbow Museum,
Calgary.

29 (Top) courtesy National Museum of Man,
National Museums of Canada (2); Lande
Collection Dept. of Rare Books, McGill University
Libraries/photo Mike Haimes; ROM; (bottom)
courtesy Glenbow Museum, Calgary.

30 (Top right) Mary Evans Picture Library,
London; Aldus Books Ltd., London; Naval
Museum of Madrid/photo by Oronoz;
PAC C-16105; National Art Gallery, Wellington,
New Zealand.

30–31 National Museum of Science & Technology
© Rand McNally & Company, R.L. 79-GP-19/
photo by John Evans.

31 Bodleian Library, Oxford; Aldus Books Ltd.,
London; National Gallery of Canada, Ottawa;
National Portrait Gallery, London (2); BBC
Hulton Picture Library, London.

32 Parks Canada; Ron Webber; PAC C-1080.

33 WNB/photo Rod Stears; WNB.

34 WNB #429/photo Rod Stears; Canadian
Pacific Corporate Archives; PAC C-605.

35 Glenbow–Alberta Institute; detail "The Taking
of Vimy Ridge, Easter Monday, 1917" by Richard
Jack, Canadian War Museum.

37 *Interprovincial Migration* courtesy Canadian
Imperial Bank of Commerce.

38 © Allan Harvey/IBC (2).

39 Courtesy Mark London, Heritage Montreal;
Vancouver Public Library; © John de Visser/IBC;
George Hunter.

44 Agriculture Canada; courtesy Allis-Chalmers.

47 Vancouver Public Library; Canadian Forestry
Service.

50–51 Courtesy Placer Development Ltd.

51 Courtesy Luscar Ltd. (2).

53 (Top) © D. Carriere/Geographical Visual
Aids, Wiarton; (left) Nova Scotia Power
Corporation; courtesy Alcan Canada Products
Ltd./photo by Karl Sliva.

54 PAC C-82808; MacMillan Bloedel; Canada
Packers/photo Robert C. Ragsdale; © E. Otto/
Miller Services.

55 General Motors of Canada; Daniel Wiener;
Doris Mowry.

56 Transport Canada; Lowry Photography; B.C.
Ferry Corporation; NFB Photothèque; BCPR Inc.;
B.C. Ministry of Forests; MacMillan Bloedel;
Canadian Pacific.

57 (Top right) TransCanada Telephone System;
Canadian Pacific; Telesat Canada; Northern
Transportation Co. Ltd./photo Ranson
Photographers, Edmonton; Transport Canada;
(bottom) Canadian National.

67 Reader's Digest Library of Modern
Knowledge.

77 PAC; Aéro Photo Inc. (3).

79 National Air Photo Library, Land Sat.; Aéro
Photo Inc.

ILLUSTRATORS: Jim Bruce, George Buctel,
Peter Buerschaper, Alan Daniel, Louis Delorme,
Diane Desrosiers, Howard S. Friedman,
Jean-Claude Gagnon, Réal Lefebvre,
Andris Leimanis, Anker Odum, Elayne Sears.

PRODUCTION

TYPESETTING: Reader's Digest Text Processing
   Center
MAPS: Aéro Photo Inc., in conjunction with
   The Reader's Digest Association (Canada) Ltd.
COLOR SEPARATION: Herzig Somerville Ltd.
PRINTING: Montreal Lithographing Ltd.
BINDING: Harpell's Press Co-operative
BINDING MATERIALS: Boise Cascade (Pajco
   Division) and Columbia Finishing Mills
PAPER: Rolland Inc.

INSIDE BACK COVER: The Land and the People. A luminous
depiction of the distribution of population in Canada.